AMERICANA

AMERICANA

THE AMERICAS IN THE WORLD, AROUND 1850 (OR 'SEEING THE ELEPHANT' AS THE THEME FOR AN IMAGINARY WESTERN)

———————

JAMES DUNKERLEY

VERSO

London · New York

First published by Verso 2000
© James Dunkerley 2000
All rights reserved

Verso
UK: 6 Meard Street, London WIV 3HR
USA: 180 Varick Street, New York, NY 10014–4606

Verso is the imprint of New Left Books

ISBN 1–85984–753–6

British Library Cataloguing in Publication Data
A catalogue record for this book is available from the British Library

Library of Congress Cataloging-in-Publication Data
Dunkerley, James.
 Americana : the Americas in the world around 1850 / James Dunkerley.
  p. ; cm.
 Includes bibliographical references and index.
 ISBN 1–85984–753–6
  1. America—Civilization—19th century.   2. Latin America—History—1830–1898.
 3. United States—History—1849–1877.   4. Civilization—American influences.
 5. United States—Relations—Latin America.   6. Latin America—Relations—United
 States.   7. Space and time—History—19th century.   8. Culture conflict—America—
 History—19th century.   9. Imperialism—America—History—19th century.   I. Title.
 E18.83.D86 2000
 970.04—dc21   00-032472

Front endpaper: 'El Camuati'. The first stock exchange in Argentina,
pictured here in 1854, drew its nickname from a water rodent that built a sack-like nest.
Back endpaper: Veterans of the Mexican War, Chester, South Carolina.

Designed and typeset by Illuminati, Grosmont
Printed and bound in Great Britain by Bath Press Ltd, Avon

To the memory of Gwyn A. Williams

Nid draw ar bell-bell draeth y mae,
Nac obry 'ngwely'r perlau chwaith,
Ond mil-mil nes, a ber yw'r daith
I ddistaw byrth y byd di-wae.

To John Hiatt

Steam rising from the sidewalk
of New Orleans after an evening rain ...
As you headed up St Charles
to catch a streetcar named Desire,
young couple struggling in the doorway.

To the memory of Graciela Liendo de Aguilar

Ripujqa ripunqachavi
sonqonta rumiyachispa
Qhepakujpamin llakiypa
uminanta yuyarispe

CONTENTS

DRAMATIS PERSONAE

THE DEFENDANTS/PLAINTIFFS

John Mitchel
Myra Clark Gaines
Mariano Donato Muñoz

THE JUDGES

Bolivian Supreme Court: President – Basilio de Cuellar
Baron Lefroy and Richard Moore
Judge Pitot
US Supreme Court: Chief Justice – Roger Taney

THE LAWYERS

James Monahan and Mr Henn
Sir Colman O'Loghlen and Robert Holmes
Francisco Alvarez Toledo
Daniel Webster and Greer Duncan; Caleb Cushing

THE SOLDIERS AND SAILORS

Col. Bellechasse
Manuel Isidoro Belzu
Edmund Pendleton Gaines
Mariano Melgarejo
Frank/Francisco Burdett O'Connor
Barrington Reynolds
John Riley
Antonio López de Santa Anna
Winfield Scott
Herbert Schomberg
Francisco Solano López
Zachary Taylor
William Walker
James Wilkinson

The Lovers

Zulime Carrière/Desgrange/Clark/Gardette
Marianne Caton, Marchioness Wellesley
Captain Chabrié
Jerome Desgrange
Paul Gauguin
Elisa Lynch
Francisca Ruyloba
Juana Sánchez
Harriet Taylor
Niña Yrena

The Farmer

John Brabazon

The Politicians

Lord Aberdeen
James Buchanan
John C. Calhoun
W.C.C. Claiborne
Lord Clarendon
Albert Gallatin
Charles Gavan Duffy
François Guizot
Thomas Jefferson
James Madison
Thomas Meagher
Feargus O'Connor
Lord Palmerston
Sir Robert Peel
James Polk
Juan Manuel de Rosas
Lord John Russell
Domingo Faustino Sarmiento
William Smith O'Brien

The Diplomats

George Bancroft
Fanny Calderón de la Barca
Frederick Chatfield
Daniel Clark

Hinton Helper
Lord Howden
Robert Livingston
John Lloyd

THE HISTORIANS

Henry Adams
Lucas Alamán
H.L.V. Ducoudray Holstein
Eric Hobsbawm
Johan Huizinga
Lord Macaulay
Jules Michelet
Richard Morse
Tomás O'Connor d'Arlach
Edmundo O'Gorman
D.C.M. Platt
W.H. Prescott
Arthur Whitaker
Gwyn A. Williams

THE WRITERS

Harriet Beecher Stowe
Gioconda Belli
Jorge Luis Borges
Ernesto Cardenal
James Fenimore Cooper
Charles Dana
Charles Darwin
Charles Dickens
Horace Greeley
Nathaniel Hawthorne
Juana Manuela Gorriti
Heinrich Heine
Søren Kierkegaard
Herman Melville
Frederick Law Olmsted
Pablo Neruda
Allen Ginsberg
Richard Rodríguez
Flora Tristán
Anthony Trollope
Walt Whitman

The Political Theorists/Activists

Juan Bautista Alberdi
Thomas Carlyle
Frederick Douglass
Ralph Waldo Emerson
Margaret Fuller
Francis Lieber
Karl Marx
John Stuart Mill
Henry David Thoreau

The Priests

Father Antoine
Jedidiah Morse
William Miller
Pio IX
Padre Zefferini Muzzani

The Merchants

The Hodgsons
Tomás Manning
The Shepherds

LATIN AMERICA IN 2000

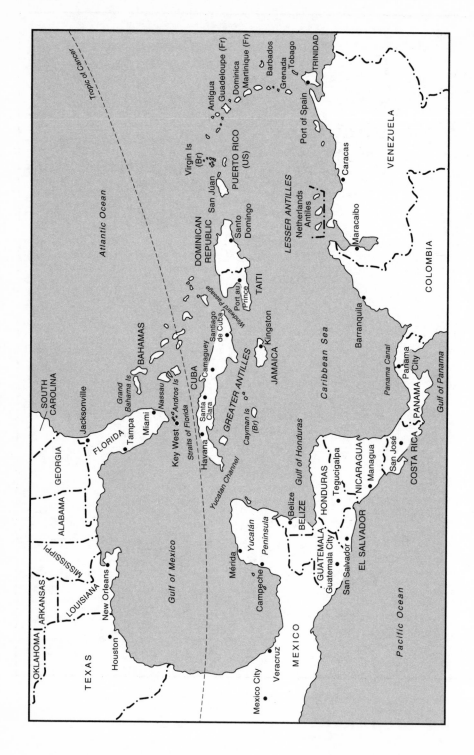

THE CARIBBEAN AND CENTRAL AMERICA IN 2000

LATIN AMERICA IN 1830

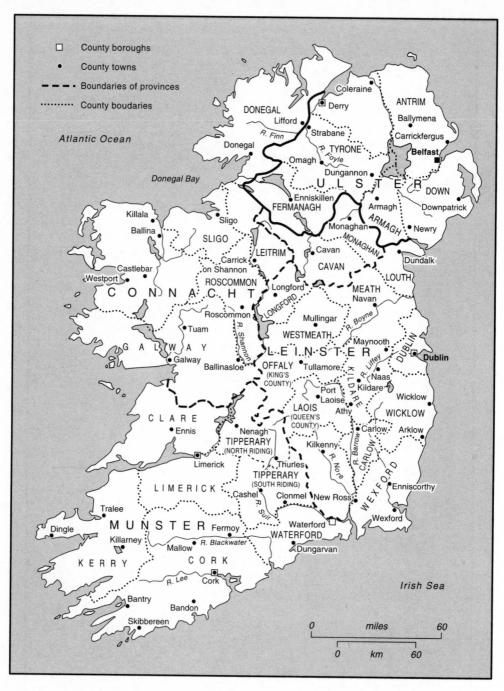

MODERN IRELAND: TOWNS, COUNTIES AND PROVINCES

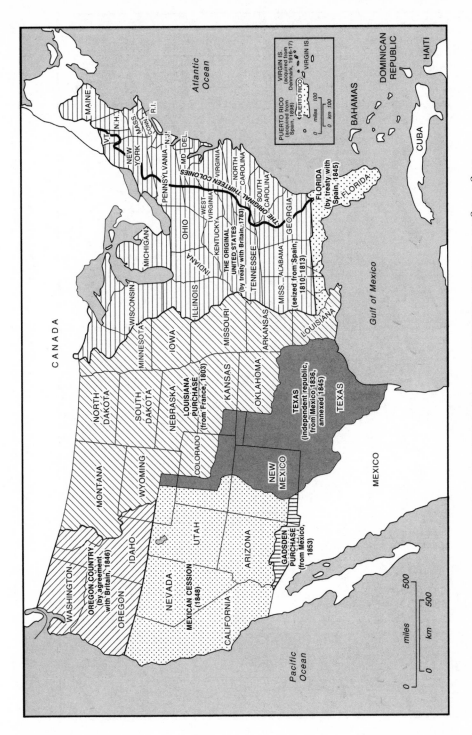

TERRITORIAL GROWTH OF THE UNITED STATES, 1783–1853

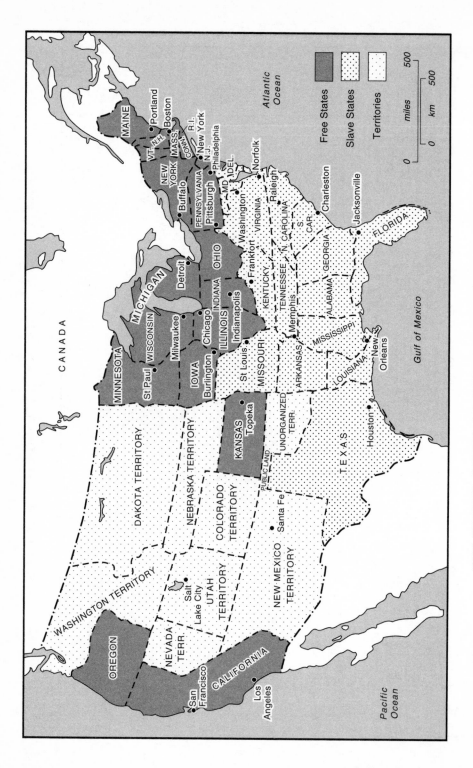

THE UNITED STATES ON THE EVE OF THE CIVIL WAR

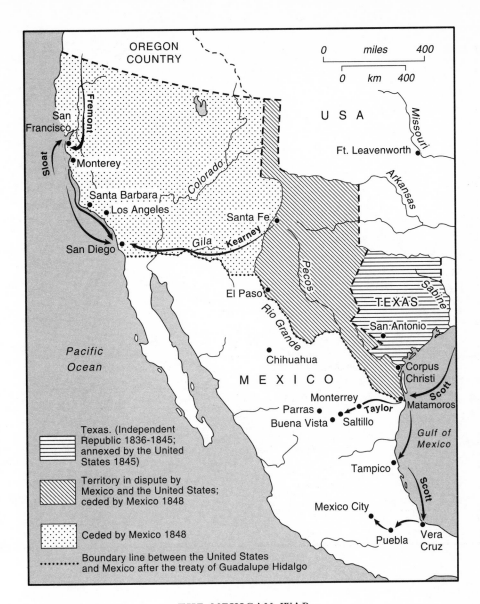

OREGON
COUNTRY

USA

Ft. Leavenworth

Missouri

Arkansas

San
Francisco

Fremont

Monterey

Sloat

Santa Barbara

Los Angeles

Colorado

Santa Fe

Kearney

San Diego

Gila

Pecos

TEXAS

Sabine

El Paso

Rio Grande

San Antonio

Pacific
Ocean

Chihuahua

MEXICO

Corpus
Christi

Scott

Monterrey

Matamoros

Parras

Taylor

Saltillo

Buena Vista

Gulf of
Mexico

Tampico

Scott

Mexico City

Vera
Cruz

Puebla

0   miles   400

0   km   400

Texas. (Independent
Republic 1836-1845;
annexed by the United
States 1845)

Territory in dispute by
Mexico and the United States;
ceded by Mexico 1848

Ceded by Mexico 1848

Boundary line between the United States
and Mexico after the treaty of Guadalupe Hidalgo

THE MEXICAN WAR

NICARAGUA

PREFACE

The book before you is unusual in its format and approach. Its origins, though, are quite normal: the desire to emulate and honour a teacher; the change in world politics after the fall of the Berlin Wall; the stimulus of a good concert; and sensible advice from a policeman.

The teacher was Gwyn A. Williams, who was a professor of history at the University of York when I was an undergraduate there in the early 1970s, and who died in 1995, before this book had developed beyond some disparate ideas and vague fancies. When he taught me Gwyn was substituting a fierce and esoteric Marxism with a no less passionate but much more poetic Welsh nationalism. Temperamentally inclined to be anecdotal and biographical, he was intellectually drawn to things structural and cyclical. The result was a wonderful manner of lecturing in which different narratives and voices exchanged through a series of ambushes, sometimes revealed and sometimes artfully laid by his strong stammer. This form of expression made for rather less successful books, where one sensed that Williams's keenness to get on to the next idea and his desire to address quite different constituencies only accentuated an already staccato style.

Gwyn Williams introduced me to the study of the Americas by encouraging an intellectual as well as an emotional response to the experience of defeat. He was forever quoting Romain Rolland's stricture on 'the optimism of the will and the pessimism of the intelligence', and when in September 1973 our hopes for a better world were severely battered by Pinochet's coup in Chile, Williams demanded that we did not just chant slogans, still less drown out the nightmare in a cloud of dope. He challenged us to behave like Gramsci's 'organic intellectuals' and, by drawing on a discipline imposed by ourselves rather than any proletarian experience, study history to find an explanation and so avoid a repetition of so terrible an occurrence. My job was to look at the related defeat of Che Guevara by the Bolivian army in 1967, starting a love affair which accounts for the third court case in this book being set in that country rather than any other of the twenty-odd national systems of Roman law that existed in the Latin America of 1850.

Although his celebration of the *sans-culottes* and radical British artisans of the 1790s formed the basis of Gwyn Williams's prior reputation as a scholar, by 1973 he was moving on to television and back to Wales. The first of these transitions took the form of preparing an Open University course on France in 1848–51, and he tested many of his ideas on his students, who, because those ideas involved Karl Marx and professors on the barricades, took to them warmly. The books on Wales came later, skidding backwards and forwards between Merthyr Tydfil, Pennsylvania and points south-west. A lifetime of archive-burrowing hit the page in a patchwork portrait of peripatetic Celts in search of freedom and fortune, sometimes pursuing mythical Welsh-speaking indians, sometimes taciturn and disappointed, but always ten genera-tions ahead of the clever-clogs who believed that they were heralding the future when they gushed about 'globalisation'.

The stories of the authentic pioneers had particular appeal for me because the first years of my life were spent in a mid-Wales village, Eglwysfach, in a cottage next to a furnace built in 1755 at the start of the industrial revolution that, Williams plausibly claimed, drew its greatest resources and its premier victims from the Welsh valleys. Those tactile memories of the first phase of life may have been kept especially vivid because I associate them with what was in the 1950s so much more exotic than in the 1990s — the sound of a language other than English being spoken by a community in the British Isles. Far more than French, Spanish and Italian, in which he happily joked and versified, it was Williams's fluency in Welsh that guaranteed his allure for the students and authenticated his communion with a past that the other lecturers might understand but could never feel with the same intensity.

The sound of Welsh entrances me, but I have never been able to understand more than a few words, and there was no way that I could revisit that side of Gwyn's work. So the Celts in this book are Irish, sparking off another love affair — much more recent and somewhat promiscuous in that as soon as I started to study that new history, I realised that it was also brim-full of non-Celts, non-Catholics and non-conformists. The novice's natural inclination was to back away from a dark past which was still taking its toll of human life when this text was started. Such diffidence, however, was neutralised by the memory of a picket by the International Socialists against a lecture given by Williams in which he expounded the 'two nations theory' of Irish history that lay at the doctrinal heart of the British and Irish Communist Organisation, the tiny sect of intense misfits endowed with self-consuming genius to which Gwyn was then paying his comradely quota. We all went into the talk anyway, and we left it believing, with equable enthusiasm, no less in the different identities of the Catholic and Protestant traditions than in the need to get the imperialist British troops out of a place in which they never belonged. My support in the pages that follow for the idea that Ireland is really an American country located in the wrong continent is by no means original — the diasporas of the eighteenth and nineteenth centuries ensured its continuous displacement — but it has taken all the encouragement of a lawyer from Omagh and an author–editor from Dublin to keep me on the trail and make sure that I honoured my Hibernian hunches.

The collapse of European communism in 1989 naturally undermined many of the assumptions that left-wingers (communist and non-communist alike) had managed to nurture through a string of lesser defeats. With almost equal predictability it encour-aged a thoroughly unreflective triumphalism on the other side of mental barricades that had in many ways ceased to exist. As a result, interpretation of the stark new reality rapidly became the property of intellectuals whose plangent neologisms reeked as much of opportunism as of a disturbing disposition for Gallic theory. Marx, who no sane person was reading any more anyway, was definitively banished to the Ultima Thule of human consciousness – unpowerful as well as unfashionable and unreadable. These were just the conditions of adversity to stimulate another 'return to the sources', not only to the foundational texts of Marxism but also to the man himself and the times in which he lived. What was it that had been lost?

Here was such a big question that it could not be answered adequately except for a relatively short period of the past. This was especially the case if one was to apply the question to that part of the world – never-communist America (*pace* Cuba, the last dose of innoculation), the northern part of which was in Marx's time deemed to represent the future just as much as it is now. The text that follows is, then, something of a detective story spun out of a return to the Americas of the mid nineteenth century. It has been constructed in the light of the evaporation of communist claims to the future that had their theoretical origins in those years, but it has not been at all hard to steer clear of glum gravity; indeed, I probably should have been less irreverent. On the other hand, I can only apologise to Canada and Canadians for displacing them entirely from a comparative study of the continent. This is most unsatisfying intellectually – a contrast of three experiences promises much greater reward that that of two – as well as sentimentally disappointing – my father grew up in northern Alberta and a beloved uncle was born there. However, the practical difficulties proved too great, so at least I was saved from the dangers of believing that Parkman could be followed down that particular trail.

The intellectual ramifications of the end of the Cold War in the British and US university systems have often provided a doleful counterpoint to the institutional embrace of a neo-liberal culture that knows the price of everything and the value of nothing. That was once a world of 'dismal science' that Thomas Carlyle spurned with unalloyed contempt and that John Stuart Mill never defended, but nobody today is reading them either. The former is far too splenetic for contemporary tastes, the latter even more difficult to follow and much more tiresome than Marx. If the 'end of history' is agreeably and authoritatively proclaimed to be at your doorstep, why stoop needlessly to discover it for yourself? The proposition that history is – amongst other things – sexy, poetic and emancipatory is very hard to press home in a climate so distinct from that in which Gwyn Williams taught. The effort to advance such a case here is made not just through recourse to the natural mystery and drama of court cases but also by dealing with economics through an attention to textiles, clothing and fashion (and sometimes cuisine too). In the same vein, I have deliberately focused upon treason, betrayal and traitordom, which (like love and hate) are not well treated by the pertinent academic discipline, political science, where a tendency to champion measurement gets badly in the way of understanding core human activities.

Only the first of the court cases transcribed below was opened with a formal charge of treason, but all three involve manifold betrayal, and despite wide differences of legal culture all three rest centrally on the power of precision in the written and spoken word. As a lawyer, President Clinton knew this well enough when he decided upon an engagingly narrow interpretation of the term 'sexual relations' preliminary to the material ejaculation that would betray him forensically, require courtroom testing of his original semantics, and lead to impeachment. Chief Justice Chase, who in 1868 presided over the only other case of impeachment, may not have been in the Supreme Court to hear the appeal of Myra Clark in 1852, but his colleague Samuel Nelson was present, establishing (and then changing) doctrine by trying a case that depended crucially on the 'word of honour' of a man who escaped charges of treason against the USA by the skin of his Sligo-born teeth.

Very often the rule of law seems distinguishable from that of men only by dint of its fastidious pedantry and orotund over-confidence in procedure. But the translation, interpretation and judgement of human deeds – including those of speaking and writing – in that other world still provide the rest of us with as much comfort as tedium. For many – not just those who after 11 September 1973 would loathe him forever – the sight of Augusto Pinochet being taken as an arrested man into a court of law was a thoroughly fitting coda to the fall of the Berlin Wall, offering some balm for the memory of those who did not live to see either event. Pinochet, of course, dictated his own laws and appointed his own judges; a decade after the tyrant left office some of his men were still comfortably ensconced in the Chilean supreme court. Moreover, as the cases presented here amply demonstrate, the law can be an ass driven by querulous tossers. The rule of law is, then, a relative concept, and it is a huge mistake to believe that a fair hearing and fine judgement of complex cases is synonymous with the values and institutions of liberal democracy.

The language of the mid nineteenth century was not paced by telephones or television. Its distension, meandering parentheses and unhurried compilation of subordinate clauses may well strike a reader at the start of the twenty-first century as better fitted for the courts of law than even a marginally profane academic book. In fact, the world of bungos, dorys and revenue-cutters (small boats) proves to be close to our own in most of its vocabulary, but the combination of complex expression and strong opinion can be unnerving to the contemporary mind. Having spent four years in the company of such discourse, I may have presumed too much on the reader of today in emulating and quoting it at such length. Compare the compositional vanities at the start of this book with the way that the US lawyer–diplomatist Hinton Helper opened his memoirs, published in St Louis in 1879, with a 'single remark' directed to the reader:

> If by any possibility it be true, as, with a slight tinge of credibility, it was once reported, that there are certain people in this world – people not generally reckoned in the category of idiots – who sometimes read the body of a book before perusing even the title-page, the preface or any other pertinent prefixture, I have to request that no one of them, nor any one else, will ever presume to take such an unwarrantable liberty with this volume; as a perfect knowledge of its preliminaries, as indeed the preliminaries of every publication, is absolutely essential to a proper understanding of the subsequent portions.[1]

---

1. Hinton Helper, *Oddments of Andean Diplomacy*, St Louis, Mo., 1879, p. i.

Few authors could dissent from such an injunction. But, confident in the knowledge that nobody in the present epoch would be so precipitate in their treatment of the prefixtures, I give my assurance that the competition to this sentence up ahead repays initial patience and soon loses its challenge.

The idea of mixing idioms was encouraged by a concert given one lovely evening in the spring of 1995 by Elvis Costello and the Brodsky Quartet at the London Lighthouse. The combination of a rock voice and classical strings seemed at first simply adventurous, even awkward. However, it quickly became clear even to the untrained ear that this was not at all avant-garde but, rather, a deeply traditional balladeering, which the music of the industrial era has rendered alien and problematic. The form of dissonance encouraged one to think of different times and temporalities; it was a peculiarly moving experience to undergo in a home populated by young men expecting an early death from AIDS.

Aside from that, Costello – an Anglo-Irishman who has pinched a very famous American name and done well in spite of it – seemed to be making his point most effectively not by advertising it baldly but by coming at it from angles and by donning guises. He was certainly performing with a 'postmodern' palate of irony, difference, mobility, disconnection and deconstruction, but the message I clearly received was one about cogent human agency within coherent historical structure. There was no gap between the form of the musical narrative and its substance. Costello was not proclaiming, 'what I want to argue is…'. As the audience became enveloped he was actually arguing it.

The policeman who took me off the straight and narrow was Colonel Alberto Mariño, who had graduated as a detective in 1939 and whom I met in La Paz fifty years later. Mariño was living with his wife in conditions of some penury – in two rooms at the back of a ramshackle *casona* or tenement in the old centre of the city. I needed his advice because I had drawn a blank in an investigation on an unexplained drowning in Lake Titicaca that I had rather rashly agreed to undertake on behalf of a British woman. In a case that bears striking resemblance to the mysterious drowning of Montana Governor Thomas Francis Meagher in the Missouri eighty years before, in 1954 a man had supposedly fallen from the steamer *Inca*, which was moored at the small Bolivian port of Guaqui. The man, a Welsh-born employee of the Peruvian Corporation, had a grave in the Anglo-American cemetery at Pura Pura, but there was no record of the death in the archive of the British embassy, and none of the people who had known him was prepared to talk to his daughter. She asked for my assistance when, after several years of making enquiries, she was telephoned by a man claiming to be her father but refusing any further information. By contrast, everybody was very eager to help me – the stevedores at the docks to whom I showed the photograph of the missing man; the British ambassador, who regretfully denied that the man might have been working for the secret intelligence service; and Colonel Vizcarra, the current head of CID, who just as regretfully explained that there were no records prior to 1959, when the central police station was burnt out during an uprising by the Falange.

I found the link to Colonel Mariño when I checked the press reports and read that he was the detective who had taken charge of the case. Now, though, face-to-face, he assured me that there must be some mistake. He had heard about the case but had played no part in it himself. He had a good memory – Colonel Vizcarra had told me this too – and he had written a memoir of his best cases; the report was wrong. I explained the background and laid out, to the colonel's evident relish, the logical deductive and inductive lines of reasoning I had rehearsed in London with the daughter. 'But', he said, 'you're confusing honesty with the truth. That's the first thing a detective is taught to avoid.' Although he – like everybody else with whom I had discussed the case – was keen to get down to its bare bones with an exhumation, the colonel could not resist giving a lecture on how different narratives could move in and out of the material and spiritual worlds, pass each other in the night, dissolve in incomprehension and still yield a perfectly satisfactory result. 'Just don't think in straight lines all the time', he advised me, 'they never do.'

This admonition seemed a little odd coming from a retired policeman, until Mariño told me that his dearest friend had been Jaime Saenz, the writer of the remarkable odyssey *Felipe Delgado*, who in his life and his books strove to efface the presence of the author by conceding authority to others. This, he understood, was a task that could never be completed, but it was still important to cleave to that axiom of Columbus: 'It is essential to navigate; it is not essential to live.' The case of the man in the lake is, so far as I can tell, still open. Those in the text that follows lie – like the history in between them – in a deeper past and have been subjected to all sorts of opinion and judgements, but they too could usefully be seen as not yet quite closed.

Note

The exchange rate of the US dollar to the pound sterling in 1850 was 4.8 to one. I have used the modern term 'ambassador' freely to describe diplomatic representatives unless the distinction between minister, chargé d'affaires, plenipotentiary, special envoy, consul, agent or attaché is of importance.

Abbreviations

AHR	American Historical Review
BFSP	British and Foreign State Papers
BLAR	Bulletin of Latin American Research
HAHR	Hispanic American Historical Review
LARR	Latin American Research Review
JLAS	Journal of Latin American Studies
MECW	Marx–Engels Collected Works

A Little Time (and Space)

MARKING TIME

I decided ... to steal an atomic submarine, an affair, which, quite naturally, was hushed up by the press. I telephoned the commander of one of our atomic submarines at Brest, pretending to be the Minister of the Navy and telling him he had been given an important promotion. I also told him his successor would be arriving almost at once to take over. Indeed, someone wearing an officer's uniform did turn up, exchanged the appropriate documents with the former commander and took over the ship. The other officer then left. The new captain called the crew together and told them they were to have a week's special leave to celebrate the promotion of their former captain. This was greeted with cheers. Everyone left the ship except the cook, who nearly foiled the whole plan by claiming he was simmering a ratatouille. In the end, he too left the ship. I took off my borrowed cap and telephoned a gangster who wanted to get hold of a nuclear submarine.

I like to think that I was that cook on the sub, but I know that there must be plenty of contenders for the post. They would be composed of young intellectuals of the late 1960s and early 1970s who laboured under the influence of the author of this statement, the French radical philosopher Louis Althusser.[1] Awkward apprentices charged with menial tasks on the ship of state of 1968, we would not have wanted to abandon the ratatouille – even under the lure of furlough – before 'getting it right'.

For those attracted to the detail of the past, both in its own terms and for understanding the political present, Althusser offered a bleak challenge. He appeared to be saying that history could only be 'general' in nature and so properly expressed in an exclusively abstract or philosophical manner. Given the dreadful density of the language employed at that time by French radical philosophers, this was a most depressing prospect:

> There can ... be no question of relating the diversity of ... different temporalities to a single ideological base time, or of measuring their *dislocation* against the line of a single continuous reference time ... [thinking of] these dislocations as backwardnesses or forwardnesses *in time* ... it is only in the specific unity of the complex structure of the whole that we can think

---

1. *The Future Lasts a Long Time*, London 1993, pp. 348–9. The reverie was recounted by Althusser in 'The Facts', written in 1976, before he strangled his wife, although he had been mentally unwell for many years. In some ways it doesn't matter whether it derives from pottiness or playfulness, and, as Johan Huizinga suggests, one could readily understand this quotation within an ancient tradition: 'Sophistry, technically regarded as a form of expression, has all the associations with primitive play.... The sophism proper is closely related to the riddle. It is a fencer's trick.' *Homo Ludens*, London 1949, p. 148. I owe this reference to Santiago Fortín, who claims that the construction of his *Uqbar Entreambasaguas: Una Recopilación Semi-Sinóptica*, Tarata 1996, was based on 'very little physical sex; oceanic quantities of Colchagua merlot; continual re-readings of Gesualdo Bufalino's *Night's Lies*'; and an aural diet of Falla's *Atlántida*; *Here at Black Mesa Arizona* by Lunar Drive; and Little Axe's *The Wolf that House Built*. As for the present text, the reader might like to read the trials whilst comparing the *Irish Melodies* edited for Novello by Michael Balfe (born Dublin 1808) with the mazurkas of Louis Moreau Gottschalk (born New Orleans 1829) and Modesta Sanjinés Uriarte (born La Paz 1832). A 'bigger' piece of music, composed in 1850, Schumann's Cello Concerto in A minor, might serve as a general backdrop.

the concept of these backwardnesses, forwardnesses, survivals of development which *co-exist* in the structure of the real historical present: the present of the *conjuncture*.

Even worse than this, though, was the repeated charge of 'empiricism' laid by Althusser and his followers against any academic work which engaged substantively with the past:

> We must take seriously the fact that the theory of history, in the strong sense, does not exist, or hardly exists as far as historians are concerned; that the concepts of existing history are therefore nearly always 'empirical' concepts … that is, cross-bred with a powerful strain of ideology behind [their] 'obviousness'. This is the case with the best historians, who can be distinguished from the rest precisely by their concern for theory, but who seek this theory at a level on which it cannot be found, at the level of historical *methodology*.[2]

However, Perry Anderson has made a particularly telling criticism of Althusser's strictures over time:

> Time as *chronology* is a single homogeneous continuum. There is nothing in the least 'ideological' about this concept of temporality, which forms the scientific object of such institutions as the Greenwich Observatory. Time as *development* is differential, heteroclite, discontinuous. The two senses of the word are engraved in every-day language as, approximately, 'clock-time' and 'musical time'.[3]

A rather different but popular variant of this approach has more recently been given by Stephen Jay Gould:

> At one end of the dichotomy – I shall call it time's arrow – history is an irreversible sequence of unrepeatable events. Each moment occupies its own distinct position in a temporal series, and all moments, considered in a proper sequence, tell a story of linked events moving in a direction. At the other end – I shall call it time's cycle – events have no meaning as distinct episodes with causal impact upon a contingent history. Fundamental states are immanent in time, always present and never changing. Apparent motions are parts of repeating cycles, and differences of the past will be realities of the future. Time has no direction.[4]

According to Cornelius Castoriadis, time as a social construction is as much a conundrum as it is a dichotomy:

> Every society exists by instituting the world as its world, or its world as the world, and by instituting itself as part of this world. In this institution, of the world and of society by society, the institution of time is always an essential component. But do we know why time is instituted as separate from space as well as … from *what* is produced in it? The man of commonsense shrugs his shoulders at this philosophical hairsplitting: *there is* time, humans see themselves grow, change, die; they observe the sun and the stars as they rise and set, and so on. We know this as well as he does. But why is it, then, that these indubitable humans have posited and represented to themselves throughout the course of history in such indubitably different manners what so indubitably 'there is'?[5]

---

2. *Reading Capital*, London 1970, pp. 104, 106, 110.
3. *Arguments within English Marxism*, London 1980, p. 75.
4. *Time's Arrow, Time's Cycle: Myth and Metaphor in the Discovery of Geological Time*, Harmondsworth 1988, pp. 10–11.
5. *The Imaginary Institution of Society*, Oxford 1997, pp. 186–7.

Of course, the notion that there are many different times and different concepts of time is old hat for anthropologists, whose object – 'the other' – is often most vividly depicted in these terms.[6] Moreover, narrow precision and broad approximation are not very useful poles for different systems of measurement and behaviour. At the start of this century the playwright J.M. Synge reported of his visit to the Aran Islands off the west of Ireland,

> When I was walking with Michael someone often came up to me to ask the time of day. Few of the people, however, are sufficiently used to modern time to understand in more than a vague way the convention of the hours, and when I tell them what o'clock it is by my watch they are not satisfied, and ask how long is left before the twilight.[7]

There is something of a logical flaw in this statement, and one wonders why the islanders were unable to deduce the answer from the conditions about them, however it was expressed. Perhaps they wanted an excuse to peep at Synge's watch?

Yet a thousand years earlier in central Mesoamerica (present-day Mexico, Guatemala and Belize) a no less rural and 'natural' society had elaborated an extremely complex system out of the 'dawn of life', which, according to Nancy Farris, manifested

> an intense interest, bordering on obsession, in measuring and recording the passage of time … among the best-known representations of cyclical time … is the *katun* round … an endlessly recurring sequence of thirteen twenty-year periods, called *katuns* (the Maya plural is *katunob*), each with its designation and characteristic events. Thus, the *katun* round serves as both history and prophecy, a guide to the future as well as a record of the past. The same pattern of events discernable for *katun* '10 Ahau' will be repeated each time that the 260-year cycle is completed and 10 Ahau comes round again. The equivalent concept in our own calendrical system would associate, say, drought within the decade of the 90s in each century and expect that droughts will occur in the 1990s, and the 2090s, as they did in the 1690s, the 1790s, and so on.… Yet there is also evidence that the Maya were perfectly capable of sorting out chronology.… They combine genealogies with historical narratives of conquest, migrations, and accessions to power, all in sequential order.… The coexistence of linear and cyclical conceptions of time and the past is by no means confined to the Maya and may well be the norm. What needs explaining is *how* they coexist.[8]

At the turn of the twenty-first century there are millions of Maya for whom this interaction is still very conscious, aided by 'daykeepers', who 'know how to interpret illnesses, omens, dreams, messages given by sensations internal to their own bodies, and the multiple rhythms of time'.[9] But these societies are increasingly driven by one of those rhythms – the tighter 'clock time' that Norbert Elias calls 'tempo' and sees as lying at the heart of the 'civilising process':

---

6. Alfred Gell, *The Anthropology of Time: Cultural Constructions of Temporal Maps and Images*, Oxford 1992; Johannes Fabian, *Time and the Other: How Anthropology Makes its Object*, New York 1983.

7. *Collected Plays and Poems and The Aran Islands*, London 1992, p. 271.

8. 'Remembering the Future, Anticipating the Past', in Diane Hughes and Thomas Trautman (eds), *Time: Histories and Ethnologies*, Ann Arbor 1995, pp. 110–11.

9. Dennis Tedlock (ed.), *Popol Vuh*, New York 1985, p. 13. For a full discussion, see Enrique Florescano, *Memory, Myth and Time in Mexico*, Austin, Tex. 1994.

This 'tempo' is ... nothing other than the manifestation of the multitude of intertwining chains of interdependence which run through every single social function people have to perform, and of the competitive pressure permeating this densely populated network ... a function situated at a junction of so many chains of action demands an exact allocation of time: it makes people accustomed to subordinating momentary inclinations to the over-riding necessities of interdependence; it trains them to eliminate all irregularities from behaviour and to achieve permanent self-control.[10]

Perhaps. That, at least, is the tendency. But it is still manifested most unevenly, and Americans of Hispanic as well as Mayan descent are frequently depicted as being at variance with it because, '[they] do not regulate their lives by the clock as Anglos do. Both rural and urban people, when asked when they plan to do something, give answers like: 'Right now, about 2 or 4 o'clock.'[11]

This is not to say, of course, that clocks were not part of the Central American landscape in the mid nineteenth century. In 1849 the new US ambassador to Nicaragua, Ephraim George Squier, reported of the last Franciscan friar in the town of León,

The Padre Cartine is a learned man, in the continental acceptation of the term two centuries ago. That is to say, he reads Latin and the Fathers, and is familiar with the Natural History of Pliny – the latest book on the subject which which he is acquainted, and which is his sole authority. The Padre is withal a mathematician, has a Latin edition of Euclid, and reads it once a year by way of amusement, and to refresh his memory.... The furniture of the house was plain and simple, and, I believe, all of the Padre's own manufacture. Upon a low bench extending around two sides of the room was the most incongruous assortment of clocks, of every date, pattern and country, from a tall cupboard contrivance of the last century, dingy with age, to a little German or French concern, which ticked spitefully from the opposite wall. There were cases without clocks, and clocks without cases; besides a wilderness of weights, cords, pulleys, wheels and springs; for the Padre was so passionately fond of clocks that he not only kept an extensive variety of his own to tinker, but borrowed all of his neighbours', and encouraged the distant visitors to bring him theirs for gratuitous cleansing and repair.... The Padre observed that they attracted my attention, and com-menced a philosophical lecture on horology, which I hastily brought to a close by suggesting a walk through the old convent.[12]

Forty years later, the great poet from León, Rubén Darío, left his homeland for the first time, and, arriving in Chile, found himself overawed by the sheer size and modernity of the place, but when Squier was writing there was much greater similarity between the two societies. Santiago could boast a handful of clocksmiths, yet once the sun set, its tempo as well as its security (always important in Chile) lay in the voices of the *serenos* (nightwatchmen), whom the regulations required to report to barracks by sunset and to be at their posts by the start of vespers. In the 1820s they had cried the time every fifteen minutes, but by the 1840s they stuck to the top of

---

10. *The Civilizing Process*, Oxford 1994, p. 457. I am using this quotation to make a point rather than to paraphrase Elias, whose *Time: An Essay*, Oxford 1992, is amongst the best writing on this subject.

11. Julian Pitt-Rivers (ed.), *Mediterranean Countrymen*, Paris 1963, p. 179.

12. E.G. Squier, *Nicaragua: Its People, Scenery, Monuments*, New York 1860, pp. 358–9.

the hour: 'Eight o'clock and raining.' For the British visitor Maria Graham this had been a delightful anachronism in the 1820s, and according to Vicente Pérez Rosales, looking back on the 1840s after a long life transformed by his experience in the Gold Rush, the *serenos* had become almost mythical by the standards of Chile itself:

> [N]obody has ever been able to discover if the origins of their name derived from the tranquillity of a clear night or, perhaps, from the calm with which they endured the downpours on stormy nights. It was their essential duty to frighten the devil, act as a clock and serve as a mobile barometer.... One day a large crowd of boys and onlookers rushed into my parents' house carrying a tray on which there was a mysterious object hidden beneath an ancient napkin. What could it be? Why did the good matrons of the neighbourhood hurry in with such excitement? It was nothing other than the boot of the devil in shape and spirit, with worn-down nails, a collapsed heel and a strong smell of sulphur! The paper of the time said that the previous night, ... the devil, crossing the Plaza de la Compañía on horseback ... was so startled by the inspired 'Ave María' shouted by the *sereno* on the hour that he had flown off, lost his stirrup, and amidst curses, his boot had fallen into the street below.[13]

What we might call 'hurried clock-time' is a relatively recent development. On an international level it was effectively put in place by the Washington International Meridian Conference of 1884. For the previous fifty years there had been only a gradual adherence to Greenwich Mean Time by British towns, obliging the railways to adopt an integrated timetable according to their own uniform hour, which often differed from that of the towns through which the tracks ran; many trains were missed. At the end of 1847 Ralph Waldo Emerson, on a lecture tour of England, wrote from Manchester to Henry David Thoreau (who had just completed his two-year retreat to nature on Walden Pond and was re-engaging with 'civilisation' by helping Emerson's wife run their large house at Concord):

> Yesterday the *time* all over the kingdon was reduced to Greenwich time. At Liverpool, where I was, the clocks were put forward twelve minutes. This had become quite necessary on account of the railroads which bind the country into swiftest connexion, and require so much interlocking, intersection, and simultaneous arrival, that the difference of time produced confusion. Every man in England carries a little book in his pocket called 'Bradshaw's Guide', which contains timetables of every arrival and departure at every station on all the railroads of the kingdom. It is published anew on the first day of each month and costs sixpence.[14]

It is, though, one thing to ordain social change and quite another to ensure that it comes into effect. Eleven years later, differential clock-time was still to be encountered, and sometimes it produced interesting consequences for the law, as in the case of *Curtis* v. *March* at Dorchester Assizes, on 25 November 1858, when

---

13. *Recuerdos del Pasado*, quoted in René Peri Fagerstrom, *Historia de la función policial en Chile: apuntes y transcripciones*, n.p. 1982, p. 45. Twenty years earlier Maria Graham wrote: 'It was so long since I had heard a watchman that I could scarcely believe my ears when the sound of "Ave purissima las onzes de la noche y sereno" reached me as I was undressing.' *Journal of a Residence in Chile* (1824), New York 1969, p. 200.

14. Emerson, Manchester, to Thoreau, 2 Dec. 1847, in Eleanor Tilton (ed.), *The Letters of Ralph Waldo Emerson: VIII. 1845–1859*, New York 1991, p. 136.

the judge took his seat at 10 a.m. by the clock in the court, but as neither the defendant nor his lawyer were present he found for the plaintiff. The defendant's counsel then entered the court and claimed to have the case tried on the grounds that it had been disposed of before 10 o'clock by the town clock, whereas the clock in the court was regulated by Greenwich time, which was some minutes before the time in Dorchester. On appeal, the assize judge's decision was reversed, on the ground that '10 o'clock' is 10 o'clock according to the time of the place.[15]

Thoreau would surely not have been impressed by either of these examples. For him,

> It matters not what the clocks say or the attitudes or labours of men. Morning is when I am awake and there is dawn in me.... Time is but the stream I go a-fishing in. I drink at it, but while I drink I see the sandy bottom and detect how shallow it is. Its thin current slides away, but eternity remains.[16]

Furthermore, of all the manifestations of material 'progress' against which Thoreau was warning, the 'iron horse' of the Fitchburg Railroad, which passed along one side of Walden Pond, was probably second only to unreflective social compliance with mental and physical acceleration as a target of Thoreau's invective. It is telling that he illustrates the poverty of political economy with a defence of walking (a form of recreation that today must be more ignored and scorned in the USA than in any other country on earth) against rail travel:

> One [man] says to me, 'I wonder that you do not lay up money; you love to travel; you might take the cars and go to Fitchburg today and see the country.' But I am wiser than that. I have learned that the swiftest traveller is he who goes a-foot. I say to my friend, Suppose we try who will get there first. The distance is thirty miles; the fare ninety cents. That is almost a day's wages. I remember when wages were sixty cents a-day for labourers on this very road. Well, I start now on foot, and get there before night; I have travelled at that rate by the week altogether. You will in the meanwhile have earned your fare, and arrive there some time tomorrow, or possibly this evening, if you are lucky enough to get a job in season. Instead of going to Fitchburg, you will be working here the greater part of the day. And so, if the railroad reached around the world, I think that I should keep ahead of you; and as for seeing the country and getting experience of that kind, I should have to cut your acquaintance altogether.'[17]

Walt Whitman, by contrast, embraced the present and enunciated all its ambivalent gifts with characteristic gusto:

> Endless unfolding of words of ages!
> And mine a word of the modern, the word En-Masse.
> A word of the faith that never balks,
> Here or henceforward it is all the same to me. I accept Time
>   absolutely.

---

15. Derek Howse, *Greenwich Time and the Discovery of Longitude*, Oxford 1980, pp. 113–14, quoted in G.J. Whitrow, *Time in History*, Oxford 1988, pp. 164–5.
16. *Walden, or Life in the Woods* (1854), London 1992, pp. 80, 87.
17. Ibid., pp. 46–7.

It alone is without flaw, it alone rounds and completes all,
That mystic baffling wonder alone completes all.

I accept Reality and dare not question it.
Materialism first and last imbuing.[18]

Different attitudes to time within any society are naturally of considerable consequence to law and order. Writing in 1821, when there was no railway but a rapidly expanding factory system that demanded disciplined labour, John Foster bemoaned the proclivities of the English poor:

Several hours in the day to be spent nearly as they please. And in what manner ... is this precious time expended by those of no mental cultivation? ... We shall often see them just simply annihilating those portions of time. They will for an hour, or for hours together ... sit on a bench, or lie down on a bank or hillock ... yielded up to their vacancy and torpor ... or collected in groups by the roadside in readiness to find whatever passes there occasions for gross jocularity; practising some impertinence, or uttering some jeering scurrility at the expense of the persons going by.[19]

On the other side of the Atlantic, the introduction of artificial light in the 1840s challenged 'natural' customs of work, provoking workers in Peterboro, New Hampshire, to issue a resolution in October 1844:

...that although the evening and the morning is spoken of in Scripture ... no mention is made of an evening in the morning. We therefore conclude that the practice of lighting up in the morning and thereby making two evenings in every 24 hours is not only oppressive but unscriptural.[20]

There is, of course, always risk and contest in interpreting the scriptures, but few were quite as precise as the New England ex-soldier and farmer William Miller, who, reading the Book of Daniel in his King James Bible with chronological annotations by Archbishop Ussher of Armagh, calculated 'that in about 25 years from that time [1818] all the affairs of our present state would be wound up'. Miller's approach was all clean lines: he accepted Ussher's date of 457 BC for the warning of the Archangel Gabriel to Daniel, and converted into years the 'days' left to his people 'to finish the transgression and make an end of sins'.[21] The answer was 2,300 years, but the rather bigger question was when did this period begin?

---

18. From 'Song of Myself', in *Leaves of Grass* (1855), London 1993, p. 46.

19. John Foster, *An Essay on the Evils of Popular Ignorance*, London 1821, pp. 180–85, quoted in E.P. Thompson, 'Time, Work Discipline, and Industrial Capitalism', *Past and Present*, 38, 1967, p. 90.

20. Quoted in David Roediger and Philip Foner, *Our Own Time: A History of American Labor and the Working Day*, New York 1989, p. 51.

21. Daniel 8:14 reads,

And he said unto me, Unto two thousand and three hundred days; then shall the sanctuary be cleansed.

The complete verse 24 of chapter 9 reads:

Seventy weeks are determined upon thy people and upon thy holy city, to finish the transgression, and to make an end of sins, and to make reconciliation for iniquity, and to bring in everlasting righteousness, and to seal up the vision and prophecy, and to annoint the most Holy.

Did it begin with Nebuchadnezzar's dream? No. For if it had, it must have been fulfilled in the Year AD 1697. Well, then, did it begin when the Angel Gabriel came to instruct Daniel into the seventy weeks? No, for if then, it would have been finished in the Year AD 1762. Let us begin it where the Angel told us, from the going forth of the decree to build the walls of Jerusalem in the troublous times, 457 years before Christ. Take 457 from 2,300, and it will leave 1843; or take seventy weeks of years, being 490 years, from 2,300 years, and it will leave 1810 after Christ's death. Add his life (because we begin to reckon our time at his birth), which is 33 years, and we come to the same AD 1843.[22]

There is scant room for slippage in calculus of this type, and although on 2 March 1843 Horace Greeley's *New York Tribune* issued a special second edition refuting Miller's mathematics, an appreciable movement had built up behind his homespun eschatology. It only collapsed once the (recalculated and postponed) end failed to arrive on 22 October 1844. For believers this was the 'Great Disappointment', a word used by Miller in its strict, literal sense: 'although I have been twice disappointed, I am not yet cast down or discouraged.... God has been with me in spirit, and has comforted me. ... My mind is perfectly calm, and my hope in the coming of Christ is as strong as ever.'[23]

None the less, one suspects that for the Peterboro workers such 'disappointment' occasioned appreciable relief and maybe even some reassessment of the merits of biblical bargaining in industrial relations.

The relationship between industrial development and the public institutionalisation of time did not always run on straight lines. Late in 1857 the municipal council of Ambato in Ecuador argued strongly against the holding of a market on a weekday rather than a Sunday:

It is an incontrovertible principle ... that the days on which one cannot work cause a loss in public wealth.... The [Sunday] market means that we can use all the six useful days of the week.... Transferring the market to an ordinary day, the artisan would have only five working days left, one of the remaining days being used for the sale of his products, and the other [Sunday] being given over to vice and complete idleness.... If Sunday commerce was prohibited ... not even a tenth of the population would attend mass.[24]

Four years earlier, in arguing energetically for the Ten Hour Act in the British parliament, Lord Macaulay had placed a quite different interpretation on the usefulness of Sunday:

That day is not lost. While industry is suspended, while the plough lies in the furrow, while the Exchange is silent, while no smoke ascends from the factory, a process is going on quite as important to the wealth of nations as any process which is performed on more busy days. Man, the machine of machines, the machine with which all the contrivances of the Watts

22. William Miller, *Evidence from Scripture and History of the Second Coming of Christ about the Year 1843*, Boston 1841, p. 54, quoted in Edwin Gaustad (ed.), *A Documentary History of Religion in America to the Civil War*, Grand Rapids, Mich. 1993, p. 374.

23. Miller to Himes, 10 Nov. 1844, in S. Bliss, *Memoirs of William Miller*, Boston 1853, p. 277.

24. Quoted in Rosemary and R.J. Bromley, 'The Debate on Sunday Markets in Nineteenth-Century Ecuador', *JLAS*, 7:1, 1975, p. 98.

and the Arkwrights are useless, is repairing and winding up, so that he returns to his labours on the Monday with clearer intellect, with livelier spirits, with renewed corporal vigour.[25]

Such logic was even applicable to slave labour, where some time had to be made 'free' simply to restore the physical capacity of workers in bondage. It was, however, even more vital to get slaves working according to the movement of the clock. One slaveholder from Alabama reported in 1852 that his slaves were obliged to

> rise in time to be at their labours by light. Their breakfast hour is eight o'clock ... which requires fifteen minutes.... In the winter they have one hour, and summer three, to rest, in the heat of the day.... I require them to retire at nine o'clock precisely. The foreman calls the roll at that hour, and two or three times during the night, to see that all are at their places.[26]

By the end of the US Civil War over two-thirds of white Southern heads of family owned a clock or watch or both, but Mark Smith argues persuasively that the response of the slaves who were freed by that war was 'not ... a time discipline, but ... something that may be termed time-obedience', which, unlike time-discipline, 'was not internalized, but was rather enforced by time-conscious planters'.[27] There is an academic debate over the degree to which slaves internalised the values of their owners, but there is little disagreement over the fact that those owners placed a considerable store on time, at least with regard to the labour of their personal property. In the early 1850s Frederick Law Olmsted recounted meeting in Alabama a planter who,

> having been from home for six weeks, his impatience to return was very great, and was constantly aggravated by the frequent and long-continued stoppages of the boat. 'Time's money, time's money!' he would constantly be saying, while we were taking on bales of cotton – 'time's worth more'n money to me now; a hundred per cent more 'cause I left my niggers all alone; not a dam white man within four mile on 'em ... I set them to clairin', but they aint doin' a dam thing – not a dam thing, they aint; that's wut they are doin', that is – not a dam thing. I know that as well as you do. That's the reason time's an object. I told the capting so when I cam aboard; says I, "Capting", says I, "time is the objective case with me." No, sir, they aint doin' a dam solitary thing; that's wut they are up to.... But I'll make it up when I get thar, now you'd better believe.'[28]

Perhaps it is stretching a point to note that Herman Melville – who was discharged from the US navy on 14 October 1844, one week before the world was due to end – begins the modernist subversion of his own 'novel' *Pierre* with a second-hand lecture on chronology that has as its core an international, millennial alienation:

25. G.O. Trevelyan, *The Life and Letters of Lord Macaulay*, London 1876, II, pp. 119–20.

26. *De Bow's Review*, XIII, 1852, pp. 193–4, quoted in Mark M. Smith, 'Time, Slavery and Plantation Capitalism in the Ante-Bellum American South', *Past and Present*, 150, 1996, p. 152.

27. Smith, 'Time, Slavery and Plantation Capitalism', p. 145.

28. *The Cotton Kingdom* (1853–54), New York 1953, pp. 216–17.

Now in an artifical world like ours, the soul of man is further removed from its God and the Heavenly Truth, than the chronometer carried to China is from Greenwich. And, as that chronometer, if at all accurate, will pronounce it to be twelve o'clock high-noon, when China local watches say, perhaps, it is twelve o'clock midnight, so the chronological soul, if in this world true to its great Greenwich in the other, will always in its so-called intuitions of right and wrong, be contradicting the mere local standards and watchmakers' brains of this earth.

Bacon's brains were mere watch-maker's brains; but Christ was a chronometer; and the most exquisitely adjusted and exact one, and the least affected by all terrestrial jarrings, of any that have ever come to us. And the reason why his teachings seemed folly to the Jews was because he carried that Heaven's time in Jerusalem, while the Jews carried Jerusalem time there. Did he not expressly say – My wisdom (time) is not of this world? But whatever is really peculiar in the wisdom of Christ seems precisely the same folly today as it did 1850 years ago. Because, in all that interval his bequeathed chronometer has still preserved his original Heaven's time, and the general Jerusalem of this world has likewise preserved its own.[29]

As Melville was on his way to his masterpiece (albeit one the public of his day strenuously resisted recognising), James Fenimore Cooper was well aware that, with *The Last of the Mohicans* published twenty years earlier, his moment had passed. In 1846 he wrote to Charles Gayarré,

My time ... is nearly done. At 57 the world is not apt to believe a man can write fiction, and I have long seen that the country is already tired of me. Novelties are puissant in this country, and new names take the place of old ones so rapidly that one scarcely learns to distinguish who are in favor before a successor is pointed out.[30]

Although the main theme of Cooper's final book, *The Ways of the Hour*, published in 1850, is the manipulation of juries, beneath its rather mannered murder mystery there courses this motif of time expressed as the tyranny of fashion.

In a recent, densely difficult but rich book, Peter Osborne seeks a theoretical reconciliation between two other broad strands of 'time-watching'.[31] The first draws its central features from the human life cycle and existential experience, which is best exemplified in philosophical terms by the work of Martin Heidegger, but in this context might better be rendered in verse, by Heinrich Heine, who was confined by illness to his bed – his 'mattress-grave' – from 1848 until death came in February 1856:

Hours, days, eternities – they glide by like snails;
these huge grey snails stick their horns out far.
Sometimes in the desolate emptiness, sometimes
in the sea of mists, a light gleams,
sweet and golden like the eyes of my dear one.
But in the same instant this joy turns to dust.[32]

29. Herman Melville, *Pierre or The Ambiguities* (1852), Harmondsworth 1996, pp. 211–12.

30. Cooper, Cooperstown, to Gayarré, 14 Dec. 1846, in *Letters and Journals of James Fenimore Cooper*, Cambridge, Mass. 1968, V, p. 178.

31. *The Politics of Time: Modernity and the Avant-Garde*, London 1995, pp. xi–xii.

32. 'Aus der Matratzengruft' (1853–54), in *Selected Verse*, trans. Peter Branscombe, Harmondsworth 1968, pp. 235–6.

On this there could be no better comment than that made by the Argentine writer Jorge Luis Borges in his poem 'Paris 1856':

> A long prostration has addicted him
> To presuming on death; he would not dare
> Enter the chattering daylight now
> And venture among men. Broken, unhinged,
> Heinrich Heine thinks of that slow river
> Time, which ferries him across the long
> Dimness and which divides him from
> The painful fate of being a man,
> A Jew. He thinks of the fragile songs
> Whose instrument he was, although he knows
> The tune is not the tree's, not the bird's –
> The tune is time's and comes from his pale days.
>   They cannot save you, your larks, your doves,
>   Nor all your golden knights and famous flowers.[33]

The second approach considered by Osborne endeavours to account for temporalisation through cultural form and finds its most accomplished expression in the writing of Walter Benjamin. In his preface Osborne defends the idea of historical totalisation and so necessarily identifies chronology as 'historicism'. He agrees with many of the criticisms made of Althusser both by Anderson and by Paul Ricoeur, but one wonders if, following Althusser, he is not instinctively taking chronology as a finale rather than as a starting-point.[34] The following passage from Ricoeur, it seems to me, both fortifies Osborne's argument and yet need not disturb those narrators or chronologists who want to stick to their stories:

> On the one hand, the epistemology of narrative, whether it considers narrative in the sense of history-writing or of story-telling, scarcely questions the concept of time which is implicit in narrative activity. It takes for granted that narratives occur *in* time, i.e., within a given temporal framework, and it uncritically identifies this given temporal framework with the ordinary representation of time as a linear succession of abstract 'nows'. On the other hand, the phenomenology of time-experience usually overlooks the fact that narrative activity, in history and in fiction, provides a privileged access to the way we articulate our experience of time.... [My] main thesis ... will be that ... narrativity is the mode of discourse through which the mode of being which we call temporality, or temporal being, is brought to language.[35]

---

33. Translated by Richard Howard and César Rennert in *Selected Poems*, Harmondsworth 1971, p. 195.
34. Osborne, *Politics of Time*, pp. xi–xii.
35. 'The Human Experience of Narrative', in Mario Valdés (ed.), *A Ricoeur Reader: Reflection and Imagination*, Hemel Hempstead 1991, p. 99. In his analysis of Althusser Ricoeur stresses the similarities between Althusser's conception of ideology as non-historical (because it is omni-historical) and Freud's understanding of the unconscious as timeless (*zeitlos*) because it is prior to any temporal order or connections as a consequence of being prior to the level of language. Paul Ricoeur, 'Althusser's Theory of Ideology', in Gregory Elliott (ed.), *Althusser: A Critical Reader*, Oxford 1994, p. 60.

It may, though, simply be that theorists need to see empirical work as a loitering with intent to the grievous bodily harm that is empiricism. Whatever the case, it requires the particularly restless loitering of a Gwyn Williams to write a book which asks *When was Wales?* as its introit and closes three hundred pages later, empirically and dynamically, with the proposition that

> Wales has always been now. The Welsh as a people have lived by making and remaking themselves in generation after generation, usually against the odds, usually within a British context. Wales is an artefact which the Welsh produce. If they want to. It requires an act of choice.[36]

CHRONOLOGIES

The present text has chronology unashamedly at its starting-point, taking the years 1845 to 1855 as its framework. The oddity of choosing eleven years can only be explained by the banal belief that this order of numbers is more expressive of a decade than is the accurate formulation '1845–54' (which would also provide greater visual symmetry). Such a whim is, none the less, probably understandable and tolerable at the start of a new millennium – its dawning inevitably celebrated at midnight on 31 December 1999 (rather than at that time in 2000 or 2032) and in a society where the phenomenology of cyberspace is happily reconciled with a creation myth derived from the execution of a young Middle-Eastern story-teller.

As should be clear from some of the examples already given, even the chronological framework adopted here is not rigid or binding. If history is indeed lived forwards and read backwards, then events in the 1840s may form part of processes of the 1820s or of the 1860s as well as being 'now'. Each of the three trials presented here demonstrates the importance of such a reach, suggesting that the mid-century slot is simply an excuse for looking at the whole. This, though, is not my aim, and I hope to make something of the very ordinary proposition that these years were not only like all others in which humans live, love and die (and so leave some good stories) but can also be seen as distinctive in themselves and in relation to the 'conjuncture' of today. They were certainly associated by Louis Althusser himself more with rupture than with continuity. In a rare foray into the treatment of substantive and specific history, he once devoted much energy to the proposition that these years saw the transformation of Karl Marx from a radical humanist into a rigorous scientist of society. For Althusser Marx's work underwent an 'epistemological break' in 1845, and

---

36. Gwyn A. Williams, *When was Wales?*, Harmondsworth 1985, p. 304.

although it was not until 1857 – with the writing of the *Grundrisse* (*Outlines of a Critique of Political Economy*) – that Marx's work became fully mature in Althusser's view, he is more than willing to identify a 'moment' in which something happened.[37]

Gwyn Williams arrives at a not dissimilar conclusion by a different route, locating Marx's shift in 1850 through the experience of accounting for the failure of the 1848 revolution in France and that of studying economics in London. Williams, who follows David Fernbach's close reading of Marx's *Class Struggles in France*, identifies a clear break, forced by political events, between the first three chapters, written between January and March 1850, and the short chapter 4, which appeared in November of that year. The summer had been spent in the British Museum studying economics, and the style changes abruptly after p. 122 from a racing local narrative ('March 10 1850 bears the inscription: *"Après moi le deluge"'*) to a cool, structuralist appraisal of macroeconomics that moves from Paris to Mexico and the Gold Rush (p. 123).[38]

It is tempting to read into this 'rupture' some resonance of the diametrically opposed 'leap of faith' espoused by the Danish thinker Søren Kierkegaard, who was five years older than Marx and whose 1849 book *The Sickness unto Death* propounded transcendental acknowledgement of death as the discovery of authentic life:

> in human terms death is the last thing of all, and in human terms hope exists only so long as there is life; but to Christian eyes death is by no means the last thing of all ... there is in death infinitely more hope than in ... not merely life itself but life at its height of health and vigour ... the sickness unto death is despair.[39]

Nearly a century later Heidegger was able to detach this 'recognition' from the Christian idiom within which Kierkegaard had presented it, and Freud (who was born a year after Kierkegaard died) could reiterate the Reality Principle by echoing it in classical form: '*Si vis pacem, para mortem.* If you want to endure life prepare yourself for death.'[40] Althusser, who borrowed heavily from Freud and who in his final years expressed enthusiasm for Heidegger, would surely have engaged with that epigram: 'Freud has discovered for us that the real subject, the individual in his unique essence,

---

37. In the introduction to *For Marx* Althusser outlined the following classification of Marx's writings:

   1840–44:   the early works
   1845:   the works of the break
   1845–57:   the transitional works
   1857–83:   the mature works

The break, which, according to Althusser, began with the *Theses on Feuerbach*, 'divides Marx's thought into two long essential periods: the "ideological" period before, and the scientific period after', and it is based on Marx's 'founding the theory of history', most notably in *The German Ideology*. *For Marx*, London 1969, pp. 33–5.

38. The page references are to the English edition published in Moscow in 1972. Gwyn A. Williams, 'Interpretations of the French Revolution: Karl Marx and Alexis de Tocqueville', in *France 1848–1851*, Milton Keynes 1976, pp. 110–13. David Fernbach (ed.), *Marx: The Revolutions of 1848*, Harmondsworth 1973, introduction.

39. *The Sickness unto Death* (1849), Harmondsworth 1989, pp. 37–8, 41.

40. 'Thoughts for the Times on War and Death' (1915), in Sigmund Freud, *Civilization, Society and Religion*, Harmondsworth 1985, p. 89.

has not the form of an ego, centred on the "ego", or "consciousness" or an "existence" ... that the human subject is decentred.'[41]

In all events, contemporary recognition of Kierkegaard as a precursor of existentialism is matched by his adoption by proponents of postmodernism, perhaps the most fashionable style today because it contains both a recognition and a repudiation of chronology – an imperfect ideology in both its tense and its lack of ambition.[42]

Today the combined image of a rehabilitated Kierkegaard – who died at the age of forty-two, as much from unpopularity as from overwork – and an abandoned Marx helps to underscore Althusser's notion of conjuncture in a more directly political sense.[43] A comparison of *The Sickness unto Death* with the *Communist Manifesto*, written the previous year, demonstrates why these authors had little to say about each other although, of course, Marx and Engels open their tract with a spectre 'haunting Europe', and it is worth recalling that on one occasion – in the 1844 Manuscripts – Marx did address the subject of death directly:

> *Death* appears as the harsh victory of the species over the *particular* individual, and it seems to contradict their unity; but the particular individual is only one *determinate species being*, and as such mortal.

This is part of an early argument that a human being is, and cannot but be, a social being – an argument that, despite its ungainly formulation, was never dropped, is now part of the mainstream, and validates two entwined types of temporality.[44]

---

41. Louis Althusser, *Lenin and Philosophy*, London 1971, pp. 200–201. Jacques Derrida reports of Althusser: 'how many times did he say to me during the last years in hospital: "Listen, you've got to talk to me about Heidegger. You've got to teach me Heidegger"?', 'Politics and Friendship: An Interview with Jacques Derrida', in E. Ann Kaplan and Michael Sprinker (eds), *The Althusserian Legacy*, London 1993, p. 190.

42. M.J. Matustick and Merold Westphal (eds), *Kierkegaard in Post/Modernity*, Bloomington, Ind., 1995.

43. The glossary prepared by Ben Brewster for both *Reading Capital* and *For Marx* defines conjuncture thus: 'The central concept of the Marxist science of politics (cf. Lenin's "current moment"); it denotes the exact balance of forces, state of overdetermination of the contradictions at any given moment to which political tactics must be applied.' Althusser took the term 'overdetermination' from Freud and used it intensively, not to signify displacement of psychic energy but, rather, to indicate the reflection of a contradiction within a complex unity of contradictions. Kierkegaard, for his part, by no means inhabited the religious sphere as exclusively as some contemporary literature infers. A few days before his death he told his friend Emil Boesen, 'The doctors don't understand my illness. It is psychological. Now they want to treat it in the usual physicians' manner. It is bad – pray for me that it is soon over.' *Papers and Journals: A Selection*, Harmondsworth 1996, p. 652.

44. *Marx–Engels Gesamtausgabe*, 1st edn, Frankfurt 1927–, vol. 2, part 1, p. 392:

> Der *Tod* erscheint als ein harter Sieg der Gattung über das *bestimmte* Individuum und ihrer Einheit zu widersprechen; aber das bestimmte Individuum ist nur ein *bestimmtes Gattungswesen*, als solches sterblich.

This translation draws on that in *Karl Marx: Early Writings*, ed. Lucio Coletti, Harmondsworth 1975, p. 351, and one done anew on my behalf by Harry Lubasz, who also supplied the following explanation, adding, 'whether the equation "species" = "society" holds up under closer scrutiny is a fair question'. Dr Lubasz kindly undertook this task for me because I was – and remain – bemused by Kenneth Minogue's view that in this passage Marx 'tells us ... death is merely a "biological event"... There would thus seem to be no real value in a particular human individual.' 'Ideology and the Collapse of Communism', *Political Studies*, XLI, 1993, p. 12.

Moreover, just as the passing of the twentieth century and second millennium of the 'Common Era' has enlivened sensitivity to periodisation, so too has the termination of the Cold War and the rapid unravelling of the polarised settlement of 1945–49 enhanced a sense in which history is certainly not all *longue durée* and often better understood as short-term 'crisis'. The puncturing of the Berlin Wall in the autumn of 1989 had a far greater impact on the population of the planet than has any impending turn of one (only partly globalised) calendar. The collapse in the West of official communism – followed in pretty short order by that of lesser variants – may not have exactly given birth to postmodernism, but it certainly fed and clothed the clammy youth. Furthermore, it has undeniably strong claims upon the paternity of 'endism', which might be seen as a mutation of American supremacism made nervously shrill by the close coincidence of the conquest of communism and that of the calendar.[45] In a review of a superior, European study of 'post-history', Malcolm Bull summarises the position with a neatness that is as compelling as it is fashionable:

> Of the eschatologies of Christianity, Kant and Marx, only one remains: the ideals of Marxist messianism and Kantian progress are now widely perceived to have been discredited by the bloody history of the twentieth century, but the same events have given the religious alternative renewed credibility. It is Christian millenarianism that has survived to compete with post-history as a guide to the present and a map of the future.[46]

Harold Bloom – for whom 'the American Christ tends to be the Jesus of the Resurrection, rather than of the Crucifixion or the Ascension' – also has a point when he notes that

> The fall of the Soviet Union into another wretchedly imperial Russia has deprived our American Protestant diviners, like the Reverend Pat Robertson, of an apocalyptic rough beast, which the Iranian juggernaut now can replace. American Christian Fundamentalism, and the Islamic Shi'ite fundamentalism of Iran, are rival heirs of the Zoroastrian imaginings of the Last Things.[47]

Bloom is not entirely relaxed about the fact that there are in the USA 10 million 'premillenarianists' – people who expect Jesus to return, in his resurrected body, in order to preside over a thousand-year kingdom on earth – in addition to the 100 million who simply anticipate a Second Coming without any necessary Kingdom of God ensuing in this world, but he still adheres passionately to a gnostic calling:

---

45. In this discussion we can clearly distinguish the camp-followers from the pioneer, Francis Fukuyama, whose *The End of History and the Last Man*, London 1992, caused a genuine politico-intellectual event, as recognised by Perry Anderson, *A Zone of Engagement*, London 1992. For those without stomachs strong enough for the Book of Revelation, see Kerichi Ohnae, *The End of the Nation State*, San Francisco 1996; Jeremy Rifkin, *The End of Work*, London 1995; Lewis Blackwell, *The End of Print*, Lynchburg, Tenn., 1997; Peter Noever (ed.), *The End of Architecture*, New York 1995; George Brockway, *The End of Economic Man*, New York 1991; *et cetera usque ad nauseam*.

46. Review of Lutz Niethammer, *Posthistoire*, London 1992, in *London Review of Books*, 11 March 1993.

47. *Omens of the Millennium*, London 1996, pp. 3, 29–30.

... psychoanalysis was and is a shamanism; its affiliations with occultism or parapsychology are far more authentic than its supposed links to biology.... Freud's creation is a mythology, reared upon the central drives of love and death ... [he] absolutely declined to see that *to interpret is to prophesy*.[48]

Meanwhile, Rev. Robertson has, indeed, kept his eye on slightly more traditional targets than the USSR:

In Third World Countries that practice idolatry, the idols are representatives of demonic power, and their worship often involves actual demon possession. The barbaric acts that have been committed in the name of the idols range from assassinations committed by followers of Kali in India, to human sacrifices by the Mayans in Mexico.... The Bible warns us that in the end times a world dictator will arise whose enormous statue will be energized by Satan in league with a false religious system to do signs and wonders.[49]

Yet, regardless of one's disposition for manicheanism or how one assesses the precise shifts in an unstable balance of world forces, the proposition that it is worth adopting both a chronological and a conjunctural approach to history is today not really very daring or dangerous.[50]

Neither, of course, is it at all original for, as we move towards the more circumscribed terrain of what Althusser calls 'historical methodology', the ground is positively littered with interpretations, hypotheses and arguments about periodisation, ages, times and epochs, with titles invariably displaying a preference for dates. This is true of Marx, whose nimble sense of irony led him to adopt the terminology of the French revolutionary calendar – halted by Napoleon Bonaparte ('the tragic uncle') on 1 January (9 Nivôse) 1806 – for the title of his 1852 pamphlet on the political crisis of 1848–51 in that country: *The Eighteenth Brumaire of Louis Bonaparte* ('the comic nephew'). It is even more the case for a direct participant in those events, Jules Michelet (1798–1874), who arguably occupies a position for today's historians similar to that held by Kierkegaard in the eyes of cultural theorists. Michelet effectively opened his career with two *Tableux de l'Histoire Moderne* – one synchronic and the other chronological – for the years 1453 to 1789, consolidated it with the six-volume *Moyen Age* (1833–44), and closed it with *Temps Modernes* (1857–67) and *Histoire du XIXe Siècle* (1872–73), even if he is still most famous for *Révolution* (1847–53).

Michelet positively 'lived' history as a sensuous duty of management on behalf of the dead. His championing of *le peuple* in the French Revolution is to Marx what Edward Thompson was to Althusser, and, although they criticise and go beyond his central category, one can find in the work of Richard Cobb and George Rudé a more

---

48. Ibid., pp. 109, 123.

49. Pat Robertson, *The New World Order: It Will Change the Way You Live*, Dallas 1991, p. 235.

50. It strikes me that this is true even if – taking the example of Marx – one believes his work to have undergone no 'breaks' at all, or to have been an effective silence from *Theses on Feuerbach* (1843) to *Capital* (1867). Similarly, the public image of Darwin with respect to the years I have chosen is effectively one of a blank gap between *The Voyage of the Beagle*, the second edition of which was issued in 1845, and *On the Origin of Species*, published in 1859, and yet this 'silence' has echoed ever since.

openly acknowledged influence. Gwyn Williams closes his survey of popular movements in France and Britain during the 'first' revolution in France by evoking 'Michelet's old artisan who never forgot "the sun of 1793"'.[51] However, Michelet's enduring influence rests as much on his visionary qualities as on his powers of evocation:

> For Michelet, relations between men and women are … not at all based on the differences between the sexes: male and female are moral figures intended to judge conventionally certain historical states or phenomena. History is male, Syria is female. But in erotic terms, there is only a spectator and his spectacle; Michelet himself is no longer man or woman, he is nothing but Gaze.… The ideal movement of love is not, for Michelet, penetration but juxtaposition, for it is not sex but seeing which gives its measure.[52]

There is here a strong similarity with the speculative thought of Jacques Derrida, which is currently very popular:

> The relationship [to the other] would not be a-sexual, far from it, but would be sexual otherwise: beyond the binary difference that governs the decorum of all codes, beyond the opposition feminine/masculine, beyond homosexuality and heterosexuality, which come to the same thing.… I would like to believe in the masses, this indeterminate number of blended voices, those mobile non-identified sexual marks.[53]

Although he is not directly invoked, Michelet seems to be the guiding influence behind *An Intimate History of Humanity* (1994) by Theodore Zeldin, who elsewhere quotes two injunctions made by the professor at the height of the 1848 revolution – that the movement should socialise not property but men's minds, so as to create *une grande amitié*; and that 'the trouble with men of letters … was that they wrote for other men of letters.… The masses were still isolated, divided by a hundred different parties. The young should seek them out. They should translate for them the messages of the geniuses.'[54]

A sharp contrast to Michelet's methodology may be found in that of the Tilly family, who explain with disconcerting candour how they came to identify a 'Rebellious Century' in France, Germany and Italy over the years 1830–1930:

> Our motives mix cowardice, convenience, and calculation.… We needed a period, or a set of periods, recent enough to make that documentation manageable, comparable enough that we could treat the world conditions impinging on each country as singular, yet spanning a

---

51. *Artisans and Sans-Culottes*, London 1989, p. 114. See also George Rudé, 'Interpretations of the French Revolution', in Harvey Kaye (ed.), *Selected Essays of George Rudé: The Face in the Crowd*, Atlantic Highlands, N.J., 1988; Richard Cobb, *The People's Armies*, New Haven, Conn., 1987.

52. Roland Barthes, *Michelet*, New York 1987, pp. 152–3.

53. Interview with Christine McDonald, *Diacritics*, 12:2, 1982, p. 76. For Noel O'Sullivan, the fact that Toril Moi ends her study *Sexual/Textual Politics*, London 1991, with this quotation indicates approval for a form of thought where 'politics disappears from sight, being replaced by a naive, almost mystical faith in the natural harmony which, it is assumed, will automatically be brought about by deconstruction'. 'Political Integration, the Limited State, and the Philosophy of Postmodernism', *Political Studies*, XLI, 1993, p. 35.

54. Theodore Zeldin, *France, 1848–1945: Ambition, Love and Politics*, Oxford 1973, pp. 483, 658. It is perhaps unsurprising that Michelet is treated with interest and some benevolence by the 'discourse' school of historiographers: Hayden White, *Metahistory: The Historical Imagination in Nineteenth Century Europe*, Baltimore 1973, pp. 135–62; Jacques Rancière, *The Names of History*, Minneapolis 1994, pp. 42ff.

considerable amount of urbanization and industrialization, as well as violent conflict which might have been linked to the urbanization and industrialization. We feared to take on the French Revolution or the Nazi seizure of power.[55]

It would be difficult to find an approach more at odds with that of the Mexican thinker Edmundo O'Gorman, who, ninety-nine years after the 1848 revolution, confronted 'the need to focus historical events in the light of an ontological perspective, i.e., as a process producing historical entities instead of a process, as is usually assumed, which takes for granted the being of such entities as logically prior to it'.[56]

Writing three years before O'Gorman, but in a year that was critically different by virtue of being 'consumed' by World War II, Lewis Namier adopts a similar approach in different language:

> In 1848 the subversive social forces were not equal to the task.... The 'Revolution of the Intellectuals' exhausted itself without achieving concrete results; it left its imprint only in the realm of ideas.... John Stuart Mill sadly reflected on the feelings which make men indifferent to the rights and interests 'of any portion of the human species, save that which is called by the same name and speaks the same language as themselves. These feelings are characteristic of barbarians'.... Thus in the *Volkerfrühling* ['springtime of nations'], 'nationality', the passionate creed of the intellectuals, invades the politics of central and east-central Europe, and with 1848 starts the Great European War of every nation against its neighbours' ... I shall be discussing problems which ninety years later, in 1938–9, were to become a touchstone of German mentality.[57]

The ideas relating to the conflict that Namier most stresses – that between 'constitutional development' and 'national movements' – were scarcely less prominent in the British experience than in that of continental Europe. And some 150 years later they continue to be to the fore of ideology on a far wider plane. Moreover, even at the start of 1848 – within days of the overthrow of the old order and when he was still thrilled by events – Mill counselled caution:

> I am hardly yet out of breath from reading and thinking.... The republicans have succeeded because *at last* they had the good sense to raise the standard not of a republic but of something in which the middle classes could join, viz. electoral reform – then the madness of Louis Philippe and Guizot in forbidding, at the last moment, the reform banquets in Paris, stirred up the people.... The whole thing is very well taken here. Nobody seems the least uneasy or terrified at the idea of the French republic. Indeed, they do not seem half as much alarmed as there is reason to be. The dangers are first of war. Secondly, communism has now for the first time a deep root.[58]

---

55. Charles, Louise and Richard Tilly, *The Rebellious Century: 1830–1930*, London 1975, p. vii.

56. *The Invention of America*, Bloomington, Ind., 1961, p. 4. O'Gorman – of Irish, Warwickshire and Coyoacán stock – is referring here to his *Crisis y Porvenir de la Ciencia Histórica*, published in Mexico in 1947.

57. *1848: The Revolution of the Intellectuals*, London 1944, pp. 31, 33. The original lecture on which this booklet is based was given on 12 July 1944, five weeks after D-Day and a month after the first V-1 landed on Bow, London.

58. Mill, London, to Henry Chapman, 29 Feb. 1848, in F.A. Hayek (ed.), *The Earlier Letters of John Stuart Mill, 1812–1848*, Toronto 1963, II, pp. 731–2.

In a similar vein, it makes eminently good sense for John Saville to open (and end) his detailed survey of the first months of that year in Great Britain with a review of developments in Ireland and France.[59] On the other hand, Eric Hobsbawm closes the first book of his four-volume series on modern history in 1848 by moving to a fully global perspective from one that had been rooted in Europe around the idea of a 'dual revolution' – political in France and industrial in Great Britain – from the late 1780s. Up until 1848 a large part of the world 'was transformed from a European, or rather a Franco-British, base'.[60] The next volume, *The Age of Capital*, opens with the powerful proposition that the dominant theme after 1848 is 'the extension of the capitalist economy to the entire world, and hence the impossibility of any longer writing a purely European history; it would be absurd to write its history without paying substantial attention to other continents.'[61]

Hobsbawm subsequently consolidated a vision of a 'long nineteenth century' (from 1789 to 1914) and a 'short twentieth century' (from 1914 to 1991), and it is in keeping with the style of the *Annales* school, for which he has evident sympathy, that he can use precise dates to make sense of long periods.[62] Of the post-war British Marxist historians Hobsbawm is probably the most understanding of Althusser's suspicion of the link between human agency and a more or less explicit 'essentialism':

> The dominance of the past does not imply an image of social immobility. It is comparable with cyclical views of historic change, and certainly with regression and catastrophe (that is, failure to reproduce the past). What it is incompatible with is the idea of continuous progress.[63]

---

59. *1848: The British State and the Chartist Movement*, Cambridge 1987. In terms of association of dates with events, one might place the last third of 1848 in '1849' since these months were incomparably more placid than the spring and summer, as reflected in the fact that 200 of the 271 pages of Raymond Postgate's study relate to the period between January and August. *Story of a Year: 1848*, London 1955.

60. *The Age of Revolution: 1789–1848*, London 1962, p. xv.

61. *The Age of Capital: 1848–1875*, London 1975, p. xiii. It is not a necessary consequence that 1848 scarcely appears at all – let alone as a decisive point of rupture – in Hobsbawm's *Nations and Nationalism since 1780*, Cambridge 1990. As a communist, Hobsbawm understandably lay emphasis on the fact that,

> in and after 1848, the possibility of pushing the revolution to the left, by means of a political vanguard transforming its character, moved to the centre of [Marx's] thinking; it is this phase that was to form the starting point for Lenin … [who] his opponents liked to say was a Jacobin

Echoes of the Marseillaise, London 1990, p. 41. But elsewhere in the same text he traces a rather different lineage: from Babeuf's *Conspiracy of Equals* (1795) via Buonarroti's history (1818) through Auguste Blanqui to the 1871 Commune, the last surviving leader of which, Zéphryn Carnélinat, died in 1932 a member of the French Communist Party. Ibid., p. 103.

62. *The Age of Extremes: The Short Twentieth Century, 1914–1991*, London 1994, pp. 3, 584. Despite its reputation and its third but last sentence – 'I am by temperament a "structuralist", little tempted by the event, or even by the short-term conjuncture which is after all merely a grouping of events in the same area' – we might note that the most celebrated book emanating from the *Annales* school has the life of a king in its title, contains plenty of direct and reported speech, a plethora of dates by the day, and much lively and informal prose, all at the service of depicting a fifty-year period, albeit one over a wide area and with much background. Fernand Braudel, *The Mediterranean and the Mediterranean World in the Age of Philip II*, Paris 1949/London 1973. For Marc Bloch, who was executed by the Germans a month before Namier gave his 1848 lecture, 'historical time is a concrete and living reality with an irreversible onward rush. It is the very plasma in which events are immersed, and the field within which they become intelligible'. *The Historian's Craft* (1954), Manchester 1992, p. 23.

63. 'The Social Function of the Past: Some Questions', *Past and Present*, 55, 1972, p. 6.

None the less, Hobsbawm's writing on both centuries, even in more recent and catastrophic voice, has never suppressed the presence – and has frequently accentuated the texture – of human action. His empirically voiced mapping of a politico–cultural complex is, in fact, more British than continental in style, and is particularly apt for the longer century in which the British reach is unparalleled. Indeed, even the most parochial of British historians is drawn to a global perspective by the expansion of the economy into global 'lift-off'. The virtually uncontested authority of the British navy, the centrality of free trade to domestic politics, or the importance of India have all made it extremely difficult even for those with resolutely insular enthusiasms, such as W.L. Burn (whose chosen period of 1852–67 was constitutionally given), not to raise their eyes:

> What I sought was a generation which, while recognizably distinct, did not represent discontinuity in relation to what had gone before and what came after. The England of 1852–67 seemed to meet my needs. No one returning to it after a long absence abroad was likely to feel that he had strayed into another world. Most of the old landmarks were still there for him to recognize. Yet it was not the same England as that of 1842 or 1872. Something of the passions, of the ingenuous and romantic emotions, which had found expression in Chartism, in Tractarianism, in the bitter controversies over the corn laws and the sugar duties, in dozens of utopian schemes, had abated.[64]

In short, there is plenty of Great Britain to talk about outside the island, even if this talk is merely narrative of British presence elsewhere. The attention given to the Great Exhibition of 1851 stands as a strong illustration of this, whether in rather direct anniversarial rendition, as by Asa Briggs – 'It was a year of national festival, the climax of early Victorian England, the turning point of the century.... *Punch* depicted an old Tory ... hanging an Exhibition notice outside his house: "ici on ne parle pas français"' – or in more modish dissection of globalised 'consumption culture', as by Thomas Richards:

> Until the Exhibition the commodity had not for a moment occupied centre-stage in English public life; during and after the Exhibition the commodity became and remained the still center of the turning earth, the focal point of all gazing and the end point of all pilgrimages.[65]

The eloquent and rather moving pages of intellectual biography with which *Pour Marx* opens show no indulgence to Stalinism, but their target is not so much 'le contagieux et implacable système de gouvernement et de pensée [qui] proroquait ces délires' – the Althusserian prose is in the classical tradition – but 'the conditions of theoretical void' in which French Communism grew up and which Stalinism helped to conceal behind that 'primacy of politics' which was in any case congenial to the French.

'The Structure of Capital', in Elliott (ed.), *Althusser: A Critical Reader*, p. 4.

64. *The Age of Equipoise*, London 1965, pp. 15–16. In the introduction to his *Age of Paradox*, published in 1953, and covering the years 1841–51, John Dodds says, 'It could be called, with equal truth, an Age of Bewilderment, an Age of Hope, an Age of Anxiety, an Age of Accomplishment, an Age of Enthusiasm, an Age of Desperation' (ibid., p. xv). This last, perhaps, for title-seekers of every type?

65. Asa Briggs, *1851*, London 1951, pp. 3–4; Thomas Richards, *The Commodity Cultures of Victorian England*, London 1991, p. 18.

And even in that burgeoning era of conservatism and consumption, foreigner commanders were prey to English ambushes. General Pinochet's apprehension by the Metropolitan Police in Ocober 1998 was a good deal more gentle than the treatment meted out in August 1850 to the Austrian Field-Marshal von Haynau, known as 'the Butcher' for his repression of the revolutionary movements in Italy and Hungary:

> On a visit to the great brewery of Barclay and Perkins he was recognised by the workmen, who ran out with brooms and sticks crying, 'Down with the Austrian butcher!' He received very rough treatment; missiles were thrown at him and his clothes nearly torn off his back; he was even dragged along by his luxuriant moustaches. In terrified flight, he ran into a public house and barricaded himself in one of the bedrooms. The crowd by this time had grown to several hundred, and it was only with the help of the police that the old man was rescued.... The episode was reported in great detail, and a good deal of secret satisfaction in many quarters. Barclay and Perkins refused to discipline their men for the attack. The most they would do 'in order that the excitement may be allayed in every possible manner', was to obliterate Haynau's signature from the visitors' book.[66]

US TIME

The North American historiography is somewhat less clear-cut, although this is hardly because of a lack of 'decisive moments'. The discovery on 24 January 1848 of gold flakes by workers at Sutter's mill on the Sacramento river, California, prompted a 'rush' which over the next two years multiplied US production of the precious metal nearly sixty-fold whilst world production quadrupled. Eight days after the discovery – on 2 February – US negotiator Nicholas P. Trist signed an agreement with the government of Mexico at the village of Guadalupe Hidalgo which formally terminated the state of war that had obtained between the two countries for some two years. By this treaty Mexico gave up all claims to Texas above the Rio Grande (one-third of that state) and ceded to the United States California and New Mexico (the present states of California, Nevada, Utah, most of New Mexico and Arizona, and parts of Oklahoma, Colorado and Wyoming). In return, Mexico received $15 million and the US assumed responsibility for civil claims of $3.2 million against the Mexican government. President Polk, whose appreciable expansionist appetite had been further whetted, initially balked at Trist's deal, but he soon recognised it – as did Congress – for the extraordinary opportunity that it was. The material and diplomatic foundations had been laid for a Californianism that would not just propel the United States'

---

66. Dodds, *Age of Paradox*, p. 441.

westward and continental mission in the nineteenth century but also underpin a twentieth-century projection of 'America' from which contemporary notions of 'globalisation' cannot be divorced.

Yet early in his celebrated and influential book *Battle Cry of Freedom* James McPherson quotes the sage of Concord, Ralph Waldo Emerson, as saying, 'the United States will conquer Mexico, but it will be as a man swallows the arsenic, which brings him down in turn. Mexico will poison us.'[67] The reason for this was far less the 'imperialist' cause and conduct of the war – although Emerson and, more famously, Henry David Thoreau found those repugnant enough – than the question of whether the conquered territory would become slave-states or free-states, how this would be decided, and what would be the consequence for the balance of sectional power within the union. Thus, David Potter opens his study of the origins of the US Civil War of 1861–65 with the arrival in Washington of Nicholas Trist's envoy, the New Orleans journalist James Freane, bringing the treaty of Guadalupe Hidalgo to Washington on the evening of Saturday, 19 February 1848. Potter's book – which was incomplete at his death in 1971 – carries the title of Hinton Helper's 1860 pamphlet, and so purposefully reads history forward and, like many in the crowded field which it still leads, courts the danger of effacing the 'now' of those pre-war years by treating them as simply time spent on the inexorable road to Fort Sumter.[68]

Even historians such as John Ashworth and William Freehling, who are currently engaged in very different forms of strategic reinterpretation of the Civil War over two generations and more, have ended the first part of what both plan as two-volume studies in 1850 and 1854 respectively. The first of these dates marks the portmanteau compromise designed by Henry Clay and sealed by Stephen Douglas. Under this deal California was admitted to the Union as a free state, the borders of slave-state Texas were rearranged, Utah and New Mexico territories had no restrictions on slavery, and the slave trade was abolished in Washington, DC, but the Slave Fugitive Act (which gave extensive powers to slave-owners) was further strengthened. The second date (1854) is that of the Kansas–Nebraska crisis, during which Douglas attempted, with much less success, to resolve a more developed expression of the same fundamental problem through incorporating the territory west of Missouri and Iowa but deferring the question of slavery to local decision ('popular sovereignty').[69] (Since this

---

67. *Journals of Ralph Waldo Emerson*, VII, p. 206, quoted in James McPherson, *Battle Cry of Freedom: The Civil War Era*, New York 1988, p. 51.

68. David Potter, *The Impending Crisis: 1848–1861*, New York 1976. In their introduction to the text completed by Dan Fehrenbacher, Henry Steele Commager and Richard Brandon Morris note that the 1850s 'was indeed a history of the impending crisis but ... had a life of its own' (ibid., p. vii). They do not, however, explain the origin of the book's title.

69. John Ashworth, *Slavery, Capitalism and Politics in the Antebellum Republic: Commerce and Compromise, 1820–1850*, Cambridge 1995, which takes an approach focused on Marx, is critical of both Potter and McPherson for ignoring black resistance to slavery (p. 7), and seeks strongly to qualify the arguments for the 'idealist' provenance and development of abolitionism (e.g. pp. 189–91); William W. Freehling, *The Road to Disunion: Secessionists at Bay: 1776–1854*, New York 1990, which provides rich elaboration of two early observations over nearly 600 pages:

move effectively terminated the Missouri Compromise of 1820 – whereby Missouri was admitted as a slave-state, Maine as a free one, and it was agreed that there would be no slavery north of 36 degrees 30 minutes – it might be seen as a moment of significant rupture in its own right, but it is still a story rarely told without an ending in 1861 or 1865.)

Another, related approach – which equally marginalises the years 1845–55 as a coherent period – is that based on 'Jacksonianism', viewed broadly as the first full expression of a white male democracy, largely shorn of insular patterns of deference, still attached to the Jeffersonian identification of independence with self-employment, rude, pious and often nativist in character. Taken as an 'era' by Glyndon Van Deusen, this lasts from 1828 to 1848; adopted as an 'age' by Arthur Schlesinger, it endures until the Civil War and even beyond.[70] Historians of a more dissident disposition – in terms of both politics and chronology – have also tended to the *longue durée*. In their post-Vietnam textbook *The Free and the Unfree* Peter Carroll and David Noble adopt the entire period between the ratification of the Constitution and the Civil War as a natural unit for sub-division into the themes of north and south society; the organisation of space (although this includes the important religious question); and political development and schism.[71] The dean of an earlier generation of radicals, William Appleman Williams, adopted a resolutely heterodox approach in *The Contours of American History* (1966) by identifying three essential periods: mercantilism (1740–1828); *laissez nous faire* (1819–96); and corporate capitalism (1882–). Typically at pains to avoid making 'reality too complex – too "thisey and thatey"', Williams divides each phase into sub-periods: 'the triumph of the rising order; a new reality for existing ideas; the adaptation of the accepted order; the transformation of reality and the inception of new ideas; the fulfillment of the passing order'. Under this logical dispensation the years at the centre of the nineteenth century fall between the adaptation of *laissez nous faire* and its transformation with the inception of the ideas of corporate capitalism.[72]

Whenever someone declaims on *a* South, premodern, egalitarian republican or whatever, ask them which South is meant, and when? ... As Marxists rightly emphasize, slaveholders' class relationship with black dependents generated a world view about dependency which transcended race and led to haughtily hierarchical conceptions of the ideal white society too. As non-Marxists rightly counter, upper class political relationships with white citizens generated a viewpoint about equality which emphasized race and reserved haughty hierarchy for non-whites.

Ibid., pp. viii, 572.

70. Glyndon G. Van Deusen, *The Jacksonian Era: 1828–1848*, New York 1959; Arthur M. Schlesinger, *The Age of Jackson*, Boston 1945.

71. *The Free and the Unfree: A New History of the United States*, New York 1977.

72. *The Contours of American History*, New York 1966/1988, pp. 22–3. In his popular history *The Bold and Magnificent Dream: America's Founding Years, 1492–1815*, New York 1978, Bruce Catton adopts a rather less original periodization, making the 1812 war with Britain a decisive event:

Americans had fought the world's greatest power to a standstill ... the sense of achievement deriving from those victories had more than supplied whatever Americans might have been lacking in self-confidence or security. Now their independence was unqualified and complete.

Maybe it is not so strange in the case of the USA that as soon as one moves away from politics a greater sense of 'progress' may be claimed over the middle of the nineteenth century. In studying the cholera epidemics of 1832, 1849 and 1866 Charles Rosenberg took 'snapshots' of different approaches to the same problem over a generation. Thus, while in 1832 sanitation in most North American cities was provided by hogs, which 'roamed everywhere', by 1866 materialism had displaced the piety of Jacksonian America:

> A more critical and empirical temper had begun to replace the abstract rationalism of an earlier day. In medicine … thoughtful physicians scorned those concepts which could not be expressed in tables and percentages … cholera, a scourge of the sinful to many Americans, had by 1866, become the consequence of remediable faults in sanitation.[73]

In 1849, by contrast, there is a very mixed picture, as Appleman Williams might have expected. The health reformer Joel Shew propagated the slogan 'TEMPERANCE IN ALL THINGS', but 'you might live to a ripe old age' until, 'like a clock, worn out with eating time, the wheels of weary life stand still' only through a combination of adequate study and God's blessing.[74] One physician from Philadelphia was still so attached to the practice of bleeding that he extracted a full sixteen fluid ounces from his own arm, gave himself a good dose of castor oil and then administered 'the inevitable calomel'. At the same time, Chicago's *Herald of the Prairies* announced that cholera was one of the means by which Jehovah swept 'with the besom of destruction nations degraded by superstition, and sift[ed] as chaff from wheat the vicious out of mixed populations … shall there be evil in the city and the Lord hath not done it'.[75]

Yet the president of the neighbouring Wisconsin State Medical Society was only addressing one challenge when he hoped that none of his members would allow 'himself to be satisfied that the result was one of God's providence'. Closing fast on his other flank were the free traders, who, bolstered by popular appetite for a dizzying range of patented purges, tonics and hydropathic treatments as well as distrust of the medical profession – by 1851 fifteen states had removed all restrictions upon the practice of medicine – trumped all evolutionary presumptions with radical logic:

> We go in for the 'largest liberty', without pretending to decide which system is best. [Liberals everywhere] desire that medicine, like theology, should be divorced from the State, and that, as in different sects of religionists, the various medical systems shall be treated alike … we go in for free-trade in doctoring.[76]

The fear of disease – and of none more than tuberculosis – varied much less than did the putative clinical and political cures. The concern expressed by James Fenimore

---

Ibid., p. 464. This approach is reflected in Arthur Shaffer's historiography, *The Politics of Writing History: Writing the History of the American Revolution, 1783–1815*, Chicago 1975.

73. *The Cholera Years: The United States in 1832, 1849 and 1866*, Chicago 1968, p. 5.

74. Quoted in Thomas R. Cole, *The Journey of Life: A Cultural History of Aging in America*, Cambridge 1992, p. 108.

75. *Herald of the Prairies*, 18 July 1849, quoted in Rosenberg, *Cholera Years*, pp. 196–7.

76. *Daily Times*, Cincinnati, quoted in ibid., p. 161.

Cooper to his son Paul in 1845 is representative of parental anxiety everywhere throughout the century:

> ...write me distinctly what your symptoms are. And *all* of them. The mere taste in the mouth of which you speak is far more likely to come from the stomach, or even the head, than from the lungs.... Have you fever, night sweats, stricture of the breast, or any other decided symptoms? ... Write to me *distinctly*; not in general terms, at once, on this subject, and leave Cambridge at once if you entertain any serious doubts and find the climate bad.... You have not the least of a pulmonary appearance, though your constitution is not robust. The five or six years that are to follow are all important to you.[77]

By now I hope it is evident that I am treating the United States as precisely that – a unit comprised of a plurality – even though prior to 1865 the term was used more in the plural than the singular sense. The unity is justified by federal institutions in executive, legislative and judicial spheres, all of which operated and were extensively tested throughout this period. Diversity within the union was – as already indicated – one of the most acute sources of pressure, friction and negotiation as the frontier expanded south and westwards and tensions rose, primarily between the group of states that upheld slavery at the foundation of the republic (Maryland, Delaware, Virginia, North Carolina, South Carolina, Georgia) and those that abolished it after 1783 (New Hampshire, Massachusetts, Rhode Island, Connecticut, New York, Pennsylvania, New Jersey), with each section being augmented by the creation of new members. (Slave: Kentucky 1792; Tennessee 1796; Louisiana 1812; Mississippi 1817; Alabama 1819; Missouri 1821; Arkansas 1836; Texas 1845; Florida 1846. Free: Vermont 1791; Ohio 1803; Illinois 1816; Indiana 1818; Maine 1820; Michigan 1837; Iowa 1846; Wisconsin 1848; California 1850.)

The debate over the reach and quality of this unity is rich and energetic, and has increasingly focused on whether even 'the South' itself can properly be treated as a whole. For the purposes of comparison with the rest of the continent it is essential to recognise the uneven character and development of both the states that formed the original union and those that came to comprise it prior to 1861. A general comparison between the USA and Latin America in 1850 is certainly plausible in terms of population – approximately 24 and 30 million respectively. So, for instance, might be one between Ohio (1.5 million) and Chile (1.4 million) on the same grounds (both being 'free-states'). Such a comparison would have to be based on very different grounds in 1850 than in 1900 because of the changed institutional as well as economic conditions of the USA, but even in 1850 it was a qualitatively distinct relation to, say, that between Chile and Venezuela for the simple reason that Ohio formed a subordinate part of an institutionalised polity and economy without which its parochial limits, practices and prospects cannot be properly understood, even if that outer world was sometimes only dimly comprehended or accepted.

---

77. Cooper, Cooperstown, to Paul Fenimore Cooper, 22 Oct. 1845, in *Letters and Journals*, V, p. 89.

It is an anachronism to approach the USA of 1850 as if it were that of 1900 or 1950, but it is far more misguided to see the federal–state relationship at any time as merely an Anglo-Protestant variant of the common culture and political forms in the south of the continent. The vanities and ambitions of political sovereignty in Latin America indubitably outstripped its reality. None the less, Chile and Venezuela shared less than did Ohio and Tennessee simply because of the separate republican identities of the Latin American polities, even though the two US states belonged to different sections and would, within a dozen years, be at war with each other over slavery and Constitution. At the same time, it is surely right to note the specific importance of this period within the USA for Texas, which was a republic for nearly a decade before its (long anticipated) incorporation into the Union in 1845, and for California, more rapidly and directly annexed and more comprehensively transformed by economic development.

Within the USA opinion divided over how Texas and Mexico should be seen in terms of the past and the future. For Emerson, writing in January 1844, 'the question of the annexation of Texas is one of those which looks very differently to the centuries and to the years … it will in the course of ages be of small import by what particular occasions it was done. It is a secular question.'[78] In March 1846, with Texas annexed and the threat of armed conflict with Mexico very sharp, John Calhoun used the same approach precisely to oppose going to war, telling the US Senate that the mission of Anglo-America to transform the continent was possessed of natural qualities and so required the patience and nerve to wait:

> War would but impede the fulfillment of this high mission, by absorbing the means and diverting the energies which would be devoted to the purpose. On the contrary, secure peace, and time, under the guidance of a sagacious and cautious policy, 'a wise and masterly inactivity', will speedily accomplish the whole.[79]

Calhoun was in the minority even before the war broke out, and after it began he had to struggle with those, like George Bancroft, who accept that 'an honourable peace would doubtless be best', but still counselled President Polk that, 'if Mexico will not have it, then our duty is manifest – to hold the country and await the counsels of futurity'.[80]

Lastly, of course, there is the simple matter of the span of human life and passage of generations; the question of memory and the ever-thinning ranks of the old who personify history. By the time of the Mexican War there was alive only one leading political figure of that generation which had founded and consolidated the republic – Albert Gallatin, treasury secretary to Jefferson and Madison and now eighty-seven

---

78. *Journal*, VI, pp. 389–90, quoted in John Q. Anderson, 'Emerson on Texas and the Mexican War', *Western Humanities Review*, XIII:2, 1959, p. 191.

79. Speech to Senate on proposed abrogation of joint occupancy of Oregon, 16 March 1846, in *The Essential Calhoun*, New Brunswick, N.J., 1992, p. 128.

80. Bancroft, London, to Polk, 18 Nov. 1847, in M.A. De Wolfe Howe, *The Life and Letters of George Bancroft*, London 1908, I, p. 28.

years of age. Yet four days before the draft treaty of Guadalupe Hidalgo arrived in Washington, Gallatin reiterated his resolution to campaign against any annexation of land through conquest:

> I write with great difficulty, and I become exhausted when I work for more than four or five hours a day. Ever since the end of October all my faculties, impaired as they are, were absorbed in one subject; not only my faculties, but I may say my feelings. I thought of nothing else. Age quod agis![81]

Some three decades earlier Jefferson himself – already past the average expectancy of life – reckoned that the individual suffering which attended a life led into another historical epoch was too high. Writing in 1816 to John Adams, his predecessor in the presidency, he reflected,

> Putting to myself your question: would I agree to live my 73 years over again for ever? I hesitate to say ... from 25 to 60, I would say Yes; and might go further back, but not come lower down. For, at the latter period, with most of us, the powers of life are sensibly on the wane, sight becomes dim, hearing dull, memory constantly enlarging its frightful blank and parting with all we have ever seen or known, spirits evaporate, bodily disability creeps in palsying every limb, and so faculty after faculty quits us and where then is life?[82]

Much comment is customarily (and understandably) made of the fact that Adams and Jefferson, the second and third presidents of the USA, died on the same day, Jefferson expiring at around noon and Adams before nightfall on 4 July 1826 – the fiftieth anniversary of Congressional approval of the Declaration of Independence drafted by Jefferson. However, Henry Adams, the president's great-grandson and arguably the most brilliant US historian of the nineteenth century, alighted on another date and death: that of John Quincy Adams (1767–1848), son of the second president, himself the sixth holder of that office, and the first to be elected via popular vote:

> The end of this first, or ancestral and Revolutionary, chapter, came on February 21 1848 – and the month of February brought life and death as a family habit – when the eighteenth century, as an actual and living companion, vanished. If the scene on the floor of the House [of Representatives], when the old President fell, struck the simple-minded American public with a sensation unusually dramatic, its effect on a ten-year-old boy, whose boy-life was fading away with the life of his grandfather, could not be slight.[83]

It is probably for reasons of style that Adams omits to mention that his grandfather died two days later, without recovering consciousness from the stroke that felled him. The other image associated with this event – that of the prostrate Adams being carried to the Speaker's chair – could perhaps only be left out by a scion of such a presidential line.

---

81. Henry Adams (ed.), *The Writings of Albert Gallatin*, Philadelphia 1879, I, p. 677.

82. Jefferson, Monticello, to Adams, 1 Aug. 1816, in Lester J. Cappon (ed.), *The Adams–Jefferson Letters*, Chapel Hill, N.C., 1959, pp. 483–4.

83. *The Education of Henry Adams* (1918), Harmondsworth 1995, pp. 24–5. In 1826 news travelled slowly. Sensing that he was reaching his end, Adams declared that he was able to draw comfort from the fact that Jefferson was still alive.

LATIN AMERICAN TIME

We will be looking at some of the main issues in the historiography of Latin America shortly, but the question of chronology can be briefly considered here, although it is even less clear than in the case of the United States. The generally accepted view is best represented and has been most eloquently propounded by Tulio Halperín Donghi, who sees this period as marking a delayed, slow and partial recovery from the independence struggles of 1810–25:

> At the start of the 1840s Latin America appeared finally to have absorbed the impact of ever diminishing changes, and to have learned to adjust to a system that – if it was not an exemplary form of liberal and enlightened reformism – at least offered some indications that it might work. At the end of the decade this resigned acceptance of a Latin America created by the dissolution of the Iberian empires gave way to a new exploration – simultaneously frightened and hopeful – of future alternatives.[84]

This image of recovery with only a tentative sense of 'forwardness' is also depicted by David Bushnell and Neill Macaulay, who, in a chapter headed 'A Quickening of Pace' in a book tellingly entitled *The Emergence of Latin America in the Nineteenth Century*, suggest that

> the mood of Latin America, or at least of the middle and upper sectors of the population, changed again about mid-century, as most countries entered a period of around 25 to 30 years in which economic growth provided a renewed basis for optimism and liberal reformers generally seized the political initiative.[85]

Of course, in 1850 there could be little sense that any recognised stability and growth might last for three decades, and even today historians prefer to look backward. Halperín's *Aftermath* approach is shared by the *Cambridge History of Latin America* – which defines the period of 1830–70 as 'After Independence' – and by most popular surveys and textbooks, even for Brazil, which underwent a quite distinct political experience between independence from Portugal and the establishment of a republic in 1889.[86]

---

84. *Reforma y Disolución de los Imperios Ibéricos: 1750–1850*, Madrid 1985, p. 375. This view lies at the heart of Halperín Donghi's general history, originally published in 1967 and by far the most influential in Latin America over the last twenty-five years: 'very slowly after 1850, Latin America began to harvest the fruits of political independence'. *The Contemporary History of Latin America*, Basingstoke 1993, p. 115. A more focused version of the same approach may be found in *The Aftermath of Revolution in Latin America*, New York 1973. It is, however, less evident in the special quincentenary issue of the *JLAS*, 'The Colonial and Post-Colonial Experience', for which Halperín Donghi was the guest editor and in which Frank Safford's chapter on political order in the early republics covers the conventional period of 1830–70.

85. *The Emergence of Latin America in the Nineteenth Century*, Oxford 1994, p. 181.

86. Leslie Bethell (ed.), *Cambridge History of Latin America*, III, originally published in 1985 and entitled *From Independence to c. 1870*, covered the entire early republican period. An edited paperback version, entitled *Spanish America after Independence, c. 1820–c. 1870*, issued in 1987, captures more directly the editorial

Under such conventions the 1840s and 1850s lack any firm 'identity' of their own, and could be seen as little more than a characterless hiatus between independence and the clear divergence from colonial tradition, adoption of free trade, and engagement with the physical infrastructure and political behaviour of 'modernity' that is usually dated from the 1870s. Indeed, some historians concerned with culture and ideas – *mentalités* (which doesn't translate well) – find little or no value in such a periodisation and relegate independence to a firmly subordinate position. For Mark Szuchman there exists a prolonged 'middle period' throughout the eighteenth and nineteenth centuries

> beginning with the consolidation of the patterns brought about by the conquerors' forced reconstitution of Amerindian traditions and ending at the point when significant imports of infrastructural elements and consumer goods resulted from massive foreign loans and investments.[87]

For Richard Morse there are more sub-divisions of the *longue durée*, and they can also be rather more precisely dated, although this schema is no less revisionist of orthodox historiography: Indigenous, to 1520; Spanish, 1520–1760; Colonial, 1760–1920; and National, 1920–.

> The term 'colonial' … serves in the new schema to characterize the period when the creole, Catholic culture and institutions of Spanish America lay open to influences and pressures of the western world and which were on the whole ineffectually mediated to the ethos of the formative Spanish period.[88]

David Brading's magisterial study *The First America: The Spanish Monarchy, Creole Patriots, and the Liberal State* takes the conventional starting date of 1492 – which by itself and through much contested anniversarialism should underline the salience of chronology and periodisation – but ends it in 1867, a Mexican variant of the '1870' conventionally adopted for the sub-continent as a whole. Brading's book is constructed by interlinking essays that lead towards and embellish but only tangentially promote a historical interpretation outlined elsewhere:

> … both independence and the first phase of state-building in Spanish America were justified by the familiar theories of European liberalism, which is to say, by the doctrines of popular

---

interpretation. The popular histories of Latin America for Penguin by George Pendle and Edwin Williamson understandably reflect the scholarly consensus, although Pendle's emphasis on the exhaustion of *caudillismo* and Williamson's on economic reactivation, both from the 1850s, express developments within it. Pendle, *A History of Latin America*, Harmondsworth 1963; Williamson, *Penguin History of Latin America*, Harmondsworth 1992. The corresponding US textbook devotes a chapter entitled 'Dictators and Revolutions' to the period 1830–70. Benjamin Keen and Mark Wasserman, *A History of Latin America*, Boston 1988.

87. Mark Szuchman (ed.), *The Middle Period in Latin America: Values and Attitudes in the 18th and 19th Centuries*, Boulder, Colo., 1989, p. 13.

88. 'Independence in a Patrimonial State', in Joseph Tulchin (ed.), *Problems in Latin American History: The Modern Period*, New York 1973, p. 12. The full version of this essay was originally published in Louis Hartz (ed.), *The Founding of New Societies*, New York 1964. As we will see, Morse's periodisation forms part of a much wider contrarian thesis.

sovereignty and the right to self-government. But this type of political theory was soon supplemented by classical republicanism, which found expression in the culture of patriotic heroes and the elevation of the *patria* as the focus of social identity. It was only at the start of the twentieth century that nationalism emerged in Latin America.... In the first instance, nationalists such as Rodó and Vasconcelos reacted against modernity, embodied in the United States, and appealed to history and culture to preserve their countries from US domination. But the forces of modernisation already operating, thanks to foreign investment, trade and immigration, drove nationalists to enlist in the grand task of state-building.[89]

One strong incentive to break with the orthodox chronology lies in the encourage-ment it can give to a natural vision of development – an almost clinical picture of malady/treatment/recuperation/retrieved health – in the passage from colony through political independence to economic modernisation. In a reading of this type the 1840s and 1850s are simply 'quiet' moments in an inevitable trajectory in which – to pick up Hobsbawm's point – there could be no 'catastrophes' or movements backwards, only progress of a greater or (as in this case) slower velocity.

Such an image is understandably nurtured by some of the views of that time, such as the buoyant celebration of progress in provincial Mexico made by the *Registro Yucateco* in 1846:

> We have literary, scientific, commercial and political journals. There are today in Mérida philanthropic societies, reading groups and scientific academies. Pioneering businesses have triumphed; we have a stagecoach network, cafés, hotels and recreational associations. Primary education has acquired new energy; the government is improving and makes efforts to develop agriculture; roads have been built and repaired. In short, we are on the road to progress.[90]

Six years later Mexico's foremost historian of the early nineteenth century, Lucas Alamán, could write that since 1808 the country had

> changed its name, its territory, the composition of the influential sector of society, the form of government, custom and practice, and not only because of the great revolutions ... but also as an effect of the complete change that the entire world had undergone in the same period.

Yet Alamán was at complete odds with the view taken by his Yucatecan compatriots. He saw no progress at all – not regression or even stasis – but a direct deterioration of the human condition, and for more reasons than the taking of part of his country by the USA:

> To see in so few years this immense loss of territory; this ruin of the economy ... this annihilation of a brave and energetic army deprived of proper equipment and resources, and, above all, the complete extinction of public spirit, which has made the idea of national

89. 'Nationalism and State Building in Latin American History', in Eduardo Posada-Carbó (ed.), *Wars, Parties and Nationalism: Essays on the Politics and Society of Nineteenth-Century Latin America*, London 1995, p. 107; *The First America: The Spanish Monarchy, Creole Patriots, and the Liberal State, 1492–1867*, Cambridge 1991.

90. Quoted in Marie Lapointe, *Los Mayas Rebeldes de Yucatán*, Zamora, Michoacán, 1983, p. 32.

character disappear. There are no Mexicans in Mexico, and looking at the country which has collapsed into infamy and decrepitude without ever having enjoyed more than a glimpse of the lushness of being juvenile or having shown any signs of life other than violent commotion, it would seem that there is every reason to agree with the great Bolívar that independence has been brought at the cost of all the assets that America possessed before.

Furthermore, if there was one particular culprit, it was the materialism bred of the Enlightenment – the very ethos associated with 'progress' and epitomised by the invading USA:

> All this has come about as a consequence of the irreligious and anti-social philosophy of the eighteenth century. Nothing now mattered except money, the acquisition of which became the exclusive objective of all, by any means deemed acceptable … and since nobody feels obliged to place their fortune at the service of their country, when a weak government needs financial support at the nation's most critical hour, it finds nothing but hardened hearts and closed purses.[91]

This view was not so distant from that of Domingo Faustino Sarmiento, who, as Halperín Donghi reminds us in the first sentence of *The Aftermath*, 'liked to compare the disconcerting trajectory covered by Latin America from the time of the declaration of independence until the middle of the nineteenth century with the forty years' wandering of the Israelites in the desert'.[92] Maybe Sarmiento – who was a 'big head' in the worst as well as best sense of the term – had figured himself as an Argentine Moses from his twenties, but it is clear from his most famous text, *Facundo* (1845), that he was not expecting the majority of the population to find a sense of direction (and so deliverance) on their own:

> The mass of men are incapable of distinctly comparing one epoch with another; the present moment is the only one embraced by their observation; and for this reason no one has yet observed this destruction and decadence of the cities; just as the visible progress of the people of the interior to total barbarism escapes notice.[93]

It might be argued that Argentina and Mexico are – for very different reasons – special cases and not representative of the general pattern of a region of some twenty states that had yet to acquire the tag of 'Latin America', even if we limit ourselves to the ex-colonies of Spain. In the former case the overthrow of the tyrant Rosas in 1852 constitutes a critical moment, and in the latter the US invasion of 1846 not only dispossessed the state of much territory but also weakened central authority so much that popular opposition, liberal reform and further foreign intervention readily followed. There is also a case for adding Nicaragua to these examples – less because the filibusters of the 1850s led by William Walker created chaos than because their aggressive intervention changed the nature of the local conflict and had the eventual

---

91. *Historia de Méjico*, V, Mexico 1852, pp. 903–4, 919.
92. Halperín, *Aftermath*, p. vii.
93. The standard English translation of *Facundo* is *Life in the Argentine Republic in the Days of the Tyrants; or Civilisation and Barbarism*, New York 1868, p. 63.

effect of reducing it.[94] Moreover, Nicaragua had already been made vulnerable by the turmoil of the California Gold Rush, for which it formed part of the main route for several years, and it soon became the site of strenuous rivalry between Washington and London. Some aspects of this experience were to make a recognisable return in the 1930s and 1980s, when the geopolitical importance of the country was similarly distinct from that of the rest of Central America notwithstanding the existence of the Panama Canal.

INDIGENOUS TIME

With respect to the indigenous peoples of the Americas – and, indeed, those indigenous to other lands who would become 'Americans' – we already know that chronology and periodisation involve greater complications and demand exceptional care and sensitivity. Perhaps it is safest just to treat these years as formally similar to or 'coeval' – 'equally old; existing at the same time', according to the *Oxford English Dictionary* – with the dominant European system. But even outside of anthropology this is a risky strategy, threatening simply to invert the self-centredness of the colonial vision.[95] Olivia Harris has lucidly argued with respect to the arrival of the Europeans in the continent that the matter is not so clear-cut:

> The 'naturalness' by which we assume that events which were of momentous significance for European historiography and the construction of the European identity have the same status in the historiographical imagination of those conquered and subjugated by these same Europeans, needs to be unpicked. It is, therefore, salutary to bear in mind that in some instances indigenous peoples seemed to have expressed indifference or at least evinced very little surprise at the arrival of the Europeans.[96]

If such an argument can be made about the initial conquest it is likely to have greater salience still for a time of ostensibly less rupture. Correspondingly, of course,

---

94. Bradford Burns's history of early Nicaragua runs from 1798, the date of 'the first cogent statement of the Nicaraguan patriarchal elites of their vision', to 1858, when he sees 'the first signs of the emergence of a viable nation-state. Anarchy characterized the decades between them.' Walker certainly increased the anarchy but he did not create it. E. Bradford Burns, *Patriarch and Folk: The Emergence of Nicaragua, 1798–1858*, Cambridge, Mass., 1991, p. 1.

95. Fabian sees 'physical' and 'typological' types of interpretative time as distancing devices that deny coevalness and represent 'a persistent and systematic tendency to place the referent(s) of anthropology in a Time other than the present of the the producer of the anthropological discourse'. *Time and the Other*, p. 31.

96. '"The Coming of the White People". Reflections on the Mythologisation of History in Latin America', *BLAR*, 14:1, 1995, p. 18.

what trades low in the market of white historiography might sell high elsewhere; the grey 'in-betweenness' of these transitional Euro-centric years covering a real or mythical life and death epoch in an autochthonous vision. And, as Harris reminds us, 'Myth cannot simply be associated with the static, the timeless, the past-oriented, but may also invoke archetypal moments of rupture, a contrast between before and after, the sense of a beginning.'[97]

In short, a formidable task of translation and revalorisation must precede any analysis, even when dealing with conflict between indigenous and European peoples, let alone the universe of 'hybridity' which has come to displace the easy – if fierce – dichotomies that previously prevailed in academic as well as political interpretation. The very fact that, for instance, the Mohawk, Chickasaw, K'ekchi, Aymara and Araucanian peoples are only seen as commonly 'Indian' through European eyes means that any uniform 'Indian History' is a European artefact. Yet the multiple indigenous histories do share a varied experience of engagement with the Anglo-Iberian forces, and this is important enough to take as at least one index of chronology.

These wholesale caveats do not apply quite so strongly to the case of Ireland, but that experience is probably of a more compacted character than any other. (It is also potent illustration of the need not to play too freely with the term 'European' in the American context; this period saw an array of aggressive nativisms, only some of which were directed against the tribes and slaves.) In recent years Irish historiography has undergone a quite extensive bout of revisionism, aimed principally at the stark certainties of a nationalist hagiography and demonology. But none of the impressive 'cliometrics' (statistical historiography) or sophisticated reappraisal has dislodged two central characteristics attributed to the famine of 1845–50: the speed of its onset and the scale of the human devastation caused by it.[98] Even the most sceptical account must, it would seem, recognise this as a historic event without parallel in the country's history.

On 16 July 1845 the *Dublin Evening Mail* reprinted a report from the *Tyrone Constitution* that 'wheat, barley, oats and flax are all good – the hay will be a prime

---

97. Ibid., p. 15.

98. In the present context the most useful contrast is less between modern, 'professional' and archaic, 'political' histories than in the different interpretations of two contemporary historians – Mary Daly and Cormac Ó Gráda – the former adopting an approach described by the latter as 'dispassionate and sanitized'. Mary Daly, *The Great Famine in Ireland*, Dublin 1986, and 'Revisionism and the Great Famine', in D. George Boyce and Alan O'Day (eds), *The Making of Modern Irish History: Revisionism and the Revisionist Controversy*, London 1996; Cormac Ó Gráda, *The Great Irish Famine*, London 1989, *Ireland: A New Economic History: 1780–1939*, Oxford 1994, and introduction to R. Dudley-Edwards and T. Desmond Williams (eds), *The Great Famine*, Dublin 1986. None the less, Ó Gráda's analysis is strong on statistics, and he works closely with the 'technical' economic historians Peter Solar and Joel Mokyr. Neither author is mentioned with respect to the Famine in the bibliographical essay of R.F. Foster, *Modern Ireland 1600–1972*, Harmondsworth 1988, which is perhaps the most accomplished general text emanating from the 'new wave'. See also Foster's 'We are all Revisionists Now', *Irish Review*, 1, 1986. Terry Eagleton, who is critical of an overly judicious tone in the writing of Daly and Foster on the Famine, comments that 'the revisionist historians' admirable broad-mindedness seems to stop mysteriously short of John Mitchel or Patrick Pearse'. *Heathcliff and the Great Hunger*, London 1995, p. 22.

crop, and potatoes are better in appearance than at any former period', fully in keeping with the good yields earlier in the decade.[99] On 23 August the *Dublin Evening Post* reported that heavy rains had damaged the potato crop; but on 9 September it reassured its readers that the recent failure of the US crop would itself have no effect in that country and, 'happily, there is no grounds for any apprehensions of the kind in Ireland'.[100] A fortnight later this was shown to be thoroughly incorrect, and by early October the scale of the blight for the country's staple crop evidently presaged a major disaster for a population that had come to depend on it. The 1846 crop failed too, and to such a degree that a ravaged and demoralised rural population planted only a third of the 1845 acreage for 1847, when the harvest was not so badly affected. The next year's crop failed, and that of 1849 was partially blighted.

When it was clear that the 1846 crop had failed, *The Vindicator* of Belfast, a town directly affected more acutely by disease than by famine itself, offered a pungent assessment of world needs:

> Russia wants liberty, Prussia wants a constitution, Switzerland wants religion, Spain wants a king, Ireland alone wants food. The public cry in every other country argues an advance in the social system; the public cry in ours betokens and presupposes a state of misery unknown on the other side of civilization.... It is a cry not heard where civilization is unknown. The red man of America flies before the advance of social life – slays the bison that grazes the prairie over which he roams, and fattens on untaxed, spontaneous plenty.[101]

This image was not true any longer for large parts of America, but it was intrinsically plausible and must have seemed increasingly persuasive over the following months as the paper's (highly privileged) readership read daily reports such as that sent in from County Sligo in January 1847:

> An inquest was held on the 12th instant, upon the body of Thomas M'Manus, of Kilmactranny. Verdict – 'Deceased came to his death by hunger and cold'. This wretched creature was observed by a man lying in a muddy ditch; he was raised up, and the man went to two or three houses in the neighbourhood, and asked the people to admit deceased, but they refused, alleging that he had typhus fever. He then carried deceased to a haggard and placed him upon some straw, where he was found dead on the following morning and horribly mutilated. We copy the evidence of Thomas Burrows, Esq., M.D. – 'Examined the body of Thomas M'Manus; both the legs, as far as the buttocks, appeared to have been eaten off by a pig...' There was not a particle of food found in deceased's stomach or intestines. Those who saw the body were of opinion, from the agonized expression of M'Manus' countenance, that he was *alive* when the pig attacked him.[102]

It was a few months after this dreadful incident that Henry Thoreau ended his seclusion in a hut on the banks of Walden Pond, Massachusetts. Although Thoreau never travelled abroad and remained in the woods during the worst years of the

---

99. Quoted in John Killen (ed.), *The Famine Decade: Contemporary Accounts 1841–1851*, Belfast 1995, p. 30.
100. Quoted in ibid., p. 35.
101. *The Vindicator*, 3 Oct. 1846, quoted in ibid., pp. 71–2.
102. *The Vindicator*, 20 Jan. 1847, quoted in ibid., p. 99.

Famine, he – like *The Vindicator* – was able to percive the awful contradiction in Ireland's condition:

> It is a mistake to suppose that, in a country where the usual evidences of civilisation exist, the condition of a very large body of the inhabitants may not be as degraded as that of savages. I refer to the degraded poor, not to the degraded rich.... I could refer you to Ireland, which is marked as one of the white or enlightened spots on the map. Contrast the physical condition of the Irish with that of the North American Indian, or the South Sea Islander, or any other savage race before it was degraded by contact with the civilised man. Yet I have no doubt that that people's rulers are as wise as the average of civilised rulers. Their condition only proves what squalidness may consist with civilisation.[103]

Between the censuses of 1841 and 1851 the population of Ireland declined by nearly 20 per cent, from 8.18 million to 6.56 million people. The most detailed and sober of modern calculations agree on excess deaths of at least a million, effectively over a period of five years.[104] The population loss as a whole was at least 2.5 million, up to 250,000 people leaving the country each year for the decade after the Famine started. Moreover, the flow did not stop. In 1911 the population of Ireland was 52 per cent of that of 1841, and four times as many people of Irish descent lived in the Americas than in Ireland itself. This is a most radical catastrophe in Eric Hobsbawm's sense of a failure to reproduce the past. In Terry Eagleton's words:

> Ireland's disaster was a kind of inverted image of European turmoil, one which you suffer rather than create, which strips culture to the poor, forked Beckettian creature and which, in threatening to slip below the level of meaning itself, offers to deny you even the meagre consolations of tragedy. What lingers on, in such contaminated remnants of the epoch as the language itself, would seem less tragedy than the very different culture of shame. During the Famine, starving families boarded themselves into their cabins, so that their deaths might go decently unviewed. After the event, there were villages which could still speak Irish but didn't; it was considered bad luck.[105]

The Famine is also what converts Ireland from a generally Atlantic country into a peculiarly American one within Europe, assuredly sustained by a superabundance of myth but also validated by the fact that well over a million Irish people became Americans – or started to become Americans – at this point, comprising a third of the population of New York in 1855.[106] Domingo Faustino Sarmiento reported of his visit to that city in 1847,

---

103. *Walden*, p. 31.

104. For a detailed analysis, see Cormac Ó Gráda and Joel Mokyr, 'New Developments in Irish Population History, 1700–1850', *Economic History Review*, XXXVII:4, 1984, pp. 473–88; Ó Gráda, *Ireland: A New Economic History*, pp. 213–35. For brief, accessible surveys, see Ó Gráda, *Great Irish Famine*, pp. 61–2; Christine Kinealy, *This Great Calamity: The Irish Famine*, Dublin 1994, pp. 167–74.

105. *Heathcliff and the Great Hunger*, p. 21.

106. The 8th US census of 1860 counted 1.6 million people of Irish birth (500,000 in New York) out of a total foreign population of 4.9 million. Although the US censuses did not ask about religious affiliation, those in Canada did, and on the basis of this and the high flow of cross-border migration Donald Akenson argues that 'the bulk of the Irish ethnic group in the United States is at present, and probably always has been, Protestant'. *The Irish Diaspora: A Primer*, Belfast 1993, p. 219.

In the afternoons I would go near the dock where the unhappy Irish came up from below like rats from caves. They were half naked and emaciated, their spirits animated by the hope of seeing an end to their miseries in the promised land. There were old women in their sixties emigrating, and a blind beggar played the pipes in the afternoon so that the filthy, skinny and dishevelled ladies could dance. The little ragamuffins, naked or covered with rags, were not hindered from loitering near the dancers. These people looked like convalescents from a hospital or inmates in a house of correction. Some looked as though they were quite ready to die, and indeed six or eight were flung into the ocean on some days without this in any way affecting the attendance at the afternoon dance.[107]

Read from the outside, no other ethnic group already in or arriving at the continent in these years underwent such an acute experience-as-event, rather than process. The indigenous peoples of North America were under continuous pressure from the east, but this varied in form and intensity. If there is a single event subsequently associated with it in 'the popular mind' it is probably the defeat of General George Custer on the Little Bighorn river in June 1876. This, of course, illustrates the dangers identified by Olivia Harris in terms of its inverted triumphalism. However, the consequences in this instance were very real and perceived as such by the Sioux and Cheyenne tribes of the northern plains, whose dwindling resistance was snuffed out at the snow-bound camp of Wounded Knee, South Dakota, on 29 December 1890. However complex and convoluted the projection of 'Indians' by Hollywood and television might sometimes have been in the Cold War era – Crazy Horse, one of the victors of Little Bighorn, decisively refused to be photographed, whereas our image of the Wounded Knee leader Little Foot is that of a frozen corpse of an ill old man – it almost invariably placed Little Bighorn above Wounded Knee. Before the late 1960s there was no mass audience for a text like Dee Brown's *Bury My Heart at Wounded Knee* (1970), which was by no means the first book – popular or academic – of its type but struck a powerful chord in its closing rendition of the massacre of some 300 exhausted, distressed and largely unarmed people – two-thirds of them women and children – by 470 members of the 7th cavalry supported by a battery of Hotchkiss guns.[108]

Brown's book begins with the Civil War and so is a story of almost unremitting tragedy – echoed to the south by the prolonged and theatrical advertisement of the subdued Chiricahua Apache leader, Geronimo. The nineteenth century opened in similar fashion, further to the east, with the failure of the Shawnee leader, Tecumseh, to establish a confederacy of Native Americans after a long peripatetic organisational and ideological campaign from his Tippecanoe base near Lake Michigan. Tecumseh was killed in 1813 during the war between the US and Britain, which he attempted to exploit in order to halt settler pressure on lands both in the old north-west and in the south. As was later to occur in the Civil War, this conflict divided the tribes internally and externally, General Andrew Jackson defeating Edward Pakenham's British

---

107. Michael Rockland (ed.), *Sarmiento's Travels in the United States in 1847*, Princeton 1970, p. 213.
108. See, in particular, Ralph K. Andrist, *The Long Death: The Last Days of the Plains Indians*, New York 1964; and the work of Angie Debo, especially *A History of the Indians of the United States*, Norman, Okla., 1970, and *Geronimo*, Norman, Okla., 1976.

forces at New Orleans in January 1815 with the help of Cherokee braves. It was also Jackson, though, who as president introduced in 1830 the central statutory basis for Indian 'removal', which, as it pressed persistently westward during the middle years of the century, simultaneously opened a white frontier and brought an indigenous world to a close.

The Indian Removal Act authorised the president to mark off lands west of the Mississippi, 'not included in any state or organised territory', in exchange for lands held by the Indians in the east, and he was charged by the act 'solemnly to assure the tribe or nation with which the exchange is made, that the United States will forever secure and guaranty to them, and their heirs or successors, the country so exchanged with them'.[109] It is more characteristic of the mid-century years than those of Tecumseh, which opened it, and Little Foot, which closed it, that this challenge was met with initial repudiation, graduated negotiation, partial compliance and occasional demands in the courts for white adherence to signed agreements. The experience – which certainly did not exclude armed conflict – was scarcely less severe since knowledge of the more or less explicit European disavowal of treaties with the tribes retreating from the east progressively diminished the trust of the indigenous population further to the west in this means deployed to 'civilise' them. Yet even when full contact was made with the Indians of California in the 1850s, the encounter had yet to acquire a fully ethnocidal nature.

In 1831 Jackson's act was subjected to an indirect but important challenge in the Supreme Court:

> This bill is brought by the Cherokee nation, praying an injunction to restrain the state of Georgia from the execution of certain laws of that State, which, it is alleged, go directly to annihilate the Cherokees as a political society, and to seize for the use of Georgia the lands of the nation which have been assured to them by The United States in solemn treaties repeatedly made and still in force.
>
> If Courts were permitted to indulge their sympathies, a case better calculated to excite them can scarcely be imagined. A People once numerous, powerful and truly independent, found by our ancestors in the quiet and uncontrolled possession of an ample domain, gradually sinking beneath our superior policy, our arts and our arms, have yielded their lands by successive treaties.

Despite his sympathy for the plaintiffs and a sharp dissenting opinion from Justice Thompson, Chief Justice Marshall delivered a majority opinion that rejected the plea of the Cherokees on the grounds that the Supreme Court was not competent to rule between Georgia and them as they did not constitute a 'foreign nation' as understood by the Constitution. Indians, the Court decided,

> may … be denominated domestic dependent nations. They occupy a territory to which we assert a title independent of their will, which must take effect in point of possession when

---

109. Quoted in Francis Paul Prucha, *The Great Father: The United States Government and the American Indians*, Lincoln, Nebr., 1984, p. 206.

their possession ceases. Meanwhile, they are in a state of pupilage. Their relation to the United States resembles that of a ward to his guardian.

In his dissenting minority opinion Mr Justice Thompson stated:

> The progress made in civilization by the Cherokee Indians cannot surely be considered as in any measure destroying their national or foreign character, so long as they are permitted to maintain a separate and distinct government; it is their political constitution that constitutes their *foreign* character, and in that sense must the term *foreign* be understood as used in the Constitution. It can have no relation to local, geographical or territorial constitution. It cannot mean a country beyond sea.... The Cherokee territory being within the chartered limits of Georgia does not affect the question. When Georgia is spoken of as a state, reference is had to its political character, and not to boundary.[110]

The next year the Court was presented with a similar case and took a different line:

> The Cherokee nation ... is a distinct community, occupying its own territory, with boundaries accurately described, in which the laws of Georgia can have no force, and which the citizens of Georgia have no right to enter, but with the assent of the Cherokees themselves.[111]

Jackson, however, purposefully ignored this ruling and thereby ensured the active relocation of the five 'civilised tribes'. The Chickasaws were moved from Mississippi, the Creeks from Alabama, and the Seminoles from Florida in 1832; the Cherokees from Georgia in 1835, whilst the Choctaws were the first to cede their lands, in Mississippi, in 1830. All were allocated lands in the Indian Territory, covering present-day Oklahoma and parts of Kansas and Nebraska. In the south there was resistance from the Seminoles until 1842; in the north the Fox and Sauk people, having suffered defeat in the Black Hawk War of 1832, were removed from Wisconsin and Iowa. Thus, when Stephen Douglas sought in January 1854 to detain the crisis around slavery – and to promote a trans-continental railroad – with his Kansas–Nebraska bill, this measure affected major tracts of supposedly inviolable Indian territory and contibuted to a second expropriation within twenty years of some fourteen tribes in those territories, from which they now lost nearly 17 million acres.

Some sense of the different cultures, needs and sense of time at stake may be gleaned from the following exchange between Governor Alexander Ramsey of Minnesota and Chief Red Iron of the Sisseton Sioux in December 1852:

---

110. Quoted in Wilcomb E. Washburn (ed.), *The American Indians and the United States: A Documentary History*, New York 1973, IV, pp. 2554-5; 2584. Article III, Section 2 of the Constitution states:

> The Judicial Power shall extend to all Cases, in Law and Equity, arising under this Constitution, the Laws of the United States, and Treaties made, or which shall be made under their Authority; to all Cases affecting Ambassadors, other public Ministers and Consuls; to all Cases of admiralty and maritime Jurisdiction; the Controversies to which the United States shall be a Party; to Controversies between two or more States; between a State and Citizens of another State; between Citizens of different States; between Citizens of the same State claiming Lands under Grants of different States, and between a State, or Citizens thereof, and foreign States, Citizens or Subjects.

111. Ibid., p. 2622.

Governor: 'Your Great Father has sent me to represent him, and what I say is what he says. He wants you to pay your old debts, in accordance with the paper you signed when the treaty was made, and to leave that money in my hands to pay these debts. If you refuse to do that I will take the money [for the annuity of the tribe] back.'

Red Iron: 'You can take the money back. We sold our land to you, and you promised to pay us. If you don't give us the money I will be glad, and all our people will be glad, for we will have our land back if you don't give us the money. That paper was not interpreted or explained to us. We are told it gives about 300 boxes [$300,000] of our money to some of the traders. We don't think we owe them so much. We want to pay all our debts. We want our Great Father to send three good men here to tell us how much we do owe, and whatever they say we will pay; and that's what all the braves say. Our chiefs and our people say this.' All the Indians present responded, 'Ho! Ho!'

Governor: 'That can't be done. You owe more than your money will pay, and I am ready now to pay your annuity, and no more, and when you are ready to receive it, the agent will pay you.'

Red Iron: 'We will receive our annuity, but we will sign no papers for anything else. The snow is on the grounds, and we have been waiting a long time to get our money. We are poor; you have plenty. Your fires are warm. Your tepees keep out the cold. We have nothing to eat. We have been waiting a long time for our moneys. Our hunting season is past. A great many of our people are sick, for being hungry. We may die because you won't pay us. We may die, but if we do we will leave our bones on the ground, that our Great Father may see where his Dakota children died. We are very poor. We have sold our hunting grounds and the graves of our fathers. We have sold our own graves. We have no place to bury our dead, and you will not pay us the money for our lands.'[112]

Not all tribes suffered equally or reacted in similar manner; there may be an 'Indian history' but it is best understood as being composed as one of separate peoples. Chitto Harjo, a Creek, recalled the first phase on the new lands in unambiguous terms: 'I was living well out here with my people. We were all prospering. We had a great deal of property, all over this country.... We had laws that were living laws, and ... I was living here in peace and plenty with my people; we were happy.'[113]

In 1851 an unprecedented council of northern tribes (Sioux, Shoshone, Crow, Cheyenne, Arapaho) produced an 'internal' accord without an acute sense of imminent danger, as expressed by Cut Nose of the Arapaho:

I will go home satisfied. I will sleep sound, and not have to watch my horses at night, or be afraid for my women and children. We have to live on these streams and in the hills, and I would be glad if the whites would pick a place for themselves and not come into our grounds.[114]

A similar council, including Comanches and Kiowas, reached an agreement not to molest the vital westward Santa Fe trail in 1853. Even the killing of the Sioux chief, Bear that Scatters, and the retaliatory annihilation of thirty US troopers near Fort

---

112. H.H. Jackson, *A Century of Dishonor*, Boston 1893, Appendix 6, quoted in Wayne Moquin and Charles Van Doren (eds), *Great Documents in American Indian History*, New York 1995, pp. 164–5.
113. Quoted in Debo, *History of the Indians*, p. 149.
114. Quoted in ibid., pp. 165–6.

Laramie in 1854 failed to provoke wider conflict. Again, it is the Civil War that constitutes the obvious general watershed, not least by making neutrality impossible for the settled tribes of the south as well as withdrawing regular troops from many forts. However, in terms of the inter-racial consquences we might identify a new phase as starting on 26 December 1862, when thirty-eight Minnesota Sioux were hanged for murder. It is at this point that President Lincoln, who had served in the Black Hawk War, eventually authorised the single largest legal execution in US history after widespread destruction and the killing of hundreds of settlers that summer.[115]

No census before 1850 counted Indians, and it is only with the 11th census of 1890 – the year of Wounded Knee – that the native population received attention remotely to the same degree as that accorded to the three categories that had hitherto dominated demographic measurement: white, free coloured and slave, immigrant. One can, however, sketch a tentative image of numbers and movement from earlier reports, estimates and extrapolations, almost all of which identify a population of from 300,000 to 320,000 between 1830 and 1880.[116] In 1867 240 distinct groups were identified – including, for example, fourteen sub-groups of the Sioux nation – but at least forty had disappeared entirely from the eastern states. Even in 1850 no more than 10 per cent of the indigenous population was living east of the Ohio River; by 1860, of the 295,000 Indians retaining their tribal character in agencies or reservations, less than 6,000 lived in the original states of the Union, where ten times that number had lived a generation earlier. (All 44,000 members of the 'civilised tribes' were now in the west.)[117] Removal had produced a comprehensive result. By 1850 there were more Irish than Indians in the space that is today the USA, and that place was rapidly becoming seen as one of arrival, not departure. On occasions these two peoples would meet, and sometimes to distinct advantage. Tom Meagher, having resigned as general commanding the Irish Brigade in the Unionist army and been appointed governor of Montana, put the crack before the bullet when faced with raids by young Blackfoot bloods:

---

115. Lincoln was presented with a list of 303 men condemned to death by Henry Sibley and General John Pope, who had earlier declared to Sibley,

> It is my purpose to utterly exterminate the Sioux if I have the power to do so.... Destroy everything belonging to them and force them out to the plains, unless, as I suggest, you can capture them. They are to be treated as maniacs or wild beasts, and by no means as people with whom treaties or compromises can be made.

The president had all the cases subjected to close review and told the Senate that he was, 'anxious not to act with so much clemency as to encourage another outbreak ... nor with so much severity as to be cruelty'. His commuting of the sentences of some 270 men was based on both procedural review and a distinction between those who had killed in cold blood and in battle. Prucha, *Great Father*, p. 445. The Sioux were removed from Minnesota the following March.

116. *11th Census of the USA, 1890*, Washington 1894, p. 5.

117. *7th Census of the USA, 1850*, Washington 1853, p. xciv, which compares the size and location of groups identified in 1825 by the secretary of war's office with those of 1853 by the commissioner of Indian affairs; *11th Census*, p. 18. (The 8th census excluded Indians retaining tribal relations.)

If anyone can carry it to a successful issue he is as good at a palaver as at a fight, and his eloquence is just of the character to suit the Indians. He will quiet them by talking their heads off – a much less costly and more humane process than that of exterminating them.[118]

The racial control of space at the other end of the continent – now known as the Southern Cone – followed a quite similar pattern over the nineteenth century, although it is perhaps telling that the indigenous chiefs of the pampa desisted from taking Tecumseh's course of siding with his enemy's enemy, and instead offered to treat with the Spanish authorities in Buenos Aires when it was raided by the British in 1806. The position is not best understood by taking the contemporary states of Argentina and Chile as a starting point. Only a small portion of the latter state, between the Bío Bío and Tolten Rivers (and the towns of Concepción and Valdivia), lay in the hands of the Araucanian people, who were divided into four main, and sometimes conflicting, groups – Abajinos, Costinos, Arribanos, Huilliches – with a total population of perhaps 150,000 in 1850. On the other side of the Andes indigenous people controlled the entire southern landmass of the continent from Tierra del Fuego to within a day's ride of the colonists' principal towns of Buenos Aires, Córdoba and Mendoza. The 'Argentina' that was only to acquire a formal identity in 1862 hitherto halted in an arc between these settlements, which until the 1830s were far more concerned with defence against Indian raids (*malones*) than expanding the frontier. The pampa was universally known as 'the desert' and hardly considered as an economic resource. The main groups occupying this vast expanse were the Ranqueles, Salineros, Pampas, Telhueches and Pehuenches, numbering no more than 100,000 and engaged in a nomadic subsistence economy that included the rustling and trading of cattle and horses to the 'Christians' of Chile.

In August 1833 Charles Darwin, exploring between the Colorado and Negro Rivers – the limit of white patrols at that time – encountered the insecurity of life on the frontier:

'When not far from our destination, my companion ... spied three people hunting on horseback. He immediately dismounted, and watching them intently, said, 'They don't ride like Christians, and nobody can leave the fort'. The three hunters joined company, and likewise dismounted from their horses ... My companion said, 'We must now get on our horses; load your pistol', and he looked to his sword. I asked, 'Are they Indians?' – 'Quien sabe? If there are no more than three, it does not signify'. It then struck me that the one man had gone over the hill to fetch the rest of his tribe. I suggested this; but all the answer I could extract was 'Quien sabe?' His head and eye never for a moment ceased scanning slowly the distant horizon. I thought his uncommon coolness too good a joke, and asked him why he did not return home. I was startled when he answered, 'We are returning, but in a line so as to pass near a swamp, into which we can gallop the horses as far as they can go, and then trust to our own legs; so that there is no danger'. I did not feel quite so confident of this, and wanted to increase our pace. He said, 'No, not until they do'.[119]

---

118. *New York Herald*, 31 May 1867, quoted in Thomas Keneally, *The Great Shame: A Story of the Irish in the Old World and the New*, London 1998, pp. 466–7.
119. *Voyage of the Beagle*, Harmondsworth 1989, pp. 92–3.

The three figures eventually transpired to be white women collecting ostrich eggs.

On the Pacific side of the Andes the Araucanians had violently and successfully resisted Spanish advances on their territory since the mid sixteenth century, and the Bío Bío was to all intents and purposes a military front-line, albeit one dormant for prolonged periods. However, at mid century both it and the trans-Andean pampa were subjected to rising pressure from both economic and political sources. In Chile a stable authoritarian regime sought to secure the integrity of a republic within which an autonomous territory posed a decided threat even if it did facilitate the commerce of cheap cattle. On the trans-Andean plain an initial effort by Governor Juan Manuel Rosas – who shared several qualities with Andrew Jackson – to clear Indians off the lands as far south as the Rio Negro in 1831–33 had succeeded in no more than establishing a few outposts, protecting Rosas' own considerable estates to the south of Buenos Aires, and securing a generally reliable agreement with the Salinero *toki* (chief), Juan Calfucura. However, when Rosas was overthrown in 1852, the victory which seemed to open the construction of a 'civilised' Argentina also upset the fragile frontier, heralding three decades of growing conflict.

This began under Bartolomé Mitre in 1855 with a futile effort to subjugate the Indians through traditional military means; it reached its peak in the guerrilla-counter-guerrilla ('*malón contra malón*') campaign of 1868–72; and it ended with the carefully prepared and sternly executed 'scorched earth' offensive of General Roca in 1879–82. That campaign also put paid to any lingering hopes of Araucanian independence, because nobody on either side of the Andes or the racial divide was under any illusion as to the close economic, ethnic and politico-military linkages between the two spheres. In 1868 the Chilean writer Benjamín Vicuña Mackenna explicitly expressed his support for fiercer military tactics in these terms:

> As for emigration to the Pampas, I just hope that it's already happening, and so saving us the large amounts of blood and cash that will otherwise be necessary … they can put up their hovels wherever they want when they make common cause with the Indian of the Pampa, the most horrible member of the human race.[120]

A dozen years later the Argentine officer J.M. Olascoaga, who in 1870 had served under the veteran Chilean frontier commander Colonel Cornelio Saavedra, was in no doubt from his experience with the Araucanians that the campaign on the pampa had to be without quarter:

> [The Santiago government] understood that if Saavedra's scheme came to fruition the Araucanians would remain suppressed within Chile as a separate and autonomous government, and as a consequence responsibility for the thousands of rustled cattle would fall upon the civilized authorities.[121]

---

120. *La Conquista del Arauco*, Santiago 1868, quoted in Leonardo León, 'Alianzas militares entre los indios Araucanos y los grupos indios de las Pampas: La rebelión Araucana de 1868–1872 en Argentina y Chile', *Nueva Historia*, 1:1, 1981, p. 23.

121. *Estudio Topográfico de la Pampa y Río Negro*, Buenos Aires 1881, quoted in ibid., pp. 29–30. Olascoaga

Saavedra and his Argentine counterpart, Colonel Alvaro Barros, were tough officers but also men who were scrupulous in their actions, generally respected by the indigenous leadership and not without some sympathy for them – somewhat like the late colonial governor of Chile, Ambrosio O'Higgins.[122] However, by the time General Roca was preparing 'the conquest of the desert' he was under heavy pressure to secure new land for farming, and he possessed barbed wire and Remington rifles with which to confront Indians still dependent on their *bolas* and lances. Moreover, attitudes were little changed from those described half a century earlier by Darwin (who erred in thinking that the warfare 'is too bloody to last; the Christians killing any Indian, and the Indians doing the same by the Christians'):

> Every one here is fully convinced that this is the most just war because it is against barbarians. Who would believe in this age, in a Christian civilized country, that such atrocities were committed? The children of the Indians are saved, to be sold or given away as servants, or rather slaves, for as long a time as the owners can deceive them; but I believe in this respect there is little to complain of.[123]

In the case of Araucania there was no 'final offensive'. Although many 'Chilean' Indians surely participated in the resistance against the white Argentine advance across the pampa in the early 1880s, the decision of the Arribano *toki*, Quilapán, to negotiate following the parliament of Purén in 1871 marked a decisive shift away from armed conflict. The Chilean campaign of 1868–71 involved much greater division and manipulation of the native groups than occurred in Argentina, and it was notably less bloody. One incident within it which is usually treated as *opéra bouffe* but has more than anecdotal weight was the arrival in Chile in 1869 of Orélie Antoine de Tounens, a fifty-year-old adventurer from Hourgnac in the Dordogne who in 1860 had himself crowned the first king of Araucania, and who at the end of 1861 offered the main chiefs support in their independence struggle. Betrayed by his interpreters, Aurelio Antonio the First was arrested, deemed by a judge to be too demented to plead, and placed in an asylum. Orélie Antoine was presumptuous enough to declare the existence of his kingdom on the ground that 'Araucania does not depend on any other state', but he was kind enough to make his monarchy constitutional as well as hereditary. (He remained a bachelor without issue, which rather suggests that he

---

was writing in the aftermath of Roca's victory. Leaving Buenos Aires in April 1879, the general was able to report by the end of that year the capture of five *caciques* (headmen) and the death of one (Baigorrita of the Ranqueles); the capture of 1,271 warriors, wounding of 1,313 and killing of another 1,049 (little effort was made to spare fighters who were not leaders); and the removal of 10,513 women, children and old people. In effect, all the fighters of the Ranquel people had been eliminated, and the entire population uprooted. *Informe del Ministro de Guerra, 1879*, cited in Jorge Paez, *La Conquista del Desierto*, Buenos Aires 1970, p. 110.

122. *Ambrose O'Higgins*, born Ballynure, County Antrim, 1720 or 1725. Moved to Cádiz, 1749; to Chile, 1761. Colonel of cavalry, 1777; Governor of Concepción, 1786; Governor of the Kingdom of Chile, 1788–96. Abolished obligatory Indian labour, 1791; held parliament with Indian leaders at Negrete, February 1793. Viceroy of Peru, 1796–1800. Died, 1801. *Bernardo O'Higgins*, born 1778 the illegitimate son of Ambrosio and Riquelme Mesa, was Supreme Director of the newly independent Chile, 1817–23. Died in Peruvian exile, 1842.

123. *Voyage of the Beagle*, pp. 111–12.

didn't become a king in order to get a queen, but he eventually appointed a successor, and the pantomime continues in Paris, where there is – of course – an Academie des Hautes Etudes Araucaniennes). The inventory made of Orélie Antoine's belongings by Inspector Jervasio Sanhuezo in January 1862 seems to indicate a quite serious monarchical disposition for dominion through dress:

> Inventory of items belonging to the Frenchman who has been arrested in the indigenous territory – he who goes by the name of Orélie Antonio [*sic*] the First – which property has been discovered in his luggage. A mattress and a pillow. A shawl of cloth. A pair of trousers. A jacket, and another jacket. Two more pairs of trousers. A shirt. A packet of silk handkerchiefs. A piece of cloth. A package. Two banderas. A shirt. A packet of snuff and a handkerchief. A pair of trousers. A black frock-coat. Shoes. Another packet. A frock-coat, and another frock-coat. A dress coat. A pair of trousers. Three waistcoats, shorts, handkerchiefs, scarves. Another package. A shawl. A shirt, another shirt, and a pair of slippers. Another bundle, dirty clothes. A dictionary. Old shoes and other useless bits of junk. A suitcase. A packet of manuscripts in French. Another suitcase with clothes, both locked up, and the key is in the possession of the Frenchman. And since there was nothing further to note, this inquiry was suspended. Nacimiento, 5 January 1862.[124]

He was sent back to France and penned three books there, returning to reclaim his title just as Quilapán, who had indulged the earlier bout of royalism, had broken off negotiations with Santiago. This time the Chilean government sensibly put a price on the head of de Tounens, whereupon he speedily retraced his steps. (Two final restorationist escapades, in 1874 and 1876, were thwarted by the Argentine government, this colourful globe-trotting pest expiring in 1878.)

The Chileans had reason enough to be concerned about the '*territorio libre*' between Concepción and Valdivia, but any possible intrusion by foreign powers posed an additional threat, especially since French troops had recently put Maximilian, the Archduke of Austria, on the imperial throne of Mexico for three years, the British maintained a strategic interest in Nicaragua through the fiction of a Miskito kingdom (of which more later), and the Spanish, who still held Cuba and Puerto Rico, had formally been at war with them a decade earlier. In the event, the Araucanian people held on – as Mapuches – whilst the indigenous presence in the pampa and Patagonian regions of Argentina was eradicated. A negligible Irish population in both states makes the numbers game inappropriate.[125]

---

124. Quoted in Armando Braun Menéndez, *El Reino de Araucanía y Patagonia*, Buenos Aires 1967, p. 25. One is put in mind of the triumphant entry of the caudillo Rafael Carrera to the city of Guatemala in February 1838 dressed in 'a pair of coarse frieze trousers and a fine coat with gold embroidery belonging to [defeated] General Prem ... for a chapeau the new general wore a woman's hat with a green veil, the property of Prem's wife'. Hubert Bancroft, *History of Central America, 1808–1887*, San Francisco 1882, 3 vols, III, p. 131. This passage also evokes the comment of Carlyle's creation Prof. Teufelsdrokh:

> Perhaps not once in a lifetime does it occur to your ordinary biped, of any country or generation, be he gold-mantled Prince or russet-jerkined Peasant, that his Vestments and his Self are not one and indivisible; that *he* is naked without vestments, till he buy or steal such.

Thomas Carlyle, *Sartor Resartus* (1833–34), London 1987, p. 45. The question of clothing is far too important to escape reconsideration. In September 1998 the 'Royal Patagonian Navy' raised the flag of the kingdom on the Minquiers, unoccupied rocks south of Jersey which France had transferred to Britain in 1953.

The only place in the Americas south of the Río Grande where these mid-century years witnessed extensive armed conflict along racial lines was from 1847 to 1854 in the Yucatán, where, as we have seen, the citizens of Mérida had expressed such great optimism in 1846. The 'War of the Castes' was not simply a revolt by the Maya leadership against Hispanic state and society; as in South America, its origins were also firmly rooted in control of land and the payment of tribute. Yet it occurred in the last stages of the Mexican–American War, the collapse of central governmental authority provoking an attempt to secure independence exactly according to the fears of Lucas Alamán (who was writing before the war ended). This, though, was no '1848' in the sense of European radicalism. On 24 February 1848, the most revolutionary day of the 'days' of the revolution in France, Tocqueville noted in his diary:

> As I left my bedroom the next day, the 24th February, I met the cook who had been out; the good woman was quite beside herself and poured out a sorrowful rigmarole from which I could understand nothing but that the government was having the poor people massacred. I went down at once, and as soon as I had set foot in the street I could for the first time scent revolution in the air ... I remember for the first time saying what had long been on the tip of my tongue: 'Believe me, this time it is not another riot, but a revolution.' [126]

That same day Jacinto Prat, a rebel leader in Yucatán, sent a letter to the priest Canuto Viejo which expresses a no less ominous atmosphere but a quite distinct radical voice:

> My most venerable Sir and Priestly Father here upon the earth, first God, because we know that he descended from his sacred sky to redeem the entire world. Most respectable Sir, I received your honourable communication and that of the saintly Bishop that you sent me

---

125. The Chilean census of 1854 did not distinguish Irish from British nationals, there being 1,940 Britons registered in the country. However, the total immigration into Chile between 1849 and 1860 was only 1,238. In the case of Argentina the records show some 1,400 Irish entering between 1845 and 1855, but in the 1860s these numbers were to remain static and would be overtaken by the establishment of an important Welsh colony in Chubút, to the south of the main area of the 'desert war'. Juan Carlos Korol and Hilda Sábato, *Como fue la inmigración irlandesa en la Argentina*, Buenos Aires 1981; Eduardo Coghlan, *El Aporte de los Irlandeses a la Formación de la Nación Argentina*, Buenos Aires 1982; Glyn Williams, *The Desert and the Dream: A Study of Welsh Colonization in Chubút, 1865–1915*, Cardiff 1975.

126. Alexis de Tocqueville, *Recollections*, New York 1971, pp. 46, 48. Marx, writing from the other side of both the Channel and the political fence, emphasises the fact that in 'the February days they fought for and won the bourgeois republic', and later qualifies even this: 'the republic dates from May 4, not February 25'. *Class Struggles in France* (1850), Moscow 1972, pp. 35, 48. The 24th, however, was the day that the people in arms invested the institutions of the French state. When Marx wrote *Class Struggles in France* – some eighteen months before the *Eighteenth Brumaire* and in an earlier section which Gwyn Williams would surely have identified as 'pre-shift' – he made the same essential analysis but in a wider frame and in more vivid language:

> The February Revolution was the *beautiful* revolution, the revolution of universal sympathy, because the antagonisms which had flared up in it against the monarchy slumbered *undeveloped*, harmoniously side by side, because the social struggle which formed its background had won only an airy existence, an existence of phrases, of words. The *June Revolution* is the *ugly* revolution, the repulsive revolution, because deeds have taken the place of phrases, because the republic uncovered the head of the monster itself by striking off the crown that shielded and concealed it. *Order!* was the battle cry of Guizot.

Ibid., pp. 51–2.

on the 18th of the present month, and having [told] all my boys its contents, I wish to inform God, your venerable self, and the Bishop as well, that it is the truth that I place in your superior knowledge: that if it were not for the damage that the Spanish gentlemen began to cause us, here in the village of Tihosuco, these people would not have risen up, and if they have done so it is only to defend themselves from the death which the Subdelegate Don Antonio Trujeque started to inflict upon us. When these indians saw the outrages used to detain them in the plaza of Tihosuco, then, Sir, they rose up. It was also he who began the burnings, destroying the village of Tepich, and started to screw the poor indian, like fucking animals at pasture. On the orders of Señor Trujeque many were killed, without us knowing whether the Superior Government might have given the order for us to be killed, and for this reason we shall not stop until the government makes a statement, and not a penny of tribute will be paid; and if the tribute were to be stopped then all the Indians would cease their uprising ... otherwise this matter will be decided by life or death because I no longer possess any other means. I would also suggest, venerable Sir, that I will know what to do when you reply to this letter. I further inform you, Sir, that the rite of baptism will cost three *reales*, that of marriage ten, for the Spaniard just as for the Indian, and mass will be according to the traditional stipend ordained by our custom, as will the last rites and burial. This is the last thing I have to express to your appreciable and venerable self.[127]

A sense of why matters had reached this point despite the earlier optimism of the Mérida elite is given by John Stephens, who six years earlier had encountered in the Yucatán a fiercely hierarchical society regimented by dress and upheld by a combination of religious ministration and physical violence:

Early in the morning we were roused by loud bursts of music in the church. The *cura* [priest] was giving them the benefit of his accidental visit by an early mass. After this we heard music of a different kind. It was the lash on the back of an Indian. Looking out into the corridor, we saw the poor fellow on his knees on the pavement, with his arms clasped around the legs of another Indian, so as to present his fair back to the lash. At every blow he rose on one knee, and sent forth a piercing cry. He seemed struggling to restrain it, but it burst from him in spite of all his efforts. His whole bearing showed the subdued character of the present Indians, and with the last stripe the expression of his face seemed that of thankfulness for not getting more. Without uttering a word, he crept to the major domo, took his hand, kissed it, and walked away.

Later Stephens reports,

Society in Yucatan stands upon an aristocratic footing. It is divided into two great classes: those who wear pantaloons, and those who do not, going in *calzoncillos*, or drawers. The high-handed regulation of the ball of etiquette was aimed at them ... the excluded taking their places at the railing ... the pig butcher was admitted in drawers, but as assistant to the servants, handing refreshments to the ladies he had danced with in the morning.[128]

Elsewhere there was no catastrophic *pachakuti* – the term used in the southern Andes to describe 'the termination and reversal of an established order, whether past,

127. Quoted in Moisés González Navarro, *Raza y Tierra: La Guerra de Castas y de Henequén*, Mexico 1970, pp. 308–9.

128. John L. Stephens, *Incidents of Travel in Yucatan*, New York 1843, I, p. 82; II, p. 71.

present or future'.[129] However, if this term is used in a rather wider sense – to mean 'when the world turns round' or 'a shift in earth/space-time' – one could say that almost all the native peoples of the south of the continent stood between one *pachakuti*, the replacement of European monarchical empires by national (and largely republican) governments, and another in the extensive exposure of their markets to international capitalism.[130]

Barely a week after the events in Paris and the dispatch of Jacinto Pat's threatening message the *United Irishman* published in Dublin a stirring call by the radical Ulsterman John Mitchel, for whom the first weeks of 1848 promised almost millennial opportunity:

> The earth is awakening from sleep: a flash of electric fire is passing through the dumb millions. Democracy is girding himself once more like a strong man to run a race; and slumbering nations are arising in their might, and 'shaking their invincible locks'. Oh! my countrymen, look up, look up! Arise from the death-dust where you have been lying, and let this light visit your eyes also, and touch your souls. Let your ears drink in the blessed words, 'Liberty! Fraternity! Equality!' which are soon to ring pole to pole. Clear steel will, ere long, dawn upon you in your desolate darkness; and the rolling thunder of the people's cannon will drive before it many a heavy cloud that has long hidden from you the face of heaven. Pray for that day; and preserve life and health that you may worthily greet it. Above all, let the man amongst you who has no gun, sell his garment and buy one.[131]

Mitchel, though, as we will see, badly misjudged the moment, not least because of economic conditions.

ATLANTIC SPACE

Gwyn Williams argues something rather similar for an earlier period when he says that 'Politics in Wales begin with the American Revolution.' This is primarily because – as 'a matter of central intellectual and spiritual importance', let it be noted – industrial capitalism

---

129. Sabine MacCormack, 'Pachacuti: Miracles, Punishments, and Last Judgement: Visionary Past and Prophetic Future in Early Colonial Peru', *AHR*, 93, 1988, p. 961.'Not one major rebellion rocked Peru between 1815 and the late 1860s'. Paul Gootenberg, 'Population and Ethnicity in Early Republican Peru: Some Revisions', *LARR*, 26:3, 1991, p. 144.

130. For a full consideration of the term, see Thérèse Bouysse-Cassagne and Olivia Harris, 'Pacha: En Torno al Pensamiento Aymara', in Thérèse Bouysse-Cassagne, Olivia Harris, Tristan Platt and Verónica Cereceda, *Tres Reflexiones sobre el Pensamiento Aymara*, La Paz 1987. The word may also be used to describe a millennium. Fernando Diez de Medina, *Pachakuti y Otras Páginas Polémicas*, La Paz 1948.

131. *United Irishman*, 4 March 1848, quoted in John Newsinger, *Fenianism in Mid-Victorian Britain*, London 1994, p. 11.

directed the Welsh towards the Atlantic which was being increasingly shaped, as a living historical experience for a generation, by the new commercial and maritime power of Britain and by those two decades of disturbing political impulse radiating from the new imperial democracy of the USA and the populist, terrorist democracy of France.[132]

Such is the backdrop against which he considers the Madoc legend of a tribe of Welsh Indians as well as tracing the American journeys of Cambrian Jacobins and dissenters, like Methodist John Evans of Waunfawr, who in 1792 nearly became embroiled in the Kentucky adventures of General James Wilkinson, lost a land grant on the Mississippi to floods, failed as a surveyor and, having taken to drink in New Orleans, died at the age of twenty-nine in the house of the Spanish governor of Louisiana, Gayoso.[133] Such stories – both real and invented – matter to us here less because of the timing (although that is important) than because of the space involved. They are set in an *Atlantic* scene and are given special meaning by Williams because, whilst being equally 'American' and 'Welsh', they are best understood as being both together. This trans-oceanic focus reflects his enthusiastic engagement with what by the early 1960s had become known as the 'Palmer–Godechot thesis'.

In 1955 R.R. Palmer and Jacques Godechot gave a paper to the International Congress of Historical Sciences that argued for a combined political history of Europe and America in the late eighteenth century based around the ocean in a manner not dissimilar to that done for the Mediterranean in an earlier epoch by Fernand Braudel. From such a viewpoint the French Revolution was part of a wider movement against the established order throughout the states bordering on the Atlantic. This was, of course, at the peak of the Cold War – NATO was only half a dozen years old – and many European historians of radical disposition 'were deeply suspicious of the term *"Atlantic"*, since it seemed designed to reinforce the Western contention that the United States and western Europe belonged together against eastern Europe'.[134] For some, the Palmer–Godechot thesis meant that 'the French Revolution loses its

---

132. *The Search for Beulah Land*, London 1980, pp. 7, 10.

133. *Madoc: The Making of a Myth*, London 1980. On 3 August 1799 the United States consular representative in New Orleans, one Daniel Clark, wrote to Evans's friend Dr Samuel Jones:

> The inclosed letter from you to Mr John T. Evans fell lately into my hands and I was induced to open it that ... I might advise his friends of the fate of that unfortunate man who died not long since in this City after being for some time deprived of his reason. Chagrin and disapppointment in his Views contributed, I fear, to hasten his end.

Search for Beulah Land, p. 177. As the persevering reader will discover, I have a reason for illustrating both Clark's kindness and the manner in which he expressed it. The English translation by Sir Idris Bell of the ancient Welsh poem 'Crwyo' given in the dedication reads:

> Not in far depth of space enfurled.
> Nor where the great sea-pulses beat,
>   But here beside us, at our feet,
> The portals of the happy world.

134. Hobsbawm, *Echoes of the Marseillaise*, p. 95. Hobsbawm quotes the observation of Sir Charles Webster at the same congress:

> The Atlantic was not suggested as a 'region' until the Second World War. The rapporteurs had failed to emphasise sufficiently the unity of the world. For this reason the Atlantic Community might be

particular identity and becomes merely a phase in a wider and more general cycle'.[135] Yet, as Anne Pérotin-Dumon has noted, such an international perspective forced 'earlier generations of French historians to ask themselves when and how they left the nationalist ghetto within which the history of "their" revolution was confined'.[136] Moreover, as Palmer later argued, the adoption of a supra-national scenario entailed less a reduction in the importance of local conditions than their reconsideration in a wider context:

> At Quebec in 1797 a man was hanged, drawn and quartered as a dangerous revolutionary. At Quito, in what is now Ecuador, the first librarian of the public library was tortured and imprisoned for political agitation. A republican conspiracy was discovered in Bahía in Brazil, in 1798. A Negro at Buenos Aires testified that Frenchmen in the city were plotting to liberate slaves in an uprising against the Spanish crown. In the high Andes, at the old silver town of Potosí, far from foreign influence on the coasts, the governor was horrified to discover men who toasted liberty and drank to France. The British government, in 1794, a year before occupying Cape Town, feared that there were too many 'democrats'.... All of these agitations, upheavals, intrigues and conspiracies were part of one great movement ... revolutionary aims and sympathies existed throughout Europe and America. They arose everywhere out of local, genuine and specific causes, or, contrariwise, they reflected conditions that were universal throughout the western world. They were not imitated from the French, or at least not imitated blindly.[137]

Godechot was initially more cautious with respect to the idea of imitation and to the chronology, which he restricted to the 1790s. However, his subsequent focus on the counter-revolution enriched the debate by highlighting the trans-national reach of reaction, which had taken a Bonapartist as well as a monarchical shape by the time Spain's colonies were ready to demand independence.[138]

In the present 'globalised' climate, when everything on the planet is linked to everything else without hesitation or embarrassment, such a perspective seems hardly adventurous, even quaint. Yet the specific characteristics of 'Atlanticism' have continued to be the subject of debate. In part this has surely derived from those general problems

---

a temporary phenomenon. It was created by the policy of the USSR and if this changed it might change also.

Ibid., p. 134.

135. George Rudé, 'Interpretations of the French Revolution', in *Selected Essays*, p. 102.

136. 'The Atlantic Empires in the Eighteenth Century', *International History Review*, Nov. 1984, p. 551.

137. *The Age of the Democratic Revolution: A Political History of Europe and America, 1760–1800*, Princeton 1959, I, pp. 6–7. The most recent political history of the continent adopts a chronology that permits a comparison of the US, Haitian and Latin American revolutions: Lester Langley, *The Americas in the Age of Revolution 1750–1850*, New Haven, Conn., 1996.

138. *La Grande Nation: L'Expansion Révolutionnaire de la France dans le Monde de 1789 a 1799*, 2 vols, Paris 1956; *Counter-Revolution: Doctrine and Action, 1789–1804*, London 1972; *France and the Atlantic Revolution of the Eighteenth Century, 1770–1799*, London 1971. Williams makes a similar point:

> The conservative response to the Revolution was unnaturally 'early' (Burke's *Reflections* came out in 1790) precisely because Church and King had already mobilised against threats to the Glorious Constitution (revered with an almost American zeal!) before the events in France had made any real impact.

Search for Beulah Land, p. 19.

of comprehending and expressing space identified by Kristin Ross: 'The difficulty is also one of vocabulary, for while words like "historical" and "political" convey a dynamic of intentionality, vitality and human motivation, "spatial", on the other hand, connotes stasis, neutrality and passivity.'[139]

Difficulties of this type might be thought less acute for maritime space, which is in perpetual movement for those who see it from the shore and is the vital site of movement for those temporarily 'at sea'. Something of this real and imagined world was imparted to Flora Tristán by one of the crew taking her from Bordeaux to Valparaiso in 1833, but even then the onset of a culture of settlement, security and system was plainly visible:

> The *true sailor*, as Leborgne used to say, has neither family nor country. His language does not belong to any nation: it is compounded of words of every tongue. He has nothing but the clothes on his back, he lives from day to day and gives no thought to the future. When in port he squanders in a few days on prostitutes all the money he so painfully earned in months at sea. He deserts whenever he can and signs on again the next day with the ship that needs him, be it English, Swedish or American. He is content to see the world without seeking to understand it. He is just an instrument for navigation, as indifferent to his destination as the anchor itself. If the sea spares him and he survives into an old age, he settles wherever his final voyage leaves him. There he begs his bread and eats it in the sun, gazing lovingly at the sea, the companion of his youth. In the end, lamenting his failing strength, he dies in hospital. Such is the life of the *true sailor*. Leborgne was my model, but as everything degenerates in our society, men like him are becoming rarer every day. Nowadays sailors marry, take a well-stocked chest with them, and desert less often because they do not want to lose their belongings and the money they have earned. They take pride in learning their profession and are ambitious to do well. When their efforts come to nothing they end up toiling in small boats and barges in seaports.[140]

The shifting Atlantic matrix has always proved highly problematic in terms of those who occupy different sides (or ends) of it. For some, such as J.G.A. Pocock, there is a premium to be placed upon common ideological or philosophical origins in trans-oceanic matters: 'what renders [1776] "American" is its role in the creation of a continental republic and nation'. Yet Pocock considers this a 'truly British revolution, one which even involves a revolt against being British', and, in fact, the first revolution to occur within a British political system, since Great Britain did not exist in 1641 or 1688.[141] This is a motif to which we shall have to return and, of course, it exists no less strongly for those Americans of Spanish or Portuguese descent. In the mid nineteenth century, when the question of revolt was effectively displaced by the movement of persons and commodities, the linkage could more readily be celebrated as a commonality of heritage as well as a commercial boon:

---

139. *The Emergence of Social Space: Rimbaud and the Paris Commune*, Basingstoke 1988, p. 8, quoted in Doreen Massey, 'Politics and Space/Time', *New Left Review*, 196, Nov./Dec. 1992, p. 75.

140. Flora Tristán, *Peregrinations of a Pariah* (1838), London 1986, p. 36.

141. J.G.A. Pocock (ed.), *Three British Revolutions: 1641, 1688, 1776*, Princeton 1980, pp. 4, 265. Pocock makes a critically important point that is ignored in almost all the literature: that if 1776 was the first such case, then the Irish Revolution, which he dates from 1912 to 1922, was the second. Ibid., p. 266.

For all practical purposes the United States are far more closely united with this kingdom than any of our colonies, and [with us they] keep up a perpetual interchange of the most important good offices: taking our manufactures and our surplus population and giving us in return the materials of industry, of revenue and of life.[142]

Such an image of bi-polarity – almost of a bridge – is easily assimilated and has popular resonance, whether applied to the Anglo or Latino shorelines.[143] However, the richest Atlantic literature is multilateral in reach, based at the very least on a triangle that touches Africa as well as Europe and America. In the same year as Palmer and Godechot propounded their thesis Philip Curtin published his study of ideas in post-emancipation Jamaica, drawing attention to what he called a 'South Atlantic system', which had been built on slavery and which locked Africa and the Caribbean firmly into American and European orbits.[144] The chronological features of such a system are particularly taxing. For Peggy Liss it was best viewed between the Treaty of Utrecht and the first pan-American congress in Panama: 'Never again has the outlook of entrepreneurs, intellectuals, and patriots been so in accord throughout the Atlantic world as it was from 1713 to 1826, when few of them gave any thought to the fragility of progress or to resources as limited.'[145]

---

142. *The Times*, 4 July 1851, quoted in Frank Thistlethwaite, *The Anglo-American Connection in the Early Nineteenth Century*, Philadelphia 1959, p. 3. Thistlethwaite's survey of the international organisations dedicated to the abolition of slavery and the promotion of peace, temperance and free trade as well as feminism leads him to argue that 'we are dealing with a genuine Atlantic community', but he sees this as linked between the USA and Britain, not Europe, and it ends with the US Civil War, after which the USA no longer possessed the attributes of a colony and had become a metropolitan state. Ibid., pp. 87, 172–4.

143. This image is used in a recent collection: María Pérez de Mendiola (ed.), *Bridging the Atlantic: Towards a Reassessment of Iberian and Latin American Cultural Ties*, Albany, N.Y., 1996. However, the editor opens the book with a quotation from Heidegger to warn against too simplistic a reading of the metaphor:

> A bridge does not just connect banks that are already there. The banks emerge as banks only as the bridge crosses the stream.... One side is set off against the other by the bridge. With the banks, the bridge brings to the stream the one and the other expanse of the landscape lying behind them.

Politics, Language, Thought, New York 1975, p. 152, quoted in ibid., p. 1. In 1841 Richard Cobden made a speech arguing that British foreign policy ought to be made as if the Atlantic were the Thames, but he was inclined to pontificate about free trade, and even at that time many would have thought this a bridge too far.

144. *Two Jamaicas: The Role of Ideas in a Tropical Colony, 1830–1865*, Cambridge, Mass., 1955. Braudel later employed the term 'Atlantic economy world'. *Afterthoughts on Material Civilization and Capitalism*, Baltimore, Md., 1977.

145. *Atlantic Empires: The Network of Trade and Revolution, 1713–1826*, Baltimore 1983. When he began his study of the 'modern world-system' in the early 1970s Immanuel Wallerstein projected four volumes divided by chronology: 1450–1640, early condition of the European world-system; 1640–1815, consolidation; 1815–1917, conversion into global enterprise; 1917–, consolidation of world capitalism. Fifteen years later he published his third volume: *The Second Era of Great Expansion of the Capitalist World Economy, 1730–1840s*, San Diego 1989. Working on a very different scale, Estyn Evans shares Liss's concern for both culture and environment. He identified in Atlantic Europe 'a pastoral heritage, in which the ties of clan and kinship were strong enough to resist, in the main, the growth of feudal society'. Correspondingly, with perhaps 250,000 people of Ulster origin in North America by the end of the eighteenth century,

> The cultural landscape of a large part of the United States is characterized by the single homestead and the unincorporated hamlet, and by a system of land-use dominated by a corn-and-livestock economy, which was pioneered in the Old West by the Scotch-Irish. Among them the claims of family and kin were stronger than those of community. Economically, it was a wasteful system, often bringing rapid environmental deterioration.

Ireland and the Atlantic Heritage, Dublin 1996, pp. 59, 100.

However, having provoked a vibrant debate, Liss has revised her dates, now starting in 1650 (on the main grounds of the decline of Spain, the shift in American economic focus from Peru to Mexico, and the supplanting of piracy by contraband) and ending in 1850 (on the main grounds of Latin American political independence and the radical diffusion of trade by the industrial revolution).[146] This span gives a higher profile to Latin America and the Caribbean, but it is driven more by economics than politics and arguably takes us only to the precipice of modernity.

Paul Gilroy, by contrast, draws on the eighteenth-century history of Marcus Rediker and Peter Linebaugh to propound the most energetically contemporary of Atlanticist theses.[147] Gilroy's book begins with a review of the British academic tradition of cultural studies, considering the appetite for postmodernity in the light of the argument that 'racial slavery was integral to western civilization' and that 'much of the supposed novelty of the postmodern evaporates when it is viewed in the unforgiving light of the brutal encounter between Europeans and those they conquered, slaughtered and enslaved'.[148] This is an important point that still needs to be registered in some refined academic circles, but it is less original than Gilroy's central thesis — that there is no specifically and integrally African, American, Caribbean or British black culture, only an amalgam, a Black Atlantic consciousness, which is thereby a counter-culture of modernity. It seems that such a culture was being distilled from the mid nineteenth century at least, but cultural forms are less precisely measured than trade flows, and in this case periodisation is secondary to contemporary politico-analytical concerns. Within these there is a fitting reliance upon popular music as much as on literature to illustrate social interaction through space, and a corresponding quickness of pace runs through the book. However, it is important that Gilroy's preferred image is of a ship

---

146. Many of these revisions stem from the commentary of John TePaske in *International History Review*, Nov. 1984, and were incorporated into the introduction of Franklin Knight and Peggy Liss (eds), *Atlantic Port Cities: Economy, Culture and Society in the Atlantic World, 1650–1850*, Knoxville, Tenn., 1991, which is, however, limited to the Americas. For our present purposes the extension from 1826 to 1850 is most consequential, and within this period perhaps the introduction of steamships and a progressive escape from the constraints of wind and current is the maritime aspect that had greatest social impact. However, in terms of the Atlantic as a site of history a very strong case can be made for the suppression of the slave trade as the dominant feature of the mid nineteenth century, in which case one would push on to 1855 or 1860. For a complementary collection that includes consideration of Ireland, see Nicholas Canny and Anthony Pagden (eds), *Colonial Identity in the Atlantic World, 1500–1800*, Princeton 1987.

147. Marcus Rediker, *Between the Devil and the Deep Blue Sea: Merchant Seamen, Pirates, and the Anglo-American Maritime World 1700–1750*, Cambridge 1987. In a spirited article much influenced by their own different styles, Linebaugh criticised the early work of E.P. Thompson and Eric Hobsbawm on the English working class for being too nationally centred:

> just as the accumulation of international capital depends on the exploitation of Atlantic labour, so 'pauses' or 'arrests' in the process of accumulation [which Thompson and Hobsbawm were seeking to explain] are the results of the many-sided oppositions of living labour brewing within and among the modes of production.

'All the Atlantic Mountains Shook', *Labour/Le Travailleur*, 10, Autumn 1982, p. 92. There are plenty of Irish, Afro-American and slaves peopling Linebaugh's own book, *The London Hanged: Crime and Civil Society in the Eighteenth Century*, London 1991.

148. *The Black Atlantic: Modernity and Double Consciousness*, London 1993, p. 44.

– almost certainly a sailing ship – not an aeroplane, which could never be associated with the slaving middle passage of the Atlantic commercial triangle and which plays a marginal role in the traditional iconography of the oceanic world.

Slavery was overwhelmingly associated with the Atlantic. By 1850 it had been abolished in Canada and the British and French Caribbean, but it persisted in Cuba, Puerto Rico, Brazil (a semi-continent without a Pacific coastline) and the south-eastern coastal states of the USA. On the Pacific coast, by contrast, it was almost completely non-existent. It is, of course, the case that the Pacific dimensions of North America were at that stage barely chartered; despite thirty years' service in the US navy, Commodore Perry, whose 1853 expedition to Japan would open a critical new international theatre, had never even gazed upon that ocean until his appointment to the East India Squadron.[149] However, from a northern standpoint the annexation of California and the Gold Rush mean that America could no longer be understood from a purely Atlantic perspective. To the south a Pacific dimension had coexisted with that of the Atlantic from the first years of Spanish imperialism in the Americas in the sixteenth century. If anything was new there in the nineteenth century it was an Asiatic element as indentured Chinese labourers were drafted in to fill the spaces vacated by emancipated slaves and opened up anew by the guano boom of the mid-century years.

All the Mesoamerican states of that time had shores on both oceans, possessing a corresponding pattern of racial settlement and attractiveness to great (British) and burgeoning (US) powers in pursuit of authority by naval means. The geopolitical importance of Nicaragua, for example, was a direct effect of the economic importance acquired by California. However, this Pacific factor was still too new to have a non-European political character. The turmoil in Nicaragua was most infamously exploited by the young filibusterer William Walker, a second-generation American of Scottish descent who attempted to impose English as the official language of the republic and whose eventual execution was facilitated by the British navy. Reviled in Latin America as the personification of Anglo-American 'manifest destiny', a disturbing symbol of the political fragility of the region, Walker also stands for that plasticity of place that prevailed when neither of the Americas had completed their European history.

A dozen years after Walker was shot and the isthmus of Central America returned to a disorder of its own making, Hinton Helper, who had so emphatically prophesied the catastrophe to befall the USA, found himself engaged in an unusual legal case – to secure for the New York mapmaker Joseph Colton payment from Bolivia for a map of the nation commissioned in 1858. Colton had been obliged to wait a long time for the agreed fee ($25,000) for his reduction of Bolivia's millions of acres to five feet by six, reproduced 10,000 times. Helper, never a patient man, drafted for Colton

---

149. Samuel Eliot Morison, *'Old Bruin': Commodore Matthew Calbraith Perry*, Boston 1967, p. 261.

a rather ominous reminder to Leopold Markbreit, the US ambassador in Bolivia: 'Sir, One of the ablest writers of antiquity, well known and deservedly honored in Hebrew literature, has assured us that there is a time for everything; and if that assurance be true, then there is a time when nations, like individuals, should pay for maps.'[150] Legend has it that four years before the Bolivians contracted Colton, Queen Victoria had responded to some reported slight on their part by erasing the country from the map of the world. No British ambassador was posted there between 1854 and 1906, and the country was effectively 'forgotten'. For many, not just in Ireland but also in Latin America, such an exeat from the imperial gaze would have seemed a great blessing. In the meantime Bolivia lost its seaboard to Chile and all the maps had to be changed anyway.

---

150. Helper, New York, to Markbreit, 17 June 1872, in Helper, *Oddments of Andean Diplomacy*, St Louis, Mo., 1879, p. 55.

FIRST CASE

The Queen v. John Mitchel, The Commission Court, Green Street, Dublin[1]

PRESIDING JUDGES: The Right Hon. Baron Lefroy and the Right Hon. Justice Moore[2]

Saturday, 20 May 1848

BARON LEFROY – Gentlemen of the Grand Jury of the City of Dublin, I am now in a condition to address you upon the case which this morning appeared to the Court not ripe for your consideration.… The case, as I stated to you then … appeared on the face of the calendar in a very ambiguous light. That case is the case of a prisoner of the name of John Mitchel.[3] … You now have to consider the case of a well-defined known offence against the law, which under the late Act is described with an accuracy and precision, which will leave you comparatively no difficulty in the discharge of the duty you have to fulfil.…

The Act in question was passed on the 22nd of April, in the present year. I call your attention to the date of passing it for reasons which you will see presently. I will first read to you that section of the Act upon which the bill about to be sent to you is framed.…

---

1. This case, like the two that follow, has been edited with emphasis upon narrative within the context of law, rather than on a rigorous description and interpretation of the law, of which I am incapable. The principal sources are Edward Cox (ed.), *Reports of Cases in Criminal Law Argued and Determined in all the Courts in England and Ireland: III. 1848–50*, London 1850, pp. 1–36, for the proceedings of 22, 23 and 25 May 1848, and John Hodges, *Report of the Trial of John Mitchel for Felony*, Dublin 1848, for those of 20, 26 and 27 May 1848. Since these sources together amount to over 130 pages of closely printed text, my condensation has clearly been radical.

2. *Thomas Langlois Lefroy* (1776–1869) of Limerick and a Flemish Protestant background. Trinity College Dublin (TCD), 1780; called to the Irish bar, 1797; KC, 1806; elected a Tory MP for Dublin universities, 1830, voting with Peel against Melbourne; 1841 to Irish Court of Exchequer; Lord Chief Justice of Queen's Bench, 1852–66. Died Newcourt, near Bray. *Richard Moore* (1783–1857) of Grenane, County Waterford. Called to the bar, 1807; KC, 1827; Solicitor General for Ireland, August 1840–September 1841; Attorney General for Ireland, July 1846–December 1847. Judge of Queen's Bench, 1847 until death.

3. *John Mitchel*, born County Londonderry, 1815, third son of Rev. John Mitchel, Presbyterian minister of Dromalane, Newry. Educated TCD; solicitor, 1840; joined Repeal Association, 1843; wrote for radical repeal paper *Nation*, 1845; established the Irish Confederation, 1846, leaving in December 1847 to set up the *United Irishman*. As indicated by the *Dublin Mail* of 16 November 1836, Mitchel had already experienced at least one run-in with the law:

> James Verner, Esquire, of Ballybot, in the county of Armagh, near Newry, having discovered that his daughter, Miss Jane, aged fourteen years, had eloped from his house, set on foot an immediate inquiry, and ascertained that she was induced to commit this brash act by a John Mitchel, a law student about twenty-one years of age, son of a clergyman in his neighbourhood. He traced the fugitives to Dundalk, Drogheda and Dublin, where he learned they had sailed for Liverpool. Having obtained a warrant, he proceeded to the last mentioned place, and there ascertained they had gone to Chester, in which city he overtook them, brought back his daughter and left Mr Mitchel in custody. Peace Officer M'Donough of the Head-Police Office was immediately dispatched for the prisoner, with whom he arrived here last Saturday, and he was committed to Kilmainham Jail, to abide his trial at the ensuing assizes in the county of Armagh. It may be necessary to mention by the 10th George the Fourth, one of Robert Peel's excellent acts, it is a misdemeanour to take any girl under sixteen years of age from her parent, lawful guardian, or even her putative father.

That if any person or persons whatsoever, after the passing of this Act, shall, within the United Kingdom or without, compass, imagine, invent, devise, or intend to deprive or depose our most Gracious Lady, the Queen, her heirs or successors from the style, honour or royal name of the Imperial Crown of the United Kingdom, or of any other of Her Majesty's dominions or countries, or to levy war against Her Majesty, her heirs or successors, within any part of the United Kingdom, in order by force or constraint to compel her or them to change her or their measures or counsels, or in order to put any force or constraint upon, or in order to intimidate or overawe both houses or either house of Parliament, or to move or stir any foreigner or stranger with force to invade the United Kingdom or any other of Her Majesty's dominions or countries; and such compassings, imaginations, inventions, devices, or intentions, or any of them, shall express, utter, or declare by publishing any printing or writing, or by open and advised speaking, or by any overt act or deed, every person so offending shall be guilty of felony, and being convicted thereof, shall be liable, at the discretion of the Court, to be transported beyond the seas for the term of his or her natural life, or for any term not less than seven years, or to be imprisoned for any term not exceeding two years, with or without hard labour, as the Court shall direct.

... Now, this law, gentlemen, I have to observe to you, is not altogether a new law, for the provisions of the Act are to be found in other Acts long antecedent to it, in substance and in terms, but only under a different character, and subject to different penalty. In fact, the matters which by the late Act are made felonies, and punishable by transportation or imprisonment, previous to this Act, at least in England, were high treason, and punishable of course by death. Certainly that was the law in England; a doubt existed whether that was the law in Ireland, and one of the objects of the present Act was to remove that doubt.... The present Act removes all doubts with respect to Ireland, and applies the same provisions to Ireland as to England.... It is therefore neither a new law nor can it be looked on as a law of extreme rigour and severity; on the contrary, it is a law mitigatory, lowering the category of the offence, and mitigating most materially the punishment which is to attend it....[4]

Mitchel was released from Kilmainham after eighteen days, without trial. He and Jane, always known as Jenny, eloped again in January 1837, marrying at Drumcree – now of sad repute for the events of 1996 and 1998. Sons John (ten) and James (eight) attended the present trial in the company of their mother. Another boy, Willie, and two girls, Henrietta (Henty) and Mary (Minnie), were born prior to the trial, and a third girl, Isabel, in 1852. It was widely reputed that Jenny was not the natural daughter of Captain James Verner, who died aged sixty-seven in July 1847, and that she and her brother Richard were born before he married their mother Mary Ward. It is probably for this reason that the *Dublin Mail* makes the reference to 'putative father'. There was, however, no legal dispute over inheritance. Rebecca O'Conner, *Jenny Mitchel: Young Irelander*, Dublin 1985, p. 53.

    4. Under the statute for high treason (25 Edw.3, stat.5, c.2) the sentence was that the guilty prisoner

      be taken from the bar of the court, where he now stands, to the place from whence he came, the gaol, and that he be thence drawn on a hurdle to the place of execution, and that he be there hanged by the neck until he be dead, and that afterwards his head shall be severed from his body, and his body shall be divided into four quarters, to be disposed of as Her Majesty shall think fit.

Kevin Nowlan lucidly explains the political context of Baron Lefroy's remark:

    The British government was in the unhappy position of being unable to decide what should be done in Ireland, at a time when Chartism threatened to become a serious menace in Britain. A possible way of meeting the immediate problem for maintaining order was, however, suggested by Lord Campbell, a former Irish Chancellor and the future Lord Chancellor of England.

The Politics of Repeal: A Study in the Relations between Great Britain and Ireland, 1841–1850, London 1965, pp. 189–90. Campbell's memo to Lord John Russell was chillingly confident:

    Since we separated I have been turning in my mind the proper mode for dealing with the Irish 'Confederates'.... After the opinions given by the Chancellor and the Attorney General in Ireland

You will observe that the Act does not require that these compassings, or purposes, or intents should be carried out into effect; but it does require that there should be such a manifestation of the intent as the Act specifies. The object of the Act, as I have already stated, is not to punish treason, or those felonious compassings when carried out into actual treason; but the wise, and I would say, the merciful purpose of the Act is to intercept treason – to stop it short while it yet rests in intent, and only in such a manifestation as ascertains the existence of the intent, but before it ripens into all its awful and mischievous effects. The Act, therefore, though it does go to punish the intent, and in that respect might perhaps be deemed an act of severity, when it comes to be considered, is in truth an act of mercy and wisdom....

Monday, 22 May 1848

AFFIDAVIT – Martin Francis O'Flaherty, of no. 84 Lower Gardiner St, in the city of Dublin, attorney for the defendant in this case, maketh oath and saith, that he, the deponent, on Wednesday last, the 17th of May instant, personally, and through others, applied to Nathaniel A. Hamilton Esquire, as also the under-sheriff's clerk for the city of Dublin, for a copy of the common jury panel summoned to serve at the approaching commission ... and that he was refused the same; saith, that he has been advised, and believes, that a timely inspection and examination of said panel will be absolutely necessary for the proper defence of the said defendant, to enable him to exercise with due effect his legal right of challenge to such persons as may be objectionable upon said panel; saith he, this deponent, has been informed and believes that a copy of the indictment ... will also be requisite for the proper conduct of his defence....

SIR COLMAN O'LOGHLEN[5] – If the Court do not permit the defendant to have a copy [of the indictment], he will be obliged to get a short-hand writer to take note of it, and it

---

all notion of prosecuting for high treason under the existing laws must be abandoned, and I do not think that it would be expedient simply to extend 36 Geo. 3, c. 7, to Ireland. The Whig party strongly (and I think reasonably) objected in 1796 and in 1817 to the new offences created by that Act being made high treason, contending that we should abide by the old 'Statute of Treasons', 25 Edw. 3, and when the punishment of death has been abolished in France for all political offences, a clamour might be excited if you were to propose that Irishmen should now for the first time be liable to be hanged, beheaded, drawn and quartered for what they have hitherto been allowed to do with impunity. Besides, you have no desire to proceed against them capitally, and, prosecuting them according to the forms prescribed in high treason you give them the last chance to escape.

My plan is this. Repeal 36 Geo. 3 and 57 Geo. 3, making it perpetual, and frame a new Act for the whole of the United Kingdom by which these offences (a conspiracy to levy war, etc.) shall be made *felony*, punishable with transportation for fourteen years or life. Thus, while you would have the glory of mitigating the severity of the penal code, you would be armed with the effectual means of sending Messrs Mitchel, Meagher and Smith O'Brien to Botany Bay.

Reproduced in G.P. Gooch (ed.), *The Later Correspondence of Lord John Russell, 1840–1878*, London 1925, pp. 227–8. The bill was introduced by the Whig administration on 7 April 1848, was passed on the 19th by a vote of 295 against 40, and received the royal assent on the 22nd. The Irish MPs made largely formal protests, the only sharp opposition coming from William Smith O'Brien, who was being tried under the old statute for sedition before the introduction of the new bill, and who was acquitted by the vote of a single juror on 15 May, two days after John Mitchel was arrested and charged under the new law. For a general survey that is as readable as it is opinionated, see Denis Gwyn, *Young Ireland and 1848*, Cork 1949.

5. *Sir Colman O'Loghlen*, born 1819, eldest son of Sir Michael O'Loghlen, judge of County Clare. Educated University College London; called to the London bar, 1840; QC, 1852; Chair of Carlow Quarter Sessions, 1856–59, and Mayo Quarter Sessions, 1859–61; MP for Clare, 1863–77; Judge Advocate General,

will be the duty of the Clerk of the Crown to read it *slowly* and *distinctly* (see 1 Lewin's Cr.C.207, n.) to enable him to do so. The object of the prisoner in seeking copies of the former panels is to be in a position to challenge the array if it appears that a different class of jurors have been empanelled to try this case from that usually empanelled for trials at this court; or if it appears that the names of the jurors have been placed on the panel in such a way as to prejudice the prisoner. I do not impute such conduct to the sheriff; all we seek is to get such information as is necessary to enable us to exercise a constitutional right, without which, in the words of Lord Denman, trial by jury would be 'a delusion, a mockery, and a snare'.

BARON LEFROY – This motion must be refused. The law is clear and express upon the point, as laid down by Lord Hale (2 Hale, P.C. 236) Hawkins (1 Hawkins, P.C. 369) and Foster (Disc. of High Treason, 228) and the practice is stated accordingly by Lord Kenyon (*Rex* v. *Holland*, 4 T.R. 692–3). No case to the contrary has been cited to us to show that a prisoner, in this stage of proceedings, is entitled to a copy of the indictment....

[The prisoner being then put forward to the bar:
    The indictment was, at the request of Sir Colman O'Loghlen, read out slowly, and at full length, so as to enable a short-hand writer to take note of it.
    The reading of the indictment having been concluded, the prisoner was again called on to plead, upon which Sir Colman O'Loghlen requested as a matter of favour that Mr Mitchel might not be compelled to plead until tomorrow, as he meant to move that the indictment be quashed, on the ground that it charged two distinct felonies, which might have been made been the subject of separate indictments. He was not then prepared to argue the question; but the case of *Young, in error*, v. *The King* (3 T.R. 89, 106) was an authority in favour of the objection upon which he meant to rely.
    The Attorney-General[6] 'assented to the prisoner's not being called upon to plead until the following day, upon the understanding that the motion to quash the indictment should be proceeded with the first thing on that day.]

Tuesday, 23 May 1848

SIR COLMAN O'LOGHLEN – I have now on behalf of Mr Mitchel to move that the indictment in this case be quashed, as it charges the prisoner with two distinct felonies – compassing to deprive and depose the Queen from the style, honour and royal name of the Imperial crown of the United Kingdom; and compassing to levy war, in order by force and constraint to compel Her Majesty to change her measures and counsels. The practice is, when the objection is taken before plea, to quash the indictment, and when,

---

1868, presenting the bill that enabled Roman Catholics to become Lord Chancellor. Died suddenly on the Holyhead to Kingstown mailboat, July 1877. According to the Dictionary of National Biography, 'his unassuming manner and good nature made him universally popular'.
    6. *James Henry Monahan* (1804–78) of Galway. Graduated in science from TCD, 1823; called to the bar, 1826, Connaught Circuit; QC, 1840; defended the leader of the Repeal movement, Daniel O'Connell, 1844; Solicitor General, 1846; won Galway Borough parliamentary seat in February 1847 and, opposed by repealers, lost it in the general election of August 1847; Attorney-General for Ireland, December 1847. Prosecuted leading repealers William Smith O'Brien and Thomas Meagher (see note 10 below) for sedition in March 1848, the former being acquitted on 15 May and the latter, by the votes of two jurors, on the 16th. Presided over a special commission for trial of Fenians at Cork and Limerick in 1867.

after plea, to put the prosecutor at his election.... All the reasons given by Mr Justice Buller, in *Young* v. *The King*, apply in this case. A prisoner is not to escape punishment because he has committed two felonies, but, because he might choose to challenge in one case and not in the other, he ought not to be tried at the same time for both....

BARON LEFROY – We do not think it necessary to call on the Attorney-General in this case.... Here is no repugnancy in the different offences charged, they constitute but one *corpus delicti*, laid different ways. The overt acts are the very same which are charged in support of all the counts, except the last two [of ten]. If the prisoner is prepared to meet them as applied to one, he is prepared to meet them as to the rest....

JUDGE MOORE – I concur in the opinion which has been pronounced by my brother Lefroy....

[Motion refused....

The prisoner, being so advised by his counsel, pleaded not guilty, and the following day was fixed by the court for his trial.]

Thursday, 25 May 1848

[The jurors upon the panel having been called, and more than a full jury having answered to their names, on behalf of the prisoner the following challenge was tendered to the array of the panel:

> ...the said John Mitchel challenges the array of the said panel ... because the said panel was arrayed by the said Henry Sneyd French, sheriff ... or the person or persons employed by him to array the same, in a partial and favourable manner to our said Lady the Queen, and to the prejudice of him the said John Mitchel, and also because the said panel was not arrayed by ... the sheriff ... from the jurors' book of the county of the city of Dublin for the current year ... French ... did, in arraying said panel, omit the names of certain persons (which said names the said John Mitchel is unable to set forth, the same being of record in the office of the Clerk of the Crown of the county of the city of Dublin, and the said John Mitchel being refused access thereto)....

The Attorney-General, after deliberation for some time with other counsel for the Crown, stated that he took issue upon the challenge and called upon the court to appoint triers.]

MR HOLMES[7] – I have now to repeat the application which was made yesterday in the absence of the Attorney-General ... that the trial be postponed in consequence of the absence of a material witness for the prisoner in support of this challenge to the array.

---

7. *Robert Holmes* (1765–1859) of Belfast. Called to the bar, 1795; married Emma Emmett, sister of Robert (b. 1778), who, having been told by Napoleon that he would invade England in 1803, invested £3,000 of his own money and borrowed £1,400 from a Mr Long to buy pikes and guns and led a disorganised rising in Dublin on 23 July 1803. The revolt rapidly collapsed, and Emmett was hanged for treason in September, provoking the death 'by brain fever' of his sister. Holmes, who was not involved in the plot, was detained for several months. The author of pamphlets against the Union, he rejected offers of senior state posts and remained on the outer bar throughout his career. The head of one of the most successful law practices in Ireland, he signed up for Mitchel's defence at the age of eighty-three, and he only retired in 1852, to live in London with his only child Elizabeth, married to George Lenox-Coyningham, Chief Clerk to the Foreign Office.

The motion is founded on the affidavits of Mr O'Flaherty, the prisoner's attorney, and Mr Singleton, his clerk. The former states…

> that immediately after the trial was fixed yesterday, deponent caused subpoenas to be issued against several persons, and amongst others, against Stephen Monahan, Esq., who is clerk to the Attorney-General … that he, the deponent, has strong ground for producing the said Stephen Monahan as such witness, and that this application is not made for the purpose of delay or for the purpose in any way of vexatiously embarrassing the crown, but for the *bona fide* purpose of having the said Stephen Monahan examined.…

The affidavit of Mr Singleton states that…

> suspecting that the said Stephen Monahan was keeping out of the way lest he might be served with said summons, [he] made several inquiries at different places to ascertain if such was the fact, but could gain no intelligence of him; in consequence of which this deponent again applied this morning at the said residence of the said Stephen Monahan, when he was informed by the man-servant belonging to said house that the said Stephen Monahan had left town by the eleven o'clock train on Monday morning, for the purpose of proceeding to the fair of Loughrea in the county of Galway, but would return in a couple of days.

It should be the desire of the Crown that the panel should be not only perfectly chaste but above suspicion. If the Crown produce this gentleman, we are ready to proceed at once.

THE ATTORNEY-GENERAL – They want the Crown to do a thing which is impossible. If they had taken any pains they might have secured the attendance of the gentleman by serving him with a summons.

MR HOLMES – How could we summon the witness until a day was fixed for the trial? It is necessary to state in the summons the day the trial is to take place. The moment we ascertained the day the court had fixed, we at once proceeded to serve this gentleman. We have heard that he is in the county of Galway, and that he is expected back in a few days. He is the clerk to the Attorney-General; the Attorney-General must be better informed on the subject than we can possibly be. I submit, therefore, that this application ought to be granted.…

THE ATTORNEY-GENERAL – Nothing would induce me to resist this application if I were not perfectly satisfied that it is made on the allegation of the absence of a person as a witness who could not be examined as a witness for the prisoner, and, who, in fact, knows nothing whatever of the subject of the challenge. It is new doctrine to me that you cannot summon a witness until a day is fixed for the trial.…

[Motion refused.

The Court proposed to appoint as triers the foreman of the county of Dublin grand jury and the grand juror next to him on the list, which nomination not having been objected to by the Attorney-General or the counsel for the prisoner, Thomas James Quinton, Esq., the foreman, and William Worthington, Esq., the next to him on the list … were accordingly sworn 'well and truly to try the challenge to the array in this case, and a true verdict give according to the evidence'.

Peter Slevin, a witness, called in support of the challenge, having stated that he had looked through the panel, was then asked by Sir Colman O'Loghlen the following question

– Are you able from your information to state how many Roman Catholics there are on the panel?]

THE ATTORNEY-GENERAL – I object to that question.

BARON LEFROY – You know that it is a perfectly irrelevant question.

SIR COLMAN O'LOGHLEN – We press the question; we say that on this panel there are only 28 Roman Catholics out of 150 jurors on this panel; we also say that there are on the jurors' book two-thirds Roman Catholics to one-third Protestants; there are on this panel only about one-sixth Catholics to five-sixths Protestants. In the case of *Adams and Langton* (Report of Marylebone Special Commission, p. 239), which was tried by Bushe C.J. and Sir William Smith, B., there is a passage in the charge of the Lord Chief Justice to the triers upon a challenge to the array, which applies strongly to our objection in the present case. He says, 'Your duty is to try whether this is an impartial panel, or has it been so constructed as to deprive the prisoner of a fair trial? If persons have been left off the panel, or corruptly placed or postponed in such a manner and to such an extent that as would deprive the prisoners of impartial jurors, or throw them into the power of jurors prejudiced against them, this is not an impartial panel, and you will find accordingly.' Now, my lords, I say that applies perfectly to our case; we are prepared to prove that whilst the proportion of persons qualified to be jurors is two-thirds Catholics and one-third Protestants, the proportion here upon the panel is five-sixths Protestants and one-sixth Catholic.[8] From this fact we assert that the sheriff has not made out an impartial panel. If he had, it would be different from what it is. If made out according to the proportion of Catholics and Protestants there would be on it two-thirds Catholics and one-third Protestants. But putting the question of religion altogether out of the question, if the names are classified alphabetically, if a small proportionate number of those names begin with the letter L, and a very large number are classed under the letter M, and that

---

8. On 23 May, two days before Mitchel's defence team of O'Loghlen and Holmes raised the issue of the array of the jury, the prime minister, Lord John Russell, was confronted by an Irish MP, Keogh, who requested

> the returns of the names and the description of the 48 special jurors, drawn by ballot to serve on the case of *The Queen* v. *William Smith O'Brien, Esq., MP*, in the Queen's Bench in Ireland, and of the 24 who afterwards, on the reduction of the list, were struck off the number, distinguishing those struck off by the crown and by the traverser; and also specifying which of the 48 were members of the Roman Catholic religion. And the like return in the case of *The Queen* v. *Thomas Meagher*.

Stating directly that Catholics had been excluded from the 680-strong jury panel, Keogh quoted back to Russell his own criticism of Peel's policy in 1844:

> …the Government of Ireland was maintained by force and not by opinion. Why had they no reason here to fear Government? Because the verdict of a jury stood betwixt every man and tyranny – because trial by jury secured for every Englishman his just rights.

Russell replied that he still held those convictions and that 'the exclusion of Roman Catholics, as such, unless they were members of Repeal Associations, and had distinguished themselves by the violence of their conduct in such associations, would be an extremely wrong and unjustifiable proceeding.' He then stalled, insisting that Clarendon, the Lord Lieutenant, had been assured by Attorney-General Monahan 'that there had not been – at least by his direction – any Roman Catholic left out of the jury merely on the grounds of his being a Roman Catholic'. Hansard, *Parliamentary Debates*, XCIII, pp. 1320–25. Six days later, the trial having concluded, the state had refined the presentation of its case. In response to Keogh's assertion that all Catholics were excluded from Mitchel's jury, Russell read out a letter written by Monahan:

it was found that on the panel, out of the names taken from the two letters, two-thirds were taken from the less numerous letter L, and but one-third from the more numerous letter M, I ask, would it not look suspicious? But if the disproportion is shown to be a great deal more unequal even than that, is it not natural to draw the inference that fair means have not been used? We now offer this evidence to show that in this instance there is reason to believe that unfair means have been used in the formation of the panel.

MR HENN, QC[9] – The case to which Sir Colman O'Loghlen has referred is substantially an authority against his objection to the array.

BARON LEFROY – I should like to know what the requisite proportion is to make an impartial panel?

MR HENN – The question here is whether the array has been made in a corrupt manner and from a partial motive. The challenge to the array in *Rex* v. *Adams and Langton* has formed a precedent for the greater portion of the challenge which has been put in here to-day. In charging the triers in that case, Bushe C.J. says,

> I might say that it has not appeared to this moment of what religion the prisoners are. And it would be an affectation not to assume that they are Roman Catholics, and we know from the crown books that they are charged with an offence connected with the existing in-surrection; but when I look at the words of the challenge I cannot imagine to myself how the evidence we have heard … can apply to the question before us, unless we are bound to identify the insurrection, and the crimes it has produced, with the religion of the prisoners – an insult and calumny directed against my Roman Catholic fellow-subjects in which I cannot consent to participate.

These observations apply with greater force here. It does not appear what the religion of the prisoner is. And I say with the learned judge that it would be an insult to Roman Catholics entitled to serve on juries, to say that they would find a verdict on account of their religion....

BARON LEFROY – Suppose there were a great many rich men on the panel, and a poor man was to be tried, or that there were a very many poor men on the panel, and a rich man was to be tried, would it be an impartial panel?

> In answer to your letter requiring my instructions relative to the … setting aside [of] jurors on the part of the crown in the case *The Queen* v. *Mitchel*, I beg to say it is not, and never was, my wish or intention that any juror be set aside on account of his religious opinions. I do not think the instructions given by previous law officers, that jurors were not to be set aside on account of their political opinions, was ever intended to apply to a case like the present, in which a party is to be tried for a political offence, and is openly supported and countenanced by certain political associa-tions. I have, therefore, no hesitation in saying that in the present and similar cases you should set aside on the part of the crown, without regard to their religious opinions, all persons whom, from the inquiries you have made, and the information you have received, you find to entertain political opinions according with those of the prisoner.

Ibid., XCIC, p. 1.

9. Henn, for whom I have been unable to find further personal details, closed for the eight-strong prosecution team. He and Monahan dominated the effort, but Whiteside and Smyly interjected a couple of times (not reproduced here) against the venerable Holmes and O'Loghlen, supported by Messrs Piggott and O'Hagan.

Mr Holmes — I would say not.

Baron Lefroy — That case has been already decided the other way by Lord Tenterden, who has pronounced an opinion that it is not an objection....

The Attorney-General — I contend that the sheriff is not bound to put his hand into a ballotting box and take out the names of the jurors by chance; if he selects the names honestly and fairly from the jurors' book that is all that can be required of him.

Sir Colman O'Loghlen — But that is just the question to be tried upon this challenge....

[H.S. French, Esq., the high sheriff of the city of Dublin, and Mr Hamilton, his returning officer, were examined in support of the challenge by the prisoner's counsel, and cross-examined by the counsel for the Crown. They stated that they had prepared the panel, but distinctly negatived the charges of partiality and corruption in the formation of it, or that they had received any suggestion on the subject from anyone connected with the prosecution, or that they selected out of the jurors' book the names upon it from a knowledge of the religion or politics of the parties.

The Attorney-General submitted that the allegations contained in the challenge had been refuted by the evidence adduced in support of it, and that there was no evidence to go to the triers to sustain the challenge, and therefore declined making any further observation upon the issue to be tried....

The triers found against the challenge.

The panel was then called over, and after twenty peremptory challenges on behalf of the prisoner, and 39 jurors being set aside on behalf of the Crown, the jury was sworn:

John Whitty, Foreman	Halwood Clarke
William Fletcher	Richard Yoakley
Robert Thomas	Edward Rothwell
William Horatio Nelson	Jason Sherwood
Frederick Rambaut	Thomas Bridgford
William Mansfield	John Collier

It being then five o'clock, the trial was adjourned on the motion of the Attorney-General until the following morning, the prisoner's counsel not objecting.]

Friday, 26 May 1848

The Attorney-General — The charge ... gentlemen, that we bring forward against Mr Mitchel on the present occasion is this, that he did, since the passing of this Act, 'compass, imagine, invent, devise, and intend to deprive and depose the Queen from the style, honour and royal name of the Imperial Crown of the United Kingdom'. And that he did also 'compass, invent, devise and intend to levy war against Her Majesty within the United Kingdom, in order by force and constraint to compel her to change her measures or counsels; and that such his intention he did express and declare by publications in a newspaper of which he is the editor, publisher and proprietor'....

A meeting was held in Limerick, which was called or described as 'a *soirée* to the prosecuted patriots'. That meeting, gentlemen, was held on Saturday, the 30th of April; and at that meeting Mr Mitchel, Mr Smith O'Brien, and Mr Meagher attended as the guests to whom this entertainment was given.[10] In the course of that evening Mr Mitchel delivered a speech, the publication of which speech in his own newspaper on Saturday the 6th of May, is one of the articles upon which we rely, as a printing and publishing by him within the words of the Act of Parliament, expressing and declaring such the imaginations, inventions, and devices that he had previously formed. And the question – and I believe the only question that will be left to you by the Court will be this, whether in point of fact this article and the article in the other paper … do not clearly express and declare such the intention of Mr Mitchel; that intention being a deposition of Her Majesty the Queen….

Gentlemen, the first of these articles is the report of a speech delivered by him at the meeting at Limerick on this occasion. It is right I should apprise you, although it does not make any difference, that it purports to be a report taken from another paper, namely a report taken or abridged from *The Limerick Reporter*. But, gentlemen, it is not for the publication of that document as taken from another paper we proceed. We do not make the subject-matter of our proceeding any of the speeches, however seditious, that may have been delivered at the meeting; but we rely on this publication, as a publishing, expressing and printing of an article, containing the sentiments delivered by Mr Mitchel himself at that meeting which, of course, he adopts by this, his publication. The article is as follows:

Mr Mitchel having been loudly called on, then rose amidst a hurricane of applause and said: Mr Chairman and citizens of Limerick, my first duty is to thank you, which I do cordially and sincerely, for the generous reception you have this night given to those who have been selected for prosecution by the British Government – a reception which, notwithstanding what has occurred outside that door, must be called a triumphant one.

As far as I can judge, what occurred outside that door was this, it so appears in a subsequent portion of the speech of Mr Mitchel that a portion of the people of Limerick, who did not approve of the course pursued by Mr Mitchel, had hooted him and not given him the reception which perhaps he had some reason to expect. He says:

I have seen nothing in all this mob violence to make me despond for a moment. The people *are* the true source of legitimate power. That howling multitude outside are a thousand times preferable to the howling legislators of England, who yelled against Smith O'Brien (*cheers*).

---

10. *William Smith O'Brien* (1803–64) of County Clare. Educated at Harrow and Cambridge; MP for Ennis, 1826–31, for County Limerick, 1835–48. Joined Repeal Association 1844, leading it during O'Connell's imprisonment, and leaving it when the freed O'Connell negotiated with the Whig government. Jailed in the cellar of the House of Commons on the order of the Speaker for refusing to attend a committee – the first MP to be so detained for 200 years. A founder of the Irish Confederation in January 1847 with Mitchel and Meagher, in December of that year he split with Mitchel because of his emphasis on violent methods. Smith O'Brien reached an agreement with Mitchel that they would not appear on the same platform, and in April 1848 neither knew beforehand of the invitation to the other. It clearly served neither party in this court case to lay great stress on the fact that the Limerick meeting was broken up by O'Connellites, Smith O'Brien being badly injured. *Thomas Francis Meagher* (1823–67) of Waterford. Educated at Stonyhurst; co-founder of the Confederation, broke with Mitchel in February 1848 when Meagher stood in the Waterford by-election, which Mitchel thought would raise false expectations in parliamentary tactics. By mid-March, following the February revolution in France, both Smith O'Brien and Meagher were calling for the formation of a National Guard and coming closer to Mitchel's advocacy of insurgency, notwithstanding the prolonged and severe effects of the Famine as well as the marked ambivalence of the clergy.

I am no drawing-room democrat, who can discourse of the powers and virtues of the people only while they are smiling and cheering around me. Mob law itself in Ireland is far better than Government law – that well-ordered and civilized system that slays its millions of human beings within the year. I tell you that rather than endure one other year of British domination, I would take a provisional government selected out of the men that are bellowing there in the street.

Now, gentlemen, let me ask you what did Mr Mitchel mean by alluding to a provisional government? What meaning will be given by his able counsel to that sentiment in this publication? What, gentlemen, is the meaning of a provisional government? What does the history of the times we live in tell us? Where then was there, and where alone, a provisional government? Where, but in the kingdom of France? Within a very short period before this article was published, the people of France had overthrown the monarchical government of the country, and established a republic.[11] If there are other expressions in this speech of which there shall be any doubt, I think that this expression, that he would prefer a provisional government formed of the mob that was hooting outside the door rather than endure one other year of the British Government of misrule, as he called it, will leave very little doubt in your minds as to what the true meaning, character, and intention of Mr Mitchel and of this publication is. He says:

Sir, I fear that I am unfortunately the cause of your meeting this night being disturbed (*no, no*). I think, however, the matter arises out of a misapprehension. There is a great difference surely between bearing testimony to one's approval of a man's general conduct and identifying oneself with all his acts (*hear*). It is one thing to offer encouragement and support to a person singled out by Government (which is the enemy of us all), as the especial object of its vengeance; and it is quite another thing to adopt for your own every particular sentiment, saying and doing of the individual in question. This difference I feel bound to note and acknowledge tonight; and I do so with alacrity and gratitude. You need not fear, my friends, that I will misinterpret the compliment that has been paid me in inviting me to your city on this occasion. You need not fear that I have accepted your invitation in order that I might thrust any particular opinions of my own down your throats (*hear, hear*), or in order to induce a belief that there is between me and your distinguished guests – Smith O'Brien and Thomas Meagher – a more thorough identification than there is or needs to be. We don't want this thorough identification (*hear*). Some of the things I have done and written these gentlemen have both condemned, as believing either that they are wrong in themselves or that the time had not come for them. And I cannot be even with my friends in this matter – I am not able to repudiate any of their public acts. Can I repudiate, for instance, the last

11. By now the impact on Europe of the events of February 1848 in Paris should be evident. However, it is worth stressing that they also had a strong, if short-lived, influence in US political circles, where European republicanism was fully celebrated and formed the ideological basis of lobbying on behalf of the Irish 'state prisoners'. In March, having visited Paris, the US ambassador to London, George Bancroft, wrote to Edward Everett, Professor of Greek and President of Harvard College,

Wonderful times there! Greece colonized. Her colonies became republics, and the mother state threw off monarchy too. Of the six great civilized states, two are now republics, and more will follow.… Of what use to Spain is a queen who does but renew the barren impurities of a Messalina? … Smith O'Brien has gone over to Ireland, eager for power, and willing to be a martyr if he can gain glory by it.… There were riots in Edinburgh, Glasgow, Manchester and London, but civil force as yet has suppressed them; and fashionable doctrine is that riots save a rebellion.

Bancroft, London, to Everett, 10 March 1848, in M.A. De Wolfe Howe (ed.), *Life and Letters of George Bancroft*, London 1908, I, p. 31.

speech of Mr O'Brien in the British parliament – one of the noblest, clearest statements of Ireland's case – the very haughtiest, grandest defiance flung in the face of Ireland's enemies that ever yet fell from the lips of man (*loud cheers*)? Or can I condemn the alternative put by Mr Meagher, who says, 'when the last constitutional appeal shall be made, and shall fail, then up with the barricades and invoke the God of battles'?

That, gentlemen, Mr Mitchel says is the sentiment of Mr Meagher that he cannot find fault with – 'when the last constitutional appeal shall be made, and shall fail, then up with the barricades, and invoke the God of battles'. He says:

> Can I repudiate this – who holds that constitutional appeals are long since closed against us, and that we have even now no resource except – when we have the means and the pluck to do it – the barricades and the God of battles?'

May I ask, gentlemen, respectfully, my very able, respected and learned friend who will follow me as the counsel of Mr Mitchel, may I ask him to inform you what construction can be put on that paragraph save the one which I take the liberty of suggesting? It appears, gentlemen, from this statement of Mr Mitchel, that the doctrine preached by one of his associates or friends was this: that when the last constitutional appeal should fail, then it was time to 'up with the barricades and invoke the God of battles'. Mr Mitchel states his own opinion to be that the time for constitutional appeals was past, 'and that we have even now no resource except – when we have the means and the pluck to do it – the barricades and the God of battles'. You gentlemen no doubt recollect – it is a portion of the history of the world – that this allusion is borrowed from the then recent revolution that was effected in France. He says, 'No, all the seditions and treasons of these gentlemen I adopt and I accept and I ask for more.' Here, gentlemen, he gives his own construction of the sentiment he expresses. He says:

> No, all the seditions and treasons of these gentlemen I adopt and and I accept and I ask for more (*hear, hear*). Whatever has been done or said by the most disaffected person in all Ireland against the existence of the party which calls itself Government – nothing can go too far for me. Whatever public treasons there are in this land, I have stomach for them all (*loud cheering*). But, sir, have we not had in Ireland somewhat too much of this adopting and avowing, or also repudiating and disavowing, what has been said or done by others? Might we not perhaps act with advantage less as parties and more as mere men, each of us on his own individual responsibility (*hear, hear*)? For myself, although an active member of the Irish Confederation, I declare that I do not belong to the Young Ireland Party, or to any party. I have found myself unsuited to party ties and trammels altogether. I have been found not to draw quietly either in single or double harness (*hear, hear and laughter*). I very soon quarrelled with the old repeal Association; and as for the Confederation, it has once or twice nearly quarrelled with me. Not many weeks ago the council of the Confederation, headed by Smith O'Brien and Mr Meagher, thought it necessary to disavow my proceedings. Very well; what harm can come of it? I merely retorted in the most good-humoured way in the world, by setting them at defiance; and things went on afterwards more smoothly than ever (*cheers and laughter*). In short, I have long felt that I belong to a party of one member – a party whose basis of action is to think and act for itself – whose one fundamental rule is to speak its mind (*cheers*). Its secretary, committee, librarian and treasurer are all one in the same person; and in its proceedings I can assure you there remains the most unbroken unanimity (*continued laughter*).
>
> Seriously, sir, I know of no other way of ensuring both honest unanimity and independent cooperation than this way of mine; and with these views and sentiments you may be sure

I am not likely to misconceive the motive of your kindness in asking me to join your party tonight. I am here, I believe, as your guest on one account alone. You will say whether I state it truly. I am not here as a Jacobin (which I am not), nor as a Communist (which I am not), nor even as a Republican (which I am) (*loud cheers*), but simply and merely because I am a bitter and irreconcilable enemy to the British Government (*hear, hear*).… It is fortunate, I think, that those who have taken a forward part in rousing our people to these hopes and efforts are first to bear the brunt of danger. It is better that they should be called to encounter it in the courts of justice first than that it should fall on a people not yet prepared in the field. But while we meet the enemy in the Queen's Bench, we have a right to call upon you to sustain us by a firm and universal avowal of your opinion. On the constituents of Smith O'Brien especially devolves this duty. While the British Parliament calls his exertions 'treason' and 'felony', it is for his constituents to declare that in all this treason and felony he is doing his duty by them (*cheers*). And more than this: it is your duty further to prepare systematically to sustain him, if it come to that, in arms.

Now, gentlemen, may I ask what meaning is intended to be conveyed by this statement.… For what purpose, may I ask, were those arms to be used? Were those arms to be used, or is it possible that they were intended to be used, for any purpose except that which I take the liberty of suggesting? If there was any other purpose, I ask my learned friend who is to follow me to state to you what that purpose was. He then, gentlemen, goes on, and I think states very clearly his intention:

> May I presume to address the women of Limerick (*hear, hear and loud cheers*). It is the first time I have ever been in the presence of the daughters of those heroines who held the breach against King William; and they will understand me when I say that no Irishwoman ought so much as to speak to a man who has not provided himself with arms.

May I ask, respectfully, for what purpose were those arms to be provided? Does he not state himself in the previous part to sustain Mr Smith O'Brien in arms against the Government of the country, 'the public enemy of the country'? He says:

> No lady is too delicate for the culinary operation of casting bullets (*laughter*). No hand is too white to make up cartridges (*hear, hear and cheers*). And I hope, if it be needful to come to the last resort, that the citizens of Limerick, male and female, will not disgrace their paternal and maternal ancestors.

For what purposes were the ladies of Limerick to make up these cartridges and to cast bullets? …

I will not, gentlemen, trespass upon your patience by again going over this speech which I have now read.… If, gentlemen, a provisional government is to be formed in Dublin, what, may I ask you, is to become of Her Majesty as Queen of the United Kingdom? The two things, gentlemen, are utterly and altogether inconsistent and incompatible. If that was not the object, must it not, at all events, have been the other – of levying war against the Government in order, by an armed force, to compel a change in the constitution? That, gentlemen, is the nature of the publication in the first paper, upon which we call for your verdict. That paper was published on the 6th of May.…

Gentlemen, if that article stood alone I do not anticipate that any doubt could be entertained of what the feelings, opinions and intentions of Mr Mitchel were. But in order to remove all doubt Mr Mitchel in the very succeeding number of his paper published two other articles in which the intention of establishing an Irish republic, the

time of its establishment, the mode of its establishment, is in express terms expressed ...
it is a letter purporting to have been written by himself addressed 'To the Protestant
farmers, labourers and artisans of the north of Ireland'....

A JUROR – What is the date of it?

THE ATTORNEY-GENERAL – It is published in his newspaper of the 13th of May.... I think
it appears from some portions of this letter that Mr Mitchel himself was from the north
of Ireland:

> MY FRIENDS – Since I wrote my first letter to you, many kind and flattering addresses have
> been made to you by exceedingly genteel and very rich noblemen and gentlemen.... Lord
> Clarendon, the English governor, congratulates you on your 'loyalty', and your 'attachment
> to the constitution', and seems to calculate, though I know not why, upon a continuance
> of those exalted sentiments in the north. Lord Enniskillen, the Irish nobleman, for his part,
> cautions you earnestly against Popery and the Papists, and points out how completely you
> would be overborne and swamped by Catholic majorities in all public affairs.
>
> My Lord Enniskillen does not say a word to you about what is, after all, the main
> concern, the *tenure of your farms*; not one word.... Lord Enniskillen knows too (or, if he did
> not, he is the very stupidest Grand Master in Ulster) that an ascendancy of one sect over
> another is henceforth *impossible*. The fierce religious zeal that animated our fathers on both
> sides is utterly dead and gone. I do not say whether this is for our advantage or not; but at
> any rate it is gone: nobody in all Europe would now so much as understand it; and if any
> man talks to you now of religious sects, when the matter in hand relates to civil and political
> rights, to administration of government or distribution of property – depend on it, though
> he wear a coronet on his head, he means to cheat you.
>
> In fact, religious hatred has been kept alive in Ireland longer than anywhere else in
> Christendom, just for the simple reason that Irish landlords and British statesmen found
> their own account of it; and so soon as Irish landlordism and British dominion are finally
> rooted out of the country, it will be heard of no longer in Ireland, any more than it is in
> France or Belgium now.[12]
>
> But then, 'Protestants have always been *loyal* men.' Have they? And what do they mean
> by 'loyalty'? I have never found that, in the north of Ireland, this word has any meaning at
> all, except that we, Protestants, hated the Papists, and despised the French. This, I think, if
> you will examine it, is the true theory of 'loyalty' in Ulster. I can hardly fancy any of my
> countrymen so brutally stupid as to really prefer high taxes to low taxes – to be really proud
> of supporting 'the Prince Albert' and his lady, and their children, and all the endless lists of
> cousins and uncles that they have in magnificent idleness at the sole expense of the half-
> starving labouring poor. I should like to meet the northern farmer or labouring man who
> would tell me, in so many words, that he prefers dear government to cheap government;
> that he likes the House of Brunswick better than his own house; that he would rather have
> the affairs of the country managed by foreign noblemen and gentlemen than by himself and
> his neighbours.

---

12. No useful purpose is served by comment on the main point in this passage, but it is worth noting
the observation of Arthur Griffith, who edited Mitchel's *Jail Journal* for publication in Dublin in 1913, that
his policies had often been misrepresented and were:

> 1) to hold the harvest; 2) to pay no rent; 3) to pay no poor rate; 4) to boycott all those who did;
> 5) to resist distraint and eviction or the carrying away of the harvest by destroying roads etc.; 6) to
> boycott those who purchased distrained chattels or took evicted farms; 7) to arm the people
> everywhere and use arms where they might effectively be used against the evicters.

John Mitchel, *Jail Journal*, ed. A. Griffith, Dublin 1913, p. 457.

Now, gentlemen, I come to the part of this letter which clearly and plainly expresses the whole object of Mr Mitchel, and the nature of this publication:

> I tell you frankly that I, for one, am not 'loyal'. I am not wedded to the Queen of England, nor unalterably attached to the House of Brunswick. In fact, I love my own barn better than I love that house. The time is long past when Jehovah *anointed* Kings. The thing has long since grown an monstrous imposture, and has been already, in some civilized countries, detected as such and drummed accordingly....
>
> Give up for ever that old interpretation you put upon the word 'Repeal'. Repeal is no priest movement; it is no sectarian movement; it is no money swindle, nor 'eighty-two' delusion, nor puffery, nor O'Connellism, nor Mullaghmast 'green cap' stage-play, nor loud-sounding inanity of any sort, got up for any man's profit or praise.[13] It is the mighty passionate struggle of a nation hastening to be born into new national life; in the which unspeakable throes, all the parts and powers and elements of our Irish existence – our confederations, our Protestant repeal associations, our tenant-right societies, our clubs, cliques, and committees, amidst confusions enough, and the saddest jostling and jumbling, are all inevitably tending, however unconsciously, to one and the same illustrious goal – *not* a local legislature, *not* a return to our 'ancient constitution', not a golden link, or a patchwork parliament, or a College-green chapel-of-ease to St Stephen's, but an Irish republic, one and indivisible.... In *arms*, my countrymen, in arms. Thus, and not otherwise, have ever nations of men sprung to liberty and power.

... What, gentlemen, the line of the defence will be, that may be taken by the able counsel of Mr Mitchel, I cannot, of course, anticipate. That he may possibly endeavour to persuade you that these articles do not bear the meaning that we impute to them, perhaps will be attempted. That, gentlemen, if I am right, is the only question that you will have to try; and if I am right, that is the only proper subject-matter of defence. At the same time, of course, counsel for a gentleman in the situation of Mr Mitchel are not confined very frequently, or do not confine themselves, to what ultimately will be the proper subject-matter of the defence of their client. They very frequently, and none with greater power or ability than my learned friend, Mr Holmes, appeal to the passions, appeal to the prejudices if they have any, appeal to the feelings of a jury; and very frequently, by great eloquence, endeavour to lead away the minds of the jury from the question that they have really to try. My friend and colleague, Mr Henn, will, of course, reply to any argument of that description, or to any argument bearing upon the question that may be brought forward by Mr Holmes in his defence of this gentlemen.

There is, however, gentlemen, one matter of defence which I trust you will excuse me anticipating. It may be alleged and stated that the Government, of which I am the servant, have endeavoured unfairly or improperly to empanel the jury who are now to try this important case against Mr Mitchel. You, gentlemen, were present here in court

---

13. Mitchel's 'eighty-two' reference is to the convention of directly elected delegates from the 40,000-strong Irish volunteers held at Dungannon in 1782 which unanimously declared that 'a claim of any body of men, other than the King, Lords and Commons of Ireland, to bind this kingdom is unconstitutional, illegal and a grievance', thereby obliging the Irish parliament to pass a Declaration of Independence, nullifying, until the Act of Union of 1800, the rights of the English parliament to legislate for Ireland whilst retaining a joint crown. Although a similar measure had been withdrawn in 1779 because of the military reverses suffered in America, it is reasonable to suppose that the process and resolution of the American War of Independence had an influence in opening the nineteen years of 'Grattan's Parliament' in which a sovereign constitution coexisted with the inalienable identity of the crowns of Ireland and England.

yesterday, and are aware an attempt was made to satisfy the Court and the jury, or rather the gentlemen who were appointed triers, that an effort had been made by the Crown to interfere with the right and duty of the sheriff in empanelling a jury. The complaint, gentlemen, against that jury panel was this: that that jury panel did not contain a sufficient number, or the proportion, of Roman Catholic jurors which it ought to have....

I am myself – I have always been from conviction, from education, and from habit, and shall always continue – a Roman Catholic. That I should be supposed capable of objecting to my Roman Catholic fellow-countryman on account of the religion which he entertains; or that the Government, of which I am the servant, should object to a Roman Catholic juror on the ground that he professes the Roman Catholic religion, is a calumny on that Government which every act of theirs gives the most flat and ample contradiction to. The very circumstance of that Government promoting me, a Roman Catholic, to one of the highest offices that I am capable of filling; the fact of that very Government promoting to the highest offices within their gift in this country distinguished members of the profession to which I belong is, I trust, a sufficient answer to the insinuation that men were excluded from the jury simply and solely, or at all, because they professed the Roman Catholic religion....

Mr Holmes – May it please your lordships, gentlemen of the jury, I am in this case counsel for the prisoner, John Mitchel.... I will avow that I feel proud to have been selected upon this occasion by Mr Mitchel as his counsel because I believe him in my heart to be an honest man, sincerely believing in, and attached to, the principles which he avows, and which there is no doubt he avows boldly; and although the Government of this country may fear him, or hate him, they cannot despise him....

There was a challenge to the array, in this case, upon the part of the accused man, who, from information we had got, false perhaps, had reason to believe that those whose duty it was to empanel an impartial jury, had not in all instances done so, particularly with respect to placing Roman Catholics upon the panel. Well, the issue was tried, and the triers found upon their oaths that it was a fair and impartial jury – a fair and impartial jury upon the oaths of those triers! What do I find then? That from that fair and impartial jury, declared upon the oaths of those two respectable men to be a fair and impartial jury between the Crown and the accused, the Crown – or the officers of the Crown – struck off that fair and impartial jury nine and thirty men, eighteen of them being Roman Catholics. Can that be denied? ... I say no more upon that subject.

In this case, gentlemen of the jury, the prisoner, John Mitchel, stands charged with two distinct offences: and it is somewhat remarkable that in support of these distinct offences the same identical evidence is given to support both. The Attorney-General will be very satisfied, no doubt, if you give your verdict upon both of them, or either – no matter which – like the foreman of the Grand Jury in finding the bills against the prisoner. He first declared they found him guilty of sedition. 'Oh, sedition,' said the Attorney-General, 'this is not an indictment for sedition.' 'Oh well, then,' said the foreman, 'we find him guilty of treason.' 'Treason! Oh, he can't be guilty of treason, he is only indicted for felony.' 'Oh, well then felony, or what you like,' says the foreman of the Grand Jury. So Mr Attorney-General would be very well satisfied if you choose between the two charges. He only wants one finding; that will satisfy him; he does not care which, and he applies the same evidence precisely to both cases, and leaves it to you to distinguish them, and to apply that evidence, as well as you can, to both or either of them....

The first charge against the prisoner is that he compassed, imagined, invented, devised or intended to deprive or depose our most gracious Sovereign the Queen, from the style, honour or royal name of the Imperial Crown of the United Kingdom; and that these intentions, and so on, were evidenced by the overt act of his printing and publishing various articles in the newspapers which have already been read to you.

Now, my lords, I really may be very dull, but I do not rightly comprehend this part of the Act of Parliament, 'to depose the Queen from the style, honour or royal name of the Imperial Crown of the United Kingdom'. I can understand deposing the Queen from the throne perfectly well – I can understand banishing Her Majesty out of her own dominions perfectly well – but I do not for the life of me understand what is meant by the words 'to depose her' – they do not say to deprive even – but to 'depose her from the style, honour or royal name of the Imperial Crown of the United Kingdom' … ?

What is the other charge? It is 'devising, intending, and so on, to levy war against Her Majesty, her heirs or successors, within any part of the United Kingdom'. That is not, however, the offence complete; it must be 'in order by force or constraint to compel her to change her measures or counsels'. What measures or counsels? Is there the slightest evidence here of what measures or counsels it is that these publications are calculated to force or constrain her to alter? What are they? Are the jury to grope in the dark? Are these publications calculated to force her to change her measures with France, or her measures with America, or her measures with any other country on the earth? What are the measures even in this country which they charge the prisoner with wanting her to change, or what counsels? I cannot understand that. What have been the measures during this session of Parliament passed for the improvement of Ireland? The poor law. That is the only measure which I know of; and has Mitchel endeavoured to oppose or interfere with that? Not in the least.…

Gentlemen of the jury, it is not my duty here to tell you – and if I did tell you, you would not believe me – that there are not very, very strong expressions used by my client in these publications. There are, and he avows them; and many of them I myself avow; and it will be impossible to try this case fairly between the Crown and the accused without my calling your attention to something of the history of Ireland, and the present state of Ireland – impossible. And I tell you, in the first place, Ireland is an enslaved country, and I will prove it. A great mistake, in my opinion, is entertained by many persons that there cannot be slavery, that no man can be a slave, except he is in chains, or is subject to the lash of the planter who flogs the negro. Some men seem under this false impression. Slavery, gentlemen, the slavery of a people consists in this – that they do not make the laws themselves by which they are governed, but those laws are made for them either by another nation or another individual; and I say boldly and broadly –

BARON LEFROY – We are very reluctant, Mr Holmes, to interfere, but we hope you will not place the Court in an embarrassing situation, by giving utterance to that which, if it appeared to the Court as objectionable as the matter we are trying, would really make us guilty of a great breach of duty if we sat quietly by and listened to.

MR HOLMES – I would be the last man in the world to ask the Court, or to press upon the Court, what I did not feel I had a right to do; and I think that it is impossible in this case to do justice to my client without doing justice to Ireland (*cheers*).

BARON LEFROY – The police who are in attendance have received orders to take into custody immediately any person who should be guilty of such an outrage upon public decorum and the order that should be preserved in a court of justice, as that which we have just witnessed. If the offence is repeated the police will certainly be directed to take into custody the parties so offending, and it will be the duty of the Crown to commit them to gaol.

MR HOLMES – I hope with all my heart your lordship will do so.

BARON LEFROY – It is an interruption to yourself as well as to the Court...

MR HOLMES – Gentlemen of the jury, I care not how you are empanelled or put into that box. I address you as what I believe you to be, honest men and Irishmen. I will now state to you (for take nothing on my assertion), but I will state to you on the highest authority – what it is that constitutes the liberty of a people. In what does the liberty of a people consist? It consists in the right and power to make laws for its own government.... And what does Blackstone say upon this – and he is a great authority upon constitutional questions? He cannot be suspected of leaning too much in favour of popular rights. He says, 'That it follows from the very nature', and he is speaking of Ireland and her dependence upon England, 'it follows from the very nature and constitution of the dependent state, that England should make laws for Ireland ... dependence being little else than the obligation to conform to the will or laws of the superior person or state upon which the inferior depends.... Ireland thus conquered, planted and governed, it must necessarily conform to her, and be bound by such laws as the superior state thinks proper to prescribe.' That is the doctrine of a commentator on the laws of England – a standard work....

What is this Act of Union? Ireland is said to be represented in the English Parliament by one hundred members, I think; the English Parliament consists of five hundred – five to one – five to one. Does Ireland, will any man say, will my able friend answer this question and say that Ireland now makes laws for herself; and that she is now free? There never was, I venture to assert, in the history of nations, so flagrant an act of injustice as that act of passing the Union – the Act of Union in this country.... I do say boldly and broadly, as a man and as a lawyer, that that Act of Union is only binding on the people of Ireland as a thing of expediency. Men will often submit to a certain order of things rather than run any risk or danger (and it is often wise and humane to do so) of subverting by force of arms what has been unjustly established; and, therefore, it may be a very expedient thing, and no man ought, but on strong grounds, to endeavour to subvert by force the present order of things. But when the question is the right, then I boldly assert, that an enslaved people – enslaved contrary to the law of Providence – has the right, if necessary, by force of arms to obtain liberty even at the hazard of life itself. I say life – for what is life? Is it worth any thing without liberty? What man, even here, would leave this country and go to Russia?

BARON LEFROY – We cannot possibly, Mr Holmes, sit here and allow you to preach that doctrine to the people – the Court sitting by and appearing to acquiesce in it – that any man has a right by force of arms to obtain a repeal of this Act. Objectionable as it may be, we cannot listen to it without observation.

MR HOLMES – I certainly do entertain that opinion, my lord.

BARON LEFROY – That may be your private opinion, but we cannot suffer the case of the prisoner to be put to the jury upon the ground that he had a right by force of arms to obtain that repeal.

MR HOLMES – I do not say that he has the right.

BARON LEFROY – Any man, you said.

MR HOLMES – I said the people; and it ought to be a great majority of the people, so as not to leave any doubt. I did not say an individual. I deny it.

BARON LEFROY – We cannot admit that any subject can, consistently with his allegiance, or any individual, or the whole body of the people – we cannot admit the right of force of arms as a matter of right. And how can that abstract question possibly justify your case, unless you mean to show that it bears on the present case?

MR HOLMES – I do ... Blackstone lays it down distinctly, my lords. I must revert to that doctrine. He lays it down distinctly that the English people have a right – you will find it, my lords, in vol. i, page 147 – to have arms, and to use arms against oppression. He lays that down distinctly and in so many words, and I am not wantonly or wildly here preaching doctrines of my own. I say they are founded upon legal and constitutional grounds and principles, and I would not presume to address your lordships on any other. But I have authority for every word I utter – I have historical facts for every word I utter.

Oh! But surely we find that these doctrines of Mr Mitchel and others are condemned? Yes, condemned by the high and the wealthy. Do we not find every day addresses upon addresses, and is not this an argument that this country is not friendly to a repeal of the Union? And it is proved, forsooth, by the number of loyal addresses which are now sent forward to the present Lord Lieutenant, declaring the unalterable attachment of those who sign them to the institutions of the country. Yes, gentlemen of the jury, there are men, and they are chiefly to be found in what are called the better ranks of society – excellent men, moral men, kind men, courteous men – but yet if all mankind were like them we should have such thing as liberty in the world. Peace in their time is their first prayer and highest aspiration....

Gentlemen of the jury, I speak not here merely for my client – I speak for you and your children, and your children's children – I speak not here for myself. My lamp of life is flickering and must soon be extinguished, but were I now standing on the brink of the grave, and uttering the last words of expiring nature, I would say, 'May Ireland be happy, may Ireland be free.' It rests with you, gentlemen of the jury, this day, by your verdict of acquittal; it rests with you to contribute your parts towards making Ireland happy and free. I call upon you, as you value truth, as you value justice, as you value public good, as you value manly bearing and personal honour, as you value and love the country of your birth and the land of your fathers, I call upon you, by your verdict of acquittal in this case, to do your parts towards making Ireland happy and free.

MR HENN – May it please your lordships – gentlemen of the jury – it now becomes my duty, on the part of the Crown, to make some observations to you upon the case now before you. And after the very extraordinary display which you have just witnessed, I certainly feel considerably embarrassed with the task I have to undertake. Gentlemen, it was a display extraordinary for the talent which it evinced, extraordinary for its eloquence, extraordinary for its energy and zeal, and not less extraordinary, in my judgement, proceeding from a gentleman of great information and great talent, in that from the commencement to the end of that eloquent appeal he has not addressed to you one topic bearing upon the real question which you upon your oaths have to try.

Unable as I am to compete with him, I shall show you that where there was colour of argument, it was purely sophistry. I will undertake to demonstrate that he has not laid before you truly the question at all; he has, in part of that very eloquent speech, assumed the question to be utterly different from what it is; and he has wisely abstained altogether from calling your attention either to the real question at issue or to the evidence which has been offered by the Crown in support of the charges contained in the indictment....

Have you any difficulty in understanding those charges? Have you been misled by what I might call (perhaps it is wrong so to do) the quibbles of my learned friend? ... I will ask you this one, plain and simple question: is it possible for anyone to compass, imagine or invent to deprive the Queen of the United Kingdom of that portion of her dominions called Ireland, without deposing her from the name, style and honour of the Imperial Crown of the United Kingdom? ...

Gentlemen of the jury, is it here that we are to discuss the question, whether Ireland has or has not a proper number of representatives in Parliament? What power have you, gentlemen, or my learned friend, or the judges on the bench, to decide that question? It is the established law of the land – the constitution is fixed and settled – and as you value the peace, tranquillity and prosperity of your country, let me implore you not to be misled by the energetic address of my learned friend, or induced to entertain for a moment the opinion that it is justifiable by force to procure an alteration in the law. Is every man to set up his own opinion?

Mr Holmes – I did not say every man; I said the people.

Mr Henn – My friend says not each man, but the people. What is it that constitutes the people? If you take every man in Ireland, as the constitution now exists, Ireland is but a portion of the United Kingdom, as Scotland or as York is; and, gentlemen, it is monstrous to say that any persons, no matter in what numbers, are justified in resorting to force to procure a change in the law. Resistance is a different thing. I do not deny that. In certain cases they may be justified in resorting to force to resist an attempt to deprive them of their rights; but I say that it is utterly inconsistent with the constitution of this country that the people, or any portion of the people, can resort to force to procure an alteration in the existing laws....

Gentlemen, am I in a court of justice? Is there a government existing? Can it be tolerated that as long as that Government exists any person can be permitted to preach such doctrines as these, and to circulate amongst the subjects of the country inducements to excite them to forget their allegiance, to throw off the allegiance they owe to the sovereign of the country, to rush into open rebellion, to arm themselves, and in all the horrors of a civil war to seek to establish 'a republic, one and indivisible', which can only be effected by the abolition of all Government, the denial of the Queen's authority, and the utter destruction of all those laws which preserve our liberties and our lives?

I ask you, does not that publication of itself demonstrate to you that his object was to depose the Queen from her royal name, style and dignity of the United Kingdom? I ask you, how is it possible he could accomplish his object, which was not 'a return to our ancient constitution' under one common sovereign but 'a republic, one and indivisible'? I ask you, as men of common sense, how could that be done without deposing the Queen from her name, style and dignity of the Imperial Crown of the United Kingdom? Is there an imaginable mode in which it could be done? Does that publication then establish, beyond all doubt, to the meanest capacity, the charge that he did compass the deposition of the Queen from her royal name, style and dignity of the Imperial Crown of the United Kingdom? ... No matter what the political opinions or the religious sentiments, which have been improperly introduced here, of any person in the community – satisfy your consciences and I am sure that you will satisfy the ends of justice and, therefore, those who prosecute for the Crown.

Summing Up

Mr Justice Moore – Gentlemen of the jury, it now becomes my duty to advert to the charge that has been brought against the prisoner at the bar, and to offer you such observations as occur to me upon the nature of that charge, and the evidence that has been adduced in support of it. Gentlemen, you have very properly been told by the counsel for the prisoner that this is a case of deep importance. The prisoner is charged with a very heinous offence. If he be innocent of it, it is, of course, of deep importance that he ought not to be found guilty or subjected to the consequences of guilt. But, gentlemen, on the other hand, if he be guilty, it appears to me to be of deep importance to the law, to the due administration of justice, and to the peace, tranquillity and well-being of this country that the man who has deliberately violated the law – if he has done so – should be made to undergo the consequences attached to that violation.

Gentlemen of the jury, a great deal of this case will depend – indeed, I may say the entire of it – upon the construction that is given to the documents that have been laid before you in evidence. And, gentlemen, it is my duty to tell you that the construction of those documents rests altogether and exclusively with you. The law has intrusted a jury with the construction of documents in a case like the present. The law has cast upon the jury the responsibility and due discharge of that duty. The law expects that that duty will not be discharged capriciously or lightly. And though it is for you, and you alone, to express what your opinion is upon the true construction, import and meaning of the documents that have been laid before you, the law expects that you will do so according to the best of your sense and of your judgement, and upon that alone....

Gentlemen of the jury, the counsel for the prisoner has introduced to you some irrelevant topics. He began with expressing his opinion, and I find no fault with him for doing so, as to the honesty and sincerity of his client. I am sure he would not have expressed any such opinion did he not honestly and conscientiously entertain it. But, gentlemen, let Mr Mitchel be honest, let him be sincere, let him have put foward those publications with the utmost honesty of purpose and sincerity of intention, yet what has that to say if those publications are in reality found to be in violation of the provisions of an Act of Parliament? And it is a principle that can never be allowed in a court of justice that a man is to say, 'It is true, I have violated an Act of Parliament, I have committed a crime, I am subject to the consequences of that crime, but in the opinion of my counsel I am an honest man, and I have brought forward what I did with the utmost sincerity of purpose.' Gentlemen, I am bound to tell you on that topic also ... the effect of an opinion of such a man as Mr Holmes – so able, so estimable, and standing so high as he always has done – you are bound to disregard and dismiss from your consideration....

I should have been very glad if the very learned and able counsel for the prisoner had not been guilty of any greater irrelevancies of topic than those to which I have just adverted. But, gentlemen, I regret to say that he has, in my judgement, and I believe I may say in the judgement of my brother judge, introduced a great variety of topics perfectly foreign and irrelevant to the questions you have to decide, and many of them topics which in no court of justice ought to have been introduced. He has told you that Ireland is an enslaved country; he has gone into the history of the Union; he has gone into the history of the country before the Union; he has denied the competency of the Irish parliament to pass an Act for the passing of the Union. Why, gentlemen, let me ask? What have these topics to do with the question which you are sworn to decide, to which I shall presently call your attention – that single question being whether the prisoner at the bar is guilty of violating the provisions of a particular Act of Parliament?

Gentlemen, let the Union be good, let it be bad, let the means by which it has been passed be right or proper, whether there was or was not corruption in the passing of the Act of Union, what has constituted – as has already been put to you by the counsel for the Crown – what has constituted this court, or you in the jury-box, as the tribunal to decide upon that? There is no issue in the case at all resting upon any such subject; and I cannot account for my learned and able friend, the counsel for the prisoner, holding as high a position as a man ever did, resorting to such topics. Because, gentlemen, when he concluded his speech he demonstrated to you that he was unable to say one single syllable upon the publications which formed the subject-matter of this indictment....

Gentlemen of the jury, there is in this case that very remarkable circumstance that probably never existed in any other case, and certainly never existed in any case with which I am acquainted. The Crown has, in the indictment, attached certain meanings to certain passages contained in those publications. The Attorney-General in his opening statement read to you the passages, and stated to you the meaning which he thought the passages bore. The able counsel for the prisoner never once adverted to those publications, and never made a single observation for the purpose of showing that the Attorney-General, either in the indictment or in his statement, had put a wrong interpretation on either of those papers. Therefore, gentlemen, if it was a case in which any thing would, or ought, to be taken against, or to the prejudice of the prisoner, you have this remarkable fact – that the counsel for the prisoner, the first in the land, has felt himself unable to offer to you any observations upon the contents of these documents beyond stating that he did not understand the Act of Parliament. And he has not attempted to assign a meaning different to that which has been attributed by the Crown to them. That, however, ought not to determine this case or influence your minds. The counsel for the prisoner has taken the course which, in his judgement, he thought most beneficial to his client. But, gentlemen, if he abstained from adverting to the purport and meaning of the publications in question, that is no reason why you are to take for granted that the meaning given by the Crown is the true and correct one ...

Gentlemen, if you think, after a careful and deliberate revision and review of all these publications, you can safely and conscientiously come to the conclusion that Mr Mitchel did not intend both or either of the intents that have been attributed to him, you ought without hesitation to find him not guilty. If, gentlemen, you think that the intents are not clear; if you think that they are ambiguous; if you think the expressions used are of a doubtful nature, and the conviction is not brought home to your minds as to what he compassed and intended, in like manner you would be bound to give him the benefit of that doubt.

But, if after a careful review and revision of all the passages of these publications, to which a meaning has been assigned in the indictment and by the counsel for the prosecution, and no opposite meaning has been attempted by the counsel fore the prisoner, you come to the deliberate conclusion that they do sustain the allegations in the indictment, and that as honest men, in the exercise of your judgement, you can lay your hands on your hearts and say, we do think these expressions demonstrate the intent with which the prisoner at the bar is charged, I would not insult you for a moment, by fancying that honest men like you would hesitate in that solemn and sacred duty which has been intrusted to you, which you are bound to execute under the solemn obligation of an oath.

[At twenty past four the jury retired.

At ten minutes to six, the judges sent the sheriff to inquire whether the jury had agreed on their verdict.

After a short time the sheriff returned and stated that the jury had not agreed, but that there was a probability of their doing so.

At ten minutes to seven the jury came into court and answered to their names.]

THE CLERK OF THE CROWN – Gentlemen, have you agreed on your verdict?

THE FOREMAN – We have.

THE CLERK OF THE CROWN – How say you, is the prisoner guilty or not guilty?

THE FOREMAN – Guilty.

BARON LEFROY – Let the prisoner stand by till to-morrow.

Saturday, 27 May 1848

THE CLERK OF THE CROWN – Put forward John Mitchel.

SIR COLMAN O'LOGHLEN – I have to apply to your lordships that the issue and verdict in this case be read. If your lordships have no objection we wish to have the verdict, as handed in last night by the jury, read.

THE CLERK OF THE CROWN – The verdict I have entered is 'Guilty'.

SIR COLMAN O'LOGHLEN – What is the issue and finding exactly?

THE CLERK OF THE CROWN – 'Your issue is to try and inquire whether John Mitchel, given in charge, is guilty or not. Verdict – Guilty, for self and fellow jurors.'

BARON LEFROY – We have called on this case this morning in order to give time, if there should be, either on the part of the prisoner or on the part of the Crown, any application to be made to the Court relating to it. Therefore we thought it better to call it on first; and we will now proceed to dispose of the case.

THE CLERK OF THE CROWN – John Mitchel, have you any thing to say why the sentence of the Court should not be passed upon you?

MR MITCHEL – I have. I have to say, my lord, that I have been found guilty by a packed jury, by the proceedings of a partisan sheriff, by a jury not empanelled according to the laws even of England – empanelled not by a sheriff but by a juggler. That is the reason why I object to your sentencing me to any punishment.

THE HIGH SHERIFF – My lords, I claim the protection of the Court.

MR MITCHEL – That is the reason why I object to sentence being passed on me.

BARON LEFROY – Well, I shall make no further observation upon that; but I owe it to the jury to state that upon the evidence, furnished thus by yourself, no juror who had the slightest regard to the oath could possibly have come to a different conclusion.... Has there been attempted, in the course of this trial, any explanation, any interpretation, any apology for these publications, or any thing tending to show, or to raise, doubt upon their bearing the interpretation that is put upon them by the indictment? ...

No interpretation was offered, no meaning was ascribed, no effort was made, in the least, to show that you were not guilty in the sense imputed in the indictment. The line of defence, not only impliedly, but expressly stated, that although you might be statutably guilty, yet you were justified in what you did. The Court, though we did not interpose to put a stop to that line of defence, yet we cannot but desire –

MR HOLMES – What I said, with the greatest respect, my lords, was that though the prisoner was statutably guilty, he was not, in my opinion, morally guilty.

BARON LEFROY – I should be very glad indeed to find that I had mistaken altogether the drift of that defence ... and so far as the learned counsel has corrected the view that I was taking of it, I am exceedingly glad to adopt his correction – I shall say no more upon it. I only adverted to it to absolve the Court from the possible suspicion that we could sit here and acquiesce in a line of defence which appeared to us at the time ... as objectionable as that for which the prisoner stood at the bar.

MR HOLMES – My lord, I am answerable for that under the Act of Parliament.

BARON LEFROY – Mr Sheriff, it is strange that the number of police I see in court cannot keep order.

THE HIGH SHERIFF – Police, if you see the slightest ebullition of feeling from any person, remove him from the court.

BARON LEFROY – No, but make a prisoner of him. I have been somewhat withdrawn from the observations which I meant to have confined to your own case ... I wish you to understand that that we have with the utmost anxiety, and with a view to come to a decision upon the measure of punishment which it is our duty to impose in this case, postponed passing the sentence until this morning.

We have examined it with the utmost deliberation, and with the utmost anxiety to duly discharge the duty which we owe the prisoner – of not awarding a punishment beyond the just measure of the offence – as well as the duty which we owe to the Queen and the public. The sentence of the Court is that you be transported beyond the seas for the term of fourteen years....

MR MITCHEL – May I address a few words to the Court?

BARON LEFROY – Certainly.

MR MITCHEL – The law has now done its part, and the Queen of England, and the Crown and the Government in Ireland are now secure, pursuant to Act of Parliament. I have done my part also. Three months ago I promised Lord Clarendon, and his Government in this country, that I would provoke him into the courts of justice, as places of this kind are called; that I would force him, publicly and notoriously, to pack a jury against me, to convict me, or else that I would walk a free man out of this court, and provoke him to a contest in another field. My lord, I knew I was setting my life on that cast; but I knew in either event the victory should be with me, and it is with me. I presume neither the jury nor the judges, nor any other man in this court, imagines that it is a criminal who stands in this dock. I have shown what law is made of in Ireland. I have shown that Her Majesty's Government sustains itself in Ireland by packed juries, by partisan judges, by perjured sheriffs –

BARON LEFROY – The Court cannot sit here to hear you arraign the jurors of the country, the sheriff of the country, the administration of justice, the tenure by which the Crown of England holds this country. It cannot sit here and suffer you to proceed thus, because the trial is over. Everything that you had to say previous to the judgement, the Court was ready to hear, and it did hear as much as you were pleased to offer. It cannot suffer you to stand at that bar to repeat, I must say, very nearly a repetition of the offence for which you have just been sentenced.

MR MITCHEL – I will not say anything more of that kind. But I wish to say this, my lord –

BARON LEFROY – Anything you wish to say we will hear; but I trust that you will keep yourself within the limits which even your own judgement must suggest to you.

MR MITCHEL – I have acted in all this business, from the first, under a strong sense of duty. I do not repent of anything I have done. And I believe that the course which I have opened is only commenced. The Roman, who saw his hand burning to ashes before the tyrant, promised that three hundred should follow out his enterprize. Can I not promise for one, for two, for three, aye, hundreds?

BARON LEFROY – Officer, remove the prisoner.

[Mr Mitchel was then removed, and great confusion ensued from the efforts of his friends to shake hands with him.]

POSTSCRIPT

The court reporter's work done, Mitchel himself takes up the story:

May 27, 1848. On this day, about four o'clock in the afternoon, I, John Mitchel, was kidnapped, and carried off from Dublin, in chains, as a convicted 'felon'. I had been in Newgate prison for a fortnight. An apparent *trial* had been enacted before twelve of the castle jurors in ordinary – much legal palaver, and a 'conviction' (as if there were *law*, *order*, *government*, or *justice* in Ireland). Sentence had been pronounced, with much gravity, by that ancient Purple Brunswicker, Baron Lefroy – *fourteen years' transportation* – and I had returned to my cell, and taken leave of my wife and two poor boys. A few minutes after they had left me a gaoler came in with a suit of coarse grey clothes. 'You are to put on these', said he, 'directly.'[14]

In the event, the authorities, who never failed to recognise Mitchel as a 'gentleman' but who were also worried at the impact on the large crowd waiting in Green Street, permitted him to keep his own clothes. There is some sense that John, and certainly his wife Jenny, expected that he would be sprung as he was taken through the streets to the steamer *Shearwater* on the first leg of his transportation. But Mitchel's comrades had judged – surely rightly – that sympathy and ebullience in the street were one thing, and a secure escape quite another. Having failed to convict Smith O'Brien and Meagher, Clarendon's administration had placed considerable importance on the Mitchel case, and the deployment of troops and police surrounding the court reflected this. Nevertheless, the severity of the sentence – unprecedented, of course, for a 'felony' of this type, but also imposed when political mobilisation in Europe was at its peak – almost certainly had a counter-productive impact. In Oldham and Nottingham there appeared banners – 'Mitchel and Liberty' and 'Mitchel should be free' – and in early June an irate MP asked the secretary of state for the Home Department,

> Whether he had heard, and if so whether the report was true, that John Mitchel, when put on board the *Shearwater* steamer to be conveyed to Spike Island, was entertained by the officers of that ship, that he was placed at their table, took part of their mess, and was treated by them, not as a convicted felon, but as a passenger.[15]

The MP was Sir William Verner, member for Armagh and brother of Jenny Mitchel's father, James. Henceforth the Verner family would repudiate the Mitchels, taking great pains to deny that Jenny was a blood relation. In reply to Verner, the secretary of state was glad to inform the House that Mitchel had been invited to breakfast, but only by the assistant surgeon, and that he asked the first lord of the admiralty to look into the matter. In reality, Mitchel had been cordially treated by the captain, Basil Hall, who had offered him sherry, apologies and interesting conversation on the Chilean and Peruvian revolutions (on which a book had been written by the author of the same name).

From his own account, Mitchel was treated correctly by almost all his British captors for the next five years or so. But he was never a physically strong man – in time asthma would be replaced by tuberculosis – and the first nine months of his transportation, on HMS *Scourge* and in Bermuda, were especially taxing. This did little, however, to temper Mitchel's critical faculties, which were juiced up by a civilised supply of literature. By mid-Atlantic he was stuck into Macaulay's essays:

> He is a born Edinburgh Reviewer, this Macaulay, and, indeed, a type-reviewer – an authentic specimen-page of nineteenth century 'literature'. He has the right omniscient tone and air, and the true knack of administering reverential flattery to British civilization, British prowess,

---

14. *Jail Journal*, Glasgow 1876, p. 21.
15. Hansard, *Parliamentary Debates*, XCIX, p. 471.

honour, enlightenment, and all that, especially to the great nineteenth century and its astounding civilization, that is, to his readers. It is altogether a new thing in the history of mankind, this triumphant glorification of a current century upon being the century it is. No former age, before Christ or after, ever took any pride in itself and sneered at the wisdom of its ancestors; and the new phenomenon indicates, I believe, not higher wisdom, but deeper stupidity.[16]

Here Mitchel echoes the timbre of Macaulay's protagonist Carlyle, whose introduction to Ireland in the summer of 1846 he and Gavan Duffy had presided over, and who, notwithstanding his own famous intemperance and despair for Ireland, was readily able to spot Mitchel's dangerous disposition:

Dined at the Mitchels' with a select party, and ate there the last truly good potato I have met with in the world. Mitchel's wife, especially his mother (Presbyterian parson's widow of the best Scotch type), his frugally elegant small house and table pleased me much, as did the man himself, a fine elastic-spirited young fellow, whom I grieved to see rushing on destruction, palpable, by attack of windmills, but on whom my persuasions were thrown away. Both Duffy and him I have always regarded as specimens of the best kind of Irish youth, seduced, like thousands before them in their early day, into courses that were at once mad and ridiculous.... Poor Mitchel! I told him that he would most likely be hanged, but I told him too they could not hang the immortal part of him.[17]

None the less, this stage of the voyage does give us a rare expression of Mitchel's introspection, where one can discern a distinct Presbyterian brake upon the fierce anarchic, individualist inclinations of his thought and prose as he ruminates upon time of a less 'conjunctural' type:

Only for the present I am advisedly letting my intellect lie, basking in the sun, dozing in the shade, grazing upon every green thing. But I never dream of *killing Time* for fourteen years – if it come to that Time would kill me – fourteen years would be too many for me. An occasional half-hour, to be sure, you may kill if you take him unaware, but to slaughter Time by whole lustra and decades is given to no mortal. Therefore, I intend, after having been at grass awhile, to cultivate friendly relations with Time – a thing to be done by *working* only – to get Time on my side instead of living *against* him, so that I may use poor Walter Scott's proverb, 'Time and I against any two.'[18]

---

16. *Jail Journal*, p. 20.

17. Quoted in James Froude, *Thomas Carlyle: A History of His Life in London, 1834–1881*, I, London 1897, p. 429. A fierce critic of British dominion in Ireland, Carlyle did not hold back from extending his (widely shared) contempt for the dying Repeal leader O'Connell to his Ulster audience, which most Scots would have seen as their own:

I saw Conciliation Hall and the last glimpse of O'Connell, chief quack of the then world; first time I had ever heard the lying scoundrel speak – a most melancholy scene to me altogether; Conciliation Hall something like a decent Methodist Chapel, but its audience very sparse, very bad and blackguard-looking; brazen faces like tipsters, tavern-keepers, miscellaneous hucksters, and quarrelsome male or female nondescripts the prevailing type; not one that you would have called a gentleman, much less a man of culture; and discontent visible among them. The speech, on potato rot, most serious of topics, had not one word of sincerity, not to speak of wisdom, in it. Every sentence seemed to you a lie, and even to know that it was a detected lie.

Ibid., pp. 427–8.

18. *Jail Journal*, p. 73.

Mitchel wrote these words on 2 September 1848 in Bermuda. Four days earlier he had heard of the arrest of Smith O'Brien, Meagher and their principal associates. Within weeks of Mitchel's trial it had been plain that the Irish potato crop was again blighted (that in 1847 had been less severely affected). On 25 July the government had suspended *habeas corpus* for eight months, two days later arresting Fintan Lalor, whose radical proposals on the land question had been a seminal influence on Mitchel. Two days after that, 29 July, Smith O'Brien, ever brave but without either gift or inclination for combat, found himself surrounded by some one hundred followers and fifty constables at Ballingarry, County Tipperary.

Certain of their prospects if arrested and now obliged to make a stand, Smith O'Brien, Terence McManus and James Stephens decided to have barricades erected. The police desisted from entering the village and retreated to a cottage about a mile north of it, at Boulagh Commons. The house was owned by a widow, Mrs Mc-Cormack, who was out at the time, but her five children – all under ten years – were in when Sub-Inspector Trant and his forty-six men took over the building and began breaking up furniture in preparation of a defence. Mrs McCormack, Smith O'Brien and McManus went up to the house, and O'Brien, climbing on to the window sill, talked to the police, asking them, 'as an Irishman and a soldier too', to hand over their arms, which they refused. He then gave them five minutes to make up their minds, at which point somebody in the crowd outside shouted that the police should be attacked and stones were thrown – a shot possibly fired. The police shot back, expending 230 rounds over an hour. Two of the crowd were killed, several wounded, and all retreated, Smith O'Brien in some style, formally declaring that he never turned his back on the enemy.

This was the real culmination of the Irish campaign of the 1840s against the Union, a campaign that coincided not only with the revolutions of 1848 in continental Europe but also with a famine caused by three catastrophic failures of the potato harvest in four years and resulting in the deaths of possibly a million people and the emigation of nearly as many even at this stage. It is, then, both right and wrong to dwell on the messy, parochial and unheroic nature of the 'Battle of Widow Mc-Cormack's Cabbage Patch' – the phrase consistently used by *The Times* to disparage the independence movement.[19] This certainly contrasted with the striking rhetoric that Mitchel, above all others, had issued, paying the most minimal attention to practical consequences. Yet one can conceive of far more horrible outcomes, and it is possible to see in the actions of Smith O'Brien and Trant a representative desire to avoid unhampered physical aggression.[20]

---

19. There was a paltry riot in a cabbage-garden – the country entirely refused its adhesion to the Smith O'Brien dynasty – not even a pig was injured; the bubble burst, and the foolish persons who had amused themselves with playing at treason found themselves within the grasp of the constables.
The Times, 13 March 1856.

20. My sketch here is drawn most immediately from the short but vivid account given in Robert Kee, *The Most Distressful Country*, London 1972, pp. 283–7. Kee is not untypical in his interpretation of these events, which is as sober as his narrative is sprightly.

Whatever the case, words had finally gone to acts, and it was no longer possible to make recourse to the new treason–felony statute. Between 28 September and 23 October Smith O'Brien, Meagher, McManus and Patrick Donohue were tried for high treason at Clonmel, Justice Moore being one of their three judges.[21] On 7 October Smith O'Brien was found guilty and sentenced to be hanged, drawn and quartered. On 22 October the young Tom Meagher was convicted and purposefully avoided the suggestion that a plea for mercy might be countenanced:

> Judged by the law of England, I know this crime entails the penalty of death; but the history of Ireland explains this crime and justifies it.... I hope to be able with a pure heart and perfect composure appear before a higher tribunal – a tribunal where a judge of infinite goodness, as well as of justice, will preside, and where, my Lords, many – many of the judgements of this court will be reversed.[22]

On 23 October the others were similarly sentenced. In November and again in January 1849 they appealed their sentences, principally on the same grounds as Mitchel's defence – that English treason law did not apply to Ireland and that copies of the indictment and lists of the witnesses and jury had not been delivered to them ten days before the trial, thus absolving them from the requirement to plead.

Sir Colman O'Loghlen acted for Smith O'Brien, and to no greater immediate avail than he had for Mitchel. However, the government itself was in no better a political position than it had been over Mitchel because of the sentence of death, which it was effectively impossible to execute. Moreover, O'Loghlen and his team were able to turn the law against the state by adopting a politically brilliant – if potentially suicidal – opposition to the commuting of the death sentences to transportation. The strong legal grounds for this objection were that the courts lacked the power in such cases to exercise the prerogative of mercy. Hoist by its own petard, the government was eventually obliged, in June 1849, to put another bill through parliament, further complicating the entire treason–sedition–felony statutory position with the 'Transport for Treason (Ireland) Act'. Thus, the four eventually made their way to Tasmania, in Mitchel's wake.

---

21. The indictment in this case carries a marginally more medieval phraseology, accusing the defendants thus:

> ...being subjects of our said Lady the Queen, not having the fear of God in their hearts, nor weighing the duty of allegiance, but being moved and seduced by the instigation of the devil, as false traitors against our said Lady the Queen, and wholly withdrawing the love, obedience, fidelity and allegiance which every true and lawful subject ... ought to bear ... on the 17th day of July ... and on divers other days between that day and the 30th ... with force and arms at the parish of Ballingarry, in the said county of Tipperary, together with a great multitude of false traitors whose names are to the said jurors unknown, to the number of five hundred or more, arrayed and armed in warlike manner, with guns, pistols, pikes, clubs, bludgeons and other weapons ... did then and there unlawfully, maliciously and traitorously levy and make war ... and did then and there erect certain obstructions composed of cars, carts, pieces of timber and other materials erected and built to a great height, that is to say to the height of five feet and upwards.

Cox (ed.), *Reports of Cases in Criminal Law*, III, pp. 362–3.

22. Quoted in Thomas Keneally, *The Great Shame: A Story of the Irish in the Old World and the New*, London 1998, p. 82.

In April 1849, as the Russell ministry was contriving to extricate itself from this debacle, Mitchel, whose health had deteriorated markedly in Bermuda, was put aboard HMS *Neptune* with the destination of the Cape of Good Hope. This voyage took him via the coast of Brazil, where the issue of the slave trade was not yet settled and relations with Great Britain remained very tense. This naturally provided occasion for Mitchel to inveigh against the pretences of British abolitionism:

> Few persons, except some serious old women, are such fools as to believe that the British government keeps on foot that African armament with any view to humanity at all, or conscience, or Christianity, or any of the fine things that they pretend in Parliament. They have just two motives in it: *one* is to cut off the supply of labour from the sugar-growers of Brazil and Cuba, or to make it so dear to them that they cannot compete with the planters of Jamaica and Barbados; and the *other* is to maintain British 'naval supremacy' and the piratical claim of a right to search ships, and accustom the eyes of all who sail the sea to the sight of the English flag domineering over everything it meets, like a bully, as it is.[23]

If, as we will discuss below, there might be more than a grain of truth to some of these contentions, Mitchel wandered into much less secure territory when he blamed abolitionists in general, and the British in particular, for compounding the horrors of the slave trade precisely by trying to suppress it:

> When slavers are chased by a humanity pirate, and in danger of being taken, they simply pitch all the negroes into the sea, together with the loose planks that make the slave deck, and then lie to and invite the British officer on board. He finds no slaves and by the terms of the treaties must let the ship go free.[24]

This charge is not without factual support, of course, but it both extends and conceals Mitchel's own support of slavery – a position that at the turn of the twenty-first century seems to sit very ill with both his upbringing and his radical politics. However, it is less obviously in contradiction with nationalism *per se*, and certainly not so when that nationalism is pitted against a British government making much of its abolitionism on the international stage, even with the USA. Here again, Mitchel was close to Carlyle, and at the height of his campaign in February 1848 he had not hesitated to reveal his convictions: 'Every man (except a born slave, who aspires only to beget slaves and die a slave) ought to have arms.'[25] One might, perhaps, interpret

---

23. *Jail Journal*, p. 155.
24. Ibid.
25. *United Irishman*, 12 February 1848, quoted in D. George Boyce, *Nationalism in Ireland*, 3rd edn, London 1995, p. 173. In his edition of the *Jail Journal* (see note 12) Arthur Griffith refers (pp. xi–xii) to Mitchel's later polemic over slavery with the Rev. Henry Ward Beecher – brother of the author Harriet Beecher Stowe – and states bluntly, 'slave-holding is not a crime, and nobody ever thought it a crime until near the end of the eighteenth century'. As Mitchel cheerfully recognised, the Congregationalist minister served up some rhetorical medicine no less potent than his own:

> I can not hide from myself that there is yet remaining for you a dismal age, a desolate and cheerless solitude of infirmities. Time, that would have carried you onward, garlanded with achievements, worthy of a man living for men, and surrounded by the living sympathies of loving hearts, now will drift you to a polar existence ... sorrowfully we must leave you, like some false and hideous image,

such a view as a concurrence with the Aristotelian theory of 'natural slavery' that was less than singular in the mid nineteenth century, but it should be noted that Mitchel scarcely possessed progressive views in other areas:

> What to do, then, with all our robbers, burglers and forgers? Why, hang them, *hang* them. You have no right to make the honest people support the rogues, and support them better than they, the honest people, can support themselves. You have no right to set a premium upon villainy, and put burglars and rickburners upon a permanent endowment.[26]

It is a little surprising that Mitchel declined the opportunity to land at Pernambuco and witness, albeit fleetingly, the social system he endorsed (even if he would have found the penalties in the criminal code pretty feeble):

> I have heard the tolling of South American bells, noted the time by a South American clock yet never set foot on South American ground. This authentic vision has passed before my face – whether in the body or out of the body, I cannot tell – and is gone. The wind's wings have wafted it; the deep has opened and swallowed it. Adieu! Adieu![27]

In fact, Mitchel was to return to the continent within three years. Detained off the Cape of Good Hope because the colonists refused to permit the landing of convicts, he reached Tasmania in April 1850, and was joined there by Jenny and the children in June 1851. This was made possible by a collection that raised over £2,000 on Mitchel's conviction. It was in Tasmania that the Mitchel's youngest child, Isabel, was born, and a good part of the Confederation's leadership was reconvened there in exile. Indeed, under the circumstances the time spent in Tasmania (Van Diemen's Land until 1855) had its compensations for all the political prisoners, but Mitchel perhaps benefited most rapidly by recovering from a state of physical health that had become dangerously decomposed during the long voyage. When he first arrived his old friend John Martin found him 'wretchedly thin and weak and exhausted in appearance, and he could hardly walk a few yards without panting'. None the less, 'he is in good spirits and as fierce as ten lions, and bullies me outrageously'.[28] Largely restored in health and with his family reconvened, Mitchel came to represent something of an object of envy for his old ally and antagonist Smith O'Brien, who could write that 'there are few politicians in the world from whose opinions I dissent so widely as from those of John Mitchel', and yet when he saw Mitchel, Jenny and the children together,

---

around which, for the moment, chattering priests of oppression have burned incense, but soon to be cast out, even by them, a detested and desecrated idol, forgotten of men and remembered only of vermin-like lizards that crawl darkling beneath the twilight of poisonous weeds.
Quoted in O'Conner, *Jenny Mitchel*, pp. 195–6.

26. *Jail Journal*, p. 125. Terry Eagleton could have been basing his observation that Mitchel had a 'self-lacerating hatred' on passages such as this. *Heathcliff and the Great Hunger: Studies in Irish Culture*, London 1995, p. 21.

27. *Jail Journal*, p. 157.

28. Quoted in Blanche Touhill, *William Smith O'Brien and His Revolutionary Companions in Exile*, Columbia, Miss., 1981, p. 70.

commented, 'I fancy that I could be *almost* happy if I were surrounded, even in this colony, by the same elements of happiness.'[29]

However, none of the Irish political prisoners had any vocation to settle in Australia. (Gavan Duffy emigrated there voluntarily in 1855, becoming prime minister of Victoria and receiving a knighthood in 1873.) In 1853 Mitchel easily exploited the freedoms of being a political prisoner by openly surrendering his 'ticket of leave' (parole) to escape, Thomas Meagher having done so and gone to New York the previous year. Although he attempted to escape once, Smith O'Brien was the only one of those transported for their role in 1848 not to surrender his 'ticket of leave' and abscond to the USA. (He was pardoned in 1856.)

By the summer of 1853 the entire Mitchel family was in California, having holidayed in Tahiti. It was evident, though, that the heart of both the politics and the community that interested Mitchel was in the east of the USA, which could only be reached with any security and dispatch by passing through Nicaragua. As a result, Mitchel was to catch a brief glimpse of the extraordinary situation prevailing on the Atlantic coast of that state, where

> The British have never, it seems, formally given up their protectorate of the Mosquito 'Kingdom' and its sambo sovereign. A flagstaff stands here, with a piece of bunting flying therefrom, displaying in the corner the Union Jack, and on the field some device representing the sovereignty of the most gracious Gallinipper, who holds his court, and drinks as much rum as he can get credit for at Bluefields ... to keep a foothold on the soil of Central America, the Downing Street men keep up the protectorate, as if to mock at American Republicanism, they insist on a poor, diseased, abject, drunken idiot Indian being called His Majesty the King. Great is the assertion of principle.[30]

This was easy stuff, at least compared with taking a position on the rights of the USA to Cuba, discussed energetically with a fellow-passenger on the steamer *Prometheus* on the Caribbean leg of the trip and in the wake of Colonel Crittenden's abortive expedition to support the revolt of Narciso López against the Spanish:

> 'After all', I asked, 'have the Americans a right to Cuba?'
> 'No, but the Cubans have a right to Cuba, even as the Irish have a right to Ireland; and Spain holds it against the right owners with a monstrous garrison, as England holds Ireland against *you*. Would a filibuster expedition of Americans to Ireland, to aid you and your friends in driving out the British, appear to you an act of piracy and robbery?'[31]

Mitchel's delight at this retort may be set alongside his admiration for William Walker, the filibusterer who took over Nicaragua, attempting to impose the English language

29. Quoted in ibid., p. 134. On another occasion Smith O'Brien wrote, 'Mitchel has throughout the whole period of his captivity displayed a fortitude well worthy of the lofty tone of defiance which he displayed both before and during his trial.' Ibid., p. 132.

30. *Jail Journal*, p. 310.

31. Ibid., pp. 312. The López revolt was easily crushed in August 1850 and followed by mass executions that shook US opinion. One need hardly dwell on the continued salience of the dilemma touched here with regard to international intervention and self-determination.

as well as slavery, two years later. Even after Walker's death in 1860, Mitchel was happy to acquiesce in the plans of his son Johnny to join a new expedition being prepared for Sonora (Mexico) by one of Walker's 'generals', Frederick Henningsen, although this eventually came to nought.[32] Here we can see a political prospectus that is not directly determined by antipathy to Great Britain, although even in those cases – such as when Mitchel offered unreserved homage to the Russian Tsar for going to war with the British in the Crimea – it is noteworthy that he often amazed and depressed his closest nationalist comrades.[33]

Although the family decided to settle in the USA, Mitchel's attachment to the causes of Ireland and slavery, and his profession as a journalist, made for a peripatetic and unsettled existence even before the rupture of the Union and the outbreak of Civil War. Having set up a paper, *The Citizen*, in New York together with Tom Meagher in 1854, he soon found himself at loggerheads with his erstwhile comrade, and they split up, never to be reconciled again. Meagher established the *Irish News* in New York, and Mitchel founded the *Southern Citizen*, first in Washington and then in Knoxville, where he encountered little or no opposition to his views on the 'peculiar institution' of the South: 'I consider negro slavery the best state of existence for the negro, and the best for the master; and if negro slavery in itself be good, then the taking of negroes out of their brutal slavery in Africa and promoting them to a humane and reasonable slavery is also good.' Indeed, Mitchel's paper actively participated in the slave industry by running advertisements for sale of human property:

SALE OF NEGROES – ON THE FIRST Monday in February Next I will offer for sale, in Knoxville, six valuable NEGROES, one third cash and balance in six and twelve months. The same may be purchased private. J.I. Dixon.[34]

In 1860 Mitchel managed to become a US citizen, although he opposed a union that would suppress slavery. Meagher, by contrast, was anxious to take up arms to defend that union. However, the ever-restless Mitchel was absent when the war broke out. Having been persuaded of the family logic promoted by Jenny that they be close to their daughters, he moved with her and their son Willie to Paris weeks before the

---

32. O'Conner, *Jenny Mitchel*, pp. 245–6. Ms O'Conner does not provide a full scholarly apparatus in a book that is as full of useful information as it is idiosyncratic in its style:

> A sister of Charity in a becoming habit could have been seen as a rewarding life for Henty. She was not the stuff to make a good wife or a useful old maid aunt. She was too much like her uncle, William Mitchel; it was pronounced 'Neither of them had an ounce of common sense'. (The judgement is John Mitchel's. Who was not overly blessed with that commodity, so a grain of salt in the pot calling the kettle black is advisable.)

Ibid., p. 265. Ms O'Conner was seventy-five when she published this book privately. On occasion, the apparent transcription of the speech patterns of an elderly Knoxville lady tripping on Irish memorabilia produces more *delirium* than *tremens*, but even the reader beleagured by her persistent failure (refusal?) to address politics has to take the rollicking narrative in good part. For something of an antidote, see Brendan O'Cathaoir, *John Blake Dillon, Young Irelander*, Dublin 1990.

33. *Jail Journal*, p. 355; O'Cathaoir, *Dillon*, p. 131. In the spring of 1854 Mitchel travelled to Washington to offer Russian Ambassador Stockl an Irish alliance in the forthcoming war with Great Britain.

34. Quoted in Keneally, *The Great Shame*, p. 308.

fighting started. Once news of war reached them, Willie insisted on joining James in the 1st Virginia Regiment, and his father could scarcely stop him or resist the desire to return himself:

> So there is another break-up of our household.... Two trembling and saying their prayers in Ireland; two passing anxious hours in the Paris convent; two in camp and garrison beyond the Atlantic; and two making ready to penetrate the Yankee blockade in disguise and by way of New York.[35]

By the time Mitchel reached New York in September 1862 all his three sons were under arms in the Confederate cause, James being wounded in the thigh and losing two fingers at the Second Battle of Manassas, Bull Run. Willie, who served as an enlisted man in the same regiment, was also at Fredericksburg at the end of that year, set against the Irish Brigade under the command of Thomas Meagher, who had recently returned from a much-publicised trip to Costa Rica and whose appointment as general had been a largely political move by Lincoln that some have argued caused more military nuisance than it was worth.

Meagher, whose reputation for carousing and organising horse races was as high as that of his personal bravery, was always a controversial general. Thomas Keneally makes a spirited case for his tipsiness being a convenient stick with which political and military enemies could beat him, and he was undoubtedly prejudiced by the simple fact of commanding Irish volunteers (largely from New York and Massachusetts) under McClellan when the Unionist campaign was at its most disorganised. One can readily imagine a prim Yankee staff officer taking against a report from a commander who describes his own unit, the 69th New York, 'pouring in an oblique fire upon [the Confederates] with a rapid precision and an incessant vigour'. Moreover, there was little that Meagher could do at the Battle of Fredericksburg, where the brigade, charging to the cry of 'Erin Go Bragh!' (Ireland Forever!), was cut up like all the other units of a Unionist army that lost 13,000 men in a miserably commanded encounter:

> The Irish Brigade ... comes out from the city in glorious file, their green sunbursts waving ... every man has a sprig of green in his cap, and a half-laughing, half-murderous look in their eyes. They passed just to our left, poor fellows, poor, glorious fellows, shaking goodbye to us with their hats! They reach a point within a stone's throw of the stone wall. No farther. They try to go beyond, but are slaughtered.[36]

Mitchel was not on the battle-field with James and Willie firing on Meagher's men, but he watched it start from a distance, and he had not shirked risks in evading arrest in New York, and hiding out in the Maryland woods before slipping through the Unionist line to reach Richmond. His poor eyesight – constantly aggravated by proof-reading – meant that instead of serving on the staff of General Beauregard, he

---

35. Quoted in ibid., pp. 363–4.
36. Quoted in ibid., p. 385.

did so as a volunteer ambulanceman, which undoubtedly exposed him to most harrowing experiences.

Indeed, it is at this point in John Mitchel's excited life that an accumulation of tragedy threatened to halt the momentum of radical engagement. In May 1863 his eldest daughter Henrietta (Henty), who had – much to Mitchel's consternation – converted to Catholicism and was on the verge of becoming a nun, died at the Convent of the Sacré-Coeur in Paris, whilst her mother was revisiting Ireland. In July Willie, regimental standard-bearer in 'Pickett's Charge' at Gettysburg, was killed. His body was never identified, and for several years his mother lived in hope of his return. Mitchel himself, meanwhile, was not only propounding the Southern cause but also vocally criticising the Confederate government of Jefferson Davis in *The Examiner*, which he had joined having rapidly split with the officialist *Enquirer*.

It is, though, only with the death of his eldest son, Johnny, that he appears to have experienced some kind of crisis. Johnny, an artillery major, was serving at the besieged Confederate Fort Sumter, which guarded Charlestown harbour and had become a vital symbol of Southern resistance, when he was hit by cannon-fire on 20 July 1864. The telegraph message was immediately relayed to his father, who walked all night before going home to tell his wife that she had lost her third child in the space of fifteen months. It is not surprising that this death prompted a rare expression of pragmatism, Mitchel working a network he found it hard not to antagonise in order to get James transferred from the staff of General Gordon in Robert E. Lee's army.

Yet even by the time that this was achieved, the holding of the second Confederate congress in November 1864 had dragged Mitchel firmly back into the political fray. His challenge of a duel to Senator Henry S. Foote of Tennessee was somewhat stymied when Mitchel's second, Congressman William Swann, found Foote and his wife in a state of undress at their hotel when he tried to deliver the challenge. Eventually the matter, which revolved around Foote's ideas for a ceasefire and re-entry into the Union, returned to the pages of the press, but even there the strength of sentiment that Mitchel could arouse was vividly illustrated by Parson Brownlow, Governor of Tennessee:

> We know Mitchel well. He is the concentrated embodiment of all that is arrogant, vile, mean and rebellious – of all that is treason and fiendish by nature – the Irish brute. This depraved tool of a rotten but dying despotism, this representative of an English prison, this representative of hell in the garb of a man, this blink-eyed insulter of decency, this sponger of traitors for a living, this defunct patriot, this censorious incarnation of all that is damnable, this beast John Mitchel is not able at home or abroad, to damage any man by his tongue or pen.[37]

The making of Governor Brownlow's point is its own palpable rebuttal.

Mitchel, though, still faced a real enemy in Tom Meagher. He scorned the very notion of the Unionist Irish Brigade:

---

37. Quoted in O'Conner, *Jenny Mitchel*, p. 302.

there are more Irish in the army of the Confederate states (in proportion to the population) than in that of Lincoln's. It is true, they flaunt no green banners nor *Sunbursts*, nor shout *Fontenoy!* Nor *Remember Limerick!* They are content to fight simply as Virginians or as Georgians.

When, in May 1863, Mitchel had reported on Meagher's resignation of his commission he had a more than plausible reason to provide: 'he *cannot* recruit *his brigade*…. This fact … proves to us what we have believed before, that the Irish of the Federal States are entirely sick of the war.'[38]

Meagher gave as good as he got. When petitioning the Johnson administration for a post after the war he deliberately contrasted his loyal conduct with that of Mitchel. He did eventually receive a position – the governorship of Montana territory – but only as an interim appointment. Moreover, the Fenian sympathiser and Democrat supporter who had served as a Unionist commander became an even more controversial figure than he was almost bound to be when he convoked elections for a legislature in the territory. On the day that he died, 1 July 1867, Meagher had been the subject of death threats in the settlement of Fort Benton, where he had gone in search of a consignment of rifles that he had requested to help resist Blackfoot and Sioux raids but which some thought he would use for other ends. That night, passengers on the steamer *Thomson* moored on the Missouri heard two cries and a splash. Meagher was not found in his cabin and had evidently plunged into the river. There was much talk that he had fallen into the swollen river by accident, having collapsed in a drunken stupor. However, there were witnesses to his sobriety that night, he was quite badly ill with gastro-enteritis, and more than a few would have him disappear. Since his body was never found, the matter remains a mystery.[39]

When Lee surrendered the Army of Northern Virginia to Grant in April 1865 Mitchel and his son James, who had followed the Confederate government to Danville, returned to Richmond, the destruction of which had been witnessed by Jenny and her two daughters although their own house on 5th and Canal Streets survived the conflagration. Throughout her life in North America Mrs Mitchel had refused to own slaves – or hire black workers – but, like her husband, she was convinced that the race could not survive the collapse of slavery. If the sight of black units liberating Richmond, and Mitchel's own logical declaration that 'if a Negro is fit to be a soldier of the Confederation, he is not fit to be a slave' were at odds with this conviction, they did little to unsettle deep beliefs.

Mitchel now adventurously headed for New York, where he started work for the *Daily News*, but in June Grant issued a warrant for his arrest for treason against the Union. He was immediately apprehended and sent to Fort Monroe, Virginia, to join Jefferson Davis in exclusive and much-publicised incarceration. His status as martyr

---

38. Quoted in ibid., pp. 388, 398.
39. Keneally, *The Great Shame*, pp. 470–72, Meagher County, Montana, includes a good portion of the Lewis and Clark National Forest.

was instantaneously revived, and he received the unreserved support of the Fenian movement:

> I suppose that I am the only person who has ever been a prisoner-of-state of the British and the American government one after the other. It is true that the English government took care to have special Act of Parliament passed for my incarceration; but our Yankees disdain in these days to make any pretence at law at all.[40]

The very severe conditions in this, his third, jail worsened what could now be recognised as tuberculosis. In October his poor health, together with the trouble being kicked up by the important Irish community of New York, obliged the government to do a deal – Mitchel would be released if he took the amnesty oath of loyalty and left the country for a period. Whilst the family planned its move to Brooklyn, Mitchel went to Paris as an agent for the Fenian cause with the job of selling Republic of Ireland bonds. He didn't even try, resigned, and took what might be said to be the second holiday of his life: 'one cannot forever live astride the Atlantic Ocean'. When he returned to New York, in 1867, he even desisted for three years from suing the government for illegal arrest, and he counselled James against plans for an adventure in Latin America. In January of that year Mitchel expressed to Mortimer Moynahan, a leader of one of the factions of the Fenian movement, sentiments that reflected his own pessimism and which many felt he should have had in 1848 (just as many felt of the Provisional IRA after it suspended its 1994 ceasefire);

> I now believe less than ever in the existence of any formidable organization, either in Ireland or in England. And I am more than ever convinced that while England is at peace with America and France, all invasions and insurrections will be in vain. It is not that I stand out for 'civilized' warfare. The Irish have a clear right to strike at England anywhere and anyhow, in Canada, in Ireland, in London, by steel or gunpowder or firewood. But I hold that those who undertake any such warfare at present, whether civilized or uncivilized, must perish and perish in vain.[41]

The last year of John Mitchel's life gives the lie, though, to any notion that he might confront illness and old age in a spirit of moderation and quietude. Late in 1874 he accepted the proposal to stand as Home Rule parliamentary candidate for Tipperary even though he harboured strong reservations about this new movement, as he told Patrick 'Nicaragua' Smyth, who had accompanied him in exile:

> In fact, I am savage against that helpless, driftless concern called 'Home Rule' and nearly as vicious against your … simple repeal. But if I were under any obligation (which I am not) to put my own oar at all into the puddle of Irish politics I would rather – as I have told John Martin – pull in your boat than his.[42]

---

40. Quoted in ibid., p. 411.
41. Quoted in William D'Arcy, *The Fenian Movement in the United States, 1858–86*, New York 1947, p. 226.
42. Quoted in ibid., p. 360.

The legal advice – perhaps not entirely to be relied upon by this stage – was that although Mitchel had received no pardon, he only stood in danger of arrest for violating his parole in Tasmania. He had not been molested on a short private trip in 1872, and as a US citizen – albeit one at sharp and public odds with his own government – he would enjoy a significant measure of diplomatic protection. Moreover, the British were left in no doubt that Mitchel would never take up the seat he proposed to fight. He duly left New York on 6 February 1875, won the seat, unopposed, on the 16th, and landed at Queenstown the next day.

Once he arrived in Ireland, it was plain that John Mitchel was a very frail man, and he was shielded from the public by his now reconciled elder brother, William. ('Am I dying, William? For that would be a very serious business for me.') This protection became doubly necessary because on the 18th Disraeli easily carried a motion in the Commons declaring Mitchel incapable of being elected – not just of taking up his seat – because he was an undischarged felon. A new writ for an election was issued on 4 March, and a Conservative candidate, Captain Stephen Moore of Barne, near Clonmel, was put up under the protection of a platoon of soldiers. On the 11th Mitchel was taken quietly to his home town and put to bed in his childhood room at Dromalane, the exultant crowd waiting to meet him at Limerick junction carrying off the first old man to alight from the train. In the poll of 12 March – the first to be held under extended franchise and with the secret ballot – Mitchel beat Moore by 3,114 votes to 746. The matter would have to return to the courts.

The case was held at the Irish Court of Common Pleas on 26 May under Judge William Keogh, a Catholic but an ardent opponent of nationalism. Moore's counsel argued that the electors knew fully well that Mitchel, as a felon and an alien, was not acceptable to parliament. The case for the defence was led by the 24-year-old John Dillon, a student of medicine – as cross-examination soon revealed – a son of Mitchel's Young Ireland comrade, John Blake Dillon, and himself to become an MP and a major figure in national politics until 1918. Dillon and his witnesses had fun in challenging the argument of Moore's counsel:

> WITNESS E. BRENAN (Mr Dillon)
> Did you read this notice before you handed it to the voters?
> I did.
> Do you know what an alien is?
> Of course I do; a man convicted, of course.
>
> WITNESS S. CRADDOCK (Mr Dillon)
> This notice states that Mr Mitchel was an alien. Do you know what is meant by his being an alien?
> I do not, indeed, and nor do I care.[43]

---

43. Quoted in ibid., p. 370.

The revenge for the jury-packing of twenty-seven years earlier may have been of little political consequence, but it gained some further sweetness when the case, which was inevitably lost and went to appeal, provoked the Appeal Court judges to complain to parliament that it was not for them to decide its procedures.

Mitchel could not savour this spectacle. He was dead. On the morning of 20 March, just a week after his famous victory, he tried to rise from his bed and collapsed immediately. The funeral three days later was conducted from his father's pulpit – the old meeting-house building had been pulled down in 1853 – and Mitchel lies buried in the first Presbyterian graveyard on High Street, Newry. His memorial stone was carefully designed by Jenny and paid for by a trust chaired by Charles Dana, the celebrated political editor of the *New York Tribune*, who wrote that Mitchel 'not only spoke the truth at all times, but he spoke the whole truth by a kind of moral necessity. He knew no reserve and no disguise, and, we may say, no prudence in this regard … his sincerity was perfect and his courage fearless.'[44] *The Times* commented:

> The wild revolutionist whose appeals to his countrymen were marked with traits of savage and ferocious violence, who seemed to scruple at the use of no means, however truculent and sanguinary, to effect the overthrow of the hated British rule in Ireland, was, in his personal and domestic relations one of the most gentle and tender-hearted of his kind…. His public life has been a terrible mistake, unfortunate for his country and still more calamitous for himself. There was a presentiment that under the show of unabated mental energy and inflexible resolution which he assumed, there was the wreck of physical powers, and that it would be found, as it has been, that he came home, not to renew a hopeless war against the British Government, but to die.[45]

John Martin, Mitchel's constant friend in liberty and imprisonment for over thirty years, insisted on attending the funeral although he was unwell. He caught bronchitis and died on the 29th. Mitchel's daughter Isabel died soon after him, stricken by severe post-natal depression. Jenny settled in Brooklyn and helped to bring up her grandson. She died at 10.30 p.m. on 31 December 1899. Given the travails she had experienced over seventy-nine years, there is no reason to suppose that she expired in awe of a twentieth century only ninety minutes away. She is buried in Woodlam Cemetery. James died in 1908, whilst registering to vote.

In his autobiography, W.B. Yeats recalls the return to Ireland at the very end of the century of Charles Gavan Duffy, Mitchel's first political mentor, very soon an opponent, and for many years thereafter a senior figure in Australian public life:

---

44. Quoted in Keneally, *The Great Shame*, p. 554. The meeting-house ruins stand next to the Convent of the Poor Clares; the Mitchel family are virtually the only occupants of its modest and beautiful graveyard. At present there is no public access, but permission to enter may be sought from Alexander Hannah and Sons, Painting and Decorating Supplies, 20 Water Street. I am most grateful to Brad Hannah for showing me the cemetery.

45. *The Times*, 24 March 1875.

No argument of mine was intelligible to him, and I would have been powerless, but that fifty years ago he had made an enemy, and though the enemy was long dead, the enemy's school remained. He had attacked, why or without result I do not remember, the only Young Ireland politician who had music and personality, though rancorous and devil possessed.[46]

At some public meeting of ours, where he spoke amidst great applause, in smooth, Gladstonian periods, of his proposed Irish publishing firm, one heard faint hostile murmurs, and at last a voice cried, 'Remember Newry', and a voice answered, 'There's a grave there!' and a part of the audience sang, 'Here's to John Mitchel that is gone, boys, gone; Here's to the friends that are gone.' The meeting over, a group of us, indignant that the meeting we had called for his welcome should have contained these malcontents, gathered around him to apologise. He had written a pamphlet, he explained: he would give us copies. We would see that he was in the right, how badly Mitchel had behaved. But in Ireland personality, if it be but harsh and hard, has loves, and some of us, I think, may have gone home muttering, 'How dare he be in the right if Mitchel is in the wrong?'[47]

---

46. In his memoirs, published in 1898, Gavan Duffy claimed full reponsibility for promoting Mitchel, and then commented,

> ...nothing is more unjust or more egregiously inconsistent with his earlier declarations than what John Mitchel wrote of me in his later years in his 'Jail Journal' ... to Dillon and myself it seemed plain that the accidental explosion of a French Revolution in February had not made his proposal in January of a peasant war any way more reasonable, and his extravagance was likely to damage the public cause.... It was plain he was determined to take an individual course and preach an individual policy. He did so, with the result of creating a profound impression and attracting universal attention upon himself.... He scoffed at State trials ... he disparaged preparation as needless.

My Life in Two Hemispheres, London 1898, II, pp. 192, 262.

47. W.B. Yeats, *Autobiographies*, Dublin 1995, pp. 225–6.

CULTURES IN CONTENTION

HISTORIOGRAPHIES

There is something benign and slightly altruistic in the image of textbooks. They are there to help, provide useful context, identify the 'five main points' of an issue, and indicate the next step, should a student prove so bold as to venture beyond this initial synthetic introduction. Because of their bite-sized, user-friendly nature, textbooks can, of course, damage your health, but respect is due to any author who defies the tyranny of academic specialism, jilts the jargonised exchange of esoteria that so often passes for debate, and purposefully addresses a broader audience. Textbooks matter because, aside from very rare cases, their influence is surreptitious and often far more extensive than that wrought by the most famous titles.

One of the leading English-language textbooks on Latin American politics is *Politics and Social Change in Latin America: Still a Distinct Tradition?*, edited by Howard Wiarda, first published in the US in 1974, and only removed from the Westview catalogue in 1996 after three editions. It must have sold very well indeed, but a summary inspection reveals this collection of essays to be a heavy-handed affair. Although Wiarda himself wrote three of the sixteen chapters, it matters rather more that his enthusiasm for the work of Richard Morse and Glen Dealy led him to include two chapters from each with entire paragraphs and passages being repeated, reborrowed or minimally rewritten. (They could almost sue themselves for plagiarism.) The whole effect is one of argument through insistence rather than persuasion, but this is perhaps suitable for a textbook, and the argument itself has dominated US academic debate on Latin American political culture despite being very unpopular in left-wing and liberal circles.

The post-war lineage of what Morse calls a 'historiocultural' explanation of the social and political distinctiveness of Latin America starts with his own essay 'Toward a Theory of Spanish American Government', published in 1954, and flows through a second, more refined and influential chapter in Louis Hartz's *The Founding of New Societies*, nearly a decade later.[1] That chapter approached the parts of the continent colonised by the Iberian powers from a viewpoint very much in harmony with Hartz's own conviction that 'the outstanding thing about the [Anglo-]American community in Western history ought to be the non-existence of those oppressions (of the Old World) ... that the American community is a liberal community'.[2] The best

---

1. 'The Heritage of Latin America', in Louis Hartz (ed.), *The Founding of New Societies*, New York 1964, pp. 123–77. An edited version of 'Towards a Theory' appears in the Wiarda collection. Morse was thirty-two when the article was published, and it is worth noting that his later reputation rests as much on his work on Brazil – which cannot readily be enveloped into a *Spanish* American tradition – and urban history as on his interpretation of political culture. A greater sense of the intellectual milieu in which it appeared can be gained from a briefing written by another Brazilianist, Charles Wragley, as a training document for the Department of State in 1953: 'An Introduction to Latin American Culture', in *The Latin American Tradition: Essays in the Unity and Diversity of Latin American Culture*, New York 1968.

2. Louis Hartz, *The Liberal Tradition in America: An Interpretation of American Political Thought since the*

example of Morse's work, however, is to be found in *New World Soundings*, where he develops an interpretation that we have already mentioned with respect to debates over chronology and which argues that feudalism was far less important as an early influence in Hispanic America than had previously been thought:

> ... for Spain and its overseas realms feudalism was a recessive force and patrimonialism a dominant trait of the polity ... the norms of legal or rational domination were conspicuously reasserted after circa 1760 ... the fragmentation of Spanish America during the independence wars caused temporary reversion to charismatic domination reminiscent of the era of European Conquest; and ... the ethos of patrimonialism survived this interlude of decentralization and ruralization, and it still conditions Latin American reception of industrial capitalism and political rationality.[3]

For Morse the primary factor in this centralist and corporate continuity is religious:

> It is of enduring consequence that our country was founded in revolt against Catholicism, against the layered and corporative society, against casuistical justice, against tolerance of sin in the human community, against private eccentricity and affective release – against the whole medieval world that Huizinga created for our century and that is still largely a reality for Hispanic peoples. Seventeenth-century Ibero-America stood for everything that Anglo-America had set itself fiercely against. History is not so capricious that this situation has radically changed. Our present *doctrinal* diversity and toleration obscure for us the fact that we are integrally a Protestant nation, insensitive and vaguely hostile to the *sociological* and psychological foundations of a Catholic society.[4]

Before we consider this forceful statement both in its own terms and those of 1845–55 it is worth noting Huizinga's agreement with Morse on the general importance of religion, if not necessarily his militant denominationalism: 'Anyone who wishes to understand [North] America must first carry over his concept of Democracy from the political and social field to the cultural and generally human. The best way to do this continues to be reading Walt Whitman.'

But for those without a copy of *Leaves of Grass* to hand Huizinga provides an illustrative anecdote:

> All during the spring [of 1926] America was filled with news of the mysterious disappearance of an evangelist, Mrs Aimee Macpherson, who had maintained a tabernacle at Los Angeles with many ... I almost said customers ... Mrs Macpherson drowned while swimming at the beach. Or did she really drown? That was the question. In any event she disappeared, and her mother continued the business for a while on the same footing. When she had gone long enough so that her return was doubtful, a memorial service was held in Angelus Temple, her building. The subject of the address was that so many of God's chosen have been taken from earthly life in mysterious ways. Her mother, Mrs Kennedy, told how Enoch

---

Revolution, New York 1955. Controversial even in the depths of the Cold War, Hartz defended his thesis that America was 'born liberal' and stayed so in full recognition of the fact that, 'now a whole series of alien cultures have crashed in upon the American world, shattering the peaceful landscape of Bancroft and Beard'. For Hartz, the 'hidden origin' of socialist thought everywhere is to be found in the feudal ethos. 'The *ancien régime* inspires Rousseau; both inspire Marx.' Ibid., pp. 5–6.

    3. 'Claims of Political Tradition', in *New World Soundings*, Baltimore 1989, p. 106.

    4. 'On Grooming Latin Americanists', in ibid., p. 175.

walked with God, and God took him away. How no one had been a witness to Moses' death, how Jesus' body had disappeared from its grave, and how the apostle Philip had suddenly been transported to a distant region. Dr Charles A. Shreve then observed how much Mrs Macpherson's disappearance recalled these and other biblical examples, and how profane history also furnished other examples, like the disappearance of Lord Kitchener. The service was made 'more realistic' by having each of the biblical figures named appear upon the stage in proper garb, except for Christ, whose appearance was represented by angels. Finally a student of the Temple Bible School read an article on the disappearance of Christ's body as it would have been reported in a present-day newspaper if there had been any newspapers published in Jerusalem at the time, with the aim of demonstrating the futility of the work of reporters. A 'monster memorial service' was announced for fourteen days later. Whether this was held or not I do not know for about that time Mrs Macpherson returned with a tale of being kidnapped.[5]

Morse, who criticises US Latin Americanists for being humourless, institutionalised purveyors of social science and who ends his own book with a spoof essay 'McCluhan-aima', would take this story in good part. However, one could not be sure of such a reaction from other advocates of what we might call the 'culturalist' thesis dividing Anglo from Latin America. Wiarda opens his textbook with a compound explanation of Latin America that manifests such confidence that one doubts if any 'ludic' comment might elicit qualification or hesitation:

> Our biases and ethnocentrism have helped ... to perpetuate some fundamental misunderstandings of Latin America ... [which] has its own social and political institutions and its own ways of achieving change, and it is both presumptuous of us and detrimental to a proper understanding of the area to look at it exclusively through the prism of the USA or Western European developmental experience.... Latin American systems have their roots in the ancient Greek notion of organic solidarity; in the Roman system of a hierarchy of laws and institutions; in historical Catholic concepts of the corporate, sectoral, and compartmentalised organisation of society based on each person's acceptance of his or her station in life; in the similarly corporate organisation (army, church, town, nobility) of Iberian society during the late medieval era; in the warrior mentality and the walled enclave cities of the period of the reconquest of the Iberian peninsular from the Moors; in the centralised systems of the early modern Spanish and Portuguese states; and in the absolutist, scholastic Catholic political culture and institutions of the Inquisition and the Counter-Reformation.[6]

---

5. Johan Huizinga, *America: A Dutch Historian's Vision, from Afar and Near* (1928), New York 1972, pp. 239–41. The notion of 'relative displacement' of politics-as-ideology to religion, sport and – after Huizinga's visit – film and television is a typical European preoccupation encouraged by American enthusiasm for political institutions.

6. *Politics and Social Change in Latin America: Still a Distant Tradition?*, 2nd edn, Boulder, Colo., 1982, p. 5. In his latest book, postdating the transition from authoritarian government in both Europe and Latin America, Wiarda warns the reader that in those regions '*forms* and *meanings* of democracy are often at variance with our own'. He then introduces a new question of identity which will surely perplex many of his readers:

> Spain and Portugal ... have now reached a living standard about 60–65% that of most of the rest of Western Europe; indices of poverty and other social indicators are similarly about two-thirds the European level. But if Spain and Portugal are only two-thirds European, they are one-third something else. What is the other third? Could it be that Spain and Portugal are two-thirds European and still one-third Latin American? Or Third World?

Iberia and Latin America, London 1996, p. 4. Wiarda is on leave as professor of political science at the University of Massachusetts at Amherst, research scholar at the Center for Strategic and International

The main message of this breathtaking sentence – in a textbook, after all – has more recently been given a promiscuously illustrated treatment by the Anglophile Chilean scholar Claudio Véliz, who borrows from Archilochus (via Isaiah Berlin) a metaphor – 'The fox knows many things, but the hedgehog knows one big thing' – through which to consider the vulpine Anglos ('independent, pluralistic and adaptable') and the prickly Hispanics ('single-minded, systematic, rationalistic').[7] Véliz's earlier work had concentrated firmly on what he called the 'centralist tradition' in Latin America but that is of less interest to us here because he identifies a 'liberal pause' in that tradition from the mid nineteenth century to at least 1930 and arguably beyond:

> The 'liberal pause' began in the mid nineteenth century, started to crumble with the Great Depression of 1929, revived for a while during the Second World War and its aftermath, and came fitfully to its end during the economic malaise of the late sixties and early seventies. For the past half century – with the expected variations from country to country – Latin America has been finding its way back to its centralist mainstream. Regardless of the intentions of revolutionaries and reformers, every major reconstruction has resulted in increased central control.[8]

In terms of this *oeuvre* a 'pause' of eighty years and upwards is quite allowable, but whereas Morse and Véliz identify at least some change, it would appear that, like Wiarda, Glen Dealy saw little or none, even in 1984:

> Latin Americans maintain that union comes from unity, not from diversity – *Ex unibus unum*, not *E pluribus unum*, has been and still is their motto. Their political beliefs are based on the

Studies (CSIS) in Washington, and Professor of National Security at the National Defence University in Washington. I leave it strictly to the reader to discern any link between the professor's ideas, his sundry places of employ, and the general trajectory of US geopolitical strategy over the last three decades.

7. *The New World of the Gothic Fox: Culture and Economy in English and Spanish America*, Berkeley 1994. Berlin uses the metaphor as the title for his essay on Tolstoy's view of history, *The Hedgehog and the Fox*, London 1953. Véliz has other variables – gothic and baroque – and makes several early qualifications to his use of the metaphor, but the publication of his book postdated that of a collection of interviews between Ramin Jahanbegloo and Berlin:

> R.J. … Why did you make this classification?
>
> I.B. I never meant it very seriously. I meant it as a kind of enjoyable intellectual game, but it was taken seriously. Every classification throws light on something else, this one was very simple.
>
> R.J. So you don't justify your classification?
>
> I.B. What do you mean by justification? Hedgehogs and foxes? It is not exhaustive. Some people are neither foxes nor hedgehogs, some people are both.
>
> R.J. Let us take Pushkin for example, why do you consider him an arch-fox?
>
> I.B. Pushkin is not a man who tries to interpret everything in the light of some all-embracing system. That's what hedgehogs do. He simply reacts as he reacts, he describes what he describes, writes what he writes. I mean, he expresses himself in many directions. Whereas hedgehogs are always trying to connect, always trying to represent things as in some sense fitting or not fitting into some simple pattern in which they passionately believe.

Ramin Jahanbegloo, *Conversations with Isaiah Berlin*, London 1992, pp. 188–9. On this basis Claudio Véliz and the rest of the 'historioculturalists' are hedgehogs *sans pareils*.

8. *The Centralist Tradition of Latin America*, Princeton 1980, p. 9. Noting that this 'pause' leaves only thirty years of independent Latin American history to be part of the centralist continuum, Ian Roxborough views Véliz's interpretation as 'seriously deficient'. 'Unity and Diversity in Latin American History', *JLAS*, 16:1, 1984, p. 5.

corporatist, medieval and Renaissance political theory that predated the contractarian thought of John Locke. The corporatists believe that society is best governed with some collective goal in mind. Latin Americans have always agreed with St Thomas Aquinas that 'it is the common good that unites the community'.[9]

Ten years earlier, in the wake of the Chilean coup, Dealy had likewise, and rather more understandably, seen

no indication that Latin Americans want to change this world outlook ... Latin America is a land of unity, of concord, of order. The travel brochures are wrong: however diverse it might look to a tourist, the people of these lands have a unity of tradition.[10]

One wonders, however, if there is a strong predisposition *not* to see any vestige of liberal democracy down South. It is one (laudable) thing to alert any unsuspecting North American to the fact that everyone else might not be like them; it is rather different to argue that

as a nation we have the power to influence that [Latin American political] choice: we can foul it up with visions of sugar pluralisms dancing in our heads, or we can accept and support a monistic style of government that is in keeping with their past and with our interests.[11]

And in the early 1990s, when all Latin American countries were free of military dictatorship, Dealy makes a similar point in a different way:

... foreigners who pity the Latin American woman's 'plight' should realize the full implications of their critique. To insist that gender parity should occur is to argue that a historically Catholic Two Morality people adopt the priorities and reforming ways of a Protestant One Morality society ... however meritorious in themselves, as exports to Latin America United States feminism and Protestantism alike are faces of cultural imperialism.[12]

Such an unqualified statement should remind us that identification of 'difference' or 'the other' is far from the exclusive property of fashionable liberal or radical circles.

---

9. 'Pipe Dreams: The Pluralistic Latins', in *Politics and Social Change*, p. 281. This piece was originally published in *Foreign Policy*, 57, Winter 1984–85.

10. 'The Tradition of Monist Democracy in Latin America', in *Politics and Social Change*, p. 60. This piece was originally published in the *Journal of the History of Ideas*, July 1974.

11. Ibid. There is a strong similarity here with the projection of the Arab world by Harold Glidden: 'it is a notable fact that while the Arab value system demands absolute solidarity within the group, it at the same time encourages among its members a kind of rivalry that is destructive of that solidarity.' Edward Said remarks of such views – which were similarly directed at influencing US foreign policy – 'On the one hand there are Westerners, and on the other there are Arab-Orientals; the former are (in no particular order) rational, peaceful, liberal, capable of holding real values, without natural suspicion; the latter are none of these things.' *Orientalism*, London 1978, p. 49.

12. *The Latin Americans: Spirit and Ethos*, Boulder, Colo., 1992, p. 14. In this, his latest text, Dealy adopts the ungainly concept of *caudillaje* to explain the 'mode of life' in Latin America to the persistently uncomprehending gringos:

Caudillaje has been defined as the 'domination (*mando*) or government of a caudillo', an individual 'who doesn't just try to get along (*convivir*), but to dominate'.... Caudillaje society originates in the amalgamation of Christianity and classical culture achieved by Aquinas in the thirteenth century.

Ibid., pp. 58, 211.

Indeed, the culturalist argument is often conservative in both upper and lower cases; here so in the most Burkean of voices. Ronald Reagan, who discovered to his agreeable surprise in 1982 that Latin America was diverse, appointed Professor Jeane Kirkpatrick as his ambassador to the United Nations largely on the basis of an article in which she argued that

> traditional autocracies are, in general and in their very nature, deeply offensive to modern American sensibilities. The notion that public affairs should be ordered on the basis of kinship, friendship, and other personal relations rather than on the basis of objective 'rational' standards violates our conception of justice and efficiency.... One reason why some modern Americans prefer 'socialist' to traditional autocracies is that the former have embraced modernity and have adopted modern modes and perspectives.... Nowhere is the affinity of liberalism, Christianity and Marxist Socialism more apparent than amongst liberals who are 'duped' time after time into supporting 'liberators' who turn out to be totalitarians.[13]

Richard Morse at least is able to see why the approach that he has adopted is so readily associated with, and sometimes put at the service of, 'the dead hand of an authoritarian and archaic political culture'.[14] Yet whether, as in his work, the literature admits to some influence of the Enlightenment, the American Revolution and that in France on Latin America, or – as in the writings of Dealy and O. Carlos Stoetzer – it asserts their irrelevance; whether its exponents admit to important moments of rupture or not, the scale of interpretations of this type presents challenges that are not simply political in nature.[15] After all, how many Anglo students of Latin America could, following the consumption of a few cool beers, persuasively deny having

---

13. 'Dictatorships and Double Standards', *Commentary*, Nov. 1979, p. 42. Reagan, it will be recalled, returned from a tour of Latin America in 1982 to announce, 'I didn't go down there with any plans for the Americas or anything. I went down to find out from them and [learn] their views. You'd be surprised. They're all individual countries.' He did get Bolivia and Brazil muddled up, but it was a start.

14. For Morse this is why Latin Americans don't like the historiocultural approach, although they are 'more hospitable to flights of fancy'; North Americans don't like it because it 'elude(s) empirical demonstration'. 'Notes towards Fresh Ideology', in *New World Soundings*, pp. 133–4.

15. Stoetzer opens his study in admirably candid fashion:

> This study seeks to prove that the Revolution which began in Spanish America in the years after 1808, and especially in 1810, and continued for the next 15 years had little to do with either the Enlightenment or the North American or French revolutions. It attempts to show, rather, that it had a profoundly Spanish and medieval foundation, and that the political thought which unleashed it was scholasticism.

The Scholastic Roots of the Spanish American Revolution, New York 1979, p. ix. He ends with equal clarity:

> ... the common struggle of Spaniards and the Spanish Americans against the Napoleonic usurpation meant a link to the other medieval concept of the tyrant, the *tyrannus ab origine* [those who attempt to rule without legal title], which allowed the people, as in the case of the *tyrannus a regimine* [those who abused authority legally granted to them], to take matters into their own hands.

Ibid., p. 260. The core of this argument – if not its fully expressed ambition – is reproduced in John Lynch (ed.), *Latin American Revolutions, 1808–1826*, Norman, Okla., 1994, pp. 241–6. Stoetzer shares much common ground with an early piece by Glen Dealy that manifests more empirically interesting and modulated claims than his later writing: 'Prolegomena on the Spanish American Political Tradition', *HAHR*, 40:1, 1968. For a very different view, see David J. Robinson, 'Liberty, Fragile Fraternity and Inequality in Early Republican Spanish America: Assessing the Impact of the French Revolution', *Journal of Historical Geography*, 16:1, 1990.

entertained one or more of all the ideas stated above? Sometimes, when faced with a check list like Wiarda's it is simply best to say nothing, stay calm and then move very slowly backwards out of the room. It is, though, a good thing that not everyone has done this.

Frank Safford, an impeccably schooled historian of the nineteenth century but not himself above a provocative generalisation,[16] finds the idea of 'corporatism' at the heart of Wiarda's work entirely anomalous for the century after independence since the corporate bodies established by Spain in the Americas were breaking down almost everywhere, with the partial and delayed exception of Mexico.[17] Safford is completely baffled by Dealy's application of 'monism' – understood as a rejection of individualism – to the nineteenth century, 'which was pre-eminently an era of individualism, in Spanish America as well as the rest of the Atlantic World'.[18] He palpably has greater time for Morse's work but still finds it static and unwarranted in its marginalisation of 'geography, economic and social structure factors'.[19] Charles A. Hale describes both Morse and Véliz as determinist, differing only in their chronological fixing of the Spanish cultural mainstream, the two lacking precisely that kind of empirical interrogation of the nineteenth-century ideas themselves which Morse says he is not really interested in doing.[20] For Hale,

> I would never maintain that liberalism as a value system based on utilitarian ethics made much headway in nineteenth-century Latin America. Yet liberalism as a set of rationally formed political and social precepts did, so long as one defines liberalism properly in its peculiar Hispanic manifestation.[21]

---

16. In Latin America 'to a greater degree than in the United States, work has been viewed by most sectors as a necessary evil rather than as a means of self-fulfillment'. *The Ideal of the Practical: Colombia's Struggle to Form a Technical Elite*, Austin, Tex., 1976, p. 3. For the second third of the nineteenth century Safford uses the term 'neo-Bourbon', suggesting some proximity at least to Morse's ideas.

17. 'Political Order in Post-Independence Spanish America', *JLAS*, 24, Quincentenary Supplement, 1992, p. 86.

18. Ibid., p. 85.

19. 'Politics, Ideology and Society in Post-Independence Spanish America', in Leslie Bethell (ed.), *Cambridge History of Latin America*, III, Cambridge 1984, p. 417. Safford's discussion of Morse in this chapter is arguably the most extensive made of any living non-Latin American in the entire Cambridge History (of eleven volumes to date). Morse himself contributed an extraordinarily learned and characteristically original chapter – 'The Multiverse of Latin American Identity, *c.* 1920–*c.* 1970' – to volume X, the piece reconnoitering over a far wider chronological plain ('circa' is interpreted with gentlemanly generosity) and providing the proper space to Brazil. In a telling review that is as much of the essay as of the volume as a whole, Tulio Halperín Donghi comments,

> It is as if, after decades of going against the grain of Latin American historiography, and reacting to his marginality by practising the *Narrenfreiheit* that he feared was the only kind of freedom his more conventional colleagues were ready to tolerate from him, the recent changes in the historiographic scene had finally allowed him to be himself.

JLAS, 29:1, 1997, p. 223.

20. 'The Reconstruction of Nineteenth Century Politics in Spanish America: A Case for the History of Ideas', *LARR*, VIII, 1973. The prospectus outlined in this article is greatly advanced in Hale's chapter – 'Political and Social Ideas in Latin America, 1870–1930' – in Bethell (ed.), *Cambridge History of Latin America*, IV, Cambridge 1984, as well as in his monographs on Mexican liberalism.

21. 'Reconstruction', p. 62. Something of the same approach, which I call 'empirical pragmatism', is manifested by J.H. Elliott in his (not unfriendly) exchange with Claudio Véliz:

These are generous responses. In reviewing Wiarda's textbook Jorge Domínguez was more direct about the concept of corporatism – 'by trying to account for so much variation it explains nothing' – and Henry Schmidt clearly suffered on behalf of the *Hispanic American Historical Review* in his survey of Dealy's book:

> There is no treatment of nationalism, identity, ethnicity, social justice, cosmopolitanism, modernization or women as integral to the Latin American spirit; among social characteristics, no inclusion of solitude, fatalism, joy, myriad forms of love, irony, humour, non-religious spirituality, moral and aesthetic values, universalism and, yes, thrift and practicality ... as flawed a construction as Rodó's theory of the hemisphere.[22]

Big ideas naturally attract – and usually deserve – big criticisms. Yet there has to be a limit to the knock-about stuff. It might be useful to break momentarily away from this set of texts and take note of some similarly 'long-range' interpretations made of the British and North American corners of the Atlantic triangle. In 1975 J.G.A. Pocock published a monumental study in which

> it is asserted that certain enduring patterns in the temporal consciousness of medieval and early modern Europeans led to the presentation of the republic, and the citizen's partici-pation in it, as constituting a problem in historical self-understanding, with which Machiavelli and his contemporaries can be seen both explicitly and implicitly contending ... the 'Machiavellian moment' denotes the problem itself. It is a name for the moment in conceptual-ised time in which the republic was seen as confronting its own temporal finitude, as at-tempting to remain morally and politically stable in a stream of irrational events conceived as essentially destructive of all systems of secular stability.[23]

In his thirty-page review of Pocock, J.H. Hexter remarks, 'one would be ill-advised to try to hold one's breath until that moment passes' since it stretches for even longer than Véliz's 'pause' – 'in an enormous panoramic survey for 22 centuries from Plato to the foothills of European Marxism and American "manifest destiny"'.[24]

> In his last published book, *L'Identité de la France*, Fernand Braudel urged the claims of comparative history, 'a history that seeks to compare like with like – the conditions of all social science if truth be told'. But what constitutes 'like'? Every historian who sets out to compare two or more societies is liable to discover very quickly that the like, on closer inspection, turns out to be unlike. While differences may in fact prove to be more illuminating than similarities, all such comparisons ... tend to be elusive.

New York Review of Books, 17 Nov. 1994. For those who feel that such an approach has to lead to spineless relativism (and anybody else) I recommend Les McCann's version of Gene McDaniels's 'Compared to What'.

22. *HAHR*, 55:3, 1975, p. 563; *HAHR*, 74:4, 1994, p. 696.

23. *The Machiavellian Moment: Florentine Political Thought and the Atlantic Republican Tradition*, Princeton 1975, pp. vii–viii.

24. *History and Theory*, 16, 1977, p. 306. In his famous feud with Christopher Hill, Hexter addressed a problem that is 'solved' through metaphor by Berlin, by non-engagement on the part of Elliott, and by multiple engagement on the part of Morse. He divides historians into 'splitters' and 'lumpers':

> Historians who are splitters like to point out divergences, to perceive differences, to draw distinc-tions. They shrink away from systems of history and from general rules.... Lumpers do not like accidents, note likenesses, instead of separateness, connection. The lumping historian wants to put the past into boxes, all of it, and not too many boxes at that, and then to tie all the boxes together into one nice shapely bundle.

One, it would appear, pretty much favoured by social scientists. Hexter, one assumes, stands aloof from this dichotomised pathology. *On Historians*, Cambridge, Mass., 1979, p. 242.

But Pocock's focus is precisely on *ideas* – not a society, still less behavioural norms – for which, in fact, the 350 years that he actually covers might seem a very modest span. (In practice, Hexter was more worried by Pocock's admittedly very difficult style of writing and his omission of non-classical republican ideas and the tradition that 'supposed liberty was a collection of rights belonging to free men regardless of the structure of society'.[25])

In a very different – and opposing – book, which might fairly be described as arguing the other side of the coin to the 'historioculturalists' of Latin America, Alan Macfarlane's *The Origins of English Individualism* (1978) opens with an appraisal of anthropological literature on 'peasants', surveys English history from the thirteenth to the eighteenth centuries, and rejects the 'traditional' chronology of 'feudal/peasant (1450–1650) ... capitalist/peasant (1750–1850) ... capitalist/modern' on the grounds of a dearth of early examples of 'community', a much higher and earlier profile of 'individualist' economic behaviour, and excessive use in the modern literature of analogy with contemporary examples.[26] In her review of this controversial text Joyce Appleby has less to criticise in its technique than in its deepest assumptions:

> What Macaulay shares with Marx and Weber is the conviction that at some time England experienced a period of decisive change, breaking not only with the rest of Europe but with its own past as well. For Marx the rupture came in the sixteenth century with the capitalist mode of production. With Weber it took the rational principle carried by the Protestant reworking of Christianity, while Macaulay looked to the time when God and Alexander Pope created the Newton of the Enlightenment. Macfarlane dismisses all three claims for change because the social habits of ordinary English men and women have not varied over time. Historians may well chafe at his procrustean conclusion. Not only is there severe reduction of interpretative options, but there also lurks, unexorcised, the sociological assumption that the form of society dictates events. Instead of seeing men and women selectively coping with concrete and changing situations, Macfarlane presents his English individuals frozen in a cultural holding pattern for six hundred years.[27]

Here, then, the balance between ideas and activity, between structure and agency, is thrown into as much dynamic contention as is that between rupture and continuity which confronts us in the Anglo/Latin American contrast.

---

25. *History and Theory*, 16, 1977, p. 336. For this lineage, which Hexter sees as complementary rather than alternative to that of Pocock, he identifies, *inter alia*: the Petition of Right (1628); the Habeas Corpus Act (1679); the Bill of Rights (1689); the United States Declaration of Independence (1776); and the US Constitution (1787), together with the first ten amendments.

26. *The Origins of English Individualism: The Family, Property and Social Transition*, Oxford 1978. Which researcher in the archives has not at some moment not felt like Macfarlane as he worked through the seventeenth-century papers of Ralph Josselin?

> My training led me to expect that, living before the watershed of the industrial revolution, his social and mental and economic life would appear very remote, very different from my own. It would still carry many of the overtones of the earlier medieval period from which the country was just emerging. I was startled to find, on the contrary, how 'modern' his world was; his family life, attitudes to children, economic anxieties, and the very structure of his thought was very familiar indeed.

Ibid., p. 3.

27. *AHR*, 84, 1979, p. 1047.

The 'historioculturalists' of Latin America tend away from social science. Morse and Dealy explicitly repudiate its presumptions and style. After all, their visible premises require argumentation about history; they are palpably averse to measurement, and sometimes even to empirical verification. Yet the scale of their inquiry, its general attitude to detail and variation, the confidence of its voice, and, above all, the values it so explicitly promotes bind them much more closely than they could accept to a tradition which, as described by Dorothy Ross, will be easily recognisable to both non-social scientists and non-North Americans:

> American social science bears the distinctive mark of its national origin. Like pragmatism or Protestant fundamentalism or abstract expressionism, social science is a characteristic product of modern American culture. Its liberal values, practical bent, shallow historical vision, and technocratic confidence are recognizable features of twentieth-century America. To foreign and domestic critics, these characteristics make American social science ahistorical and scientistic, lacking in appreciation of historical difference and complexity. To its supporters, the drive for scientific method, freedom from the vagaries of history, and practical utility in American society have been praiseworthy goals marred by too-frequent lapses, but they have been equally singled out as its characteristic features. What is so marked about American social science is the degree to which it is modeled on the natural rather than the historical sciences and imbedded in the classical ideology of liberal individualism.[28]

Ross's book is a study of the intellectual development of 'American exceptionalism', a long-standing current of enormous political influence which has been succinctly defined as 'the notion that the United States was created differently, developed differently, and thus has to be *understood* differently – essentially on its own terms and within its own context'.[29] The term originates with Tocqueville, who did not employ the noun in recounting his visit to the USA in 1831 but laid the basis for its future use in his forceful espousal not just of specificity but of exclusivity:

> The position of the Americans is … quite exceptional, and it may be believed that no democratic people will ever be placed in a similar one. Their strictly Puritanical origin, their exclusively commercial habits, even the country they inhabit, which seems to direct their minds from the pursuit of science, literature and the arts, the proximity of Europe, which allows them to neglect these pursuits without relapsing into barbarism, a thousand special causes, of which I have only been able to point out the most important, have singularly concurred to fix the mind of the American upon purely practical objects. His passions, his wants, his education, and everything about him seem to unite in drawing the native of the United States earthward; his religion alone bids him to turn, from time to time, a transient and distracted glance to heaven. Let us cease, then, to view all democratic nations with the example of the American people, and attempt to survey them at length with their own features.[30]

---

28. *The Origins of American Social Science*, Cambridge 1991, p. xiii.
29. Byron E. Shafer (ed.), *Is America Different? A New Look at American Exceptionalism*, Oxford 1991, p. v.
30. *Democracy in America*, New York 1990, II, pp. 36–7.

Here, once more, we face the paradox of demonstrating that a phenomenon is incomparable. One means of avoiding this difficulty recently employed by Rogers Smith is to talk of a common culture constituted of multiple traditions, including, of course, those of women, blacks, Indians and immigrants for whom white, liberal, Christian, republican patriarchy contains as many threats as it does affirmations (if not more).[31] Joyce Appleby has suggested that 'one by one the props under the notion of American exceptionalism [at least as a notion that was applied to the colonial period] have disappeared'.[32] Ian Tyrrel sees this as lying to appreciable degree with the logical difficulty of making comparisons as well as taking for granted the primacy of the national unit for analysis.[33] However, in response to Appleby, Jack Greene, one of the most sure-footed 'historioculturalists', has pointed out that whatever its intellectual state, exceptionalism retains considerable popular appeal and political potency. And more recently Seymour Martin Lipset has 'reaffirmed' exceptionalism as an academic interpretation precisely through comparative methodology, unruffled reliance upon mass surveys, and a conviction that 'America continues to be qualitatively different ... exceptionalism is a two-edged sword; it does not mean better. This country is an outlier. It is the most religious, optimistic, patriotic, rights-oriented and individualistic.'[34]

The tradition of the tradition seems set to continue too, then. Although the North American 'historioculturalists' of Latin America have not particularly sought to locate themselves within this 'exceptionalist' intellectual lineage, they may usefully be understood to be occupying part of its terrain.

Perhaps the most prominent exception to exceptionalism amongst North American historians was Herbert Eugene Bolton (1870–1953), who described his Wisconsin upbringing as very much within the populist expression of the 'American creed':

> My early environment and outlook were typically Yankee 'American', that is to say, provincial, nationalistic. My unquestioned historical beliefs included the following: Democrats were born to be damned; Catholics, Mormons and Jews were looked upon askance. The Americans licked the English; they licked the Indians; all good Indians were dead; the English came to America to build homes; the Spaniards merely explored and hunted gold; Spain failed in the New World; the English always succeeded; their successors, the Americans, were God's elect; American history all happened between the 49th parallel and the Rio Grande; the Americans virtuously drove the Mexicans out of New Mexico, Colorado, Texas, Arizona and the rest, and thereby built a great empire. Every one of these concepts is false in whole or in part, but it took me half a lifetime to discover it.[35]

---

31. 'Beyond Tocqueville, Myrdal and Hartz: The Multiple Traditions in America', *American Political Science Review*, 87:3, Sept. 1993.

32. 'Value and Society', in Jack P. Greene and J.R. Pole (eds), *Colonial British America: Essays in the New History of the Early Modern Era*, Baltimore 1993, pp. 5–6.

33. 'American Exceptionalism in an Age of International History', *AHR*, 96:4, 1991.

34. *American Exceptionalism: A Double-Edged Sword*, New York 1996, p. 26. Essentially a collection of revised essays, this volume contains Lipset's chapter in the Shafer collection, but for a full sense of Lipset's historical approach it is better to consult *The First New Nation: The United States in Historical and Comparative Perspective*, London 1964.

35. Quoted in *Selected Writings of Lewis Hanke on Latin American History*, Tempe, Fla., 1979, p. 357.

Bolton went on the University of California in 1911, specialising in what are known as the 'Spanish Borderlands' of North America, and also taking a close interest in the Indian history of those regions. In 1920 he wrote a textbook which deliberately treated the colonisation of North America in a comparative fashion, thereby downplaying what might be called 'Anglo triumphalism'. However, Bolton is perhaps best known for his 1932 presidential address to the American Historical Association, when he forcefully identified a

> need for a broader treatment of American history, to supplement the purely nationalistic presentation to which we are accustomed.... American history [cannot] be adequately presented if confined to Brazil, or Chile, or Mexico, or Canada or the United States ... similar distortion has resulted from the teaching and writing of national history in other American countries.[36]

In the North this appeal largely fell on deaf ears, and the reaction in the South was perhaps best represented by Edmundo O'Gorman, who repudiated less Bolton's liberal internationalism than the 'materialist' sense of unity that he had sought to put at its service without recognising the spiritual distinctiveness of the South. If Bolton succeeded in founding a 'school' of thought at Berkeley – he supervised over 100 PhD and 300 master's theses – his own work was strongly empirical and is today generally seen as quite elitist and lacking the theory or reach to match the prospectus he had laid out.[37] None the less, until the onset of international historiography in the post-war period, and particularly from the 1960s, Bolton's approach stood in marked contrast to a 'differentialist' tradition within what are today called 'Latin American Studies' in the USA.

Although the author of the following statement is not known for sure, the likelihood is that it was either Edward Everett, president of Harvard (1846–49) and US secretary of state (1852), or his elder brother Alexander, US ambassador to Spain (1825–29) and commissioner to China (1845–47), or Jared Sparks, professor of history at Harvard (1838–49) and then Everett's successor as president (1849–53).[38] The article

---

36. Quoted in ibid., p. 353. Prior to his address Bolton had written (with Thomas Maitland Marshall) *The Colonization of North America 1492–1783*, New York 1920; *The Spanish Borderlands: A Chronicle of Old Florida and the Southwest*, New Haven, Conn., 1921; *Outpost of Empire: The Story of the Founding of San Francisco*, New York 1931.

37. Hanke's response is quite representative. See also David J. Weber, *The Spanish Frontier in North America*, New Haven 1992, pp. 353–6. O'Gorman may have a point. Directly having written this sentence, I went out into the Holloway Road, north London, where I was handed a leaflet advertising Mrs Adams, Spiritual Adviser, Healer and Spell Breaker.

> I am superior in readings of palm, face, crystal ball, Ora [sic] and Wizard. I can and will analyze your past, present and future. I have the influence of the most divine holy spirit to destroy any unnatural forces that are harming you through love, health, business, exams, lawsuits and even alcohol. My guard, oils, candles, powders, incense and prayers will do any job that needs to be done without fail.

0171 281 5208 (mobile 0958 317273).

38. José De Onis attributes the authorship to Edward Everett in *The United States as Seen by Spanish American Writers, 1776–1890*, New York 1952, p. 91, but Lewis Hanke suggests that it was Sparks, who was editor of the *North American Review* at the time. However, Sparks was followed as editor by Alexander

was written in 1821, towards the end of the Latin American independence wars and when very few people in New England had a sense of the southern part of the continent, but the tone is not so distant either from that of Bolton's upbringing or – until the final statement – from some of the sharper 'historioculturalist' theses.

> We have here no concern with South America; we have no sympathy, we can have no well founded political sympathy with them. We are sprung from different stocks, we speak different languages, we have been brought up in different social and moral schools, we have been governed by different codes of law, we profess radically different forms of religion.... How can our mild and merciful peoples, who went through their revolution without shedding a drop of civil blood, sympathize with a people that are hanging and shooting each other in their streets, with every fluctuation of their ill-organized and exasperated factions? ... We are told it to be a maxim clearly established in the history of the world, that none but the temperate climates, and the climates which produce and retain the European complexion of skin in its various shades, admit of the highest degrees of national civilization.[39]

Some 120 years later, in the midst of a world war fought between eminently 'temperate' powers, Samuel Flagg Bemis could write with no less confidence,

> It is a scientific fact of political, economic and social geography, that the areas of best and of second-best climatic energy coincide geographically with the more impressive evidence of human civilization, such as maximum wheat yield, maximum of professional occupation, maximum of industrial production, greatest number of schools and colleges, of automobiles and of telephones per capita, maximum of railway networks, and best human health. All these imply social progress and political stability ... a necessary basis of modern civilization.[40]

Far closer to the author of the *North American Review* in terms of historical time but qualitatively more modulated in her expression than both these assured North American authors, the Franco-Peruvian Flora Tristán – balking at London's 'eight months of winter and four months of bad weather' – made a similar point:

> Moral differences in people may well be due to differences in climate. In the south, where perception is keen and imagination intuitive, the pace of life is rapid but interspersed with long interludes of reverie and yearning. In the north, the mind is slower to respond to the promptings of the senses; investigation is calm and careful, action slow and steady. But it is a gradual progression from the Negro to the Laplander; as one goes north, the pressure of human needs increases, physical pleasure and pain become almost the sole preoccupation of

---

Everett, who at least had some experience of Hispanic matters whereas Sparks only learned Spanish in 1824–25. H.B. Adams, *The Life and Writings of Jared Sparks*, New York 1893, II, p. 292.

    39. 'South America', *North American Review*, XXXI, 1821, pp. 422–43.

    40. *The Latin American Policy of the United States*, New York 1943, p. 6. I owe this reference to Charles Bergquist, *Labor and the Course of American Democracy: US History in Latin American Perspective*, London 1996. In that book, which adopts a critical 'inter-American' approach of the type for which I am striving, Bergquist goes on to discuss theories of US expansionism, such as that of Walter LaFeber, who, drawing on the frontier thesis of Frederick Turner, suggests that expansionism abroad derived in part from the closing of the internal western frontier that we have here been watching open up. (The US Census Bureau formally declared the frontier closed in 1890.) It would seem that almost any thesis based on the frontier is contradictory with one based on climate, especially if we follow Dale Carter's lead and find the 'final frontier' in space, or in the imagination of that space. *The Final Frontier: The Rise and Fall of the American Rocket State*, London 1988.

Man, whereas in the south, prodigal Nature allows the soul to bask in self-contemplation; awareness of life's blessings and misfortunes is less acute, and people are more open to the influence of mysticism than in the north.[41]

As a rule, identification of some tropicalist obstacle has not been a dominant motif in understanding Latin America. But one can appreciate the merits of such a naturalist determinism when it is placed alongside an example of directly social characterisation, such as the reflections of another Harvard history professor, Clarence Haring, on his trip south in 1925/26, at the same time as Huizinga was visiting the States:

> The Latin American finds it difficult to understand an attitude of disinterestedness. In public affairs he is rarely able to subordinate self to the public welfare. He cannot engage in enterprise, whether politics or sport, without striving himself always to occupy first place, hold the centre of the stage, *seem* to be directing affairs ... the Anglo-American, on the other hand, more practical and realistic, has the qualities of mind that make a better engineer, a more aggressive man of business; he receives a training that produces more experienced physicians, more genuine scholars. While his politics are by no means free from graft and corruption, there is a sufficiency of altruism and of a spirit of public service in the community effectively to leaven the whole lump.[42]

RELIGION AND ROME

Right at the end of his book *New World Soundings* – the very last words of the spoof 'McLuhanaima' – Richard Morse, writing in 1976, celebrates the fifty-fourth anniversary of the invention of the Morse Code. We know that we're being teased because it was on 24 May 1844 that Samuel Finley Breese Morse sent the first telegraph message, from Washington to Baltimore: 'What hath God wrought!' Professor Morse was, of course, born in 1922, and one might well suppose that he shares blood as well as name and a proper respect for religiosity not only with Samuel Morse but also with his formidable father, the Reverend Jedidiah Morse (1761–1826). It is fitting, then, that we open this section with the strict Calvinist minister at Charlestown, Massachusetts.

---

41. *The London Journal of Flora Tristán, 1842*, London 1982, pp. 21–2.
42. C.H. Haring, *South America Looks at the United States*, New York 1928, p. 64. Richard Kagan uses another work by Haring – *Trade and Navigation between Spain and the Indies in the Time of the Hapsburgs* (Cambridge, Mass., 1918) – to illustrate an excellent essay, published after the present text was completed: 'Prescott's Paradigm: American Historical Scholarship and the Decline of Spain', in Anthony Molho and Gordon S. Wood (eds), *Imagined Histories: American Historians Interpret the Past*, Princeton 1998.

Jedidiah was probably most sharply remembered by the Unitarian masters of Harvard for staging an energetic but ultimately futile campaign against the appointment of the moderate Henry Ware to the chair of divinity in 1808, and he continued to harass the liberals for nearly twenty years through his journal *Panoplist*. Morse's authority stemmed in good measure from his opposition to the slave trade and his missionary work amongst the tribes.[43] However, his wider fame rested on his political and intellectual activity in the late 1790s. In May 1798 Jedidiah claimed in two sermons to have discovered a clandestine society of subversives operating under a name derived from their Enlightenment ideals – the *Illuminati*. The next year he told his congregation,

> I have now in my possession complete and indubitable proof that such societies exist, and have for many years existed, in the United States. I have, my brethren, an official, authenticated list of the names, ages, places of nativity, professions etc. of the officers and members of the society of *Illuminati* … consisting of *one hundred* members, instituted in Virginia by the *Grand Orient* of FRANCE.… You will perceive, my brethren … that we have in truth secret enemies … whose professed design is to subvert and overturn our holy religion and our free and excellent government … the industrious circulation of baneful and corrupting books, and the consequent wonderful spread of infidelity, impiety and immorality.[44]

A strong Federalist, Morse was here, it should be noted, identifying a plot against the administration of John Adams prior to the election of Thomas Jefferson, widely seen as pro-French, with Aaron Burr as vice-president, the next year. However, Jedidiah's early practice of the 'paranoid style of American politics' is surely secondary to that of geography, where his reputation rests more soundly, albeit with the occasional judgement over which, I am sure, Richard Morse has long since chuckled:

> *Peru* … Among all the inhabitants of Peru, pride and laziness are said to be the most prominent passions. Avarice may likewise be attributed to them with a great deal of propriety.… *Brazil* … The Portuguese live here in the most effeminate luxury. The portrait drawn of the manners, customs and morals of that nation in America, by judicious travellers, is very far from being favourable.[45]

Jedidiah travelled no further than Georgia, but we should note the authority given to travellers' accounts, which stretched well into the telegraphic era, even as we recognise that resort to them entails exposure to much 'Euroimperialism, androcentrism and

---

43. Franklin Bowditch Dexter, *Biographical Sketches of the Graduates of Yale with Annals of the College History: IV, July 1775–June 1792*, New York 1907, p. 297. Jedidiah Morse, *A discourse delivered at the African meeting house, in Boston, July 14 1808: in grateful celebration of the abolition of the African slave trade, by the governments of the United States, Great Britain and Denmark*, Boston 1808.

44. Quoted in Vernon Stauffer, *New England and the Bavarian Illuminati*, New York 1918, p. 283, cited in Seymour Martin Lipset and Earl Rabb, *The Politics of Unreason: Right-Wing Extremism in America, 1790–1970*, London 1971, pp. 36–7. Morse had apparently got hold of a copy of John Robison, *Proofs of a Conspiracy to Overthrow All the Governments in the World*, published in Great Britain the previous year. Thanks to Robin Blackburn for this reference.

45. Jedidiah Morse, *The American Gazeteer* (1797), New York 1971 (unpaginated and with far too many pages to count).

white supremacy' amongst other traits that are today sometimes anachronistic, sometimes impolite, sometimes repugnant.[46]

Samuel Morse also practised politics, and to scarcely better result. In 1835 he
collected into a volume the letters he had written under the pseudonym 'Brutus' to
the *New York Observer* promoting the view that the Holy Alliance was conspiring to
subvert American democracy through Catholic immigration:

> What then shall be done? Shall Protestants organise themselves into a political union after
> the manner of the Papists, and the various classes of industry and even of *foreigners* in the
> country? Shall they form an Anti-Popery Union, and take their places among this strange
> medley of conflicting interests? And why should they not?[47]

The following year Morse sought municipal office on a nativist platform and was
soundly defeated. If he had tried ten years later he would have had a much better
chance, not only because of his personal fame but also because the levels of immigration by Catholics had increased markedly even before the Irish Famine took
hold. Amidst the resulting xenophobia the Whigs were encouraged to make a tacit
alliance with the nativists.

There is general agreement that at the time of the first US census (1790), which
did not ask about religious affiliation, there were a mere 35,000 Roman Catholics of
a total white and black population of 3.9 million. According to John Ellis, these
people 'had existed through a century and a half as an insignificant minority in a state
of practical outlawry'.[48] Of largely German background and concentrated in Maryland and Philadelphia, their status was not immediately improved by independence –
Canadian Catholics had been given religious freedom in 1774 – when several states
banned Catholics from office; it was only after the first constitutional amendment that
federal restrictions began to loosen. However, at state and local level political controls
remained in force until the 1820s.[49] (Of course, until emancipation in 1829 no British

---

46. Mary Louise Pratt, *Imperial Eyes: Travel Writing and Transculturation*, London 1992, p. xi.
47. *Foreign Conspiracy against the Liberties of the United States*, New York 1835, pp. 125–6, quoted in
Sydney E. Ahlstrom, *A Religious History of the American People*, New Haven, Conn., 1972, p. 563. According
to David Brion Davis,

> Samuel F.B. Morse analyzed the Catholic conspiracy in essentially the same terms his father had
> used in exposing the Society of the Illuminati, supposedly a radical branch of freemasonry.... What
> distinguished the stereotype Mason, Catholic and Mormon was the way in which they were seen
> to embody those traits that were precise antitheses of American ideals. The subversive group was
> essentially an inverted image of Jacksonian democracy and the cult of the common man; as such
> it not only challenged the dominant values but stimulated those suppressed needs and yearnings that
> are unfulfilled in a mobile, rootless and individualistic society.

'Some Themes of Counter-Subversion: An Analysis of Anti-Masonic, Anti-Catholic and Anti-Mormon
Literature', *Mississippi Valley Historical Review*, XLVII, 1960, pp. 207–8. There is a huge difference between
the views of Samuel and Richard Morse, but it is worth noting that whilst the latter's patrician finesse is
not an ordinary American voice, the views it expresses chime far more readily with popular attitudes in the
USA than do those of the 'progressive' academics whom he provokes. Perhaps, as Halperín suggests (see
note 19), Morse was marginalised within his profession, but like Jedidiah and Samuel, he was with the
masses.
48. *American Catholicism*, Chicago 1969, pp. 41, 43.
49. Ray Billington, *The Protestant Crusade 1800–1860: A Study of the Origins of American Nativism*, Chicago

Catholic could vote or stand for election or hold commissions in the army or navy or qualify for ministerial office.) The accelerating levels of immigration over the next two decades, together with the annexation of Mexico, increased the Roman Catholics in the USA to 1.5 million when the total population was 23 million (1850). Unsurprisingly, 'no Popery' started to take hold on national politics, the refusal in 1844 of Philadelphia Catholics to have the Protestant Bible in their schools provoking a series of bloody riots, destruction of houses and the full deployment of the militia. In February 1846 the *American Protestant Magazine* issued a plea:

> O Lord God, thou hast commanded us to wait upon thee and to call upon thee in the day of trouble, and thou hast promised to hear and answer us ... be thou our sun and shield, that if popery is destined to gain the ascendency in our Land, we may be armed to meet and triumph over its attendant evils; may we remember that not only from seeming but from real evils thou canst and will enduce good; that in leading thy Church triumphantly over all her enemies thou art glorifying thyself.[50]

The previous year the Presbyterian Board of Foreign Missions had declared in its annual report,

> The papal crusade is against the truth, wherever it is found – the warfare is against the liberties of the world. We cannot, therefore, avoid this contest unless we deem the truth, and everything dear to the Christian and to Man, not worth contending for. In such a contest there can be no neutrals, it is between Christ and Anti-Christ, and there is no middle ground.[51]

Such sentiments did not change formal constitutional liberties, but neither did they promote the kind of tolerance and pluralism that the 'historioculturalists' have as abiding so intimately with Protestantism.[52] The great fixer of the Whig party, Thurlow Weed, reflected in 1854, 'Between the Catholic and Protestant world there has been, and there is to be, we suppose, perpetual warfare. The excited and ultra on either side will go on probably to the end of time mistaking fanaticism for religion.'[53]

1964, pp. 20–23. It is worth stressing that even at this stage there were almost certainly more Irish Protestants than Catholics in the USA, but that is not how it was felt then or, indeed, later. Accepting this fact, Andrew Greeley excludes the Protestants entirely from his book *Irish Americans*, New York 1981, not only on the grounds that they have a 'very different culture and historical experience of American life' but also because so few studies have been made of them.

50. Quoted in ibid., p. 250.

51. Quoted in ibid., p. 274.

52. However reluctantly, it should be registered that in a footnote Dealy seems to undermine the entire argument of his book:

> Fear of communism has been much greater in Protestant-ethos societies than in Catholic-ethos societies, no doubt due to the former's One Morality system, despite its pluralistic pretenses. It cannot accommodate diverse public orthodoxies without private values also being threatened. US political pluralism is singularly non-pluralist, ideologically speaking, when compared with Catholic polities in Europe and the Americas.

Latin Americans, p. 37. There really is no polite way of asking what political pluralism means if it doesn't include ideology, even in the USA.

53. *Life of Thurlow Weed*, Boston 1884, II, pp. 224.

Now, though, these two 'worlds' contended within the same polity. They were scarcely on comparable terms – the US Catholic Church held its first plenary meeting at Baltimore in May 1852 having only 1,800 churches throughout the USA, when the state of Ohio alone had 4,000 churches belonging to over twenty denominations (130 belonging to the Catholics). There was no American-born archbishop and only nine of the bishops had been born in the country. The Irish dominated the clergy in terms of seniority, and it was correspondingly easy for militant Protestants to paint the faith as foreign and imported.[54]

It should, though, be stressed that anti-Catholicism was by no means a North American preserve. In Britain very similar sentiments were excited by the vote in 1845 to give the Catholic college at Maynooth a permanent endowment instead of the annual grant that had been paid since Union in 1801. In a letter to Daniel O'Connell, Sir Culling Eardley Smith expressed a direct and impolite view of the relationship between Catholicism and political freedom as well as the Liberator's own probity:

> There have not been wanting those who have questioned the genuineness and probable permanence of your liberality. They believe that your religion is averse to liberality. They have mentally traversed Catholic Europe, and they have observed that, exactly in proportion as your priests possess power, they use it against freedom … this proportion of tyranny to Romanism cannot be accidental … that the genius of your faith must be essentially illiberal; that you are a friend of freedom simply by accident.[55]

Such sentiments were by no means limited to 'back-benchers'. Five years later, when Pius IX restored the British hierarchy – very far from the most provocative act of this pontiff to Protestants in Great Britain – Lord John Russell wrote to the bishop of Durham,

> There is an assumption of power in all the documents which have come from Rome; a pretension of supremacy over the realm of England, and a claim to sole and undivided sovereignty, which is inconsistent with the Queen's supremacy.... The liberty of protestantism has been enjoyed too long in England to allow of any successful attempt to impose a foreign yoke on our minds and consciences.... The honour paid to saints, the claim of infallibility for the Church, the superstitious use of the sign of the cross, the muttering of the liturgy so as to disguise the language in which it is written, the recommendation of auricular confession, the administration of penance and absolution.[56]

Russell's sense is not just one of defence of the secular – post-Reformation – state but also of that religious demeanour which Emerson captured so well:

---

54. Ahlstrom, *Religious History*, p. 546; *8th Census of the USA, 1860*, Washington 1864, p. 871. The British census of 1851 registered a total of 34,467 places of worship, divided between the main denominations thus: Churches of England and Ireland 14,077; All Scottish Presbyterians 160; Congregationalists 3,244; All Baptists 2,789; Quakers 371; Unitarians 229; Moravians 32; Wesleyan Methodists 11,007; Calvinist Methodists 937; Roman Catholics 570; Mormons 222; Jews 53. Reprinted in Harold Hanham (ed.), *The Nineteenth-Century Constitution: Documents and Commentary*, Cambridge 1969, pp. 432–5.

55. Quoted in E.R. Norman, *Anti-Catholicism in Victorian England*, London 1968, pp. 148–9.

56. Quoted in ibid., pp. 159–61.

The Anglican church is marked by the grace and good sense of its forms, by the manly grace of its clergy. The gospel it preaches is 'By taste are ye saved'. It keeps the old structures in repair, spends a world of money in music and building; and in buying Pugin and architectural literature. It has a general good name for amenity and mildness. It is not in ordinary a persecuting church; it is not inquisitorial, not even inquisitive, is perfectly well-bred, and can shut its eyes on all proper occasions. If you let it alone, it will leave you alone.... Nature, to be sure [has] her remedy. Religious persons are driven out of the Established Church into the sects.[57]

Yet this was only generally true, and it was always brought at the price of occasional rememberance of persecution as well as cathartic admonition. As ever, the most pugnacious resolution came from the pulpit. Preaching on Guy Fawkes Day 1850 William Bennett demonstrated that a parson from Walthamstow could match the brethren of the New World in Cromwellian fulmination:

And does not the past history of the Romish Church confirm every one of these charges? If she does not persecute, and slay, as once she did, it is because she has not the *power*; but she is striving with all her might and all her craft, to regain her lost power. The claws of the beast, on which she sits, have been closely pared; she waits till they grow again ... she changes not, this is her confession and her boast. Can we forget our own deliverance from the invading Spanish Armada, sanctioned and blessed by the Pope, and bearing to our shores a freight of torturing instruments; but, dissipated by the winds of Jehovah, shattered and wrecked before it reached our shores? And from that traitorous and all but successful plot, of which we are reminded by this day?[58]

The Black Legend of both sides of the Atlantic had conspiracy and treason at its very core. One can readily understand, for instance, that the jurors who found John Mitchel guilty of a serious crime against the Crown also saw him as betraying his faith.

But to whom? At a certain point conspiratorial logic can regress no further, can identify no finite enemy, encountering just betrayal-as-departure/removal/non-belonging. It is the incredulity which this awakens that Cardinal Newman registered as a core component of the Christian schism. However, Newman, who left the Anglican for the Roman Catholic Church in October 1845, could find no easy answer in explaining the 'Position of my Mind Since 1845':

---

57. Ralph Waldo Emerson, *English Traits* (1856), Cambridge, Mass., 1994, pp. 126, 129.
58. Quoted in Norman, *Anti-Catholicism*, pp. 172–3. In September 1656 Cromwell told the second protectorate parliament,

Why, truly, your great Enemy is the Spaniard. He is a natural enemy. He is naturally so; he is naturally so throughout, by reason of that enmity that is in him against whatsoever is of God. 'Whatsoever is of God' which is in *you*, or which may be in you; contrary to that which *his* blindness and darkness, led by superstition, and the implicitness of his faith in submitting to the See of Rome activate him unto.... It would not be difficult to call to mind the several Assassinations designed upon that Lady, that great Queen: the attempts upon Ireland, the Spaniards' invading of it; their design of the same time upon *this* Nation – public designs, private designs, all manner of designs, to accomplish this great and general end.

Thomas Carlyle (ed.), *Oliver Cromwell's Letters and Speeches*, IV, London 1873, pp. 208–10. For those liable to be irritated by Carlyle's interjections, this passage may also be found in Ivan Roots (ed.), *Speeches of Oliver Cromwell*, London 1989, p. 81.

Sometimes, when [Protestants] reflect upon it ... [they] remark on the wonderful discipline of the Catholic priesthood; they say that no Church has so well ordered a clergy, and that in some respects it surpasses their own; they wish they could have such discipline among themselves. But is it an excellence which can be purchased? Is it a phenomenon which depends on nothing else than itself? Or is it an effect which has a cause? You cannot buy devotion at a price. 'It hath never been heard of in the land of Chanaan, neither hath it been seen in the Theman. The children of Agar, the merchants of Meran, none of those have known its way.' What then is that wonderful charm, which makes a thousand men act all in one way, and infuses a prompt obedience to rule, as if they were under some stern military compulsion? How difficult to find an answer, unless you will allow the obvious one, that they believe intensely what they profess![59]

It was not difficult to hear of papal conspiracies in the USA through the 1850s.[60] Nevertheless, victory over Mexico and the Gold Rush drew much of the sting of religiously driven nativism. According to C.S. Ellsworth, 'At the beginning of the war many Protestants predicted that the Roman Catholics would prove to be traitors in a war against a Catholic country. Their fears were entirely groundless.' The pastoral letter issued by the hierarchy was as reassuring to the state as it was predictable in its content by insisting that obedience to the Pope was 'in no way inconsistent with your civil allegiance, your social duties as citizens, or your rights as men.... You can bear witness that we have always taught you to render to Caesar the things that are Caesar's, to God the things that are God's.'[61]

Sometimes, as in the case of the Episcopalians, a Protestant denomination adopted an effectively neutral response to the war. Sometimes, as with the Methodists, it generally supported it. Sometimes, as in the case of the Unitarians, it opposed the conflict but with hesitation. Perhaps it was only the Congregationalists who entirely and unambiguously denounced the war and the US role in it:

While Humanity is outraged, our country disgraced, the Laws of Heaven suspended, and those of Hell put in force, by the conduct and continuance of the Mexican war, we shall not cease (to attempt at least) to rouse the public mind to a sense of the awful guilt brought upon this nation by what has deservedly been called 'the most infamous war ever recorded upon the page of history'.[62]

But the war was over in a matter of months, and the really enduring issue of economic, political and moral controversy throughout these decades was that of slavery, and slavery was an issue over which Protestantism was internally fractured with much more critical consequences.

---

59. John Henry Newman, *Apologia Pro Vita Sua* (1864), Harmondsworth 1994, p. 242. The quotation is from Baruch 3: 22–3.

60. 'The two systems are diametrically opposed: one must and will exterminate the other.' Edward Beecher, *The Papal Conspiracy Exposed, and Protestantism Defended in the Light of Reason, History and Scripture*, Boston 1855, p. 27.

61. Quoted in C.S. Ellsworth, 'The American Churches and the Mexican War', *AHR*, 45, 1940, p. 302.

62. *Boston Recorder*, 21 Jan., 12 July 1847, quoted in ibid., p. 318.

Although the 'historioculturalists' very occasionally mention this critical feature, it is presented as a characteristic and unproblematic pluralism, in binary opposition to unitarian Catholicism, not as a sectarian source of theological and political complication. Seymour Martin Lipset, in a rather distinct strain, argues that North American Protestantism was internally secularised, and 'only Catholicism, viewed by many Protestants not as a different set of religious beliefs but as an alien conspiracy seeking to undermine the American way of life, was outside the pale'.[63] The Cold War analogies here need not be laboured. But before we switch to the 'externalities' demanded by this attitude it is worth registering the bemusement of the Italian Jesuit Giovanni Grassi, whose observations of 1818 are quoted by Lipset to illustrate the peculiar lack of intensity of North American religiosity:

> Every sect there is held as good, every road as correct, and every error as the insignificant weakness of poor mortals ... Although how can one speak of sects? Those who describe themselves as members of one or another of the sects do not thereby profess an abiding adherence to the doctrines of the founders of the sect.... Thus the Anglicans of today no longer take much account of their Thirty Nine Articles, nor the Lutherans of the Confession of Augsburg, nor the Presbyterians of the teachings of Calvin or of Knox.... Among the peculiarities of America, not the most extreme is that of finding people who live together for several years without knowing each other's religion. And many, when asked, do not answer, 'I believe', but simply, 'I was brought up in such a persuasion'.[64]

For Domingo Faustino Sarmiento this attribute was a thoroughly laudable aspect of US civil society:

> The Americans prefer the admirable and conciliatory principle of not discussing religion or politics with anyone except those who are of their own sect or persuasion. This system is based on an obvious understanding of human nature. The Yankee orator strives to confirm his followers in their beliefs rather than to convert his opponents, who meanwhile are dozing or thinking of their business.[65]

Tocqueville, who stated that 'there is no country in the world where the Christian religion retains a greater influence over the souls of men than in America', identified a similar disposition at the same time as he defended Catholicism – 'erroneously regarded as the natural enemy of democracy'.[66] The young Francis Parkman – yet to

---

63. *First New Nation*, p. 165.

64. Quoted in ibid., p. 153.

65. Michael Rockland (ed.), *Sarmiento's Travels in the United States in 1847*, Princeton 1970, p. 150.

66. *Democracy in America*, I, p. 300. Tocqueville casts some light on the 'historioculturalists' as well as on American Protestantism when, in a chapter entitled 'What Causes Democratic Nations to Incline Towards Pantheism', he states,

> When the conditions of society are becoming more equal and each individual man becomes more like the rest ... the human mind seeks to embrace a multitude of different objects at once, and it constantly strives to connect a variety of consequences with a single cause. The idea of unity so possesses man and is sought by him so generally that if he thinks he has found it he readily yields himself to repose in that belief. Not content with the discovery that there is nothing in the world but a creation and a Creator, he is still embarrassed by this primary division of things and seeks to expand and simplify his conception by including God and the universe in one great whole.

find himself on the Oregon Trail – describes for us just such a phenomenon taking place within the process of 'Americanisation' when he was sailing off Italy in 1843:

> As I lounged about the deck in the morning, utterly unable to hold any intercourse with any on board except by signs, a sleek-looking fellow came up and accosted me in English. We soon got deep into conversation. My new acquaintance proved to be Guiseppe Jackson, a Sicilian with an English grandfather, who had been a cook at the Albion, and at Murdoch's Tavern, had frequently been to Fresh Pond – knew some of the Cambridge students, and was now on his way to Mr Marston's in Palermo. I was right glad to see him, cook though he was. He made me a very good interpreter. In the course of our conversation he made some remark about 'the Pope, that fool'.
>   'What?' said I, 'Do you speak so of the Pope? Are you not a Roman Catholic?'
>   'Ah! I was till I live in America. I was all in the dark – you understand what I say – till I come there. Then my eyes open; I say dat for the Pope and his old red cap. Ah! Once I was afraid to think of him.'
>   'You are no longer a Catholic; what religion do you believe in now?'
>   'Oh! No religion in particular.'
> I congratulated him on so happy a conversion from the error of his ways.'[67]

In a more mature but equally spirited vein, Parkman's critique of Catholicism derived from a broad suspicion of priesthood (itself extremely variegated within the Protestant tradition):

> … while he, the priest, yields reverence and obedience to the Superior in whom he sees the representation of the Deity, it behooves him, in his degree, to require obedience from those whom he imagines that God has confided to his guidance. His conscience, then, acts in perfect accord with the love of power innate in the human heart. These allied forces mingle with a perplexing subtlety; pride, disguised even from itself, walks in the likeness of love and duty; and a thousand times on the page of history we find Hell beguiling the virtues of Heaven to do its work. The instinct of domination is a weed that grows rank in the shadow of the temple, climbs over it, possesses it, covers its ruin, and feeds on its decay. The unchecked sway of priests has always been the most mischievous of tyrannies; and even were they all well-meaning and sincere, it would be so still.[68]

Parkman was true to his age in being unsympathetic – or even blind – to the alternative psycho-social explication of the Roman Catholic Church's division of power, here presented in the idiom of modern Marxism by Terry Eagleton for the case of Ireland, which is largely applicable to the Americas:

> The Church is, in effect, an oligarchy; but within its structures prelate and peasant are linked by a common vision in a social order with all the Byzantine apparatus of a political state yet all the intimacy of a family. In this stratified yet corporate society, intellectuals (theologians) and the masses (laity) share the same faith at different levels: what the former articulate as

---

Ibid, II, p. 31. For a discussion of this, see Ralph C. Hancock, 'The Uses and Hazards of Christianity in Tocqueville's Attempt to Save Democratic Souls', in Ken Masugi (ed.), *Interpreting Tocqueville's America*, Savage, Md., 1991.

67. Mason Wade (ed.), *The Journals of Francis Parkman*, New York 1947, I, pp. 127–8.

68. 'Historic Progress', quoted in David Levin, *History as Romantic Art: Bancroft, Prescott, Motley and Parkman*, Harcourt, N.Y., 1959, p. 109.

doctrine, the latter live out as pious observance. Yet, true to Gramsci's generous sense of 'intellectual', even the simple faithful must be capable of mastering their catechism and defending the faith, in a Church which has traditionally set a high premium on human reason. Louis Althusser, himself a former Catholic, insists that ideology is less dismembered consciousness than material practice; and the Catholic Church, whose faith is more a matter of ritual gesture than agonized inwardness, is a case in point.[69]

Old Spain

As we have seen, the Pope and priesthood were not the only problem. Protestant demonology has been most potent precisely when directed against Hispanic Catholicism – a matter of great significance for Latin America and those 40 million US citizens (equivalent to more than the population of Uruguay, Paraguay and Argentina combined) who are Roman Catholics today. Even in the sympathetic eye of Waldo Frank the impulse of the creed goes beyond the normal targets of the Black Legend:

> Spain's purpose in the colonies had been Catholic. The worlds must become one world, under the rule of a king who was the will of Rome – the body of God. Bolívar's plan was for a Catholic transfiguration. From the great creed he retained the notion of an organic unity of states – of a body expressing the world's spirit.[70]

The British traveller Clements Markham reflects a quite standard view of this history when, as background to his visit to Cuzco in 1856, he tells us that

> swarms of clergy, both secular and regulars, flocked to Peru, thirsting for plunder, and for the blood of the poor Indians. First came the Dominicans, who spread the religion of Christ with fire and sword.... It is a mistake to suppose that the Inquisition was a Popish institution in all its bearings. It was a peculiarly Spanish institution, at least in its worst and most fearful form.[71]

Prior to his trip Markham had read William Hickling Prescott's *History of the Conquest of Peru*, published in 1847, and he visited Prescott before sailing south. Prescott, who suffered intermittently from blindness, himself never travelled to Latin America, but his books, based on detailed documentation and written with carefully calculated romantic charge,[72] sold very widely and had a considerable influence over the Northern image of Spanish America:

---

69. *Heathcliff and the Great Hunger: Studies in Irish Culture*, London 1995, p. 76.
70. *America Hispana: A Portrait and a Prospect*, New York 1931, p. 8.
71. *Cuzco: A Journey to the Ancient Capital of Peru*, London 1856, pp. 140, 295–6.
72. Before he started writing his book on Peru Prescott wrote himself a memo that to some might indicate good writerly sense and to others a tension between specious authorial sovereignty and the innate lure of a dispersed object:

The Castilian, too proud for hypocrisy, committed more cruelties in the name of religion than was ever practised by the pagan idolators or the fanatical Moslem. The burning of the infidel was a sacrifice acceptable to Heaven, and the conversion of those who survived amply atoned for the foulest offences. It is a melancholy and mortifying consideration that the most uncompromising spirit of intolerance – the spirit of the Inquisitor at home, and of the Crusades abroad – should have emanated from a religion which preached peace on earth and good will towards man![73]

Language such as this dismayed conservative Catholics, such as Lucas Alamán, to whom Prescott had to offer rather weak disclaimers (on the brink of war between their countries):

It is true you think I savour something of the old Puritan acid in my anti-Catholic strictures. A Roman Catholic Dublin review speaks of it as doubtful from my writings whether I am a Catholic or a Protestant. A Baltimore Catholic journal condemns me as a deist. The Madrid translator of *Ferdinand and Isabella* condemns me for my hostility to the Inquisition. So I think between them all I may pass for a liberal Christian.[74]

However, many amongst the Latin American elite did not share the view that they were inevitably enveloped in a seamless web of catholicity. Andrés Bello, who had done much diplomatic work for independence in London, led those for whom Prescott's work was welcome because, amongst other things, it published documentation that rightfully belonged to Americans but was retained by Spain, which was only now recognising its ex-colonies as independent republics.[75] Yet Bello's was a cautious

---

Be very brief when theme not very interesting. Don't be prolix in scenes like each other. Variety, variety is the secret of interest. Expectation is another. Development of passion and personal character another ... I must not be prolix in trivialities. Keep leading points in view and work up to them. If the narrative is somewhat *fragmentary* each fragment may have its peculiar unity and interest – and all be bound together in a natural *liaison* – like the course of events in nature.

Memo of 23 April 1845, in C. Harvey Gardiner (ed.), *The Literary Memoranda of William Hickling Prescott*, Norman, Okla., 1961, II, p. 145. For documentation Prescott had owed much to material sent from Spain by Pascual Gayangos and Martín Fernández de Navarrete, director of the Royal Academy of History in Madrid, about whose death in October 1844 Prescott was informed by Gayangos in terms that would touch any historian's heart:

On the evening that he died, finding himself alone in his bedroom after having received extreme unction, he managed to get up without being heard by anyone and tottered into his study. He was found there by his daughters and when they asked him what he was doing he replied that he was bidding farewell to his books.

Gayangos, Madrid, to Prescott, 15 Oct. 1844, in Roger Wolcott (ed.), *The Correspondence of William Hickling Prescott, 1832–1847*, Cambridge, Mass., 1925, p. 509.

73. *History of the Conquest of Peru*, London 1847, p. 92.

74. Prescott, Boston, to Alamán, 30 March 1846, in Wolcott (ed.), *Correspondence of Prescott*, p. 583. Some months earlier Prescott was putting a rather different line to Alamán when he heard that the Spanish translation of his *Conquest of Mexico* '[made me] talk like a good son of the Pope! I think in that case I have a right to have my Protestant heresies at least preserved in a Note at the bottom of the page in the original English.' Ibid., p. 533.

75. Bello reviewed and reproduced long passages of Prescott on Peru in the April and May 1848 issues of *Revista de Santiago*. *Obras Completas de Andrés Bello*, Caracas 1957, XIX, pp. 263–93. Bartolomé Mitre, to be first president of the united Argentina a dozen years later, read the book in Valparaiso in 1851 and found it 'one of the finest histories that have been written on the new world; reading it is a true pleasure'. *Correspondencia Literaria, Histórica y Política del General Bartolomé Mitre*, Buenos Aires 1912, p. 25.

liberalism, and he was inclined to dialectical reflection as well as heroic vision. He rejected the rigid anti-Hispanism of the young intellectuals – of several nations – who strove in early republican Chile to develop a secular continentalism: 'It is the Iberian element that has allowed us to prevail against the Mother country. Spanish culture has clashed against itself.... The veterans of the legions of transatlantic Iberia were defeated and humiliated by the caudillos improvised by young Iberia.'[76]

Bello's main antagonist in this respect was his own pupil José Victorino Lastarria, who viewed the independence struggle in an entirely different light:

> The revolution of 1810 split the great Spanish family into two branches, and it did so in such a profound and radical way that the two parts became not simply distinguished the one from the other but placed at opposite extremes in the conditions of their existence and progress.... Spanish civilization dedicated itself to, and indeed still maintains within its own territory, the opposite principle – that of the enslavement of the human spirit. Spanish politics, religion, legislation and customs took the intelligent and moral being – man – and reduced him to nothing.[77]

Although Lastarria did depict the Anglo-Saxon tradition far more favourably, the very robustness of his repudiation of Spain underscores the fact that Spanish Americans did not need to make recourse to such a comparison in order to reject the 'empire of fanaticism'. Nor, indeed, did many Spaniards then or later take such rejection as an 'alien' act; it was, as illustrated by Unamuno's response to Sarmiento, a recognisable expression of self-deprecation:

> Whenever I hear Sarmiento's invectives against Spain, I say to myself: 'But this man says against Spain what we Spaniards who most love it say! True, he speaks badly of Spain, but he speaks badly of Spain as only a Spaniard can; he speaks badly of Spain, but he does it in Spanish, and in very correct Spanish.'[78]

For George Bancroft, who had served as Polk's secretary of navy and who read Prescott's work when United States ambassador in London, its prose was a thrilling expression of the democratic and Anglophone vocation that was to emerge in his own history of the United States:

> Go forth, then, language of Milton and Hamden, language of my country, take possession of the North American continent! Gladden the waste places with every tone that has been rightly struck on the English lyre, with every English word that has been spoken well for liberty and for man ... the lips of the messengers of the people's power shall proclaim the renovating tidings of equal freedom for the race![79]

---

76. *Opúsculos literarios i críticos*, Santiago 1850, p. 119, quoted in Efrain Kristal, 'Dialogues and Polemics: Sarmiento, Lastarria and Bello', in Joseph Criscenti (ed.), *Sarmiento and His Argentina*, Boulder, Colo., 1993, p. 67.

77. 'América' (1867), in *Obras Completas*, Santiago 1909, III, pp. 229–31, 217–19.

78. Miguel de Unamuno, 'Domingo Faustino Sarmiento', *Ensayos*, Madrid 1919, VII, p. 105.

79. Quoted in Levin, *History as Romantic Art*, p. 82. In view of this sentiment, Bancroft might well have been dismayed by Carlyle's assessment of him to Emerson: 'A tough Yankee man; of many worldly qualities more tough than musical; among which it gratified me to find a certain undercurrent of genial humour.'

On the other hand, the anonymous reviewer of Prescott's history in London's *Quarterly Review* concentrated on his treatment of the Inca empire, upon which the author reflected with a candour unusual even for him:

> It is not easy to comprehend the genius in the full impact of institutions so opposite to those of free people.... The New World is the theatre on which those two political systems, so opposite in their character, have been carried into operation. The empire of the Incas has passed away and left no trace. The other great experiment is still going on – the experiment which is to solve the problem, so long contested in the Old World, of the capacity for self-government. Alas for humanity if it should fail![80]

Rather than take constitutional umbrage, the European response of the *Review* is nearly one of detached agnosticism:

> Mr Prescott could not but be struck with the contrast between the ancient institutions of South America and those of his own country. In the former case there seems to have been the least possible freedom, and that freedom among the least possible number of people; and yet, if human happiness consist in security of life and property, in the certainty of subsistence and clothing, in order and peace, the great Benthamite test of 'the greatest happiness of the greatest number' seems to have been more nearly approached than in countries of much higher civilization. In the latter, in the United States, the great experiment of allowing the least possible power to the government, and the most absolute individual freedom, is the basis of the social system. Mr Prescott would willingly hold the balance with a steady hand; and even he, as is shown by a few pregnant words ... cannot contemplate without some awe the solution of this problem of which our children may see the issue.[81]

Although written in the spring of 1847, this is a prescient perception of the particular problem communism represented for America as well as being a restatement of one of the classical dilemmas of politics. For our purposes the fact that subsequent historiography has revealed the Inca empire to be rather less efficient in economic terms – and arguably less so in political ones, too – than Prescott believed to be the case is not really relevant. Prescott was learned enough to be awestruck by the alternative to his own creed, but not so much so as to be dislodged from his convictions. Before the collapse of the Soviet Union Cuba posed for those North Americans predisposed to reflect on their own polity a challenge that was dissimilar in only one essential particular – it was no historical echo but aggressively contemporaneous. (Once the Cuban claims to welfare could be seriously challenged, the issue devolved into a familiar neo-colonial conflict that was no less vital in political terms but much less challenging to the imagination.)

In fact, Karl Marx borrowed from Prescott's *Conquest of Mexico* a quotation from Peter Martyr for his *Critique of Political Economy* (1859),[82] and in a letter of 1854 to

---

Carlyle, London, to Emerson, 13 Nov. 1847, *The Correspondence of Thomas Carlyle and Ralph Waldo Emerson, 1834–1877*, London 1883, II, p. 154.

80. *Conquest of Peru*, pp. 157–8.
81. *Quarterly Review*, 81, June/Sept. 1847, p. 338.
82. 'Blessed money which furnishes mankind with a sweet and nutritious beverage and protects its innocent possessors from the infernal disease of avarice, since it cannot long be hoarded nor hidden

Engels he reveals a much more blunt bigotry than was ever expressed by the purblind Bostonian:

> The Spanish are already degenerate. But a degenerate Spaniard, a Mexican, is an ideal. All the Spanish vices, braggadocio, swagger and Don Quixotry, raised to the third power, but little or nothing of the steadiness which the Spaniards possess. The Mexican guerrilla war was a caricature of the Spanish, and even the *sauve qui peut* of the regular armies infinitely surpassed. But then the Spaniards have produced no talent comparable to that of Santa Anna.[83]

A few years after Prescott completed his book Francis Lieber published one of the first systematic works on political science in North America – *On Civil Liberty and Self-Government* (1853). Lieber focused less on the terms of the Constitution than on the social conditions for liberty, which he saw as a check on undue interference from either individuals or masses or the government. In some ways a forerunner of the modern US 'political culture' school, and late in his life the author of important handbooks on the rules of war, Lieber expresses a less attractive but surely more common admixture of prejudice and political preference in his attitude to Spain:[84]

> You speak well of the Spaniards.... I have never been to Spain, but what I do know of the Spaniards, and by seeing one of their colonies, does not allow me to agree with you. I dislike the nation. I dislike the garlicky, gold-chained individuals, and I dislike their carica-ture politeness. What have they done in history? What have they made of religion? They have developed the darkest of all institutions, the Inquisition, with a consistency, a cruelty, an infamy which surpasses every unhallowed tendency into which other people have been betrayed. They have established systems of government in their colonies so inferior to those which existed among the unconquered heathens that the ruins of the broken-down civili-zations put the Christians to shame to this day. They were cruel and faithless, as no other nation has been for any length of time; their cupidity has prostrated religion on a scale so gigantic that other nations appear like pigmies compared to them in this great vice of the white race. They have left the law wholly undeveloped; they have contributed nothing to science.[85]

What we have here is another rant in a private letter; but it is more than that too. The Spanish have betrayed both Christianity and the white race; their 'civilisation' is inferior to that of the heathen Indians. Here in unmoderated language of the mid nineteenth century we can find some at least of the motifs that would attend the

---

underground!' *De orbe novo* (1530), dec. 5, cap. 4, quoted in Prescott, *History of the Conquest of Mexico*, London 1850, I, p. 123, and cited in Marx, *A Contribution to the Critique of Political Economy* (1859), London 1971, p. 154.

83. Marx, London, to Engels, 2 Dec. 1854, in *MECW*, XXXIX, London 1982, p. 504.

84. *Francis Lieber*, born Berlin 1800; 1819 restricted to Jena for political reasons; 1823 tutor in Rome to son of Niebuhr; to Boston 1827; editor *Encyclopaedia Americana*, 1829–33; translator, De Tocqueville and Beaumont, *On the Penitentiary System in the United States*; *Manual of Political Ethics*, 1838–39; 1857 chair, Columbia College, New York; *Guerrilla Parties Considered with Reference to the Laws and Usages of War* (1862); *Instructions for the Government of Armies in the Field: General Orders*, 1863; 1870–72 served on Mexican Claims Commission; died 1872.

85. Lieber, Columbia, South Carolina, to George Hilliard, Jan. 1850, in Thomas Perry (ed.), *The Life and Letters of Francis Lieber*, London 1882, p. 239.

debate over the 500th anniversary of 1492. What, of course, is entirely lacking is the nuance and complication of the Spanish religious identity – complexities that were on view in Spain itself at that time and took an even more compound form in the Americas. In this regard the English prejudice of Richard Ford is somewhat more revealing:

> It will be better to avoid all religious discussions whatever, on which the natives are very sensitive. There is too wide a gulf between, ever to be passed. Spaniards, who, like the Moslem, allow themselves great latitude in laughing at monks, priests and professors of religion, are very touchy as regards the articles of their creed; on these, therefore, beware of even sportive criticism; con el ojo y la fé, nunca me burlaré. The whole nation, in religious matters, is divided only into two classes – bigoted Romanists or infidels: there is no via media. The existence of the Bible is unknown to the vast majority, who, when convinced of the cheats put forth as religion, have nothing better to fall back on than infidelity. They have no means of knowing the truth; and even the better classes have not the *moral courage* to seek it; they are afraid to examine the subject – they anticipate an unsatisfactory result, and therefore leave it alone in dangerous indifferentism; and even with the most liberal – with those who believe everything except the Bible – the term *hereje* (heretic) still conveys an undefined feeling of horror and disgust that we tolerant Protestants cannot understand. A *Lutheran* they scarcely believe to have a soul, and almost think has a tail.[86]

Pius IX was the first Pope to have visited the New World, having been a member of the papal mission sent by Pius VII to the Río de la Plata and Chile in 1823 in an effort to reconcile Rome with the emerging American republics. The mission had little effect since a year later the new Pope Leo XII issued an encyclical, *Etsi iam diu*, offering fulsome support to the Spanish king and the American royalists just as they stood on the verge of defeat. As a result, the deep divisions of both clergy and hierarchy caused by fifteen years of conflict were compounded by a categorical political error on the part of the Pontiff. The severity of the rupture needs to be registered, even if only to demonstrate that traditions can endure when institutions undergo acute crises. The Spanish American Church lost up to half its secular clergy with a greater proportion of the orders leaving either the continent or their vows behind. By 1850 the largest national Church, that in Mexico, had only 3,320 secular clergy and 1,295 regulars – a total of 4,615 male religious – less than half the number of fifty years earlier and representing a ratio of under one per 1,000 souls. There were just under 2,000 female religious in fifty-eight convents.[87] The assets and income of this establishment have been estimated at $100 million – perhaps a quarter of the national economy – but much of this was shortly to be expropriated ('privatised' in the demotic of Thatcherism) by a resurgent liberalism that had, as elsewhere, raised a

---

86. Richard Ford, *A Handbook for Travellers in Spain*, London 1845, I, p. 68.

87. Jan Bazant, *Alienation of Church Wealth in Mexico*, Cambridge 1971, pp. 7–13. Payment of the tithe in Mexico was made voluntary – and fell substantially – in 1833, and subsequent Conservative governments made no attempt to restore it. 'The liberals used the Church as a source of revenue in accordance with political conviction, whereas their opponents did the same in spite of it.' Ibid., p. 5.

reformist voice that varied in intensity and degree of secularism but posed a much more resilient threat than the 'historioculturalist' account allows for.

In his survey of Ecuador, Colombia and Venezuela, Malcolm Deas finds the incomplete hold of the Church under the late colony further weakened following independence:

> In Venezuela as a whole the Church was not strong; its dioceses were not rich, and it had little hold on the *pardos* [people of mixed race], the slaves or the *libertos* [free blacks]. The missions in the east had been destroyed, and the more clerical western states carried as yet little weight in the nation's affairs. Most of rural Venezuela was not amenable to control through this institution. In New Granada too its strength was patchy: mestizo Colombia had given many colonial examples of hostility to the Church. Little of the hot country had been thoroughly catechized – Tolima, the Cauca valley, the Pacific and Atlantic coasts were never subject to the same degree of ecclesiastical control as the uplands of Boyacá, Cundinamarca and Pasto. Similar distinctions can be made within Ecuador.... Much is usually made of the domination of rural life by *hacendado* and priest, but such rhetoric has ignored the many areas where the power of both was weakened, had never existed, or was hedged about with many natural limitations.[88]

It might be thought that the sole exception to this pattern would be found in Cuba, where the Church was not only protected by the monarchy (and 40,000 troops) but also bolstered – at least temporarily – by clergy in enforced or voluntary exile from the mainland republics. Yet even if the island had eighty parishes – from the church pulpits of which slave sales were announced – the image of a renovated and resplendent Romanism could not be further from reality. Travellers found that although Cuba remained under European rule, the society of the island was quite distinct. In 1844 John Wurdemann reported,

> On the whole, there is more toleration of religious opinion here than in many European Catholic communities; certainly far more than in Germany and Ireland. No one can hold property or practise any of the professions without first acknowledging in writing that he is Apostolical, Roman Catholic; but those who have tender consciences leave out the middle term, and it is winked at. The term *judío*, Jew, is also applied to foreigners, including Spaniards, more in jest than derision, and without any particular reference to its sectarian application; and I have not met with as much inimical feeling in the Creoles towards Protestants as the sects of the latter manifest towards the Catholics in our northern states.[89]

In 1851, when US ambitions on Cuba were at an unprecedented peak – raising the distinct possibility of purchase or annexation – a similar account of insular religiosity was published by John Taylor in London:

> It is unnecessary perhaps to remind [my readers] that Cuba is, most strictly speaking, a Catholic country, though its being a country of Catholics may be apocryphal enough, for

---

88. 'Venezuala, Colombia and Ecuador: The First Half-Century of Independence', in Bethell (ed.), *Cambridge History of Latin America*, III, p. 515.

89. *Notes on Cuba*, Boston 1844, p. 165, quoted in Louis A. Pérez (ed.), *Slaves, Sugar and Colonial Society: Travel Accounts of Cuba, 1801–1899*, Wilmington, Del., 1992, p. 156.

I declare that during my whole residence I do not know of an instance of *men* going to church.... As for *fasts*, it is a most remarkable matter that in regard to the island of Cuba, the Pope every year regularly goes through the form of granting a general indulgence on that score to all its inhabitants; giving them free leave to eat meat during the whole of Lent, and on every Friday throughout the year. As I do not imagine it would be any way more difficult to keep a fast there than in Italy, I confess I am at a loss to account for His Holiness's kindness in any other way than by supposing he 'knows his neighbours' ways', and that in any case the 'olla' would be cooked. In the meantime the *Government* professes to be as strictly Roman Catholic as ever, and the Bible is rigorously interdicted at the Customs Houses.[90]

Richard Madden, who in the 1830s helped supervise the freeing in Havana of intercepted slaves and in the 1850s oversaw the Loan Fund Board in Dublin, could find on the Caribbean island only two estates where slaves could attend mass on a Sunday, and only one plantation which had a chaplain; this was no longer a 'priest-ridden society'.[91] At the end of the 1850s Anthony Trollope (who had also served the British state in Ireland) shared Madden's amazement at that eminently non-Protestant institution, the lottery – 'not ... an amusement but an occupation. The public lotteries offer the daily means to everyone for gratifying this passion.' As opposed to Mexico, where churches used them to raise income, the lottery in Cuba was a state monopoly, but it was not only because of this that Trollope considered 'Roman Catholic worship [to be] at a lower ebb in Cuba than almost anywhere else'.[92] He found degeneration from the popularity of cock-fighting – only outlawed in Britain in 1849 – to the comprehensive corruption of the colonial administration. As a consequence the novelist saw a Cuban future as lying with the United States:

> What love can [the Cuban] have for Spain? He cannot even have the poor pride of being slave to a great lord. He is the lacquey of a reduced gentleman, and lives on the rails of those who despise his master. Of course the transfer would be grateful to him.... The Havana will soon become as much American as New Orleans.[93]

And within the USA Trollope was no less confident that Catholicism would wither culturally and economically, but not physically:

> Surely one may declare as a fact that a Roman Catholic population can never hold its ground against one that is Protestant. I do not speak of numbers, for the Roman Catholics will increase and multiply, and stick by their religion, although their religion entails poverty and dependence; as they have done and still do in Ireland. But in progress and wealth the Romanists have always gone to the wall when the two have been made to compete together.[94]

In the republics of the isthmus Trollope found a different kind of society, but not one so ruptured as to be militantly secular or so traditional as to be truly pious:

---

90. *The United States and Cuba*, London 1851, pp. 294–7, quoted in ibid., pp. 163–4.
91. Richard Madden, *The Island of Cuba*, London 1849, p. 110.
92. Anthony Trollope, *The West Indies and the Spanish Main* (1860), London 1968, p. 154.
93. Ibid., pp. 140, 143.
94. Anthony Trollope, *North America* (1862), London 1987, I, p. 75.

I certainly should not say that the Costa Ricans are especially religious people. They are humdrum in this as in other respects, and have no enthusiasm either for or against the priesthood. Free-thinking is not the national sin; nor is fanaticism. They are all Roman Catholics, most probably without exception. Their fathers and mothers were so before them.[95]

In line with those of other Latin American republics, the constitution of Costa Rica – in this case that of 1847 – proclaimed, 'The State professes the Catholic, Apostolic, Roman Religion, the only true one; it protects the same by wise laws, and does not permit the public exercise of any other.'[96] And even if the private celebration of other creeds was indulged, the state – through the columns of *Mentor Costarricense* – was not above putting the case for a Catholicism of republican democracy, not monarchical tyranny:

> We are Catholics; and this is fully consonant with the democratic and republican opinions which we uphold. The dogma of Catholicism is assuredly that which forms the best type of citizen. Under the doctrines taught by the Christian religion the wise man is equally subject to the strictures of the faith as is he who is ignorant; the sophisticated just as the vulgar; the rich man must comply as does the poor.... If Catholicism requires the faithful to obey it does not prepare them for inequality.[97]

This might be thought to be stretching a point, and in Central America it was an equality of poverty that struck most Protestants. However, in the case of George Squier such a reality – in San Juan del Norte, Nicaragua in 1849 – produced not dismay but millennial imagery:

> We sauntered ... through the town, looking into the doorways, catching occasional glimpses of the domestic economy of the inhabitants, and admiring not a little the perfect equality and general good understanding which existed between the pigs, babies, dogs, cats and chickens. The pigs gravely took pieces of *tortillas* from the mouths of babies, and the babies as gravely took other pieces away from the pigs. B— observed that this was as near an approach to those millennial days when the lion and the lamb lie down together as we should probably live to see, and suggested that a particular 'note' should be made of it for the comfort of father Miller and the Second Advent Saints in general.[98]

Although he may have been overly influenced by comparison with Padre Cartine, the lone Franciscan clocksmith of León, Squier thought the Nicaraguan clergy both ill educated and highly influential in a nominally Catholic society where many in the

---

95. *West Indies and the Spanish Main*, pp. 281–2.
96. Article XXXVII, reprinted and translated in *BFSP, 1846–47*, XXXV, London 1860, p. 49. Article XVI of the Honduran constitution of 1848 stated,

> The religion of the state shall be the Christian, Catholic, Apostolic, Roman, the public exercise of every other being prohibited. Its high authorities shall protect it by wise laws; but neither these authorities nor any other shall interfere in any manner with the private exercise of other modes of worship.

In *BFSP, 1847–48*, XXXVI, London 1861, p. 1088.
97. No. 85, 2 April 1845, in *Mentor Costarricense 1842–46*, San José 1978.
98. E.G. Squier, *Nicaragua: Its People, Scenery, Monuments*, New York 1860, p. 31. William Miller died in 1849 whilst Squier was still in Nicaragua.

elite, including priests, had greater scepticism than faith. Yet, having met a volunteer schoolmistress who tells him that her payment would be in heaven, the Boston Methodist remarks, 'How little do the sectaries and bigots of our own country know of the devotion, and fervent, unselfish piety of many of those who they so unsparingly denounce as the impious monsters of a debased religion!'[99]

Squier could also be sure of an attentive audience back in Massachusetts for his observation about local habits that would be the envy of many New England social campaigners:

> The Spanish people, in all parts of the world, are temperate in their habits. Those in Nicaragua in this regard do not disrespect their progenitors. Strong liquors are little used except among the lower orders of the population ... I do not remember to have seen a single respectable citizen drunk during the whole of my residence in the country.[100]

However, as befits a diplomat, Squier is himself better at 'translating' cultural traits than at passing judgements. His account of the celebration of 4 July in Managua by US citizens in 1849 reveals a calm recognition of the equivalence of secular and religious celebration in a manner that would have shocked less liberal compatriots:

> We all breakfasted together, and drank patriotic toasts, and sang Yankee Doodle, and were altogether appropriately patriotic, to the great delectation of the quidnuncs of Managua, who gathered in crowds around the open doors and windows. They were properly instructed as to the nature of 'the day we celebrated' – that it was the great feast of St Jonathan, whereupon they hurrahed for the saint, and even proposed to ring the church bells in his honour.[101]

Sometimes, however, the experience of 'popular religion' was more shocking to visitors. The French-born non-Christian Flora Tristán was more than a little dismayed by a typically carnivalesque procession in Arequipa, Peru, the home town of her family:

> On 24 September there was a grand procession to celebrate the Feast of Our Lady of Ransom. This is the only sort of entertainment the people have, and it gives an idea of what the pagan bacchanals and saturnalia must have been. Even in the Dark Ages the Catholic Church never exposed such scandalous spectacles to the public gaze. The procession was headed by bands of musicians and dancers, all in the most ludicrous costumes: the Church hires negroes and *sambos* [persons of mixed negro and Indian blood] for a small sum to take part in this religious farce and dresses them up as pierrots, harlequins and clowns with crude coloured masks to cover their faces. There must have been forty or fifty of them, writhing and gesticulating in the most shameless and indecent fashion, arousing the excitement of the coloured women and negresses who lined the route and calling out obscenities to them. The women for their part tried to guess the identity of the dancers. This ugly rabble with its shouts and unrestrained laughter made me turn away in disgust. Then the Virgin appeared, magnificently dressed in velvet and pearls, with diamonds on her head, neck and hands. She

---

99. Ibid., p. 216.
100. Ibid., p. 255.
101. Ibid., pp. 207–8.

was carried by twenty or thirty negroes and behind her walked the Bishop and clergy. Next came the monks from all the monasteries, and the official part of the procession ended with the civic dignitaries, followed by a noisy surging mass of people whose minds were far removed from any thought of prayers. It is from these festivals, remarkable for their splendour, that the Peruvians derive their chief happiness, and I fear it will be a long time before their religion has any spiritual meaning for them.[102]

The young Ayrshire traveller Robert Dunlop was also being a bigot more of European than Protestant character when he reported of his 1846 travels in the region that one could not compare

> the degraded and childish superstition which at present exists in Central America with the Roman Catholic Church in Ireland, Germany or even Italy, which probably differs much less from the purest reformed Church than that of Central America does from them.[103]

However, in a striking description of the eruption of the Nicaraguan volcano of Cosiguina for three days in January 1835 Dunlop furnishes us with a clue as to why the local people were so devoted to the ceremonial, festivities and general recreational possibilities that even the most primitive religion allowed:

> The astonished people supposed that the day of judgement had come, and rushed to the churches, throwing themselves on the floors before the images of the saints; others confessed their sins and implored mercy; all was terror and dismay; and, to complete the horror of the scene, a terrific darkness, deeper than the most obscure night, continued for 43 hours.... During this time there were continued noises, louder than the most terrific peals of thunder, accompanied by lightnings, which played in all directions, rendering the darkness more terrible, and such immense quantities of ash fell as in some parts to cover the earth three feet deep.[104]

There are few volcanoes in Ayrshire or Massachusetts. All the same, everyone there dies eventually, and, as Squier reflects after observing the funeral of Bishop Desiderio de la Cuadra of León, it is simply that the 'American way of death' is distinct to that further south:

> In most instances the funeral ceremony has few of those gloomy accessories which our customs prescribe.... Theirs is a happier conception. Death mercifully relieves the infant from the sorrows and dangers of life; and withers the rose on the cheeks of youth that it may retain its bloom and fragrance in the more genial atmosphere of Heaven.[105]

---

102. Flora Tristán, *Peregrinations of a Pariah* (1838), London 1986, pp. 107–8.

103. *Travels in Central America: Being a Journal of Nearly Three Years' Residence in the Country*, London 1847, pp. 349–50. A decade later the North American William Wells reported of Nicaragua,

> Public holidays are artistically combined with religious ceremonies, the two being inseparable. At the celebration of certain saints' days and the observance of special rites of the Church one finds cockfights, bullfights, music, fairs, fireworks and dancing. It will be seen that all the diversions of the people, by being linked to submission to the Catholic faith, are powerful instruments in the hands of the clergy, who take advantage of the innate superstition of the race and the monopoly they have over education.

Exploraciones y Aventuras en Honduras, 1857, San José 1978, p. 55.

104. Dunlop, *Travels in Central America*, p. 16.

105. Squier, *Nicaragua*, p. 365.

This is not, of course, a static contrast, nor one exclusively between the two great European stands of Christianity. Waman Puma reports that when the Spanish arrived in Peru the local population believed that

> the dead go directly to Puquinapampa and Corapona. There they meet together and it is said that there is enjoyed much feasting and conversation between the dead men and the dead women; and that when they leave there they go to another place where they endure much work, hunger, thirst and cold, and when it is hot the heat is too great.[106]

Today, Olivia Harris tells us, centuries of Church insistence upon burial in consecrated ground, and campaigns against such idolatrous practices as mummifying and disinterring corpses for reburial in their own fields and hills, have produced an attitude amongst the Laymi of southern Bolivia in which

> the dead are viewed with a repugnance which is never fully transcended. The absence of monuments or shrines to the dead is perhaps an indication of their ambiguity ... they are unable to harness fully the potential power of the dead for the reproduction of their own society.[107]

Amongst the Choctaw of Mississippi there was great reluctance to speak one's own name or even that of close kin, but

> an even stricter taboo forbade them to name their dead. United States Commissioner Claiborne found in allocating land, that the only way in which parents could be induced to present claims for their deceased children was by asking them to arrange their families in line according to ages; they invariably left a vacancy where the deceased would have stood.[108]

Robert Dunlop would probably have found such a disposition more familiar than he did the management of the cemetery at Guatemala City, which, while less impressive than those in New Orleans – perforce built above ground because of the height of the water table – shares the qualities of design that make such an attraction for tourists from the 'Protestant North'.

> The principal burial ground is a square of about 300 yards, enclosed by thick stone walls 15 feet high; in the wall are some thousand niches, in which those who are interred in coffins are placed, the charge being $4 each; as soon as the niche is filled, the entrance is plastered up and the name and date written outside. These niches are calculated to be filled in six years' time, when the first filled will be opened, and gradually all the rest, the bones being thrown into square holes built on purpose at the four corners of the cemetery, to make room for new occupants; those, however, who can pay $20 are entitled to a piece of ground for a separate grave, which is not to be touched, and they may, if they choose, fence it in. Those who are too poor even to pay the $4 are interred in the ground in the centre, generally without coffins, but their bones will be dug up as soon as the ground is required again.[109]

106. *Nueva Corónica y buen gobierno* (1613), Paris 1936, p. 294, quoted in Olivia Harris, 'The Dead and the Devils among the Bolivian Laymi', in Maurice Bloch and Jonathan Parry (eds), *Death and the Regeneration of Life*, Cambridge 1982, p. 45.

107. Ibid., p. 49.

108. Angie Debo, *The Rise and Fall of the Choctaw Republic*, Norman, Okla., 1961, pp. 18–19.

109. Dunlop, *Travels in Central America*, p. 84.

On his trip up through Nicaragua and El Salvador Dunlop had been taking calomel for his fevers whilst treating the boils breaking out over his body with chalk and egg white. It was the fever that got him first – at the age of thirty-one on New Year's Day 1847 – a few weeks after he had written this description of what would be his own final resting place.

Neither the strangeness of the cultures into which it had insinuated itself nor the crises suffered after independence affected the Roman Catholic Church in Latin America so profoundly that it lost its traditional vocation. Whilst it may not have always been able to impose its writ, it capitulated nowhere and in some places retained considerable influence. In May 1850 *El Amigo del Pueblo*, published in Santiago de Chile by the young radical Francisco Bilbao, declared,

> The clerics ... possess an aristocratic outlook, and from this stems their determination to block anything that might assist the progress of the poor.... If they want to have the respect of the poor they must abandon their attitude of condescension, avarice and ambition. They should forget the comforts of the opulent life in order to re-engage with and attend to the miserable existence of the poor; they should offer words of comfort and hope, and not adopt execrable statements and scandalous positions; they should put aside their sumptuous silk garb and reduce the inflated expenditure incurred in an indolent life.

Bilbao, who had been influenced by 1848 and held positions quite close to those of European 'utopian socialism', 'defended the idea of a God of absolute liberty and the socialist character of the image of the realm of God whilst, on the other hand, he rejected a Catholicism which he saw as oppressive and terrorist, dedicated to the idea of blame and suffering'.[110]

It was for sentiments stronger than these – effectively the equation of Christianity and the Spanish empire with barbarism – that Bilbao had been charged with blasphemy in 1844, but the experience of persecution and exile had produced some moderation in his language at least. (It is perhaps telling that the sedition charges against him were dropped by the state whilst the Church accusations of heresy were upheld.)[111] In all events, Bilbao was certainly no match for the likes of Monseñor Joaquín Larraín Gandarillas, who, writing from Georgetown at the end of 1851, urged a stiffening of resolve to a supporter of the Chilean government, which was in the midst of suppressing a rare opposition revolt with great difficulty (and British assistance):

> Please do not fail to urge your friends in the cabinet to act as conservatives and as a government for that is what they are – a conservative government.... I expect our conservatives to take a lead and go on the offensive, and not to lose all the advantages that their position gives them.... They should both publicly and privately insist that socialism and communism

---

110. Miguel Salinas, 'La Iglesia Chilena ante el Surgimiento del Orden Neocolonial', in Enrique Dussel (ed.), *Historia General de la Iglesia en América Latina*, Salamanca 1994, IX, p. 315. The quotation from *El Amigo del Pueblo* (14 May 1850) is cited by Salinas on the same page.

111. On 15 December 1853 Lammenais wrote Bilbao a letter in markedly more forceful language: 'You can be certain that nothing can be expected of Spanish America whilst it remains under the yoke of a clergy soaked in the most revolting doctrines, whose ignorance is without limit, and who are both corrupt and corrupting.' Quoted in ibid., p. 314.

undermine the two bases of the social order – authority and property – and that they can only be defeated by religion.[112]

This, moreover, was quite moderate stuff when set alongside the response of the Arequipa priest Pedro Gual to requests for greater religious tolerance from the Peruvian hierarchy. Gual, like Larraín, saw the adoption of such an attitude as opening a path down which every stripe of 'anabaptist and insurrectionary' would beat their way into the southern Andes:

> ... the disciples of Luther and other reformers who give the most voluptuous example of sensuality, teaching that it is licit for the married man to obtain divorce, to abandon his wife and children and marry with as many others, successively or simultaneously, as he may wish.... There will enter into our Catholic nations the Egyptians, the Greeks, the Spartans, the Indians, the Chinese and other idolatrous people, who will build temples to all their detestable deities, in whose honour they will publicly make prostitutes of virgins, sacrifice men to the sun and women to the moon, and offer up the blood of innocent children taken out of their homes at the points of daggers.[113]

At the other end of the subcontinent Dr Basilio Zeceña had a month earlier preached an independence day sermon in the metropolitan cathedral of Guatemala City that likewise bemoaned the lack of government resolution in upholding 'Christian principles' since the end of the colony:

> ... they permitted immoral books, full of anarchical maxims, to circulate freely; and in the hands of the ignorant and hot-headed, but under-educated, youths this caused more harm to society than a sharpened dagger in the hand of the most insolent and daring assassin. They zealously propagated poorly understood ideas of liberty and equality, and carried them to the hut of the innocent shepherd, awakening in this way the powerful force that lay dormant in the arms of the peasants.[114]

The *Gaceta de Guatemala* had already stipulated the better path:

> A moral and religious education and a well-founded enlightenment are in our eyes the best things we can do for a people such as ours. To mark respect for constituted authority, the necessity of working to live, and the obligation of respecting the opinions of others are the surest means, although slow, of civilizing the ignorant masses. To preach to them constantly of liberty, equality etc. is to lead them to insurrection, and to give them arms that they will turn against us, making practical and positive the doctrines that we have carelessly taught them.[115]

In view of this, it is perhaps unsurprising that Hubert Bancroft could write so unreservedly of the death, in 1865, of Rafael Carrera, the caudillo who since 1838 had presided over Guatemala:

---

112. Larraín, Georgetown, 5 Dec. 1851, to José Hipólito Salas, quoted in ibid., p. 306.

113. *El Equilibrio entre las Dos Potestades*, Barcelona 1852, II, quoted in Frederick B. Pike, 'Heresy, Real and Alleged, in Peru: An Aspect of the Conservative–Liberal Struggle, 1830–1875', *HAHR*, 47:1, 1967, p. 66.

114. Quoted in R.L. Woodward, *Rafael Carrera and the Emergence of the Republic of Guatemala*, Athens, Ga., 1993, p. 260.

115. *Gaceta de Guatemala*, 21 Feb. 1850, quoted in ibid., p. 265.

Carrera died in the full conviction that he had been the instrument of providence in saving society and good order in Guatemala. He had been so assured by his supporters, and had come to believe it, in the face of the fact that he had been guilty of heinous crimes and was notoriously immoral. So die those who pass hence from the murderers' gallows under the banner of the cross, and with priestly consolation.[116]

For Bancroft, the concordat signed in Rome in October 1852 between Guatemala and the Vatican would have been repugnant enough on the basis of the titles allocated to the Central American signatory:

> Don Fernando de Lorenzana, Marquis of Belmonte, Knight of the Sacred Equestrian Order of Jerusalem of the Holy Sepulchre of our Lord Jesus Christ, Commander of the Pontifical Order of Saint Gregory the Great, of the military class, Knight Grand Cross of the same order, of the civil class, Commander of the Royal Order of Francis I of the Two Sicilies, and Minister Plenipotentiary of Guatemala to the Holy See....

But it was the meat of the agreement which really offended New England susceptibilities:

> Article I. The Catholic, Apostolic, Roman religion shall continue to be the religion of the Republic of Guatemala, and it shall always be maintained with all the rights and prerogatives which it ought to enjoy according to the law of God and the provisions of the sacred canons.
>   II ... all education will be according to Catholic doctrine, and nothing contrary is to be taught.... III. Bishops have the right of censorship over all books and writings relating to dogmas, ecclesiastical discipline or public morals, and will receive the support of the courts.... XXIII. His Holiness consents that the Bishops, Capitular Vicars and other ecclesiastics should [express the following form]: 'I swear and promise to God, upon the Holy Gospels, to obey and to be faithful to the Government established by the Constitution of the Republic of Guatemala, and I promise also not to mix myself personally, or by counsel, in any project that may be contrary to national independence or to public tranquillity.'[117]

For those, such as the Argentine Juan Bautista Alberdi, who were grappling with the dilemmas posed by the application to Catholic societies of models of political economy associated with Protestantism or by the challenge of establishing the rule of law in polities where *caudillismo* enjoyed popular support and international respect, Bancroft's certainties were simply insufficient, even for catharsis.

> 'God save me from believing that Catholicism is inadequate for liberty; it is my religion, that of my forefathers, of my people. But, yes, I do believe that it is not the only creed capable of favouring the development of human freedom, nor is the religious element the only foundation of civilization.... It is the first, and the most important, but it is not the only one.... England is happy because of her customs, because of the work ethic and the skills of her statesmen just as much as because of the religious education of the people ... the English family is not a monastery. Religion is an issue on Sunday, and for the six days of the week it is honest dedication to toil that prevails.... Let us be religious, let us be believers and Christians to be free; that is all very good. But not without remembering that we also need

116. *History of Central America, 1808–1887*, San Francisco 1882–87, 3 vols, III, p. 284.
117. *BFSP, 1855–56*, XLVI, London 1865, pp. 1077–82.

good public and private customs, of reserve and morality in family life, of the habit of hard work and development of the mind. Let us be Catholics, as our fathers were before us, and as befits our race; but not forgetting that there are also other *profoundly religious* peoples who are not Catholics.[118]

Alberdi, then, holds to an article of faith which the 'historioculturalists' believe is misguided, if not futile. Whilst he shares with them a recognition of faith as tradition, he also believes in change and development. This will come not from major religious transformation or secularisation *per se* but, rather, from emulating the secular habits of Northern Civilization. The main obstacle facing such a prospectus – the extraordinary historical power saturating popular culture and attitudes – is well illustrated by Alberdi himself as he expresses his feelings upon approaching the coast of Spain for the first time in May 1844:

> Spain, whatever your misdeeds towards us, you are our Mother. I want in this instant to wash from my soul all vestige of emnity, and to gaze upon the peaks of your mountains with the same eyes which my parents would have done so. Ha! When their eyes closed in the distant valleys of our continent you were their last thought of love and lost hope.[119]

For the more hard-headed – not just Lastarria but also Sarmiento – this was sentimentalism of the most dangerous stripe. It is true that Alberdi soon tired of Spain and became homesick for America, but he never disparaged Spain with the same facility displayed by Sarmiento, nor did he seek to tarry in the USA, which is where Sarmiento was when he gave vent to expressions of almost equal intensity:

> Why was it the Anglo-Saxon race that discovered this piece of the world which is so well suited to its industrial instincts, whilst South America, a land of gold and silver mines and gentle and submissive Indians, has fallen to the Spanish race – a region aptly suited to its proud laziness, its backwardness, and its industrial ineptitude? Is there not order and premeditation in all of these cases? Is there not Providence? Oh, my friend, God must be the explanation for these things![120]

The fact that it was very hard to catch Sarmiento in such proximity to a genuine religious sentiment was one criticism made of him and his understanding of Argentina by Esteban Echeverría, the true poet of this 'generation of '37' seemingly doomed to perpetual exile by Rosas. Echeverría recognised in Sarmiento's writing plenty of 'spiritual reflection' – there is religious imagery in abundance – but little 'dogma' (or programme), and for him, it seemed, religious questions elicited 'at best an ironic smile', which was a thoroughly misguided response when Rosas's sway depended upon the compliance of a mendacious clergy. Echeverría's own prescriptions for Argentina were a heady mix of maximalist idealism and celebration of platine custom

---

118. 'Examen de las Ideas del Señor Frías', *Obras Completas de J.B. Alberdi*, Buenos Aires 1886, III, p. 362.
119. Quoted in Jorge Mayer, *Alberdi y su Tiempo*, Buenos Aires 1963, p. 279.
120. Rockland (ed.), *Sarmiento's Travels in the United States*, pp. 118–19. It is worth reminding ourselves that Sarmiento was in the USA whilst it was conquering Mexico but before gold had been discovered in California.

and practice, but he was clear-sighted enough to ask his fellow-intellectuals to consider the position of the ordinary folk of Buenos Aires: 'What authority will morality have in their eyes if it lacks the divine seal of religious approval?'[121] This was also the view of Father Anthony Fahey, who in November 1849 wrote from Buenos Aires to the *Dublin Review* to protest at a 'libellous' article it had printed against Rosas:

> ...this upright magistrate, who extends so much and is so enlightened to all the inhabitants of the country – who has restored the reign of order, the splendour of the Catholic religion ... all that is stated in regard to supposed crime and assassinations of a Mazhorca society ... all that is said of the profanations of Churches and sanctuaries, and other suppositions of this stamp ... are but a tissue of contemptible falsehoods.[122]

Fahey was here struggling against the tide since, of all Rosas's acts, it was the execution of the pregnant Camila O'Gorman which was the most infamous.

It might be true that '*las ideas, señor, no tienen patria*' – as the Chilean statesman Manuel Montt told Sarmiento when he proved uncharacteristically reticent about writing in and about a country other than his own – but Echeverría baulked at the enthusiasm of his comrades to draw models from abroad, whether the USA or Europe:

> How important to us are the political and philosophical solutions reached in Europe when they have an objective entirely different from that which we seek? Do we, by any chance, live in that world? Would Guizot make a good minister if he were ensconced in the fortress of Buenos Aires?[123]

This was written in 1846, when the extent of the accumulating weaknesses of Guizot's administration in Paris was far from clear. None the less, Guizot's reputation abroad remained remarkably high even after the revolution of 1848. In large measure this was because of his historical and administrative writings prior to holding office. Yet even as late as 1851, when Guizot was secluded at Val Richer in political retirement – Echeverría having died in January of that year at the age of forty-five from *le mal du siècle*, tuberculosis – Alberdi did not hesitate to quote approvingly from a letter sent by the French dignitary to another Argentine, Ismael Frías:

> I believe ... that the principal, if not the exclusive, cause of our social troubles is to be found in the intimate state of the soul. Assuredly, of all the forms of society and government, the democratic form is the one that most requires firm beliefs and strict behaviour in order to subsist. A people that does not constantly look to God, and find him above it as well as within it, can neither govern itself nor, indeed, be governed.[124]

Were these lines not written by François Guizot, overthrown elderly European statesman, one might easily think them a classic expression of modern North American political morality.

---

121. 'Ojeada Retrospectiva' (1846), in *Dogma Socialista*, Buenos Aires 1915, pp. 45–6.
122. Fahey, Buenos Aires, to *Dublin Review*, 7 Nov. 1849, quoted in T. Murray, *The Story of the Irish in Argentina*, London 1919, pp. 129, 131.
123. Ibid., pp. 89–90.
124. Guizot, Val Richer, to Frías, 22 Aug. 1851, quoted in 'Examen de las Ideas del Señor Frías', p. 369.

CIVILISATIONS AND BARBARISMS

In 1846 – just as Echeverría was warning his compatriots off unquestioning obeisance to Guizot – Bohn's of Covent Garden published Hazlitt's translation of *The History of European Civilization* by Guizot, which had originally been issued in France in 1828. For Guizot Europe was distinct because of the pluralism of its inheritance, taking from Rome the tradition of the municipality/commune, from the Christian Church its recognition of moral law above human legislation (and so separation of spiritual and temporal powers), and from Germany the bond between warriors and leaders. The competition between and amalgamation of these practices, ideas and institutions took place over a period of 'historioculturalist' dimensions – five or six hundred years – and was largely resolved at the end of the eighteenth century through 'the struggle between absolute temporal power and absolute spiritual power'.[125] Guizot's survey exercised a strong influence over Tocqueville, John Stuart Mill and Marx, who had, of course, been expelled from France by him and so must have felt doubly attracted by the idea that the scholar from Nîmes represented one of the highest expressions of bourgeois decay.[126] In Guizot's view civilisation could not simply be gauged by material progress or even social development; it had also to embrace 'the development ... of man himself ... internal and moral development' – a position which, as we have just seen, he, a Protestant educated in Geneva, continued to uphold over twenty years later.[127]

Such an approach – adopted when industrial development to any significant degree was confined to Great Britain – enabled Guizot to search for the constituent features of civilisation across a wide range of variables. Thus, in his first lecture – the book is a collection of fourteen – he sets up four models, all of which retain a recognisable application over 170 years later: an aristocratic republic where physical life is very comfortable but intellectual and moral development tightly suppressed; a tough but endurable economic regime in which moral and spiritual views are cultivated but individual liberty stifled; a high degree of individual liberty but an equally great incidence of disorder and social inequality with the strong prevailing in a general

---

125. François Guizot, *The History of Civilization in Europe* (1828), Harmondsworth 1997, pp. 244–5.

126. Guizot appears in the third line of the *Communist Manifesto*, menaced by the 'spectre of communism', immediately behind the Pope, the Tsar and Metternich. In March 1852 Marx wrote to Joseph Weydemeyer in New York that his critics should first read 'the historical works of Thierry, Guizot, John Wade and others ... [to] acquaint themselves with the fundamentals of political economy'. In 1894 Engels wrote to a correspondent in Breslau that, 'while Marx discovered the materialist conception of history, Thierry, Miguet, Guizot and all the English historians up to 1850 are evidence that it was being striven for'. *Marx–Engels: Selected Correspondence*, Moscow 1975, pp. 63, 442. In was in his capacity as minister of the interior that, on 25 January 1845, Guizot ordered Marx to quit France within twenty-four hours. Although there was now a railway to Brussels, the Red Prussian contrived not to leave the country until 2 February.

127. *History of Civilization in Europe*, p. 245.

climate of aggression; finally, great individual liberty, low and transient inequality, low economic development and a marginal sense of community, which does not progress from generation to generation. None of these models corresponds, in Guizot's view, to civilisation, but Europe had passed through them at some stage since the fall of the Roman Empire, and one could find strong features of these permutations of liberty, equality and material welfare still persisting in Asia and Africa (America is not mentioned in this connection).[128] If anything, Guizot's lectures – which closed with the French Revolution but offered Latin American readers a modern alternative to the classical canon that had held sway under the colony – were a disincentive to emulation and promoted only the most general of models.

Two years later, in 1830–31, another set of lectures were delivered, by G.W.F. Hegel in Berlin, on 'The Philosophy of History'. Hegel, now at the end of his life, had given a preliminary version of these ideas nearly a decade earlier, and the series remains consistent with the character of his mature thought, in which a primacy is given to the state as an expression of collective freedom. Like Guizot, Hegel was a Protestant, but unlike the French thinker's major work, Hegel's devotes some attention – based on very thin reading – to the Americas. Some of these lines are worth quoting if only to indicate that many of the sentiments of the travellers cited here were close to those of one of the greatest and most influential minds of the age even if most of them preferred to describe in concrete detail rather than analyse in the abstract the *Volksgeiste* (spirit of peoples), understood as the manifestation of an animating principle of collectivities in their religion, science, art, morals, and so on:

I will not deny the New World the honour of having emerged from the sea at the world's formation contemporaneously with the Old; yet the archipelago between South America and Asia shows a physical immaturity.... Of America and its grade of civilization, especially in Mexico and Peru, we have information, but it imports nothing more than that this culture was an entirely national one, which must expire as soon as Spirit approaches it. America has always shown itself physically and psychically powerless, and still shows itself so. For the aborigines, after the landing of the Europeans in America, gradually vanished at the breath of European activity. In the United States of North America all the citizens are of European descent, with whom the old inhabitants could not amalgamate, but were driven back. The aborigines have certainly adopted some arts and usages from the Europeans, among others that of brandy-drinking, which has operated with deadly effect. In the South the natives were treated with much greater violence, and employed in hard labours to which their strength was by no means competent.... A wild and passionless disposition, want of spirit, and a crouching submissiveness towards the Creole, and still more towards a European, are the chief characteristics of the native Americans ... the inferiority of these individuals in all respects, even in regard to size, is very manifest: only the quite southern races in Patagonia are more vigorous in their nature, but still abiding in their natural condition of rudeness and barbarism.... America is therefore the land of the future, where, in the ages that lie before us, the burden of the World's History shall reveal itself – perhaps in a contest between North and South America. It is a land of desire for all those who are weary of the historical lumber-room of Old Europe. Napoleon is reported to have said: 'Cette vieille Europe

128. Ibid., pp. 15–16.

m'ennuie.' It is for America to abandon the ground on which hitherto the History of the
World has developed itself. What *has* taken place in the New World up to the present time
is only an echo of the Old World – an expression of a foreign life; and as a Land of the
Future, it has no interest for us here, for, as regards *History*, our concern must be with that
which has been and that which is.[129]

As Ortega y Gasset observed a century later, this is a bitter-sweet message.[130] America
is pre-historical; coeval with Europe in terms of its natural origins but physically
immature and in social terms amounting to nothing more than a pale reflection of
the old other. The only elements that are indigenous or autochthonous are barbaric
and doomed to expire in the face of mimetic Europeanism. Yet America, for all the
absence of an independent past and present, can be the future, can be itself in the
future. This message and method would be retrieved and energetically considered
from the mid twentieth century by thinkers such as Leopoldo Zea and Edmundo
O'Gorman.[131] But even today it requires an absolute elision of history and philosophy
– a requirement that the truths of the latter are set by the circumstances of the former
– and in the mid nineteenth century, on the interface of romanticism and positivism,
such a dialectical idealism could not find a distinctive voice. What, however, was not
absent amongst the embattled intellectuals of the South was a disposition to overcome
the past, either by denouncing it as barbarism or by recognising it as history – as a
valid precursor to present change and so the start of the future.

Discussing the word 'civilisation', Guizot noted,

> It is common sense which gives to words their ordinary signification, and common sense is
> the characteristic of humanity. The ordinary signification of a word is found by gradual
> progress, and in the constant presence of facts; so that when a fact presents itself which
> seems to come within the meaning of a known term, and it is received into it, as it were,

---

129. G.W.F. Hegel, *The Philosophy of History* (1831), New York 1899, pp. 81, 86–7.

130. José Ortega y Gasset, 'Hegel y América' (1928), in *El Espectador: VII–VIII*, Madrid 1972, p. 33.
Writing in 1949 in response to Arnold Toynbee's *Study of History*, Ortega gave full expression to his
Hegelian vocation:

> differing radically from Toynbee, you will remember that I have left present-day America outside
> our consideration because in my judgement it represents a historic phenomenon completely apart
> from our civilization and one which demands being treated by itself. I think that America, North,
> Central and South, is a human fact still intellectually virgin, on which *no single basic word* with any
> real meaning has yet been said; or, what is the same thing, that it is an immense and most original
> human reality, which, precisely because it is so original, so different from the others, has not yet
> been either seen or made clear.

An Interpretation of Universal History, New York 1975, p. 141.

131. For O'Gorman,

> It was the Spanish part of the invention of America that liberated Western Man from the fetters of
> a prison-like conception of his physical world, and it was the English part that liberated him from
> subordination to a European-centred conception of the historical world. In these two great liberations
> lies the hidden and true significance of American history … since the spiritual being with which
> America was endowed … consists in the possibility of becoming another Europe, it follows that,
> in its essence, the history of America is the way in which that possibility has been actualized.

Invention of America, Bloomington, Ind., 1961, pp. 145, 141. Leopoldo Zea, *The Latin American Mind*,
Norman, Okla., 1963.

naturally ... scientific definitions are, in general, much more narrow, and, hence, much less accurate, much less true, at bottom, than the popular meanings of the terms.[132]

Domingo Faustino Sarmiento had great sympathy with this sentiment, finding formal definitions most unsatisfactory:

> Salva's dictionary – the Academy's is not always accurate any more – defines the word 'civilization' as 'that degree of culture which nations or persons acquire when they pass from primitivism to the beauty, elegance and sweetness of voice and manner appropriate to a cultivated people'. I would call this 'civility'. For neither an affected way of speaking nor extremely delicate manners represent moral and physical perfection or the abilities which a civilized man develops in order to subject nature to his desires.[133]

However, when dealing with barbarism, which was his principal concern, the challenge was harder still, precisely because it entailed dealing with a different language – for the ancient Greeks the *barbaroi* were those who could not speak their tongue – a language in which 'common sense' is fundamentally alien to the likes of Guizot and Sarmiento. Perhaps it is for this reason that throughout his life Sarmiento made greater recourse to images of dress and animal behaviour than to reported speech in an effort to symbolise this force. At the age of seventy-three he recounted in a speech how an experience as a youth of fifteen had marked him for life:

> I was a merchant in 1826 when I first went to Chile. I was standing in the doorway of my store across the street from what today is, as if by Providence, the Sarmiento School of San Juan ... watching six hundred men arrive at the neighbouring barracks ... with the triumphant air that dust and intoxication can give. What a sight! They were riding spirited steeds, taken from artificial meadows. In order to shelter themselves on the plains from the rough brush [*chaparral*] they used the enormous chaps of the region consisting of two tough protectors of rawhide for keeping legs and even the head safe from the two-headed, dartlike thorns. The noise produced by this apparatus is impressive, and much of the contact and collision evoke the sound of shields and weapons in contact. The spirited horses, perhaps more domesticated than their riders, were frightened by these noises and strange encounters. On the unpaved streets, we spectators watched a dense cloud of dust advance, pregnant with muttering, yelling and cursing, and laughing; here and there dusty faces appeared between tangles of hair and rags, looking almost bodiless because of the wide chaps, as if cherubs or half-centaur devils. This is my version of the road to Damascus, of liberty and civilization. All the ills of my country suddenly became evident: Barbarism![134]

Some forty years earlier Sarmiento had introduced a very similar motif into the first chapter of *Facundo*. First he quotes from Scott's *Life of Napoleon*:

> 'The vast plains of Buenos Ayres', he says, 'are inhabited only by Christian savages known as Guachos' (gauchos, he should have said), 'whose furniture is chiefly composed of horses' skulls, whose food is raw beef and water, and whose favourite pastime is running horses to

---

132. *History of Civilization in Europe*, pp. 14–15.
133. Rockland (ed.), *Sarmiento's Travels in the United States*, p. 133.
134. 'En los Andes (Chile)', speech of 8 April 1884, *Obras Completas*, XXII, Buenos Aires 1956, p. 238 cited in Natalio R. Botana, 'Sarmiento and Political Order', in Tulio Halperín Donghi, Iván Jaksic, Gwen Kirkpatrick and Francine Masiello (eds), *Sarmiento: Author of a Nation*, Berkeley 1994, pp. 103–4.

death. Unfortunately', adds the good foreigner, 'they prefer their national independence to
our cottons and muslins'. It would be well to ask England to say at a venture how many
yards of linen and pieces of muslin she would give to own these plains of Buenos Ayres!

Two pages later one feels that Sarmiento would gladly have flogged off the pampa for
a roll of calico:

> The inhabitants of the city wear European dress, live in a civilized manner, and possess laws,
> ideas of progress, means of instruction, some municipal organization, regular forms of govern-
> ment etc. Beyond the precinct of the city everything assumes a new aspect; the country
> people wear a different dress, which I will call American, as it is common to all the peoples;
> their habits of life are different, their wants peculiar and limited. The people comprising
> these two distinct forms of society do not seem to belong to the same nation. Moreover, the
> countryman, far from seeking to imitate the customs of the city, rejects with disdain its
> luxury and refinement; and it is unsafe for city people to use their dress, their jackets, their
> cloaks, saddles, or anything European, in the countryside. Everything which the city contains
> that is civilized is blockaded in there, proscribed beyond its limits, and anyone who might
> dare to appear in the rural districts wearing a frock-coat or mounted on an English saddle
> would provoke ridicule and brutal assault from the country people.[135]

Many students of *Facundo* have pointed out that Sarmiento's fascination with the
countryside and nature as a whole encloses a much deeper sense of ambivalence than
suggested by the blunt dichotomy here. Alberdi – who lived in Buenos Aires from the
age of fourteen but had spent his childhood in provincial Tucumán – pointed out that
agriculture in the platine region comprised a great deal more than stock-raising, even
if pastoralism still outstripped crop-raising, and that it was the gaucho who not only
funded the capacity of the city to buy into its trans-continental identity but also
underwrote the economic capacity of the Rosas regime, which was not upheld
exclusively by repression.[136]

But one doesn't have to be an epigone of Raymond Williams – whose own
analysis of the urban–pastoralist polarity is, in fact, sartorially rather modest – to
recognise that Sarmiento is on to something.[137] Here, in *Recuerdos de Provincia*, he is
describing his colonial ancestor Doña Antonia Albarracín a couple of paragraphs after

---

135. *Facundo*, pp. 12, 14. My reference here is to Mrs Mann's 1868 translation, which dispenses with the
traditional title, although I have amended it somewhat. The corresponding pages in Roberto Yahni's Madrid
edition of 1990 are 65, 66–7.

136. *La Barbarie Histórica de Sarmiento* (1862), Buenos Aires 1964. Kristin Ruggiero reports a joke told to
her by a 'gringo' of Italian descent in an Entre Rios village in the 1980s:

> One day in the Chaco a gringo moved into an estancia next door to a creole. Next day the gringo
> went to introduce himself. The creole asked him what he was going to do there, and he replied that
> he was going to grow wheat. The creole declared that nothing would come of it. The gringo
> couldn't understand this because an agronomist had assured him that wheat would grow there, so
> he said, 'Oh well, I'll grow corn.' 'Corn doesn't grow here either,' said the creole. 'Well, I'll grow
> cotton then,' replied the gringo, undaunted. 'Cotton doesn't grow here either,' said the creole.
> Exasperated, the gringo despaired, 'But I was told if I planted–' 'Oh,' said the creole with sudden
> understanding, 'if you're going to *plant!*'

'The Legacy of Civilization and Barbarism', in Criscenti (ed.), *Sarmiento and His Argentina*, p. 186.

137. In *The Country and the City*, London 1973, Williams draws a chapter title, 'Nature's Threads', from
Cowper's *Yardley Oak* (1791):

vilifying Rosas for having executed the eight-month pregnant Camila O'Gorman 'like a dog'. The effect – whether deliberately designed or less consciously achieved – is to contrast the 'brutal savagism' of Rosas (the 'heir of the Spanish inquisition in his persecution of learned men and foreigners') with the domestic quietude and opulence of the San Juan aristocracy of a now distant era:

> At dinner time, an orchestra of violins and harps, composed of six slaves, played sonatas for the delight of her guests. And at night two slave-girls first prepared [Doña Antonio's] bed with a silver bed-warmer, perfuming the rooms, and then proceeded to undress their mistress of the rich skirts of brocade, damask or melanie which she wore at home.... On high days her person was adorned with rich fabrics embroidered with gold – now preserved in the chasubles of Santa Lucía – and covered with clouds of Dutch lace, with which she wore enormous topaz drop-earrings, a coral choker, a rosary of aventurines, precious stones of coffee and gold separated into groups of ten by golden lemons twisted into spirals as big as eggs.[138]

The colours paraded before us are yellow through green and blue (the two colours of the Unitarian opposition to Rosas) to brown (aventurine is a gold-spangled brownish glass). There is very little red. Red was the colour of Rosas, Federalism and the *mazorca*, the vigilante arm and secret police of the regime:

> The Argentine colours are blue and white; the clear sky of a fair day, and the bright light of the disk of the sun: 'peace and justice for all.' ... But now, in the very heart of the Republic, the colour red appears on the national banners, in the dress of the soldiers, and in the cockade which every native Argentine must wear under pain of death ... until the last century it was the custom in all the countries of Europe for the executioners to be dressed in red ... red is the symbol of violence, blood and barbarism.[139]

Echeverría's powerful novella *El Matadero* (The Slaughter-House) is understandably dominated by red, but it is not the only colour and it is not present simply as the colour of blood. Floods have deprived Buenos Aires of a supply of red meat for over a fortnight. The impact on one of the world's most fiercely carnivorous societies is acute: 'some doctors declared that if the absence of meat continued half the population

---

Nature's threads,
Fine, passing thought, e'en in her coarsest works,
Delight in agitation, yet sustain
The force that agitates, not unimpaired,
But worn by frequent impulse, to the cause
Of their best tone their dissolution owe.

This verse is persuasively presented as a brief, transformative break in a poem of melancholy custom – 'an intermediate reflection, which seems to catch the dialectic of just the change that was being widely experienced' (ibid., p. 71). One would not, however, have to make great strides – in terms of either Cockney slang or simile – to read these lines directly in terms of fabric and costume without displacing the same sense. This was the year in which the frock-coat began to replace cut-away tails for men, and the large 'Gainsborough' hat for women was, so to speak, eclipsed. In 1795 Pitt slapped a tax on hair-powder, thereby promoting a tonsorial revolution even as he laboured mightily to smother a political one.

138. *Recuerdos de Provincia* (1850), Buenos Aires 1952, pp. 42, 44. My attention was drawn to this passage by Tulio Halperín Donghi, 'Sarmiento's Place', in Halperín Donghi et al. (eds), *Sarmiento: Author of a Nation*, p. 24.

139. *Facundo*, pp. 137–9.

would suffer fainting fits because their stomachs were so accustomed to its juices'. However, the shortage also raises doubts about the abilities of the Rosas regime, and it challenges the authority of the Church, which has refused to lift the Lenten ban on meat,

> which starts a kind of intestinal war between the stomachs and the consciences, stirred up by uncontainable appetite and the no less uncontainable admonitions of the clerics ... to which one had to add the state of the intestinal flatulence of the inhabitants produced by fish, vegetables and other foods they were not able fully to digest.[140]

Echeverría's text is shown to be truly visceral in its invective against the lower orders of *porteño* society when a herd of steers is finally driven to the abbatoir and killed amidst a huge crowd that (literally) bays for blood, tears apart the carcasses, and smothers itself in the offal and juices of the dead and dying animals, heedless of the death of a child in their midst. Many – if not most – of the participants are black or mulatto, Echeverría's fear and loathing of the masses manifesting a strong racist strand, albeit one of a markedly urban character to complement Sarmiento's equally animalised Indian half-castes of the countryside.[141] However, black is also a feature of this pungent short story in that the mob is able to identify a passing rider as a Unitarian by virtue of the fact that he wears no badge of mourning for Encarnación Ezcurra, Rosas's wife, who died on 19 October 1838 and for whom the nation was ordered into formal mourning for two years. (The rider also lacks a red cockade and a moustache to accompany his beard – two other clear signals of political and cultural opposition.) Young and proud, the horseman stands his ground and answers the taunts of the crowd, asserting his aristocratic principles and returning the insults. The previous detailed scenes of gleeful disembowelling set the reader up for a dreadful end, but it is a mark of both Echeverría's skill and his appreciation of the complex realities of the town from which he was shortly to be banished for life that he resists the obvious closure. Although the crowd demands death, this is an almost automatic response to the *rosista* slogan which identified the very aristocratic proponents of civilisation as savages themselves: '*Mueran los salvajes unitarios!*' Moreover, a judge who is present tries to contain the popular bloodlust and cultivate some political theatre out of the scene through ritualised interrogation and denigration. The prisoner, however, refuses to buckle physically or mentally, and suffers a haemorrhage which is caused as much by his noble fury as by the wounds inflicted by his captors.

When John Brabazon, born in Mullingar, County Westmeath, arrived at Buenos Aires at the age of eighteen a few months after the start of the Famine in December 1845 he had to learn quickly how to negotiate this tough, alien society. However, the upset he suffered on his first night was neither so unusual nor so particular to that place as to merit more than disingenuous remembrance:

---

140. *El Matadero* (1838), Madrid 1995, p. 95.
141. In 1838 the total population of Buenos Aires was 62,228, of whom roughly a quarter (14,932) were 'black' (either '*pardos*' or '*morenos*') and 4,000 were 'foreigners'.

That night a friend, who was young, invited me to the theatre, but instead took me to a house of ill-repute, where I found myself surrounded by girls. And since my friend had disappeared, leaving me alone, and I didn't know how to speak Spanish, I began to panic. I gave them all the money I had on me, not knowing how much it was really worth because it was my brother Tom who had changed the little that I had brought from Ireland.[142]

Early on Brabazon himself does a stint in the *matadero*:

I had to be at my post at dawn, before the skinners and tanners arrived. My job consisted of taking off in a cart the guts and other refuse – something that was very unpleasant because quite often the waste would flow over the sides of the wagon, being as slippery as mercury.[143]

Eventually, like many of the settlers from Westmeath, he sets up to raise sheep near Chascomús. It was an exceptionally demanding life, interrupted by roving bands of soldiers, deserters and bandits – for whom all foreigners were good targets but the 'English' particularly so – and the fierce forces of nature, which Sarmiento imagined in such detail and with which the shepherd is far less associated than is the gaucho/ cowboy. Brabazon is a European, and so forms part of Alberdi's rescue-package of immigration for Argentine civilisation – 'to govern is to populate' – but the Irishman is neither educated nor a town-dweller and so forms part of Sarmiento's 'barbarism'. He liked to watch Rosas's troops parade on Sundays (although he found the infantry poorly shod), and in describing the clothes he wore to a dance at Arroyo Chico in January 1848 he leads us through a wardrobe of almost completely barbarian costume:

On that occasion I wore my fine riding boots, a pair of pants without any adornment, a *chiripá* with a wide fringe which reached to my knees; a belt with silver buttons (which the creoles call *tirados*) and a pampa strip, which is another belt that one uses beneath the *tirados*, with pretty tassles; a red shirt with a black collar and sleeves. I also had two beautiful silk handkerchiefs, one around my neck and the other around the buttons. We had a most agreeable evening during which I gave to a handsome lass who danced with me the hand- kerchief which had been a present from my sister Jane, which was embroidered with my name, and which I told her she could keep until we danced again, and so she would not forget me.[144]

We learn nothing more about this memento or its effects, but Brabazon married Honor MacDonnell in 1851. The next year, whilst he was taking her family to Buenos Aires for protection from the effects of the fighting at Los Caseros, where Rosas was finally defeated and overthrown, he faced the greatest threat to his life. This was posed by fleeing Federal troops, who halted the small group and demanded civilian clothing in which to make their getaway.

---

142. Eduardo A. Coghlan, *Andanzas de un Irlandés en el Campo Porteño (1845–1864)*, Buenos Aires 1981, pp. 15–16.

143. Ibid., p. 37.

144. Ibid., p. 68. *Chiripá* derives from the Quechua *chiripac* ('for the cold') and is a broad, poncho-like garment drawn between the legs to form loose knee-length trousers – a kind of heavy version of the Indian *khadi*.

I climbed up on to the wagon and began to show them our things and also to offer them some women's petticoats, saying that this was all that we had. One of these individuals then lost his temper and said that he was going to cut the 'Englishman's' throat because we were mocking them by offering female clothes. The others, though, said that they should leave 'the Englishman' alone.[145]

So healthy is the present appetite for transvestism in certain sophisticated academic circles that one almost feels tempted to ruminate over whether Brabazon was indulging an extravagant and risky cross-dressing fantasy, but I suspect that if he isn't embellishing a tale with the safety of hindsight, he was a naturally jocund (and lucky) individual in a bit of a fix. Sarmiento, who followed the army that won the day at Caseros in a uniform of his own design, might have appreciated Brabazon's gesture. Alberdi, who admitted to a feminine character and who had edited *Modas*, a fashion magazine for women, until it was closed in 1838 by Rosas for promoting European styles, would have done so with much greater energy. Indeed, in September 1845 Alberdi had taken on a rare criminal case in Santiago that involved some female impersonation:

> Señor Manuel Cifuentes, member of Congress and resident of Campañillas, had been attacked in his bedroom and killed by machete blows to the head. It was quickly discovered that at the time he had been in the company of Carmen Peña, a former sweetheart whom he had abandoned, when her father, José Pastor Peña, effected entry dressed as a woman in order to demand reparation. The nature of the event, the status of the victim, and the fact that Carmen was expecting a child by the said Cifuentes all generated great popular interest. The dead man's family appointed Gabriel Ocampo as their attorney, and Mariano Sarratea designated as defence lawyer Dr Alberdi, a young jurist, full of vivacity and movement in his writings, very capable of defending a case with enthusiasm and zeal.... Alberdi soon recognised the difficulties of the case and sought the assistance of José Barrios Pazos and Manuel Carvallo. The case, so passionate and full of incident, was attended by an immense public. In order to swing public opinion in favour of Carmen Peña Alberdi arranged to have her publish an open letter and for José Pastor Peña to issue a defence entitled 'My Deeds and their Causes', in which he recounted the intimate details of the drama – 'a page of George Sand set in Chile' – a most unusual ploy which enfuriated the judge. In court Alberdi focused on the relations between Cifuentes and Carmen, explaining Peña's attack in terms of his feelings as a father. 'This is an act of honour, well or badly understood, with or without title; it is love in itself; it is the heart of a father torn asunder for the modesty of a beloved daughter.' He presented an original analysis of the social causes of the crime and the feelings of the protagonists, although Lastarria described the defence as romantic, 'because he didn't smell of snuff or wear a wig or toga'. But Peña's background was bad, and his disguise, the wounds to the back of Cifuentes' head, and the social commotion stirred up all proved to be insuperable obstacles. The judge of the case and then the appeal court absolved Carmen but condemned José Pastor to the death penalty.[146]

There is a touch of Robert Holmes's 'go-for-broke' approach in Alberdi's tactics in and out of court here, but it is hard to see how he could have defended barbaric acts

---

145. Ibid., p. 121.
146. Mayer, *Alberdi y su Tiempo*, p. 329. Thoreau, whom Emerson described as 'the bachelor of thought and nature', once remarked, 'They say that there is a *Lady's Companion* that pays, but I could not write anything companionable.' William Condry, *Thoreau*, New York 1954, p. 38.

other than by seeking to explain them in other terms. This was something that he had been obliged to relearn when he arrived in Chile and was sent by the Bulnes government to serve as secretary to the Intendant of Concepción, a place that shocked him to the core:

> As of yesterday I am sad, terribly sad. Nothing, nothing consoles me. This provincialism suffocates me; every affectation, every misunderstanding, everything retrograde and opposed to my ideas. Accent, behaviour, conversation, all of it bores me.... Why do you live badly? Why is your house dirty and untidy? Why do you eat badly? Why are you slothful, ignorant and small-minded? Is the government really responsible for this? Does it stop you having decent inns, comfortable lodgings? Who stops you doing good?[147]

As might be deduced from the prominent self-interested elements of this outburst, Alberdi was back in the capital within weeks. Yet, alongside his implacable idealism (and the disappointment that tracked so tightly in its wake) Alberdi possessed a droll comprehension of the popular mind. This is, perhaps, nowhere better captured than in his response to the anecdote used by Sarmiento to open *Facundo* (in all but the English edition):

> Towards the end of 1840 I left my native land, banished in shame, crippled, covered in bruises, wounds and blows received the day before in one of those bloody orgies staged by the soldiery and the *mazorca*. Upon passing by the baths of Zonda, upon the coat of arms of the fatherland which in happier days I had painted in a salon, I wrote in charcoal these words: '*On ne tue point les idées*'. Upon hearing of this, the government sent a commission to decipher the hieroglyphics, which had been reported to contain ignoble outbursts, insults and threats. When they were given the translation, they said, 'Well, what does it mean?'[148]

Maybe, as Jaime Concha has suggested, Sarmiento was saying, 'they have not killed my ideas', and this, in turn, was longhand for 'they have not killed me'.[149] But for Alberdi the critical issue is the answer to the government's question:

> On his way into exile, when passing by the baths of Zonda, he took the opportunity of a rest to register his protest. On a sign, beneath the coat of arms, he wrote, '*On ne tue point les idées*', words that wakened deep suspicion until a humorous amanuensis decoded the enigma and translated the graffito: 'One day I'll get my own back, you Sons of Bitches!'[150]

Apocryphal or not, Alberdi's version flushes out the Sarmiento whom he had come to see as little more than another caudillo-in-the-guise-of-civiliser. Alberdi did not pursue his feud with Sarmiento purely out of personal animus but because he was appalled when Sarmiento turned against Urquiza, treating the man who had over-thrown Rosas as no better than the original tyrant. Likewise, when Sarmiento, now as president himself in the 1860s, had the provincial warlord El Chacho executed as a

---

147. Mayer, *Alberdi y su Tiempo*, p. 318.
148. *Facundo*, Madrid 1990, pp. 35–6.
149. 'On the Threshold of *Facundo*', in Halperín Donghi et al. (eds), *Sarmiento: Author of a Nation*, pp. 146–8.
150. Mayer, *Alberdi y su Tiempo*, p. 303.

criminal, Alberdi protested that this was a convenient and flimsy excuse for a political assassination: 'For Sarmiento terror is a means of government – not just that of [Facundo] Quiroga and Rosas, but of every government. This is a gross and dangerous sophism, especially in a young country.'[151] Here Alberdi not only reveals the manipulation that can easily be made of the civilisation–barbarism polarity by those convinced that they incarnate the former. He also replaces the dichotomy with a continuum and suggests, at least for his own day, a zone of some equivalence. In Alberdi's view Sarmiento cannot distinguish between society and government, and this difference was huge even though he believed that the form of government would only change fundamentally with social transformation. The age of conquest had long since passed; civilisation was no longer about forcibly suppressing barbarism.[152]

When president in the 1860s, Sarmiento charged Colonel Lucio Mansilla with 'pacifying' the Ranquel people. This was a task that Mansilla – who had family ties with Rosas, who had recently witnessed terrible scenes in the Paraguayan war, and who loathed what he called 'civilisation without mercy' – sought to accomplish by negotiation and treaty. However, his counterpart, the chief Mariano Rosas, was understandably suspicious of the terms of any deal, not least because, as Mansilla wryly recounts, the political arrangements of the republic were quite different to those of the tribe:

'Tell me, brother', he asked me, 'what's the name of the president?'
'Domingo Faustino Sarmiento.'
'Is he a friend of yours?'
'He's a close friend.'
'And what if you should stop being friends – what would happen to the peaces that you've signed with us?'
'Well now, brother, nothing. Because I am unable to fight with the president, even if he were to punish me. I am only a poor colonel, and it is my duty to be obedient. The president has much power; he commands the whole army. Anyway, if I go away another commander will be sent, and he will have to do what General Arredondo says, just as I do.'
'And this Arredondo, is he a friend of the president?'
'A very good friend.'
'More of a friend than you are?'
'I can't say, brother, because, as you know, friendship is something that you can test but cannot measure.'
'Tell me, brother, what is the constitution called?'
At this point I knew that I had really lost the script. But if the president could be called Domingo Faustino Sarmiento why, for this barbarian, should the constitution not also be called by another name? Still, I was flummoxed.
'The constitution, brother … the constitution … is just called that, you see, the constitution.'
'So it doesn't have another name?'
'That's its name.'

---

151. 'Facundo y su Biografía', p. 116, quoted in Celina Lacay, *Sarmiento y la Formación de la Ideología de la Clase Dominante*, Buenos Aires 1986, p. 16.
152. 'Acción de Europa en América', *El Mercurio*, Santiago, 10 Aug. 1845, in *Obras Completas*, III, Buenos Aires 1886, pp. 83–4.

'So, it only has one name and the president has two?'

'Yes.'

'Is the constitution good or bad?'

'Brother, some say it's good, others that it's bad.'

'Is the constitution your friend?'

'Of course, a very close friend.'

Perhaps, in the light of experiences such as this, it is unsurprising that Mansilla's reflections on civilisation echo those of Thoreau as much as Alberdi's:

> Civilisation consists – if I am going to give a precise picture of it – in a number of things. In using detachable collars, which are the most economical, wearing patent shoes and kidskin gloves; in that there are many doctors and many patients, many lawyers and many lawsuits, many soldiers and many wars, many rich people and many poor people. Under civilisation many newspapers are published and many lies circulate; many buildings are constructed with many rooms and few comforts. The government is made up of many people – the president, ministers, members of congress – and governs as little as possible. Under civilisation there are a great many hotels, and they're all bad, all very expensive.[153]

In the 1840s Sarmiento did not, in fact, make an explicit case for civilisation through the military conquest of barbarism, but in his eyes this was scarcely necessary since nature would anyway take its course:

> There is no possible amalgam between a savage and a civilised people. Wherever the latter sets its foot, deliberately or otherwise, the former is obliged to surrender land and its existence; and sooner or later it has to disappear from the face of the earth.[154]

Such an argument might be seen as more persuasive for Anglo America than for the South, where 350 years of coexistence between Indians and Europeans would appear to require more qualification (unless, of course, one does not consider the Spanish and Portuguese civilised). British commentators were more inclined to seek gradations and qualifications. For John Parish Robertson, who spent four years in Paraguay under the severe rule of Dr Francia, 'America, when first discovered, was peopled by savages, in the common acceptance of that phrase; though savages, I allow, with various grades of removal from absolute barbarism.'[155] Similarly, Sir Arthur

---

153. Lucio Mansilla, *Una Excursión a los Indios Ranqueles* (1870), Mexico 1947, pp. 213, 48. Later Mansilla was prevailed upon to become the godfather of the daughter of Mariano Rosas:

> The little girl was dressed in her best and most luxurious clothes, a beautifully tailored work of brocade with gold and jewel decorations that seemed exceptionally fine. Instead of shoes, she wore catskin riding boots. Civilization and barbarism were hand-in-hand. But what dress was this? Where did it come from? Who had made it? ... The sleeves were in the style of Mary Stuart. This didn't come from the backlands.... Curiosity overcame my sense of apprehensive repugnance and I asked disingenuously, 'Where did my *compadre* find this dress?' 'Oh', he said ... 'this is the dress of the Virgin of the town of La Paz ... we took it on one of our raids and gave it to the general.'

Ibid., p. 333. I owe this reference to Malcolm Deas, who has a peerless eye for such matters, and who recalled the incident the instant I mentioned the small matter of clothing.

154. *Obras Completas*, II, Buenos Aires 1948, p. 218.

155. *Letters on Paraguay*, I, London 1839, p. 187.

Helps thought that 'The Indians, if they have not been highly civilized, have at least been somewhat Christianized'.[156]

By the mid nineteenth century the social categorisation of Colombia by its elite was manifesting the influence of economic liberalism, which tended to modify by expansion the 'natural' dichotomies inherited from the colony:

> The first division was between the 'savage' (for the most part forest Indians) and the 'civilized', which included sedentary Indians and Afro-Colombians as well as Europeans and mestizos. The 'civilised', in turn, were divided into those who lived 'decently', in terms of housing and clothing, and worked hard in order to obtain such '*comodidades*', and those who were satisfied with survival at a lower level of material consumption and could not be induced to undertake systematic work. By and large, as elite writers saw it, the white and mestizo populations fell into the category of the meritoriously working and consuming, while Indians and Afro-Colombians in general revealed their deficient 'civilisation' by being content with low levels of material consumption.[157]

For some, such as the engineer and pioneering geographer Colonel Agustín Codazzi, subscription to ideas of racial predestination went against 'the justice of God and the unity of the human family'. On the other hand, in his report from the province of Tunja in 1851, Manuel Anzícar was able to glimpse a future republican prosperity through miscegenation:

> ... the indigenous race forms the smaller number of inhabitants, it being admirable how rapidly it was crossed with and been absorbed by the European, since half a century ago the province of Tunja presented a compact mass of Indians and very few Spanish families. Today one notes in the new generation the progressive improvement of the castes: the children are white, blond, of fine and intelligent features and better built bodies than their elders.[158]

As the influence of 'racial thinking', like that of Gobineau, began to converge with ideas of progress and science, the notion of 'in-betweenness' took on a more assertively biologised form, at least in the South.

In the North, where the balance between the races was entirely different and where inter-racial intimacy was so infrequent as to be aberrant, the only serious options under consideration by the political elite were behavioural transformation or apartheid-through-relocation. That did not, however, erase all dilemmas and doubt as to identity and the nature of providence or progress. Some features of this are captured brilliantly by Herman Melville in his depiction of the 'in-betweenness' of Queequeg in *Moby-Dick*, as recounted by Ishmael:

> Upon waking next morning about daylight, I found Queequeg's arm thrown over me in the most loving and affectionate manner. You had almost thought I had been his wife. The counterpane was of patchwork, full of odd little parti-colored squares and triangles; and this

---

156. *The Spanish Conquest in America* (1855), London 1904, p. 299.

157. Frank Safford, 'Race, Integration, and Progress: Elite Attitudes and the Indian in Colombia, 1750–1870', *HAHR*, 71:1, 1991, p. 24.

158. *Peregrinación de Alpha por las provincias del Norte de la Nueva Granada en 1850–51*, Bogotá 1956, p. 342, quoted in ibid., p. 28.

arm of his tattooed all over with an interminable Cretan labyrinth of a figure ... looked for all the world like a strip of that same patchwork quilt. Indeed, partly lying on it as the arm did when I first awoke, I could hardly tell it from the quilt, they so blended their hues together; and it was only by the sense of weight and pressure that I could tell that Queequeg was hugging me.... I lay only alive to the comical predicament. For though I tried to move his arm – unlock his bridegroom clasp – yet, sleeping as he was, he still hugged me tightly, as though naught but death should part us twain.... When, at least, his mind seemed made up touching the character of his bedfellow, and he became, as it were, reconciled to the fact; he jumped out upon the floor, and by certain signs and sounds gave me to understand that, if it pleased me, he would dress first and then leave me to dress afterwards, having the whole apartment to myself. Thinks I, Queequeg, under the circumstances, this is a very civilized overture; but, the truth is, these savages have an innate sense of delicacy, say what you will; it is marvellous how essentially polite they are.... Queequeg, do you see, was a creature in the transition state – neither caterpillar nor butterfly. He was just enough civilized to show off his outlandishness in the strangest possible manner. His education was not completed. He was an undergraduate. If he had not been a small degree civilized, he probably would not have troubled himself with boots at all; but then, if he had not been still a savage, he never would have dreamt of getting under the bed to put them on.[159]

Melville provokes laughter here, I feel, in order to dissipate the anxiety of his reader, rather than that of the author himself, who neither suppresses the sexual subtext nor – with years as a sailor and experience in the South Seas – would need to, except to protect the squeamish sensibilities of a New England audience that he was finding it hard to hold. Yet Melville can only offer understanding – a most tender understanding – of the 'other', and no effort is enough to transform this understanding into salvation. As C.L.R. James argues,

> Queequeg is a distinguished personality. But he is a savage, a cannibal. If in addition to his grand physique, his skillful work, and his noble character, he were a civilized human being, then there would be some hope for the world which Melville sends to its doom. But splendid as he is, the primitive Queequeg cannot save society.[160]

Here, as for Alberdi, civilisation is the future and it is for those who have the means of 'getting there'. In a novel this is doubly imagined; in the present case it takes the voice of resignation, not only because Queequeg will die but also because all the crew of the *Pequod* – bar the narrator – must do so. In the same vein, it says much that the sole reference to the work of Karl Marx to be found in Emerson's writings is a copied quotation from an article in the *New York Daily Tribune*: 'The classes and races too weak to master the new conditions of life must give way.' Before this Emerson writes, 'Fate.'[161]

---

159. *Moby-Dick, or The Whale* (1851), Harmondsworth 1992, pp. 28–31.

160. 'The American Intellectuals of the Nineteenth Century', in *American Civilization* (1950), London 1993, p. 74. Perhaps because he was partly writing this text in order to evade deportation from the USA at one of the most miserable moments of the Cold War, the ex-Trotskyist James uses 'safer' passages from Melville than the one I have quoted to illustrate a similar point. It didn't help, and he was soon on his way to Brixton.

161. Lewis Feuer, 'Ralph Waldo Emerson's Reference to Karl Marx', *New England Quarterly*, 33, Sept. 1960, pp. 378–9. The original article, 'Forced Emigration', was published on 22 March 1853.

Resignation is, nevertheless, quite distinct from the advocacy of civilisation as the future, which, although based upon a projection, is a vehicle for the fiercest type of politics: that which pretends it is nature. To some, both North and South, such a choice between the nature of the past and that of the future seemed very harsh. Even if in his letters to George Squier, Francis Parkman was content to refer to Nicaragua as 'the land of El Vomito', to its inhabitants as 'greasers', and to life there as 'unpalatable to the best stomached antiquarian', he resented having to jump one way or another.[162] In a review of the novels of James Fenimore Cooper, Parkman is unconvinced by that author's depiction of Indians, whom he sees as being so softened as to become 'superficial ... falsely drawn'. Leatherstocking, by contrast, Parkman finds thoroughly compelling:

> There is something admirably felicitous in the conception of this hybrid of civilization and barbarism, in whom uprightness, kindliness, innate philosophy, and the truest moral perceptions are joined with the wandering instincts and hatred of restraint which stamp the Indian or the bedouin.

None the less, in assigning meaning to Leatherstocking, Parkman comes to accept that he himself is composing a threnody:

> Civilization has a destroying as well as a creating power. It is exterminating the buffalo and the Indian, over whose fate too many lamentations, real or affected, have been sounded for us to renew them here. It must ... eventually sweep from before it a class of men, its own precursors and pioneers, so remarkable both in their virtues and their faults, that few will see their extinction without regret.[163]

Yet once one moves beyond heroic hybridity to the heart of North American Indian society even these caveats are set aside, almost every shade of opinion concurring that the laws of nature were at work. Stated in the unapologetic language of De Bow's Review, the Indian's 'race is run, and probably he has performed his earthly mission. He is gradually disappearing, to give place to a higher order of beings. The order of nature must have its course.'[164] Thirty years before this, in a report to Secretary of War John C. Calhoun, Rev. Jedidiah Morse had insisted that the Indians were

> an intelligent and noble part of our race, and capable of high moral and intellectual improvement.... They are a race who on every correct principle ought to be saved from extinction, if it be possible to save them.... It is too late to say that the Indians cannot be civilized [even

---

162. Parkman, Boston, to Squier, 13 May 1849; 15 Oct. 1849; 6 Sept. 1850, in W.R. Jacobs (ed.), *Letters of Francis Parkman*, I, Norman, Okla., 1960, pp. 60, 64, 75. In fairness to Parkman, it should be noted that 'el vómito' was the contemporary term for yellow fever in Latin America, but one senses that Parkman enjoyed the *double entendre*.

163. *North American Review*, LXXIV, 1852, pp. 147–61, quoted in R.H. Pearce, *The Savages of America: A Study of the Indian and the Idea of Civilization*, Baltimore 1965, p. 208.

164. *De Bow's Review*, XVI, Feb. 1854, pp. 147–8, quoted in Alden T. Vaughan, 'From White Man to Redskin: Changing Anglo-American Perceptions of the American Indian', *AHR*, 87, 1982, p. 953.

if] the work of educating and changing the manners and habits of nearly half a million Indians, as they are now situated, is acknowledged to be great and arduous and appalling.[165]

However, by the 1840s the Indians were being treated unambiguously as a different race, and after the experience of removal their 'extinction' was seen less as physical elimination than as the obliteration of a distinct social and cultural identity – as social death. What Morse, the devout and devoted Congregationalist, had viewed as an unavoidable challenge was now seen as beyond the agency of individuals and in the hands of uncontainable forces. Even Thoreau, for whom the kind of sentiments espoused by *De Bow's Review* were usually repellent, and for whom Indian society was fascinating precisely because of its closeness to nature, was in line on this matter:

> For the Indian there is no safety but in the plow. If he would not be pushed into the Pacific he must seize hold of the plow-tail and let go his bow and arrow, his fish-spear and his rifle. This is the only Christianity that will save him! The Indian, perchance, has not made up his mind to some things which the white man has consented to; he has not, in all respects, stooped so low; and hence, though he loves food and warmth, he draws his tattered blanket about him and follows his fathers rather than barter his birthright. He dies, and no doubt his Genius judges well for him. But he is not worsted in the fight; he is not destroyed. He emigrates beyond the Pacific to more spacious and happier hunting grounds.[166]

Thoreau here goes beyond Parkman by recognising that the Indians did have a degree of choice in defeat and social death; they are not unaware of their destiny. David Levin comments on a similar effort by the Transcendentalist historian George Bancroft to square the troubling circle of conflicting laws of nature in order to be able to have a secure view of historical progress:

> Arguing that the Indian had never had a right to his lands would have denied him the rights of Nature, denied that the 'gifts of mind and heart' were universally diffused, and denied the unity of the [human] race. At the same time, the destinarian method gave the historian the same sentimental advantages enjoyed by dramatists and historical romances. He could now sympathise with both sides. The Indian could be the heroic child of Nature destined to death or exile in the cause of human freedom; serving history by touching the reader's heart.[167]

In this Bancroft is joined – in pithier manner – by Parkman, but not, in my view, by Thoreau, who on a personal level strenuously avoided all romance once he had been rejected by Ellen Sewall. Moreover – in romantic terms – it proves hard to think of him acquiescing in such metaphysical expediency when one knows that the only intelligible words of the last sentence he spoke were 'Indian' and 'moose'.[168] Dickens,

---

165. Quoted in Francis Paul Prucha, *The Great Father: The United States Government and the American Indians*, Lincoln, Nebr., 1984, pp. 155–7.

166. Undated journal entry quoted in Robert F. Sayre, *Thoreau and the American Indians*, Princeton 1977, p. 21.

167. Levin, *History as Romantic Art*, p. 131.

168. Robert D. Richardson, *Henry Thoreau: A Life of the Mind*, Berkeley 1986, pp. 57–62, 389; Condry, *Thoreau*, pp. 26, 108. In the same spirit as the above sentence, I note that in the week it was written there was published in the *Guardian* a column by Bill Condry in which, some 43 years after his book on Thoreau

who was sensible of almost all routes to the reader's heart (and who admitted that he would be a Transcendentalist if he lived in Boston), needed only to read the Indian signatures on the treaties kept at Harrisburg in order to draw conclusions as disconsolate as Thoreau's:

> I was very much interested in looking over a number of treaties made from time to time with the poor Indians, signed by the different chiefs at the period of their ratification, and preserved in the office of the Secretary of the Commonwealth. These signatures, traced of course by their own hands, are rough drawings of the creatures or weapons they were called after. Thus, the Great Turtle makes a crooked pen-and-ink outline of a great turtle; the Buffalo sketches a buffalo; the War Hatchet sets a rough image of that weapon for his mark.... I could not but think – as I looked at these feeble and tremulous productions of hands which could draw the longest arrow to the head in a stout elk-horn bow, or split a bead or feather with a rifle-ball – of Crabbe's musings over the Parish Register, and the irregular scratches made with a pen, by men who would plough a lengthy furrow straight from end to end. Nor could I help bestowing many sorrowful thoughts upon the simple warriors whose hands and hearts were set there, in all truth and honesty, and who learned in course of time from white men how to break their faith, and quibble out of forms and bonds.[169]

(and the last of his own life), he resolutely upheld the Thoreauvian tradition for a 'post-industrial' Britain:

> *Machynlleth*. Chiffchaffs and willow warblers were singing in the leafing birches and the year's first redstart showed himself beautifully on a hawthorn spray as we walked past the ruins of the old slate quarry. Decades have passed since this moorland quarry closed, and what was an industrial scar has healed as the huge heaps of waste slate have been partly clothed with trees.... Next month parts of the wood will be coloured with carpets of bluebells, and white with the flowers of wild garlic. But though the valley, with its paths and footbridges, is a walker's paradise, a question mark hangs over it because its oakwood, not protected by any conservation body, is up for sale. The hope is that the Woodland Trust will be able to raise enough money to save it from all threat of exploitation. So if you feel moved to help it keep the philistines away, please send a donation.

Guardian, 19 April 1997. As Condry points out, Thoreau left his shanty on Walden Pond, which is now a nature reserve, in September 1847 without sentiment – then or later, when the shed was used to store tools and the bean-patch grown over.

169. *American Notes for General Circulation* (1842), Harmondsworth 1985, p. 189. In their useful notes to the *Notes* John Whitley and Arnold Goodman provide a succinct explanation of Transcendentalism, within the ranks of which we can number not only Emerson and Thoreau but also William Henry Channing and William Ellery Channing, Margaret Fuller, Bronson Alcott and Orestes Brownson:

> In reaction against eighteenth-century rationalism, the Transcendentalists turned to Kant, who, in *The Critique of Pure Reason* (1781), declared that the 'transcendental' knowledge in the mind of men was innate. This was translated as meaning that intuition surpassed reason as a guide to the truth. The immanence of God coexisted in the universe and the individual, whose mind was a microcosm of the Oversoul of the universe. From this followed the Transcendental belief in self-reliance and optimistic individualism.

Ibid., p. 338. It is, though, worth noting that Thoreau never read Kant or Hegel, and he was only familiar with Guizot's study of Washington – not that of European civilisation – whilst he consumed everything written by his early mentor Emerson, including the 1842 essay 'The Transcendentalist':

> It is well known to most of my audience that the Idealism of the present day acquired the name of Transcendental from the use of that term by Immanuel Kant, of Konigsberg, who replied to the skeptical philosophy of Locke, which insisted that there was nothing in the intellect which was not previously in the experience of the senses, by showing that there was a very important class of ideas or imperative forms which do not come from experience, but through which experience was acquired; these were the intuitions of the mind itself.

Although, as has been seen, the treaties were quickly reinterpreted, extensively manipulated and openly broken, they are not best seen as the product of some conspiratorial 'trick'. Their white authors may have subscribed more faithfully to the spirit of their missionary assumptions than to the letter of the detailed stipulations, but breaking the latter was as much a function of changing conditions as it was of any prepared ambush. Thus, in November 1844 Secretary of War William Wilkins could report to the president on the Indians in terms of a positive confluence of white supremacism and Indian moral evolution:

> In the course of the progress under our moral enterprise for their civilization, they must eventually attain the sagacity to look out for individual and social rights, and that degree of general intelligence to entitle them to the full extension of all the privileges of American citizens. When that time shall arrive, there will be no obstacle to political association by reason of any natural or acquired repugnance to the blood of the original American.[170]

A year later Wilkins's successor, William Marcy, felt obliged to identify differences between the tribes, noting that the recent annexation of Texas brought Washington much closer to the Comanches:

> These Indians in their habits and character are unlike those who dwell on our borders or within our territories. They are fierce and warlike, have no fixed abodes, are generally mounted on horseback and habituated to plunder; they annually rove over a large extent of country, make fearful incursions into the settlements within their range; and regardless of life, frequently add murder to rapine. The fear of chastisement is the best, if not the only reliable security for their good conduct.[171]

In his next report, by contrast, Marcy stressed both sides of the argument for separatism and relocation. A treaty 'under negotiation' with the Winnebagos, he promised,

> will entirely free Iowa from an Indian population, and open for unobstructed setlement and cultivation a large extent of valuable country fast coming into demand.... The removal thence to their new homes will free our citizens in that State from a fruitful source of annoyance, and the Indians from the bad influences incident to the proximity to a white population.[172]

Four months before Marcy's confident projections Peter Wilson, a member of the Cayuga tribe – now reduced to less than a dozen families – gave an impassioned address to the New York Historical Society in which he reminded his audience of the origins of the present expansionist confidence:

Ralph Waldo Emerson, *Selected Essays*, Harmondsworth 1982, p. 246; Robert Sattelmeyer, *Thoreau's Reading*, Princeton 1988.

    170. Wilkins, Washington, to Pres. William Harrison, 30 Nov. 1844, in *BFSP, 1844–45*, XXXIII, London 1859, p. 171.

    171. Marcy, Washington, to Pres. James Polk, 29 Nov. 1845, in *BFSP, 1845–46*, XXXIV, London 1860, p. 175.

    172. Marcy, Washington, to Polk, 5 Dec. 1846, in *BFSP, 1846–47*, XXXV, p. 109.

The Empire State, as you love to call it, was once laced by our trails from Albany to Buffalo – trails that we had trod for centuries – trails worn so deep by the feet of the Iroquois that they became your roads of travel, as your possessions gradually eat into those of my people.... Have we, the first holders of this prosperous region, no longer a share in your history? Glad were your fathers to sit upon the threshold of the Long House. Had our forefathers spurned you from it, when the French were thundering from the opposite to get a passage through and drive you into the sea, whatever has been the fate of other Indians, the Iroquois might still have been a nation, and I, instead of pleading here for the privilege of living within your borders, I might have had a country.[173]

RACE, CUSTOM AND DIFFERENCE

The existence of slavery placed all blacks in a significantly different relationship to both 'whiteness' and 'civilisation' to that held by Indians. Although as individuals they might have been in a better condition than the 'civilised tribes', free blacks were still tied by their race to a state of bondage. (Indeed, up to the Civil War the leaders of the Cherokee, Chickasaw, Choctaw and Creek nations themselves held slaves.) We will look later at the arguments around this in greater detail, but it is here worth registering the distinctive positions of the two great 'race questions' of the nineteenth century that subsequently became elided. However strong sentiment within the white population was concerning the Indians, this never matched that felt, expressed and given political voice – on both sides – with regard to slavery. At this stage there were only slight community links between Indians and blacks, as a result of removal, very tight social control over the 85 per cent of blacks (3.2 million) who were enslaved, the sheer imbalance in numbers (roughly 3.6 million blacks to 300,000 Indians), and the dispersion of accultured Indians and fugitive slaves. If for many outsiders the fate of the Indian peoples of the Americas was sadly predestined, that of North American civilisation and the black population was less predictable but likely to be even more tragic. Arthur Helps saw slavery as qualitatively worse than the conquest of the Indians, which was 'a page of [Spain's] eventful history to which every Spaniard may with just pride refer, as evincing a provident humanity which great nations in later ages have so often failed to imitate'. By contrast,

> The world still has, and long will have reason, to deplore that ... the entrance into America of the civilized inhabitants of Europe should have been accompanied by the introduction of a subject race from another continent, whose enforced presence has since proved a dire obstacle to the maintenance of concord and to the general growth of civilization.[174]

---

173. Quoted in L.H. Morgan, *League of the Hodensaunec or Iroquois*, New York 1901, pp. 104–5, cited in Wayne Moquin and Charles Van Doren, *Great Documents in American Indian History*, New York 1995, p. 159.
174. Helps, *Spanish Conquest in America*, pp. 301–2.

At some variance with the views he expressed in *Facundo*, Sarmiento regretted the fate of the 'extraordinary, instinctive' Indians of the North at the hands of the 'INDIAN HATER', but he devoted much more space to explaining that

> everyone today is afraid that this colossus of a civilization, so complete and so vast, may die in the convulsions which will attend the emancipation of the Negro race, a menacing possibility and yet as foreign to American civilization in its essence as it would be foreign to the laws of the universe if one of those thousands of comets that wander through space should crash against our planet some day and make it explode ... slavery in the United States today is quite without a solution. There are four million Negroes and within twenty years there will be eight. Redeem them? Who will pay the $1,000 million they are worth? Free them? What can be done with this black race that is hated by the white race? ... Today slavery is supported by doctrine because it has been made the soul of the society which exploits it.... There will be a racial war within a century, a war of extermination, or a black, backward and vile nation alongside a white one, the most powerful and cultivated one on earth.[175]

Even after the outbreak of the Civil War Anthony Trollope neither saw nor was disposed to see the merits and possibilities of the abolition of slavery, and he was writing late in 1861, some four years before the introduction of the 13th Amendment to the Constitution on 18 December 1865 that emancipated all slaves:

> As a rule, the men of the north are not abolitionists. It is quite certain that they were not so before secession began. They hate slavery as we in England hate it; but they are aware, as also we are, that the disposition of four million black men and women forms a question which cannot be solved by the chivalry of any modern Orlando. The property vested in these four million slaves forms the entire wealth of the South. If they could be wafted by a philanthropic breeze back to the shores of Africa – a breeze of which the philanthropy would certainly not be appreciated by those so wafted – the South would be a wilderness.[176]

Nineteenth-century attitudes to race are, of course, very different to those of the turn of the twenty-first century. What today is deemed retrograde racism and so effectively banned from public expression in many societies was very often associated with a reflective and 'scientific' appraisal of human progress. But this should not be taken as meaning that – including or excluding the question of slavery – recognition of race was unproblematic or discussion of it uncontroversial within dominant white Atlantic society, especially in terms of its being a constituent of civilisation. In scholarly circles the debate over whether the British were really Teutons or Celts was well established, would long continue, and had a clear application to notions of 'American Civilisation'.[177] This was also a period when Madame de Stael's celebrated division of Europe into Latin clarity and Germanic obscurity had yet to be displaced by less culturalist, more biological, theses although few long-range theories of descent pretended to more than symbolic authority. Despite years of exile in the USA, the

---

175. Rockland (ed.), *Sarmiento's Travels in the United States*, pp. 190, 273, 304–6.
176. *North America*, I, pp. 169–70.
177. Charles Beard, *The Rise of American Civilization*, New York 1942.

hero of the Venezuelan independence war, General José Antonio Paez, never lost the habit of that time in calling the Spaniards 'Goths'.[178]

The Chilean historian Benjamín Vicuña Mackenna gave vent to a similar complaint when he noted that 'the Saxon race was unanimous in its insolent contempt for the peoples of Latin origin, the contempt of the Vandal in the presence of the Roman, but alas! a bent and senile Roman'.[179] Vicuña was one of many thousands of Chileans who made their way to California after 1848, and this barbed comment reflects his experience there in 1853. Vicente Pérez Rosales, an authentic '49er' who went north to make his fortune, recounts an experience that seems to have been quite common in the early days of the Gold Rush:

> I was with my friend, Gillespie, under the shade of a pine tree near the ruins of Sutter's Fort when we heard yells coming from a man who was being held on top of a wagon. I thought I recognized the voice, and I jumped up in alarm and called to Gillespie, 'They are killing a friend of mine. We must run over there and save him.' Luckily we got there in time. I can still see poor Alvarez with the noose around his neck and the attached rope thrown over the branch of the tree, and with his feet tied to the cart which was ready to be driven away. He was going to be drawn and quartered! I was thought to be a Frenchman in California, and I knew the name of Lafayette was venerated by even the most uncouth American. So I invoked that magical name and declared Alvarez was the only protector the French had in Chile, that he had even saved my life, and that I would vouch for his honesty. My friend nodded emphatically to everything I said, and the hand of God intervened: Alvarez was lowered from the gallows. The reason for this quick and barbaric justice was the character of our countryman: he was always getting his nose in everywhere. I do not know what he was doing with that group of men headed for the mines; but a shovel was lost, and as there were no other aliens among them but this 'descendant of Africans', as the Yankees called the Chileans and the Spaniards, they accused him of the theft. Without any further ado the barbarians became the jury. They were ready to do what they normally do to thieves. For five days the poor fellow was out of his mind and in the grip of convulsions and stupor. Once he recovered he left us, and I never heard of him again.[180]

---

178. R.B. Cunninghame Graham, *José Antonio Paez*, London 1929, p. 75. One gets some sense of why the general might have been content not to 'update' his vocabulary or world-view from a description of a visit he made to Philadelphia in October 1850:

> Paez and his companions toured the gingham mills, examined the machinery, drank 'Twenty Dollar Champagne (the best in the country)' and were tendered a speech by Joseph R. Chandler, the city's representative in Congress, which, not surprisingly, named Paez as the 'Washington of the South'. The General, whose English was rudimentary at best, appeared much affected. Mr Brown, involved in the Venezuelan importation of dry and fancy goods, possibly had an eye on the future and Paez's return to the helm of his misguided country. Upon their return [to the city], the visitors went to see the Eastern State Penitentiary in Brown's coaches and visited a Masonic Lodge. The evening wound up at Mr Riché's in Clinton Street and the heroic recipient of Philadelphian hospitality left next morning at nine. Unfortunately, the General had forgotten to say goodbye to two of his principal hosts, who were also left with a bill for $40 worth of public music, the authorities having neglected to provide for it and afterwards refusing to do so.

Francis James Dallett, 'Paez in Philadelphia', *HAHR*, 40:1, 1960, pp. 101–2.

179. *Páginas de mi Diario Durante Tres Años de Viaje*, Santiago 1856, quoted in De Onis, *The US Seen by Spanish American Writers*, p. 146. Vicuña Mackenna had been exiled by Montt for his participation in the uprising of 1851.

180. 'Viaje a California: Recuerdos de 1848, 1849, 1850', *Revista Chilena*, 10, 1878, translated in Edwin Beilharz and Carlos López (eds), *We Were 49ers! Chilean Accounts of the Californian Gold Rush*, Pasadena 1976, pp. 63–4.

It was not only the 'alien' targets of such actions who construed them as barbarian. The following year Bayard Taylor – later to be US ambassador to Germany – described a group of California-bound passengers on a riverboat at Lafayette City (every relation) in terms that scarcely celebrated their civilisation:

> Our deck became populous with tall, gaunt Mississipians and Arkansans, Missouri squatters who had pulled up their stakes yet another time, and an ominous number of professed gamblers. All were going to seek their fortunes in California, but few had any definite idea of the country or the voyage to be made before reaching it. There were among them some new varieties of the American – long, loosely-jointed men, with large hands and limbs which would still be awkward, whatever the fashion of their clothes. Their faces were lengthened, deeply sallow, overhung by struggling locks of straight black hair, and wore an expression of settled melancholy. The corners of their mouths curved downwards, the upper lip drawn slightly over the under one, giving to the lower part of the face that cast of destructiveness peculiar to the Indian. These men chewed tobacco at a ruinous rate, and spent their time either in dozing at full length on the deck or going into the fore-cabin for 'drinks'. Each of them carried arms enough for a small company and breathed defiance to all foreigners.[181]

In such circumstances quite who constituted a 'foreigner' must often have been a whimsical calculation, for even in 1850 it was possible to make the kind of observation produced by Luis Alberto Sánchez a century later:

> If somebody argues that it is impossible to compare the huge distance that exists between the descendants of Europe who are settled in Argentina and those of Africa who live in Haiti with that which exists between the various states of the Union, I would reply by pointing out the Irishman from Boston, the Dutchman from Pennsylvania, the Jew of Chicago or the Bronx, the Negro from Harlem ... the mestizo of New Mexico or Oklahoma, a cowboy of Arizona, and Italian-American from 'Little Italy', and then ask how much one can really talk about homogeneity.[182]

As we have seen, the differences between the immigrant communities were often serious, sometimes as a result of the pressures of recent settlement, sometimes because of enduring prejudice of the type expressed by Charles Murray:

> The Irish in America – in every state from Maine to Louisiana, where they are certainly not oppressed, and are free from tithes, from heavy taxes, from ecclesiastical burthens, from want, in short from every subject of complaint and grievance in Ireland – are still the most improvident, quarrelsome, turbulent population of this continent.[183]

---

181. Bayard Taylor, *Eldorado*, I, New York 1850, p. 8.
182. Luis Alberto Sánchez, *Examen Espectral de América Latina* (1945), Buenos Aires 1962, pp. 15–16.
183. *Travels in North America*, London 1841, p. 169. Thirty years later, the entrepreneur Henry Meiggs remarked, upon the completion of a railway line in Peru, that his Chilean workers were far superior to the Irish navvies, who were 'capable even of assaulting those who direct them'. Walt Stewart, *Henry Meiggs: Yankee Pizarro*, Durham N.C., p. 202, quoted in V.G. Kiernan, *The Lords of Human Kind: European Attitudes to the Outside World in the Imperial Age*, Harmondsworth 1972, p. 317. Kiernan's is a marvellous book, full of rich detail, blissfully free of elitist neologisms and false piety. For suggestive studies of how the Irish proved able to assimilate notwithstanding attitudes such as Murray's, see Theodore Allen, *The Invention of the White Race*, London 1994; Noel Ignatiev, *How the Irish Became White*, London 1995.

Perhaps Murray thought that the ability of (most of) the Irish to speak English encouraged such behaviour?[184] Yet in the isthmus of Central America – through which virtually all the non-Chileans bound for California in the 1850s had to travel – prejudice was more than usually aroused, had little to do with language skills, and could be awakened by the least expected encounter. On his way from the port of Puntarenas to the Costa Rican capital of San José, Anthony Trollope reports of his halt at the inn of Esparta that,

> On entering the public sitting room a melodiously rich Irish brogue at once greeted my ears, and I saw seated at the table, joyous in a semi-military uniform, The O'Gorman Mahon, great as in bygone pre-Emancipation days, when with head erect and stentorian voice he would make himself audible to half the County Clare.[185]

One feels that Trollope, who is, of course, 'doubly abroad', here expresses an ambivalence identified by Terry Eagleton – that, 'if Ireland is raw, turbulent, destructive, it is also a locus of play, pleasure, fantasy, a blessed release from the tyranny of the English reality principle'.[186] However, Mahon wasn't in Costa Rica just to show off. Together with the young Prince Polignac, and at the service of the entrepreneur Félix Belly, he was endeavouring to persuade President Juan Mora of the merits of a trans-isthmian canal, which would closely affect Costa Rican affairs as well as the entire geopolitical and economic climate of the Caribbean. The involvement of these two global adventurers in any such scheme certainly reflects the high degree of un-certainty and risk involved. Even after the construction of the Panama railroad in 1855 there was huge potential for a canal, not only to reduce costs and increase capacity in the transit but also to diminish the contact time and opportunities for trouble between travellers and local inhabitants.[187] As described by Hubert Bancroft, this was clearly a 'two-way process'. In January 1854 the consuls of the USA and several European and Latin American states

---

184. New Orleans would, of course, be the main exception here. There, Murray noted,

> The prevailing language seems to be that of Babel – Spanish, Portuguese, French, English mixed with a few wretched remains of Choctaw ... and all these are spoken in the loudest, broadest and strangest dialects, especially in the markets.

Travels in North America, p. 189.

185. *West Indies and the Spanish Main*, p. 264.

186. *Heathcliff and the Great Hunger*, p. 9.

187. *Charles James Patrick Mahon*, born Ennis, County Clare, March 1800, better known in the traditional style as The O'Gorman Mahon; MA TCD, 1826; instrumental in O'Connell's 1828 campaign for the Ennis parliamentary seat which preceded Catholic Emancipation. According to the *Dictionary of National Biography*,

> Not content with ordinary electioneering tactics, he exploited to the full the eccentric resources of his own picturesque personality. On the opening of the polling in the court-house he suspended himself, from a gallery above the heads of the gaping crowd, attired in extravagant national cos-tume, and with a medal of the 'Order of Liberators' on his breast. In a whimsical speech he declined to obey the high sheriff's direction that he should remove the badge.

Himself MP for County Clare 1847–52, when he lost by thirteen votes; 1857–71, apparent service in the international bodyguard of the Tsar of Russia, Chilean navy and armies of Uruguay, Brazil, the North in the US Civil War, and as a colonel of Chasseurs for Napoleon III in the Franco-Prussian War. According to the *Dictionary of Irish Biography*, 'the details of his life are difficult to establish with certainty due to lack

addressed a protest to the governor of Panamá against the neglect of his government to afford protection to passengers crossing the isthmus, notwithstanding that each passenger was made to pay the sum of two dollars for the privilege of landing and going from one side to the other.... They said it was notorious that no passenger arrived at either side of the route without being abused, robbed or otherwise maltreated; many had been wounded, and not a few murdered; hardly a party passed without their luggage being plundered; women were insulted and even outraged.[188]

Governor Urrutia replied that the gaol was full and that he had just executed three criminals, but this did not stop the expatriate community from setting up a vigilante band under one Ram Runnels, who oversaw plenty of extra-judicial lynching and undoubtedly contributed to the rising tension that finally blew up in the riot of 15 April 1856. Bancroft offers polite recognition of some of the contributory factors:

It must be confessed that the impression caused by the influx of foreigners, parading the streets, many of them armed with bowie-knives and revolvers, often excited by intoxication and gambling to acts of lawlessness, was not a favourable one.... Once an American rode a mule into the cathedral and tried to make it drink from the baptismal font. Fortunately, Theller, an American resident, interfered. Often the dirty, red-shirted fellows would stride into chapels and light their cigars at the altar.[189]

However, his description of the riot itself reveals a racial dimension that was frequently present in these Central American conflicts:

The trouble originated in the act of a drunken man named Jack Oliver, who seized a piece of water-melon from a fruit-stall and refused to pay for it. Simultaneously and without preconcertation, fights occurred between parties of passengers and the coloured population in various parts of the town. The city was soon in commotion. Residents retired to their homes and barred themselves in. The fights lasted about three hours, when the foreigners were driven into the depot. The negroes, who had formerly been humble and submissive to the whites, remembered on that day the abusive treatment often received by them at the hands of the transient foreigners.... Fortunately, the rabble was bent more on plunder than slaughter. It is said that even the wounded had the boots pulled from their feet.[190]

None the less, the casualty toll of fifteen Americans dead and sixteen wounded against two locals dead and thirteen wounded reflects the fact that the Colombian

---

of reliable sources', and he appears in no biographical dictionary of the American countries mentioned here. It is, though, sure that he admitted to Gladstone that he had fought thirteen duels – his duelling pistol had two ominous notches – and that he promoted Willie O'Shea and introduced him to Parnell, whom he considered to have taught Irishmen 'how we can successfully combat the hereditary antagonism which exists in the Saxon mind against everything appertaining to the welfare of this country'. Re-elected MP for Clare in 1879 at the age of eighty, he died in Chelsea in 1891 whilst the sitting MP for Carlow. *Camille Polignac*, born 1832 the third son of Prince Jules Polignac; French army service through Crimean War to 1859; to Central America 'to study plant life'. Fought on Confederate side in US Civil War; distinguished service at Battles of Mansfield and Pleasant Hill; 1864 Major General; March 1865, sent to seek aid of Napoleon III for Confederacy; Commander, First French Division, Franco-Prussian War; led several surveying expeditions to Algeria. Died November 1913.

188. *History of Central America*, III, p. 518.
189. Ibid., p. 530.
190. Ibid.

garrison sympathised and sided with a crowd reported as shouting 'Death to the whites!'

The question of slavery and the slave trade was, as will be seen, the source of prolonged diplomatic conflict between Britain and Brazil and Spain, causing extensive naval activity. London struggled to avoid similar difficulties with the USA, but even in the free states of the North there was resentment at the British conflation of moral rectitude and naval supremacy over this issue. Francis Parkman, resolutely unsympathetic to the British, expresses this in an anecdote about a jarring but probably representative encounter between some Americans and British officers on a transatlantic steamer in 1844:

> When they approach the Americans there is a perceptible rising of the chin, and a redoubled stiffness of carriage. Their eyes seem bent on vacuity, but they will glance down an instant disdainfully at the variety of uncouth attitudes of the group – then as they turn away, one will curl his lip and whisper to the other. Green bawls out to the Colonel's son: 'Billy, you don't understand how to be comfortable. Here, let me show you the way to enjoy yourself like an American and a freeman.' So he lifts one of his long legs up to Billy's head, and reaches the other out to the railings of the deck. 'Well, I swow!' says another, 'you do things first rate, I calculate, and no mistake. *We* don't live under a despotic government, I guess!' And this man tries to emulate Green by stretching both feet across his neighbour's lap. 'Yes', says the next man, 'freedom's the word – to all but the niggers! I wish we kept those cattle in the north – a good thing to exercise a man of a cold morning, and give him an appetite for breakfast. I'd lash mine till they roared again.' 'I'd roast mine alive,' says another, taking out a penknife to pick his teeth, 'if they didn't behave.' 'I'd raise a breed for the doctors,' adds another.' They sell well, and it don't cost anything to raise them, because the thinner the body is, the better it is to dissect.' All this being uttered in a loud voice, the Englishmen could not help hearing. Unlike some of their countrymen, they began at last to 'smell a rat' – so, casting a look of disdainful ire on the grave countenances of the Americans, they descended with stately steps, to the lower deck.[191]

Older and wiser, Prescott was more analytical and less anecdotal about the English when, in June 1850, he visited them for the first time in thirty-three years:

> There is a shyness in an Englishman, a natural reserve which makes him cold to strangers and difficult to approach. But corner him in his own house, a frank and full expansion will be given to his feelings that we should look for in vain in the colder Yankee, and a depth not to be found in the light and superficial Frenchman.

But there is a pretty comprehensive caveat in store for those (many) islanders keen to get out of the front door:

> The Englishman, the cultivated Englishman, has no standard of excellence borrowed from mankind. His speculation never travels beyond his own little-great island. That is the world to him. True, he travels – shoots lions among the Hottentots, chases the grizzly bear over the Rocky Mountains, kills elephants in India and salmon on the coast of Labrador – comes home and very likely makes a book. But the scope of his ideas does not seem to be enlarged

---

191. Wade (ed.), *Journals of Francis Parkman*, I, pp. 234–5.

by all this. The body travels, but not the mind ... how little sympathy they show for other people or institutions, and how slight the interest they take in them.[192]

Emerson was even more dedicated to such reportage, free of the burdens of proof or the vanities of objectivity that would afflict future generations oppressed by social science. Visiting Britain in 1833, in the wake of the Reform Act, and then at the end of 1848 to witness the aftermath of the tumultuous events of the spring and summer, he glimpsed the island-in-Europe at rather good times for registering both its continuity and its ruptures. This suited his style of rolling statements and counter-statements calculated to play Lyceum audiences on both sides of the Atlantic that were keen to have the combined experience of their convictions reaffirmed, their curiosity enlivened, and their imagination consciously stirred. It is, of course, a travesty to attempt a 'representative' condensation of the nineteen lectures on 178 printed pages of Emerson's *English Traits*, but their popularity at least could be advanced as an excuse for doing so:

> The English composite character betrays a mixed origin. Everything English is a fusion of distant and antagonistic elements. The language is mixed; the names of men are of different nations — three languages, three or four nations — the currents of thought are counter: contemplation and practical skill; active intellect and dread conservatism; world-wide enterprise and devoted use and wont; aggressive freedom and hospitable law, with bitter class-legislation; a people scattered by their wars and affairs over the face of the whole earth, and homesick to a man; a country of extremes — dukes and chartists, Bishops of Durham and naked heathen colliers — nothing can be praised in it without damning exceptions, and nothing denounced without salvos of cordial praise.... England tends to accumulate her liberals in America and her conservatives in London.... In Ireland, are the same climate and soil as in England, but less food, no right relation to the land, political dependence, small tenantry, and an inferior or misplaced race.... The English uncultured are a brutal nation.... Dear to the English heart is a fair stand-up fight. The brutality of manners in the lower class appears in the boxing, bear-baiting, cock-fighting, love of executions, and in the readiness for a set-to in the streets, delightful to the English of all classes.... The English delight in the antagonism which combines in one person the extremes of courage and tenderness. Nelson, dying at Trafalgar, sends his love to Lord Collingwood, and, like an innocent schoolboy who goes to bed, says, 'Kiss me, Hardy', and turns to sleep.... There is a necessity on them to be logical.... They are impatient of genius, or of minds addicted to contemplation, and cannot conceal their contempt for sallies of thought, however lawful, whose steps they cannot count by their wanted rule.... For they have a supreme eye to facts, and theirs is a logic which brings salt to soup, hammer to nail, oar to boat ... following the sequence of nature, and one in which words make no impression.... they are impious in their skepticism of a theory, but kiss the dust before a fact.... They have no Indian taste for a tomahawk-dance, no French taste for a badge or procession. The Englishman is peaceably minding his business, and earning his day's wages. But if you offer to lay hand on his day's wages, on his cow, or his right in common, or his shop, he will fight to the Judgement. Magna-charta, jury-trial, *habeas corpus*, star-chamber, ship-money, Popery, Plymouth Colony, American Revolution, are all questions involving a yeoman's right to his dinner, and, excepting as touching that,

---

192. Gardiner (ed.), *Literary Memoranda of William Hickling Prescott*, II, pp. 204–6. Amongst those Prescott met in England (and so might have had in mind when drafting this passage) were Macaulay, Peel (a week before his death) and Lord John Russell.

would not have lashed the British nation to rage and revolt.... I know not where any personal eccentricity is so freely allowed, and no man gives himself any concern of it.... They hate innovation. Bacon told them Time was the right reformer; Chatham, that 'confidence was a plant of slow growth'; Canning, to 'advance with the times'; and Wellington that 'habit was ten times nature'.[193]

Maybe the voice here is that which Unamuno recognised in Sarmiento: familiar in its criticism, distant in its affinity?

Whatever the reservations and criticisms, Europe remained an essential point of reference. Echeverría didn't want Guizot's ideas borrowed by Argentines, but, equally, he did not hesitate to agree with Hegel in stating that 'Europe is the centre of the civilisation of centuries and of human progress'; it had at least to be studied.[194] Alberdi lived out a contradiction similar to this – and to that embraced by Sarmiento – when he wrote in 1845,

> America is a European discovery. The European Columbus discovered it; the European Isabel funded its development; the Europeans Pizarro and Cortés colonised it with the non-indigenous people who occupy it today. It was the European Valdivia, and not a Chilean, who founded Chile. America's own name is European – given to it by the European Américo Vespucci.... The indigenous people do not figure, have no place in our political order. We who call ourselves Americans, are nothing but Europeans born in America.[195]

Yet Alberdi wrote for effect no less well than did Sarmiento. Nine months before he penned this, holed up in Paris, he had yearned for home as strongly as any Englishman:

> How beautiful America is! How consoling. How sweet. I know that, now that I've seen these hellish countries; these countries of egoism, of insensibility, of gilded vice, of ennobled prostitution. We greatly overvalue that which we do not know; we give far more value to Europe than it deserves.

More important, perhaps, than this ectopian recognition of positively Pauline proportion – and even than the attendant virulence displayed towards the French – was Alberdi's much more studied and reflective reponse to meeting in reality another legend, the long exiled founding father of Argentina, General San Martín:

> I stood still, full of happy surprise at the prospect of seeing this great American celebrity whom I had so wanted to know ... at last he entered, his hat in his hand, with the modesty and timidity of an ordinary man. How different I found him to the idea I had formed on the basis of hyperbolic descriptions which had made me one of his American admirers. I expected him to be very tall, and yet he was just a little higher than average. I thought that he would be an Indian, as he had so often been depicted to me, and here he was, a man whose skin was no more dark than his bilious humour could make it. I had imagined him to be stout, and although he is surely fatter than when he waged war in America, to me he

---

193. *English Traits*, pp. 27–8, 29, 34, 37, 44–5, 48, 58, 62.
194. *Dogma Socialista*, Montevideo 1851, p. 143.
195. 'Acción de la Europa en América', *El Mercurio*, 10 and 11 August 1845, in *Obras Completas*, III, Buenos Aires 1986–87, pp. 80–82.

Ephraim George Squier, pictured in Peru
a dozen years after his stay in Nicaragua.

Parisian barricades, February 1848.

Kennington Common, London, 10 April 1848.
The huge Chartist demonstration was addressed before noon
by Feargus O'Connor, probably on the stage-cart at centre.

Frederick Law Olmsted,
pictured before the US Civil War.

Anthony Trollope,
writer on Central America
and the Caribbean better
known for his novels.

The first known (1845) photographic portrait of a 'Red Indian',
Kahkewaquonaby of the Mississauga, was actually of a man half-Welsh
and also known as the Reverend Peter Jones.

Little Six (Shakopee) of the Mdewakanton Dakota, pictured in mid 1858.
Little Six was hanged as a leader of the 1862 Sioux revolt.

A group of Kickapoos
migrating to Mexico.

A gaucho dwelling in the Argentine pampa – home of the 'barbarians'
whom Sarmiento sought to eliminate.

John Mitchel before his arrest for treason in May 1848.

Mitchel, aged by transportation
and chronic illness.

William Smith
O'Brien and Thomas
Francis Meagher
under detention
before their 1848
trial for treason.

Meagher in the USA.

Anglo-Hibernian relations
in the partisan view of *Punch*.

HEIGHT OF IMPUDENCE.

Irishman to John Bull.—"SPARE A TRIFLE, YER HONOUR, FOR A POOR IRISH LAD TO BUY A BIT OF——
A BLUNDERBUSS WITH."

Broadway, New York, in 1861 – fertile territory
for the first American flâneurs.

Rio de Janeiro in 1863.

Buenos Aires in 1865.

Domingo
Faustino Sarmiento.

Rubén Darío's birthplace in Metapa, Nicaragua.

Eliza Lynch.

Juan Bautista Alberdi.

San Martín, photographed in
his French exile about the time
that Alberdi met him.

'El Supremo', Dr José Gaspar
Rodríguez de Francia.

Francisco Solano López.

Ralph Waldo Emerson.

Henry David Thoreau.

appeared slim. I was anticipating a grave and solemn man, but before me was one who was sprightly and at ease.... I was impressed by the tenor of his deep and manly voice, which he used without the slightest affectation.[196]

San Martín was not the man whom Alberdi was expecting, but the reality isn't too bad and seems proximate to the myth; the grass is not always greener on the other side of the present or of the sea. Alberdi, though, is not really looking for it in that way; he simply arrives with his preconceptions. He does not approach Paris as a *flâneur* – the city wanderer who, in Walter Benjamin's words, 'goes botanizing asphalt ... the street becomes a dwelling for the flâneur; he is as much at home among the façades of houses as a citizen is in his four walls'.[197] Paris had yet to be transformed by Haussmann, but it was still comparable in size, speed and multiple potential for anonymity to London in a way that was not true of Lausanne, whence Dickens complained in 1846,

> I cannot express how much I want [those streets of London]. It seems as if they supplied something to my brain, which it cannot bear, when busy, to lose. For a week or for a fortnight I can write prodigiously in a retired place ... and a day in London sets me up again and starts me. But the toil and labour of writing day after day without the magic lantern is *immense*.... My figures seem disposed to stagnate without crowds about them.[198]

For Sarmiento the joy of Paris was to be part of that urban crowd:

> *Flâner* is a thing so holy and respectable in Paris, it is a function so privileged that no one dares interrupt it. The *flâneur* has the right to stick his nose everywhere. If you stop in front of a crack in the wall and look at it attentively, some enthusiast will come along and stop to see what you are looking at; a third joins you, and if eight gather, then everyone who passes stops, the street is blocked, a crowd forms.[199]

Within this fluid freedom to create individual and collective social space came erotic possibility unknown in village society and rare in small town life. But the new experience is not so much put into practice as imagined, in a manner not dissimilar to that intimated by Michelet and yearned for by Derrida. Benjamin finds this in Baudelaire's sonnet 'À une Passante', in which the poet glimpses a tall, slender woman 'amid the deafening traffic of the town' and receives from her eyes 'the pleasure that kills':

> A flash ... then night! O lovely fugitive,
> I am suddenly reborn from your swift glance;
> Shall I never see you till eternity?

196. Mayer, *Alberdi y su Tiempo*, pp. 288, 285. Alberdi turned against the French the kind of characterisation sometimes used by Anglo against Latin Americans:

> The Frenchman is a totally vain and despotic being who seeks not good but to establish his own domination; he is entirely lacking in respect, and his vanity is wholly for display. He loves drama and spectacle; when he does something good it will be done in public, in front of an audience; he would not do good in secret.

197. Walter Benjamin, *Charles Baudelaire*, London 1973, pp. 36–7.
198. Quoted in ibid., p. 49.
199. D.F. Sarmiento, *Viajes en Europa, África y América* (1849), quoted in Pratt, *Imperial Eyes*, p. 192.

Somewhere, far off! too late! *never*, perchance!
Neither knows where the other goes or lives;
We might have loved, and you knew this might be![200]

For Walter Benjamin,

This sonnet presents the crowd not as the refuge of a criminal but as that of love which eludes a poet. One may say that it deals with the function of the crowd not in the life of a citizen but in the life of an erotic person. At first glance this function appears to be a negative one, but it is not. Far from eluding the erotic in the crowd, the apparition which fascinates him is brought to him by this very crowd.[201]

The American version of this experience-as-poetry is Anglo, not Latin: Walt Whitman's 1860 'To a Stranger', written in and out of New York. However, this poem is distinct in at least two ways – it encourages a homosexual reading and, as a function of Whitman's strong preference for the second-person in order to hold his reader(s), we become directly involved and so cannot so readily be lost in the throng:

'Passing stranger! you do not know how lovingly I look upon you,
You must be he I was seeking, or she I was seeking, (it comes
    as of a dream,)
I have somewhere surely lived a life of joy with you,
All is recall'd as we flit by each other, fluid, affectionate,
    chaste, matured,
You grew up with me, were a boy with me or a girl with me,
I ate with you and slept with you, your body has become not yours
    only nor left my body mine only,
You gave me the pleasure of your eyes, face, flesh, as we pass, you
    take of my beard, breast, hands in return,
I am not to speak to you, I am to think of you when I sit alone or
    wake at night alone,
I am to wait, I do not doubt I am to meet you again,
I am to see to it that I do not lose you.[202]

Whitman, of course, has realised his dream and will not lose us precisely by having written his poem. Would it be possible, though, to present this as a recognisable and common experience in Santiago, with a population in 1845 of 60,000 and where the newspaper with the highest circulation, *El Mercurio*, sold only 1,000 copies a day? The poems by Baudelaire (1857) and Whitman (1860) were written when the populations of Paris and New York City were over a million (that of London was already over 3 million). Thirty years later – at the end of the nineteenth century – Buenos Aires would have reached half that level, albeit sharing with the New York of 1860 that particularly dynamic anonymity bestowed by the fact that half the population was foreign-born. The same was true of Rio de Janeiro, which by 1849 had over 200,000

---

200. 'To a Passer-by', translated by C.F. MacIntyre, quoted in Benjamin, *Baudelaire*, p. 45.
201. Ibid.
202. 'To a Stranger', part of the 'Calamus' series of the third edition of *Leaves of Grass* (1855), London 1993, p. 112.

inhabitants. Of this city population at least 60,000 were blacks, who, if they were not enslaved, were overwhelmingly engaged in the trades and services that made them part of 'the crowd' but hardly free to be *flâneurs* at their leisured will. However, economic and demographic expansion was already beyond the capacity of the city's infrastructure, producing new slums and directly inverting the street–house relation identified by Benjamin:

> Although householders strove energetically to maintain the boundaries that secured domestic space, the forces of the street seemed always to encroach. Householders faced the dilemma that, in order to constitute their households, they had to bring servants who belonged to the disorderly outside world into the intimate confines of their homes. Being neither family nor wholly unknown, servants occupied an ambiguous and suspicious place between the two. And so the essential paradox formed: for house to function, it had to render itself chronically vulnerable to the dangers of the street.[203]

Thus, although Dumas and Balzac did paint the new and fascinating dangers of Paris streetlife in American terms, these were those not of transatlantic towns but of the continental countryside, and particularly the image purveyed by Cooper:

> The poetry of terror of which the American woods with their hostile tribes on the warpath encountering each other are so full – this poetry which stood Cooper in such good stead attaches in the same way to the smallest details of Parisian life. The pedestrians, the shops, the hired coaches, or a man leaning against a window – all this was of the same burning interest to the members of Peyrade's bodyguard as a tree stump, a beaver's den, a rock, a buffalo skin, an immobile canoe, or a floating leaf was to the reader of a novel by Cooper.[204]

None the less, it is easy to exaggerate the scale and speed of urbanisation – even in 1900 there were only thirteen towns in Latin America with a population over 100,000; less than a fifth of the US population lived in cities in 1860. It is correspondingly tempting to overemphasise the impact of the new urban sites upon the mind. Thoreau usually walked for four hours a day in the countryside, finding arrowheads for real, daydreaming as expansively as any but also with a recall and resolute lack of glamour that make his reflections a fitting finale for Simon Schama's *Landscape and Society*. There Schama quotes a passage from Thoreau's journal where he wonders if he might be, among others, a mail-carrier in Peru, a Siberian exile, a settler on the Columbia river or, perhaps, a Robinson Crusoe. Thoreau responds that he would do none of these things because 'our limbs indeed have room enough but it is our souls that rust in a corner. Let us migrate interiorly without intermission, and pitch our tent each day nearer the western horizon.' And later he insists that, 'It is vain to dream of a wilderness distant from ourselves. There is none such. It is the bog in our brain and bowels, the primitive vigor of Nature in us that inspires that dream.'[205]

203. Sandra Lauderdale Graham, *House and Street: The Domestic World of Masters and Slaves in Nineteenth-Century Rio de Janeiro*, Cambridge 1988, p. 27.

204. Balzac, quoted in Benjamin, *Baudelaire*, p. 42.

205. H.D. Thoreau, *Journal*, Princeton 1981, I, pp. 118–19, and R.L. Rothwell (ed.), *Henry David Thoreau: An American Landscape*, New York 1991, pp. 126–7, quoted in Simon Schama, *Landscape and Memory*,

This is probably a worthy admonition rather than a confident assertion. Certainly, if we accept Renata Mautner Wasserman's notion of the exotic, such a wilderness must always be found both inside and outside:

> The exotic, for centuries a mode in which strangeness is translated for the West, constitutes ... a mediating entity. The exotic arises as a sign of interest on the part of the self in that which is not self. It is not, however, the complete other; it is the acceptable, complementary, renewing other. The exotic mediates between the defining self and a more radical otherness, which at the limit would fall outside the grammar of the defining discourse.[206]

On this understanding there was absolutely nothing exotic about Sarmiento's real-life visit to the islands of Juan Fernández off Chile, where the marooned Alexander Selkirk had given Defoe his model for Robinson Crusoe. All Sarmiento found was a group of North American castaways on a utopian enterprise soured by recrimination and being subverted by a regime of 'fasting on Thursday, hearing mass on Saturday, and working on Sunday' without any sign of Man Friday.[207] By contrast with that observed presence and registered drudgery – deflating an entire imagined world – one grasps from the description of Governor Rosas's hold over Buenos Aires sent to Palmerston by the British envoy Lord Howden in May 1847 the importance of absence and the attractions of invisibility:

> In an old unacknowledged monarchy, claiming to exist by divine right, or in some Asiatic tyranny established by the sword, one can conceive the agency of mystery in augmenting respect or diminishing rivalities; but it is difficult to explain ... the same means obtaining the same end in a Government purely democratic in principle, and governed by a man with no claim beyond that freely conceded to him by the will of his equals. I was witness yesterday to a verification of this, which is remarkable. It was the anniversary of the birth of the republic, a day on which the whole town turned out into the streets; every window was dressed with flags; there was a solemn mass in the cathedral; there were salutes from all the batteries; the Representatives of the people, Ministers and Magistrates, all came forth. One would have thought it the day of all others when an elected chief must at least have shown himself, if not have endeavoured to conciliate popularity. On such a meeting of the people, from whatever cause, the Emperors of Russia or Austria, or the Sultan at Constantinople, *must* have appeared. The most extraordinary part of this is that the troops, above two-thirds of which were volunteers, composed of shopkeepers and men of substance, all with arms kept in their houses, defiled past the windows of Rosas, *which were shut*, and they there burst

---

London 1995, pp. 577–8. Nicholas Green underscores precisely the combination of urban and rural experiences and imagery: 'it was in and through the type of modern urbanisation crystallised in 1830s and 1840s Paris that conditions for a new discourse on nature were laid down.' *The Spectacle of Nature: Landscape and Bourgeois Culture in Nineteenth-Century France*, Manchester 1990, p. 5. According to Angel Rama,

> During the [nineteenth] century, no Latin American Thoreau went to inhabit the solitude of nature and write a diary about its glories. Latin American writers lived and wrote in cities and, if possible, capital cities, remaining resolutely urban people, however much they sprinkled their works with naturalistic details required by the literary vogue of local colour.

The Lettered City, Durham, N.C., 1996, p. 61.

206. *Exotic Nations: Literature and Cultural Identity in the United States and Brazil, 1830–1930*, Ithaca, N.Y., 1994, pp. 13–14.

207. *Viajes*, p. 10, cited in Pratt, *Imperial Eyes*, pp. 190–91.

out into the most enthusiastic vociferations of life to him, and death to his enemies, as if offering incense to the unknown God.[208]

This was the man who, when he was overthrown half a dozen years later, presented himself at the house of the British consul Captain Robert Gore. Discovering that Gore was out, Rosas ordered a bath be drawn, took a nap, and then, reassured with suitably equestrian imagery, the alarmed diplomat who returned home to find it occupied by the most hunted man in the country:

> My friend, don't worry yourself. Look, here the English flag flies, a flag that I've taught them to respect. They're not going to come in here, these people that I've taught to ride, whom I've saddled up, on whom I've put spurs and who I've bucked about. It is not they who have turned against me; it's the brutes.[209]

SOUTHERN ARCADIA

In terms of control, inaccessibility and mystique the example of Rosas must be rated modest beside that of Paraguay, particularly when it was under the dominion of José Gaspar Rodríguez de Francia (1814–40) but also during the regimes of Carlos Antonio López (1844–62) and his son Francisco Solano López (1862–70), who took the country into a catastrophic war against an alliance of Argentina, Brazil and Uruguay (1865–70). Before the republican era Paraguay's reputation rested firmly on its Jesuit missions, broken up with the expulsion of that order from the continent in 1767. That reputation – revived in recent years by the film *The Mission* – is best captured by the title of Cunninghame Graham's book on it: *A Vanished Arcadia*.[210] Indeed, Paraguay is almost an Arcadia within an Arcadia, lost in time and exceptionally difficult to find. When the young Edward Hopkins contrived to ascend the River Paraguay as far as Asunción in November 1845 he reported to US Secretary of State James Buchanan, 'I have discovered that, on no map of the civilised world that I have seen, are the confines of Paraguay correctly delineated.'[211] He was surely correct, and it is likely

---

208. Howden, Buenos Aires, to Palmerston, 26 May 1847, reprinted in Kenneth Bourne and Donald Cameron Watt (eds), *British Documents on Foreign Policy: Latin America 1845–1914*, London 1991, I, p. 45.

209. Mayer, *Alberdi y Su Tiempo*, p. 400. Other versions have Rosas cowering in the bedroom. Opinion is also divided as to how good a horseman the governor really was, but most authorities agree that he was a very poor general. He was put on board a British warship late on the same night.

210. R.B. Cunninghame Graham, *A Vanished Arcadia: Being Some Account of the Jesuits in Paraguay, 1607–1767* (1901), London 1988.

211. Hopkins, Asunción, to Buchanan, 30 Nov. 1845, in W.R. Manning (ed.), *Diplomatic Correspondence of the United States: X. Inter-American Affairs, 1831–1860*, Washington 1938, p. 65.

that Richard Gott is equally so when he boldly opens his book *Land Without Evil*: 'This is a book about places you have never been to, about a history you have never read, and about people you have never heard of.'[212]

It is for this reason, one imagines, that Paraguay has proved so attractive to utopians of every class. For four years it was home to Elisabeth Nietzsche, Friedrich's younger sister and so true to the Nazi cause that Hitler attended her funeral and sent German soil to be placed on the grave of Bernhard Förster, her husband, who had poisoned himself at the Aryan colony – 'Nueva Germania' – they had set up on the Rio Aguaraya (and where there still is a settlement).[213] Seven years later 'New Australia' was established between San José and Ajos (Coronel Oviedo, on what is now Ruta II) by a group of 600 drawn from strikers of the Queensland Shearers' Union and their families under the leadership of the radical journalist William Lane. Lane had been tried for conspiracy in that state under 6 George IV, c. 129 – an act then repealed in Great Britain – by a jury drawn from a panel of 500, of whom 254 were challenged by the Crown and 255 by the defence. He was a man completely in the mould of John Mitchel, and it is not surprising that the libertarian promise of the commune evaporated almost immediately.[214]

Gott's utopian vision is less contestable and more widely shared. It resides in the conviction that,

> the people of the watershed were better off in the nineteenth century than they are in the twentieth. They were far better off in the eighteenth century than in the nineteenth. And in the sixteenth and seventeenth centuries, in spite of the disruptions of conquest and slavery, the people were infinitely better off than in the eighteenth. One does not need to be a retrospective utopian to perceive that the early accounts of the state of the local population, written by the Spanish conquistadores in the sixteenth century, are infinitely more optimistic than anything written by a visiting journalist today.[215]

---

212. *Land Without Evil: Utopian Journeys Across the South American Watershed*, London 1993, p. 1.
213. Ben Macintyre, *Forgotten Fatherland: The Search for Elisabeth Nietzsche*, New York 1993.
214. At the Rockingham conspiracy trial Lane declared,

> I take it that Tyranny itself has no claim upon us and that no tyrannical class has any claim upon us either. As far as they are concerned, any blow struck against them is a blow justified before it is struck – for they who rule by Force, and by Force alone, can claim no consideration if by Force their outrageous claims are questioned.... The Queensland Government denies to the Queensland people the right of self-government, and is thus as much a tyranny as is the Russian Government. It is only because of the toleration of the people that this tyrannical ruling by Force is not changed by Force.

Quoted in Gavin Souter, *A Peculiar People: The Australians in Paraguay*, Sydney 1968, p. 10. The association of the governance of Queensland with that of Tsarist Russia strikes one as absurdly extravagant until one recalls the profoundly reactionary premiership of J. Bjelke Petersen (1968–83).

215. Gott, *Land Without Evil*, p. 4. The book is also about the missions of Chiquitanía and Moxos, which are in present-day Bolivia. Objection to Gott's interpretation is likely to rest just as much on his choice of criterion – the degree of optimism of outsiders – as on his presentation of slavery as only a 'disruption'. Yet one could judge both to be infelicities of expression and still agree with his basic thesis. Whatever the case, this passage brings strongly to mind Engels's early comments about English popular life before the introduction of machinery:

> So the workers vegetated through a passably comfortable existence, leading a righteous and peaceable life in all piety and probity; and their material position was far better than that of their

However severely posterity had dealt with the people of Paraguay by the mid nineteenth century, Hopkins was of the opinion that isolation had served them well but could and should come to an end:

> The state of the case is simply this. No Government of the Civilized world knows anything about Paraguay, my own when I left the United States perhaps least of all. As to coming here, to gain information of her fitness to be an independent power, it is only necessary to pass through the heart of the country as I have done, to learn conclusively that she is more worthy of her rights in the family of nations than any other republic on this Continent save our own.[216]

If Hopkins had a point about ignorance of the country, it was sharper still a decade earlier, when John and William Parish Robertson wrote:

> Paraguay was a land which, when we took up the subject, was enveloped in a vague and misty celebrity. Most people who had read anything of the world knew that there was a beautiful and fertile region of that name, a long way inland in some part or another of South America; that it produced a sort of tea [yerba] … that it had been the seat of the Jesuits … and that it had at last come under the rule of a strange and incomprehensible person, called Dr Francia.[217]

The solitary dictator Francia was known to Paraguayans at the time as the *Caraí-guazú* (great señor) and to almost everybody else then and later as 'El Supremo'. Well before his death in 1840 (when he immediately became 'El Difunto') Francia had established a unique fame, but not as some impulsive, sensual caudillo of a pathologised type that could be freely assigned across the continent. Dr Francia was an intellectual, and one surrounded by farmers in a country surrounded by enemies, real or imagined. He continues to command attention because although he all but sealed the country off from the rest of the world, he did not sequester himself in learned contemplation on his small farm at Ybiraí as if it were a tropical Walden. His engagement with power and his construction of a state offers a challenge to all intellectuals and academics – Anglo and Latin alike – who presume to offer political prescription from without.

Francia was exaggerating little when he complained that, 'I find myself here drowning, unable to breathe, in the immense accumulation of attentions and cares that fall

---

successors. They did not need to overwork; they did no more than they chose to do, and yet earned what they needed. They had leisure for healthful work in garden or field, work, which, in itself, was recreation for them, and they could take part besides in the recreations and games of their neighbours, and all these games – bowling, cricket, football etc. – contributed to their physical health and vigour. They were, for the most part, strong, well-built people, in whose physique little or no difference from that of their peasant neighbours was discernable. Their children grew up in the fresh country air, and, if they could help their parents at work, it was only occasionally; while of eight or twelve hours work for them there was no question.

The Condition of the Working Class in England (1844), *MECW*, IV, London 1975, p. 308.

216. Hopkins to Buchanan, in Manning (ed.), *Diplomatic Correspondence*, X, p. 66. Hopkins's language was almost certainly influenced by his keenness to win a commercial concession; eight years later, having set up a tobacco factory, his enthusiastic meddling resulted in expulsion from the country.

217. J.P. and W.P. Robertson, *Letters on Paraguay*, London 1839, III, p. 4.

upon me alone.'[218] Yet, together with his clerk Policarpo Patiño, the Treasurer Gabriel Benítez, a secretary and an assistant, El Supremo proved able to administer a society of 300,000 people over twenty-six years in a manner only dreamt of in think-tanks, novels and moments of condensed inebriation.[219] In describing the manner of this rule, John Hoyt Williams reminds us that omnipotence depends upon capacity as well as that critical element of absence which, whether enforced or voluntarily arranged, enthrals the ruled:

> El Supremo personally trained his cavalry in the use of the sabre, granted permission for an Indian of Atirá to marry a white woman, ascertained the exact number of nails in the inventory of Fort Orange, awarded 102 pesos to a French resident whose anchor had been melted down by the state, sent wine to churches near Concepción, tested a repeating pistol and found it too complicated for his troops, lowered the price of salt in the capital, donated state yerba to the people of Saladillo, and denied permission for a 'quatroon' to marry in Villa Rica. It would not be surprising if he handled these actual problems all in the space of a few minutes on a Monday morning. Scarcely a decision was made in Paraguay by anyone but the Caraí, and his monastic habits and life-style were dictated by his own strongly felt need to attend to all affairs of state personally, no matter their minute nature. From dawn to late evening he worked in Government House, resting briefly during the siesta period with his cup of yerba and a strong black cigar, perhaps discussing affairs with his record keeper or strolling the large patio in his formal black frock coat each day, after his brief siesta, Francia would ride through the streets of Asunción, normally accompanied by a single watchful sergeant of grenadiers. The people of the capital, aware of this ritual, and also addicted to their own, much longer siestas, were rarely to be seen at midday, and he often rode through the deserted streets, his horse's hooves echoing as if in a corridor.[220]

Francia, like all Paraguayans, spoke both Guaraní and Spanish, but his bookishness, knowledge of English and French, and his ascetic vocation made him not just an intellectual but also a kind of supra-national figure, and one frequently assailed as epitomising a new calculation in autocratic violence. For the Robertsons, who spent four years under the thumb of El Supremo,

> the peace and quiet of Paraguay are as the stillness of the grave. What originated in a deeply laid plot of oppressive tyranny has been consummated by a universal system of terror. By the most ruthless cruelty, by the sternest despotism, Francia established and now maintains his

---

218. Francia, Asunción, to Subdelegate at Ytapúa, 22 Aug. 1830, quoted in John Hoyt Williams, *The Rise and Fall of the Paraguayan Republic, 1800–1870*, Austin, Tex., 1979, p. 82.

219. Francia, of course, is the subject of one of the greatest Latin American novels of the twentieth century, *Yo el Supremo* by Augusto Roa Bastos (1974) – a text with copious and extended factual footnotes and in some danger of losing readers because it belongs to the currently unpopular 'great dictator' genre. By taking the voices of both Francia and Patiño, Roa Bastos fortifies the sense of clerical obligation. Engels, who knew a thing or two about management, once boasted to Marx in less than libertarian vein:

> With six clerks I could organise an infinitely more simple, better arranged and most practical branch of administration than I could with sixty government councillors and financial experts ... office workers are used to continuous mechanical activity, they are less pretentious, less given to dawdling, and it is easier to get rid of them if they are unsuitable.

Engels, Manchester, to Marx, 20 July 1851, in *Marx–Engels: Selected Correspondence*, p. 53.

220. Williams, *Rise and Fall of the Paraguayan Republic*, p. 82.

sway; crimes of a dye so deep, of a character so appalling as to make human nature shudder and recoil, have stained his course as he has advanced in his relentless and bloody career.[221]

Such language is not so dissimilar to that used to denounce the violation of human rights by the military dictatorships of the 1970s, and Francia certainly jailed, exiled and executed Paraguayans and foreigners at will if not quite on a modern scale. At least a hundred people were killed under his regime – some seventy at the end of June 1821 by a series of firing squads held daily in the patio of Government House – and many more were held in the dungeons for years. This undoubtedly instilled fear as well as removing opponents, and there was a corresponding insecurity as to whether Francia, when not seen or heard of for some time, might have died or was simply laying a trap. It is telling that the Robertsons open the second volume of their book with the dismayed observation that 'the Doctor's death so currently repeated three months ago, we now know has not taken place'.[222] Carlyle thought that Francia had probably killed forty people, and yet in a typically wild essay of 1843 on the dictator for the *Foreign Quarterly Review* he talks of 'rigour', not 'terror', and he sees the population of the country as deserving El Supremo, so the doctor's enlightened despotism receives some understanding:

> Certainly, as we say, nothing could well shock the constitutional feeling of mankind as Dr Francia has done.... [He] was, perhaps, too awful a practical phenomenon to be calmly treated in the literary way.... [Yet the population,] it must be owned, is not yet fit for constitutional liberty. They are a rude people; lead a drowsy life, of ease and sluttish abundance – one shade, and but one, above a dog's life, which is defined as 'ease and scarcity'. The arts are in their infancy; and not less the virtues.... Such men cannot have a history, though a Thuycidides come to write it. Enough for us to understand that Don This was a vapourising blockhead, who followed his pleasures, his peculations, and Don That another of the same; that there occurred fatuities, mismanagements innumerable; then discontents, open grumblings, and, as an accompaniment, intriguings, caballings, outings, innings ... [so] of Francia's improvements there might as much be said as of his cruelties or rigours; for, indeed, at bottom, the one was in proportion to the other.[223]

Suspicious and unmerciful and yet capable of sudden pragmatism, the stern Francia was anathema to the likes of Sarmiento because he exceeded even Rosas in his distrust of foreigners – any foreigners, not just Europeans. Yet Francia, the prototype republican technocrat, was definitively not a promoter of the type of barbarism

---

221. J.P. and W.P. Robertson, *Letters from Paraguay*, II, p. 9. Pressing their point on the reader, the Robertsons note that these are

> facts which relate not to some negro chieftain of a savage tribe of Africans but to a lawyer, scholar, a political chief, who in all probability exercises *at this moment* absolute sway over a country larger than Great Britain; a country which, for three centuries, was ruled by a civilized European power.

Ibid., p. 11.

222. Ibid., p. 3.

223. Thomas Carlyle, 'Dr Francia', *Foreign Quarterly Review*, 62, 1843, reprinted in *Critical and Miscellaneous Essays*, London 1869, VI, pp. 69–139, this quotation being drawn from pp. 81–2, 99, 108 and 119 of that edition.

associated by Sarmiento with the backlands, even if, as Carlyle noted, he was occasionally inclined to 'withdraw to his *chacra* [farm] … there to interrogate nature'.[224] (Sarmiento, it might be noted, died in 'barbarian' Asunción, propped up by a window waiting for his beloved Aurelia Vélez Sarsfeld, but expiring before she arrived.).

In practice, Francia's regime protected Paraguay from its neighbours, and from two groups described by the Robertson brothers. The first was the old creole elite – Carlyle's Dons This and That – depicted here strutting their stuff on the day of *Besamanos*:

> old and antiquated Spanish court dress, which I believe had in some cases been handed down from father to son, since the first conquerors of Paraguay, were to be seen in all directions. They were worn by shopkeepers, merchants and some of the better landed proprietors of the old school. The prevailing fashion was very much in the Dr Vargas style, being a coat of great amplitude of cuff, pocket and flap, of 'Paño de San Fernando', the best and most costly superfine of Spain, with monstrously large flat buttons, and tails reaching to the calf of the leg. The rest of the dress was in keeping with this well-preserved heir-loom. Then come the *doctores* in court suits of black of an equally ancient cut; a few (among these Generals Yegros and Cavallero) in fantastic, medley and very tight regimentals; and a few more young men, like myself, who had been to Buenos Aires and adopted the modern European fashion.[225]

The second group was the Indians, against whom Francia's system of forts was an essential defence. The Indians that the Scots travellers describe here had arrived downriver at the Argentine town of Santa Fé to sign with the Christian authorities of that province a treaty of the type that El Supremo never trusted:

> About 15 of these caciques rode into town, and very much excited my curiosity. They were a fine set of men, well made, and a dark copper-colour. They were mounted on beautiful horses, gaudily comparisoned; and their own persons are adorned, after a barbarous fashion, with a profusion of morris-bells, beads, and short silver tubes, laid in rows and devices over their ponchos and mantles. Their uncouth caps were stuck full of many-coloured feathers; they were scantily clothed in dyed and partly-striped cotton-manufactures of their own; and some of them wore silver ornaments bored through their lips and ears. Their weapons were old swords, clubs and bows and arrows. The ratification of the treaty was proclaimed by repeated discharges of artillery which greatly pleased the barbarians; and copious draughts of aguardiente administered to them at the same time pleased them still more. They swung on their horses, raised horrid yells, or, dismounting, they half-danced, half-staggered on the ground.[226]

In our own day, with body piercing in such vogue, such a depiction of the barbarian-as-jewellery seems rather more sympathetic than that of the barbarian-as-despot, but Carlyle's approach of seeing the need for the one to deal with the other is probably just as applicable in this case as it was for the placid plutocrats of the old order.

---

224. Ibid., p. 109.
225. J.P. and W.P. Robertson, *Letters from Paraguay*, III, pp. 14–15.
226. Ibid., II, p. 195.

The Paraguayan state of Dr Francia was both amended and extended by López *père et fils*. If suspicion and insistence upon riverine sovereignty remained at the heart of political management, there was also an increasingly open attitude to external assistance, particularly from Europe. At no stage, however, was there any reduction in reliance upon the military system. Francisco Solano López was placed in charge of this at the age of nineteen, quickly recognised the importance of appearances for discipline, and displayed a Francia-like attention to detail in writing to his father on this matter in 1846:

> There is a shortage of clothing for our troops, because that which was distributed earlier has been worn out very rapidly by all the marches we have undertaken, and there has been no opportunity to repair it. Accordingly, I would be most grateful if, when Your Excellency might find it convenient, you could send me as quickly as possible: for the cavalry baize shirts, but for the infantry they can be of linen. This lasts them longer and is less expensive. I very dearly request Your Excellency that, when you might find it convenient, you might arrange for me to be sent those visored helmets that are in the barracks, because we are very poorly uniformed in this place, the companies and squadrons being completed scrambled up, some having caps and others different types of hats, which greatly tarnishes their appearance. If I am sent the aforementioned helmets, even if they might be as heavy as some say – which I doubt is the case – I can see the means by which to improve matters.[227]

There was, though, another side to this 'garrison state' – one that absolutely forbade absence on the part of its servants, whose desertion was punished with a severity that went beyond removal of a uniform acquired so assiduously in the first place. In September 1848 Francisco Solano López informed his father of a case for which he evidently felt no need to hold any consultation:

> The undersigned General in Chief has the honour to address Your Excellency in order to inform you that, having deserted from this camp on the 6th inst., Antonio Cañete, a soldier of the third company of the second batallion and an inhabitant of Itauguá, was captured on the 10th of the same by the garrison of Itatí in the gulleys of the Paranamí. An indictment was drawn up accordingly, and as a result the crime of desertion abroad was found to be fully proved, with the punishment for the said crime being applicable with the full rigour

---

227. Francisco Solano López, Villanueva, to Pres. Carlos Antonio López, 7 July 1846, in J.I. Livieres Argaña (ed.), *Con la Rúbica del Mariscal: Documentos*, Asunción 1970, pp. 101–2. It is a mark of the efficiency of the López regime that at the end of the month the son could write to his father thanking him for the delivery of the clothing. Nowadays one is only allowed to admire the military appearance if one is very camp or very normal, but in the nineteenth century it was an almost universal occupation, particularly for travellers. In Guatemala, it will be remembered, Carrera staged his victorious entry into the capital decked out in dress of fantastic, medley and distinctly unregimental fashion (Señora de Prem's hat etc.), and from Robert Dunlop's account this set a mode amongst the troops:

> The soldiers are a most ill-looking set of ruffians, whose appearance in the streets of London would ensure them a place in the watch-house. Carrera had adopted the British colour [scarlet] for clothing his troops, but the red jackets are few in number, and only put on upon feast days, and other extraordinary occasions; and even then, the strange figures of the men, all clothed in jackets of one size, none of which of course fits the wearer, makes them look like a band of robbers who had dressed themselves in stolen clothes. The officers dress themselves, according to fancy, in strange nondescript uniforms, the most respectable resembling English footmen out of place.

Travels in Central America, p. 83.

of the ordinances. For the satisfaction of public revenge and as an example to others, it was ordered that he be stripped of his uniform in the square of his unit, shot straight away, and his body strung up for five hours, as established by article five of the ordinances of 18 January last.[228]

The effect of such measures was not difficult to discern. Edward Hopkins reported to Washington that 'the moment you cross the Paraguayan border, your knives and pistols you may throw away, the most perfect security existing all over the land'.[229] Addressing Spanish Foreign Minister Calderón de la Barca, the young General López made the same point but in a wider political context, emphasising the fact that although Paraguay had once formed part of the old viceroyalty of Buenos Aires and shared some religious origins with the other provinces,

> there was no moral or political comparison.… Paraguay removed herself from their community, keeping herself entirely separate from their affairs … and from this separation the Republic gained the benefit and advantage of having a stable government, which was moderate and progressed peacefully, providing law and order, owing no debts at home or abroad.[230]

Separation did not simply mean withdrawal, could not depend upon removal alone, and had not done so even under Francia. The restrictions on foreign commerce were lifted appreciably in the early 1850s but disputes over freedom of transit grew as a result. Moreover, the removal of Rosas in 1852 clarified and stabilised the regional balance of power less than anticipated. What benefited Uruguay did not necessary improve the position of Paraguay, and it proved more necessary than ever to fend off Brazilian pressure. For this the occasional execution of deserters before troops in uniform headwear was necessary but insufficient preparation. It was essential to make foreign treaties and alliances, and to acquire modern technology and weaponry.

In June 1853 Francisco Solano López departed for London, where he placed an order with Blyth's of Limehouse for a new steam warship, the *Tacuarí*, at a cost of £50,000. He then proceeded to Paris for a much anticipated visit to Napoleon III. Here accounts vary somewhat, but the most seemly have him on the platform of the Gare de St Lazare catching the eye of a *passante*, the eighteen-year-old Eliza Lynch. Born in Cork in 1835, Eliza later presented her background in terms that made her easy meat for the many writers who set out to vilify her. But she was certainly separated from the husband, M. Quatrefages, whom she had married in London and

228. Francisco Solano López, Villanueva, to Pres. Carlos Antonio López, 23 Sept. 1848, in Argaña (ed.), *Con la Rúbica del Mariscal*, p. 241. The concept of a garrison state was developed by Harold Lasswell at the start of World War II in a bleak essay that conceived of a world 'in which the specialists in violence are the most powerful group in society'. *The Analysis of Political Behaviour*, London 1947, p. 146. A less rigid reading could include the Paraguay of 1814–70, although the term has increased salience for the whole of the Southern Cone in the 1970s.

229. Hopkins, Asunción, to Buchanan, 30 Nov. 1845, in Manning (ed.), *Diplomatic Correspondence*, X, p. 64.

230. Francisco Solano López, Paris, to Varela, 5 Jan. 1854, in Argaña (ed.), *Con la Rúbica del Mariscal*, p. 182.

lived with in Algeria for nearly three years, and she evidently was not content with the wistfulness of a *flâneuse* since she took the portly General to bed that same night.[231] Cunninghame Graham's attitude is typical: 'From the first Madame Lynch seems to have set her mind on two objects. She was to get her lover to marry her, and the next to make him the greatest power in South America.'[232] According to this school, López – who never married Eliza but recognised her five sons as his own – was entirely in her thrall and progressively dragged his small country towards war under her influence. Such an interpretation is reassuringly blinkered and inherently implausible, even for understanding a society and regime as tightly organised as that of Paraguay. Yet if by the 1860s López found himself assailed by a dynamic and complex international crisis for which his limited diplomatic skills were far from sufficient, it is also true that Eliza had played her part in national life for the previous dozen years:

> Some writers give Eliza Lynch the whole credit for the introduction of the vogue for rich materials, modern jewellery and various details of feminine coquetry, but in this there is certainly exaggeration. Anyone who examines the bills of lading from the time before in-dependence to 1840 will find, even with the restriction of trade by isolation and blockade in Francia's days, blond lace, satin, velvet, embroidered muslins and perfumes in the lists, though admittedly these treasures were imported only in small quantities and remained the privilege of a tiny minority until after 1855.... Although it was severely repressed during the long period of Francia's rule, we cannot ignore this element of luxury or caprice that had been present since colonial days. On the other hand, if Eliza did not introduce certain items in the luxury class, it cannot be denied that she played a part in their rapid diffusion.... The common people, or at least a part of them, gave up the *typoi* for printed cottons. The change was due not only to the allure of colour and variety, which naturally appealed to popular taste, but also the cheapness of these textiles in comparison with the hand-made local cloth.... Eliza Lynch introduced the taste for cosmetics, and the traditional meagre list of powders and perfumes broadened its scope. The seller of these feminine trifles in Asunción was, in fact, Eliza's hairdresser, Jules Henry, who imported 'making-up pomades' and also stocked perfumed gloves, essences and sandalwood fans.... Champagne had already begun to figure in bills of lading from 1845, but Eliza Lynch, who was a great drinker of it, was its most effective populariser.[233]

It is understandable that those who delight in depicting Eliza Lynch as a grasping courtesan and *femme fatale* should find it hard to recognise the tragedy that ensued as she buried with her own hands her lover and eldest son, the fifteen-year-old Colonel Juan Francisco, after they were killed by Brazilian cavalry at Cerro Corá in 1870; was

---

231. In her *Exposición y Protesta*, issued in Buenos Aires in 1875 to clear her name, Eliza notes that her poor reputation derived from the supposition of her adultery with López, when, in fact, her marriage to Quatrefages was null and void because 'it had not been undertaken according to the formalities of the law'. She then says that their separation was caused by her ill health, that Quatrefages married another woman in 1857 and had children, strongly suggesting that the original marriage was never consummated. Juan E. O'Leary, *El Mariscal López*, Asunción 1970, pp. 34–6. For the most piously salacious – and so rather good – account, see Alyn Brodsky, *Madame Lynch and Friend*, London 1975.

232. *Portrait of a Dictator: Francisco Solano López*, London 1933, p. 102.

233. Josefina Plá, *The British in Paraguay*, Richmond 1976, pp. 193–4.

expelled to Europe; lost law suits in Edinburgh to retrieve her property; wandered through Palestine; and died destitute back in Paris at the age of fifty-three.[234]

A few days before López first caught sight of the young Eliza Lynch in Paris he had paid a courtesy farewell visit to Queen Victoria, who had retired to Osborne House, her home on the Isle of Wight, prior to Christmas. In his report of this piece of protocol to Foreign Minister Benito Varela, López registers the revolution in travel and time wrought by the steam engines on both land and water:

> The Queen received me with the warmth and generosity that is her mark. Replying to my farewell speech, she asked me to assure the President of the Republic of the keen interest she takes in Paraguay and that His Excellency can always count on the good offices of England.... As it was already getting dark I saw that I would be obliged to stay at some inn on the island although I had wanted to reach Southampton in time to be able to return to London through the night. I understand that an attaché had informed Her Majesty of my concern since she did not hesitate to place her private launch at my disposal for the trip to Southampton ... where I arrived at 5.30 p.m. At 7 p.m. I took the steam train, arriving in London at 11 p.m., that is, only twelve hours after having left it and having completed a round-trip of more than eighty leagues.[235]

Within a year of López's return to Paraguay it was decided that the country should have a railway, not for speed of personal travel but for the transport of yerba and development of industry. Plans were drawn up by William Whitehead, and the track laid between Asunción and Villarica under the supervision of George Paddison and three other British engineers; Blyth and Co. again provided the essential materials.[236] Such a modest line dedicated to freight hardly challenged the pace of life symbolised by the siesta that was such a public and private feature of the Francia era, but it provided some contrast – and one drawn from abroad – to 'natural' cycles. Few Northerners, now accustomed to the railroad and a notion of work-through-haste, would have responded to the siesta as equably as did George Squier when invited by his Nicaraguan host to recline for some hours:

> A siesta was strongly commended to us after dinner, and hammocks were strung for the whole party. It was indispensable, our host told us, in this climate, and he wondered how

---

234. Brodsky ferreted with a penetrative puritanism into both Eliza's life and her version of it, to the extent that he is able to deny that she was interred in a pauper's grave, even telling us the name of the last of sixteen persons who were buried on top of Madame Lynch up to 1900, with the strong inference that the remains eventually interred in the National Pantheon with the full pomp of the Paraguayan state in 1964 belonged not to Eliza but to one Estelle Martín. *Madame Lynch*, pp. 267–8. One cannot but ruminate upon the parallels and counterpoints of this life with that of the likewise Cork-born Eliza Gilbert, who in 1851 published her memoirs under the name of Lola Montez. 'Lola' went through several permutations of international fame as a dancer – celebrated in particular for the erotic routine 'El Oleano' – and seduced, amongst others, Liszt, Peel's son and, with great political consequence, King Ludwig I of Bavaria, for whose abdication she was widely blamed. After the revolutions of 1848 she spent the Gold Rush years in California, moving with a theatre troop to Australia when gold was discovered there. Getting religion, she died in New York under the name of 'Mrs Heald' in 1861. Bruce Seymour, *Lola Montez: A Life*, New Haven, Conn., 1996.

235. López, London, to Varela, 8 Dec. 1853, in Argaña (ed.), *Con la Rúbica del Mariscal*, pp. 134–5.

236. Plá, *British in Paraguay*, pp. 49–52, 107–112, 163–4.

it could be omitted in El Norte. Life, in his opinion, without a siesta after dinner, must soon become a wearisome affair, and he quoted some verses from a native poet that were conclusive upon the subject; so we yielded and lay down; the people left, the doors were closed, and all was silent – even the pigeons were still. Two hours passed in a dreamy pleasurable way, with just enough of consciousness to enjoy the sensation of novelty and ease.[237]

The passage to California did entail periods of enforced idleness on boats and, for some years, the trip required those dashing along time's arrow towards the gold fields to witness, like Squier, time's cycle as they passed through Nicaragua. A few were tempted. Yet for the great majority 'Rush' represented not just one frantic journey but a disposition, almost an ideology. As Vicente Pérez Rosales witnessed it, 'No one walked, they flew.'[238]

Observation and commentary on North American manners by foreigners had been made newly controversial by Frances Trollope and Captain Marryat in the 1830s, but this did not prevent Dickens and Sarmiento from engaging in the same activity a decade later, with Emerson and others repaying them in good coin. Velocity and diet stood high on the list of remarkable strangenesses for both authors, Dickens displaying a Gladstonian prissiness about what we would today call 'fast food':

I may venture to say, after conversing with many members of the medical profession in America, that I am not singular in the opinion that much of the disease that does prevail, might be avoided if a few common precautions were observed. Greater means of personal cleanliness are indispensable to this end; the custom of hastily swallowing large quantities of animal food, three times a day and rushing back to sedentary pursuits must be changed.[239]

Sarmiento, who came from a society where meat was an unquestioned staple, responds more as an amused epicure – just as North Americans do today when confronted by a British sandwich – but still one whose norms of civility, let alone civilisation, have been seriously transgressed:

---

237. *Nicaragua*, p. 93.

238. *Diario*, p. 303, quoted in De Onis, *United States as Seen by Spanish American Writers*, p. 124.

239. *American Notes*, p. 292. In a study of 1841 – the year before Dickens visited the USA – William Neild undertook a survey of the domestic economy and diet of Lancashire cotton workers, only the most comfortable of whom could spend as much on meat as on bread, with the poorest – a mechanic's assistant – spending three times as much on bread as on meat. A couple of years later Engels wrote,

> The better-paid workers, especially those in whose families every member is able to earn something, have good food as long as this state of things lasts; meat daily, and bacon and cheese for supper. Where wages are less, meat is used only two or three times a week, and the proportion of bread and potatoes increases. Descending gradually, we find the animal food reduced to a small piece of bacon cut up with the potatoes; lower still, even this disappears, and there remains only bread, cheese, porridge and potatoes until on the lowest round of the ladder, among the Irish, potatoes form the sole food.

Condition of the Working Class in England (1844), in *MECW*, IV, p. 372. In such circumstances it is not so surprising that even a well-heeled member of the British diplomatic service should be impressed by the presents given by Rosas to the company of the ship in which he arrived at Buenos Aires: '400 pounds of beef, a large quantity of vegetable and fruit, three sheep, three pigs, six turkeys and some fifty or sixty partridges'. Hood, Buenos Aires, to Aberdeen, 18 July 1846, in Bourne and Cameron Watt (ed.), *British Documents: Latin America 1845–1914*, I, p. 19.

[There] instantly begins a racket of plates, knives and forks colliding with each other which goes on for five minutes, letting all the world know for half a league around that eating is going on at a hotel. It is impossible to follow with the eye the events of the meal in the midst of all this uproar despite the activity and skill of 50 or 100 servants who try to give a certain style to the uncovering of dishes and pouring of tea and coffee. The American has two minutes set aside for lunch, five for dinner, ten for a smoke or to chew tobacco, and the rest of the day for staring at the newspaper you are reading, the only one that interests him because it belongs to somebody else.... The Yankee *pur sang* eats all his food, desserts and fruits from the same plate, one at a time or all together. We saw one fellow from the FAR WEST, an unsettled land like the Phoenicians' Ophir, begin his meal with great quantities of fresh tomato sauce taken straight and scooped up on the top of his knife! Sweet potatoes and vinegar! We were frozen with horror, and my travelling companion was filled with gastronomical indignation: 'And will not heaven rain down fire upon them?' he asked. 'The sins of Sodom and Gomorrah must have been minor compared to the ones the Puritans commit every day.'[240]

It is probably as well that the slightly built Flora Tristán never fulfilled her project of visiting the United States, because although she ate almost as fast as the Yankees, she ate little, and no meat. Yet her description of the meals of the republican aristocracy of southern Peru reminds us of the customs rejected by 'American consumption' wittingly or otherwise:

I found these banquets unimaginably tedious. Two courses are served, sometimes three, and one has to partake of everything in order not to offend against the rules of etiquette. I had to explain over and over again that I did not eat soup or meat, and that my diet was usually confined to vegetables, fruit and milk. People stay at table a good two hours, during which conversation alternates between praise of the food and fulsome compliments addressed to the master of the house. Here as in Arequipa they are in the habit of passing titbits around on the end of a fork, but this custom is dying out. The amount I have seen eaten on these occasions is truly prodigious. As a consequence, by the end of the meal nearly all the guests are unwell and in such a state of stupor that they are incapable of uttering a word. No doubt about it, these banquets are as bad for the mind as they are for the health.[241]

Henry Thoreau was not himself a complete vegetarian, but he had very little time for reflexive carnivorism prevalent in the North, and even less for the ethos of hurry, which he chastised precisely with an analogy drawn from the railway:[242]

---

240. Rockland (ed.), *Sarmiento's Travels in the United States*, pp. 147–8. Twenty years later Anthony Trollope found both procedural and substantive points to make on this subject:

The greatest luxury at an English inn is one's tea, one's fire and one's book. Such an arrangement is not practicable at an American hotel. Tea, like breakfast, is a great meal at which meat should be eaten, generally with the addition of much jelly, jam and sweet preserve; but no person delays over his tea-cup. I love to have my tea-cup emptied and filled with gradual pauses, so that time for oblivion may accrue, and no exact record be taken. No such meal is known at American hotels.

North America, I, p. 61.
241. Tristán, *Peregrinations*, p. 279.
242. For Thoreau,

the practical objection to animal food in my case was its uncleanness; and, besides, when I had caught, and cleaned, and cooked and eaten my fish, they seemed not to have fed me essentially ... [but] the repugnance to animal food is not the effect of experience ... it is an instinct.... One farmer says to me, 'You cannot live on vegetable solely, for it furnishes nothing to make bones

[The nation] lives too fast. Men think that it is essential that the *Nation* have commerce, and export ice, and talk through a telegraph, and ride thirty miles an hour, without a doubt, whether they do it or not; but whether we should live like baboons or like men, is a little uncertain. If we do not get out sleepers and forge rails, and devote days and nights to the work, but go to tinkering our *lives* to improve *them*, who will build railroads? And if railroads are not built, how shall we get to heaven in season? But if we stay at home and mind our business, who will want railroads? We do not ride on the railroad; it rides upon us. Did you ever think what those sleepers are that underlie the railroad? Each one is a man, an Irishman, or a Yankee man. The rails are laid on them, and they are covered with sand, and the cars run smoothly over them. They are sound sleepers, I assure you.... Hardly a man takes a half-hour's nap after dinner, but when he wakes he holds up his head and asks, 'What's the news?' as if the rest of mankind has stood his sentinels.[243]

Thoreau here identifies an important displacement between the individual – who is unconsciously a sleeper by subscribing to public hurry – and the collectivity, which vindicates occasional post-prandial somnambulence by creating 'news' in the meantime. A siesta, then, is OK if not everyone is at it, which, of course, they were in Nicaragua and Paraguay (even Dr Francia).

Thoreau also reminds us – just in case Professor Bemis's notion of a 'temperate' climate has been taken too literally – of the particularly Northern need to keep warm. In doing so he not only speaks from bitter experience – in the 1830s a tenth of a student's costs at Harvard were taken up by firewood (six cords a year; $22.50) – but also reveals a little of the lineage back from Transcendentalism to Unitarianism to Calvinism which gave moral confidence to his radical 'common sense':

The grand necessity, then, for our bodies, is to keep warm, to keep the vital heat in us. What pains we accordingly take, not only with our food, and clothing, and shelter, but with out beds, which are our night-clothes, robbing the nests and breasts of birds to prepare this shelter within a shelter as a mole has its bed of grass and leaves at the end of its burrow! ... Let him who has work to do recollect that the object of clothing is, first, to retain the vital heat, and, secondly, in this state of society, to cover nakedness, and he may judge how much of any necessary or important work may be accomplished without adding to his wardrobe. Kings and queens who wear a suit but once, though made by some tailor or dressmaker to their majesties, cannot know the comfort of wearing a suit that fits. They are no better than wooden horses to hang the clean clothes on. Every day our garments become more assimilated to ourselves, receiving the impress of the wearer's character, until we hesitate to lay them aside.... No man ever stood lower in my estimation for having a patch on his clothes; yet I am sure that there is a greater anxiety, commonly, to have fashionable, or at least clean and unpatched clothes, than to have a sound conscience.[244]

---

with'; and so he religiously devotes a part of his day to supplying his system with the raw material of bones; walking all the while he talks behind his oxen, which, with vegetable-made bones, jerk him and his lumbering plough along in spite of every obstacle.

Walden, or Life in the Woods (1854), London 1992, pp. 191, 8–9.

243. Ibid., pp. 82–3. Thoreau followed his own existential injunction to the end. According to Sam Staples, the Concord gaoler who visited his former prisoner on his deathbed, he found 'a man dying with so much pleasure and peace'. Quoted in Condry, *Thoreau*, p. 108.

244. Ibid., pp. 12, 19. Thoreau's grandfather had died of a cold caught whilst patrolling the streets of Concord against anti-Catholic rioters. The information on wood is given in Richardson, *Henry Thoreau*, p. 9.

Emerson, on the other hand, identified an interactive relationship between outer garments and inner mind:

> When the young European emigrant, after a summer's labour, puts on for the first time a new coat, he puts on much more. His good and becoming clothes put him on thinking that he must behave like people who are so dressed; and silently and steadily his behaviour mends.

If this was more prescriptively reactionary than Thoreau, Emerson was still able to register – from a suitably judicious distance – a gendered difference which could be merely tasteful but might be truly transcendent: 'I am not ignorant – I have heard with admiring submission the experience of the lady who declared that, "the sense of being perfectly well dressed gives a feeling of inward tranquillity which religion is powerless to bestow".'[245]

In 1847 there arrived in the USA from Buttenheim, Bavaria, an eighteen-year-old, Levi Strauss, whose design and mass production of trousers and jackets from serge imported from Nimes provided a brief renaissance for the Salvadorean indigo industry, a popular and democratic resolution to Thoreau's dilemma, and an American style which has endured for over 150 years, the last thirty of which as a globalised and ungendered statement of leisured informality (and uniformity). A century after Strauss's arrival a large part of the Indian sub-continent became independent under the leadership of M.K. Gandhi, for whom *Walden* was a major – possibly unique – literary influence, who adopted as much as anything its strictures as to simplicty of dress (*satyagraha* relates more to *Civil Disobedience*), and who had the book translated into fifteen languages and widely distributed by the state.

It is a moot point whether Thoreau, who thought that 'the mass of men serve the State ... not as men mainly, but as machines', would have approved of this.[246] But perhaps he would have acquiesced in any means to improve popular literary taste: 'Most men have learned to read to serve a paltry convenience, as they have learned to cipher in order to keep accounts and not be cheated in trade; but of reading as a noble intellectual exercise they know little or nothing.'[247]

This might be thought rather high-minded when the USA formally had the highest literacy rate in the world, at 90 per cent. In Britain 37 per cent of men and 48 per cent of women were unable to sign the marriage register in 1843.[248] However, it is important to place capacity and consumption in perspective. Very few books were as popular as Margaret Fuller's *Woman in the Nineteenth Century*, which, priced at 50 cents, sold out its print-run of 1,000 within a fortnight in 1845. The Transcendentalist

---

245. 'Social Aims', in Ralph Waldo Emerson, *Complete Works*, Boston 1893, VIII, pp. 87–8. For Sarmiento US white society was already sartorially homogeneous: 'Americans do not wear jackets or ponchos, but have a dress common to all.' Rockland (ed.), *Sarmiento's Travels in the United States*, p. 132.

246. *Civil Disobedience* ['Resistance to Civil Government'] (1849), New York 1993, p. 3.

247. *Walden*, p. 92.

248. Jane Rendall, *The Origins of Modern Feminism: Women in Britain, France and the United States, 1780–1860*, London 1985, p. 140.

journal *Dial*, which Fuller edited, never had a circulation of over 300 whilst the popular *Graham's Magazine* exceeded 50,000. Thoreau's first book, *A Week on the Concord and Merrimack Rivers* (1849), sold only 200 copies of a 1,000 print-run, obliging the author to make pencils to pay off the debt he had incurred (on Emerson's bad advice).[249] Even *Walden*, long in preparation and well trailed in New England literary circles, only sold 750 copies in its first year. Poetry books, of course, very rarely log sales into three digits, but in view of its subsequent status as master of the national canon, it is worth noting that the first edition of Whitman's *Leaves of Grass* sold less than a hundred. On the second (1856) he not only put his name but also as an endorsement Emerson's private praise that he stood on the threshold of a great career. Yet the next year Whitman could find no publisher for a third edition. Books generally remained a very expensive article to buy, and membership of subscription libraries was beyond the financial power of most working people.

It is correspondingly easy to overestimate the reach of North American education in this epoch. Even in New England there was in the 1840s only one college student for every 1,294 people (in 1985 the ratio was one for every nineteen). If Harvard might be seen as the pinnacle of that 'system', Robert Richardson reminds us that it had 432 students, eleven professors, seven instructors, nine proctors (residential supervisor and teaching assistant combined), a bursar, steward and librarian.

> The curriculum was largely fixed and generally detested, consisting of three years of Greek, three of Latin, two of math, one of history, three of English, and two years of one modern language.... Perhaps the worst aspect of the college was the hated marking system ... [under which] every aspect of college life was graded and marked. Every student received a mark on a scale of eight every day for recitation. Themes and other assignments counted for so many points each. The totals, which were used to determine class rank, upon which in turn rested the scholarship awards, were subject to all sorts of deductions, including disciplinary ones such as an absence from chapel or class or curfew violation.... All instructors and monitors sent their marks weekly to 'Old Quin' [President Josiah Quincy] who, more a headmaster than a college president, added up the scores himself.[250]

Subsequent generations must have benefited greatly from the fact that this academic propensity for numerical calculation was partially displaced from the judgement of students to the methodology of the social sciences (although contemporary grade point averages can still run to three decimal places, and they are increasingly being adopted by managers of British universities too pusillanimous or witless to resist this sublime Americanism).

In the South of the continent there was nothing to match Anglo America in terms of newspapers and journals, and literacy rates bore absolutely no comparison (even though none was properly measured until well into the twentieth century). In a recent study of Chile in the second quarter of the nineteenth century Iván Jaksić has

---

249. Robert Sattelmeyer, 'Thoreau and Emerson', in Joel Meyerson (ed.), *The Cambridge Companion to Henry David Thoreau*, Cambridge 1995, p. 31.
250. Richardson, *Henry Thoreau*, pp. 9–10.

identified 152 different newspapers, of which only nine published more than 1,000 issues and only sixteen more than 100. Yet in 1845 the government in Santiago spent 13,527 pesos subsidising seven papers – an expenditure that was not modest in the terms of the day and that would hardly have been agreed if these papers were not read and did not have influence.[251] The likes of Sarmiento and Alberdi were set to write for an immediate purpose by their patrons and editors, and Rosas had his own *Archivo Americano* under Pedro De Angelis to answer back. Robert Dunlop may have been correct when he claimed that 'reading is rarely resorted to in Guatemala, the only amusement of the men being gambling and making love to the fair sex, and of the women, intriguing and scandal'.[252] Yet the University of San Carlos was not much meaner as an isthmian institution than was Harvard for New England, and even a relatively impoverished college, such as that in San José, Costa Rica, could muster in its library works by De Tocqueville, Destutt de Tracy, Condillac, Montesquieu, Bentham (the collected works), Humboldt, Thiers, Constant, Franklin, Holbach and Puffendorf, as well as more familiar authors writing in Spanish.[253]

Dickens was very widely read in the USA through the popular magazines, and on his visit he was lionised as an author (as well as being scrutinised by the press and pirated by copyright thieves). Yet despite the extravagant accolades, his *American Notes* leave a distinctly sour taste. Much of this, as he candidly admits, was due to a habit that seemed to flourish within civilisation but which he found revolting:

> As Washington may be called the headquarters of tobacco-tinctured saliva, the time is come when I must confess, without any disguise, that the prevalence of those two odious practices of chewing and expectorating began about this time to be anything but agreeable and soon became most offensive and sickening. In all the public places in America this filthy custom is recognised. In the courts of law, the judge has his spittoon, the crier his, the witness his, the prisoner his; while the jurymen and spectators are provided for, as so many men who in the curse of nature must desire to spit incessantly. In the hospitals, the students of medicine are requested, by notices upon the wall, to eject their tobacco juice into the boxes provided for that purpose, and not to discolour the stairs.

And, when he visited the Senate,

> I was surprised to observe that even steady old chewers of great experience are not always good marksmen, which has rather inclined me to doubt that general proficiency with the rifle, of which we have heard so much in England. Several gentlemen called upon me who, in the course of conversation, frequently missed the spittoon at five paces; and one (but he was certainly short-sighted) mistook the closed sash for the open window, at three.[254]

---

251. 'Sarmiento and the Chilean Press', in Halperín Donghi et al. (eds), *Sarmiento: Author of a Nation*, pp. 41, 50–54.

252. *Travels in Central America*, p. 86. Here the term 'making love' is meant in the sense of 'courting' – itself a term in some danger of extinction in estuarised English, where shags are no longer the exclusive preserve of ornithologists and tobacconists. On the other hand, it could well be that Guatemalan males were more often engaged in sexual than literary intercourse (in the modern sense).

253. *Mentor Costarricense*, 78, 1 Feb. 1845.

254. *American Notes*, pp. 160, 169. In 'Romanzero' Heine wrote,

Little of the modern polemic against the burning of the same leaf possesses such humour, perhaps because it is now so part of the mainstream that it is available for full puritanisation, perhaps because one simply does not play with fire. In any event, Guizot would surely have conceded to sputum a place in civilisation, which he depicted in both liquid and pluralist terms:

> Civilization is a sort of ocean, constituting the wealth of a people, and on whose bosoms all the elements of life of that people, all the powers supporting its existence, assemble and unite. This is so true ... even [for] facts, which from their nature are odious, pernicious and which weight painfully upon nations...[255]

Sarmiento came to the same conclusion with explicit regard to the USA, accepting the argument that its flaws were part of its civilisation:

> In the United States, civilization holds sway over such numbers that, slowly, improvement is coming about. The influence of the gross masses on the individual forces him to accept the customs of the majority, and creates, finally, a kind of national consensus which may turn into pride and chauvinism. Europeans make fun of these rude habits, which are more superficial than profound, and the Americans, for the sake of argument, become obstinate and justify them as going hand in hand with liberty and the American way of life. I do not mean to defend or excuse these characteristics. Still, after examining the chief nations of Christendom, I have come to the conclusion that the Americans are the only really cultured people that exist on this earth and the last word in modern civilization.[256]

HTTP://WETNESS.WOMEN.WHITMAN

When E. George Squier reached Nicaragua's Caribbean coast in 1849 he was confronted with sights which he described in a detail that was scarcely necessary for his diplomatic dispatches:

> Most of the women had a simple white or flowered skirt (*nagua*) fastened above the hips, with a *guipil* or sort of large vandyke, with holes through which the arms were passed, and which hung loosely down over the breast. In some cases the *guipil* was rather short, and exposed a dark strip of skin from one to four inches wide, which the wanton wind often made much broader. It was very clear that false hips and other civilized contrivances had not

---

I sometimes think I'll go to America, that huge freedom-stall
inhabited by churls who believe in equality –
But I'm put off by a country where people chew tobacco, where
they play skittles without a king, where they spit without a spittoon.

Translated by Peter Branscombe in *Selected Verse*, Harmondsworth 1986, p. 193.

255. *History of Civilization in Europe*, p. 13.

256. Rockland (ed.), *Sarmiento's Travels in the United States*, p. 151. This despite exposure to a habit on which Sarmiento dwelled almost as long as had Dickens on matters salivary:

reached here, and it was equally clear that they were not needed to give fullness to the female figures which we saw around us.[257]

As the US minister moved further inland he came across more examples of such uncivilised sensuality to engage and excite his modern masculinity. When crossing Lake Nicaragua his boat was surrounded by teenage girls whose nakedness in the water would not in itself be so strange – even in Britain swimming costumes were not required by municipal baths until the 1870s, although there was strict segregation – but whose unselfconsciousness evoked more than a narrowly libidinal response:

> They looked laughingly up in our faces for a moment, exclaiming 'California!', then ducked under and were away. It seemed to us, while they stood drying their wet locks on the beach that no sculptor could desire fairer models for his studio; nor the painter a more effective group for the 'Bath of the Naides'. We were in an auspicious period; these days of primitive simplicity are passing away, if, indeed, they are not already past.[258]

Two thousand miles to the south the Leicestershire naturalist Henry Bates encountered on the banks of the River Pará a scene that drew a less wistful but not incomparable response:

> several handsome women, dressed in a slovenly manner, barefoot or shod in loose slippers; but wearing richly-decorated ear-rings, and around their necks strings of very large gold beads. They had dark expressive eyes, and remarkably rich heads of hair. It was a mere fancy, but I thought the mingled squalor, luxuriance and beauty of these women were pointedly in harmony with the rest of the scene; so striking in the view was the mixture of natural riches and human poverty.[259]

It is very likely that before he left for Nicaragua Squier had read Herman Melville's *Typee*, published to great controversy three years earlier. Unlike the later *Moby-Dick*, this text, sub-titled 'A Peep at Polynesian Life' and largely based on Melville's experience as a sailor beached in the Marquesa Islands, was fully populated with women, whose appearance and behaviour not only chimed with a burgeoning Anglo imagery of tropical abandon but was also remarkably similar to that subsequently described by Squier:

> In the United States you will see evidence everywhere of the religious cult which has grown up around that nation's noble and worthy instruments of its wealth: its feet. While conversing with you, the Yankee of careful breeding lifts one foot knee-high, takes off his shoe in order to caress his foot, and listens to the complaints that his overworked toes make. Any four individuals seated around a table will infallibly have their eight feet on top of it unless they can get seats upholstered in velvet, which, because of its softness, the Yankees prefer to marble.

Ibid., p. 149.

257. Squier, *Nicaragua*, p. 29. Squier was plainly less interested in the clothing than what filled it: 'The women of pure Spanish stock are very fair, and have the *embonpoint* which characterizes the sex under the tropics.' Ibid., p. 129.

258. Ibid., p. 102.

259. H.W. Bates, *The Naturalist on the River Amazon* (1863), London 1969, p. 4. Bates was here writing about mid-1848.

We were still some distance from the beach, and under slow headway when we sailed right into the midst of these swimming nymphs, and they boarded us at every quarter; many seizing hold of the chain-plates and springing into the chains; others, at the peril of being run over by the vessel in her course, catching at the bob-stays, and wreathing their slender forms about the ropes, hung suspended in the air. All of them at length succeeded in getting up the ship's side, where they clung dripping with the brine and glowing from the bath, their jet-black tresses streaming over their shoulders, and half-enveloping their otherwise naked forms. There they hung, sparkling with savage vitality, laughing gaily at one another, and chattering away with infinite glee. Nor were they idle the while, for each one performed the simple offices of the toilette for the other. Their luxuriant locks, wound up and twisted into the smallest possible compass, were freed from the briny element; the whole person carefully dried, and from a little round shell that passed from hand to hand, anointed with a fragrant oil.[260]

Melville teases us for another page or so before leaving the scene, which, in fact, opened a series of ugly misunderstandings that were typical of such encounters and which have prompted Victor Kiernan to remark that 'more than any other region the Pacific refutes any hypothesis of race relations being improved by free sex relations. If respect and esteem between two races do not grow by daylight they will not grow by moonlight'.[261]

It is worth mentioning – even at the risk of exasperating the serious reader – that in a further extended passage Melville describes his favourite 'beauteous nymph', the delicately tattooed Fayaway, not only in terms of her direct physical desirability but also in comparison to the indirect, semi-hidden attractions of a Peruvian woman:

Her free pliant figure was the very perfection of female grace and beauty. Her complexion was a rich and mantling olive, and when watching the glow upon her cheeks I could almost swear that beneath the transparent medium there lurked the blushes of a faint vermillion.... Her full lips, when parted with a smile, disclosed teeth with a dazzling whiteness; and when her rosy mouth opened with a burst of merriment, they looked like the milk-white seeds of the 'arta', a fruit of the valley, which, when cleft in twain, shows them reposing in rows on each side, imbedded in the red and juicy pulp. Her hair of the deepest brown, parted irregularly in the middle, flowed in natural ringlets over her shoulders, and whenever she chanced to stoop, fell over and hid from view her lovely bosom.... Her feet, though wholly exposed, were as diminutive and fairly shaped as those which peep from beneath the skirts of a Lima lady's dress.[262]

Building another scene – said to be an invention because it broke a Marquesan taboo – where Melville has Fayaway cast aside her robe whilst standing in a canoe, he observes, 'How captivating is a Peruvian lady, swinging in her gaily-worn hammock of grass, extended between two orange-trees, and inhaling the fragrance of a choice cigarro.'[263] Although attractively languid and indulging in a recreation normally reserved for men in the North, the woman from Peru occupies the middle distance in this

260. Herman Melville, *Typee* (1846), Harmondsworth 1972, pp. 48–9.
261. *Lords of Human Kind*, p. 265.
262. *Typee*, pp. 133–4.
263. Ibid., p. 191.

erotic landscape. She is not exposed like the nymphs of the Marquesas and Nicaragua; she attends to her own pleasures, and that is what we enjoy. When Melville, no longer dedicated to the task of literary arousal, describes Lima in *Moby-Dick*, he depicts it as having 'taken the white veil' – nearly the complete opposite of brown nakedness, and firmly on the 'civilised' side of any erotic frontier.[264]

Yet, as argued by Judy Mabro in her collection of European travel writing on the Middle East, the veil afforded yet one more opportunity for the expression of male prejudice and sexual fantasy.[265] Are not Squier and Melville doing rather more than describing (and embellishing) their experiences? Do they not represent a North American variant of the European attitude towards 'the Orient' which has attracted such critical attention over the last twenty years? In the words of Joanna De Groot,

> Oriental societies were frequently characterized by reference to the way in which women were treated, by descriptions of the laws and customs affecting women, by references to polygamy, veiling, and the seclusion of women, or by fascinated anecdotes of harems, dancing-girls, and sexual encounters.... Through these safely seductive and exotic scenarios, western middle class men could recover enjoyment of a sexuality which had become problematic in their own homes, just as some did through involvement with working-class women, a parallel which Flaubert realized when commenting on his recollections of Parisian brothels while in bed with Kucuk Hanem.[266]

Moreover, although De Groot notes that Flaubert describes being in the Red Sea as like 'lying on a thousand liquid breasts', she does not mention that he also wrote back to France, 'here one admits one's sodomy ... we have considered it our duty to indulge in this form of ejaculation'.[267] And such licence – whether paraded as duty or simply indulged because of the freedom so to do – is often presented as embodying more than a *frisson* of danger. In Rana Kabbani's view,

> The eroticism that the East promised was mysterious and tinged with hints of violence. The Oriental woman was linked, like a primitive goddess, with cycles of the supernatural. Cleopatra possesses knowledge of magic and poisonous prescriptions long before the need for death arises. Scheherazade lives on the edge of the sword, its blade is what her narrative must defeat, its shadow what makes her tale so captivating. Salome's dance is sexual and macabre at once. Her beauty is linked to the darker elements, complicit with the corruption that John the Baptist's words uncover.[268]

Yet, as Doris Sommer has argued with respect to gender relations and politico-literary culture *within* the Americas, it is less the erotic qualities of danger and cruelty than those of romantic endeavour and transgression which prevail.[269] Alberdi may not

---

264. *Moby-Dick*, p. 210.
265. *Veiled Half-Truths: Western Travellers' Perceptions of Middle Eastern Women*, London 1991.
266. '"Sex" and "Race": The Construction of Language and Image in the Nineteenth Century', in Susan Mendus and Jane Rendall (eds), *Sexuality and Subordination*, London 1989, pp. 104, 110.
267. Ibid., p. 105. Francis Steegmuller (ed.), *The Letters of Gustave Flaubert, 1830–1857*, London 1980, pp. 111, 121.
268. *Imperial Fictions: Europe's Myths of Orient*, London 1986, p. 68.
269. *Foundational Fictions: The National Romance of Latin America*, Berkeley 1991.

himself have been very turned on by Melville's nubile nymphs but he was fully aware of the contribution that sexual attraction could make to his mission of civilising Spanish America through blood (which meant through insemination):

> we will conquer instead of being conquered. South America has an army for this purpose, its beautiful and amiable women of Andalusian origin and improved under the splendid sky of the New World. Remove the immoral impediments that sterilize the power of America's fair sex and you will have effected the change in our race or our racial character.[270]

Sommer also notes that Sarmiento – in what was surely not an unguarded moment of writing – describes the Argentine pampa as

> ready for the man who dares to make her productive [as she] flaunts her smooth, infinite, downy brow without frontiers, without any landmarks; it's the very image of the sea on land ... the land waiting for the command to bring forth every herb-yielding seed after its kind.[271]

The modern variant of this voice, in Neruda, is more direct but equally gender-specific/exclusive:

> When I look at the shape
> of America on the map,
> my love, it is you I see:
> the height of copper on your head,
> your breasts, wheat and snow,
> your slender waist,
> swift throbbing rivers, sweet
> hills and meadows
> and in the cold of the south your feet end
> its geography of duplicated gold ...
>
> and the red thickness
> of the bush where
> thirst and hunger lie in wait.

---

270. Mayer, *Las 'Bases' de Alberdi*, p. 406.

271. *Facundo*, p. 3, quoted in *Foundational Fictions*, p. 61. In my edition of Mrs Mann's translation 'flaunts' ('ostenta') is rendered 'displays', and 'downy brow' ('velluda frente') as 'velvet-like surface', but Sommer's point that 'velludo' has strong associations with pubic hair is well taken. Sarmiento was an 'Orientalist' in the sense of Edward Said's 1978 book (*Orientalism*, Harmondsworth) and Rana Kabbani's of 1986 (*Imperial Fictions: Europe's Myths of Orient*, London, republished in 1994 without any apparent recognition of feminist and other criticisms of the term for its univocal political qualities and narrow methodological possibilities). On 22 August 1841 Sarmiento opened an article in *El Mercurio* with an epigram penned by Aimé Martin at the time of the occupation of Algeria (which Sarmiento had visited):

> Man cannot lower woman without himself falling into degradation; and by elevating her he improves himself. Societies are turned to brutes in her arms, or they are civilized at her feet. Let us take a look around the globe: we observe these two great divisions of the human race, the Orient and the West. Half of the ancient world remains motionless and without thought, under the weight of a barbarous civilization: women there are slaves. The other half marches toward equality and light: women are free and honoured.

Quoted in Elizabeth Garrels, 'Sarmiento and the Woman Question', in Halperín Donghi et al. (eds), *Sarmiento: Author of a Nation*, p. 279.

And this my spacious country welcomes me,
little America, in your body.[272]

It may be more familiar, but poetic reaffirmation of belonging through sexual
rapport and symbolism is by no means the exclusive property of the male voice, even
if such confidence and direct language are rare before the twentieth century, when
the nations were not yet fully made. Gioconda Belli's amatory declaration to her
country opens with a tender post-coital sigh and an amused reflection on gender that
Neruda did not have to negotiate:

> Ah, Nicaragua
> You're my man
> with a woman's name!
> You please me.
>
> You please me across all your forests,
> valleys and mountains.
> Your heat and the reverberating rays of the sun on your roads
> please me.
> Your great bristling chest pleases me,
> there I hear the volcanoes and the thunder of magma.
> The furious breathing of your skies pleases me
> when it rains and drenches.
> You please me by the way you possess me,
> filling me with grass, sadness and laughter
> from head to toe.
>
> I love you,
> I'm hopelessly in love
> and if I left you it wasn't for long,
> it wasn't to forget the bonds, the limes,
> it wasn't to forget that which should not be forgotten.
>   I am with you, my Nicaragua
>   my man
>   with a woman's name![273]

For outsiders desire for possession is unlikely to assume language such as this,
which actually lies closer to the fornicatory form often used for dismissive abuse.
Indeed, desire from the outside is much more likely to take the form of denial. In the

---

272. 'Little America' in *The Captain's Verses* (1953), New York 1972, p. 111.
273. From 'Linea del Fuego' (1974–78), in *El Ojo de la Mujer*, Managua 1991, p. 86. Belli also writes
strongly from the body outwards:

> To explore a body through the night
> Is to travel the world
> To cross without a compass
> Gulf islands, peninsulars, and dams against the enraged waters.
> It is no easy task but it gives pleasure –
> Don't believe that you can do it in a day
> Or a night opened out on the sheets.
> There are in the pores enough secrets to fill many moons.

'Pequeñas lecciones de erotismo', from 'De la Costilla de Eva' (1986), in ibid., p. 273.

Nicaragua of 1856 beset by foreign filibusterers the antics of the Masaya madame Ramona Barquero gave rise to a popular ditty which made the most of the fact that a screw can go both ways:

> Ah! Poor Mamá Ramona,
> She's been screwed.
> By lying with the Yankees
> She showed the devil she's no prude!
>
> Ah! Poor Mamá Ramona,
> With the Yankees she felt whorey.
> They grabbed her tits
> And now can't finish the story.
>
> From faraway came the Yankees.
> From faraway came those bastards
> To screw our Nicaragua.
> Those thieves are real dastards.[274]

Freud's model of sublimation – broadly, the expression of the sexual instinct through non-sexual activity – is perhaps too engagingly simple to explain the full gamut of foreign policy (when it is run by priapic personalities such as Palmerston and Kennedy), but David Slater has recently sought to apply the approach of Lacan to this field:

> The desire to possess, to take hold of the other society, is reflected in the three registers of Lacanian analysis – the imaginary, the symbolic order, and the real. In Lacanian theory, the discourse of the Master (or self-identical ego) promotes consciousness, synthesis, and self-equivalence by establishing the control of master signifiers which order knowledge according to their own values. For example, in the Cuban case, the desire of the United States to penetrate and possess the other was justified through the master signifier of bringing Cuba into the orbit of US and Western civilization.[275]

Read in this light, the sentiments expressed in April 1849 by James Buchanan to Secretary of State John Clayton, whilst firmly in the realm of the 'imaginary' – not least because he was not appointed to the embassy in Madrid he thought he had been promised – are positively tumescent in their anticipation of seduction:

> We must have Cuba. We can't do without Cuba, and above all we must not suffer its transfer to Great Britain. We shall acquire it by a coup d'état at some propitious moment, which from the present state of Europe may not be far distant. How delighted, then, am I to feel that you have selected a diplomatist and fit for the work – one who, possessing no vanity himself and knowing when to speak and when to be silent, is so well calculated to flatter the pride of the Dons – who by the gentle arts of insinuation and persuasion can gradually prepare the queen mother, the ministers and courtiers for the great surrender – and who

---

274. Quoted in E. Bradford Burns, *Patriarch and Folk: The Emergence of Nicaragua, 1798–1858*, Cambridge, Mass., 1991, pp. 214–15.

275. David Slater, 'Spatialities of Power and Postmodern Ethics – Rethinking Geopolitical Encounters', *Environmental Planning*, 15, 1997, p. 66.

above all is a perfect master both of the language of Louis le Grand and of the knight of rueful countenance. Cuba is already ours. I can feel it in my finger ends.[276]

Here the sense of jealousy links the 'real' and 'imaginary' aspects of possessiveness in international affairs rather tightly. Of course, Buchanan's confidence was misplaced, and it became less and less easy to 'have' Cuba in terms of formal annexation of territory. This was partly as a result of the deep-seated anti-colonial ethos in US political culture, partly because increased opposition within Cuba to Spanish rule enhanced Madrid's defensiveness and drew attention to a complicating internal element, and partly because – whether or not still preoccupied with the 'internal frontier' to the exclusion of expansionism abroad – the United States was unready for such a major undertaking until at least the 1880s. When the invasion/penetration finally came, in 1898, it led to both feigned independence and incomplete possession – a loveless marriage, perhaps, based on an initially violent tryst and the inequitable contract of the Platt Amendment, by which Uncle Sam assigned all conjugal rights to himself. If the metaphor has not already gone soft, one might suggest that since 1961 Cuba has been, at the very least, the object of Washington's wet dream, protected in the world of the 'real' precisely because it is an island surrounded by water.

Although the exceptional case of Cuba presents an unusually high consonance between the 'imaginary' and the 'real' in political and physical/spatial spheres, there are good grounds for resisting any simple 'Orientalist' reading of Anglo–Latin American relations. As Julia Kushigian has argued, the problems with this notion of imperialist cultures comfortably pathologising their dominions go beyond simplistic theses about the collusion of knowledge and power, or the narrow binary opposition upon which such theses almost invariably rest. Hispanic society possesses its own Orientalist tradition, which since the early seventeenth century became increasingly detached from political power, and from the nineteenth century developed in America a strand that, in the guise of modernism, reached for more than the merely exotic, seeking the eliptical-within-the-exotic.[277] This is one of the more prominent features in Borges's writing although it is perhaps most compelling when he places it in harness with nineteenth-century material drawn as much from the Mississippi as from life on the platine pampa.[278]

---

276. Buchanan, Washington, to Clayton, 17 April 1849, in J.B. Moore (ed.), *Works of James Buchanan*, Washington 1908–11, VIII, pp. 360–61. Buchanan's immodesty stemmed in part from his own experience as secretary of state during the Mexican War, but it had evidently been boosted by Clayton's ingratiating overture three days earlier: 'What will you give me to recall Romulus Saunders from Spain? Speak out – do not be bashful. Shall I try to buy Cuba after you made such a botch of that business? Do you still wish like Sancho to have an island?' Quoted in ibid., p. 356.

277. Julia Kushigian, *Orientalism in the Hispanic Literary Tradition: In Dialogue with Borges, Paz and Sarduy*, Albuquerque 1991.

278. For a marvellous appraisal of the short story 'The South', in which Johannes Dahlmann travels half-wounded, half-lucid, towards his austral destiny in the company of *The Thousand and One Nights*, see Beatriz Sarlo, *Jorge Luis Borges: A Writer on the Edge*, London 1993, pp. 42–8.

One might see some shared features in the post-Orientalist emergence of 'sub-altern studies', which identifies hitherto unrecognised possibilities of power lying beyond the 'real' in ambivalence and hybridity. This perspective seeks to unveil parallax worlds of comprehension and experience in a way which questions the winner/loser finality of 'zero-sum politics' so often associated with the publicly powerful and powerless.[279] In some ways that genre is best seen as a subset of postmodernism, but its interpretative focus on the formally weak offers a refreshing opportunity to escape from the intellectually deadening effect of 'victim culture' without losing any sense of the inequity and injustice within which new combinations of the 'imaginary' and the 'symbolic' are continually renegotiated – sometimes with more than surreptitious impact upon the 'real'. In short, the baby is not evacuated with the bathwater. Without such a sensibility where does anybody find the woman of the nineteenth century except on the plinth of male desire, in the stockade of domestic drudgery, or on the wild shores of maddening protest?

In a brief but powerful essay, the modern novelist Luisa Valenzuela traces the journey made by Gioconda Belli between words and bodies by taking up the Latin motif '*hic sunt leones*' (here be lions) inscribed on those parts of ancient maps where the territory was unknown:

> '*Hic sunt leones*' seems now to be written the length and breadth of the woman's body, and all over the body of her literary work.... There are lions ready to jump at the first instigation, in that precise moment when words are not controlled any more and truths can be uttered by means of our bodies, without our even being aware of them ... writers are meant for that: to look and then tell what they have seen. But that look is usually more interior than exterior, goes more towards the invisible than the visible, so when women have looked between their legs not to find the phallus, they have really seen much further away, further in and further back.... This feminine language ... this obscure discourse coming from the depths of the guts, can be defined as a fascination with the disgusting. It has to do with mud and very visceral feelings and perhaps unnamed menstrual blood and love for warm viscosities.[280]

The language of the nineteenth century very rarely allowed for such direct and literal expression, but one can identify a related affinity for fluids, for the kind of 'oceanic feeling' that Freud failed to find in himself, which he presented as 'religious ... even if one rejects every belief and illusion', and with which he introduces us to the 'reality principle'.[281] For Margaret Fuller, whose *Woman in the Nineteenth Century*

279. A good example of this approach towards literary studies is Homi K. Bhabha (ed.), *Nation and Narration*, London 1990, in which Doris Sommer presents a condensed version of her thesis for Latin America.

280. 'The Other Face of the Phallus', in Bell Gale Chevigny and Gari Laguardia (eds), *Reinventing the Americas: Comparative Studies of the Literature of the United States and Spanish America*, Cambridge 1987, pp. 242–4.

281. One comes to learn a procedure by which, through a deliberate action of one's sensory activities and through suitable muscular action, one can differentiate between what is internal – what belongs to the ego – and what is external – what emanates from the outer world. In this way one makes the first step towards the introduction of the reality principle which is to dominate future development.

(1845) addressed the question of gender firmly within the Transcendentalist paradigm and at a time of sharp reversals to the advances made by women in the early republic,[282] the first fluid to be identified in this regard was electrical:

> The electrical, the magnetic element in woman has not been fairly brought out at any period. Every thing might be expected from it; she has far more of it than man. This is commonly expressed by saying that her intuitions are more rapid and more correct. You will often see men of high intellect absolutely stupid in regard to the atmospheric changes, the fine invisible links which connect the forms of life around them, while common women, if pure and modest, so that a vulgar self do not overshadow the mental eye, will seize and delineate these with unerring discrimination ... Male and female represent the two sides of the great radical dualism. But, in fact, they are perpetually passing into one another. Fluid hardens to solid, solid rushes to fluid. There is no wholly masculine man, no purely feminine woman.[283]

> This differentiation, of course, serves the practical purpose of enabling one to defend oneself against sensations of unpleasure which one actually feels or with which one is threatened. In order to fend off certain unpleasurable excitations arising from within, the ego can use no other methods than those which it uses against unpleasure from without, and this is the starting point of important pathological disturbances. In this way, then, the ego detaches itself from the external world. Or, to put it more correctly, originally the ego includes everything, later it separates off an external world from itself. Our present ego-feeling is, therefore, only a shrunken residue of a much more inclusive – indeed, an all-embracing – feeling which corresponded to a more intimate bond between the ego and the world about it. If we may assume that there are many people in whose mental life this primary ego-feeling has persisted to a greater or lesser degree, it would exist in them side by side with the narrower and more sharply demarcated ego-feeling of maturity, like a kind of counterpoint to it. In that case, the ideational contents appropriate to it would be precisely those of limitlessness and a bond with the universe – the same ideas with which my friend elucidated the 'oceanic feeling'.

'Civilization and Its Discontents' (1929), in *Civilization, Society and Religion*, Harmondsworth 1985, p. 255. Freud's interlocutor was a man, but Jimmie Killingsworth refers to this 'oceanic feeling' as 'interuterine', which might perhaps meet our present purposes, and is a key insight to the stanzas of 'Song of Myself' that he is analysing (and that we will discuss in a moment), but that quite wrongly attributes an aspect of gender to this specific passage of Freud's. *Whitman's Poetry of the Body: Sexuality, Politics and the Text*, Chapel Hill, N.C., 1989, p. 5.

282. Man is a being of two-fold relations, to nature beneath, and intelligences above him. The earth is his school, if not his birth-place: God his object: life and thought, his means of interpreting nature, and aspiring to God.

  Only a fraction of this purpose is accomplished in the life of any one man. Its entire accomplishment is to be hoped only from the sum of the lives of men, or man considered as a whole.

  As this whole has one soul and one body, any injury or obstruction to a part, or to the meanest member, affects the whole. Man can never be perfectly happy or virtuous, till all men are so.

  To address man wisely, you must not forget that his life is partly animal, subject to the same laws with nature.

  But you cannot address him wisely unless you consider him still more as a soul, and appreciate the conditions and destiny of soul.

  The growth of man is two-fold, masculine and feminine.

  As far as these two methods can be distinguished they are so as
    Energy and Harmony
    Power and Beauty
    Intellect and Love.

Woman in the Nineteenth Century (1845), Oxford 1994, p. 112.

283. Ibid., pp. 66, 75. Reporting from Paris for the *New York Daily Tribune* in 1847, Fuller wrote that, although beautiful, American women did not match the French for presence: 'the magnetic fluid that envelopes them is less brilliant and exhilarating in its attractions'. *The Portable Margaret Fuller*, New York 1994, p. 401.

Fuller frequently resorts to nature in order to make a social point. The first example is dry and warm:

> Even among the North American Indians, a race of men as completely engaged in mere instinctive life as almost any in the world, and where each chief, keeping many wives as useful servants, of course looks with no kind eye on celibacy in women, it was excused in the following instance.... A woman dreamt in youth that she was betrothed to the Sun. She built her a wigwam apart, filled it with emblems of her alliance, and means of an independent life. There she passed her days, sustained by her own exertions, and true to her supposed engagement. In any tribe, we believe, a woman, who lived as if she were betrothed to the Sun, would be tolerated, and the rays which made her youth blossom sweetly, would crown her with a halo in old age.... I would have [woman], like the Indian girl, dedicate herself to the Sun, the Sun of Truth, and go nowhere if his beams did not make clear the path. I would have her free from compromise, from complaisance, from helplessness, because I would have her good enough and strong enough to love one and all beings, from the fulness, not the poverty of being.[284]

The next is cold, wet and somewhat more prosaic in its association between the inner and the outer:

> The praises of cold water seem to me an excellent sign in the age. They denote a tendency to the true life. We are now to have, as a remedy for ills, not orvietan, or opium, or any quack medicine, but plenty of air and water.... Every day we observe signs that the natural feelings on these subjects are about to be reinstated, and the body to claim care as the abode and organ of the soul, not as the tool of servile labor, or the object of voluptuous indulgence. A poor woman who had passed through the lowest grades of ignomiwny seemed to think she had never been wholly lost, 'for', said she, 'I would always have good underclothes'; and, indeed, who could doubt that this denoted the remains of private self-respect in the mind?[285]

In describing a trip outside Mexico City in 1840, the Edinburgh-born wife of the Spanish ambassador, Fanny Calderón de la Barca, conflates this motif of chaste cleanliness with the energetic animalism portrayed by Melville and Squier, as if to ratify Fuller's own point about the overlapping properties of masculinity and feminity (although she doesn't apply this to the men in her report):

> San Bartolo is a small, scattered Indian village, with a church, and is remarkable for a beautiful spring of water, that jets cold and clear from the hard rock, as if Moses had but just smote it; for its superb tall pine-trees; for the good looks and cleanness of the Indian women, who are for ever washing their long hair in the innumerable clear streamlets formed by the spring.... Some of the young women were remarkably handsome, with the most beautiful teeth imaginable, laughing and talking in their native tongue at a great rate, as they were washing in the brooks, some their hair and others their clothes. The men looked as dirty as Indians generally do.... A sister of the woman who takes charge of the hacienda where we live is one of the most beautiful I have ever beheld. Large eyes, with long dark lashes, black hair nearly touching the ground, teeth like snow, a dark but glowing complexion, a superb figure, with fine arms and hands, and small beautifully formed feet.[286]

---

284. *Woman in the Nineteenth Century*, pp. 65, 78.
285. Ibid., p. 109.
286. Madame Calderón de la Barca, *Life in Mexico* (1842), London 1987, pp. 367–8.

Madame Calderón de la Barca herself occasionally bathed in warm springs. Some-times, 'my curiosity to try its temperature was very soon satisfied', the heat forcing her to slump out on the mattress provided alongside, but occasionally the natural springs provided prolonged pleasure, as at Cuincho:

> We stopped here to take a bath, and found the temperature of the water delicious, about the ordinary temperature of the human body. The baths are rather dark, being enclosed in great stone walls, with the light coming from a very small aperture near the roof. A bird, that looked like a wild duck, was sailing about in the largest one, having made its entry along with the water when it was let in. I never bathed in any water which I so much regretted leaving.[287]

The present age is awash with literature in which the aquatic element swamps out the reality principle, not least by imagined regression to 'polymorphously perverse' childhood.[288] As a result of this and the prominence of the water motif in classical mythology it is tempting to 'naturalise' the phenomenon and see it as ever prominent, whereas Peter Gay suggests that, whatever the movements of the inner mind over the ages, the mid nineteenth century witnessed a particularly strong upsurge in public interest:

> It was water even more than the woods or the hills, water yielding the most primitive of stimulation buoying up the body and caressing the skin, that Kingsley celebrated most rhapsodically: 'the purple veil of water', to say nothing of the 'fiery sea'. Others, as disparate as Amiel and Whitman, found bathing, or just lolling in the wet element, a keenly sensual experience, at once refreshing and stirring. Indeed Amiel could associate Venus Anadyomene, the goddess of love rising from the sea, with a cold bath he recorded in his private journal. Similarly, Flaubert has Emma Bovary, that doomed bourgeoise, 'stretch her limbs lazily', as she bathes in the amorous, hopelessly banal words of her lover Rodolphe. The founding of the hydropathic establishments in the United States of the 1840s, and later, institutionalized this water eroticism. Women who frequented them, like [Harriet] Beecher, found them places where they could freely discuss their bodies and, more or less artlessly, enjoy them. As the *Water Cure Journal* sketched the treatment in 1846: 'A large coarse blanket is spread upon a mattress. The patient lies down upon it, as in the wet sheet, and is closely packed from neck to toe and covered with a number of other blankets.' Then, 'having duly sweated, the patient is unpacked, and steps into a shallow bath, preferably a plunge bath'. Now, 'this transition from copious perspiration to cold water is not only perfectly innocuous, but

---

287. Ibid., pp. 262–3, 480.
288. In her own response to 'phallogocentrism' (the privileging of the phallus and the word as the sources of power) Toril Moi celebrates the work of Hélène Cixous, for whom

> 'water is the feminine element *par excellence*; the closure of the mythical world contains and reflects the comforting security of the mother's womb. It is within this space that Cixous's speaking subject is free to move from one subject position to another, or to merge oceanically with the world.'

Cixous's prose may lose something in translation, but it would seem to justify Moi's comment:

> We are ourselves sea, sand, coral, sea-weed, beaches, tides, swimmers, children, waves…. Hetero-geneous, yes. For her joyous benefits she is erogenous; she is the erogeneity of the heterogeneous: airborne swimmer, in flight, she does not cling to herself; she is dispersible, prodigious, stunning, desirous and capable of others, of the other woman that she will be, of the other woman she isn't, of him, of you.

'Medusa', quoted in Toril Moi, *Sexual/Textual Politics*, London 1998, pp. 116–17.

highly sanitary. A powerful reaction, and a high degree of exhilaration and vigour are the result.' One might well believe it. This sort of treatment provided some of the enjoyment of intercourse, and was much safer.[289]

It was in 1846 that Harriet Beecher Stowe – exhausted by childbirth, a brush with cholera, and ten years of a demanding marriage – had checked herself into the Brattleboro Water Cure in Vermont and stayed for well over a year. The diet, fresh air and exercise, as well as the bathing, restored her precarious health, and seemingly did so with some of the sensuality indicated by Peter Gay. Most of the 400 patients who attended Brattleboro that year were women, and the relaxed intimacy in the baths was always between people of the same sex. In the case of Beecher – and quite possibly others too – the husband left behind chafed at the absence of a sexual partner that taking the water cure entailed: 'If your health were so far restored that you could take me again to your *bed and board*, that would be the surest.' However, Calvin Stowe was breaking far fewer taboos of that day than this by responding to eighteen months of wifely absence by sleeping with a man. In February 1847 he wrote to Harriet that, 'When I get desperate, and cannot stand it any longer, I get dear, good kind-hearted Brother Stagg to come and sleep with me, and he puts his arms round me and hugs me to my heart's content.' Another acquaintance, Mr Farben of Newton, Massachusetts, 'kisses and kisses upon my rough old face, as if I were a most beautiful young lady instead of a musty old man ... he says that it *is almost as good as being married*'.[290]

Walt Whitman not only liked to bathe himself but also deployed aquatic imagery in some of his most powerfully sexual stanzas. His work was a lifelong endeavour of holding self by expressing it through a variety of what Toril Moi calls 'subject positions'. In the middle sections of 'Song of Myself' – the 52-section poem that formed the core of the first edition of *Leaves of Grass* (1855) – he makes no bones about this or the power it endows:

> I am the poet of the Body and I am the poet of the Soul,
> The pleasures of heaven are with me and the pains of hell are with me,
> The first I graft and increase upon myself, the latter I translate into a new tongue.
> I am the poet of the woman the same as the man,
> And I say it is as great to be a woman as to be a man,
> And I say there is nothing greater than the mother of men.

It is as himself in the guise – or 'subject position' – of either gender that he yields to the 'oceanic feeling' in the following section:

> You sea! I resign myself to you also – I guess what you mean,
> I behold from the beach your crooked inviting fingers,
> I believe you refuse to go back without feeling of me,
> We must have a turn together, I undress, hurry me out of sight of the land,
> Cushion me soft, rock me in billowy drowse.
> Dash me with amorous wet, I can repay you.

---

289. Peter Gay, *The Bourgeois Experience Victoria to Freud: II. The Tender Passion*, Oxford 1986, pp. 279–80.
290. Quoted in Joan D. Hedrick, *Harriet Beecher Stowe: A Life*, New York 1994, pp. 180–81.

Earlier, writing with empathy for the hidden gaze and the dreams it distils, he depicts a woman as an invisible 'twenty-ninth bather':

> Twenty-eight young men bathe by the shore,
> Twenty-eight young men and all so friendly,
> Twenty-eight years of womanly life and all so lonesome.
>
> She owns the fine house by the rise of the bank,
> She hides handsome and richly drest aft the blinds of the window.
>
> Which of the young men does she like the best?
> Ah the homeliest of them is beautiful to her.
>
> Where are you off to, lady? for I see you,
> You splash in the water there, yet stay stock still in your room.
>
> Dancing and laughing along the beach came the twenty-ninth bather,
> The rest did not see her, but she saw them and loved them.
>
> The beards of the young men glisten'd with wet, it ran from their long hair,
> Little streams pass'd all over their bodies.
>
> An unseen hand also pass'd over their bodies,
> It descended tremblingly from their temples and ribs.
>
> The young men float on their backs, their white bellies bulge to the
>   sun, they do not ask who seizes fast to them,
> They do not know who puffs and declines with pendant and
>   bending arch,
> They do not think whom they souse with spray.

Even at the end Whitman is only looking on, but in her mind's eye his woman is herself actively participating; she is not watching another woman love the men, or the men souse each other. Rather like Melville's lady from Lima, she is in the middle distance – she is depicted in the third person, addressed briefly in the second, and then described again in the third; she has twenty-eight men with whom to take her pleasure but, under interrogation, one proves more special, limiting the sense of promiscuity. At one level Whitman is making sex public, but at another it remains hidden, both in the woman's imaginings and in the possibility of reading the poem innocuously. Here at least the conventions of representation are not fully overthrown, even if they are surely jarred.[291] Water provides the perfect alibi for everyone concerned.

In contrast to Melville's accomplished literary translation of his residence in the Marquesas into chaste profit, Paul Gauguin lived out his last years on the islands in

---

291. *Leaves of Grass*, pp. 44–5, 35. For the commentary here I owe much to Michael Warner, 'Whitman Drunk', in Betsy Erkkila and Jay Grossman (eds), *Breaking Bounds: Whitman and American Cultural Studies*, Oxford 1996, p. 42, although there, discussing a different poem, Warner makes the rather different point that Whitman frequently sought to make sex public. In the same volume Vivian Pollack notes that Whitman pays scant attention to the eroticism of maternity, although his heterosexual lovemaking always leads to childbirth. Ibid., p. 99. Elsewhile Erkkila has written, '[i]f at times Whitman's work seems to reinscribe the conservative sexual ideology of his time, his poems had and still do have a galvanizing effect on women readers'. *Whitman the Political Poet*, New York 1989, p. 314, quoted in Sherry Ceniza, 'Women's Responses to the *Leaves of Grass*', in Ezra Greenspan (ed.), *The Cambridge Companion to Walt Whitman*, Cambridge 1995, p. 113.

open scandal as he sought an authentic 'savagism' in his art and the arms of his teenage lover. Gauguin's fine painting of the androgynous *Man with an Axe* decorates the cover of the latest Everyman edition of *Typee*, and his written descriptions of both Tahiti and the Marquesas understandably share Melville's attention to physicality, even when clothing was being worn.

> Here and there some of the women, hidden by stones, squatted in the water, their skirts lifted to their waists, cleansing their hips soiled by the dust of the road, refreshing the joints that had become irritated by the walk and the heat. Feeling in good shape again, they resumed their way to Papeete, bosom to the fore, the tips of the breasts like two pointed shells protruding under the muslin dress, with all the suppleness and grace of healthy animals, they give off all around them a blend of animal odour and perfumes of sandalwood and *tiaré*: *Teine merahi noa noa* ('Now very fragrant'), they say.[292]

When John Mitchel visited Tahiti in 1854 his response was rather different, appreciating most of the bodies but none of the imperialist garb with which they were covered:

> We walk along the beach, which is also the main street of Papeete: meet hundreds of men and women − a tall, well-made, graceful and lazy race. The women have great black eyes, long, smooth black hair; and on every glossy head a wreath of fresh flowers. They wear nothing but the *parien*, a long robe of some bright-coloured fabric (made for them in world-clothing Manchester), gathered close around the neck, and hanging loose to the feet, without even a girdle. I am not reconciled to this dress, though they generally have forms that no barbarity of drapery can disguise − nor to their wide mouths, though their teeth are orient pearls.[293]

Constitutionally incapable of treating such matters as merely secondary, Gauguin was unafraid to reveal − and even promote − a sexual life that was viewed as absolutely licentious in *fin-de-siècle* France. One finds in his accounts not, as in Melville, a simple fade before penetration − the age of Verlaine and Rimbaud had, after all, passed in the interim − but, rather, a tugging away from the easy phallic associations of assured masculinity towards a more complex identity. He once wrote in a newspaper, 'I must confess that I am myself a woman, and that I am always prepared to applaud a woman who is more daring than I, and is equal to a man in fighting for freedom of behaviour.'[294]

In one − not unrepresentative − passage of his journal Gauguin presses a point almost completely contrary to that conjured up by Melville's description of the nymphs:

> Among peoples that go naked, as among animals, the difference between the sexes is less accentuated than in our climates. Thanks to our cinctures and corsets we have succeeded in making an artificial being out of woman.... On Tahiti the breezes from forest and sea strengthen the lungs, they broaden the shoulders and hips.... There is something virile in the

---

292. 'Noa Noa' (1893), in Daniel Guérin (ed.), *Paul Gauguin: The Writings of a Savage*, New York 1996, p. 78.
293. *Jail Journal*, Glasgow 1876, p. 304.
294. Quoted in Stephen F. Eisenman, *Gauguin's Skirt*, London 1997, p. 100.

women and feminine in the men.... Man and woman are comrades, friends rather than lovers, dwelling together almost without cease, in pain as in pleasure, and even the very idea of vice is unknown to them.[295]

As Stephen Eisenman has pointed out, this observation may not derive exclusively from experience since it is in keeping with sentiments expressed (to a woman) nearly a decade earlier:

If ... you want to be someone, to find happiness solely in your independence and your conscience ... you must regard yourself as Androgyne, without sex. By that I mean that heart and soul, in short all that is divine, must not be the slave of matter, that is the body. The virtues of a woman are exactly the same as the virtues of a man.[296]

Gauguin appears to be occupying almost the same space as Margaret Fuller, but if he derived any inclination for a progressive attitude to women and sexuality from reading, it was surely from his own grandmother, Flora Tristán, whom he never met and about whom he was very proud. A few months before his death in 1903 Gauguin wrote,

Memories! That means history. That means a date. Everything in it is interesting – except the author. And you have to tell who you are and where you come from. Making a confession – ever since Jean-Jacques Rousseau that has been no slight affair. If I tell you that by the female line I descend from a Borgia of Aragon, [and a] viceroy of Peru you will say that it is not true and I am pretentious. But if I tell you that the family is a family of sewer cleaners, you will hold me in contempt.... My grandmother was quite a woman. Her name was Flora Tristán. Proudhon said she had genius. Not knowing anything about it, I rely on Proudhon. She created a whole lot of socialist things, among others the Union ouvrière. The grateful workers erected a monument to her in the cemetery in Bordeaux. She probably didn't know how to cook – a socialist bluestocking, an anarchist.... What I can be sure of, however, is that Flora Tristán was a very lovely and noble lady.[297]

Nevertheless, the passage of Tristán's writing that is most redolent of her grandson's style and persona is one that Gauguin could not have read – a letter to her Polish friend Olympe Chodzko that is an unusually candid expression of the difficulty she experienced throughout her life over the limits of sexual activity:

perhaps you are playing with me – if so, beware! For a long time I have wanted to be loved passionately by a woman – oh, how I would have liked to be a man, so that I could have a woman's love. I have reached the point where no man's love is enough for me; perhaps

---

295. Quoted in ibid., p. 115.
296. Quoted in ibid., p. 116.
297. Guérin (ed.), *Writings of a Savage*, pp. 230–32. Gauguin was not inventing – the Tristán de Moscosos could claim blood ties with Cesare Borgia (and so with his sister Lucrezia). Flora's uncle, Pio de Tristán y Moscoso of Arequipa, was the last Spanish viceroy of Peru, then, having embraced republicanism, president of South Peru under Marshal Santa Cruz's Peru–Bolivia Confederation in the 1830s. He long outlived Flora, and, as we shall see, when Gauguin says of her, 'at one point she went to Peru to see her uncle', he laconically suppresses a critical encounter in both their lives. (Don Pio had Flora's account of it publicly burnt in the plaza of Arequipa.) Marx and Engels refer briefly to Tristán at the start and end of *The Holy Family* (1845), and although the tone there is quite sympathetic, one imagines that they saw her as simply one more 'utopian socialist'.

a woman's love would give me what I seek for a woman's heart and imagination are so much stronger than a man's, and her mind is much richer in resources. But perhaps you will tell me that as physical attraction cannot exist between two people of the same sex, this passionate exalted love you dream of can never be realised between one woman and another? Yes and no – there comes a time in life when the senses change places, or to put it another way, the brain takes them all in its embrace ... for me, love, *true* love, can exist only between souls. It is all so simple: two women can love in this way, so can two men. I am only trying to tell you that just now I feel an ardent desire to be loved, but I am so ambitious, so demanding, so fastidious and so greedy that nothing I am offered ever satisfies me.[298]

FEMINIST FOREPIECES

Both Tristán and Gauguin had disastrous marriages, and the grandson was writing out of bitter experience as well as under her influence when he observed,

> If ... this institution, marriage, which is nothing other than a sale, is the only one declared to be moral and acceptable for the copulation of the sexes, it follows that all who do not want or who cannot marry are excluded from that morality. There is no room left for love. Treated this way, woman becomes abject; she is doomed either to get married if fortune permits or to remain a virgin, which is such an unnatural condition, so monstrously indecent and unhealthy.[299]

Yet even for the 14-year-old Tehamana who shared his bed in the South Seas Gauguin employs the terminology of the institution and reveals a deeper dread than that of form: 'At night my wife seeks my caresses. She knows that I am afraid of her and she abuses my fear.'[300] In a similar vein, reflecting on her voyage to Peru in 1833, his grandmother wrote,

> I had loved twice: the first time, I was still a child. The young man to whom I gave my affection was worthy of it in every way, but his soul lacked strength, and he died rather than disobey the proud father who spurned me. The second time, the man on whom I lavished my whole affection was one of those cold, calculating beings who regard a great passion as madness. He was *afraid* of my love; he feared that I loved him *too much*. This second betrayal broke my heart, and I vowed never to be the cause of similar suffering in others.[301]

298. Tristán, London, to Chodzko, 1839, quoted by Jean Hawkes, introduction to *The London Journal of Flora Tristán or The Aristocracy and the Working Class of England* (1842), London 1982, pp. xxxiv–xxxv.

299. Guérin (ed.), *Writings of a Savage*, p. 177. 'My grandfather married, so did my father, so did I. We are respectable people. Otherwise, what would the neighbours say?' Ibid., p. 179. Gauguin's father died whilst landing at Callao harbour in November 1849 when Paul was eighteen months. The next six years of his life were as a child of a single mother in Lima, very much in the company of women, under the protection of Don Pio.

300. Ibid., p. 196.

301. Tristán, *Peregrinations*, p. 18.

In September 1838, shortly after this statement was published, the second of these men, Flora's estranged husband André Chazal, shot her in the back outside her house. She survived, but the bullet remained lodged in her chest, and the wound almost certainly contributed to her death four years later, at the age of forty-one, when, stricken by typhoid during an exhausting campaign to establish a national workers' union, she collapsed in a Bordeaux street. Chazal was sentenced to twenty years' hard labour for the attempt, but he had earlier won possession of the couple's son and had only been forced to yield up their daughter, Aline (Gauguin's mother), whom he had kidnapped, following a charge of attempted rape upon her. Flora could not herself escape his hatred since divorce was prohibited in France between 1816, when Napoleon's Code Civil was suppressed, and 1884. (Her campaign for the Union ouvrière was preceded by one for the revival of the divorce law of the revolutionary era.) Although she was eventually able to win custody of her children, this was only under the most desperate of circumstances. Some, such as George Sand, believed Tristán to be a negligent mother, but the legal battle for her independence and that of her children was more affected by the prejudicial view that in leaving her husband she had to all intents and purposes forfeited claim on the children.[302] Moreover, even under the Code the position of a married woman was entirely subordinate to her husband: she could have no other domicile than his (article 108); he owed her protection and she owed him obedience (article 213); he administered all her personal property (article 1428).[303] Of course, under common law at that time in Great Britain and the USA married women equally had no civil existence, and so could neither own property nor sue (or be sued), divorce or claim rights over their children, although there is evidence of some variation and latitude in New England as well as those parts of France where the influence of Roman law was particularly deep.[304]

---

302. Both Tristán and Sand (Aurore Dudevant) campaigned for the re-establishment of divorce, but Sand refused to support the introduction of the female franchise. She did, however, pay for the education of Aline after the death of her mother – a woman for whom Sand had little time, but whose daughter she described with tenderness:

> … a young girl seemingly as affectionate and as pleasing as her mother was imperious and quick-tempered. This child has the air of an angel; the sadness in her beautiful eyes, her mourning, her obvious loneliness, her modest and affectionate manner, all touched my heart. Did her mother love her? Why were they separated? What marriage to a cause can make a mother forget and leave so far away from her in a dressmaker's establishment a creature so charming and adorable? I would much rather spend money on her future than on establishing a monument to her mother, whom I never cared for despite her courage and her convictions. She was too vain. When people die, everybody pays lip-service to their memory. It is right to respect the mystery of death, but why lie?

Quoted in David Sweetman, *Paul Gauguin: A Complete Life*, London 1995, p. 19. The monument in the Carthusian cemetery in Bordeaux was erected largely on the basis of workers' subscriptions. Although the Union failed to take off, in some cities, particularly Lyons, it enjoyed temporary success. Flora's book *The Workers' Union* was published in 1843. An extraordinary work, including songs, summaries, advice, an appeal to the bourgeoisie and an opening address to 'men and women of faith, love, intelligence, strength, action', it is scarcely in the Marxist mould. A fine English translation by Beverly Livingston was published in 1983 (Urbana, Ill.).

303. Sandra Dijkstra, *Flora Tristán: Feminism in the Age of George Sand*, London 1992, p. 8.

304. Rendall, *Origins of Modern Feminism*, p. 5. New Jersey gave all adult women – married or single, propertied or not – the vote between 1776 and 1807.

In the light of this experience there is a cruel irony in the fact that Flora Tristán suffered so because her own parents' marriage in Spain had not been officially consecrated and so could not be formally recognised. (Moreover, when France went to war with Spain her father's property in that country was confiscated by the state.) Nearly three decades later, when she travelled to Peru in an effort to persuade her uncle Pio to release her deceased father's share of the considerable family estate, she felt obliged to keep secret her own (already failed) marriage (and so, of course, the existence of her children). Yet this formidable woman proved no match for a patriarch who could extend a modest annuity and expressions of tenderness whilst reposing with comfortable formality upon the law in refusing to recognise Flora's legitimacy and right to any inheritance:

> Mademoiselle and my estimable niece,
>
> I received your dear letter with as much surprise as pleasure. I knew from General Bolívar's visit here in 1823 that at the time of his death my beloved brother Mariano de Tristán had a daughter.... I have examined the birth certificate you sent me and I am fully convinced that you are my brother's acknowledged daughter, although the document is not authenticated and signed by three lawyers, as it should have been, to certify that the signature of the priest who issued it is genuine. As for your mother and her status as the legitimate spouse of my deceased brother, you yourself admit and confess that the manner in which the nuptial blessing was bestowed is null and void and has no validity in this country or anywhere in Christendom. Indeed, it is extraordinary that a cleric who claims to be so respectable, like M. Roncelin, should have allowed himself to proceed to such an act, seeing that the contracting parties had not observed the proper formalities. It is also quite irrelevant that when you were baptised he declared that you were legitimate, as is the document which you tell me was sent from Bilbao by M. Adam, in which ten persons from that city state that they knew and regarded your mother as the legitimate spouse of Mariano: all that this proves is that she was granted this status purely and simply as a matter of propriety. Moreover, in the correspondence I maintained with my brother until shortly before his death, there is strong, albeit negative, proof of what I affirm: my brother never once mentioned this union, an extraordinary fact when we had no secrets from one another ... let us accept, then, that you are only the natural daughter of my brother, which does not make you any less worthy of my consideration and tender affection.[305]

When she published her account of this affair Tristán had firmly adopted a public politics of protest and campaigning in preference to a private policy of seduction, but

---

305. *Peregrinations*, pp. 73–4. Flora's father died in 1808 when she was three. In reponse to this letter, she comments,

> If my uncle had the nobility of character to give me a hundred thousand francs, I would have accepted so generous a gift with the keenest gratitude; but when, in order to obtain this sum, I saw myself compelled to compromise my independence, I preferred to remain poor because I set too high a value on my freedom of thought.

This despite the fact that

> I can safely say that I have experienced every misfortune except one, I have never been in debt. Fear of falling in debt has always dominated my actions, and by carefully calculating my expenditure in advance, I have managed never to owe anybody a sou.

Ibid., pp. 151, 256. There are 'silent periods' in Flora's life in which she is thought to have worked as a governess, in Britain and Belgium as well as France.

at the time she was still vulnerable to the attractions of the latter. Perhaps Flora was reawakened to its possibilities by the overtures made by Captain Chabrié on the 133-day voyage from Bordeaux to Valparaiso – overtures to which (as she reports it) she responded with such inconsistency as to indicate a profound insecurity about the qualities of friendship between men and women.[306] However, later in her account Flora reveals that she was perfectly capable of calculation in terms of combining the personal and the political. Here she reflects on Colonel Escudero, aide to Francisca Zubiaga de Gamarra, the warlike wife of ex-President Gamarra:

> I had plenty of time to get to know him and I realised that he was perhaps the only man in Peru capable of seconding my ambitious plans. I suffered at the misfortunes of the country I had come to look upon as my own; I had always had a passionate desire to contribute to the good of the world, and I have always wanted an active and adventurous life. I imagined that if I could inspire Escudero with love for me, I would gain great influence over him. Then once again my inner conflict revived and I was in mental torment; the idea of an association with this witty, daring, carefree man appealed to my imagination. If I take a chance with him, what does it matter if I do not succeed, when I have nothing to lose? ... His tender glance and melancholy smile lent his face a lofty and poetic air which quite carried me away. With such a man it seemed to me that nothing would have been impossible. I have the deep-seated conviction that had I become his wife I would have been very happy.... I was *afraid of myself*, and I judged it prudent to escape this new danger by flight, so I resolved to leave immediately for Lima.[307]

It was there that Flora finally encountered 'Pancha' Gamarra, the young woman from Cuzco who, having spent five years in a convent as a novice, gave some substance to the preceding daydream by marrying General Gamarra, exercising great influence over him, and even fighting in the battles that won and kept him in presidential office

---

306. '"Then you accept me as your friend?" "How can you ask such a thing?" And I kissed him on the forehead in a gesture of gratitude which made my tears flow'(p. 23). 'How many delightful evenings I spent in this way, plunged in the sweetest reverie! M. Chabrié told me of the sorrows he had encountered in his life, especially the last encounter which had so cruelly broken his heart. He suffered, so did I, and this established a close and unsuspected bond between us. Each day M. Chabrié loved me more, and each day I felt inexpressibly happy in the knowledge that he loved me' (p. 34). 'Thank you, Chabrié, I shall treasure the memory all my life. Go, then, dear friend, and since the thought of me can make you so happy, let me assure you that the friendship I feel for you is far greater than the love you have had from other women' (p. 38). 'I was hoping to make him understand that my friendship could be as sweet to him as the love of other women had been. This was not arrogance on my part; I had acted in good faith, but I was completely mistaken' (pp. 41–2). 'My dear Flora, you are so naive you astonish me! Let me tell you, my child, there is no such thing as friendship in the world, only self-interest in the wicked and love in the good' (p. 43). 'The kind young man did not know that for me Chabrié too was *dead*' (p. 56). 'There were two selves inside me, one physical responding to questions and conscious of the exterior world, the other spiritual, with its own life of visions, memories and premonitions' (p. 57). 'I promised that I would be his wife and stay with him in America, to share his lot for better or worse. The poor man, delirious with joy, was too agitated to notice the profound sorrow which overwhelmed me' (p. 63). 'At last he left me, and I collapsed utterly exhausted. I never saw him again. His last words to me were: "I hate you as much as I loved you ..."' (p. 117).

307. Ibid., p. 232. Flora depicts herself as taking a leading role in the politico-military crisis prevailing in Arequipa at the time of her visit, but her account is rendered implausible by her slight command of Spanish and her 'outsider' status, even if her beauty and energy would certainly have commended her to the local *jefes*.

on four occasions. In fact, Flora conversed with her aboard the *Jean Henriette*, docked in Callao harbour prior to leaving for Valparaiso, where she was being sent into exile (and death from tuberculosis the next year at the age of thirty-one). Palpably surprised to find the former first lady decked out in a sophisticated gown and much jewellery, Flora's reaction elicited a telling response from the disgraced Amazon:

'You must find me very ridiculous in this grotesque costume, my dear Florita, you dress so simply yourself; but now you have passed judgement on me, you probably realise that these clothes are not mine. It was my poor sister who persuaded me to wear them, to please her and my mother and all the rest of them; these good people imagine that my luck will change if I consent to wear European clothes. So I yielded to their entreaties and put on this gown which hampers my movements, these stockings which feel cold to my legs, this big shawl which I am afraid of burning with the ash of my cigar. I like clothes that are comfortable for riding…. You are admiring my hair,' continued this alarming woman with the eagle eyes, 'well, my dear Florita, in a career where my strength has often fallen short of my courage, my position has been threatened more than once, and to compensate for the weakness of our sex I have had to retain its attractions and exploit them as need arose in order to enlist the support of women.'[308]

If Pancha Gamarra's escape from the convent had eventually ended in this – the enforced discomfort of alien luxury – it needed spelling out to Flora, who often forgot that she was not the only person with a complex interior world. In Arequipa she asked her cousin Dominga, who had also escaped from a convent, why,

'when you are so beautiful, so charmingly dressed, you are more unhappy now than when you were in that gloomy convent, shrouded in your nun's veil?' The young woman threw back her proud head and, looking at me with a sardonic smile, she said: 'You call me *free*? In what country can a frail creature oppressed by a wicked prejudice be called *free*? Here, Florita, in this room, in her pretty silk dress, Dominga is still the nun of Santa Rosa. Through courage and perseverance I managed to escaped from my *tomb*, but the woollen veil I took is still here on my head, it separates me for ever from the world…. I shall always be a nun!' And I, I muttered under my breath, I shall always be *married*![309]

Perhaps it was because she was less personally involved that Fanny Calderón de la Barca, who was very happily married but found the attractions of the cloister for girls as unappealing as did Flora Tristán, was able to seek a fuller explanation for it in Mexico:

I have now seen three nuns take the veil; and, next to a death, consider it the saddest event that can occur in this nether sphere; yet the frequency of these human sacrifices here is not so strange as might at first appear. A young girl, who knows nothing of the world, who, as it too frequently happens, has at home neither amusement nor instruction, and no society abroad, who from childhood is under the dominion of her confessor, and who firmly believes that by entering a convent she becomes sure of heaven; who moreover finds there a

---

308. Ibid., pp. 294–5. Tristán was greatly impressed by the *rabonas*, female camp-followers of the armies of the *caudillos* who constituted an autonomous logistical force, practised a rough mass democracy, and would also have been an important constituency for *la Mariscala* Gamarra.

309. Ibid., p. 240.

number of companions of her own age, and of older women who load her with praises and caresses – it is not, after all, astonishing that she should consent to insure her salvation on such easy terms. Add to this the splendour of the ceremony, of which she is the sole object; the cynosure of all approving eyes. A girl of 16 finds it hard to resist all this. I am told that more girls are smitten by the ceremony than by anything else, and I am inclined to believe it, from the remarks made on these occasions by young girls in my vicinity. What does she lose? A husband and children? Probably she has seen no one who has touched her heart. Most probably she has hitherto seen no men, or at least conversed with none but her brothers, her uncles, or her confessor. She has perhaps also felt the troubles of a Mexican ménage. The society of men! She will still see her confessor, and she will have occasional visits from reverend padres and right reverend bishops.'[310]

The ensuing description of a service for a girl taking the veil lends weight to Madame Calderón's views on the powers of the ceremony, especially on adolescents, although, as she points out, many were obliged to take this course by economic duress or family pressure:

Suddenly the curtain was withdrawn, and the picturesque beauty of the scene baffles all description. Beside the altar, which was in a blaze of light, was a perfect mass of crimson and gold drapery; the walls, the antique chairs, the table before which the priests sat, all hung with the same splendid material. The bishop wore his superb mitre and robes of crimson and gold.... In contrast to this, five-and-twenty figures, entirely robed in black from head to foot, were ranged on each side of the room prostrate, their faces touching the ground, and in their hands immense lighted tapers. On the foreground was spread a purple carpet bordered round with a garland of freshly-gathered flowers, roses and carnations and heliotrope, the only thing that looked real and living in the whole scene; and in the middle of this knelt the novice, still, arrayed in her blue satin, white lace veil and jewels, and also with a great lighted taper in her hand. The black nuns then rose and sang a hymn, every now and then falling on their faces and touching the floor with their foreheads.... The novice was then raised from the ground and led to the feet of the bishop, who examined her as to her vocation, and gave her his blessing, and once more the black curtains fell between us and them. In the *second act*, she was lying prostrate on the floor, disrobed of her profane dress, and now covered over with a black cloth, while the black figurines kneeling around her chanted a hymn. She was now dead to the world.... Again she was raised. All the blood had rushed into her face, and her attempt at a smile was truly painful.[311]

Flora Tristán spent three 'wearisome' days visiting the convent of Santa Rosa, where Dominga had been enclosed, in the company of her aunt and cousins:

310. *Life in Mexico*, pp. 189–90.

311. Ibid., pp. 193–4. At least some women, none the less, must have entered the order fully aware of the consequences and on grounds similar to those presented by the great seventeenth-century poet Sor Juana Inés de la Cruz (Juana Ramírez):

'And so I entered the religious order, knowing that life there entailed conditions (I refer to super-ficial, not fundamental, circumstances) most repugnant to my nature; but given the total antipathy I felt towards marriage, I deemed convent life the least unsuitable and most honourable I could elect if I were to ensure my salvation. To that end, first (as, finally, the most important) was the matter of all the trivial aspects of my nature ... such as wishing to live alone, and wishing to have no obligatory occupation to inhibit the freedom of my studies, nor the sounds of a community to intrude upon the peaceful silence of my books.

Quoted in Octavio Paz, *Sor Juana: Her Life and Her World*, London 1988, p. 109.

The grave nuns accompanied us as we left with the same formalities they had observed on our arrival. At last we stepped across the threshold of the massive oaken gate, bolted and barred like the gate of some citadel, and no sooner had it closed behind us than we all began to run down the long wide street crying, 'God! What happiness to be free!' All the ladies were weeping, the children and the slaves were dancing in the street, and I confess I was breathing more easily.

However, taking refuge from a revolution in the Santa Catalina convent some days later, she encountered a reception of an entirely different order — one that would seem to ratify Fanny Calderón de la Barca's observations about innocence, albeit in a much less despondent mood:

What a deafening noise, what joyous cries when I entered! 'La francesita! La francesita!' I heard on all sides. Hardly was the gate open than I was surrounded by at least a dozen nuns all speaking at once and laughing and jumping for joy. One pulled off my hat, another took my comb, a third tugged at my leg-of-mutton sleeves, because, they said, such things were indecent. Yet another lifted up my skirt from behind, because she wanted to see how my corsets were made. One took down my hair to see how long it was, another took hold of my foot to examine my boots from Paris; but what excited the most wonder was the discovery of my drawers. The dear girls are very naïve, and, without a doubt, their questions were far more indecent than my clothes![312]

Such an encounter stood in stark contrast to the behaviour of the veiled aristocratic ladies of the capital, compared to which, according to the palpably envious Tristán, 'there is no place on earth where women are so *free* and exercise so much power'.[313] The principal reason for this was the anonymity provided by a secular veil — the *manto*, which, worn over head and shoulders together with a skirt known as the *saya*, simultaneously hid its owner, drew attention to her, and endowed her with the qualities of a *flâneuse* in this city based on recognition:

To make an ordinary *saya* it takes between 16 and 18 yards of satin and some lightweight silk or cotton fabric for the lining. In exchange the seamstress brings you a narrow skirt which reaches from waist to ankles and is so tight that it allows just enough room to put one foot in front of the other and to take very little steps. Thus you are encased in this skirt like a sword in a sheath. It is entirely pleated from top to bottom with very narrow pleats so finely worked that it is impossible to see the stitches. However, these pleats are so firmly made and give the skirt such elasticity that I have seen 15-year-old *sayas* which were still flexible enough to reveal the whole shape of the body and to give with every movement of the wearer.... The *manto* is always black. It completely covers the bust and most of the head, leaving only one eye revealed.... Oh how enchanting they are, with their beautiful black *saya* shining in the sun; how graceful the movements of their shoulders are, as first they draw their *manto* right over their face, then slyly draw it aside! What fine supple figures they have and how sinuously they sway as they walk![314]

---

312. *Peregrinations*, pp. 192–3.
313. Ibid., p. 269.
314. Ibid., pp. 270–71.

It might almost be Melville penning this, but Tristán, whilst evidently enchanted with the appropriation of sensual freedom in public by the complete extension of the private sphere, describes it fully in order more efficiently to issue a Fulleresque moral stricture:

> Men follow them out of a burning desire to see their features, which they so carefully hide from view; but it takes an expert to follow a woman in a *saya*, as the costume tends to make all women alike … a woman, if she wants to go out … slips on her *saya* … lets down her hair, puts on her *manto* and goes wherever her fancy takes her; she meets her husband in the street, and he does not recognise her; she flirts with him, leads him on … gives him a rendezvous, leaves him, and immediately starts a new conversation with an officer passing by … but while this kind of beauty may excite the senses, only spiritual, moral and mental qualities can prolong its reign … when [woman] fails to recognise her mission, when instead of being the inspiration of man and improving his character, she seeks only to seduce him, her authority disappears with the desire she has aroused.[315]

Throughout these passages Tristán seems to be straining to hold herself back; this injunction is almost a memorandum to herself. The account is more than usually contradictory since she appears to believe that the *saya* infects the rest of a Limeña's life with freedom – 'in every situation the woman of Lima is always *herself*'. Yet, apart from the fact that this temporal veil, much like that of the convent, was only worn by those of the upper classes, Flora finds the women of the elite uneducated, un-interested in books and 'ignorant of everything that is happening in the world', which may well preserve a stable identity but were not qualities she elsewhere propounded in the cause of freedom, for either gender.

Sarmiento argued that Christ's repudiation of the Jewish custom of divorce was one of his core teachings on equality between the sexes and the best source of defending the position of women. Yet he enjoyed and approved of the *saya y manto* on grounds not dissimilar to those outlined by Tristán – they afforded a measure of independence, increased confidence and social skills, and broke the tedium of domestic existence.[316] As noted by Elizabeth Garrels, Sarmiento's most celebrated work, *Facundo*, contains no really memorable female figures nor any significant effort to explain their absence except as sundry victims of barbarism (or, occasionally, as inflexible mothers encouraging it).[317] This would fit with his frequently expressed conservative views on

---

315. Ibid., pp. 272, 274.

316. Speech in Paris, 1 July 1847, quoted in *Los Discursos Populares de Domingo Faustino Sarmiento, 1839–1883*, Buenos Aires 1883, cited in Laura Monti, '"Woman" in Sarmiento', in Criscenti (ed.), *Sarmiento and his Argentina*, p. 93. There is, though, nothing quite like the outlook of a middle-aged English male for evacuating almost all fun from the scene. This is General William Miller on the *saya y manto* in the 1820s:

> … there is another class of visitors peculiar to South America, called *tapadas*, or muffled-up females, who are frequently of a rank, or intimacy, to entitle them to an invitation, but who, being elderly, or unprovided with a proper dress, or not liking the trouble of dressing, or slightly indisposed, or in deep mourning, or from some other cause, prefer to attend in the character of unseen spectators. Some go thus disguised in consequence of not being of a rank in life to appear otherwise, and it is maliciously supposed that some few attend for the purposes of flirtation.

John Miller (ed.), *Memoirs of General Miller*, London 1829, I, p. 401.

317. 'Sarmiento and the Woman Question', in Halperín Donghi et al. (eds), *Sarmiento: Author of a Nation*, p. 287.

the 'natural' sexual division of labour, but Doris Sommer stresses a more complex feature of the later *Recuerdos de Provincia*:

> Sarmiento's repeated denial of his paternal lineage and of his father's personal importance. The son seems to have engendered himself upon the body and the genealogy of his mother, whose identity is sometimes and purposefully confused with that of the motherland. The superfluous father is infantilized, or feminized, which amounts to the same thing, so that Sarmiento can replace him in the familial text.[318]

In fact, these two transformations could amount to very different things, but in this case it seems that Sarmiento is simply being promiscuous in the means employed to clear more space to occupy for himself. A similar approach was employed by Thomas Carlyle, who always denied hating blacks, but, as Catherine Hall has shown, sought to challenge the abolitionist motto 'Am I not a man and a brother?' by channelling his hostility through a condescending feminisation: 'I decidedly like poor Quashee, and find him a pretty kind of man. With a pennyworth of oil, you can make a handsome glossy thing of Quashee.'[319]

John Stuart Mill responded immediately to Carlyle's polemic because

> The words of English writers of celebrity are words of power on the other side of the ocean; and the owners of human flesh, who probably thought that they had not an honest man on their side between the Atlantic and the Vistula, will welcome an auxiliary.[320]

Twenty years later, when these two celebrities were still locked in conflict, Mill would reverse the equation, treating the condition of women in terms of slavery:

> In early times, the great majority of the male sex were slaves, as well as the whole of the female. And many ages elapsed, some of the ages of high cultivation, before any thinker was bold enough to question the rightfulness, and the absolute social necessity, either of the one slavery or of the other. By degrees such thinkers did arise: and (the general progress of society assisting) the slavery of the male sex has, in all countries of Christian Europe at least (though, in one of them only within the last years), been at length abolished, and that of the female sex has been gradually changed into a milder form of dependence. But this dependence, as it exists at present, is not an original institution, taking a fresh start from considerations of justice and social expediency – it is the primitive state of slavery lasting on, through successive mitigations and modifications occasioned by the same causes which have

---

318. *Foundational Fictions*, p. 81. This passage draws upon Carlos Altamirano and Beatriz Sarlo, 'La Estrategia de *Recuerdos de Provincia*', in *Literatura/Sociedad*, Buenos Aires 1983.

319. Carlyle, *Occasional Discourse on the Nigger Question*, London 1853, p. 311, quoted in Catherine Hall, *White, Male and Middle Class*, Cambridge 1992, p. 273. A slightly less aggressive version of this tract – with 'Negro' in the title and no attributed authorship – was published as an article in *Fraser's Magazine* in December 1849. Elsewhere in this piece of calculated offensiveness Carlyle comments, 'our beautiful Black darlings are at least happy'. For discussion of what Hall describes as Carlyle's association of masculinity with strength, independence and action, see Norma Clarke, 'Strenuous Idleness: Thomas Carlyle and Man of Letters as Hero', in Michael Roper and John Tosh (eds), *Manful Assertions: Masculinities in Britain since 1800*, London 1991.

320. 'The Negro Question', *Fraser's Magazine*, XLI, Jan. 1850, p. 31, quoted in Hall, *White, Male and Middle Class*, p. 274.

softened the general manners, and brought all human relations more under the control of justice and the influence of humanity. It has not lost the taint of its brutal origin.[321]

Mill adheres only erratically to his own injunction not to generalise about 'nature', and it is not long before he makes the point that

> Men do not want solely the obedience of women, they want their sentiments. All men, except the most brutish, desire to have, in the woman most nearly connected with them, not a forced slave but a willing one, not a slave merely, but a favourite. They have therefore put everything in place to enslave their minds.[322]

Later he returns to this question of the degree of compulsion required in the defence of the institutions of marriage and slavery:

> I should like to hear somebody openly enunciating the doctrine (it is already implied in much that is written on the subject) – 'It is necessary to society that women should marry and produce children. They will not do so unless they are compelled. Therefore it is necessary to compel them.' The merits of the case would then be clearly defined. It would be exactly that of the slaveholders of South Carolina and Louisiana. 'It is necessary that cotton and sugar be grown. White men cannot produce them. Negroes will not, for any wages which we choose to give. *Ergo*, they must be compelled.'[323]

In an essay that by today's standards is about twice as long as it need be, Mill makes a third pass through these motifs, noting the link between betrayal of a common male and that of a sovereign or state in his consideration of the common law:

> By the old laws of England, the husband was called the *lord* of the wife; he was literally regarded as her sovereign, inasmuch that the murder of a man by his wife was called treason (*petty* as distinguished from *high* treason), and was more cruelly avenged than was usually the case with high treason, for the penalty was burning to death … meanwhile the wife is the actual bondservant of her husband: no less so, as far as legal obligation goes, than slaves commonly called.… She can do no act whatever but by his permission, at least tacit. She can acquire no property but for him; the instant it becomes hers, even by inheritance, it becomes *ipso facto* his. In this respect the wife's position under the common law of England is worse than that of slaves in the laws of many countries; by the Roman law, for example, a slave might have his peculium, which to a certain extent the law guaranteed to him for his exclusive use.[324]

In a very rare footnote Mill makes an almost as rare excursus from the Atlantic site of his essay to qualify the 'Orientalist' perspective of the day on gender and power, again suggesting that Flora Tristán's 'woman behind the throne' scenario had some salience:

> If a Hindoo principality is strongly, vigilantly, and economically governed, if order is pre-served without oppression; if cultivation is extending, and the people prosperous, in three

321. 'The Subjection of Women' (1869), in J.S. Mill, *On Liberty and Other Writings*, Cambridge 1989, p. 123.
322. Ibid., p. 132.
323. Ibid., p. 144.
324. Ibid., p. 147.

cases out of four that principality is under a woman's rule. This fact, to me an entirely unexpected one, I have collected from a long official knowledge of Hindoo governments. There are many such instances: for though, by Hindoo institutions, a woman cannot reign, she is the legal regent of a kingdom during the minority of the heir; and the minorities are frequent, the lives of the male rulers being so often prematurely terminated through the effect of inactivity and sensual excesses ... the example they afford of the natural capacity of women for government is very striking.[325]

It was, though, to North America that Mill looked for advances in the feminist cause. Late in 1850 he wrote to Harriet Taylor,

> I have been put in spirits by what I think will put you in spirits too. You know some time ago there was a convention of women in Ohio to claim equal rights [Salem, April 1850]? Well, there has just been a convention for the same purpose in Massachusetts – chiefly of women but with a great number of men, including the chief slavery abolitionists Garrison, Wendell Phillips, the Negro Douglass etc. The *New York Tribune* contains a long report – most of the speakers are women – and I never remember any public meetings or agitation comparable to it in the proportion good sense bears to nonsense. While as to tone it is almost like ourselves speaking – outspoken like American, not frightened and servile like England – not the least iota of compromise, asserting the whole of principle and claiming the whole of the consequences, without any of the little feminine concessions and reserves.[326]

In fact, from the Seneca Falls conference of July 1848 onwards Frederick Douglass held to the view that, for tactical reasons, black men should be given the vote before women. Yet at that meeting and thereafter Douglass insisted upon the linked oppression of slaves and women:

> Many who have at last made the discovery that negroes have some rights as well as other members of the human family, have yet to be convinced that woman is entitled to any. Eight years ago, a number of persons of this description actually abandoned the anti-slavery cause, lest by giving their influence in that direction, they might possibly be giving countenance to the dangerous heresy that woman, in respect to rights, stands on an equal footing with man. In the judgement of such persons, the American slave system, with all its concomitant horrors, is less to be deplored than this *wicked* idea.[327]

Margaret Fuller's Transcendentalist voice does tend to soften the slavery motif in *Woman in the Nineteenth Century*, but it still recurs more naturally in the context of New England than in that of the old:

> It may well be an Anti-Slavery party that pleads for woman, if we consider merely that she does not hold property on equal terms with men; so that, if a husband dies without making a will, the wife, instead of taking at once his place as head of the family, inherits only a part

---

325. Ibid., p. 171. Mill worked for the East India Company and the Indian Civil Service from 1823 to 1858. Later in this essay the 'Orientalist' strain envelopes that of feminism: 'An Oriental thinks that women are by nature peculiarly voluptuous; see the violent abuse of them on this ground in Hindoo writings.' Ibid. pp. 182–3.

326. Mill, London, to Taylor, 29 Oct. 1850, in Francis Mineka and Dwight Lindley (eds), *The Late Letters of John Stuart Mill, 1849–1873*, Toronto 1972, p. 49.

327. 'The Rights of Women', in *The North Star*, 19 and 20 July 1848, reproduced in *The Oxford Frederick Douglass Reader*, Oxford 1996, p. 100.

of his fortune, often brought him by herself, as if she were a child, or ward only, not an equal partner.... In slavery, acknowledged slavery, women are on a par with men. Each is a work-tool, an article of property, no more![328]

Here, then, not only is the woman reduced to a child for the purposes of inheriting property, but her 'free' status puts her – in terms of gender equity – in a position worse than that of her slave sister, if seen from the perspective of property. Writing at the same time, Marx and Engels trace a similar pattern in *The German Ideology*. Yet they lack the historical depth of Mill or the political edge of Fuller when they identify a division of labour within the family that sets up the first property relationship, in which 'wife and children are the slaves of the husband'.[329] The fact that a very similar formulation appears in the first volume of *Capital* (1867) suggests that with respect to his understanding of gender relations Marx underwent no 'epistemological break'.[330] For her part, Fuller was able to take possession of her inheritance from Kant in postulating a less overtly radical course for women than Marx sketched for the proletariat of both sexes:

> I have urged upon the sex self-subsistence in its two forms of self-reliance and self-impulse, because I believe them to be the needed means of the present juncture. I have urged on woman independence of man, not that I do not think the sexes mutually needed by each other, but because in woman this fact has led to an excessive devotion, which has cooled love, degraded marriage, and prevented either sex from being what it should be to itself and to the other. I wish woman to live, *first* for God's sake. Then she will not make an imperfect man her god, and thus sink into idolatory. Then she will not take what is not fit for her from a sense of weakness and poverty. Then, if she finds what she needs in a man embodied, she will know how to love, and be worthy of being loved. By being more a soul, she will not be less a woman, for nature is perfected through spirit. Now there is no woman, only an overgrown child.[331]

Again we are given the equivalence between grown and ungrown woman. It draws our attention back to the development of the inner life of the mind rather than to the outer material world, although Fuller moves between them with all the energy (and less of the bother) of Flora Tristán. Like George Sand, Margaret Fuller never publicly

---

328. *Woman in the Nineteenth Century*, pp. 16, 38. The response of the British establishment to Fuller may be gauged from a 1852 review of her book in the *New Quarterly*:

> Margaret Fuller was one of those he-women, who, thank Heaven! for the most part figure and flourish, and have their fame on the other side of the Atlantic ... we think it is not a nice book for English ladies, and not an entertaining one for English gentlemen.

Quoted in Paula Blanchard, *Margaret Fuller: From Transcendentalist to Revolution*, New York 1978, pp. 341–2. Fuller herself was nowhere near as predictable. Her review of Melville's *Typee* for the *New York Daily Tribune* of 4 April 1846 suggested that village sewing societies would 'find this the very book they wish to have read while assembled at their work'. Quoted in Hershel Parker, *Melville: A Biography, 1819–51*, Baltimore 1996, p. 413.

329. *The German Ideology* (1845–46), ed. C.J. Arthur, London 1970, p. 52.

330. 'Within a family ... there springs up naturally a division of labour, caused by divisions of sex and age, a division that is consequently based on a purely physiological foundation.' *Capital*, I, London 1974, p. 332.

331. *Woman in the Nineteenth Century*, p. 117.

campaigned for the female vote.[332] However, it should be noted that at the Seneca Falls Convention of 1848 (when Fuller was in Europe), which drew up a 'Declaration of Sentiments' that opened with the self-evident truth that 'all men and women are created equal', the only resolution not to be passed with unanimous support was that presented by Elizabeth Cady Stanton and Frederick Douglass: 'It is the duty of the women of this country to secure for themselves their sacred right to the elective franchise.' Whereas votes affirming women's right to speak, and preach, in public were passed unopposed, this issue was sharply disputed on tactical and strategic grounds, and it would be an anachronism to foist on either Sand or Fuller some percentage degree of a contemporarily 'correct' feminism.[333]

Fuller's politics shift and sharpen at the end of her life and under the experience of the revolution and counter-revolution in Rome of 1848–49, during which time she worked in a republican military hospital and gave birth, at the age of thirty-nine, to a son. In *Woman in the Nineteenth Century* her platform is broad and loose, noting the prior influence of certain individual women – she mentions Mesdames Pompadour and DuBarry, who may well have served as fleeting models for Tristán – and the 'moral power' that is possessed by women and which can be translated into rejection of 'the glittering baubles, spacious dwellings and plentiful service' proffered by men in exchange for submission.[334] This gendered 'emotional hegemony' provides the most consistent strand of her text; it is a war of position within society that she recommends, not one of manoeuvre against the state. Critical to such a prospectus of moral and emotional resistance was the core Transcendentalist understanding of, on the one hand, the integral subordination of the individual to the collectivity, and, on the other, the development of the collectivity through the improvement of the individual. For Fuller this depended upon a capacity for withdrawal:

> If any individual live too much in relations, so that he becomes a stranger to the resources of his own nature, he falls, after a while, into a distraction, or imbecility, from which he can only be cured by a time of isolation, which gives the renovating fountain time to rise up. Within society it is the same.[335]

The temporary nature of this need precludes the option of the convent, and it could be argued to do so for marriage as well, but Fuller never pressed the institutional issue. Thoreau, by contrast, did, making his refusal to pay the poll tax to fund the Mexican War a matter of exclusion: 'I simply wish to refuse allegiance to the

---

332. Fuller does not address Tristán's work, but she, like Walt Whitman, greatly admired Sand's *Consuelo*, of which she wrote in the *New York Daily Tribune*, 'the book is entirely successful, in showing how inward purity and honor may preserve a woman from bewilderment and danger, and secure her a genuine independence'. Ibid., p. 216. Fuller met Sand in Paris in 1847 and, notwithstanding Sand's reputation as an adulteress, reported, '[It] made me happy to see such a woman, so large and developed a character.... I never liked a woman better.' Ibid., p. 234.

333. Rendall, *Origins of Modern Feminism*, p. 300. See, for instance, Naomi Schor's introduction to the 1994 Oxford University Press edition of Sand's *Indiana* (1832), p. xv.

334. *Woman in the Nineteenth Century*, pp. 37, 111.

335. Ibid., p. 77.

State, to withdraw and stand aloof from it effectually. I do not care to trace the course of my dollar, if I could, till it buys a man or a musket to shoot one with.'[336]

This is a retreat not so different from that to Walden Pond, but the powerful image was not quite the idealist vanity some have suggested. As the political crisis of the republic focused on slavery, marginalising and then all but excluding other social issues, the idea of withdrawal from the federal union either in the form of states or as individual citizens, expressed respectively by the likes of John C. Calhoun and Wendell Phillips, entered mainstream political and social discourse.[337]

Fuller did not witness this process, during which the orotund generalisations of the Transcendentalist 1840s were overtaken by a rhetorical vehemence outstripping even her own rapid radicalisation. She died on 19 July 1850, when the ship in which she was returning to the USA from the defeat of the Roman republic, the *Elizabeth*, was wrecked in a fierce storm on a sandbar a few hundred yards off Fire Island, New York, the weight in its hold of the Italian marble for a statue of Calhoun hastening the disintegration of the craft. She, her companion Giovanni Ossoli and their son of twenty-two months Angelo drowned, together with several others. Fuller's body and her manuscript on the revolution in Rome were never found.

Five days after the wreck Henry Thoreau reached the scene to look for any remains and hear from the many witnesses on shore and ship. He wrote to Emerson,

> At flood-tide about 3 and a half o'clock when the ship broke up entirely – they came out of the forecastle and Margaret sat with her back to the foremast with her hands on her knees – her husband and child already drowned – a great wave came and washed her off.[338]

Two days later Thoreau wrote to Charles Sumner, whose younger brother's body had not been found, in order to let him know that he had looked at part of a skeleton on the beach but that he knew too little of anatomy 'to decide, as so many might, whether it was that of a male or a female'. All his immersion in nature had preserved for Thoreau innocence on such a basic matter, but it also gave his letter a poetic ring:

> There lay the relics in a certain state, rendered perfectly inoffensive to both bodily and spiritual eye by the surrounding scenery, a slight inequality in the sweep of the shore.... It reigned over the shore. That dead body possessed the shore as no living one could.[339]

---

336. *Civil Disobedience*, (1849), New York 1993, p. 15.
337. Wendell Phillips:

> Thank God, I am not a citizen. You will remember, all of you, citizens of the United States, that there was not a Virginian gun fired at John Brown. Hundreds of well-armed Maryland and Virginia troops rushed to Harper's Ferry, and – went away! Sixteen marines, to whom you pay $8 a month – your own representatives ... with the vulture of the Union above them – your representatives! It was the covenant with death and agreement with hell, which you call the Union of thirty states, that took the old man by the throat with a pirate hand.

Speech in New York, 1 Nov. 1859, in Louis Filler (ed.), *Wendell Phillips on Civil Rights and Freedom*, Lanham, Md., 1982, p. 109. We will return in greater detail to the case of Calhoun.
338. Quoted in Richardson, *Henry Thoreau*, p. 212.
339. Quoted in ibid., p. 213.

In 1852 Emerson (apparently under some duress) and others issued the *Memoirs of Margaret Fuller Ossoli*, which carved up her writings, drew the least radical portrait that was plausible, and introduced what they saw as her physical ugliness and personal forwardness with a marked meanness of spirit: 'It is to be said that Margaret made a disagreeable first impression on most persons, including those who became afterwards her best friends, to such an extent that they did not wish to be in the same room as her.'[340] Nathaniel Hawthorne is widely accepted to have harboured a dislike for Fuller – some commentators speak of hatred – his private notebook stating that she was

> without the charm of womanhood ... she had a strong and coarse nature, which she had done her utmost to refine; but of course it could only be superficially changed ... she was a great humbug ... she had stuck herself full of borrowed qualities ... she set herself to work on her strong, heavy, unpliable and, in many respects, defective and evil nature ... but ... she could not recreate or refine it.[341]

By basing the person of Zenobia in *Blithedale Romance* on Fuller, drawing attention, as did other men, not just to her intellect and feminism but also to the shape of her person and the challenging confidence of her sexuality, Hawthorne suggests a rather different, but possibly complementary, reaction.[342] Maybe these posthumous comments reflect long-contained bitterness at Fuller's strength of character, maybe they express a more recent disapproval at her conduct, not least in loving a Latin man? Whatever the case, one can reasonably conclude that she lived as she wrote, existed as she professed, and challenged the effete Massachusetts intelligentsia no less acutely than had Flora Tristán the pompous provincial aristocrats of Arequipa.

---

340. (R.W. Emerson, J.W. Clarke, W.H. Channing), *Memoirs of Margaret Fuller Ossoli*, London 1852, I, p. 270, quoted by Donna Dickenson, introduction to *Woman in the Nineteenth Century*, p. x. On 23 July 1850 he wrote,

> The morning papers add no syllable to the fatal paragraphs of last night concerning Margaret Fuller; no contradiction and no explanation. At first I thought I would go myself and see if I could help in the inquiries at the wrecking ground, and act for the friends. But I have prevailed upon my friend, Mr Henry D. Thoreau, to go for me and all the friends. Mr Thoreau is the most competent person that could be selected; and in the dispersion of the Fuller family, and our uncertainty how to communicate with them, he is authorised by Mr Ellery Channing [married to Margaret's sister] to act for them all. I fear the chances of recovering manuscripts and other property, after five or six days, are small and diminishing every hour.... Mr Thoreau is prepared to spend a number of days in this object.

Emerson, Concord, to Marcus Spring, in Eleanor Tilton (ed.), *The Letters of Ralph Waldo Emerson: VIII. 1845–1859*, New York 1991, p. 254.

341. Quoted in Oscar Cargill, 'Nemesis and Nathaniel Hawthorne', in Joel Myerson (ed.), *Critical Essays on Margaret Fuller*, Boston 1980, p. 178. For an alternative view, see Austin Warren, 'Hawthorne, Margaret Fuller and "Nemesis"', in the same volume.

342. She should have made it a point of duty, moreover, to sit endlessly to painters and sculptors, and preferably to the latter; because the cold decorum of the marble would consist with the utmost scantiness of drapery, so that the eye might chastely be gladdened with her material perfection in its entireness ... what was visible of her full bust – in a word, her womanliness incarnated – compelled me sometimes to close my eyes, as if it were not quite the privilege of modesty to gaze at her.

Blithedale Romance, (1852), Harmondsworth 1983, p. 44. Zenobia is 'a female reformer ... in her attacks on society', and she dies of drowning.

Singing Sex

Henry Thoreau, it seems, met Walt Whitman just once – in November 1856 – in the company of others at the poet's lodgings, which made the visitor stiff and uncomfortable. Thoreau subscribed – with rather greater consistency, one suspects, than many – to prevailing notions of 'spermatic economy': 'The generative energy, which, when we are loose, dissipates and makes us unclean, when we are continent invigorates and inspires us.'[343] Unsurprisingly, then, he found Whitman hard to take – 'He does not celebrate love at all. It is as if the beasts spoke.' Yet he was able to recognise the poet's stature, and to do so generously: 'even on this side [sensuality] he has spoken more truth than any American or modern that I know. I have found his poem [*Leaves of Grass*] exhilarating, encouraging.... We ought to rejoice greatly in him.'[344]

Emerson, whose imprimatur Whitman had so brazenly purloined, suggested that he prune the sex out of *Leaves of Grass*, but as the poet later remarked, if he had done so he 'might just as well have cut everything out'. Besides, 'the dirtiest book in all the world is the expurgated book. Expurgation is apology – yes, surrender – yes, an admission that something or other was wrong.'[345]

Whitman was nothing if not incontinent. He is the poet who thrusts liquid lists at us:

> A woman waits for me, she contains all, nothing is lacking,
> Yet all were lacking if sex were lacking, or if the moisture of the right man
>   were lacking.
> Sex contains all, bodies, souls,
> Meanings, proofs, purities, delicacies, results, promulgations,
> Songs, commands, health, pride, the maternal mystery, the seminal milk.[346]

If 'identity' is today a word tested almost to destruction, Whitman was one of those presiding at the initiation rites of individualism, at a time when our contemporary culture of the self as sacred was not unimaginable but still too prey to charges of heresy to be taken on its own terms: 'nothing, not God, is greater to one than one's self'.[347] Here two mental worlds are separated by a few letters. An individualism

---

343. All sensuality is one, though it takes many forms; all purity is one. It is the same whether a man, eat, or drink, or cohabit, or sleep sensually. They are but one appetite, and we only need to see a person do any one of these things to know how great a sensualist he is. The impure can neither stand nor sit with purity. When the reptile is attacked at one mouth of his burrow, he shows himself at another. If you would be chaste, you must be temperate.

Walden, pp. 195–6.

344. Quoted in Richardson, *Henry Thoreau*, p. 349.

345. Quoted in Peter Gay, *The Bourgeois Experience, Victoria to Freud: I. Education of the Senses*, Oxford 1984, p. 414.

346. 'A Woman Waits for Me', *Leaves of Grass*, pp. 90–91.

347. 'Song of Myself', ibid., p. 77.

permissible to 'the nineteenth century' is preserved by 'to', which ensures the primary sense of subjective assessment, and so of fallibility. Exchange the conjunction for the preposition, though – the 'than' for the 'to' – and one has a twentieth-century expression of the self asserted two confident syllables earlier as fact. These two little words, however, can easily be shunted to the back of the mind in a heady verse of clearer declaration than meaning about those big-hitters, God and self. If nothing else, the line demonstrates the opportunities for (mis)reading Whitman's work both in 1855 and today, when it is harder to miss the carnal and profane elements.

This creative grey area is generated by a sense of Whitman striving to say everything and yet being restrained from doing so by both the rectitude of the Emersonian notables he needed to please and the still uncertain pieties of a populace with which he so identified as an 'American, one of the roughs'. When it appeared, *Leaves of Grass* was described in *Putnam's Monthly* as 'a mixture of Yankee transcendentalism and New York rowdyism', and, as Jonathan Arac has shown, to achieve this it was necessary to fuse the vision of the vernacular with the sounds of Puritanism – the language not of the street, nor of the drawing-room, but of the newspaper.[348] We may be pulled in two directions, but they are not opposite each other, and the result is distinctively American, quite un-British.

If seventy years later Huizinga believed that 'Crossing Brooklyn Ferry' expressed the essence of the United States, in the wake of World War II C.L.R. James found the decisive element of the poem in the fact that Whitman himself is outside the scene:

> Others will enter the gates of the ferry and cross from shore to
>   shore,
> Others will watch the run of the flood-tide;
> Others will see the shipping of Manhattan north and west, and
>   the heights of Brooklyn to the south and east;
> Others will see the islands large and small.[349]

For James, Whitman

himself is not a part of it. *He wants to be, terribly wants to be*, and here this American separates himself from his European counterparts. He, and this is a fundamental part of the modern character, product of the whole country, is an isolated individual. But he craves *free association* with his fellows.[350]

Sometimes this utopia can only be reached through 'sleeping sensually'. 'I wander all night in my vision' runs the opening line of 'The Sleepers' (1855), the first section of this dream-poem ending with lines that allow for Whitman to be either male or female, either the recipient or agent of ejaculation:

---

348. 'Whitman and Problems of the Vernacular', in Erkkila and Grossman (eds), *Breaking Bounds*.
349. 'Crossing Brooklyn Ferry', *Leaves of Grass*, p. 141.
350. *American Civilization*, Oxford 1993, p. 55.

> Darkness, you are gentler than my lover, his flesh was sweaty and
>   panting,
> I feel the hot moisture yet that he left me.
>
> My hands are spread forth, I pass them in all directions,
> I would sound up the shadowy shore to which you are journeying.
>
> Be careful darkness! already what was it touched me?
> I thought my lover had gone, else darkness and he are one,
> I hear the heart-beat, I follow, I fade away.

The opening of the next section – 'I descend my western course, my sinews are flaccid' – suggests the orgasm of male autoeroticism, and it opens a transcendental nocturnal tour of a world passing through democratic tranquillity and sensual amity:

> The sleepers are very beautiful as they lie unclothed,
> They flow hand in hand over the whole earth from east to west as
>   they lie unclothed,
> The Asiatic and African are hand in hand, the European and
>   American are hand in hand,
> Learn'd and unlearn'd are hand in hand, and male and female are
>   hand in hand ...
> The scholar kisses the teacher and the teacher kisses the scholar, the
>   wrong'd is made right,
> The call of the slave is one with the master's call, and the master
>   salutes the slave ...
> I will stop only a time with the night, and rise betimes,
> I will duly pass the day O my mother, and duly return to you.[351]

Here it is less important how precisely Whitman comes to his reverie than what it reveals to him. The only 'you' in 'The Sleepers' is darkness, on which to 'roll myself ... as upon a bed', and this was not such a great strain on either public morals or popular imagination. By 1860, though, Whitman, in a context not only of personal fame but also of political breakdown, has taken illocutionary expression much further, both in the classical terms of cheating death by talking to us from beyond the grave and implicating us more directly in an uncertain physical union. Thus, in 'Whoever You Are Holding Me Now in Hand',

> ... thrusting me beneath your clothing,
> Where I may feel the throbs of your heart or rest upon your hip,
> Carry me when you go forth over land or sea;
> For thus merely touching you is enough, is best,
> And thus touching you would I silently sleep and be carried
>   eternally.[352]

The laconic reading – that the poet is pleasing the reader with his verse – runs smoothly alongside that of a virtually metaphor-free fuck into the future.

---

351. 'The Sleepers', *Leaves of Grass*, pp. 370, 374–5.
352. Ibid., p. 103.

For Borges, Whitman can only be understood in the context of the temptation to write 'the book of books' and as a writer who has been continually misunderstood through a false identification of 'Whitman, the man of letters, with Whitman, the semi-divine hero of *Leaves of Grass*'. At the same time, Borges almost despairs of the 'foolish' reaction to Whitman's vocabulary and style that takes these as indivisible from that which they are deployed to explain:

> Walt Whitman, the man, was editor of the *Brooklyn Eagle*, and he found his fundamental ideas in the pages of Emerson, Hegel and Volney. Walt Whitman, as a poetic personality, developed these through contact with America, illustrated in imagined experiences in the bedrooms of New Orleans and the battlefields of Georgia. This process does not, of course, necessarily entail a lie. A false fact may be essentially true.... Whitman's strategy yields a personal relationship with each future reader, who is confused with him and talks with the other, with Whitman.... Thus he is transformed into the eternal Whitman, into that friend, into the old American poet of the nineteenth century, into the legend, into one of us, and also into happiness. The task was huge and almost inhuman, but the victory was no less great.[353]

Doris Sommer is more interested in this achievement than in any 'misunderstanding' upon which it must rest:

> ... by supplying this perfect self as the ideal lover for each of his readers, Whitman invites the reader–lover to be co-author. The empty and unpredictable spaces in the poems promise free and equal erotic exchange, and therefore also promise to level the traditional hierarchy of writer over reader.[354]

One necessary element of this perfect construction that now dominates the reading of Whitman's work is his 'homosexuality' – a term that is dated by the *Oxford Dictionary* from 1897 and was not understood or lived by him in any limited sense of genital behaviour. Although not directed specifically to Whitman's work, Eve Kosofsky Sedgewick's comment is certainly applicable:

> ... the relations of the known and the unknown, the explicit and the inexplicit around homo/heterosexual definition ... have the potential for being peculiarly revealing ... about speech acts.... It is a rather amazing fact that, of the very many dimensions along which the genital activity of one person can be differentiated from that of another (dimensions that include preference for certain acts, certain zones or sensations, certain physical types, a certain frequency, certain symbolic investments, certain relations of age or power, a certain species, a certain number of participants, etc., etc.), precisely one, the gender of object choice, emerged as from the end of the century, and has remained, as *the* dimension denoted by the now ubiquitous category of 'sexual orientation'.[355]

---

353. Jorge Luis Borges, 'Nota sobre Walt Whitman', in *Otras Inquisiciones*, Buenos Aires 1960, pp. 163–4. A rather more blunt treatment is given in Borges's *An Introduction to American Literature*, Lexington, Ky., 1971, pp. 30ff.
354. 'Walt Whitman as the Liberal Self', in Chevigny and Laguardia (eds), *Reinventing the Americas*, p. 69.
355. *Epistemology of the Closet*, Harmondsworth 1990, pp. 3, 8.

In this sense we ought to distinguish the context in which Whitman wrote from the bulk of that in which he has subsequently been read. None the less, it may still be generally true, as argued by Tom Yingling, that

> American utopias have always had to imagine sexual relations and a sexual division or nondivision of their communities as one of the things that defined them as different from the dominant culture, as one of the terms of contest for utopia. Roland Barthes claims that 'utopia begins' when 'meaning and sex become the objects of free play ... liberated from the binary prison'.[356]

And Sommer takes a similar view of the

> scandal of displacing heterosexual love with homoeroticism [which] is obviously related to Whitman's appeal for the reader's surrender, to the socially equalizing quality of his free verse.... Homosexual love, then, becomes an allegory for a unhierarchical and truly democratic relation.[357]

Whitman's achievement in Allen Ginsberg's 'Love Poem on Theme by Whitman' (1954) is simple. It is, first, to be 'reborn' in the USA of the 1950s by 'Whoever You Are Holding Me Now in Hand', and, secondly, to have his style praised through emulation and (just) permissible modernization:

> 'legs raised up crook'd to receive, cock in the darkness driven tormented
>   and attacking
> roused up from hole to itching head,
> bodies locked shuddering naked, hot hips and buttocks screwed into
>   each other
> and eyes, eyes glinting and charming, widening into looks and abandon,
> and moans of movement, voices, hands in air, hands between thighs,
> hands in moisture on softened hips, throbbing contraction of bellies
> till the white come flow in the swirling sheets...[358]

But the true utopian victory is in 'A Supermarket in California' (1955):

> Where are we going, Walt Whitman? The doors close in an hour.
> Which way does your beard point tonight?
>   (I touch your book and dream of our odyssey in the supermarket
> and feel absurd.)
>   Will we walk all night through solitary streets? The trees add shade to shade,
> lights out in the houses, we'll both be lonely.
>   Will we stroll dreaming of the lost America of love past blue automobiles
> in driveways, home to our silent cottage?
>   Ah, dear father, graybeard, lonely old courage-teacher, what America
> did you have when Charon quit poling his ferry and you got out on a smoking
> bank and stood watching the boat disappear on the black water of Lethe?[359]

---

356. 'Homosexuality and Utopian Discourse in American Poetry', in Erkkila and Grossman (eds), *Breaking Bounds*, p. 138. The quotation is from *Roland Barthes by Roland Barthes*, New York 1977, p. 133.
357. 'Walt Whitman as the Liberal Self', pp. 80–81.
358. *Collected Poems 1947–1985*, Harmondsworth 1995, p. 115.
359. Ibid., p. 136.

Here, as Yingling puts it, 'some have better things to do with their time than invest in an illusionary "America"'.[360] In the depths of the Cold War – and in the very heartland of the 'dream' – Ginsberg takes Whitman 'in hand' and turns away from the supermarket to *walk*, with almost Thoreau-like decision, past the cars. It is night, of course, but it is not for that reason that they are lonely; they are alone in more than a physical sense.

Five years earlier Neruda had published *Canto General*, where, for Doris Sommer, his admiration 'for the master … displaced Whitman's narcissism with love for others … ironically, by re-placing self-love with the hierarchy-producing secondary narcissism of hero-worship'.[361] But *Canto General* is just as much a work of denunciation as of celebration, Neruda's accusations of betrayal against President González Videla being typical of this voice:

> And so it has been. *Betrayal* was Chile's
>   Government.
> A traitor has bequeathed his name to our history.
> *Judas* flourishing a grinning skull
> sold out my brother and sister,
>   poisoned my
>   country,
> founded Pisagua, demolished our star,
> profaned the colors of a pure flag.[362]

One can find the same charge in Whitman's 'Blood-Money', penned in a few days in March 1850 against Daniel Webster for his congressional defence of the strengthening of the Fugitive Slave Act at the service of maintaining the Union. This is an 'early poem', not in its sense of outrage or physicality but in the language, which is not so distant from the jeremiads of Jedidiah Morse:

> Old olden time, when it came to pass
> That the beautiful god, Jesus, should finish his work on earth,
> Then went Judas, and sold the divine youth
> And took pay for his body.
>
> Curs'd was the deed, even before the sweat of the clutching hand
>   grew dry;
> And darkness frown'd upon the seller of the like of God,
> Where, as though earth lifted her breast to throw him from her,
>   and heaven refused him
> He hung in the air, self-slaughtered…
>
> Witness of anguish, brother of slaves,
> Not with thy price closed the price of thine image
> And still Iscariot plies his trade.[363]

---

360. 'Homosexuality and Utopian Discourse in American Poetry', p. 144.
361. 'Walt Whitman as the Liberal Self', p. 68.
362. 'González Videla: Chile's Traitor (Epilogue) 1949', in *Canto General*, trans. Jack Schmitt, Berkeley 1991, p. 201.

Whitman the incontinent is a continental poet. There is no Latin equivalent. Even if Sommer's judgement on Neruda is deemed harsh, he still forms part of a Southern pattern, which is to follow Whitman and so, as Borges says, to react to him. This pattern, which has become a tradition, was opened in both prose and poetry by José Martí, who upon the issue of his collection *Ismaelillo* in 1882 wrote to Charles Dana (then editing the *New York Sun*): 'I have just published a little book, not for profit but as a present for those I love, a present in the name of my son who is my master. The book is the story of my love affair with my son; one tires of reading of so many love affairs with women.'[364]

That relationship between father and son is one to which Whitman did not give great weight, although, as Borges counsels, we should be cautious about assuming any immediate relation between experience and poetic expression. It has surely been very convenient for the cultural policy of Fidel Castro's notably homophobic regime that Martí directed his amatory energies in that direction, and Sylvia Malloy believes that Martí reads Whitman so narrowly as to make him a 'fiend'. Whatever the case, Martí certainly grasped Whitman's capacity to genitalise the heart and to take tenancy of different genders and sexualities:

> This man loves the world with the fire of Sappho. His world is a gigantic bed, and the bed an altar. He gives nobility to the words and ideas that men have prostituted with their secrecy and false modesty. One source of his originality is the herculean strength with which he flings down ideas to the ground as if to violate them, when all he wants to do is kiss them with a saintly passion ... when he sings the divine sin in 'Children of Adam' ... he trembles, shrivels, swells and overflows, goes mad with pride and satisfied virility.[365]

Martí's celebration of Whitman may be seen by some as a wilfully heterosexual reading, but Borges, whose reading of the poems was trimmed by his prosaic image

---

363. 'Blood-Money' in T.L. Brasher (ed.), *Collected Writings of Walt Whitman: The Early Poems and the Fiction*, New York 1963, pp. 47–8. Contrast this barely veiled damnation of Webster with section 10 of 'Song of Myself' in which the poet cares for a fugitive slave, the stanza closing with almost casual mention of a gun:

> Through the swung half-door of the kitchen I saw him limpsy and
>   weak ...
> And remember perfectly well his revolving eyes and his
>   awkwardness,
> And remember putting plasters on the galls of his neck and ankles;
> He staid with me a week before he was recuperated and pass'd
>   north,
> I had him sit next me at table, my fire-lock lean'd in the corner.

Leaves of Grass, p. 35.

364. *Obras Completas*, XXI, quoted in Sylvia Malloy, 'His America, Our America: José Martí Reads Whitman', in Erkkila and Grossman (eds), *Breaking Bounds*, p. 83. The translation is Malloy's.

365. 'Walt Whitman, the Poet' (1887), in *Critical Writings on Art and Literature*, New York 1982, p. 178. Malloy comments of this essay, 'at the beginning ... the feminine signified the trivial, the derivative ... it escalate[s] to signify a force to be destroyed by, and in the name of heterosexual virility'. She does, however, end by giving Martí credit for being the only Latin American 'to consider, in Whitman, the erotic together with the political, and to register his anxiety, even his panic, before that explosive alliance'. 'His America, Our America', p. 90.

of the individual penning them, proves much less prey to any such transgression. As Fernando Alegría has reflected, 'Studying Whitman in the poetry of Hispanic America is like searching for the footprints of a ghost that can be felt everywhere but is nowhere to be seen.'[366] Yet if he is to be found anywhere, even will-o'-the-wisp, it is in Borges's translations, which are scarcely cleaned-up and display a sensuality absent from his own original work, perhaps because he was convinced of Whitman's chaste and reserved character.[367]

The case against Neruda has been assembled by Paul Julian Smith, but with reference to the *Odas elementales*, not *Canto General*, and in terms of Neruda's intellectual inheritance from Marx rather than Whitman. In Smith's view, metaphorical material in *Capital*, particularly that relating to the commodity form, personifies the object in terms of gender, and this is echoed in the odes of the Chilean Communist. One example he mentions is the wanton Maritornes from *Don Quixote*:

> What chiefly distinguishes a commodity from its owner is the fact that it looks on every other commodity as but a form of appearance of its own value. A born leveller and cynic, it is always ready to join not only soul but also body with any and every other commodity, even if the latter were more repulsive than Maritornes herself.[368]

---

366. *Walt Whitman en Hispanoamérica*, Mexico 1954, p. 9, repeated in 'Borges's "Song of Myself"', in Ezra Greenspan (ed.), *Cambridge Companion to Walt Whitman*, Cambridge 1995, p. 208.

367. Amongst the several verses of translation cited by Alegría is this one from 'Song of Myself', which Borges renders frankly:

> Recuerdo cómo nos acostamos una mañana transparente de estío,
> Cómo apoyaste la cabeza sobre mis caderas y la volviste a mí dulcemente,
> Y abriste mi camisa sobre el pecho y hundiste tu lengua hasta tocar
>   mi corazón desnudo,
> Y te estiraste hasta tocarme la barba, y luego hasta tocarme los pies...

368. *Capital: A Critical Analysis of Capitalist Production*, I (1867), London 1974, p. 89.

> ... at harvest-time a lot of the reapers come in here in the mid-day heat. There's always one of them who can read, and he takes up one of those books. Then as many as thirty of us sit around him, and we enjoy listening so much that it saves us countless grey hairs. At least I can say for myself that when I hear about those furious, terrible blows the knights deal one another, I get the fancy to strike a few myself. And I could go on listening night and day.' 'I agree absolutely,' said the landlady, 'for I never get any peace in my house except when you're listening to the reading. You're so fascinated then that you forget to scold for once.' 'That's right,' said Maritornes, 'I'll tell you I enjoy hearing them too. They're very pretty, particularly the parts when some lady or other is lying in her knight's embrace under some orange-trees, and there's a damsel keeping watch for them, dying of envy and frightened to death. It's all as sweet as honey, I say.

Miguel de Cervantes Saavedra, *The Adventures of Don Quixote* (1604–14), Harmondsworth 1950, pp. 277–8. Marx was just as fond of Shakespeare: 'The reality of the value of commodities differs in this respect from Dame Quickly, that we don't know "where to have it"'. *Capital*, I, p. 54. And one might add one from the section on the relative form of value:

> A coat as such no more tells us it is value, than does the first piece of linen we take hold of. This shows that when placed in value-relation to the linen, the coat signifies more than when out of that relation, just as many a man strutting about in a gorgeous uniform counts for more than when in mufti.

Ibid., p. 58.

Neruda's female lover lives in a 'real', material world, but she is no less objectified than were the figures in the lyrical tradition which Neruda claimed to have rejected. Just as Marx seeks only to jest or enliven the boring voice of economics in his use of metaphor, so Neruda, approaching from the other side, remains blind:

> His fluency derives from his blindness, and the prestige of his (male) perspective from its habitual repression of a divergent (female) point of view. His appeal to the reader (like that of the State to its subjects) is both seductive and repressive, an 'interpellation' which seeks to recreate the addressee in its own image, to naturalize the cultural and to universalize the specific.[369]

In addition to the fact that Neruda excludes homosexuals from the poet–reader relationship, he is here seen to fix the position and power of the sexes in a manner quite the opposite of Whitman's. Furthermore, he fossilises that position. For Paul Julian Smith much of this insufficiency of voice derives from the poet's technique, but that is framed by a wider shortcoming of his ideology:

> Like woman ... Latin America marks that threshold of marginality beyond which theory fears to tread ... Defined by Marx himself as invisible, empty, ahistorical, and irrational, Latin America exemplifies the point at which Marxism is no longer Marxist, but idealist. By staking its claim, none the less, to autonomous agency and identity the continent calls into question one tenet taken for granted by many Marxists: the claim of dialectical materialism to universal applicability. In the case of both woman and Latin America, the subject term speaks back to the dominant order using the language it has received from that order.[370]

It may be that Smith is exploiting Marx's virtual 'silence' on Latin America too readily in order to foist onto him the views expressed by Hegel in the *Philosophy of History*. Only under certain circumstances – quite often legal ones – is silence properly taken as assent, and Marx, who certainly read Spanish, did manage to disagree with quite a lot of Hegel's thought, as Althusser often reminds us.[371] Equally, it has to be said that in the wake of the collapse of communism the insufficiencies of Marxism for explaining either part of the Americas no longer constitute the same kind of preoccupation or target as once they did. None the less, Marx certainly did make recourse to analogies of gender at critical explanatory moments, as in the opening chapter of *The Eighteenth Brumaire of Louis Bonaparte*, written early in 1852 to explain the coup staged the previous December by Bonaparte:

---

369. Paul Julian Smith, *The Body Hispanic: Gender and Sexuality in Spanish and Spanish American Literature*, Oxford 1989, p. 155.

370. Ibid., p. 142.

371. Liebknecht remembered,

> How he scolded me one day because I did not know ... Spanish! He snatched up *Don Quixote* out of a pile of books and gave me a lesson immediately.... And what a patient teacher he was, he who was in other respects so fiery and impatient! The lesson was cut short only by the entrance of a visitor. Every day I was examined and had to translate a passage from *Don Quixote* or some other Spanish book until he judged me capable enough.

S.S. Prawer, *Karl Marx and World Literature*, Oxford 1978, p. 208. Marx evidently followed pan-American affairs quite closely, and there are references of some detail to Peru, Mexico and Brazil in the first chapters of *Capital*.

A nation and a woman are not forgiven the unguarded hour in which the first adventurer that came along could violate them. The riddle is not solved by such terms of speech, but merely formulated differently. It remains to be explained how a nation of 36 millions can be surprised and delivered unresisting into captivity by three *chevaliers d'industrie*.[372]

Moreover, he himself was not above insisting that silence was a sign of assent,[373] and in an unusually passionate letter to his wife Jenny he readily reversed the process by depicting his enemies as too slow-witted to paint '"the relationship of production and exchange" on one side and myself at your feet on the other' in some second-rate theatrical production. This lover of Heine and Shakespeare and Cervantes was also one of his wife in the romantic tradition: 'love – not of Feuerbachian man, not of Moleschott's metabolisms, not of the proletariat, but love of one's darling, namely you, makes a man into a man again.'[374] We should, though, take a brief glimpse at the one text of Marx's – short and obscure though it is – which devotes itself exclusively to a Latin American topic.

Marx and Bolívar

In mid February 1858 Friedrich Engels, who was running the family business in Manchester, received from Karl Marx a letter that contained all the usual gossip about continental politics and worries about money:

For three days I shall now be on tenterhooks until I know whether or not my bill, which does not appear to have been dispatched from here until several weeks AFTER ITS DRAWING, has been honoured. At the very best I shan't be able to draw anything more on the *Tribune* against the articles I have sent in until the matter is … settled. My estimate of the last goods dispatched … was badly out. Moreover, a longish article on 'Bolívar' elicited objections from Dana because, he said, it is written IN A PARTISAN STYLE and he asked me to cite my

---

372. *The Eighteenth Brumaire of Louis Bonaparte* (1852), Moscow 1972, p. 15.
373. [In August 1852] the rumour had reached Marx that on his American trip Kinkel had referred to Engels and himself as 'two down-and-outs who had been thrown out of the London pubs by the workers'. He wrote to Kinkel: 'I await your explanation by return. Silence will be treated as an admission of guilt.' Kinkel did reply by return that he wanted nothing more to do with Marx in view of Marx's article in the *Revue* attacking him while still in gaol. Marx should not, he continued, trust hearsay, but if he chose to do so, the due processes of law were open to him. Convinced that Kinkel would not look at anything with a Soho postmark, Marx 'got Lupus in Windsor to post a letter to him, written on paper in the shape of a *billet doux* with a bunch of roses and forget-me-nots printed on it in colour'. The letter named Marx's sources … and claimed that Kinkel's letter provided, 'a new and striking proof that the said Kinkel is a common and cowardly priest'.
David McLellan, *Karl Marx: His Life and Thought*, London 1973, pp. 256–7.
374. This version taken from ibid., p. 274. There is a fuller and different translation in Saul Padover (ed.), *The Selected Letters of Karl Marx*, New York 1979, pp. 106–7, which is reproduced in Mike Gane, *Harmless*

AUTHORITIES. This I can, of course, do, although it's a singular demand. As regards the PARTISAN STYLE, it is true that I departed somewhat from the tone of a cyclopaedia. To see the most dastardly, most miserable and meanest of blackguards described as Napoleon I was altogether too much. Bolívar is a veritable Soulouque.[375]

The exasperation – and the use of capital letters – was entirely typical of Marx, but here he is making a really very rare admission of a shortcoming, if not exactly guilt. Moreover, he was sensible to make the admission, although Dana eventually published the piece in its original form despite his criticism and having called Marx's bluff. Even a cursory and uninformed glance at the general style of the thirteen-page article, 'Bolívar y Ponte', submitted to the *New American Cyclopaedia* would seem to justify the editor's reaction:

> The Spanish prisoners of war, whom Miranda used regularly to send to Puerto Cabello, to be confined in the citadel, having succeeded in overcoming their guards by surprise, and in seizing the citadel, Bolívar, although they were unarmed, while he had a numerous garrison and large magazines, embarked precipitately in the night, with eight of his officers, without giving notice to his own troops, arrived at daybreak at La Guayra, and retired to his estate at San Mateo. On becoming aware of their commander's flight, the garrison retired in good order.... Ribas, from whom Bolívar had derived his reputation, having been shot by the Spaniards after the capture of Maturín, there appeared in his stead another man on the stage, of still greater abilities, who, being as a foreigner unable to play an independent part in the South American revolution, finally resolved to act under Bolívar. This was Louis Brion.... [Bolívar] left the post in the night of April 5, informing Colonel Freites, to whom he transferred his command, that he was going in search of more troops, and would soon return. Trusting this promise, Freites declined the offer of a capitulation, and, after the assault, was slaughtered with the whole garrison by the Spaniards.... On the false accusation of having conspired against the whites, plotted against Bolívar's life, and aspired to the supreme power, Piar was arraigned before a war council under the presidency of Brion, convicted, condemned to death, and shot.... Scattering as he did his superior forces, they were always beaten in detail.... Bolívar marched toward Pamplona, where he spent about two months in festivals and balls ... Dr Roscio, fascinating him with the prospects of centralized power, led him to proclaim the 'republic of Colombia'.... Notwithstanding his vastly superior

---

Love? Gender, Theory and Personal Relationships, London 1993. Gane rejects the view of Christine Di Stephano which insists narrowly on Marx's 'combative, heroic and hence masculine' style (in Lyndon Shanley and Carole Pateman (eds), *Feminist Interpretations and Political Theory*, Oxford 1991). His discussion of the early years, together with that of the image painted by Marx of the black Madonna, is refreshing and suggestive but the chapter does not really address the question of metaphor and simile in the 'mature' economic works.

375. Marx, London, to Engels, 14 Feb. 1858, in *MECW*, XL, London 1984, pp. 165–6. Faustin Elie Soulouque (1785–1867), a Haitain general who, born a slave, took power in 1848, had himself crowned emperor in 1852, invaded Santo Domingo, and was widely caricatured in Europe and the USA as the epitome of 'black barbarism' until his overthrow in January 1859. In 1856 *Men of the Time* commented of Soulouque's rise to power that

> he triumphed in consequence of his displaying a terrible energy of character. Perfidious counsellors drove him into a course of vengeance, having for its object nothing less than the extermination of the whole coloured race, who form a fifth of the population of Hayti.... The name of Emperor expresses nothing Napoleon-like at Hayti; it supposes only an authority better respected than that of the president.... Faustin Soulouque is completely black, and though upwards of 65 years of age, he does not appear to be more than 50.

forces, Bolívar contrived to accomplish nothing during the campaign of 1820.... The enemy's position seemed so formidable to Bolívar, that he proposed to his council of war to make a new armistice, which, however, was rejected by his subalterns.... His position had meanwhile become strengthened, what with the formal recognition of the new state on the part of England, what with Sucre's conquest of the provinces of Upper Peru, which the latter united into an independent republic, under the name of Bolivia. Here, where Sucre's bayonets were supreme, Bolívar gave full scope to his propensities for arbitrary power, by introducing the 'Bolivian Code', an imitation of the *Code Napoléon*.... An attempt to assassinate him in his sleeping room at Bogotá, which he escaped only by leaping in the dark from the balcony of the window, and lying concealed under a bridge, allowed him to introduce a sort of military terrorism. He did not, however, lay hands on Santander, although he had participated in the conspiracy, while he put to death General Padilla, whose guilt was not proved at all, but who, as a man of colour, was not able to resist.[376]

Marx, of course, could be said to be the most criticised author in modern history, and not just for his global interpretation but also for simply 'getting facts wrong'.[377] At the same time, although Bolívar's judgements and actions over fifteen years of continental warfare and politicking could scarcely have avoided instances of sharp practice, dubious rectitude, ruthlessness and opportunism, he was, by the time Marx penned this article, widely acknowledged and celebrated as the founding father of regional and national independence in all the fledgeling states of Spanish America. It is hardly surprising, then, that the essay has received a hostile response, automatically winning an entry in the *Critical Bibliography of the Detraction of Bolívar* despite the fact that the author of that book had not actually read what Marx had written.[378] In a more telling critique, Carlos Uribe identifies with painstaking detail some sixty-six separate 'errors', some of them very slight – 'Bolívar y Ponte' was the name of the Liberator's father – some of them disputable, but many evidently derived from a tendentious presentation. For Uribe,

> The evidence allows us to suggest that Marx had set about destroying a myth, and this myth had two aspects. The first was that of collective liberation as the work of a single personality, of a charismatic individual, of the 'man of providence'. Secondly, there was the myth of 'nationality' in the manner of Mazzini – the idea of the creation of new nations as a result of the emancipation struggle against oppression by the great metropolitan powers.[379]

---

376. 'Bolívar y Ponte', *MECW*, XVIII, London 1982, pp. 219–33. First published in *The New American Cyclopaedia*, III, New York 1858. Spanish translations may be found in José Aricó, *Marx y América Latina*, Lima 1980, and Carlos Uribe Celis, *Bolívar y Marx: Dos Enfoques Polémicos*, Bogotá 1986.

377. See, for example, Richard F. Hamilton, *The Bourgeois Epoch: Marx and Engels on Britain, France and Germany*, Chapel Hill, N.C., 1991.

378. M.A. Osorio Jiménez, *Bibliografía Crítica de la Detracción Bolivariana*, Caracas 1959, which, by way of compensation, quotes from Angel Francisco Brice:

> Marx's essay does not appear to be the work of a fully informed writer but, rather, of an author of fiction who is endeavouring to construct a framework in which class struggle might make some sense, because he gives particular stress to the fact that Bolívar was a child of the Mantuan families of the Venezuelan creole nobility.... Marx saw in the Liberator a bourgeois and so he had to be disparaged.

Ibid., p. 238.

379. Uribe Celis, *Bolívar y Marx*, pp. 89–90. Simón José Antonio de la Santísima Trinidad Bolívar, born Caracas, 24 July 1783. Following the early deaths of his father (1786) and mother (1792), tutored by Simón Rodríguez, follower of the French *philosophes* and admirer of Locke and Hume. 1798, appointed sublieutenant

In this interpretation the need for Marx to propound, however implicitly, the superiority of the class struggle over that of national liberation was the main motive for the disparagement of Bolívar. Earlier explanations that Marx was simply revealing his unrevolutionary Eurocentrism or that his sources were few and weak might be true, says Uribe, but they are matters of secondary importance. As it stands, this is a most persuasive position. After all, the next year Marx wrote: 'The mythopoeic power of popular fantasy has always shown itself in the creation of "great men". Simón Bolívar is undeniably the most convincing illustration of this.'[380] One might, none the less, take cognisance of the circumstances of the writing of the essay, if only to confirm the mundane realities that lay behind Marx's authorship of both works like this of apparently ephemeral importance as well as those like *Capital*, which was under preparation at the same time and would occupy a central place in the twentieth century.

From Marx's arrival in London, on 24 August 1849, until at least a decade later, he and his family lived in poverty and conditions of general adversity. When Jenny joined him at the end of September she was seven months pregnant, but her mother had given her some money, enabling them to rent two rooms off the King's Road, Chelsea, at the very high rate of £6 a month. Initially, what was planned as a very brief exile – possibly prior to moving to the USA – seemed propitious:

> On 5 November, while the people were shouting 'Guy Fawkes for ever!' and small masked boys were riding the streets on cleverly-made donkeys and all was in uproar, my poor little Heinrich was born. We call him Little Fawkes in honour of the great conspirator.[381]

Furthermore, the British state was rather more indulgent of talkative continental radicals than of their Irish counterparts. As Home Secretary Sir George Grey patiently explained to the Austrian ambassador, whose spies were telling him that 'the Marx party' in London was discussing regicide: 'under our laws, mere discussion of regicide, so long as it does not concern the Queen of England and so long as there is no definite plan, does not constitute sufficient grounds for the arrest of the conspirators'.[382]

---

in militia; 1799, travels to Spain via Mexico; 1802, visits France; May 1802, marries María Teresa Rodríguez in Madrid. Jan. 1803, Maria Teresa dies in Caracas; Bolívar returns to Spain, witnessing coronation of Napoleon, May 1804. 1805–6, travels in France, Italy and Germany, returning to Venezuela after three months in the USA. July 1810, diplomatic mission to London on behalf of independence movement. July 1811, declaration of Venezuelan independence, military campaign opens. 1815, named Captain General of Confederation of New Granada; publishes *Jamaica Letter*; 1816, exile in Haiti; 1819 liberation of Bogotá and publication of *Angostura Address*. 1821, victory of Carabobo consolidates independence of Venezuela; Bolívar enters Caracas for first time in seven years. 1822, Royalist defeat at Pichincha yields Quito to Patriots; Bolívar faces down San Martín, leader of southern Patriot forces, at Guayaquil interview. 1824, declared dictator of Peru; 1825, Bolivia named after him; 1826, address to Congress of Bolivia, returns to Bogotá to suppress separatist movements. 1828, declared dictator of Gran Colombia; 1829, suppresses revolts in Peru; first serious signs of tuberculosis. March 1830, renounces presidency of Colombia, retires to Cartagena. Dies at Santa Marta 17 Dec. 1830.

380. 'Dr Vogt', *MECW*, XVII, London 1982, p. 328. This statement was made in the context of a discussion of the Hungarian leader Kossuth. Earlier in the same tract Marx refers to Col. Johan Bangya, a member of the Austro-Hungarian secret police, as 'the Simón Bolívar of the Circassians'. Ibid., p. 219.

381. Jenny Marx, *Reminiscences*, p. 225, quoted in McLellan, *Marx*, p. 227.

382. Quoted in ibid., p. 231. However, the Home Office was prepared to fund the passage to the USA of refugees from Austria and Prussia.

It is also true, as David McLellan has shown, that Marx, the greatest critic and adversary of capitalism, was an appalling manager of his own finances. The impoverishment of the Marx family was in good part due to his political activity and commitments (the funding of newspapers, organisation of meetings, support for refugees) and the pressures of raising five children in exile, but it also stemmed from pride – a refusal to accept help from anyone who was not family, aside from Engels – and a lack of financial control and planning. McLellan notes that in the early 1850s, when prices were falling, the rent for the two-room flat at 28 Dean Street, Soho (occupied by the family from 1850 to 1856), was £22 a year whilst Marx's income was £150, a sum considered at least adequate for a lower middle-class family.[383] Yet this family was tightly yoked to a demanding political struggle on the margins of British culture, and it lacked either social or physical defences against the diseases that rampaged through London in the mid nineteenth century. Heinrich, known as Guido, died within a year, and both his elder brother Edgar and his younger sister Franziska perished in the Dean Street flat. Those children who survived were either born abroad (Jenny and Laura) or were brought up in the eight-room house on Haverstock Hill, some three miles north-west from the city centre (Eleanor) or left the family altogether (Freddy Demuth, Marx's illegitimate son with the housekeeper Helene Demuth, who was fostered out and survived until 1929). Writing to Joseph Weydemeyer in New York in 1850, Jenny recounted a scene typical of the early years of what would prove a permanent residence in the city:

> As wet-nurses here are too expensive I decided to feed my child [Guido] myself in spite of continual terrible pains in the breast and back. But the poor little angel drank in so much worry and hushed-up anxiety that he was always poorly and suffered horribly day and night. Since he came into the world he has not slept a single night, two or three hours at the most and that rarely. Recently he has had violent convulsions, too, and has always been between life and death. In his pain he sucked so hard that my breast was chafed and the skin cracked and the blood often poured into his trembling little mouth. I was sitting with him like that one day when our landlady came in. We had paid her 250 thalers during the winter and had an agreement to give the money in the future not to her but to her own landlord, who had a bailiff's warrant against her. She denied the agreement and demanded the £5 we still owed her. As we did not have the money at the time ... two bailiffs came and sequestered all my few possessions – linen, beds, clothes – everything, even my poor child's cradle and the best toys of my daughters, who stood there weeping bitterly.... We had to leave the house the next day. It was cold, rainy and dull. My husband looked for accommodation for us. When he mentioned the four children nobody would take us in. Finally a friend helped us, we paid our rent and I hastily sold all my beds to pay the chemist, baker, the butcher and milkman who, alarmed at the sight of the sequestration, suddenly besieged me with their bills.[384]

Engels almost always helped out – sometimes sending in different envelopes a banknote cut in two – and in the early days this was often at the cost of his own

---

383. Ibid., p. 264.
384. *Reminiscences*, pp. 237ff., quoted in ibid., p. 228.

discomfort. But if any person was responsible for stabilising the Marx family finances, it was Charles Dana, the foreign and managing editor of the *New York Tribune* (which had daily, weekly and monthly editions). Himself born to an impoverished New Hampshire family in 1819 – and so an almost exact contemporary of Marx – Dana had schooled himself well enough to matriculate at Harvard, but poor eyesight halted his studies, and he only received a degree twenty years after his class of 1843 had graduated. Dana had been a companion of Margaret Fuller and Nathaniel Hawthorne on the Brook Farm commune, joining Horace Greeley's paper in 1847, when it had been running for six years and built up a circulation of over 100,000 with its high-minded, intellectual copy, aversion to scandal and attention to hard news – in 1854 the *Tribune* had fourteen reporters in New York, twenty in the rest of the States and eighteen abroad. When, at the start of 1848, Europe was thrown into revolutionary turmoil, Dana, still not yet thirty, hurried to the continent as a correspondent. It must have been then that he got to know of John Mitchel and acquired his enduring sympathy for the Irish republican cause. He certainly met Marx, in Cologne, and was very impressed, although his own views were much less radical.

Dana first gave Marx work as a correspondent in 1852, and by 1854 – when the annual rent on the north London house stood at £36 – income from the articles sent to (and sometimes published in) New York netted £160. Although Marx was uncertain of both the terms and the schedules of payment – which explains his frequent concern over drawing bills – the family was able in that year to take its first holiday, and until 1856 enough of his material was being printed so that, combined with other journalism, he could both keep the wolf from the door and devote appreciable time to what was becoming known as 'the Economics'. Marx had obtained a reader's ticket to the British Museum in June 1850 and, starting with the back numbers of the *Economist*, began a study of economics that would form the core of his work for the rest of his life, although in April 1851 he told Engels that he was soon coming to the end of it:

> I am so far advanced that in five weeks I will be through with the whole economic shit. And that done, I will work over my Economics at home and throw myself into another science at the Museum. I am beginning to be tired of it. Basically, this science has made no further progress since A. Smith and D. Ricardo, however much has been done in individual and often very subtle researches.[385]

Given that it was to be sixteen years until *Capital* was published, one might say that the generation of that work owed a great deal to Charles Dana and the *New York Tribune*, although, by the same token, Marx's journalistic chores often distracted him from his major political and intellectual project. The relationship, moreover, was never easy and frequently tense. Dana had firm views of his own, and he often thought Marx's articles too polemical or partisan. Marx's views on Russia, especially, were felt excessive, and Dana was prone to withdraw his by-line or transfer material into

---

385. Marx, London, to Engels, April 1851, quoted in ibid., p. 283.

editorials; sometimes their different positions would appear in separate parts of the paper. Neither were matters helped much by Marx's lack of organisation, keenness to cash bills of credit, and short temper. By January 1857 relations had become so poor that he wrote to Engels with more than the habitual tone of desperation:

> I really have monumentally bad luck! For the past three weeks or so Mr Dana has been sending me the daily *Tribune* – obviously with the sole intention of showing me that they aren't publishing *any more* of my stuff.... Having for some four years printed all my things (and yours too) under their own name, the curs have succeeded in eclipsing the name I was making for myself among the Yankees and which would have enabled me to find another paper.... As soon as I draw something they will make it a pretext to get rid of me once and for all ... so here I am without any prospects, and with growing domestic liabilities, completely stranded in a house into which I have put what little cash I possessed and where it is impossible to scrape along from day to day as we did in Dean Street. I am utterly at a loss as to what to do, being, indeed, in a more desperate situation than five years ago.[386]

Dana's response was most peculiar in view of his past problems with Marx, but it was convenient to him and probably motivated by kindness: he proposed to Marx a contract to write articles for the *New American Cyclopaedia*, to which he had been appointed editorial director. Early in April 1857 he offered the entries on military and economic matters to Marx, who immediately forwarded the letter to Engels – known as 'the General' for his interest in military affairs – for advice and support. Engels's candid response gives us an idea of the attitude they took towards the task:

> [The] pay is quite profitable, even at $2 per large page; a lot of the stuff will only have to be copied or translated, and the longer articles won't involve a great deal of work. I shall take a look at one or two English encyclopaedias straight away to see what military articles they contain, but then concentrate on *Brockhaus* which, after all, not only provides a better basis but is also more complete and is evidently looked upon by Dana as a model ... which articles will you be taking on? Take as many ... as you can ... even though the work won't be very interesting (most of it, at any rate), I'm immensely tickled by the whole thing since it will mean an enormous LIFT for you ... especially as Dana was threatening to put you on half-pay.[387]

Marx agreed, promising to write to Dana the next day: 'the thing has come as a godsend.... It also reassured my wife, which is important in her present SITUATION.'[388]

In the event, Engels, who was thoroughly bored in Manchester, did virtually all the entries because he wanted to give Marx time in which to concentrate on his economic work. Moreover, as Marx's letter to Engels of February 1858 amply illustrates, this work may have provided a modicum of financial security, but it was incredibly tedious:

> New Bs are: Bidassoa (battle of), Blenheim (ditto), Burmah (war in), Bomarsund (siege), Borodino (battle), Brescia (assault), Bridgehead, Bulow, Buda (siege of), Beresford, Berme.

---

386. Marx, London, to Engels, 20 Jan. 1857, *MECW*, XL, p. 93.
387. Engels, Manchester, to Marx, 22 April 1857, ibid., pp. 122 ff.
388. Marx, London, to Engels, 23 April 1857, ibid., p. 125.

When Dana says, 'MOST OF THEM I ASKED YOU BEFORE', he is mistaken, and is confusing your list of Bs with *his own*. All he himself ordered was: Barbette, Bastion, Bayonet, Barclay de Tully, Battery, Battle, Bem, Benningsen, Berthier, Bernadotte, Bessieres, Bivouac, Blindage, Blucher, Blum, Bolívar, Bomb, Bombadier, Bombardment, Bonnet, Bosquet, Bourienne, Bridge (pontoon), Brown (Sir George), Brune, Bugeard. (The ass has received the lot.) ... It's a lengthy business where PERCUSSION CAPS are concerned because there are so many different types of gun-locks to be listed. I'd have already finished the job if it hadn't been for the new order from Dana. I'll send you all the rubbish at the same time.[389]

As can be seen, Marx had started on the Cs, and the reason for this was that of the 'original Bs' he had contributed only two – Bernadotte and Bolívar. A fortnight later he got Dana's letter of complaint about the latter.

Working in the Reagan era and on the cusp of *perestroika*, the London-, New York-, and Moscow-based editors of the English-language edition of the *Collected Works* of Marx and Engels provide their own explanation for the tone of Marx's article, and, in view of the comments of Uribe and others about source material, it is worth quoting this extensively.

Marx wrote the article on Bolívar at a time when the history of the Latin American countries' war of independence (1810–26) had not yet been adequately studied. Books and memoirs by European adventurers who had taken part in the war out of mercenary motives were widely read at the time. Many of these authors, having failed to achieve their aims in Latin America, gave a distorted idea of the war of independence. Examples of such books are *Memoirs of Simón Bolívar*, by H. Ducoudray Holstein, who was at one time Bolívar's chief of staff and had become his personal enemy, *A Narrative of the Expedition to the River Orinoco and Apuré* by G. Hippisley, an English deserter from Bolívar's army, and *Memoirs of General Miller* by John Miller, which dealt unscrupulously with the notes of William Miller (John Miller's brother) who fought for the independence of Peru. Marx's excerpts from the first two books are extant. The third is mentioned in Marx's preparatory materials for the article and in the article itself. The authors of these books attributed numerous imaginary vices to Bolívar (perfidy, arrogance, cowardice) and greatly exaggerated his actual shortcomings (love of the spectacular and ambition). Bolívar's struggle against federalist and separatist elements and for the unification of Latin American republics was presented as a striving for dictatorship. There were also downright factual inaccuracies, such as Ducoudray Holstein's statement that in 1810 Bolívar refused to take part in the struggle for the independence of Venezuela, or the allegation that his participation in Miranda's arrest was motivated by personal considerations (in fact he was convinced of the latter's presumed betrayal). In reality, as later objective researches confirmed, Simón Bolívar played an outstanding role in Latin America's struggle for independence, rallying for a time the patriotic elements among the landowning creoles (Latin Americans of Spanish descent), the bourgeoisie and the masses, including Indians and Negroes. His activity, contradictory though it was, helped to liberate several Latin American countries from the Spanish yoke, to establish republican forms of government, and to carry out progressive bourgeois reforms. Marx only had the above-mentioned sources at his disposal. Hence his one-sided view of Bolívar's personality in this article, in his letter to Engels of February 14, 1858, and in *Herr Vogt* written later.... His attitude to Bolívar was to a certain extent determined by the fact that the sources he used exaggerated Bolívar's striving for personal power, and over-emphasised the Bonapartist features of his policy, against which Marx and Engels waged a relentless struggle. Nevertheless, Marx pointed out the progressive

---

389. Marx, London, to Engels, 1 Feb. 1858, ibid., pp. 588–9.

aspects of Bolívar's activity, such as his liberation of Negro slaves, and on the whole appreciated the revolutionary anti-colonial struggle for national liberation in Latin America. There is an entry in Marx's notebook on the dispatch of 'Bolívar' to New York on January 8, 1858, together with some articles beginning with C by Engels. In his letter to Marx of January 25, Charles Dana acknowledged receipt of the articles. At Dana's request Marx had also enclosed a list of sources used.[390]

One can explain the rather weasel words of the politically correct passages here by the fact that the *Collected Works* was as much a political project subsidised by the Communist Party of the Soviet Union as it was a historico-intellectual project undertaken by a committee. However, their appraisal and explanation of the sources is quite misleading. Of course, the bibliography on the independence wars was not nearly as rich as at the end of the century, let alone today. It was, after all, the retention of Spanish records that so incensed Bello, and that required Prescott to receive so many transatlantic parcels. But it is quite absurd to say that a reader of the British Museum in the late 1850s had access to only these three titles, even if that reader did not understand – as Marx did – Spanish, French and German. These were the three titles that he chose, and it is scarcely an innocent matter for such well-informed individuals to confuse an act of choice with one of necessity. Morever, any reader of the committee's explanation in *MECW* volume XL can turn without let or hindrance to volume XVIII to discover for themselves that Marx cites Miller just once – although it is arguably the most tendentious sentence (on Miranda's arrest) in 500 pages – Hippisley not at all, and Ducoudray almost always, finishing the entire piece with a quotation from him on Bolívar's character. In short, Marx, as might be expected from Engels's earlier comments about 'technique', has relied on/copied from a single author, and the one who best suited his own prejudices. Given the nature of the task to hand, this might surprise only those still totally in the thrall of 'the Moor', but if one looks a little closer at Ducoudray and his writing even the most cynical mind must wonder a little at Marx's choice of 'authority'.

In fact, we know very little of Henri La Fayette Villaume Ducoudray Holstein (1763–1839). In the frontispiece of his book, published in 1829 in New York and 1830 in London, he (or his publishers) described himself as 'after the year 1800, attached to the staff of Napoléon Bonaparte'; which attachment must have been distant to the point of disappearance since he is not mentioned once in the seven volumes of Oman's *History of the Peninsular War*, he has no entry in the *Biographie Universelle*, or in the *Dictionnaire de Biographie Française*, or even in Jean Tulard's exhaustive *Dictionnaire Napoléon*. However, he might possibly have been the son of Alexandre-Jacques Ducoudray, whose date of birth and entry in the *Dictionnaire de*

390. *MECW*, XVIII, pp. 584–5, n. 280. A condensed version of this note is given with the letter of 14 Feb. 1858 where Marx notes Dana's complaint. *MECW*, XL, p. 614. The Ducoudray book, for instance, is today in the libraries of Columbia University, Harvard and Congress. I cannot tell if that was the case in 1858, but if it were, it seems unlikely that even the punctilious Dana would have spent much, if any, time checking it. None of the material cited above is included in Aricó's *Marx y América Latina*, which, in my view, would have been greatly fortified by its inclusion and discussion.

Biographie would fit with the age and known character of Henri. It is an entry which reads nicely in the original:

> *Ducoudray* (Alexandre-Jacques Chevalier, dit le chevalier). On ne sait, a vrai dire, rien de cet auteur fécond, sinon qu'il naquit a Paris en 1744 et qu'il fut, un temps, mousquetaire du roi.... *Nouveaux essais historiques sur Paris*, 7 volumes ... ouvrage pornographique; beaucoup de pieces de circonstance et des poésies fugitives.[391]

On the title page of his own book Ducoudray baldly states that, as a general, he was Bolívar's 'Chief of Staff'. In fact, the record shows that he joined the army, with the rank of colonel, in December 1815, and in February 1816 temporarily occupied the post of assistant chief of staff. Twelve weeks later Bolívar wrote to him:

> Colonel Ducoudray,
>
> This is the third time that you have sent me a request to leave the army. Since I have been of the persuasion that the services you offer are important for the Republic I have rejected this request on two previous occasions. However, the reasons you specify in your last communication have convinced me to accept it, despite my reservations. You are therefore removed from the army. Colonel Soublette, who will replace you as interim assistant chief of staff, will place your papers in the archive. Please be so good as to deliver them to him.[392]

The formal tone masks the fact that, as Ducoudray himself reports, Bolívar refused even a formal greeting to the Frenchman, with the words, 'I will not shake hands with a man who deserves to be shot without ceremony.' The 53-year-old Ducoudray had apparently encouraged his compatriot Brion to replace Bolívar, and his six months of service had witnessed frequent clashes with the 26-year-old Colonel Carlos Soublette, who would twice serve as president of Venezuela, and who appears in a passage which is typical of Ducoudray's book and the tone it gave Marx's essay:

> General Bolívar is, like all his countrymen, the Caraguins, greatly attracted to the fair sex, and has usually with him one, two or more mistresses in his retinue, besides those whom he takes a fancy to in passing from one place to another. These amours last ordinarily four and twenty hours or a week; but Miss Pepa made a rare exception to the general's customary habits ... as soon as he was appointed Commander in Chief by the assembly at Aux Cayes, he wrote to Miss Pepa, who resided with her mother and sister at St Thomas's, to come and join him without delay. He expected them daily with great anxiety, and deferred the departure of our expedition from one day to another, during more than six days. At last, Commodore Brion, growing impatient, declared to him frankly that it was high time to embark, and that he would not and could not wait any longer ... but the entreaties of General Bolívar prevailed at last, and he consented to wait. The complaisant Paez, Anzoátegui and Soublette made a formal toilette, put themselves in uniform, and sailed back to Aux Cayes in the fast-sailing armed schooner, the *Constitution*, in search of Miss Pepa. They were rewarded for their readiness to comply with the desires of their master; Anzoátegui was promoted to the rank of lieutenant-colonel, commander of the bodyguard of General Bolívar, and Soublette, adjutant-colonel, attached to the staff. When I and others of the foreigners

---

391. *Dictionnaire de Biographie Française*, p. 1298.
392. Bolívar, Carúpano, to Ducoudray, 23 June 1816, in *Escritos del Libertador*, IX, Caracas 1973, p. 267.

heard this curious news, we were greatly mortified at such a proceeding and declared loudly that we would leave a commander who compromised the welfare of so many thousands for such a motive. When Brion heard this determination, he urged me in very strong terms to remain, and said that if I was to leave the expedition, all the other foreigners would, undoubtedly, follow my example.... His entreaties were so urgent that I at last yielded.[393]

Shortly after this 'incident' there ensued, on 2 May 1816, a naval engagement between the revolutionaries and the royalists off the Isle of Margarita. This is how the encounter was described in the official *Bulletin of the Army of Liberation*, signed by General Santiago Mariño, the real chief of staff:

> At 11 in the morning, gunfire having been exchanged, the Commander [Brion] directed that the schooner *La Constitución* attack the [Spanish] brig from the starboard, and *La Comandanta* opened fire with its heavy cannon from the port side on the brig, which responded with both artillery and small-arms fire. The schooner *La Constitución* directed its cannonade on the brig's port side, and as soon as they closed, our infantry opened fire, overpowering the enemy in a matter of minutes notwithstanding the most tenacious resistance. At this juncture the Commander [Brion] was wounded, and Frigate Captain Renato Beluche took command of both *La Comandanta* and the whole squadron, and, under very fierce fire, *La Comandanta* boarded the enemy, who tried without success to repulse her. Having taken the quarter-deck, our valiant marines drove the enemy back to the hold and hauled down the Spanish flag. The captain of the vessel was found dead with a bullet in the head, also the pilot and surgeon. On the deck there were 42 dead and 31 wounded, many others having drowned by throwing themselves into the sea.[394]

Mariño's account reads like a contrived mix of military precision and propaganda, as might be expected from an official publication on the morrow of a victorious engagement in which a senior officer was badly wounded. Daniel O'Leary, who was not present, who later married Soublette's sister, and who by 1825 was Bolívar's 'principal aide-de-camp', gives a laconic version which, in terms of historical scale rather than human experience, probably captures the importance of the event aright:

> On 2 May in the morning there was a clash at the height of *Los Frailes*, near the Isle of Margarita, between an armed schooner and a brig of His Catholic Majesty, which, after fierce resistance, was overcome. The Spanish Commander Don Rafael Iglesias died in the fight, and Brion was wounded.[395]

Neither of these accounts was available to Marx, who read Ducoudray's singular version – the only one to place Bolívar at the scene:

---

393. H.L.V. Ducoudray Holstein, *Memoirs of Simon Bolívar*, London 1830, pp. 308–10.

394. *Boletín del Ejército Libertador de Venezuela*, 1, 3 May 1815, in *Escritos del Libertador*, pp. 114–6.

395. *Memorias del General Daniel Florencio O'Leary: Narración*, I (1879–88), Caracas 1952, p. 359. The Cork-born O'Leary first became an aide to Bolívar at the age of nineteen, upon the death of Anzoátegui in 1820. He accompanied Bolívar on his only trip to Bolivia in 1825, when he was at the height of his powers, and remained loyal to the tuberculosis-stricken commander to the end, describing the Liberator's death in December 1830 as 'the last embers of an expiring volcano, the dust of the Andes still on his garments'. R.A. Humphreys (ed.), *The 'Detached Recollections' of General D.F. O'Leary*, London 1969, p. 48. O'Leary had a way with words, and could readily have pumped up any scene, had he wished. He was the British diplomatic representative at Bogotá from 1843 until his death in February 1854. Louis Brion was killed in 1821, at the age of thirty-nine.

... how did General Bolívar behave in this pretty hot and close action, which lasted more than four hours? As soon as he heard that Brion had ordered the necessary preparations for an attack, he took me aside and spoke as follows: 'But, my friend, do you not think that the Spaniards will resist and fight to the last? Do you think that our schooner is strong enough to fight alone? Do you not think that if I were wounded or killed our expedition would be totally lost?' ... I was giving the necessary orders to our officers to arm with muskets and cartridges, when Bolívar came hastily and took me by the arm, saying, 'Now I have found an excellent place ...' He showed me the long-boat, which, in armed vessels, is generally fixed over the cabin windows. He jumped in, called García [his intendant], ordered his pistols and sword, and told him to load two balls in each pistol, which García did in my presence, looking at me and laughing. This position, which Bolívar chose for himself, was surely the safest place in the vessel; then, in sitting as he did in the long-boat, his head and whole body was safely protected by the thickness and strength of the beam which supports the rudder of the vessel.... We suffered much during the action from the musket-fire of about 100 men of the Spanish regiment *La Corona*, who fired from the rigging into our vessel, and wounded and killed about fifty of our officers and men. But when our number increased, and their brave commander fell, himself mortally wounded, they lost all hope; and about thirty of them stripped off their clothes and jumped overboard, in hope to save their lives by swimming to the three rocks, which lay a gun-shot distance from us. At this moment, General Bolívar, having all this time been sitting very safe in the long-boat behind his beam, perceived these naked unfortunate men swimming at a very short distance from him; he took his pistol and killed one of them – took the second and fired at (but missed) another! When all was over, and the brig was taken, he jumped out of his boat, came with a radiant face to me and said, 'My dear friend, you fought bravely, but I too have not been inactive; I killed my man, but unfortunately missed the second'.... Such was Bolívar, in the action of 2 May 1816. I was there; I saw him, he spoke to me, and I commanded, in his place, our corps of officers and volunteers, who will testify to the truth of my plain statement, if they are now living, and not interested, and out of his reach.[396]

Perhaps Karl Marx, who had some horse sense as well as a life-consuming vocation, saw that Ducoudray had commandeered the craft in the same manner as accomplished at Brest by Louis Althusser. He certainly makes no mention of this engagement, but one can only assume that he does trust the judgement of Ducoudray – who, once the days of valour were over, settled in Haiti as a music teacher – because, as has been mentioned, he ends his essay by quoting the Frenchman's description of Bolívar. This the reader can be spared. Instead, let us take a look at another assessment available to Marx from the memoirs of William Miller, who, being an officer in the southern army of San Martín, had no reason whatsoever to like Bolívar, yet who draws his account in part from Bolívar's favourite general, Sucre, and who presents it with something like objectivity. However, it certainly is not the 'scientific' objectivity which the editors of the *Collected Works* so respected and which – despite its very low profile in North America – bears much responsibility for the resurgence of a radical relativism that today offers every liar the veil of simply being 'discursively sovereign'.

The person of Bolívar is thin, and somewhat below the middle size. He dresses in good taste, and has an easy military walk. He is a very bold rider, and capable of undergoing great fatigue. His manners are good, and his address unaffected, but not very prepossessing. It is

---

396. Ducoudray, *Memoirs*, pp. 313–16.

said that, in his youth, he was rather handsome. His complexion is sallow; his hair originally very black, is now mixed with grey. His eyes are dark and penetrating, but generally downcast, or turned askance, when he speaks; his nose is well-formed, his forehead high and broad, the lower part of his face is sharp; the expression of his countenance is cavernous, lowering, and sometimes rather fierce. His temper, spoiled by adulation, is fiery and capricious. His opinions of men and things are variable. He is rather prone to personal abuse, but makes ample amends to those who will put up with it. Towards such his resentments are not lasting. He is a passionate admirer of the fair sex, but jealous to excess. He is fond of waltzing, and is a very quick, but not very graceful, dancer. His mind is of the most active description. When not more stirringly employed, he is always reading, dictating letters etc. or conversing. His voice is loud and harsh, but he speaks eloquently on most subjects. His reading has been principally confined to French authors; hence the Gallic idiom so common in his productions. He is an *impressive* writer, but his style is vitiated by an affection of grandeur. Speaking so well as he does, it is not wonderful that he should be more fond of hearing himself talk than of listening to others, and apt to engross conversation in the society he receives. He entertains numerously; and no one has more skillful cooks, or gives better dinners; but he is himself so very abstemious, in both eating and drinking, that he seldom takes his place at his own table until the repast is nearly over, having probably dined in private upon a plain dish or two. He is fond of giving toasts, which he always prefaces in the most eloquent and appropriate manner; and his enthusiasm is so great that he frequently mounts his chair, or the table, to propose them. Although the cigar is almost universally used in South America, Bolívar never smokes, nor does he permit smoking in his presence. He is never without proper officers in waiting, and keeps up a considerable degree of etiquette. Disinterested in the extreme with regard to pecuniary matters, he is insatiably covetous of fame.[397]

One can see why Marx would not like either such a person or what they represented. It was, one imagines, not so difficult to 'work outwards' from instinct and the assessment of an individual's psychology to a wider political analysis, reaching beyond even the pressing contemporary problem of 'bonapartism' to the 'essential' question of economic structure. In this respect Engels had already laid down a compelling line of interpretation in his response to the Mexican war:

In *America* we have witnessed the conquest of Mexico and have rejoiced at it. It is also an advance when a country which has hitherto been exclusively wrapped up in its own affairs, perpetually rent by civil wars, and completely hindered in its development, a country whose best prospect had been to become industrially subject to Britain – when such a country is forcibly drawn into the historical process. It is to the interest of its own development that Mexico will in future be placed under the tutelage of the United States. The evolution of the whole of America will profit by the fact that the United States, by the possession of California, obtains command of the Pacific.

Yet even Engels, accustomed to the existence of only one industrial 'empire', ends his paragraph by raising some doubts about the confident logic with which it opens:

But again we ask: 'Who is going to profit immediately by the war?' The bourgeoisie alone. The North Americans acquire new regions in California and New Mexico for the creation of fresh capital, that is, for calling new bourgeois into being and enriching those already in existence: for all capital created today flows into the hands of the bourgeoisie. And what

---

397. *Memoirs of General Miller*, II, pp. 331–3.

about the proposed cut through the Tehuantepec isthmus? Who is likely to gain by that? Who else but the American shipping owners?[398]

By the end of 1861, with the outbreak of civil war in the USA and a more clearly defined 'balance of world forces', Marx, writing for the *New York Tribune*, could adopt what today would be recognised as a more orthodox 'anti-imperialist' position. None the less, one suspects that it took the reported involvement of Palmerston – almost on a par with Louis Napoleon in Marx's demonology – in planning an intervention in Mexico for the 'political' to be placed above the 'economic' in Marx's analysis:

> Authoritative interference on behalf of order! This is very literally the Holy Alliance slang and sounds very *remarkable* indeed on the part of England, glorying in the non-intervention principle! And why is 'the way of war, and of declaration of war, and all other behests on international law' supplanted by 'an authoritative intervention in behalf of order'? Because, says the *Times*, there 'exists no government in Mexico'. And what is the professed aim of the expedition? 'To address demands to the constituted authorities at Mexico'.... Palmerston and the *Times*, then, are fully aware that there 'exists a government in Mexico'; that the Liberal Party, 'ostensibly favoured by England, is now in power'; that 'the ecclesiastical rule has been overthrown'; that Spanish intervention was the last folorn hope of the priests and bandits; and finally, that Mexican anarchy was dying away. They know, then, that the joint intervention, with no other avowed end save the rescue of Mexico from anarchy, will produce just the opposite effect, weaken the constitutional government, strengthen the priestly party by a supply of French and Spanish bayonets, rekindle the embers of civil war, and, instead of extinguishing, *restore* anarchy to its bloom.[399]

The tense ambivalence between the merits of accepting capitalist expansion – being part of 'the historical process' – and those of upholding independent republican politics was never to disappear from the Marxist assessment of Latin America. After the Russian Revolution matters became even more complicated because, of course, Latin America could now be 'intervened' in from another source – with alien ideas from the Slavic centre of an internationalist creed for which the independent republics were scarcely any more deserving of specific respect than they were for global capitalist entrepreneurs. In the 1920s the young Peruvian radical Eudocio Ravines was brought face to face with all these complications when, in Buenos Aires on his first spell of exile, he was taken to meet the celebrated socialist Juan B. Justo:

> He received us cordially but questioned us closely.
> 'Anti-imperialist,' he said. 'That means against imperialism, eh? You're the Peruvian?' He asked, turning towards me. 'Well, they tell me you are active and willing to sacrifice. That's good. When a man gives himself, he should do it ungrudgingly. But they say you don't sleep, and that's bad. You'll work better if you sleep. Now about imperialism, what is imperialism?'
> 'The last stage of capitalism.'
> 'Says Lenin,' answered Justo. 'But what do you say? Don't merely repeat bad translations

---

398. 'The Movements of 1847', *Deutsche–Brusseler Zeitung*, 23 Jan. 1848, *MECW*, VI, London 1975, p. 527.
399. 'The Intervention in Mexico', *New York Daily Tribune*, 23 Nov. 1861, in Karl Marx and Frederick Engels, *The Civil War in the United States*, New York 1937, pp. 29, 32–3.

from the Russian. If we are living the last, or as the Russian really says it, the highest, stage of capitalism, what comes next?'

'Socialism,' my friend Kaufman answered firmly.

'Ah, but socialism and bolshevism are not the same things. Socialism is, above all, freedom, the rights of man, respect for life and dignity. If this is lost it isn't socialism.' Then he turned to me again. 'Does imperialism hurt your country?'

'Yes', I answered, 'as it hurts Panama and Cuba with the Platt Amendment – Mexico, Santo Domingo and Haiti with war and occupation.'

'Have you read Marx?' he asked.

'No.'

'And Lenin?'

'No, I haven't.'

'Well, read them and you will learn that for Lenin imperialism is an economic phenomenon. Are there many foreign businesses in your country – imperialistic ones?'

'Yes, there are several.'

'Do they pay wages?'

'Yes.'

'Well, well. And do the great landlords pay wages?'

'They do on the coast.'

'Well, those are the capitalist haciendas. What about the highland ones?' asked Justo.

'There they don't pay wages.'

'Well, now, tell me, which seems to you better for the people?'

'Neither,' I answered.

'So both systems seem bad to you?'

'Yes, because in neither case do the people live decently.'

'Well, you'll make a good socialist some day. But don't talk about imperialism, that's not the problem.'

When we left him, Kaufman was angry because Justo had seemed to believe in the progressive role of imperialism in backward countries. This, Kaufman thought, was absurd. 'This man,' he said, 'is an intellectual. A student of Marx.'[400]

For Martí, Marx had a good point but pursued it too hard. Addressing a meeting in New York on 29 March 1883 in honour of Marx, who had died on the 13th, he spoke candidly:

Look at this large hall. Karl Marx is dead. He deserves to be honoured for declaring himself on the side of the weak. But the virtuous man is not the one who points out the damage and turns with generous anxiety to put it right; he is the one who teaches the gentle amendment of the injury…. Karl Marx studied the methods of setting the world on new foundations, and wakened those who were asleep, and showed them how to cast down the broken props. But being in a hurry, with his understanding somewhat clouded, he did not see that children who do not have a natural, slow, and painful gestation are not born viable, whether they come from the bosom of the people in history, or from the wombs of women in the home. Here are the good friends of Karl Marx, who was not only a titanic stimulator of the wrath of European workers, but also showed great insight into the causes of human misery and the destiny of men, a man driven by a burning desire to do good. He saw in everyone what he carried in himself: rebellion, the highest ideals, struggle.[401]

---

400. Eudocio Ravines, *The Yenan Way*, New York 1951, pp. 17–18.

401. 'The Memorial Meeting in Honor of Karl Marx', in José Martí, *Inside the Monster: Writings on the United States and Imperialism*, New York 1975, pp. 184–5.

Simón Bolívar was, of course, himself an internationalist, at least in the sense that he envisaged a 'continental' politics. Moreover, as he declared in a letter written to his fairweather ally Santander in October 1825 from Potosí, he recognised that such a vision depended not only upon capacity for leadership but also upon recognition of the economic foundation of international relations:

> I am weary of commands, yet never less so than at this time, when flattery overwhelms me with her favours and I at last begin to see the fruits of the seeds that we have planted. But, dear friend, remember that from 1813 to 1826 makes a full fourteen years. The Liberator of North America was not in office that long – nor should I continue in office any longer, lest some should say that I am more ambitious than he…. Brazil will be protected by England, in order to reduce Portugal to dependency. To that end everything will be peacefully settled in Brazil through Mr Stewart, the British ambassador who has just arrived there. It was this reasoning that prompted me yesterday to make such a strong reply to the plenipotentiaries from La Plata. Brazil has insulted us and has so far failed to give us any satisfaction; hence, I deem it politic to complain bitterly of her conduct. If we permit ourselves to be insulted by a weak country, we shall be respected by none nor shall we deserve to be nations … should the Brazilians seek further quarrels with us, I shall fight as a Bolivian, a name that was mine before I was born.[402]

Here Bolívar 'naturalises' the high politics of the state by personalisation more directly even than does Martí. This is hardly surprising, given that an entire 'nation' had just been brought into being in his name; one would expect him to fight for it, even if his mention of 'dependency' contains recognition of a greater power. Indeed, Bolívar shared Marx and Engels's views on British power, although he did not use the term 'capitalism' or even refer explictly to economics. Writing to General Sucre as he left Bolivia, he employed instead a figure of speech that might well have been deployed with irony by Marx in *Capital*, had he known of it:

> Politically, alliance with Great Britain would be a greater victory than Ayacucho, and once it is realised you may be certain that our future happiness is assured. The series of blessings that will result … if we ally ourselves with the Mistress of the Universe is incalculable. I am beside myself with joy and happiness at the very thought that our interests and politics may be linked with those of Great Britain.[403]

Of course, most seductions feel this good at the start, when the nature of 'dependency' is merely sensually dreamed as one of reciprocity within nuptial bliss.

---

402. Bolívar, Potosí, to Santander, 21 Oct. 1825, in Vicente Lecuna and Harold Bierck (eds), *Selected Writings of Bolívar*, II, New York 1951, pp. 541–3.

403. Bolívar, Oruro, to Sucre, 22 Jan. 1826, in ibid., p. 563.

Second Case

SECOND PART

Myra Clark Gaines, Appellant

v.

Richard Relf and Beverly Chew, Executors of Daniel Clark, et al.

Supreme Court of the United States
February 1852[1]

Omnibus has literas, Inspecturis Sulutem in Domino

Ego infrascriptus sacerdos Catholicus et Apostolicus, pastor Ecclesiae S. Petri Apostoli, hinc Praesentibus, notum facio et attestor omnibus et singulis, quorum interest, quod die sexta mensis Julij, A.D. 1790, in matrimonium conjunxerum Jacobum Desgrange et Barbara m. Orci. Testes praesentes fuerunt Joannes O'Connell, Carolus Bernardi et Victoria Bernardi. In quorum fidem, has manu propria scripsi, vigilloq. muniri. Datum Neo Eboraci, vulgo New York, hac die 11d mensis Septembris A.D. 1806.

GULIELMUS V. O'BRIEN
Pastor Ecclesiae S. Petri ut supra.
Reg. pag. '45.' [*sic*]

Nous, Gabriel Rey, général divisionaire, commissaire des relationes commerciales de France à New York, certifione que Monsieur Guillaume V. O'Brien, dont la signature est apposé a l'extrait de mariage en l'autre part, est prêtre et curé de l'Église Catholique de Ste Pierre, en cette ville de New York, et qu'en cette qualité foi doit être a jouter à sa dite signature tant en jugement que hors.

En témoin de quoi nous avons signé le présente et scellé fait apposer le timbre du commissariat à New York, le 13 Septembre, 1806. REY. [*sic*]

★

---

1. The source for this case is Stephen K. Williams (ed.), *Reports of Cases Argued and Decided in the Supreme Court of the United States*, XIII (incl. Howard 12), Newark 1883, pp. 1071–1124. Falling in the official law term of December 1851, the suit was heard throughout February 1852 and decided on 1 March 1852. Evidence and testimony generated by this case from 1802 was included in the Supreme Court hearing. Since litigation begun in 1836 was not finally resolved by the court until 1891 after fifteen hearings (in addition to at least seven appearances in State and Federal courts in Louisiana), the interested reader would be wise to go first to the secondary sources: Nolan B. Harman Jnr, *The Famous Case of Myra Clark Gaines*, Baton Rouge 1946; Perry Scott Rader, 'The Romance of American Courts: Gaines v. New Orleans', *Louisiana Historical Quarterly*, 27:3, Jan. 1944, pp. 1–314; John S. Kendall, 'The Strange Case of Myra Clark Gaines', *Louisiana Historical Quarterly*, 20:1, Jan. 1937, pp. 5–42; Carl S. Swisher, *The Oliver Wendell Holmes devise History of the Supreme Court of the United States: Vol. VI. The Taney Period, 1836–64*, New York 1974.

Ellen Guinan was the niece of William V. O'Brien, and resided with him from the time that she was nine years old until he died, being about twenty years. O'Brien was the pastor of the church for thirty years, viz: from 1784 to 1814, when he died. She had been accustomed to see him write several times a day, and testified that the whole of the above certificate was in his handwriting. She also deposed as follows:

13. *Question*. Do you know the persons named in the body of this exhibit, Joannes O'Connell, Carolus Bernardi and Victoria Bernardi?
Answer. I have heard of them, and think they are dead, but never knew or saw them that I know of.

14. *Question*. Did you know Jacobum Desgrange and Barbara M. Orci, named in the body of the exhibit?
Answer. I did not – never have known them.

15. *Question*. Do you know whether the books or records of St Peter's church were at any time destroyed?
Answer. I heard they were.

16. *Question*. When did you hear they were, and on what occasion?
Answer. A gentleman from Ireland, Mr Cruise, who married the sister of Sir John Johnston, of Johnstown and Warrenstown, in Ireland, came to inquire about the marriage of one of his family, whom he had understood was married by my uncle. I told him to go to the church, as we had given up uncle's books after his death to Bishop Connelly, Catholic Bishop of this city. He came back and told us that he had found that the books had been destroyed by fire.

17. *Question*. About how long ago was it that you thus heard that the books were destroyed?
Answer. To the best of my recollection, about thirteen or fourteen years ago.

★

THE YEAR 1802
T.M.T
No. 141

Criminal proceedings instituted against Geronimo [also known as Jerome] Desgrange for bigamy.

The vicar-general and governor of the bishopric, judge.
Francisco Bermudez. Notary.

DECREE. In the City of New Orleans, the 4th day of September 1802, Thomas Hasset, canonical presbytary of this holy cathedral church, provisor, vicar-general, and governor of the bishopric of this province:

Says, that it has been publicly stated in this city, that Geronimo Desgrange, who was married in the year 1794, to Maria Julia Carrière, was at that time married, and is so even now, before the church, to Barbara Jeanbelle, who has just arrived; and also that the said Desgrange, having arrived from France a few months since, he caused another woman to come here, whose name will be obtained. It is reported in all the city, publicly and notoriously, that the said Geronimo Desgrange has three wives, and not being able to keep secret such an act, as scandalous as it is opposed to the precepts of our holy mother church, his excellency has ordered, that in order to proceed in the investigation, and to the corresponding penalty, testimony be produced to substantiate his being a single man, in order to consummate his marriage with said Carrière; that all persons shall appear who can give any information in this matter....

And also, as it has been ascertained that the said Desgrange is about to leave with the last of these three wives, let him be placed in the public prison, during these proceedings, with the aid of one of the gaolers; this decree serving as an order, which his excellency has approved, and as such it is signed by me, notary.

Signed, Thomas Hasset.

Before me, Francisco Bermudez.

New Orleans, in the same day it was passed to the Capitular House and audience hall of Don Franc'o Caisergues, alcalde of this city, and in his jurisdiction, and I notified to his worship the preceding decree, of which I have taken note.

Signed, Francisco Bermudez.

TESTIMONY. Testimony of Doña Barbara Jeanbelle. In the City of New Orleans, on the 6th of September 1802, appeared before Mr Thomas Hasset, presbytary canon of this holy cathedral church, provisor, vicar-general and governor of the bishopric of this province and the Floridas. Doña Barbara Margarita Jeanbelle de Orsy, who was sworn to tell the truth, and the following questions were then put to her:

1st. If she knows Geronimo Desgrange; how long, and where did she know him.

Answers: That she has known him for sixteen years and she was acquainted with him in New York.

2nd. Being asked whether it is true that she was married to the aforesaid Desgrange, in what place, in what church, how long ago, in what parish, by what clergyman, and who were the witnesses,

Answers: No, although it was her intention to marry the aforesaid Desgrange; but as the latter was going away, she changed her mind; nevertheless, she obtained the permission of her father to go to Philadelphia for that purpose, and that while there Desgrange begged of her to come to this City to consummate the marriage, to which she did not consent; this took place about eleven years and a half ago.

Being asked whether she was acquainted with Desgrange in France, after the period above stated, and if she has ever spoken to him on the subject,

Answers: That last year she saw him in Bordeaux, and that she did not again speak to him of the marriage, because they were both of them married.

Being asked that, if she says she is married, with whom is she married, how long since, in what place, by what clergyman, and who were the witnesses,

Answers: That she is married to Don Juan Santiago Soumeylliat, about ten years ago, in the City of Philadelphia, by a Catholic priest, and that Mr Bernardy and his wife were witnesses.

Being asked if she has any document to prove it,
Answers: That she has no document to prove it.

Being asked if she has heard it publicly said that Desgrange has been married to two women before or since her arrival in this City,
Answers: That she never heard anything of what is asked until last night, when she was told that it was said that she was one of his wives, and she says that what she has declared is the truth; and the testimony having been read to her – which was interpreted by Don Celestino Lavergne and Don Antonio Fromentin – she declared it was what she had said, and she now ratifies it; that she is thirty-four years old.

Signed: B.M. Zambell De Orsi. Hasset. Lavergne. Fromentin.
    Before me, Francisco Bermudez.

Testimony of María Yllar, on the same day, month and year ... who, being sworn to tell the truth, the following questions were propounded to her.

Being asked whether she is married or not, how long it is since she arrived in this City, and with what object,
Answers: That she is the widow of Juan Dupor, *alias* Poulé, who died two years ago, to whom she was married about —— years; that she has never had any other husband, neither before nor since; that she arrived here two days ago, and that her object was to gain a livelihood, having been informed it was a good country for seamstresses.

Being asked if she knows Geronimo Desgrange, how long, and if she was invited or told by him to come to this City, and with what object,
Answers: That she knew Geronimo Desgrange in France about eight months ago, and it was he who had told her to come to this City, where she could gain a better livelihood than in her own country.

Being asked whether she was promised marriage to the said Geronimo Desgrange, or if she had entered into any private contract with reference to matrimony, or any other contract with him,
Answers: That she has not had any contract of the kind with the said Desgrange because she knew before her departure from France that he was married in Louisiana....

Being asked if she had promised the said Desgrange to accompany him in the voyage he is going to make to France,
Answers: That far from accompanying Desgrange during his voyage, she thinks of remaining in the house of Cornelius Ploy, *alias* Flamand, to whom she has been recommended by the said Desgrange, for the purpose of gaining her livelihood by sewing, as the said Flamand is a tailor by trade.

Being asked if she has heard it publicly said that Desgrange has been married to two women before or since her arrival in this City,

Answers: That before her arrival she had heard nothing of the matter; but since she has been here she has heard it said publicly that Desgrange has been married three times; she swears that what she has said is the truth, and that she is twenty-five years old; she does not sign, not knowing how to write.

Signed: Hasset, Fromentin, Lavergne.
   Before me, Bermudez.

Testimony of Maria Julia Carrière. Then appeared before his excellency Maria Julia Carrière, who, through the interpreters, was duly sworn to tell the truth, and the following questions were propounded to her.

Being asked whether she was married or single,
Answers: That she is married to Geronimo Desgrange, since the 4th of December 1794.

Being asked whether she heard, before or since her marriage, that her said husband was married to another woman,
Answers: That about a year since she heard it stated, in this City, that her husband was married in the north, and, in consequence, she wished to ascertain whether it was true or not, and she left this City for Philadelphia and New York, where she used every exertion to ascertain the truth of the report, and she learned only that he had courted a woman, whose father not consenting to the match, it did not take place, and she married another man shortly afterwards.

Being asked whether she had recently heard that her husband was married to three women, if she believed it, or does believe it, or has any doubt about the matter which renders her unquiet or unhappy,
Answers: That although she has heard so in public, she has not believed it, and the report has caused her no uneasiness, as she is satisfied that it is not true; she also swears that she is twenty-two years old.

Signed, Marie Zulime Carrière Desgrange, Hasset, his mark, Celestino Lavergne, Antonio Fromentin.
   Before me. Francisco Bermudez.

Testimony of Geronimo Desgrange, in the City of New Orleans, on the 7th day of September 1802 ... in the presence of interpreters....

Being asked whether he knows Barbara Tanbel de Orsi, how long, and in what place,
Answers: That he first knew her in New York about eleven years ago, and afterwards in Philadelphia.

Being asked that, if he was married to her, to state in what place, before what clergyman, how long ago, and who were the witnesses,
Answers: That he never was married to her although he wished to do so, and had asked the consent of her father, but he refused it, as deponent was poor....

Being asked if he knows María Yllar, to state how long he has known her, in what place, and with what motives,

Answers: That in the month of December, of last year, he knew her when she was in a boarding-house, where she was employed as a servant, in Bordeaux, where the respondent lived.

Being asked if he made any arrangements with the aforesaid to accompany him to this City, to state what that arrangement was, and what object she had in coming here,

Answers: That he made no arrangement nor agreement with the aforesaid; and the reason she is here is that, having asked him whether this country held out better inducements than Bordeaux, in order to gain a livelihood by sewing, he advised her to come, as it would prove more advantageous to her....

Being asked why Maria Julia Carrière, his wife, went to the north last year,

Answers: That the principal reason was that a report had circulated in this City that he was married with another woman; she wished to ascertain whether it was true, and she went....

Being asked whether it is true that, in order to satisfy his wife and the public, he offered to bring with him or to procure documents to prove his innocence in this matter, and that if he have them, to show them,

Answers: That taking it for granted that this charge would naturally fall, his wife being satisfied of his innocence, and no judge having required the showing of such documents, he has used no exertions to obtain them; and that he is forty-two years old.

Signed: J. Desgrange. Hasset, his mark. Antonio Fromentin, Celestino Lavergne.
     Before me, Francisco Bermudez.

DECREE. Not being able to prove the public report, which is contained in the original decree of these proceedings, and having no more proofs for the present, let all proceedings be suspended, with power to prosecute them hereafter, if necessary, and let the person of Geronimo Desgrange be set at liberty, he paying the costs.

Signed, Thomas Hasset.
     Francisco Bermudez.

★

Mr Justice CATRON delivered the opinion of the court:[2]

This case comes here by appeal from the decree of the Circuit Court of the Eastern District of Louisiana, where the bill was dismissed.

     The complainant sues as the only legitimate child of the late Daniel Clark, who died in the City of New Orleans the 13th of August, 1813.[3] No account is prayed against

---

2. Chief Justice Roger Taney (Maryland, appointed by Pres. Jackson 1836, died 1864) did not sit because a relative held property relating to the case. Justice John McLean (Ohio, appointed by Jackson 1829, died 1861) was absent because of illness. As a result, the Justices hearing the case were: John Catron (Tennessee, appointed by Jackson 1837, died 1865); Peter Daniel (Virginia, appointed by Van Buren 1841,

Daniel Clark's executors; but the complainant seeks to recover the property sold by them, consisting of land and slaves, on the ground that her father could not deprive her, as his legitimate child, of more than one fifth part of his estate by a last will, according to the laws of Louisiana as they stood in 1813. And she maintains that the sales made by Chew and Relf were made without any orders of court to authorise them and therefore they are void....

The respondents claim under a will made by Daniel Clark in 1811, by which he devised all his property, real and personal, to his mother, Mary Clark, and appointed Richard Relf and Beverly Chew his executors; and to whom Mary Clark made a power to sell Daniel Clark's estate for purpose of raising money to pay his debts. Chew and Relf, acting as executors of Daniel Clark, and also as attorneys of Mary Clark, did sell the property in controversy for the purpose of paying the debts of the testator....[4]

On the 2nd of July, 1844, the then complainants, Gaines and wife[5] ... filed the following:

Your oratrix alleges that she is entitled to the one moiety of the estate of which the said Daniel Clark died possessed, by reason of a conveyance thereof made to her by M.Z. Gardette, the widow of the said Clark and the mother of your oratrix, on the 7th day of May 1836, and which is hereunto annexed, marked A.B. ... and the mother of your oratrix did there-after, on the 20th June 1844, further convey to her all her interest in said estate ... the whole of said estate having been acquired during the coverture of said Clark and wife.

The first and most important of the issues presented is that of the legitimacy of the complainant. It is raised by the following pleadings.

---

died 1860); John McKinley (Virginia, appointed by Van Buren, 1837, died 1852); Robert Grier (Pennsylvania, appointed by Polk 1846, resigned 1870); Samuel Nelson (New York, appointed by Tyler 1845, resigned 1872); and James Wayne (Georgia, appointed by Jackson 1835, died 1867). The lawyers for the appellant were Messrs Reverdy Johnson and John Campbell (who, appointed a Supreme Court Justice by President Pierce in 1853, was unable to sit on further hearings of this case) and for the appellees Messrs Duncan and Webster, who – being Daniel Webster the Whig leader, member of Congress since 1811, and now serving his third term as secretary of state – gave the case an unusually high profile. Indeed, although they were aged (both were to die within months), Webster and Henry Clay – no less prominent a Whig notable and ex-secretary of state – remained closely involved with the case, with which Clay had an indirect attachment since 1807.

3. *Daniel Clark*, born County Sligo, 1766, educated at Eton. Settled in New Orleans, 1786. Merchant partnership with Daniel Coxe, trading largely through Philadelphia, established in 1791. In 1795 built a working model of Eli Whitney's cotton gin on the basis of a newspaper description. His principal private houses in the city were on Royal Street and on the Bayou Road, near Bayou St John, where he died in 1800.

4. *Beverly Chew*, from Virginia, one-time Collector of the Port of New Orleans, where he had died in 1851. *Richard Relf*, from Philadelphia, one-time Cashier of the Lousiana State Bank, died New Orleans, October 1857, aged eighty-one. Both were partners of Clark, to whom they owed $400,000, according to an inventory of 1811, used as evidence in the Supreme Court hearings of 1841.

5. *Myra Gaines née Clark*, born New Orleans 1805 and brought up until 1832 as Myra Davis, married William Wallace Whitney, of Binghampton, New York, in September 1832 at the home of her foster-father, Captain Samuel Boyer Davis, in Wilmington, Delaware. Once informed of her true father, Myra and Whitney went to New Orleans, where, in 1835, Whitney was arrested for libel against Beverly Chew, only being released upon payment of bail of $25,000. When they returned to pursue the case in 1837, Whitney died of yellow fever. There were five children from this marriage, two dying in infancy and one, Julia, at the age of sixteen. Myra's six grandchildren issued from William Whitney and Rhoda Christmas née Whitney. In 1839 Myra became the third wife of *General Edmund Pendleton Gaines*, born 1777, of Culpeper County, Virginia. Appointed ensign in 1795 on the recommendation of W.C. Claiborne, then congressman from Tennessee. Promoted on account of his record in the 1812 war against the British and subsequent

She alleges that her father, Daniel Clark, was married to Zulime née Carrière in the City of Philadelphia in the year 1802 or 1803; and that she is the legitimate, and only legitimate offspring of that marriage.

The defendants deny that Daniel Clark was married to said Zulime at the time and place alleged, or at any other time and place. And they further aver that at the time said marriage is alleged to have taken place, the said Zulime was the lawful wife of one Jerome Desgrange.

If the mother of the complainant was the lawful wife of Jerome Desgrange at the time Zulime is alleged to have intermarried with Daniel Clark then the marriage with Clark is merely void; and it is immaterial whether it did or did not take place. And the first question we propose to examine is … whether said Zulime was Desgrange's lawful wife in 1802 or 1803.

A formal record of the marriage between Desgrange and Marie Julie Carrière, obtained from the cathedral Catholic church at New Orleans, is before us. That it is a true record of said marriage is not controverted. Marie Julia is designated Zulime, by a soubriquet or nickname, which is proved to have been a common custom in Louisiana at the time. The marriage was solemnized in due form on the 2nd day of December 1794. This is admitted on the part of the complainant. The parties cohabited together as man and wife for seven or eight years. This is also conceded by both sides. To rebut and overcome the established fact of this marriage it is alleged that previous to Desgrange's marriage with Zulime he had lawfully married another woman, whom was living when he married Zulime and was still his wife; and that therefore this second marriage was void. And this issue we are called upon to try.…

The first witness whose testimony will be referred to was Madame Despau, sister of Zulime.[6] Her testimony has been taken three times: first in 1839, then in 1845, and again in 1849.

In 1839 she says:

I was well acquainted with the late Daniel Clark of New Orleans. He was married in Philadelphia in 1803, by a Catholic priest. One child was born of that marriage, to wit Myra Clark, who married William Wallace Whitney. I was present at her birth and knew that Mr Clark claimed and acknowledged her to be his child. She was born in 1806. I neither knew, nor had any reason to believe that any other child, besides Myra, was born of that marriage. The circumstances of Zulime's marriage with Daniel Clark were these. Several years after her marriage with Desgrange she heard he had a living wife. Our family charged him with the crime of bigamy in marrying said Zulime. He at first denied it, but afterwards admitted it and fled from the country.

---

management of the Creek Indians, Gaines had made a name for himself by arresting ex-Vice-President Aaron Burr, charged with treason, whose trial he attended in 1807. In the Mexican War of 1846–48 he became involved in a sharp conflict with Secretary of War Marcy over conscription, but was acquitted of insubordination. In a pre-nuptial agreement, Myra promised to pay Gaines $100,000 should her claim be upheld and he committed himself to funding the litigation. Gaines died of cholera in New Orleans in June 1849. In fact, neither of Myra's husbands died in the city's great epidemics – yellow fever (1831, 1853, 1858, 1875) and cholera (1832) – estimated to have killed at least 100,000 people between 1793 and 1905.

6. *Sophie Veuve Despau née Carrière*, born 1778, ex-wife of William Despau, a New Orleans planter, resident in Louisiana, Philadelphia, Cuba and, eventually, as a teacher, Biloxi, Mississippi. As indicated here, Sophie had given testimony three times – on the final occasion when she was seventy-two years old – for Federal Court hearings, but by this stage Myra's claim had come before the Supreme Court four times: *Ex Parte Myra Clark Whitney* (1839); *Gaines* v. *Relf* (1841); *Gaines* v. *Chew* (1844); *Patterson* v. *Gaines* (1848).

These circumstances became public, and Mr Clark made proposals of marriage to my sister, with the knowledge of all our family. It was considered essential first to obtain record proof of Desgrange having a living wife at the time he married my sister; to obtain which, from the records of the Catholic church in New York (where Mr Desgrange's prior marriage was celebrated), we sailed for that city. On our arrival there we found that the registry of marriages had been destroyed. Mr Clark arrived after us. We heard that a Mr Gardette, then living in Philadelphia, was one of the witnesses to Mr Desgrange's prior marriage. We proceeded to that city and found Mr Gardette. He answered that he was present at said prior marriage of Desgrange, and that afterwards he knew Desgrange and his wife by this marriage; that his wife had sailed for France.

Mr Clark then said: 'You have no reason longer to refuse being married to me. It will, however, be necessary to keep our marriage secret till I have obtained judicial proof of the nullity of your and Desgrange's marriage.'[7] They, the said Clark and the said Zulime, were then married. Soon afterwards our sister, Madame Caillavet, wrote to us from New Orleans that Desgrange's wife, whom he had married prior to marrying Zulime, had arrived at New Orleans. We hastened our return to New Orleans. He was prosecuted for bigamy, father Antoine,[8] of the Catholic church, taking part in the proceedings against Desgrange. Mr Desgrange was condemned for bigamy ... and was cast into prison, from which he secretly escaped by connivance, and was taken down the Mississippi River by Mr Le Breton D'Orgenois where he got into a vessel, escaped from the country and, according to the best

---

7. This may strike a modern reader as distinctly strange, but in the eighteenth and early nineteenth centuries clandestine marriages were common, being numbered in their thousands in England, where until 1753 legally binding marriages 'did not have to be performed in church, by a clergyman of the Church of England, according to the rites laid down in the Book of Common Prayer', and where there was no system of legalised divorce until 1857. Lawrence Stone, *Uncertain Unions and Broken Lives*, Oxford 1995; R.B. Outhwaite, *Clandestine Marriage in England, 1500–1850*, London 1995. Perhaps the most infamous case at the time of these events was that of the Swiss political philosopher Benjamin Constant, who hid his secret marriage of 1808 from the formidable Madame de Staël for nearly a year. The nature of 'engagement' and the status of 'fiancés' was at that time qualitatively different to those of the present day (even if 'bundling' – joint pernoctation – was often permitted provided it did not result in pregnancy). There were correspondingly tighter strictures of the common law in Anglo-Saxon systems and sharper applications of the reforms of the Council of Trent in the Roman system. In the case of Santiago de Chile, for instance, some eighty cases of broken engagement vows were taken before the ecclesiastical tribunals between 1756 and 1856 (fifty-nine broken by men), and twenty-nine of the eighty cases of illicit union brought before them involved clandestine marriage, suggesting a much higher level in society as a whole. Eduardo Cavieres and René Salinas, *Amor, Sexo y Matrimonio en Chile Tradicional*, Valparaiso 1991, pp. 91, 102. According to Richard Boyer, even after the Council of Trent, which increased the emphasis on banns and marriage being in the sight of the Church, 'clandestine marriages, once they slipped through, were supposed to be binding (especially when a woman had lost her virginity), when checked for impediment and confirmed with a nuptial mass or blessing'. *Lives of the Bigamists: Marriage, Family and Community in Colonial Mexico*, Albuquerque 1995, p. 73.

8. *Antonio Ildefonso Moreno* (1748–1829), from Granada, Spain. Arrived in New Orleans as a Capuchin friar in 1781; expelled by Governor Miró, 1790; returned with Bishop Penalver, 1795; suspended by Archbishop Carroll in 1807 for refusing to recognise the authority of any priest sent to take charge of the city. In 1806 the US governor of the Territory of Louisiana, William Claiborne, wrote to the secretary of state,

> We have a Spanish priest here who is a very dangerous man; he rebelled against the Superiors of his own church and would even rebel, I am persuaded, against this Government.... This seditious priest is a Father Antoine; he is a great favourite of the Louisiana ladies; has married many of them, and christened all their children; he is by some citizens esteemed an accomplished hypocrite, has great influence with the people of colour and, report says, embraces every opportunity to render them discontented with the American government.

Claiborne, New Orleans, to Madison, 8 Oct. 1806, quoted in Charles Gayarré, *History of Louisiana: The American Domination*, New York 1866, p. 154.

of my knowledge, never afterwards returned to Louisiana. This happened in 1803, not a great while before the close of the Spanish government in Louisiana.[9]

Mr Clark told us that before he could promulgate his marriage with my sister, it would be necessary that there should be brought by her an action against the name of Desgrange. The anticipated change of government created delay; but at length, in 1806, Mr James Brown and Eligius Fromentin,[10] as the counsel for my sister, brought suit against the name of Desgrange in the city court, I think, of New Orleans. The grounds of said suit were that Desgrange had imposed himself upon her at a time when he had a living lawful wife. Judgement was rendered against Desgrange. Mr Clark still continued to defer promulgating his marriage with my sister, which very much fretted and irritated her feelings. Mr Clark became a member of the United States Congress in 1806. Whilst he was in Congress my sister heard he was courting Miss C., of Baltimore.[11]

She was much distressed, though she could not believe the report, knowing herself to be his wife. Still, his strange conduct in deferring to promulgate his marriage with her had alarmed her. She and I sailed for Philadelphia to get proof of his marriage with my sister. We could find no record, and were told that the priest who married her and Mr Clark had gone to Ireland. My sister then sent for Daniel W. Coxe; mentioned to him the rumor; he answered that he knew it to be true that he (Clark) was engaged to her (Miss C.). My sister replied that it could not be so. He then told her that she would not be able to establish her marriage with Clark if he were disposed to contest it. He advised her to take counsel, and said he would send one.

---

9. By the treaty signed in Paris on 30 April 1803 the USA obtained the Louisiana territory through payment of approximately $15 million to France, thereby acquiring – on the US interpretation and Talleyrand's compliance – the entire Mississippi valley west of the river, and effectively doubling the territory of the United States of America by adding the lands today covered by the states of Louisiana, Arkansas, Colorado, Iowa, Kansas, Minnesota, Missouri, Montana, Nebraska, North and South Dakota, Oklahoma and Wyoming.

> Napoleon, the First Consul of France, sold something he had neither the moral nor the legal right to sell. The United States ministers, Robert R. Livingstone and James Monroe, bought something they were not authorised to buy, and spent seven and a half times what they were authorised to spend on something else. President Thomas Jefferson, after the Louisiana purchase, did not believe that he had the right under the United States Constitution to receive what he had bought. And two British banking houses – Baring and Co. and its Amsterdam affiliate, Hope and Co. – bought the American stock, issued to pay Napoleon, who used the ready funds to continue the war against England.

Walter G. Cowan, John C. Chase and John Wilds, *New Orleans Yesterday and Today*, Baton Rouge 1983, p. 120.

10. *Eligius Fromentin*, French Jesuit priest sent as a missionary to New Orleans. Renounced vows and married; studied law; elected as US Senator for Louisiana 1813, serving full six-year term. 1821, judge of New Orleans Circuit Court; 1822, federal judge. Died of yellow fever, 6 Oct. 1822, twenty-four hours after his wife had expired of the same disease.

11. If Daniel Clark didn't marry Zulime he never married anybody. It is only in the report of the 1861 case that Miss C. is clearly revealed to be a Miss Caton, almost certainly a daughter of the English-born Richard Caton, a leading Baltimore merchant who probably knew Clark through the Association for Cotton Manufacture, which he set up. Caton, however, had four daughters, three of whom married into the British peerage. As a result, the secondary and biographical literature is very confused, but it is my hunch that Zulime's competitor for Clark's affections was the eldest daughter Marianne, born in 1788 and renowned in both the United States and Britain as a great beauty. The widow of Richard Patterson, Marianne was wed in 1825 to Richard Wellesley, Earl of Mornington and the Duke of Wellington's eldest brother, previously the Governor of Bengal (for which he received poor notices from Mill), ambassador to Spain, and currently serving as Lord Lieutenant of Ireland (the family's seat was Dangan Castle, County Meath). The marriage was very unhappy. Following her second husband's death in 1842, Marianne, now Marchioness Wellesley, became Lady of the Bedchamber to Queen Adelaide, and died at Hampton Court Palace on Christmas Eve 1853.

A Mr Smyth came and told my sister that she could not legally establish her marriage with Clark, and pretended to read her a letter in English (a language then unknown to my sister) from Mr Clark to Mr Coxe, stating that he was about to marry Miss C. In consequence of this information, my sister Zulime came to the resolution of having no further connection or intercourse with Mr Clark, and soon afterwards she married Mr Gardette, of Philadelphia.

The witness further states that she became acquainted with Desgrange in 1793.[12] He was a nobleman by birth, and married Zulime when she was thirteen years old. Zulime had two children by him, a boy and a girl; the boy died, the girl is living (1839); her name is Caroline and she is married to Dr Barnes.[13] Witness was present at the birth of these children. The marriage of Zulime was a private one. Besides the witness, Mr Dorsier of New Orleans, and an Irish gentleman, a friend of Mr Clark, from New York, were present at the marriage. A Catholic priest performed the ceremony....

The next most important witness is Madame Caillavet, another sister of Zulime.[14] She was also three times examined. Her first deposition was taken at New Orleans in May 1835, in which she states:

I did reside in the City of New Orleans about the year 1800, and for many years previous; my residence continued there until I went to France, about the year 1807.

I was acquainted with Daniel Clark, late of the City of New Orleans, deceased. My acquaintance with him commenced about the year 1797; my intimacy with him, growing out of his marriage with my sister, continued during my residence in New Orleans.

I was not present at the marriage of Zulime née Carrière (who is my sister) with Mr Clark, but it is within my knowledge, both from information derived from my sisters at the time, and from statements of Mr Clark made to me during his lifetime, that a marriage was solemnized between them....

In her last deposition Madame Caillavet states:

There was born of this marriage one, and only one child, a female named Myra, who was put by Mr Clark, while an infant, under the charge of Mrs Samuel B. Davis, in whose family she was brought up and educated. Having suffered from hired nurses, she was nursed, through kindness, for some time after her birth, by Mrs Harriet Harper, wife of William Harper, the nephew of Colonel Samuel B. Davis. Mr Clark stated to me, frequently, that Myra was his lawful and only child. This child is the same person who was married to William Wallace Whitney; and who is now the wife of General Edmund B. Gaines, of the United States army. I have always understood that the marriage between my sister and Mr Clark was a private one, and that it was not promulgated by Mr Clark in his lifetime, unless

12. *Jerome Desgrange*, born 1760, originally from Bordeaux. Established as a confectioner and distiller on Royal and St Philip streets of New Orleans in the early 1790s. It is likely that Zulime met him at his shop, effectively a café, as she probably did Daniel Clark.

13. *Caroline Barnes née Clark*, born in Philadelphia, brought up under the supervision of Daniel Coxe, boarding with the Alexander family, Trenton, New Jersey, and then, upon Clark's death, at Mrs Baisley's school near the home of Clark's mother, Mary, in Germantown, Philadelphia. Mary Clark, who was the principal beneficiary of Daniel's 1811 will, died in June 1823, having made Caroline the beneficiary of her own will. However Caroline, whose husband was a dentist, was only technically part of the case in 1840 and evidently did not wish to get involved in the affair, either on her own behalf or in support of Myra. She died in 1844 without issue.

14. *Rose Caillavet née Carrière*, born in Louisiana, probably in 1772, and so appreciably older than Zulime, eventually resident in Mississippi.

he did so in a last will, made a short time previous to his death. I have heard that such a
last will was made, but it was believed to have been suppressed or destroyed after his death.

... Respondents introduced the following evidence:

On the 26th of March, 1801, Madame Caillavet, Madame Lasabe, and Madame Despau
joined in a power of attorney, authorizing Jerome Desgrange, their brother-in-law, to
proceed to Bordeaux, in France, and there recover any estate or property belonging to
them, as co-heiresses of their father and mother.[15]

At the same time, Desgrange made a general power of attorney to his wife, Donna
Marie Zulime, to act for him in all his affairs in his absence. She acted under the power,
and sold several slaves, and did other acts, which appear in notarial records. In each of
these acts she styles herself 'the legitimate wife and general attorney of Don Geronimo
Desgrange'.

In July 1801, Desgrange wrote to Clark the following letter:

Bordeaux, July 1801.

My Dear Sir and Friend – Although, uncertain whether you are at New Orleans, I
hasten to seize the opportunity of the sailing of the Natchez to furnish you with some news.
I hope my letter will find you in good health. When one has such a friend as you, we cannot
feel too deep an interest in him.... I have taken the liberty to inclose under cover a package
for my wife, which I beg you to remit to her. Permit me, my dear friend, to reiterate my
acceptance of the kind offer you made before I left, and should my wife find herself embarrassed in any respect, you will truly oblige me by aiding her with your kind advice. I expect
to leave in a few days to join my family. I hope to return to Bordeaux in two or three
months, to terminate my affairs here and to make preparations to meet you. I have been
some days engaged in a lawsuit for the purpose of recovering an estate belonging to my
wife's family ... I have not heard from my wife, which renders me very uneasy as to going
to Providence before I hear from her. It is said that peace will be declared by the end of the
year, but I have my fears whether we will enjoy that happiness. Hoping to have the pleasure
of hearing from you soon.

I am, most truly, your friend,
Desgrange.

The respondents introduced the deposition of Daniel W. Coxe of Philadelphia. He had
been the partner in trade of Daniel Clark, in their New Orleans house, from the time
Clark started out as a commission and shipping merchant. They were nearly of the same
age; both proud, intelligent, and ambitious of success; equals in rank, and intimate in their
social relations, as a common interest and constant intercourse could make them. This
abundantly appears by their correspondence, introduced into the record before us.

Coxe states that in 1802 Madame Desgrange presented herself to him in Philadelphia
with a confidential letter from Daniel Clark, which stated that the bearer was pregnant
and would soon be delivered of a child; and that he, Clark, was the father of it. And the
letter requested Coxe to put her under the care of a respectable physician and to furnish
her with money during her confinement and stay in Philadelphia. That Coxe, accordingly,

---

15. Madame Lasabe, Zulime's third sister, was never a witness in this case and does not – so far as I can
discern – appear anywhere else in the record. Although she authorised the power of attorney, she may well
not have been living in New Orleans by this time or she may simply have decided – rather like Caroline
Barnes – to play no part in the affairs of her sister.

employed the late Dr William Shippen to attend her at her accouchement. That he, Coxe, procured a nurse for her; and removed the child on the day of its birth to the residence of the nurse; that this child was Caroline Barnes, who, before her marriage, always went by the name of Clark.

The first nurse was Mrs Stevens; afterwards the child was placed, at Clark's request, with Mr and Mrs James Alexander, of Trenton, New Jersey, and continued there until 1814 or 1815. After this (her father being dead), she was placed at Mrs Baisley's school in Philadelphia. She remained with Mrs Baisley several years, and acted during part of that time as a teacher, and, Coxe thinks, continued there until she was married. She was under Coxe's supervision all the time, from her birth until her marriage; and was supported at the expense of Clark until his death. She was at all times, during his life, recognized by Clark as his child, and caressed as such when he was at Philadelphia....

Coxe states:

I also think it proper to state that in the year 1808, after Madame Desgrange had returned to Philadephia from New Orleans (a second time), and when lodging in Walnut Street, she sent for me, and during a private interview with her, at Mrs Rowan's, where she was lodged, she stated that she had heard that Mr Clark was going to be married to Miss C., of Baltimore, which, she said, was a violation of his promise to marry her, and added that she now considered herself at liberty to connect herself in marriage with another person; alluding, doubtless, to Dr Gardette, who, at the moment of this disclosure, entered the room, when after a few words of general conversation, I withdrew, and her marriage to Mr Gardette was announced a few days later.

The complainant's principal witnesses are Madame Despau and Madame Caillavet. Madame Despau swears that in 1802 or in 1803, Madame Desgrange and herself went to New York for the purpose of ascertaining whether Jerome Desgrange had previously been married, where Clark overtook them; that no church record of the marriage could be found in the Catholic chapel at New York; but hearing that Mr Gardette, of Philadelphia, knew something of the matter, they went there, and Gardette informed them that he was present at the first marriage; and that Clark and Zulime were then married. And that soon afterwards, they received a letter from Madame Caillavet informing them that Desgrange's first wife had come to New Orleans, and they immediately returned there; where Desgrange was prosecuted by his first wife, convicted and imprisoned, and that he fled the country and never returned to it....

It is true beyond question that these witnesses did know that their sister went north to hide her adultery; that she did delude her absent husband, that she did impose upon him the mendacious tale that her sole business north was to clear up doubts that disturbed her mind, about his having another wife. These facts they carefully conceal in their depositions; and on the contrary swear that she went north to get evidence of her husband's bigamy and imposition on her.

When they swore positively that Caroline was the child of Desgrange they did not know that he had been in France, and his wife in New Orleans, and that they had not seen each other for a year before the child was born; and Madame Despau could not be ignorant that Clark claimed it as his, and that the mother admitted the fact to Coxe....

It is clear – as we think – that at the time Desgrange left for Europe he and his wife were on terms of intercourse and ordinary affection, and certainly not separated; and that the cause of their separation is found in the connection formed by Clark and Zulime in Desgrange's absence.

In support of the consistency of these witnesses, stress is laid on the fact so strong was the rumour of Desgrange's having two other wives besides Zulime, that he was arrested, imprisoned, and tried on the rumor. This is certainly true; the record of his prosecution establishes the fact. But what circumstances are brought forth to show that there was any plausible ground for such rumor and such prosecution? Desgrange was a man somewhat advanced in life. He kept a humble shop for selling liquors and confectionery; this seems to have been his sole business. His wife Zulime was about twenty years old, and uncommonly handsome.[16] He seems to have been a lone man in New Orleans, and his friends were his wife and her relations. In the face of these facts it is assumed that he brought from France an additional wife, and that another followed him....

The early times and the unintelligent condition of much of the population of New Orleans at that day must account for this absurd public opinion, and the proceedings founded on it.

It is palpable that the witnesses Despau and Caillavet swear to a plausible tale of fiction, leaving out the circumstances of gross reality. These originated beyond question in profligacy of a highly dangerous and criminal character, that of a wife having committed adultery, and been delivered of an illegitimate child, in the absence of her husband, not only on his lawful business, but on her's, and at her instance....

The complicated and curious circumstances that surrounded this charge of bigamy against Desgrange ... are easily enough understood now. A clew is furnished to unravel

---

16. According to Rader,

> Many witnesses gave it as their opinion that [Zulime] was remarkably beautiful. Their testimony was their conclusion from having seen and known her; they did not state her size or weight, or the colour of her eyes or hair, or the shape of her nose or lips. But one witness testified that in physical form she was 'unusually charming and attractive'.

Rader, 'Romance', p. 23. Myra, of course, was widely described, but one must harbour reservations about some of the sources, for example, E.F. Ellet:

> Mrs Gaines is of the medium height, slender but well rounded and symmetrical in form. Her brown hair is thick and clusters in short curls; her eyes are dark and brilliant; her complexion is fair and clear; her features are regular, and she is beautiful beyond criticism. Full of life and animation, fresh in feeling and impulsive, with a store of information and a mind well cultivated, possessing rich humour and spirit, with manners cordial, piquant and winning, she was a universal favourite in society, and had a court of gentlemen about her wherever she moved.

Court Circles of the Republic, or the Beauties and Celebrities of the Nation, cited without full reference by Rader, 'Romance', p. 176. This chimes with the tone of the *Washington National Intelligencer*, of 1 February 1848, describing the scene as Mr Justice Wayne delivered a (temporarily) favourable verdict:

> The form of the lovely and accomplished Mrs Gaines was bent forward, catching every sound as it fell; while every eye was riveted upon her, and every heart throbbed in unison with her own. As the Judge proceeded it became manifest that there was an earthly tribunal before which the rights of the child, the mother, and the wife would be protected, and *every heart* was moved.

Somewhat less affecting is the image hatched years later before the Georgia Bar Association by one of her counsel: 'She was under five feet in height, thin, wiry, with small, bright, restless eyes, very red hair streaked with white and worn in bunches of little curls on either side of her forehead.' Quoted in Kendall, 'Strange Case', p. 39. According to Sir Charles Murray, who visited New Orleans at the time Myra first undertook litigation,

> The general character of Creole beauty is a dark but clear and transparent complexion, black eyes fringed with long eyelashes, and finely pencilled eyebrows; a nose neither Greek nor Roman, but delicately formed, and very fine '*taille*' although apt to run rather early too far into the '*aimable embonpoint*' ... much attention to hair.

Travels in North America during the Years 1834, 1835 and 1836, London 1841, pp. 187-8.

the mystery, why it was that an humble shopkeeper should be of sufficient consequence to excite public indignation, be the object of general and gross reproach, and for his name afterwards to appear in the columns of the only newspaper then published in New Orleans, an extract from which the complainant has given in evidence. There an account was given of Desgrange's alleged crime of bigamy, and the enormity of his conduct in marrying Zulime née Carrière, whose artless innocence he so basely imposed upon.

The mystery is explained by the fact now presented, that in Desgrange's absence to France his wife formed a connection with Clark, and the child Caroline came of that illicit connection. On Desgrange's return home, Madame Caillavet notified her sisters to return in haste, as Desgrange's first wife was in New Orleans. Mesdames Despau and Desgrange forthwith returned, and at this time it was that Desgrange was so fiercely assailed by public opinion, and very soon after arrested on general rumor and tried for bigamy. The reports, to which these witnesses swear, obviously originated with, and relied upon by Madame Desgrange, her sisters and friends to harass and drive Desgrange from the country so that his wife might indulge herself in the company of Clark, unincumbered and unannoyed by the presence of a humble and deserted husband. And this was, in fact, accomplished, for Desgrange did leave the country soon after he was tried for bigamy, and Clark did set up Desgrange's wife in a handsome establishment, where their intercourse was unrestrained.[17]

In 1805 when Desgrange came again to New Orleans, his wife immediately sued him for alimony ... speedily got judgement against him for $500 per annum; on the same day issued execution, and drove him away again....

The great basis of human society throughout the civilized world is founded on marriages and legitimate offspring; and to hold that either of the parties could, by a mere declaration, establish the fact that a marriage was void would be an alarming doctrine....

In England, by the statute law, copies from parish registers are received to prove marriages; but the paper produced must be a sworn copy of the parish register, and not a certificate of the officiating clergyman; nor will a copy of a foreign register be received in evidence on proof that it is a true copy.

If it were allowable in this country to give such certificate in evidence, where every clergyman of all denominations can perform the ceremony of marriage, and where it is performed by justices of the peace in many states, it would open a door to frauds that could not be guarded against....

The power of attorney from Desgrange to his wife; and the one from his wife and sisters to him, to pursue and recover their property in France; his letter to Clark of July

---

17. Although Judge Catron had not sat when Myra's case previously came before the Supreme Court in 1848, he does not appear to have made much effort to shield his prejudices. Two days after his opinion was delivered, the Tennessee jurist wrote to James Buchanan (Polk's secretary of state and himself president in 1861, when the case returned to the Supreme Court):

> The ladies have been edified by hearing Mrs Gaines' suit – and on Monday they heard the opinion in such like phrases as these: that the plan of driving off Des Grange [sic] (Mrs Gaines' mother's first husband) so as to enjoy the society of Clark unencumbered, and without restraint, originated beyond question in profligacy highly criminal; that of committing adultery in the absence of Des Grange to France ... as Byron said to Murray, when he sent from Italy Don Juan to be published – 'it is full of passion and profligacy, and will be read by half the men and *all* the women'. They are albut [sic] dead to see it in print. Of course, the little woman makes the smoke come off the water – Your Obedient Servant.

Buchanan Papers, quoted in Swisher, *History*, pp. 765–6.

1801; the proof of his absence from his absence for more than a year before Caroline was born; the record of the suit for alimony, prosecuted in 1805, by his wife against Desgrange, together with Daniel W. Coxe's evidence, as it now stands, fortified, as it is, with letters showing dates, consistency and accuracy, are all new; and make up a defense altogether conclusive.

The following is the result of our conclusions:

That the complainant's two principal witnesses Madame Despau and Madame Caillavet are not worthy of credit....

That the certificate of William V. O'Brien is inadmissible and must be disregarded....

That the record of Desgrange's prosecution for bigamy overthrows the feeble and discredited evidence introduced by complainant to prove the bigamy by Desgrange by marrying Marie Julia née Carrière in 1794; and establishes the fact that Desgrange was her lawful husband in 1802 or 1803, when complainant alleges Daniel Clark married her mother; and that therefore complainant is not the lawful heir of Daniel Clark, and can inherit nothing from him. And consequently that the complainant can take no interest under her mother, by the conveyance set forth in the amended bill, she not being the widow of Daniel Clark.

The question decided concludes this controversy; nor shall we go farther into it.

The harshness of judicial duty requires that we should deal with witnesses and evidences, and with men's rights, as we find them; and it is done so here. But we sincerely regret that it could not be satisfactorily done without making exposures that would most willingly have been avoided.

It is ordered that the decree of the Circuit Court be affirmed, and the bill dismissed.

Messrs. Justices WAYNE and DANIEL dissented.

Mr Justice WAYNE delivered the following dissenting opinion:

I dissent from the judgement just given, and I will give my reasons for doing so as briefly as I can. But it will be necessary to occupy some time. I believe that the case of the complainant has been proved beyond a reasonable doubt, as the law requires it to be done....

I think it has been proved that Myra Clark Gaines is the only child of her father, Daniel Clark, by his marriage with her mother Zulime Carrière. That when the marriage took place, the parties were willing to contract, able to contract, and that they did contract marriage in Pennsylvania, according to the laws of that state, in the year 1802. I also think that there was nothing then or now in the laws of Pennsylvania which lessens in any way the validity of that marriage....

By what principle is it, I ask, that the unsworn declarations of Clark, now repeated by Mr Coxe, have been used to discredit Madame Despau's sworn evidence concerning a transaction in which Coxe discloses Clark to have been the criminal transgressor, and Madame Despau, at most, only the attendant of a frail sister to aid her in her travail and to shelter her and her family from disgrace?

... This is putting the narrative of Mr Coxe in the strongest light against Madame Despau upon a presumption only, however, that she knew Caroline to be the child of Clark and that she was not the child of Desgrange. I say 'knew', apart from the intuitive perception, which is not evidence, which women have in such matters – and especially concerning such as we are speaking of – bringing them to a conclusion with the quickness of instinct which is only uncertainly reached by men – and after a comparison of the facts with the instincts of their own nature, without that of women to help them....

Here, then, we have from Mr Coxe, Clark's confession of an offense (subjecting him to stripes and the galleys) used to discredit a sworn witness guiltless of any offense against the law in relation to other facts ... and who in relation to the fact related by Mr Coxe may have been as much the victim of Clark's contrivance as Zulime had been of his seduction....

The next objection to Madame Despau's credit is made on account of her alleged want of character. It is said that she was unchaste, and the defendants were allowed to put in proof a paper or record of a separation between herself and her husband upon his prosecution for a divorce, upon which a judgement was given in his favor, which cut her off on account of his charges of her infidelity, from any interest in the property which he had, to a part of which she would otherwise have been entitled.[18]

I confess my inability to see, even supposing it to have been altogether regular, as an adjucation in a competent tribunal – which it is not – how this paper was received as evidence in this case, either against the witness or against the complainant....

Madame Despau cannot be discredited by anything contradictory to her evidence, or by anything exterior from it, or by any contradiction of her by any other witness. It is admitted by all of my brethren in all of her examinations. No witness disproves any fact

18. Greer Duncan, the New Orleans-based lawyer for Relf and Chew, had done his homework as diligently as had Myra and her team, unearthing the divorce papers for Sophie and William Despau that show the latter to have filed for a separation in June 1805. In his petition Despau alleges 'incompatibility of humor and several other reasons, the recital of which would be too afflicting'. In May 1808 the Third District Court of New Orleans was persuaded that Sophie's share of Despau's property should be forfeited because she had twice travelled 'clandestinely' to 'North America'. These papers were backed up by testimonies which Myra's lawyers described as 'the loose statements of a rout of witnesses who say she was reported to be a *galante femme*; that nothing good was said of her; that she was spoken of in the same terms as her sister', and also implying that she had been Daniel Clark's mistress. Some thirty-two character witnesses on behalf of Sophie were called by Myra's team. Certainly, in addressing the court, Daniel Webster sought to paint the Carrières as being equally disreputable, his notes for the case containing lines from Ovid's *Metamorphoses*: 'facies non omnibus una. Nec diversa tamen, qualem decet esse sororum.' (Not altogether the same features, nor yet different; but such as would be natural in sisters.) A.J. King (ed.), *The Papers of Daniel Webster: Legal Papers. The Federal Practice*, III, Hanover, N.H., 1989, p. 1042. Despite her evidence suggesting strongly to the contrary, one cannot completely discount an early liaison between Sophie and Daniel. The importance of Webster's inference here is that the ecclesiastical law obtaining in Louisiana was particularly precise and rigid on the question of sex with siblings. Indeed, a Chilean man seeking to nullify his marriage under canon law in Santiago had based his entire submission on these grounds:

being very young and inexperienced, in 1843 I visited my future wife and had illicit relations with her sister. Immediately putting a halt to this incorrect behaviour, I stopped visiting the house and went to California. On my return, in 1852, I visited her again. There was in that house the most appalling licence. There were four women, and in the midst of the orgy and complete laxity, I had carnal relations with all of them on many and repeated occasions, but particularly with my wife. After four years of this arrangement, we came to Santiago, and within three days there was widespread recognition of the marriage without any consideration of the grounds upon which it was invalid. And even then, relations with the sisters continued.

The case was predictably dismissed – as were many based upon claims of prior '*cópula ilícita*' – because of the absence of proof other than that presented by the interested parties. Cavieres and Salinas, *Amor, Sexo y Matrimonio*, p. 82. Those who might accept plural intra-domestic affairs as more than a common(?) male fantasy might enjoy Fernando Trueba's film *Belle Époque*.

stated by her. Her character for veracity rose above the attempt to assail her general reputation. It is not shown that she ever made statements out of court contrary to her testimony at the trial, and it is shown that the scandals against her, as they are reported by the witnesses of the defendant, are made more improbable by the exemplary life sustained and carried by her through forty years into a respected old age....

The defendants rely upon the validity of Desgrange's marriage to Zulime, upon the secrecy of her intercourse with Clark, or of their alleged marriage – upon their not having lived together in open cohabitation as man and wife – upon Clark's subsequent courtship of other females with offers of marriage; upon Zulime's marriage with Gardette in 1808 without any attempt to prove her marriage with Clark, or to dissolve it by legal means or to enforce it with the proofs which she had of it, when she discovered his infidelity to her....

They also rely upon certain papers to be found in the record. There is in the record a certificate of a marriage between one Jacobus Desgrange and one Barbara née D'Orci, in every other particular corresponding with the relation which these persons had been in to each other in the year 1790, excepting in this – that Desgrange was afterwards known as Jerome, and not as Jacobus, and it will be admitted that the facts just recited ... are sufficient to establish the bigamy of Desgrange when he married the complainant's mother....

My views have been given upon the credit of Madame Despau and upon the testimony relating to the bigamy of Desgrange. I turn now to that upon which the defendants rely to disprove it. Their first paper is termed the ecclesiastical proceedings in a prosecution against Desgrange in 1802 for bigamy....

It is not used to show that he is a bigamist, for the paper contains only an inter-locutory order, suspensive of further action, until the inquiry shall be resumed. But it is used because, it is said, there is in this paper a declaration by Zulime of her disbelief of the charge against Desgrange, and that she was then his wife....

Now, this ecclesiastical record, as it is called, is either a transaction which official persons are required to keep or it is the judgement of a foreign court. Whether one or the other, the certificates of the bishop ... are not sufficient to make it testimony....

The Catholic church in Spain, and the Spanish ecclesiastical authorities in New Orleans, had a political character and did exercise an undefined jurisdiction in criminal matters of a certain description. And records may have been kept of its transactions. But since the cession of Louisiana to the United States the Catholic society in New Orleans has not had any political connection with that institution. There has not been any regular association or hierarchy of Catholic Christians there since the change of government....

Courts cannot recognize any private association of persons or sect of Christians as legitimately the successors of the political authorities of Spain for the custody of documents of a public nature.... I speak with a proper sense of the sacred characters which they fill, but I cannot judicially recognize them to be the successors of the public authorities of Spain in Louisiana....

I proceed now to show the misuse which has been made of this paper and its worthless-ness as testimony.... It positively leaves Desgrange under a criminal prosecution for bigamy. The order given in it is not an acquittal. It suspends proceedings only for further investigation, and releases Desgrange from jail because, up to this time, his guilt had not been proved. In other words, the evidence was thought sufficient to subject him to another trial, and not enough for a final judgement against or for him. Such is the paper. It cannot, then, be used for any other or larger purpose....

But I pass on, as hastily as I can, to another objection to the use of this deposition, and one more interesting than those which have already been stated.

It is that by the law of Louisiana, as it then was and still is, Zulime could not be a witness in the criminal prosecution against Desgrange, supposing her to be his wife, as the defendants assert her to have been. A husband may not be a witness for his wife, or the wife for the husband, in a criminal proceeding. A wife may impeach marriage to obtain a sentence of nullity; she may be a witness to certain facts in relation to those impediments deemed by law sufficient to annul a marriage. But neither by the civil nor by the common law can she be a witness for or against her husband, when he is prosecuted for any offense which the law punishes in his person....

I will now notice two other points which were urged in the argument of this case.

It was said the complainant could not recover, even if it was proved or admitted that her mother and father were married, because there had not been, before that marriage took place, a sentence of the nullity of the marriage with Desgrange. The other was, supposing Zulime to have been then free to marry and that she did marry Clark, it was a clandestine marriage, which has no civil effects according to the law of Louisiana to give to the issue a right of inheritance....

The 8th Book, Tit. 20, Law 4, *Nueva Recopilación*, as translated and cited, reads thus:

> Should a woman, *either married*, or even only publicly *betrothed*, before Our Holy Mother the Church, commit adultery, although she should ALLEGE AND SHOW that her marriage is NULL AND VOID, either on account of near relationship by consanguinity, or affinity within the 4th degree, OR BECAUSE ONE OF THE SPOUSES WAS PREVIOUSLY BOUND BY ANOTHER MARRIAGE, or had made a vow of chastity, or was about entering a religious community, or had some other reason − YET FOR ALL THIS she is not to be allowed to do what is forbidden; and she cannot prevent her husband from bringing a suit for *adultery*, both against HER and the ADULTERER, as if THE MARRIAGE WERE NOT A TRUE ONE. We decree against such persons − WHOM WE CONSIDER AS HAVING COMMITTED ADULTERY (*que habemos por adulteros*), the law of the *fuero* be strictly followed, which treats about *adulterers*, and is the first law of this title.

I write diffidently upon such subjects, but not without due care. The result of my examination is that the law just given has no bearing on this case....

I shall cite from the institutes of Asa Y. Manuel, illustrated by Palacios, having the original work and Johnson's translation before me. And I do so because I find the translation introduced into White's *Recopilacion* is frequently cited in Louisiana and is so by one of the learned judges who sat on this case in the Circuit Court:

> While the marriage is not dissolved by the sentence of the church, the father, the adulteress, her brother, paternal and maternal uncles were legitimate accusers of the adulterer, and for sixty days after a dissolution either of them may accuse.
>
> Whilst the marriage continued, if the adultery is publicly scandalous, anyone belonging to the town may accuse, and for four months afterwards.
>
> If the husband dies, the accusation may be made in six months after, computing from the day when the crime was committed.

So, whilst the married persons were united, five months were allowed for the accusation, unless force was used, and then the ravisher might be charged at any time within thirty years.

An accusation made after the times stated might be avoided by the accused by such an exception. It was another available exception if the wife could prove she had committed the offense with the consent of her husband; so if, knowing the adultery, he continues to cohabit with his wife. Nor could he accuse after having said before the judge that he did not wish to accuse his wife. After accusation and an acquittal for want of proofs, the prosecution could not be renewed. A husband of bad habits and dissolute character could not accuse....

In conclusion upon this point, the law declares that bigamy makes a marriage void as if it had never been, replaces the parties as they personally were before such a connection, and though it may be expedient to have a sentence of its nullity declared for the purpose of restoring rights of property, it is not necessary to enable the party imposed upon to marry again....

There was but one way to get rid of the force of the complainant's evidence in support of her legitimacy. It was to assail the integrity of her witnesses. The way in which that was attempted, I have shown in respect to Mesdames Despau and Caillavet. It has succeeded with the majority of the judges who have tried this cause with me. But I feel authorized to say that in all my experience in the profession I have never heard witnesses so assailed before and upon such illegal testimony; not insufficient, but inadmissibly introduced into this cause for that purpose. My brother Daniel thinks as I do....

Besides, these witnesses have been said to be unworthy of credit, when in the most important particulars of their testimony, concerning Clark's marriage with the mother of the complainant, and of her legitimacy, they are confirmed by other disinterested witnesses to whom Clark admitted both – not once, but several times on different occasions.

These persons are strangers to the parties in this suit in all those relations of life which might be supposed to incline them to favor either. They have not any connection with each other, except in those social relations which made them companions and intimate friends of Clark. They have lived apart at remote distances for many years since the death of Clark, knowing nothing of his child, except as she was seen by them in her infancy, receiving publicly the caresses of her father and hearing from him his acknowledgement that she was his legitimate child.

Boisfontaine tells us that Clark frequently told him, after Zulime's marriage with Gardette, that he would have made his marriage with her public if that barrier had not been made, and frequently lamented to him that it had been made, but that she was blameless. But this witness shall speak for himself. His testimony is taken from the record without the change of a word.[19]

Pierre Baron Boisfontaine, who, being duly sworn to declare the truth on the questions put to him in this cause, in answer to the ... interrogatories says:

I was acquainted with Daniel Clark for between nine and ten years; I knew him as the father of Myra Clark. She was born in my house, and was put by Mr Clark, when a few days old, with my sister and brother-in-law, Samuel B. Davis. I was Mr Clark's agent for his various plantations – first the Sligo and the Desert, then the Houmas, the Havana Point, and when he died, of the one that he purchased of Stephen Henderson. He respected our misfortunes, knowing that our family was rich and of the highest standing in Santo Domingo before the Revolution.

---

19. In addition to the testimony of Boisfontaine, the circumstances of Myra's birth and Daniel's death at Bayou St John are revealed by that of Colonel Joseph D.D. Bellechasse, Mrs Harriet Smyth – previously Mrs Harper, who suckled Myra – and Chevalier François Dusuau De la Croix, who recounted that in his one conversation with Clark about Myra, Daniel had referred to his daughter as 'natural'. These witnesses, however, agreed on all other points made by Boisfontaine.

The mother of Myra Clark was a lady of the Carrière family. Not being present at any marriage, I can only declare it as my belief Mr Clark was her husband.... It was represented to me that this lady married Mr Desgrange in good faith; but it was found out some time afterwards that he already had a living wife, when lady née Carrière separated from him. Mr Clark, sometime after this, married her at the North.

When the time came for it to be made public, interested persons had produced a false state of things between them. And this lady being in Philadelphia, and Mr Clark not there, was persuaded by a lawyer employed, that her marriage with Mr Clark was invalid, which believing, she married M. Gardette. Some time afterwards, Mr Clark lamented to me that this barrier to making his marriage public had been created. He spoke of ... Myra's mother with great respect, and frequently told me after her marriage with M. Gardette, that he would have made his marriage with her public if that barrier had not been made, but that she was blameless. He said he would never give Myra a step-mother....

After the birth of his daughter Myra, Mr Clark acknowledged her to me as his own, constantly, and at various places. He was very fond of her, and seemed to take pleasure in talking to me about her. When he communicated to me that he was making his last will, he told me that he should acknowledge her in it as his legitimate daughter. The day before he died, he spoke to me about her with great affection, and as being left his estate in his last will. The day he died he spoke of her with the interest of a dying parent, as heir of his estate in his last will. She is still living, and is now the wife of William Wallace Whitney (1835)....

About fifteen days before Mr Clark's death, I was present at his house, when he handed to Chevalier De la Croix a sealed packet, and told him that his last will was finished and was in that sealed packet. About ten days before this, he had told me that it was done. Previous to this, commencing about four months before his death, he had often told me he was making his last will. He said this in conversations to me on the plantation and at his house; and I heard him mention this subject at Judge Pitot's. I frequently dined at Judge Pitot's, with Mr Clark, on Sundays. The day before he died he told me that his last will was below in his office room, in his little black case. The day he died he mentioned his last will to me....

I was present at Mr Clark's house, about fifteen days before his death, when he took from a small black case a sealed packet, handed it to Chevalier De la Croix, and said, my last will is finished. It is in this sealed packet with valuable papers; as you consented I have made you in it the tutor to my daughter. If any misfortune happens to me, will you do for her all you promised me; will you take her at once from Mr Davis? I have given her all my estate in my will, an annuity to my mother, and some legacies to friends – you, Pitot and Bellechasse are the executors....

Previous to this ... he told me that Chevalier De la Croix had consented to be Myra's tutor in his will, and had promised, if he died before doing it, to go at once to the North and take her from Mr Davis; that she was to be educated in Europe. He told me that Chevalier De la Croix, Judge Pitot and Colonel Bellechasse were to be executors in his will.[20]

---

20. In another hearing, according to oral testimony, the main clause of the 1813 will read thus:

   I do hereby acknowledge that my beloved Myra, who is now living in the family of Samuel B. Davis, is my legitimate and only daughter, and that I leave and bequeath unto her, the said Myra, all the esate, whether real or personal, of which I may die possessed, subject only to the payment of certain legacies, hereinafter named.

Gaines v. Hennen, 14 February–14 March 1861, in Reports of the Supreme Court of the United States, 24 Howard (65 US), p. 783. The will of 1811 admitted to probate and executed by Relf and Chew read thus:

   Daniel Clark. In the name of God: I, Daniel Clark, of New Orleans, do make this my last will and testament.

Two or three days before his death I came to see Mr Clark on plantation business. He told me he felt quite ill. I asked him if I should remain with him; he answered that he wished me to. I went to the plantation to set things in order that I might stay with Mr Clark, and returned the same day to Mr Clark, and stayed with him constantly until he died. The day before he died, Mr Clark, speaking of his daughter Myra, told me that his last will was in his office room below, in the little black case; that he could die contented, as he had ensured his estate to her in his will. He mentioned his pleasure that he had made his mother comfortable by an annuity in it, and remembered some friends by legacies....

About two hours before his death, Mr Clark showed strong feelings for said Myra, and told me that he wished his will to be taken to Chevalier De la Croix, as he was her tutor as well as one of the executors in it. And just afterwards, Mr Clark told Lubin, his confidential servant, to be sure, as soon as he died, to carry his little black case to Chevalier De la Croix.

After this, and in a very short time before Mr Clark died, I saw Mr Relf take a bundle of keys from Mr Clark's *armoire*, one of which, I believe, opened the little black case. I had seen Mr Clark open it very often. After taking these keys from the *armoire*, Mr Relf went below. When I went below I did not see Mr Relf, and the office door was shut. Lubin told me that when Mr Relf went down with the keys from the *armoire*, he followed, saw him then, on getting down, go into the office room, locked the office room door. Almost Mr Clark's last words were that his last will must be taken care of on said Myra's account....

When, after Mr Clark's death, the disappearance of his last will was the subject of conversation, I related what Mr Clark told me about his last will in his last sickness. Judge Pitot and John Lynd told me that they read it not many days before Mr Clark's last sickness; that its contents corresponded with what Mr Clark had told me about it; that when they read it, it was finished, was dated and signed by Mr Clark, was an holographic will, was in Mr Clark's handwriting; that in it he acknowledged the said Myra as his legitimate daughter and bequeathed all of his estate to her, gave an annuity to his mother, and legacies to some friends; that the Chevalier De la Croix was tutor of Myra; Chevalier De la Croix, Colonel Bellechasse, Judge Pitot were executors.

Judge Pitot and John Lynd are dead. The wife of William Harper told me she read it. Colonel Bellechasse told me that Mr Clark showed it to him not many days before his final sickness; that it was then finished. Colonel Bellechasse and the lady who was Madame Harper are living....

My name is Pierre Baron Boisfontaine; my age about fifty-eight. I have been some time in Madisonville. The place of my family abode is near New Orleans, opposite side of the river. I was eight years in the British army. I was several years agent for M. Clark's plantations. Since his death I have been engaged in various objects. I now possess a house and lots, and derive my revenue from my slaves, cows etcetera. I am in no manner connected with, or related to, any of the parties of this suit. I have no interest in this suit.

Those of us who have borne our part in the case will pass away. The case will live. Years hence, as well as now, the profession will look to it for what has been ruled upon its

---

Inprimis. I order that all my just debts be paid.

Second. I leave and bequeath unto my mother, Mary Clark, now of Germantown, in the State of Pennsylvania, all the estate, whether real or personal, which I may die possessed of.

Third. I hereby nominate my friends, Richard Relf and Beverly Chew, my executors, with power to settle everything relating to my estate.

(signed) Daniel Clark.

Ne Varietur. New Orleans. 20th May 1811.

J. Pitot, Judge.

In *Patterson* v. *Gaines* (1848), Williams (ed.), *Cases in Supreme Court*, XII, p. 544

merits and also for the kind of testimony upon which these merits were decided. The majority of my brothers who give the judgement stand, as they may well do, upon their responsibility. I have placed myself alongside of them, humbly submitting to have any error into which I may have fallen corrected by our contemporaries and by our professional posterity.

The case itself presents thought for our philosophy, in its contemplation of all the business and domestic relations of life.

It shows the hollowness of those friendships formed between persons in the greediness of gain, seeking its gratification in a disregard of all those laws by which commerce can only be honestly and respectably pursued....

It shows if the ruffian takes life for the purse which he robs, that a dying man's agonies soothed only by tears and prayers for the happiness of a child, may not arrest a fraudulent attempt to filch her name and fortune.

We can learn from it, too, that there is a kindred between virtue and lasting respectability in life, and that transgressions of its proprieties or irregular yieldings to our passions in forming the most interesting relation between human creatures, are most likely to make them miserable and bring ruin upon children.

I do not know from my own reasoning that the sins of parents are visited upon children, but my reason does not tell me that it may not be so. But I do know, from one of those rays shot from Sinai, that it is said for the offense of idolatory:

> I, the Lord God, am a jealous God, and visit the sins of the fathers upon the children unto the third and fourth generation of them that hate me, and show mercy unto thousands of those who love me and keep my commandments.

It may be so for other offenses. If it be, let the victim submissively recognize him who inflicts the chastisement, and that it may be the beginning of a communion with our Maker, to raise the hope of a richer inheritance than this world can give or take away.

POSTSCRIPT

Perhaps Mr Justice Wayne produced such a *tour de force* to end fifty-eight pages of written opinion simply because, as his biographer puts it, he 'tenaciously espoused a litigant's cause'.[21] Maybe he felt that, having won previous cases in the Supreme Court, Myra had been dealt a particularly unfair judgement by the four justices headed by Catron, who alone voted against her in 1844 and did not sit in 1848, when there was no dissenting opinion. Possibly, having consistently supported her claim throughout its time in court, Wayne felt able to play to an appreciable gallery. Whatever the case, it is perhaps predictable that one of the principal targets of the

---

21. Alexander A. Lawrence, *James Moore Wayne, Southern Unionist*, Chapel Hill, N.C., 1943, p. 127.

Judge's final strictures – Zulime Carrière/Desgrange/Clark/Gardette – was not in court to hear it although she was still alive and living in the United States. It is, though, one of the multifarious enigmas of this case that Zulime was never called to the witness box to give evidence despite living in the jurisdiction of the courts involved for fifteen years.[22]

Having married the ubiquitous Gardette in August 1808, Zulime lived with him in Philadelphia before the couple moved to France. They had three children – whom Zulime was now able to keep – and it would seem that time and circumstance at least enabled her to overcome the reputation of being, as the witness Courcelle put it, 'coquette et légère'.[23] Gardette died in 1831, and Zulime returned to New Orleans with her family in 1838, by which time, of course, Myra knew of her existence. Clearly, Zulime, by surrendering to Myra her claim on Clark's estate, could no longer be suspected of being a fortune-hunter, and in 1849 it was she and her son James who unearthed and passed to Myra the 1806 certificate of the Desgrange–D'Orci marriage. Yet she sat in the Circuit Court briefly on just one day, and her voice is virtually absent from the entire proceeding.

Perry Scott Rader, for thirty-five years the Reporter of the State Court of Missouri and the first serious student of this case, presents a plausible explanation as to why Zulime was not called to the witness box. Myra, for her part, would scarcely wish to put her mother through the indignity of a cross-examination in which all the consequences of the not unnatural foibles of an attractive and energetic young person would be subjected to ruthless exploitation. After all, even on the most innocent initial reading of the evidence Zulime and Jerome were both married to three people without ever having been legally separated from any of them. On the other hand, the lawyers for the defence must have seen little advantage in calling Zulime, apart from the sympathy for her that cross-examination might arouse. She would assuredly testify that Desgrange was the father of Caroline; that he had finally confessed to having a living wife at the time he married her; that she consequently married Clark in 1802 or 1803; and that Coxe was lying in his account of Caroline's birth and what happened in Philadelphia in 1808.[24]

---

22. According to Rader, a commission was once served but never used. 'Romance', p. 61.
23. The records of the lower courts had J. Courcelle saying,

> Clark was never married as far as I know. I have said he was never married because the population was so small that we knew everything that took place. I knew Madame Desgrange. I have been in certain circles where her reputation was spoken of lightly, but I cannot give any positive testimony about it. She was very *coquette et légère*.

Another, E. Carraby, put a rather different spin on the matter:

> Clark and Madame Desgrange lived together in an illicit connection. I mean this was the general report. Her reputation was well known enough not to have been misunderstood by Clark. Mr Clark was a too high-minded man to contract marriage with his paramour.

Cited in ibid., pp. 116–17. In 1806 the population of New Orleans was given as 17,000 (including 6,300 whites; 8,400 slaves and 2,300 free blacks).
24. Ibid., pp. 60–62.

Other than her (translated) response to Father Hasset's brief interrogation, Zulime's life is presented here by others. But even as she and Myra discover documents, listen to testimony and reconstruct events to mitigate the ultimate 'purloined letter' – a stolen will – we might take heed of Poe's injunction, and look at what we have before us rather than bemoan the silences.

The Lolita image has a strong Southern motif, most famously and compulsively in Faulkner (Lena Grove, Eula Varner, Yettie Snopes, Caddy Compson), more recently in films by Louis Malle (Brooke Shields in *Pretty Baby*) and Alan Parker (Lisa Bonet in *Angel Heart*). But to cast Zulime this way would be an anachronism in two senses. First, simply because although she was thirteen when she first married, she was a woman in her twenties at the time of her liaison with Clark. Secondly, because contemporary Northern mores about age, sex and marriage are not applicable to eighteenth-century Louisiana. (The age of consent in the United States through most of the nineteenth century was either not stipulated or ten; in Britain it was twelve until 1875; in France, Japan and Italy it was twelve until the 1930s – all for girls; in Spain it remains at twelve for both sexes and both hetero- and homosexuals.) There is in the record very little emphasis upon Zulime's age at marriage, and although Judge Catron does sympathise with Jerome's middle-aged condition, the point there is to indicate the relative disparity of age and attractiveness rather than Zulime's absolute youth. It not so much 'intercourse' as 'unrestrained intercourse' that got the judge's goat.

Beyond this, and the fact that no member of the *menage à trois* could appear as a wholly innocent party, it is notable that Zulime has the support of her family and a hearing in the community. It may well be that New Orleans was a sultry entrepôt where brazen behaviour was meteorologically accelerated, but in 1800 it still carried all the tyrannies of village society founded upon personal prejudice. If years later the lawyers for Relf and Chew could line up pious witnesses to finger the Carrière women as strumpets, one wonders why the Church so readily heard the case, why the three elder sisters had made respectable matches, and why Dr Gardette felt able publicly to tie a knot that Daniel Clark was so squeamish about (and as much so in Philadelphia as in New Orleans).

Rose and Sophie tell Zulime's story as well as might be expected from memories in their eighth decade. It may have been – as Messrs Duncan and Webster argued – a well-rehearsed, self-serving fib, but it is one that bites back against both the society of fifty years before and the salacious expectations of the audience in court. Whether or not the old ladies had come completely to identify with the version they told on behalf of their sister, there is something admirable in the story and the tenacity with which it is recounted. Zulime's reputation was not to be enhanced by its serial examination and defence; Zulime herself had little to gain from litigation; only their niece Myra had a lot riding on it, and she could have let bygones be bygones if material comfort were the only consideration. Zulime, however, was only able to draw on Judge Wayne's tirade for her consolation. In 1853, before the case came back to court, she died, aged seventy-two, in New Orleans.

Myra, a widow of forty-seven with an accumulating number of enemies in that city, was no more daunted by legal defeat than had been her mother by marital misadventure. Her funds were low but sufficient to continue litigation. None the less, the temper of US politics was quickening decisively in the 1850s, and the case could no longer be approached solely in terms of its own merits and legal mechanisms. All the justices taking hard positions on it were Southerners, so there is little question of the expression of some 'yankee morality' against Southern voluptuary. But, aside from the local New Orleans issue of property rights, the case had always possessed political connections and resonance.

In some respects it is more difficult to comprehend the actions of Daniel Clark than it is to understand those of his lover/wife and daughter. Even at a great distance and with scant information that has been continually refiltered through the adversarial logic of the courts one spots enigmas and harbours doubts. At closer quarter these naturally grow, but perhaps less in terms of sex and wealth than in those of political power.

Referring to Clark's 'public life' in trade, diplomacy and politics, Arthur Whitaker describes him as

> a mole-like individual who burrowed his way through the life of his generation in the South-west, leaving many surface indications of his activity but seldom giving any sign of what the activity was all about. It cannot be proved that he was a rascal, and yet one would hardly employ such terms as honor, probity and fidelity in describing him.[25]

There can be little doubt of Daniel Clark's ambition, of his willingness to realise it through charm, or of his perspicacious pragmatism. Yet he was living in exceptionally volatile times, when his home town was right at the heart of continental politics and directly influenced by those of Napoleonic Europe. As a trader in a 'foreign' land, the ownership of which changed twice (from Spain to France to the USA) in three years (1800–03), he simply had to be a wheeler-dealer to stay afloat. But, as Whitaker suggests, Daniel was not just a survivor; he was a champion opportunist.

If the Supreme Court of the United States spent such time and was so indecisive in finding evidence to 'condemn' Clark, it is hardly surprising that Whitaker was also stumped. Furthermore, this sense of foggy ambivalence is not just the product of the passage of time. Clark excited fierce sentiments amongst his contemporaries, but they too failed to deliver a consolidated judgement. Indeed, they failed even to bring him to trial. However, in the first weeks of 1807 President Thomas Jefferson surely considered such a possibility – on a charge of treason for conspiring to break up the Union.

---

25. Arthur Whitaker, *The Mississippi Question, 1795–1803*, Gloucester, Mass., 1962, p. 92. From the sources he used Whitaker must have known of Myra's case, but he mentions it nowhere in this detailed monograph. For a magisterial treatment of the world into which Clark had moved, see David J. Weber, *The Spanish Frontier in North America*, New Haven, Conn., 1992.

This was because Clark was closely linked to the extraordinary adventures of Jefferson's first vice-president, Aaron Burr, who was eventually tried alone and acquitted on the defence that he had merely been seeking to invade and take over Mexico.[26] The evidence around that case, though, reveals Clark as a figure who stood briefly right at the centre of the affairs of Louisiana and the Mississippi system, understood not as today's state of the Union but as the entire middle third of the territory of the United States.

Daniel's life in the South began with considerable advantages. Whilst his parents stayed in Philadelphia, at the age of twenty he joined his uncle, also Daniel, at Natchez in what was to become the Mississippi Territory. Daniel senior had been a colonel in the British army, and on his retirement he acquired from the Spanish a grant of extensive lands on this frontier as well as in western Florida.[27] The uncle clearly carried a martial air into his civilian career, being proposed to the secretary of state as a judge in 1797 because he 'would do honor to the Bench; his austerity and uncommon respectability of person petrifies every rogue that is brought into his presence – this is Mr Daniel Clark'.[28]

It was possibly under avuncular advice that young Dan travelled down the river to New Orleans and got himself a job in the office of the Spanish governor, Miró. At the same time he established his mercantile business in partnership with Daniel Coxe, who was based in Philadelphia. In all events, Daniel senior appears to have been an acute judge of character and a consistent supporter, transferring his property to his nephew's name in 1796 and recommending him wholeheartedly to General James Wilkinson, the Commander of the US Western Army:

> I received a letter from my nephew Dan … desiring I would solicit your interest with the executive of your nation to appoint him consul at New Orleans, where he now, at the desire of Mr Ellicot and Capt. Guion, acts as vice-consul. Daniel is a young man of nice honor, and, as a trader of fair character, extremely well effected towards the United States. He speaks French and Spanish, and from a natural aptitude and an experience of ten years, he has acquired great commercial knowledge, and a general acquaintance with the people, with whom he is a favorite.[29]

---

26. *Aaron Burr*, born Newark, New Jersey, 1756. Military officer and lawyer. US Senate, 1791; lost election to presidency, 1796; became third vice-president of the USA, 1801, after narrowly failing to win the presidency. 1804, fugitive in New Jersey for killing in a duel Alexander Hamilton, an author of the constitution, senator from New York and Washington's treasury secretary. Disdainful of duels more than he was of Burr, Hamilton had not aimed at his adversary. Notoriously spendthrift and free with his favours, Burr – a widower – married for the second time when he was seventy-seven, but his new wife, Madame Jumel, divorced him for adultery within the year. He died in September 1836.

27. *Daniel Clark* (senior), born Sligo. Commanded a royal regiment of Pennsylvania. Spanish land grants in western Florida, 1786, and upper Mississippi, 1787. An affiliate of the Coleraine-born Virginian merchant Oliver Pollock, whose considerable trade in the south-west benefited from the influence of Alexander O'Reilly, governor of Louisiana, 1769–70, later commander of the garrison of Cuba, and originally from Beltrasna, County Meath. Clark was *alcalde* of Natchez and a member of the Permanent Committee overseeing the transfer of the Mississippi territory to the USA. He died in 1800. His papers for the period of 1795 to 1800 are at the University of Texas.

28. Andrew Ellicot, Mississippi Limits Commissioner, Natchez, to Pickering, 24 Sept. 1797, in C.E. Carter (ed.), *The Territorial Papers of the United States: The Territory of Mississippi, 1798–1817*, Washington 1937, V, p. 7.

Here Daniel senior was calling in a favour because he had himself introduced Wilkinson to Governor Miró, who permitted the Kentucky-based officer to trade tobacco down the river through New Orleans for a period. Although Wilkinson was a senior member of the military, he was notoriously temperamental and his political influence very unreliable. Daniel did not at that stage get the job, despite the fact that he was being backed by Mississippi Governor Winthrop Sargent, also indebted to his uncle, who spent the last weeks of his life defending that embattled politician.[30]

Daniel certainly sought the prestige of the post of consul, but he had a greater economic need for the authority it conferred. Under the reforms of the Bourbon monarchy and whilst Great Britain remained at war with Spain, North Americans were permitted to trade through New Orleans, but their position was precarious and dependent upon the payment of '*douceurs*' to compliant officials for the protection of commerce worth well over $1 million by the turn of the century.[31]

As a result, on 1 May 1798 Clark took the considerable step of presenting to the Spanish intendant, Juan Vicente Morales, a 'memorial' in which he described himself as the US vice-consul when he had no such formal appointment, and Spain, in any case, refused to recognise such posts in its colonies. In this memorandum Clark proposed that American ships should be allowed to carry Louisiana produce from New Orleans to US and other foreign ports paying the same 6 per cent export tax as did Spanish vessels, and that Spanish ships should be permitted to take cargoes from the American deposit without payment of extra export duties. This proposal – effectively that the exports of Americans and Spaniards be placed on the same footing

---

29. Daniel Clark sr, Natchez, to Wilkinson, 28 Mar. 1798, quoted in James Wilkinson, *Memoirs on My Own Time*, Philadelphia 1816, II, appendix VII. As we shall see, Wilkinson later sought to publicise every unflattering aspect of Daniel jr, and he published this letter in that light.

30. In November 1799 Sargent wrote to Secretary of State Timothy Pickering,

> Mr Clark's intelligence and information will so eminently capacitate him…. [His] respectability, influence and zeal may probably render him a very suitable Character for the office [of consul in New Orleans] if the same may be agreeable to him, but I am uninformed if he intends continuing at Orleans or to return to his plantation in this territory.

Sargent, Natchez, to Pickering, 12 Oct. 1799, in Dunbar Rowland (ed.), *The Mississippi Territorial Archives, 1798–1803*, Nashville 1905, pp. 177–8. Colonel Clark described Sargent as of 'austere appearance, not even anxious for popularity, and wanting that kind of affability which is necessary to draw the people about his person'. Clark, Clarkesville, to Claiborne, 18 June 1800, in ibid., p. 314. Yet Sargent, having read this comment, subsequently wrote to Chief Justice Marshall,

> My respected Friend Colo. Clark deceased – whose Elogium and worth have been so long and so well established, and whose situation as Commanding the Militia and presiding over the Courts of Justice rendered him more and better conversant in the Administration of the Government than almost any other man … Devoted the last moments of a life passed in honor to the bearing of a strong Testimony against that Obloquy and Odium which had been produced by the unprincipled Clamor of Malevolence.

Sargent, Natchez, to Marshall, 25 Aug. 1800, in ibid., pp. 275–6. See also D. Clayton James, *Antebellum Natchez*, Baton Rouge 1968.

31. In January 1798 Clark wrote to his partner Coxe, 'We are here without a consul and his presence is highly necessary to prevent and put a stop to the numerous abuses which the Spanish Government force the Americans to submit to.' Clark, New Orleans, to Coxe, 13 Jan. 1798, quoted in 'Despatches from the US Consulate in New Orleans, 1801–3', *AHR*, XXXII, 1927, p. 803. Daniel Clark was eventually ratified by the Senate as US Consul to New Orleans on 26 January 1802.

– would appear to have been doomed since similar requests had been rejected at the negotiation of the Treaty of San Lorenzo in 1795, when the frontier between the USA and Louisiana was agreed and the right of US citizens to deposit goods at New Orleans conceded.

However, on 2 May 1798 – in what is surely record time for Spanish imperial bureaucracy – Morales presented Clark's paper to the chamber of commerce for consideration. On 11 June the colonial authorities not only agreed to the proposal but conceded even more, allowing all neutrals to trade on the same terms as the Spanish. Clark had gained something beyond the grasp of John Jay (co-author of the *Federalist Papers* and governor of New York) and Thomas Pinckney (ambassador to Spain) when they negotiated San Lorenzo. This unexpected deal explains why Governor Sargent and Secretary of State Pickering thought so highly of Clark, but before too long others came to suspect the nature of his relationship with Morales.[32]

There are strong grounds for believing that Clark had used his time in the employ of the Spanish governor to acquire not just language and administrative skills but also profitable friendships. That with Morales was not always easy, and Daniel was prudently ambivalent about it in his dispatches, but it yielded to Clark perhaps his single richest piece of real estate: the Maison Rouge claim of 100,000 acres in the Ouchetta country of western Florida. Some of Daniel's friends took shares in a much larger tract – the Bastrop claim of 1.2 million acres – which, like the Maison Rouge, had been granted by Governor Carondelet in 1795 on condition that the claimants settled the lands, and which had also been declared void when this condition was not met.[33] (Vice-President Burr, who was notorious for his property speculations, eventually bought 350,000 acres of the Bastrop claim for $5,000 in cash and $30,000 in credit.)

These properties in western Florida were not immediately threatened by the transfer of Louisiana from Spanish control, but they had been made without the sanction of the US Limits Commission, and in 1803 the Spanish governor, Folch, who doubted Morales's right to grant or sell the lands, ordered a halt to surveying. As a result, many purchasers found themselves with incomplete titles, but Daniel Clark was not among them.[34] When Louisiana passed into new hands the new governor, William Claiborne, pointedly asked for official investigations into the status of Clark's property and reported his speculation to Washington.[35]

---

32. Whitaker, *Mississippi Question*, p. 93. Morales's response to Clark is reprinted in Arthur Whitaker (ed.), *Documents Relating to the Commercial Policy of Spain in the Floridas*, Deland, Fla., 1931, pp. 201–3.

33. J.O. Marshall and R.D. Calhoun, 'The Maison Rouge and Bastrop Spanish Land "Grants"', *Louisiana Historical Quarterly*, 20:2, April 1937.

34. Claiborne, New Orleans, to Secretary of State James Madison, 16 Aug. 1805, in Dunbar Rowland (ed.), *Official Letter Books of W.C.C. Claiborne, 1801–1816*, Jackson, Miss., 1917, III, p. 170.

35. In 1806 Claiborne wrote to Madison,

> Neither of these two claims have been laid before the Board of Commissioners … many citizens are of opinion that they ought not, at this time, to be considered as valid, either in Law or Equity. The Grants are said to contain certain conditions, which neither party complied with…. I have esteemed it a duty to suggest the expediency of employing a lawyer to investigate before the Board these particular claims.

Morales, maximising the opportunities provided by transfers of sovereignty, removal of archival records, and uncertain chains of command, could not, however, buck market forces entirely. He insisted to the Marquis Casa Yrujo, the disapproving Spanish ambassador in Washington, that he had the authority to make the grants but pointed out that the Florida land would become virtually valueless unless it was believed that what had happened in Louisiana would also occur in Florida – a United States takeover:

> ... it would be expedient to allow this belief to circulate, but it would be still more profitable to persuade the people that, when the cession [of western Florida] shall be allowed to take place, Spain, before making it, will take care to ... confirm ... all the sales or grants of land previously made by her officers in all the ceded territories.[36]

The culture of favours naturally depends upon reciprocity, and opportunities for this abounded once Morales, who based himself in New Orleans, contemplated the prospect of living in a state of which Clark, as consul, was – for a short while, at least – the senior representative. Daniel, however, was plainly aware of the dangers when he wrote to Madison in October 1803:

> The Intendant Morales, who is immensely rich in ready Money, wishes much to stay and will rather accept the Consulship of Louisiana, which he has applied for, than return to Spain. Although I am perhaps the only Man in the country he would render a Service to disinterestedly – and on account of Services rendered me [I] have an attachment to him – yet I think his obtaining the consulship, which he solicits merely to have a pretext to stay, would be of injury to the Trade of the Place, as he would never fail to give advice [to] all the Spanish Contraband Traders, who would frequent the Port, which would considerably diminish an advantageous intercourse ... A refusal will disgust him and in that case he will probably prefer settling in some of our large Cities rather than go to Europe so that his Fortune may be placed beyond the reach of accident.[37]

This assessment was probably accurate, but it amounted to little less than a personal betrayal of Morales by Clark, who openly admits the existence of past obligations (if not their precise nature). Was he being a disinterested patriot or washing his hands of a friend who was of little further use, threatened to embarrass him, and had already provided for himself well enough?

Claiborne, New Orleans, to Madison, 11 July 1806, in Carter (ed.), *Territorial Papers*, IX, pp. 679–80. In fact, Treasury Secretary Albert Gallatin had already instructed Commissioner Allan McGruder to investigate Clark's claim, assessed at 378 square miles. Gallatin, Washington, to McGruder, 8 July 1805, in ibid., p. 469. A few months earlier General Wilkinson reported to Secretary of War Dearborn,

> Almost the whole of the Americans, English and Irish here, with many Frenchmen and Spaniards, are engaged on this speculation, and every valuable spot between the Mississippi and Mobile will doubtless be granted away – our ex-consul stands at the head of the list.

Wilkinson, New Orleans, to Dearborn, 3 Jan. 1804, in ibid., p. 151.

36. Morales, New Orleans, to Casa Yrujo, 20 December 1804, quoted in Gayarré, *History of Louisiana*, p. 69.

37. Clark, New Orleans, to Madison, 13 Oct. 1803, in Carter (ed.), *Territorial Papers*, IX, p. 80.

Support for the latter interpretation – which would surely be favoured by Professor Whitaker and Judge Catron – lies in the action taken by Morales a year earlier (October 1802), when he effectively closed the Mississippi to American traffic by cancelling the US right of deposit in New Orleans. Morales's justification for this measure was that the Treaty of Amiens, which had (temporarily) halted the war in Europe, required the cancellation of privileges granted to Americans in their status as neutrals.[38] Morales appeared to have taken this extraordinary step on his own initiative, but it was not until May 1803 that orders to rescind it reached New Orleans from Madrid.

Perhaps more than any other single act, Morales's closure of the Mississippi trade sealed the fate of Louisiana (and, in time, that of western Florida). For Madison, who scarcely needed persuading of the strategic importance of the region, 'The Mississippi is [to our Western Citizens] everything. It is the Hudson, the Delaware, the Potomac, and all the navigable rivers of the Atlantic states into one stream.'[39]

This observation was made in a dispatch to the US embassy in Madrid requiring it to obtain a reversal of Morales's measure, but in the medium term New Orleans plainly had to be acquired outright. At the time of the closure the formal owner was France, which had secretly acquired the territory in 1800 and was strongly suspected by Washington to have done so from May 1801. It is not clear whether Daniel Clark had himself already reached this conclusion, but he was not present to counsel Morales against his move since two months earlier he had left on his own initiative for Paris and was engaged in lobbying the staff appointed by Bonaparte to replace the Spanish authorities.[40]

For Whitaker this trip symbolises Clark's lack of attention to his consular duties – in the nineteen months between assuming his post in August 1801 and February 1803, when he returned from Europe, Daniel was in New Orleans for no more than four months.[41] For the French – and particularly Pierre Clément Laussat, the incoming prefect, who was 'doorstepped' at his Paris house by Clark clutching a sheaf

---

38. *State Papers and Correspondence bearing on the Purchase of the Territory of Louisiana*, Washington 1903, pp. 54–5.

39. Madison, Washington, to Pinckney, Madrid, 27 Nov. 1802, in *American State Papers: Foreign Affairs*, II, Washington 1832, p. 527.

40. On the eve of his departure in August 1802 Clark told Madison that he was going to Europe because 'a business of very considerable importance calls me suddenly to England', that the New Orleans authorities would not recognise his position, that Vice-Consul Hulings could undertake all necessary tasks, and that there was no problem if the secretary of state wanted his resignation. Clark, New York, to Madison, 16 Aug. 1802, in *The Papers of James Madison: Secretary of State Series*, Charlottesville, Va., 1995, III, pp. 487–8. It may be significant that from June the Spanish were once again charging extra duties on American cargoes, and Clark clearly felt that he had lost influence. Clark, New Orleans, to Madison, 22 June 1802, in ibid., pp. 330–31. Perhaps Morales had dropped Clark first? Even before the Treaty of Amiens Clark had told Madison that Morales was only contemplating the closure of the port if it was not going to be transferred to the United States. Clark, Philadelphia, to Madison, 22 Mar. 1802, in ibid., p. 58. In all events, in March 1803, once Daniel had returned from France – but before the US purchase was agreed – he told Madison that Morales was 'too rich, too sensible and too cautious' to have closed the river on his own authority. Clark, New Orleans, to Madison, 8 Mar. 1803, in 'Despatches', p. 331.

41. Whitaker, *Mississippi Question*, p. 323.

of letters of introduction from Laussat's closest friends – it provided an early taste of his disconcertingly forward charm.[42]

For Washington, his presence held out some slender hope that Bonaparte's staff might divulge some of their intentions at a time when the Spanish officials in New Orleans were displaying open aggression against the United States.[43] For us, though, there is an extra interest in Clark's movements in that they can help an assessment of the testimony of Mesdames Despau and Caillavet, and give some indication as to whether Daniel was the father of Caroline and as to the likelihood that Daniel and Zulime were married in Philadelphia in 1802 or 1803.

If the evidence of the trials is combined with that given by Clark's correspondence as a consul, certain parts of the testimony given by Zulime's sisters can be discounted. Daniel and Zulime could not have married in Philadelphia in 1803 because Clark was not at that city at any time during the year. Indeed, they could not have married there after August 1802 because Daniel left on the 7th of that month on his European trip. He was in town from January until 22 April, but Zulime arrived there after he had left.[44] It is possible, however, that they married in January 1802 – when we know that Daniel was in Philadelphia and Zulime absent from New Orleans – or in July, which is more likely if we accept Sophie's account of 'rushing back' to confront the returned Desgrange, whose trial for bigamy was in early September.

---

42. Laussat says that Clark impressed him as being very supple, witty and ambitious, was apparently on intimate terms with the Spanish officials; and having made a good thing of the intimacy, wished to establish the same relations with the incoming French government. Laussat says that he replied to Clark in a friendly but non-committal way, and there the colloquy ended.

Whitaker, *Mississippi Question*, p. 321. Clark evidently felt the same about Laussat, telling Madison upon the Frenchman's arrival,

> The Prefect's language with respect to the United States is soft and conciliatory ... a perfect contrast to what he made use of it in Europe. He put me in mind of our Conversation at Paris, and laughingly told me I had fled before him. He inquired about my Fortune and advised me to divide my negroes and put half of them on the French territory ... said that I had done wrong to break up my commercial establishment.

Clark, New Orleans, to Madison, 27 Apr. 1803, in 'Despatches', p. 338.

43. In November 1802 the US Ambassador to Paris, Robert Livingston, introduced Clark to General Victor, just appointed as commander of the French garrison to be sent to Louisiana. Livingston had made no progress in discerning what France intended to do with the territory it had acquired but did not yet directly control. However, in Clark's company Victor spoke very freely, indicating that the French did not intend to respect the Americans' right of deposit at New Orleans, and intimating that New Orleans was of limited value without control of Natchez, which was in US territory. Upon hearing this, Livingston went immediately to Joseph Bonaparte to secure French respect of both the Treaty of San Lorenzo and the deal struck by Clark in June 1798. Livingston, Paris, to Madison twice on 11 Nov. 1802, in *American State Papers: Foreign Affairs*, II, pp. 526–7.

44. Laussat described Clark as 'possessed by restlessness ... he bustled around a great deal in order to seem important, and in doing so often made foolish mistakes'. Pierre Clément de Laussat, *Memoirs* (1831), Baton Rouge 1978, p. 94. Henry Adams described him as 'eccentric in his movements'. *History of the United States of America* (1890), New York 1931, III, p. 300. But Adams at least recognised Clark's needs as a merchant, and it was just as much these as any political agenda that determined Daniel's itineraries. That for 1802 ran thus: Jan. – arrives in Philadelphia from Havana; Apr. – leaves Philadelphia for New Orleans; June – leaves New Orleans for New York; August – sails from New York to Liverpool; Oct. – London; Nov. – Paris; Dec. – leaves Liverpool for New Orleans. Daniel had his own schooner, *The Comet*, but he often used other ships, perhaps even the sloop *Carrière*, which worked out of New Orleans and Mobile.

There is a much better chance that Daniel was the father of Zulime's child Caroline, who was born at some point between late April and early July 1802. Certainly, as Judge Catron emphasised, the father could not have been Jerome Desgrange. We know that Zulime and her sisters signed over to Desgrange a power of attorney to manage their parents' estate on 26 March 1801. Desgrange's letter to Clark expressing concern about Zulime was written in early July 1801, so he could not have left New Orleans later than May. Even if Caroline had been born in April 1802, Desgrange was definitely not her father. In August 1801, though, Daniel and Zulime were together in New Orleans.

It is also worth noting that when Desgrange returned to New Orleans at the start of September 1802 Zulime began her suit for bigamy without any prompting from Clark, who had been out of New Orleans since June. It seems likely, then, that Zulime, having handed over her clandestine baby to Coxe and having seen Clark for no more than four weeks in the previous nine months, still harboured some expectations of her returning husband. Yet she found Desgrange accompanied by the young María Yllar.

There can be little doubt that the liaison between Zulime and Daniel was known of in New Orleans, but the evidence that is readily available provides no precise link and is simply reflective of Daniel's general reputation. Moreover, it should be borne in mind that as consul, the city's richest man, and an active intermediary between the United States, French and Spanish interests, Clark was a very controversial figure and the obvious target of more or less malevolent gossip. There is, though, a rather persuasive tone to the comments made of him by the captain of the port, Benjamin Morgan, to the chandler, Mr Price, in August 1803:

> I have no personal emnity to Mr Daniel Clark; on the contrary, we are good friends. But as I regard the welfare of this young country, which I shall now most probably continue to live in, it is my wish he may not be appointed to this important office [of governor]. You know a good deal of him, and it is only necessary to put you in mind that he is deficient in dignity of character and sterling veracity to fill the office.... He is liked by very few of the Americans here but those dependent on him. Claiborne is also unsuitable.[45]

Clairborne it was, none the less, whom Jefferson appointed as Louisiana's first governor that month:

> To be appointed on the part of my Government to receive the island of Orleans, the province of Louisiana and the public property, archives etc., I should esteem as the highest honor which could be conferred upon me, and I know of no other mission which would be so grateful to my feelings.[46]

---

45. Morgan, New Orleans, to Price, 18 Aug. 1803, in Carter (ed.), *Territorial Papers*, IX, p. 9.
46. Claiborne, Natchez, to Madison, 12 Aug. 1803, in ibid., p. 14. *William Charles Coles Claiborne*, born Sussex County, Virginia, 1775. Clerk to Congress, 1790; governor of Mississippi Territory, 1801.

All the indications are that Daniel Clark would have felt the same way, and Claiborne's appointment must have been a very bitter blow for him. Madison, however, plainly felt that Daniel's intelligence was more than matched by his personal ambition: 'Clark's remarks are judicious, but I think he might have assumed the proper course to be assumed, taking care to foster individual expectations as little as possible.'[47] Laussat arrived later in the year, and in his memoirs he remembers Daniel in the following terms:

> To tell the truth, he really did not know what he wanted. He readily accepted affection and flattery from others, as well as their prejudices and animosities of the most contradictory kind; and he fluctuated between them. Even though he repeatedly said that he did not seek any prominent position, he found it strange that anybody else but he had been charged with the confidence of his government, and he did not disguise his grudge.[48]

On Claiborne, Laussat, whose anti-Americanism was frequently berated by the French ambassador Pichon, was scarcely less sharp: 'With estimable qualities as a private man, [he] has little intellect, a good deal of awkwardness, and is extremely beneath the position in which he has been placed ... understands [not] one word of French or Spanish.'[49]

These judgements receive some support from Claiborne's own explanation, two years later, of Clark's distance from him: 'Mr Clark's opposition to me may be attributed to ... disappointment [and] an unwillingness on my part (immediately upon my arrival) to be controuled by his opinion and aversion to his views as well private as public.'[50]

Something of the difference between the two Americans is caught in their responses to a questionnaire sent by Jefferson after Louisiana had been purchased. Amongst over twenty questions, the president asked if the people were litigious and how they would respond to the novelty of trial by jury. Claiborne responded,

> At present the people of Louisiana are represented to me as being Mild and Submissive people, not by any Means prone to litigation. But such is generally the character of Men under Arbitrary Government. In the 'calm of despotism' the more violent passions of the Vassal find few opportunities of Indulgence. But when their present shackles are removed, and a Rational System of Free Government shall acknowledge and protect their Rights, the change of disposition which may accompany so sudden a transition from the condition of Subjects to that of Free Men will probably be considerable ... some of the oldest and most respectable Inhabitants of this territory are of opinion that in civil cases the Trial by Jury will at first be unpopular, and I have heard this reason assigned: 'That Men who have long appealed for Justice to great Personages, whom they looked up to as wise and learned, cannot at first, without reluctance, submit to the decrees of men no better than themselves.'[51]

47. Madison, Washington, to Jefferson, 20 Aug. 1803, in J.M. Smith (ed.), *The Republic of Letters: The Correspondence between Thomas Jefferson and James Madison, 1776–1826*, New York 1995, pp. 1279–80.

48. Laussat, *Memoirs*, p. 94.

49. Quoted in Gayarré, *History of Louisiana*, p. 10.

50. Claiborne, New Orleans, to Madison, 22 May 1806, in Rowland (ed.), *Claiborne Letter Books*, III, p. 305.

51. Claiborne, Natchez, to Madison, 24 Aug. 1803, in ibid., p. 22.

Clark, far more familiar with the society, responds with greater economy but not without a modicum of ideological assurance for Washington:

> The people generally are far from litigious; they are afraid, as they express it, *des démélés avec la justice*. There are, however, characters of the opposite Cast. The nature of most suits are personal contracts, women's rights to dowers. There are very few suits respecting rights to land or personal quarrels ... in a little Time when the French could be made to comprehend the nature of trial by Jury the effect would be of a most satisfactory kind.[52]

In fact, Clark's dispatches as consul from 1801 right up to the formal transfer of the territory on 20 December 1803 are rather more detailed and professional than this excerpt might suggest. Yet even after his return from Europe in February 1803, one senses beneath the surface an anxiety to keep absolutely abreast of moves on the part of the Spanish and the French as well as the government that he represented with respect to Louisiana.

It should be recalled that the Spanish cession of the territory to the French at the Treaty of Ildefonso (1800) was secret, and it was not until May 1801 that Washington learnt of the move. As late as August 1802 Jefferson was telling Treasury Secretary Albert Gallatin 'that Louisiana is to be possessed by France is probable; that any man in America has undoubted authority that it will be so I do not think'.[53] Moreover, the Spanish, fully aware of the wealth of a colony that they were surrendering under appreciable pressure, hesitated to effect the transfer, obliging Napoleon to promise them in July 1802 that he would never cede the territory to a third party.[54] On this basis practical steps were begun to start the handover, and as soon as he knew of the French appointments – General Victor as commander, Laussat as prefect – Daniel Clark made for Paris to meet them.

However, Bonaparte's aim to establish an empire in North America was not exclusively determined by events in Europe, which included the peace reached at Amiens as well as Spanish submission. Indeed, this matter was eventually determined on Saint Domingue (Haiti), where these years witnessed social and political convulsions of enormous consequence, not just for Caribbean slave-owners like Daniel Clark but for the balance of power on a world scale.

The principal development of importance to us was the dispatch in December 1801 of a substantial force under Bonaparte's brother-in-law General Leclerc to obtain the submission of Toussaint L'Ouverture, the leader of the post-revolutionary regime and the most important figure associated with the abolition of slavery. Moreover,

---

52. Clark, New Orleans, to Madison, 8 Sept. 1803, in ibid., p. 38. In the event, the Louisianans accepted trial by jury for criminal cases but strenuously resisted all efforts to supplant their civil code, so that, as George Dargo puts it, the territory became 'a civil law island in a sea of common law'. *Jefferson's Louisiana: Politics and the Clash of Legal Traditions*, Cambridge, Mass., 1975, p. 171.

53. Jefferson, Monticello, to Gallatin, 20 Aug. 1802, in Henry Adams (ed.), *The Writings of Albert Gallatin*, Philadelphia 1879, I, p. 92.

54. R.B. Mowat, *The Diplomacy of Napoleon*, New York 1971, pp. 140–41. Alexander De Conde, *This Affair of Louisiana*, New York 1976. For a critical survey of the historiography, see Elizabeth Carlo, 'The Louisiana Purchase and the Historians', Dept. Government, University of Manchester 1995.

there is much to indicate that Leclerc's principal mission was, in fact, to take possession of Louisiana, the trip to Saint Domingue being both a preliminary subordinate
task and something of a feint to distract the United States and Spain.[55]

However, Leclerc's arrival off Cap Saint Domingue in February 1802 was met with
resistance, and throughout the first half of the year there ensued a bloody and confused campaign of subjugation, insurgency and temporary surrenders by Toussaint and
his principal lieutenants Dessalines and Christophe. In March the Treaty of Amiens
restored Martinique to France, and Bonaparte moved quickly to re-establish slavery
there. In June Leclerc's army of occupation in Saint Domingue was hit by yellow
fever and, assailed by continuous guerrilla attacks, clearly lost the initiative. In August
news of the restitution of slavery in Guadeloupe provoked wholesale social revolt in
Saint Domingue, the embattled Leclerc's dispatches expressing despair. When, in
November, he himself died of yellow fever, so had 24,000 out of 34,000 French
troops deployed on the island, 8,000 being hospitalised.[56]

Although a campaign of the utmost barbarism, yielding death rates of twentieth-
century proportions, continued for a further year before independence was declared,
Napoleon recognised that Haiti was already lost to the French. When James Monroe
arrived in Paris in April 1803 as plenipotentiary to join Ambassador Livingston in
negotiating at least New Orleans, part of western Florida, and maybe more, Bonaparte's
regional ambitions were so badly damaged that he no longer harboured any designs on
North America. He could therefore move rapidly to sell the entire Louisiana Territory,
which – even if it was not mapped as extensively as the US wanted, as France accepted,
and as it eventually came to be – was without doubt the sale of the century. Yet when
the deal was signed on 30 April 1803 it was not at all clear that the Spanish, who still
controlled the territory and formally protested at its sale (which broke Bonaparte's
assurances to them), would accept it. Indeed, as we have seen, the US Constitution
did not allow for such an event, so even congressional approval was uncertain.

In the light of this background one can without too much difficulty imagine
Daniel Clark returning to New Orleans in late February 1803 quite convinced but

55. On 4 June 1802 Napoleon wrote to Admiral Denis Decres, 'My intention is that we take Louisiana
with the shortest possible delay, that this expedition be organised in the greatest possible secrecy, and that
it have the appearance of being directed towards Saint Domingue.' Quoted in Laussat, *Memoirs*, p. 114. See
also Mowat, *Diplomacy*, p. 141.

56. C.L.R. James, *The Black Jacobins: Toussaint L'Ouverture and the San Domingo Revolution*, London 1980,
pp. 289–377. In his final exile in St Helena Bonaparte accepted that the Leclerc expedition had been one
of his greatest mistakes: 'I ought to have been content to govern it through the intermediary of Toussaint.'
Quoted in Mowat, *Diplomacy*, p. 93. According to Napoleon's private secretary Bourienne,

> The expedition to St. Domingue was one of Napoleon's greatest errors. Almost every person whom
> he consulted endeavoured to dissuade him from it.... Bonaparte often experienced bodily pain ...
> these pains ... affected him most acutely on the night he dictated to me the instructions for General
> Leclerc.

Louis Antoine Fauvelet de Bourienne, *Memoirs of Napoleon Bonaparte* (1834), New York 1906, II, pp. 91,
93. James is surely right to identify the resumption of slavery on Guadeloupe and Martinique as a critical
factor.

not certain of future US dominion. After May, when the news of the purchase arrived, he enjoyed a further two months harbouring legitimate expectations of the governorship. This probably caused him some difficulty with Zulime for, having returned to find Desgrange come, tried and gone, his own position promising, and with their affair having already yielded one child, he was surely asked for a public and formal commitment. And yet, in addition to the question of local reputation, Zulime spoke no English and was unschooled; Daniel may well have thought that she would not make a suitable wife for a governor. He could, of course, have also reflected that as a travelling man he himself stood to be betrayed as Desgrange had been, deservedly or otherwise. The clandestine marriage – real or invented – bisected his fears and needs perfectly in the short term, even if it stored up a host of problems for the future.

Some calculation of a similar nature can be discerned in a peculiar letter that Daniel sent, together with supporting documentation, to Secretary of State Madison within a week of his return to Louisiana:

> Should you think the documents of sufficient importance to require my presence in Washington to elucidate any part of them, I shall immediately sacrifice all public business of my own and hasten there … although for four or five years past I had a perfect conviction that the intrigues of the Spaniards in the western country were not for the time dangerous on account of the incapacity of the Governors of this province and their want of pecuniary means. Yet fearful of what might happen in the future should more enlightened and ambitious chiefs preside over it, I could not last year resist the temptation of revealing my suspicions of what had formerly done in this way to the President at an interview with which he honored me….
>
> I even went so far as to assert that a person supposed to be an agent from the State of Kentucky had been here at the end of 1795 and beginning of 1796 to negotiate on the part of that state, independent of the General Government, for the navigation of the Mississippi, before the result of the Treaty of San Lorenzo was known…. But as [the President] made no other inquiry of me respecting it than merely in what year the thing happened, it struck me that he must have other information on the subject, and that he thought it needless to hear anything more about it.
>
> By great accident I have lately learned something which induces me to suppose that any information he may have received respecting the measure alluded to has been incorrect and given with the view of misleading him. I request that you will mention the subject anew to him, that you may know how far I am right in my suspicions. The information I obtained on the subject could not, from the way it was obtained, be accompanied with what would be proof to convict the person concerned or I should have openly accused him in the face of the world. But to me it amounts to a moral certainty of his guilt, and my conduct to him showed, on all occasions, how much I detested his object and his person.
>
> The same want of proof positive sufficient to convict him prevents me from naming him. But if inquiry is diligently made about the influential character from Kentucky who at that period was so long at Natchez, what his business was, and what was the idea entertained of him, enough will doubtless be discovered to put our Government on its guard against him and others of his stamp, and against all machinations in that quarter in the future.[57]

---

57. Clark, New Orleans, to Madison, 8 Mar. 1803, in *Annals of Congress: 10th Congress, 1st Session, Jan.– April 1808*, Washington 1852, cols 2743–5.

It is not unusual that an allegation about secret deals with a foreign power be guarded in tone and artfully scripted, but here Clark is purposefully putting both Jefferson and Madison in a corner whilst protecting his own flank. He must have had reason to repeat the revelation now to Madison, having made it to Jefferson in 1802. Equally, he was not confident enough to name the person in league with the Spanish, apparently because they were still engaged in illicit activity and posed a threat, possibly to him personally.

Neither the president nor the secretary of state made any response to Clark. Both men were acutely aware that the Spaniards in Louisiana resented the purchase; their first priority was to secure the transfer of the territory to the USA rather than concern themselves with underhand dealings prior to the San Lorenzo treaty of 1795, let alone that of 1803. It was in this light that Daniel Clark was encouraged to raise a militia of Americans in New Orleans throughout the summer of 1803, and, upon being elected its commander in the autumn, he was cautiously included by Jefferson (who seems to have been more favourably disposed towards him than was Madison) in the preparations for the transfer:

> I think Clark might be trusted with a general hint of the possibility of opposition from Spain, and an instruction to sound in every direction, but with so much caution as to avoid suspicion, and to inform us whether he discovers any symptoms of doubt as to the delivery, to let us know the force Spain has there, where posted, how the inhabitants are likely to act if we march a force there, and what numbers of them could be armed and brought into opposition against us.[58]

The next month Clark was brought into Madison's plans for a coup should the Spanish refuse to implement the first part of the hand-over by ceding the city to the French prefect, Laussat:

> Should a *coup de main* be resolved, there may be a call on your assistance … a cooperating movement of the well disposed part of the inhabitants will be of essential advantage, and it is desirable that it should be in concert with the military counsels …[59]

These 'counsels' were the responsibility of General James Wilkinson, who was the military commander accompanying Claiborne in the receipt of the territory.[60]

In the event, nothing untoward did occur. On 3 November the Senate ratified Monroe's treaty with Talleyrand by twenty-six votes to six, and by the 5th the main

---

58. Jefferson, Monticello, to Madison, 14 Sept. 1803, in Smith (ed.), *Republic of Letters*, p. 1286. Earlier in the month Albert Gallatin had suggested to Jefferson that Clark be involved 'if he can be trusted to that extent'. Gallatin, Washington, to Jefferson, 5 Sept. 1803, in Adams (ed.), *Writings of Albert Gallatin*, I, p. 153.

59. Madison, Washington, to Clark, 31 Oct. 1803, in Carter (ed.), *Territorial Papers*, IX, pp. 95–6.

60. *James Wilkinson*, born Calvert County, Maryland, 1757. Fought at Trenton and Princeton under Washington; Captain, 1777; 1781, forced to resign lucrative position as clothier general because of irregular accounts; 1783, elected to Pennsylvania state assembly. Appointed to military command in Kentucky, 1784. Started trading with New Orleans in 1787. Rejoined regular army, 1791; 1792, Brigadier General. Died 28 Dec. 1825 in Mexico City, in the house of US Ambassador Joel Poinsett whilst on a mission to collect debts owed to the USA by Mexico.

US forces were in position for the take-over. Claiborne and Wilkinson remained upstream at Natchez, and Daniel recounted to Madison a most lacklustre first transfer ceremony: 'Except the noise of the cannon not a sound was heard. The most gloomy silence prevailed, and nothing could induce the numerous spectators to express the least joy or give any sign of satisfaction on the occasion.'[61] The French transfer to the United States a month later was noisier but also without incident. There being no French troops, the salute for Claiborne and Wilkinson was again given by Spanish gunners – part of a garrison of 250 which remained in the town for some time.

This, though, did not presage a tranquil opening to US administration of the city and territory. Indeed, almost from the start Claiborne was struggling to maintain his grip. Laussat reports a illustrative incident just two weeks after the transfer:

> During the night of 8 January [1804] an unfortunate potential for trouble broke out between the French and Anglo-Americans at the regular public ball. Two quadrilles, one French, the other English, formed at the same time. An American, taking offence at something, raised his stick at one of the fiddlers. Bedlam ensued. Claiborne remained quiet until Clark roused him. Unable to express himself in French, Claiborne appeared embarrassed and weak. He yielded at first, then endeavoured to reassert his authority. In the end he resorted to persuasion rather than to vigorous measures in order to silence the American, who was a simple surgeon attached to the troops. The French quadrille resumed. The American interrupted it again with an English quadrille and took his place to dance. Someone cried, 'If the women have a drop of French blood, they will not dance.' Within minutes the hall was completely deserted by the women. The Marquis of Casacalvo [the ex-Spanish governor], who was present, continued to play cards, laughing up his sleeve. He had gumbo served to the two or three women who came to him for protection, and he maliciously played his hand.[62]

A fortnight later Clark took the liberty of writing to Madison.

---

61. Clark, New Orleans, to Madison, 3 Dec. 1803, in 'Despatches', pp. 355–6, n. 43. Laussat, who, having served as prefect for only a month, stayed on in New Orleans as French commissioner for limits, later wrote:

> The *Telegraph* of January 11 [1804] had published a letter written under the pseudonym 'The Philadelphian'. It refuted the assertion that at the moment when the French flag had been lowered, everywhere, except for a scattering of applause coming from a group of Americans, tears and sadness were manifest, and it took this opportunity to insult the company of French citizens. The printer was immediately summoned to reveal the name of the author. He declared that Relf, an associate of Relf and Chew Co., commonly assumed to be Mr Clark's commercial house, had brought it in. They looked up Relf; he denied the letter.… Clark was apparently the real author, but nobody claimed authorship.

Laussat, *Memoirs*, p. 93.

62. Laussat, *Memoirs*, p. 92. Claiborne was obliged to field almost all the complaints provoked by the 'Americanisation' of New Orleans. In June 1805 he complained to Judge Pitot, whom he had appointed mayor, that it was not the governor's duty to police the theatre, and he was himself obliged to placate the mother superior of the Ursuline convent, who had protested,

> Holy Sister,
> I am honored with your Letter of this Morning, and its Contents shall receive my immediate attention. I greatly regret that a Representation at the Theatre should have been marked with indecency and disrespect towards your Amiable community, and I shall use my influence to prevent a repetition of an occurrence every good Citizen must lament.
> I renew to you holy Sister Assurances of my great Respect and sincere Esteem.

I have foreborn to write to you because my functions ceased ... but I think it necessary to intrude once more on you and mention that at an entertainment given to our Commissioners by M. Laussat he unreservedly informed Governor Claiborne that Bonaparte, previous to the departure of General Victor from Paris, had told him that he might count on war with Great Britain in less than twelve months after his arrival in Louisiana, and that he must immediately after a knowledge of that event take possession of Canada.... When Claiborne asked him how he was going to get there, he said, 'through your country'.[63]

It is not obvious how many messages Clark wanted to convey to Madison in this unsolicited letter, but thereafter the emnity between Clark and Claiborne remained fierce. Moreover, it was not merely personal. As the episode recounted by Laussat shows, the new regime engendered predictable social and racial tensions, but it also prompted economic and political conflict. With the loss of access to Mexican silver there was an immediate dearth of specie, and the creoles distrusted the paper money Claiborne set up a bank to issue. There was deep concern at the prospect of the slave trade being ended, anger at the introduction of English as the official language, a demand for the immediate conferral of statehood, and disquiet that Claiborne's position gave him judicial powers subject to less constraint than had been those of the Spanish governor. By July 1804 a series of protest meetings had consolidated a substantial opposition movement to Claiborne, and Daniel Clark was elected to take a memorial to Washington.

Before this spate of protest activity in June and July 1804, Daniel had retired to his plantation at Bayou Sarah, some 250 miles upstream, to avoid both the sickly season and an increasingly fractious and sour political scene. There was in New Orleans little sympathy for Claiborne outside of the cluster of American civil and military officials, but Daniel knew to his cost how much the awkward governor had the confidence of Jefferson and Madison. The challenge and price of opposition were high enough to require calm contemplation before they were assumed. When he returned, though, the gloves were off, and Clark, without any official position, was in the unusual position of having to go public. His enemies in power, on the other hand, conducted their campaign against him through confidential correspondence with Washington.

Claiborne, almost always measured and painstaking in his judgements, told Madison in June,

Mr Daniel Clark also manifests much discontent at the proceedings of the Government. This gentleman, I am inclined to think, is of the opinion that his services at New Orleans have

---

Claiborne, New Orleans, to Sister Thérèse de Saint Xavier Farján, 8 June 1805, in Rowland (ed.), *Claiborne Letter Books*, III, p. 85. In order to keep a sense of balance it is worth noting the impressions of a British visitor thirty years later:

The society, like the town, is divided into two distinct portions, the American and the Creole, and they do not mingle much together; the former being composed mostly of persons actively and constantly engaged in making fortunes, have little time for gaiety.... I should judge from what I have seen that the gayest and merriest part of New Orleans is to be found in the Creole society.

Murray, *Travels in North America*, p. 187.

63. Clark, New Orleans, to Madison, 24 Jan. 1804, in 'Despatches', pp. 358–9.

not been sufficiently rewarded, and I view him as very inimical to the present Administration. From the first period of my arrival to the present day, Mr Clark ... [has] made great exertions to injure me here.[64]

By November the governor had become more blunt:

I deem it my duty positively to assure you that Mr Clark is an Enemy of the Government of the United States. He is particularly intimate with Moralis, largely concerned in the Florida purchases, and in my opinion Decidedly in the Spanish interest.[65]

General Wilkinson, for his part, told the president in confidence that Clark, with whom he maintained an outward friendship,

is rather an Englishman at heart ... he is unpopular and too assuming here ... his cunning and overbearing pretensions [possess] capacities to do more good or harm than any other individual in the province. He pants for power, and is mortified by disappointment.[66]

Wilkinson might have painted Clark thus simply because of Claiborne's open dislike of the man or maybe in a fit of pique when in his cups. After all, Laussat had described the general as 'long known here in the most unfortunate manner. [He] is a rattle-headed fellow, full of odd fantasies. He is frequently drunk and has committed a hundred inconsistent and impertinent acts.'[67] Two years later Turreau, the French ambassador, reported to Paris,

General Wilkinson is 48 years of age. He has an amiable exterior. Though said to be well informed in civil and political matters, his military capacity is small. Ambitious and easily dazzled, fond of show and appearances, he complains rather indiscreetly, and especially after dinner, of the form of government which leaves officers few chances of fortune, advancement and glory, and which does not pay its military chiefs enough to support a proper style ... he seems to hold to the American service only because he can do no better.[68]

Indeed, it is not beyond the bounds of possibility that Wilkinson, a comfortably married man, was acting out of some compressed envy at Daniel's arrangement with Zulime. Claiborne, on the other hand, who lost his wife, Clarissa Duralde, in 1804 was, as we have seen, much more likely to have found it an unacceptably vulgar liaison. None the less, even he was not above some light flirtation. In a rather endearing post-scriptum to Treasury Secretary Albert Gallatin, Claiborne recounted a conversation in New Orleans 'with a very interesting young lady':

I expressed an opinion that she was not as partial to the *American* as to the *French* character. She declared, 'that in many respects the *former* was more amiable than the *latter* character.

64. Claiborne, New Orleans, to Madison, 3 June 1804, in Carter (ed.), *Territorial Papers*, IX, p. 242.

65. Claiborne, New Orleans, to Madison, 5 Nov. 1804, in ibid., p. 320. Intendant Morales had changed his name to John V. Moralis.

66. Wilkinson, New Orleans, to Jefferson, 1 July 1804, in ibid., pp. 253, 255.

67. Quoted in Gayarré, *History of Louisiana*, p. 11.

68. Turreau, Washington, to Talleyrand, 9 Mar. 1805, quoted in Adams, *History of USA*, II, pp. 406–7. In 1802 Wilkinson's pay was $225 per month, but by 1811 he was in debt to the War Department to the tune of $7,891.03. James R. Jacobs, *The Beginning of the US Army, 1783–1812*, New York 1947, p. 254.

The French love with more ardour, but the Americans with more constancy; the French make more affectionate husbands, but the Americans are the best fathers; the French love their country, but the Americans are attached to their Government; the French act from feeling but the Americans consult their judgement. To conclude, the French evidence much bravery and enthusiasm, but the Americans display most firmness and perseverance.' I replied that she justly appreciated the American character. 'But', continued the young lady, 'You Americans will all take another bottle.' This unexpected accusation so confused me that I could make no reply, and added the lady, 'You, I observe, cannot deny it.' Her goodness, however, was such as to admit that there were some exceptions.[69]

A state of ill-concealed hostility persisted for a year without any major shift in the balance of power in either town or territory. However, the animosity between Claiborne and the city fathers of both creole and American background offered tempting bait both to those foreign powers with interests in the region – not just France and Spain but also Britain – and to those elements in the USA that were disillusioned with 'Jeffersonian democracy', which had included sharp reductions in military expenditure, or to those who remained unpersuaded by the prospect of a single union of states extending westwards from the Atlantic seaboard of North America. The palpable weakness of Spain and rising disorder in its colony of Mexico encouraged in certain circles the notion of an annexation of the northern Spanish colonies in America, including Texas, and their integration with the western states of the USA. Ex-Vice President Aaron Burr, amongst others, envisaged a new state, pledged to the maintenance of the slave trade, committed to an Anglophone culture and alliance, and yet unhampered by any egalitarian anarchy of the type feared by some as the natural consequence of a continued Jeffersonian regime. Whether as the logistical centre for a thrust south and west into Spanish territory or as the bottleneck of the trade of the western states of the USA, New Orleans was a vital strategic centre.

As we have seen, Daniel Clark wrote to Madison as early as March 1803 warning of ambitions – if not conspiracies – along these lines. Yet by mid 1805, with US control of New Orleans having yielded him no personal advancement or influence in Washington, and with an unpopular local administration, Clark may well have considered alternatives to the new and unstable status quo. In all events, at the end of June 1805 Burr, who had been on a caravan of ill-disguised and poorly organised campaigning since having killed Hamilton the previous year, arrived at New Orleans and presented himself to Clark. The ex-statesman bore a letter of introduction to Daniel from Wilkinson that was fully in keeping with the general's formidable standards of flamboyance, not least when it came to dark hints:

---

69. Claiborne, New Orleans, to Gallatin, 11 Aug. 1806, in Carter (ed.), *Territorial Papers*, IX, p. 680. One wonders if the lady chatting Claiborne up might have been Suzette Bosque, who became his second wife. Wilkinson reported that when in Havana in the spring of 1800 he looked on Spanish women 'with strong emotions of admiration and desire'. Quoted in James R. Jacobs, *Tarnished Warrior: Major-General James Wilkinson*, New York 1938, pp. 192–3.

My Dear Sir,

This will be delivered to you by Colonel Burr, whose worth you know well how to estimate. If the persecutions of a great and honorable man can give title to generous attentions, he has claims on all your civilities and all your services. You can not oblige me more than by such conduct, and I pledge my life to you it will not be misapplied. To him I refer you for many things improper to letter, and which he will not say to any other. I shall be at St. Louis in two weeks, and if you were there, we could open a mine, a commercial one at least. Let me hear from you. Farewell, do well and believe me always your friend.[70]

Much was subsequently made of the phrase 'improper to letter', but as Daniel pointed out, Wilkinson's style was one of conspiratorial melodrama whoever his correspondent.[71] Equally, whilst it was plain that Clark was one of Burr's main hosts – a point not missed by Claiborne in his reports to Madison and confirmed by Daniel's loan of a servant and two horses for Burr's journey back to Natchez – Claiborne himself received the ex-vice president, who seems to have held the entire city in his thrall for a fortnight.[72] (Nevertheless, Daniel Clark does not appear in Gore Vidal's fictionalised version of Burr's long life and ambitious conspiracies.[73])

There was, however, a more telling charge that Burr had gone to New Orleans principally to confer with the 'Mexican Association', a 300–strong body that was promoting the annexation of that colony. Daniel Clark always denied membership of the association, and his frequent trips to Spanish territory would have made public participation most inadvisable, but many assumed that he was closely involved and may even have been at its head.[74]

---

70. Wilkinson, Natchez, to Clark, 28 May 1805, quoted in James Parton, *Life of Aaron Burr*, New York 1892, II, p. 42.

71. The things which it was improper to *letter* to me are pretty plainly expressed about the same time [by Wilkinson] to General Adair. The letter is dated Rapids of Ohio, May 28th 1805, 11 o'clock, and contains these expressions: 'I was to have introduced my friend Burr to you, but in this I failed by accident. He understands your merits, and reckons on you. Repair to me and I will tell you *all*.'

Daniel Clark, *Proofs of the corruption of General James Wilkinson, and of his connexion with Aaron Burr, with a full refutation of his slanderous allegations in relation to the character of the principal witness against him*, Philadelphia 1809, p. 89.

72. 'During Colo. Burr's continuance in this city he was marked in attention to Moralis and was in habits of intimacy with Livingston, Clark and Jones.' Claiborne, New Orleans, to Madison, 6 Aug. 1805, in Carter (ed.), *Territorial Papers*, IX, p. 489. Clark said (*Proofs*, p. 94) that he entertained Burr

as well as to do honor to the recommendation he brought as because I was pleased by his society.... I showed him the civilities usual on these occasions. In this I was not singular. He dined, I believe, with Governor Claiborne, and I know received the greatest attentions from several of the principal inhabitants.

73. Inventing Burr's memoirs, Vidal has the Colonel make a quite convincing case:

Between us lay an unfurled map of the Floridas.

Aware that I had seen it, Jefferson declared, 'It is our view that the Floridas are an integral part of the recent purchase of Louisiana. Certainly Western Florida to the Perdido River is ours.' Jefferson talked for some time of his famous acquisition. He had every reason to be pleased with his remarkable good luck. I say good luck because if the slaves of Santo Domingo Island had not overthrown their masters, Bonaparte would not have been forced to commit a vast amount of money and troops to the pacification of that island when he was on fire to begin the conquest of Europe ... Jefferson unrolled the map of Louisiana. He was jubilant. 'And to think it is only a beginning.'

Gore Vidal, *Burr*, New York 1973, pp. 295, 355.

74. Adams, *History of USA*, III, p. 227; Thomas Abernethy, *The Burr Conspiracy*, New York 1954, p. 25.

If this point is unlikely ever to be resolved, Clark was certainly ambivalent about the two loquacious, indebted and grand-standing officers with whom his attachments appeared to be coming far too public and threatening. Whatever his own ambitions and problems with Claiborne, Clark was anxious to remain the third man in the shadows. In early September 1805 he wrote Wilkinson such a disingenuous letter that it must have been drafted in the knowledge that if it wasn't stolen, it would anyway be leaked:

> Many absurd and wild rumors are circulated here, and have reached the ears of the officers of the late Spanish government respecting our late vice president. You are spoken of as his right-hand man, and even I am now supposed to be of consequence enough to combine with Generals and Vice Presidents. At any time than the present I should amuse myself vastly at the folly and fears of those who are affected with these idle tales; but being on the point of setting off for Veracruz on a large mercantile speculation I feel cursedly hurt at the rumors, and might, in consequence of Spanish jealously get into a hobble.... Were I sufficiently intimate with Mr Burr and knew where to direct a line to him I should take the liberty of writing to him.... Recollect that you, if you intend to become Kings and Emperors, must have a little more consideration for vassals ... and if Congress take the land for want of formalities we shall then have no produce, and shall make a very shabby figure in your courts.[75]

It is interesting that two years after the transfer of the territory Clark still refers to the US courts as 'yours'. Moreover, when he returned from Mexico, which he visited twice in the next six months (September to December 1805 and February to April 1806), he reported to Wilkinson in a much more up-beat tone:

> I have been twice, since I last wrote to you, to the *Land of Promise*, but what is more surprising I have got back safe from it after being reported to the Vice Roy as a person dangerous to the Spanish government.... I have made some money and acquired *more knowledge* of the country.[76]

Later Clark admitted that he had used these trading trips to assess the possibilities of a military assault on Veracruz and was convinced that this could be successfully achieved without any involvement of the US government.[77] However, the idea that he was not just indulging in some recreational militarist speculation for private gain is supported by Burr's conversations in Washington with British Ambassador Anthony Merry, who informed Foreign Secretary Lord Mulgrave on 25 November 1805 that Burr was seeking a loan of £10,000, 'and if it should be requisite a name, he desired that the transfer might be made out in the name of John Barclay of Philadelphia and Daniel Clark of New Orleans'. Furthermore, in the same conversation Burr requested the support of British warships, 'which it was necessary should cruise off the mouth of

75. Clark, New Orleans, to Wilkinson, 7 Sept. 1805, quoted in Parton, *Burr*, II, p. 48.

76. Clark, New Orleans, to Wilkinson, 7 Sept. 1806, quoted in Abernethy, *Burr Conspiracy*, p. 30.

77. Clark, *Proofs*, pp. 94–5. Daniel was only a lieutenant in the militia, and although his uncle had been a colonel, it might be doubted whether he was capable of making a professional appraisal of such a large undertaking.

the Mississippi at the latest by 10th of April next, and to continue there until the commanding officer should receive information from him [Burr] or from Mr. Daniel Clark'.[78]

Any distant possibility of such intervention was removed by the death of Prime Minister Pitt in January 1806. By the time 'free trade' had collapsed under Bonaparte's 'continental system' (November 1806), provoking clashes between British and US warships in June 1807, Aaron Burr was already under arrest and on trial. Daniel Clark, by predictable contrast, had escaped the closing noose and was shortly to be providing evidence against Wilkinson, the other alleged leader of this, the first conspiracy against the integrity of the Union.

One critical development in this shift of allegiance was Clark's election to the US House of Representatives in May 1806, restoring at least some of his status, providing him with a platform and opening the political opportunities that had been blocked in New Orleans. When faced with this result of the election, Claiborne wrote to Madison,

> I do not know the course the delegate may pursue. He possesses Talents, and may, if he chuses, be serviceable to the Territory.... [He] will, most unquestionably, say much and do much with a view to my injury ... all I ask is that before [this is] believed, I may have the opportunity of explaining and justifying my conduct.[79]

In the event, Clark, who only spoke on the record on half a dozen occasions in two years, said nothing openly against Claiborne. However, he was anxious to protect his own interests whilst away from New Orleans and asked Wilkinson to keep him informed of developments.[80]

Whether this request was entirely innocent is unclear, but by the early autumn of 1806, when he was about to embark for Washington, Clark evidently reckoned Burr's plot to have minimal chances of success. At the same time, though, it would not have been judicious to have been the first to denounce it in public. Instead, Daniel found

---

78. Merry, Washington, to Mulgrave, 25 Nov. 1805, reprinted in M.J. Kline and J. Wood Ryan (eds), *Political Correspondence and Public Papers of Aaron Burr*, Princeton 1983, II, p. 944; Adams, *History of USA*, pp. 229–30.

79. Claiborne, New Orleans, to Madison, 21 May and 21 June 1806, in Rowland (ed.), *Claiborne Letter Books*, III, pp. 303–4, 339–40.

80. Dear Sir,
    I have within these three or four weeks past found it necessary, in order to oppose Governor Claiborne's creatures and schemes with success, to accept the appointment of Delegate from this country to Congress. You well know the burden I have taken on. Let me, therefore, beg your assistance and write me confidentially as soon as possible as may serve the good Cause. If you could possibly favor me with a copy of the Commissioners' correspondence and transactions at the period of the delivery of this country with your remarks, it might be of great service, and I could, without letting the source be known, make a precious use of the information.... If there is beside anything which can be undertaken with a view to serve yourself, only hint it. You know my ardent disposition and that I do not easily abandon what I undertake ... my nomination has been a severe shock to [Claiborne] and his Gang. They are much chop-fallen, and all the first Character and best men here are united against them.

Clark, New Orleans, to Wilkinson, 16 June 1806, in Carter (ed.), *Territorial Papers*, IX, pp. 660–61.

excuses in September not to travel up-river to see Wilkinson, and, according to Colonel Bellechasse, before leaving the city in October,

> he called together a number of his friends, and informed them of the views and intentions imputed to Colonel Burr, which were then almost the sole topic of conversation, and which, from the reports daily arriving from Kentucky, had caused a serious alarm. And he advised them all to exert their influence with the inhabitants of the country to support the Government of the United States and to rally round the Governor (although he thought him incapable of rendering much service as a military man). This would be the best method of convincing the Government ... of the attachment of the inhabitants of Louisiana and of the falsity of all the reports circulating to their prejudice.[81]

The rumour that reached Natchez a few weeks later, when Clark was in Washington, was lucidly passed on by Judge Thomas Rodney to his son:

> The Design of the Conspiracy is said to be to unite Kentucky, Louisiana, the Floridas and part at least of Mexico into an Independent Empire. The Spanish Governors of those Provinces are to act in concert with the Conspirators of our Country to Effect this purpose with the Patronage and Protection of Great Britain. And that they expect a British fleet to aid them, which is to arrive at the mouth of the Mississippi within two or three months at the farthest. Colonel Burr, General Wilkinson and Daniel Clark are said to be the leaders.[82]

Wilkinson knew that Burr's resources amounted to no more than the sixty men and nine flat-bottomed boats which had been moving at the colonel's erratic whim down the river from Kentucky in the late autumn. With the rumours now so widespread and precise, Wilkinson lost his nerve, writing what very nearly amounted to a confession to Jefferson on 25 November. But in order both to justify his action and to prompt the president into action, Wilkinson greatly exaggerated the size of Burr's force and painted a picture of an imminent seizure of power in New Orleans.[83] In fact, it was not until 10 January 1807 that Burr, who was at Chickasaw Bluffs (now Memphis, Tennessee), saw in a newspaper a copy of a letter which he had written in cipher to Wilkinson in July and which Wilkinson had now published to prove his allegation. Burr realised that the game was up and took to a half-hearted flight.

Wilkinson's act of betrayal yielded him immediate results. A grateful Jefferson ordered him to take military command of Louisiana and secure the region. Claiborne was obliged – against his better judgement – to acquiesce in the general's imposition of virtual military rule in New Orleans, where the merchants were threatened with a closure of the river if they did not cooperate. For Claiborne the conspiracy seemed to confirm his convictions about Clark. On the morning of 5 December he wrote to Madison,

---

81. Quoted in Clark, *Proofs*, p. 145. Claiborne was colonel and commander of the militia whilst in 1803 Daniel had led the first impromptu force without a rank.
82. Rodney, Natchez, to Caesar Rodney, 21 Nov. 1806, quoted in Abernethy, *Burr Conspiracy*, p. 202.
83. Adams, *History of USA*, III, p. 309.

If [dismemberment of the Union] be the object of the conspirators, the delegate to Congress from this territory, Daniel Clark, is one of the leaders. He has often said that the Union could not last, and that, had he children, he would impress early on their minds the expediency of a division between Atlantic and Western states.[84]

However, later on that day Claiborne learnt from Bellechasse of the meeting held in October when Clark had counselled loyalty, even to his own political foe. As a result, the governor, who may have been apprehensive about Daniel's new influence in Washington but who was an upright man, wrote immediately to the secretary of state,

In a former letter, I mentioned my suspicions of Mr Clark, and the causes which excited them; but upon further inquiry, I can find nothing to justify an opinion that he is a Party in the existing conspiracy. I have, therefore, to request that the letter in which his name was introduced be considered confidential.[85]

Wilkinson must have been extremely nervous playing at least three parties off against each other, and he himself had good reason to be grateful for Bellechasse's intervention since it made his ties to Clark less dangerous and reduced the chances of his own involvement being revealed from that quarter: 'Thank God your advice to Bellechasse – if your character were not a sufficient guarantee – would vindicate you against any foul imputation.'[86]

And then, to compound his double-dealing, the general informed Daniel, 'It is a fact that our fool [Claiborne] has written to his contemptible fabricator [Jefferson] that you had declared if you had children you would teach them to curse the United States as soon as they were able to lisp.'[87]

Of course, the fact that Myra was now born – if yet barely able to lisp – places Wilkinson's deceptions in proper context. However, the general's appetite for conspiracy did not subside even after Burr's eventual arrest – by Lieutenant Gaines at Fort Stoddard – in February. In March 1807 Wilkinson wrote to Clark,

Cet bête [Claiborne] is at present up to the chin in folly and vanity. He cannot be supported much longer, for Burr or no Burr, we shall have to revolt if he is not removed speedily. The moment Bonaparte compromises with Great Britain will be the signal for a general rising of French and Spaniards; and if the Americans do not join in, they will not oppose. Take care! Suspicion is abroad; but you have a friend worth having.[88]

In the event, Burr's trial yielded neither further confessions – Daniel was not called upon to testify for the defence or prosecution – nor a guilty verdict. The

---

84. Claiborne, New Orleans, to Madison, 5 Dec. 1806, quoted in Gayarré, *History of Louisiana*, p. 161.

85. Claiborne, New Orleans, to Madison, 5 Dec. 1806, in Rowland (ed.), *Claiborne Letter Books*, IV, p. 42. Dunbar Rowland clearly developed great affection for William Claibourne when editing his correspondence, and, responding to his subject's request to Madison, he omits from his volume the earlier letter mentioned here.

86. Wilkinson, New Orleans, to Clark, 10 Dec. 1806, quoted in *Proofs*, p. 151.

87. Ibid.

88. Wilkinson, New Orleans, to Clark, 20 March 1807, quoted in *Proofs*, p. 151; Adams, *History of USA*, I, p. 322.

reasons for this were not unconnected with the fact that two years earlier Burr had, as vice-president, presided over the impeachment of Mr Justice Samuel Chase, whom Jefferson had assiduously sought to remove from the Supreme Court. Against expectations, Burr regulated that trial sternly and fairly enough for the judge to be acquitted. At his own trial, which the president staged at his home town of Richmond, Burr was faced with a jury of fourteen Republicans and two Federalists, who knew that the trial judge, Chief Justice John Marshall, had been subject to threats from Jefferson and had himself declared that 'it would be difficult or dangerous for a jury to acquit Burr, however innocent they might think him'. But the colonel was well defended by Henry Clay (who would later take a strong interest in Myra's case) and given a scrupulously correct trial by Marshall. At the end, the jury produced an extraordinary verdict: 'we the jury say that Aaron Burr is not proved guilty ... by any of the evidence entrusted to us'. The disorganised group assembled in Kentucky could not be definitively tied to Burr by documentary evidence or – as stipulated by the Constitution – by at least two witnesses (who could, of course, have been Clark and Wilkinson).[89]

In view of its relevance to Mitchel's case as well as to the background to Myra's, it is worth quoting from Judge Marshall's opinion:

> Crimes so atrocious as those which have as their object the subversion by violence of those laws and those institutions which have been ordained in order to secure the peace and happiness of society, are not to escape punishment because they have not ripened into treason. The wisdom of the legislature is competent to provide for the case; and the framers of our constitution, who not only defined and limited the crime but with jealous circumspection attempted to protect their limitation – by providing that no person should be convicted of it, unless on the testimony of two witnesses on the same overt act, or a confession in open court – must have conceived it more safe that punishment should be ordained by general laws ... than it should be inflicted under the influence of those passions which the occasion seldom fails to excite.[90]

---

89. Section four of article two of the Constitution states: 'The President, Vice President and all civil Officers of the United States, shall be removed from Office on Impeachment for, and Conviction of, Treason, Bribery, or other High Crimes and Misdemeanors.' Section three of article three states:

> Treason against the United States, shall consist only in levying War against them, or in adhering to their Enemies, giving them Aid and Comfort. No Person shall be convicted of Treason unless on the Testimony of two Witnesses to the same overt Act, or on Confession in open Court.

90. Quoted in G.L. Hoskins and H.A. Johnson, *Oliver Wendell Holmes devise History of the Supreme Court of the United States: Vol. II. Foundations of Power: John Marshall, 1801–15*, New York 1981, p. 260. Marshall's judgement also established an important doctrine which assisted Burr and would certainly have offered easy meat to John Mitchel's lawyers had he been tried for treason in the USA in 1865:

> All those who form the various and essential military parts of prosecuting the war, which must be assigned to different persons, may with correctness and accuracy be said to levy war ... and to commit treason under the constitution. It will be observed that this opinion does not extend to the case of a person who performs no act in the prosecution of the war – who counsels and advises it – or who, being engaged in the conspiracy, fails to perform his part.

Quoted in ibid., p. 280.

Burr campaigned hard to get an unambiguous acquittal but never succeeded. Three years later he visited Paris in an effort to persuade Bonaparte to retake Louisiana, and he also seems to have suggested provoking a war between Britain and the USA. Of course, two years later just such a conflict did break out, and its most famous battle was fought at New Orleans in 1815, days after peace had been signed in the Netherlands. General Andrew Jackson's victorious defence of the city against superior forces commanded by General Packenham (Wellington's brother-in-law) subsequently became an important component of the folklore of 'a people armed' and the ideology of a popular militia founded upon the prowess of independent, arms-bearing citizens.[91]

By that stage Daniel Clark had been dead for eighteen months. However, he had long before settled scores with his two foes – the public opponent Claiborne and the private enemy Wilkinson.

In May 1807 Clark openly criticised the leadership and organisation of the New Orleans militia in Congress, and Claiborne, commander of the force, felt obliged to challenge Daniel to a duel even though his brother-in-law had recently been killed in such a fight. The engagement was held at Manchac on 8 June 1807, and Claiborne was wounded in the thigh, seriously enough to keep him in bed for several weeks and, apparently, to assuage at least some of Daniel's contempt. Claiborne continued as governor and Clark retired from politics when he was not re-elected the next year.

However, before he left the House of Representatives, Daniel, who by now may well have thought that he had nothing left to lose, decided to resurrect the matter of the traitor which he had raised to no avail with Jefferson and Madison some six years earlier. After Burr's trial he let it be known that he had access to evidence against Wilkinson, but he refused either to present it or to indicate what it was without being obliged to do so by a vote of the House, in order that the executive would be formally forced to divulge the documents he had sent them before.

---

91. Governor Claiborne played his part with a deft appeal to the Chief of the Caddo Indians:

> Friend and Brother! I arrived at this Post three sleeps past, and learn from our friend Dr Sibley that you only left it last month. I should rejoice to have met you here, that we might have shaken hands in friendship, and smoked and conversed under the shade of the same tree. Seven years ago, Brother, we had a conference at this place, Natchitoches, and mutually promised to keep the path between our two nations white. We have been long in authority and know from experience the blessings of peace.... Brother, the United States are like the oaks of the forest. A great body with many branches. The people of the United States are composed of 18 families. Each family has a chief, but the great beloved Man of all is your father, the President, who stands in the place of the great Washington.... Brother! Seven years ago you told me your nation had but one enemy, the Osages. And I am sorry to learn that you are still at war with those people. I have often heard of the Osages. In the vast hunting grounds where the Great Spirit has placed a sufficiency of Buffaloe, Bear and Deer for all the Red Men, the Osages, I hear, have already robbed the hunters of all Nations, and their chiefs wage War to acquire more skins. Among the white people, brother, there is also a nation of Osages. Beyond the sea, there lies a people called the English, who may really be considered white Osages. On the big water which the Great Spirit made large enough for the use of all men, the English have already plundered every people.

Talk by Claiborne to Great Chief of the Caddo, 13 Oct. 1813, in Rowland (ed.), *Claiborne Letter Books*, VI, pp. 275–6.

On 20 January 1808 Jefferson replied to Congress that Clark had indeed presented some papers, and that accusations had been made about certain activities during the presidencies of Washington and Adams. However, the papers, which had not been burnt as Clark had initially requested, could not be located.[92] It seemed as if the president, who owed Wilkinson a favour for revealing Burr's plans, had neatly blocked further investigation.

None the less, on 4 February Jefferson reported that the papers had been found by the chief clerk of the State Department, and he laid edited transcripts before Congress.[93] Amongst the quite considerable material identifying Wilkinson as 'agent 13' at the service of Spain well after he rejoined the US army in 1791 was the matter of the payment of $9,640 to him by Governor Carondelet in January 1796. This sum was sent up the Mississippi in silver coin secreted in barrels of sugar and coffee. However, when Wilkinson did not immediately receive the shipment, he suspected that his commander, General Wayne, was suspicious about his loyalty, and he protested to Carondelet's succesor Gayoso in characteristic style:

> [Thomas] Power will explain to you the circumstances which justify the belief of great treachery that has been practised with respect to the money lately sent to me. For the love of God and friendship, enjoin great secrecy and caution in all our concerns. Never suffer my name to be written or spoken. THE SUSPICION OF WILKINSON IS WIDE AWAKE.[94]

Wilkinson had not, in fact, been betrayed over his money, which General Wayne's men failed to locate and which finally turned up – albeit slightly shorn to the gratifyingly tidy sum of $9,000 – at Montgomery Brown's store in Frankfort, Kentucky.[95] Although Daniel Clark's time in the Spanish governor's office enabled him to show that the money could scarcely be payment for tobacco, as Wilkinson claimed, the authorities in Havana had no interest in seeing the general go to the wall, and they duly produced the affidavits that allowed Jefferson to provide him with some protection from Congress.

When, later in 1808, Wilkinson was tried by a court martial, he was acquitted on much the same grounds, although Daniel's evidence was voluminous enough to be published the following year in an octavo volume of nearly two hundred pages – the 'Proofs'. The material it contained was sufficiently damning that some of Wilkinson's supporters claimed that it had been forged, and even some contemporary scholars have felt that the general was 'fitted up'.[96] However, Wilkinson got the opportunity to

---

92. *Annals of Congress: 10th Congress. First Sesssion. 20 Oct. 1807 to 25 April 1808*, Washington 1852, cols 2726–8.

93. Ibid., cols 1563, 2743ff.

94. Wilkinson, Fort Washington, to Gayoso, 22 Sept. 1796, quoted in ibid., col. 1258.

95. Jacobs, *Beginning of US Army*, p. 186.

96. On 8 July 1808, while the general's court martial was under way, *The Baltimore Whig* accused Clark of having forged the signature of Thomas Power, Wilkinson's agent, 'the handwriting being compared and recognised by several respectable gentlemen ... demonstrates that Mr. Clark is capable of resorting to the most detestable practices'. One concludes, though, that the paper was not entirely unbiased given that on the 20th it described Wilkinson's acquittal as 'manna to every democratic taste ... rue and wormwood to the palate of federalism'. It took a slightly different tack on 1 July 1809:

publish his own version of events in his *Memoirs*, where he confronts the question as to why Daniel Clark decided, with the Burr trial over and the dangers of prosecution past, to accuse him.

For James Madison this was evidently a source of potential embarrassment, threatening to revive debate over the administration's handling of the spying case. Upon first publication of Wilkinson's defence in 1811 Madison wrote anxiously to Jefferson to ask if the general had disowned the anonymous letter printed in Clark's book or if he would 'say anything relevant to the subject'. In reply Jefferson reveals not only how little interested he was in the detail of the case but also his attitude to Wilkinson's activity since the early 1790s:

> The letter which I wrote lately to Wilkinson was one of necessity written to thank him for his book which he sent me. He says nothing in his letter of the anonymous letter in Clark's book to which you allude. I have never seen Clark's book, and know nothing of its contents.... Whatever previous communications might have passed between Burr and Wilkinson on the subject of Mexico, I believe that on the part of the latter it was on the hypothesis of the approbation of the government. I never believed Wilkinson would give up dependence on the government, under whom he was the first, to become secondary and dependent.[97]

On this last point at least, Jefferson's judgement of Wilkinson's character seems fully vindicated. It does not, though, explain why Daniel Clark turned against the unreliable general. For Professor Abernethy this is the central enigma of the case, and although we know that Daniel's own explanation – that Wilkinson had traduced him in letters to Jefferson and Madison – is correct, it is hardly persuasive.[98]

Wilkinson's own version of events is convincing not because the man himself deserves much credit as a straight-talker, nor even because he produced it after Clark had died, but simply because its main message fits with other facts, many of which Wilkinson could not have known or understood, even if it is boxed around with invention and mean abuse. Since it fills a large piece of the puzzle about Daniel's private affairs it is worth quoting at some length:

> Daniel Clark ... a man! soaring above *vulgar prejudices* and distinguished for political depravity and moral turpitude. This gentleman who had always been my professed friend and obsequious servant, as his correspondence will testify, was suddenly converted into a remorseless enemy, and the world remains to be informed of the causes of the sudden revolution in the conduct of Mr. Clark. 'Tis true, his connection with Colonel Burr has been proved by the strongest

---

> In some of the letters of Mr Clark that writer presents himself as a curious Character; as a person who can play any part to obtain his object, capable of canting, whining etc., to dive into the views of men. And in other letters, there is an equivocal squinting at Burr's project.

These quotations are given in Thomas Robson Hay, 'Some Reflections on the Career of General James Wilkinson', *Mississippi Valley Historical Review*, XXI:4, 1935, which broadly revindicates the general. For a Spanish viewpoint, see J. Navarro Latorre and F. Solano Costa, *Conspiración Española? 1787–1789*, Zaragoza 1949. Over 300 documents relating to the Wilkinson–Clark dispute are housed at the Historical Society of Pennsylvania, Philadelphia.

97. Madison, Washington, to Jefferson, 1 April 1811; Jefferson, Monticello, to Madison, 7 April 1811, in Smith (ed.), *Republic of Letters*, pp. 1663–5.

98. Abernethy, *Burr Conspiracy*, p. 264.

circumstantial evidence, and is credited by the candid part of society; but the ember of *traitorous revenge*, which lay smothered in his bosom, was blown into flames by incidents, which it has become my duty to explain, however delicate the task....

In November 1807, whilst Mr. Clark was running this career [as a congressman] and receiving the homage of distinguished characters, I visited Annapolis, accompanied by Dr. Carmichael, of the Mississippi Territory, and Captain Murray, of the army. At this time, trusting to Mr. Clark's professions and deportment, I had no cause to doubt the sincere attachment which he avowed. He had attended Mr. Burr's trial at Richmond, on the summons of the prisoner ... professed he did not know for what he was summoned, and did not appear before the court. But the style in which he was spoken of, at Annapolis, excited the astonishment of my companions, who had known him eight or ten years, and was [*sic*] well acquainted with his *real character* and *circumstances*. From his riches the conversation glided to his personal merits and accomplishments, and when mention was made of his gallantry, and the havoc he was making among the hearts of our charming countrywomen, it produced some pleasantry from these gentlemen, which did not appear to injure Mr. Clark and yet would not have recommended him.

During this visit, I dined with one of the most distinguished and respectable characters of our country, who, after tea, took occasion to ask me whether I knew Mr. Clark in New Orleans, and proceeded to inquire into his circumstances. Not knowing at the time that Mr. Clark was even an acquaintance of the family, I was struck by the inquiry, and from my knowledge of his habits of finance it occurred to me that he had borrowed, or was about to borrow, money from the inquirer, for whom I had, since the year 1775, cherished an undeviating respect and attachment, and, of consequence, I felt it my duty to satisfy his inquiries. But not before I had adverted to my standing with Mr. Clark and the delicacy of the subject and the propriety of treating it confidentially, which was acquiesced in.

I then stated, with great candour, that Mr. Clark had inherited a cotton estate from an uncle, which, with judicious management, would produce a revenue of $12,000 per annum; that I possessed no further knowledge of his circumstances, but that he was a merchant of great enterprise, and that I had, the preceding month of March, been offered in New Orleans his note at nine months on a discount of about one-third. The gentleman with whom I was conversing remarked that this was '*a very bad sign*', and nothing further was said. It is proper to observe that a third gentleman was in the room, who in the course of the conversation drew near and attended to what passed.

Soon after this visit to Annapolis I arrived at Washington and, to my surprise, learned that Mr. Clark was addressing a very young and charming daughter of the third gentleman to whom I have alluded, which caused me unfeigned concern, not only for the interesting object of his attentions, and the ancient and honorable family with which he sought an alliance, but also lest he should be informed of the conversation which had casually occurred at Annapolis and be led to misinterpret my motives. A few days after I was advised that this had taken place and that Mr. Clark was highly incensed.[99]

The third gentleman was, of course, Richard Caton, father of Marianne. In the end, Wilkinson succeeded in spiking Daniel's chances in love as well as undermining his credit. We know from the evidence of his last days, when he was dying of yellow fever, that this blow had told against our anti-hero.

★

---

99. Wilkinson, *Memoirs*, II, pp. 3–24.

There is no open reference to this background in the Supreme Court hearing of 1852, but all of the justices – most of whom were Jacksonians by appointment or disposition – and many of the lawyers were increasingly involved in the controversy over the nature of the Union, states' rights and the political as well as legal consequences of slavery, the 'personal property' mentioned in Clark's will. In 1857, all nine justices were involved in the Dred Scott case, perhaps the single most important legal decision contributing to the Civil War.[100] John Kendall is characteristically outspoken on this aspect, but one finds his view inferred at least in other commentary:

> Apparently our most exalted tribunal did not know its mind. Or shall we conclude that the animosities of the period preceding the Civil War had something to do with the Supreme Court's actions? After all, wasn't Myra Clark a victim of those proud, slave-owning aristocrats?[101]

Whether she was or not, Myra knew that she had to engage in local politics if her suit were to be revived. She had persistently lost in the Circuit Court before Judge McCaleb, and so it was again in March 1856, when that court rejected the ruling of fifteen months earlier by the local probate court that Daniel Clark's 1813 will could be admitted. This was a major setback because it was inceasingly clear that, under Louisiana law, Myra's claim would only be won if it could be proved *both* that she was legitimate and that she was a beneficiary under a valid will. Neither on its own would be sufficient.

In December 1856 a partial advance was made when the Louisiana Supreme Court ruled that the 1813 will could be formally admitted to probate, but this was by no means the same thing as conceding Myra's claim. In the meantime, Myra had taken the risk of openly backing the candidacy of Edwin Merrick for the office of Chief Justice of Louisiana, despite his fiercely anti-Roman Catholic views and platform. When Merrick won office, he heard the case himself in 1860 and ruled in Myra's favour. The inevitable appeals from those liable to lose their property meant that the case returned – as '*Gaines* v. *Hennen*' – to the federal Supreme Court, where it was heard in February 1861, on the cusp of both Lincoln's presidency and the Civil War.

By this stage Myra was in severe debt and had even had her luggage impounded for non-payment of hotel bills, but hers was now a *cause célèbre* that attracted a huge audience and with it the free services of the greatest lawyers. In this instance her

---

100. The Dred Scott decision was given on 6 March 1857. Dred Scott, born around 1800, was a slave whose owner had died in 1843 and who had tried to buy his freedom. In 1846, with help from white friends, Scott had filed a suit in a Missouri court claiming that his residence in Illinois and Wisconsin had given him the status of a free man. When the case was referred to the Supreme Court it ruled decisively against him. All the justices filed an opinion, except one who concurred completely with Chief Justice Taney, and each ruled that Scott remained a slave, but on quite different grounds. Taney's opinion, which stood as that of the court, was that Scott lacked standing in court because he was not a citizen, and one could only become a citizen by birth or naturalisation. Negroes 'had for more than a century been regarded as ... so far inferior that they had no rights which the white man was bound to respect'. Moreover, residency in a free state did not confer freedom, and Congress had acted to deprive citizens of property in slaves.

101. Kendall, 'Strange Case', p. 26.

advocate was Caleb Cushing, attorney general in the Pierce administration, renowned poet and scholar – he had translated Alberdi – now over sixty, but still energetic. Cushing directly attacked the twin objectives of legitimacy and the authenticity of the lost 1813 will. Whereas in 1852 the testimony of Boisfontaine and the others on the latter had been projected rather late, defensively and somewhat subordinate to the question of Zulime's marriages, it was now given greater prominence. Relf – the implied thief of the will – was now, of course, dead. But there was no substantial new evidence beyond that presented in 1852, which Myra and Whitney had gathered from their trip to Cuba in the mid 1830s, when they consulted the documentation removed from New Orleans by the Spanish and listened to the testimony of Colonel Bellechasse, who had settled in Matanzas many years before. The issue revolved once more about questions of law.

It might be thought that Boisfontaine – to whom Daniel Clark had given his house in Royal Street in 1809 – Mrs Smyth, Bellechase and De la Croix were scarcely 'disinterested' witnesses. Moreover, although Washington was a Southern city in a state of exceptional tension over slavery and the Union, it may not have done the case any harm to indicate that Daniel's slave Lubin – the supposed witness to Relf's perfidy – was to have been given his freedom under the 1813 will. On this, though, as on the nature of marriage, divorce and bigamy under Roman and common law, Cushing did the business:

> In his summing-up of the case I have rarely heard anything that surpassed it. His voice was not loud, but deep and firm, and every word caused a singular power. In gesture he was very sparing, using his left hand mostly, and closed, with the exception of the third finger, which was thrust straight out.... At the close of Mr Cushing's remarks, he closed his books as coolly as if in his own library, stepped across the room to the right, and shook hands with some ladies who had been listening.[102]

Judge Wayne was over seventy and under considerable pressure as a unionist from Georgia.[103] Now it was he who read the majority opinion and Catron who spoke for the dissenting minority. And, as in 1852, Wayne stinted on neither length nor his palpable attraction to Spanish history.[104] His ruling was that although it was possible –

102. Quoted in Claude M. Fuess, *The Life of Caleb Cushing*, New York 1923, II, p. 295. After their meeting in June 1855, Alberdi described Cushing as 'of regular height, affable, with a fine head, a daring and penetrating eye'. Jorge Mayer, *Alberdi y su Tiempo*, Buenos Aires 1963, p. 493.

103. *James Moore Wayne*, born 1790, Savannah. Educated, Princeton; fought against British, 1812–15; Congress, 1829–35. Supported Jackson over removing Indians from white jurisdiction; defended legal rights of slave-owners but did not advocate slavery. Died 1867.

104. Wayne's opinion in the 1861 case covers twenty-four double-columned pages. In one of his several digressions, he told the court:

> The inquisition, as it had existed for more than one hundred years in France and Italy, was introduced into Spain by Gregory IX, about the middle of the 13th century. It encountered no opposition there. It at first attained a prevalence and extension larger than it had exercised before, and was on the increase when Spain became a united kingdom under Ferdinand and Isabella. They were authorised by the bull of Sextus IV to establish the inquisition in their States. And then it was invested with jurisdiction of heresies of all kinds, and also of sorcery, Judaism, Mahomedanism, offenses against nature, and polygamy, with power to punish them, from temporary confinement

even likely – that Daniel Clark was the biological father of Caroline, she had been Desgrange's daughter by law; that if either of Myra's parents had contracted marriage in good faith, no adulterous bastardy was involved, and Daniel at least had done so; and that the 1813 will was validated by the testimony of the witnesses to Clark's death, who explained its disappearance – and thereby invalidated the will of 1811 – as well as relating its contents.

> This court ... doth now here order, adjudge and decree ... that Myra Clark Gaines ... is the only legitimate child of Daniel Clark ... and that under and by virtue of the last will and testament of the said Daniel Clark, the said Myra Clark Gaines is ... entitled to all the estate, whether real or personal, of which he ... died possessed; subject only to the payment of certain legacies therein named.'[105]

Catron, Grier and Chief Justice Taney all dissented. For Catron the principal issue was now one of property rights. In a clear statement that ignored the many arcane issues raised by Wayne, he addressed the consequences of the majority opinion:

> This will [of 1811], from the time it was probated in 1813, stood as the true succession of Daniel Clark for more than forty years. An immense estate in lands and personal property has been acquired under it, by all classes of innocent purchasers, without any suspicion of the fact that other and better title existed. It is admitted ... that each purchaser who bought in 1820, and every subsequent purchase under the first one, bought for a full price, paid the purchase money, and got a regular conveyance for the land purchased....
>
> Daniel Clark was known and recognised in New Orleans as an unmarried man.... His father was then dead, and Mary Clark, his mother, recognised as his undoubted heir. He addressed and made propositions of marriage to ladies of his own rank after it is pretended he had married Madame Des Grange. Those who purchased in 1820, including judges of the highest rank residing in the spot, could not doubt the validity of Mary Clark's title and power to sell the lands they bought and paid for....
>
> The evidence shows ... the claim is grossly unjust. Clark's failure was very large: his estate was wholly insolvent. The purchasers have, in fact, paid his debts to a large amount. Many of them are yet unpaid. The purchasers have built houses and raised families on the property now sought to be recovered. A city has been built upon it. It has probably increased in value five hundred fold since 1820; much of it certainly has.[106]

---

and severe penances to the *san benito* and the *auto de fé*. Before that time the inquisition had exercised a capricious jurisdiction, both as to persons and to creeds. Encyclopaedia Britannica, 8 ed., 11th vol., artic. *Inqui*, page 386.

Four pages later he concluded that Hasset, the presbyter canon, had operated outside the law fifty-eight years earlier, and so none of the evidence relating to the Desgrange bigamy trial was admissible. '*Gaines v. Hennen*', in Stephen K. Williams (ed.), *Reports of Cases Argued and Decided in the Supreme Court of the United States*, XXIV, Newark 1884, p. 779. It is surely more reflective of the wilfulness of the court reporter than the merits of the legal opinion to hand that whilst all of Wayne's long opinions are set down scrupulously, in 1849 Howard wrote, 'The Reporter is compelled to omit the arguments of Mr Johnson and Mr Jones, the counsel for Gaines and wife, as their insertion would make the report of this case too long.' Stephen K. Williams (ed.), *Reports of Cases Argued and Decided in the Supreme Court of the United States*, XII, Newark 1883, p. 566.

105. Williams (ed.), *Reports of ... the Supreme Court*, XXIV, p. 779. Bellechasse was the witness who provided most detail of these 'certain legacies': $2,000 to Mary Clark; $500 a year to 'Caroline Desgrange' until she came of age, when she was to be paid $5,000; another $5,000 to the son of Judge Pitot; $5,000 to a son of Mr Du Buys; Lubin, his freedom.

106. Ibid., pp. 794–5.

Catron acidly observed that in fifteen years Myra's lawyers had never called upon Zulime to confirm her marriage to Clark and so the legitimacy of her daughter, and he pungently reasserted the main points of his opinion of 1852. The last word in this case, though, went to Mr Justice Grier, who struck a loser's note of despair much less prolix and somewhat less apocalyptic than Wayne's of a decade earlier:

> I wholly dissent from the opinion of the majority of the court in this case, both as to law and the facts. But I do not think it necessary to indicate my opinion by again presenting to the public view a history of scandalous gossip which has been buried under the dust of half a century, and which a proper feeling of delicacy should have suffered to remain so. I therefore dismiss the case, as I hope for the last time, with the single remark that if it be the law of Louisiana that a will can be established by the dim recollections, imaginations or inventions of anile gossips, after 45 years, to disturb the titles and possessions of *bona fide* purchasers, without notice, of an indefeasible title, '*Haud equidem invideo, miror magis.*'[107]

The property question was naturally of immense consequence, but it could not be practically engaged because, of course, within weeks of the ruling war broke out, Louisiana seceded from the Union and the matter remained purely academic for the better part of five years. (It little mattered that Louisiana, like the other states of the Confederacy, insisted that its secession would not prejudice civil cases in federal courts.) Moreover, the court had only ruled that Myra could recover her property; it had not determined what rents or damages she might claim. And the precise state of Daniel Clark's property fifty years after his death remained very unclear.

At the end of the eighteenth century Clark had bought – in addition to his sugar and cotton plantations – some marshy, uninhabited land on the edge of the town, the limits of which were then what is today known as the French Quarter. In the early nineteenth century this land was transformed into what is now the first eight blocks of Canal Street (from the River Mississippi to Dauphine Street), being settled by the new American citizens of the city and becoming the very residential heart of New Orleans. Even by 1836 some one hundred purchasers were affected by Myra's suit, the figure rising to well over 400 by the time of the 1861 hearing. At the end of that case it was widely reported and popularly believed that the property affected was worth $35 million and that Myra had collected $6 million.[108]

The population and economic activity of both Louisiana and New Orleans had evidently multiplied over the years. The settlement of less than 10,000 in 1796 had grown to 80,000 in 1812, just before Daniel died, and 700,000 (including 300,000 slaves) in 1860, as Myra was going to court. At that time New Orleans trade was worth $135 million a year.[109] Property values had increased correspondingly, but the estimates of that directly affected vary widely and are not based on primary documentation.

---

107. Ibid., p. 796. This might be translated today as, 'I am more astonished than I am annoyed.'
108. *Appleton's Cyclopaedia of American Biography*, New York 1888, p. 572.
109. Bennett Wall, Judith Kelle Schafer and Light Townsend Cummins, *Louisiana: A History*, 2nd edn, Arlington Heights, Ill., 1990, p. 139.

In the event, this was of secondary importance since Myra, once she had finally obtained ownership, refused to sell the houses, and thereby guaranteed the occupancy of the owners who had become tenants. In a famous meeting at which representatives of these families thanked her for this decision she is supposed to have responded:

> You have persecuted me for more than forty years as I hope no other human being has ever been persecuted, or ever will be. Four attempts have been made on my life, and I have suffered greatly in heart and mind. Yet notwithstanding all this, mercy now asserts itself in my soul, and I say to you, in this hour of triumph, that I freely forgive you. Return to your homes, and in due time, I will bring an appeal to the City of New Orleans to give you full and free claim to the property.[110]

The appeal was never made in Myra's lifetime, but mention of it indicates the importance of the case to the city corporation, ensuring that it continued to occupy the courts for many years to come.

This was primarily because Daniel Clark owned other land – some 144 acres bounding what are now Esplanade Avenue and Bayou St John – which Relf and Chew had sold for $4,760 in 1821 to Evariste Blanc, and which he, in turn, had sold to the city authorities for $25,000 in 1834. The city had converted a substantial part of the lot into sewerage and drainage works, and so became a direct litigant in the case (although it had also been represented in some of the private cases). The broad legal and moral victory won by Myra clearly stems from the 1861 hearing, but the issue of the Blanc Tract, as it was known, was not resolved then. Indeed, definitive adjudication over this property was not reached until 1890, on the basis of its value when last sold plus forty-six years' interest – a total of $566,707 – the only precise sum that hard public evidence shows to have been paid to Myra and her heirs. Indeed, in her last years it was upon the Blanc Tract that Myra's inheritance really rested.

As to Judge Catron's point about Daniel Clark's insolvency, there can be little doubt that in 1812–13 the British navy had dealt a severe blow to the Mississippi trade and Louisiana production. Clark evidently had some big debts. But he was also a creditor, not least, it will be recalled, of Relf and Chew, to the tune of $400,000. The 1811 inventory of his estates, liquid assets, town property and slaves exceeds $5 million in the prices of the day. One of the legal objections in the case of 1844 was that 133 slaves known to be owned by Clark were not properly accounted for in the inventory.[111] Without stronger evidence for his indebtedness the suggestion of bankruptcy is less persuasive than is one of a predictably poor performance by a large plantation enterprise under wartime conditions. Of course, the time that the case had

---

110. Gustavus Myers, *Great American Fortunes*, New York 1882, cited in Kendall, 'Strange Case', pp. 34–5. According to Kendall, this was written on the basis of Myra's own information. She never wrote her account, and herself only testified on one occasion in court for formal purposes.

111. Stephen K. Williams (ed.), *Reports of Cases Argued and Decided in the Supreme Court of the United States*, XI, Rochester, N.Y., 1901, p. 635.

spent in court makes all subsequent calculation of assets rather abstract, but it is likely that Myra's costs over forty years matched her receipts as well as depleting her inheritances from Whitney and Gaines.

Although her children and grandchildren settled in Brooklyn, once she had won her case Myra spent most of her time in New Orleans. She occupied none of the hundreds of houses that had been ruled as her legal property, and instead stayed as a lodger of a Mrs David at 150 Thalia Street. It was at that address that she died on 9 January 1885, attended by Dr W.H. Holcombe and her son-in-law J.Y. Christmas. One account has her buried in New York; another – as by her express wish to lie alongside her father – in the Clark vault in St Louis No. 1 Cemetery, where, it is said, no evidence of his remains was found when the tomb was opened.[112]

What is certain is that two days after her death a woman called Evans, who had been a friend of Myra's years before, offered for probate in the New Orleans Civil District Court what purported to be a holographic will executed by her on 8 January – one day before her death – and leaving a third of her estate to 'my excellent friend Juliet Perkins'. At the same time, another will – dated 3 January – was presented by Mr Christmas. This left all of her estate to her natural heirs.

On 21 February 1885 the court rejected the will presented by Evans, who was later charged with forgery and fled the country. The Blanc Tract case had yet to be settled, and even after it had been, it was not until 1894 that the heirs had resolved differences amongst themselves and distributed their legacies. By then electric street cars operated in the city centre, and Jelly Roll Morton, the father of jazz, was four years old. It was a hundred years since Zulime Carrière had married Jerome Desgrange – a peculiarly personal and meridional nineteenth century, but an almost exact one.

112. Kendall, 'Strange Case', p. 36; Harmon, *Famous Case*, p. 451.

POLITICAL ECONOMIES

EXPLANATIONS OF EMPIRE

Late in July 1845, George Hamilton-Gordon, the fourth Earl of Aberdeen, four years into his second spell as foreign secretary, received a letter from Robert Falk, a Liverpool merchant. The missive told the kind of story and made the type of claim with which Aberdeen was familiar. It recounted a tale of misadventure in enterprise that obliged the Foreign Office – like any ministry of foreign affairs – to investigate and verify the complaint, and, if necessary, act upon it. Although it is hard to argue that the experience of the *Hibernia* was in any way representative, it is suggestive enough to be followed at a little length.

After the obligatory opening niceties of addressing a member of the nobility and senior member of the government, Falk starts his account:

> About two years ago, the British brigantine *Hibernia*, of Liverpool, belonging to one of our first Liverpool merchants, James Dempsey Esq., and myself, was sent from this on a trading and fishery voyage to the Pacific Ocean, under the superintendence of a son of Mr Dempsey, Henry Dermott Dempsey, as supercargo, being fitted out in a very superior manner, and furnished with the new patent diving apparatus, so much used now in this country by Government for submarine works. She was employed all last year in pearl-fishing and trading upon the western coast of South America, and when at Lima in November last, the super-cargo, Henry D. Dempsey, hearing of the loss of a vessel with a large quantity of treasure on board near the Lobos Islands, close to Lambayeque in Peru, he made for that part of the coast, thinking that as his diving apparatus was the only one in South America, he would earn an excellent salvage previous to returning to Europe with a cargo of saltpetre, which he had been ordered to buy for owners' account in that neighbourhood.
>
> The lost vessel being already entirely broken up, nothing but some chains were recovered by the *Hibernia*, after a fruitless and arduous attempt of several weeks. The vessel then returned to Lambayeque and it will be necessary to state that during her attempt to rescue the treasure from a depth of thirty yards under water, she had on board not only a Custom-House officer and the owners of the lost treasure, but also a Customs licence.
>
> The vessel no sooner entered the Port of Lambayeque than the supercargo … and the crew were placed under arrest by the Captain of the Port, an embargo laid on the vessel, under some spurious pretence of violation of regulations; and the vessel subsequently con-demned by the Customs, they having allowed the same to run full of water. They not only seized the ship's papers, but actually took away the sails and inventory, depriving her of everything.
>
> Against this arbitrary and indefensible proceeding the supercargo appealed to the Courts of Lambayeque, which reversed the sentence. The other parties, not satisfied with this, took the matter to Truxillo, where they gained their point; and the supercargo then thought it his duty to go the Supreme Court of Peru, at Lima, where, after paying fees and law expenses to the amount of several hundred pounds sterling, the proceedings were smashed, the Court advising a new investigation, which is now proceeding.
>
> In the meantime, the vessel, if returned, will be perfectly useless to me; and I trust that Her Majesty's Government will see the necessity of protecting the commerce of this country, in distant parts, by compelling the Peruvian government not only to disavow the scandalous proceedings of their officer, but also to make immediate restoration of the value of the property they have robbed me of:

- the value of the brigantine *Hibernia* (a coppered vessel, only three years old, with her outfit, interest and expenses, up till today) is £2,800;
- to which have to be added the law expenses incurred till now, and the supercargo's passage home: £200;
- and the freight she would have made upon the cargo of saltpetre to Liverpool, which the supercargo had orders to buy, and which would have come to an excellent market: £2,000.
  Making together: £5,000.

I trust that Her Majesty's Government will, by the next West Indies mail, instruct the Admiral commanding the squadron, Her Majesty's ships in the Pacific, to repair to Lima, to demand repayment of the above sum from the Peruvian government, and such other damages as the unjustifiable arrest of a British vessel call for, and if not complied with immediately, take such steps as will enforce its payment.

It might be thought that Mr Falk, having attributed all blame to the Peruvians, calculated his own losses in the most generous manner, and indicated the level of punitive sanction he considered appropriate, would rest content. Yet whilst Aberdeen had overseen the annexation of Hong Kong, authorised the Second Afghan War, and presided over the colonisation of the Natal and Gambia, he was not Lord Palmerston. Perhaps the merchant knew that the foreign secretary was inclined to caution, and Falk seems to have feared that Aberdeen might not discharge his obvious imperialist duty, and so added two final paragraphs to his letter:

I may mention that the Commander of a United States man-of-war being at Lambayeque when this transaction took place, and knowing the whole of the circumstances from personal investigation, stated that if such an insult had been offered to any vessel belonging to his flag he would have immediately used main force in settling the question.

Mr Dempsey as well as myself are known personally to several members of your Lordship's house, as well as to many honourable members of the other House of Parliament, which may be a guarantee to your Lordship that we would not state but what will bear the strictest investigation.[1]

Inside a week a copy of this letter had been sent to William Pitt Adams, the British ambassador in Peru, together with a request for precisely the type of investigation Falk reckoned his case could withstand. In October he himself wrote again to the Foreign Office with the information that the Supreme Court of Peru had exonerated the supercargo, but he continued to urge his case even as he tacitly recognised the need to reduce the size of the claim:

Through this illegal detention, the whole of the objects of the voyage have been frustrated. An otherwise profitable voyage has been changed into an exceedingly disastrous one, and even if the damages I claim, say 3,000 pounds, are paid to me, I shall be a considerable loser.[2]

Falk's eventual losses threatened to be greater still because young Dempsey had himself applied to the ambassador for help in February, when he was arrested, and Mr

---

1. Falk, Liverpool, to Aberdeen, 22 July 1845, in *BFSP, 1846–47*, XXXV, London 1860, pp. 1280–81.
2. Falk, Liverpool, to Viscount Canning, 6 Oct. 1845, in ibid., p. 1283.

Adams began immediately to make inquiries. Rear-Admiral Sir George Seymour on HMS *Collingwood* at Callao – commanding the very squadron Falk wanted ordered into action – was forwarded by his US counterpart a report from Lieutenant Hewison of USS *Shark* (stationed in Lambayeque). This report did not tally at all with the sentiments attributed to him by Falk and cast doubt on the propriety of the activities of Dempsey, whom Hewison described as a mate who had taken over when the captain of the *Hibernia* died off Panama. A month later Adams received another account from Captain Thomas Baillie of HMS *Modeste* (at sea), who had been at the port shortly after Dempsey's detention and had successfully requested Sub-Prefect Juan de Díos Díaz to speed up his trial, explaining that this had been delayed by the need to have the ship's logbook translated in order to verify its exact movements. Also amongst the sixteen documents enclosed with the final report sent in December 1845 by Adams to Aberdeen was a letter of that June from the Peruvian Ministry of Foreign Affairs confirming that the original sentence of confiscation of the *Hibernia* had been overthrown on appeal, and another from British Vice-Consul Barton in Callao – the port for Lima – informing the ambassador that Dempsey had sold the *Hibernia* in September and that her register had been returned to Liverpool.

Adams's report duly reached London on 10 February 1846:

> The British brigantine *Hibernia*, under control of the supercargo, Mr H. Dempsey, a son of the owner, sailed from Callao on the 14th of November, 1844, with a regular clearance for the port of Lambayeque; but instead of going direct to the port, she went to the Lobos Islands in search of treasure from a wreck, without having obtained the permission either of the Custom House or the owners of the treasure, such proceeding being contrary to the law. She remained at those islands from 19th of November 'till the 10th of January, 1845, when she went to Lambayeque; but in order to prevent the transaction from being known, the date of the sailing licence from Callao was fraudulently altered. She then obtained a licence to go to the Lobos … and this second voyage is correctly described in Mr Falk's letter to your Lordship of 22nd of July, as being undertaken under a proper licence….
>
> On the second arrival of the *Hibernia* at Lambayeque, her first voyage had become officially known, as well as the alteration of the Callao clearance; the vessel was therefore seized by the authorities, and Mr Dempsey detained on shore. Mr Falk's letter states correctly that the sails were taken on shore; but he omits to add that this was done in consequence of an attempt of the master to get the vessel under weigh and escape; in proof of which I have the honour to refer to the dispositions of two seamen taken before Mr Vice-Consul Barton. It is equally true that the vessel was allowed to run full of water, but Mr Falk has failed to inform your Lordship that the leak was first discovered immediately after a visit paid to the vessel by the master, supercargo, and carpenter, and that, upon pumping her out, two auger-holes were found in her bottom, for which the carpenter was sent a prisoner to Callao, and is now on bail awaiting his trial on a charge of scuttling the vessel. In this state she was saved from sinking by the United States' schooner of war *Shark*.[3]

In fact, it was Hewison who, with the agreement of the Captain of the Port of Lambayeque, took Bernard Hood, the carpenter, to be detained in Callao. Small wonder, then, that nearly a year after making his original claim, Falk received a

---

3. Adams, Lima, to Aberdeen, 3 Dec. 1845, in ibid., pp. 1284–5.

distinctly cool response from Under-Secretary Henry Addington: 'The forms of law may have produced some unnecessary, though not unusual delay, in bringing the case to a conclusion; but neither in form nor in substance has there been sufficient cause for a remonstrance to the Peruvian Government.'[4]

No doubt Henry Dempsey had some explaining to do to his father and his partner upon return to Liverpool (or maybe they already had his measure and were just chancing their luck). But what strikes one most about this case is less the bravado of a wealthy young man abroad than the comportment of the states of Peru, Great Britain and the USA. Whilst the latter two powers possessed an impressive military presence and political authority in Peruvian waters and territory, the former did not desist from arresting a British subject, and although the court cases had clearly involved some exchange of money, the British authorities accepted their procedures and findings. On the one hand, it could be argued that this case illustrates the extraordinary power of the British and US on the Pacific coast of South America in the 1840s. On the other, it could be used to demonstrate the restraint of that power, recognition of local sovereignty, and a reluctance by the Anglo-Saxon state to back its entrepreneurs abroad under all circumstances.

This latter position would surely have been upheld by D.C.M. Platt, a British historian who from the 1960s dedicated much energy to the argument that in the mid nineteenth century

> the range of government action on behalf of overseas trade permitted by the *laissez faire* tradition of the time was extraordinarily narrow; official demands on behalf of British interests overseas never went beyond equal favour and open competition; non-intervention in the internal affairs of foreign states was one of the most respected principles of British diplomacy; and force, while often called for in the protection of British subjects injured by government action abroad, was rarely and only exceptionally employed for the promotion of British trade and investments.[5]

Moreover, the *Hibernia* case appears to bear out Platt's insistence that, 'if there was one principle that was axiomatic in Her Majesty's Government's treatment of claims, it was that justice must first be sought and denied before the local tribunals'.[6] However, Platt's views on the British use of force and respect for local form were less controversial than his argument that British investment abroad was, until at least 1860, very risky, inconsistently profitable and far less powerful and exploitative than the prevailing literature suggested. For Platt, the son of a senior executive of Shell, the fashionable *marxisant* assumptions about 'imperialism' had greatly underestimated the degree of uncertainty and competition affecting capitalist enterprise before the 1880s,

---

4. Addington, London, to Falk, 27 June 1846, in ibid., p. 1301.
5. 'The Imperialism of Free Trade: Some Reservations', *The Economic History Review*, XXI:2, 1968, p. 297.
6. 'British Diplomacy in Latin America since Emancipation', *Inter-American Economic Affairs*, 21:3, 1967, p. 31.

especially outside the British Isles; and unlike many of his critics, he insistently placed entrepreneurs and investors in their domestic context:

> Trade to a market at the end of the world, in days before regular steam services and the telegraph, was no place for the amateur. 'Panics' of alarming proportions convulsed the British money market in 1825, 1837, 1847, 1857 and 1866, and a host of minor, more localized crises intervened. The whole period was distinguished not by steady pressure for overseas trade outlets and for opportunities for investment, but by a series of short booms followed by disastrous slumps and by long 'slow' periods, in which confidence was shattered and commercial men, banks, and investors looked out for any safe, unadventurous employment for their capital.... It took a substantial return to tempt a careful man into a new and distant overseas market, 5 and a half to 7 and a half per cent in addition to the standard 4 per cent per annum which the capital would have earned on the market without individual exertion. High freights and insurance premiums, unfamiliar markets, political disturbances, uncertain communications, fluctuation of currencies, scarce and erratic remittances put a premium on size, reserves and experience.[7]

In making this case, Platt was responding to a highly influential article written some twenty years before by two Cambridge academics, John Gallagher and Ronald Robinson, specialists in Asia and Africa, who had argued that 'the usual summing up of the policy of the free trade empire as "trade, not rule" should read "trade with informal control if possible; trade with rule where necessary"'.[8] For Gallagher and Robinson, the idea of an 'informal empire' made sense of the entire Victorian period, which had long been presented in both liberal and Marxist literature as comprising an early free trade, non-colonialist phase and a later, annexationist and openly imperialist cycle, starting from around 1870. Some years before Platt, Oliver MacDonagh argued persuasively that Gallagher and Robinson had overreacted to a narrowly politico-constitutional construction of imperialism and thereby attributed too great an 'imperialist' quality to free trade, the most powerful advocates of which, Richard Cobden and John Bright,

> were both anti-imperialist, whatever the form of empire, and quick to discover and denounce all forms of informality. They hunted down confusions of 'free trade' with mere increases of commerce or with the favourable 'opening up' of markets; and they predicted with no little accuracy the consequences of casual interventions.[9]

Platt accepted but made scant reference to the ideological issue pressed by MacDonagh. What riled him most were the assumptions in the theory of informal empire that had, by the early 1970s, been adopted by a new generation of academics subscribing to what was being termed 'dependency theory'. Indeed, when Christopher Platt inveighed against Gallagher and Robinson for assuming the readiness of London to uphold British paramountcy by whatever means, or the expansionist 'logic'

---

7. 'Further Objections to an "Imperialism of Free Trade", 1830–60', *The Economic History Review*, XXV:1, 1973, pp. 85–6.
8. 'The Imperialism of Free Trade', *The Economic History Review*, VI:1, 1953, p. 5.
9. 'The Anti-Imperialism of Free Trade', *The Economic History Review*, XV:3, 1962, p. 500.

of British merchants, or the subordination of primary producers to Albion's 'workshop of the world', his comments were seen as far more applicable to André Gunder Frank's *Capitalism and Underdevelopment in Latin America*, written in 1965. This text had exerted great influence outside the academy with its clear, radical argument that the British had won key sectors of the Latin American elite to free trade ideology, captured almost all of the surplus from the export sector, greatly restricted the opportunities for the internal development of Latin America by displacing local entrepreneurs, and intervened by force when opposed. For Frank,

> Trade and the sword were readying Latin America for metropolitan free trade by eliminating the competition of Latin American industrial development; and, with the victory of outward-oriented economic interest groups over the inward-oriented ones, ever more of the Latin American economy and state as well had to be subordinated to the metropolis.[10]

Platt rejected this interpretation as resting on 'the absurdities in attributing a modern neo-colonial relationship ... to a period and to trades where primary products were not, as yet, in demand' and when British trade with Latin America was very modest.[11] For him the argument was based not only upon anachronistic inductive reasoning but also upon disreputable scholarship, Frank's historical sources being entirely secondary and what seemed to Platt to be a shabby confection of nationalists conjuring up a creation myth and Marxists endeavouring to fit the non-colonial experience of nineteenth-century Latin America into Lenin's catch-all categories.

Platt's insistence upon the complex internal reality of Latin America was an important corrective to the tendency to assume an almost automatic application of external power. But it was not a reality that he himself had either much interest in or capacity for exploring. In the 400 pages of text – one book and six articles – that he wrote on this subject over the decade to 1977 he referred to just two Spanish-language sources on twelve occasions amongst more than 1,200 citations to British official, company and travel literature.[12] At the very least this meant that he did not properly test one of the main theses of the dependency school – that the economies of Latin America remained hamstrung by residues of the colonial system until well after independence. It also explains why Platt and the more doctrinaire *dependista* analysts, such as Gunder Frank, share a firmly externally oriented focus; they simply disagreed about the reach and efficacy of foreign capital. For Platt, Latin America only started to develop when improvements in its transport systems allowed European demand for primary goods to have a real impact upon production.

---

10. *Capitalism and Underdevelopment in Latin America*, Harmondsworth 1971, pp. 315–16.

11. 'Further Objections', p. 84. Gunder Frank opened and closed his text with admirable candour:

> I believe ... that it is capitalism, both world and national, which produced underdevelopment in the past and still generates underdevelopment in the present ... the only way out of Latin American underdevelopment is armed revolution leading to socialist development.

12. The two sources are Academia Nacional de Historia, *Historia Argentina Contemporánea, 1862–1930*, Buenos Aires 1966, and David Cosío Villegas (ed.), *Historia Moderna de México*, Mexico 1965.

In 1980 Platt turned his attention to a direct – and ill-tempered – critique of dependency theory itself. This might have come earlier but he had been seriously ill in the mid 1970s, giving the polemic a rather old-fashioned feel, not least because one of his targets was *Dependency and Development in Latin America* by Fernando Henrique Cardoso and Enzo Faletto, written in Santiago in 1965–67 but not translated into English until 1979. Cardoso and Faletto's book was methodologically more nuanced than Gunder Frank's work, and although its nineteenth-century sections relied exclusively on the historical analysis of a single author – Tulio Halperín Donghi – they explicitly allowed for variation within the Latin American experience according to both region/state and time. The worst generalisation that Platt could hang on them was the observation that 'the predominance of the linkage with the peninsular metropoli – Spain and Portugal – during the colonial period, the dependency later on England, and lastly on the USA is of transcendent importance'.[13]

In fact, Cardoso had already himself complained vehemently at the distortion and mythologisation of 'dependency theory' – a unifying term he disliked – particularly in the USA, where

> there was a preoccupation with the denunciation of forms of 'foreign aid' – the intervention of the CIA in foreign policy, the invisible and Machiavellian hand of the multinationals, etc. – a politically legitimate preoccupation that emphasized real aspects of the contemporary historical process. Little by little, however, this ended by re-establishing the priority of the *external* over the internal (which may be well-founded), and it led in the end to the elimination of the dynamic proper to dependent societies as a relevant explanatory factor (which is not acceptable).[14]

At the same time as Cardoso protested at the failure to take Latin America seriously in its own terms, his main historical source, Halperín Donghi, expressed exasperation at 'ever more frequent use of categories of analysis taken from Marxism with total indifference towards the historical framework for which they were developed'.[15] In short, the attempt to provide a strategic understanding of the economic history of Latin America was being parodied and politicised not only by conservatives like Platt but also by those on the left, especially in North America.

Of course, academics have ever been prone to protest when their sophisticated theories and diligent analysis are distorted by wrong-headed emulation and enthusiastic sloganisation; it is almost worse than the use of parody for criticism. But in the present case the embracing of dependency theory (of any type) in the USA was particularly

---

13. 'Dependencia y desarrollo en América Latina', in José Matos Mar (ed.), *La Dominación de América Latina*, Buenos Aires 1968, p. 163, quoted in D.C.M. Platt, 'Dependency in Nineteenth-Century Latin America', *LARR*, XV:1, 1980, p. 114.

14. 'The Consumption of Dependency Theory in the United States', *LARR*, XII:3, 1977, p. 14. This essay makes no mention of Platt's work.

15. '"Dependency Theory" and Latin American Historiography', *LARR*, XVII:1, 1982, p. 121. Cardoso and Faletto acknowledged that 'almost all the information in this chapter [on the nineteenth century] is based on the excellent book by Tulio Halperín Donghi, *Historia Contemporánea de América Latina*'. *Dependency and Development in Latin America*, Berkeley 1979, p. 30.

understandable since it provided a clear and direct critique of 'modernisation theory', a much more openly ideological and prescriptive form of liberal analysis than that upheld by Platt, the reclusive Oxford professor. That approach is best exemplified by W.W. Rostow's 1960 text *The Stages of Economic Growth: A Non-Communist Manifesto*, which postulated a model of 'development' based on five distinct stages of growth established by historical experience since Britain's 'take-off' in 1783–1802 (and that of the USA in 1830–50). Rostow regarded 'the process of development now going on in Asia, the Middle East, Africa and Latin America as analogous to the stages of pre-conditions and take-off of other societies, in the late eighteenth, nineteenth, and early twentieth centuries'.[16] Although the Rostovian prospectus had these backward regions playing a role in their own 'modernisation', it had little truck with the notion that the more advanced economies had previously played any part in impeding such development. Its prescriptions rested equally on a repudiation of the Soviet model, a celebration of the record of liberal capitalism and a recognition of natural 'resource endowments', which were also at the heart of Platt's explanation as to why at the end of the nineteenth century Latin America was so different from Anglo-America:

> The obstacles to autonomous industrial growth were formidable. Latin America lacked skilled labor; skilled labor could be imported, but only at uncompetitively high rates. Latin America suffered from an endemic shortage of industrial fuels: oil was not extracted until the end of the nineteenth century; wood was in short supply; coal (which was scarce in workable quantities) was imported at prices that, inclusive of transport, rose to as much as four times its cost at the Welsh pithead. Domestic markets were small and scattered, too small for mass production; railways (after the 1860s) gradually opened markets of sufficient size to absorb local production of consumer goods, but demand was never enough to support the manufacture of capital goods. Exploitable raw materials were in short supply, iron in particular. Capital was scarce, if not for small plants at least for large-scale industry. In regions of relatively sparse population, like Argentina and Chile, there were absolute shortages of labor, skilled or unskilled, which permanently restricted opportunities for industrial development. With handicaps such as these, domestic manufacturing was slow to develop in Latin America with or without the machinations of the metropolis.[17]

There is some irony in the fact that, responding to this almost naturalistic *tour de force*, Stanley and Barbara Stein, who were Platt's main targets, score their most telling points less by facing down his scorn for their theoretical ambitions than by showing how his numbers were open to question, undervaluing the extent of British trade with Latin America as well as the importance of mining and the export of precious metals.[18] The natural obstacles remained formidable, but both internal and external commerce mattered and promised much more than Platt's vision could allow. Correspondingly, it would be misguided to view the Iberian portion of the continent during the nineteenth century as condemned to backwardness by both nature and its

---

16. *The Stages of Economic Growth: A Non-Communist Manifesto*, Cambridge 1960, p. 139.
17. Platt, 'Dependency in Nineteenth-Century Latin America', p. 123.
18. Stanley J. and Barbara H. Stein, 'Dependency in Nineteenth-Century Latin America: Comment', *LARR*, XV:1, 1980; *The Colonial Heritage of Latin America: Essays on Economic Dependency in Perspective*, New York 1970.

culture, seeing it as much an economic failure as the USA was an industrial success. Although by 1900 it was possible unreservedly to celebrate the latter, this was still quite a recent phenomenon, and the culture of 'exceptionalism' made it hard simply to instruct other parts of the world to follow the North American example, shining though that was. For much of the nineteenth century the US economy had been in debt, and it manifestly had become an industrial power on the basis of both internally and externally led growth.[19]

Half a century earlier, in 1850, more still lay in the balance, even if we remain agnostic about the singularity of the North American experience and the character and causes of that undergone in the central and southern parts of the continent. For Christopher Platt, Latin America was at least ten years (and maybe thirty) away from fulfilling the conditions for 'take-off'. For Cardoso and Faletto, though, this was the point of recovery from both the wars of independence and the most onerous legacies of the colony:

> In the years following 1850, almost all the Latin American countries entered a period of greater prosperity. The economic order at the international level was better organised around the metropolitan powers. Trade, which until that time had been relatively small in volume, began to grow. The gold rush in California and a little later in Australia not only increased trade but also gave rise to waves of migration that affected the American countries ... the importation of consumer goods, principally textiles, on which Latin America had depended until 1850 and which often has adverse effects on the balance of payments, became less important.[20]

TRADE

At the start of an article on why Mexico did not fulfil what was arguably its economic potential in the nineteenth century, John Coatsworth makes a pithy observation:

> all the numbers in this article are, without exception, inaccurate; however, that is not a valid argument against their use. Literary estimates typically contain fewer errors (we all know that Mexico was 'poorer' than its northern neighbor), but only because they use a ridiculously wide range of values.[21]

---

19. Douglass C. North, *The Economic Growth of the United States, 1790–1860*, New York 1966, p. 81; Stanley Lebergott, *The Americans: An Economic Record*, New York 1984, p. 64.

20. *Dependency and Development in Latin America*, pp. 54–5. Platt seems to have backdated the phase of profitability of British capital in Latin America from 1880 to 1860 between his articles of 1968 and 1973 for *The Economic History Review*. In 1980 he settled on 1870 as the point of change, but less because of evolving conditions in Latin America than because of the reduced opportunities for investment in the domestic railway industry. 'British Portfolio Investment Overseas before 1870: Some Doubts', *The Economic History Review*, XXXIII:1, 1980, pp. 4, 8.

21. 'Obstacles to Economic Growth in Nineteenth-Century Mexico', *AHR*, 83, 1978, p. 80. Not quite

The particular pertinence of this warning for Latin America at that time is re-inforced by the candid confession of President Tomás Mosquera when presenting the budget to the Colombian Congress in March 1846:

> I have no reliance in the exactness of these accounts, because so far from there having been any improvement in the method of keeping accounts in the National Exchequer, it has become complicated by several partial reforms. The credit and debit sides of the year do not agree; and the numerous indirect expenses authorised by the laws in the department of the home debt [have meant] that instead of specie, cancelled Government bonds have been paid in.[22]

Even in the case of Britain – by far the most advanced commercial power in the world – we depend heavily upon the guidance and 'guestimates' of experts on trade figures since many goods are poorly measured by volume, and between 1789 and 1854 it was the declared rather than current value of goods traded abroad that was recorded. Moreover, until 1859 British records did not include the importation of precious metals, thereby seriously underrepresenting the trade of Mexico, Peru and Chile – a point on which the Steins were right to correct Platt.[23] Equally, almost all of the measuring undertaken by state and business in the mid nineteenth century was of goods and money; people were occasionally counted for non-fiscal reasons, but the censuses were only held with regularity in the USA, and everywhere they confronted huge logistical problems. Brazil's first national census was held in 1872; in Peru there was no full head-count between 1791 and 1876. In regimented Paraguay just one was undertaken between 1785 and 1872, the new dictator Carlos Antonio López ordering a national census in 1845. By 1847 20,000 pages of information had been amassed, but these contained very different definitions of age, race and community status – sometimes gender was entirely omitted – by the parish priests charged with the tally.[24] Sometimes it paid to count heads accurately – for instance, slaves in the Southern USA, where the size of the (non-voting) slave population affected the number of representatives in Congress – or to distinguish finely between types of person – for example, between foundational (originario) and additional (forastero) members of Andean communities for the purposes of tribute payment. Both the state and civil society also had a high interest in the surveying of land, which was occasionally taxed, often granted to individuals, frequently sold between them, and sometimes withheld from the market by indigenous and religious communities. Throughout the continent the practice of granting lands for colonisation or payment of military service was rarely accompanied by surveys, and cadastral information was usually slight and in-

---

the same, then, as Dr Johnson: 'That, sir, is the good of counting. It brings everything to a certainty, which floated before in the mind indefinitely.'

22. Message to Constitutional Congress, 1 March 1846, *BFSP, 1846–47*, XXXV, p. 712.

23. Rory Miller, *Britain and Latin America in the Nineteenth and Twentieth Centuries*, London 1993, pp. 72–3.

24. John Hoyt Williams, 'Observations on the Paraguayan Census of 1846', *HAHR*, 56:3, 1976, pp. 424–5.

secure. In the USA the federal policy of granting lands at a fixed price – $1.25 an acre after 1820, with a minimum of eighty acres to be bought – had the effect of removing the factor of quality from the equation, but even where such matters were dutifully measured, recorded, reported and filed, secure tenure on and of the ground was hardly guaranteed.[25] And, as Warren Dean shows for Brazil, the paperwork could always be adjusted to tally with the fluid state of play in the world outside:

> It was not difficult for private individuals to cover their encroachments with an appearance of legality. Until the general registry was closed or given up, sometime between 1857 and 1862, depending on the locality, a simple false statement of occuption prior to 1850 could be added to the parish ledger. In this fashion, for example, José Teodoro de Souza, emigrating from Minas Gerais to São Paulo in 1856, staked out five posses [squatted holdings] in the region of Campos Novos de Paranapanema containing 800 square leagues (13,360 square miles) with the help of a fellow migrant who was the political boss of Botucatu. Even after the closing of the registry, new pages might still be sewn into the ledgers, or blank spaces might be discovered. Ledgers get lost or accidentally ruined. In a yet simpler subterfuge, a statement could be made to a notary that one was buying a posse belonging to a squatter who had resided on the claim before 1850. The squatter might be a confederate or wholly fictitious. Since few of the legitimate holdings were properly validated, sales such as these were not especially remarkable.[26]

The example of Brazil might be exaggerated, but it is not exceptional. Even in Chile, particularly well ordered then as now, those with farms in the central valley who could not afford legal fees were most vulnerable to claims on their land, whereas for those with sufficient social standing to seek a mortgage,

> the landowner's word or his signature in the company's books was usually the only guarantee required – or rather it was, however inadequate, the best security a lender could get.... A credit system based on verbal pledge depended upon public reputation and mutual faith.... There is no way to determine the total amount of credit extended during these years as most of it was not recorded in the public records.[27]

In effect, if the case of Daniel Clark's will was exceptional, it is only because there is some record of its loss and, like Dickens's case of Jarndyce and Jarndyce, it occasioned disputation of unusual length (unlike that required to sort out Harry Dempsey's antics). And, of course, it was not just the fortunes of individuals that were at stake; entire communities and cultures existed in a world of parallax between precise, recorded measurement and open, often oral, approximation. As has been suggested, the latter realm was not necessarily more tenuous and malleable than the former, even if present-day sensibilities urge that conclusion. The measured world lived in only partial distinction to that which was untouched by what Carlyle dubbed 'the dismal science'; and we do not have to subscribe to all claims made by that

---

25. Lebergott, *The Americans*, pp. 79–80; Malcolm Deas, 'The Fiscal Problems of Nineteenth-Century Colombia', *JLAS*, 14:2, 1982, p. 300.

26. 'Latifundia and Land Policy in Nineteenth-Century Brazil', *HAHR*, 51:3, 1971, p. 622.

27. Arnold J. Bauer, *Chilean Rural Society from the Spanish Conquest to 1930*, Cambridge 1975, p. 88. Mario Góngora and Jean Borde, *Evolución de la propriedad rural en el valle de Puangue*, Santiago 1956.

TABLE I American countries/colonies: population and exports, 1850 and 1870

Country		Exports ($1,000)	Population (thousand)	Exports per capita ($)
Argentina	1850	11,310	1,100	10.3
	1870	29,667	1,793	16.5
Bolivia	1850	7,500	1,374	5.5
	1870	12,916	1,495	8.6
Brazil	1850	35,850	7,230	5.0
	1870	83,880	9,808	8.5
Central America	1850	5,874	1,818	3.2
	1870	11,270	2,312	4.9
Chile	1850	11,308	1,443	7.8
	1870	27,625	1,943	14.3
Colombia	1850	4,133	2,200	1.9
	1870	18,600	2,819	6.6
Cuba	1850	26,333	1,186	22.2
	1870	67,000	1,459	45.9
Dominican Republic	1850	500	146	3.4
	1870	1,200	242	5.0
Ecuador	1850	1,594	816	2.0
	1870	4,133	1,013	4.1
Haiti	1850	4,499	938	4.8
	1870	7,425	1,150	6.5
Mexico	1850	24,313	7,662	3.2
	1870	21,276	9,100	2.3
Paraguay	1850	451	350	1.3
	1870	1,582	221	7.2
Peru	1850	7,500	2,001	3.7
	1870	25,834	2,568	10.1
Puerto Rico	1850	6,204	495	12.5
	1870	6,421	667	9.6
Uruguay	1850	7,250	132	54.9
	1870	13,333	286	46.6
Venezuela	1850	4,865	1,490	3.3
	1870	11,961	1,752	6.8
Latin America	1850	159,484	30,381	5.2
	1870	344,123	38,628	8.9
Canada	1850	16,325	2,546	6.4
	1870	77,132	3,790	20.4
USA	1850	162,000	23,192	7.0
	1870	400,000	39,818	10.0

Source: Derived from Victor Bulmer-Thomas, *Economic History of Latin America*, Cambridge 1994, pp. 38, 432–3. (Exports are three-year averages.)

science, even in Britain, because Carlyle was right in declaring that 'cash payment is not the sole nexus of man to man'.[28]

Table 1 provides a limited but useful snapshot of the population and exports of the American continent in the third quarter of the nineteenth century – the first period for which it is possible to assemble a set of partially reliable figures. (Since exports were not significantly taxed, these figures are less prone to distortions caused by under-reporting and contraband than were imports.) While no single country in Latin America comes close to matching the size and performance of the USA, taken as a whole, the two sections of the continent stood closer on these terms in 1850 than they ever would subsequently.

It is now generally accepted that by 1850 cotton was no longer the strategic staple export for US economic development. None the less, cotton exports were still very important beyond the states of the slave-based plantations of the South, which had Great Britain as their main market. In 1845 cotton accounted for half of all US exports; in 1855 it represented some 30 per cent.[29] In the 1840s two-thirds of the US cotton crop was being sold to the United Kingdom, which drew three-quarters of its imports of raw cotton from the United States between 1845 and 1855; the level of dependence was high on both sides. As can be seen from table 2, in 1855 the USA was selling goods worth over £30 million to Britain, more than double the level of a decade earlier. Latin American exports had increased by nearly the same proportion, but by 1855 they were only a third of the US level and accounted for less than 7 per cent of British imports. However, the extent of British exports to Latin America lends some weight to the dependency thesis since although Britain was formally selling rather less to the subcontinent than it was buying from it, this figure was itself some 10 per cent of total British exports. Moreover, it does not include re-exports from London's colonies in the West Indies as well as from Cuba, which would have made it appreciably higher. Indeed, allowing fully for this, the Steins reckon that during the 1840s British exports to Latin America and the foreign Caribbean very nearly matched those to the USA.[30]

On the other hand, table 2 shows clearly that commerce between Latin America and the USA was extremely modest up to the Civil War, effectively being confined to Brazil and Cuba (Spain). Given that in 1855 the dollar exchanged at five to one pound sterling, it can be seen that the absolute value of commerce between the

---

28. 'Gospel of Mammonism' (1850), in Alan Shelston (ed.), *Thomas Carlyle: Selected Writings*, Harmondsworth 1971, p. 277.

> Counting the house was a habit of mine. The question of how many people were present in a particular place seemed important to me, perhaps because the recurring news of airline disasters and military engagements always stressed the number of dead and missing; such exactness is a trickle of electricity to the numbed brain.

Don De Lillo, *Americana*, London 1990, p. 4.

29. North, *Economic Growth of the United States*, p. 233.

30. 'Dependency in Nineteenth-Century Latin America: Comment', p. 144. For a later, judicious assessment of the volume and value of south Atlantic trade, see Miller, *Britain and Latin America*, pp. 70ff.

TABLE 2 British and US trade in the Americas

(i)		BRITISH TRADE *(annual average; £1,000, excl. formal re-exports)*			
		1824/26	1834/36	1844/46	1854/56
Canada	import	3,801	3,320	5,449	5,740
	export	1,675	2,132	4,280	4,326
USA	import	6,061	13,223	14,058	30,282
	export	5,695	9,438	7,162	20,078
West Indies	import	8,577	7,946	5,937	8,709
	export	4,123	4,117	3,866	3,947
Latin America	import	3,109	3,380	4,905	9,698
	export	5,009	5,047	5,634	8,940

(ii)		US TRADE, 1830–1900 *($ million)*							
		1830	1840	1850	1860	1870	1880	1890	1900
Canada	export	3	6	10	23	25	29	40	106
	import	–	1	5	24	36	33	39	39
Cuba	export	5	6	5	12	14	11	13	26
	import	5	9	10	32	54	65	54	31
Mexico	export	5	3	2	5	6	8	13	36
	import	1	1	1	2	3	7	23	29
Brazil	export	2	2	3	6	6	9	12	12
	import	2	5	9	21	25	55	59	58
Total	export	72	124	144	334	471	836	858	1,394
	import	63	98	174	354	436	668	789	850

Sources: B.R. Mitchell, *British Historical Statistics*, London 1988, p. 497; US Department of Commerce, *Historical Statistics of The United States*, II, Washington 1975, pp. 904–6.

northern and southern parts of the continent was only a fraction of that across the Atlantic. In this respect at least, then, there was a genuine gap between the US practice and ideology of commercialism wryly observed by Dickens:

> ... all kinds of deficient and impolitic usages are referred to the national love of trade; though, oddly enough, it would be a weighty charge against a foreigner that he regarded the Americans as a trading people ... the love of trade is assigned as a reason for that comfortless custom of ... married people persons living in hotels ... the love of trade is a reason why the literature is to remain unprotected. 'For we are a trading people, and don't care for poetry.'[31]

---

31. *American Notes for General Circulation* (1842), Harmondsworth 1985, p. 287. The comment on literature was provoked by the widespread pirating of Dickens's own books.

TABLE 3 British trade with Latin America, 1850–60 (£1,000, annual average)

Country	Exports	Imports
Argentina	900	1,285
Bolivia	–	57
Brazil	3,620	2,500
Chile	1,420	1,914
Colombia	480	500
Central America	280	214
Cuba/Puerto Rico	1,340	3,214
Dominican Republic/Haiti	210	100
Ecuador	–	43
Mexico	580	300
Peru	1,070	3,285
Uruguay	430	600
Venezuela	350	–

Source: D.C.M. Platt, *Latin America and British Trade, 1806–1914*, London 1972, pp. 317–20. (The export figures are calculated from 1854, when reporting of current values began.)

This, though, was all about selling at home, not abroad, which, if Dickens had half a case, was just as well for the Latin Americans since he comes close to equating 'love of trade' with 'smart-dealing', 'which gilds over many a swindle and gross breach of trust; many a defalcation, public and private, and enables many a knave to hold his head up with the best'.[32]

Table 3 breaks down British trade with Latin America by country. It is based on Platt's figures and so probably understates the values, but that is less important than the question of distribution, which largely reflects British demand for specific commodities – coffee (Brazil, Central America), sugar (Brazil and Cuba), tobacco (Cuba), wool, hides and skins (Argentina and Uruguay), guano (Peru), and copper (Chile).

Mention must also be made of mining and the export of silver, which still formed the basis of most coinage even as the Gold Rushes altered almost overnight the balance of production of the world's leading precious metals. Mexican production of silver had recovered quickly after independence, and although it dropped in the 1840s as a result of the war with the USA, it remained a core element of the regional and national economy – US silver production was very small – just as lesser amounts were to those of Peru, which was exporting over £1 million worth of bullion and specie annually to Britain in the early 1840s, and Bolivia (often appearing under 'Chile' in export statistics because of re-exports), and as gold was to Colombia. Of course, silver could be retained and minted as specie within the national economy, which was a

---

32. Ibid., p. 286.

TABLE 4   Gold and silver

(i)	World production, 1831–55	
	gold (*thousand oz*)	silver (*million oz*)
1831–40	652	19
1841–50	1,761	25
1851	4,049	110
1852	6,709	106
1853	7,227	87
1854	6,309	81
1855	6,639	82

(ii)	Gold and silver output, selected countries (*tonnes*)			
	USA		AUSTRALIA	CHILE*
	silver	gold	gold	silver
1845	1.2	1.5		36
1846	1.2	1.7		41
1847	1.2	1.3		41
1848	1.2	15		50
1849	1.2	60		71
1850	1.2	75		92
1851	1.2	83	10	80
1852	1.2	90	86	86
1853	1.2	98	93	57
1854	1.2	90	71	69
1855	1.2	83	87	62

(iii)	Silver production, Mexico and Bolivia (*tonnes*)	
	MEXICO	BOLIVIA
1821–30	3,209	610
1831–40	4,203	660
1841–50	2,330	366
1851–60	2,229	359

* 'Chile' as export source usually includes Bolivia as well.

Sources: Pierre Vilar, *A History of Gold and Money*, London 1976, p. 351; B.R. Mitchell (ed.), *International Historical Statistics: The Americas and Australasia*, London 1983, pp. 425, 437; Laura Randall, *A Comparative Economic History of Latin America, 1500–1914*, New York 1977, I, p. 22; Adolf Soetbeer, *Edelmetall-Produktion*, Gotha 1880, pp. 78–9.

source of satisfaction both to those who still subscribed to mercantilist ideas and to employees of the state, particularly the military, for whom the direct transition from mineral to money promised to be distinctly profitable. During this period silver maintained its value relative to gold – approximately 15:1 – but whilst the US Coinage Act of 1792 had adopted this ratio, it was only in 1848 that the gold dollar could actually be minted as reserves soared. (The Mexican peso, it is worth noting, held its value against the US dollar between 1840 and 1860.) As we have seen, there was a certain Latin American, particularly Chilean, presence in the Californian economy after its annexation from Mexico, and the main ports of the Pacific benefited from the upsurge in commerce (and prices) caused by the Gold Rush. At the same time, one should not allow the politically driven falls in Mexican and Bolivian output to obscure the modest general renaissance of silver that is indicated in table 4. Of course, gold and silver are exceptionally prone to smuggling – regardless of the tax regime – and since they were anyway omitted from British official records, 'it is difficult to escape the conclusion that a considerable portion of Britain's exports were paid for with precious metals omitted from the British import statistics'.[33]

There is little dispute over the general British predominance in shipping, even after the 1849 repeal of the Navigation Acts which had restricted much inter-continental trade into British ports to vessels flying the national flag. (One should, though, note the critical reciprocity treaty of 1827 with the USA, that with Brazil of the same year, and those with Buenos Aires and Peru of 1825 and 1837 respectively.) In 1845–49 70 per cent of tonnage entering British ports was national; in 1855–59 the level was down to 61 per cent. In 1846 only 3 per cent of the tonnage entering Great Britain from South America flew a foreign flag. However, over two-thirds of the tonnage embarked from the USA – and 23 per cent of that from the 'foreign' West Indies – was of non-British, overwhelmingly US, ownership.[34] Nor was this competition confined to the north Atlantic; between 1849 and 1851 253 US ships accounted for 21.6 per cent of the total tonnage clearing the port of Buenos Aires, just behind the British share of 22.8 per cent.[35]

From the early 1840s there was a progressive introduction of iron-hulled, screw-driven steamships – in 1850 Margaret Fuller could have waited to cross the Atlantic in such a craft – and wooden vessels had reached the limits of their size, but the quality of steel was not yet high enough to make steam boilers fully reliable. Moreover, poor distribution of fuels and very high capital costs meant that sailing vessels were often still competitive.[36] This was particularly the case for long trans-oceanic voyages involving several cargoes – many of the 3,000 ships dispatched with guano from Peru

---

33. Miller, *Britain and Latin America*, p. 73.
34. Sarah Palmer, *Politics, Shipping and the Repeal of the Navigation Laws*, Manchester 1990, p. 54.
35. Jonathan C. Brown, 'A Traditional Marketing System: Buenos Aires, 1810–1860', *HAHR*, 56:4, 1976, p. 610.
36. F.E. Hyde, *Cunard and the North Atlantic, 1840–1973*, London 1975, pp. 28–9.

between 1850 and 1860 had previously cleared Australian and US ports, and some would be chartered a year or more in advance, even though it was only a trip of eighteen weeks to Liverpool from Callao (where they were obliged by the Peruvian authorities to call twice in completion of customs formalities).[37]

In that instance the firm of Anthony Gibbs held a trading monopoly conceded – sometimes on very fragile grounds – by the Peruvian government, allowing the house to keep freight rates relatively constant, but in the north Atlantic US freight rates fell by almost a half between 1847 and 1851 in the wake of the repeal not only of the Navigation Acts but also the British Corn Laws in 1846. The latter measure may be seen as a result of both the famine in Ireland and the powerful free trade campaign of the Anti-Corn Law League. For Douglass North, 'the first big impetus to westward expansion [in the USA] was the demand for wheat and corn resulting from the Irish famine' – a demand that helped to triple the shipment of flour and grain from Chicago between 1845 and 1847 as Ireland was transformed from a net exporter of 485,000 tons to an importer of 743,000 in the same period.[38]

In the South trade was sometimes interrupted by naval blockades, Buenos Aires being particularly affected by European efforts to control the precarious balance of power in the Plate region. Although skilled captains sometimes succeeded in running those imposed by Brazil (1825–28), France (1838–40), and Britain and France (1845–48), conflict between London and Rosas had already reduced British exports to Buenos Aires to £593,000 in 1845 before the blockade drove them down to a mere £187,000 the next year.[39] Unsurprisingly, the fifty-two British merchants in the city protested – 'our worst enemy could not desire to inflict greater injuries upon us' – pleading, in contrast to Mr Falk, for the navy to be called off.[40] Whatever may have been the higher geopolitical objectives of the Foreign Office, the use of armed force against Rosas had resulted in rapid devaluation of the paper currency he had issued, thereby almost halving the value of British property and debts held in Buenos Aires. Even when the blockade had been lifted this problem endured; the complaint made by Baring's George White in 1852 sounds every bit like that of a banker from the 1980s:

> This wretched currency is in every respect injurious to the community, not being based on tangible security and having only a fictitious and conventional value; the fluctuations are enormous and trade is thus to a considerable extent reduced to the level of a mere speculation. This is particularly the case as regards the sale of imports, which are sold commonly on long credit, six months and sometimes more. A sale may be made on apparently favourable grounds,

---

37. W.M. Mathew, *The House of Gibbs and the Peruvian Guano Monopoly*, London 1981, pp. 117–22.

38. North, *Economic Growth of the United States*, pp. 207, 262; P.M. Austin Bourke, 'The Irish Grain Trade, 1839–48', *Irish Historical Studies*, XX, 1976–77, p. 168. In 1845 Great Britain imported 2.25 million hundredweight of wheat (100,000 from the USA); in 1847 the figure rose to 8.2 million (1.8 million from the USA). Mitchell, *British Historical Statistics*, p. 229.

39. John Lynch, *Argentine Dictator: Juan Manuel Rosas, 1829–1852*, Oxford 1981, p. 285.

40. Quoted in David McLean, *Diplomacy and Informal Empire: Britain and the Republics of La Plata, 1836–1853*, London 1995, p. 87.

and when the time for payment comes, the variation in the currency will not improbably be such as to give an entirely different result.[41]

Perhaps, then, it is understandable that Britain ran a trade deficit with Argentina in the 1850s. Equally, it should be borne in mind that British traders accounted for only a fifth of the merchant houses of Buenos Aires, and that Argentine salted beef found its main markets in the slave plantations of Cuba and Brazil – some 23,000 tons a year in the 1840s, conveyed by ships from those states that outstripped in numbers and tonnage the British vessels even after the lifting of the blockade.[42] Regional trade was more important than dependency theorists allowed for, and that with non-industrial states, such as Italy and France, also mattered: taken together with trade with Cuba and Brazil, this commerce accounted for a third of Argentine exports in 1850. Equally, Sarmiento had a point about costume and culture: Argentine demand for British cottons and linens was very modest – behind that of Brazil, Chile, Peru and Cuba – whereas its consumption of woollen goods from that country was the highest in the subcontinent.[43] Between his arrival in Argentina from Ireland at the end of 1845 and his sixtieth birthday in 1887 the sheepfarmer John Brabazon had readily been able to swap his chiripá for a fine European frock-coat, but one central reason for this was a tenfold increase in exports of wool and sheepskins, an increasingly 'merinoised' country taking a third of the European and North American markets.[44]

   The case of Buenos Aires is, nevertheless, exceptional because it was a port city in frequent conflict with London. Perhaps more representative of the region as a whole was Cali, a town of 14,000 in the Cauca valley of Colombia which had not a single commercial house in 1849, or Tarija in southern Bolivia, which exported 'virtually nothing', produced none of its own clothing, and where, according to the prefect, General Francisco O'Connor, 'every man who possesses 300 pesos calls himself a merchant.... [They] make a yearly trip to Salta and return with textiles for making clothes' or with European-style clothes themselves to exchange for cattle with the Chiriguano people.[45] In Valparaiso, by contrast, two-thirds of the seventy-three active wholesale concerns were British, French or German, whilst a quarter of the 243 retailers registered in Santiago and Valparaiso were foreign-owned.[46] Although the leading merchants were British, this was a generally competitive 'export-led development', whereas in Peru foreign firms were prohibited from the retail trade and

---

41. Quoted in Vera Blinn Reber, *British Mercantile Houses in Buenos Aires, 1810–1880*, Cambridge, Mass., 1979, p. 31. Between the institution of the paper peso by Rosas in 1845 and his overthrow in 1852 its exchange rate with an ounce of gold varied from 109 to 414 whilst sterling stayed constant.
   42. Brown, 'Traditional Marketing System', p. 608.
   43. Miller, *Britain and Latin America*, p. 75.
   44. Hilda Sabato, 'Wool Trade and Commercial Networks in Buenos Aires, 1840s to 1880s', *JLAS*, 15:1, 1983, pp. 58–9.
   45. Quoted in Erick D. Langer and Gina L. Hames, 'Commerce and Credit on the Periphery: Tarija Merchants, 1830–1914', *HAHR*, 74:2, 1994, p. 292; Richard P. Hyland, 'A Fragile Prosperity: Credit and Agrarian Structure in the Cauca Valley, 1851–87', *HAHR*, 62:3, 1982, p. 381.
   46. Bauer, *Chilean Rural Society*, pp. 38–9.

financing state activity until 1848. And such an exclusion was reaffirmed in Mexico as late as 1843 on the grounds that, 'in foreign states most advanced in civilization, retail trade by foreigners is subject to restriction in divers ways, Mexicans not being permitted to enjoy any reciprocity in this respect'.[47] 'Free trade' was still understood in some parts simply to mean 'freedom to trade'.

In the case of Peru the shift from a generally protectionist policy and attitude coincided with the start of the boom in guano, the sea-bird excrement used for fertiliser that was concentrated in huge quantities on several offshore islands, principally the Chinchas and Lobos groups. From July 1849 until December 1861 the firm of Anthony Gibbs retained the exclusive contract for overseas sales, which in Britain amounted to 1,810,704 tons at an average retail price of £11 a ton. In this period the house made an average annual profit of £92,000, enabling it to lend both to the state and in the private market in a manner well beyond the ability of the hundred or so local firms, which, indeed, were its main clients since Peru had no bank until the Gibbs contract expired:

> The merchants who find themselves pressed by the maturing of their debts procure hides, iron, cochineal, cotton, wool, bark, silver bars, etc., for dispatch to Europe; these articles are not sufficient to make up the sums owing, for exports unfortunately do not measure up to imports, so they have recourse to the house of Gibbs for bills.... The Gibbs firms makes all the profits from guano available to the Government; but that money only enters the national coffers by virtue of bills drawn in favour of the merchants who pay in Peruvian, or better still, Bolivian currency. The Gibbs agents sign drafts at 42 or 43 pence per peso – 48 pence represent par – and as a penny makes two centavos, it follows that the merchants lose five or six pence and the Government gains 10 or 12 on the exchange. The agents award themselves a halfpenny for the service of issuing bills against funds belonging to the State.[48]

This was banking and good business; it derived from from a monopoly based precisely on an ability to link the 'centre' and the 'periphery'. There is scant evidence of any prolonged discontent with it amongst the parties concerned in Lima. Indeed, the principal critics of the contract between Gibbs and the Peruvian state were British farmers. When, in 1850, General Ramón Castilla (president 1845–51, 1855–62) asked Gibbs about the possibility of raising the price of guano, they replied, 'at a time when the abolition of the Corn Laws has terrified the farmers ... a rise in price would be very inopportune and would greatly risk the popularity of huano [sic]'.[49] The following year Palmerston, who was being put under strong pressure by the agricultural lobby, wrote to Ambassador Adams instructing him to press Lima for a

---

47. Decree of 23 Sept. 1843, reprinted in *BFSP, 1846–47*, XXXV, p. 1108.

48. Luis Mesones, *El Ministerio de Hacienda del Perú en sus relaciones con los administradores del huano en Europa*, Besançon 1859, pp. 116–17, quoted in Mathew, *House of Gibbs*, p. 134.

49. Gibbs, Lima, to Castilla, 16 Dec. 1850, quoted in ibid., p. 138. In the hands of some forty moneylenders, retail interest rates in Lima varied between 40 and 70 per cent in 1850. P.E. Pérez-Maillana Bueno, 'Profesiones y Oficios en la Lima de 1850', *Anuario de Estudios Americanos*, XXXVII, 1980, p. 227.

reduction in the price. Adams's reply shows that recitations of classical economics were the monopoly of no party:

> I have used the arguments with which Your Lordship supplied me in favour of the diminution of the price of Guano on every occasion but am generally reminded of the irreversible law of supply and demand which England has so amply developed, and I have little reason to think Peru will ever be persuaded to forego [*sic*] the full advantage of the monopoly with which Nature has endowed her except in obedience to that law and by open competition with such other discoveries or inventions as may supplant her in the Market.[50]

Since all known alternative deposits, such as those at the African island of Ichaboe, had rapidly been exhausted, this was a distinctly unpalatable message for the farming interest only five years out from the comforts of protection. The imperialist option had, in fact, already begun to surface. In April 1851 Thomas Wentworth Buller, a large Devon farmer, former naval officer and critic of Ricardo, wrote to Palmerston raising doubts about the legitimacy of Peru's claim to the Lobos islands, and, in a manner very akin to that of Robert Falk, urged the dispatch of a British warship to verify the possession and protect British vessels: 'If, as an agriculturalist, I submit to all the disadvantages of Free Trade, it is but just and reasonable that I should expect a share of its advantages, the greatest of which would be the obtaining of this most valuable manure at a moderate price.'[51]

The question of Peru's ownership of the Lobos was not seriously followed up by the Foreign Office. However, the farming lobby kept up its pressure, particularly in Scotland, where, it would seem, guano was especially vital to the turnip crop; the *Glasgow Herald* opined that, even if the Lobos did belong to Peru, 'it is never to be conceived that the Government of that country is to be allowed to keep under lock and key deposits of such immense importance to the universal human family'.[52] Hopes of pressing the claims of this internationalist fraternity rose in February 1852 when the Russell government fell and was replaced by a Tory administration headed by Lord Derby, still sympathetic to protection. In June Derby received a deputation 'of the most influential character' headed by Buller, the Dukes of Buccleuch and Richmond for the squirearchy, John Hudson representing tenant farmers, and Robert Hildyard on behalf of the shipping interest:

> All the well practised arguments were produced: some spoke in moderate terms, others more vehemently. John Hudson asserted that guano at £6 [it then stood at £9.5.0 a ton] would give more benefit to the farmers than any fair duty that might be placed on corn imports. This, according to *The Times*, 'was received with loud cries of "hear"' ... and 'produced a marked sensation'. Derby listened and then gave the deputation an account of the history and organisation of the trade and of British negotiations with Peru on guano ... he insisted that Peru was the sole and rightful owner of the Lobos islands and that this had been accepted by a Law Officer of the Crown as far back as 1834. The British, whether they liked

---

50. Adams, Lima, to Palmerston, 20 Nov. 1851, quoted in Mathews, *House of Gibbs*, p. 152.
51. Buller, Whimple, to Palmerston, 18 Apr. 1851, quoted in ibid., p. 150.
52. *Glasgow Herald*, 7 June 1852, quoted in ibid., p. 158.

it or not, were entirely in Peru's hands as far as guano was concerned; she exercised a monopoly and knew that the farmers were still eager to buy the fertiliser, high prices notwithstanding. 'The attention of the Government would be devoted to impressing on the Government of Peru the advantages that must result from a largely increased demand, but he feared that it would be a difficult piece of diplomacy to convince them'. The deputation then withdrew, 'a good deal disappointed with the result of the interview'.[53]

Such an image of genteel dissension may accord with Christopher Platt's rejection of 'informal empire' but it is not a proper picture of the guano trade as a whole, which was 'primitive' in more ways than one. The millions of tons of bird-shit were first dug and carted by convicts and captured deserters alongside forced labourers, and then by slaves, but these were emancipated by Castilla in 1854. The main source of labour from 1849 onwards was indentured workers from China, and although the numbers were relatively small – perhaps 800 at any one time – the conditions were truly appalling. A North American visitor reported as many as thirty floggings a day, another observer wrote of the 'horrible howling constantly heard on the islands', and in 1853 the eminent Peruvian Nicolás de Piérola stressed to his government that 'it is in the interests of good order, humanity and religion that the wretched Chinamen of the middle island be treated with less severity'.[54] The next year a US sailor drew attention to the alternative to opium as a means of escaping the daily obligation to shift at least four tons – some eighty barrow-loads – a day for the pay of a shilling a week:

> In the month of November [1853] I have heard 50 of the boldest of them joined hands and jumped from the precipice into the sea. In December there were 23 suicides; this is from one in authority; in January quite a number, but I have not learned how many. I was a few days since on the South Island, and there saw two of the most miserable starved creatures. They had swam across on their wheelbarrows, and fully determined to die.[55]

In 1854 Lord Clarendon, the new foreign secretary, made reference to 'shocking atrocities' on the Chinchas. There is, though, evidence that complaints produced some change in a regime that had seemingly reached the point of systematic suicide through cruelty, and in the late 1850s coolie labour was supplemented by free waged workers.

It is also important to note that life at sea was far from easy or free of risk as well as affecting a great many people – sailing ships were labour-intensive. (According to the British census of 1841, 256,162 people, or 1 per cent of the British population, were related to the maritime industry, 180,000 being seamen.[56]) In 1846 public outrage at the death of a soldier who had been given 150 lashes forced Wellington, still commander-in-chief, to head off a campaign for the total abolition of flogging in the

---

53. Ibid., pp. 159–60.
54. Quoted in W.M. Mathew, 'A Primitive Export Sector: Guano Production in Mid-Nineteenth-Century Peru', *JLAS*, 9:1, 1977, pp. 44–5.
55. Quoted in ibid., p. 47.
56. Palmer, *Politics, Shipping and the Repeal of the Navigation Laws*, p. 11.

William Hickling Prescott.

The only known photograph of Margaret Fuller.

Flora Tristán.

Gauguin's descendants at his tomb in the Marquesas.

La Saya y Manto modelled in Lima.

Walt Whitman.

Horace Greeley shortly before he hired Karl Marx.

Jenny and Karl Marx.

Signed portraits of Simón Bolívar and Antonio José de Sucre.

Myra Clark Gaines.

This engraving by Favret de Saint Memin
is inscribed 'Clarke', and is believed to be
the sole existing likeness of Daniel Clark.

General Edmund
Pendleton Gaines.

Mr Justice James Moore Wayne.

Chief Justice Roger Taney.

Canal Street, New Orleans, pictured around 1845, before Myra Clark had won back these buildings as her lawful property.

The US Supreme Court when Myra finally won her suit. Mr Justice Catron is inset. Seated from second left are Justices Davis, Swayne, Grier, Wayne, Chase, Nelson, Clifford, Miller, Field.

Punch lampoons the pretensions of US democracy.

Sale of Slaves and Stock.

The Negroes and Stock listed below, are a Prime Lot, and belong to the ESTATE OF THE LATE LUTHER McGOWAN, and will be sold on Monday, Sept. 22nd, 1852, at the Fair Grounds, in Savannah, Georgia, at 1:00 P. M. The Negroes will be taken to the grounds two days previous to the Sale, so that they may be inspected by prospective buyers.

On account of the low prices listed below, they will be sold for cash only, and must be taken into custody within two hours after sale.

No.	Name.	Age.	Remarks.	Price.
1	Lunesta	27	Prime Rice Planter,	$1,275.00
2	Violet	16	Housework and Nursemaid,	900.00
3	Lizzie	30	Rice, Unsound,	300.00
4	Minda	27	Cotton, Prime Woman,	1,200.00
5	Adam	28	Cotton, Prime Young Man,	1,100.00
6	Abel	41	Rice Hand, Eyesight Poor,	675.00
7	Tanney	22	Prime Cotton Hand,	950.00
8	Flementina	39	Good Cook. Stiff Knee,	400.00
9	Lanney	34	Prime Cottom Man,	1,000.00
10	Sally	10	Handy in Kitchen,	675.00
11	Maccabey	35	Prime Man, Fair Carpenter,	980.00
12	Dorcas Judy	25	Seamstress, Handy in House,	800.00
13	Happy	60	Blacksmith,	575.00
14	Mowden	15	Prime Cotton Boy,	700.00
15	Bills	21	Handy with Mules,	900.00
16	Theopolis	39	Rice Hand, Gets Fits,	575.00
17	Coolidge	29	Rice Hand and Blacksmith,	1,275.00
18	Bessie	69	Infirm, Sews,	250.00
19	Infant	1	Strong Likely Boy	400.00
20	Samson	41	Prime Man, Good with Stock,	975.00
21	Callie May	27	Prime Woman, Rice,	1,000.00
22	Honey	14	Prime Girl, Hearing Poor,	850.00
23	Angelina	16	Prime Girl, House or Field,	1,000.00
24	Virgil	21	Prime Field Hand,	1,100.00
25	Tom	40	Rice Hand, Lame Leg,	750.00
26	Noble	11	Handy Boy,	900.00
27	Judge Lesh	55	Prime Blacksmith,	800.00
28	Booster	43	Fair Mason, Unsound,	600.00
29	Big Kate	37	Housekeeper and Nurse,	950.00
30	Melie Ann	19	Housework, Smart Yellow Girl,	1,250.00
31	Deacon	26	Prime Rice Hand,	1,000.00
32	Coming	19	Prime Cotton Hand,	1,000.00
33	Mabel	47	Prime Cotton Hand,	800.00
34	Uncle Tim	60	Fair Hand with Mules,	600.00
35	Abe	27	Prime Cotton Hand,	1,000.00
36	Tennes	29	Prime Rice Hand and Cocahman,	1,250.00

There will also be offered at this sale, twenty head of Horses and Mules with harness, along with thirty head of Prime Cattle. Slaves will be sold separate, or in lots, as best suits the purchaser. Sale will be held rain or shine.

'Personal property' advertised for sale.

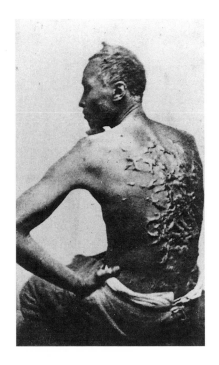

Gordon, an ex-slave in Anglo-America,
photographed to display the
outer scars of bondage.

A slave family
in Anglo-America.

Frederick Douglass.

'The Cast-Iron Man':
John C. Calhoun in 1849.

'Black Dan': Daniel Webster, portrayed by Southworth and Hawes
around the time he challenged Myra Clark's case.

armed forces by instituting fifty lashes as a maximum. He was supported by Russell, and the American experience of abolition at the end of the 1840s suggests that flogging was so central to the system that it could not simply be removed without causing serious dilemmas:

> The punishment of whipping entered so largely into the code heretofore, existing since the foundation of the navy, that its abolition has left in the hands of the authority few other sanctions than those of death and imprisonment; and its single prohibition, without any other changes in the system, leaves the offender still exposed to the extreme penalty of human law, to which stripes were in many instances only a milder alternative.... Thus, Article 20: If any person in the navy shall sleep upon his watch, or negligently perform the duty assigned him, or leave his station before regularly relieved, he shall suffer death, or such other punishment as a court martial shall ajudge; or, if the offender be a private, he may, at the discretion of the Captain, be put in irons or flogged not exceeding 12 lashes.[57]

Of course, merchant captains never possessed this range of sanctions, even though the behaviour and discipline required of all sailors was very similar. Their comportment on land was viewed by the authorities as generally dysfunctional, if not precisely barbaric:

> The sailor is, in general, upon shore a helpless being. Between himself and all around him there is a palpable incongruity. He has come off a long cruize, and has earned some 300 or 400 dollars. He has no home – often no friends but his comrades. He knows no thrift – no saving economy; has no adviser. His only look-out is for some pastime, and his idea of that is confined to sensual enjoyment. Every one is familiar with his history in his brief sojourn on shore. He is a victim of that class of persons who pander to his appetites, and who plunder him of his earnings.[58]

Not all sailors, then, were so cultured as Herman Melville, and even he had to desert to have his appetites pandered to *gratis* by Fayaway. When, in the spring of 1852, Thomas Wentworth Buller began to publicise his campaign for the annexation of the Lobos islands through the columns of the *Times*, the Earl of Malmesbury, who was briefly foreign secretary, received an anxious letter from Captain Andrew Snape Hamond. In his long and detailed screed Hamond recounted the case of a British captain who had tried to load an unauthorised cargo of guano off the Chinchas in 1843, only to be wounded in a clash with Peruvian troops, jailed and then set at liberty, although his vessel was condemned as a prize. The tale was bloodier than that occasioned by Henry D. Dempsey, but Captain Hamond's main point was to warn the government against giving any encouragement at all to 'free enterprise' by mariners. It was a point he drove home to Malmesbury with a homily illustrating the risks of seafaring that Professor Platt might have added to his list in objection to some hydraulic imperialist 'logic':

---

57. William Graham, Secretary of the Navy, to Pres. Fillmore, 30 Nov. 1850, in *BFSP, 1849–50*, XXXIX, London 1863, p. 136.

58. John P. Kennedy, Secretary of the Navy, to Pres. Fillmore, 26 Aug. 1852, in *BFSP 1851–52*, XLI, London 1863, p. 99.

The end of this miserable man deserves to be recorded. Having returned to Valparaiso, of course penniless and homeless, accompanied by his son, a youth of 14 or 15, he managed to ingratiate himself with a worthy, honest-hearted Scot, of the name of Mackensie, commander of a fine ship on the point of sailing for England, and telling him an artful tale of his woes and losses, succeeded in inducing him to grant both himself and his son a passage (*gratis*) home. Little did the poor fellow know what a despicable villain he was harbouring. On the passage home this monster in human form, having found out that a considerable freight was on board, decided upon murdering his benefactor and taking possession of the ship.

For this purpose he gained over a portion of the crew to assist him in carrying out his wicked design; and in the dead of night, watching his opportunity, he stabbed the man at the wheel to the heart, and having flung him over the side, he shouted out to the captain, who was asleep in his cabin, to come upon deck, as a man, he said, had fallen overboard. The poor captain, suspecting no evil, jumped upon deck in his shirt, and as he did so, this monster struck him on the head with an axe as he ascended the companion-ladder, and after a death struggle, the captain was over-powered and likewise thrown overboard. The vessel now being in the hands of the mutineers, all those who did not take the oath of secrecy were at once dispatched, and their bodies thrown into the sea.

Apparently reckless as to consequences, this depraved villain now assumed the most despotic sway over the rest of his confederates in crime, and ruled them with ungovernable brutality. This was too much to be borne, and the men, having watched their time, they seized him when asleep, bound him and his son back to back together, and threw them alive into the sea. The mutineers navigated the shop to the neighbourhood of Halifax, Nova Scotia, where they ran her ashore, and dispersed themselves into the country. Circumstances most providentially were brought to light which enabled the authorities at Halifax to discover the crime of which these miserable men had been guilty, and I believe they all expiated their guilt upon the gallows.

Such, my Lord, was the fatal result of the misconduct of the captain of an English merchant-ship in attempting to take a cargo of guano off the coast of Peru without permission of the authorities.

As a postscript Hamond names the captain as a Fielding and the last ship to suffer under his command as the *Vitula*.[59]

TARIFFS AND TEXTILES

During the 1840s free trade was transformed in Great Britain from a single-issue campaign into a comprehensive ideology. It was, furthermore, an ideology with a strong popular component even if − as in the USA and Latin America − it remained controversial. It is not easy to get a fine sense of the fault-lines between free trade and protection of the 1840s and 1850s over 150 years later, following the collapse of communism, in a period when 'liberal economics' has − amidst a quite regular cycle

---

59. Hamond, Freshwater, to Malmesbury, 20 April 1852, in *BFSP, 1854–55*, XLV, London 1865, pp. 1190–91.

of booms and slumps – enjoyed much greater prestige than protectionism. This is particularly the case with regard to the competing claims of export-led and protectionist paths to growth, development and 'modernity' in the modern world. The vogue in Latin America for 'import substitution industrialisation' from the 1930s to the 1970s is now widely deemed a failure, albeit one that carried significant short- and medium-term gains for the poorer strata of society. Today, it would seem that, outside the US, more people acquiesce in 'market economics' than actively celebrate it, but the global vernacular has free trade as an almost constant nostrum, and protection is now a policy without a defensible ideology. This was not the case in 1850.

There is little evidence from that time to show any significant portion of the populations of the USA or Latin America – except some of the tribes undergoing removal – being threatened by famine. Subsistence can mean a multitude of things but it always includes basic food security, which, as we will see, was generally secure in the Americas, and which may best be seen as a pre-industrial, pre-capitalist phenomenon. By the 1840s such security was, by contrast, under tangible threat in the British Isles, and not solely in Ireland. The price of flour was extremely erratic, rising 27 per cent between 1836 and 1841, and then falling back nearly as far over the next four years as a result of particularly good harvests and the space that they gave Peel for tinkering with the protective tariff as he came under pressure from Chartism as well as the Anti-Corn Law League.[60] However, an analysis of the diet of the families of Manchester workers in the 1840s in terms of the daily allowances of protein, calories, iron and vitamin C recommended today by the British Medical Association and the US National Research Institution shows that 'only the best paid of the regularly employed workers achieved a diet which would now be regarded as adequate for health'.[61] In 1844 Richard Cobden asked Parliament,

> will it be believed in future ages that in a country periodically on the point of actual famine – at a time when its inhabitants subsisted on the lowest food, the very roots of the earth – there was a law in existence which virtually prohibited the import of bread?[62]

What might have been seen as self-serving hyperbole was, within a year, revealed as prescient rhetoric, but in March 1845 – before the famine struck Ireland – Cobden was winning strong parliamentary support for the case against agricultural protection on the basis of remarkable and yet somehow plausible assertions, such as the fact that more goods had been exported to Brazil in one year than had been consumed by the entire rural labour force of England.[63] There had now coalesced over this issue a 'cross-class alliance' between manufacturing entrepreneurs, the professional middle classes and the urban proletariat out of which each sector could perceive a distinct

---

60. John Burnett, *Plenty and Want: A Social History of Food in England from 1815 to the Present Day*, 3rd edn, London 1989, p. 42.
61. Ibid., p. 58.
62. John Bright and James E. Thorold Rogers (eds), *Speeches of Richard Cobden*, London 1870, I, p. 164.
63. John Morley, *The Life of Richard Cobden*, London 1896, I, p. 321.

advantage but which was perhaps best represented in the popular calculus reported by
Cobden to the House of Commons:

> At a meeting held at Oldham, a workman got up in the body of the hall. He had been
> thinking, he said, on the subject of the Corn Laws for twenty years; as there was no possi-
> bility that he should ever see Sir Robert Peel, as he never came down into that neighbourhood,
> and as he, the speaker, could not bear the expense of a journey to London, he begged Mr
> Cobden to convey to the Prime Minister the following train of thought: 'When provisions
> are high, the people have so much to pay for them that they have little or nothing left to
> buy clothes with; and when they have little to buy clothes with, few clothes are sold; and
> when few clothes are sold, there are too many to sell; and when there are too many to sell
> they are very cheap; and when they are very cheap, there cannot be much paid for making
> them; and consequently the manufacturing working man's wages are reduced, the mills are
> shut up, business is ruined, and general distress is spread through the country. But when as
> now the working man has the said 25 shillings [the fall in the price of wheat] left in his
> pocket, he buys more clothes with it, ay, and other articles of comfort too, and that increases
> the demand for them, and the greater the demand, you know, makes them rise in price, and
> the rising in price enables the working man to get higher wages and the master better
> profits. This therefore is the way I prove that higher provisions make lower wages, and cheap
> provisions make higher wages.[64]

The abolition of the Corn Laws in 1846 did not, of course, halt the Irish Famine.
Nor did it transform the human condition in the industrial centres of England – the
1855 price of bread in London was 80 per cent higher than that in 1845. Attention
shifted vehemently from the conditions of commerce to those of production and
tenure of land. As free trade increasingly came to stand for a supply and demand
rationale of the status quo rather than a democratic redistributionism, *laissez faire*
acquired a dark, naturalistic aspect that John Mitchel was not slow to parody in
August 1847, as the Famine completed its second year:

> Now, my dear surplus brethren, I have a simple, a sublime, a patriotic project to suggest. It
> must be plain to you that you are surplus, and must somehow be got rid of. Do not wait
> ingloriously for famine to sweep you off – if you must die, die gloriously; serve your
> country by your death, and shed around your name the halo of a patriotic fame. Go; choose
> out in all the island two million trees, and thereupon go and hang yourselves.[65]

Mitchel, we know, had an innate talent for driving to the harshest source of things.
But it should be remembered that his audience could read on the same page of the
Belfast News-Letter an advertisement for Jamaican coffee at 1s 8d a lb placed by Hudson and Faren, declaring, 'we know of no method so well calculated to establish a
good trade, and secure the confidence of a discerning public, as a genuine article at
a low price. Upon this principle we have based our business, and have only to appeal
to our gratifying and remunerating success', and a letter from Dr John Dilworth of
Portadown, who reported that at the start of March,

---

64. Ibid., p. 313.
65. *The Nation*, 21 Aug. 1847, quoted in Chris Morash, *Writing the Irish Famine*, Oxford 1995, p. 65.

I called on a family named McClean – found the house like a pig-sty – having fled from Lurgan poor-house where fever and dysintery prevailed.... Want sent the poor man to bed. I gave him some assistance, but he died a few days after. The wife almost immediately after, met the same melancholy fate; and a daughter followed her parents to the grave.... On the Thursday after, I repeated my visit; oh! what a spectacle! a young man, about fourteen or fifteen, on the cold damp floor – off the rubbish – dead! without a single vestige of clothing – the eyes sunk – the mouth wide open – the flesh shrivelled up – the bones all visible – so small round the waist, that I could span him with my hand.[66]

Two years later, in August 1849, when it was still far from clear that the potato crop would not fail for yet more years, Carlyle wrote to Emerson after making a second tour of Ireland:

What the other results of this Irish tour are to be for me I cannot in the least specify. For one thing I seem to be farther from speech on any subject than ever; such masses of chaotic ruin everywhere fronted me; the general fruit of long-continued universal falsity and folly; and such mountains of delusion yet possessing all hearts and tongues.... Alas, alas! The Gospels of Political Economy, of Laissez-Faire, No Government Paradise to all comers, and so many fatal Gospels of this blessed 'New Era' will first have to be tried and found wanting.[67]

Although Carlyle was not wont to dwell on the detail of a subject he found so distateful, the question of free trade arose in two quite distinct areas: the attitude of the authorities towards relief, where the evidence suggests it did impede the speed and scale of intervention after the lifting of protection; and the degree to which food supplies were affected by continued exports, where the evidence is much less emphatic.[68] It was, though, Cobden who had stood at the head of the mass demonstrations

---

66. *Belfast News-Letter*, 2 April 1847.

67. Carlyle, Chelsea, to Emerson, 13 Aug. 1849, in *The Correspondence of Thomas Carlyle and Ralph Waldo Emerson, 1834–1877*, London 1883, II, pp. 182–3. Carlyle, it might be recalled, had eaten his last decent potato for many a month when dining with the Mitchels in 1846 (First Case, p. 85). In December 1848 he had to rely on Emerson for help:

The fact is, potatoes having vanished here, we are again, with motives large and small, trying to learn the use of Indian meal; and indeed do eat it daily to meat at dinner, though hitherto with considerable despair.... Is there by nature a *bitter* final taste, which makes the throat smart, and disheartens much the apprentice in Indian meal, or is it accidental and to be avoided? ... Let some oracle speak. I tell all people, our staff of life is in the Mississippi Valley henceforth, and one of the truest benefactors an American Minerva who could teach us to cook this meal.

Ibid., pp. 169–70. Emerson later sent Carlyle a barrel of maize that had not been kiln-dried to prevent mustiness in shipping. Steamship transport provided far more predictable voyages and so did not require a process that effectively killed off the starch.

68. Cormac Ó Gráda, *Ireland: A New Economic History, 1780–1939*, Oxford 1994, pp. 193, 200. In October 1845 James Wilson, editor of the new doctrinaire free trade journal *The Economist*, wrote of Ireland,

The accounts we receive depict the country as thrown into a state of the deepest despair.... What! the Government do nothing to relieve a famine, when duty on wheat of 18/– a quarter, and on other grain in proportion, stands between it and the famished buyer.... It is impossible to calculate the amount of evil which may be averted, and of positive good which may be secured by an immediate and bold removal of all existing impediments to a free supply of food.

A few weeks later he insisted on the corollary critique – that of the provision of financial assistance:

'Why' (says the charitable), 'it will enable the poor, and those whose little crops have failed, to buy food, which otherwise they could not buy.' Very true – but it will enable them *only to buy that food which, but for this charitable aid, others not so assisted would have bought*: that is, it will enable them to

of the autumn of 1845 demanding the opening of the ports so that the Irish people might be fed, and once this was achieved, his stock and that of his policy stood at their zenith. The tariff lifted, he toured continental Europe to great acclaim. Visiting a pottery works at Seville, 'I found all the workpeople drawn up in a crowd, and they gave me several lusty cheers being led on by some English workmen. Over the door of the manufactory was inscribed in porcelain characters "Cobden for Ever".' A few days earlier he had been asked for advice by the Spanish minister of finance, and his reply might be taken as indicative of the type of policy he would have proposed for the American republics:

> I told him I would charge such duties on foreign goods as would destroy the trade of the smuggler – that if the prohibition [of foreign traders] were removed, and excessively high protective duties substituted, it would only facilitate smuggling. I told him I would guarantee him four times the present customs revenue if he would let them be framed for a number of years upon the understanding that the rate of duties might be lowered at discretion, but that in no case should they be raised. He professed to agree with me, but spoke of the difficulties in the way of lowering the tariff – that the moment the government propounded a measure the very papers and political parties which now professed to be in favour of free trade would turn against them.[69]

Cobden visited the USA twice, in 1835 and 1859, noting on the second occasion that the trip from New York to Niagra took him fifteen hours by train instead of a week by carriage twenty-four years before. Every bit as class-conscious as Dickens, he observed that when he dined with President Buchanan in the White House,

> The few men servants are either Irish or German, the old housemaid is from Derbyshire in England. Native American Citizens will not (at least the better part of them) undertake the duties of a menial servant, even for their president. They will attend upon horses, or even pigs, but will not on the person of their fellow-man ... Comparing class with class the people of the United States are raised to a much higher level than in any country. Writers and travellers fall into a great unfairness in comparing the middle and upper classes, with whom alone the tourists and the book-writing class associate in Europe, with the *whole people* whom they meet at the table d'hôte and in the railway cars in the United States – there are no second- or third-class carriages.[70]

On this second visit Cobden also found that the issue of free trade had been completely eclipsed by that of slavery, which he appears to have accepted as the

---

take the bread out of the mouths of certain others of their countrymen. It will not augment the quantity of food to be distributed – it will only vary the distribution of it.

The Economist, 18 Oct.; 29 Nov. 1845, quoted in Ruth Dudley Edwards, *The Pursuit of Reason: The Economist, 1843–1993*, London 1994, pp. 55, 57. In 1836 six miles of railway had been constructed in Ireland by private companies; by 1845 only seventy. Thereafter the government began to subsidise railway development – to the tune of £2.4 million by 1865, when traffic was still unprofitably low. R.D. Collison Black, 'Economic Policy in Ireland and India in the Time of J.S. Mill', *The Economic History Review*, XXI, 1968, p. 332.

69. Miles Taylor (ed.), *The European Diaries of Richard Cobden, 1846–1849*, Aldershot 1994, pp. 71–2, 69–70.

70. Elizabeth Hoon Cawley (ed.), *The American Diaries of Richard Cobden*, Princeton 1952, pp. 180, 208.

dominant political issue. The question of free trade could not be raised in the USA with the same fervour as in Britain, and it was very rarely treated as some supercilious abstraction of supply and demand since attitudes in North America, as in Peru, depended as much on the availability of credit and capital as on differentials in industrial production. In the 1850s the memory was still sharp of the failure of the US Bank in February 1841 and the subsequent refusal of many states to service debts raised in Europe. (The Senate had rejected federal responsibility for these foreign debts in March 1840.) As Leland Jenks put it, 'It was highly embarrassing for an American to be in London in the winter of 1842/43' (perhaps as much as it was to be a Mexican in New York in 1994/95). When Duff Green, the federal government agent, went to Paris in mid 1842 in search of a loan to cover the shortfall in customs receipts caused by the collapse of imports, he was haughtily admonished by Rothschild: 'You may tell your government that you have seen who is at the head of the finances of Europe, and that he has told you that they cannot borrow a dollar, not a dollar.'[71] Jenks's explanation for this state of affairs largely vindicates the states, which were certainly prey to citizens reluctant to 'write down their hopes of sudden gain', and goes beyond the issue of trade flows in themselves:

> It had been easy for England to expand merchandise and defer payment by means of a credit transaction. What was difficult was to get the investment of capital to produce means of its repayment. What was difficult was to stir backward regions by its application to produce a surplus of goods for export. That the American South was doing. It was the result of a more highly concentrated market for its goods.... Industrial England had outrun the world. Her plant – the railways at least, which had drawn labor from the soil while improving its capital value – and her population, had outgrown the means of subsistence and the markets for their produce. England faced a crisis of more moment than a money panic, whose conditions were altered but whose gravity was not lessened by the suspending of the Corn Laws in 1846, and their final repeal. And the root of the evil was a dearth of money, affecting chiefly her relations with the commercially backward countries.[72]

The Cotton South of the USA was generally and understandably sympathetic to free trade – described by Jenks as a 'political abracadabra whose frequent repetition shut off the past in soothing oblivion' – whilst in the industrial and free-farming North there was far greater scepticism about the 'British fetish'. There was, though, no absolute sectional division over the issue. The tariff of 1832 that had nearly led South Carolina to leave the Union had received the support of all congressmen from three Southern states (Mississippi, Tennessee and Maryland) and that of a majority of those from four more (Alabama, Kentucky, North Carolina and Virginia). There were not only producer interests at stake but also those of consumers as well as political trade-offs in an environment where the slight overall economic advantage to the Cotton South in lower duties was pitched against manufacturing industry's need for

71. *The Migration of British Capital to 1875*, London 1927, pp. 104–6.
72. Ibid., pp. 108, 158.

higher tariffs. Free trade tended to be defended more in terms of ideology, most naturally by Calhoun:

> Mr Calhoun was very glad to hear the Senator from Kentucky [Henry Clay] at last coming round to this sound doctrine ... that those articles ought to be imported which can be obtained upon cheaper terms than they can be produced at home ... the whole tendency [of the protective system] is to force labor and enterprise from their natural channels.[73]

In the words of Thurlow Weed – writing from London in 1851, when US conditions were much more auspicious – the contrasting protectionist view is expressed through wry pragmatism:

> There is a fable, I believe, of a fox who, having lost his own tail, persuaded his friends that tails were quite useless. England has got to the end of Protection, and is now endeavoring to persuade America, a nation that possesses, like England, all the elements required for manufacturing independence, that as she can manufacture for us, we should abandon the Protective policy. She does not tell us, however, that when, deluded by the popular theory of Free Trade, we shall have withdrawn the pressure of American competition, John Bull, generous as he is, will consult his own rather than our interests, in his prices.[74]

Although Cobden had anticipated this perfectly rational position, he does not appear to have envisaged it being based upon economic – as opposed to political – logic:

> We came to the conclusion that the less we attempted to persuade foreigners to adopt our trade principles, the better; for we discovered so much suspicion of the motives of the English that it was lending an argument to protectionists abroad to incite the popular feeling against the Free Traders, by enabling them to say: 'See what these men are wanting to do; they are partisans of Englishmen, and they are seeking to prostrate our industries at the feet of their perfidious nation'.... To take away this pretence we avowed our total indifference whether other nations became free traders or not; but we should abolish Protection for our own sakes, and leave other countries to take whatever course they liked best.[75]

This might be thought the disingenuousness of a single-minded campaigner, but it may just reflect a pre-hegemonic innocence.

The United States maintained a balancing act between the positions of Calhoun and Weed, depending on commodity. The very high tariff rates of the 1820s and 1830s were lowered somewhat in the next two decades – and freight rates fell further still – but in 1845 imported raw cotton was still charged 68 per cent and manufactured cotton at 49 per cent; clayed sugar at 105 per cent, and refined at 92 per cent; pig-iron at 49 per cent, and bars at 36 per cent.[76] Moreover, as already noted, customs duties were central to federal revenue, and they were often seen primarily in those

---

73. Speech in US Senate, 18 Aug. 1841, excerpted in Clyde N. Wilson (ed.), *The Essential Calhoun*, New Brunswick, N.J., 1992, p. 216.
74. *Life of Thurlow Weed including his autobiography and a memoir*, 2 vols, Boston 1883–84, II, p. 202.
75. Cobden to Van Maeren, 5 Oct. 1856, quoted in Morley, *Life of Cobden*, I, pp. 309–10.
76. Lebergott, *The Americans*, p. 141.

terms rather than as an instrument of commercial policy. In his message to Congress at the end of 1846 Polk stressed the convergence of these virtues in a defence of a reduction of the tariff so as to make it more consistent:

> With such rates of duty as those established by the existing law, the system will probably be permanent; and capitalists who have made, or shall hereafter make, their investments in manufactures, will know upon what to rely. The country will be satisfied with these rates because the advantages which the manufacturers still enjoy result necessarily from the collection of revenue for the support of Government ... lower and more permanent rates of duty, at the same time as they will yield to the manufacturer fair and remunerating profits, will secure him against the danger of frequent changes in the system.[77]

Four years later, in the full wake of British repeal, Fillmore had shifted the emphasis somewhat:

> All experience has demonstrated the wisdom and policy of raising a large portion of revenue for the support of Government from duties on goods imported. The power to levy these duties is unquestionable, and its chief object, of course, is to replenish the Treasury. But if, in doing this, an incidental advantage may be gained by encouraging the industry of our citizens, it is our duty to avail ourselves of that advantage.[78]

However, in the USA the matter went much deeper than the relative incidental advantage to state or producer. The disposition towards industrial protectionism had descended from Hamilton to Clay as a political legacy, being supported by the rationale of national defence – now against England – and the need to expand the domestic market. An alternative *laissez faire* tradition represented by Jefferson and Jackson possessed an equally populist appeal in its emphasis upon the natural qualities of labour, a critique of aristocratic political economy, and the restriction of the law to the defence – not acquisition – of property.[79] However, by the 1840s industrialisation on both sides of the Atlantic accentuated the role of labour within these sometimes competing, sometimes converging ideological cultures. According to James Huston,

> The free trade concepts of supply and demand, equilibria in the market place, the division of labor, the mobility of resources, the elimination of government involvement in business affairs, the sanctification of property rights, and, to some degree, the role of marginal returns in business expansion had gained a wide acceptance in England and the United States. Protectionists did not usually quarrel with these axioms.... [But they] were horrified by one aspect of the free trade paradigm: the analysis of labor and its fate.[80]

---

77. Polk, Message to Congress, 8 Dec. 1846, in *BFSP, 1845–46*, XXXIV, London 1860, pp. 272–3.
78. Fillmore, Message to Congress, 2 Dec. 1850, in *BFSP, 1849–50*, XXXVIII, London 1860, p. 206.
79. James L. Huston, 'The American Revolutionaries, the Political Economy of Aristocracy, and the American Concept of the Distribution of Wealth, 1765–1900', *AHR*, 98, 1993, pp. 1097–8.
80. 'A Political Response to Industrialisation: The Republican Embrace of Protectionist Labor Doctrines', *The Journal of American History*, 70:1, June 1983, p. 37. There was widespread support in the North for the conviction expressed by Horace Greeley that 'protection is the shortest and best way to real free trade'. *New York Daily Tribune*, 23 April 1851.

Huston argues that this has largely been ignored in analyses of the adoption of the protectionist cause in the 1850s by the new Republican Party. It provided a popular base to complement the core free soil component at the same time as it sharpened nationalist appeal and revived some traditional convictions: that wages had to be high to protect republicanism in commercial societies; that aristocracies deliberately reduced domestic wages in order to compete abroad; and that it was madness to compete on its own terms with a nation that purposefully depressed wages. On the other hand, the critique of *de facto* industrial 'wage slavery' was commonly to be found within a defence of *de jure* chattel slavery and commercial freedom. It took a complete maverick like George Fitzhugh to defend slavery in the USA by attacking at the same time (and in Carlylean mode) British wages, emancipation and free trade:

> We despise this flood of crocodile tears which England is shedding over the free negroes of the West Indies, whilst she has not one tear to shed for her laboring poor at home, who are ten times worse off than the free negroes.... The free trade or competitive philosophy is an admitted failure, and most of the literature in Europe is employed in exposing and condemning it.... Slavery to capital, so intolerable in densely-settled countries, where lands are monopolised by the few, can never be felt at the North [of the USA] until our vast possessions in the West are peopled to the Pacific, and a refluent population begins to pour back upon the East. Then, like Western Europe, the North would have a laboring population slaves to capital, 'slaves without masters'. Famine would become perennial and revolution the common order of the day as in Western Europe.... The spirit of trade and commerce is universal, and it is as much the business of trade to devour the poor as of whales to swallow herrings.[81]

Attitudes towards foreign commerce in Iberian America were not couched so directly in ideological terms, but nor were they entirely liberated from the legacies of the colonial monopoly on trade or free from distrust of foreigners. Paraguay was the only country that could rival Japan in this sense, but by 1854, when Rear-Admiral Sir James Stirling succeeded in signing a convention with Japan to allow British ships the right for the first time to visit two designated ports in order to take on supplies, Carlos Antonio López was instituting in Asunción a regime markedly more liberal than that at Nagasaki:

1. Ships shall anchor within Two-sima, and there await the directions of the Governor.
2. No firearms to be discharged.
3. No person to land on any of the islands.

---

81. 'Southern Thought', *De Bow's Review*, XXIII, 1857, quoted in D.W. Faust (ed.), *The Ideology of Slavery: Proslavery Thought in the Antebellum South, 1830–1860*, Baton Rouge 1981, pp. 267–8, 282. The combining of an economistic estimation of the closing of the western frontier with a moral/cultural defence of slavery stood at the core of Fitzhugh's iconoclastic writing. In the book derived from these articles he moves from quoting Carlyle's pamphlet *The Present Time* to assert,

> The social forms of the North and the South are, for the present, equally promotive of growth and prosperity at home, and equally beneficial to mankind at large, by affording asylums to the oppressed, and by furnishing food and clothing to all. Northern society is a partial failure.

But it would only fail completely when the labour market became saturated by returning colonists and/ or continued immigration from abroad. *Cannibals All! or Slaves without Masters* (1857), Cambridge, Mass., 1960, p. 11.

4. No soundings to be taken, nor boats to be pulling about.

5. Should any communication be desired, a boat of the upper officers shall be called; but no communication shall be held with merchant-boats, and no exchange of articles to take place, or trading of any sort.[82]

By the mid 1850s most of the countries in the centre and south of the continent had signed treaties with Britain in the style of that concluded between London and Tegucigalpa in 1856:

> Article II. The two High Contracting Parties being desirous of placing the commerce and navigation on the liberal basis of perfect equality and reciprocity, mutually agree that the citizens of each may frequent all the coasts and countries of the other, and reside therein, and shall have the power to purchase and hold all kinds of property which the laws of the country may permit any foreigner, of whatsoever nation, to hold, and to engage in all kinds of trade, manufactures, and mining upon the same terms with native subjects or citizens....
>
> Article V. No higher or other duties shall be imposed on the importation into the British dominions of any article the growth, produce or manufacture of the Republic of Honduras, and no higher or other duties shall be imposed on the importation into the Republic of Honduras of any article the growth, produce or manufacture of the British dominions, than are or shall be payable on the like article being the growth, produce or manufacture of any foreign country.... No prohibition shall be imposed on any article.[83]

Nobody seriously entertained the notion that entrepreneurs from San Pedro Sula and Sheffield were about to enter the market of the other on any perfect basis of equality, but the idea of recriprocal treatment was essential to an ideology that was now so warmly embraced that it was being enshrined in the charters of the republics: the new Mexican constitution of 1857 followed that of 1853 designed for Argentina by Alberdi in expressly outlawing any prohibition of imports. It was now rare to encounter a rebuttal of the arguments for comparative advantage in the manner made by the attractive Colonel San Román in the 1830s when conversing with Flora Tristán:

> 'We shall close our ports to all those foreign vessels which compete to infest our country with goods so cheap that even the black slaves strut about in their cloth. You know that Peruvian industry can never flourish in the face of such competition, and as long as people here can obtain things they need from the foreigner for next to nothing they will never buckle down to producing them themselves.'

---

82. Regulations of the Port of Nagasaki, Oct. 1854, in *BFSP, 1853–54*, XLIV, p. 66. These ordinances have the great merit of simplicity and clarity. One marvels at the negotiating skills of the US diplomats who signed the 1856 trade treaty with Siam wherein the following items are excluded from tax:

> ivory; gamboge; rhinoceros horns; best cardamoms; bastard cardamoms; dived mussels; pelicans' quills; dried betel nut; krachi wood; white sharks' fins; ditto black; lukkraban seed; Peacock's tails; buffalo and cow bones; rhinoceros hides; hide cuttings; turtle shells; soft ditto; bêche de mer; fish maws; birds' nests uncleaned; kingfisher feathers; cutch; Beyché seed (*Nux Vomica*); Pungtarai seed; Gum bengamin; angrai bark; agrilla wood; ray skins; old deers' horns; soft or young ditto; deer hides, fine; ditto common; deer sinews; buffalo and cow hides; elephants' bones; tiger bones; buffalo horns; elephant hides; tiger skins; armadillo skins; sticklac; hemp; dried fish; *Flaheng*; ditto, *Plasalit*; sapan wood; salt meat; mangrove bark; rosewood; ebony; and rice.

Treaty of 29 May 1856, in *BFSP, 1855–56*, XLVI, p. 399.

83. Friendship, Commerce and Navigation Treaty between Great Britain and Honduras, 27 Aug. 1856, in *BFSP, 1855–56*, XLVI, pp. 158–62.

'Colonel, you cannot train manufacturers as you train soldiers, nor can you raise factories as you raise armies, by force.'

'This system is not as difficult to put into effect as you seem to think; our country furnishes all the raw materials – flax, cotton, silk, wool of incomparable fineness, gold, silver, lead and so on; as for machinery, we shall import it from England, together with workers from every corner of the earth.'

'A bad system colonel! Believe me, you will never encourage competition and love of work by isolating yourselves.'

'And I believe, mademoiselle, that necessity is the only spur which will compel our people to work; besides, our country is in a better position than any country in Europe, for we have no large army or navy to maintain, no huge debt to support. We are, therefore, in a favourable position to develop our industry, and when peace is restored and we have prohibited the consumption of foreign goods, there will be nothing to prevent the factories we set up from prospering.'

'But you forget that for a long time to come the cost of labour will be higher here than in England. You have only a small population; would you have it employed in producing cloth, watches, furniture and so on? If so, what will become of agriculture, which is already backward enough, and the exploitation of the mines which you have been forced to abandon for want of labour?'

'As long as we have no factories, the foreigners will continue to carry off our gold and silver.'

'But, colonel, gold and silver are what this country produces, and more than anything else they would lose their value if you could not exchange them for products from outside. I repeat, the time for setting up factories has not yet arrived; before you even think of such a thing you should instil in your people the taste for luxury and the comforts of life, create needs for them in order to make them work; and it is only through the free importation of foreign merchandise that you will succeed.'[84]

By 1850, in the first year of the Gibbs contract, it would seem from the columns of Lima's press that Flora's prospectus was bearing some fruit, the elite at least chafing at unsavoury duties:

> As French wines are pleasant to our tastebuds, and as crossing the public avenues in a beautiful English carriage serves our recreation, we spend our money in the most spontaneous manner on these objects of taste and comfort … but the law of higher duties forces us to drink that *Lanchas* wine (so unpleasant to the tongue!) and to pass through the parks in those bothersome carts called balacines.[85]

Here we find more than the interests of the superior consumer at stake – or even those of the importing merchant houses – because many artisans used imported components in local manufacturing. Also, of course, not all foreign goods were luxuries. There was a constituency for free trade, and within a year a complaint based upon consumer choice had mutated into a much more profound proposition:

> Industry whose products cannot compete with foreigners should disappear. If paper or textiles cannot be made better or cheaper in this country, then we should neither manufacture paper

---

84. *Peregrinations of a Pariah* (1858), London 1986, pp. 236–7.
85. *El Comercio*, 22 July 1850, quoted in Paul Gootenberg, 'The Social Origins of Protectionism and Free Trade in Nineteenth-Century Lima', *JLAS*, 14:2, 1982, p. 352.

nor textiles. If furniture, shoes etcetera (however cheapened subsistence is) cannot compete with foreigners who pay 20 per cent at customs then we ought not to make furniture or footwear in Peru.[86]

No region could compete with British textiles. In the interior of Colombia effective protection was provided less by tariffs than through the lack of coin with which to build even a credit-based demand, and by very high transport costs: 35–65 cents per ton-mile in dry weather (and up to 95 cents in the rainy season), compared with 1851 US railway rates of 4 cents per ton-mile and canal rates of a penny.[87] Yet even there the local industry was inhibited by the competition, and sales of British cottons and linens contributed towards the lack of specie. In Chile, where the major centres of population were much more accessible, there were still in 1854 some 80,000 weavers and spinners engaged in local – almost always household – textile production. Within a decade their numbers had fallen by nearly three-quarters in the face of a flood of British imports that were not only cheaper but also of better quality: 'to hold back this flood would have required an enforced tariff and political will that are difficult to imagine given the class interests of the most powerful political groups in the country'.[88]

There was some strong early resistance from the elite in Mexico, but this was on the wane before the war with the USA, and by 1856 80 per cent of its imports from Britain were textiles. Lucas Alamán and others had promoted the local industry in the 1830s through the Banco de Avío, which was itself funded by a fifth of the customs revenue; raw materials were locally available; European specialist craftsmen were employed to greater effect than Platt supposed; foreign merchants quite often entered into joint partnerships with local entrepreneurs (not least because of the tight regulations to which they were subjected); and a sizeable middle class experienced such erratic political conditions that its capacity to purchase even cheap imports varied wildly.[89] Also, of course, the large population of Mexico – some 8 million people in 1850; over a third of that of the USA – contained a quite high residual demand from the poor for local goods, particularly clothing, which in the highlands of Oaxaca, no less than on the pampa of Buenos Aires or the Sierra Real of the Andes, was more an element of culture than a commodity. Indeed, in the historic indigenous centres of Mexico there seems to have been less of a gender divide in attitudes towards imported attire than that amongst the Chiriguanos of southern Bolivia, where women were far

86. *El Comercio*, 4 July 1851, quoted in ibid., p. 354.

87. Anthony McFarlane, 'The Transition from Colonialism in Colombia, 1819–1875', in Christopher Abel and Colin Lewis (eds), *Latin America: Economic Imperialism and the State*, London 1985, p. 112; Frank Safford, 'The Emergence of Economic Liberalism in Colombia', in Joseph L. Love and Nils Jacobsen (eds), *Guiding the Invisible Hand: Economic Liberalism and the State in Latin American History*, New York 1988, p. 36.

88. Arnold J. Bauer, 'Industry and the Missing Bourgeoisie: Consumption and Development in Chile, 1850–1950', *HAHR*, 70:2, 1990, p. 234.

89. Guy Thomson, 'Protectionism and Industrialization in Mexico, 1821–1854: The Case of Puebla', in Abel and Lewis (eds), *Latin America: Economic Imperialism and the State*; Walther L. Bernecker, 'Foreign Interests, Tariff Policy and Early Industrialization in Mexico, 1821–1848', *Ibero-Amerikanisches Archiv*, 14:1, 1988, pp. 71–88.

more reluctant than men to don European apparel.[90] Evidently, it was not just in the Andes that

> the cloth with which the bodies of the women were wrapped (the *aqsu*) was considered to be more than a garment that protected and adorned the wearer. It formed an outer skin that stood in metonymic relationship to the self; in other words, it was considered to be an integral part of the person who wore it. The *aqsu* forms an outer surface that simultaneously conceals and reveals an interior.[91]

Yet even in the provincial towns of the Andes this was coming to be seen as something more traditional than natural. A report of 1853 from Cochabamba, nestled beyond two mountain ranges and hundreds of miles from the sea, reflected the scale of the British 'invasion' in a zone with a once vibrant textile industry and still strong Quechua culture:

> English goods are in the *greatest demand on account of their cheapness and comparative excellence.* Cotton goods especially of all descriptions are in general use such as maddapolans (white shirtings), grey domestics, trowserings, prints, jaconets, jeans, mock and fine quiltings, handkerchiefs, shawls, thread, relseteens, lace, etc. Woollen goods of all descriptions, baizes, 'pellon cien hilos' (Rawson and Edwards are preferred), 'feijudas', fancy doc skins, casimeres, 'paño de verano', casimere shawls, alpacas, merinos, the last two for dresses, flanel etc.[92]

Issues of identity are often subsumed to the vagaries of 'fashion', which exercised a tyranny of delights just as actively before the epoch of Levi Strauss as in the era of the designer label. Sometimes taste was politically driven, and however great the overall success of British products, individual merchants still had to have their cloth cut and coloured correctly in order to survive in a highly competitive market. At the start of the Rosas regime importer James Hodgson wrote emphatically from Buenos Aires to Thomas Broadbent, his manufacturer in Manchester:

> Red, pink and scarlet ground print are now all the rage here – these being the popular or *Federal Party* colours and what is more: to every appearance, as far as can be seen forwards, they are certain to remain, and accordingly you must exclusively in a measure run upon such and carefully avoid both in ground and prominent objects thereupon, the colours of *Sky Blue* and *Green*, which are the anti-party colours.[93]

Table 5 shows the scale of the British export success as well as its early cause in low and falling prices. Although the factories of Lancashire were under some technical competition from the north-east of the USA, they possessed substantial inherited

90. Bernardino de Niño, *Etnografía Chiriguana*, La Paz 1912, cited in Erich Langer and Gina L. Hames, 'Commerce and Credit on the Periphery: Tarija Merchants, 1830–1914', *HAHR*, 74:2, 1994, p. 294.

91. Penny Dransart, 'Pachamama: The Inka Earth Mother of the Long Sweeping Garment', in Ruth Barnes and Joanne B. Eicher (eds), *Dress and Gender: Making and Meaning*, New York 1992, pp. 145–6.

92. Lloyd, Tacna, to Russell, 15 Apr. 1853, FO 11/15, cited in Hans Huber Abendroth, 'Comercio, manufactura y hacienda pública en Bolivia entre 1825 y 1870', in Rossana Barragán, Dora Cajías and Seemin Qayum (eds), *El Siglo XIX: Bolivia y América Latina*, La Paz 1997, p. 339.

93. Hodgson, Buenos Aires, to Broadbent, 15 April 1836, quoted in Reber, *British Mercantile Houses*, p. 86.

TABLE 5   British textile trade with Latin America

(i)	Exports to Latin America, 1814–56 (*annual average, £1,000*)				
	total	cottons	linens	woollens	% GB exports
1814/16	2,476	1,353	89	426	5.2
1824/26	5,009	2,825	366	751	12.6
1834/36	5,047	3,206	270	720	10.9
1844/46	5,634	3,037	524	1,023	9.7
1854/56	8,874	4,522	593	1,266	8.8

(ii)	Price and volume of British cotton and linen trade			
	COTTON PRICE		EXPORT VOLUME PIECES	
	raw cotton (*pence/lb*)	pieces (*pence/yd*)	cotton (*million lb*)	linen (*1,000 yd*)
1830	6.88	7.62	445	61,920
1835	10.25	6.53	558	77,977
1840	6.00	4.95	791	89,373
1845	4.13	3.96	1,092	88,402
1850	7.00	3.63	1,358	122,343
1855	5.63	3.24	1,938	118,040

Sources: Miller, *Britain and Latin America*, p. 73; Mitchell, *British Historical Statisics*, pp. 356, 760.

advantages, forcing down costs so far that between 1830 and 1850 the overall value of cotton goods exported to Latin America increased very modestly although the volume rose by more than two-and-a-half times. At times the wholesale price of British textiles in Latin America was so low that today its sale would be described as 'dumping'.

By around 1850 the price of cotton pieces had stabilised, and increases in export earnings derive much less from an expansion in the volume of goods shipped. Market share – particularly at the lower end, it would seem – was already secured: in 1840 Latin America took a third of all British exports of cotton cloth, with a per capita consumption seven times that of the world average.[94] These are the official figures; they exclude all flows of contraband, which were even greater in the sub-continent than in the Spanish case to which Cobden had directed his advice. Estimates of smuggling at a quarter or a half of the level of officially measured, regulated and taxed levels have been proposed for Mexico and Venezuela, indicating an even greater

94. Miller, *Britain and Latin America*, pp. 73–4.

market for foreign goods.[95] For Peru, where protection loses its strength in the late 1840s – at the same time as Mexico – Paul Gootenberg argues,

> contraband was very much a political problem rather than being technically impossible to eliminate. This task, to raise production to the efficient level of capacity, demanded a consistent state protectionist commitment over the transition period, a time when pressures would erupt from consumers who could not be supplied with those goods fast or cheaply enough.[96]

Nowhere was this successfully undertaken. Rosas altered the rate of duty according to political circumstances and occasional crashes, but he was unpersuaded by the strategy of protection even though customs revenue accounted for at least two-thirds (and often 80 per cent) of government income when there was no blockade.[97] In Mexico, as we have seen, there was an effort both to promote cotton and to fund the state from customs duties on foreign trade. Barbara Tenenbaum believes that this was at the root of the instability of that republic at least until the war with the USA, at which time the military budget and income from port taxes were roughly the same, at 6 million pesos, which was also the size of the annual deficit from 1840 to 1856.[98] The textile industry did contrive to hold some ground but only partly for reasons of mercantile policy or direct subsidy, and the other requirement stipulated by Gootenberg – maintenance of consistent policy over time – was more absent from Mexico than any other state of the region: between 1821 and 1856 it was ruled by fifty-three separate governments and hundreds of different ministers under four constitutions. These, of course, are just numbers, but John Coatsworth, who has already alerted us to their two-edged qualities, concurs with Tenenbaum's assessment of what they added up to. For him, 'inefficient economic organisation' in Mexico meant

> an ensemble of policies, laws, and institutions that magnified, instead of reduced, the gap between private and social benefits of economic activity. During most of the nineteenth century activities which could have contributed to economic growth were never undertaken because they promised too small a return to potential owners and producers.[99]

Coatsworth views most of the early Latin American republics in such a downbeat vein:

> They could tax the diminished output of stagnating economies, but they could not do much else – define and defend borders, monopolize the use of force, discipline bureaucracies to public purposes, assume rather than delegate public functions, build infrastructure, educate and train the labor force. Indeed, the effort to accomplish even a few of these goals usually

---

95. David Walker, *Kinship, Business and Politics: The Martínez del Rio Family in Mexico 1823–1867*, Austin, Tex., 1986, p. 13; M.E. González Deluca, 'Los intereses británicos y la política en Venezuela en las últimas décadas del siglo xix', *Boletín Americanista*, p. 103, cited in ibid., p. 72.

96. Gootenberg, 'Social Origins', p. 347.

97. Carlos Marichal, 'Liberalism and Fiscal Policy: The Argentine Paradox, 1820–1862', in Vincent C. Peloso and Barbara A. Tenenbaum (eds), *Liberals, Politics and Power: State Formation in Nineteenth-Century Latin America*, Athens, Ga., 1996, p. 94.

98. *The Politics of Penury: Debt and Taxes in Mexico, 1821–1856*, Albuquerque 1986, pp. 179, 181.

99. 'Obstacles to Economic Growth', p. 92.

proved fruitless, because conservative regimes so often neglected, or even opposed, the fundamental constitutional and policy reforms needed to consolidate bourgeois principles of government.[100]

These, by contrast, were already firmly established in the USA.

LAND OF PLENTY (FOR SOME)

The figures used by John Coatsworth to compute the growth of GDP per capita between 1800 and 1850 would not have to be hugely inaccurate to unsettle the picture of starkly contrasting Anglo prosperity and Latin stagnation. A yearly average of 0.8 per cent for the UK and 1.1 per cent for the USA, on the one side, stand against representative figures of 0.4 per cent for Brazil, zero for Colombia and –0.7 per cent for Mexico, on the other. The differential is less emphatic still for the period between 1850 and World War I, but the much higher Anglo starting point matters a lot and the USA maintains a clear and growing lead. Coatsworth's explanation for the 'Anglo success' side of the equation is familiar enough: capitalist growth enabled immigrants and native workers to enjoy income and social mobility (whereas Latin America's rural population would experience economic growth as personal and economic disaster). It was also accompanied by sufficient political stability – punctuated by one quite short, if exceptionally violent, civil war – to give

> a relative inclusiveness to the US political system and its decentralized governing structures. It is also related to the phenomena of widespread property ownership, early public commitments to certain kinds of social spending (especially on education), and a lesser degree of concentration of wealth and income.[101]

Coatsworth goes on to refer to slavery, which, of course, prevailed as a system in the two most productive Latin economies – Brazil and Cuba – just as much as in the South of the USA. Indeed, in Richard Graham's opinion one could quite accurately describe Brazil in the terms used for the antebellum US South by Douglass North:

> the production for an international market of a single market staple, a tropical or semi-tropical crop; the plantation system based on the labour of slaves on large estates; the geographical shift of the crop associated with allegedly worn-out soils and impelled by surging prices; the presence of a large and relatively forgotten population that was neither slave nor

---

100. 'Notes on the Comparative Economic History of Latin America and the United States', in W.L. Bernecker and H.W. Tobler (eds), *Development and Underdevelopment in America: Contrasts of Economic Growth in North and Latin America in Historical Perspective*, Berlin 1993, pp. 21–2.
101. Ibid., p. 27.

planter; low investment in human capital; few large cities; a small local market for industrial goods; a lack of industrialization; and the location outside its borders of both the principal sources of capital and the controlling centres of its commercial life.[102]

However, Graham argues that it is wrong to believe that slavery explains the other features shared between the Southern states of the USA and Brazil, which he shows to be lagging behind the slave section of North America in a number of key areas. Moreover, even Douglass North – sometimes criticised for overemphasising the role of cotton in US growth – does not see that crop as the prime cause for the success of the economy after 1845; for him development is thereafter the product of industrialisation in the north-east, the creation of a new market for agricultural produce from the expanding west, and the discovery of gold in California.[103] A combination of availability of land, a revolution in transport and industrial technology, immigration and the Gold Rush lies at the heart of the traditional historiography of US economic transformation in the mid nineteenth century.[104] The figures in table 6 for changing per capita income over the years 1840 to 1860 are somewhat more reliable than those for Latin America and they indicate a general pattern of expansion, whether one views the picture in terms of free or slave section or by sub-region within each. There is a strong suggestion of a dynamic economic collaboration and complementarity, even as the two sections polarised over the political and ideological issues accentuated by such integration.

Only a modest proportion of the investment behind this growth was furnished by the country's 700 chartered banks, which had been notoriously unstable in the first decades of the century. Although 500 of them held some kind of account in New York, these institutions remained parochially organised because the banknotes that were widely used for local currency depreciated in terms of the national dollar coin the greater the distance from the issuing institution. Banks rarely refused to honour their notes but they sometimes exchanged them at less than par, despite their legal obligations. The Constitution had confronted the question of paper money with absolute silence, and it is not very surprising that banking on a national scale lacked systematic organisation before the Civil War. Until then taxes had to be paid in coin, and even in 1855 the new criminal code of Nebraska declared that any person attempting to form a bank would be imprisoned and fined 'not less than $1,000' – presumably readily to hand.[105] A decade elapsed between the expiring of the charter of the second Bank of the United States and the creation of the Independent Treasury

---

102. Richard Graham, 'Slavery and Economic Development: Brazil and the United States South in the Nineteenth Century', *Comparative Studies in Society and History*, 23:4, 1981, p. 622. In this paraphrase Graham loses some of North's detail, notably that north-eastern capital financed the purchase–transfer of slaves to the south-west as well as the purchase of land there. *Economic Growth of the United States*, pp. 128–30.

103. *Economic Growth of the United States*, pp. 69–70.

104. Peter Temin, *Causal Factors in American Economic Growth in the Nineteenth Century*, London 1975.

105. *Nebraska History*, 6, Oct.–Dec. 1923, p. 112, quoted in Lebergott, *The Americans*, p. 121.

TABLE 6   USA: per capita income by region, 1840 and 1860 (*1860 $*)

	Total population		Free population	
	1840	1860	1840	1860
USA	96	128	109	144
NORTH	109	141	110	142
North-east	129	181	130	183
North Central	65	89	66	90
SOUTH	74	103	105	150
South Atlantic	66	84	96	124
East South Central	69	89	92	124
West South Central	151	184	238	274

North-east: Maine, New Hampshire, Massachussetts, Rhode Island, Connecticut, New Jersey, Pennsylvania, New York, Vermont. *North Central*: Ohio, Michigan, Indiana, Illinois, Wisconsin, Minnesota, Iowa, Missouri, Kansas, Nebraska, South Dakota, North Dakota. *South Atlantic*: District of Columbia, Delaware, Maryland, Virginia, North Carolina, South Carolina, Georgia, Florida. *East South Central*: Kentucky, Tennessee, Mississippi, Alabama. *West South Central*: Louisiana, Arkansas, Oklahoma, Texas.

Source: R.W. Fogel, *Without Consent or Contract: The Rise and Fall of American Slavery*, New York 1989, p. 85.

by the federal government in 1846 – a clearing house was only established in New York in 1854 – and these were ten years of exceptional internal expansion.

Between 1845 and 1855, by contrast, the USA only registered a surplus in its foreign merchandise trade in 1847. Its aggregate overseas indebtedness rose from $213 million to $356 million, and foreign investors accounted for less than 5 per cent of capital formation.[106] It was a rather different proposition to finance trade, but after 1841–42 many British investors looked on the USA in pretty much the same light as Platt has them viewing Latin America. According to Joshua Bates of Baring's, 'there never was a Country so disgraced in point of credit as The United States of America'.[107] The states had, as a result of that crisis, drawn back from public finance. The federal government, whilst it continued to receive banknotes as well as to run a modest budget surplus – 10 per cent over $40 million expended in 1850 – was too delicately poised and tightly circumscribed to intervene substantially in the market for money. Credit, therefore, tended to be private, local and quite socialised, most obviously through store-keepers, very probably through a much higher commerce in kind than the statistics could register, and through middle-class investment in money-lending. Here we encounter once again the old saws about Protestant thrift and disposition for theological defence of profit; lenders could justify their interest rates no less than did

---

106. North, *Economic Growth of the United States*, p. 220.
107. Quoted in David Kynaston, *The City of London: A World of its Own, 1815–1870*, London 1994, p. 116.

godly producers their mark-ups. But there were also plenty of borrowers – like frontier farmers on heavy mortgages and awaiting the harvest or cattle sales – who were equally up for scriptural support, even redress. The midwest states of the North were particularly prone to legislation against usury, and nominal interest rates were kept quite low, but the black market was very different, and loan-sharks were always circling. Debt, like cholera, could easily be given a biblical aspect, although George Fitzhugh stood alone in deriving a comprehensive radical economy from the Old Testament:

> We think we have discovered that Moses has anticipated the Socialists, and that in prohibiting 'usury of money, and of victuals, and of all things that are lent on usury', and in denouncing 'increase' he was far wiser than Aristotle, and saw that other capital or property did not 'breed' any more than money, and that its profits were unjust exactions levied from the laboring men. The Socialists proclaim this a discovery of their own. We think Moses discovered it and proclaimed it more than 3,000 years ago – and that it is the only true theory of capital and labor, the only adequate theoretical defence of Slavery – for it proves that the profits which capital exacts from labor makes free laborers slaves, without the rights, privileges, or advantages of domestic slaves, and capitalists their masters, with all the advantages, and none of the burdens and obligations of the ordinary owners of slaves.[108]

To some people viewing the USA from outside, its financial system, and particularly the use of paper money by local banks, lay at the heart of its successful economy. As part of his prolonged campaign to establish a bank in Colombia, William Wills in January 1854 set out for the readers of Bogotá's *Gaceta Oficial* an estimation of the global money stock of 1849 in terms of millions of pesos:

	PAPER	COIN
USA	170	80
Great Britain	200	90
France	125	50
Rest of Europe	500	150
Rest of World	250	150
Total	1,245	520

For Wills these figures provided a conclusive lesson:

> See how the quantity of money in notes that circulates in the world is twice that of gold and silver. In New Granada [Colombia] there circulates not a single banknote or government promissory note at par, nor will they until such time as there is a balance between public revenue and expenditure and the funding of public credit. This is one of the big secrets of our poverty and the lack of capital available for hard-working and honest men engaged in diligent enterprise who have to submit to the yoke of usury, which absorbs all their profits and, in any reverse of fortune, condemns them to live in awful prostration and industrial impotence, perhaps unto death, at least until the infirmities of old age have rendered them useless.[109]

---

108. *Cannibals All!*, p. 13.
109. *Gaceta Oficial*, Bogotá, 9 Jan. 1854, reproduced in Malcolm Deas (ed.), *Vida y opiniones de Mr William Wills*, Santafé de Bogotá 1996, II, p. 202.

Some within the USA might not have thought the contrast with their own experience to be so stark. There was, however, widespread recognition at home and abroad of the importance of popular subscription to a labour theory of value and property. From the early years of independence an emphasis on 'the fruits of labour', reward for individual effort and the property rights that accrued had tended to complement the paper-money cause since it preserved the produce of labour (whereas the conservative 'hard money' advocates argued that this was only possible in conditions of constant value).[110] Yet sharp differences within white US society over practical policies of this type very seldom spilled over into doubt over the options described by John Stuart Mill in 1850:

> The economics of society may be grounded on the principle of property or on that of community. The principle of property I understand to be that what any individuals have earned by their own labour, and what the law permits to be given by others, they are allowed to dispose of at pleasure, and are not ... bound to hold it in trust for the public or for the poor. This is a great advance, both in justice and utility, above the mere force of law, but far inferior to the law of community; and there is not and cannot be any reason against the immediate adoption of some form of this last, unless it be that that mankind are not yet prepared for it.[111]

In the communities of the USA property amounted to a great deal more than law. One important element of the attack on slavery was that slaves could not enjoy the fruits of their labour, and that 'to labor solely for the benefit of other men is repugnant to every principle of the human heart'.[112] But against this stood the formidable argument that all assets which had been legally received as property remained so, and any attempt to distinguish on moral grounds between types of property would undermine the system as a whole. In January 1845 this position was candidly expressed in a letter to an English abolitionist by James Henry Hammond, who owned 147 slaves on his South Carolina plantation and would become governor of the state:

> The wisdom of ages has concurred in the justice and expediency of establishing rights by prescriptive use, however tortious in their origin they may have been. You would deem a man insane whose keen sense of equity would lead him to denounce your rights to the lands you hold, and which perhaps you inherited from a Saxon or Norman conqueror, and your lands were originally wrested by violence from the vanquished Britons ... the means, therefore, whatever they may have been, by which the Africans now in this country have been reduced to slavery, cannot affect us, since they are our property, as your land is yours, by inheritance or purchase or prescriptive rights. You will say that man cannot hold *property in man*. The answer is, that he can and *actually does* hold property in his fellow all the world over, in a variety of forms, and *has always done so*.[113]

---

110. Huston, 'American Concept of the Distribution of Wealth', pp. 1081–8.

111. Mill, to Frederick J. Furnivall, 19 Nov. 1850, in F.E. Mineka and D.N. Lindley (eds), *The Later Letters of John Stuart Mill, 1849–1873*, Toronto 1972, p. 50.

112. Noah Webster, 1793, quoted in Huston, 'American Concept of the Distribution of Wealth', p. 1099.

113. Hammond, Silver Bluff, to Clarkson, 28 Jan. 1845. 'Two Letters on Slavery in the United States', reprinted in Faust, *Ideology of Slavery*, p. 171.

Moreover, the normally eccentric Fitzhugh was fully in the mainstream of pro-slavery thought in his attitude to human-as-property: 'Labor pays all taxes, but labor in slave society is property, and men will take care of their property. In free society labor is not property, and there is nothing to shield the laborer from the grinding weight of taxation.'[114]

The condition and cost of workers of every type was a vital issue in an economy undergoing such rapid change. In 1850 more than half of a total workforce of 8.2 million (including 2 million adult slaves) was employed in agriculture, and only 1.2 million in manufacturing industry. However, the industrial labour force had quad-rupled over the previous decade in a rate of increase than would not be repeated until the twentieth century.[115] The very distinct pattern by which free rural workers and immigrants became 'proletarianised' for some or all of the year is explained by Carville Earle and Ronald Hoffman in terms of the differential between wages in agriculture and industry, with the former very much determined by the demands of the crops involved. For these historians the analogy between the USA and Brazil is based less on slavery and the plantation regime of the nineteenth century than on a shared experience of inexpensive labour subsidising industrial development: in the United States from 1800 to 1860, and in Brazil from the 1930s.[116] What Earle and Hoffman term 'the transfer wage' – the rate of pay capable of attracting rural labourers into the factory, workshop or railroad crew – was appreciably higher in the South of the USA than the North. Broadly, this was because the amount of labour time required for the cultivation of cotton was considerable, providing free workers with employment for most of the year and pushing wage rates up to over $100 a year, when the cost of working a slave was between $50 and $60.[117]

In the grain-belt of the old north-west (today's midwest), by contrast, the rural labour force could often not find work for more than four or five months in the year – at rates of between $14 and $18 a month in the 1850s. It was, then, correspondingly cheaper to attract them into urban jobs. For Earle and Hoffman, US industrialisation in the middle years of the nineteenth century owed much to the experience of hundreds of thousands in a position similar to that of Lucian Enos, who wrote to his parents from Wisconsin in October 1843,

> I have not found a place for the winter yet for it is rather hard to hire out to work by the month through the winter season. Though I have not hired out for the winter, I have worked about a month ... and shall work some more either by the month or by chopping some cordwood.[118]

---

114. 'Southern Thought', quoted in ibid., p. 283.
115. Lebergott, *The Americans*, p. 66.
116. 'The Foundation of the Modern Economy: Agriculture and the Costs of Labor in the United States and England, 1800–1860', *AHR*, 85, 1980, p. 1082.
117. Ibid., p. 1067.
118. Quoted in ibid., p. 1071.

On the rural side this cycle followed the seasons – in the midwest between 10 and 20 per cent of the rural population moved at harvest time – and was especially severe in winter: in 1851 7,500 common labourers in Cincinnati (6.5 per cent of the total population) needed shelter and welfare from the city. And the effect was to depress Northern industrial wages in general. In the South the high 'transfer wage' discouraged any shift from slave to free labour in agriculture; it kept industrial costs up, and also helped to depress local demand for manufactured products since slaves possessed very little disposable cash and were generally provided with only four rough cloth suits and a pair of shoes a year. Similarly, wage rates in the railway industry varied significantly between the North and South: unskilled construction workers on the Louisiana state railroad could command $312 a year whereas wages on the Illinois Central a decade later were $248. This was only one element in a complex and fluid economic scenario, but it must have been a factor in the much less extensive construction of railways in the South: of the total track of 14,518 km laid by 1850, only 3,347 km was in the South and of that 1,958 km in the cotton belt (Alabama, Georgia, Louisiana, Mississippi and South Carolina).[119] Of course, wage rates depended on other variables as well, particularly whilst the western frontier remained open, but even aside from the special case of California, they were slow to converge and only reached modest differentials in the last years of the century. In all events, the antebellum South remained an overwhelmingly agricultural and rural society. In 1860 only five cities of the section had more than 50,000 inhabitants, and only one of these – New Orleans, with a population of 168,675 – was in the Deep South. This was still larger than Chicago (110,000), but Chicago had not existed in 1830 and only had 29,000 people in 1850.

At the centre of the argument presented by Earle and Hoffman is the idea that US entrepreneurs were more interested in suppressing the costs of labour than in increasing productivity through technical innovation. Even if one allows for the holding of both objectives in parallel, the former was achieved with some success. The low immigration rates from England (as opposed to Great Britain as a whole) indicate that wage rates there were of a comparable order; Earle and Hoffman suggest an even broader transatlantic similarity in the conditions for developmental 'take-off':

> Is it a coincidence … that the wage share of Illinois in 1860 resembles that of the developing nation of Venezuela in the 1950s? … [We would suggest] an evolutionary process wherein labor subsidizes capital investment for some time but then improves its position as labor supply becomes less elastic and, we would add, as seasonal market imperfections are removed.[120]

Edward Pessen – more concerned to compare the two sections than the South with Latin America – is in broad agreement, at least in terms of the workers' standard of living:

---

119. Graham, 'Slavery and Economic Development', p. 626.
120. Earle and Hoffman, 'Foundation of the Modern Economy', p. 1080.

Evidence bearing on the conditions of white Northern as well as black Southern labor demonstrates that during the middle decades of the nineteenth century the real wages of Northern workingmen declined and their living conditions remained bleak, their job security was reduced, their skills were increasingly devalued, and in many respects their lives became more insecure and precarious.[121]

In fact, it is not very daring to suggest that in 1850 the condition of the average white North American was worse – and that of the average non-slave Latin American was better – than the image broadcast by the schools of exceptionalism and dependency. It is a commonplace that, even in capitalist industrial societies, figures for the overall size and growth of an economy constitute very poor indicators of how wealth is distributed within it. However, in the case of the USA the tendency to assume lower levels of inequity and higher levels of social mobility – 'the egalitarian thesis' – amounts to much more than convenient economic inference:

> The logic of the egalitarian thesis – denying as it does the existence of great extremes of wealth or poverty – and ... the unostentatious style of the American rich and their tendency at all times to 'play down their wealth' evidently blinded even the most brilliant contemporary observer to the reality.[122]

Amongst the brilliant observers, of course, was Alexis de Tocqueville, popularly associated with the recognition and celebration of an 'egalitarian' society even as he identified such an ideology as anathema to most Americans, who were prey to levelling business cycles:

> I am aware that among a great democratic people there will always be some members of the community in great poverty and others in great opulence; but the poor, instead of forming the immense majority of the nation, as is always the case in aristocratic communities, are comparatively few in number, and the laws do not bind them together by the ties of irremediable and hereditary penury.
> The wealthy on their side, are few and powerless; they have no privileges that attract public observation; even their wealth, as it is no longer incorporated and bound up with the soil, is impalpable and, as it were, invisible. As there is no longer a race of poor men, so there is no longer a race of rich men; the latter spring up daily from the multitude and relapse into it again.... I do not mean that there is any lack of wealthy individuals in the United States; I know of no country, indeed, where the love of money has taken stronger hold on the affections of men and where a profounder contempt is expressed for the theory of the permanent equality of property. But wealth circulates with inconceivable rapidity, and experience shows that it is rare to find two succeeding generations in the full enjoyment of it.[123]

We can be confident that Tocqueville was not including blacks in this consideration. In the North blacks were a very small minority whose economic fortune might well have been worsened by racial prejudice, but that would not have greatly affected the overall distribution of wealth. In the South, by contrast, 95 per cent of black people

---

121. 'How Different from Each Other Were the Antebellum North and South?', *AHR*, 85, 1980, p. 1124.
122. Edward Pessen, *Riches, Class and Power Before the Civil War*, Lexington, Ky., 1973, p. 26.
123. *Democracy in America*, New York 1990, II, p. 252; I, p. 51.

were slaves and, as we have seen, treated as being themselves property (trading in the 1850s at an average price of some $1,000). Whatever the controversy over their own conditions, their personal value affected the overall distribution of wealth – an idea that strains and offends the modern imagination. At the same time, it should be recognised that only a quarter to a fifth of Southern white families owned slaves, and of those who did more than a half owned five slaves or fewer. Only 10 per cent of white families owned more than ten slaves, and less than one-half of 1 per cent held 100 people or more in slavery.[124] Considered purely from the viewpoint of the distribution of wealth, this indicates not only great disparities within the South but also a major differential between the two sections:

> Had slaves been treated as part of the potential property-owning southern population to which they actually belonged, instead of being treated as property pure and simple, the total wealth of the antebellum South would have been diminished by several billion dollars ... the addition of nearly 4 million very poor black people to the number of potential property-owners in the South would have increased its rate of inequality ... although not everywhere to the same extent.[125]

If, on the other hand, the factor of slavery is removed entirely from the equation – in an effort, effectively, to compare the state of the white populations of North and South that held the same broad assumptions about capital, wages, markets and inheritance – it has been suggested that the distribution of wealth before the Civil War was quite similar.[126]

Even this distribution was most inequitable. On the eve of the Civil War the poorest 50 per cent of free adult males North and South 'held less than 1 per cent of real and personal property' whilst the richest 1 per cent owned 27 per cent of the country's wealth. Moreover, in the 'Cotton South' wealth was intimately associated with the possession of personal property. In 1860 the average wealth of owners of slaves in these states (Alabama, Mississippi, Louisiana) was $24,748, nearly fourteen times that of those who did not own slaves. Unsurprisingly, slaveholders accounted for over 93 per cent of the agricultural wealth of a region responsible for three-quarters of US cotton production.[127] Table 7 reinforces this image of a general inequity in rural wealth but with the Southern plantation system encouraging concentration of property more than did the grain farms of the midwest in the north.

In the North the wealthy might have been less publicly identifiable, as Tocqueville argued, but in the large urban centres their background was still more traditional than arriviste: 66 per cent of the richest people in Boston and 60 per cent of those in Philadelphia were merchants or brokers; manufacturers accounted for 2 per cent and

---

124. Pessen, 'How Different?', p. 1132.
125. Ibid., p. 1131.
126. Lee Soltow, *Men and Wealth in the United States, 1850–1870*, New Haven, Conn., 1975, pp. 149–58.
127. Pessen, 'How Different?', p. 1130; Peter Kolchin, *American Slavery*, Harmondsworth 1995, p. 180.

TABLE 7   Concentration of US rural wealth, 1860 (%)

(i)	Share of top 10% of farms	
	value	wealth
Cotton South	62.3	58.6
North-west	39.0	58.6
Illinois	40.4	37.7
Indiana	39.3	37.8
Ohio	35.5	36.9

(ii)	Share of cotton and slaves by improved acreage	
acres	cotton	slaves
0–49	5.9	3.0
50–99	8.3	6.8
100–199	14.2	16.9
200–399	23.7	26.9
400–599	15.1	15.2
600–799	9.3	9.3
800–999	5.8	5.4
1000–1249	7.1	6.3
1250+	10.6	10.3

Source: Gavin Wright, *The Political Economy of the Cotton South: Households, Markets and Wealth in the Nineteenth Century*, New York 1978, pp. 26, 28.

5 per cent, respectively.[128] Moreover, as suggested by table 8, although the middle classes were starting to make their presence felt, distribution was still very imbalanced. But how do these statistics relate to the daily life of ordinary Northern city folk? After all, poverty has an absolute as well as relative aspect; and even if the 'egalitarian thesis' is exaggerated or mistaken, it is this substantive quality of life that was the principal preoccupation of those directly involved.

The impressionistic evidence suggests that Earle and Hoffman have a strong point about the existence of a relatively low 'transfer wage' for un- and semi-skilled labour – in New York, say $1 a day – but also that it was possible to eat better than in Great Britain on such pay, even if payment of a higher than an average rent liquidated any savings. For skilled workers, artisans and employees on $10–20 a week, saving was a distinct possibility. Frederick Law Olmsted, who investigated the matter quite closely in his efforts to test the Southern claims of a North 'wage slavery', reckoned that in

128. Pessen, *Riches, Class and Power*, p. 50. Even allowing for some slippage between reported categories, industrialists accounted for less than 15 per cent of the city counsellors and aldermen of New York City, Brooklyn, Boston and Philadelphia. Ibid., p. 287.

TABLE 8 Concentration of US urban non-corporate wealth

Wealth ($)	Population (%)	Est. total ($)	Share (%)
NEW YORK CITY, 1845			
55,000+	I	88,804,000	40
20–55,000	3	55,000,000	26
BOSTON, 1848			
90,000+	I	47,778,500	37
35–90,000	3	34,781,800	32
4–35,000	I 5	40,636,400	32
-4,000	8I	6,000,000	4

Source: Pessen, *Riches, Class and Power*, pp. 34, 39.

the mid 1840s a north-eastern mechanic, joiner or shoemaker could purchase with one week's pay: 2 bushels (16 gallons) of corn, 1 bushel of wheat, 5 lb sugar, 12 lb tea, 10 lb beef, 25 lb pork, 1 turkey, 3 lb butter, 1 lb coffee, 1 bushel potatoes.[129] It is also worth noting recent estimates of very high consumption of lean meat in the South – 150 lb of pork and 50 lb beef per capita a year – making for a much more comfortable subsistence than had previously been credited.[130]

One should treat all these items of consumption of victuals seriously since food prices, being at the core of everyday existence, are reported more accurately than most. Quality, of course, is a rather different matter, especially in an epoch prior to the regular imposition of public standards. As we have seen from the Irish press, the USA was often depicted as a place of abundance, but the representation and the reality could sometimes diverge spectacularly. Staying at the Commercial Hotel in Vicksburg, Missouri, in March 1854, Olmsted himself experienced this when, arriving a little late in the dining hall, he was presented with a glorious bill of fare:

SOUP
Oyster

FISH
Red

BOILED

Jole and Green	Ham	Corned Beef
Bacon and Turnips	Codfish, egg sauce	Leg mutton, caper sauce
Barbecued rabbits		Boiled tongue

129. *The Cotton Kingdom* (1853–54), New York 1953, p. 487.
130. S.B. Hilliard, *Hog Meat and Hoecake: Food Supply in the Old South, 1840–1860*, Carbondale, Ill., 1972, p. 105, quoted in Forrest McDonald and Grady McWhiney, 'The South from Self-Sufficiency to Peonage: An Interpretation', *AHR*, 85, 1980, p. 1106.

Roast

Veal	Roast pig	Muscovie ducks
Kentucky beef	Mutton	Barbecued shoat
Roast bear meat		Roast pork

Entrées

Fricasee pork	Calf feet, mushroom sauce	Bear sausages
Harricane tripe	Calf head, wine sauce	Browned rice
Giblets volivon	Calf feet, madeira sauce	Mutton omelett
Beef's heart fricasee	Cheese macaroni	Cod fish, baked
Chicken chops, robert sauce	Beef kidney, pickle sauce	Stewed mutton
	Chicken breast, madeira sauce	

Fruit

Almonds	Raisins	Pecans

Vegetables

Boiled cabbage	Turnips	Cold slaugh
Hot slaugh	Pickled beets	Creole hominy
Crout cabbage	Oyster plant fried	Parsneps gravied
Fried cabbage	Sweet potatoes spiced	Carrot
Sweet potatoes baked	Cabbage stuffed	Onions boiled
Irish potatoes mashed	Irish potatoes browned	Boiled shellots
Scalloped carrots	Boiled turnips	White beans

Pastry

Currant pies	Lemon custard	Rice pudding
Cocoanut pie	Cranberry pies	Sliced potato pie
Cheese cake	Irish pudding	Orange custard
Cranberry shapes	Green peach tart	Round cake
Grape tart	Green peach puff paste	Huckleberry pies
Rheubarb tarts	Plum tarts	Calves' feet jelly
	Orange jelly	

To Irish eyes in particular this would have seemed a marvellous feast in the waiting, but Olmsted's disappointment exceeded that of diners today, so often obliged to discount the luscious adjectives and imaginative translations from/into French employed in restaurant menus:

> ... beginning with the soup, and going on by the fish to the roasts, the first five dishes I inquired for – when at last I succeeded in arresting one of the negro boys – were 'all gone'; and as the waiter had to go to the head of the dining room, or to the kitchen, to ascertain this fact upon each demand, the majority of the company had left the table before I was served at all. At length I said I would take anything that was to be had, and thereupon was provided immediately with some grimy bacon and greasy cabbage. This I commenced eating, but I no sooner paused for a moment than it was suddenly and surreptitiously removed, and its place supplied, without the expression of any desire on my part, with some other Memphitic chef d'oeuvre, a close investigation of which left me in doubt whether it was that denominated 'sliced potato pie' or 'Irish pudding'.[131]

---

131. *The Cotton Kingdom*, pp. 334–5.

Olmsted's uncomfortable experience was surely not uncommon, but it took place in a society where there were, as Francis Lieber put it, 'thousands of men without property who have quite as great a stake in the public welfare as those many who possess a house or enjoy a certain amount of revenue'.[132] They were not only able to eat but also, as Tocqueville insisted, never so far from acquiring property and improving their state as were the poor of Europe. Although it may seem a paltry gain by today's standards, the reduction of the working day from thirteen to ten hours constituted a major improvement in the human condition, especially taken in harness with the widespread fall of prices of both food and consumer durables. One item that did not fall was wood – already expensive in the cities of the north-east in the 1830s and becoming more so as the supplies of this bulky fuel (and material for construction) were pushed further into the distance. But development of the sheet-iron cylinder stove hugely reduced the wood required for cooking and heating compared with the open hearth; the number of families possessing a stove rose from 1 per cent in 1830 to 65 per cent in 1860. The impact on the iron production and construction industries was substantial (but probably less than that caused by the expansion of the agricultural frontier and the ever-rising demand for pig-iron for horseshoes and farm implements[133]).

In the more measurable terms of saving to set up a small farm – the reality of hundreds of thousands and the dream of millions in the 1850s – the risks were higher than the costs. As we have seen, they included Indian raids and fragile tenure as well as insecure loans. But by mid century it was not difficult to acquire cultivable frontier land for 50 to 80 cents an acre and, if borrowed at 10 per cent, the price of a holding could be raised for a total cost of $100, the grubstake for which an ordinary labourer might save in two years. In the towns, by contrast, it was reckoned possible to save $50 a year on earnings of $250, with a savings rate of 12–15 per cent.[134] Yet perhaps a third of the free population had a dollar or less to their name and, poor even by European standards, they stood at the heart of pro-slavery rhetoric aimed at 'free industry'.[135] The means for improvement through work and borrowing were almost always visibly available, and so served to uphold traditional convictions about the fruits of labour, but they were also far from universally realised.

The idea of an open market in land for the free black and white population had an exhilarating strength and stood in stark contrast to the closed, hierarchical and quasi-monopolist systems in Europe. This, of course, was especially true with respect to Ireland, where two generations of subletting, subdivision, 'tenancies at will', and absentee ownership had created a system much more retrograde than that in England.

---

132. *On Civil Liberty and Self-Government*, Philadelphia 1859, pp. 176–7.
133. The average farm worked three horses, needing new shoes each five weeks, which, allowing for nails and the retrieval of some cast-shoes, amounted to a consumption of 32 lb a year per farm. Lebergott, *The Americans*, pp. 71, 137. In 1860 Ohio had almost as many horses as cows – 463,000 against 544,500.
134. Ibid., p. 86.
135. Soltow, *Men and Wealth*, p. 188.

J.S. Mill, whom Marx was forever slagging off in footnotes for a shallow recycling of Ricardo's theories, was able to strike such a firm line on the land question in Ireland precisely because of his Ricardian conviction that rent was a pure surplus. In October 1846 he was clear that 'the great economical evil of Ireland is the cottier-tenant system ... neither the economic nor the moral evils admit of any considerable alleviation while that baneful system continues.'[136] Two years later, following John Mitchel's transportation, he energetically expanded this criticism:

> The cause of Irish disaffection is not demagogism. It is no creation of Mr O'Connor or Mr Mitchel. These, and such as these, are the more or less able and active, and skilful organs of dissatisfaction ... but do not create it.... The causes of Irish disaffection are many and various; the greatest of them being that several millions of the Irish people having nothing to support them but potatoes for two or three months every year [and] not enough of these, even when the crop has not failed; all the remainder of what the land produces ... being taken, under the name of rent, by about 8,000 persons.... A people may be lazy or imprudent under any system, but they must be so under the customs as to the occupation of land which exist in Ireland. When land is let by competition, it may almost be said by auction, to peasants cultivating for food and not for profit, then if those peasants are superabundant in numbers, their competition makes them engage for rents impossible to be paid; and the utmost that can be paid becomes the landlord's by right, leaving the tenant still in debt to him.... To extinguish a system by which, under the name of sanctions of property, the land with all it produces exists for the sole benefit ... of a handful of persons who neither by their labour, their skill nor their accumulations contribute in any way to its productiveness, is difficult ... but not impossible and *must* be done.'[137]

Recent 'revisionist' history has raised serious questions about the accuracy of this picture and suggests a more complex state of play, but it is so easy to evacuate the baby with the bathwater. Before the Famine over 30,000 people were leaving Ireland every year; the system was failing in terms of distribution long before it failed to keep people alive. The 1849 Unencumbered Estates Act responded to the widespread collapse of estates by easing constraints on raising capital and accelerated the market in land so that by 1850 'most of Ireland was organised into large farms'.[138] Many of those who had emigrated before the Famine are identified by Forrest McDonald and Grady McWhiney as taking their Celtic pastoralist traditions to the Southern states of the USA, where they maintained a low-productivity, consumption-oriented, hog-raising culture beneath and within the plantation system:

> Virtually all, even those who owned no land, owned animals. No one actually needed to own land, for the open range prevailed throughout the South. Animals were simply branded or clipped and turned loose to graze the land – anybody's land, for fencing laws prohibited the enclosure of any space not actually under cultivation and required farmers to fence their

---

136. *Morning Chronicle*, 10 Oct. 1846, in A.P. Robson and J.M. Robson (eds), *Collected Works of John Stuart Mill: XXIV. Newspaper Writings, 1835–1847*, Toronto 1982, p. 889.

137. 'What Is To Be Done in Ireland?', in A.P. Robson and J.M. Robson (eds), *Collected Works of John Stuart Mill: VI. Essays on England, Ireland and the Empire*, Toronto 1982, pp. 501–2.

138. Michael J. Winstanley, *Ireland and the Land Question, 1800–1922*, London 1984, p. 16.

crops against the animals of others, rather than the other way round. When the larder got low, the plain folk stuck another hog. For vegetables, almost no tillage was necessary, since green gardens in the Southern soil and climate, once planted, grew wild, reseeding themselves year after year.... The system made the South lavishly self-sufficient – lavishly, that is, by the plain folk's own preferred standards, which required only an abundance of leisure, tobacco, liquor and food.[139]

In fact, land was owned by a greater proportion of white males in the South than in the North – less than two-fifths of heads of household in the north-east owned or leased farms in 1860.[140] It was not only because between 1845 and 1853 the territory of the USA increased by 844,237 square miles (to 3 million square miles) that land prices varied considerably. Land grants in the west were vulnerable to early intrusion by speculators; in the east the market had long been dependent on soil quality and water-courses as well as the tracks of the new railways and the pattern of urbanisation. Richard Cobden noted that outside Chicago, 'the soil is of the best quality for wheat, and would let in England for £2 an acre. Here it is on *sale* from 40/– to 50/– with long credit and with a railroad running through it'.[141] During his 1853 train journey to Charleston Frederick Olmsted had occasion to discuss land with the elderly gentleman sat opposite:

'You are a farmer?'
    'Yes.'
    'Well, I am a farmer too.'
    'Be ye – to New York?'
    'Yes; how much land have you got?'
    '125 acres; how much have you?'
    'Just about the same. What's your land worth here?'
    'Some on't – what we call swamp-land, kinder low and wet like, you know – that's worth $5 an acre; and mainly it's worth a dollar and a half or two dollars – that's takin' a common trac' of upland. What's yours worth?'
    'A hundred and fifty to two hundred dollars.'
    'What?!'
    'A hundred and fifty to two hundred.'
    'Dollars?'
    'Yes.'
    'Not an acre?'
    'Yes.'
    'Good Lord! Yer might as well buy niggers to onst. Do you work any niggers?'
    'No.'
    'May be they don't have niggers – that is slaves – to New York.'

---

139. 'The South from Self-Sufficiency to Peonage', pp. 1105–6, 1107–9. This adventurous analysis suggests much lower labour inputs in the South by both slave and free workers than does the literature of the 1960s and 1970s. In the fifteen years prior to the Civil War a total of 67 million hogs were marketed in the South, and if the authors are correct about the high levels of domestic consumption, the total pig population would have been very much greater than that.

140. Between 1789 and 1860 the wealthiest 5 per cent of landlords held between a third and two-fifths of all land. Alan Kulikoff, *The Agrarian Origins of American Capitalism*, Charlottesville, Va., 1992, pp. 44, 47; Pessen, 'How Different?', p. 1132.

141. *American Diaries*, p. 151.

'No, we do not. It's against the law.'

'Yes, I heard t'was, some place. How do yer get yer work done?'

'I hire white men – Irishmen, generally.'

'Do they work good?'

'Yes, better than negroes, I think, and don't cost nearly as much.'

'What do you have to give 'em?'

'Eight or nine dollars a month, and board, for common hands, by the year.'

'Hi Lordy! and they wake up right smart, do they? Why you can't get any kind of a good nigger less'n twelve dollars a month.'

'And board?'

'And board 'em? Yes; and clothe, and blank, and shoe 'em too.'[142]

Olmsted's Irish workers might well have been recent rural immigrants – nearly 150,000 people a year had been leaving Great Britain and Ireland each year for the previous five years, and not even the most buoyant of urban economies could accomodate this new supply of labour, much of which was unskilled (see table 9). By 1860 there were half a million Irish people in New York state, and of the total US foreign-born population of 4.1 million, 1.6 million were from Ireland.[143] In the first instance, of course, many of them – generally not the poorest – would save not so much to set up their own farms as to send money back home – annual remittances rose from $1.4 million in 1847 to $8.4 million in 1854.[144] Often these funds were to cover the fare from Liverpool, which was officially £20 in second class but could be as low as £2 in steerage during the early years since the British government provided no direct assistance to emigrants until the 1849 Poor Law Amendment Act, and thereafter it helped fewer than 20,000 people.[145]

London did, however, attempt to impose some order on the regime of the vessels transporting the emigrants on what was often a very dangerous voyage (albeit one infinitely less perilous than that still being experienced by slaves in the south Atlantic):

> … breakfast 8–9 a.m.; decks to be swept before breakfast; all beds to be rolled up; deck to be swept after every meal; five out of every 100 emigrants – males of over 14 – to be sweepers each day; dinner at 1 p.m. and supper at 6 p.m.; fires out at 7 p.m.; three lamps dusk to 10 p.m. and one kept through the night; two washing days a week, but never between deck…. XVII. On Sunday mornings the passengers shall be mustered at 10 o'clock a.m. and will be expected to appear in clean and decent apparel. The Lord's Day shall be observed as religiously as circumstances will admit…. XXI. All gambling, fighting, riotous or quarrelsome behaviour, swearing or violent language shall be at once put a stop to. Swords and other offensive weapons shall, as soon as the passengers embark, be placed in the custody of the master.[146]

---

142. *Cotton Kingdom*, p. 171. Olmsted's South Carolinian interlocutor himself neither owned nor hired slaves.

143. *8th Census of the USA*, p. xxix. Only 100,000 of these Famine immigrants went to the Southern states.

144. North, *Economic Growth of the United States*, p. 235.

145. Hyde, *Cunard*, p. 40; Christine Kenealy, *This Great Calamity: The Irish Famine, 1845–1852*, Dublin 1994, p. 310.

146. Order in Council, 6 Oct. 1849, in *BFSP, 1848–49*, XXXVII, London 1862, pp. 229–30.

TABLE 9   Immigration to the USA

(i)	BY DECADE			
	1821–30	1831–40	1841–50	1851–60
Ireland	50,724	207,381	780,719	914,119
Great Britain	25,079	75,810	267,044	423,974
Germany	6,761	152,454	434,626	951,667
Total	143,439	599,125	1,713,251	2,598,214

(ii)	FROM IRELAND, 1845–55 (*1,000s*)	
	1845	45
	1846	46
	1847	106
	1848	113
	1849	159
	1850	164
	1851	221
	1852	160
	1853	163
	1854	102
	1855	50

Sources: *8th Census of the USA*, p. xxv; Mitchell, *British Historical Statistics*, pp. 137–8; *International Historical Statistics: The Americas*, pp. 85, 89.

Fights, though, were nothing compared to disease, which killed thousands, whose committal to the sea meant that their presence in the continent is limited to the memorials at Quebec, Montreal and Grosse Isle. When Sarmiento saw corpses being tipped overboard in New York harbour, he was witnessing the final point on a long watery trail of death.

By 1849 the mortality levels of the emigrants during the transatlantic voyage had been reduced from those of the first years of the Famine, and, as we have seen, the Irish presence had begun to affect the religious, political and ethnic balance of the cities of the North. Even in the South concern about their numbers was spreading. In 1860 there were only 80,000 foreign-born people (28,000 Irish) in Louisiana. And yet nearly a decade earlier the *Morehouse Advocate* declared,

> The great mass of foreigners who come to our shores are laborers, and consequently come in competition with slave labor. It is to their interest to abolish slave labor; and we know full well the disposition of men to promote all things which advantage his own interests. These men come from nations where slavery is not allowed, and they drink in abolition

sentiments from their mothers' breasts; they (all the white race) entertain an utter abhorrence of being put on a level with blacks, whether in the field or in the workshop. Could slavery be abolished, there would be a greater demand for laborers, and the price of labor must be greatly enhanced. These may be termed the internal evidences of the abolitionism of foreigners.[147]

Although we have heard the case for a high 'transfer wage' in the South as being complementary to the retention of slavery, the argument here seems plausible in terms of obtaining work. At the same time, recent immigrants were generally anxious for social acceptance, which required support for the law. And support for the law in this period meant recognition of slavery in the South and of the Fugitive Slave Law in the North. In 1854 the bulk of the militia protecting the court-house where fugitive slave Anthony Burns was on trial was composed of Irishmen, whose sensitive position is reflected in the protestation of Thomas Sweney, owner of the *American Celt*:

> At this time, when so much opprobium is heaped on Adopted Citizens, it is astonishing to behold the alacrity with which papers heretofore *professing* to be particularly friendly to us, join in the hue and cry against us – take, for instance, the item in the Boston *Daily Times* of this morning, in which it is stated that John C. Cluer, one of the alleged abolitionist rioters, is an Irishman. Now, it is known to the Citizens of Boston in general, and to the reporter of the Times in particular, that John C. Cluer is a Scotchman. Since the passing of that questionable enactment, the Fugitive Slave Law, it has been openly and violently resisted, and violated in this city and elsewhere, by the descendants of Puritans only – but in no instance have Irish Adopted Citizens cooperated with them. The Citizens of Boston, of Irish birth, have taken a solemn oath to sustain the Constitution and Laws of this glorious Union – and to their honor be it spoken, they never have, and never will be found to act inconsistently with the proper observance of that solemn obligation.[148]

However, neither this sentiment nor the examples of Daniel Clark, an owner of many slaves, and John Mitchel, more openly supportive of the 'peculiar institution' even than Carlyle, is representative of the general attitude of the Irish in America to slavery. Frederick Douglass found early enlightenment about his condition as a slave in the words of Sheridan:

> I met with one of Sheridan's mighty speeches on and in behalf of Catholic emancipation. These were choice documents to me. I read them over and over again with unabated interest. They gave tongue to interesting thoughts of my own soul, which had frequently flashed through my mind, and died away from want of utterance. The moral which I gained from the dialogue was the power of truth over the conscience of even a slaveholder. What I got from Sheridan was a bold denunciation of slavery, and a powerful vindication of human rights.

Not long after – in the early 1840s – Douglass's duties took him to the Baltimore waterfront:

---

147. Quoted in Olmsted, *Cotton Kingdom*, p. 232.
148. *The Liberator*, 11 June 1854, quoted in Albert J. Von Frank, *The Trials of Anthony Burns*, Cambridge, Mass., 1998, p. 137.

I went one day down on the wharf of Mr Waters; and seeing two Irishmen unloading a scow of stone, I went, unasked, and helped them. When we had finished, one of them came to me and asked me if I were a slave. I told him I was. The good Irishman seemed to be deeply affected by the statement. He said to the other that it was a pity so fine a little fellow as myself should be a slave for life. He said it was a shame to hold me. They both advised me to run away to the north; that I should find friends there, and that I should be free.[149]

Thirty miles from the Mason–Dixon Line, Baltimore was the most northerly city with slaves – in 1850 over a seventh of Maryland's 583,000 people were enslaved – and although the tightening of the Fugitive Slave Act in that year made escape very much harder, this was still a different world from that in New Orleans, 1,460 miles away at the other extreme of the section.[150] At the turn of the century Daniel Clark could – with favourable winds – travel between them inside a couple of weeks, but most took the arduous and much longer land route across to Louisville and Fort Massac and then down the Mississippi. Even in 1850 there was only a railway for a few miles north out of New Orleans, and the trip from Baltimore required travel on five different lines, two stage-coaches and two steamships. By 1840 the railroads of the east were able to transport passengers at 15 m.p.h. – three times the speed of the stage-coach – and they required only 8.5 lb. of force to move a ton of freight (against 145 lb needed from horses on a common road).[151] The advantages had been manifest immediately and the New York Central, Erie, Pennsylvania and Baltimore and Ohio systems were quickly established. Nevertheless, railway construction was very expensive and the market for capital in the early 1840s was, as we have seen, most erratic. In 1850 the eastward rail-link from Chicago only reached Detroit; ten years later – in the wake of the Gold Rush as well as the Mexican War – four lines connected Chicago with New York. Now the trip between New Orleans and Baltimore could also be made entirely by rail.

There were political and logistical as well as economic reasons behind this expansion. In December 1850 President Fillmore reported that the country's inland mail routes amounted to 176,672 miles (including 18,417 post offices) and cost $2.7 million to sustain (letters travelled at 3 cents if prepaid or 5 if not). The need to improve communications in terms of speed and security as well as cost was no less

---

149. *Narrative of the Life of Frederick Douglass, an American Slave* (1845), Harmondsworth 1986, pp. 84–6.

150. 'Even Playing-Cards, – they want to take a Shilling the Pack. If *your* Parliament go ahead with this, we'll have a Summer like the World has never seen.'
'Not my Parliament,' Mason alertly.
'Do I take it, then, that you own no Property, whatever 'tis you're from, Sir?'
'What Rooms in my Adult Life have not been rented to me,' Mason reckons, 'have been included in the terms of my employment.'
'Then you're a serf. As they call it here, a Slave.'
'Sir, I work under Contract.'
'Someone owns you, Sir. He pays for your Meals and Lodging. He lends you to others. What is that call'd, where you come from?'
Thomas Pynchon, *Mason and Dixon*, London 1997, pp. 405–6.

151. Lebergott, *The Americans*, p. 109.

TABLE 10   Railway track (*km*)

	1840	1845	1850	1855	1860
USA	4,535	7,456	14,518	17,674	49,288
Canada	25	25	106	1,411	3,323
Cuba	82	82	440	440	682
Jamaica		23	23	23	23
Mexico			13	16	32
Brazil				14	223
Panama				76	76
Peru				24	87
Argentina					69

Source: Mitchell, *International Historical Statistics: The Americas*, pp. 656, 661.

evident after Morse's invention of the telegraph than before it. Railroads could not always be built alongside telegraph lines, but it was already clear that the combined construction of the two would yield more than convenience. Telegraph lines were, though, very vulnerable to destruction by hostile Indians. In 1851 Fillmore was informed by his secretary of war of the escalating costs of maintaining the south-west garrisons. In 1845 the most isolated was Fort Scott, 90 miles from a steam-boat landing and readily reachable by wagon-train without great cost. By 1851 the Indianola depot for most of the Texas and New Mexico forts was 540 miles from New Orleans by water, 420 miles by wagon from Fort Worth, and 803 miles from El Paso. Total military transport costs had risen from $130,000 to $2 million, and those of forage (a cost of animal transport that is too easily ignored today) had also increased vertiginously – from $100,000 to $1.3 million. Acquisition of new territory after the Mexican War had led to the expansion of the army's budget by $4.5 million but the number of troops had risen by only 2,000 to 11,000 in all.[152]

By the outbreak of the Civil War there was still no railway line much further west than Houston (St Joseph, Missouri, in the North). The way to California was either via Nicaragua and Panama or by wagon-train (north via the Mormon trail through Fort Laramie towards Salt Lake City and then by the Oregon trail to Portland or the California trail to San Francisco; through Kansas to Santa Fe and then by the old Spanish trail to Los Angeles; or south through the Oxbow route passing through Texas to San Diego), and this would not be free of serious risk for decades.

As can be seen from table 10, by 1860 the USA possessed more than ten times the track laid in the rest of the continent – forty times that laid in Latin America – but

---

152. Fillmore, Message to Congress, 2 Dec. 1850, in *BFSP, 1849–50*, XXXVIII, p. 212; C.M. Conrad, Secretary of War, to Fillmore, 29 Nov. 1851, in *BFSP, 1850–51*, XL, London 1863, pp. 193–6.

it was not until May 1869 that the Continental Pacific and Union Pacific lines were joined at Promontory, Utah to form the first trans-continental railroad.

California, then, was always far away. The gold found there seemed to most only to augment the blessings of Providence upon a nation that had just defeated Mexico in war. Ten months after the discovery at Sutter's Mill and the signing of the Treaty of Guadalupe Hidalgo, President Polk told Congress,

> It was known that mines of the precious metals existed to a considerable extent in California at the time of its acquisition. Recent discoveries render it probable that these mines are more extensive and valuable than was anticipated. The accounts are of such an extraordinary character as would scarcely commend belief, were they not corroborated by the authentic reports of officers in the public service.

However, as the senior public servant, Polk was himself obliged to indicate some consequences of both reality and narrative:

> … all other pursuits but that of searching for the precious metals are abandoned. Nearly the whole of the male population of the country are gone to the gold districts. Ships arriving on the coast are deserted by their crews, and their voyages suspended for want of sailors. Our commanding officer there entertains apprehensions that soldiers cannot be kept in the public service without a large increase in pay.

Prices were spiralling out of control; there was no mint in California; and the monthly steamer service from Panama was completely inadequate.[153] Three years later Fillmore was concerned that the strength of Californian inflation would affect the balance of payments of the nation as a whole:

> Unless some salutary check shall be given to these tendencies, it is to be feared that importations of foreign goods, beyond a healthy demand in this country, will lead to a sudden drain of the precious metals from us, bringing with it, as it has done in former times, the most disastrous consequences to the business and capital of the American people.[154]

Given that economic disaster had occurred less than a decade before, the proposal to alleviate this position by decreasing the size of plots put up for sale seems a distinctly frail response. As can be seen from table 2, Britain did indeed increase its exports to the USA, but this was more than matched by US sales into the British market. Californian wages remained high, but by 1860 they were only two to three times those paid in the midwest.

In 1860 13 per cent of the US population had been born abroad, but nearly half of California's 300,000 people were immigrants (33,000 of them from Ireland). Most would have been drawn to the west by exotic accounts whereby California was America and more, but the experience was frequently much more prosaic than the tales told, even for the likes of Benjamín Vicuña Mackenna, who arrived in 1853 with much already to his name:

---

153. Polk, Message to Congress, 5 Dec. 1848, in *BFSP, 1847–48*, XXXVI, London 1861, pp. 798–9.
154. Fillmore, Message to Congress, 2 Dec. 1851, in *BFSP, 1850–51*, XL, p. 172.

I had come to San Francisco with 2,000 sacks of Chilean wheat as a cargo. My consignee sold them all in a few hours at $29 and a half a sack. They had cost only $8 in Valparaiso, so that made us a profit of $35,000. But I, who thought I knew so much about San Francisco, discovered I knew nothing. In the first place, the pilot lost two of my anchors in the mouth of the bay and made me pay $80, or 50 cents a day for each unit of the ship's tonnage. The towing of the ship two or three miles cost $50 more. When I finally tied up to one of the hundreds of public or private piers in the bay, the owner, a butcher, told me there would be no charge provided I bought all the meat for the crew from him. The ship was unloaded, but the bill for a month came to $249, or about 5 cents a day for each of the ship's 250 tons.

When we got moored at the pier, the customs service sent on board an inspector whom we had to feed as well as paying $6 a day. After the cargo was sold, other men came to make an official quality inspection. Every sack was as good, bad or very bad, according to the amount of damage each sack showed. One ounce of damaged flour got the whole sack stamped as bad; but our official, a man of the highest rank in the service, marked a large part of the cargo as very bad, and there was a $8 difference between that and the good. He had obviously been bribed by the purchaser.[155]

Maybe Vicuña Mackenna was jumping to conclusions, but Dickens would probably have called this 'sharp practice', and Christopher Platt could hardly have been more lucid in enumerating the tribulations of commerce in alien lands, be they administered by Anglo- or Latin Americans. California was, of course, a lottery and a violent one in more ways than this; there were many losers. It is not so surprising that, writing in 1854, at the end of his Journal, John Mitchel should report the excitement of those who were not going to but returning from California:

This morning, the heights of Nevisink, then Sandy Hook, Staten Island, Long Island. We steam rapidly up the outer harbour. My wife and I walking on deck, enjoying and admiring the glee of some of our New York acquaintances on board, as the great ocean avenue to their native city opens before them, after years of absence in California. They eagerly point out every known feature in the vast bay; and ask me to admit that it is the most beautiful bay in the world.[156]

ON THE ROAD TO SOMEWHERE

Everybody now knows that after 1850 Latin America did not develop like Anglo-America. Nor, of course, did any other place on earth. One does not have to subscribe to the theses of exceptionalism to see that the comparison is only good for certain purposes and cannot usefully be taken beyond a certain point. For the six generations that lived between then and now the economic differences between the

---

155. Edwin A. Meilharz and Carlos U. López (eds), *We Were 49ers! Chilean Accounts of the California Gold Rush*, Pasadena, Calif., 1976, p. 201.

156. *Jail Journal*, Glasgow 1876, pp. 319–20.

two parts of the continent mattered a bit in the North and quite a lot in the South, but not, perhaps, as much as we like to think today. For all the Alberdis and Sarmientos promoting the future there were millions of 'plain folk' for whom 'modernity' was both an absurdity, because it was to occur after their death, and an irrelevance, because daily survival constituted an end (and often a joy) in itself. In many ways the 'now' of 1850 looked very different in Panama to that in Paraguay as thousands poured through the former on their way to uncertain fortunes in California whilst the latter excluded foreigners precisely to preserve the stability of the past. Yet the existentialist commonality both between these two small states and between them and the USA was greater and richer than some evolutionist perspectives allow.

Such a claim would appear to be completely misguided if we work on the basis of simple averages. In 1845 the average per capita income in Mexico was $56 and that in Brazil $72, compared to $274 in the USA and $323 in Great Britain.[157] But, in addition to the very different local purchasing power of their currencies, there were important variations inside Latin American societies, which, in the case of Mexico, included a quite sizeable and influential middle class. In the state of Querétaro, for instance, about a fifth of the population in 1844 was in receipt of an income of over $365 (a dollar a day), with members of the merchant and professional middle class earning over $1,000 a year. Comparable figures for Sinaloa and Mexico City suggest that perhaps a third of the population was 'middle class' in terms of relative income and the sense that its condition was merely one of insecurity, not permanent misery.[158] The distribution is not the same as in the USA, but neither is it one of absolute polarisation between rich and poor. This middle sector was also the group most directly hindered by the colonial legacy and, as John Coatsworth suggests, the one least understood in dependency theory:

> Latin America did not need autarky (or a more exalted place in the developing international division of labor), as the dependistas have argued. Instead, the region needed new governments founded on the bourgeois principles of equal legal rights for adult male 'citizens', a modern regime of bourgeois property rights, judicial systems capable of enforcing the sanctity of private property and contracts, and policymaking institutions that would accord priority to responding to the needs of the rich and successful (whether well-born or not).[159]

By 1850 these 'preconditions' had been 'absent' from Latin America for a century in the sense that they were increasingly prevalent in Great Britain and the USA. It was not just recurrent political conflict but the public culture within which it took place that one must add to the physical obstacles and poor transport in explaining the 'backwardness' of the Mexican economy or its 'failure' to develop a capitalism based on local investment, political participation and a range of skills. Such a failure in

---

157. Coatsworth, 'Obstacles to Economic Growth', p. 82.
158. Torcuato Di Tella, 'The Dangerous Classes in Early Nineteenth-Century Mexico', *JLAS*, 5:1, 1973.
159. 'Notes on the Comparative Economic History of Latin America and the United States', p. 18.

terms of economic development has widely been ascribed to a 'feudalism', but, as Coatsworth argues, that is seriously to misrepresent the position by applying to Latin America a term that has been derived from an earlier European period and to do so without proper consideration of whether the characteristics associated with that term really obtained in the Americas (at any time):

> Mexico's landowners enjoyed none of the privileges of the old European nobility, either before independence or after. Spanish raison d'état – principally the fear of an American nobility rising to claim sovereignty over New World populations – prevented any such development. Indian access to land came from the crown in the form of corporate, and thus inalienable, land grants to villages. The crown never countenanced legal obligations between Indian villagers and landowners, save those regulated by royal decree and administered by royal officials.[160]

This was the bitter-sweet institutional legacy received by the republics in the 1820s. It was founded upon absolutism, affected broad popular interests, and could not be overturned by any amount of rhetoric borrowed from other revolutions – either that which had been aimed at an entirely distinct imperial system (the USA) or that which overthrew a completely different economic structure (France). Moreover, as has been suggested, the legacy was compounded by two decades of political instability, which was itself the result of ten years of widespread destruction in the wars against Spain (the absence of which provided Brazil with a formidable advantage). Alberdi was open in his recognition of a fact that Sarmiento would only admit tacitly: Rosas was successful because he was popular, he was popular because he secured order, and the order he secured owed little or nothing to bourgeois freedoms. In Mexico Lucas Alamán favoured industrialisation much more than did Rosas, and he was prepared to uphold a protectionist policy to develop textile manufacturing, but Alamán refused to disamortise the corporate lands of the Church, which he saw as the glue holding society together, and holding it together precisely against a destructive democracy. In both cases it did not suit the elite to implement (or the masses to support) more than discrete elements of some 'bourgeois programme', but this did not mean that it was completely absent. The mix of freedoms and fears was simply different, and it existed in a context that would not subsequently be sacralised as the antecedent essential to success.

The anxieties and weaknesses were real enough. Manuel Ibañez happened to be a conservative Colombian landowner, but the fears he expressed in the wake of an abortive insurrectionary movement in 1851 were quite typical of those of property-owners of every ideological stripe when they found themselves bereft of guarantees:

> Imagine your haciendas laid waste, your country houses burnt, your homes assaulted by gangs led on occasion by public authorities; here a timid woman is violated, there a man is cruelly whipped, further away another is murdered; he that stays behind is beaten; he that flees is pursued; no one can walk the streets or roads without the danger of being robbed,

---

160. 'Obstacles to Economic Growth', p. 96.

abused or insulted; he that resists or defends himself is taken to the jail as a conspirator; he that protests is inscribed in the terrible book of the [Sociedad] Democrática.[161]

From the perspective of confidence it does not matter much that the picture painted here is deliberately exaggerated for effect or that such conditions prevailed only occasionally. As the reflective conservative Sergio Arboleda argued,

Because of this [lack of confidence] capital investments are not made in a visible way nor are they employed in industries from which they cannot be withdrawn easily; because of this, capital has been directed preferentially into foreign commerce in order to safeguard it from the revolutionary exploitations of the interior; because of this, our best branches of industry have not been perfected, because no one wants to expose himself to the losses caused to those industries in a country that gives no guarantees from one day to the next; in the same way, the prices of domestic products have not gone down because consumers must pay for the risk endured by invested capital; and because of this, ultimately, timid men have tried to place their fortune in urban real estate because the revolutionaries, so they say, cannot carry off the buildings.[162]

Arboleda, in his turn, is able to project the factor of political instability well beyond all others, probably because he was writing in the immediate wake of the expulsion of the Jesuits, abolition of clerical privileges, separation of Church and state, division of Indian communal lands, abolition of slavery and overhaul of commercial regulation – all of which occurred between 1850 and 1853 and all of which might readily be included in some 'bourgeois programme'. None the less, Arboleda was surely correct in his identification of the general response to risk. There were plenty of landlords like 'Don Federico' of Granada, Nicaragua, whom George Squier described as 'having gone through several revolutions, securely locked in, eating and sleeping as usual': more secure, perhaps, than we might imagine but still completely unproductive.[163] Given that the first twenty years of Nicaraguan independence witnessed eighteen holders of supreme executive office and seventeen battles in which 1,200 people lost their lives, it is quite understandable that the general view of the day was that slow economic growth was less a matter of lacking capital than of suffering from too much fighting.[164]

Political instability usually meant increased military conscription, forcing peasants to flee their work or lands in order to evade the press-gangs, reducing the number of troops serving as police and so inviting more crime. At the same time, of course, it entailed forced loans and appropriation of forage for the cavalry as well as the looting

161. *Nuevas observaciones sobre la administración del general José H. López en la Nueva Granada*, Lima 1853, p. 18, quoted in Richard P. Hyland, 'A Fragile Prosperity: Credit and Agrarian Structure in the Cauca Valley, Colombia, 1851–87', *HAHR*, 63:3, 1982, p. 382.

162. *La república en la américa española* (1857), quoted in ibid.

163. *Nicaragua: Its People, Scenery, Monuments*, I, New York 1852, p. 138.

164. Alejandro Marue, *Efeméridades de los hechos notables acaeidos en la república de Centroamérica*, Guatemala 1895, pp. 141, 151, cited in Héctor Lindo Fuentes, *Weak Foundations: The Economy of El Salvador in the Nineteenth Century, 1821–1898*, Berkeley 1990, p. 50; Tulio Halperín Donghi, 'Economy and Society', in Leslie Bethell (ed.), *Spanish America after Independence, c. 1820–c. 1870*, Cambridge 1987, p. 9.

that often attended the aftermath of clashes between troops whose commanders rarely had sufficient cash to hand for regular pay, let alone bounty. If this sort of disruption was not fully comparable with the insecurity of Indian raids on the US frontier, there was greater similarity in the hazards to production posed by banditry and brigandage. Here the focus is less on the landlord than the peasant or rural poor, in whose ranks that evasive but potent figure, the 'social bandit', was discerned in the 1930s by the Peruvian judge Enrique López Albujar thirty years before Eric Hobsbawm developed his suggestive and controversial thesis of a primitive rebellion encapsulated within apparently 'ordinary' crime. López Albujar had little sympathy for the likes of Arboleda and Ibañez, and he attributed the lack of crime in certain areas precisely to the lack of landlords:

> In Moquegua there are no haciendas, which is the same as saying there are no landlords, no swindling hacienda wage clerks, no labour contractors, foremen, nor a naked, irrevocable and absolute domination over water supplies. Water is not deliberately wasted. Neither is production high at the cost of low wages. Perpetual chains of debt to a landlord are absent. People labour freely, without desperate and exhausting needs, but with the faith that they are working for themselves. Even the poorest labourer owns something, a shack in which to live. He does not have the constant fear of eviction from the hacienda, so condemning him to a life of brigandage.[165]

Although this, too, was an idealised picture, it is far more likely to have prevailed in the Peru of 1850 than that of 1920. Banditry was almost always a localised phenomenon, but highwaymen could still cause great upset to trade. The experience of Fanny Calderón de la Barca in the Mexico of the 1840s was far from rare:

> We came ... to a pretty lane, where those of our escort who were in front stopped, and those who were behind rode up and begged us to keep close together, as for many leagues the country was haunted by robbers. Guns and pistols being looked to, we rode on in serried ranks, expecting every moment to hear a bullet whizz over our heads ... We examined as well as we could the robbers' domicile, which was an old half-ruined house, standing alone in the plain, with no tree near it. Several men, with guns, were walking up and down before the house – sporting-looking characters, but rather dirty – apparently either waiting for some expected *game*, or going in search of it.... The well-armed men ... accompanied us ... in the name of ——, so well known in these parts that once when his carriage was surrounded by robbers, he merely mentioned who he was and they retreated with many apologies for their mistake ... but woe to the solitary horseman or the escorted carriage that should pass thereby.[166]

The position was more precarious still on the borderlands of Araucania, where, as we have seen, the *malones* (plundering raids) against settler estates and townships made any enterprise insecure. However, by the early 1850s Indian raids were probably more

---

165. *Los caballeros de delito*, Lima 1936, p. 96, quoted in John Dawe and Lewis Taylor, 'Enrique López Albujar and the Study of Peruvian Brigandage', *BLAR*, 13:3, 1994, p. 254; E.J. Hobsbawm, *Primitive Rebels*, Manchester 1959; *Bandits*, Harmondsworth 1972.

166. *Life in Mexico* (1842), London 1987, pp. 322, 152–3.

extensive and destructive in North America than South. Following the Gadsden Treaty of 1853, whereby the USA purchased a further belt of Mexican territory and undertook to offer protection from Apache intrusions, the Sánchez Navarro family lodged a huge compensation claim for 'Indian depredations' suffered over the previous five years. According to their submission, the Apache had killed 43 peons and 98 shepherds, driving off 12,918 lambs, 7,106 mules, 100 asses, 204,212 sheep, 2,080 goats, 111,867 cattle and 1,230 unspecified animals, together valued at $865,165.89. The precision of these numbers must have aroused the suspicion of the US commissioners since the Sánchez Navarros received not a cent of their claim, but there can be little doubt that a large border enterprise such as this – 12 farms with 4,000 peons in 1846 – was very vulnerable and would have suffered significant losses.[167]

Lack of law and order was certainly a serious problem, but by 1850 it was no longer the primary cause of slow economic growth and it is better seen as an effect of the fragile legitimacy of the states established in the wake of independence:

> Republican governments were to face yet greater political resistance to raising revenue; they had no mystery or majesty, they had to sacrifice some 'colonial' resources for the sake of modernity, they were nearly always partisan and often patently feeble, sometimes corrupt. In such circumstances tax-evasion appeared to many to be a civic duty, and one must remember that none of these governments existed in a political vacuum. Viceroys were apprehensive about the possible effects of innovation, and republican presidents all the more so.[168]

It was conservatism of this type that frustrated William Wills's efforts to set up a bank in Colombia:

> The arguments that have been used against the establishment of a bank include:
> – the lack of stability of our social institutions and confidence in the government;
> – the state of bankruptcy in which the Treasury finds itself;
> – the doleful state of public credit;
> – the defective nature of our legislation with respect to civil procedures in the case of bankruptcy, and the obstacles against any rapid settlement of creditors' claims on the property of the insolvent;
> – the risks posed by an excessive emission of paper money, which would cause fluctuations in price, a lack of confidence, insecure credit, and commercial crises;
> – the notion that banks increase usury at the same time as they tend to reduce other credit and discount transactions to individuals;
> – the ease with which bankrupt, fraudulent or misguided merchants could undertake imprudent speculations in an effort to maintain a fictitious credit;
> – lastly, the political influence of such a powerful institution.[169]

Wills's frustration may have been sharpened by the modest success of the Caja de Ahorros opened in Bogotá in 1846 allowing quite ordinary folk to salt away a few

---

167. Charles A. Harris, *A Mexican Family Empire: The Latifundio of the Sánchez Navarros, 1765–1867*, Austin, Tex., 1975, p. 199.
168. Deas, 'Fiscal Problems of Nineteenth-Century Colombia', pp. 293–4.
169. *Vida y Opiniones de Mr William Wills*, II, p. 178.

reales at an interest rate of 5 to 10 per cent, with the result that over the next decade the average deposit rose from 692 to 1,219 reales. Yet by 1854, when Wills was writing, there were only 1,057 depositors with total savings of less than 1 million reales.[170] This was no competition at all for the Church, which was the country's traditional 'trustee, banker and financial custodian'. The attacks on the Church in the early 1850s that so frightened Sergio Arboleda were to a large degree a reaction to the fact that

> credit, as both a symbol of value and a symbol of trust, was interwoven with the bonds of faith and authority embodied by that institution ... in a society where wealth was concentrated in the hands of the few; where the domestic market forces were enfeebled by isolation and scarcely transcended the limits of a subsistence economy; where fixed capital (in land) vastly overshadowed liquid capital (cash) as a determinant of wealth; and where external sources of capital – governmental, commercial or foreign – were remote, any movement forward, any progress could succeed only by way of major attacks on the economic influence of the Church.[171]

This did not, however, mean that all the rhetoric about clerical backwardness, abuses and inefficiency was either correct or disinterested. Colonial restrictions on lending had been lifted in Colombia in 1835, and the subsequent failure of a secular financial system to emerge cannot be explained exclusively by ecclestiastical inertia and manipulation. In the case of Mexico, where the Church was wealthier still, Coatsworth argues that the standard liberal and left-wing view that it represented an obstacle to growth is incorrect:

> By the time of independence (until 1833 when the tithe was abolished as a legal obligation for the citizenry), Church revenues from this source had already dropped to negligible sums ... the Church did invest a sizable portion of its revenues in mortgage loans to private entrepreneurs.... In addition, it acted as fiduciary agent for trust funds left in its care. The Church invested a large portion of its net income and all of the trust capital it managed, usually at 6 per cent interest on the security of real property. Because it charged a low, non-market interest rate, the Church dominated the mortgage-lending market.... It performed like a modern development bank, charging taxpayers to subsidize the accumulation of private capital.... Most Church estates after independence were rented to individuals, so the efficiency of these properties did not depend on Church management at all.[172]

At the same time, Mexico's secular 'development bank', the Banco de Avío set up by Lucas Alamán in 1830, lasted only twelve years and spent less than a million pesos on a dozen textile factories despite having access to the customs revenue of the state.[173] In Chile the wealthy mineowner Pedro Félix Vicuña had tried without success

---

170. David Sowell, 'La Caja de Ahorros de Bogotá, 1846–1865: Artisans, Credit, Development and Savings in Early National Colombia', *HAHR*, 73:4, 1993, pp. 625–6.

171. Hyland, 'A Fragile Prosperity', p. 387.

172. 'Obstacles to Economic Growth', pp. 89–90.

173. Walther L. Bernecker, 'Foreign Interests, Tariff Policy and Early Industrialization in Mexico', *Ibero-Amerikanisches Arkiv*, 14:1, 1988, p. 81.

to set up a bank as early as 1828 on the grounds that it should be the 'fourth branch of our political organisation' and was vital to national sovereignty. There, copper mineowners were dependent on advances from *habilitadores*, but although these merchants could issue credit through purchase of futures – and did so at rates of up to 36 per cent annually – they were like the cotton factors in the US South in lacking a bank's ability to issue notes or hold deposits. A great many of them went bust, but, as in Colombia, there was still a widespread fear of paper money – the example of Rosas was not so distant – and a marked reluctance on the part of the state to authorise banks of issue and deposit.[174] In the case of Brazil two banks had been founded, in Rio (1838) and Bahía (1848), but they were forbidden by the Crown to print notes, and they had lost all independence within twenty years. Throughout this period,

> interest rates reflected the scarcity of credit. Like much else concerned with the export economy, they were a worse problem in the northeast and north than in the southeast. From midcentury through the 1880s in the southeast they ranged from 6 to 10 per cent annually for merchant houses and from 8 to 14 per cent for planters, but in the northeast from 9 to 18 per cent for merchant firms and from 18 to 24 per cent for planters. Shortages of currency would send such rates temporarily higher. In certain localities, under especially unfavourable conditions, rates for planters climbed to more than 70 per cent.... Overall, Brazil's agricultural credit problem remained unsolved during the nineteenth century.[175]

In Latin America, then, as in the USA, the space in the nexus that is now filled so naturally by banks, building societies, thrift institutions and credit cards was generally covered by wholesale and retail merchants. When he died in 1854, Juan de Dios Trigo, a prominent merchant of Tarija in Bolivia, left an estate of 14,909 pesos, over half of which was in the form of his customers' debts, compared to the one-fifth in the form of merchandise stock (largely fabrics, clothing and buttons). Trigo's colleague of English birth John Lord died three years later, having imported goods from Tacna to the value of 35,233 pesos, leaving 17,245 in customer debt and only 2,100 pesos in land. He was evidently a most successful wholesaler, and very few of his customers owed as little as the 10 pesos 4 reales listed from Francisco Burdett O'Connor, probably the richest landlord in the department.[176]

These examples suggest that until at least 1855 the domestic sources of credit were sufficient to ensure the maintenance of a string of provincial agro-commercial economic circuits, some mining enclaves and a few export sectors into the international market (coffee from Costa Rica as well as from Brazil). This, though, was not 'take-off'. It is also very doubtful whether fiscal pressure from states and governments was bleeding off resources that might otherwise have constituted a significant accumulation of

---

174. Steven S. Volk, 'Mine Owners, Moneylenders, and the State in Mid-Nineteenth-Century Chile: Transitions and Conflicts', *HAHR*, 73:1, 1993, pp. 83–5.

175. Eugene Ridings, *Business Interest Groups in Nineteenth-Century Brazil*, Cambridge 1994, pp. 132–3.

176. Langer and Hames, 'Tarija Merchants', pp. 295–7.

capital. As has been noted, taxes tended to be on trade, particularly on imports, and they suffered from an evasion consonant with slight legitimacy. The indigenous tribute or poll tax, collected in parts of Mesoamerica and the Andes, was more stable because it was perceived as a guarantee of communal rights, but the revenue from this too was often completely drained by the military budget.

Rosas, who had no taxable Indians in his jurisdiction, regularly spent all the custom-house revenue on his army, but he succeeded in cancelling the entire internal debt by 1851. It was the foreign debt, contracted in 1827, that went unnegotiated and unserviced.[177] In Colombia, where taxes on foreign trade yielded much less, charges on alcohol and cattle at the abbatoir remained correspondingly high. There, as in Buenos Aires, the government had multiplied the means by which it could borrow from its own citizens, but

> the history of the foreign debt ... is essentially a simple one. For reasons of diplomatic urgency the country contracted debts that it subsequently could not pay on the terms agreed. Governments could not devote to that end the proportion of their income that would have been required, and Colombia had nothing to offer in the way of bienes nacionales that was acceptable.[178]

If the US was able to recover from its default in 1841–42 in a matter of a few years, it took Argentina thirty to renegotiate that of 1827 and Colombia until 1861 to service bonds issued in 1826. In October 1845 – before Gibbs had signed the contract for guano – Peruvian President Castilla could celebrate political tranquillity and the obedience of the army, but he had to admit that

> the state of the public treasury is lamentable. In fact, it is necessary to confess that it does not exist. Its defective state is the result of disturbances which more than once have over-whelmed the Republic. Its different branches mortgaged for some time to come; laden with payments which it will be difficult to meet; claims made upon it even before means can be found to satisfy them; it offers a picture of desolation which afflicts me beyond measure. Many families exhibit to the Government their misery and their claims, and the Government can only show them the public coffers, empty.[179]

Gibbs were later able to operate in Peru because they collected the guano revenue directly themselves, but it took the signing of their 1849 contract to reopen the negotiation of a debt defaulted on twenty-three years earlier, no foreign banker risking a penny on the country in the interval. Over the following twenty-five years,

---

177. D.C.M. Platt, 'Foreign Finance in Argentina for the First Half-Century of Independence', *JLAS*, 15:1, 1983, p. 30. In this essay Platt makes a rare concession to nationalist arguments in recognising the low profile of international finance in early Argentine economic development – a line that, of course, fits well with his wider thesis of aversion on the part of investors and bankers in Britain to foreign risk. The 1827 loan – nominally for £1 million – was renegotiated in 1857. Carlos Marichal, *A Century of Debt Crises in Latin America*, Princeton 1989, p. 59.

178. Deas, 'Fiscal Problems of Nineteenth-Century Colombia', p. 318.

179. Castilla, message to Congress, Lima, 22 Oct. 1845, in *BFSP, 1845–46*, XXXIV, pp. 1244–5.

by contrast, the Peruvian government received seven international loans worth nearly £52 million, less than half of which was dedicated to financing its prior obligations. This was the exceptional reward bestowed by guano – the total government borrowing of Argentina, Brazil and Mexico combined stood at less than £55 million over the same period – and the region did not restore its reputation as a borrower until foreigners began to make significant investments during the final decades of the century.[180]

Nowadays few scholars would dispute the view that,

By 1850, thirty years after independence, Mexico was unique in Latin America in retaining intact the structure of traditional manufacturing while possessing the outlines, and some of the substance, of a modern manufacturing sector established over the previous two decades.

There is also general acceptance of the fact that, even in the case of Mexico,

The mid-1850s proved to be the peak in this early development of modern manufacturing, which ... declined in relative importance over the rest of the century, as opportunities for foreign investment in mining and agriculture became increasingly important. Traditional cottage industry, it seems, declined in absolute terms from the mid-century.[181]

For Claudio Véliz the failure to develop a manufacturing sector derived from a lack of industrial culture at all levels of society in Latin America – a view perhaps shared by his fellow Chilean Neruda, who uses the word 'industry' not once through-out his work.[182] For Arnold Bauer the fact that by 1882 thirty-nine of Chile's fifty-nine 'millionaires' had made their money as mineowners, bankers and entrepeneurs only to invest it in rural estates reflects rather more than 'the attraction of a place in the country and the ownership of a proper estate where archaic working relations and obedient workers remained anchored in the seventeenth century'. He sees it as representing the equivalent of the South beating the North in the US Civil War.[183] A decade before that Civil War occurred, the US naval officer William Herndon was struck by a not dissimilar thought upon his arrival at the hacienda of Quicarán near Cerro de Pasco in Peru:

I was strongly reminded of the large farmhouses in some parts of Virginia: the same number of servants bustling about in each other's way; the children of the masters and the servants all mixed up together; the same hospitable welcome to all comers; the same careless profusion.

---

180. Marichal, *A Century of Debt Crises*, p. 80.

181. Guy P.C. Thomson, 'Protectionism and Industrialization in Mexico, 1821–1854: The Case of Puebla', in Abel and Lewis (eds), *Economic Imperialism and the State*, p. 123. According to Walther Bernecker,

   ... the assertion that Mexican industrialization in this early phase failed is correct; nevertheless, it succeeded in providing employment and an outlet for domestic and ... foreign investment in an economy where other investment opportunities (excepting risky speculation) were still lacking.

'Foreign Interests, Tariff Policy and Early Industrialization', pp. 87–8.

182. Claudio Véliz, *The Centralist Tradition of Latin America*, Princeton 1980, p. 274.

183. 'Industry and the Missing Bourgeoisie: Consumption and Development in Chile, 1850–1950', *HAHR*, 70:2, 1990, pp. 242–3.

The inhabitants of such a society were by no means less possessed of a sense of local and national space than the 'Southerners' to their north. When one of Herndon's travelling companions fell ill as they ascended the Cordillera Occidental of the Andes,

> I made a speech to some curious loafers about the tent, in which I appealed to their pride and patriotism, telling them that I thought it strange that so large a town as San Mateo, belonging to so famous a country as Peru, could not furnish a sick stranger, who could eat nothing else, with a few eggs. Whereupon a fellow went off and brought us a dozen, though he had just sworn by the Pope that there were no such things in the village.[184]

Of course, most rural societies uphold mutually reinforcing sentiments of parochial intimacy and suspicion of strangers, but in the case of Latin America this, as has already been suggested, was often translated into a stark image of comprehensive 'feudal' backwardness. That association was certainly encouraged by the sheer size of some of the estates created after independence, whatever the prior relationship of landlords with communal property. The huge holdings of the Sánchez Navarros were not unique. In his first year as governor of Buenos Aires Rosas was making land grants of four or five square leagues (26,000–32,500 acres) to 'impoverished' families; a greater acreage still was awarded in 1834 and 1835 to troops owed back-pay; and 1,500 square leagues were sold in May 1836 to reduce the government's debts. Although these tracts were overwhelmingly unsurveyed lands conceived as pastorage, located on the frontier of the 'desert', and prey to *malones*, they represented a critical extension of 'property' in itself as well as increasing the opportunities for a concentration of wealth. Under Rosas nearly 4.5 million acres were distributed to the troops, and after his fall this system was not only retained but also included the expropriation of his own considerable estates: between 1852 and 1864 some 18.5 million acres were sold or granted by the government. Since Rosas had abolished the system of emphyteusis (the Roman custom of hereditary lease introduced in Buenos Aires after independence), this represented a massive alienation of state land.[185] There was no longer any Crown to preside jealously over powers of property. Perhaps this new system might, indeed, merit the term 'feudal'?

Marc Bloch reminds us of one aspect of the beneficium or fief in Western Europe a millennium earlier:

> Since estates regularly distributed by the lord to his followers were much more in the nature of pay than of reward, it was essential that they should revert to him without difficulty as soon as the service ceased to be rendered; at the latest, therefore, when the tie was broken by death ... such grants of land, by definition temporary and, originally at least, devoid of any 'warranty' [had precedent in] neither the official Roman law nor Germanic custom, with their rigid systems of bilateral leases.... Nevertheless in the Empire, under the influence

---

184. *Exploration of the Valley of the Amazon* (1854), New York 1952, pp. 61–2, 22–3.
185. A.F. Zimmerman, 'The Land Policy of Argentina, with Particular Reference to the Conquest of the Southern Pampas', *HAHR*, 25:1, 1945, pp. 13–15.

of powerful individuals there [came] into existence as a matter of private arrangement a great many pacts of this kind, which were naturally associated with the patron–client relationship.'[186]

Only some of these features are shared with the distribution/market of land through-out the Americas in the mid nineteenth century, and we should also note that Euro-pean feudal society retained the autonomy of the peasant commune, independent towns and an ambiguity – through the system of *primus inter pares* – at the heart of sovereignty.[187] Even if interpreted very broadly, those features are hard to discern in the wake of 250 years of absolutist-imperialist monarchy in the South. Similar expressions of deference, dependence and servility were, as we have seen, to be found in the estate-centred hierarchy of rural Chile – and they were readily encountered in the more densely populated Andean and Mexican countrysides – but it was precisely the lack of control of the Argentine elite over rural workers that so exercised Sarmiento. For Tulio Halperín Donghi, Sarmiento's resort to immigration as the answer to this lack of organic hierarchy belied a core weakness of Argentine liberalism – its incapacity to fashion a peasant society on the pampa as the foundation of the new nation. This might be thought understandable of Buenos Aires province at least, which, in terms of per capita value of foreign trade at the time of independence, was more integrated into the world market than Great Britain.[188]

It was not, though, a shortcoming unique to Argentina. The Brazilian elite was infused with a quite similar pessimism about the possibility of control over the native workforce, although the continued existence of slavery there encouraged the conviction that it was just as much freedom as local custom which militated against a tradition of work. In a congressional debate of 1843 the deputy Manuel Antonio Galvao ex-pressed in direct manner a point quite similar to that made by McDonald and McWhiney about the Southern states of the USA:

> Work? You want to oblige these simpletons to work? Are these the people that the noble deputy is very seriously going to talk political economy to, inviting them to pick up a hoe and go to work? For them there are many forests, full of fruit and game ... [And even if expelled by the police] who is to stop these inhabitants of the forests from going a few leagues further on, from disappearing into the forest and making their clearing when the fog comes, so that the police won't see the smoke, and then remaining there two years planting and contenting themselves with their manioc bread?[189]

On the Argentine pampa supply and control of workers was, in fact, less acute a problem because cattle-raising was not labour-intensive, and the rhythms of pastoralism were consonant with high levels of both dependence and autonomy. Certainly, as Alberdi argued, the 'barbarism' of the gaucho did not impede, and did much to

186. *Feudal Society* (1940), London 1965, pp. 163–4.

187. Perry Anderson, *Passages from Antiquity to Feudalism*, London 1974, pp. 148–51.

188. 'Liberalism in Argentina', in Love and Jacobsen (eds), *Guiding the Invisible Hand*, pp. 102–4; *Proyecto y construcción de una nación: Argentina, 1846–1880*, Caracas 1980; Jonathan C. Brown, 'The Bondage of Old Habits in Nineteenth-Century Argentina', *LARR*, XXXI:2, 1986, p. 5.

189. Quoted in Dean, 'Latifundia and Land Policy', p. 612.

promote, the construction of the formidable ranching enterprises that transformed the economy of Buenos Aires in mid century. At the apex of this system was the Anchorena family, whose holdings of 6,330 square kilometres in 1852 outstripped those of the Sánchez Navarros, although they contained many fewer tied workers. Under Juan José Anchorena the family had acquired half this property through purchase and renting of state lands (*tierras baldías*) in emphyteusis by the time Rosas came to power, but it was his sale of the *baldíos* that consolidated the two main estates (Pila and Mar Chiquita) and enabled the acquisition of three more, of which two – Pergamino and Tordillo – exceeded 1,500 square kilometres.[190] Jonathan Brown estimates the size of the Anchorena herd to be around 50,000 head at that time – less than that of the Sánchez Navarros in terms of quantity of animals but much more valuable. The fact that in 1830 alone Juan José Anchorena bought 999 cows, 123 bulls and steers, 397 calves and 453 horses gives weight to Brown's description of the family as 'one of the largest and wealthiest landed empires in the Americas. The extent of their cattle operations presaged by at least 50 years the large cattle ranches in the western United States.'[191]

When Nicolás Anchorena died in 1856 he left, in addition to his lands, 7.5 million pesos fuertes (silver pesos, equivalent to a dollar or four shillings). Like Juan José, Nicolás would surely have given financial assistance to the Rosas regime, even as they gave as wide a berth as possible to the governor's paper currency and were paid by the *mataderos* in thirty-day letters of credit. With a slaughtering season between December and April and herds of some 250 head on each tropa (drive) of no more than 450 kilometres – compared with drives of up to 2,000 kilometres in the USA in the 1870s – the Anchorenas could deliver 1,000 head of cattle to the abbatoir every month for nigh-on half the year. We should not be surprised to discover that their rate of return was probably over 15 per cent in the 1850s, when Chilean landlords could barely manage 4 per cent and those in northern Mexico registered between 6 and 12 per cent.[192]

Under Rosas the Anchorenas paid their hands between 12 and 14 pesos a month; the foremen earned 25, and all workers received full board, tobacco, paper, *yerba*, salt, flour and ponchos on top of their pay. This would underpin a life much better than that of a dog – 'scarcity and ease' – attributed to the population of Paraguay by Carlyle. It was also rather better than the earnings of the peons of the Sánchez Navarros, whose pay of five pesos covered twenty gallons of corn, seven quarts of beans, a bottle of wine, a yard of coarse frieze and a pound of meat.[193] However, a closer reconstruction by Harry Cross of the standard of living on the hacienda del

190. Jonathan C. Brown, 'A Nineteenth-Century Argentine Cattle Empire', *Agricultural History*, 52, 1978, pp. 163–4.

191. Ibid., pp. 163, 166.

192. Ibid., pp. 176–7.

193. Harris, *Mexican Family Empire*, p. 217.

Manguey in Zacatecas, Mexico, in this period suggests that estate labourers were better off than these figures suggest. Cross finds these people – not untypical of the country's rural poor – to be critically protected by the maize ration that was the responsibility of their landlord. Paying no rent, they were able to purchase enough beans and meat to exceed today's recommended calorie intake for a daily cycle of sleeping eight hours, undertaking light activity for ten, light work for three, with another three dedicated to 'moderate labour' (walking at 4 m.p.h., weeding and hoeing, loading and stacking bales, scrubbing floors).[194]

Cross also notes that there was often a surplus to cover expenditure on tobacco and alcohol, and he suggests that over a sixty-year period family size was deliberately regulated to preserve or improve the standard of living. In fact, the general pattern in Mexico, as for most of the continent, was for the price of food and basic necessities to stay stable or fall during the mid-century decades. This seems to have been as true of the towns as of the countryside. In the case of Lima, Paul Gootenberg finds a long period – between 1830 and 1860 – of declining food prices, with as much as a third of family income (regardless of class) being spent on meat as real income increased up to the early 1850s. Of course, such deflation also affected the income of producers and those local artisans competing against cheap imports, but Gootenberg plausibly suggests that its impact was 'democratic'.[195]

Carlyle's pungent one-liners usually contained the germ of their own qualification, if not outright contradiction. This is nicely illustrated by Fanny Calderón de la Barca as she records her first impressions of Mexico:

> Tortillas, which are the common food of the people, and which are merely maize-cakes mixed with a little lime, and of the form and size of what we call scones, I find rather good when very hot and fresh-baked, but insipid by themselves. They have been in use all through this country since the earliest stages of its history, without any change in the manner of baking them, excepting that, for the noble Mexicans in former days, they used to be kneaded with various medicinal plants, supposed to render them more wholesome. They are considered particularly palatable with *chile*, to endure which, in the quantities in which it is eaten here, it seems to me necessary to have a throat lined with tin.
>
> In unpacking some books today, I happened to take up *Sartor Resartus*, which, by a curious coincidence opened of itself, to my great delight, at the following passage: 'The simplest costume', observes our Professor, 'which I anywhere find alluded to in history, is that used as regimental by Bolívar's cavalry, in the late Colombian wars. A square blanket, twelve feet in diagonal, is provided (some were wont to cut off the corners, and make it circular); in the centre a slit is effected, 18 inches long; through this the mother-naked trooper introduces his head and neck; and so rides, shielded from all weather, and in battle from many strokes (for he rolls it about his left arm); and not only dressed, but harnessed and draperied.' Here then we find the true 'Old Roman contempt for the superfluous' which seems rather to meet the approbation of the illustrious Professor Teufelsdrokh.[196]

---

194. 'Living Standards in Rural Nineteenth-Century Mexico: Zacatecas, 1820–1880', *JLAS*, 10:1, 1978, pp. 5–9.

195. 'Prices in Nineteenth-Century Peru', *HAHR*, 70:1, 1990, p. 38.

196. *Life in Mexico*, p. 66. Had Fanny possessed the Oxford University Press 1987 edition of Carlyle's work, it would have fallen open at p. 40.

Carlyle's own first experience of 'Indian corn' had produced an ambivalence nearly as fierce as that which he displayed towards simplicity, but he was clear at least in his outright antipathy to the haste in life produced by the 'dismal science' of economics. Today, of course, 'Mexican food' has been subsumed to 'fast food' as efficiently as the Northern platters that Frederick Olmsted was too slow to order in Vicksburg. In 1848, by contrast, it stood at the heart of a distended and modulated domestic cycle, constituted much more than mere comestible matter, and was still strange enough for Anglos that the Ohio volunteer Samuel Ryan Curtis felt it worthwhile to provide – albeit in a rather off-hand manner – a detailed description:

> We stopped at a ranch, the best we saw in the route. The main building was a one-storey brick, with two rooms below; and the back of these, a large shed or piazza. We were invited into the south room which was about half full of corn in the husk. The other half was full of men, women and children. They were a little shy at first, but soon became assured after they perceived our arms were not designated to operate against them. We got corn to feed our horses, seated ourselves in the midst of them, and passed around segars to men and women who all participated in smoking as all good Mexicans always do. The group is a fair sample of the inside of a Mexican house, and I may as well describe it. The fire place is occupied with a small fire, surrounded with skillets and small kettles. On the left on her hunkers (if there be such a word) is an old woman engaged in washing corn. On the right side of the chimney are two more women, in a similar posture; one is taking hominy or shelled corn from a Mexican crock and grinding it on a stone. The stone is constructed from solid granite, and made to stand before her inclined, so that the ground meal or 'batter' runs down to the lower end of the stone. It is then taken up in her hands and passed over to the woman on the right, who rolls it out into a very thin pan cake, and puts it on a griddle to bake. After it remains for a few moments on the iron plate it is taken up by the woman with her fingers and thrown onto the fire where it is smoked and dried a moment more. The cake is called a 'tortillia' and is very good eating. Nearer to us, on the right, is a very old man apparently 90 or 100 years old; on the left, opposite, is a dark Mexican, who seems to oversee every thing; he is about 30 years old. All the intervals of this picture are filled up with little girls and boys of all sizes, who all seemed delighted to see us.
>
> We all wanted dinner, and we were soon provided with what they, no doubt, regarded as something extra. Our table was arranged in the back shed. It was about two feet by four, covered with a cotton cloth. We were told to sit, and soon the center of the table was adorned with a plate of tortillias. I was much embarrassed to know if we were to commence or wait for more. It was a moment of terrible suspense. If we wait and no more is designed, it will indicate a dissatisfaction and mortify the family. If we commence on this alone and more is coming, they will regard us as voracious boobies. I continue to pass a moment in adjusting my chair, and addressing a little black-eyed girl that had crept up on a bench close on my left. Our suspense was however soon relieved by the presentation to all of us with a saucer of egg and onion boiled and mixed together. Here was a fair foundation to start on, and we all 'with one accord', took a tortillo, tore it in pieces with our hands, and commenced dipping the end of it in our egg. Being very hungry, we found it an easy matter to dispense with knife and fork, even in eating soft eggs. We had hardly commenced when another saucer was presented with a kind of hashed meat and pepper; also semi-fluid. I would have given a dollar for a spoon or knife, and really found myself quite fortunate in finding in my pocket a small pen knife. It was interesting to see the means each of us contrived to convey provisions to our gaping mouths without interposing our fingers. The Mexicans seemed much amused, and gathered around, as the crowd does at a caravan to see the animals feed.

Six weeks later, having tasted even richer fare in a middle-class dining room, Curtis was ready to augment a novice's attention to detail with an equanimity born of growing familiarity: 'I regard the difference of modes a very trifling matter which all countries seem foolishly addicted to. What can be the difference to a philosophical mind whether we commence with beans or end with them?'[197]

SLAVERY DAYS

Between September 1850 and August 1853 Karl Marx's studies in the British Museum led him to fill twenty-four notebooks on economic subjects – the *Grundrisse* that would mutate into the *Contribution to the Critique of Political Economy* (1859) and, eight years after that, *Capital*. Like most reading-notes and analytical drafts, these passages are very pedestrian, no thought being given to any reader (for whom Marx would provide at least some metaphorical relief in Capital), but early in the first notebook one of the core elements of Marx's economic thought is lucidly laid out:

> The product becomes a commodity; the commodity becomes exchange value; the exchange value of the commodity is its immanent money-property; this, its money-property, separates itself from it in the form of money, and achieves a general social existence separated from all particular commodities and their natural mode of existence.[198]

Here Marx is concerned to explain the nature of 'money', but the more enduring aspect of his analysis concerns the transformation of the product from use value – say, a table to be sat at – to exchange value – say, a bargain at $150 – and the social processes of production and consumption underlying this passage. In 1849, prior to

197. J.E. Chance (ed.), *Mexico under Fire, being the diary of Samuel Ryan Curtis, 3rd. Ohio Volunteer Regiment, during the American military occupation of northern Mexico, 1846–47*, Fort Worth, Tex., 1994, pp. 49–50. Curtis's lunch at the Matamoros house of the lawyer Menchaca was on a scale likely to dismay Flora Tristán and Henry Thoreau:

> The first dish was a kind of vermicelli without the soup. Plates were removed and kind of hash containing onions, tomatoes and the like vegetables in a semi-fluid form was handed to us in clean plates. Next came a compound – a kind of fricasee or stew (I am no conniseur [sic] in culinary sciences). Next a compound which differed in having a kind of red gravy and green gravy was also passed to us in a sauce dish. Next came another stew of kid which was cooked with the blood of the animal. After this came a plate of beans, *frijoles*, then a saucer of custard. Next preserves and finally a cup of strong coffee with sugar but neither milk nor cream. During the repast claret wine was freely circulated and the whole party was in the gayest humor imaginable. The servants were very alive and obedient.

Ibid., pp. 71–2.

198. *Grundrisse: Introduction to the Critique of Political Economy*, Harmondsworth 1973, pp. 146–7.

his prolonged economic research and whilst still directly embroiled in political agitation, Marx had raised some of these issues in speeches and articles, particularly in a series known as 'Wage Labour and Capital'. There he takes up the most peculiar type of property of all – human property:

> What is a Negro slave? A man of the black race. The one explanation is as good as the other. A Negro is a Negro. He only becomes a slave in certain relations. A cotton-spinning jenny is a machine for spinning cotton. It becomes *capital* only in certain relations.[199]

The slave, then, is a human being possessed of use value and exchange value. Whereas by the late 1850s Marx had indeed come to identify the core characteristic of waged workers as lying in their own sale of their labour power to the capitalist, it is the sale and purchase of the slave by others that most starkly expresses a relation which Marx depicted as an antagonism, even for inanimate property:

> the commodity exists doubly, in one aspect as a specific product whose natural form of existence ideally contains ... its exchange value, and in the other aspect as manifest exchange value (money), in which all connection with the natural form of the product is stripped away again – this double, *differentiated* existence must develop into a *difference*, and the difference into *antithesis* and *contradiction*.[200]

Small wonder that, having completed the *Contribution*, Marx should write in January 1860 to Engels:

> In my opinion, the biggest things that are happening in the world today are, on the one hand, the movement of the slaves in America started by the death of John Brown, and on the other, the movement of the serfs in Russia.... I have just seen in the *Tribune* that there has been been a fresh rising of slaves in Missouri, naturally suppressed. But the signal has now been given. If things get serious by and by, what will become of Manchester?[201]

Although Marx almost instinctively raised the international capitalist connection – not least, one imagines, because of Engels's own business interests in what was still the heart of the world textile industry – he no longer envisaged a direct and rapid resolution in favour of the oppressed: the rising is 'naturally suppressed'. One reason for this was the very 'naturalness' of the slave system in much of the South, even as it provoked a furiously vocal minority in the North, threatening the existence of the

---

199. 'Wage Labour and Capital', in *Marx–Engels: Selected Works*, London 1968, pp. 80–81. It is my sense that this passage is one that escaped the confident editorialising undertaken by Engels for the English edition in 1891:

> I feel certain of acting as he would have done in undertaking for this edition the few alterations and editions which are required ... this is not the pamphlet as Marx wrote it in 1849 but approximately as he would have written it in 1891.... My alterations all turn on one point. According to the original the worker sells his *labour* to the capitalist for wages; according to the present text he sells his labour *power*.

Ibid., p. 65.
200. *Grundrisse*, p. 147.
201. Marx, London, to Engels, 11 Jan. 1860, in Karl Marx and Friedrich Engels, *The Civil War in the United States*, New York 1961, p. 221.

Union. The 'peculiar institution' was such a part of the landscape that millions did not treat it as abnormal and contradictory (or possessed of a *differentiated* existence). Something of this 'naturalness' can be gleaned from the description of Frederick Olmsted of a slave auction in Richmond, Virginia, in the summer of 1853, just as Marx was completing his notebooks. Olmsted's New York sensibilities are both explicitly expressed and implicit in his fascination with the detail of a transaction that dehumanised precisely through its attention to the bestial qualities of the people up for purchase:

> The sight of the negroes at once attracted the attention of Wide-awake. Chewing with vigour, he kept keenly eyeing the pair, as if to see what they were good for. Under this searching gaze the man and boy were a little abashed, but said nothing. Their appearance had little of the repulsiveness we are apt to associate with the idea of slaves. They were dressed in a gray, woollen coat, pants and waistcoat, coloured cotton neck-cloths, clean shirts, coarse woollen stockings, and stout shoes. The man wore a black hat; the boy was bare-headed. Moved by a sudden impulse, Wide-awake left his seat, and rounding the back of my chair began to grasp at the man's arms, as if to feel their muscular capacity. He then examined his hands and fingers; and, last of all, told him to open his mouth and show his teeth, which he did in a submissive manner. Having finished these examinations, Wide-awake resumed his seat, and chewed on in silence as before.
>
> I thought that it was but fair that I should now have my turn of investigation, and accordingly asked the elder negro what was his age. He said he did not know. I next inquired how old the boy was. He said he was seven years of age. On asking the man if the boy was his son, he said he was not – he was his cousin. I was going into other particulars, when the office-keeper approached and handed me the note he had been preparing, at the same time making the observation that the market was dull at present, and that there could never be a more favourable opportunity of buying. I thanked him for the troubles which he had taken, and now submit a copy of his price-current:

Best Men	18 to 25 years old	$1,000–1,300
Fair	ditto	$950–1,050
Boys	5 feet	$850–950
Ditto	4 feet 8 inches	$700–800
Ditto	4 feet 5 inches	$500–600
Ditto	4 feet	$375–450
Young Women		$800–1,000
Girls	5 feet	$750–850
Ditto	4 feet 9 inches	$700–750
Ditto	4 feet	$350–450

> ... 'Now, gentlemen', said the auctioneer, putting his hand on the shoulder of the boy, 'here is a very fine boy, seven years of age, warranted sound – what do you say for him? I put him up at $500; $500' (speaking quick, his right hand raised up, and coming down down in the open palm of his left), '$500. Any one say more than $500?' (560 is bid.) '$560? Nonsense! Just look at him! See how high he is.' (He draws the lot in front of him, and shows that the little fellow's head comes up to his breast.) 'You see he is a fine, tall, healthy boy. Look at his hands.'
>
> Several step forward and cause the boy to open and shut his hands – the flexibility of the small fingers, black on the one side, and whitish on the other, being well looked into. The hands, and also the mouth, having given satisfaction, an advance is made to $570, then to $580.

'Gentlemen, that is a very poor price for a boy of this size.' Addressing the lot – 'Go down, my boy, and show them how you can run.' The boy, seemingly happy to do as he was bid, went down from the block and ran smartly across the floor several times, the eyes of every one in the room following him.

'Now that will do. Get up again.' The boy mounts the block, the steps being rather deep for his short legs; but the auctioneer kindly lends him a hand. 'Come, gentlemen, you see that this is a first-rate lot.' $590 – 600 – 610 – 620 – 630 are bid. ' I will sell him for $630.' Right hand coming down on left. 'Last call: $630 once; $630 twice.' A pause, hand sinks. 'Gone!'[202]

Marx had read Olmsted's work and was evidently affected by the power of its detail. In the first volume of *Capital* he cites another of the New Yorker's passages at length in order to illustrate an existential feature of the wastefulness of the slave labour process which he himself described in only partly theoretical language:

The labourer here is, to use a striking expression of the ancients, distinguishable only as instrumentum vocale, from an animal as instrumentum semi-vocale, and from an implement as instrumentum mutum. But himself takes care to let both beast and implement feel that he is none of them, but is a man. He convinces himself with immense satisfaction that he is a different being, by treating the one unmercifully and damaging the other con amore. Hence the principle, universally applied in this method of production, only to employ the rudest and heaviest implements and such as are difficult to damage owing to their sheer clumsiness.[203]

This image of harshness closely combined with inefficiency chimes with that widely held today. Yet it begs a series of questions about the economic logic and character of the system, especially because it coexisted in the same polity as a burgeoning manufacturing industry run along lines as capitalist as any described by Marx. Over a number of decades the world's largest and richest community of historians has produced a stream of detailed and often contradictory studies on the existential and ethical as well as the economic nature of the system that had to be destroyed to ensure the modern existence of their nation-state. The enduring importance of the study of slavery naturally relates to its unique position within American life, and this was even more true before it was eliminated, as a Free Soil convention at Buffalo in August 1848 was told in no uncertain terms:

If we are wrong on the Tariff, it can be righted in twelve hours. If we are wrong on Banks, it can be righted by legislation. But if we are wrong on the subject of slavery, it can never be righted. It will reach down to posterity, inflicting curses and misery upon generations yet to come.[204]

Something of such a legacy evidently remains, giving particular resonance to the study of the subject in the USA, but, as British historian Howard Temperley indicates,

---

202. *Cotton Kingdom*, pp. 594–9.
203. *Capital*, I (1887), London 1974, p. 191, n. 1. Marx quoted from Olmsted's *A Journey in the Sea Board Slave States* of 1856.
204. Quoted in Martin Klammer, *Whitman, Slavery and the Emergence of Leaves of Grass*, University Park, Penn., 1995, p. 61.

it has a much wider importance and was never a phenomenon exclusive to that republic or the British colony before it:

> From the point of view of those concerned with the mainstream of Western social and economic development slavery is apt to appear an anomaly. Morally and socially it seems regressive – an anachronism, a throw-back to the beliefs and practices of earlier times. Yet there is substantial evidence that, as a method of production, it was often very successful, providing both cheap goods and a high level of profit. It is thus a phenomenon which is remarkably hard to characterize, an awkward exception to the rules. For this reason not only historians but economic theorists and social philosophers have kept coming back to it to see how this aberrant institution can, or just conceivably might, be related to the general pattern of Western development.[205]

James Oakes makes a similar point with respect to political form:

> ... the political structures of slave societies have not reflexively mirrored the intrinsic tyranny of the master–slave relationship but have been shaped by the institutional inheritance and social relations of the non-slave populations – the 'insiders'. This is why slave societies have flourished in a variety of political formations: the autocracy of the Roman empire, the royal bureaucracies of Spanish America, and the republican democracies of Periclean Athens and the Old South. One of the few political systems with which slavery was generally in-compatible was feudalism, and the reasons for this are instructive. In medieval Europe the social and political hierarchies were fused into a single structure, and the prevailing ideology reflected that fusion. In theory, seigneurialism incorporated the lowliest serf into an explic-itly hierarchical but 'organically' unified society. By contrast, slaves were culturally and politically ostracised, and slavery was formally separated from the political structures.'[206]

As a consequence of factors such as these, the scholarly literature includes an exceptional range of analytical and methodological controversies as well as strong political undertones. One can sense the influence not only of the campaign for civil rights in the 1950s and 1960s but also that of the liberal critique of 'totalitarianism' in the wake of World War II and during the Cold War. Slavery is probably the single most important issue in post-war US historiography, and, with books dedicated to assessing the debate themselves being overtaken within a few years, no brief summary can hope to capture its full character.[207]

It is, none the less, worth registering the fact that the debate undertaken in the 1840s and 1850s by the likes of Garrison, Olmsted and Helper, on the one side, and Fitzhugh, Calhoun and Hammond, on the other, could never be repeated in the same human and historical terms once hundreds of thousands had died over the issue. Although it left the fate of previous generations of slaves completely unaffected, it was subsequently unacceptable openly to revindicate chattel slavery in any public forum of mainstream American life. All the same, by the early twentieth century academic as well as popular writers were raising serious doubts about the harshness, efficiency and

---

205. 'Capitalism, Slavery and Ideology', *Past and Present*, 75, May 1977, p. 94.
206. 'The Political Significance of Slave Resistance', *History Workshop Journal*, 22, 1986, p. 91.
207. Peter Parish, *Slavery: History and Historians*, New York 1989; Kolchin, *American Slavery*.

profitability of the system. Thus, in 1918 Ulrich Phillips, drawing primarily on owner-related sources, could depict it as both less oppressive than the abolitionists had insisted and less economically efficient than claimed by supporters of slavery. Such a picture would have been harder to propagate a generation earlier, and it may well have been encouraged by the experience of World War I, which set new precedents of magnitude for both inefficiency and human destructiveness. The work of Kenneth Stampp and Stanley Elkins in the 1950s was of a different scholarly order and raised political issues related to their own times as well as to a century earlier. Stampp's work not only focused on the experience of the slaves themselves but also presented it as one of unambiguous oppression, whilst Elkins, much influenced by the recent experience of Nazism, argued that the system had operated for so long with so few revolts precisely because of the acquiescence of the slaves, whose compliant infantilism bespoke a psychological collapse. Although these lines of interpretation might be seen as diametrically opposed – and Elkins, in particular, was soon subjected to sharp criticism – they were essentially at one in perceiving the slaves as 'culturally rootless people'.[208]

From the 1960s there was rising academic interest in the political economy of the system, producing a notable convergence between the theoretical concerns of the Marxist canon, which was quite strongly represented in this area throughout the Cold War, and the technical methodologies of liberal economics. The former were primarily concerned with the lived experience and macro-economic conceptualisation of slavery: was it fully, partially or not at all capitalist? For Elizabeth Fox Genovese and Eugene Genovese, the system was 'hybrid', 'the bastard child of merchant capital', whilst James Oakes, writing within the same interpretative tradition, moved from an emphasis on the capitalist coherence and dynamic pursuit of profit of the slaveholders to making a distinction between the market determination of the relations of exchange and the non-market determination of the relations of production in the South.[209] Like Oakes, the British historian John Ashworth repudiates the neo-classical appraisal of slavery in terms of its elemental assumptions about economic behaviour, and he also places great importance on slave resistance.[210] These scholars form part of

---

208. Kenneth M. Stampp, *The Peculiar Institution: Slavery in the Antebellum South*, New York 1956, p. 364; Stanley Elkins, *Slavery: A Problem in American Institutional and Intellectual Life*, Chicago 1959. Twenty years later, John Blassingame commented on Elkins's use of the analogy with the concentration camp that,

> While the concentration camp differed significantly from the plantation, it illustrates how, even under the most extreme conditions, persecuted individuals can maintain their psychical balance.... If some men could escape infantilism in a murderous institution like the concentration camp, it may have been possible for the slave to avoid becoming abjectly docile in a much more benign institution like the plantation.

The Slave Community: Plantation Life in the Antebellum South, New York 1979, p. 331.

209. Elizabeth Fox Genovese and Eugene Genovese, *Fruits of Merchant Capital: Slavery and Bourgeois Property in the Rise and Expansion of Capitalism*, New York 1983, p. 5; Eugene Genovese, *Roll Jordan Roll: The World the Slaves Made*, New York 1974, pp. 286, 292. James Oakes, *The Ruling Race: A History of American Slaveholders*, New York 1982; *Slavery and Freedom: An Interpretation of the Old South*, New York 1990.

210. *Slavery, Capitalism and Politics in the Antebellum Republic: Commerce and Compromise, 1820–1850*, Cambridge 1995.

a generation that was not only critically aroused by Genovese but also provoked by Stanley Engerman and Robert Fogel's *Time on the Cross*. Published in 1974, this text immediately stirred controversy by projecting slavery as a competitive and profitable system in good measure because it was based on an efficient labour force. Moreover, Fogel and Engerman argued that the slaves' efficiency owed much more to their adoption of their masters' work ethic than to the application of the whip.[211] Although based on 'cliometrics' – the processing and extrapolation of historical data through micro- and macro-economic models (which filled an entire supplementary volume) – the book appeared to blend Phillips's arguments for mildness with Stampp's for efficiency and Elkins's for psychological adaptation even as it explicitly rejected the arguments of each on its own. The claims of *Time on the Cross* for a more 'scientific' methodology, which included repudiation of the assumptions and calculations employed by Olmsted and Helper, were themselves subjected to such criticism that Fogel and Engerman won only limited support for an interpretation that was intrinsically unpopular amongst liberal circles and especially so in the wake of the Vietnam War. Yet, fifteen years later, writing in a more popular vein (albeit with the statutory companion texts), Fogel only modestly qualified the thesis, which by no means had the support of all adherents to the cliometric method.[212]

In some senses *Time on the Cross* marked the end of a debate that had largely been conducted in terms of dichotomies. Those reacting to the book increasingly came to emphasise the complexities of a system that was no longer satisfactorily understood just in terms of input–output ratios, moral stridency and enunciations of values. Acceptance of the difficulties in distinguishing between economic and non-economic motives has been paralleled in the academic literature by an enhanced interest in the 'weapons of the weak' and the extent to which an inner and outer dependency of slaves on their masters was matched by daily strategies for improving their lot.[213] If Hollywood had, over twenty-five years, only advanced from Mandingo to Amistad, a much more nuanced and less sententious picture had been built up within the academic literature, post-revisionist hybridity syndrome sometimes even threatening

---

211. *Time on the Cross*, Vol. 1: *The Economics of American Slavery*; Vol. 2: *Evidence and Methods*, Boston 1974.

212. For a critique from within the broad camp of political economy, see Herbert G. Gutman, *Slavery and the Numbers Game: A Critique of Time on the Cross*, Urbana, Ill., 1975. Rejection on rather broader terms was made by Thomas Haskell, most publicly in 'The Time and Tragical History of *Time on the Cross*', *New York Review of Books*, 2 Oct. 1975. See Haskell's *The Culture of the Market*, Cambridge 1993, for a refined review of many of the major interpretative claims made for change in the mid nineteenth century. Fogel's later work, which serves both as a textbook and a review of the debate he did so much to ignite, is *Without Consent or Contract: The Rise and Fall of American Slavery*, New York 1989. For an example of technical economics employed in support of a thesis different to that of Fogel and Engerman, see Gavin Wright, *The Political Economy of the Cotton South: Households, Markets and Wealth in the Nineteenth Century*, New York 1978, which makes telling points about the manner in which agriculture in the North and South is compared in *Time on the Cross*, and questions the usefulness of extrapolating from the 1860 census as well as the role of economies of scale in the supposed strengths of Southern agriculture.

213. Although this term is associated with a major work of social anthropology on peasantries, it can equally well be applied to slaves: James C. Scott, *Weapons of the Weak: Everyday Forms of Peasant Resistance*, New Haven, Conn., 1985.

to smooth all edges. The fact that so few revolts occurred after that led by Nat Turner in 1831 was no longer explained by simple docility or taken as indicating a lack of resistance. Some, such as Peter Parish, stressed the sober calculus made by the slaves:

> The infrequency of armed slave insurrections ... testified to ... their realism.... Many of the conditions which encouraged revolts elsewhere – a large slave majority in the population, a concentration of slaves on very large plantations, a preponderance of African-born or of young males in the slave population – were not present in the South.[214]

Peter Kolchin takes this line of reasoning further still in his rebuttal of the idealised image of a 'slave community' bonded by oppression:

> Slaves lacked any kind of institutional body like the Russian peasant commune, which represented a whole village or estate and made decisions on behalf of all peasants. Decisions to flee or confront authorities were not reached communally, through collective deliberation, but individually, through private deliberation; indeed, slaves planning to escape usually took care *not* to inform others and thus risk their chances at freedom. Although occasionally a large group of slaves, unexpectedly caught by a slave patrol in a forbidden night-time revelry, might put up spirited if futile resistance, virtually never in the antebellum South did all the slaves on a plantation decide collectively to go on strike or run away, as serfs often did in Russia. The pattern of slave resistance in the antebellum South thus points to a complex environment that permitted extensive cooperation among slaves but at the same time severely limited the kinds of communal behaviour that were possible.[215]

In short, the heroism of Frederick Douglass as a runaway was typical in that he acted alone but atypical in that relatively few slaves made the break at all. Equally, while Douglass's narrative has stood the test of time because he displayed individual valour, for others seeking refuge, such as Anthony Burns and Peter and Vina Still, the personal passage to freedom involved horrible complications, lapses of nerve and a disturbing trespass of the daily mutation of the truth that necessarily existed under slavery into the very account of escaping it. These are not new voices – the words of all were published in one form or another by the end of 1856 – but the contemporary ear, acutely attuned to arguments attenuated by complexity, hears them clearly. At the time, of course, the complications of life under slavery were recognised on all sides. Abolitionists were by no means insensitive to the dilemmas of fugitives, even as they inveighed fervently against the *realpolitik* of compromise conducted by Clay and Webster in 1850. In the South the law had to be adjusted to a state of social power where only one section of society could be relied upon to speak the truth. At Burns's trial in May 1854 his defence attorney, Charles Mayo Ellis, explained the admission that he allegedly made whilst in custody in terms of Southern legal doctrine:

> The master has an almost unlimited control over the body and mind of his slave. The master's will is the slave's will. All his acts, all his sayings are made with a view to propitiate his master. His confessions are made, not from a love of truth, not from a sense of duty, not

---

214. *Slavery*, p. 69.
215. *American Slavery*, p. 162.

to speak a falsehood but to please his master, and it is in vain that his master tells him to speak the truth and conceals from him how he wishes the question answered. The slave will ascertain, or which is the same thing, think that he has ascertained, the wishes of his master and moulds his answer accordingly. We therefore more often get the wishes of the master, or the slave's belief of his wishes, than the truth. And this is so often the case that the public justice of the country requires that they should be altogether excluded [as witnesses].[216]

The complications and controversies attending the scale of slavery in the antebellum USA has less to do with the accuracy of the numbers involved than with what they might mean. Table 11 shows the overall numbers of those held in bondage, their distribution in the fifteen slave states, and their proportion of the total and black populations. The number of slaves continued to grow right up to the Civil War, when, at nearly 4 million, they accounted for an eighth of all inhabitants and were eight times more numerous than free blacks. According to Peter Parish, there was no general breeding programme amongst owners – the marriage of slaves was not formally recognised in the USA – but since owners acquired new property when their slaves gave birth, they 'enjoyed the fruits of coition without coercion'.[217] The birth rate of slaves was quite high, but their life expectancy was lower than that of whites: in 1860 3.5 per cent of slaves and 4.4 per cent of whites were over the age of sixty, lending some weight to Fogel and Engerman's thesis that slaves were generally the object of careful husbandry on the part of their owners.

With respect to geographical distribution, on the other hand, there has been much criticism of Fogel and Engerman's contention that the internal slave trade was slight and that over three-quarters of the slaves who moved from the Old/Upper South to the Deep/New or Cotton South did so in the company of their masters and as migrants. Michael Tadman estimates that two-thirds of interregional movement was through sale, and Parish puts its level in the 1850s at 250,000. On Tadman's reckoning, a slave child born in the 1820s in the Upper South would have had a one-in-three chance of being 'sold South' by the time of the Civil War.[218] It can be seen from table 11 that at the start of the 1850s the 'old' states of Virginia, the Carolinas and Georgia still held 1.5 million slaves, but there were already half this number in Alabama, Mississippi and Louisiana, where they accounted for nearly half the total inhabitants. Given that the slave population of those states and South Carolina was rising faster than average, it seems that the market was indeed freely at work.

Even in the Deep South, however, the slaves never came close to dominating the population, or the 'world', as in Saint-Domingue or Jamaica, where at emancipation twenty years earlier a third of all slaves were held on plantations which had 199 workers or more. By contrast, the 1850 median holding in the Deep South was

---

216. Quoted in Von Frank, *Trials of Anthony Burns*, pp. 142–3.
217. *Slavery*, p. 57.
218. Michael Tadman, *Speculators and Slaves: Masters, Traders and Slaves in the Old South*, Madison 1989, p. 45, cited in Kolchin, *American Slavery*, p. 97; Parish, *Slavery*, p. 56.

TABLE 11   US slave population

(i)		TOTAL	
	total pop.	slaves	free blacks
1770	2,100,000	450,000	32,000
1820	9,638,000	1,540,000	234,000
1830	12,866,000	2,001,000	320,000
1840	17,096,000	2,490,000	386,300
1850	23,192,000	3,204,000	434,000
1860	31,443,000	3,954,000	488,000

(ii)		BY STATE (1850)		
	total	slave	slave/pop. (%)	slave/black (%)*
Alabama	771,623	324,844	42.1	99.11
Arkansas	209,897	47,100	22.4	87.36
Delaware	91,532	2,290	2.5	95.38
Florida	87,000	39,310	45.2	91.49
Georgia	906,185	381,682	42.1	92.02
Kentucky	982,405	210,981	21.5	80.81
Lousiana	517,762	244,809	47.3	90.17
Maryland	583,034	90,368	15.5	89.82
Mississippi	606,185	309,878	51.1	91.61
Missouri	682,044	87,422	12.8	80.93
North Carolina	869,039	288,548	33.2	93.06
South Carolina	668,507	384,984	57.6	94.74
Tennessee	1,002,717	239,878	23.9	86.37
Texas	212,592	58,161	27.4	86.32
Virginia	1,421,661	472,528	33.2	85.75
DC	51,687	3,687	7.1	70.71
Total	9,663,870	3,186,470	32.97	88.5

* 1860.

Sources: Bureau of the Census, Historical Statistics of the United States, I, Westport, Conn., p. 18; derived from 7th Census of the USA, 1850, Washington 1855, p. ix; 8th Census of the USA, p. xiii.

thirty-five slaves, and in Virginia and North Carolina it was only 18.5.[219] This would suggest a more popular and less oligarchic pattern of slaveholding on the part of whites, with some 385,000 out of a total white population of 8 million (1.5 million families) possessing personal property. Of these slaveholders, half owned five or fewer unfree workers. Although two out of every three white families in the South as a whole did not own slaves at all, the rate of ownership was still fifteen times that of people who held stocks and shares throughout the entire USA in 1949, and in some states, like Mississippi and South Carolina, half of the white families were slaveholders. As Kolchin points out, the system was much greater than the number of owners.[220] This, then, was a system that could simultaneously possess an oligarchic and a popular character. Both could be seen in the fact that three-quarters of the members of the legislatures of the Deep South were slaveholders, and table 7 shows that the concentration of agricultural wealth was higher in the slave plantations of the South than in the North.

The Fugitive Slave Act stood at the heart of the 1850 compromise which sustained the slave-incorporating Union for a final tense decade. The key Southern component of that compact, the law went well beyond that of 1793 by denying alleged fugitives a jury trial, providing special commissioners a fee of $10 for the certified delivery of an alleged slave, and empowering federal marshals to oblige citizens to assist in its enforcement. Those who violated the provisions of the act were liable to a fine of $1,000 and imprisonment for six months. Such terms almost encouraged the kidnapping of free blacks. More importantly, they transformed the issue of slavery from a generally unstable political coexistence between the sections into one whereby this was to be continually tested as a criminal question within the jurisdiction of people for whom the peculiar institution was almost always alien, usually awkward and sometimes anathema. As so often with acts of seamless expediency, the act solved a short-term problem by sharpening the cost of irresolution in the medium term, heightening sectional differentiation and augmenting the dilemmas for a Northern majority inclined to the most peaceful coexistence possible.

Stanley Campbell argues that, 'while most citizens residing in the North were opposed to the institution of slavery, only a few citizens in isolated communities engaged in active opposition to the Fugitive Slave Law'.[221] Nevertheless, the controversy over the Kansas–Nebraska Act in 1854 had so sharpened opinions that when Anthony Burns was arrested in Boston that May, all available state and federal forces

---

219. Lewis Gray, *History of Agriculture in the Southern United States to 1860*, I, Washington 1933, pp. 530–31. According to John Boles, in 1850 73.4 per cent of slaveholders owned less than ten slaves, but an equal 73.4 per cent of slaves lived on properties numbering more than ten slaves. *Black Southerners, 1619–1869*, Lexington, Ky., 1983, p. 107.

220. *American Slavery*, p. 180; Otto Olsen, 'Historians and the Extent of Slaveownership in the Southern United States', *Civil War History*, 18, 1972, pp. 101–16, cited in Parish, *Slavery*, p. 28.

221. *The Slave Catchers: Enforcement of the Fugitive Slave Law, 1850–1860*, Chapel Hill, N.C., 1970, pp. vii–viii.

had to be mobilised to prevent him from being released. Massachusetts Senator Edward Everett was in no doubt over the importance of the affair:

> A change has taken place in this community within three weeks such as the preceding thirty years had not produced. While the minds of conservative men were embittered by the passage of the Nebraska bill, the occurrence of a successful demand for the surrender of a fugitive slave was the last drop which made the cup run over.[222]

When, in 1845, Frederick Douglass first published a narrative of his life, he was obliged to omit all detail of his escape from slavery because 'others would thereby be involved in the most embarrassing difficulties', and 'such a statement would most undoubtedly induce greater vigilance on the part of slaveholders'.[223] But even without such detail his account, and hundreds like it which appeared over the next fifteen years, provoked a Southern backlash because they threatened to erode the ignorance and sense of hopelessness of the type felt by Douglass himself prior to his escape:

> We could see no spot, this side of the ocean, where we could be free. We knew nothing about Canada. Our knowledge of the north did not extend farther than New York; and to go there, and be forever harrassed with the frightful liability of being returned to slavery – with the certainty of being treated tenfold worse than before – the thought was truly a horrible one, and one which it was not easy to overcome.[224]

The year before Douglass's book was published the new state of Texas had strengthened its law on runaway slaves, offering $50 for the capture of each head plus payment of $2 for each thirty miles of their transportation to the nearest sheriff's office. These incentives enhanced the existing provisions which punished those who harboured fugitives with a fine of up to $500 and six months in jail, obliged owners to pay $10 to those who returned slaves, and empowered sheriffs to auction captured fugitives after a month in custody.[225]

The tightening of the federal law in 1850 was not, then, simply an ideological and political trade-off; it reflected rising apprehension on the part of the slaveholders at the threat posed by those helping runaways. The advertisement placed by J.T. Schonwald in a North Carolina paper in June 1855 was quite representative in its offer of a greater reward for the conviction of accomplices than for the return of the fugitive:

$200 REWARD

Ran away from the employ of Messrs Holmes and Brown, on Sunday night, 20th inst., a negro man named YATNEY or MEDICINE, belonging to the undersigned. Said boy is stout built, about 5 feet 4 inches high, 22 years old, and dark complected, and has the appearance, when walking slow, of one leg being a little shorter than the other. He was brought from Chapel Hill, and is probably working either in the neighborhood of that place, or Betty's

---

222. Everett, Boston, to Joseph S. Cottman, 15 June 1854, quoted in Jane H. and William H. Pease, *The Fugitive Slave Law and Anthony Burns: A Problem in Law Enforcement*, Philadelphia 1975, p. 51.
223. *Narrative*, p. 137.
224. Ibid., p. 123.
225. *BFSP, 1844–45*, XXXIII, London 1859, pp. 594–6.

Bridge, in Bladen County. The above reward will be paid for evidence sufficient to convict any white person of harboring him, or a reward of $25 for his apprehension and confinement in any jail in the State, so that I can get him, or for his delivery to me in Wilmington.[226]

In terms of the rates of pay for farmhands, offers like this represented a very good deal, in addition to the excitement of the chase. Just as Sarmiento fixed the tracker (rastreador) as a core personality in the culture and system of justice of the Argentine pampa, so stood the bounty-hunter in the buoyant sub-culture of apprehension that prevailed even well inside the US frontier. In the early 1850s the *Fayetteville Observer* was advertising dogs for tracking fugitives at a price range of $75 to $300 (the upper end of which approached the cost of a small slave girl at the Richmond auction witnessed by Olmsted), but it was probably easier to hire in a professional such as David Turner, who advertised his services in the *West Tennessee Democrat*:

BLOOD-HOUNDS – I have two of the FINEST DOGS for CATCHING NEGROES in the southwest. They can take the trail TWELVE HOURS after the NEGRO has passed, and catch him with ease. I live just four miles southwest of Bolivar, in the road leading from Bolivar to Whiteville. I am ready at all times to catch runaway negroes. March 2 1853.[227]

If only a small minority of slaves even attempted to break free, the following account of what would appear to be a quite ordinary state of affairs on a Virginia plantation, sent in 1847 to the owner John H. Cocke by his overseer George Skipwith, shows why many more must have been tempted to flee:

I have a good crop on hand for you, borth of cotten and corn. this you know could not be don without hard work. i have worked the people but not with out reason. and i have whiped none without a caus. the persons whome i have correct i will tell you their names and their faults. Suky who I put to plant som corn and after she had been there long anuf to have been don i went there and she hardly begun it i gave her four or five licks over her clothes i gave isham too licks over his clothes for covering up cotten with the plow. i put frank, isham, Evally, Dinah, Jinny evealine and Charlott to sweeping cotten going twice in a roe. and at a Reasonable days work they ought to have plowed seven accers a peice. and they had been at it half a day. and they had not done more than one accer and a half and i gave them ten licks a peace upon their skins i gave Evlyann 8 or 10 licks for misplacing her hoe. and that was all the whiping i have done from the time i pitched the crop untell we commenced cutting oats.[228]

The Fugitive Slave Law took slavery north in an unprecedented manner and provided a political rallying point for the states of the South, but, of course, those states still remained quite diverse in many other respects. Some of these, such as the relatively and absolutely low number of slaves in certain states (but never a low proportion of slaves to free blacks), can be seen in table 11. Others, such as the distribution of slave labour by crop, are hardly less consequential. According to the

---

226. Quoted in Olmsted, *Cotton Kingdom*, p. 123.
227. Quoted in ibid., p. 124.
228. Skipwith, Hopewell, to Cocke, 8 July 1847, reproduced in John Blassingame (ed.), *Slave Testimony*, Baton Rouge 1978, pp. 66–7.

1850 census, of the 2.5 million slaves engaged in agriculture, 1.8 million worked in
the cotton fields; 350,000 on tobacco; 150,000 on sugar; and 125,000 on rice (in 1860
a third of all owners with over 300 slaves were rice growers). These were quite
different crops to plant, cultivate and harvest, imposing labour regimes of variegated
skill and rigour. Urban slaves were likely to be engaged in an even wider variety of
employment, directly or as hands hired out. But between 1840 and 1860 both their
relative and absolute importance fell – from 18 to 7 per cent of the population of the
eight largest Southern cities (59,400 to 57,000) – not least because they were hard to
control and treated with increasing suspicion for their greater access to literacy, free
blacks and immigrants.

Today such distinctions might appear almost totally irrelevant, but at the time they
could be vital. Frederick Olmsted's travels gradually instilled a sensitivity to this 'local'
factor within his unbending abolitionism. In South Carolina he struck up conversation
with an aged free black from North Carolina selling tobacco with his son:

'Well, I've been thinking myself, the niggers did not look so well here as they did in North
Carolina and Virginia; they are not so well clothed, and they don't appear as bright as they
do there.'

'Well, master, Sundays dey is mighty well clothed, dis country; 'pears like dere an't
nobody looks better Sundays dan dey do. But Lord! workin' days, seems like dey haden no
close dey could keep on 'um at all, master. Dey is a'mos' naked, wen deys at work, some
on 'em. Why, master, up in our country, de wite folks – why, some on 'em has ten or twelve
niggars, dey doan' hev no real big plantations, like dey has heah, but some on 'em has ten
or twelve niggars, may be, and dey juss lives and talks wid 'em; and dey treats 'um most as
if dem was der own chile. Dey doan' keep no niggars dey can't treat so; dey won't keep 'em,
won't be bothered wid 'em. If dey gets a niggar and he doan behave himself, dey won't keep
him; dey juss tell him, sar, he must look up anudder master, and if he doan find hisself one,
I tell 'on, when de trader cum along, dey sells him, and he totes him away. Dey allers sell
off all de bad niggars out of our country; dat's de way all de bad niggars and all dem no-
account niggars keep a cumin' down heah; dat's de way on't, master.'

'Yes, that's the way of it, I suppose; these big plantations are not the best thing for
niggers, I see that plainly.'

'Master, you wan't raise in dis country, was 'on?'

'No, I come from the North.'

'I tort so, sar; I knew 'on wan't one of dis country people; 'peared like 'on was one of
my country people, way 'on talks; and I loves dem kine of people. Won't you take some
whisky, sar? Heah, you boy! Bring dat jug of whisky dah, out of my waggon; in dah – in
dat box under dem foddar.'

'No, don't trouble yourself, I am very much obliged to you, but I don't like to drink
whisky.'

'Like to have you drink some, master, if you'd like it. Yon's right welcome to it. Pears like
I knew you was one of my country people. Ever been in Greensboro, master? dat's in
Guildford.'

'No, I never was there. I come from New York, further north than your country.'

'New York, did 'on, master? I heard New York was what dey calls a free state; all de
niggars free dah.'

'Yes, that is so.'

'Not no slaves at all; well, I expect dat's a good thing, for all de niggers to be free.
Greensboro is a right comely town; t'aint like dese heah Souf Car'lina towns.'[229]

For the great abolitionist Wendell Phillips the existence of slavery united all parts of the South in one single category: 'The South is one great brothel, where half a million of women are flogged to prostitution.'[230] On the question of comparisons between slave and non-slave jurisdictions, Phillips took as his target the recently deceased Daniel Webster, whose 'Seventh March' speech in favour of the 1850 compromise (and so of the new fugitive slave law) had provoked such fury amongst the free-soil community:

> As Daniel Webster, when he was talking to the farmers of western New York, and wished to contrast slave labor with free labor, did not dare compare New York with Virginia – sister States, under the same government, planted by the same race, worshiping at the same altar, speaking the same language: identical in all respects, save that one in which he wished the seek the contrast. But, no. He compared it with Cuba [*cheers and laughter*] – the contrast was so close! [*Renewed cheers*] Catholic – Protestant; Spanish – Saxon; despotism – municipal institutions; readers of Lope de Vega and of Shakespeare; mutterers of the Mass – Children of the Bible! But Virginia is too near home![231]

Here Phillips not only shows the compatibility of a range of prejudices with abolitionism but also how the Anglo–Latin dichotomy could be exploited by all parties in the dispute over slavery. Webster, in his three-hour senate speech – 100,000 copies of which were sold before the month was out – had made a strenuous defence of the Union and insisted on the local nature of slavery because

> there is not at this moment within the United States, or any territory of the United States, a single foot of land, the character of which, in regard to its being free territory or slave territory, is not fixed by some law, and some irrepealable law, beyond the power of the action of the government.[232]

During that speech John Calhoun, slumped out by pneumonia and within three weeks of death, interjected, 'No, Sir! The Union can be broken', which sentiment lay at the heart of his own bleak words, read out by Senator Mason of Virginia three days earlier:

> I refer to the relation between the two races in the Southern section, which constitutes a vital portion of her social organization. Every portion of the North entertains views and feelings more or less hostile to it. Those most opposed and hostile regard it as a sin, and consider themselves under the most sacred obligation to use every effort to destroy it. Indeed, to the extent that they conceive they have power, they regard themselves as implicated in the sin, and responsible for not suppressing it by the use of all and every means. Those less opposed and hostile, regard it as a crime – an offence against humanity, as they call it; and,

---

229. *Cotton Kingdom*, pp. 164–5.
230. Speech of 27 Jan. 1853 to Massachusetts Anti-Slavery Society, in Louis Filler (ed.), *Wendell Phillips on Civil Rights and Freedom*, Lanham, Md., 1982, p. 37.
231. Ibid., p. 59.
232. Quoted in Merrill D. Peterson, *The Great Triumvirate: Webster, Clay and Calhoun*, New York 1987, p. 463. Four days later William Seward responded to Webster in a speech that many Northerners thought Webster himself should have made, but Seward's reference to a 'higher law than the Constitution' was no longer in Webster's repertoire.

although not so fanatical, feel themselves bound to use all efforts to effect the same object; while those who are least opposed and hostile, regard it as a blot and a stain on the character of what they call the Nation, and feel themselves accordingly bound to give it no countenance or support. On the contrary, the Southern section regards the relation as one which cannot be destroyed without subjecting the two races to the greatest calamity, and the section to poverty, desolation, and wretchedness; and accordingly they feel bound, by every considera-tion of interest and safety, to defend it.[233]

Six years earlier, in an ill-tempered exchange with the British ambassador, Sir Richard Pakenham, Calhoun had elaborated upon the South's viewpoint. Writing as secretary of state, he tellingly refers to the USA in the plural:

> While they conceded to Great Britain the right of adopting whatever policy she might deem best, in reference to the African race, within her own possessions, they on their part claim the same right for themselves.... With us, it is a question to be decided, not by the Federal Government, but by each member of this union by itself, according to its own views of its domestic policy, and without any right on the part of the Federal Government to interfere in any manner whatever.... [I do] not, however, deem it irrelevant to state that, if the experience of more than half a century is to decide, it would be neither humane nor wise in [the Southern states] to change their policy. The census and other authentic documents show that, in all instances in which the states have changed the former relation between the two races, the condition of the African, instead of being improved, has become worse. They have been invariably sunk into vice and pauperism, accompanied by the bodily and mental afflictions incident thereto – deafness, blindness, insanity and idiocy, to a degree without example; while, in all other states which have retained the ancient relation between them, they have improved greatly in every respect, in number, in comfort, intelligence and morals, as the following facts, taken from such sources will serve to illustrate:
>   The number of deaf and dumb, blind, idiots and insane of the negroes in the states that have changed the ancient relations between the races is 1 out of every 96; while in the states adhering to it, it is 1 out of every 672; that is, 7 to 1 in favour of the latter.... In addition, it deserves to be remarked that in Massachusetts, where the change in the ancient relation of the two races was first made (now more than sixty years since), where the greatest zeal has been exhibited on their behalf, and where their number is comparatively few (but little more than 8,000 in a population of upwards of 730,000), the condition of the African is amongst the most wretched. By the latest authentic accounts, there was 1 out of every 21 of the black population in jails or houses of correction; and 1 out of every 13 was either deaf and dumb, idiot, insane or in prison. On the other hand, the census and other authentic sources of information establish the fact that the condition of the African race throughout all the states where the ancient relation between the two races has been maintained, enjoys a degree of health and comfort which may well compare with that of the labouring population of any country in Christendom; and, it may be added, that in no other condition, or in any other age or country, has the Negro race ever attained so high an elevation in morals, intelligence or civilization.[234]

Argumentation along lines such as these complemented recourse to the sanctity of property in Southern discourse. But, of course, the argument was by no means

---

233. 'Speech on the Admission of California – and the General State of the Union', 4 March 1850, in Ross M. Lence (ed.), *Union and Liberty: The Political Philosophy of John C. Calhoun*, Indianapolis 1992, pp. 582–3.

234. Calhoun, Washington, to Pakenham, 18 Apr. 1844, in *BFSP 1844–45*, XXXIII, pp. 238–9.

limited to the South of the United States. Writing five years later, Carlyle ducked and weaved around the same motifs as he despaired at the fact that the British West Indies had been '"emancipated" ... into a *Black Ireland*; "free" indeed, but an Ireland and black!' For Carlyle, as for Calhoun, it was precisely the *institutionalised* combination of the races that worked:

> This certainly is a notable fact: the Black African, alone of wild-men, can live among men civilised. While all manner of Caribs and others pine into annihilation in presence of the pale faces, he contrives to continue; does not die of sullen irreconcilable rage, of rum, of brutish laziness and darkness, and fated incompatibility with his new place; but lives and multiplies, and evidently means to abide among us, if we can find the right regulation for him.[235]

The quite opposite view – that people of African descent in the Americas would benefit most from a return to their place of origin – was popular with a significant strand of US opinion that supported gradual abolition. This was the position of Henry Clay, the leading architect of pacts to preserve the Union in the post-Jeffersonian era. Opening the Senate debate which would lead to the 1850 compromise, the 73-year-old Kentuckian approached slavery in terms of nature and the Constitution. He attacked the free-soilers for insisting that slavery not be introduced to territories conquered from Mexico because such insistence was unnecessary and deliberately provocative:

> What do you want? You want that there shall be no slavery introduced into the territories acquired from Mexico. Well, have you not got it in California already, if admitted as a state? Have you not got it in New Mexico, in all human probability, also? What more do you want? You have got what is worth a thousand Wilmot provisos. You have got nature on your side.[236]

---

235. 'Occasional Discourse on the Nigger Question', in *Miscellaneous Essays*, VI, London 1869, p. 182. Sentiments such as this elicited two quite similar responses to Carlyle's work. From William Wells Brown, who had escaped to London from Slavery in Missouri:

> As a writer Mr Carlyle is often monotonous and extravagant. He does not exhibit a new view of nature, or raise insignificant objects into importance; but generally takes commonplace thoughts and events, and tries to express them in stronger and statelier language than others. He holds no communion with his kind but stands alone, without mate or fellow.... He exists not by sympathy, but by antipathy.... He cares little what he says, so long as he can say it differently from others.

And from Karl Marx:

> To Thomas Carlyle belongs the credit of having taken the literary field against the bourgeoisie at a time when its views, tastes and ideas held the whole of English literature totally in thrall.... Carlyle's style is at one with his ideas. It is a direct violent reaction against the modern bourgeois pecksniffery, whose enervated affectedness, circumspect verbosity and vague, sentimentally moral tediousness has spread from the original inventors, the educated Cockneys, to the whole of English literature.

Paul Jefferson (ed.), *The Travels of William Wells Brown* (1855), Edinburgh 1991, p. 167; *MECW*, X, London 1980, pp. 301–2.

236. Quoted in Peterson, *The Great Triumvirate*, p. 457. On 6 August 1846 David Wilmot, a Democrat from Pennsylvania, added an amendment to Polk's appropriation bill for $2 million to fund the Mexican war: 'neither slavery nor involuntary servitude shall ever exist in any part of [territory acquired from Mexico]'.

For Clay, then, the climate, soil and productive record of the lands ceded under Guadalupe Hidalgo rendered the issue of slavery a practical irrelevance, and he – a slaveholding senator from a slave state – returned the challenge to the free-soilers by insisting that federal sanctions be restored to the 1793 Fugitive Slave Law, which had been progressively watered down in the states of the North. He would, indeed, 'go with the furthest senator from the South to impose the heaviest sanctions on the recovery of fugitive slaves'.[237] (It was this sentiment that the New England abolitionist community had been expecting Webster to rebut but which he effectively reaffirmed.) Behind Clay's initiative lay his conviction that

> Slavery may be terminated in different modes. It may by the law; it may by the sword; but it is by the operation of natural causes to which I look for its ultimate extinction ... whenever the population shall be three or four times as great as it is – when we measure time, not by individuals or the particular lives of persons, but by the period of national existence – when the time arrives ... when the price of labor, the wages of manual labor, shall be so reduced that it will be too burdensome and expensive on the part of owners of slaves to raise them for the sake of the labor they perform, then it will become the interest of the slave states and slaveholders to resort to another fund than that which is afforded by slaves.... It took two centuries and more to bring from the shores of Africa her sons, the descendents of whom are now in slavery in the United States. It may take two centuries to transport their descendents to such an extent as not to create apprehension as to the few who remain.

Clay's support for the American Colonization Society and the repopulation of Liberia by Americans of African descent rested on a social vision very close to that held by Calhoun:

> With regard to the free people of color, do you not all know (I wish to say nothing but what is warranted by daily experience) that it is not their fault that they are a degraded set? It is not their fault that they are more addicted to crime and dissolute manners than any other portion of the population of the United States. It is the inevitable result of the law of their condition.... Will they not be benefited by going to Africa?
> ... The white men of the North and the South will be benefited; the slaves of the South will be benefited. We all know what corrupting influences are exercised over the slave population by the dissolute free people of color, who lead off and seduce them. Intoxicating liquors are sold to them, and they are induced to commit acts of petty larceny against their masters ... all will be benefited by the separation which is proposed ultimately to be effected by the Colonization Society. And, gentlemen, if we quit our country and go to that, how much is there to animate the Christian bosom, and encourage us in the prosecution of this great scheme in which we are engaged? There is a whole continent, with millions of inhabitants in a state of utter barbarism. The very people of color, then, sent thither, will, in the end – not in two or three years, but ultimately, as surely as civilization and Christianity are destined to triumph over barbarism – be their deliverers.[238]

---

237. Quoted in ibid., p. 458.
238. Speech to Annual Meeting of the American Colonization Society, Washington, 21 Jan. 1851, in *BFSP, 1850–51*, XL, pp. 600–603.

Hard though it may be for the modern eye to discern, Clay's position is not the same as the natural hierarchy of race and gender championed by the *New York Herald* in 1852, because he allows a couple of centuries for change, whereas the paper could not conceive it over any amount of time: 'How did woman first become subject to man, as she is now all over the world? By her nature, her sex, just as the negro is and always will be, to the end of time, inferior to the white race, and, therefore, doomed to subjection.'[239]

Seven years later Hinton Helper's massively circulated *Impending Crisis* prophesied the collapse of slavery, but Helper shared the views of the *Herald* on race, and if his expression in later life was entirely unhampered, that does not make it any less reflective of an important current of US public opinion:

> ... this is the man, the vile man of Africa, the Ethiopian of grovelling nature, unsightly skin, and noxious stench, with whom certain very contemptibly foolish and knavish politicians would have you and me and other decent people, of Olympian and Heliconian descent, fraternize and coalesce upon terms of equality.... The bare proposition for miscegenation, or for long continuance together in the same society, with any arrangement or regulation whatever, the mere thought of such a thing, in any conceivable form of accommodation, is repugnant and demoralizing to the last degree. In my humble but mature judgement there is nothing in the antecedents of the negro, nor in his present or prospective character or condition, which justifies us in regarding him otherwise than as an ill-starred alien of most pestilent and pernicious presence, to be tolerated only so long as a fair opportunity may offer for getting rid of him effectually and for ever.[240]

This was not an exclusively Southern view (nor exclusive within the South), and the critical divisions over slavery did not bear as centrally on the question of race as they would have done in the second half of the twentieth century. Nevertheless, relatively few proponents of the American system of human bondage promoted it like George Fitzhugh, as an ideal form of social security: 'Domestic slavery must be vindicated in the abstract, and in the general, as a normal, natural and *in general* necessitous element of civilized society, without regard to race or color.'[241] Much more common was the anti-intellectual fusion of pragmatism, 'common-sense' and religious imprimatur served up by James Hammond to his British correspondent Thomas Clarkson:

> I must say that I am no more in favor of slavery in the abstract than I am of poverty, disease, idiocy or any other inequality in the condition of the human family; that I love perfection, and think I should enjoy a millennium such as God has promised. But what would that

239. Quoted in Eric Foner, *Slavery and Freedom in Nineteenth-Century America*, Oxford 1994, p. 11.

240. Helper, Dakar, to Senator Augustus Merriman, 29 June 1877, in *Oddments of Andean Diplomacy*, St Louis, Mo., 1879, pp. 293–4. Helper's appointment as ambassador to Buenos Aires by Lincoln in 1861 might be thought a deserved reward for his booklet, but if it it seems not to have greatly improved the unionist cause in the southern cone, it did at least afford the irascible lawyer the opportunity of getting down to a little miscegenation of his own; in 1863 he married María Luisa Rodríguez.

241. 'Southern Thought', in Faust, *Ideology of Slavery*, p. 294.

amount to? A pledge that I would set about eradicating those apparently inevitable evils of
our nature, in equalizing the conditions of all mankind, consummating the perfection of our
race, and introducing the millennium? By no means. To effect these things belongs exclusively
to a higher power.

And that higher power had bequeathed a sufficiency of scriptural evidence of its will.
At the heart of this lay the tenth commandment ('Thou shalt not covet thy neighbour's ... man-servant, nor his maid-servant'); Noah's curse on his son Ham and
grandson Canaan ('Cursed be Canaan, a slave of slaves shall he be to his brother');
and – of especial resonance after March 1850 – St Paul's returning of the fugitive slave
Onesimus to his owner Philemon.[242] All these allowed Hammond, a man of the
world, commercial farmer and political dignitary, to aver that,

> I firmly believe that American slavery is not only not a sin, but especially commended to
> God through Moses, and approved by Christ through his apostles.... I deny that the power
> of the slaveholders in America is 'irresponsible'. He is responsible to God. He is responsible
> to the world – a responsibility which abolitionists do not intend to allow him to evade – and
> ... he is responsible to the community in which he lives.

Furthermore, this fusion of sacred and communal responsibility created a generally
virtuous effect, not least for the slaves themselves:

> The piety of the South is unobtrusive. We think it proves but little, though it is a confident
> thing for a man to claim that he stands higher in the estimation of his Creator and is less
> a sinner than his neighbor. If vociferation is to carry the question of religion, the North, and
> probably the Scotch, have it. Our sects are few, harmonious, pretty much united amongst
> themselves, and pursue their avocations in humble peace.... We have been so irreverent as
> to laugh at Mormonism and Millerism, which have created such commotions further North;
> and modern prophets have no honor in our country. Shakers, Rappists, Dunkers, Socialists,
> Fourierists and the like keep themselves far off.[243]

---

242. When I have sent again [Onesimus]: thou therefore receive him, that is, mine own bowels. Whom
     I would have retained with me, that in thy stead he might have ministered unto me in the bonds
     of the gospel: But without thy mind would I do nothing; that thy benefit should not be as it were
     of necessity, but willingly. For perhaps he therefore departed for a season, that thou shouldest
     receive him for ever; Not now as a servant [slave], but above a servant, a brother beloved, specially
     to me, but how much more unto thee, both in the flesh, and in the Lord?

Epistle of Paul to Philemon, verses 12–16. More than a slave, but still a slave; a dear, Christian man, but
still a slave. Here one is more inclined to the academic interpretation of Peter Garnsey – 'Paul, like every
one else, accepted legal slavery. The social attitudes he betrays in addressing slaves and masters are conventional and conservative' – than to the popular commentary of William Barclay – 'If the slave has become
a dear brother, then the sting of slavery is drawn, and the principle has been stated which will end sooner
or later in emancipation.' Peter Garnsey, *Ideas of Slavery from Aristotle to Augustine*, Cambridge 1996, p. 176;
William Barclay, *The New Testament: The Letters and the Revelation*, II, London 1969, p. 136. David Brion
Davis argues for a neutral reading because the letter refers to an individual case, but one feels that he does
so primarily out of exasperation with the tortuous debates over this text in the past. *The Problem of Slavery
in Western Culture*, 2nd edn, New York 1988, p. 86. For a suggestive modern discussion of the use of the
term 'slavery' in the book of Exodus and the rest of the Pentateuch, see Michael Walzer, *Exodus and
Revolution*, New York 1985.

243. 'Letter to an English Abolitionist', in Faust, *Ideology of Slavery*, pp. 172–5, 180, 185–6.

This is a claim that Fogel and Engerman took seriously in terms of slave inculcation of mainstream Protestant values. However, it is best seen in the light of self-justification and the slave culture of appeasement of their masters' expectations. It is surely also true that the sacred world

> created the necessary space between the slaves and their owners and … the means of preventing legal slavery from becoming spiritual slavery. In addition to the world of the masters which the slaves inhabited and accommodated to, as they had to, they created a world apart which they shared with each other and which remained their own domain, free of control of those who ruled the earth.[244]

Moreover, Hammond's presentation of the South as a community of sober, consensual non-conformity scarcely tallies with the evidence, even when it is provided by whites. In northern Mississippi Frederick Olmsted brought up the question of religion with his slaveholding host:

> 'Are your negroes Baptists or Methodists?' I inquired of our host.
> 'All Baptists; niggers allers want to be ducked, you know. They ain't content to be just titch'd with water; they must be ducked in all over. There was two niggers jined the Methodists up here last Summer, and they made the minister put 'em into the branch; they wouldn't jine 'less he'd duck 'em.'
> 'The Bible says baptize, too,' observed Yazoo.
> 'Well, they think they must be ducked all under, or t'aint no good.'
> 'Do they go to meeting?'
> 'Yes, they hev a meeting among themselves.'
> 'And a preacher?'
> 'Yes; a nigger preacher.'
> 'Our niggers is mighty wicked; they dance!' repeated Yazoo.
> 'Do you consider dancing so very wicked, then?' I asked.
> 'Well, I don't account so myself, as I know on, but they do, you know – the pious people, all kinds, except the 'Piscopers; some 'o them, they do dance themselves, I believe. Do you dance in your country?'
> 'Yes.'
> 'What sort of dances – cotillions and reels?'
> 'Yes; what do you dance?'
> 'Well, we dance cotillions and reels too, and we dance on a plank; that's the kind of dancin' I like best.'
> 'How is it done?'
> 'Why, don't you know that? You stand face to face with your partner on a plank and keep a dancin'. Put the plank up on two barrel heads so it'll kinda spring.'

Not even his considerable reserves of wry condescension could protect Olmsted from being both enraptured and bewildered by a New Orleans church service attended by just three other whites:

---

244. Albert J. Raboteau, *Slave Religion: The 'Invisible Institution' in the Antebellum South*, New York 1978, quoted in Parish, *Slavery*, p. 82.

The text was, 'I have fought the good fight, I have kept the faith; henceforth there is laid up for me a crown of glory'; and the sermon was an appropriate and generally correct explanation of the customs of the Olympian games, and a proper and often eloquent application of the figure to the Christian course of life. Much of the language was highly metaphorical; the figures long, strange and complicated, yet sometimes, however, beautiful. Words were frequently misplaced, and their meaning evidently misapprehended, while the grammar and pronunciation were sometimes such as to make the idea intended to be conveyed by the speaker incomprehensible to me. Vulgarisms and slang phrases occasionally occurred, but evidently without any consciousness of impropriety on the part of the speaker or his congregation.

As soon as I had taken my seat, my attention was attracted by an old negro near me, whom I supposed for some time to be suffering with some nervous complaint; he trembled, his teeth chattered, and his face, at intervals, was convulsed. He soon began to respond aloud to the sentiments of the preacher, in such words as these: 'Oh yes!' 'That's it, that's it!' 'Yes, yes, glory yes!', and similar expressions could be heard from all parts of the house whenever the speaker's voice was unusually solemn, or his language and manner eloquent or excited.

Sometimes the outcries and responses were not confined to ejaculations of this kind, but shouts and groans, terrific shrieks and indescribable expressions of ecstasy – of pleasure or agony – and even stamping, jumping and clapping of hands were added. The tumult often resembled that of an excited political meeting; and I was at once surprised to find my own muscles all stretched, as if ready for a struggle – my face glowing and my feet stamping – having been infected unconsciously, as men often are, with instinctive bodily sympathy with the excitement of the crowd.[245]

In the autumn of 1852, writing from refuge in Canada, the runaway ex-slave Henry Bibb sternly addressed Albert Sibley, who had owned him sixteen years before in Kentucky, to make a strong point clearly:

For more than twenty years you have been a member of the Methodist Episcopal church – a class leader and an exhorter of that denomination, professing to take the Bible as your standard of Christian duty. But, Sir, know ye not that in the light of this book, you have been acting a hypocrite all the while? ... Oh! What harmony there seems to be between these twin sisters: the Fugitive Slave Law and the Methodist Episcopalian Church. Listen to the languages of inspiration: 'Feed the hungry, and clothe the naked'; 'Break every yoke and let the oppressed go free'; 'All things, whatsoever, ye would that men should do unto you, do ye even so unto them, for this is the law and the prophets.'

While, on the other hand, your church sanctions the buying and selling of men, women and children; the robbing men of their wives, and parents of their offspring – the violation of the whole of the decalogue, by permitting the profanation of the Sabbath; committing of theft, murder, incest and adultery, which is consistently done by church members holding slaves and which form the very essence of slavery. Now, Sir, allow me with greatest defer-ence to your intelligence to inform you that you are miserably deceiving yourself, if you believe that you are in the straight and narrow path to heaven whilst you are practising such abominable violations of the plainest precepts of religion.[246]

---

245. *Cotton Kingdom*, pp. 349–50, 241–3.
246. Bibb, Windsor, Ontario, to Sibley, 23 Sept. 1852, in Blassingame (ed.), *Slave Testimony*, pp. 50–51.

LATIN BONDAGE

One of the leading theses of Stanley Elkins's 1959 book *Slavery: A Problem in American Institutional and Intellectual Life* was that, in contrast to Anglo-America, the essential humanity of the slave was fully and legally recognised in Latin America.[247] In taking this view Elkins was following the lead of Frank Tannenbaum and Gilberto Freyre. Tannenbaum's influential *Slave and Citizen: The Negro in the Americas*, published in 1947, sought to fill one major gap in the Bolton approach to the development of the continent as a whole by emphasising the extent to which this was based on slavery. But whilst he was right to identify this formal feature of the Spanish codes derived from the *Siete Partidas*, Tannenbaum was wrong in assuming that North American law denied the slave a moral personality. Equally, he understated the degree to which Latin culture upheld the Aristotelian view of 'natural slavery', and he overestimated the extent to which the Spanish and Portuguese systems remained stable and patriarchially unconcerned by shifting economic circumstances.[248]

Freyre, on the other hand, provided Elkins with a view of the Brazilian system that almost idealised the 'big house' around a motif of high levels of miscegenation and the existence of a spectrum of 'colour' that stood in contrast to some stark North American racial polarisation. Although Freyre, writing in the early 1930s, recognised that sexual relations between masters and slaves were authoritarian in nature and often involved sadistic cruelty, David Brion Davis is far from alone in identifying the lasting impression of his sprawling book as an 'idyllic picture ... where slaves and freemen pray and loaf together, and where masters shrug their shoulders at account books and prefer to frolic with slave girls in shaded hammocks'.[249] And it is an impression drawn directly from a text which, in straining for effect, may have rather over-egged the description for a Protestant palate:

> Slothful but filled to overflowing with sexual concerns, the life of the sugar-planter tended to become a life that was lived in a hammock. A stationary hammock, with the master

---

247. *Slavery*, pp. 27ff.

248. Sidney Mintz, review, *American Anthropologist*, XLIII, June 1961, pp. 579–87; Arnold Sio, 'Interpretations of Slavery: The Slave Status in the Americas', *Comparative Studies in Society and History*, VII, April 1965, pp. 289–308. For a comparative approach based on the same period rather than common points of economic development, see Herbert S. Klein, *Slavery in the Americas: A Comparative Study of Virginia and Cuba*, London 1967. Twenty years later Klein issued a textbook that applied the comparative method more loosely to the southern section of the continent – *African Slavery in Latin America and the Caribbean*, New York 1986 – where he argued that 'the [real] comparison is ... not between slave groups across political boundaries but within each country between its slave and free populations' (ibid., p. 158). For the debate in the 1960s, see Laura Foner and Eugene D. Genovese (eds), *Slavery in the New World: A Reader in Comparative History*, Princeton 1969; Eugene D. Genovese, 'The Comparative Focus in Latin American History', *Journal of Inter-American Affairs*, 12, July 1970.

249. *The Problem of Slavery*, p. 224.

taking his ease, sleeping, dozing. Or a hammock on the move, with the master on a journey or a promenade beneath the heavy draperies or curtains. Or again, a squeaking hammock with the master copulating in it. The slaveholder did not have to leave his hammock to give orders to his Negroes, to have letters written by his plantation clerk or chaplain, or to play a game of backgammon with some relative or friend. Nearly all of them travelled by hammock, having no desire to go by horse; and within the house they permitted themselves to be jolted about like jelly in a spoon. It was in the hammock that, after breakfast or dinner, they let their food settle, as they lay there picking their teeth, smoking a cigar, belching loudly, emitting wind, and allowing themselves fanned or searched for lice by the pickaninnies, as they scratched their feet or genitals – some of them out of vicious habit, others because of venereal or skin disease.[250]

Until at least the mid 1970s, when the elderly Freyre had occupied public office under military rule, his optimistic view of a Brazilian national character based on an 'ethnic potpourri', or 'multiracialism', enjoyed widespread acceptance, not least because it stressed the indigenous and African contributions to Brazilian society and extracted a modicum of intimate comfort from a history of conquest and subjugation:

> Conquerors, in the military and technical sense, of the indigenous populations, the absolutist rulers of the Negroes imported from Africa for the hard labour of the *bagaceira* [sugar plantation], the Europeans and their descendants meanwhile had to compromise with the Indians and the Africans in the matter of genetic and social relations. The scarcity of white women created zones of fraternization between conquerors and conquered, between masters and slaves. While the relations between white men and coloured women did not cease to be those of 'superiors' with 'inferiors', and in the majority of cases those of disillusioned and sadistic gentlemen with passive slave girls, they were mitigated by the need that was felt by many colonists of founding a family.… What a latifundiary system based on slavery accomplished in the way of creating an aristocracy by dividing Brazil into two extremes, of gentry and slaves, with a thin and insignificant remnant of free men sandwiched in between, was in good part offset by the social effects of miscegenation. The Indian woman and the mina or Negro woman, in the beginning, and later the mulatta, the cabrocha (dark-skinned woman), the quadroon, and the octoroon, becoming domestics, concubines, and even the lawful wives of their white masters, exerted a powerful influence for social democracy in Brazil.[251]

An interpretation such as this, focused so tightly on social 'mitigation', flourished for decades in good measure because of its contrast with the US experience. But it was increasingly criticised as historically insecure, misleading and blinkered in its

---

250. *The Master and Slaves* (1933), Berkeley 1986, p. 429. It should, though, be recognised that in the preface to the first English edition, Freyre wrote,

> The two expressions that make up the title – the Portuguese *casa-grande* (that is, big house or mansion in English) and the African *senzala* (slave-quarters) – have here a symbolic intention, the purpose being to suggest the cultural antagonism and social distance between masters and slaves, whites and blacks, Europeans and Africans … without for a moment forgetting the fact that the antagonism and distance of which we are speaking had their force broken by the interpenetration of cultures and by miscegenation – the democratic factors of a society that would have remained divided into two irreconcilable groups – we cannot view with indifference the aristocratic effect of these interpersonal and interregional relations.

Ibid., p. xvi.
251. Ibid., pp. xxxix–xxx.

TABLE 12   Latin American slave populations

State/region	Date	Slaves	Free blacks	Emancipation
Argentina	1810	8,500		
	1887	8,000		1/5/1853
Bolivia	1846	1,391	26,550	6/8/1861
Brazil	1770	700,000		
	1850	2,500,000		
	1872	1,700,000	4,300,000	13/5/1888
Central America	1801	8,925		24/4/1824
Chile	1778	12,000		
	1823	4,000		24/7/1823
Colombia	1800	70,000	140,000	
	1836	38,940		
	1851	16,468		1/1/1852
Ecuador	1800	8,000		
	1851	2,839	42,000	25/7/1851
Mexico	1793	9,500		
	1821	3,000	624,461	27/9/1822
Paraguay	1782	3,945	6,893	
	1864	20,000	24,000	2/10/1869
Peru	1812	89,241	41,256	
	1854	17,000		5/12/1854
Uruguay	1803	899		2/5/1853
Venezuela	1805	87,800	440,000	
	1854	35,000		24/3/1854

Sources: Leslie Rout, *The African Experience in Spanish America*, Cambridge 1976, pp. 95, 134; Herbert S. Klein, *African Slavery in Latin America and the Caribbean*, New York 1986, pp. 295–7.

amateur anthropology.[252] For our purposes it is best to follow Roberto Schwarz's generous scepticism about any notion of Brazilian 'essence' or 'national character', but this need not entail rejection of either the importance of slavery in Brazil or its distinct pattern of race relations.[253]

As can be seen from table 12, in 1850 2.5 million slaves were held in Brazil – a third of the total population, a sizeable proportion of the number in the USA, and over twice as many as in Cuba – the region's third main slave economy (table 13).

---

252. For alternative views, see, for example, C.R. Boxer, *Race Relations in the Portuguese Colonial Empire, 1415–1825*, Oxford 1963; Stanley Stein, *Vassouras: A Brazilian Coffee County, 1850–1900*, Cambridge, Mass., 1957; Thomas Skidmore, *Black into White: Race and Nationality in Brazilian Thought*, 2nd edn, London 1990, and 'The Myth-makers: Architects of Brazilian National Identity', in R. González Echeverría and E. Popó-Walker (eds), *Cambridge History of Latin American Literature*, Cambridge 1996, II; G. Reid Andrews, *Blacks and Whites in São Paulo, 1888–1988*, Madison 1991.

253. *Misplaced Ideas: Essays on Brazilian Culture*, London 1992.

TABLE 13   Caribbean slave populations

Region/state	Date	Total pop.	Slave pop.	Free blacks	Emancipation
Anglo-Caribbean	1770	500,000	428,000		
	1807		775,000	51,150	
	1830		665,000	81,130	1/8/1834
French Caribbean	1791		450,000		
	1831		183,000	55,000	
	1838		169,000	75,000	
	1848		163,000		27/4/1848
Cuba	1792	272,300		54,152	
	1827	704,487	286,900	106,694	
	1841	1,007,624	436,500	152,900	
	1861	1,396,530	370,500	227,843	7/10/1886
Puerto Rico	1834	357,086	41,818	126,399	
	1860	583,181	41,736	241,015	
	1872	618,000	31,635	257,709	22/3/1873
Dutch Caribbean	1770	90,000	70,000		
Suriname	1863		33,000		1/7/1863

Note: French Caribbean 1791 includes Saint-Domingue (Haiti and Santo Domingo); slavery was abolished in Haiti (1810 pop. 600,000) on 29/8/1793, and Santo Domingo was administered by Haiti without slavery from 1822 to independence in 1844. Dutch Caribbean included Curaçao, Aruba, Bonaire, St Eustatius, part of St Maarten and Suriname. Although Curaçao had been an important entrepôt for the trade in the eighteenth century, it had no plantation itself.

Sources: Robin Blackburn, *The Overthrow of Colonial Slavery, 1776–1848*, London 1988, pp. 5, 422–4, 487; Nicolás Sánchez Albornoz, *The Population of Latin America*, Berkeley 1974, p. 139; Klein, *African Slavery in Latin America*, pp. 295–7.

Moreover, as we shall see, from 1837 until early 1851, the number of people being forcibly transported from Africa to Brazil each year ran into tens of thousands, despite the formal outlawing of the international slave trade under national law in 1831. Yet Freyre's vision of an absolutely polarised economic society is incorrect. In contrast to the US South, where slaves comprised 32 per cent of the population (44 per cent in the cotton states), in Brazil they constituted only 15 per cent (37 per cent in the province of Rio de Janeiro). As can be seen from table 14 (which compares the US position on the eve of the Civil War with that in Brazil at its first census), Brazilian slaves were heavily outnumbered by free blacks and persons of colour. On the other hand, we should note that the 80,000 slaves who lived in Rio in 1849 made it the single largest urban concentration of unfree people in all the Americas (even in 1860 fewer than 15,000 slaves lived in New Orleans).

On the other hand, one must note that in Brazil whites – as defined and discerned by the census-takers – formed less than half of the total population, whereas in the

TABLE 14 Population of Brazil (1872) and USA (1860) by race

	Brazil	US South
Black and mulatto slaves	1,510,810	3,953,696
Free blacks and mulattos	4,245,428	261,918
Total blacks and mulattos	5,756,238	4,215,614
Whites	3,787,289	8,097,463
Total population	9,543,527	12,313,077
% of blacks and mulattos free	74	6
Free blacks and mulattos as % of total population	44	2

Source: Graham, 'Slavery and Economic Development', p. 652.

US South they were double the number of blacks. Moreover, this balance obtained despite the influx into Brazil of newly enslaved people (*bozales*), whose presence contributed to the retention of slavery until 1888 – longer than anywhere else in the hemisphere.[254] At mid century the number of slaves held in Brazil was roughly ten times that in all the rest of mainland Latin America, being approached only by the case of Cuba, which, like Brazil, was still a monarchy in this period. Most of the Spanish American republics proceeded to decree a general manumission in the 1850s if they had not already done so at independence.

Although the total number of slaves in Brazil began to fall with the effective ending of the slave trade in 1851, the coffee crop, which depended on slave labour, was only marginally less important to the national economy (41 per cent of exports in 1846–50) than was cotton to that of the USA (46 per cent). As a result, many features of daily life were markedly similar to those in the US South. For instance, the slave auction witnessed by Thomas Ewbank in Rio in 1846 appears almost identical to that in Richmond described by Olmsted seven years later:

> A hammer in his right hand, the forefinger in his left pointing to a plantation hand standing confused at his side, he pours out a flood of words. The poor fellow had on a canvas shirt, with sleeves ending at the elbows and trowsers of the same, the legs of which he is told to roll above his knees. A bidder steps up, examines his lower limbs, then his mouth, breast and other parts. He is now told to walk towards the door and back, to show his gait. As he was returning, the hammer fell, and he was pushed back within the railing. Another, who had but four toes on one foot, was quickly disposed of. The clerk next went behind the railings

254. Graham, 'Slavery and Economic Development', p. 635.

and brought forward a woman – a field-hand. She was stout and seemed older than reported in the catalogue. Dressed as sparsely and plainly as the men, she too was examined and told to walk to and fro. When near the door, a bidder interrogated her, but on what I could not comprehend. His last remark was translated plainly by her raising her skirt to expose her legs. They were much swollen. Two hundred and fifty milreis was the sum she bought.[255]

In contrast to the USA, where virtually no slaves were imported from abroad after 1808 (and where in 1861 the seceding states signally desisted from restoring the international trade), the personal property up for sale in Brazil originated from both that country and Africa. There is today little scholarly dispute over the importance of importing and trading slaves, which was at the time such a cause for British protest and even raised concerns amongst US officials:

> There are only three ways of making a fortune in Brazil – either by the slave trade, or by slaving, or by coffee commission house. The foreign merchants alone engage in the latter, and to be a Brazilian 'man of consequence' all have to partake more or less, directly or indirectly, in the two former. And all who are of consequence do partake in them both. Here you must be rich to profit by usury, and to be rich you must engage in the slave trade. The slave traders, then, are either the men in power or those who lend to the men in power and hold them by the purse strings. Thus the government itself is in fact a slave trading government against its own laws and treaties.[256]

Recent historiography has, however, registered important differences of emphasis on the relative capacity of Brazilian slavery to usher in modernisation. For Richard Graham,

> In Brazilian historiography it has become almost a truism that industrialization and slavery were mutually antagonistic. Indeed, the ending of the slave system there is generally explained by citing internal contradictions that became more and more intense as slave labor itself produced the wealth that undid the foundations of slavery ... [and] lessened the attractiveness of slave labor, which could best be used at rough and repetitive agricultural tasks rather than skilled industrial ones.... The North American experience casts doubt on most of these generalizations.[257]

On the other hand, Seymour Drescher, also treating the subject through comparison with the USA, suggests that what was achieved in the USA without fresh infusions of slaves from abroad was beyond the capability of the Brazilian system, where the total slave population was still falling and yet modern infrastructure slow to develop – quite the reverse of the experience of even the Southern US states prior to 1860:

> In the second half of the nineteenth century, Brazilians, especially those who travelled abroad, increasingly measured themselves against a broader West, in which the long-term weaknesses of their society became more manifest with each passing decade. In this respect, the significant

255. *Life in Brazil* (1853), Detroit 1971, pp. 282–4, cited in Mary Karasch, *Slave Life in Rio de Janeiro, 1808–1850*, Princeton 1986, pp. 48–9.

256. Minister Wise, Rio, to Buchanan, 9 Dec. 1846, quoted in Leslie Bethell, *The Abolition of the Brazilian Slave Trade*, Cambridge 1970, p. 289.

257. 'Slavery and Economic Development', pp. 631–2.

comparisons were not those of the marketplace such as crop output, productivity, profits, the net worth of slaveholders, or the aggregate wealth of the nation. What was important was Brazil's relative dearth of railroads, canals, towns, factories, schools and books. The echoes of Alexis de Tocqueville's contrast between the bustle of free societies and the stagnation of slave societies in the United States resonated among the Brazilian elite. Long before 1850, it was clear that Brazil's demographic dependency on Africa was the most critical ingredient in slavery's viability as an economic system.[258]

This, quite understandably, was the settled conviction of British Caribbean planters, whose slaves had been emancipated (with compensation) from 1834 and whose sugar now had to compete directly with that produced in Cuba and Puerto Rico as well as Brazil. At a meeting held in June 1849 in the parish of St Andrew, Jamaica, Robert Osborn was evidently reflecting the convictions of his audience when he declared,

> That under the present system of British duties, if the planters of Cuba, Porto Rico and the Brazils are permitted to evade the treaties entered into by their respective Governments with Great Britain for the suppression of the slave trade, are allowed to import slaves in unlimited numbers from Africa, and are suffered to enforce from their slaves 16 hours' labour out of every 24, the planters of this thinly populated colony cannot with any hope or prospect of success continue to cultivate their estates, or to arrest the downward tendency of the affairs of this fine and once prosperous and important exporting island to a state of irremediable ruin.[259]

Here there was a felicitous coincidence of self-interest (over protectionism), philanthropy (over the inhumanity of the slave trade) and belligerent sentiment (over employment of the navy). Indeed, it had been a familiar refrain in Britain since even before emancipation that if consumers wanted cheap sugar (and free trade) they would, in the words of Bristol MP Richard Vyvyan, have to pay 'a bounty upon the slave labour of foreign colonies, such as the Brazils and the Spanish islands'.[260] By the late 1840s the production of Jamaica had indeed suffered severely from the emancipation of the colony's slaves, and the planters were not engaged in an entirely idle culture of complaint. This is another argument developed by Drescher, one of the leading exponents of the view that the decline of the British West Indies was closely connected with the abolition of their slave trade in 1807, which, together with the ending of slavery itself, is best seen not as a rational – let alone planned – capitalist reaction to an economic obstacle but as a more complicated phenomenon in which the ideological, religious and ethical components of abolitionism acquire greater prominence. That debate over the relative economic logic and altruism of British abolitionism predates the scholarly polemic over the efficiency of US slavery and also resonates of deeper historiographical differences, which in this case are less tied to matters of methodology.[261]

---

258. 'Brazilian Abolition in Comparative Perspective', *HAHR*, 68:3, 1988, pp. 436–7.

259. 'Memorial of a Meeting of Clergy, Magistrates and Other Inhabitants of St Andrew, Court House, at Half-Way Tree, 5 June 1849', in *BFSP, 1849–50*, XXXVIII, pp. 333–4.

260. House of Commons, 30 May 1833, quoted in Temperley, 'Capitalism, Slavery and Ideology', p. 104.

261. The central text in this regard is Eric Williams, *Capitalism and Slavery*, Chapel Hill, N.C., 1944, which argued, 'when British capitalism depended on the West Indies, [the capitalists] ignored slavery or defended it. When British capitalism found the West Indian monopoly a nuisance, they destroyed West

What, however, is not seriously contested is the depth of abolitionist sentiment, whatever its convergence with economic interest. Sometimes, in fact, this convergence was less with the interests of production than with those of consumption or prohibition, particularly alcohol and tobacco. Although even the most pious of Victorians could not seriously envisage boycotting cotton, the popular cause of temperance was closely allied with that of abolition and pacifism. As with most such campaigns, the ardour of upholding high principle sometimes burnt out all practical sensitivity, as when L.A. Chamerovzov confronted 28-year-old David Holmes, a slave who had escaped from Virginia to London late in 1852:

> 'And so you smoke tobacco, David.'
> 'Yes, Sir. I've smoked it ever since I was that high,' indicating by a sign the height of a little boy of eight or ten years old.
> 'Did it ever occur to you, David, where and how that tobacco is grown?'
> 'Well, we raised a lot in Virginia.'
> 'Yes; where you were a slave, and where you have left many of your brethren in slavery.'
> 'Yes, Sir.'
> 'What do you think becomes of all the tobacco, and cotton, and sugar and rice that is grown by slaves, David?'
> 'I guess it's a good deal of it sold; most all I should say.'
> 'Well, don't you see how the buyers, the consumers of slave produce, help to keep up slavery? It's because the slave-owners find a market for the products of their slaves' labour; perhaps by some one you know. But if there were no one to buy it when it was grown, what use would there be in growing it?'
> 'I see that, Sir. I never thought of that before.'
> 'Well, David, now you have it before you, turn it over in your mind, and next time you come, let me know what you think about it.' ...
> In about twelve days, he came again....
> 'And how about the tobacco, David?' said we.
> 'It's very hard, Sir,' he said, 'I can't a'most do at all. I've been used to it so long.'
> 'Yes, David, I'm sure what you say is true. But I'm asking you what you think – you know – smoking tobacco that is grown by slaves.'
> 'Well, Sir, I do think it's right down wicked; raley now.'
> 'I'm glad to hear you say so, David. And what do you think then you ought to do?'
> 'I can't say I'm sure, Sir. But I'll tell you what I have done.'
> 'What's that, David?'
> 'I – I've – I've quit smoking it,' sobbed David, but with such a brightened countenance that we felt it had been with him a conscientious act.'[262]

Indian slavery' (ibid., p. 169). This interpretation is criticised most narrowly on the grounds that evidence of discontent with the sugar monopoly followed emancipation, but a later school, represented by Drescher in the USA and Roger Anstey in the UK, lays much greater emphasis on ideological and political factors. Seymour Drescher, *Econocide: British Slavery in the Era of Abolition*, Pittsburgh 1977; Roger Anstey, *The Atlantic Slave Trade and British Abolition, 1760–1810*, London 1975; Howard Temperley, *British Antislavery, 1833–1870*, London 1970. In the case of Brazil this approach is reflected in the work of Robert Conrad, *The Destruction of Brazilian Slavery, 1850–1888*, 2nd edn, Malabar 1993. Robin Blackburn has now completed the bulk of a major project of historical reinterpretation that seeks to synthesise for the Americas as a whole and within the framework of revolutionary change the key elements of the structuralist- and agency-led explanations: *The Overthrow of Colonial Slavery, 1776–1848*, London 1988; *The Making of New World Slavery: From the Baroque to the Modern, 1492–1800*, London 1997.

262. *Anti-Slavery Reporter*, 1 Feb. 1853, pp. 27–8, quoted in Blassingame (ed.), *Slave Testimony*, pp. 301–2.

Of course, by its very nature, the abolitionist cause scarcely lent itself to half-heartedness or strenuous expression of moderation. Whatever economic arguments that could be mustered in its support were normally enveloped in tight moral wrapping, and there were few opponents of slavery who fastened exclusively on its supposed economic inefficiency in simple input–output terms. Indeed, the fact that Hinton Helper's *Impending Crisis* did precisely this probably commended it as campaign material to the Republican Party in 1859 because by that time many voters in the North of the USA were familiar with *Uncle Tom's Cabin* and lesser examples of a genre that was reaching the limits of its constituency and capacity to convert. What was needed was a more 'objective' and 'scientific' appeal to those unpersuaded by the need to alter a system – however morally questionable – that was so deeply rooted in part of their society. By the same token, though, some economic criticism was almost always to be found enclosed within repudiations of slavery founded on ethical grounds. An idea of how these elements might interchange on both sides of the argument is given by Flora Tristán, who towards the end of her visit to Peru visited a sugar plantation at Chorillos which was unusually – perhaps uniquely – large for that country, having a slave population of 900. The owner, one Lavalle, complained to Flora that he once held 1,500 slaves but that three-quarters of the children died before the age of twelve and the suppression of the slave trade meant that he could not obtain fresh supplies.

'Such a death rate is frightening, and must give you cause for concern about your business. But how is it that there is no balance between the births and the deaths? This is a healthy climate and I would have thought that the negroes would do just as well here as they do in Africa.'

'You are right about the climate but you do not know the negroes. Many of the women miscarry and the rest let their children die out of sheer laziness. You can get nothing out of them unless you use the whip.'

'Do you think that if they were free their needs would be enough to make them work?'

'In this climate their needs are so few they would not have to work very hard. But, then, it is my belief that no man, whatever his needs, can ever be persuaded to work regularly unless he is forced to do so; most of our Indians still do next to nothing and live in idleness and poverty; our missionaries have to beat them to make them cultivate the land. It is the same with the negroes; you French have already tried the experiment with Santo Domingo. Now that you have freed your slaves they will no longer work.'

'I agree with you that whether a man is white, black or red, he will not take easily to work when he has not been brought up to it; but slavery corrupts man because it makes him loathe work, so that it is impossible to prepare him for civilisation. I grant that Spanish laws regarding slaves are far more humane than those of any other nation, but the root of the evil is the same everywhere: slavery is a permanent condition. The slave has to work such long hours that it is impossible for him to exercise his right to purchase his freedom. If the products of his labour were to lose their value I am certain that slavery would change very much for the better.'

'How so, mademoiselle?'

'If the price of sugar bore the same relation to the cost of labour that produces it as prices bear to labour costs in Europe, the master, having no compensation for the loss of his slave, need not make him work so hard and would take better care of him.'

'Mademoiselle, you speak of negroes like someone who knows them only from fine speeches of philanthropists in parliament, but unfortunately it is only too true that you cannot make them work without the whip.'

'If that is so, monsieur, I can only pray for the ruin of your refineries, and I believe my prayers will soon be answered. A few years more, and the sugar beet will replace your sugar cane.'

'Oh, mademoiselle, if you have nothing worse than that to bring against us! Your sugar beet is just a joke, only good for sweetening cow's milk in winter.'

'Laugh if you like, monsieur, but in France we can already do without you. The sugar we produce is as good as yours; what is more, it has the supreme merit, in my eyes, of bringing down the price of sugar from the colonies, and I am convinced that this alone can bring about the improvement in the lot of the negroes and the eventual abolition of slavery.'

Flora's point about beet sugar was not much stronger than that on the correspondence between price and labour cost – by mid century world production of beet was only 95,000 tons (of which France produced 38,000). That of cane sugar, by contrast, was nearly 1 million tons and in strong demand, but its price did continue to fall, and almost as rapidly as consumption rose. On the other hand, Tristán's programme of abolition through competitive undermining of slave-based industries was more worldly than sacrificial consumer boycotts of the type suffered by the doubly oppressed David Holmes. Equally, Flora had only to witness some of Lavalle's slaves to discern a different explanation for their behaviour:

It was late when we left; as we were passing a sort of shed where the negroes were still at work, the bell for angelus sounded, and they all fell upon their knees, pressing their faces against the earth. They all looked sullen and miserable, even the children. I tried to talk to one or two, but all I could get out of them was *yes* or *no*, uttered in a flat toneless voice.

I went inside a cell where the negresses were imprisoned. They had let their children die by neglecting to give them milk; both of them were crouching completely naked in a corner. One was eating raw maize; the other, who was young and very beautiful, turned her large eyes upon me in a look which seemed to say: I let my child die because I knew he would never be free like you, and I would sooner have him dead than a slave. The sight of that woman upset me.[263]

It is now broadly accepted that organised abolitionism in France was as elitist in the 1840s as it had been in the 1790s – Napoleon, of course, had restored the system in 1802 – and it certainly drew less popular interest and support than in the UK and USA. Flora Tristán was not unusual in supporting both a phased process of abolition and a transitional form of community organisation and shared property derived from the theories of Charles Fourier.[264] Indeed, on the eve of the 1848 Revolution such a proposal even commended itself to elements of the slaveholding plantocracy of the French Caribbean islands which were justifiably fearful that developments in the metropolis were leading to the complete elimination of their personal property. Tristán's

---

263. *Peregrinations*, pp. 282–3; 286.
264. Lawrence Jennings, *French Reaction to British Slave Emancipation*, Baton Rouge 1988; Seymour Drescher, 'British Way, French Way; Opinion Building and Revolution in the Second French Slave Emancipation', *AHR*, 96, 1991.

gradualist scenario – which, as in the case of Margaret Fuller, might be associated with her caution over the question of female suffrage – was consistent with her use of the term 'slave' in *The Workers' Union* to describe the state of Ireland and that of women whilst omitting discussion of the system of bondage in the Caribbean and Algeria in her passionate emancipatory plea to the French working class.[265] The slave population of the French Caribbean was not only less than half of that of Cuba but it was also in slow decline (table 13). Equally, Señor Lavalle's jibe about Saint Domingue/Haiti was familiar outside as well as within the Americas, and it had a particularly sharp resonance in France. It may well be true that 'even without the 1848 Revolution, French slavery would soon have come to an end', but this did not appear so obvious a few years earlier, and the emancipation that the Revolution brought about not only encouraged emulation elsewhere in the region but also significantly increased the pressure on Spain and Brazil – the two powers to uphold the system beyond the 1860s.[266]

Much of this new pressure came through the greater freedom of action that developments in France gave to the British campaign against the slave trade in the Atlantic. This fact is easily overlooked because in many respects the events of early 1848 in France came as an unalloyed disappointment to London, and, with Palmerston again serving as foreign secretary from August 1846, it scarcely seemed as if the British needed further encouragement in that quarter. Indeed, even Palmerston's temporising predecessor, Lord Aberdeen, had leant so heavily on Brazil through 'his' act of August 1845 – which treated the Brazilian slave trade as piracy on the high seas in a contravention of international law comparable to the 1996 Helms–Burton Act – that the British ambassador in Rio, Lord Howden, felt able to intervene personally and physically in individual cases.[267] In November 1847 Howden wrote to Palmerston,

---

265. Late in 1840 Fuller wrote to the abolitionist Maria Chapman,

> The Abolition cause commands my respect, as do all efforts to relieve and raise suffering human nature. The faults of the party are such that it seems must always be incident to the partizan spirit. All that was noble and pure in their zeal has helped us all. For disinterestedness and constancy of many individuals among you I have a high respect.

In her June 1845 review of Douglass's *Narrative*, she declared,

> He knows how to allow for motive and influence. Upon the subject of religion he speaks with great force, and not more than our own sympathies can respond to. The inconsistencies of slaveholding professors of religion cry to Heaven. We are not disposed to detest, or refuse communion with them. Their blindness is but one form of that prevalent fallacy which substitutes a creed for a faith, a ritual for a life.

Quoted in Bell Gale Chevigny, *The Woman and the Myth: Margaret Fuller's Life and Writings*, New York 1976, pp. 238, 342.

266. Drescher, 'British Way, French Way', p. 733. At several points in this article Drescher seems so eager to correct what he sees as Robin Blackburn's image of emancipation as 'a revolutionary tableau, with all lines of action converging harmoniously on a central point' (p. 713, n. 14) that he passes over evidence of his own that this was not entirely untrue and that, however messy the picture immediately before and after the events of spring 1848, the position was decisively altered by the mobilisation of February.

267. The debate in London over this matter in mid 1845 was as complex as it was charged. In May the government's law officers, while accepting that the Anglo-Portuguese treaty of 1817 had expired, informed the Peel administration that the first article of the Anglo-Brazilian treaty of 1826 (of indefinite duration)

Some weeks ago a little Negro girl, about ten years old, entered my house in the country; whether she had lost her way, or took refuge there voluntarily, it was impossible to know, as the girl was evidently just imported, frightened at everything and everybody, and not speaking a word of Portuguese. Three days afterwards a man of the name of Leitte, a neighbour of considerable wealth, but of notorious bad character, came to my cottage and claimed the girl as his slave.

I told this person that I could not give up the girl to him in that summary way, as I believed her to be a newly-imported slave, and that therefore he had no right to her, but that I would send her down to the Legation in the town (about eight miles off) at a certain hour, and that if he could there prove that she was born in the country, and that he had a legal right to her, she should be delivered to him on a promise that she should not receive punishment for absenting herself.

Mr Leitte seemed much discontented at this, saying that I had much better give up the slave to him, who would treat her well, than to the Government which was composed of a set of villains (his own words), who, instead of giving her liberty, would sell her again and divide the produce.

I, however, refused to do so, and I sent the girl away from the cottage at the time appointed, accompanied by three persons. Hardly had they proceeded a quarter of a mile from the house when a body of blacks, headed by a white overseer, all armed with pikes and bludgeons, rushed out of the thicket, threw down and held the persons who were accompanying the Negress, and the white overseer, putting the little girl over his shoulder, they all returned into the thicket whence they had issued.

One of the persons who were thrown down had the presence of mind to run to a height whence the house inhabited not far off by M. Leitte could be seen, and shortly after the white overseer and twelve Negroes were perceived entering into an unfinished building adjoining. The person then ran back and acquainted me with what had happened.

As I was perfectly well aware that no effectual means would be taken of bringing to punishment the perpetrators of this outrage, if I went through the long and always unsuccessful course of a complaint to the police, I was determined to take the matter into my own hands, somewhat irritated, I confess, at an outrage like this being committed almost in sight of my windows. I went to the house, which was not far from my own, where the gang had entered, and on the person, a woman, who was with me, identifying the overseer who had held his hand over her mouth, I went alone up to him, in the midst of all his Negroes, and with a considerable crowd of Brazilians at the gate, collared him, tied his hands behind

---

bestowed upon the Crown 'the right to order the seizure of all Brazilians found upon the High Seas engaged in the slave trade, of punishing them as pirates, and of disposing of their vessels ... as *bona piratoram*'. On the other hand, Sir Thomas Wilde, a former attorney general, told the House of Commons that the 1826 treaty had not been matched by any municipal law passed by the Brazilian legislature:

> They [the British] might punish their own subjects as pirates for any offence they pleased, but could they pass a law to punish as pirates the subjects of another nation, for committing an act against the subjects of a third nation? They had no more right to make a law binding on the subjects of Brazil than they had on the subjects of China or any other nation; and they had no right to punish them for an alleged act of piracy which was not piracy by the law of that country.

However, late in July, Stephen Lushington, an admiralty judge expert in the slave trade, interpreted the first clause of the 1826 treaty to mean that the Brazilians accepted that the trade could be so deemed, indicating that this need not depend on more than agreement to municipal *regulation*, which was implicit in the absence of open reference to legislation. Such advice, that Great Britain could try and punish Brazilian subjects as well as confiscate their property, not only helped Peel to push the bill through the Commons on 31 July but would later, through Palmerston's extended application, contribute to the final eradication of the slave trade into Brazil. None the less, the 1845 act was bitterly resented by even the most committed of Brazilian abolitionists. Bethell, *Abolition*, pp. 263–5.

him, and made him walk before me into town, where I informed the Minister for Foreign Affairs of what had happened, and put the man at his disposal.

The Minister for Foreign Affairs sent an account of the transaction to the Minister for Justice, who sent for M. Leitte, and desired him to produce the Negress; but the Negress was stated to have run away again, and was not forthcoming. M. Leitte had sent her to a friend of his at Santos by the steam-boat that plies on the coast. The Government then intimated to M. Leitte that if the girl did not make her appearance, he should be sent out of the country. M. Leitte is a native-born Portuguese.

The day before yesterday the little Negress arrived at Rio, and was sent to me by Senhor Saturnino, who requested me to take charge of her for a short time and make a formal request that she should be taken care of by the Government and considered free, being evidently a newly-imported slave. I, in consequence, made this application, and I yesterday gave her up, after having received a receipt for her, acknowledging her freedom.

It is a source of satisfaction to me to have been an accessory in snatching this poor girl from Slavery, although she be but a unit of the 50,000 unfortunate creatures who have been landed on this coast during the present year. I must add, in justice to Senhor Saturnino, and it gives me great pleasure to do so, that I received every assistance from him for the recovery of the child. I do not expect that M. Leitte will receive any punishment; he has many friends among the English merchants because he owes them money, and they have entreated the Brazilian government, which requires no pressing, not to send him away. Considering the little chance I had of obtaining any redress commensurate with the offence, I have thought it better to push the matter no further, and to content myself with obtaining the freedom of the Negress.

Despite the fact that Howden's actions barely fell within the bounds of acceptable diplomatic conduct, Palmerston's response was predictable enough:

> I have the satisfaction to acquaint your Lordship that Her Majesty's Government highly approve the humanity which prompted your proceeding, and the spirit and decision with which you acted. It will be well that your Lordship should ascertain how the girl is eventually disposed of.[268]

There can be found in the reports of both Howden and Tristán a sense of resistance on the part of slaves – even a little girl of ten separated from her family and thousands of miles from her home – which is not violent but which is also not best described as 'passive'. Non-compliance required initiative and bore a cost everywhere. Yet by the time of Flora's visit, slavery in Peru, which had once been among the strongest systems in mainland America, was in advanced decline; within twenty years it would be abolished without major social conflict. This accelerated the residual impetus to escape bondage by open and legal means – a process that occurred everywhere but tends to be seen as exceptional because in the USA manumission had become a rarity in the decades before the Civil War. Christine Hunefeldt paints a rather different picture of Peru in the early nineteenth century:

---

268. Howden, Rio, to Palmerston, 12 Dec. 1847; Palmerston, London, to Howden, 31 December 1847, in *BFSP, 1847–48*, XXXVI, pp. 613–14. Howden, previously Sir John Caradoc, was the grandson of the archbishop of Dublin and the son of his namesake, who had been amongst the leaders of the suppression of the 1798 uprising in Ireland. Sent to Brazil after thirty years of military service, he was promoted to lieutenant-general in 1859.

Despite the complex and manifold universe of internal conflict and faction, the priority of the slave population remained clear: freedom. All efforts aimed at obtaining it, and the most important methods were negotiation and the daily wage. Negotiation occurred in two ways. The first was a gradual lowering of the slave's purchase price; the second was the accumulation of money. In the end, a reduced purchase price and savings would come together in the acquisition of freedom. Many times this goal involved the intervention of relatives, *cofradía*, Church and state. Clearly, the possibility for negotiation was greater when the owner was a woman. As the weakest elements of the society – and many *limeñas* compared their own lives to that of slaves – women relied more heavily on slave labor and perhaps had other sympathies. The two methods might combine. The vast realm of negotiation included a variety of factors: a slave's good behavior, a master's declared will, the number of children a couple had, whether a slave had been born into the master's possession.[269]

In view of this it was perhaps unsurprising that by 1840 10 per cent of marriages registered in Lima involved slaves, and of these more than half were with a partner who was free.[270] In fact, the illegitimate offspring of Peruvian slaves were sometimes sold in order to encourage marriage, which had the support of both civil law and the Church. Of course, not all adult slaves wished to be married or could rely upon family support. Moreover, negotiation depended upon trust and was vulnerable to manipulation, as illustrated by the case of Patricio Negrón, whose efforts to obtain freedom in 1840 were complicated in a manner that has a ring of predictability about it:

> Being a slave originally from the city of Ica, I was brought up in a manner appropriate to my condition and according to the talents that were discovered in me. Nature more actively inclined me to the work that should occupy women. I washed and took care of the linen with skill, cooked and ran a house as the best housekeeper might do. Never did any aspect of my integrity, conduct or social behavior give occasion for remark. However, displeased with my master, I came to this city, and he arrived soon after in search of me – he wished to take me away by force. However, Doña Estefa Palacios, who understood well the importance of my services, lent me 200 pesos to free myself, in such a way that I managed to release myself from servitude. The owner received the money for my freedom, returned to his estate, and I remained in Doña Estefa's service.
>
> My work earns more than 24 pesos monthly. However, the *señora* did not give me anything. She planned a trip to Ica and took me with her. There I served her for the period of four months that included the arrival, stay and return. There I gave her from the total amount of 200 pesos she lent me 47 pesos and 7 reales, but she did not give me a penny for those four months. I gave her 11 pesos on the one hand, and 8 on the other, according to her receipt ... and the said *señora* owes me for all the time I served her without payment. Finally, she tells me that I have to give her the money or a guarantee.[271]

In Cuba at this time manumission was extremely rare and actively resisted by the authorities. The civil law expressly forbade marriage between the races, and although the Church supported it as a means of limiting concubinage, the granting of licences was exceptional.[272] Indeed, at mid century the Cuban regime of slavery was probably

---

269. *Paying the Price of Freedom: Family and Labor among Lima's Slaves, 1800–1854*, Berkeley 1994, p. 35.
270. Ibid., p. 145.
271. Quoted in ibid., p. 76.
272. Verena Martínez Alier, *Marriage, Class and Colour in Nineteenth-Century Cuba*, Cambridge 1974, p. 63.

the fiercest in all the hemisphere. As everywhere, the official regulations prescribed in some detail rules and treatment that could in practice readily be ignored, evaded, exceeded or abused:

6. Masters shall necessarily give their slaves in the country two or three meals as they may think best, provided that they may be sufficient to maintain them and restore them from their fatigues, keeping in mind that six or eight plantains or its equivalent in sweet potatoes, yams, yuccas and other edible roots, eight ounces of meat or salt fish, four ounces of rice or other pottage or meal is standardized as daily food and of absolute necessity for each individual.

7. [Masters] shall give them two suits of clothes a year in the months of December and May, each consisting of a shirt and pants of nankin or linen, a cap or hat, and a handkerchief; in December shall be added alternately a flannel suit one year and a blanket for protection during the winter the next....

11. Until they reach the age of three years [slave children] shall have shirts of striped gingham; from the age of three to six they may be of nankin. The girls of six to ten shall be given skirts or long dresses, and the boys of six to fourteen shall be provided with trousers. After these ages the dress shall be like the adults.

12. In ordinary times slaves shall work nine or ten hours daily, the master arranging these hours as best he can. On sugar plantations during harvest time, the hours shall be 16, arranged in such a way that the slave shall have two hours in the day to rest and six a night to sleep....

20. Any individual of whatever class, color and condition he may be is authorized to arrest any slave if he is met outside of the house or lands of his master; if he does not present the written license he is obliged to carry; or if, on the presentation, it shows the bearer has manifestly changed the route or direction described or if the leave of absence has expired. The individual shall conduct said slave to the nearest estate, whose owner shall receive him and secure him and notify the slave's master, should he be from the same district, or the pedaneo (district magistrate), so he may give notice to the interested party in order that the fugitive slave may be recovered by the person to whom he belongs.

21. Owners and overseers of the plantations shall not receive any remuneration for the fugitive slaves that they shall apprehend or deliver according to the aforesaid article, since it is a service that the proprietors are reciprocally obliged to loan and redounds to their private advantage....

24. Owners and overseers shall be charged particularly to watch vigilantly in order to restrain excessive drinking [among slaves] and the introduction of slaves from another estate and free men of color into amusements....

29. Masters of slaves shall avoid the illicit contact of both sexes and encourage marriages. They shall not prevent marriages made with slaves of other owners, and they shall give to married couples the means of living under the same roof....

31. When the master of the married male slave buys the wife, he shall also buy all her children under three years old, since according to law the mothers are obliged to suckle and nurse them until they attain that age.[273]

This was a regime designed for the production of sugar — a crop that had to be milled within two days of being cut if it was to be of any value. Its severity was

---

273. Slave Code of 1842, reproduced in Robert L. Paquette, *Sugar is Made with Blood: The Conspiracy of La Escalera and the Conflict between Empires over Slavery in Cuba*, Middletown, Conn., 1988, pp. 267–70.

remarked upon not only by most abolitionists (even Daniel Webster) but also US pro-slave ideologues, such as George Fitzhugh. The Cuban system itself never produced a defender or apologist like Fitzhugh, Hammond or Calhoun because the dictatorship of the Spanish captains-general did not require the services of such propaganda. Moreover, it would have been very hard to substantiate even the type of statistical argument served up by Calhoun for Ambassador Pakenham. Slave sickness rates habitually ran at 15 to 20 per cent, and by the end of the extraordinarily exacting harvest (*zafra*) of January to May or June (compared to sixty days in Louisiana) as many as 40 per cent of a plantation's field-slaves could be unfit for work. It did not need a very strict reading of the 1842 code to justify making slaves work for sixteen hours a day six days a week for more than a third of the year. Unsurprisingly, in the 1840s nearly 90 per cent of the island's suicides were slaves, whose final act not only gained deliverance from such travail but also deprived their masters of valuable capital stock.[274] Cuba was also sufficiently mountainous to make flight a highly risky but still possible option, permitting the formation of maroon communities in the backlands. Localised but often bloody uprisings were more common than elsewhere in the Caribbean, and certainly than in the USA. Although there were some similarities with the labour regime of Jamaica – where the insurrection led by Sam Sharp in 1831 had hastened emancipation – the continuance of the slave trade into Cuba until the 1860s meant that its slave population possessed an unusually high proportion of young men born in Africa. At least a third of a million slaves were imported into the colony between 1830 and 1860, producing not only a delicate balance between the *bozales*, *ladinos* (those who could speak Spanish) and the Cuban-born *criollos* but also marked imbalances between the sexes – as high as three males to one female on some estates. It was for good reason that Madrid not only garrisoned its most prized overseas possession with some 30,000 regular troops but also supplemented them with a militia, in which mulattos were encouraged to serve until the 'conspiracy of La Escalera' of 1844.

This was the human foundation of one of the most efficient plantation systems in the world. It was, furthermore, a system that relied and promoted a high degree of modern infrastructure and capital investment even as it exploited chattel slavery. The Havana to Bejucal railway was one of the first in the Americas, completed in 1837 with the labour of at least a thousand Irish navvies (railway workers, white and black alike, were from the start objects of suspicion about revolutionary activity). Early enthusiasm for steam power was motivated not only by a need to expand the rail network and reduce the time between cutting and milling but also – and no less vitally – by the aim of reducing reliance on inefficient and labour-intensive ox-drawn equipment. Although by mid century the bulk of mills (*ingenios*) had still to make the shift, those that had and the new railways enabled the island to increase production from 220,000 tons in 1849 to 359,397 in 1856 (21 to 25 per cent of world production, when the British West Indies had slipped back from 12 to 10 per cent and Brazil from

---

274. Manuel Moreno Fraginals, 'Africa in Cuba', quoted in ibid., p. 54.

10 to 6 per cent).[275] When Anthony Trollope visited the colony a couple of years later he remarked,

> The works at the Cuban sugar estate were very different to those I had seen at Jamaica. They were on a much larger scale, in much better order, overlooked by a larger proportion of white men, with a greater amount of skilled labour. The evidence of capital was very plain in Cuba, whereas the want of it was frequently equally plain in our own island.[276]

Trollope also considered Spain a distinctly second-rate power, but the cultural confidence exhibited in the construction of Havana's Tacón theatre (1838) was nearly as important as the subsidies creamed off slave-trading kick-backs that enabled 'Pancho' Martí to keep the place open. The social comportment of the capital's elite may have struck Anglo observers as anachronistic and the activities of the island's authorities as corrupt without parallel, but both were dependent on the macadamised roads and other engineering innovations as well as on the illicit 'handling charges' of the slave trade (reckoned by British Consul David Turnbull to be running at $17 a head in 1840).[277] In the terminology of present-day political economy, this was a limit case of 'combined and uneven development'. Santísima Trinidad, one of Cuba's most technologically advanced estates, was also infamous as a slave-breeding centre, its owner Esteban Santa Cruz de Oviedo, the father of at least twenty-six mulatto children, renowned for raping and abusing his female slaves.[278] It is perhaps just as well that we know less about Thomas Duggan as a person, but the 1846 inventory of his Saratoga mill (identified by a House of Commons select committee as an example of the kind of competitor the Anglo-Caribbean enterprises would have to copy and match) suggests that he was operating in the same league as Santa Cruz de Oviedo:[279]

LAND	1850 acres (933 in cane; 267 in pasture; 67 in garden; 100 in fallow; 433 wooded)	$55,000
CROPS	667 acres good cane; 267 acres poor cane; 25,000 plantation trees; orchard trees	$31,225
ANIMALS	25 oxen @ $59.50; 30 mules @ $34; 25 cows @ $25; 24 calves @ $5; 267 sheep @ $1	$9,929
NEGROES	4 drivers @ $600; 1 engineer @ $650; 11 1st class prime @ $550; 112 1st class able @ $150–400; 16 boys @ $50–100	$70,000
NEGRO WOMEN	6 prime wenches @ $400; 80 wenches @ $250–350; 38 girls @ $50–200	$32,380

275. Hugh Thomas, *Cuba or the Pursuit of Freedom*, London 1971, p. 126; Peter Eisenberg, *The Sugar Industry in Pernambuco: Modernization without Change, 1840–1910*, Berkeley 1974, p. 20.
276. *The West Indies and the Spanish Main* (1860), London 1968, p. 136.
277. *Travels in the West*, London 1840, p. 156.
278. Paquette, *Sugar is Made with Blood*, p. 214.
279. Select Committee on Sugar and Coffee Planting, 1848, 4th report, p. 86, reproduced in Thomas, *Cuba*, pp. 112–13.

BUILDINGS	engine house; 2 steam-engines; 4 trains	$38,000
	purging houses for 11,144 pots, tramways and hoists	$25,000
	drying and packing houses, bagasse logie, kilns and tramways	$10,000
	dwelling houses, negro quarters, hospitals, stables, wash-houses, clock-tower	$16,025
	reservoirs, wells, pumping-house	$10,045
	boundary walls and fencing	$6,133
	embankments and bridges	$2,000
	fire engines	$1,000
	34 ox-carts	$1,581
	sundries	$640
	TOTAL	$308,958

ANNUAL EXPENSES	cattle, horses and mules	$2,300
	food and clothing for negroes	$6,174
	wages of white workers	$7,340
	transport and replenishment of negroes	$21,151
	TOTAL	$37,151

RECEIPTS	226 tons white sugar	$18,326
	266 tons brown sugar	$16,996
	267 tons low-grade sugar	$15,174
	800 hogshead molasses	$2,000
	4,000 containers	$13,000
	TOTAL	$64,495

| PROFIT (less interest) | | $27,344 |

Up until 1861 it would have made quite good sense for Mr Duggan and his like that Cuba become part of the USA. In the view of Hugh Thomas, if such a move had been taken in, say, 1850, it

> would guarantee the continuance of slavery. It would restrain the English from forcing the Madrid government to abolish the slave trade but, important also, would not enforce the freedom of slaves who had entered the island since 1820 [when, under the 1817 treaty with London, Spain agreed to halt the slave trade into its colonies]. Refined sugar would be able to be sold to the US market without crossing a tariff wall while North American wheat could feed the slaves in Cuba without meeting Spanish taxes *en route*; the wheat interest of Castile would no longer be preferred nor would the merchants of Santander be able to sell their corn at high prices. Such was the political ... conflict at the heart of Cuba during what was, by world standards, her golden age as a provider of sugar.[280]

In fact, significant numbers of the plantocracy supported putting a real end to the slave trade since this would not only reduce pressure from the British and bring Cuba into line with the south of the USA but also deprive the bureaucratic apparatus around the Spanish captain-general of its primary source of income. More of the elite, however,

---

280. Ibid., p. 111.

bitterly resented London's campaign against their supply of labour, were prepared to pay pre-budgeted bribes to officials, and were critically reliant upon the military establishment and disposition for tight control maintained by the Spanish commanders (whose men easily outnumbered those of the regular armed forces of the USA).

This was especially the case after the crisis of 1843–44, generally known as the 'conspiracy of La Escalera' after the ladders onto which suspected rebels were strapped during interrogation and whipping. Whether any coordinated conspiracy existed at all remains a moot point, but there were undoubtedly plantation revolts of consequence in the spring and winter of 1843, particularly in Matanzas, and an uprising by 400 slaves in which six people died at the Triumvirato mill coincided with the arrival in November of the new captain-general, Leopoldo O'Donnell. Although his family was originally from Donegal, O'Donnell had, like his father and grandfather before him, made a career in the Spanish army. Inclined to political manoeuvre but more dedicated to personal enrichment, he derived considerable pecuniary advantage from turning a blind eye to slave cargoes. O'Donnell was also unbending in his attitude towards the discontent that he encountered upon his arrival in Cuba, and early in 1844 he began to authorise 'extrajudicial procedures' whereby planters and local militia commanders could conduct interrogations and order punishments without any legal oversight or sanction. His logic in this resonated of the 'national security doctrine' espoused by generals throughout the Americas in the 1960s and 1970s: 'When one deals with the security of the country and of crimes against the State, any means is legal and permitted, if beforehand the moral conviction exists that the desired result will be produced and that the public welfare demands it.' Judged by his own criteria, O'Donnell registered signal success. The aim of the measures, he said, was

> to return the slaves to their habitual state of discipline and servitude without grave damage to the proprietors, and at the same time to punish in a severe and exemplary manner the leaders and the whites and free blacks who have introduced this germ of unrest and in-subordination.[281]

The official toll in terms of exemplary punishment was the execution of seventy-eight persons (including thirty-eight free blacks and one white), with 3,000 being exiled or jailed for up to ten years. The real totals were probably much higher, not least because a system already rooted in violence practised it without any semblance of restraint in pursuit of information that almost all of the suspects were unable to provide. Quite a few of those subjected to *la escalera* evidently made up stories of plots to save themselves from further suffering, and many surely expired from the effects of the lash. The free blacks were widely seen as a threat but had no capital value for the proprietors, and it may well have been because their death or removal was less expensive than that of the slaves that they were so heavily persecuted – nearly 2,200 of the 3,000 punished for the conspiracy were free blacks. O'Donnell's new

---

281. Quoted in Paquette, *Sugar is Made with Blood*, pp. 220, 236.

slave regulations of 1844 decreed that all free blacks should leave the island within a fortnight, stating that in the meantime, 'on no account shall people of colour be employed as apothecaries, nor even make the simplest prescription' – an order that reflects the conviction that the rebels, recognising the uneven military odds, had settled on a programme of poisoning whites, some of whom in Matanzas would eat nothing but eggs from the shell, so fearful were they of this rumour. The free black population did fall – perhaps 1,000 left in the year after the repression, and royal regulations subsequently prohibited the entry into Cuba of free blacks – but it was impossible to transport an adult population of over 100,000, especially when it was still an important source of skilled labour (two years after the exclusion order 7 per cent of overseers and 12 per cent of plantation administrators were free blacks). Imports of slaves did, however, fall for a while, suggesting that both the planters and the authorities recognised some link between the trade and unrest.

O'Donnell's pogrom greatly lessened the threat of revolt over the final thirty years of Cuban slavery. It also marginalised those sections of the planter class who, led by Domingo Del Monte, favoured an ending of the slave trade and closer ties with the USA. These two policies were not naturally interdependent because Washington fiercely resisted the aggressive manner in which the British invigilated Atlantic shipping in pursuit of halting the trade; it was only a year into the Civil War that Lincoln reluctantly conceded the right of search on the high seas to the British. Moreover, neither policy was realised for decades to come. Spain retained its grip over Cuba through two independence wars and in the face of several financial offers from the USA, resisting pressure to ban the slave trade until 1865 (when slavery was definitively ended in the USA) and upholding the system of personal bondage until late 1886 – a full generation after North American emancipation. This pattern owed not a little to British reluctance to pursue with vigour the suppression of the Cuban slave trade because of the likelihood that it would lead to both war with Spain and a serious breakdown of relations with the USA. Instead, London turned its attention to reducing the source of supply in Africa and to eradicating the trade to Brazil.

Confronting the Slave Trade

Early in 1847 Palmerston received from Sir James Hudson, Lord Howden's number two at the Rio embassy, a report of a private conversation with the Brazilian foreign minister, Barão de Cairu, in which the politician outlined the embattled state of those who, like himself, opposed the slave trade. At the same time, the minister, who lasted barely a year in office, seemed to be sending a signal that only an external force could achieve the elimination of this 'odious commerce':

I know of none who could or would attempt it, and when 99 men in every 100 are engaged in it, how is it to be done? ... The vice has eaten into the very core of society. Who is so sought after, who is so feasted in this city as Manuel Pinto [da Fonseca]? You know him to be the great slave trader *par excellence* of Rio. Yet he and scores of minor slave dealers go to the Court – sit at the tables of the wealthiest and most respectable citizens – have seats in the Chamber as our Representatives and have a voice even in the Council of State. They are increasing in vigilance, perserverance, audacity – those whom they dare not put out of the way, they buy. No people make money so easily or spend it so lavishly – what they touch turns to gold – they carry all before them. You know my individual abhorrence of this cursed traffic – but with such men to deal with, what am I to do, what can I do? ... Where am I to begin? With my colleagues – useless. With the Council – they would not listen to me. In the Chamber – they would call me a traitor. In the streets I would be stoned. I cannot consent to be *The* Man in Brazil for whom all his countrymen would turn away with contempt and aversion. I *will not Bell the Cat*.[282]

Two years later Hudson, now himself the British envoy, reported that little or nothing had changed, estimating that 60,000 slaves had been landed in 1848 (the same number that Howden reckoned had been brought in the previous year):

The Rio Janeiro slave market is glutted – indeed it is impossible to approach this capital in any direction without meeting troops of Bozal negroes. They are landed openly ... and no measures whatever are taken by any Brazilian authority to repress the traffic. At Bahía the public sale of slaves, which was prohibited, is again in full operation and the depots are overflowing with newly-imported negroes.[283]

Six months later he raised the matter directly with Foreign Minister Paulino José Soares de Sousa:

I asked Senhor Paulino why the Brazilian law of 7 November 1831 was not put into force against the importers of slaves and why the Brazilian slaves were not seized by the Brazilian authorities now? His Excellency, with great candour, said that the slaves were not seized because the Brazilian government did not know what to do with them; but that a plan was under the consideration of the Imperial court for transporting slaves so seized to Africa.
I asked if His Excellency had considered the expense of their transport, and whether the Imperial treasury could bear it, and after discussing the point, His Excellency seemed to be of the opinion that the Brazilian treasury could not defray it. I am, therefore, inclined to think this plan quite chimerical, and, in point of fact, highly objectionable, as relieving the importers of slaves from the penalties of the Brazilian law.[284]

Palmerston plainly chafed as report after report of this nature reached his desk in the late 1840s. He was then, no less than twenty years later, of the conviction that Brazil was 'like a Billingsgate fisherwoman ... she feels the strong grip of the police-man and ... goes quiet as a lamb though still using foul-mouthed language at the corner of every street', but the Commons was in no mood to support more energetic enforcement of the 'Aberdeen Act'.[285] This was because foreign policy in general and

282. Hudson, Rio, to Palmerston, 12 Jan. 1847, cited in Bethell, *Abolition*, p. 290.
283. Hudson, Rio, to Palmerston, 9 June 1849, in *BFSP, 1849–50*, XXXVIII, p. 461.
284. Hudson, Rio, to Palmerston, 20 Feb. 1850, in *BFSP, 1850–51*, XL, p. 338.
285. Quoted in E.D. Steele, *Palmerston and Liberalism, 1855–1865*, Cambridge 1991, p. 358.

abolitionism in particular were still closely tied up with the issue of free trade and the
fall-out from the repeal of the Corn Laws. Palmerston could draw on the support of
the droll Macaulay, who noted the hypocrisy of a nation that condemned Brazilian
slavery but traded in Brazilian (and Cuban) sugar, the proposed duties on which were
continually defeated in the Commons:

> We import the accursed thing; we bond it; we employ our skill and machinery to render
> it more alluring to the eye and the palate; we export it to Leghorn and to Hamburg; we
> send it to all the coffee houses of Italy and Germany; we pocket a profit on all this; and
> then, we put on a pharisaical air, and thank God that we are not like those sinful Italians and
> Germans, who have no scruples about swallowing slave-grown sugar.[286]

Cobden, by contrast, simply asked how the British, who were the largest sellers of
slave-picked cotton textiles to Brazil, could refuse to take slave-cut sugar in return.
For him, this was not only 'lucrative humanity' but could easily lead to intervention
abroad, which he always strenuously opposed, 'even in cases where my feelings were
most strongly interested'. Cobden's principled anti-interventionism was rather less
popular, however, in both Commons and country than his assessment of Palmerston's
personal politics:

> It is said ... that the noble Lord goes abroad as the champion of liberalism and constitutional-
> ism. But I cannot fall into the delusion. I cannot trace the battle that we are taught to
> believe is going on under the noble Viscount's policy between liberalism and despotism
> abroad. I do not think that the noble Lord is more democratic than his colleagues, or that
> the right honourable Gentleman opposite [Peel]. I believe the noble Lord is of an active turn
> of mind – that he likes these protocols and conventions, and that the smaller the subject, the
> better it suits his taste.[287]

Even if Cobden was wrong about Palmerston's individual disposition, the foreign
secretary's failure to make a new strategic move on the slave trade for four years can
be explained by the sheer size of the problem he faced as well as the awkwardness of
MPs. The figures given in table 15 are subject to the same strictures about accuracy
and precision as those issued by John Coatsworth, but they are the product of a
detailed academic debate over the scale and profitability of the slave trade, and they
may taken as the best approximations available from existing evidence.[288] Of course,

---

286. Quoted in Hugh Thomas, *The Slave Trade: A History of the Atlantic Slave Trade, 1440–1870*, London
1997, p. 734.
287. Bright and Rogers (eds), *Speeches of Richard Cobden*, II, p. 227.
288. I follow Hugh Thomas in relying primarily on David Eltis, *Economic Growth and the Ending of the
Atlantic Slave Trade*, New York 1987. Eltis's figures are usefully viewed as a revision to the pioneering work
of Philip Curtin, *The Atlantic Slave Trade: A Census*, Madison 1969, which is now thought to have
underestimated the flows in the nineteenth century with the following figures for imports to the Americas
(1,000s):

	1831–40	1841–50	1851–60
Cuba	126.1	47.6	123.3
Puerto Rico	14.1	10.6	7.2
French Caribbean	3.6	–	15.0
Brazil	212.0	338.3	3.3

TABLE 15 The slave trade

(i)	Import of slaves into the Americas by decade, 1830–60 (*1,000s*)		
	1831–40	1841–50	1851–60
USA	–	–	0.3
Cuba	181.6	50.8	121.0
Spanish America	25.4	3.8	1.0
French Caribbean	0.6	–	12.5
British Caribbean	10.2	–	–
Brazil	334.3	378.4	6.4

(ii)				Slaves imported into Brazil, 1831–1853			
1831	138	1837	35,209	1843	19,095	1849	54,061
1832	116	1838	40,256	1844	22,849	1850	22,856
1833	1,233	1839	42,182	1845	19,453	1851	3,287
1834	749	1840	20,796	1846	50,324	1852	800
1835	745	1841	13,804	1847	56,172	1853	–
1836	4,966	1842	17,435	1848	60,000		

(iii)	Price of prime male bozals (*1821/25 $*)		
	AFRICA	CUBA	BAHÍA
1831–35	62.4	342.9	249.6
1836–40	47.2	364.5	249.6
1841–45	64.1	395.3	267.7
1846–50	40.4	661.5	326.1
1851–55	84.1	1,018.0	394.0

Sources: Eltis, *Economic Growth*, pp. 249, 263; Foreign Office estimates, 4/8/1864, cited in Bethell, *Abolition*, pp. 389–90.

the trade in the Atlantic had effectively become covert from the early 1830s, but although only five-strong in 1850, the Foreign Office Slave Trade Department managed with the assistance of often well-paid secret agents, as well as the services of consular officials, to assemble estimates that have stood the test of subsequent scrutiny quite well – perhaps because the flows were generally large.[289]

---

289. Naturally, one can find exceptions to this rule – consuls were of uneven quality and not always disinterested. Thus, in December 1847 Edward Porter reported that slaves landed in the province of Bahía had risen from 1,413 in 1840 to 6,501 in 1844 and 10,064 in 1847: 'the slave trade is increasing in a great degree, which may be seen accounted for by the great temptation now held out to individuals to embark in this traffic, as small shares can be obtained in the companies established here for that purpose'. By contrast, Augustus Cowper, in Pernambuco, confidently reported in February 1847 that 'the slave trade no

These figures support Barão Cairu's appreciation of the slave trade as so flourishing and important as to dominate national politics – a fact no less true for Cuba, which boosted its demand for enslaved Africans after that in Brazil was halted. For David Eltis, the eventual suppression of this impressive trade did not at all help to develop a modern Atlantic economy. Quite the reverse – bringing the trade to an end hindered the expansion of the Brazilian and Cuban economies, where sugar and coffee production was rising markedly in the 1840s, a period of high recent and actual slave imports:

> Abolition of slavery itself came gradually between 1813 and 1861 but employers could not attract Europeans in large numbers until after this. We might, however, question whether suppression, abolition or mass European immigration could have occurred when they did anywhere in temperate South America if slave prices (and access to Africa) had continued at early-nineteenth-century [levels] … the ability of the market sector fuelled with slave labour to overwhelm and absorb non-market activities was severely circumscribed by the termination of the African slave trade. The widely recognised poor performance of Brazilian measured income in the nineteenth century might have improved if Brazil had continued unfettered access to labour in Africa.[290]

It is from the mid 1840s that the prices of imported slaves begin to rise steeply, particularly in Cuba, for which Laird Bergad makes a similar point: 'planter willingness to support rising prices indicates the economic viability of slave-based sugar production … if slavery was no longer viable at this point … demand for slaves would soften and prices would decline.'[291] In the case of Brazil prices had been more stable from 1825, but after the abrupt closing down of external supply in 1850–51 they started to rise within what was now an exclusively domestic market.[292] This did not occur to nearly the same degree in the USA after the ending of the slave trade

---

longer exists, at least as far as importation is concerned'. But Cowper's reliability may be questioned on the basis of the homily that he presumed to offer Palmerston:

> An opinion appears to be gaining popularity in England, and to be extending itself to the officers of our squadron, that the armed preventative measures adopted by HMG and its allies, for the suppression of this traffic on the coast of Africa, are, to quote an expression of one of them, 'futile, mischievous and useless'; but if we consider that this wealthy province – the greatest sugar-producing and the most populous for its size in Brazil – has not imported 600 slaves in two years, and that it is nearly 12 months since a single one was landed, and that this has, in my opinion, been chiefly brought about by that intervention [they must be wrong].'

Porter, Bahía, to Palmerston, 31 Dec. 1847; Cowper, Pernambuco, to Palmerston, 12 Feb. 1847, in *BFSP, 1847–48*, XXXVI, pp. 619–20, 622–3. Pernambuco's slave population remained quite stable between 1845 and 1855 as a result of the internal market, but to declare that landings had ceased by early 1847 was at odds with all other evidence.

290. *Economic Growth*, pp. 234; 238.
291. 'Slave Prices in Cuba, 1840–1875', *HAHR*, 67:4, 1987, p. 633.
292. Consul Porter reported the following top sterling prices for Bahía:

	1825	1830	1840	1850
Males	£51 6s 8d	£52 10s 0d	£57 10s 0d	£52 19s 4d
Females	£42 0s 0d	£45 18s 0d	£45 18s 9d	£44 14s 7d

Porter, Bahía, to Palmerston, 31 Dec. 1850, in *BFSP, 1850–51*, XL, p. 430.

TABLE 16 Slave trade costs ($, Cuba, 1836–45)

SHIPPING	ship	135 tons @ $38.4 per ton ($5,184)	
		depreciation @ 7% per trip	363
		outfit	6,480
	labour	wages (18 sailors @ $37; 4 officers @ $74)	
		7.3 months	7,023
		commissions and privileges @ 5%	4,719
	other	slaves' food (52 days @ 7.3 cents)	1,419
		crew's food @ $69 per month	504
		mortality @ 16.9% (63 slaves @ $44.2)	2,785
		insurance @ 30%: ship and outfit	3,499
		cargo	6,020
		freight for trade	6,551
		ship's papers	1,638
		miscellaneous expenses	1,613
			42,614
DISTRIBUTION		commissions @ 7% retail price	6,607
		bribes @ $25 per slave	7,775
		coastal transport/maintenance @ $8 per slave	2,488
			16,870
TOTAL			59,484

Source: Eltis, *Economic Growth*, p. 273.

there because the domestic system of slavery was still so buoyant, slave birth rates were high, and new, supplementary sources of immigrant labour were soon coming on stream.

Brazilian slavery would survive for thirty-five years after the elimination of the slave trade into the country, but it was evident from the start that the economy would require an expansion of its labour force. In fact, Senhor Paulino had spoken to Hudson of the government's putative plan to export people back to Africa just as his ministry issued a report insisting that the slave trade could only be effectively suppressed as the result of successful immigration and colonisation schemes.[293] Although these were initially expected to involve Africans, a debate soon developed over the tension between the existence of slavery and the need to attract European immigrants. But in Brazil, as in the rest of Latin America, such immigration did not take off until the end of the century – well after the end of the slave trade and, indeed, that of slavery as a whole.

293. Enclosure to Hudson, Rio, to Palmerston, 20 Feb. 1850, in ibid., pp. 333–5.

Table 16 depicts the costs entailed in transporting slaves across the middle passage from Africa to market in Cuba, but the figures for Brazil in the late 1840s were of a comparable order. Rates of return and profits evidently varied according to the mortality rate of slaves (who were carefully tended in 'seasoning' quarters on their immediate arrival) as well as the successful evasion of naval patrols, but a profit margin of the order of 50 per cent is yielded by very cautious estimates of the day that allowed for low prices and half of loaded vessels being detained; most suggest much higher levels. According to Captain Richard Drake, one voyage of the Baltimore clipper *Napoleon* made in 1835 (just before the period depicted in table 16) transported 350 slaves who had been bought at $16 a head for a total cost of $20,000. Their sale in Havana at an average of $360 a head produced a profit of around $100,000. Twenty-five years later, at the end of the Cuban slave trade, the British consul in Havana, Joseph Crawford, reported to Earl Russell that a voyage costing $150,000 could expect to make $400,000 if slaves could be sold for $1,200 each. When he was himself prime minister in the 1840s Russell told parliament that the trade to Brazil was yielding profit margins of 400 per cent. Few ships, though, registered quite such success as Joaquim Pereira Marinho's eighty-ton yacht *Audorinha*, which between October 1846 and September 1848 evaded the British navy on eight successive voyages, landed 4,000 slaves, and made a clear £40,000.[294]

It is no coincidence that half the slave ships working out of Brazil at the end of the trade were US-built and -owned. Fast and modern, they were often operated on dodges that were so loosely disguised that Washington was fully aware of the scale of the involvement of its nationals:

> the vessel clears from the United States for some port in Great Britain, where a cargo of merchandize, known as 'coast goods', designed especially for the African trade, is purchased, shipped and consigned, together with the vessel, either to the slave-dealer himself or to his agents or accomplices in Brazil. On her arrival, a crew is put on board as passenger, and the vessel and cargo consigned to an equally guilty factor or agent on the coast of Africa, where the unlawful purpose originally designed is finally consummated. The merchandize is exchanged for slaves, the vessel is delivered up, her name obliterated, her papers destroyed, her American crew discharged, to be provided for by the charterers, and the new or passenger crew put in command, to carry back its miserable freight to the first contrivers of the voyage or their employees in Brazil.[295]

The US navy, which during this period stationed between three and eight craft in the Atlantic, detained only twenty-eight slave vessels between 1844 and 1854.[296]

As can be seen from table 16, sailors' wages were high, but so was the risk, and in 1850 the British consul in Havana reported that Spanish sailors were prepared to settle for wages of $18 on British vessels rather than the $40 that they could command on

294. Thomas, *Slave Trade*, pp. 725–6, 735.
295. President Tyler to Congress, 19 Feb. 1848, in *BFSP, 1845–46*, XXXIV, p. 924.
296. Thomas, *Slave Trade*, pp. 728–9. Between 1840 and 1845 sixty-four US-built ships were sold in Rio alone.

a slaver.[297] On the other side – the British navy habitually referred to 'the enemy' – it was both necessary and traditional to distribute prize money to the crews of ships which detained slavers that were subsequently condemned by admiralty and mixed commission courts. Although the deep hierarchy of the Royal Navy meant that a ship's boy could expect a meagre fraction of the money given to its senior officers (or the secret agents in Brazil, who were sometimes awarded 10 per cent of a prize), such an incentive helps to explain why between 1840 and 1850 the thirty-odd ships of the Cape and West African squadrons detained 530 vessels and so released 33,000 slaves.[298]

It was not easy to catch slavers, and success depended heavily on skilled seamanship as well as aggression. Once a vessel had been detained, however, it did not take great powers of detection to discern its purpose. The hallmarks of a slaveship carefully itemised in the Brazilian imperial decree of October 1850 were instantly recognisable to sailors of all nations and would have been the first features of western commercial organisation to be encountered by millions of Africans:

> The appearances constituting legal presumption that a vessel is employed in the trading of slaves are the following:
>
> 1. Hatches with open gratings, instead of the closed hatches which are usual in merchant-vessels.
> 2. Divisions or bulkheads in the hold, or upon deck, in greater number than is necessary in vessels employed in lawful trade.
> 3. Spare plank fitted for being laid down as a second deck.
> 4. A greater quantity of water in casks, tanks or any other receptacle than is necessary for the consumption of the crew, passengers and cattle in relation to the voyage.
> 5. A greater quantity of fetters, chains or handcuffs that are necessary for the maintenance of order on board the vessel.
> 6. A greater quantity of trays, wooden bowls or mess tubs than are necessary for the crew.
> 7. A boiler of extraordinary size, or a number of boilers greater than is necessary on board legal traders.
> 8. An extraordinary quantity of rice, manioc flour, Indian corn, kidney beans or animal food, obviously exceeding the wants of crew and passengers, not being declared in the manifest as part of the commercial cargo.
> 9. A greater quantity of mats or matting than is necessary for the persons on board.[299]

---

297. Kennedy, Havana, to Palmerston, 1 Jan. 1850, in *BFSP, 1849–50*, XXXVIII, p. 312.

298. Christopher Lloyd, *The Navy and the Slave Trade*, London 1949, p. 276. The allocation of prize money was revised in 1836, 1846 and 1854 when, as a result of the outbreak of war in the Crimea, it was reapportioned thus: 1st class (master of the fleet; inspector of steam machinery; medical inspectors) 45 shares each; 2nd class (2nd lieutenant) 35 shares; 3rd class (sea lieutenant; master; captain of marines) 28 shares; 4th class (lieutenant of marines; chaplain; paymaster; boatswain; surgeon) 18 shares; 5th class (midshipman; pilot; chief gunner's mate; ship's cook) 10 shares; 6th class (cadet; quartermaster; gunner's mate; leading stoker) 9 shares; 7th class (coxwain; sailmaker's mate; caulker's mate; musician; cooper; corporal of marines) 6 shares; 8th class (leading seaman; shipwright; able seaman; private and fifer of marines; bandsman; butcher) 3 shares; 9th class (cook's mate; ship's steward's boy; 2nd class ordinary seaman) 2 shares; 10th class (boy beyond first class) 1 share. Royal Proclamation, 29 April 1854, in *BFSP, 1855–56*, XLVI, pp. 43–5.

299. Imperial decree of 14 Oct. 1850, declaring the execution of Law of 7 Nov. 1831, in *BFSP, 1849–50*, XXXIX, p. 1069. The kind of practices described by President Tyler made it essential that any law, such as this, which declared the trading in human cargo to be piracy should also provide sanctions against the duplication of log-books and substitution of captains by 'flag' (nominal) commanders as well as treating the flight of the crew as admission of guilt.

The evidence presented to meet such requirements of proof was rarely subjected to serious challenge in the mixed commission courts and even less so when cases were tried within completely British courts. But neither was the law simply the final gloss on a contest decided by speed and force at sea, even if the high level of risk, the death of sailors as well as slaves, and the universal formal outlaw status of the trade sometimes made legal procedures seem strictly subordinate. Aberdeen's act of 1845, for instance, related to the high seas, not territorial waters – the place where slavers were most vulnerable and could best be intercepted. Its passage, therefore, made little difference to the advice that Aberdeen had sent the previous year to the embassy in Rio:

> I have now to observe to you that the Act 2 and 3 Vict., cap.73, confers no authority on a British cruizer, within the recognised territorial jurisdiction of any civilised power, to detain a vessel upon the ground of her being engaged in Slave Trade, even though destitute of proof of nationality.[300]

Reminders like this were frequently issued because the young British lieutenants dispatched from brigs and sloops of the South American squadron were prone to enthusiasm as they closed on suspicious ships. Complaints by Spanish, Cuban, Portuguese and Brazilian captains often had about them the same air as that directed to Aberdeen by Robert Falk – an initial plausibility undermined by compound one-sidedness. But this was not always so, even when little effort had been expended in diminishing the dramatic element, as in the protest of Captain José Joaquim Gomes Dos Santos about the actions directed by the British brig *Racer* (Reed) off Santos in August 1844:

> On my voyage from Rio Grande to this province, on board the Brazilian brig *Principe Americano*, of which I am the captain, and whose owner is the merchant Francisco José Godinho, with a cargo of jerked beef, I was, on the evening of the 20th of the present month to the southward of point San Antonio, and two miles from the entrance to this port, when a launch appeared, which, after hoisting the English flag, came on towards the brig, which also continued her course in the direction of the port.... The launch, however, making every effort by sailing and pulling to reach the brig, commenced firing muskets so that there are marks thereof, not only in the hull but several of the sails of the vessel have shot-holes in them.
>
> On observing this proceeding, and wishing to avoid a continuation of it, as well as any consequences which might result therefrom, and even to prevent the balls from wounding any one, I hove to, and although there was a national flag at the mizen, I showed another in the gangway; notwithstanding which, and in spite of my being little more than a mile from the batteries of the fortress, the crew jumped on board the brig, at 2 o'clock in the afternoon, and not only by force, and presenting a pistol, cocked, to my breast, but also by making use, at pleasure, of threats and insults, opened and removed the hatches, destroyed their caulking, and searched the vessel throughout; and in like manner, and using the same means, which I saw to be very easily effected, they obliged me to stand out to sea to meet the English brig-of-war, which was cruizing in the offing, when the vessel of which I am captain was again searched, and then permitted to make for this port.

---

300. Aberdeen, London, to Hamilton, 22 July 1844 in *BFSP, 1844–45*, XXXIII, p. 459.

When questioned about this by Commodore Purvis, second-in-command of the squadron, Captain Reed told him that his information was that the *Principe Americano* was detained five miles off-shore, keeping sail after blanks were fired. Live rounds were only fired under provocation: 'I have no doubt the provocation was great. Otherwise the officer, whose judgement and discretion is good upon these trying occasions, would not even have had recourse to that measure.'[301] Five days before receiving this report, the British ambassador had been handed another from the US envoy to Brazil, relating to the detention by the *Racer* of the *Sooy*, a US-built and Newport-registered ship. That time, though, the captured vessel was found to possess no papers or colours, having, according to Reed, previously landed 650 slaves at Bahía when under an American crew.[302] If there were any doubts about the word of an officer and gentleman in the case of the *Principe Americano*, the experience of the Sooy would surely have expunged them instantaneously.

The action of the *Racer* was the kind being demanded a full five years later by Carlyle, irritated by the abolitionist campaign alone, and doubly so by the fact that it was taking place in a country with the most powerful navy in the world:

> Watch the coast of Africa? That is a very long Coast; good part of the Coast of the terraqueous Globe! And the living centres of the slave mischief, the live coals that produce all this world-wide smoke, it appears, lie simply in two points, Cuba and Brazil, which are perfectly accessible and manageable.
>
> If the laws of Heaven do authorize you to keep the whole world in a pother about this question; if you really can appeal to the Almighty God about it, and set common interests, and terrestrial considerations, and common sense, at defiance in behalf of it – why, in Heaven's name, not go to Cuba and Brazil with a sufficiency of 74s and signify to those nefarious nations: 'Nefarious countries, your procedure on the Negro Question is too bad...!'[303]

Perhaps it was, indeed, that easy? In 1849 – the year in which Carlyle was writing – the British navy had a total establishment of nearly 250 ships and 36,000 men. This force included only eleven 'first-rate' ships with over seventy guns – the type that Carlyle thought would do the business – but in the prosecution of this campaign it was less the large warships (many of which were 'in ordinary', or laid up) than the new steamers that would decide the issue. On the combined Cape (Reynolds) and West African (Hotham) stations the navy kept just two fifty-gun ships and two frigates (twenty-four guns), twenty-four sailing sloops and brigs, and nine steam vessels. The South American squadron, with its command at Montevideo, comprised just four ships, and if any single vessel might be said finally to have finished off the slave trade into Brazil it was the new steam sloop HMS *Cormorant* (Schomberg), which was large enough at 1,050 tons but carried only six light guns.[304]

---

301. Enclosure to Ministry of Foreign Affairs, Rio, to Hamilton, 20 Sept. 1844; Purvis, Rio, to Hamilton, 30 Sept. 1844, in ibid., pp. 462–4.
302. Ibid., p. 465.
303. 'Occasional Discourse on the Nigger Question', p. 209.
304. Lloyd, *Navy and the Slave Trade*, pp. 143, 279, 282.

Size was not everything, and even with the support of such forces, the crews of small warships were vulnerable once they engaged with their targets, landed boarding parties and had to conduct the prize (often with prisoners and a full cargo of slaves) to port. The case of the *Felicidade* in 1845 was quite unusual because it ended up in a court in Great Britain, but it illustrates why sailors felt that they fully deserved their prize money. The matter was raised a day before the Commons passed the Aberdeen bill by Brazilian ambassador Marques José Lisboa, who predictably protested at the application of British law to foreigners, but within the legal argumentation rehearsed at the Exeter Assizes one gets a clear sense of human experience (even if this account completely effaces the suffering of the slaves):

Upon the trial of ten foreigners, of whom one was believed to be a Spaniard, and others Brazilians and Portuguese, for the murder of Mr Thomas Palmer, late midshipman on board the *Wasp*, a British cruiser, on the coast of Africa, the following facts appeared.

The *Felicidade*, a schooner fitted out for the Slave Trade, of which the witness Cerqueira was commander, and the prisoner Majaval was the cook, sailed from Bahía for Lagos, in Africa, for a cargo of slaves. Before she had succeeded in taking in any slaves, the *Felicidade* was, at the end of February, boarded and taken by Lt Stupart, an officer of the *Wasp*, accompanied by Mr Palmer and 16 men from that vessel. On 1st March, the *Echo*, a small vessel from Rio de Janeiro which had a cargo of 430 slaves, was chased by Lt Stupart in the *Felicidade*. Upon approaching the *Echo*, in the evening, Lt Stupart sent Mr Palmer, with about eight men, in a boat to the *Echo*, of which Mr Palmer took possession, remaining on board all night.

In the morning, Mr Palmer, by the orders of Lt Stupart, brought 14 of the 22 men who constituted the crew of the *Echo* on board the *Felicidade*, and Lt Stupart returned by the same boat to the *Echo*, taking with him part of the crew of the *Felicidade*, leaving Mr Palmer, with seven British sailors and two Kroomen, on board the *Felicidade*. The foreigners on board the *Felicidade*, consisting of the crew of the *Echo*, rose up and threw Mr Palmer and the rest of the English overboard, Mr Palmer and some others being first wounded; the parts which the different prisoners took in the transaction being proved only by Cerqueira, the captain of the *Felicidade*, who stated that, though on deck during the struggle, he took no part in it. It was submitted, on the part of the prisoners, that they were, at the time of the rising, detained in illegal custody on board the *Felicidade*; and that there being no other means by which they could regain their liberty, they were justified in resorting to this violent proceeding.

It was submitted to the Judge that the capture of the *Felicidade* was illegal. That vessel, having no slaves on board, was protected from capture by the Treaty of November 1826, between Great Britain and Brazil, which adopts the provisions of the Convention between Great Britain and Portugal of July 1817. Besides Article VI of that treaty, Article I of the Instructions, which form part of the convention, contains the following clause: 'Ships on board of which no slaves shall be found, intended for the purpose of traffic, shall not be detained on any pretence or account whatever.' It was contended for the prisoners that this clause constitutes a condition precedent, and forms an essential part of the Convention. It was argued for the Crown, and ruled by the Judge, that this clause was directory only, and did not make the seizure void.

It was also submitted for the prisoners that, upon Article VII of the Instructions, which runs thus: 'whenever a ship-of-war shall meet a merchant-vessel viable to be searched, it shall be done in the most mild manner, and with all the attention which is due between allied and friendly nations; and that in no case shall the search (*a visita*) be made by an officer holding an inferior rank to that of lieutenant of the navy'; that although the first part of the clause was only directory, the latter clause was essential, and formed a condition precedent, and that it had not been complied with in the case of the *Echo*.

It was argued on the part of the Crown, and ruled by the Judge, that both clauses were merely directory. It was also contended for the Crown that the sending of Mr Palmer on board by Lt Stupart, who was within hail and gave directions, was a making of the search by a lieutenant. Upon the latter point the Judge was at first with the Crown, but ultimately gave no opinion upon it, none indeed being necessary if the clause were merely directory.

It was submitted that the capture of the *Echo* was illegal on the ground that, at the time of the capture, there were no instructions on board the *Felicidade*, as required by Article VII. It was contended on behalf of the prisoners, that the capture of the *Felicidade* and that of the *Echo*, being illegal for the above causes, the prisoners were illegally removed from the *Felicidade* and illegally placed upon the *Echo*; and that they had a right to use all the means which were necessary for their liberation, and that it would have been absurd for them to attempt their liberation by any means short of those of destroying the persons by whom they were detained. The Judge ruled, and the jury were told, that whether the capture of the *Felicidade*, or whether the capture of the *Echo*, was legal or not, the fact of the *Felicidade* being in actual possession of an officer of the British navy, as such placed that vessel under the authority of the Queen of England, and that thereby Her Majesty acquired jurisdiction over all persons subject to the law of England, and rendered all such persons subject to the laws of England and bound to obey them, whether they were acquainted with these laws or no, as *ignorantia legis non excusat*; and he refused to reserve the point for the opinion of the twelve Judges, saying that when the point was so clear it was his duty not to reserve it.

The Judge also ruled that the *Felicidade* being fitted for Slave Trade, and having sailed on a slaving voyage, was a vessel carrying out the Slave Trade within the meaning of Article I of the Treaty of November 1826; and that all persons found on board that vessel, as well as those found on board the *Echo*, in which there were slaves, must be taken to be pirates to all intents and purposes, and the general enemies of mankind, whether subjects of Brazil or not.

Of the prisoners, seven were found guilty and three (all Brazilians) were acquitted. Although one appreciates that their barristers were professionally bound to dig out points of law when so few facts stood in their defence, the verdict does, at the distance of over 150 years, seem quite a fair administration of justice in the name not just of mankind but also of 430 African people made anonymous through the social death that is slavery, the equally unnamed seven British sailors who were thrown overboard, and Mr Midshipman Palmer.[305]

Mostly, of course, British officials were far less vulnerable; and sometimes they almost forgot that their jurisdiction did not encompass the entire world. In August 1849 the British consul in Havana wrote to the governor general of Cuba with respect to a very rare instance of the Spanish authorities having punished some of their number caught conniving in the trade:

> I am instructed to state to your Excellency that it is very satisfactory to Her Majesty's Government that these subordinate officers have been removed; and that Her Majesty's Government hopes these proofs of your Excellency's determination to cause the Treaty obligations of the Crown of Spain to be respected, will serve as examples to impress your officers.

---

305. Enclosure to Lisboa, London, to Aberdeen, 29 July 1845, in *BFSP, 1845–46*, XXXIV, pp. 705–7.

The Duke of Alcoy dallied a couple of days before telling Consul Kennedy, in the most diplomatic of linguistic turns, where precisely he might insert his instructions:

> Respecting the measures which, in fulfilment of existing instructions in this island, I may think it right to adopt for any purpose, it is only to Her Majesty the Queen of Spain, to whom I owe explanations and obedience, equally whether she deign to approve of my conduct or whether she may judge it erroneous; and without this in any manner or conception offending the susceptibility of the Government of Her Britannic Majesty, in compliance with whose instructions, you tell me you addressed to me your communication of the 1st inst., it is not possible for me to avoid making known to you for your information and for the use that you think fit, that it would be better in future to excuse me from being acquainted with the judgement, favourable or adverse, that I may merit in the exercise of the authority confided in me.[306]

The return of Palmerston to the Foreign Office undoubtedly heightened the imperial condescension of British diplomats, and particularly so with respect to the slave trade, which led them so readily to the high moral ground despite political battles at home throughout the 1840s over the cost and means of its suppression. The sharpest opposition to the naval campaign came from free trade MPs, led by William Hutt, the member for Gateshead whose uncle had been lost at sea and who seemed to be exclusively dedicated to halting the operation of the West Africa squadron, and more because of its expense than for reasons of international relations. By the spring of 1850 this campaign had drawn much support from the press, *The Times* describing the navy's operations in the Atlantic as 'this most stupendous folly', whilst they were dubbed a 'cruel, hopeless and absurd experiment' by the *Morning Chronicle* and 'this costly failure, this deadly farce' by the *Spectator*.[307] The *Morning Post* was in a distinct minority with its attacks on those content to acquiesce in 'the free trade in human blood'. This was a sentiment that commended itself to many radicals, but Chartism had, even under the leadership of O'Connor, stuck to a strictly insular vision which precluded active engagement in causes overseas.[308]

The Russell administration had been able to fend off the harrying of the select committee chaired by Hutt – Palmerston's appearance before it produced some marvellous exchanges – and in April 1849 only thirty-four MPs (including Cobden and Bright) voted to repeal the Aberdeen Act. But matters became much more serious from October 1849, when Rear-Admiral Barrington Reynolds replaced Admiral Herbert as commander of the South American squadron, moved it from Montevideo to Rio, and added two extra sloops. Reynolds, like Hudson, was fiercely committed

---

306. Kennedy, Havana, to Alcoy, 1 Aug. 1849; Alcoy, Havana, to Kennedy, 6 Aug. 1849, in *BFSP, 1849–50*, XXXVIII, pp. 555–6.

307. Quoted in Bethell, *Abolition*, p. 321.

308. In July 1847 O'Connor wrote in the *Northern Star*, 'Let Englishmen and Irishmen and Scotchmen work together for England, Ireland and Scotland – let Frenchmen work for France, Russians for Russia, and Prussians for Prussia. I will work only for home sweet home.' Quoted in F.C. Mather (ed.), *Chartism and Society: An Anthology of Documents*, London 1980, p. 119.

to the eradication of the trade, and his aggression was certainly encouraged by Palmerston. However, it is worth noting the impact on this relatively small force of an incident in June 1849, when a ship chased by HMS *Rifleman* ran aground and was abandoned by its crew, who left 127 shackled and terrified slaves to drown as the craft foundered in high seas. The rescue of the captives, one by one along a hawser, lasted throughout the night and required each seaman on the *Rifleman* to tend to three Africans, who needed constant rubbing down against the effects of hypothermia. It is reasonable to suppose that the company and the squadron as a whole subsequently went about their work with added determination.

The final phase of the naval campaign opened on 5 January 1850, when the *Cormorant* seized the *Santa Cruz*, which had just landed 700 slaves, and immediately destroyed it. On the 10th the *Rifleman* intercepted a ship leaving for Africa and sent it to St Helena under a prize crew. Two days later the *Cormorant* seized the *Paulina* as it left Rio; despite the fact that it was flying the US flag Captain Herbert Schomberg did not hesitate to consign it as a prize to St Helena.[309] The message to the Brazilian government was clear enough, and in early February Foreign Minister Paulino visited Hudson to discuss a new bill to outlaw the trade despite widespread indignation at the actions of the British steam sloops. News of these developments had reached London when, on 19 March, the House of Commons debated Hutt's motion for British withdrawal from those international treaties that required the operations of the navy's Africa squadron. Although when in opposition he had himself thrown much doubt on the possibility of suppressing the slave trade through military force, Russell decided to make the vote an issue of confidence, giving a vivid speech in which he referred to the suppression of the trade as 'high and holy work'. At the division 154 opposed the naval operations and 232 (including many protectionists) supported its continuation. For Philip Curtin this represented 'the last important stand of humanitarian politics', but at the time it seemed to *The Times* to be

> the promotion of an unimpeachable principle with the maintenance of a particular scheme of violence, rude and barbarous in its essence, costly in its practice, ineffective in its operation, convicted by its results and formally condemned by those who were most instrumental in bringing it into being.[310]

The paper was wrong, though, on the matter of effectiveness. Reynolds's small squadron had shaken Brazilian landlords already hit by high levels of debt and a glut in the local market for slaves caused by the rush to stock up on chattel labour prior to abolition. Whatever the subsequent interpretation by historians, the local economic incentives for ending the trade seemed to be growing, and they were certainly sharpened by the activity of the British warships. This activity was itself to become

---

309. Schomberg belonged to one of the most distinguished of British naval families and had been schooled in this work by chasing smugglers off Ireland. His activities in 1849 and 1850 ought to be included in the Jewish contribution to Latin American culture.

310. Curtin, *Atlantic Trade. The Times*, 20 March 1850, quoted in Bethell, *Abolition*, p. 324.

decisive when the Foreign Office, no doubt emboldened by the vote in the Commons, three days later advised Palmerston that it was possible to interpret the Aberdeen Act of 1845 in such a way as to permit operations not only in Brazilian territorial waters but even within its harbours and ports. In the six months to June, when this 'reading' was conveyed to Hudson, some 8,000 slaves had been landed in Brazil – a marked reduction over previous years but still nowhere near suggesting any 'natural' termination of the trade.

On 18 June Hudson went aboard HMS *Southampton* to discuss the implications of the directive with Reynolds. On the 20th he informed Paulino of its existence, the foreign minister being 'thunderstruck' and protesting that any action would prejudice his own bill and raise the spectre of war. Hudson, who nurtured a barely veiled derision for the Brazilian elite, remained unmoved, knowing that Reynolds was at the moment ordering his ships into action. On the 23rd the newly arrived *Sharpshooter* entered the port of Macaé, exchanged fire with the shore-batteries and seized a brigantine. On the 26th Schomberg took the *Cormorant* into Cabo Frio and destroyed another brigantine in sight of a large angry crowd. Three days later, steaming south of Santos, he informed the commander of a fortress of his instructions and his intention to carry them out. He was allowed to proceed unchallenged; the Brazilian military – some of whom had tacitly collaborated with the British – had clearly weighed up the odds and decided not to contest the challenge. Its government followed not long after. In the midst of an outbreak of yellow fever, Paulino pushed his bill through the Council of State on 11 July, had it adopted by the Deputies on the 17th, and adopted as law on 4 September. Although 3,287 slaves were imported into Brazil in 1851, this was a fraction of the numbers of earlier years, and the trade soon dwindled into insignificance.

At the end of his life Palmerston declared this to be one of the most satisfying achievements of his career, but at the time he did not beat about the bush with regard to the niceties of diplomacy, international law and what today would be called multiculturalism:

> These half-civilized governments … all require a dressing down every eight or ten years to keep them in order. Their minds are too shallow to receive any impression than will last longer than some such period and warning is of little use. They care little for words and they must not only see the stick but actually feel it on their shoulders before they yield to that only argument which to them brings conviction, the *Argumentum Baculinum*.'[311]

This was the type of attitude that Gallagher and Robinson believed was sometimes required to buttress the free trade which was the real core of British imperialism in the nineteenth century. Although unqualified in its disdain, it retains only a partial and temporary commitment to violent intervention. In cases such as that of Robert

---

311. 29 Sept. 1850, quoted in Christopher Bartlett, *Great Britain and Sea Power*, Oxford 1963, pp. 261–2.

Falk's Hibernia no such action was needed or wanted. Moreover, it was not simply hard-headed pragmatism at play. Those who most espoused free trade as an ideology most repudiated military intervention, but the ideological and ethical confusion over emancipation in British colonies, the question of commerce in slave-produced commodities, the forcible eradication of the slave trade, and the cost and consequences of global naval operations scrambled allegiances and alliances not only within the political elite and the industrial bourgeoisie but also among the ordinary British populace. If the academic debate around this now seems rather obscure and abstruse, this is probably because – in stark contrast to the experience of the USA – most of these developments took place at a great geographical distance, had few deep material roots in most sectors of civil society, and never came to the point of violent crisis.

THIRD CASE

CRIMINAL CASE

BROUGHT AGAINST THE PREFECT OF TARIJA, DR MARIANO DONATO MUÑOZ,[1]

FOR ILLEGALLY RELEASING ANSELMA CONDORI

SUPREME COURT OF BOLIVIA[2]
JUNE–DECEMBER 1850

Justice of the Peace, Canton of Padcaya,
23 October 1849.

To His Honour, the Judge for the Department.

Sir, with this I send to you Anselma Condori, widow of the murdered Miguel Martínez, under the supervision of the Corregidor of this Canton.[3] He who delivers the said Anselma will also give to you Facundo's hatchet. The knife cannot be located; there is nobody who can account for it. I do not send to you that belonging to Mario because my colleague is two days' ride away from this place in the mountains ... it will be delivered shortly.

May God preserve you,
  Salvador Mendieta.

★

DETENTION.
Tarija. 23 October 1849.

The present note received with the person of Anselma Condori, accomplice in the murder perpetrated against the person of Miguel Martínez with the axe sent by the judge as evidence ... On this basis an order of imprisonment is to be made against the said offenders, to be implemented by the Constable of the Court.

---

1. *Mariano Donato Muñoz*, born Chuquisaca, 12 Dec. 1823. Educated Colegio Junín; graduated Faculty of Law, Universidad de San Francisco Xavier, 18 Feb. 1844; chief clerk to Congress, 1848. Appointed prefect of the Department of Tarija, 1849. In October 1849 the Supreme Court had heard a civil case in which Justo Porcel unsuccessfully sued Muñoz for payment of debt.

2. Transcript, at forty-seven folios, held in the Archivo Nacional de Bolivia, Sucre. 'Corte Suprema', no. 165, 1850.

3. A *corregidor* was the principal executive officer of a canton. In Bolivia at this time there were two types of 'judge'. To be a *juez de paz* it was necessary to be a citizen, at least twenty-five years of age, to belong to a community and have a profession or business, and to be able to read and write. To be a *juez de letras* one was required to be at least twenty-five, to have worked as a lawyer for at least four years, and never to have committed a serious crime or misdemeanour. *Ley Orgánica y Reglamentaria de los Juzgados y Tribunales Ordinarios de la República*, Sucre 1845, pp. 2, 5.

Let their statements be taken dutifully, let them be informed of the reason for their imprisonment, and let them name a counsel for their defence. Notice to be given to the Superior Tribunal of the District, and a copy of this to the Warden of the Gaol.

At 9.15 a.m. I made the Governor of the Court aware of this order. I sign. I testify. Luis Mendieta.

★

Prefect of the Department of Tarija.
In the Capital. 22 March 1850. 41st of Independence and 2nd of Liberty.[4]

To the Warden of the Public Gaol of the City.

Upon receipt of this order, you will put at liberty Anselma Condori, made a prisoner by order of the Court. I warn and order you to ensure the most exact fulfilment of this measure, taken under my responsibility, so that no serious measures are taken against yourself or anybody who might intervene to impede it.

May God preserve you. Mariano Donato Muñoz.

★

Secretary of the Court of the District, Tarija.
24 May 1850. 41st of Independence and 2nd of Liberty.

It having been decided in session by the Supreme Court of Justice of the Republic that this Court shall prepare an indictment in accordance with article 827 of the Procedural Code,[5]

Take for me the sworn declaration of the accusing citizen, Warden Manuel Ascensio Soto, together with the note that he received for the release of the convict Anselma Condori from the ex-prefect Mariano Donato Muñoz, the declaration of the aforesaid Condori and those of the people knowing of the improper act committed by the said Muñoz.

This summary should include as evidence the orders for the imprisonment and release of the convict, distinguishing these documents from accounts of the same. Also the original sent by Muñoz to the Warden, to be added to the evidence.

---

4. Bolivia formally gained independence from Spain – the last mainland territory of the Americas to do so – in August 1825. However, it was the site of one of the first insurrections against the imperial order, in 1809 under the leadership of Pedro Murillo. The 'liberty' reference is to the establishment of the government of General Manuel Isidoro Belzu in December 1848 – the 14th administration to rule the republic.

5. Only the judge sitting in the case may set the defendant on trial free. When this is done by another person without the authority of the judge a summary of the justification will be required to explain under what higher authority this infraction was committed; and if this is insufficient that person will be prosecuted according to the laws.

Código de Procedimientos Santa Cruz, Sucre 1875, p. 91. In the early years of the republic the departments of Tarija and Santa Cruz had no higher courts and were supervised directly by the Supreme Court in the national capital, Sucre, Department of Chuquisaca, which had been the site of the Audiencia de Charcas, one of the most powerful legal bodies in the Spanish government of the Americas. The Supreme Court comprised an attorney-general, president and six ministers, each of whom served a two-year office and sat in one of two chambers. Luis Paz, *La Corte Suprema de Justicia: Su Historia y Jurisprudencia*, Sucre 1910.

All this will be sufficient to authorise the issue of a warrant. This crime being punishable by corporal penalty, the ex-prefect Dr Muñoz is to be placed under arrest immediately by the officers of the Constable of the Court. T. Rafael Vargas. Antenor Dionisio Mendieta, Clerk of the Court.[6]

On this date I passed the above order to the Constable of the Court. I sign. I testify. Alejo Guerrero Mendieta.

★

In this City of Tarija at noon of 24 May 1850 there appeared in the court a man who said that his name was Manuel Ascensio Soto, of 26 years of age, bachelor, Warden of the Public Gaol and citizen of this city, who took the oath through me before the Judge. Having examined by reading the order relative to the release of the convict Anselma Condori by the ex-prefect Mariano Donato Muñoz, which is evidence in this summary, he said in response:

> that the note signed by the ex-prefect Mariano Donato Muñoz which appears in this summary was the original … that the report given by himself to the court was the same as that which appears in this summary; that on 29 March … Muñoz appeared in the gaol and issued to him under his own responsibility an order for the release of the convict Condori, who was, in fact, put at liberty at 1 p. m. on 29 March;

> that there was present at this event Dr Nicanor Echaín, who heard the argument of the ex-judge Dr Serrano with the ex-prefect, once the prisoner had been put at liberty, concerning the charge that the latter had no authority to free her; that the prisoners of the gaol had probably seen the said Muñoz take out and release the said Condori through the window that looked onto the place where she was.

With this concluded his declaration, which, read to him, he affirmed, adding that the aforesaid ex-prefect left in the direction of Chuquisaca [Sucre] on the 15th of the present at 3 p.m. accompanied by various persons of the town;[7] that, being cautioned to be

---

6. According to article 27 of the penal code of 1843,

   Under no circumstances shall any crime or misdemeanour − except for those reserved under the military and ecclesiastical *fueros* − be punished in Bolivia in any manner except the following. *Corporal Penalties*: 1. Death; 2. Penal Servitude; 3. Public Works; 4. Permanent or temporary removal from the national territory; 5. Internment in a workhouse; 6. Imprisonment in a fortified place; 7. Confinement in a specified town or region; 8. Permanent or temporary exile to a specified town or region. *Non-corporal Penalties*: 1. Declaration of disgrace [*infamia*], as well as the declaration of being unworthy of being called a Bolivian or of having the trust of the nation; 2. Prohibition from working in a job, profession or public post, either specifically or in general; 3. Removal from a position, profession or public post; 4. Suspension from the same; 5. Arrest; 6. Subjection to special invigilation by the authorities; 7. The requirement to pay bail; 8. Public retraction; 9. Judicial redress; 10. House arrest; 11. Judicial reprimand; 12. The public announcement of a court decision; 13. House of correction for women and minors. *Pecuniary Penalties*: 1. Fine; 2. Loss of certain property.

Código Penal Boliviano, Sucre 1845, p. 9.

7. The description of Muñoz riding to Sucre (as the city of Chuquisaca was renamed in 1839 in honour of Marshal José Antonio de Sucre, the republic's second president) is repeated by several witnesses not reproduced here because of the similarity of their accounts. It clearly suggests culpability and flight, and may also have indicated dereliction of duty. Even outside times of political convulsion, the movement of persons was subject to strict formal (and sometimes real) control in the main towns:

available when required by the court, he added that he faced no impediment [to testifying] under law with Dr Muñoz.[8] I sign with his Honour, the Judge. I testify. Vargas. Manuel Ascensio Soto. D. Mendieta, Clerk.

★

Immediately there appeared in the court a woman who said her name was Anselma Condori, widow, 40 years of age, weaver, inhabitant of the valley of Orosas, whom the Warden removed from her prison, and, her oath being sworn in the legal form, was examined with respect to the proceedings and answered thus:

> that on the day of 29 March at 1 p.m. the prefect arrived in the company of the head of the monastery, Friar Zeferini Muzzani, and set her free.[9]

With this she finished her statement, which was read to her, she adding that she found herself imprisoned at that moment as an accomplice in the murder perpetrated against the person of her husband Miguel Martínez; that the prisoners Matías Sider, Mariano Mejía and Facundo Martínez had seen her put at liberty from a window in the prison when the said Muñoz and the Reverend Father came to the place where she was held.

She confirmed the sense of this statement, without impediment, and, cautioned to be ready to return at the court's convenience, she did not sign because she does not know how to. The Judge did so, to which I testify. Vargas. D. Mendieta, Clerk.

★

At 1 p. m. of the same day his Honour, the Judge, ordered to be removed from his confinement a man who said his name was Matías Sider, bachelor, twenty-eight years of age, labourer and inhabitant of the canton of Zomayapa, competent to testify. Having taken the oath properly before the Judge, he was examined and said:

> All persons who arrive at this capital are obliged to present themselves to the police within twenty-five hours, either with or without a passport. To this end all traders, wholesalers and other householders must report any guest lodged in their house. At the same time, no individual will be permitted to leave without the appropriate passport since the undersigned is solely responsible for the good order of this city. Any persons who disobey this disposition will be fined four reales in accordance with the first clause of article 179 of the Police Regulations currently in force.

El Nacional, Sucre, 17 November 1849.

8. This simply means that they were not relatives.

9. *Zeferino Muzzani*, born April 1811, San Giorgio, Lomellina. Ordained Belmonte 25 Oct. 1831. Arrived Tarija, 31 Dec. 1845. Several times declined nomination to Bishop of Santa Cruz on grounds of Franciscan vocation. Died Tarija, 23 July 1895. The Franciscan monastery of Nuestra Señora de los Angeles, established in 1606 and situated between the modern streets of Madrid, Campos, Ingavi and Colón. Tarija itself was founded in 1574, the Dominicans arriving the next year, the Augustans in 1588, the Franciscans in 1606, and the Jesuits in 1690. Although this region of South America is generally associated with the Jesuit missions, the challenge of evangelising the warlike Chiriguano people was led by the Franciscans, who established a *Colegio de Propaganda Fide* in October 1755. According to a nineteenth-century historian of the Tarija Franciscans, their monastery,

> exists today just as the Spanish fathers constructed it, [and] is in no sense elegant or sumptuous. The cells are small and low, the corridors narrow and gloomy; everything instils a holy sadness … none the less, the religious community that inhabits this place has all its needs met. There is a large garden with groves of peaches and olives, cypress trees and poplars … a comfortable sanatorium, an oratory … a well-stocked pharmacy, a bakery, a carpenter's workshop, forge and looms for weaving.

A. Corrado, *El Colegio Franciscano de Tarija y sus Misiones*, Florence 1884, p. 32.

that on 29 March at 1 p.m. the prefect appeared in the company of the Reverend Father Zeferini Muzzani at the public gaol where Anselma Condori was held, the said prefect set her free, which he could confirm on account of having seen it through a window in the company of Mariano Mejía, a prisoner like himself....

On the same day there appeared in the court a man who said his name was Nicanor Echaín, twenty-five years of age, doctor of laws, and citizen of this city ... shown the note from the ex-prefect ordering the release of Condori, he confirmed that he recognised it, and he declared that when he had questioned Muñoz as to whether the ex-prefect had the authority to release the prisoner, Muñoz had replied that it was an inveterate tradition to release a prisoner on Good Friday in the style of Barrabas, and that he knew from the same ex-prefect's own mouth that he was the author of the release of the prisoner.

★

[Attorney General Francisco Alvarez Toledo reviews and signs the Tarija summary sixteen times, 11–25 June 1850.[10]]

On 25 June 1850 at four in the afternoon, in the room of his Honour, the Dean, there appeared a man who, for the purpose of providing a preliminary statement, was cautioned by the Secretary of the Court to tell the truth, and, having so committed himself, he was asked his name, country, residence, age, civil status and occupation. He said his name was

---

10. The chamber hearing Muñoz's case comprised Judges José Pablo Heria y Baca, Basilio de Cuellar, José Eustaquio Moscoso and Dionosio Barrientos. Of these de Cuellar was the most renowned jurist, and only he and Heria y Baca had survived the closure of the court in December 1848 by the new Belzu government – 'because of the judges' lack of attention' – when it was reopened in July 1849. Attorney-General (*Fiscal*) Alvarez was new, replacing Andrés de Quintela. Although Bolivia had 450 lawyers, Muñoz was from Sucre, and would certainly have been known by Alvarez and his assistant, Gregorio Valda. The court's hearings were public, and great emphasis was laid upon formal dress. Shortly after the present case new regulations were issued in this regard:

> The Magistrates of the Supreme Court of Justice will wear the toga and the medal assigned to them under the regulations of 14 June 1841; their caps of silk with black feathers; and when they appear without the toga they will do so in formal diplomatic dress, stick with tassels, properly fringed hats plumed with black feathers.

Edict of 26 January 1853, quoted in José Agustín Morales, *Los Primeros Cien Años de Bolivia*, La Paz 1925, I, p. 444. Of course, the law is an area where control of dress by rank extended into the post-feudal age almost everywhere, but it is worth noting that in Bolivia – an economy highly dependent upon the textile trade as well as a society of strict republican aristocracy – the moral economy of dress had been a matter of debate for some time:

> Order requires that we start with the leading personalities of the Nation and then the list of public officers that follow them. No civilised nation in the world fails to respect the necessity of recognising authority with some outward sign fitting to the dignity of the magistracy. Without such an accessory there would be confusion among citizens. It would not be clear at first appearance which of the divers classes was which, and the people, who are captivated by outward show, would not respect or pay consideration to the persons set to govern over them ... as Bentham says, if there is not a certain proportion between the dignity with which a man presents himself and the means to sustain this he will enter a state of privation ... but the luxury associated with clothing today may truly be called scandalous. Even in the dance-hall European style and decoration is required simply because the hall cannot itself be in Europe. Its trinkets, candlesticks and illuminations, its drinks and everything else. The participants of both sexes evidently do not wish to be American when the entire apparatus of the banquet and objective of the guests is to emulate foreign nations.

Ana María Lema (ed.), *Bosquejo del estado en que se halla la riqueza nacional de Bolivia con sus resultados, presentado al examen de la Nación por un Aldeano hijo de ella: Año de 1830*, La Paz 1994, pp. 35, 39. For some,

Mariano Donato Muñoz, a Bolivian, citizen and resident of this city, thirty years of age, a bachelor, and presently under-secretary at the ministry of the interior.[11]

Asked if he knew Anselma Condori, if she was held prisoner, in what gaol and for what crime; who set her free, on what day, hour, month and year, he said,

> I know Anselma Condori, that she was was held in the gaol of Tarija charged with complicity in the death of Miguel Martínez. And I put her at liberty on 29 March of this year at around 2 p.m. as a result of there being congregated about the office of the prefecture – which I then directed – all the people of the city, the priests of the *Propaganda of the Faith*, the guilds and corporations. They demanded that I respect the ancient custom, observed since time immemorial, of releasing a prisoner with the name of Barrabas.
>
> For this reason, and acquiescing in the demand of each and everyone, and especially the president of the district court, Dr Julián Arze, who offered to plead the case of the chosen prisoner with the Judge, I oversaw the drawing of lots, and Condori having been chosen, I ordered that she be freed.
>
> Furthermore, in taking this step I had in mind the wide powers conferred upon me by the Supreme Chief of the Nation when he appointed me as prefect of Tarija.[12] It was in the use of these that I undertook a measure that was governmental – even political – in character because it was being demanded by the best of the citizenry, who insisted that I proceed, as had all the prefects who had preceded me, in this way to celebrate the Easter Resurrection.

---

however, the combination of social hierarchy and industrial capitalism produced a less voluntary acculturation, as recounted by Edmond Temple in the same year:

> A European speculator sent, amongst the articles, a consignment of spectacles to a Lima merchant, who, finding them a drug upon his hands, applied to a *corregidor* to aid him in disposing of them. The latter issued an order that no Indian in his district should attend divine service unless ornamented with spectacles. The consequence was the speedy sale of the whole.

Edmond Temple, *Travels in various parts of Peru, including a year's residence in Potosí*, London 1830, II, p. 104.

11. It may well be that Muñoz had added a year or two to his age, although there was no legal need to do so – he was certainly over twenty-five, the barrier for all major public offices. One should also register the importance of being a 'citizen' in an economically and racially polarised society. Although all inhabitants of the republic were 'Bolivians', birth itself conferred very few rights within the Hispano-mestizo state. At least 70 per cent of the population of around two million were indigenous, and only the senior members of the Amerindian elite would be granted rights outside of their own communities. In terms of European associations with citizenship, under the 1843 Constitution only those with capital of at least 4,000 pesos had the right to vote. In August 1850 Bolivia held its second presidential election, when 5,935 men voted for General Belzu, who stood unopposed, as had General Ballivián, also the incumbent, at the first poll of 1844.

12. *Manuel Isidoro Belzu Téllez*, born La Paz, 1808, natural son of an Arab soldier and a mestizo mother, adopted by Gaspar Belzu. Joined army, 1828. 1830, posted to Tarija, where he married the fourteen-year-old *Juana Manuela Gorriti*, daughter of General José Ignacio Gorriti, a leader of the opposition to Rosas in Salta. Juana Manuela and Belzu had three daughters but he left her in 1843 upon hearing that she was being courted by then-President José Ballivián (1805–52). Following the collapse of both relationships, Juana Manuela settled shortly thereafter in Arequipa. In her later years she became a famed continental author – her *El Mundo de los Recuerdos* is a pioneering work of Argentine literature – but never lost her devotion to the culinary arts: she introduced the *salteña* (short-crust pasty) into Bolivia and is justly re-nowned for her pan-American recipe book *La Cocina Ecléctica*, Buenos Aires 1877. When Belzu became president in 1848 Juana Manuela sent her eldest daughter Edelmira to accompany him as 'first lady'. In 1874 she herself settled in Buenos Aires, where she died in 1892. Although Belzu was supposed to have read Proudhon and Stendhal, his reputation is as a *caudillo* – the 'Mohammed of Bolivia' – who generated strong support from the lower orders of society in the north of the country through a combination of protectionist measures and anti-foreign and oligarchic rhetoric. He was not particularly popular in Sucre or Tarija although he had himself been prefect of the latter department in 1842. Celebrated by twentieth-century populists as a forebear, Belzu plainly possessed charisma. In 1864, nearly ten years after he left office, a newspaper could opine:

Asked if he knows if in the releasing of Anselma Condori there had been any accomplices or mitigating circumstances, he said: 'I spontaneously, and for the reasons I have been outlining, released the criminal Condori.' With which he affirmed his declaration, which was read to him, and he was cautioned to be available to continue it at the pleasure of the court. Signed. Mariano Donato Muñoz. Alvarez.

★

First Chamber.
Supreme Court of the Republic of Bolivia.

Under this order the Constable will call at the house of Dr Mariano Donato Muñoz and notify him that he is confined to the city bounds while the criminal proceedings against him are under way, the charge being the exceeding of the authority vested in him as prefect of Tarija by releasing the prisoner Anselma Condori. He must present himself at the Secretariat in order to make a sworn declaration, which is hereby required by this order.

Sucre. 9 July 1850.
Cuellar. Barrientos.

[Muñoz signs to confirm receipt of order.
Alvarez sees and signs the transcript of proceedings four times, 4–15 July.]

★

In the city of Sucre at four in the afternoon on the 15th inst. there appeared in the office of his Honour, the Dean of the First Chamber, a man who, for the purposes of recording his statement, was exhorted to tell the truth and then read the indictment and the names of the witnesses.

Asked if he knew the witnesses who testify against him, if the name in the preliminary statement was his, and if he affirmed and ratified all that he had declared in it, he replied,

The name of Mariano Donato Muñoz given in the preliminary statement is the same as mine, and is the one by which I am known; I affirm and ratify what I expressed in my statement, and I have nothing to add to or substract from it. I know all the witnesses in the indictment except for Sider and Mejía, and I find no fault with them.

Asked if he knew the reason for his trial, he said,

I know why I am being tried, and it is for having freed the prisoner Anselma Condori who was confined in the gaol of Tarija when I was prefect of that department.

Bolivia needs a man – there is a general demand – and she needs him now more than ever because she is prostrate, distraught and as disorientated as a planet that has left its orbit. We ask now: Who is that man? Who is the hero called upon to regenerate the father land and uphold the republic? The mysterious phoenix of freedom, the only one sought by the people, the one called by Bolivia, the athlete of democracy and the champion of the republic is Captain General Manuel Isidoro Belzu.

La Voz de Bolivia, 7 Jan. 1864, cited in Ramón Sotomayor Valdés, *Estudio Histórico de Bolivia bajo la Administración del Jeneral José María de Achá*, Santiago 1874, p. 364.

Asked why he abused his office of prefect, releasing a woman who had been convicted under due process for an atrocious crime, namely complicity in the murder of her husband, he said,

> I took this measure not with the aim of abusing my position but in response to the pressures under which I laboured at that time in Tarija. Powerful reasons drove me to yield to the insinuations of the priests of the monastery, of the then judge Dr Julián Arze, of the vice-president of the municipality citizen Domingo Arze, of various other officials and the greater part of the citizenry, including those of the Fair Sex who, with their humanitarian motives, begged that Anselma Condori should be given a pardon.
>
> I was mindful of the fact that my predecessors at the prefecture had always cleaved to this practice, and I was especially influenced by the fact that the present president of the republic, when himself prefect of that department, took a similar measure of releasing a prisoner, in different circumstances and normal times, without possessing any powers beyond those ordinarily vested in prefects. Yet I myself was placed at the head of that department with wide powers, being authorised by the Supreme Government to undertake measures of any type, without restriction.
>
> I was evidently obliged by my duty to comport myself in the same manner as the general who is our president, doing what he did. To oppose the wishes of the people by treating this measure as illegal or abusive would have effectively been to reprove his own conduct when he occupied the prefecture. I did not find a law that clearly prohibited me from taking this action, and there was no case whatsoever of one of my predecessors being charged for upholding this custom. These reasons, which I have briefly outlined, and many others that were just as powerful, persuaded me to set Anselma Condori free.

The accused was admonished that he sought to excuse the crime that he had committed by making recourse to specious explanations that could never justify his actions. The influence of the better sectors of society of the department which he commanded could not oblige him to release a prisoner over whom he had no jurisdiction, and this was no less true of what he says was his predecessors' custom because there is in the Republic no custom that over-rules the law, and only the Judge trying the case can set free the criminal being tried. He should confess his crime without covering up the truth and the facts disclosed by the documents. He replied,

> When I took over the department of Tarija I found the department completely divided by political issues. Sentiment ran against the present administration, to the extent of an insurrection against it being likely on almost any pretext, and this certainly obliged the local authorities to make use of every one of their prerogatives.[13] My mission was to reduce conflict, bring tranquillity to the region, and demonstrate that the government of General Belzu was paternal and humanitarian, and that its only object was to enhance the well-being of all sectors of society, but especially the poor and unfortunate.

---

13. The record bears Muñoz out, in part at least. Although Tarija was not one of the most turbulent or influential of Bolivia's departments – in 1846 the town had a population of 5,129 living in 364 houses; the department some 64,000 people – it had been claimed and was in 1838 invaded by Argentina. Moreover, its pastoral economy and the still unsettled Chiriguano people in the east encouraged an independent, horse-riding individual of 'frontier spirit', usually available for political manipulation. There had been a revolt in 1841, and another in November 1848, both backing the eventual presidents – Ballivián and Belzu. However, Muñoz is referring to the consequences of an uprising in March 1849, when Pedro González Avila, the military governor of the department, won the town's five police officers to his rebellious designs because it was thought that Belzu had been killed in La Paz. Once this report was discredited, Muñoz's predecessor, Domingo Arze, was readily able to muster a force to defeat the rebels – now num-

The advice of the public officials on its own would not have persuaded me. I was convinced that what was at stake was a political issue, which I had to decide in order to avoid the outbreak of public disorder. Both public opinion and my moral duty obliged me to separate that woman from the persons who, by their involvement in the matter for which she was charged and by the assuredly illicit relationship she had with one of them, threatened a bad example and made her removal expedient.

Naturally, I was not the judge in her case, but I was in possession of the powers necessary, in my judgement, to preserve public order in a country where I alone was responsible for keeping the peace. I thought that I was acting correctly and in accordance with the wishes of the Chief of the Nation. My aim in this action was to promote virtue, and I was far from intentionally breaking the law.

At this point, the hour being advanced, the confession was suspended until tomorrow, it being initialled by his Honour, the Dean and signed by the accused, to which I testify. [Illegible.] Mariano Donato Muñoz. Alvarez Toledo.

★

On the 17th of the said month, in continuation of the suspended confession, the accused was again exhorted to tell the truth, and, having assented, he was questioned once more as to why why he persists in pretending that he did not deliberately flout the law, and raises political matters, when, far from being a measure to pacify society, this was one that would upset it since it is in the interest of society that criminals be punished and that there be no impunity.

The people of Tarija, who support such maxims, could not have been so at odds with each other that the release of a delinquent woman could become the pretext for a collapse in public order. He should speak the truth, and he should not contradict himself, as he does when he asserts that public opinion obliged him to separate the criminal from persons with whom she had an illicit relationship, which version does not tally at all with the drawing of lots that he claimed in his preliminary statement to have organised.

He answered:

My duty required me to uphold order, whatever the difficulties. I knew that if I refused to bow to the wish of the people there would be discontent and unruliness, and it would be used as a pretext to commit abuses and promote upheaval. It would have been only too easy to convince a population that is strongly – even fanatically – inclined to custom and tradition, which they have always given a religious gloss, that the government and its agents were opposed to the continuation of these ceremonies and wished to outlaw them. Under such circumstances, upsetting local sentiment would have simply provoked them to insist upon their ancient rights and customs by creating disturbances.

As a result, surely it was prudent to reach an understanding with the people in order to preserve the country's peace? Supposing that I had rashly refused, prompting a breakdown in law and order, was it not I who was responsible to the government, to the entire nation?

bering some 150 – at Tarbita on 31 April. A month later the rebel General Velasco launched another attack in which the aged independence hero Eustaquio (*El Múthu*) Méndez was executed by the insurrectionists, who thereby lost much local backing. But they continued to hold on to the town until the end of June. It was following their defeat, by the Chichas Regiment on 1 July, that Muñoz was appointed to his post. Nicanor Aranzaes, *Las Revoluciones de Bolivia* (1918), La Paz 1980, pp. 101–2; Morales, *Primeros Cien Años*, I, pp. 399–400, 401–2.

Far, far fewer wrongs stemmed from lifting the sentence duly imposed by the law on a delinquent, as was the case of Condori, than would have arisen from a tumult, which would have offered unlimited opportunity for wrongdoing by the depraved in the name of the people, tradition, local custom, etc.

It is undoubtedly the duty of the chief of a department to restrict and contain the damage caused by any public event, and his starting-point ought to be that which most facilitates the exercise of his office, rather than simple obedience to the letter of the law. I saw, then, that any denial on my part would cause considerable trouble whilst, by contrast, my prudent acquiescence in the proposal would avert it. The principles of law themselves indicate that it is better to avoid an ill than to seek remedy for it, and when it is evident that two infractions are inevitable, the lesser is assuredly preferable.

With regard to the last charge against me, I find absolutely no contradiction whatsoever between what I have stated frankly in my preliminary declaration and what I have said in my interrogation. Well before Condori was set free public opinion was upset by her detention alongside persons who had illicit relations with her. As a consequence, I sought to have her removed to a different part of the same prison building, but this was too fetid and unhealthy to be inhabited, and so it was necessary to keep her where she had been.

It is also true that the first public petitions on her behalf were as much for this reason as because her sex, age, position and wretched circumstances aroused the compassion of all and affected the sensibility of anybody who saw her.[14] I wanted to give this measure all the impartiality that befits a magistrate, even though I was acting out of pure grace.

All of the prisoners were given a chance, their names being written on paper lots. One could see from the expressions of those present that they wanted fortune to smile upon the wretched Condori. The priests, the citizens present and I all excused ourselves from drawing the ticket that offered deliverance from adversity for that person whose name was written on it. A young man was called up from the crowd, and he was told to draw a lot from the hat that had been placed on the courtroom table.

I verified it in the presence of everyone, and it corresponded to Condori. This was exactly what the people wanted and what the citizens, guided by their moral sentiments, had earlier been urging.

This is the manner in which I satisfied the citizens so that it appeared that even destiny supported the wishes of the public. Moreover, the criminality of any act ought to be judged by its effect, and since Condori has now been returned to her prison, as has been widely indicated in these proceedings, the charge against me is null and void.

---

14. The 1843 Criminal Code expressly prohibited women from being sentenced to penal servitude (article 57), and there was no gaol for women in Sucre, let alone Tarija. One possible inference in this case might have led a more daring *fiscal* to charge Muñoz under article 364 of the code:

> The judge who propositions or seduces a woman with a suit in court, or who is charged before him, or who appears as a witness, will lose his post and will be permanently proscribed from practising the law, without affecting any other penalty which might be imposed for this offence.

Under article 368 all state employees were subject to removal from post if guilty of 'public and scandalous incontinence':

> 1. When the public functionary keeps a known concubine in his house; 2. When he scandalously visits the whore-house; 3. When he fails to end a friendship with a woman, having been required to do so by a competent authority upon the complaint of the parents, tutors, relatives to the fourth degree of consanguinity, or by the husband. Drunkenness and gambling are prohibited, and if repeated on three occasions in the course of a year they will be sufficient cause for the same penalty to be imposed.

This might be thought overly ambitious for a popular culture where, to employ a free translation, men were renowned for their adhesion to 'the three Cs': chicha (corn beer), cards and cunt.

Asked how many times he had been tried and for what crimes, he said: 'This is the first time, for the crime with which I am charged.'

[Alvarez signs the transcript of proceedings ten times, and Muñoz thrice, up to 25 July.]

★

The Attorney-General formally presents the indictment against Dr Mariano Donato Muñoz, erstwhile prefect of Tarija, for having exceeded his powers by ordering the release, in contravention of article 827 of the Procedural Code, of Anselma Condori, who was prisoner in the gaol of that city by order of the Judge.

He has vainly sought to find excuse for this act of last 29 March by pretending that he undertook it to ensure public order, respecting what he claims to be an ancient custom, and by using powers that he asserts were vested in him by higher authority.

The first point does not stand in his favour since there can be no custom standing counter to such a clear and precise law as this one, which the accused has not been able to deny, and since it is the duty of each prefect to uphold the law in his district.

Equally, there is no basis to the fear of disruption of public order, but, rather, there was indulgence of the improper imprecations of the priests and others supplicating for the execution of an abuse. Indeed, the peace that has been maintained since Condori was returned to gaol as a result of the order of the Judge who had tried her demonstrates vividly that the citizens of Tarija are always respectful of the law and not given to protest at the cessation of practices which stopped when the legislation of the republic expressly prohibited them.

The Attorney-General concludes by asking the Supreme Tribunal to pass a sentence of suspension from all public office for the period of seven months, a summons to pay a fine of 55 pesos, and for the accused to be placed on parole, as befits a crime of the second degree.

Sucre. 4 November 1850.
Valda.

★

SENTENCE
16 December 1850, at 9 in the morning.

In the name of the Nation and with the authority which she endows, it is declared that the crime for which Dr Mariano Donato Muñoz is charged is fully proved, and that the defendant has confessed.

Mindful of the content of clauses four and seven of article 15 of the Penal Code, we classify the offence as moderate, and in accordance with the first part of article 395 of the same Code, we sentence the accused to suspension from all public posts and employment for seven months, to a fine of 55 pesos, and to be placed on parole so that hereafter he might not commit further offences, it being stipulated that should he re-offend he will be punished with greater severity.[15]

Heria y Baca. Dionisio Barrientos. José Eustaquio Moscoso.[16]

POSTSCRIPT

It is notable that the trial of Mariano Donato Muñoz for an uncomplicated and less than horrible crime lasted a long time – from 11 June to 16 December 1850. In particular, there is a prolonged gap between the cross-examination, which finished in July, and the formal charging and sentencing, at the end of November and early in December. The reason for this was not bureaucratic intertia but political chaos.

Attorney-General Alvarez was by no means lily-livered. He brought Muñoz, a senior official of the government, to court when General Belzu was in Sucre and, apparently, at the peak of his power. Arriving in the capital in May, having toured the departments of La Paz, Cochabamba and Oruro, the president organised an election, in which he received 5,935 votes without any opposition. In August the new congress suspended the constitution of the previous regime, and proceeded to hear the claim for 150,000 pesos of Agustín Morales, whose warehouse in Cochabamba had been looted and burnt on 17 March 1849 – along with property of other supporters of ex-President Ballivián – by a mob cheering Belzu's name.

Writing eleven years after the event, Manuel José Cortés, who was distinctly unsympathetic to Belzu, describes the outcome:

> Different proposals were discussed in the chambers. The House of Deputies argued for the payment of compensation to anybody who had suffered from past political disturbances, thereby implicitly condemning Ballivián and his supporters [who had been in revolt since 1849]. On the other hand, the Senate wanted an investigation so that the looters could be identified and made to pay reparation. This was a fairer proposal than the first, but also less practical, and there was a heated debate before the vote. When this resulted in a tie, Colonel Laguna, president of the Senate, decided the matter in favour of that house. Perhaps this result, which was obviously influenced by Belzu, prompted Morales to commit a deed which he had already planned.

---

15. Article 15 of the code reads:

> The penalty ordained by the law for an offence shall be reduced in the following circumstances: 1. The offender is a minor, or lacks education or common sense; 2. The crime was inspired by destitution, love, friendship, gratitude, frivolity or a fit of passion; 3. The crime was committed as a result of threats or seductions, when these are insufficient to justify it; 4. It is a first offence, the previous behaviour of the culprit being good or of useful service to the state; 5. Sincere repentance is shown immediately after the commiting of the crime, its author voluntarily seeking to halt or repair the damage he has caused, or to help or indemnify the victim; 6. The offender voluntarily presents himself to the authorities after committing the crime, or confesses it sincerely in the trial when there is no other evidence for it; 7. The offender is provoked; 8. When the crime is committed in a state of inebriation.

Article 395 stipulates the details for fining and suspending public servants or those who have defrauded the state.

16. Although, following convention, Judge Moscoso signed the majority verdict, he disagreed with it, being of the opinion that the crime was of the third degree and so punishable by two months' suspension and a fine of 10 pesos.

The fact of the matter is that on the afternoon of the day on which Morales's petition was denied [6 September 1850], Belzu, as was his custom, took a walk through the Prado. He was accompanied by Laguna and an aide-de-camp, Ichazo. Morales and his son-in-law Benito López had been mounted since 3 p.m. It is believed that López warned Morales when Belzu left the palace. When the president reached the end of the Prado he stopped to talk to Morales, but he had barely uttered a word when Juan Sotomayor, a student whom one of Belzu's prefects had ordered to be flogged in the seminary, coolly cocked and aimed his pistol. Belzu raised his stick to defend himself but the shot was fired and the president, wounded in the head, fell to the ground.

It is not known whether Sotomayor or Morales fired the next bullet, which also hit Belzu in the head. But since Morales was mounted it seems more likely that it was the younger man. The first bullet had caused only a slight wound, but the second had flattened against the skull (almost certainly because the cartridge contained too little or poor gunpowder – a quite common occurrence in this period, when revolvers were very new, breech-loading rifles still under development, and approaching cannonballs often visible).

As soon as Belzu collapsed, his companions Laguna and Ichazo fled without offering any resistance. José Siñanis, who was accompanying the assailant Sotomayor, drew a knife and wanted to slit the president's throat, but before he could do so Morales rode in on the prone figure and tried to get the beast to kick Belzu's head. However, his animal was a pedigree bred for racing and nobly refused to tread on the human, dancing dressage-style around the unconscious figure. Thinking that the *coup de grâce* was anyway unnecessary, Morales ordered the young men away and himself galloped off to the barracks, shouting *vivas* for Ballivián and the Congress of 1848.

When he reached the main square he heard nobody shouting in his support and so began to retreat. Belzu's officers, who had been panic-stricken and made themselves scarce immediately after the assault, now began to turn on Morales. An Argentine, López, was closest to him but drew back when the rebel simply glared at him. By contrast, the noble sons of Sucre, humiliated by a brutal government, no longer looked upon Belzu as the oppressor of their country but as a wounded man drenched in his own blood, and they immediately went to his assistance.[17]

As a result of this assassination attempt power passed into the hands of the cabinet, led by Minister of War General José Gabriel Téllez, who immediately suspended the constitution, thereby halting the work of the court in which Muñoz was being tried. Téllez was a tough veteran of the independence wars from Potosí who had always been opposed to the 'oligarchic' government of ex-President Ballivián and his many supporters in Sucre. He was probably predisposed to take harsh measures; he certainly felt able so to do, and he received the support of the civilian members of the cabinet.

On 19 September Colonel Laguna, who was not only president of the Senate but also the senator for Chuquisaca, was put before a firing squad at the very spot where Belzu had been shot. He had been sentenced to death by a court martial not for

---

17. Manuel José Cortés, *Ensayo sobre la Historia de Bolivia* (1861), La Paz 1981, pp. 228–9.

cowardice but for complicity. It is, though, worth noting that it took two hearings to procure this sentence and that under the constitution there was no vice-president, Laguna's post as president of the Senate making him the formally ordained successor to Belzu if he died or remained incapacitated. This was what raised suspicions against him, but it also provided the ambitious Téllez, who was quite reasonably convinced that Belzu was at death's door, with a strong motive to get rid of Laguna for good.

The next day Belzu underwent a painful operation – chemical anaesthesia was four years old in Britain but had not yet reached Bolivia, where alcohol was still employed. The bullet, which had wounded him at the top of the jawbone and the bridge of the nose but which had not perforated his skull, was successfully removed by a team of surgeons (Drs Cuellar, Ascarrunz, Cordero and Salinas) who had just witnessed the execution of a local dignitary in the name of their patient.[18] One cannot but reflect that men less dedicated to the Hippocratic oath might have let the scalpel slip.

Following the operation, Belzu began to recover, but the repression directed by Téllez continued. On 24 September the deputies who had opposed the suspension of the constitution were arrested and only narrowly escaped execution. On 8 October the centre of Sucre was flooded with troops, and a proclamation read out requiring the surrender of Belzu's attackers within twenty-four hours on pain of death. Many houses were raided, but nobody was found for three days, when Benito López was arrested after a particularly diligent stakeout. He was promptly sentenced to death.

Cortés picks up the story:

> Fifty paces from the cell where he was read his sentence, the cannibal judges of the court that condemned him ... held a dance at which the battalion band played. The most notable ladies of the city gathered to plead for the commuting of the sentence. Téllez promised them that he would talk with the other ministers but he then ordered the palace guard not let the ministers in. In vain the women waited in the main square throughout the night, sending several representations to the government.
>
> The wretched López, full of life and at the age of illusion, calmly watched his end approach. He wrote moving letters to his elderly mother and his young wife. He received the ministrations of the Church, and he went to the firing squad without tarnishing the reputation for bravery that he had acquired in the army. After insistent requests his distraught mother was finally able to retrieve his body. Perhaps López might have been saved had the executive committee not sought to please Belzu, who, now conscious and somewhat stronger, had ordered that the execution go ahead. This was justified in the press because 'López had been decorated by Ballivián and had *been educated in that monster's school*, and because of this attachment he would always harbour bad inclinations against any government that was not led by Ballivián.'[19]

Four days later Belzu formally returned to office. Still in pain and deeply suspicious of all around him, he began a purge of the palace staff. On 27 November the

---

18. *La Epoca*, La Paz, 13 Sept. 1850.

19. Cortés, *Ensayo*, p. 234. The Rotunda chapel that today stands at the foot of Ladislao Cabrera Street was originally built at the end of the Alameda in gratitude for Belzu's survival. His bloodstained uniform and the scarf used to bandage his wound may be viewed in the Casa de la Libertad.

president of the Supreme Court, Basilio de Cuellar, and judges Juan de la Cruz Renjel and José Lorenzo Maldonado were arrested and sent into internal exile. On 4 December the president finally left the city. Twelve days after that the remaining justices of the Supreme Court passed sentence on Mariano Donato Muñoz.

Their proceedings must appear as a most paltry revenge and merely symbolic revindication of the rule of law in the wake of the feral activity of the previous weeks. It is true that the criminal code contained severe penalties not only for treason, sedition and rebellion but also for mutiny (*motín*), rabble-rousing (*asonada*) and commotion (*tumulto*). A criminal convicted for most of these offences would face the death penalty, although Bolivian law did make a significant distinction between material and intellectual authorship.[20] Moreover, it is doubtful if Benito López – even had he been properly tried before a civilian court – could have persuaded the judges that he deserved acquittal under article 35 of the code: 'The thought and decision to commit a crime, when no act has been taken to prepare or start the execution of the offence, are not subject to any penalty beyond the special vigilance of the authorities.' Words had plainly moved to deeds, and the attack on Belzu was – regardless of politics – a premeditated offence against the person from which not even the most extravagant legal code could offer excuse.

Yet notwithstanding much prima facie evidence that Morales had planned to murder the head of state, it must have appeared to many inhabitants of Sucre that they had been plunged into the depths of anarchy. For the new British chargé d'affaires, Frederick Bruce, it was less Belzu himself than the entire system within which the president operated that was to blame: 'there are no elements of stability; there is no industry, no middle class, no honour of fidelity in soldiers or officers, and revolutionary intrigues are always going on'.[21] In fact, Bruce considered his relations with Belzu to be good, and he was concerned at a possible change in government, but when he

---

20. The relevant passages of the code may have seldom – if ever – been applied in a court of law, but the offences described plainly related to observable behaviour and possess some taxonomic interest:

> 104. Every person, of whatever station, who directly and actively conspires to alter, upset or destroy the constitution of the republic, or the republican form of government established for her, or her independence or integrity, is a traitor to the fatherland and will be condemned to death.

> 105. Every person, without regard to distinction of class or *fuero* [privileged legal status] who by spoken or written word makes a direct effort to induce non-compliance with the constitution of the republic, whether in entirety or in part, will be sentenced to between one and four years. If this offence is committed in a speech, sermon or some other written work directed to the public, a corporate body or a public functionary, the author, having served the requisite penalty, will be expelled from the territory of the republic for between two and six years.

> 143. The Bolivian who by means of emissaries or correspondence, or whatever other intelligence, intrigues and conspires with one or more foreign powers, or the agents or ministers, in order to encourage or induce them to enter into war or hostilities with Bolivia or its allies is also a traitor and will suffer the death penalty.

Article 164 identified 'rebellion' as the uprising or insurrection by a 'greater or lesser' number of subjects 'refusing due obedience'. Participants fell into three classes: the ringleaders (six categories; all to suffer death); voluntary participants (four categories; two to eight years' gaol); all other participants (one to three years; loss of post and pay).

21. Bruce, La Paz, to Palmerston, July 1850, FO 11/8, no. 4.

had arrived at La Paz as the second British ambassador to the country it took him four months to find a government to which he could present his credentials.

Still, his experience was markedly better than that of his successor, John Lloyd, an engineer from King's Lynn who was awarded the post as a distinctly odd reward for collecting industrial exhibits for the Great Exhibition of 1851. Despite having spent time in Panama and twenty years in Mauritius, Lloyd was appalled by Belzu's behaviour and was careful to encode his dispatches to Lord John Russell when they touched on such matters:

> Invitations are sent to some unhappy persons who have daughters and who tremble at the vengeance of Belzu if they decline. They are forced to eat and drink. The closing scene is their disgrace and ruin, and at nine or ten o'clock may be seen the whole party returning perfectly inebriated – the president and his officers, reeling, pirouetting and dancing through the *Plaza* to the *Palacio* to the sound of ribaldry and obscene songs.[22]

It has, though, to be said that some of Lloyd's dispatches were complete nonsense, and the Foreign Office clerk annotating one of them appears not to have taken the charitable view that the ambassador was simply clumsy with his codes: 'Colonel Lloyd [the title was bestowed by Bolívar for survey work in Panama] ... must have taken leave of his senses or [be] under the influence of inebriants.'[23] Whatever the case, the fact that is remembered is that Belzu eventually expelled Lloyd, halting diplomatic relations between the two states for almost fifty years, creating the legend that Queen Victoria ordered that Bolivia be effaced from her maps, and establishing a much more real distance between two unequal economies.[24] The view from the North American legation was very similar, the US chargé, Alexander McClung, keeping a brace of pistols permanently on his desk. On the other hand, the fact that he was so often to be found talking to himself suggests that the image of a clear and absolute contrast between civilisation and barbarism might not be entirely justified.[25]

---

22. Lloyd, La Paz, to Russell, March 1853, FO 11/12, no. 12.

23. Annotation to ibid. Poor Lloyd seemed no better off when the government was not resident in Sucre since this left the city 'almost exclusively occupied by an immense number of Roman Catholic priests and clerical collegians, a few timid families and large numbers of *cholos* and indians' – scarcely congenial company for a Norfolk engineer. The despondent tone in his dispatches really deepens when his belongings are stolen: 'My application to the Police, who is also a *cholo* officer, was answered with a smile saying that the people were great robbers, particularly so with English strangers.' In March 1851 US Chargé McClung reported to Daniel Webster, 'I have no cypher in the legation, and in truth there is but little danger at any rate. The English language is a complete cypher to the whole of Bolivia except five or six foreigners.' *The Papers of Daniel Webster: Diplomatic Papers, 1850–1852*, II, Hanover, N.H., 1987, p. 655.

24. The legend – unsupported by local or Foreign Office sources – is that Belzu had Lloyd tied backwards on a mule and driven ignominiously out of La Paz in 1853. Lloyd – who had a high reputation for his learned articles on surveying and engineering topics – quickly moved on, but not out of danger. He was arrested as a spy in the Crimea following the Battle of the Alma, and he died of cholera in Therapia in October 1854.

25. Hugh de Bonelli, *Travels in Bolivia*, London 1854, II, p. 94. The Kentucky-born McClung was notoriously bad-tempered and had been obliged to resign from the US navy in 1829 after only a year's service because he had provoked so many duels. He owed his posting to Bolivia in good measure to his heroic conduct in the Mexican War. Famed as an orator, his only published work is a eulogy to Henry Clay in 1852. Aged forty-three, McClung committed suicide in Jackson, Missouri, in March 1855.

A clue may be found in Juan Bautista Alberdi's *'Bases'*, written when Belzu was president of Bolivia. For Alberdi and his politico-literary companions Belzu was little better than Rosas, not least because 'his aversion to foreigners is famous'. Bolivia, in Alberdi's view, was one of the worst cases of an American state repudiating the advances of Northern modernity and reposing on the ideology of independence derived from the initial rupture from Spain. Writing about the constitution of 1843, he is primarily concerned that it

> ... declares from the very start (article one) that the Bolivian nation is comprised of all Bolivians. Beyond Bolivians no other elements of the nation exist. The foreign population does not form part of the people. It then immediately declares the independence of the country, which was an idea that dominated our institutions in their earliest phase. But what does Bolivia mean? An 'unlimited love of freedom'. These words of Bolívar himself – he who gave this republic its existence, its name and its exclusive spirit of freedom and independence with respect to the outside world – these words are the expression of the external regime of the country: independence and isolation, without limit, without quarter.[26]

This interpretation received a quite prompt and sharp response from within the country, where the case for protection, autonomy and not relying on settlement by European immigrants and merchants was made most coherently and persuasively by José María Molina.[27]

Ironically, Alberdi's other main criticism was directed at the very elements against whom Belzu's *cholo* hordes were ranged and who should have introduced the modernisation that only Northerners could now guarantee. Alberdi shared Bruce's appraisal of Bolivia's shortcomings, but he saw many more of their causes as resting precisely in a Lilliputian constitution,

> inspired and drafted by the civilized circles of Chuquisaca [Sucre], an isolated university town of theologians and jurists characterised by subtle scholasticism, and who have included in their statutes and charters not one single measure that might lift Spanish America from the state of prostration and backwardness in which it languishes.[28]

It was not just that the law did not prevail, but that even this law was wrong and bad. So much for the labours of the founding fathers of Bolivian jurisprudence – Torrico, Urcullu and Sánchez de Velasco – against whom the likes of Mariano Donato

---

26. Jorge Mayer (ed.), *Las 'Bases' de Alberdi*, Buenos Aires 1969, pp. 201–2. The two Latin American countries that lack a seaboard at the start of the twenty-first century – Bolivia and Paraguay – share several characteristics – not least autochthonous languages and semi-autarkic economic regimes – in the nineteenth century. As implied by Alberdi, these similarities go well beyond constitutions and are rooted in social values. There are few Bolivians who would be surprised to hear of Chileans or Argentines who, upon visiting their country, become perplexed or disorientated in a manner beyond condescension over race or indulgence over poverty. Although evidently unintended as such, Alberdi's succinct observation serves very well as a celebration of the country as grandeur in adversity.

27. *Observaciones sobre el proyecto intitulado 'Bases y puntos de partida para la organización política de la República Argentina'*, Sucre 1852, reproduced in Juan Silva (ed.), 'Alrededor de las Bases de Alberdi', *Revista de la Universidad de Córdoba*, V–VI, 1928. There is also a copy of this 68-page booklet enclosed in FO 11/10, no. 14, with Colonel Lloyd's annotations.

28. Mayer (ed.), *'Bases'*, p. 201.

Muñoz were too formidable an opposition. From Washington's perspective the condition of Bolivian politics was also understood in terms of race, even if it was projected
in terms of higher principle. Secretary of State James Buchanan knew very little of
the country when he drafted the instructions for the first US ambassador, John
Appleton, in June 1848, but he was in no doubt as to the message that had to be
conveyed:

> The principal object of your mission is to cultivate the most friendly relations with Bolivia.
> The enemies of free Government throughout the world point with satisfaction to the perpetual
> revolutions in the South American republics. They hence argue that man is not fit for Self
> Government; and it is greatly to be deplored that the instability of these Republics and in
> many instances their disregard for private rights have afforded a pretext for such an unfor-
> tunate assumption. Liberty cannot be preserved without order; and this can only spring from
> a sacred observance of the law. So long as it shall be in the power of successive military
> chieftans to subvert the Governments of these Republics by the sword, their people cannot
> expect to enjoy the blessings of liberty. Anarchy, confusion, and civil war must be the result.
> In your intercourse with the Bolivian authorities you will omit no opportunity of pressing
> these truths upon them, and of presenting to them the example of our own country, where
> all controversies are decided at the ballot box.... Instead of weakening themselves by domestic
> dissensions, the Spanish race in these Republics have every motive for union and harmony.
> They nearly all have an enemy within their own bosoms burning for vengeance on account
> of the supposed wrongs of centuries, and ever ready, when a favourable opportunity may
> offer, to expel or exterminate the descendants of their conquerors. Already a war of races has
> arisen between the Indians and the Spaniards in Guatemala and Yucatán, and the civil war
> raging in Venezuela partakes largely of this character. In Bolivia it is understood that three-
> fourths of the inhabitants belong to the Indian race. How unfortunate it is that, under these
> circumstances, the Spanish race there should be weakening themselves by warring against
> each other.[29]

Before too long Muñoz would, in fact, espouse, views quite close to Alberdi's, and he
frequently issued rhetoric of the type used by Buchanan, but at the end of 1850 there
still existed reasons to doubt a simple dichotomy between brute force and legalist
fantasy.

In the first place, Muñoz was sentenced at a time when such a move can hardly be
deemed politically expedient for the judiciary since, as we have noted, he was effectively number two in the Ministry of the Interior and could be expected to return to
it. Muñoz was not a successful lawyer and was known in Sucre – a town fond of
nicknames – as 'Comepan' ('Penniless').[30] His fine was equivalent to the price of three

29. Buchanan, Washington, to Appleton, 1 June 1848, in John Bassett Moore (ed.), *Works of James
Buchanan*, VIII (1911), New York 1960, pp. 75–6. Appleton, who nearly died in a shipwreck on his way
to Bolivia, did not last long, resigning his post in May 1849, serving one term in the House of Representatives and then becoming Buchanan's secretary in the US embassy in London. A leading member of
the campaign team that won Buchanan the presidency in 1856, he was made ambassador to Russia, and
one assumes that he received no instructions on that occasion similar to those above. Resigning upon
Lincoln's election, Appleton died of tuberculosis in August 1864.

30. Alcides Arguedas, *Historia General de Bolivia*, La Paz 1980, p. 267; Antonio Paredes Candia, *El Apodo
en Bolivia*, La Paz 1977, p. 77.

horses, and he would certainly feel the lack of a salary. Hence, although the sentence might appear to be purely symbolic, it was, in fact, risky enough for those pronouncing it to give the symbolism real force.

Secondly, Muñoz was a *Chuquisaqueño*, a member of the very society thrown into turmoil by the government that he served. His personal reputation – particularly as a bachelor – had to be measured against any short-term political gain, and this was no easy task, even for a man as calculating as himself. Both he and the judges took appreciable risks in their actions, and both parties did so according to the logic of the system that they knew best, albeit without any guarantee of success.

Thirdly, and in the same light, the actions in Tarija for which Muñoz was brought to book indicated a more than passing pre-eminence of civil society over the state. The Franciscan brothers were no mugs; the library of their monastery was one of the best in the country, containing 360 books on canon law and 143 on civil law amongst its 5,000 volumes.[31] What occurred in Tarija on Good Friday 1850 was not simply a case of a parallel customary law being more efficacious than that of the state because it was possessed of deeper social roots. That instance was, rather, a dynamic and conscious hybrid of the two legal strains with justifications drawn liberally, if erratically, from both.[32]

To talk of legal pluralism is anachronistic but not essentially inaccurate. Equally, it would be misconceived to think that the violent turmoil 'at the top' of the formal political world was repeated elsewhere in society, even within that hispanic elite so dismayed by *caudillos* who would not obey laws but who had to be sponsored precisely because this was the best means of defence against greater lawlessness. For the great bulk of the population – urban and mixed race ('*cholo*' in Lloyd's parlance) as well as rural and indigenous – these comings and goings and bouts of blood-letting were rarely observed and largely indifferent in their effect.

---

31. Lorenzo Calzavarini G., 'La Biblioteca del Convento "Nuestra Señora de los Angeles" y Acción Franciscana en Tarija', in Josep M. Barnadas (ed.), *El Libro, Espejo de la Cultura: Estudios sobre la cultura del libro en Bolivia*, Cochabamba 1990, p. 47.

32. In nineteenth-century Bolivia this is perhaps most vividly illustrated in the fiscal sphere and particularly in the payment of the 'Indian tribute'. In one of his many detailed essays on this subject Tristan Platt quotes José Berdeja, the subprefect of Chayanta, explaining to the departmental prefect of Potosí in 1843 why payment of this head-tax did not always adhere to the traditional timetable of the solstices at Christmas and St John's day:

> ... the customs which distinguish this province from others are not arbitrary: the time for tribute payment depends on the double residence which forces each individual to move from one climate to another according to their work schedule. Even between the communities some make their payments at different times, according to the distance of their respective valleys, or the locations of the markets where they expend their products; so that the Chayantakas, for example, celebrate their *cabildos* [tribute-paying ceremony] on San Roque's day (16 August) while the Sicoyas can only do so at Rosario (23 October).

Quoted in T. Platt, 'Liberalism and Ethnocide in the Southern Andes', *History Workshop Journal*, 17, Spring 1984, p. 10. One reason for President Belzu's popularity is that he ended anticipatory payment of the tribute by collectors. As we shall see, Mariano Donato Muñoz had even more radical ideas.

Finally, as the reader may already have anticipated, we need to register the Hibernian dimension. Muñoz did not release Anselma Condori unseen; Irish eyes were watching. They belonged to Francisco (Frank) Burdett O'Connor, one of the most powerful and respected figures in the department of Tarija – a province is named after him – and a man who himself (if Muñoz is to be believed) acted the part of Pontius Pilate on a Good Friday since he too had held the office of prefect.

The early constitutions of Bolivia conferred nationality on foreigners who had participated in the wars of independence, and it was through his service as chief of staff of the army of liberation that O'Connor arrived in Alto Perú (as Bolivia then was) in 1825, establishing himself in Tarija almost immediately after the defeat of the Spaniards. Born in Cork in 1791, O'Connor came from a family that had emphatically put its stamp on the political life of the British Isles. His uncle, Arthur, was one of the leaders of the great Irish rebellion of 1798, narrowly escaping execution for high treason after his arrest at Margate in possession of a large sum of money, much baggage and a code (hidden in a razor box) with which to conduct correspondence between Napoleonic France and the rebel forces in Ireland.

Arthur O'Connor was in the company of a priest, James Coigley, who was found guilty at Maidstone court and hanged, but O'Connor and two other accomplices were acquitted largely because his friends in the Whig elite – including Fox, Lord John Russell (the later prime minister's father) and the playright Sheridan – testified unreservedly and inaccurately on their behalf, and not a single witness was called from Ireland.[33] Immediately the trial was finished, O'Connor was arrested on the same charge on behalf of the authorities in Dublin, a fight breaking out in the courtroom. According to Thomas Pakenham,

> The trial concluded on May 22nd with one of the strangest scenes in a British court of justice. O'Connor could be re-tried under Irish law on exactly the same charge of which he had just been acquitted under British law. Accordingly, two Bow Street runners were waiting by the dock ready to re-arrest him. But no sooner had the death sentence been pronounced on the unfortunate Coigley than O'Connor rushed from the dock to the bar, and from the bar into the body of the court, with the police in hot pursuit. The court was plunged into confusion. Outraged Whigs, including O'Connor's counsel and Lord Thanet, tried to snatch him to safety. Swords were drawn – the swords that were lying as evidence

---

33. On 22 May 1798 Sheridan wrote to his wife from Maidstone,

> My Heart's Beloved, knowing how anxious you will be, I send [this], though the Trials will be over some time tonight. Matters, we think, look good for O'Connor, but I am resolved not to be sanguine. I got to speak to him this morning. His mind is composed, but his nerves sadly shaken. He was greatly affected when his poor brother was brought into court yesterday, and when the other took his hand, he burst into tears. The usage of Roger O'Connor, who is one of the finest fellows I ever saw, has been merciless beyond example. We are all very anxious and very busy, for the counsel want assistance. Here is Fox, Gray, Erskine, Grattan, Moira, Norfolk etc.

Quoted in Walter Sichel, *Sheridan*, London 1909, II, p. 284. Lord John Russell senior became the sixth Duke of Bedford and was Lord Lieutenant of Ireland in 1806–07.

on the table. Furniture was smashed, and heads broken. O'Connor might have got clean away, but for the quick-wittedness of the judge's coachman who brought him crashing to the floor.[34]

In the end, O'Connor and the other leaders were shipped to Fort George in Scotland and held there until 1802, when he made his way to France, was appointed a divisional general in Napoleon's Dutch Brigade, bought Mirabeau's estate in Le Bignon, and married Condorcet's only daughter, Eliza, when she was seventeen and he forty-four.[35] Having met him in January 1805, the political philosopher Benjamin Constant noted in his diary,

> O'Connor is a sophisticated man [*esprit fin*]. When joking he has a lighter touch than for-eigners usually do, and so has something of the French defect of joking about one's own opinions. He is more ambitious than he is a friend of liberty, and yet a friend of liberty nevertheless, because to be so is the refuge of ambitious men who have missed success.[36]

Roger O'Connor – Arthur's elder brother and Frank's father – was detained in London immediately following Arthur's arrest and used as a witness by the prosecu-tion at the trial, but once freed from Fort George he resolved to avoid political complications. Roger is described by several authors as 'a little mad', and he was plainly unreliable. Having power of attorney over Arthur's property, he contrived to lose almost all of it in suspicious manner. He was perhaps most renowned for purchasing Dangan Castle for £40,000 (never fully paid) from the Wellesley family (the Marquis not yet having married Marianne Caton) shortly before part of it was destroyed by fire. However, his next appearance in court was in 1817 for robbing the Galway mail coach (and murdering its guard) five years earlier. An acquittal was eventually secured once the jury was persuaded by Sir Francis Burdett MP that the defendant could always rely on unlimited loans from him.[37]

---

34. *The Year of Liberty: The History of the Great Irish Rebellion of 1798*, London 1972, pp. 129–30. Pakenham's account is characteristically racy. A magisterial scholarly account is provided by Marianne Elliott, *Partners in Revolution: The United Irishmen and France*, New Haven, Conn., 1992. For Frank MacDermot, Arthur O'Connor's acquittal owed much to his brother Roger, 'one of the most plausible men living, who played a part in beguiling the Whigs'. 'Arthur O'Connor', *Irish Historical Studies*, XV, 1966–67, p. 59.

35. MacDermot makes a strong case for O'Connor fibbing pretty extensively – reducing his age, in-flating his income – in order to secure such an elevated position in 1804. Perhaps it was lucky for both him and France, of which he became a citizen in 1818, that his active service never brought him within the whiff of gunpowder expended in earnest. Ibid., p. 63.

36. *Journaux Intimes*, Paris 1952, p. 189. Arthur and Eliza had three sons. Eliza, who was free to travel to Ireland, was no match for her brother-in-law Roger, whose management of Arthur's estate defied the norms of fraternal propriety. However, after Roger died in 1834 Arthur was permitted by the Whig administration to visit Ireland and dispose of the property that remained and had been so comprehensively mishandled by his brother. Required to leave again after six months when the Tories returned to power, Arthur died at Le Bignon in April 1852, aged eighty-eight.

37. *Roger O'Connor*, born Connerville, County Cork, 1762. TCD, called to the English bar, 1784. Bought the inheritance of his elder brother Daniel (1754–1846) for £5,000 after Daniel's elopement to Bristol and loss of a suit for damages over it. Arrested for sedition in 1797 on the instigation of another older brother, Robert. Detained in London, 1798, witness in trial of younger brother Arthur, Maidstone, May 1798. Confined to Fort George; released 1801 but not allowed to enter Ireland. 1803, permitted to enter Ireland but not County Cork. Twice married – secondly, in 1788, to Wilhamena Bowen, who bore

Indeed, it was to Burdett – arguably the most popular politician in London at the start of the nineteenth century, champion of free speech and Catholic rights, and bane of the state of Pitt and Liverpool – that Roger O'Connor dedicated his book *The Chronicles of Eri*, published in 1822 and purporting to be the only true account of Ireland, 'translated from the original manuscripts in the Phoenician dialect of the Scythian language'.[38] It is unclear whether Burdett was pleased to be associated with this colourful concoction – a more 'imagined community' it would be hard to locate outside of Atlantis – but he undoubtedly deserved the author's gratitude since he had brought up O'Connor's second and fourth sons, Frank and Feargus, whilst their father was in gaol. Certainly Francisco – as Frank became in the Americas – always referred to Burdett with pride and kept his godfather's name throughout his life.

Feargus, on the other hand, did not. Apart from the fact that he had no need to emulate a Spanish matronym, his fame was won under his own name – as the most prominent of the leaders of the Chartist movement.[39] It is possible that both he and Frank helped Roger hold up the Galway mail, and Feargus evidently harboured literary ambitions like his father, although nobody ever saw *The Devil on Three Sticks*, the novel which he claimed to have written when jailed in York and which he would 'fearlessly place in competition with the works of any living author'.[40] After her visit to London in 1842 Flora Tristán described this kindred spirit as 'a vigorous, fiery orator whose brilliance is inspiring'.[41]

It would, though, be a mistake to attribute O'Connor's infamous temper and lurching judgement exclusively to family influence as he sought to engage with what

---

him four sons and three daughters and died in 1806 – he moved out of Dangan Castle, which he had bought as a 'suitable residence in which to entertain Napoleon', after the Galway mail coach trial. Lived the rest of his life in a fisherman's cottage in Ballincollig, County Cork, with a local young woman whom he called his 'Princess of Kerry'. Died January 1834, buried in the ancestral tomb of the MacCarthy's, Kilcrea.

38. For a suggestive discussion of earlier endeavours of a similar nature, see Ann Rosalind Jones and Peter Stallybrass, 'Dismantling Irena. The Sexualising of Ireland in Early Modern England', in Andrew Parker, Mary Russo, Doris Sommer and Patricia Yeagar (eds), *Nationalisms and Sexualities*, London 1992. *Sir Francis Burdett* (1770–1844), listened to the debates in the Assembly in Paris after the Revolution; married to Sophia Coutts, daughter of Thomas, the banker. Supporter of Paine and Bentham. Arrest ordered by the Speaker in 1810 for publishing speech of radical orator John Gale Jones, his house being defended for four days against the Lifeguards by a crowd led by Francis Place. Held in Tower until Parliament prorogued; re-elected MP for Westminster 1812, 1818; fined £2,000 for criticising repression at Peterloo. Represented North Wiltshire, 1837–44.

39. *Feargus O'Connor*, born Connerville, County Cork, 1794. First reported speech, 1822, against the landlords and Protestant clergy. MP for Cork 1832 as supporter of O'Connell; disqualified in 1835 for holding insufficient property. Founded *Northern Star* radical weekly, 1837. After Convention of 1839 became chief figure of Chartism (demanding manhood suffrage, annual parliaments, the secret ballot, equal electoral districts, abolition of MPs' property qualifications, payment of MPs). Published *A Practical Work on the Management of Small Farms*, 1843. He was unmarried; his speaking tours often coincided with productions given by the repertory company featuring the beautiful Louisa Nisbett. 'Unquestionably the best-loved, as well as the most hated, man in the Chartist movement.' G.D.H. Cole, *Chartist Portraits*, London 1941, p. 300.

40. *Northern Star*, 16 Jan. 1841.

41. *The London Journal of Flora Tristán or The Aristocracy and the Working Class of England* (1842), London 1982, p. 48.

Eric Hobsbawm has called 'the extraordinary feebleness of this greatest of all mass movements of British labour'.[42] Already unstable, by the time of the Muñoz trial in Bolivia Feargus O'Connor was showing clear signs of mental collapse. In June 1852 he was committed to asylum, having punched two fellow MPs in the House of Commons, and he died at the house of his younger sister Harriet in Notting Hill in September 1855.[43]

One can occasionally catch glimpses of similar character traits in Francisco Burdett O'Connor's long life in Bolivia, but his reputation was based upon his gifts of decisiveness as a regimental commander and preparation as a staff officer.[44] Promoted to a regimental command within a year of joining Bolívar's army, O'Connor was chief of staff up to the Battle of Ayacucho, which site he chose and which sealed the fate of the Spanish empire in the Americas, and early in 1825 Sucre chose him to direct the final operation of the war – the pursuit and elimination of General Pedro Olañeta, the last royalist commander to offer resistance.

At the age of thirty-three O'Connor had achieved greater feats of arms than any other member of his family, and it is perhaps unremarkable that he chose both to remain a soldier and to stay in the country that he had helped to liberate. A brief passage in his markedly unpretentious memoirs interrupts the recounting of military duties to register instant attraction to Tarija:

---

42. *Labouring Men*, London 1964, p. 381. O'Connor's own major contribution was the Chartist Land Company, established in 1846 with the plan to let out by lottery smallholdings to subscribers, and achieving 600 branches the next year. One settlement, at Heronsgate near Rickmansworth, Hertfordshire, was named O'Connorville. A House of Commons investigation in June 1848 found the company to be bankrupt, and it was closed shortly thereafter. Alice May Hadfield, *The Chartist Land Company*, Newton Abbot 1970. In January 1848 Engels wrote warmly of O'Connor:

> ... seriously concerned at the well-being of the millions in Ireland. Repeal – the abolition of union, that is the achievement of an independent Irish parliament – is not for *him* an empty word, a pretext for obtaining posts for himself and his friends, and for making profitable business transactions.

Deutsche–Brusseler Zeitung, 9 January 1848, reprinted in *Marx and Engels on Ireland*, London 1971, p. 48. However, after O'Connor urged the masses gathered at Kennington Common not to march on the House of Commons on 10 April 1848 he lost any lingering indulgence from the radicals. In November 1850 – at the same time as General Belzu was recovering in Sucre – Karl Marx wrote of O'Connor,

> He is essentially conservative, and feels a highly determined hatred not only for industrial progress but also for the revolution. His ideals are patriarchal and petty bourgeois through and through. He united in his person an inexhaustable number of contradictions, which find their fulfilment and harmony in a certain blunt common sense.

Neue Rheinische Zeitung Revue, 'Review May to October 1850', reprinted in Karl Marx, *The Revolutions of 1848*, Harmondsworth 1973, pp. 308–9.

43. His burial at Kensal Green Cemetery on 10 September was paid for by public subscription and attended by at least 15,000 people. For the last year of his life Feargus believed that he was a state prisoner and simply lodging with Dr Tuke, the owner of the asylum. There is a statue in the Nottingham arboretum.

44. 'Major O'Connor should be detached from his battalion to oversee the carrying out of your instructions to the Grenadiers as I think he is the best officer to use at the advanced posts.' Bolívar, Pativilca, to Sucre, 24 Jan. 1824, in Vicente Lecuna (ed.), *Selected Writings of Bolívar*, New York 1952, II, p. 427. Examples of correspondence to and from O'Connor during the wars of independence are best found in *Memorias del General O'Leary: Documentos*, Caracas 1879–88, vols XXI and XXII.

... it seemed to me as if I were in the clouds, the towering blue peaks of the mountains appearing like islands in the sea. I descended the ridge which bears the name 'Inca' and which is extremely long and precipitous. Once I reached its foot I found myself in the most beautiful plain.[45]

It was here – a few leagues from the final manoeuvres against Olañeta – that O'Connor settled with the objective of setting up an estate. In 1827 he married Francisca de Ruyloba, for whom he built a house on Palma Street in which to bring up their daughter Hercilia. Francisco established two farms, at Santa Anna and San Luis (Entre Rios), but he also remained on the active list of the new army of Bolivia. He was promoted to general and took a leading part in charting the largely unexplored territories of the south-east towards the Chaco Boreal.

O'Connor was not a major player in the troubled political life of the young republic, but he could scarcely avoid some involvement, if only by dint of his military rank. (It was largely in this capacity that he acted as best man when Belzu married Juana Manuela Gorriti in Tarija in 1830.) He was a supporter of protectionism but open enough in his views to report President Santa Cruz's retort to his lobbying on this policy:

'What do you want me to do, O'Connor? I am just as ready as you to protect national industry, and I will give you an example. During the sessions of congress I presented a bill requiring every Bolivian in receipt of a salary from the public purse to wear clothes made from fabric produced in this country. It was rejected without even being discussed.' 'It was very natural, sir,' I replied, 'because the majority of the deputies are involved in foreign trade.'[46]

Occupying a number of senior posts under Santa Cruz, O'Connor was closely identified with that president's short-lived effort to establish a confederation between Bolivia and Peru. His participation in the victorious battles with invading Peruvian forces at Yanacocha (1835) and Socabaya (1836), where he commanded the centre of the Bolivian army, won him promotion to general. The rigours of that especially fierce campaign damaged his health, and he retired to his farms. However, he had barely settled back with his family when an Argentine army invaded Tarija in order to enforce the longstanding claim that country had on the department. As a result, O'Connor took up arms once more, serving beneath Otto Felipe Braun – the other naturalised independence hero – at the Battle of Montenegro in 1838, when the

---

45. Francisco Burdett O'Connor, *Independencia Americana*, Madrid 1915, p. 174.
46. Ibid., pp. 331–2. In Britain Feargus was no less opposed to free trade:

Free trade is but a substitute for landed monopoly at home, and free trade is but chaunted as a means of creating a competitive power for the taskmaster, and a new source of commercial speculation for gamblers with fictitious money for real labour – have you store-houses abroad, and you have a wholesale market for the money mongers, and your necessities will form the standard of retail prices.

Northern Star, 3 Nov. 1838, quoted in Gareth Stedman Jones, *Languages of Class: Studies in English Working Class History, 1832–1982*, Cambridge 1983, p. 123.

Argentines were comprehensively defeated and Tarija secured as an integral part of Bolivia.[47] Neither O'Connor nor Braun was at the Battle of Yungay where Santa Cruz's forces were defeated the following year.

O'Connor escaped the fate of exile that faced the more prominent supporters of a president upon his overthrow, but he was placed under house arrest for a while. However, in August 1841 he set aside his protectionist instincts to lead the town of Tarija in proclaiming as president the rebel General José Ballivián, and it was a consequence of that initiative, which was not seriously resisted by the local police, that he became prefect of the department. Thereafter his role in political life was marginal, and his activities concentrated on local affairs in a region where the family of O'Connor, along with those of Paz and Trigo, was one of the most distinguished of a small paternalist hierarchy.

Francisco Burdett O'Connor died in Tarija at the age of eighty in October 1871.[48] The profile of the family name was maintained, albeit in a far more sedate manner, by Hercilia's son Tomás, who trained in law, preferred writing poetry, and made his living as a journalist.[49] (In 1994 Bolivia was represented at the Miss Universe contest in Manila by Cecilia O'Connor, L'Oréal model, admirer of Fidel Castro and worthy – if red-headed – representative of the country's bustling pulchritude.)

★

47. *Otto Felipe Braun*, born Cassel, Hesse, 1798. Served in Prussian campaign against Bonaparte, 1815. Qualified as a vet, 1818. Travelled to Santo Domingo, where he said he could live on 1,500 pesos a year but couldn't swim because of the sharks. Joined Bolívar's forces, 1820; promoted colonel, 1822. Commanding officer of Grenadiers at Ayacucho, 1824. Served as prefect of La Paz several times. Promoted marshall following his defeat of General Heredia at Montenegro. Died La Paz, December 1858. The traffic, it should be said, was not all one-way. Although he was on diplomatic duty when he left London in March 1845, *Vicente Pazos Kanki* was an authentic internationalist. Born in 1779 in Ilabaya of Aymara origin, he graduated in law from Cusco. A convinced republican, he wrote for the pro-independence press in Buenos Aires, whence he was expelled to London, where he married in 1812. Translated Gospel of St Luke into Aymara. Published *Compendio de la Historia de los Estados Unidos*, Paris 1825; *Letters on the United Provinces addressed to the Hon. Henry Clay*, Philadelphia 1819. From his reply of July 1819 it is evident that Clay's ambitions on the presidency of the USA were taking him down the Mississippi from his Kentucky homeland: 'I saw the book in New Orleans, on board the steam-boat and several other places – and I trust that it will contribute more and more to enlist the feelings and affections of the people of this country on behalf of their suffering brethren of South America.' *The Papers of Henry Clay*, Lexington, Ky., 1961, II, p. 701.

48. At this stage of proceedings one actively resists tale of audacity, but it is a matter of record that Francisco O'Connor refused to receive the last rites in his own home, was taken to have them administered at the monastery at 8 p.m., and returned home to die at 10 p.m. on 5 October 1871. Tomás O'Connor d'Arlach, introduction to *Independencia Americana*, p. 10.

49. *Tomás O'Connor d'Arlach*, born Tarija, 1853, son of Ademar d'Arlach and Hercilia O'Connor. Graduated faculty of law, Universidad San Francisco Xavier, Sucre. Married Aurora Velasco. Editor for twenty-seven years of *La Estrella de Tarija*. Senator for the department 1904–19. Books included: *El General Melgarejo: hechos y dichos de este hombre celebre*; *Doña Juana Sánchez*; *Tarija: bosquejo histórico*. Died Tarija, 1932. Rather as their great-grandfather had done, Tomás's sons altered their names so as not to lose a distinctive family identity. Jorge O'Connor d'Arlach became a career diplomat; his brother Amable, who trained as a doctor, also joined the foreign service and was for a while Bolivian consul in Liverpool. Víctor Varas Reyes recounts – via Antonio Paredes Candia – these stories of Tomás and another brother, Octavio:

> It was midnight and everyone was asleep in the O'Connor household. Suddenly Don Tomás was awoken by sounds that indicated that at least two people had effected an entry by climbing over the low wall on Palma Street. The poet got up and went downstairs, taking the burglars by surprise.

I can find no documentary link between General O'Connor and Mariano Donato Muñoz's antics of Easter 1850; there was no newspaper published in Tarija before Muñoz himself set up *El Telégrafo* in July 1850. Having proclaimed Ballivián as president in 1841, O'Connor might be supposed not to favour General Belzu and his appointees. But these matters were ever tractable and, besides, Ballivián and Belzu were not enemies in 1841, Belzu being appointed by the new president to succeed O'Connor as prefect of Tarija. Moreover, O'Connor had been Belzu's best man and patron in Tarija. It is also telling that in his final years O'Connor opposed the highly contro- versial General Mariano Melgarejo (about whom his grandson Tomás none the less wrote two quite sympathetic books).[50] Melgarejo ruled Bolivia from 28 December 1864 to 15 January 1871, and for all but the first day of this regime – the fourth longest in the history of Bolivia – one man simultaneously occupied the posts of minister of government, minister of foreign relations and minister of justice. He was Mariano Donato Muñoz.

It is not easy to keep a close trace on Muñoz over the fifteen years between his trial and his appointment as the senior manager of the Bolivian state. What can, however, be discerned is not unusual for a member of the political class of that epoch, even if Mariano usually managed to give matters his characteristic imprint.

This was certainly the case in 1853, when he was serving as prefect again, this time of the department of Cochabamba. Belzu had now been president for over five years and was confronting a particularly sharp challenge for power from the civilian free- trader José María Linares. In July 1853 pro-Linares forces successfully took over the eastern town of Santa Cruz and sent a Captain Alpiri as their emissary to Cochabamba.

'Gentlemen,' he said, 'in the room where you are now, on the table in the corner, there is a small box containing some money. If you must, take it with you, but please do so carefully and quietly. I don't want Aurora to wake up and get a fright.' 'One good turn deserves another,' said one thief to the other, and they left empty handed.

The ceremony to mark the opening of the school year was exceptionally well attended, the teachers and populace of Tarija overflowing the stalls of the '15th April' hall. In the wait before ascending the platform the director of education, Dr Octavio O'Connor d'Arlach, slowly lit his pipe and took a few contented puffs as he listened to the talk around him. Then somebody came up to him to tell him that people were getting impatient of waiting. O'Connor snapped to, put his pipe in his back-pocket, as you would a handkerchief, and requested the committee to take their seats.

Following the solemn act of inauguration, Dr O'Connor, who was standing to the right of Don Víctor Navajas Trigo, prefect of the department, began to read his annual report. Immersed in his speech, he was unaware of the mounting consternation around him. But just as he was describing with some passion the infrastructural needs of the district, he sensed both the odour of burning and the gentle elbow of the prefect in his ribs. The smell came from his trousers, which the increasingly alarmed audience could not see. The boss was unharmed, the trousers were a write-off, and the pedagogic community most gratified.

Antonio Paredes Candia, *Anécdotas Bolivianas*, La Paz 1978, pp. 108–9, 127–8. There is perhaps no social unit better than the small town to make the case for universal human consciousness, and even steely metropolitan intellectuals may occasionally relish tales of the Cork-to-Tarija nexus that they know to be so much deconstructable nostalgia.

50. Alcibiades Guzmán, *Libertad o Despotismo en Bolivia: El Antimelgarejismo después de Melgarejo*, La Paz 1918, p. 186.

Shortly after he arrived there, he was detained, found to possess a proclamation calling for rebellion, tried by a court martial, and sentenced to death.

However, the women of the city, led by the nuns of the priory, mobilised in favour of the young soldier and pleaded with Muñoz to spare him. Notwithstanding the seriousness of the crime and his own recent experience in the Supreme Court, Muñoz acquiesced. The Tarija episode had evidently whetted his appetite for granting mercy. This, it should be said, was not a property exclusive to him. The following April, when Muñoz had left this post, Captain Mariano Melgarejo, who had also been involved in the Santa Cruz uprising, was likewise saved from imminent execution by the new prefect, Dr Hernández. However, Hernández took care only to postpone the firing squad until the matter had been referred to Belzu, who, in granting the request for mercy from a commission sent from Cochabamba, told them, 'The day will come when Cochabamba will repent its ardent support for such a dangerous man.'[51]

It was in Cochabamba that Mariano Muñoz married Rosaura Quevedo, whose brother Quintin had become a prominent military officer despite the fact that the family was from Córdoba, Argentina. This link was important because within a year Belzu, wearied by revolts, had left office, handing it on to his son-in-law General Córdoba, whose softer line proved incapable of resisting the constant *linarista* challenges. In October 1857 Linares finally captured the government, opening a persecution of *belcistas* that drove Muñoz, like many others, into exile in Peru.

In 1859 Muñoz, who does not seem at all to have been a physical coward, participated in a rebellious raid into Bolivia seeking to restore Belzu. Commanded by the aged General Agreda, this small force reached as far as El Alto, on the edge of the crater containing La Paz, before it was defeated by government forces in a running four-hour fight. The rebels lost forty men, but Muñoz escaped unhurt.

His period of adversity in exile did not last long simply because Linares's repression was so unremitting that it alienated even members of his own cabinet, who naturally harboured their own ambitions, overthrowing him in 1861. Thus, by 1863 Mariano was not only back in the country but also serving as a deputy under the government of General Achá. Yet it was not long before he was accused of conspiracy – a charge he repudiated from the floor of Congress, describing Achá as the 'anchor of national salvation', and insisting that, 'I am dedicated to the constitutional cause, which the very excellent President Achá legitimately represents, and my duty and my honour oblige me to defend it and uphold it, regardless of my social station.'

These words are quoted by Alcides Arguedas, the controversial historian of the early twentieth century, pointedly to illustrate Muñoz's hypocrisy and disloyalty.[52]

---

51. Aranzaes, *Revoluciones*, pp. 120, 127.

52. Arguedas, *Historia*, p. 267. It could be argued that the strength of Arguedas's Anglophile devotion casts doubt over all his judgements:

The phrase of Rubén Darío's that 'every Englishman is an island' is taken from Emerson and captures the psychology of that strong and authoritative nation.... Valour, loyalty and particularly

Such a judgement might be thought most fair given that Muñoz was running Colonel Melgarejo's administration within twenty-four hours of that young officer having overthrown Achá in December 1864.

This is certainly the general view of Mariano Donato Muñoz, who has bequeathed to Bolivian political folklore the nickname 'Donato', signifying an eager, amoral civilian servant of military tyrants. Ramón Sotomayor Valdés, the Chilean ambassador to Bolivia at that time, was strongly of that belief, as was the silver magnate Avelino Aramayo.[53] Later historians – particularly those associated with the nationalist revolution of 1952 – tend to depict Muñoz as simply the most shameless representative of a bevy of civilians scavaging for personal reward in the wake of the latest strongman.[54]

Perhaps there was no alternative for the likes of Mariano Muñoz within the system of their day. The historian Gabriel René Moreno, who escaped it at any early age for the somewhat more mellow ambience of Chile, was, like Arguedas, convinced of its primitivism:

> [It is] composed of soldiers, spongers off the treasury, unruly and indolent plebeians, an elite bereft of culture and a sense of civic duty, a mass of stupid Indians, and timid, selfish entrepreneurs. There are two main social forces: the military praetorians and the militant plebs. Both are either Indian or mestizo, and so radically incapable of either comprehending or practising republican duties and virtue.[55]

Subscription to convictions such as these was quite common within the civilian elite of Bolivia, and it entailed a difficult choice as to the degree of real and pretended participation in public affairs by those who felt themselves to be in but not of them. As in the case of the law, there is a tendency for modern historians to emphasise the huge chasm between theory and practice in the conduct of politics. Yet, apart from running the risk of emulating René Moreno's prejudices in a safe and sanitised contemporary idiom, such an attitude ignores one of the important qualities of rhetoric – that it is a balm for its own irrelevance.

It may have been either in this sense or in a more prosaic indulgence of his own pride that in 1866 Muñoz defended his loyalty to Melgarejo when urged by the minister of education, Jorge Oblitas, to betray the *caudillo*:

---

sincerity are the natural and most prominent characteristics of the gentleman. For the English it only matters if a man is energetic, reliable and honest. Talent itself does not matter much. On the contrary, they feel disdain for the man who is intelligent but duplicitous, inclined to intrigue and ingratiation. Neither do they greatly esteem wealth, which, as a rule, is seen as the product of circumstance. Moreover, no gentleman is ever born; they are always made. Any man of any social background can acquire such status through his conduct since this is a privilege that is conferred solely by moral behaviour. A man who plots, lies and cheats and is insincere can bank up all the rewards of fortune and talent … but he will never be a gentleman.

Pueblo Enfermo, La Paz 1975, pp. 76–7.

53. Ramón Sotomayor Valdés, *La Legación de Chile en Bolivia*, Santiago 1874, p. 29; Avelino Aramayo, *Apuntes sobre el estado industrial, económico y político de Bolivia*, Sucre 1871, p. 122.

54. José Fellmann Velarde, *Historia de Bolivia*, La Paz 1970, II, p. 201; Luis Antezana Ergueta, *El Feudalismo de Melgarejo y la Reforma Agraria*, La Paz 1970, p. 39.

55. Gabriel René Moreno, *Matanzas de Yañez*, La Paz 1976, p. 87.

The enemies of public tranquillity, suffering from the blows that they have been dealt, have now resorted to even more vile methods – they have begun to sow discord in the cabinet. On the one hand, they have beguiled the incautious Dr Oblitas, encouraging him ever further in the extraordinary delusion that he could take over the reins of the state. On the other, they have spread the rumour that I was a disloyal friend of General Melgarejo and the minister who was betraying the cause of December.

No, never! That infamy is reserved for an immoral foreigner who betrayed the man he called his father and a repugnant minister who, having been elevated by General Melgarejo from nowhere to the highest of positions, came to believe that he was able to do anything that took his fancy. That infamy belongs to [General Ruperto] Fernández and to Oblitas.[56] ... I greatly prefer the modest services I render on behalf of the glorious chief who commands me to seeking a post that I know I could not keep. When the *caudillo* whom I accompany thinks my services unnecessary I shall happily retire to the bosom of my family to concern myself with the education of my dear children. I am completely satisfied with the friendship of General Melgarejo and the confidence he has vested in me.[57]

One should not dismiss the possibility that Muñoz meant what he said. After the fawning self-vindication and easy abuse of a fresh set of enemies, Mariano reveals an evident vocation to be a subordinate, even if this is the best kind of subordination – to be directly under the president and so the second in the land.

Of course, this automatically entailed more than escalating enmities and anxious personal and policy manoeuvre. It also required that loyalty be focused on the person of the chief. Of this, as he revealed to his judges in 1850, Muñoz had an instinctive understanding. The question, then, is whether such 'loyalty' is authentic, sequential and unconditional or, on the other hand, dissembled, parallel and more fearfully calculating. In the case of Mariano Donato Muñoz the evidence tends to support the first interpretation – that he backed the incumbent chief precisely because he was the chief and because support for the prevailing order was intrinsically desirable as well as personally advantageous. The twisting *realpolitik* expressed in the 1850 trial seems to have been real and to have endured.

Muñoz's opposition to Linares runs against this interpretation, but the argument is fortified by the events of March 1865 when, scarcely twelve weeks in office, Muñoz

---

56. *General Ruperto Fernandez*, an Argentine, was Linares's minister of government and the leader of the coup which removed the president – to whom the soubriquet applied – in January 1861. In November of the same year Fernández rebelled again, this time against Achá, who had been given the presidency by a constitutional convention. Driven into exile, he ended up living in Tacna, the same Peruvian city that the Muñoz family was to make its home. *Jorge Oblitas*, born Oruro, 1831; graduated in law, Sucre. A renowned orator, he was Fernández's under-secretary when Achá was overthrown, which is why Muñoz links the two as traitors. Having rebelled against Melgarejo in Potosí in April 1866, Oblitas was forced into hiding, eventually surrendering to the authorities in Cochabamba in 1867. Maybe he chose that town because of its accumulating tradition of mercifulness. In the event, he was saved from the death sentence predictably pronounced by his court martial, but this time by the representatives of the diplomatic corps rather than the city's womenfolk. Thus spared, he subsequently encouraged General Daza to stage a coup in 1876, gaining the post of interior minister as a reward. In 1880 he served in the constitutional convention that followed the overthrow of Daza himself; foreign minister in 1885; vice-president in 1887. For Arguedas he was a worse opportunist even than Muñoz. To me he seems simply to have betrayed the men he served when they were in power, which Muñoz never did.

57. Quoted in Arguedas, *Historia*, pp. 286–7.

faced a momentary but decisive and dangerous dilemma. General Belzu, whom Mariano had served in office for six years, for whom he had gone into exile, and for whom he risked his life in battle, declared himself in revolt against the Melgarejo government, of which Mariano was now the leading servant.

Having spent a decade in Europe, Belzu, who was now an elderly man but still exceptionally popular in La Paz, slipped secretly over the border with Peru. As soon as his presence was known, he attracted large crowds and expressions of support from most of the regional authorities. At the time, Melgarejo, whose regime was based on a small, peripatetic army rather than local garrisons, was in Sucre, suppressing protest at his declaration of dictatorial powers. The prefect and local commander of La Paz went into hiding, and on 22 March Belzu took command of Bolivia's largest city without a fight and amidst great celebration.

It took Melgarejo five days to march his army from Sucre, and when it arrived at La Paz Colonel Tomás Peña led two companies over to Belzu's side, demonstrating the strong preference for a local rebel over a president from Cochabamba. Muñoz, however, stayed by Melgarejo's side throughout the march from Sucre and the street fighting in which the government forces – attacking barricades with muzzle-loading Minié rifles – took the heavier casualties: 122 dead and 160 wounded. The matter seemed decided, but Melgarejo, Colonel Narciso Campero and six *cuirasseurs* fought their way into the main square and entered the palace.

Belzu's bodyguard, thinking the entrants defeated and in the process of offering surrender, hesitated long enough to be overwhelmed. Although there are several versions of what happened next, all agree that when Melgarejo and his men entered the salon in search of the old *caudillo*, the amazed Belzu had no time to say anything intelligible before he was shot and fell mortally wounded to the sound of Melgarejo's blasphemies.[58] Belzu did not live long enough to reflect upon the mercy he had extended to Melgarejo in 1854; he had been hit by a rifle fired by a soldier, not a pistol handled by a student.

The classical brutalism of the scene was cemented when Melgarejo went out onto the balcony of the presidential palace to face a crowd unaware of what had happened within and still cheering for the supposed victor of the morning. 'Belzu is dead,' he shouted, 'Who lives now?' 'Viva Melgarejo!' came the confused reply, according to most accounts. However extraordinary the circumstances, there is no reason to disbelieve this mass expression of what was, after all, a blunt reality as well as a therapautic pragmatism of the type practised professionally by Muñoz.

Pablo Neruda describes this scene in a long section – 'Bolivia (22 March 1865)' – of *Canto General*:

---

58. Ibid., pp. 269–73; Aranzaes, *Revoluciones*, pp. 202–5. Campero, who was the only participant to write to about this event, was convinced that Belzu did not expect trouble, but as Campero soon split with Melgarejo, his account is not entirely disinterested. He did, however, write it before he became president, in 1880. *Recuerdos del regreso de Europa a Bolivia*, Paris 1874, pp. 70–71.

He enters the crowd, cuts through
nameless masses, clumsily scales
the estranged throne,
and attacks the conquering caudillo. Belzu
tumbles down, his starch soiled, broken his glass
that falls scattering its liquid light,
his breast riddled forever,
while the conflagration's solitary
assailant bloody buffalo
leans his bulk against the balcony,
shouting: 'Belzu died. Who's alive?
Answer.' And from the plaza,
a hoarse earthly voice, a black roar
of panic and horror, replies: 'Viva,
sí, Melgarejo, viva Melgarejo,'
the dead man's same followers,
who celebrated the cadaver bleeding
on the palace steps: 'Viva'
shouts the colossal puppet that covers
the entire balcony with tattered clothes,
slum mud and filthy blood.[59]

That night Melgarejo was prevailed upon to allow Belzu's estranged wife, Juana Manuela Gorriti, to take possession of his remains. One can also see the hand of Muñoz behind the decision to permit a public funeral, at which there was an outpouring of grief and support for the only *caudillo* in the nineteenth century who genuinely captured the sympathy of the urban masses. In July 1865 the Buenos Aires paper *La Nación* published a private letter written by Juana Manuela Gorriti:

On 27 March, two days after the date of your letter, Belzu, my husband, the man who plunged my whole destiny into grief, victor of a combat in which the people defeated the army, was murdered by the general commanding the army. They came and told me that Belzu had been shot in the chest, and I ran through the battle; I reached the place where his unfortunate corpse lay, picked it up in my arms and in them carried him to the house, to that home that he had abandoned so many years earlier. With my hands I washed his bloody body, and laid it out. I stayed with him all the time until he was placed in the tomb.[60]

In committing himself to Melgarejo, Mariano Donato Muñoz had, in fact, increased the risks as well as the considerable rewards of his political life. This was because

---

59. Pablo Neruda, *Canto General*, trans. Jack Schmitt, Berkeley 1991, p. 159. The translation by Jesús Lara of the Quechua poem in the dedication reads:

It is easy for those who leave
to still their hearts.
For those who stay there remains
the pain of not forgetting.

60. Quoted in María Gabriela Mizraje, 'La Escritura Velada: Historia y Biografía en Juana Manuela Gorriti', paper to conference of Latin American Studies Association, Washington 1995. A generously selective account of the life of her late husband is given in 'Belzu', Juana Manuela Gorriti, *Panoramas de la Vida*, II, Salta 1993, pp. 53–62.

Melgarejo's fierce dedication to the consumption of chicha (corn beer) and, when in the Altiplano (Andean Plain), beer (his favourite brand was Bass), created an almost schizophrenic atmosphere at his peripatetic court as the president veered from sober effusions of affection and generosity to arbitrary drunken acts of exceptional cruelty, aside from that kind of impulsive action taken in and around combat, as illustrated by the killing of Belzu.[61]

At the same time, Melgarejo's wildly erratic moods instilled in him a comprehensive sense of suspicion, exemplified by a saying that may be found today as graffito on the walls of Tarata: 'Trust? Never, not even of my shirt!' For this reason the president increasingly relied upon an inner circle based on the Sánchez family, favouring General José Aurelio Sánchez, brother of his lover Juana, whose sister Rosaura was married to Melgarejo's son Severo. Mariano Donato Muñoz undoubtedly belonged to this group as well as to that collaborationist strand of the republican aristocracy that either felt that it could bend the uneducated *caudillo* to its will or was reconciled to his intemperate behaviour as the least worst option available. Perhaps Mariano privately took a view similar to that adopted by Tomás O'Connor d'Arlach, who, notwithstanding his grandfather's support for Belzu, rejected any simple demonising of Melgarejo:

> Many have compared him with the tyrants of Paraguay and the Argentine Republic, even with those of ancient Rome. We who judge him calmly – *sine amore nec odio* – and with the severe impartiality of history, do not see in Melgarejo a scheming and gloomy tyrant like Tiberius, nor the folorn, suspecting and neurotic Dr Francia, nor the madly bloodthirsty Rosas. All we see in him is … an ingenuously good man in whom passion, sensual instincts and organic compulsion had driven out the seeds of virtue that a careful education might have salvaged. As a man, as a president, he exercised absolutely no influence on the political life of Bolivia because he represented no idea or party…. He was a true soldier, ignorant of civil law and appreciative only of personal physical force.[62]

Whatever the case, Muñoz's predisposition for mercy was taxed as frequently as the regime accumulated enemies by its arbitrary violence.[63]

Melgarejo only occasionally paid any heed to his minister's intercessions, but he never punished or turned against him for making them. Barely literate, he would not

---

61. *Mariano Melgarejo Valencia*, born Tarata, Cochabamba, 13 Apr. 1820. (Melgarejo always celebrated his birthday at Easter, whenever it fell.) Illegitimate son of Ignacia Melgarejo and José Linares. Married Rosa Rojas, whose brother Nicolás served as his minister of war. Served as a trooper under Santa Cruz and staged his first insubordination as a sergeant, aged twenty. In permanent opposition to the governments of Belzu and Cordoba, but of the sixteen generals in his army, fourteen had previously served Belzu. When in power he left his wife for the toothsome 23–year-old Juana Sánchez, who was the only person other than Muñoz who was able to exercise a moderating influence over him. According to Pablo Subieta, 'Melgarejo was exceptionally brave, but his bravery did not lie in any application of reason, as in the case of Caesar. Rather it came from the outbreak of fever, the boiling of blood, the cracking of nerves … the uncontrolled activity of delirium.' Tomás O'Connor d'Arlach, *El General Melgarejo: hechos y dichos de este hombre celebre* (1911), La Paz 1996, p. 11.

62. Ibid., pp. 7–8.

63. 'Blessed with great intelligence and a warm character, [Muñoz] placated the furious *caudillo* as well as possessing a marked talent for organisation.' Alberto Gutiérrez, *El Melgarejismo antes y después de Melgarejo*, La Paz 1972, p. 107.

have read Machiavelli, intuition and experience making redundant the advice of the Florentine sage:

> ... as for how a prince can assess his minister, here is an infallible guide: when you see a minister thinking more of himself than you, and seeking his own profit in everything he does, such a one will never be a good minister ... a man entrusted with the task of government ... must never concern himself with anything except the prince's affairs. To keep his minister up to the mark the prince, on his side, must be considerate towards him, must pay him honour, enrich him, put him in his debt, share with him both honours and responsibilities. Thus, the minister will see how dependent he is on the prince.[64]

It took some time, but by the middle of 1866 there was absolutely no way out for Muñoz. If Melgarejo fell in the normal manner, he would be looking to save his own skin, not that of others.

This story has already been so fierce that a single example will suffice. In March 1865, as Melgarejo and Muñoz were coming to the end of their forced march to challenge Belzu in La Paz, they met Colonel Vicente Cortés riding away from the city. Cortés, the military commander of La Paz, had — it will be recalled — gone into hiding when Belzu entered. He had very few men at his disposal and the overriding sentiment of the townsfolk was with the rebels.

When he realised that his flight had taken him straight into the path of Melgarejo himself, Cortés, anticipating his fate, begged forgiveness at the foot of the tyrant, who only drew back from shooting him in the head at Muñoz's plea. However, an instant after this, Melgarejo turned to some soldiers and ordered them to execute both Cortés and his horse, to make an example. The troops, who had already taken the mixture of gunpowder and liquor traditionally consumed before battle, immediately shot man and beast without skill and then began clubbing them to death. Campero, who several hours later would deliver victory to Melgarejo, made no effort to hide his disgust.[65]

The horrible price of even suspected betrayal established, Muñoz was frequently tipping off his friends, and even acquaintances opposed to the regime, such as the mine-owner Aniceto Arce, of plans to move against them or even just the president's mood.[66] It is small wonder that the US ambassador, John Caldwell, made every effort to keep in with the minister[67] or that the US entrepreneur Henry Meiggs, who struck a critical deal to sell Melgarejo new breech-loading Springfields, urged his son to keep well clear of political activity in the country:

---

64. Niccolo Machiavelli, *The Prince* (1513), Harmondsworth 1961, p. 125.

65. Aranzaes, *Revoluciones*, p. 202.

66. Ramiro Condarco Morales, *Aniceto Arce*, La Paz 1985, pp. 186–7.

67. Caldwell, aged sixty, arrived in Bolivia in November 1868, when Melgarejo was at the height of his power and keen to develop links with the USA. The general feted him sumptuously – dispatches run over with mention of banquets, well-ordered confectionery and 'a variety of beers from London' – but the man scarcely needed courting. Within a month of his arrival he reported to the secretary of state: 'I think it proper to say to your excellency ... that it is impossible to find on the face of the earth a people and a government more cordial or more friendly to the people and the government of the US.' No. 8, 4

... my advice now and always is for you to take no part, nor give any opinion in the matter, and beg all in our employ to do the same, as it is very easy, by a single word, to get us all into trouble. We are foreigners and working men and have no right nor any desire to take part in the political movements of the country in which we come to gain our subsistence.[68]

★

Although Melgarejo's personality marks him out within the formidable array of Bolivian *caudillos*, the reputation of his government rests no less on its efforts to alter the historic system of land tenure in the Andean region of the country, its issue of a debased coinage, and its cession of territory to neighbouring states. In all these areas Mariano Donato Muñoz is remembered not as an emollient counsellor but as the prime mover and overseer of policy.

Property law is complex at the best of times, but that in Bolivia had always been very complicated and conflictive, not only because it encompassed both European legislation and indigenous customary law but, more importantly, because the relation between the two lay at the heart of social control and economic management. In very broad terms, the effort made immediately following independence to transform the Aymara and Quechua people into individual property-owning citizens was abandoned in the 1830s. Throughout the period up to Melgarejo's regime the indigenous communities had continued to pay tribute, which remained the mainstay of the state budget, to hold lands in common without individual title to property, and to uphold those aspects of colonial practice which complemented local custom.

There has been a lively academic debate over the degree to which land was held in communal or private form (the latter normally as haciendas).[69] Mixing quite technical analysis of censuses and cadastral surveys with varying disposition to find capitalist penetration or indigenous resistance, this rich historiography must for our present purposes be passed by. Suffice it to say that whether one accepts the thesis that communal holdings were still very widespread in the 1860s or supports a more cautious and qualified assessment of forms of land and labour, once Mariano Muñoz resolved in early 1866 to alter the status quo of centuries, he had taken a decision of great gravity for public policy.

Of course, Muñoz took his initiative against the background of a debate echoing the ideas of Alberdi and Sarmiento over race, economic development and social management. In Bolivia this debate was conducted in intellectual terms almost

---

November 1868. Caldwell, who had dropped out of West Point, found Melgarejo 'a frank, generous, manly soldier'. No. 61, 31 May 1869. When he returned to Washington he did so bearing credentials as the Bolivian ambassador to the USA; these were rejected immediately.

68. Quoted in Watt Stewart, *Henry Meiggs: Yankee Pizarro*, Durham, N.C., 1946, p. 260.

69. Luis Antezana, *Feudalismo*; Erwin Grieshaber, *Survival of Indian Communities in Nineteenth-Century Bolivia*, PhD, University of North Carolina, 1977; Herbert S. Klein, *Haciendas and Ayllus: Rural Society in the Bolivian Andes in the 18th and 19th Centuries*, Stanford 1993; Alejandro Antezana, *Estructura Agraria en el Siglo XIX*, La Paz 1992; Alejandro Ovando Sanz, *El Tributo Indígena en las Finanzas de Bolivia en el Siglo XIX*, La Paz 1985; Tristan Platt, *Estado Boliviano y Ayllu Andino*, Lima 1982.

exclusively within the elite, which was by no means united around the proposition that communal lands should be brought into the market just as their produce had been since the conquest.[70] It is true that by the middle of the decade the silver mines were recovering from a recession that had lasted almost fifty years, but there is no strong sense that social and economic forces were straining for the resolution of the agrarian question.

It was, therefore, something of a shock to those (very few) who read it when on 20 March 1866 Muñoz published a decree that stipulated that all Indians must register title to property under their name within sixty days and at a charge of 25 to 100 pesos, which would 'consolidate' their lands and relieve them of any further obligation to pay the tribute. After two months all land not so registered would revert to the state and be sold by auction.

For Muñoz,

> Justice and humanity advance with the disappearance of the indigenous tribute … the distribution and subdivision of property, the liberation of dead capital and its placing in circulation; the rapid and progressive development of agriculture, which is one of the principal sources of public wealth, the reduction of the price of basic necessities; the habits of political morality and public order which are undoubtedly engendered by private property and work; the extinction of placemanship; and the increase in employment – all this, gentlemen, is why we instituted the sale of lands.[71]

It is still difficult to obtain a fine picture of what really happened next. It is, though, plain that whilst the breathtaking ambition of the degree was not remotely matched in practical transfers of property, a very large number of people stood to be deprived of their ancestral lands, and a very small group clustered around Muñoz amassed fortunes on paper and beyond. Many Indians ended up paying the tribute twice, and the communities around Lake Titicaca in particular were provoked into a residual hostility against the regime. Perhaps most important of all, Mariano Donato Muñoz's precipitate action – with its absurd demands of an overwhelmingly illiterate and deliberately underinformed indigenous society – laid a precedent for a much more consolidated strategy based on elite consensus in the next decade.

According to Jorge Alejandro Ovando Sanz, Muñoz's move was

> the substitution of the juridical fiction of state proprietorship of communal lands by the fiction of the proprietorship of the new purchasers. These buyers did not expel the members of the communities from the lands; they did not wish to nor could they have done. Equally, they did not move to or occupy the communities, except in very rare cases, and stayed in the cities with their new title deeds in their pockets.[72]

---

70. For the case for 'alienation', see José Vicente Dorado, *Proyecto de repartición de tierras y venta de ellas entre los indígenas*, Sucre 1864. The case against is made strongly in Avelino Aramayo, *Bolivia: Apuntes sobre el congreso de 1870*, Sucre 1871.

71. Quoted in Aramayo, *Bolivia*, p. 22.

72. *Tributo Indígena*, p. 169. Aramayo argued that the sale would do nothing to develop agriculture without massive investment of new capital, and it could only be enforced by no less a massive slaughter. *Bolivia*, pp. 23–5.

We should, however, note that some 100,000 adults paid tribute as members of communities, suggesting that over 500,000 people stood to be affected, and that by the time Melgarejo fell only 13 per cent of the communities had been 'consolidated' whilst 42 per cent had nominally reverted to the state.[73] Where, in those 'rare cases' mentioned by Ovando Sanz, lands were both bought — at knock-down prices with liberal credit offered by Meiggs's Banco Boliviano — and also occupied, the germs of a civil war were sown, to emerge every time central control loosened for the next hundred years. This legacy, then, remained into the 1960s, when the name of Mariano Donato Muñoz was still recognised by Bolivian *campesinos* as that of a historic enemy.

Such a popular memory is undoubtedly enhanced by the fact that throughout that period there were freely available as curios in the shops and stalls of the country one-peso coins that carried the effigies of Melgarejo and Muñoz and the slogan '*Al Valor y Al Talento*' (To Valor and to Talent). This coin — known ever since as the 'melgarejo' — was the brainchild of Jorge Oblitas, who ordered them struck in January 1866, when he was political chief of the south of the country and so had direct control over the mint at Potosí. However, Oblitas was not just trying to curry favour with his partners; he was also seeking to raise extra cash by issuing 400,000 debased coins at face value when their intrinsic worth was no more than 80 centavos. The predictable loss of confidence and hoarding of hard coin and gold provoked by this compelled the official withdrawal of the coin from circulation in October, when departmental commissions sitting for one day received 332,000 coins in return for payment of 83,000 pesos.[74] (Oblitas, of course, had already been thrown out of his job.)

Notwithstanding this sobering experience, the government of a country that traditionally produced silver and minted coin could scarcely resist the temptation to 'create money'. Thus, Melgarejo acquired a new coining machine from Philadelphia, and in 1867 farmed out a monopoly of coin issue to Clemente Torreti, who over the next two years issued 4.5 million pesos in exchange for silver worth 3.2 million — a profit margin that even with the cabinet's cut of 8 per cent made the contractor sufficiently nervous to seek the protection of the Prussian ambassador. (Not of much use in itself since Melgarejo was a decided Francophile, but in 1870 Teutonic tutelage must have seemed particularly reassuring.[75])

Although Muñoz did not take primary responsibility for the financial management of Bolivia in these years, there is no doubt that in the small cabinet of five or six ministers that he chaired he was an avid supporter of concessions to foreign capital. Meiggs, for example, funded the purchase of the communal lands through the Banco Boliviano, which was the first ever to issue notes; he also held nitrate and guano

---

73. Alejandro Antezana, *Estructura Agraria*, p. 200.

74. Julio Benavides, *Historia de la Moneda en Bolivia*, La Paz 1972, pp. 58–9. According to US Consul Charles Rand, the value of the debased peso had fallen to 25 cents within three years although coins were still trading at 40 cents. The value of the Chilean peso throughout all this stood at 91.275 cents. Rand to Washington, no. 14, 30 September 1870.

75. Luis Peñaloza, *Historia Económica de Bolivia*, La Paz 1947, II, pp. 12–15.

concessions on very good terms. The US consuls were not boasting when they reported that Melgarejo and Muñoz had a marked preference for American goods, machinery and services.[76] For Melgarejo the new Springfield and Remington rifles were vital to the military defence of his government; for Muñoz accelerated cash flow facilitated a politics of cooptation to balance the repression of the *caudillo*.

However, it was in his capacity as foreign minister that Mariano Donato Muñoz's appetite for income was most readily satisfied and most consequential for the future of a state that was thinly populated, poorly administered and incapable of protecting an extensive frontier. The temptation – or the obligation – to trade land for cash was too great.[77] In September 1866 Muñoz negotiated a new border with Chile at 24 degrees south – an effective surrender of rich reserves of copper and recently discovered nitrates – for a down payment of 400,000 pesos and a loan of 1.3 million. There is no doubt that Bolivia was already poorly placed to establish its authority over this littoral territory, but, equally, the willingness of the Melgarejo regime to treat with Santiago could not have curbed Chilean ambitions, hastening the loss of access to the sea that eventually came with defeat in the War of the Pacific in 1880. In 1866, though, Melgarejo was appointed an honorary general in the Chilean army.

At least the treaty with Chile corresponded to recognised areas of debate and dispute over inherited borders. That signed with Brazil in March 1867 – the Muñoz–Netto treaty – opened an entirely new arena by ceding unmarked territory to the neighbouring state well beyond the unchallenged line agreed by Spain and Portugal at the Treaty of Ildefonso in 1777. By moving the east–west line from 6 degrees 52 minutes to 10 degrees 20 minutes south in Brazil's favour, Muñoz diminished Bolivia by an area greater than that of Louisiana and Cork combined. Unsurprisingly, this treaty was widely viewed as an unnecessary sale at a very low price – 400,000 pesos again, but no supplementary loan – not only of the national patrimony but also of lands to which Bolivia had no inherent right since they had also been inherited from the Spanish Crown by Peru, which complained bitterly.[78]

The treaties produced one unanticipated outcome – the calling of a congress. Both Chile and Brazil naturally required that these important international agreements be ratified by some kind of convention or parliament in order that they might have official status beyond the imprimatur of an unelected cabinet minister, however authoritative and secure he might seem. As a result, it was necessary to call elections and restore the trappings of constitutionalism after a lapse of four years.

★

---

76. Rand to Washington, no. 14, 30 September 1870.

77. It is notable that two contemporary sources insist that any Bolivian government would have been obliged to implement a foreign policy similar to that taken under Melgarejo and Muñoz simply because of the balance of regional power. Thajmara (Isaac Tamayo), *Habla Melgarejo*, La Paz 1914 (Tamayo was a member of the 1868 Convention); Juan Pablo Gómez, *Vida, Pasión y Muerte del General Mariano Melgarejo*, Lima 1872/La Paz 1980 (Gómez was a Colombian).

78. J. Valerie Fifer, *Bolivia: Land, Location and Politics since 1825*, Cambridge 1972, pp. 55–6, 96–7, 100–102; Morales, *Primeros Cien Años*, II, pp. 140, 161.

By 1868 the forces opposed to Melgarejo were starting to take on the form of a genuine political movement, but they were still too divided by personalism to pose a serious threat to this, the most aggressive and least predictable of the *caudillos*. As a consequence, Mariano Donato Muñoz was able to preside over what approximated to the working of constitutional procedure without excessive interruption or upset. Ballivián's son was allowed to stand against the president in the election and won a creditable 8 per cent of the 22,000 votes cast. Melgarejo seemed to like the idea of popular mandates, and the congress ratified the treaties with sufficiently little complaint for him to permit another session in 1870.

This was undoubtedly Muñoz's finest hour. The political temper was rising fast and the opposition was well represented in congress, but the regime was supremely confident. Muñoz used the floor of the chamber to praise Melgarejo and defend his own policies at great length and with minimal qualification before a full audience in a charged atmosphere. The proceeds of dictatorship could be paraded as if democratic, and the prerogatives of power displayed as though they were honestly acquired and earnestly discharged. Moreover, acclamation was assured – the Bolivian congress, as described shortly after by Edward Matthews (who greatly preferred it to the House of Commons), was not a place for the faint-hearted: the crowds in the gallery

> frequently interrupted the speakers with approving hurrahs for a popular sentiment, or groans, cat-calls, hisses and other lively expressions of disgust, for one that does not coincide with the mob's whim of the moment ... at several sittings I fully expected to see a free fight in the Congress Hall.[79]

Of course, it could not last. In November 1870 Campero declared himself in revolt in Potosí and threw in his lot with Agustín Morales, the man who had failed to kill Belzu in 1850 but liked Melgarejo no better for having succeeded in this fifteen years later. Melgarejo himself was now rarely sober, and in riding to meet the rebels he fell off his horse Holofernes – a Chilean grey of great size and presence but poor discipline – and dislocated a knee. The US embassy reported that without his presence the army's order and commitment flagged notably, but it had to keep moving because once the rebels retreated in Potosí, a new revolt, headed by Morales himself, flared up in La Paz.

This rebellion began in the normal way – with cash hand-outs for troops who changed sides, proclamations vilifying the regime and assuring imminent deliverance, the disappearance of the authorities into hiding, and a predictably high degree of confusion: 'A Colonel Gutiérrez, who had entered enthusiastically into the revolution, on entering the courtyard became so excited that he cried out "*Viva* Melgarejo!" – a mistake that instantly cost him his life.'[80]

---

79. Edward D. Matthews, *Up the Amazon and Madeira Rivers through Bolivia and Peru*, London 1879, p. 267.
80. Rand to Washington, no. 15, 9 November 1870.

However, when Morales assumed command, the city took on a much more ordered and committed air. Fully aware of the regime's weak points, Morales broke two taboos: he took the womenfolk of the rulers hostage, and he made no effort to control the Indian agitation that was spreading throughout the Altiplano.

Thus, Rosaura de Muñoz and Juana Sánchez were arrested, threatened with execution, and offered for ransom at 50,000 pesos and 30,000 pesos respectively – a price differential that was telling in terms of Muñoz's supposed assets, and one which was publicly and shamelessly defended by Morales's minister, Casimiro Corral.[81] At the same time, Melgarejo's exhausted forces were the first natural target of the indigenous communities, which not only withheld supplies and forage but also picked off stragglers and waited to move in on any defeated party.

By the time Melgarejo reached El Alto – on 15 January 1871 – the balance of forces was strongly against him even though his army was larger in size. The president remained deeply distracted over the uncertain fate of Juana Sánchez, and he never took direct command of his troops. Mariano Donato Muñoz probably sensed the *finis*, but he would anyway almost certainly have essayed a resolution through words rather than blood. In all events, his last act in office was an effort to halt the battle, in a letter addressed to Corral:

Alto de La Paz, 15 January 1871.
To Señor Doctor don Casimiro Corral,
Secretary General of the Revolutionary Government.

Sir,

The undersigned secretary of state has received an order from His Excellency the Captain General don Mariano Melgarejo, constitutional president of the republic, to write to don Casimiro Corral ... to communicate to him that the national army, having completed its great mission of pacifying the south of the republic, as he was able to witness on 28 November last ... is now positioned ready to complete its no less momentous task of tranquillising the north ... but before the national army makes use of its weapons in fulfilment of its sacred commitment to the fatherland, His Excellency calls upon the patriotism of all Bolivians who find themselves within the orbit of this insurrection, inviting them to make a gift to this land which we all love by setting aside their arms and avoiding the unnecessary effusion of blood which would be fruitless in seeking the objectives the rebels have proclaimed and which would sterilise the vigorous seeds of material progress and moral grandeur that have been sown.

Muñoz carried on in this vein for several more paragraphs before reaching the bottom line: Melgarejo promised that his army would enter the city peacefully; he would take no prisoners and conduct no repression; and he promised to leave the presidency within ten days.

Corral was having none of it. Having watched Melgarejo and Muñoz at work for the last six years, he was clearly intent on matching them and could harbour no

---

81. *Memoria de Secretario Jeneral del Estado, Dr Casimiro Corral, que presenta a la Asamblea Constituyente de 1871*, Sucre 1871, p. 8.

delusions over the price of failure. Although the ransom money was delivered, he did not yet release Rosaura and Juana, and he replied to Muñoz in kind:

> His Excellency Señor Morales and the other leaders of the revolution have not come here with some idea of imposing our will on the nation. We were called upon by the majority of Bolivians, and we have undertaken a solemn commitment to free them from the unspeakable tyranny of Melgarejo, who has committed terrible and bloody acts, reducing Bolivia to complete ruin with his cruelty and arbitrary decisions.
>
> You, Sir, as you are perfectly well aware, form part of a government that has committed every possible crime, engaged ostentatiously in vice, and failed to avoid or omit any mistake, insult or abuse in its administration of this country.... In the name of a generous people, in the cause of civilisation, and on behalf of His Excellency the Supreme Chief of the Revolution I now offer to General Melgarejo, and to those who apparently want to support him for another ten days, full personal guarantees against retribution and even forgiveness for the repugnant offences that they have committed.
>
> With sentiments of the highest consideration, and in the conviction that you will, along with the others, grasp this opportunity to reconcile yourself with the people, I am your obedient servant,
>
> Casimiro Corral.[82]

Just as Melgarejo had met his match in Morales, so had Muñoz in Corral. This time the barricades were stoutly defended and no chances taken. The rebels readily held their ground, the government fell, and the 'invincible army' that had held sway over the country since December 1864 was driven into headlong flight across the Altiplano to the Peruvian border thirty miles off. Many – including four generals and dozens of officers – did not make it, being captured and put to death in the communities through which they had to pass.

Corral and Morales reversed the agrarian legislation, but it would soon be replaced by more effective steps to achieve the same end. The new government could do nothing about the international treaties except rail against the minister who had signed them. And although it promised to reform the currency, that too proved an insuperable obstacle. It did, however, release Rosaura Muñoz and Juana Sánchez. Both Melgarejo and Muñoz managed to escape – Melgarejo to Chile, where he mistakenly thought he would be protected and fêted, and Muñoz back to Tacna, where he wrote a long memorandum of self-exculpation to the congress of 1871.

Although he leant some support to the ambitions of Rosaura's brother, General Quintin Quevedo, Muñoz's political days were over. The family settled in Tacna, and were in that city at the outbreak of the War of the Pacific, when their eldest son, Andrés, served as a medical orderly for the Allied Peruvian–Bolivian army. He later became a doctor, and once the family was permitted to return to Bolivia in the 1880s, his political career flourished nearly as fully as had that of his father, but in much more stable times.[83] Mariano died peacefully in La Paz in 1894, at the age of seventy-two.

---

82. Quoted in Gutiérrez, *Melgarejismo*, pp. 249–53.

Muñoz had outlived Melgarejo by more than twenty years. Lonely and vilified in Santiago, the dictator, who had just passed the age of fifty, made his way to Lima in an effort to see Juana Sánchez, who had spurned him after his overthrow and refused all contact. After several days making futile calls, Melgarejo tried to force an entry into the Sánchez household on Gallinacitos Street in the evening of 23 November 1871. As he entered the door he was shot twice in the face by Juana's brother, General José Aurelio Sánchez, Melgarejo's favourite when he was in power. He died three hours later and was given a full military funeral on 25 November, paid for by the Bolivian embassy, at the church of Nuestra Señora de la Merced.[84]

For 124 years Melgarejo's body lay intact in niche 16A of the San Eloy section of the 'Presbítero Maestro' Cemetery, a couple of miles outside the centre of Lima. Then, in June 1995 Carlos and Rosario Rodríguez led a group from Tarata – no less proud of Melgarejo for his superhuman powers than they are of another son of their small valley town, President René Barrientos Ortuño (1919–69); a dead general equally associated with occult matters – to repatriate the skull of the *caudillo*. However, once the relic had been returned to the Church of San Severino by the Centro Espiritista 'Luz, Amor y Esperanza' there was doubt and division over what precisely to do with the head of 'Hermano Erasto': inter it or put it on display.

A *cabildo* (town council) was held to decide the matter, but there was no clear majority for either option. Accordingly, it was resolved to consult Melgarejo himself, and a medium was contracted for this purpose. She held her seance in San Severino, which was packed as she crawled up the aisle to the altar, and in a rasping tenor voice announced that the head could be exhibited, but only if it was accorded proper respect. The decision was then made in a correct, democratic manner.

The skull may now be viewed – dimly behind darkly smoked glass, resting on a folded national flag – in a niche on the left of the aisle of San Severino.[85] The luxuriant hair of Melgarejo's beard remains, as do his exceptionally good teeth. Of course, it was this beard that Neruda chose as the symbol of the tyranny and as an object of vilification that no *Tarateño* could accept:

> Mark of Melgarejo,
> besotted beast, filthy scum
> of betrayed minerals,
> beard of infamy, horrendous beard
> above the embittered mountains,

---

83. *Andrés Muñoz*, born Cochabamba, 1859. Graduated in medicine, University of San Marcos, Lima. Ambulance service, War of Pacific, 1879–80. Bolivian delegate to the Panamerican Health Congress, 1888. Participated in the victorious revolution of the Liberal Party, 1898, with the rank of colonel. Dean of Faculty of Medicine, Universidad de San Andrés, La Paz. Minister of education, 1901–03; ambassador to Brazil; prefect of Oruro, 1905; senator, 1906–17; minister of war, 1917. Died Santiago, 1922.

84. Tomás O'Connor d'Arlach, *Doña Juana Sánchez* (1895), La Paz 1969, pp. 161–2; Vicente Terán Erquicia, *La Muerte del Tirano: Asesinato del General Melgarejo en Lima*, La Paz 1980.

85. My thanks to Víctor Hugo Ponce de León, who showed me Melgarejo's now ruined birthplace, the site of a more extemporised shrine.

beard dragged in delirium,
beard filled with bloodclots,
beard discovered in gangrenous
nightmares, roving beard
galloping in the pastures,
cohabiting in the parlours,
while the Indian and his burden traverse
the last sheet of oxygen,
trotting through the bled
corridors of poverty.[86]

As if in answer to Neruda's wish, a large triangular hole at the junction between the left parietal and frontal bones is testimony to the marksmanship of José Aurelio Sánchez. Plaques are beginning to appear. When I visited, the latest stated, 'Gracias, Hermanito Mariano, por los favores recibidos.'

---

86. *Canto General*, pp. 157–8.

EMPIRES AT WAR
(AND NEARLY SO)

BECOMING AMERICAN (AGAIN)

'Memories' that are retold by those who have not themselves directly lived them almost inevitably become transposed, convoluted and reinvented. They are, though, hardly less 'historical' as a result. This is clear enough in the case of official histories, endlessly recycled by the educational and entertainment industries, venerated in the offices of a state that derives much of its legitimacy from them, and so comfortably ensconced in the psyche of the majority that they can be permitted the status of myth. However, in the case of obscure and oppressed sectors of society historical memory is never so smoothly expressed, even when it embodies a more vibrant catharsis of heroism or promise of redemption. Of course, such traditions can quite readily be junked by individuals brought up within them, or they can be fitted piecemeal into the mainstream. But even 170 years after the first removal of the tribes and 140 years after the abolition of slavery in the USA it is hard to find a popular image of Indian or African Americanism without a strong component of exclusion and conflict. Indeed, these alternative histories have become so familiar that in recent years they have been provided with formal recognition by fiat through public and political 'correctness', not least because they cannot be naturally incorporated into any 'melting pot' vision of the past.

By the last decade of the twentieth century one could discern the beginnings of a similar process with respect to the US population of Mexican origin. As with the experience of Native Americans, this past involved military defeat, territorial loss and the elimination of a state. But for Mexicans the annihilation of community was not comprehensive – certainly not the social death that was slavery – and even in the era of globalisation and the North American Free Trade Area (NAFTA) there remains in place a polity that incarnates difference, symbolises independence, and serves as a rememberance of past antagonism. The contemporary image of this separation naturally has its focus on the state borders at the Rio Grande and immigration into 'the North' whereas prior to 1847 Mexico extended to Oregon, and before 1836 it included places that today go by the names of Houston, Austin and Dallas – what Carlos Fuentes calls 'airport names', wrenched from their historical roots by constant usage. Equally, as Richard Rodríguez notes,

> ... in the years following the Mexican–American War, pragmatic Americans never thought to change the Spanish names on the map, though Americans seemed to have agreed among themselves to mispronounce all Spanish names. And Americans have their leveling ways: La Ciudad de Nuestra Señora la Reina de los Angeles de Perciuncula has become, in one hundred years, L.A.[1]

---

1. Carlos Fuentes, *Myself with Others*, London 1988, p. 15; Richard Rodríguez, *Days of Obligation: An Argument with My Mexican Father*, New York 1992, pp. 121–2.

Although Rodríguez is not absolutely correct in this – in January 1847 the new Anglo-American authorities ordained that the settlement known locally as Yerba Buena be called San Francisco – his point about subliminal appropriation is a strong one, and it is poignantly driven home by the experience of his own family:

> Consider my father: when he decided to apply for American citizenship, my father told no one, none of his friends, those men with whom he had come to this country looking for work. American citizenship would have seemed a betrayal of Mexico, a sin against memory. One afternoon, like a man with something to hide, my father slipped away. He went downtown to the Federal building in Sacramento and disappeared into America.[2]

For Rodríguez himself, bred in US California and speaking Spanish with some difficulty, this Janus-like existence incorporates some of the 'historioculturalist' motifs used by Morse and Dealy but is best explained in terms of gender:

> America does not lend itself to sexual metaphor as easily as Mexico does. George Washington is the father of the country, we say. We speak of the Founding Fathers. The legend ascribed to the Statue of Liberty is childlessness.
>
> America is an immigrant country. Motherhood – parenthood – is less our point than adoption. If I had to assign gender to America, I would notice the consensus of the rest of the world. When America is burned in effigy, a male is burned. Americans themselves speak of Uncle Sam. Uncle Sam is the personification of conscription.
>
> During World War II hundreds of thousands of Mexican Americans were drafted to fight in Europe and in Asia. And they went, submitting themselves to a commonweal. Not a very Mexican thing to do, for Mexico had taught us always that we lived apart from history in the realm of *tú*.
>
> It was Uncle Sam who shaved the sideburns from that generation of Mexican Americans. Like the Goddess of Liberty, Uncle Sam has no children of his own. In a way, Sam represents necessary evil to the American imagination. He steals children to make men of them, mocks all reticence, all modesty, all memory. Uncle Sam is a hectoring Yankee, a skinflint uncle, gaunt, uncouth, unloved. He is the American Savonarola – hater of moonshine, destroyer of stills, burner of cocaine. Free enterprise is curiously an evasion of Uncle Sam, as is sentimentality. Sam has no patience with mama's boys. That includes Mama Mexico, ma'am.
>
> You betray Uncle Sam by favoring private over public life, by seeking to exempt yourself: by cheating on your income taxes, by avoiding jury duty, by trying to keep your boy on the farm. These are legal offenses. Betrayal of Mother Mexico, on the other hand, is a sin against a natural law, a failure of memory.[3]

---

2. *Days of Obligation*, p. 50. Even the renaming of Yerba Buena in 1847 was undertaken on strictly instrumentalist grounds:

> Whereas, the local name of Yerba Buena, as applied to the settlement or town of San Francisco, is unknown beyond the district; and has been applied from the local name of the cove, on which the town is built: Therefore, to prevent confusion and mistakes in public documents, in that the town may have the advantage of the name given in the public map, IT IS HEREBY ORDAINED that the name of SAN FRANCISCO shall hereafter be used.

California Star, 30 Jan. 1847, quoted in Roger W. Lotchin, *San Francisco, 1846–1856: From Hamlet to City*, Urbana, Ill., 1974, p. 33.

3. *Days of Obligation*, pp. 62–3.

In 1939, when the prime Mexican American memory of conscription remained that from the war of 1847 precisely against Uncle Sam, Carlos Fuentes was taken by his father to the old RKO-Keith cinema in Washington:

> [The film] was called *Man of Conquest* and it starred Richard Dix as Sam Houston. When Dix/Houston proclaimed the secession of the Republic of Texas from Mexico, I jumped on the theater seat and proclaimed on my own and from the full height of my nationalist ten years, 'Viva México! Death to the Gringos!' My embarrassed father hauled me from the theater, but his pride in me could not resist leaking my first rebellious act to the *Washington Star*.[4]

Eleven years later, in *The Labyrinth of Solitude*, Octavio Paz referred to 'one of the most unjust wars in the history of imperialist expansion', but also remarked that, 'if, as Ortega y Gasset said, a nation is not really a nation unless it has both a past that is capable of animating dissimilar spirits and of giving unity and transcendence to solitary efforts, then Mexico was born during the epoch of the Reform [after the war of 1847]'.[5] For Paz,

> Independence was a false beginning; it freed us from Madrid, but not from our past. To the evils we had inherited we added others that were all our own. As our dreams of modernization faded, the fascination exerted on us by the United States grew. The war of aggression of 1847 turned it into an obsession. An ambivalent fascination: at one and the same time the titan was the enemy of our identity and the unacknowledged model for what we would most like to be. In addition to being a political and social ideal, the United States was an interventionist power, an aggressor.[6]

Most explanations of their military defeat by Mexicans of the time were more painfully prosaic but essentially similar. That penned by José María Roa Barcena, who witnessed the invasion and collapse as a twenty-year-old, is quite representative:

> In the war with the USA we were in every respect in a very disadvantageous position. In addition to racial inferiority, one must add the weakness of our social and political organization, demoralization, exhaustion and impoverishment resulting from 25 years of civil war. We possessed an army that was too small, composed of troops who had been pressganged, armed with outdated weapons sold to us by England, without means of transport, ambulances or supplies. Federalism, which for the enemy was the bond that held different states together, was for us the element which had sundered ancient unity and established separate states.[7]

Although not correct in every particular and easy to interpret as a self-serving excuse for national disgrace, Roa Barcena's explanation was widely shared north of what had become the new border at the Rio Grande. In 1847 Albert Gallatin, despite being in his eighty-seventh year, was so incensed by Washington's aggression and so fearful of its impact upon republican and democratic morality at home that he penned

---

4. *Myself with Others*, pp. 8–9.
5. *The Labyrinth of Solitude: Life and Thought in Mexico* (1950), London 1967, pp. 116, 118.
6. *One Earth, Four or Five Worlds*, London 1988, p. 147.
7. *Recuerdos de la invasión norteamericana (1846–1848)*, Mexico 1947, I, pp. 341–2.

a pamphlet in condemnation of the war and revindication of the moral universe he associated with the state of Jefferson and Madison. Yet even though it was written before the end of hostilities, Gallatin's broadside presented the outcome of the war as a foregone conclusion:

> It seems certain that Mexico must ultimately submit to such terms of peace as the United States shall dictate. An heterogeneous population of seven millions, with very limited resources and no credit, distracted by internal dissensions and by the ambitions of its chiefs, a prey by turns to anarchy and to civil usurpers, occupying among the nations of the civilized world either physically or mentally, whether in political education, social state or any other respect, but an inferior position, cannot contend successfully with an energetic, intelligent, enlightened and united nation of twenty millions, possessed of unlimited resources and credit, and enjoying all the benefits of a regular, strong and free government.[8]

Here Gallatin itemises the triumphalist claims of US exceptionalism without placing them at the service of what had already become known as 'manifest destiny', or the providential imprimatur to expand westwards (and elsewhere) at the expense of other (distant or inferior) peoples. The aged statesman reminds us that it was perfectly possible to subscribe to notions of US supremacism without investing them with an imperialist vocation.

Gallatin's image, like Roa Barcena's, is one of abstractions, collectivities and general conditions. There is little pulse of that historical memory conducive to fear and loathing or the distress and love that promote patriotism even when, as Paz would have it, no nation yet exists. The 'memory' revived by the young Carlos Fuentes in the Washington cinema was less of Mexico's lack of public education or creditworthiness than of the experience of its soldiers fleeing after defeat by General Winfield Scott's army at Cerro Gordo in April 1847 (see Appendix 1 for a chronology of the war):

> They poured through the town [Jalapa] that evening and the day following ... in the wildest disorder, some mounted on donkeys, some on mules, some on foot, many of the officers without hats or swords, others wrapped in the dusty coat of a private, and all cursing, gesticulating and actually weeping like men crazed. They had been so confident of success that the reverse seemed almost heart-breaking.[9]

Five months later the death of six cadets – the *niños heroes* – amidst the bloody and chaotic defence of the capital yielded a symbol of heroism that palliated the shame and would become a keystone in Mexico's own 'official history', competing with the Alamo as a schoolbook token of abnegation and sacrifice. But if for Mexicans 'Houston' today represents the sky-scrapered city rising out of the deltalands of the San Jacinto river rather than the burly Virginian who won Texan independence at the battle of the same name, the *niños heroes* are completely unknown to most US citizens, even as the name of a metro station.

---

8. 'Peace with Mexico', in Henry Adams (ed.,) *Writings of Albert Gallatin*, Philadelphia 1879, IV, p. 557.
9. Bayard Taylor, *Eldorado*, II, New York 1850, p. 193.

Thomas Carlyle.

Lord Palmerston, photographed
in 1858 by Graham Vivian.

Juan Manuel Rosas.

Mariano Donato Muñoz
posing amiably as a minister.

General Mariano
Melgarejo (seated
centre), with his
cabinet, including
Muñoz (right).

Padre Zefferino Muzzani,
laid out for burial at the Franciscan
monastery nearly fifty years after
the release of Anselma Condori.

The Franciscan community of Tarija at the end of the nineteenth century.

General Francisco Burdett O'Connor,
pictured when Melgarejo was president of Bolivia.

Francisca Ruyloba de O'Connor, in a fine dress bought in Tarija.
This portrait was dedicated to Mariano Donato Muñoz.

Manuel Isidoro Belzu, probably in Paris after he had left the presidency of Bolivia in 1855. Ten years later Belzu would be killed by Melgarejo.

Agustín Morales, who tried to kill
both Belzu and Melgarejo.

Barricades in Calle Comercio, La Paz, January 1871,
when Melgarejo was overthrown.

James Buchanan as president.

Melgarejo's skull,
currently displayed in the
church of San Severino, Tarata.

James Polk as president.

Albert Gallatin.

Zachary Taylor.

'Old Fuss and Feathers': General Winfield Scott a decade after the Mexican War.

Antonio López de Santa Anna.

William Walker.

US volunteers in Mexico.
The figure on the right has been
identified as Captain Moses Merrill,
who appears to have 'seen the
elephant'. Merrill was killed at
Molino del Rey on 8 September
1847.

An elite family of Mexican California at the start
of the Anglo-American domination.

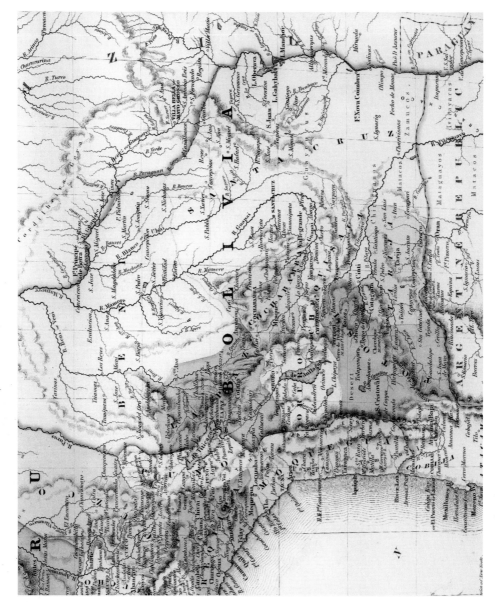

Map of Bolivia by Joseph Colton, for whom not even Hinton Helper could secure payment.

The issue is, of course, much more consequential than the general maintenance of educational standards in historical geography or sensitivity to the civic traditions of neighbouring countries. There are millions of Mexican Americans who, like Carlos Fuentes, would instinctively cry 'Viva México!' in the face of some hamfisted Holly-wood confection but who also, as inhabitants of the USA, respond like Richard Rodríguez:

> At some celebration – we went to so many when I was a boy – a man in the crowd filled his lungs with American air to crow over all ¡VIVA MEXICO! Everyone cheered. My parents cheered. The band played louder. Why VIVA MEXICO? The country that had betrayed them? The country that had forced them to live elsewhere?[10]

In 1945, when the Mexican American GIs were being demobilised, 2.5 per cent of the US population of 140 million was of Hispanic (overwhelmingly Mexican) origin. Fifty years later over 10 per cent of the 260 million inhabitants was of Hispanic descent, there being more legal immigrants from Mexico than from all of Europe combined. In 1996 163,500 of the 916,000 immigrants formally admitted to the USA came from Mexico, the 7 million Mexican immigrants in the country constituting about a third of its foreign-born population.[11] Moreover, the overall process is acceler-ating, with projections of the Hispanic share of the US population rising from 11 per cent of 270 million (29 million) in 1998 to 24.5 per cent of 393 million (96.5 million) in 2050. Of course, this growth will largely reflect expansion of the locally established population rather than new immigration, and in the 1980s and 1990s non-Mexicans accounted for nearly a half of all Hispanic immigrants.[12] None the less, the scenario is not only of a population half comprised of ethnic 'minorities' (Hispanic 24.5 per cent; Black 13.6 per cent; Asian 8.2 per cent), or of one of the largest Latin populations in the western hemisphere, but also of territory conquered from Mexico 200 years earlier being repopulated by people of the same ethnic origin as those defeated in 1847.

At that time the term *californio* was universally understood to refer to a Spanish-speaking resident of the Mexican state. By the 1860 census half of the 300,000 Californians were 'foreign-born', but it was from Europe that these people hailed (20 per cent of them from Ireland), and Mexicans comprised less than 5 per cent of all the state's inhabitants. Some 130 years later their descendants and those of the Anglo-American settlers, living in one of the world's wealthiest economies, were asked to vote on a proposition (no. 187) which reflected acute anxiety that another reversal was underway and required a strict exclusionary response of withdrawing welfare from those without the right papers:

---

10. *Days of Obligation*, p. 53.

11. Marcelo M. Suárez Orozco, 'Latin American Immigration to the United States: Some Interdiscipli-nary Observations', in Victor Bulmer-Thomas and James Dunkerley (eds), *United States–Latin American Relations: Analysing the New Agenda*, London 1999, pp. 228–9.

12. Ibid., p. 228; *Guardian*, 16 July 1998.

[The People of California] have suffered and are suffering economic hardship caused by the presence of illegal aliens in this state. That they have suffered and are suffering personal injury and damage caused by the criminal conduct of illegal aliens in this state.

That they have a right to the protection of their government from any person or persons entering this country unlawfully. Therefore, the people of California declare their intention to provide for cooperation between their agencies of state and local government with the federal government, and to establish a system of required notification by and between such agencies to prevent illegal aliens in the United States from receiving benefits or public services in the State of California.

The fact that in the early stages of the campaign over this proposition a significant proportion of the legal immigrant population favoured its implementation suggests the depth of concern in all social sectors over illegal immigration as well as some ambivalence over identity of the type expressed by Paz and Rodríguez. On the other hand, the eventual failure to secure a punitive platform based on thinly veiled racist scares reflects the existence of a Latino–liberal constituency capable of resisting the lure of chauvinist polarisation.

The lack of any historical substance in the debate over Proposition 187 is hardly surprising quite apart from the fact that it related to a narrow – if critical – issue of public policy. Mainstream Latino opinion had long since subjected Paz's ambivalence over the 1847 war to further modulation, the account in the *Hispanic Almanac* being typically judicious:

> ... in February 1845, the United States voted for the annexation of Texas, and Mexico broke off relations but stopped short of declaring war. Apparently, Mexico at this point was about to recognise Texas's independence and did not want any border problems.... Still, the issue that eventually brought the two nations into warfare was the matter of the boundary. When Texans declared their independence in 1836, they claimed the lower Rio Grande as their southern border. The Mexicans insisted that the Nueces River, a few hundred miles to the north, was the border. With the annexation, the United States accepted the Texan version of the boundary dispute.
>
> It is no secret that many Anglo-Americans wanted to fulfill their Manifest Destiny of expanding their country all the way to the Pacific coast.... In the fall of 1845 [President James K. Polk] sent John Slidell to Mexico with an offer of 25 million dollars for California, but Mexican officials refused to even see him. General Zachary Taylor was then sent across the Nueces River to set up a blockade of the Rio Grande at its mouth at Port Isabel, and Mexicans retaliated by attacking the U.S. troops on April 25 1846. Casualties ensued. President Polk immediately went to Congress and obtained a declaration of war against Mexico.
>
> Two years of war followed. That it took so long was somewhat surprising, considering Mexico's weak political position ... Nonetheless, the Mexican will to resist was underestimated, and it was difficult for an inexperienced U.S. army to fight on foreign soil.... Not all Americans supported the war. Newspapers carried reports that General Scott had admitted that his men had committed horrible atrocities.... The Mexicans refused to come to the bargaining table until they were thoroughly routed.[13]

---

13. Nicolás Kanellos (ed.), *The Hispanic Almanac: From Columbus to Corporate America*, Detroit 1994, pp. 80–81.

On the Anglo-American side the war seems barely to figure in the popular mind beyond the exploits of Texan annexation that preceded it. Even in the academic literature there is a prolonged dearth of serious work between Justin Smith's exhaustive, emphatic and enduring two-volume study of 1919 and a spate of fresh assessments in the late 1960s and early 1970s best represented by Jack Bauer's orthodox general survey. In his introduction to that volume Robert W. Johannsen devotes several paragraphs to analogies with the Vietnam War, particularly in terms of domestic political dissent. The fact that the Mexican War was 'the most reviled in American history – at least until the Vietnam War of the 1960s' may well explain both the lack of modern attention to it and the political awkwardness with which Anglo-America addresses its memory.[14] In 1973, a year before Bauer's book appeared, John Schroeder published a volume dedicated entirely to internal politial opposition to 'Mr Polk's war' in which, again linking it with the experience of Vietnam, he sought to rebut 'the popular myth ... that the American people have patriotically suspended their political differences when the nation was at war'.[15] For Schroeder, World War II is the only conflict for which this myth might genuinely hold true – a conviction probably encouraged by Samuel Eliot Morison's earlier study of dissent in the wars of 1812 and 1898 as well as that of 1847.[16]

A quarter of a century after the US withdrawal from Vietnam such similarities seem somewhat less strong, and if the 1847 war has not occupied a prominent place in the public memory of Anglo-America, this is scarcely because it was at the time subjected to widespread repudiation. In fact, such was popular support for the war in the north-west that, when asked if he would condemn the conflict as he had done that of 1812, the leading Chicago Whig Justin Butterfield replied, 'No, indeed! I opposed one war, and it ruined me. From now on I am for war, pestilence and famine.'[17] As we shall see, the war raised sharp dilemmas for those who disliked it, and whilst the optic of Vietnam is partly useful for understanding the strains on republican morality and American identity, it can too readily be exaggerated.

There is another, strong reason why the Mexican War remains poorly known inside the USA. As Edward Moseley and Paul Clark declare almost apologetically at the start of their historical dictionary, it was to be overshadowed by the far bloodier and politically consequential Civil War just thirteen years after the Treaty of Guadalupe Hidalgo.[18] The territorial gains resulting from military victory in 1847 were huge – 500,000 square miles (a million if Texas is included) or half of Mexico's landmass at independence – but on the US side the human cost of acquiring this land did not

---

14. K. Jack Bauer, *The Mexican War, 1846–1848*, Lincoln, Nebr., 1992, pp. xv–xvi.

15. John H. Schroeder, *Mr Polk's War: American Opposition and Dissent, 1846–1848*, Madison 1973, p. ix.

16. S.E. Morison (ed.), *Dissent in Three American Wars*, Cambridge, Mass., 1970. The chapter on Mexico was by Frederick Merk; that on 1812 by Morison; and that on the Spanish–American War by Frank Freidel.

17. Quoted in David Herbert Donald, *Lincoln*, New York 1995, p. 126.

18. Edward H. Moseley and Paul C. Clark, Jr, *Historical Dictionary of the United States–Mexican War*, Lanham, Md., 1997, p. xi.

approach the 620,000 deaths of the Civil War. The total US deaths in the Mexican campaign numbered 11,155, and of these only 1,700 were killed in action or died of their wounds, the great majority expiring from disease or exposure. Some 13,000 soldiers were wounded in action or discharged for disability, whilst about 9,000 deserted from a force that totalled less than 120,000 (43,000 regular troops and 74,000 volunteers) and cost a total of $98 million to deploy.[19] These numbers were indeed greater than in any conflict since independence, and they were more consequential than most general histories recognise, but they still pale into insignificance when set against the war of 1861–65. Although counted less carefully, Mexican losses were clearly much higher – possibly in the region of 20,000 dead – but themselves a fraction of those incurred in the Revolution of 1910–20.[20]

In addition to being politically embarrassing and dwarfed in terms of human cost by the Civil War, the conflict of 1847 seems from a US perspective to hark back to the Napoleonic age and almost to have caught some Mexican contagion in its lack of modernity, industrial qualities or strategic innovation. It is not celebrated as a watershed in terms of material progress or the forces of production, still less in the concatenation of political power in the western hemisphere. It makes no appearance in Michael Mann's *The Sources of Social Power* that analyses the rise of nation-states in the 'long nineteenth century' of 1760 to 1914, and Paul Kennedy's brief reference to it in *The Rise and Fall of the Great Powers* underscores its (positive) negative qualities: 'Neither conflict with the Indians nor the 1846 war with Mexico was a substantial drain upon [US] productive investment.'[21] In Eric Hobsbawm's *The Age of Revolution*, 'the USA ... acquired virtually its entire west ... by insurrection and war against the hapless Mexicans', and in *The Age of Capital*, 'Mexico lost vast territories as a result of American aggression in 1847'. But Hobsbawm notes that Karl Marx welcomed the US victory precisely because it brought historical progress and created the conditions for capitalist development.[22] In fact, Marx had little time for the anti-war convictions of Horace Greeley and Charles Dana, his employers on the *New York Tribune*, and his derision for the Anglo-American commanders did nothing to temper the idealised portrait he painted of the US forces:

---

19. Bauer, *Mexican War*, p. 397. A mortality rate from disease of 110 per 1,000 p.a. (compared with the Civil War figure of 65 and that in World War I of 16) is generally agreed despite some differences in the precise casualty statistics. Although there is no firm documentary evidence, it seems that army surgeons first used ether in this campaign. T. Irey, 'Soldiering, Suffering and Dying in the Mexican War', *Journal of the West*, XI:2, 1972, p. 285.

20. My 'guesstimate' based upon reports of losses in action given in Bauer, *Mexican War*. With the exception of the División del Norte stationed in Matamoros in the spring of 1846 and Santa Anna's large army amassed at San Luis Potosí early in 1847 most regular Mexican forces operated within quite modest logistical parameters and were less vulnerable than their enemy to disease. General Scott reckoned the Mexicans lost 7,000 killed and wounded in action.

21. Michael Mann, *The Sources of Social Power: II. The Rise of Classes and Nation–States, 1760–1914*, Cambridge 1993; Paul Kennedy, *The Rise and Fall of the Great Powers: Economic Change and Military Conflict from 1500 to 2000*, London 1989, p. 229.

22. *The Age of Revolution, 1789–1848*, London 1962, p. 136; *The Age of Capital, 1848–1875*, London 1975, pp. 119; 132.

It seems to me typical of the war that, despite wrong or inadequate orders from their CHIEF, every division and every single small body of men at all times make STUBBORNLY for their objectives, SPONTANEOUSLY exploiting every incident, so that in the end a measure of wholeness emerges. A Yankee sense of independence and individual proficiency greater, perhaps, than that of the Anglo-Saxons.[23]

As we have seen, Engels – to whom these sentiments were addressed – had six years earlier expressed them in more modulated and strategic language, celebrating the advance of 'the historical process' even when it took the form of military conquest and imperialism as well as adopting a pan-American perspective that anticipated the North American Free Trade Area by some 145 years.[24] At the time the sense of newness and a slippage of epochs was far more widely felt than is recognised today. In the wake of both the Treaty of Guadalupe Hidalgo and the European revolutions of the spring of 1848 it was unsurprising that the *New York Herald* predicted that the war would 'lay the foundation of a new age, a new destiny, affecting both this continent and the old continent of Europe'.[25] But the perception of a passing era went well beyond triumphalism of this type. In February 1847, even before the second stage of the war opened with Scott's landing at Veracruz, John Calhoun declared to the US Senate in language drawn resolutely from the eighteenth century that the conflict had closed a chapter in history and rendered the future invisible:

> Every Senator knows that I was opposed to the war; but none knows but myself the depth of that opposition. With my conceptions of its character and consequences, it was impossible for me to vote for it. When, accordingly, I was deserted by every friend on this side of the house ... I was not shaken in the least degree in reference to my course. On the passage of the act recognizing the war, I said to many of my friends that a deed had been done from which the country would not be able to recover for a long time, if ever; and added, it had dropped a curtain between the present and the future, which is to me inpenetrable; and for the first time since I have been in public life I am unable to see the future. I also added that it has closed the first volume of our political history under the constitution, and opened the second, and that no mortal could tell what would be written in it.[26]

Here Calhoun is taking a deeper draught of history than that offered in Emerson's reference to the conquest of Mexico as the ingestion of poison or in Helper's confident anticipation of an 'impending crisis'. The foreboding lies in the absence of knowledge, in the fact that all bets are now off. James Fenimore Cooper, for whom the war sharpened an already acute sense of intangibility, was grasping at straws when he praised the comfortably homespun style of the victorious General Zachary Taylor ('as yet Rough and Ready carries off all the glories of the pen'). Amongst most intellectuals

---

23. Marx, London, to Engels, 2 Dec. 1854, *MECW*, XXXIX, London 1985, p. 504.

24. See p. 239 above.

25. Quoted in Robert W. Johannsen, *To the Halls of the Montezumas: The Mexican War in the American Imagination*, New York 1985, p. 8.

26. Speech to Senate, 24 Feb. 1847, in Clyde N. Wilson (ed.), *The Essential Calhoun*, New Brunswick, N.J., p. 159.

and the public at large the overriding image of Taylor was of a backwoods man, only able to contend with modernity by dint of prolonged communion with nature. The model ensconced in the popular mind was of Cooper's invention, Leatherstocking, and this was a species clearly marked out for extinction.[27]

Destiny Manifest, Elephant Visible

President James Polk imposed a strong personal stamp on the provocation and conduct of the war against Mexico. His diary fails to hide an instinct for secrecy, an appetite for partisanship, and proclivity for personal score-settling. Yet it also reveals Polk to be entirely bereft of doubt about the rightness of the conflict. This was indeed 'Mr Polk's war', as his opponents dubbed it, by dint of his single-minded pursuit of victory when even his cabinet entertained serious doubts. And although Polk was obliged to accept the terms negotiated at Guadalupe Hidalgo by Nicholas Trist with the acquiescence of General Scott and in direct contravention of the president's own orders, these terms were not only very good for the USA, they were also the direct result of a war conducted with exceptional focus – bordering on obsession – by the chief executive.

There is, nevertheless, an important sense in which the war did not 'belong' to Polk at all and was a product of a disputed but strong mood amongst the US public as a whole. It should be recalled that prior to the election of 1844 Polk was by no means a recognised national figure, and that he had only gained the Democrat candidacy at the ninth ballot in the party convention. The Tennesseean was, then, the first successful 'dark horse' candidate in US presidential history and also the product of a platform: that for national expansionism or 'manifest destiny'. The leading contender for the Democrat nomination, Martin Van Buren, had been opposed to the annexation of Texas, and he lost the candidacy very much for this reason. Indeed, so strongly was

---

27. Johannsen, *To the Halls of the Montezumas*, pp. 115, 249. In a letter to the wife of Commodore Branford Shubrick, Cooper was engagingly direct about the importance of rhetorical ability to military command, and at the same time gave short shrift to the notion – actively propagated by General Winfield Scott – that Taylor was reliant on his chief of staff Major William Bliss for all but his instincts of command:

> Stockton, of course, will come home as soon as he can. He is rather a rum author. Old Sloat can beat him at a proclamation and give him ten. Well, we shall now see what Commodore Shubrick can do in that way. I wish they had all been sent to school to Rough and Ready, who really writes like a book. I do not believe a word about that Major Bliss writing his letters. Bliss has learned more from Taylor than Taylor has learned from Bliss.

Cooper, Cooperstown, to Mrs Shubrick, 2 May 1847, in J. Franklin Beard (ed.), *Letters and Journals of James Fenimore Cooper*, V, Cambridge, Mass., 1968, p. 210.

Polk associated with the cause that outgoing President Tyler, nominally a Whig, felt able to sign the annexation of the state into law hours before Polk entered office. This he had achieved by a close victory over the Whig candidate Henry Clay, who had opened his campaign with the declaration that annexation was 'dangerous to the integrity of the union ... and not called for by any general expression of public opinion'. Although Clay later temporised enough to raise doubts about his second point, the view from Mexico, where the election campaign was followed carefully, was very much that 'if Clay won, peace was certain'.[28]

By contrast, prudence was not an attribute closely associated with the expansionist creed to which Polk subscribed, even if he himself was a narrow and cautious man. 'Manifest destiny' was almost by its nature an ideology that rolled behind the fact of expanding Anglo settlement to the south and west. Thus, in his first message to Congress, on 2 December 1845, Polk could claim,

> This accession [of Texas] to our territory has been a bloodless achievement. No arm of force has been raised to produce the result. The sword has had no part in the victory. We have not sought to extend our territorial possessions by conquest, or our republican institutions over a reluctant people.[29]

The fighting had, of course, taken place a decade earlier, and it had been conducted by Texans, not citizens of the USA. This, though, could plausibly be depicted as a niggling detail in the heady atmosphere of late 1845, when tension on the Mexican border was sharp, the dispute with Great Britain over the limits of Oregon was high in the public mind, and resentment over European – principally British and French – 'ambitions' in the continent at an unprecedented level. Polk's address to Congress followed the publication over three days in the *New York Morning News* of a series of energetic articles written by John L. O'Sullivan, who is normally identified as the inventor of the term 'manifest destiny'. Although O'Sullivan's Kerry-born great-grandfather had served on the staff of Bonnie Prince Charlie a century earlier, he himself was less narrowly anti-British than generally insistent upon restricting European rights in the Americas. After the Mexican War O'Sullivan was twice indicted for violating the Neutrality Act through his sponsorship of secessionist raids on Cuba, but in 1845 his views were widely supported and about to receive the practical endorsement

---

28. This was the view of Justo Sierra O'Reilly, who, sent to Washington as an envoy from Yucatán, has it both ways:

> If our politicians had been perceptive enough to see things as they were and if they had recognised the legitimacy of the secession of Texas, both the war with Texas and its shameful and ruinous consequences, and the struggle with the United States, which was its inevitable aftermath, would have been avoided ... Congress turned its attention to the American problem, tiresome, solemn and terrible. It was the iron gauntlet around the collar of a weak and anaemic nation; a brutal knee in its belly; jaws ready to gnaw, mangle and devour while at the same time talking about humanity, justice and law.

Evolución Política del Pueblo Mexicano, reprinted in Ramón Ruiz (ed.), *The Mexican War: Was it Manifest Destiny?*, New York 1963, pp. 112, 114.

29. *BFSP, 1844–45*, XXXIII, London 1859, p. 200.

of many state governments as well as the federal administration. On 29 November O'Sullivan effectively condensed the Monroe Doctrine, driving it well beyond its original expression (and any construction put on it by John Quincy Adams, the initial author and twenty-five years later an unbending opponent of the Mexican War):

> We deny that the policy of our country, which refuses to allow any encroachment by the monarchies of Europe upon the free soil of America, to subject it to their arbitrary sway, and to strew over its future destiny their baleful influence ... is a just cause of war ... We say that European governments have no right upon this continent beyond the enjoyment of their present possessions, to which they are of course entitled, so long as the people who inhabit them prefer submission to alien rulers in another hemisphere to the blessed privilege of selecting their own. What further right have they? None!

Two days later he mapped out a more positive vision, although still lacing it heavily with denunciations of Europe (including the lack of freedom in Canada):

> If we have the right, then, to take our stand against 'any extension of European dominion in this continent', we hold the exercise of that right to be our duty.... Yes, duty, duty, not merely to ourselves, but to humanity and progress.... A wise and merciful Providence has guided our course, nourished our growth, increased our vigor, and each day poured new blessings upon our heads. But with all, has no 'mission' been given for us to fulfil? Has the privilege been also added to shut our eyes and stop our ears and steel our hearts to human woes and human wrongs, and man's abasement? Are we to know or seek nought but our own enjoyment? Shall we virtually say to the monarchies of Europe, leave us but the Lakes for our northern border, and the Rocky Mountains on the west, and take all else to gorge your insatiable appetite for increased dominion, rule it with the rod of rigor, and choke down the first aspiration of freedom in all its vast extent? Or shall we, with the eye of faith fixed on the glowing future, and love for our kind warm in our hearts, ask Great Britain and every other power, what need have you, three thousand miles away, of another slice of man's inheritance in the New World? Shall we not say to them, 'this territory must be secured for civilized man and free institutions; we will keep it open for settlement by all who seek it.... [The USA] never yet extended its dominion by fraud and violence; it never will. But when a people really independent of all allegiance, occupying territory contiguous to our own, apply to be admitted to our Confederacy, we cannot, we have justly no right, to refuse them. They are entitled to participate in all the blessings we enjoy.[30]

In his message Polk deployed equally unhampered rhetoric, particularly over Oregon (although he was to compromise over that issue in order to concentrate on Mexico). And with General Taylor's force having spent five bloodless months on its new Texan station it was difficult for those, like Horace Greeley, who opposed such chauvinism to make their message felt beyond the core Whig and abolitionist constituencies:

> All the gas of the Message about the 'balance of power on this Continent' and our resistance to farther European conquest and colonization is the paltriest fishing for thoughtless huzzas, worthy of a candidate for constable rather than President of the United States. When Mr Monroe declared our opposition to European conquest on this Continent, it was supposed

---

30. *New York Morning News*, 29 Nov., 1 Dec. 1845, cited in Frederick Merk, *The Monroe Doctrine and American Expansionism, 1843–1849*, New York 1966, pp. 75–7. O'Sullivan first used the term 'manifest destiny' in July 1845. James Pratt, 'The Origin of "Manifest Destiny"', *AHR*, 32, 1927.

that the Great Powers were meditating the subjugation of our sister Republics by their arms to the Spanish yoke. It was right that we should regard such a procedure with jealousy and meet it with prompt remonstrance. The principle which would justify their subjugation by foreign arms to Spain would need but little extension to authorize *our* subjugation by like force to Great Britain. But what is there like this in the present attitude of Europe toward this Continent? Is any body asserting a 'divine right' to restore revolted colonies to the parent states? Great Britain claims Oregon on just such grounds as our claim rests upon – Discovery, Exploration, Settlement, Possession. Let her claims be fairly sifted; let us invalidate them to the farthest extent practicable. But when we speak of her as an intruder here, and as impertinently intermeddling with the affairs of a Continent on which she has older and more extensive possessions than ours, we fly from argument to cant – we repudiate Evidence and resort to unprovoked Insolence. Let us have no more of this.[31]

Emerson, prone to distinguish between the 'law of things' and the 'law of men', to resign himself before the former and make judicious remonstration about the latter, noted in 1844 that 'it is quite necessary and true to our New England character that we should consider the question in its local and temporary bearings, and resist the annexation with tooth and nail. It is a measure which goes not by right, nor by wisdom but by feeling.' But when, some two years later, hostilities had opened, he reflected that 'the people are no worse since they invaded Mexico than they were before, only they have given their will a deed'.[32] The deed undertaken, Polk was correspondingly able in his next message, of December 1846, to provide this 'will' with the rationale of complaint:

The existing war was neither desired nor provoked by the United States.... After years of endurance of aggravated and unredressed wrongs on our part, Mexico, in violation of solemn Treaty obligations, and of every principle of justice recognized by civilized nations, commenced hostilities.... The wrongs which we have suffered from Mexico almost ever since she became an Independent Power ... are without a parallel in the history of modern civilized nations. Scarcely had Mexico achieved her independence ... when she commenced the system of insult and spoliation which she has ever since pursued.... Rulers superseded rulers in Mexico in rapid succession, but still there was no change in this system of depredation.[33]

This is now the leader of a nation at war, and although Polk found himself a little less harried by his opponents after the fighting started, he became so submerged in the detailed organisation of the campaign that he spent much less time in speechifying on its behalf. This seems to have been a sensible decision because popular support and acquiescence generally held up whilst the practical capacity of the armed forces of the USA lagged far behind that suggested by the rhetoric of manifest destiny.

In 1845 the regular US army had a formal enlistment of some 8,500 men, including 800 officers. In reality, some 5,500 personnel were in service at about 100 posts east

---

31. *New York Tribune*, 3 Dec. 1845, quoted in Merk, *Monroe Doctrine*, p. 80.
32. *Journal*, VI, p. 390; VII, p. 206, quoted in John Q. Anderson, 'Emerson on Texas and the Mexican War', *Western Humanities Review*, XIII:2, 1959, pp. 192, 195.
33. Polk, to Congress, 8 Dec. 1846, in *BFSP, 1845–46*, XXXIV, London 1860, pp. 242–4.

of a frontier running down from the Great Lakes along the Mississippi to western Louisiana. This establishment comprised eight regiments of infantry, two of dragoons, a corps of engineers and central quartermaster and medical services commanded by a major general (Winfield Scott) and three brigadiers (Edmund Pendleton Gaines, husband to Myra Clark; John E. Wool; and Zachary Taylor, soon to be promoted to major-general).[34] This force was not only more modest in size than those of several Latin American states but also one of the smallest of the western world in terms of its proportion to the total population of the country. It had, moreover, been so since the establishment of the republic, rising to 11,000 for the war of 1812 against Britain but being reduced to 6,000 a decade later on the familiar grounds of the wasteful, un-democratic and dangerous character of standing armies. The need to patrol a rapidly expanding frontier and invigilate Indian removal had pushed numbers up somewhat from the 1830s, but General Andrew Jackson's presidency had not been as sympathetic to institutional demands as some feared, and with desertion rates running at over 10 per cent, real enlistment nearly 20 per cent below legal strength, and the average cost of sending a new trooper to station at some $75, the army was in no state to provide an efficient guarantee of the existing western limits of the USA, let alone extend them by conducting a foreign war.[35]

As we have seen, the navy was equally modest in terms of manpower and had few modern craft at its disposal. Its numbers were restricted by law to 7,500, but in December 1845 fewer than that were enrolled in service on the four ships-of-the-line, seven frigates, fifteen sloops, five brigs, five schooners, six steamers and four storeships that constituted, at a cost of $5.8 million, the full maritime power of a state about to acquire a second oceanic seaboard.[36] At the end of the war the navy had eight steamers in service, three laid up in ordinary and five under construction through contracts that had increased the budget to over $7 million and raised the number of craft in active service to 52.[37] Its new responsibilities in the Pacific, where Commodores Sloat and Stockton had taking a leading part in the occupation of California, would maintain the pressure for expansion encouraged by the achievement of the March 1847 amphibious landing at Veracruz directed by Commodore David Conner. The first, heroic phase of the transition towards Mahan's globalised force of the late nineteenth century was represented by Commodore Matthew Perry's voyage to Japan, but this was still a symbolic achievement, and the technological advances

---

34. R.F. Weigley, *A History of the United States Army*, Bloomington, Ind., 1984, p. 597; W.A. Ganoe, *The History of the United States Army*, New York 1964, p. 196. The main posts were Fort Snelling (near St Paul), Jefferson Barracks (near St Louis), Fort Jessup (western Louisiana), and Fort Leavenworth (western Kansas).

35. The historical figures are provided by Jefferson Davis, Secretary of War, to Pres. Pierce, 1 Dec. 1853, in *BFSP, 1852–53*, XLII, London 1863, pp. 67–72.

36. George Bancroft, Secretary of Navy, to Pres. Polk, 1 Dec. 1845, in *BFSP, 1845–46*, XXXIV, pp. 191–203; John Mason, Secretary of Navy, to Pres. Polk, 10 Dec. 1847, in *BFSP, 1847–48*, XXXV, London 1860, p. 784.

37. John Mason, Secretary of Navy, to Pres. Polk, 4 Dec. 1848, in *BFSP, 1848–49*, XXXVIII, London 1862, pp. 263–4.

spurred by the Civil War would be necessary to put the navy in the same league as that of Great Britain.

The evolution of the regular army was of an entirely different order for although its numbers rose from 7,500 in May 1846 to 42,500 a year later, they were cut right back immediately upon cessation of hostilities. In 1848 the total force was reduced to 11,000, and the officer corps, which had expanded to nearly 3,000, to 945 – levels that were to remain until the late 1850s.[38] The army's victories in Mexico did little to dislodge an ideology that upheld a formal anti-militarism by celebrating a militia-based army of citizens, and great attention was paid to organising volunteer soldiers, who at their peak of 73,000 were nearly double the contingent of regulars. This was an impressive number, reflecting both popular enthusiasm for the war and a signifi-cant logistical potential of a state inexperienced in such matters. However, the raising, training and deployment of the volunteers was often a chaotic experience, and by the end of the conflict the system had lost much of its early popular and military appeal.

One of the initial attractions for volunteers was the limiting of service to twelve months. Another was the local, state-based nature of the regiments, which, according to lapsed militia practice, were required to elect their own officers, although about a third were commanded by West Pointers, and over a third of volunteer officers had previously received some military training. For Polk it was essential that the raising of the troops be a national effort:

> During the sitting of the cabinet [on 16 May 1846] I submitted to them the distribution among the States of the 50,000 volunteers to be raised. A portion of this force was assigned to each State and Territory in the Union, so as to make each feel an interest in the war.[39]

The president's initial plan was to raise 20,000 men from the west and south-west, and the final enlistment in those states exceeded 40,000. In states like Louisiana and Texas enrolment was as high as 1:20 of the white population; in those of the present midwest (Illinois, Michigan, Ohio) it fell to an average of 1:200; and in New England the total enlistment during the war of 1,057 represented a ratio of 1:2,500. In short, the pattern varied through the country, and the greatest number understandably came from the south-west.[40] A fortnight before Polk and the cabinet had agreed the number of volunteers, General Taylor, who had crossed the Rio Grande but not yet engaged the Mexicans in large formation, expressed his apprehension that the recruitment effort would get out of hand:

> I much fear so many volunteers will come we will hardly find anything for them to do; the enemies principal posissions [sic] are so far off, with deserts intervening, that it will be I fear impossible to reach them for want of transportation. I truly regret to see they are organizing

---

38. Weigley, *History of the United States Army*, p. 597. Only some of the wartime increase was achieved by expanding companies from 64 to 100 privates on five-year service, and a number of new units were created.

39. Allan Nevins (ed.), *Polk: The Diary of a President, 1845–1849*, London 1952, p. 95.

40. C.S. Ellsworth, 'The American Churches and the Mexican War', *AHR*, 45, 1940, p. 318.

a company of Taylor Guard etc at New Orleans as I have a great horror of being made a lion of.[41]

Taylor's modesty was not false, and his concern was shared by Polk, who had little confidence in his principal commander but was more worried by the ebullient and unauthorised raising of troops at New Orleans by General Gaines, the commander of the western division. Although Gaines was technically Taylor's superior, Polk, never keen to share information, had not told him of the order that Taylor's force should proceed to the Mexican border, no doubt sharpening the sensibilities of the seventy-year-old officer, who, ever on guard against the 'Mexican threat', had ordered a call-up without Washington's authorisation four times over the previous decade. When, early in May, Gaines received news of Taylor's first contacts with the Mexican División del Norte, he immediately issued a proclamation calling up patriots, and within a fortnight had raised some 12,000 men – more than half the total Polk envisaged from the entire Southern USA – to be engaged for a period of six months.[42] For General Winfield Scott this endeavour was due to 'partial insanity at least'. However, Polk – once he had halted Gaines's levy, dismissed all those who refused to serve a full year, and ordered the general back to Washington from New Orleans, where he had become a popular member of society – was inclined to be more indulgent:

> General Gaines is now a very old man and although guilty of acts which cannot be justified, and for the commission of which, if brought before a general court martial, he would without doubt be punished, yet I determined to take no further proceeding against him. His late conduct at New Orleans greatly embarrassed the government and will cost the Treasury many hundreds of thousands of dollars. He is now, however, removed from that command and cannot now repeat the mischief.[43]

For Taylor, who had himself settled deep into Louisiana life whilst on service with the division, this resolution was fair enough because Scott and the politicians in the capital were already showing themselves far too eager to pass judgement: 'I have not read or seen all the correspondence between Generals Gaines, Scott and [Secretary of War] Marcy; and if General Scott has charged General Gaines with being crazy, he can with great propriety return the compliment.'[44] (In the event, few of General Gaines's troops saw action, and although he stayed in Washington with Myra for the fourth hearing of her case before the Supreme Court in 1848, he returned to New Orleans later that year and died there from cholera in June 1849.)

So high were warlike spirits in May 1846 that Gaines did not need to expend much energy to attract thousands of volunteers to the colours. The bitter-sweet

---

41. Taylor, Matamoros, to Wood, 16 May 1846, in *Letters of Zachary Taylor from the Battlefields of the Mexican War*, New York 1970, p. 4.

42. K.B. Germany, 'Patriotism and Protest: Louisiana and General Edmund Pendleton Gaines's Army of Mexican–American War Volunteers, 1845–47', *Louisiana History*, XXXVII:3, 1996.

43. *Diary of a President*, p. 140.

44. Taylor, Matamoros, to Wood, 30 June 1846, in *Letters of Zachary Taylor*, p. 21.

qualities of this mood were expressed by William Hickling Prescott, who, having obtained such fame and fortune from his account of the 'first' conquest of Mexico, experienced sharp ambivalence at the prospect of a second:

> We are here just now in a war crisis.... It was no more than was to be expected. For how could two armed bodies lie in gunshot of each other, all prepared for an explosion, with such causes of irritation between the two nations, and not come to blows? ... But we have a happy confidence in our own superiority over every and over all the nations of Christendom combined. The South and West seem to be overrun with a dare-devil spirit that one might expect to meet with in France, but not in a money-making democracy. Yet this same war spirit has been the bane of more democracies than one, and I fear we are reserved to point a moral, if we do nothing to adorn a tale. One would suppose that millions of uncultivated acres inviting settlement and the hand of civilization that lie within our present limits might satisfy the most craving cupidity. And so it would have at the North, where we have sober business-like habits and the steadiness of one somewhat advanced in years. But in the Far West we áre wedded to a brisk young helpmate who is like to give us enough of her gambols and who most unhappily has the control of Brother Jonathan's *ménage* – for the present. But I am sick of our domestic troubles, brought on us by unparalleled folly. And I take refuge from them in Peruvian hills, where the devildoms I read of – black enough – have at least no reference to ourselves.[45]

Prescott's escapism went beyond distracting himself in Pizarro's conquest of Peru – the north-east may have been raising fewer volunteers than the southern and frontier states but it was hardly immune to outbursts of patriotism. Walt Whitman was writing for the *Brooklyn Eagle* not the *New Orleans Crescent* when, in the same week as Prescott expressed his anguish, he declared, 'Let our arms now be carried with a spirit which will teach the world that, while we are not forward for a quarrel, America knows how to crush, as well as how to expand.'[46] (Nearly two years later, in February 1848, Whitman left New York for New Orleans, his appetite for the South in no manner diminished by the subsequent experience of war.) Even in Prescott's home state of Massachusetts, Caleb Cushing, the diplomat and Hispanist who would win Myra's case for her, had little difficulty in raising a unit of volunteers once he had sunk his own money into its outfitting and maintenance. When, in June 1846, the Massachusetts Anti-Slavery Society denounced those who supported the war as 'enemies to the country, traitors to liberty and the rights of man', they did not find themselves on an easy Puritan wicket:

> Prowar 'rowdies' and 'mobbites' forced a scheduled Syracuse anti-war meeting, with the Reverend Samuel J. May as chairman, to adjourn from the Empire House and reconvene at the nearly Congregational church. Here speeches were heard and resolutions condemning the war as an immoral scheme to extend slavery were adopted. But again a large prowar mob appeared, set up a large cannon by the rear of the church, and fired it three times,

---

45. Prescott, Boston, to Sumner, 15 May 1846, in Roger Wolcott (ed.), *The Correspondence of William Hickling Prescott, 1832–1847*, Cambridge, Mass., 1925, p. 597.
46. *Brooklyn Eagle*, 11 May 1846, quoted in Bauer, *Mexican War*, p. 69.

causing the meeting to be abruptly adjourned amid the confusion of deafening noise and shattering windows.[47]

Patriotic sentiment endured well into a campaign that was to be the first fought under the Stars and Stripes as the official banner of the United States. 'The Star-Spangled Banner' was sung at parades, but it was not yet an unofficial national anthem, and 'Yankee Doodle' was still the most popular song amongst the troops. On 4 July 1846 Taylor's troops at Matamoros were played 'Hail Columbia!', read the Declaration of Independence, and given a homily on the importance of emulating their revolutionary forebears.[48] The following February at the critical battle of Buena Vista, when almost all of Taylor's forces were volunteers, the veteran General Wool rode along the line reminding his men of their good fortune to be meeting the enemy on Washington's birthday. (Despite a confused retreat by units from Illinois and Kentucky, the volunteers held off a much larger force.)

At the same time, state and regional pride retained a high profile within a wider national identity. For Thomas Tennery, born in Kentucky and raised in Illinois, it was precisely this unity in diversity that guaranteed the strength of patriotism:

> Here we are camped seven or eight thousand troops from different states; though everyone seems to have connections in each state, and it is amusing to see friends meet. Let those who are vain or ignorant enough to talk of a disunion of the United States be silent forever when they consider the ties of kindred and the feelings existing from Maine to the Rio Grande, and from Florida to Oregon.[49]

When they lost their nerve at Buena Vista, Taylor chastised Tennery's comrades, 'This is not the way for Kentuckians to behave!', and no amount of nationalism could impede the adoption of local nicknames such as the Wabash Invincibles (Indiana) or Jasper Greens (Georgian Irish).[50] That tendency may have been encouraged by the fact that for most of the war the volunteers were not issued with uniforms but given a clothing allowance of $3.50 per month. (The cavalry were paid an allowance of 40

---

47. Schroeder, *Mr Polk's War*, p. 100. After the war similar activity continued:

> During the 1848 campaign, efforts were made to establish a Taylor bloc in New York City. Earlier attempts had been disrupted by Clay Whig 'roughs'. Alexander Stephens arranged for Isaiah Rhynders, 'captain among toughs and shoulder hitters in New York' and a Taylor man, to ensure an uninterrupted speech by [Robert] Toombs in a hall in the city. The price for this was $200.00. At Rhynders' suggestion, Toombs met with some of the Rhynders boys at a favorite saloon to establish comraderie the night before his speech. The next evening Toombs' speech was interrupted by shouts of 'slaveholder' and 'a hurray for Clay'. Toombs continued speaking. Again, the cries erupted in the hall. The speaker began to question his success at establishing comraderie in the saloon the night before. Then a great row broke out, and the hall was cleared of forty trouble-makers in two minutes. Later, Toombs discovered that during the initial heckling Rhynders' men had circulated and chalked the backs of the hecklers. Then, on order, they were bodily ejected.'

William Y. Thompson, *Robert Toombs of Georgia*, Baton Rouge 1966, p. 47.

48. Johannsen, *To the Halls of the Montezumas*, pp. 52, 59.

49. D.E. Livingstone-Little (ed.), *The Mexican War Diary of Thomas Tennery*, Norman, Okla., 1970, pp. 14–15.

50. Johannsen, *To the Halls of the Montezumas*, pp. 27, 64.

cents a day if they brought their own horses.) This was a matter of some consequence not just for the provision of a basic need in very inclement conditions but also for relations between volunteers and the regulars, who were from the start kitted out by the Schuylkill arsenal in Philadelphia. A year into the war the correspondent of *The Times* found the volunteers decked out in uniform of a sort, but to a European eye it did not make a favourable – let alone a martial – impression:

> I saw hundreds of gallows-faced men, uniformed (if the dress which most of them wore could be called such) with poverty and bad taste, many of them in shirt-sleeves, armed with swords, carbines and pistols of a common kind ... all wore jackets and pantaloons of light blue; all, even the dragoons, wore flat cloth caps although several have adopted the palm hats of the country ... coarse and clownish men [these] Messiahs of Civilization.[51]

For Colonel Samuel Curtis, who had held a commission in the 1820s prior to becoming a lawyer in Wooster, Ohio, the clothing of his 678 volunteers was the source of constant irritation with the quartermasters:

> I have much anxiety and trouble to procure requisite clothing for my regiment. The clothing department, I am informed by letter from the Quartermaster General's office, cannot do anything towards clothing the volunteers. That this law does not authorise the department to do so. Under this ruling, the pay of the volunteers is much less than that of regulars ... the volunteers are obliged to clothe themselves at great disadvantage from the place of manufacture ... a suit that the Government furnishes the regulars for $6 cannot be obtained for any price, and one costing twelve to the volunteers would not be equal to it.

For the Ohio colonel the source of such an unhelpful attitude lay in the high command:

> I admit that General Taylor has had reason to rely on regulars and has had some reason to doubt the conduct of volunteers after the street brawls that have gone off in the city of Matamoros; but I fear there is that prejudice which will exist and will manifest itself each day enacted at the head of the army.[52]

What Taylor thought privately, many regular troops were happy to express openly. The *New Orleans Daily Delta* published a regular's complaint about bedbugs, fleas, mosquitoes, sandfleas, tarantulas and ants, 'but of all the varmints, these volunteer soldiers are the worst'.[53] One leading reason for views of this type was the volunteers' lack of discipline, which, according to the English observer George Ruxton, the citizen soldiers viewed as tantamount to a violation of their basic liberties: 'The American will never be made a soldier. His constitution will not bear the restraint of discipline, neither will his very mistaken notion about liberty allow him to subject

---

51. Quoted in John Q. Anderson, 'Soldier Lore of the War with Mexico', *Western Humanities Review*, XI:4, 1957, p. 325.
52. Joseph E. Chance (ed.), *Mexico under Fire: Being the Diary of Samuel Ryan Curtis, 3rd Ohio Volunteer Regiment*, Fort Worth, Tex., 1994, pp. 60, 23.
53. Quoted in Anderson, 'Soldier Lore', p. 322.

himself to its necessary control.'[54] Discipline was not readily enforced by the courts martial because they had no authority to punish troops for those offences which in the United States would be heard in civilian courts. (Although Taylor and Scott proposed measures and even drafted a law to cover this, Congress took no action during the conflict.) Nor was the position helped by the election of officers, who often engaged in popularity contests and knew that at the end of their term they could return to the ranks. Small wonder that an unbending martinet like General Wool was so disliked in the first months of the war, although after Buena Vista the merits of order and training were appreciated by thousands who had survived the two-day battle. Many incidents of disorder occurred when the US forces were concentrating at Matamoros, and they did little to strengthen a sense of national unity: when the Georgian volunteers, a fifth of whom were on the sick list, rioted in August 1846 they had to be repressed by troops from other states, in this case the 4th Illinois, several of whom were killed by their insubordinate compatriots.

The Mexican populace soon learned to distinguish the volunteer from the regular troops, whose conduct was generally seen as predictable and reliable and who were under strict orders to respect the persons and laws of local civilians – a policy that both Taylor and Scott saw as vital to victory. Perhaps the single worst incident of violence against civilians was perpetrated in February 1847 by the notoriously unruly Arkansans, who massacred up to thirty refugees from Taylor's army hiding in a cave near Agua Nueva. The volunteers only stopped firing when General Wool, whose suspicions had been aroused by the gunfire, sent a detachment to investigate. The Arkansans' commanding officer, Colonel Archibald Yell, conspicuously failed to produce a single trooper suspected of the murders, and Taylor ordered the two companies to the rear but could do nothing more. 'Such deeds', he commented, 'cast indelible disgrace upon our arms and [the] reputation of our country.'[55] Yet, for Taylor, the Arkansans were but the least manageable element of an inappropriate system, which he viewed in a manner not unlike Albert Gallatin:

> The whole system of volunteers is at best defective but made worse than it might be by the mismanagement of the same, by those who control it for political effect, which is the case in the present instance. Volunteers were never intended to invade or carry on war out of the limits of their own country, but should be used as the Constitution intended they should be for enforcing the execution of laws and repelling invasion, for which they are admirably suited.[56]

---

54. *Adventures in Mexico and the Rocky Mountains*, New York 1848, pp. 178–9, quoted in Johannsen, *To the Halls of the Montezumas*, p. 41.

55. Quoted in Bauer, *Mexican War*, p. 208.

56. Taylor, Camargo, to Wood, 3 Nov. 1846, in *Letters of Zachary Taylor*, p. 51. Even Samuel Curtis came to think along similar lines:

> I see that it is impossible for volunteers and regulars to come together on such terms of equality as should exist between them. The regular and volunteer forces must be connected in peace and war; or one of the classes must be abandoned. A representative government must depend on vounteers or militia; and when these forces come into the field they must be placed on terms of equality.

Mexico under Fire, pp. 67–8.

Many volunteer troopers themselves came to feel likewise when their initial en-thusiasm collided with brute reality and they had 'seen the elephant'. This phrase, widely used in the mid nineteenth century, signified more than experiencing disap-pointment of high expectations and could 'encompass any new, broadening, even frightening experience, without necessarily suggesting a negative quality'.[57] A surgeon who crossed the New Mexico desert as part of General Stephen Kearny's expedition confessed that, 'I have see the Elephant and I hope that I shall never be compelled to cross it again.' For 'Ruff Sam', the volunteer invented by *Spirit of the Times*, the battles of Buena Vista and Monterrey produced a similar reaction: 'Thar's where I seed the elephant I'm going to tell about – not the live elephant stuffed with straw, but the rale Mexikin elephant, horns an' all.'[58] With 270 Anglo-Americans killed and nearly 400 wounded, Buena Vista was the bloodiest battle to date in the history of the USA, and all but a handful of the 4,650 men whom Taylor pitted against Santa Anna's force of over 15,000 were volunteers (from Arkansas, Kentucky, Illinois, Indiana and Mississippi). Yet the battle was fought in spectacular mountainous terrain and on days with impressive weather. According to an Illinois officer, 'it was a beautiful battle ... the most grand and gorgeous spectacle'. A volunteer from Indiana remarked that the setting was 'truly romantic', and an officer for Massachusetts who visited the scene later wrote that 'it was one of the prettiest places in the world' despite the slaughter.[59]

Here the ambivalent sense of 'seeing the elephant' may be felt, even if it does derive from a need to reconcile oneself with the trauma of battle. Many of those who went through Buena Vista had never seen such scenery before in their lives and so were undergoing a double experience. Upon arriving in Mexico Thomas Tennery went through a kind of epiphany induced by nature that would prepare him at least in part for the sight of the elephant when, seven months later, he was wounded in both legs at Cerro Gordo:

> This evening we walked out north of the encampment to the point of the ridge, and it is truly a place for a post; we can hear the loud but distant roar of the gulf, the howl of the solitary prairie wolf, the croaking of frogs of various kinds and the chirping of hundreds of insects, mingled with splashing water in the overgrown bottom by toads, crabs and water-fowl; while to the south is the long line of encampments illuminated by a thousand candles, while the hum and noise roar like the roar of the gulf, and the retiring clouds still give out their faint flashes of light; add to this the groan of a distant steamer, the bright sheets of water with the almost viewless groves beyond them, with the calm fresh air and the blue

---

57. Here Johannsen is building on Bartlett's *Dictionary of Americanisms* (1848): *To the Halls of the Montezumas*, p. 87. According to Geoffrey Ward, the phrase might have derived from an old joke:

> When an eastern farmer heard a circus was coming, he loaded his farm wagon with produce and hurried to town. On the way, he met the circus parade, led by an elephant. His horses bolted at the strange sight, tipping over the wagon and spilling vegetables all over the road. 'I don't give a hang', the farmer said, 'for I have seen the elephant.'

The West: An Illustrated History, London 1996, p. 125.

58. Johannsen, *To the Halls of the Montezumas*, p. 87; *Spirit of the Times*, 6 Nov. 1847, quoted in Anderson, 'Soldier Lore', p. 323.

59. Johannsen, *To the Halls of the Montezumas*, p. 92.

heavens bespangled with a million gems of light. Contemplating scenes like this, the mind is lost in reverie.

Of course, such reveries were easier to float into when down in Matamoros one's comrades were dying of dysentery and cholera by the day: 'A burying today, one of F company. The king of terrors reigns without a rival save the blood of Jesus.' And not all volunteers possessed Tennery's piety to protect them against the inevitable adversities of army life:

> Inman lost his purse containing $25 in gold and 5 cents in silver, with some papers. It is thought that it was taken by some lowbreed pickpocket while he was in a crowd looking at some men who were performing some theatrical trick, but he appears not to care much and no doubt feels better by ten degrees, [his] self-respect real content, better than the conscience of the condemned down-cast imp who stole it.[60]

Matamoros provoked a quite different reaction from Colonel Curtis: 'This is Sabbath … the bell rang for Matins this morning, but how can we expect religion in such a den of thieves, robbers and assassins? I believe the place ought to be cleansed by fire!' Maybe Curtis's exasperation resulted from the diarrhoea he could not shake off, or the loss of twelve of his men from measles, or the fact that Taylor's scrupulous attention to maintaining tolerable relations with the town's inhabitants meant that he could find no billet in which to be ill:

> Major Love returned without obtaining a room. Colonel Clark said the orders of General Taylor required all the property of peaceable Mexicans to be respected. All the property belongs to Mexicans and they all pretend to be peaceable; so my quartermaster very properly under this order declaimed taking any for public use. As an officer of the state of Ohio I have often taken from the citizens of Ohio the most valuable property for public uses. It seems the rights of these Mexicans are better guaranteed than the rights of our citizens in the states would be, all of whom yield to the well-established law that all the property of citizens may be sacrificed for public uses, the state making compensation for the same.

Curtis was also not unrepresentative of volunteer opinion in his resentment at the efforts to reduce conflict over religion by a government anxious not to lose the support of the growing Catholic population in the USA and be accused of seeking a denominational conquest:

> This is Sunday. It is very warm. A great number of the regiment have gone into the city to attend Catholic church. Father McElroy sent out by the President is the only one I hear of who preaches in the English language. There is a kind of tempering whining policy in the position of our government in the matter of sending a Catholic priest to this barbarous Catholic country. Does our country wish to Catholicise the Catholics, or is the government afraid of Catholicism and do they [do] this to flatter the church with our cause? The mode strikes me as pusillanimous, and I place my private opinion for future reference only. The idea of associating our government with any sect of the Church, especially one of the most despotic and monarchistic, I regard as encroaching on our constitutional liberty.[61]

---

60. *Mexican War Diary of Thomas D. Tennery*, pp. 21, 33, 17.
61. *Mexico under Fire*, pp. 32, 30.

One is a little surprised that Curtis's congregationalist instincts and his rank did not lead him to preach a sermon of his own. Captain R.A. Stewart, a Methodist, did so to the Louisiana volunteers, who (despite the far greater profile of Catholicism in their state) thereby had no need to expose themselves to dangerously hierarchical doctrines as the price for attending divine service.[62] Moreover, Stewart managed to combine manifest destiny with a call to respect human rights by basing his sermon on Jeremiah VII, 6–7: 'If ye oppress not the stranger, the fatherless, and the widow, and shed not innocent blood in this place, neither walk after other gods to your own hurt: Then will I cause you to dwell in this place, in the land that I gave to your fathers, for ever and ever.' For Polk, the logic of asking the senior Catholic bishop in the USA – John Hughes of New York, who knew the archbishop of Mexico person-ally – for Spanish-speaking chaplains to accompany the army was not so far from that attributed to him by Curtis:

> Our object was to procure his aid in disabusing the minds of the Catholic priests and people of Mexico in regard to what they most erroneously supposed to be the hostile designs of the government and people of the United States upon the religion and church property of Mexico.[63]

Although the US government declared that 'hundreds of our army and hundreds of thousands of our people are members of the Catholic Church', most of the Catholics under arms were regular soldiers, not volunteers. The hierarchy, which was in council at Baltimore when fighting started, issued a pastoral letter that distinguished between religious and civil allegiance, and despite the voluble criticism of the convert Orestes Brownson, there was less opposition to the conflict from the Roman Catholic Church than from several protestant sects.[64] On the other hand, early expectation of Catholic treason in some hardline Protestant communities was buoyed up by the fact that a good proportion of those deserters the Mexicans organised into the 200-strong San Patricio batallion were of immigrant background and assumed to be Catholics.

It is, in fact, far from clear that the US desertion rate, which predictably included few volunteers, owed much to religious factors. At the very start of the campaign dozens of men swam across to Matamoros when it was still under Mexican control, not least because there was a positive 'pull-factor' to encourage flight from the rigours and dangers of life in the ranks:

---

62. Johannsen, *To the Halls of the Montezumas*, p. 50.

63. *Diary of a President*, p. 97. At the start of hostilities Polk drew up a proclamation to be issued by Taylor to the local population: 'Your religion, your altars and churches, the property of your churches and citizens, the emblems of your faith and its ministers, shall be protected and remain inviolate.' Quoted in Bauer, *Mexican War*, p. 85.

64. The bishops noted that obedience to the Pope was 'in no way inconsistent with your civil alle-giance, your social duties as citizens or your rights as men.... You can bear witness that we have always taught you to render to Caesar the things that are Caesar's, to God the things that are God's.' Quoted in Ellsworth, 'The American Churches and the Mexican War', p. 302.

Standing on the river bank in early morning or evening, they gaped as the young women of Matamoros came down to the river, disrobed without hesitation or embarrassment, and plunged into the stream. Swimming and splashing, their long black hair floating behind, oblivious to the spectators, they seemed like mermaids to one volunteer.[65]

Of the eighty-five members of the San Patricio batallion who were captured alive after putting up fierce resistance at the Battle of Churubusco in August 1847, only twenty-four had Irish surnames, a minority declared themselves to be Roman Catholics, just two indicated the involvement of any priest in their desertion, and thirty claimed to have wandered off whilst intoxicated.[66] Much was made of the case of the San Patricios's colonel, John Riley, formerly a sergeant in K company of the 5th infantry and before that a member of the 66th regiment of the British army in Canada. But Riley – evidently a serial deserter – seems to have had little political motivation and he escaped the executions staged at San Angel, Mixcoac and Tacubaya, where fifty members of the battalion were hanged, thirty of them at the moment that the Stars and Stripes were raised above the citadel of the captured capital. This punishment – together with the fifty lashes, branding of 'D' on the cheek and hard labour in a yoke to which sixteen others were sentenced – may be thought particularly cruel. Yet although Colonel Bennet Riley (no close relation), who presided over the main court martial, had a reputation for severity and Scott commuted several death sentences, the penalty for treason was not out of keeping with the customs of the time. Moreover, it is not surprising that only fourteen of the captured San Patricios either escaped charge or were found innocent since the unit had played a visible part in the fighting, particularly in manning a heavy battery at Buena Vista. Unlike the other 9,000 deserters, these men had not simply fled the ranks – a possibility that was widely recognised despite acceptance of some defence claims of coercion as well as entrapment by the Mexicans.[67]

Irish soldiers made up a majority of neither the San Patricios nor all deserters; many more Irish troops fought for their new country than opposed it or fled the ranks. Nevertheless, the state of popular prejudice at home made it relatively easy to stigmatise them thus, and in July 1847 Tomás Murphy, a captain in the Mexican army,

---

65. Johannsen, *To the Halls of the Montezumas*, p. 169. Of course, volunteers were no less vulnerable to temptations of this type, and they sometimes produced a felicitous combination of warlike and recreational pursuit, as when a unit of Texas Rangers staked out a hacienda with the plan of capturing some Mexican officers due to attend a ball. Once it was obvious that the enemy had absconded, the warriors from the Lone Star state themselves joined in the festivities, delighting their ex-compatriots with a display of US dances: 'They performed the "double shuffle", the "Virginny breakdown", the "Kentucky heel tap", the "pigeon wing", the "back balance lick", and the "Arkansas hoe-down" with unbounded applause and irresistible effect.' Samuel Reid, *The Scouting Expeditions of McCulloch's Texas Rangers*, Philadelphia 1860, pp. 57–8, quoted in Anderson, 'Soldier Lore', p. 326.

66. R. McCarmack, 'The San Patricio Deserters in the Mexican War', *The Americas*, Oct. 1951, p. 136. The fullest study of this subject is Michael Hogan, *The Irish Soldiers of Mexico*, Guadalajara 1996.

67. Edward Wallace, 'Deserters in the Mexican war', *HAHR*, 15:2, 1935. On 12 Sept. 1997 the Mexican state formally honoured the San Patricios as national heroes on the 150th anniversary of their execution. At the time Lance Hool was directing a film (*One Man's Hero*, starring Tom Berenger) based on the life of John Riley.

only narrowly escaped execution as a traitor at the hands of US forces.[68] On 22 September 1847, ten days after the hanging of the San Patricios, Scott warned of a Mexican conspiracy to entice more deserters from the US army with the promise of land grants in California, issuing General Order 296, the essence of which was distilled in his exhortation that 'All our soldiers professing the Catholic religion remember the fate of the deserters taken at Churubusco'. However, even as early as the Spring of 1847 the major problem facing the US commanders was less desertion than the replacement of the initial cohort of volunteers who would complete their twelve months of service in June.

Although very few politicians had expected the war to last more than a year, the consequence of relying on temporary soldiers had always been evident. In November 1846 – with Taylor controlling the North at Monterrey but lacking a decisive victory, and the decision to launch a second invasion through Veracruz agreed – the cabinet called for the raising of nine new regiments. However, these were very slow to form. Too many people had 'seen the elephant' and told the story to family and friends (after the Battle of Monterrey the New Orleans post office received 14,000 letters from Taylor's men when this abnormally literate army normally dispatched only half that number). The telegraph had made press reports even more up-to-date, and the campaign was closely covered by a profusion of regional papers, which inevitably included mention – often detailed description – of privation, disease and death even within the most boisterous propaganda. Although there was still a public disposition to support the troops in the field, this was qualitatively different to volunteering to join or replace them there oneself. In New York the recruiting sergeants were obliged to sign up men who had been rejected in the first phase of enlistment, and then they made recourse to jailbirds, for whom war-weariness was a distinctly relative sentiment. In North Carolina it proved impossible to fill the companies of the state's second regiment, which was dispatched to Mexico in small groups between February and

---

68. After the war was over navy lieutenant Henry Wise published a typical account:

> In Salamanca, where we stopped to bait and change the horses, a number of beggars surrounded the coach, and in one I at once detected the pure Milesian brogue and visage. He was whining and limping about, with a tattered hat and stick, imploring alms in the most ludicrous attempts at the Castilian tongue. 'Why, Pat, you're a deserter,' said I, from the top of the vehicle. 'Who siz that,' quoth he, evidently startled. Forgetting his infirmities, clapping on his sombrero, and clenching the stick in readiness for a fight, or flight, as he peered among the crowd; and stepping up to a miserable leper, whose face had been painfully stereotyped into a broad grin, he poked him sharply in the ribs and roared out: 'Ye lie, ye baste! I was sick in the hospital, and the gineral tuk me off in his own carridge.' 'Here, Pat, I'm your man!' 'Ah is it there ye are, liftinint! You're a paycock of a bay! Will ye give us a rial?' 'No, but if you chance to be caught by the Yankees, you'll get a rial's worthy of hearty-chokes and caper sauce,' I replied, going through a little pantomime with heels and neck for his especial benefit. 'No, be Jasus! Thim Harney blaggards will niver choke me while the Dons is so generous!' This was the last I saw or heard of Pat.

Los Gringos, New York 1850, pp. 246–7. Stories of this type put one in mind of Aubrey De Vere's observation that 'charges made against Ireland, it is true, derive a certain verisimilitude from the stories in circulation amongst you; but you cannot be ignorant that for such tales the supply, according to the ordinary laws of trade, will always be proportionate to the demand'. *English Misrule and Irish Misdeeds* (1848), London 1970, p. 44.

June 1847, and across the state line the position reported in the *Anderson Gazette* at the start of the fighting had also worsened considerably:

> We hear many with one accord making excuses. Some object to the length of time their services are required, others to the season of the year in which the call is made, or the great distance to the seat of the war; one has to attend to his merchandise and another his crop; and finally one has married a wife and therefore begs to be excused. Upon the whole, we are inclined to think, that to secure volunteers from this quarter the fighting must be post-poned 'till the coming of the frosts or be brought nearer us.[69]

This was not only a 'money-making democracy' but also Calhoun country, where few had been prepared to follow the old hawk into full opposition to the war but where equally few would continue to back it without consistently renewed good reason. In February 1847, the government, recognising this to have become the national mood, offered twelve-month volunteers a land grant of 160 acres, and although some 60,000 claims were eventually made under the act, enlistment was still slow.[70] On 6 June 1847, a year and a day after the *Anderson Gazette* published its downbeat appraisal of recruitment potential, seven regiments of volunteers, including the 900-strong 'Palmettos' of South Carolina, left Scott's army, which was reduced to just 7,113 men. Despite the important victory at Cerro Gordo, Scott was advancing on Mexico City with a most insecure line back to his source of supply at Veracruz, some 2,000 men on the sick list, and the need to garrison Puebla as well as prepare for the fierce battles expected around the capital. On 4 June a force of 700 had left Veracruz to join him, but they were almost all raw recruits, and an equal number of Mexican guerrillas, lured by the $350,000 that the column was known to be bringing to replenish the army's coffers, were closing in on the road. With teamsters too inexperienced to keep the wagon-train tight enough to be defended, the veteran commander Colonel James McIntosh was forced to halt and wait for 500 extra troops under General Cadwalader before the road could be opened to Jalapa and the US offensive restarted. A year into the campaign, it must have seemed to the senior commanders in the field that 'they had been jockeyed into a false position by an obtuse and wily control of military affairs [in Washington]. There were not enough trained men on hand, so that the volunteer had to be used, abused and sacrificed.'[71] Democratic society was not an unalloyed boon for the conduct of military campaigns, even if its merits were continually trumpeted – by Marx as much as Polk – as the reason for American superiority. Nor was it so easy as it sometimes appeared to the outside world to reaffirm the superiority of the Anglo-Saxon race through force of arms.[72]

---

69. *Anderson Gazette*, 5 June 1846, quoted in E.M. Lander, *Reluctant Imperialists: Calhoun, the South Carolinians, and the Mexican War*, Baton Rouge 1980, p. 22.

70. Ganoe, *History of the United States Army*, p. 217. In March 1847 a bounty of $12 was introduced for regulars who re-enlisted. After the war finished the War Department was processing 250 land claims a day – a rate that set it far apart from those Latin American states that likewise offered property in return for service to the state. Secretary of War Marcy to Pres. Polk, 1 Dec. 1848, in *BFSP, 1848–49*, XXXVIII, p. 241.

71. Ganoe, *History of the United States Army*, p. 225.

Finally, we should note that it was not only through force of arms that the USA prevailed. In August 1846 Stephen Kearny occupied Santa Fe without firing a shot when, against all expectations, its tough governor Manuel Armijo decided to evacuate his troops. This decision, it transpired, owed much to a conversation with his cousin by marriage, James Wiley Magoffin, the Kentucky-born son of a County Down trader who for some twenty years had exploited the Santa Fe trail well enough to have established flourishing wholesale outlets there, in Saltillo and at Chihuahua, where he had married a local woman in 1830. Justin Smith presents Magoffin rather in the same manner as Arthur Whitaker treats Daniel Clark, which is perhaps not so surprising since both were successful traders of Irish origin who were intimately involved in the transfer of foreign territory to the possession of the USA. Although there is no written record of the transaction between Magoffin, whom Polk had previously brought to Washington from Missouri to brief on this secret aspect of the campaign, and Armijo, who had a business of his own in Albuquerque, Smith is comfortable conjecting upon it:

> Undoubtedly he [Magoffin] dwellt on the impossibility of successful resistance; and probably he suggested – though Armijo's avarice required no hint on this point – that should cordial feelings prevail, the duties of the approaching merchandise, a fortune in themselves, would be paid at the Santa Fé customhouse, where the governor could handle them.[73]

Armijo was soon accused of having been bought off by US agents, but Kearny had not been given any cash for this purpose, so any deal would have been private. Whatever the case, having left a celebratory champagne and oyster dinner for his brother and sister-in-law, Magoffin rushed on to Chihuahua, where his reputation stood very high and where he presumably sought to pull off the same feat.[74] Unfortunately for Magoffin, a Mexican patrol detained his companion Henry Connelly

---

72. After the capture of Veracruz George Bancroft, who had moved to the embassy in London from being secretary of navy, wrote to the president that

> ... even Lord Palmerston, who, more than any of them, has one system of politics for England and quite a different one for the other countries, spoke to me in the very warmest language of the generosity of America toward the Irish, and of the immense superiority of the Anglo-Saxon race as displayed in our great number of victories over the Mexicans.... England is even preparing to hear of our negotiating for half, or two-thirds or even the whole of Mexico.

Bancroft, London, to Pres. Polk, 14 May 1847, in M. De Wolfe Howe (ed.), *Life and Letters of George Bancroft*, II, London 1908, p. 18.

73. *The War with Mexico* (1919), Gloucester, Mass., 1963, I, p. 294.

74. In 1841, following the abortive Texan raid on Santa Fe and when distrust of Anglo-Americans was very high, the Mexican government entrusted the pay of that town's garrison to Magoffin's wagon-train. According to Howard Lamar,

> Of the brothers – all of whom [Beriah, James, and Samuel] were notably able, lively and extremely energetic – it was evident that James was the most popular and attractive to the Mexicans. Naturally convivial, full of Irish wit and drollery, a master story-teller and lavish dispenser of hospitality and drinks, he soon became 'Don Santiago' to nearly every person of note in the Mexican border provinces.

S. Drumm (ed.), *Down the Santa Fé Trail and into Mexico: The Diary of Susan Shelby Magoffin, 1846–47*, New Haven, Conn., 1962, p. xix.

and found on him a letter from Kearny to Magoffin praising him for his role in the capture of New Mexico.

> This letter contained sufficient evidence for the Mexican officials to shoot Magoffin. Instead the Mexican officer in charge of Magoffin had become so fond of his convivial and extra-ordinarily hospitable prisoner – Magoffin later boasted that he had expended 2,900 bottles of champagne on his captors – that he handed Magoffin the upopened [sic] letter with the remark that if it was unimportant, just to pitch it into the fire.[75]

How accurate this account might be is difficult to discern. Magoffin certainly had the cash first to save his life and later to buy his freedom. Moreover, the War Department balked at the expense account of $37,780.36 that he submitted after hostilities – 'nine months' imprisonment in Chihuahua and Durango (can't be estimated)' – only inso-far as to reduce it to expenses of $17,000 and pay of $13,000. As for the letter, perhaps the best approach to adopt is that taken by Alfred Hitchcock, who employed the Scottish–Irish origin of Magoffin's name to describe mystifying red herrings.[76]

HEROES WITHOUT A CAUSE?

A sharp sense that the war of 1847 was lost by Mexico rather than won by the USA has permeated the historiography of the former ever since. The traditional perspective on both sides of the border was that the defeat flowed naturally from the political instability of the 'age of Santa Anna' (from independence to 1855) when politico-military chieftains or caudillos competed aggressively for power. At one level this instability is incontestable and can be rendered in simple numbers: between 1821 and 1855 twenty-five individuals, of whom only seven were civilians, served as president. Santa Anna himself held that office on eleven occasions. Moreover, as Michael Costeloe explains, this condition deteriorated in the decade between the secession of Texas and the war:

---

75. Ibid., p. xxviii.
76. Hitchcock explains the term when discussing *Foreign Correspondent* with Truffaut:

    François Truffaut: Isn't the MacGuffin the pretext for the plot?

    Alfred Hitchcock: Well, it's the device, the gimmick, if you will, or the papers the spies are after. I'll tell you about it. Most of Kipling's stories, as you know, were set in India, and they dealt with the fighting between the natives and the British forces on the Afghanistan border. Many of them were spy stories, and they were concerned with the efforts to steal the secret plans out of the fortress. The theft of secret documents was the original MacGuffin. So 'the MacGuffin' is the term we use to cover all that sort of thing: to steal plans or documents, or discover a secret, it doesn't matter what it is. And the logicians are wrong in trying to figure out the truth about a MacGuffin, since it is beside the point. The only thing that really matters is that in the picture the plans, documents or secrets must seem to be of vital importance to the character.

TABLE 17   Changes in senior executive posts, Mexico

	President	Minister of War	Minister of Finance	Minister of Foreign Relations	Minister of Interior
1840	0	0	0	1	5
1841	2	1	4	3	0
1842	1	0	0	0	1
1843	2	3	0	0	1
1844	4	5	4	4	1
1845	0	1	3	1	4
1846	4	6	16	7	9
1847	5	4	7	7	10
1848	2	3	6	2	3
1849	0	0	5	3	2
1850	0	0	4	0	0

Source: D.F. Stevens, *Origins of Instability in Early Republican Mexico*, Durham, N.C., 1991, p. 11.

The centralist decade was an eventful period in Mexico's always eventful history. Ten individuals had occupied the presidential palace – eight army officers and two civilians – and there were several hundred ministerial changes as various administrations came and went. The 1836 constitution, or *Siete Leyes*, had lasted four and a half years until its replacement by the *Bases de Tacubaya* in 1841, which in turn was removed in favour of the *Bases Orgánicas* in 1843, which survived, if only on paper, until the restoration of the 1824 federal charter in 1846. *Pronunciamientos* had been declared more or less continuously, and Mexico City had witnessed the human and physical devastation of warfare in 1840 and 1841 as well as the comparatively bloodless coups of 1844, 1845 and 1846. Two presidents – Bustamante and Herrera – had been arrested in person inside the walls of the national palace, and apart from the interim occupants of the presidential quarters, every president had been driven unwillingly from office as a result of armed rebellion, with the unique exception of the peaceful coup by congress against the Santa Anna–Canalizo regime of 1844. Texas had been lost forever. Yucatán was virtually independent for much of the decade.[77]

Of course, change is not intrinsically a bad thing, and change of presidents or prime ministers does not necessarily reflect instability elsewhere in the system. But there is virtual unanimity amongst historians that it was highly prejudicial to economic and social cohesion during the first three decades of the republic, weakening any prospect of orderly administration of the state, regardless of whether it was along *puro* (federalist), *moderado*, conservative or monarchist lines. Donald Stevens's tabulation of executive turnover during the 1840s (table 17) drives this point home. The impact

---

Hitchcock/Truffaut, New York 1984, p. 138. A recent example of the device may be seen in Harold Becker's *Mercury Rising*.

77. Michael P. Costeloe, *The Central Republic in Mexico, 1835–1846*, Cambridge 1993, p. 298.

of the US invasion is evident in the high turnover in 1846 and 1847, but it is also clear that defeat did not have an immediately cathartic effect on the political elite and 'the many factions ... continued their bitter rivalries, and the chaotic instability in both national and state governments remained unabated' following the campaign.[78]

Where opinion does divide is over the explanation for such disunity and conflict. According to Will Fowler, there are four indentifiable interpretative schools stressing different factors: a predatory praetorianism, where the military lacked any ideology; the institutional conditions of the post-independence army, in which pay and conditions were important determinants of political activity; military intervention as a result of circumstances created by civilian political groups; and a pre-eminence of ideology in which the civil–military divide is blurred and conducive to intrigue.[79] Perhaps it is this combination of a very desultory record and a variety of partly contradictory explanations that led Timothy Anna to remark that

> Early nineteenth-century Mexican history ... has long been the black hole of Mexican historiography. I use the term *black hole* in both its major senses as a hypothetical celestial body of such intense gravitational pull that none who draw near can resist its attraction and of such density that little light escapes, and also as a pit of such fathomless depth that the observer draws back from its infinity.[80]

It does seem plain that the combination of a strong militarist ethos, resilient civilist opposition and extensively but poorly organised regular and militia forces failed to endow Mexico with a military capacity to repel foreign invasion. The competition between the regular army and civic militias was of an entirely different order to that experienced by the US forces during the campaign. In Mexico the militia had long been used as a force in national and local political competition, and in the year before the war it had played a leading role in removing Santa Anna from office. However, the militias were frequently disbanded by governments fearful of the threat they posed – in January 1845 the volunteers of Puebla successfully resisted a siege by regular troops for a week – concerned at their association with liberal and radical currents, or just jealously protective of the regular army's privileges under the *fuero militar*.[81] This

78. Michael P. Costeloe, 'Mariano Arizcorreta and Peasant Unrest in the State of Mexico, 1849', *BLAR*, 15:1, 1996, p. 69.

79. 'Military Political Identity and Reformism in Independent Mexico: An Analysis of the *Memorias de Guerra* (1821–1855)', Research Paper no. 47, Institute of Latin American Studies, London 1996. One explanation that Fowler did not feel it necessary to include as a serious contender is that which focuses on the personality of Santa Anna, and Stevens sees this as a subset of the praetorian thesis:

> Antonio López de Santa Anna ... has been the principal scapegoat for the trials of the young nation. One man's flawed character has been blamed for Mexico's problems, as if Santa Anna's personal weaknesses infected the entire nation. The contagion has been called caudillismo.... The caudillo thesis discounts political motivations and regards caudillos as unprincipled opportunists who mimicked political discourse to hide personal ambitions.

Origins of Instability, p. 2.

80. 'Demystifying Early-Nineteenth-Century Mexico', *Mexican Studies*, 9:1, 1993, p. 117.

81. According to Linda Arnold,

'politicisation' delayed the call-up following the US annexation of Texas in March 1845 as well as contributing to the low level of enlistment once the Herrera government had, on 16 July, finally authorised mobilisation. Whatever the problems acquiring volunteers in the states of the USA, they were miniscule compared to those in Mexico, where only eleven men joined up in the capital on the first day and thirty in the first week whilst nobody at all signed up in Guanajato and San Luis Potosí. For some, such as Carlos María Bustamante, this was not at all a national calamity or 'a great evil, but a great benefit, as the soldiers are the former *cívicos*, famous for their wickedness and offenders of laws and Christian piety. This only proves the common sense of the nation, for it hates and abhors this rabble.'[82]

With a total of over 20,000 men under arms, Mexico ostensibly possessed enough regular troops to provide a stop-gap and detain Taylor's advance towards Matamoros whilst a concerted effort was made in the interior to organise national defence. However, of the 3,450 troops of the División del Norte charged with patrolling the border of 140 leagues under General Mariano Arista, only 930 were at Matamoros. Moreover, Arista, who spent the first months of 1846 plotting to overthrow the government, lacked horses, mules, powder or cash to pay scouts and so determine the whereabouts and movements of the invading army. Neither did he possess a supply of food to sustain a force of any size beyond the town.[83]

These were the circumstances that had led to the desertion of over 4,000 recruits sent to guard the Texan border over the previous four years, convincing US Ambassador Waddy Thompson (who served as governor of South Carolina during the war) that the Mexican army was in organisational and logistical terms a most inferior institution. Although Thompson's view that both its horses and its men were 'too small' might now seem a rather quaint judgement, he was surely on strong grounds in identifying a failure to engage in 'tactical evolution' since the independence war fought along Napoleonic lines. Despite erratic efforts – usually at the hands of General José María Tornel – at restoring the military academy and renewing methods, exercises continued to be based on 'mere mêlées' ending in charges by the cavalry, 'which is, therefore, the favourite corps with all Mexican officers'. Thompson's prejudice may

---

The colonial legacy of a corporate military and a system of corporate military justice persisted in Mexico through the 1850s.... Just policing the military proved an overwhelming task.... A cursory count of criminal cases that came before the national military appellate court betwen 1838 and 1854 yields 354 desertion (absent from roll call for four days) cases, 512 desertion from guard duty cases, 84 jail breaks, 315 homicide cases, 250 physical injury cases, over 800 robbery cases with many of these cases involving more than one suspect.... Most members of the military, as most ordinary folk, died without much, if any property. In fact, by the early 1840s the military judicial notary had begun to file suits against estates for nonpayment of recording fees.

'Privileged Justice? The *Fuero Militar* in Early National Mexico', paper to the Fourth Conference on Nineteenth-Century Latin American History, Institute of Latin American Studies, University of London, May 1996, pp. 8, 6, 5, 17.

82. Quoted in Pedro Santoni, 'A Fear of the People: The Civic Militia of Mexico in 1845', *HAHR*, 68:2, 1988, pp. 283–4.

83. George M. Brack, *Mexico Views Manifest Destiny, 1821–1846*, Albuquerque 1975, pp. 154–5.

have led him to underestimate the degree to which the army's conscripts were trained – he thought that one trooper in ten had handled a rifle and one in a hundred had fired one – but it is a fact that pressganging continued for five years after the war and troopers were provided with no rations, having to serve – very often through their families – as their own commissaries:

> The soldiers of the Mexican army are generally collected by sending out recruiting detachments into the mountains, where they hunt the Indians in their dens and caverns, and bring them in chains to Mexico; there is scarcely a day that droves of these miserable and more than half-naked wretches are not seen thus chained together and marching through the streets to the barracks, where they are scoured and then dressed in a uniform made of linen cloth or serge, and are occasionally drilled.[84]

With such a rank and file it is hardly surprising that many Mexican officers thought, like General Juan Alvarez, that although it would be a 'great calamity' to enter into negotiations over the US annexation of Texas, going to war over it would be a far worse option.[85] Yet, as Thompson's successor Wilson Shannon reported to Calhoun in October 1844, there was no political division over the question of Texas in Mexico similar to that occurring in the US election campaign. Both conservative and liberal currents

> created a public opinion which they cannot, if they were so disposed, easily resist or control. It is true that many intelligent Mexicans privately entertain and express opinions favorable to the amicable arrangement of the difficulties with Texas, and believe that the proposed invasion, if attempted, would result in no good to Mexico. But there are few who have the boldness to express these opinions publicly, or who would be willing to stem the current of popular prejudice by undertaking to carry them out.[86]

In short, public opinion – and one less economically based than the comparable pro-slavery sentiment in Brazil which a couple of years later would dissuade the Barão de Cairu from breaking ranks – was so strong that vital pragmatic considerations were drowned out by patriotic emotion. And yet, according to Timothy Anna, at independence, 'a "national project" was not possible until the regions played their fair share in defining it. The Mexicans had yet to create Mexico.'[87]

That the country went to war over a frontier with a seceded and annexed province suggests that such a creation was under way by 1846. That it did so through a failure of political will, having lost the territory in the first place, and with weak and unprepared forces, indicates the extent of its shortcomings. That the war was then lost undoubtedly contributed to the subsequent construction of Mexican nationhood, but

---

84. *Recollections of Mexico*, London 1847, p. 170; Ruth Olivera and Liliane Crete, *Life in Mexico under Santa Anna, 1822–1855*, Norman, Okla., 1991, pp. 159–61. For a summary of Tornel's (often illusory) reports, see Fowler, 'Military Political Identity', pp. 23–40.

85. Brack, *Mexico Views Manifest Destiny*, p. 156.

86. Quoted in ibid., p. 132.

87. 'Demystifying Early Nineteenth-Century Mexico', p. 122.

at the time there was a sense of impotence and despair within the elite. When, at the end of March 1846, Taylor arrived at the Rio Grande and General Paredes issued a declaration of war, José Fernando Ramírez, a congressman from Durango, wrote,

I am going out in the street to add to the number of imbeciles. Shortly before 4 o'clock General Valencia left the Palace for his home with a large staff accompanied by an immense number of people. At the same time people who had gone up to the towers of the cathedral and all the churches started to ring the bells furiously. Now try to believe in the sovereignty of the people! Strain your mental powers to the bursting point to find anything that can justify their actions! These citizens of ours are nothing but a flock of sheep that need the lash. They are good for nothing except to maintain a few ambitious and ignorant demagogues in power.

A year later, in the wake of the Battle of Cerro Gordo – 'a rout as complete as it was shameful' – Ramírez reflected that, 'When a nation gets to such a point of financial distress it does it no good to have a large army or to have a patriotism great enough to build an army if there were the means to support it. What happens when a nation cannot count on either a large army or patriotism?'[88] A year after that, the Treaty of Guadalupe Hidalgo signed, *El Siglo XIX* declared,

The elements of disintegration which have accumulated in the country, previously [as] internal discord and recently as foreign war, have such force and are so numerous ... that at first glance one could doubt if our republic is really a society or only a simple collection of men, without the bonds, the rights or the duties which constitute a society.[89]

Here again, though, one picks up the note of hesitation and ambiguity. Just as Mariano Otero declared that national spirit did not exist, 'for there is no nation', so he marvelled at how this 'simple collection of men' poured money into a war effort when they knew that it was in vain and their money lost for ever.[90] For what reason did the population of Veracruz, its volunteer soldiers outnumbered by three to one by a professional force and with no sensible hope of outside help, endure a bombardment of 7,000 shells for ninety hours? Perhaps, rather than Mexicans, they simply felt themselves to be steadfast townsfolk and so in honour bound to 'see the elephant' which had visited them from the sea. Likewise, Robert Johannsen's description of the Mexican cavalry at Buena Vista in February 1847 can be construed at face value – an old-fashioned mix of vainglory and adrenalin, marvellous to behold, in stark contrast to dull Yankee efficiency, and unrepresentative of any profound idea of community:

Shortly after noon on the 23rd, some 1,500 lancers, the 'Chivalry of Mexico' in bright scarlet coats, shiny buttons and snow-white belts, their horses richly caparisoned, advanced

---

88. *Mexico during the War with the United States*, Columbia, Mo., 1950, pp. 34, 124.

89. *El Siglo XIX*, 1 June 1848, quoted in Charles A. Hale, 'The War with the United States and the Crisis in Mexican Thought', *The Americas*, XIV, Oct. 1957, p. 155.

90. *Consideraciones sobre la situación política y social de la República de México en el año 1847*, reproduced in Cecil Robinson (ed.), *The View from Chapultepec: Mexican Writers on the Mexican–American War*, Tucson, Ariz., 1989, pp. 5–32.

on the American line like knights on a medieval field, crimson pennants and brightly-colored banners waving over their ranks. Sitting erect in their saddles, their brass helmets topped with flowing red and black plumes, their lances decorated with ribbons and reflecting the bright sunlight, they moved 'at an easy hand-gallop', their lines perfectly dressed, never losing their intervals or breaking their formations. Bugles sounded the charge and the horsemen chanted a song as they moved forward. The movement had a nonchalance about it that recalled the 'ideal picture of the cavalry of olden days'.[91]

Buena Vista was a bloody battle for both sides. According to Bauer, 'although the fire of the American artillery tore horrible gaps in the Mexican line – the engineers, for instance, lost half their men – the attackers kept coming'.[92] The losses reported by Santa Anna amounted to 591 killed, 1,048 wounded and 1,894 missing – a casualty toll nearly equivalent to the entire US force that took the field and including many pressganged Indian infantrymen who had been force-marched up from San Luis Potosí without any break and who were just as frightened and suggestible as those who twelve weeks later were to flee from Scott's men:

> … the soldiers are telling terrible tales that bring to mind the Conquest. Some say that the enemy soldiers are such huge, strong men that they can cut an opponent in two with a single sweep of their swords. It is also said that their horses are gigantic and very fast and that their muskets discharge shots which, once they leave the gun, divide into fifty pieces, each one fatal and well-aimed. Let us say nothing of their artillery, which has inspired fear and terror in all our troops and is undeniable proof of our backwardness in military art.[93]

To fight bravely when one feels doomed as cannon fodder is not a sure sign of 'national spirit' and might be thought a necessary and natural response. But a display of pride and refusal to buckle was evident amongst the citizens of New Mexico and California who could entertain little hope of help from regular forces and only choose whether to capitulate in style or harry the gringo in extemporised fashion. In August 1846, when Stephen Kearny occupied Santa Fe, he was told by Juan Bautista Vigil,

> The speech which you have just delivered, in which you announce that you have taken possession of this great country in the name of the United States of America, gives us some idea of the wonderful future that awaits us. It is not for us to determine the boundaries of nations. The cabinets in Mexico and Washington will arrange these differences. It is for us to obey and respect the established authorities, no matter what might be our private opinions.
>
> The inhabitants of this territory humbly and honourably present their loyalty and allegiance to the government of North America. No one in this world can resist the power of he who is stronger. Do not find it strange that there is no manifestation of joy and enthusiasm in seeing this city occupied by your military forces. To us the power of the Mexican Republic is dead. No matter what the condition, she was our mother. What child will not shed abundant tears at the tomb of his parents?[94]

---

91. *To the Halls of the Montezumas*, p. 95.
92. *Mexican War*, p. 216.
93. Ramírez, *Mexico during the War with the United States*, p. 135.
94. Quoted in L. Valdez and S. Steiner, *Aztlán*, cited in Christopher Ricks and William Vance (eds), *The Faber Book of America*, London 1992, pp. 411–12.

In contrast, as noted by Antonio María Osio, there were some grounds for mounting resistance in California a week earlier:

> The population of Los Angeles was so large that the commander general (Don José María Flores) could have recruited 300 capable men there with fine horses. However, since there were not enough weapons and munitions, he could outfit only 80 men. Meanwhile, the corvette *Cyane*, under the command of Captain Mervine, anchored in San Pedro Bay. He and about 400 men went ashore and began the nine-league march to Los Angeles. The *angelinos* had acquired a very small cannon which they would fire to celebrate special occasions. Unfortunately, the vent on the cannon was too wide, and those who wanted to play artilleryman would be injured and might even lose their thumbs when they fired it. Even though the cannon had this defect, the *angelinos*, aware that it could do more damage through its mouth than through its vent, believed that it was an excellent defence. However, it was not mounted on a gun carriage. So to make it more powerful, they mounted it on a cart made from a tree trunk and left to engage Captain Mervine's forces.
>
> Mervine had confidence in the size of his corps of well-armed soldiers, and he did not deem it necessary to unload any large pieces of artillery. He advanced to the Domínguez family ranch, where he was approached by Flores and his 80 men. Much to his dismay, Mervine began to experience the little cannon's adverse effects. He was forced to place his dead and wounded men in the large carts he had brought as a precaution or for use in the campaign. The *californios* used the few shotgun cartridges they had to fire their cannon; it performed so successfully that Captain Mervine was forced to retreat quickly to the beach.[95]

Not for long. But Stockton first took his force to San Diego, where he prepared for the capture of San Diego in a manner that Osio could hardly bear to recount:

> Because I am a *californio* who loves his country and a Mexican on all four sides and in my heart, as a point of honor, I should keep quiet about the following event or let it go unnoticed or be forgotten, but this would not be in keeping with the purpose of my narrative.
>
> When the commodore arrived in San Diego he encountered some corrupt *californios* and some Mexican traitors. They strongly hoped to improve their condition. They offered themselves and their supplies to the commodore so that he could increase his ranks and resources in the war he was fighting against the men whom they should have regarded as their brothers. They were blinded by their selfish ambition to sell a small number of cattle and horses for a good price. Señor Stockton definitely should have had misgivings about the gratuitous offers of these wretched people, but when their actions showed him that they had black shiny leather hearts, he deemed it wise to praise them. However, if those men had been Americans, Señor Stockton, a patriotic and upright man, would have hanged them like bunches of grapes from every yardarm of his frigate's main mast.[96]

In the same vein, General Scott, who had little compunction in hanging the San Patricios for treason and threatening deserters with the same penalty, was content to let his colonels hire the services of Mexican 'bandits' as guides and spies for the

---

95. Later Osio notes, 'The flag of the North Americans waved in all the populated areas of Alta California, but the Mexican tricolor still flew in a few places as it wandered about its own country, passing through the deserted fields, unable to find shelter from the bad weather.' *The History of Alta California: A Memoir of Mexican California*, Madison, Wis., 1996, pp. 234, 241.

96. Ibid., p. 236.

advance to the capital of their country.[97] Food and supplies were frequently purchased by US forces from communities which were subjected to stiff fines if they were thought to be supporting guerrillas.

In general, when the Anglo-Americans captured Mexican soldiers they released them upon the promise not to take arms again. As the war progressed and the merits of irregular warfare became more compelling, those who broke this undertaking were liable to suffer more than incarceration as prisoners of war and were sometimes shot. José María Roa Barcena provides a spirited account of one famous case that would have restored Osio's pride in his compatriots – not least because it took place months after the capital had fallen – when the stern Tyrone-born General Robert Patterson insisted on the ultimate penalty:

> On 19 or 20 November 1847, a North American advance party in the vicinity of Jacomulco fell upon some of the guerrillas of Rebolledo and apprehended and took to Jalapa the colonel himself, the lieutenant of the 11th infantry regiment, Don Ambrosio Alcalde, the lieutenant of a corps from Veracruz, Don Antonio García, and the lieutenant or captain of the National Guard of Jalapa, Don Rafael Covarrubias, and one or more other officers, leaving them under guard in two rooms of the Posada Veracruzana. They were then brought before a military commission, which judged them summarily and, finding that García and Alcalde, at the surrender of Veracruz, had given their word, before they were released, that they would not again take up arms, condemned these two officers to death. Rebolledo, Covarrubias and the other prisoners, who were not in the same situation, succeeded in getting their case postponed and were taken to the fortress of Perote, notwithstanding the fact that the judges had wanted to condemn the first of these to death because he was, to begin with, the leader of the group, and also because they were ill disposed toward him because of what seemed to be a derisive smirk on his face, which was, in fact, a permanent facial tick.
>
> Alcalde's parents, supported by Mr Kennedy – a rich and respectable Scotsman who had resided for many years at Jalapa and to whom this city had rendered notable services during all the period of the invasion – took immediate steps to solicit the commuting of that young man's sentence as well as that of his companion in misfortune. They saw the governor and military commander (Colonel Hughes, if I remember correctly) and Major General Patterson, who was there at the time; but both of them maintained that the sentence of the court martial had already been confirmed and that they had not the power to revoke it. Hughes, for his part, nevertheless suggested that the city council should solicit the commutation, and in saying so he named a commission from that body ... [which], accompanied by Mr Kennedy serving as interpreter, obtained a long and cordial audience with Patterson without, though, achieving their objective.
>
> The commission put forward the following arguments: that the [Mexican] government obliged its commissioned officers to continue in service; that these officers found themselves in a state of misery and hopelessness after the capitulation of Veracruz; that Alcalde and García were not captured in the course of guerrilla action but rather in carrying out some commission of Governor Soto; and even that Alcalde's youth should be taken into account, he being only twenty or twenty-one years old. Patterson repeated his earlier reply and added that the sentence was just because perjury on the part of the defendants had been proven. In addition, he maintained that pardon under these circumstances would be prejudicial to the Mexicans themselves because in future instances of combat no quarter would be given

---

97. Bauer, *Mexican War*, p. 247.

to prisoners in the knowledge that they could break their word with impunity. If he were to yield in this matter he would lose among his subordinates that essential prestige by which he was able to keep them within bounds. That very morning, he said, he had had two Negroes from a corps of volunteers hanged for the crime of homicide without yielding to the entreaties of their officers. If, therefore, he was now to accede to the desires of the city council, he would lose the necessary power to guarantee, as he intended, the lives and property of those living in the vicinity. Nor were the ecclesiastical authorities successful in their supplication, nor the ladies who presented themselves en masse at the house of Governor Hughes and in whose name Don José Ignacio Estera spoke out eloquently. Not even the spectacle of a lovely little girl of four months, Alcalde's daughter, held before the invaders in the arms of her mother, was able to alter the judgement.

The two condemned officers were taken out that very afternoon from the Posada Veracruzana, where they had been lodged with the other prisoners, to the chapel of the city jail, in the consistorial apartments, where their confessions were taken that night, that of García by Father Compomanes and that of Alcalde by Father Aguilar, guardian of the monastery of San Francisco. Very early the next morning they received Holy Communion, and were immediately afterwards visited by their parents and friends. Both officers were serene and resigned; they ate a light breakfast, and Alcalde had his portrait done by the painter Castillo. He asked me to have a certain article of clothing sent to him. I will never forget his sweet and tranquil voice nor his close embrace, bidding an eternal farewell. The military escort then took the condemned men out into the street, where they were marched, accompanied by a priest, to the small square of San José and placed a short distance from the wall of the barracks. Alcalde, and only at the insistence of the priest, accepted a blindfold, and fully erect, giving a cheer for Mexico, he, together with García, received the discharge of the North American rifles. In the same place in which the victims fell a modest column was later erected in their memory. Those bloody corpses, in the eyes of the people, whose reasoning is usually that which springs from the heart, were not the bodies of officers who had paid for violating their word but rather of the firm defenders of national independence who had been done to death by a foreign enemy. And now the very appearance of these two filled the people with sorrow and at the same time inflamed them with rage. Were not these worthy of envy who with their arms in their hands withdrew into the mountains and backroads, abandoning the tranquillity and security of their homes to contend with hardship and death? ...

The coffins were carried on the shoulders of the respectable people, followed by practically all the population of the area, and were taken from the church to the cemetery, passing by the first and second principal streets, in the second of which Patterson lived. The general and his chief of staff came out onto the balcony, took off their hats and stood silently and gravely at the passing of the bodies and the numerous retinue, which constituted a mute but unmistakable protest.[98]

The fact that US commanders were prepared to risk such a popular reaction when so many of their ordinances were designed to placate the Mexican public indicates the degree to which they were harried by guerrilla activity and worried about the

---

98. *Recuerdos de la invasión*, II, pp. 498–503. *Robert Patterson*, born County Tyrone, 1792; father settled in Pennsylvania following exile for leading role in 1798 insurrection; served in Pennsylvania militia in 1812 war; established grocery in Philadelphia, 1817; married Sarah Ann Eagle of Germantown, with whom he had eleven children; appointed major-general of volunteers, 7 May 1846; commanded division at Cerro Gordo and was second ranking officer in Scott's army; after war developed sugar interests in Louisiana in addition to thirty cotton mills in Pennsylvania; served as major-general in Union army but acted indecisively at the Battle of first Manassas; died 1881.

widespread adoption of irregular warfare. As early as August 1846 Taylor, who was as perceptive a commander as he was cautious, identified this danger:

> I fear the enemy will not fight us for Monterrey … my greatest apprehensions are that they will avoid us in force, attempt to harass us in small parties, attack our trains, attempting to cut off our supplies at favorable positions, destroy the corn and drive away the stock, in which cas[e] we would have to fall back on our supplies near to ar [sic] depots on the water; all of which cannot be ascertained without marching into their country.[99]

The preoccupation was well founded. Both before and after Buena Vista the US forces occupying Monterrey and Taylor's main supply line were subjected to repeated raids by guerrillas under General José Urrea in much the same way as the Veracruz road was attacked through the second half of 1847. In the wake of the Battle of Cerro Gordo (18 April), which effectively opened the road to Jalapa and beyond it to the capital, this danger was palpable as far away as Prescott's study in Boston:

> We ride on conquering and to conquer, as you see, up to the very Halls of Montezuma, and many, I should think, from the positive manner they speak of them expect to find the palace of the Old Aztec still standing. The Mexicans have missed it in fighting pitched battles, instead of trusting to guerrilla warfare. My friend General Miller, who has much experience of the Spanish American character, told me that it is only by the guerrilla that they could fight us with success, and if they pursued that system, they would be invincible. They may trouble us yet in that way, but the capital and the seaports seem destined to come into our hands. But what shall we do with them?[100]

However, there was a general attitude on the Mexican side that guerrilla warfare was 'the last hope of peoples overwhelmed by superior forces' rather than a positive strategic option.[101] Moreover, until the capital fell in mid September 1847, the abandonment of a traditional military apparatus and ambition would have dealt a terrible blow to morale and probably removed any remaining authority from the central state. In some respects, the period between September 1847 and February 1848, when the treaty was finally signed, represents a working through by the Mexican politico-military leadership of the dilemma between, on the one hand, the merits of accepting as a state formal defeat and the possibility of recomposition, and, on the other, those of pursuing a prolonged irregular campaign as an occupied nation against

---

99. Taylor, Camargo, to Wood, 23 April 1846, in *Letters of Zachary Taylor*, p. 47.

100. Prescott, Boston, to Winthrop, 30 May 1847, in *Correspondence of Prescott*, p. 642. This was General William Miller (1795–1861), who, along with his friend Frank O'Connor, had been a leading member of the patriot army in the independence of Peru and Bolivia, and whose experience in the campaigns of 1823–25 led him to reject the idea of standing armies in the sub-continent:

> … the immense extent of territory … would require innumerable garrisons … as there are very few fortified places, detached garrisons would easily be overpowered whenever the natives might choose to attack them by rising en masse.… From the great abundance in South America, and the simple mode of living, the maintaining of guerrillas or montoneros in that country is attended with less difficulty, perhaps, than in any other part of the globe.

John Miller (ed.), *Memoirs of General Miller in the Service of Peru*, II, London 1828, p. 232.

101. Ramírez, *Mexico during the War with the United States*, p. 125.

an army that might eventually be driven through attrition from the interior. This latter option was Washington's nightmare, but on the Mexican side the social and political support for it was already weakened by an all-pervasive sense of military inferiority.

There was, though, a third, much less obvious option attributed by the perceptive Nicholas Trist to the *puro* faction's advocacy of continued belligerancy after the fall of the capital. This was the desire to have the Mexican military system comprehensively destroyed and removed for ever from a political scenario in which civilian government would be guaranteed by close relations with the USA (although these seem to have been conceived of as short of annexation).[102] In the event, such a scenario would have to wait almost a century, until the establishment of the state based on the Partido Revolucionario Institucional (PRI). And it would not then take the shape of a replica of US liberal constitutionalism but of a civilist autocracy licensed by Washington and accepted by the armed forces that had been conceded a reduced but dependable *derecho de petición* in public policy. By 1848 the 'All Mexico' constituency in the United States was quite narrow, disowned even by the Polk administration (scared of being lumbered with undesirable lands and responsibilities), and disliked by most of the senior US commanders (under no illusions as to their fragile hold over the two salients they had driven into the populated heartland of the country).[103]

The US army may have been very small and overstretched before the war, but it operated as effectively as any in a transitional epoch when Napoleonic traditions would be found seriously wanting in the Crimean War and be qualitatively surpassed a decade later in the US Civil War. One important element in this – unseen on the battlefield or in the patriotic literature – was the reliable issue of pay to the troops and pensions to the veterans and disabled (no small matter in consolidating the esprit de corps of those still in service): at the outset of the campaign forty-four agencies were paying out a pension to over 20,000 ex-soldiers twice a year.[104] The pension system was deemed antiquated – the number of ex-soldiers who had died was unknown and only tentatively estimated at 10 per cent – but there was nothing approaching it in Latin America, where there were so many officers like General

---

102. Trist, Mexico City, to Buchanan, 25 Oct. 1847, cited in Pedro Santoni, *Mexicans at Arms: Puro Federalists and the Politics of War, 1845–1848*, Fort Worth, Tex., 1996, p. 215.

103. In April 1847 Secretary of State Buchanan wrote brusquely to the Tyrone-born James Shields, who had been head of the land office and risen to brigadier as a commander of the Illinois volunteers:

> You desire to annex the country on this side of the Sierra Madre mountains to the United States. This would not be in accordance with public opinion in our country. How should we govern the mongrel race which populates it? Could we admit them to seats in our Senate and House of Representatives? Are they capable of Self-Government as States of this Confederacy? Besides, the acquisition of that Territory would raise a terrible excitement on the question of slavery.

Buchanan, Washington, to Shields, 23 Apr. 1847, in *Works of Buchanan*, VII, pp. 286–7. Calhoun applied the same logic to *all* lands annexed from Mexico. One cannot but help noting the manner in which this dilemma is circumvented under NAFTA.

104. W.L. Marcy, Secretary of War, to Pres. Polk, 5 Dec. 1846 and 2 Dec. 1847, in *BFSP, 1846–47*, XXXV, p. 117; *BFSP, 1847–48*, XXXVI, London 1861, p. 771.

Francisco Burdett O'Connor – who had served for decades and never received a real in pension – that this was to become a literary theme as well as a source of political discontent.[105]

Newer and more directly relevant was the telegraph, which helped to bring news back from the troops at unprecedented velocity and enabled orders to be sent out more rapidly. However, there were no lines at all on Mexican territory and the network within the USA was not yet extensive. The passage of the news of the surrender of Veracruz on 29 March 1847 gives an idea of the scale of speed involved:

> Immediately after the surrender ceremony, the Princeton put to sea. She carried Commodore Conner and Colonel Totten. The latter had in his baggage Scott's official announcement of the seizure of the port. The steamer touched at Pensacola on April 3 from whence an express rider carried the news of the victory to Charleston, South Carolina, and from there a steamer took it to Baltimore. There it rode the telegraph wires to Washington, arriving on the tenth, two days before Totten.[106]

Furthermore, the existence of lines between Baltimore and Washington offered no guarantee that the government's analysis of information and generation of new instructions would accelerate. In mid June 1846 General Taylor was complaining at the absence of an official reponse to the Battles of Palo Alto and Resaca de la Palma, fought over a month earlier:

> It is strange, passing strange that I have heard nothing from Washing[ton] since my official report of the battles of the 8th and 9th reached there, which I have seen published in the *National Intelligencer and Union*, the receipt of them have not been acknowledged – something is going on at the general headquarters in regard to this matter that we are not aware of.

Taylor, like any general in the field, was quick to complain about his logistical back-up, which was weakest at the very start of the campaign and delayed the advance inland from Matamoros. Indeed, he initially expressed (in his inimitable style) the view that this might be the result of some deliberate manoeuvre against him:

> I am perfectly disgusted with the way they are going on, I consider this an entire breakdown in the Quartermaster department everywhere; there are more than 10,000 men here and in its vicinity, waiting, and a portion of them a month, for small steam boats and waggons to carry their provisions toward the enemy, which have been required more than a month, time enough to have sent to Liverpool for them, without having heard of or from them, up to the present time. Was I a prominent or ambitious aspirant for civil distinction or honors,

---

105. The doctor interrupted his reading of the newspapers. He looked at the colonel. Then he looked at the postmaster seated in front of the telegraph key, and then again at the colonel.

    'We're leaving,' he said.

    The postmaster didn't raise his head.

    'Nothing for the colonel,' he said.

    The colonel felt ashamed.

    'I wasn't expecting anything,' he lied. He turned to the doctor with an entirely childish look. 'No one writes to me.'

Gabriel García Márquez, *No One Writes to the Colonel*, Harmondsworth 1974, p. 17.

106. Bauer, *Mexican War*, p. 253.

I might very readily suppose there was an intention somewhere among the high functionaries to break me down.

Later – despite having received no horseshoes or nails for three months – he was inclined to adopt a more typically prejudiced view:

> It is unnecessary to animadvert on the Quartermaster's department. The system is certainly a bad one, and a large portion of its officers feeble and would be so in any relations in life, but which is more apparent in their present positions, which requires so much [more] energy and decision than in many other professions or pursuits.[107]

There was little love during the war between Taylor and his erstwhile friend Quartermaster General Thomas S. Jesup, who, having served in the corps since 1818, was almost as experienced and who could object that, 'with our depots farther from the sources of supply than Algiers is from Toulon or Marseilles, we accomplished more in the first six months of our operations in Mexico than France, the first military power in Europe, has accomplished in Africa in 17 years'.[108] This was a reasonable analogy, even if the bureaucratic checks and balances employed by the department in peacetime to cut graft did initially hold up some supplies (and when these controls were slackened in 1847 Jesup found himself conned out of $1.6 million in a scam run out of New Orleans by the corrupt chief clerk to the treasury and the banker William Corcoran).[109]

In fact, the superiority of the US forces in the field owed a great deal to their logistical support. When Jesup appraised the requirements for moving a 25,000-strong force from Veracruz to Mexico City, he reckoned on 2,893,950 pounds of supplies in 9,303 wagons and on the backs of 17,413 mules. Amongst these supplies he included 300,000 bushels of oats and 200,000 of corn as well as 100,000 horseshoes, 100 pounds of blister ointment, 5,000 quills, 300 bottles of ink and 1,000 pounds of office tape. Scott, who was to command the expedition, wanted lesser quantities, but even his professed needs amounted to nearly three-quarters of the impedimenta planned by the punctilious Jesup. Furthermore, in order to meet Scott's requirements for the bombardment and capture of Veracruz in the first place, forty-nine 10-inch howitzers and 50,000 shells were ordered, manufactured, transported to Atlantic ports and delivered to the expedition within the space of twelve weeks under the supervision of the quartermaster's department.[110]

The scale of weaponry and quantity of ammunition issued by the department in the first year of the war was correspondingly impressive: 18-pound and 24-pound siege cannon; 8-inch and 10-inch siege howitzers; 6-pound and 12-pound bronze field cannon; 12-pound and 24-pound bronze field howitzers; 12-pound mountain

---

107. Taylor, Matamoros, to Wood, 12 June 1846; Taylor, Matamoros, to Wood, 21 June 1846; Taylor, Camargo, to Wood, 23 August 1846, in *Letters of Zachary Taylor*, pp. 9, 13, 46.
108. Quoted in Johannsen, *To the Halls of the Montezumas*, p. 15.
109. Bauer, *Mexican War*, pp. 84, 272.
110. Ibid., pp. 259, 235.

howitzers; travelling forges; battery wagons; artillery harnesses; 20,000 rounds of siege artillery shells; 30,000 field artillery shells; 60,000 rounds of mortar shells; 1,000 cannonballs; 40,000 pounds of black gunpowder; 1,300 rockets; 24,000 muskets; 3,000 rifles; 2,000 carbines; 1,000 pistols; 2,000 sabres; 2,000 short swords; 12 million cartridges; 40,000 flints; a million percussion caps.[111] Here again one finds a state of transition rather than revolution, with the flintlock still in much greater use than the percussion-cap weapons, which were much more reliable even if – as Marx discovered a decade later when preparing the entry for the *New American Cyclopaedia* – there were still many different types of cap. The easily used smooth-bore musket had yet to be replaced by the more accurate rifle. Moreover, all these were muzzle-loading weapons. The breech-loading, bolt-action rifle had first been developed in 1828, but it was not adopted for military use anywhere until 1848, when the Prussian army began to use it. The repeating rifle first appeared in 1851, but two years later the British army adopted the Enfield muzzle-loader, which was 54 inches long and weighed 9 pounds, as its standard infantry weapon, and this was extensively used on both sides in the US Civil War. Steel was first made by the Bessemer process in 1856, and over the next five years repeating weapons were gradually developed, but it was only after the Civil War that these were established, the Springfield, Tyler Henry and Spencer breech-loading rifles becoming a standard feature of the modern military arsenal and quickly adopted throughout the world, including the Americas. In the war of 1847, then, the US forces had more, and more reliable, weapons than their Mexican foe, but their guns were not so much qualitatively superior as rather more advanced.[112]

There was, however, a major disparity between the skill and resources of the gunners on both sides. In the case of the bombardment of Veracruz the crucial element was quantity. Although at the turn of the century Daniel Clark had, after visiting this port-city protected by the formidable island fortress of San Juan de Ulúa, reckoned it to be vulnerable to attack from the sea, in 1846 the expectations of US commanders that a major bombardment would be necessary to secure capitulation were reasonable and widely shared. In the event, the barrage lasted for four days, during which 6,700 rounds of shot and shell, weighing a total of 500,000 pounds, were fired into the town, killing at least 100 civilians and probably as many soldiers (the figures given by the Mexican government were five times greater). Two-thirds of the shells were from the huge 10-inch mortars and heavy guns of the naval battery that had been sent ashore to augment them.[113] This intensity of firepower – and the planning that lay behind it – was of a type that presaged the Civil War. Its massive

---

111. Ganoe, *History of the United States Army*, p. 208. A howitzer is a cannon with a short barrel, steep angle of fire and low muzzle velocity.

112. Ibid., pp. 198–9; Bauer, *Mexican War*, p. 188.

113. Bauer, *Mexican War*, p. 253. Commodore Conner had thought that in order to take Ulúa and Veracruz he would need five ships-of-the-line (seventy-four guns), three frigates, four bomb vessels and some sloops. Scott initially assessed the army's needs for the operation at 10,000 men including 600 artillery-men. The decision to undertake the attack was made before these projections were reduced – an indication of the scale of Washington's commitment.

character inevitably entailed what is today termed by the military 'collateral damage', but in the mid nineteenth century there was no euphemism for the slaughter of civilians in besieged towns – a practice that would shortly be eliminated as a norm in warfare precisely by modern artillery – and the Geneva Convention lay sixteen years in the future.

The bombardment of Veracruz proved to be the sole instance of a city falling to an artillery barrage because the ordnance required for such an offensive could not be carried far inland without huge numbers of draught animals. Taylor, whose army contained sixteen of the forty batteries possessed by the army at the start of the campaign, was unable to lay siege to Monterrey because he only had one 10-inch mortar and two 24-pound howitzers. In fact, the superiority of the US artillery in the major battles was due less to the heavy guns than to the light 6-pound cannon, which could be readily manoeuvred to forward positions – the cannoneers riding on the horses rather than the limbers of the piece – to break up troop formations with canister and grapeshot, while still being accurate over 1,000 yards. At the first battle of the war, Palo Alto, such use of fragmentation-shot was so effective that only one US infantry unit had to engage the Mexican troops. At Buena Vista the military effectively saved the day with only ten guns against the Mexicans' 24-pounders, which, although manned by the San Patricios, were too cumbersome for advantage to be taken of their extra range.[114]

In Santa Anna's account of that battle, 'Taylor was driven back, losing three cannon, a field forge, three flags, and more than 2,000 dead, wounded and prisoners. He managed to escape decisive defeat on the second day.'[115] This is not wholly inaccurate, but neither is the Mexican commander's breathless description of the problems he faced in preparing an army to take the field against the Anglo-Americans:

> Previously, the general treasury of the nation had supplied the commissary of the army with the basic necessities for each soldier. Now there was no money to supply the essentials needed, and each day our needs increased.... Harassed on every side, I racked my brain for a way out. Victory was the only answer. I knew that if we did not move, we were dead.... I knew that I would have to make personal sacrifices for my country's safety, and I did not hesitate. I had the mint coin a hundred bars of silver, giving as collateral the total sum of property I owned – worth half a million pesos ... by my efforts, in January 1847, the inhabitants of San Luis Potosí could survey a well-equipped, thoroughly instructed army of some 18,000 men.[116]

As we have seen, the cavalry may have been impressive, but the equipment as well as the skills of the rest of the Mexican forces was inferior. They had plenty of shot and musket-balls, which, because they were made of copper, the American troops feared, thinking that any wound they caused would poison and mean certain death.

---

114. Ibid., pp. 57, 156; D.E. Houston, 'The Role of Artillery in the Mexican War', *Journal of the West*, XI:2, 1972.
115. Antonio López de Santa Anna, *The Eagle: The Autobiography of Santa Anna*, Austin, Tex., 1967, p. 93.
116. Ibid., pp. 90–91.

However, the artillery shot were crudely cast, their flat spots and rough surfaces reducing accuracy. Poor powder meant that, in addition to 'growling and whistling' in flight, Mexican cannonballs often fell short of their target. The blue streak that they left in clear air sometimes enabled the US soldiers to dodge incoming missiles, and there were few cases of Anglo-Americans being cut up by artillery except, as in Mervine's case at Los Angeles, when taken by surprise.[117] Equally, as Waddy Thompson had observed, the marksmanship of the Mexican troopers was weak because of lack of practice caused by low supplies of gunpowder. Their British muskets weighed over 10 pounds and were not commonly used outside formal military ranks, with the result that the inexperienced infantry often fired high. (At Tacubaya, however, the downward slope of the ground compensated for this, and the US forces were subjected to a withering fire.) It was at close quarters, in hand-to-hand combat, that most discrepancies disappeared and casualty rates converged (even when the Mexican troops were green, as at Buena Vista). The battles fought around Mexico City reflect this, although one must also take into account the fact that the local forces were in defensive positions and included proportionately more members of the urban elite and middle class than did the armies in the field.

Finally, Mexico possessed no navy worthy of the name to act as the first line of resistance or transport its troops. The government issued letters of marque to privateers in June 1846, but only two Spanish vessels were ever fitted out. As a consequence, the Mexican forces were generally deployed in reaction to US initiatives and, lacking strategic mobility, operated on the defensive. For Justo Sierra O'Reilly, the only answer was to put even greater numbers of men into the field, but the quantities required to compensate for US superiority in armaments were completely impracticable. Once victory had been missed at Buena Vista, Mexico could not win a regular war.[118]

Politics in Command

Sierra was just as disconsolately clear about the personal capacity of Santa Anna to lead his country's war effort:

> The masses, who had frequently reviled him and pulled down his statues and destroyed his trophies, now hailed Santa Anna as a messiah. He in turn had but one thought. This was to redeem himself, to become a simple soldier fighting for his fatherland. Unfortunately, the soldier could never be a general; still, he was to be the generalissimo.[119]

117. Curtis, *Mexico under Fire*, p. 105; Bauer, *Mexican War*, p. 155.
118. *Evolución Política*, in Ruiz (ed.), *The Mexican War*, p. 115.
119. Ibid.

For Jack Bauer, Santa Anna displayed obvious technical insufficiencies as a commander:

> The Buena Vista campaign represented Santa Anna's sole offensive of the war. It showed a better grasp of strategic realities and more sophisticated conception than execution. Santa Anna was not a good battlefield general. Neither he nor his troops were capable of responding to changing tactical situations.

At the time, Winfield Scott was of the same view:

> His vigilance and energy were unquestionable, and his powers of creating and organizing worthy of admiration. He was also great in administrative ability, and though not deficient in personal courage, he, on the field of battle, failed in quickness of perception and rapidity of combination. Hence his defeats.[120]

It was, though, convenient for Scott, whose opinion of Zachary Taylor was not high, to explain Buena Vista in terms of the enemy's weaknesses. The Mexican general's own account of the outcome of the battle understandably takes a different tack:

> The battle was going our way, and everyone in our camp felt that victory would be ours the following day. We were confident of our success, but how things change! Suddenly our confidence turned to grief and despair. By word of mouth, the news travelled to our camp – revolution in the capital! A special message was dispatched from the government to send the news to us. The government ordered our troops back to defend the capital and restore law and order. The minister of war was adamant; the army must return…. I ordered a junta of generals and agreed with their decision.[121]

Nobody, of course, had ordered Santa Anna about for years unless he was firmly under arrest. And at the time he was not only at the head of Mexico's largest ever army but also president of the republic. Moreover, the revolt to which Santa Anna refers took place on the 27th – four days after the battle – and had his own tacit backing. The melodramatic version presented here is a concoction of later years, when it was widely known that if, on the morrow of 23 February 1847, Santa Anna had returned to the offensive against Taylor's men he could have defeated the US army before snuffing out the revolt and so restoring 'law and order' on an infinitely greater scale. Still, it is a fact that the decree issued on 11 January by the *puro* vice-president, Valentín Gómez Farías, to raise funds for the war effort by mortgaging or selling church property had provoked another collapse in an already chaotic political situation. This, though, was less the result of machinations by maniacally ambitious and sectarian individuals than the natural playing out of ideological divisions and unstable coalitions that had persisted since the founding of the republic and which, exacerbated by the war, could not be suppressed in the name of fighting that same war.

When Mexico had broken diplomatic relations with Washington in March 1845 over the annexation of Texas, the country had been governed for some twelve weeks

---

120. Bauer, *Mexican War*, p. 218; Winfield Scott, *Memoirs of Lt. General Scott*, New York 1864, p. 66.
121. *The Eagle*, p. 93.

by the moderate federalist José Joaquin Herrera, who had led the revolt the previous December against Santa Anna's dictatorship. Herrera was subsequently elected president with wide support on 1 August and formally assumed office on 14 September. As a senior army officer suspicious of the militias associated with the *puro* radical federalists but also an opponent of monarchism and dictatorship, Herrera appeared to be a mainstream figure able to interact with and neutralise the country's principal political antagonists. In fact, his eleven-month administration was in trouble from the very start, occupying the centre with increasing inertia as the international conflict encouraged fresh permutations of opportunism in which *puros* like Gómez Farías and monarchists like Alamán sought out different alliances in order to take power. The only really new element in this scenario – and it did not last for long – was the absence of Santa Anna, who had failed to escape from the country when deserted by his troops and been held prisoner since January 1845 at Perote under a charge of treason. Even then, though, Herrera was unable to escape the complaints of the *caudillo*:

> He was not being allowed to see his wife and children, people had insulted him in the streets, he had no privacy, no servant, and 'I cannot sleep because of the thoughtless noise of the guards.' Over the next few weeks he wrote many such letters.... In a bizarre mixture of appeals for clemency, better food and the return of his wife's wardrobe, which had been confiscated, he inserted demands that his record of service to the nation be acknowledged, that his rights as a citizen be respected, and that he be allowed to keep all his assets as well as his salary. Indeed, he maintained that government owed him 89,000 pesos and he wanted it paid.[122]

Although the Herrera government would have no truck with this, at the end of May Congress voted to grant an amnesty to members of the previous regime and drop the treason charges against the ex-president in return for Santa Anna agreeing to go into perpetual exile in Venezuela. When he embarked at Veracruz on 3 June his career looked to be finished for good. However, four days later a major revolt broke out in the capital, where some rebel officers adopted the slogan 'Federation and Santa Anna!' – an indication of a shift by the radicals towards one of their oldest enemies. Gómez Farías, the *puro* leader, reckoned a revolt could be staged with a good chance of success for between 8,000 and 10,000 pesos, and the radicals' use of fierce nationalist rhetoric against the temporising government as Taylor's army moved into position on the frontier helped to improve their relations with important elements of the army. The uprising of June 1845 failed, but in such a conspiratorial culture this only encouraged pre-emptive plotting by other factions, notably conservatives, monarchists and those moderate liberals for whom the *puro* popular constituency went by a varied nomenclature – *leperada, populacho, sansculottes, canalla, chusma* – but commonly signified barbarism and threatened mob rule. By December 1845 the Herrera government was

---

122. Costeloe, *Central Republic*, pp. 259–60.

facing at least five plots, even with Santa Anna in Cuba (where he had taken up Governor O'Donnell's invitation to stay).

In the event, it was General Mariano Paredes y Arillaga, sympathetic to the monarchist cause and deeply antagonistic to the civic militias, who struck first, 'pronouncing' on 15 December. Herrera, who had held back from mobilising the *cívicos* precisely out of fear that this would provoke conservatives, was now obliged to do so, but it was too late and he left office on the last day of the year. The government of Mexico was, then, in the hands of Paredes and a conservative team when the fighting with the USA started. Gómez Farías was locked up, and initially it seemed that some monarchist system would be reintroduced. Nevertheless, the tenuous balance of power persuaded the new president not to reveal his hand immediately, and Taylor's victories at Palo Alto and Resaca de la Palma in May put paid to any effort to challenge the prevailing republican order. At the same time, the 'saviour' of December 1845 had proved no more effective than the president he replaced in directing the national war effort. As a result, Paredes was ousted in July 1846, as news of the loss of California reached the capital. It was now apparent that success on the battlefield was no less important than ideological malleability for the retention of state power.

Two governments having fallen since his own, Santa Anna arrived back at Veracruz on 16 August 1846, passing through the US blockade after an agreement that he would negotiate with Washington as soon as he retrieved power.[123] Struck by the cold reception he received on landing at the port, the general, who was a more practised and effective opportunist than any other operating in the politico-military firmament, resolved to grasp with both hands the alliance offered by the radicals. Thus, when, a month later, a man known for his firm dictatorial and conservative instincts (not to mention a proclivity for full dress uniforms) finally entered Mexico City, it was with some awkwardness that he deferred to the democratic style of his new partner, Gómez Farías. For José Fernando Rodríguez, the sight was far from appetising:

> Disregarding all the farcical stuff in the newspapers, I shall tell you that the whole affair was a decidedly democratic one: not a frock coat nor a carriage other than those of the officials. Santa Anna rode in the government's state coach, an open carriage. He sat there on the main seat, sunk down among the cushions, with the big banner of the federal constitution fluttering from its staff at its right. The size of the banner with its attached streamers and tricolored ribbons made it impossible for him.... Gómez Farías rode on the front seat, facing him and the banner. Both men were silent and seemed more like victims than conquerors. Santa

---

123. Santa Anna had conversations with Alexander Slidell Mackenzie in Havana on 6 and 7 July 1846:

> The American peace terms would be: no indemnity; settlement of the spoilation claims; United States purchase of the disputed territory and New Mexico. Santa Anna responded with a document stating his hopes for peace and his readiness to negotiate. He also offered several good suggestions for American strategy, notably the seizure of Saltillo and Tampico and the suggestion that Veracruz could be taken by landing below it and then investing the town. Santa Anna told Mackenzie that on returning to power he would govern in the interests of the masses, reduce the power and wealth of the clergy, and embrace free trade.

Bauer, *Mexican War*, pp. 76–7.

Anna was dressed in quite a democratic fashion: a long travelling coat, white trousers and no crosses or medals on his breast. So terrible was the impression all this produced on me that when the coach got to a place opposite my balcony windows, I drew back involuntarily, being seized with such a violent headache that I was no good for the rest of the day.[124]

As early as April Santa Anna had proposed such a democrat–military link-up, having the confidence to offer from his exile in Cuba to the *puro* leader

the affection of the army, in which I have many good friends, and you will give me the masses over whom you have so much influence, not because I desire to return to power, which I will need only for a brief time to become reconciled with my country and to demonstrate with greater deeds that I never intended to oppress it or tyrannize it....[125]

By the time he reached the capital in mid September, California and New Mexico were effectively lost, and Taylor was closing on the northern city of Monterrey, where General Ampudia's 7,300 men were in a weaker position than it appeared since many of them were cavalry, of marginal use for urban defence. There was, then, a pressing need for the *caudillo* to go straight away to San Luis Potosí and organise a new northern army to counter-attack the US invaders, but he stayed a fortnight in the capital, during which the consequences of his deal with the radicals began to unfurl on the streets. Again, it is the anguished Ramírez who describes the scene for us, and some of his passages are exaggerated, but it is evident that war with the USA was now being seen as providing an opportunity to stage an offensive on the old order. Two days after Santa Anna's return to the capital, Ramírez wrote to a correspondent in Durango,

The preliminary signs are not very consoling. The victorious federalists have determined upon their course of action and have assumed the most hysterical transactions. These affairs are those given prominence in the ridiculous pantomimes which the *Republicano* calls 'Federalist Society'. They are no more than a farce, a parody of the meetings held by the English and the people of the United States. Although the resolutions agreed at the assemblies will give you some idea of their nature – you have, no doubt, read them in the newspapers – it is nevertheless impossible to imagine what kind of issues have been included in the speeches; you have to understand that anyone at all has the right to get up and express his opinions. Indeed, I must tell you that among other matters discussed with utmost attention were these: first, behead Don Lucas Alamán and all those suspected of being Monarchists, even if it meant an expenditure of 200,000 pesos, according to the orator, who added that 400,000 pesos had been spent to cut off the head of an illustrious man [Guerrero in 1831, in which Alamán was allegedly involved]. It was also suggested that they could arm themselves with daggers and have a regular Sicilian Vespers bloodbath. The speaker here drew his blade to make his point.
    The second was to take over church properties and to abolish church privileges. On this subject all kinds of opinions were expressed. The third point covered the closing of the houses for novices, the reason being the alleged corruption and prostitution of the monks, who, it is said, kept mistresses. This was also an occasion for a fierce jab at the secular clergy. Point number four urged the institution of civil marriages, leaving it to the wish or the

124. *Mexico during the War with the United States*, p. 77.
125. Santa Anna, Havana, to Gómez Farías, 25 Apr. 1846, quoted in Santoni, *Mexicans at Arms*, p. 125.

conscience of each of the contracting parties whether or not the blessing of the church was to be included. The fifth point referred to the exclusion of Monarchist priests from provincial councils. The sixth dealt with intolerance; the seventh with limiting the church's general powers and, if necessary, the suppression of the confession. It was alleged that on the pretext of getting confessions the priests reveal family secrets, to the detriment of fathers, husbands etc. The eighth point incorporated a plan for excluding from public office all men who had reached a certain age; for example, the age of forty, at which age it was suggested public servants were to be dismissed.

The fifth point was voted down. The sixth scandalised some of the members with its politico-religious aspects, and they went so far as to interrupt the speaker. The seventh point aroused the ire of a gentleman of the cloth to such a pitch that he shouted, 'Down with the heretic!' All the suggestions were applauded more or less, especially the remarks against the army.[126]

Through the autumn such matters were sidelined by the need to fund the war effort as Monterrey, Tampico and Saltillo fell to the US forces in the north of the country. Although Santa Anna's claims to have subsidised the raising of the army at San Luis Potosí by mortgaging his properties were not entirely without foundation, his contribution – much greater than, say, that of Caleb Cushing to the Massachusetts volunteers – could only cover a small part of the overall expenditure. Furthermore, Santa Anna's attempts to raise private loans from entrepreneurs yielded little of substance, and on 17 September Congress was forced to introduce a bill appropriating for the military budget all port taxes, a 4 per cent tax on coinage, revenue from land sales, the tobacco monopoly, the lottery, salt deposits, official paper and the mint. At the same time, it abolished the sales tax (*alcabala*) and imposed a 50 per cent surcharge on businesses and the income taxes notionally raised by the states. On 2 October the deputies compounded the egalitarian tone of these measures by requiring all urban property-owners to donate a month's income to the defence of the nation. On paper all this looked like a comprehensive response, but virtually no money resulted from these edicts. The September taxes were rapidly repealed under sharp commercial pressure, and it proved impossible to collect revenue from owners of real estate, many of whom lacked liquid assets or simply survived off their rents.

As we have seen, the only institution in early republican Mexico with sufficient resources to lend money at modest rates of interest was the Church, the very target of the radicals. In November 1845 it had proved impossible to sustain a proposal in Congress for the seizure of the Church's estate under mortmain in order to raise 4 million pesos; the ecclesiastical protests had been more telling than anticipated. Equally, in May 1846 the conservative Paredes regime had failed to persuade the hierarchy to concede a new loan. In November of that year the new government issued a decree mortgaging Church property for 2 million pesos, and once more it was obliged to withdraw the measure, although the bishops did lend the state 850,000 as a result of the pressure. By the turn of the year Santa Anna, preparing to close on Taylor's

---

126. *Mexico during the War with the United States*, pp. 75–6.

position at Saltillo, reckoned that Church property should be mortgaged to the tune of 20 million pesos, and he wrote to the cabinet, urging that

> Congress should deal with [this] today, because any other artifices will only be mere talk, and there is no time to lose. It is not unusual for the clergy to come to the rescue of the state's expenses with its income and possessions.... I had my doubts, and for ten years I staunchly resisted dictating any measures against Church property, and I even assured the cabinet many times that I would rather have my hand cut off than sign a decree that would dispose of those possessions: the country's resources were more or less abundant, the treasury was not as drained as it is today.... As a result of these considerations I am not opposed to the loan being carried out under the aforementioned basis, and if such is the congress's august will, I will support.[127]

There could scarcely be a clearer signal, or a more pressing issue on which to drive the *puro*–military alliance forward. Nine days after Santa Anna wrote these lines, Gómez Farías duly issued a decree to raise 15 million pesos through the sale and mortgaging of Church property. The legislation was approved by Congress on the 15th. At the same time, the government reissued an order of October 1833 which forbade the clergy from addressing political issues from the pulpit. The next day meetings of more than eight persons were outlawed. However, not even the publication of Santa Anna's letter could contain the opposition in both the capital and the provinces as conservative and moderate liberal opinion rounded on the *puros* over the question of property, the *fueros* or privileges of the Church, and constitutional liberties. The cabinet split, and Gómez Farías, forced to watch as regional commanders brazenly seized port taxes for themselves as Santa Anna molested him for funds, tried to resign. Thus was the state of play when the Battle of Buena Vista was fought in late February.

Although the revolt of the *polko* liberal moderates did not take place for another four days, Santa Anna had already started backtracking on the financial question and was making for the capital both to suppress the insurgent *polkos* and to get rid of the *puros* who had helped him get back into power. On 23 March, the uprising quashed, he appointed a mixed cabinet, including some moderate liberals close to the rebels, removed Gómez Farías from office, and sent the pro-*puro* Hidalgo, Victoria and Independencia militia battalions off to the front. On the 29th he rescinded the January fiscal measures, and in return the ecclesiastical authorities extended a 1.5 million peso loan. Two days later news of the capitulation of Veracruz to Scott reached Mexico City.

Scott's landing and Santa Anna's marginalisation of the *puros* had the combined effect of reducing outward political conflict within the Mexican elite for the rest of the war. Although the *caudillo* did offer his resignation at the end of May 1847, when General Worth took Puebla, he was not finally ousted from office until 16 September – two days after the US army took control of the capital. (He would return as dictator from 1853 to 1855.) There were still imaginative and resourceful commanders in the Mexican army – the fortifications at Cerro Gordo, for instance, were expertly

---

127. Santa Anna, San Luis Potosí, to Rejón, 2 Jan. 1847, quoted in Santoni, *Mexicans at Arms*, p. 171.

engineered – but the high command was bitterly divided. In military terms this meant that there was insufficient coordination to close a pincer movement around Scott's army between Contreras and Churubusco, where the US forces were acutely vulnerable as they closed on the capital. In political terms it allowed Santa Anna to hold off any serious military challenge to his position. The opportunities for the civilian political elite were equally limited despite the fact that the *caudillo* withdrew the *puro* decree of 30 April which explicitly prohibited the executive from negotiating with foreign powers, from signing a peace treaty with the United States, and from disposing of any portion of the national territory, all of which acts were deemed to be treasonable. Santa Anna made sure that Congress was implicated in the reversal of this controversial ruling – on the grounds that it contravened the constitutional responsibility of the executive to conduct foreign affairs – but very few were so valiant as publicly to espouse the case for a settlement until the dictator was once again in exile, the capital invested by *gringo* troops, and circumstances such that a charge of betrayal could plausibly be turned against those who insisted on war at any price.

Despite the fact that there had been much deeper divisions in the USA over whether to go to war in the first place, the political conditions for the campaign of the Anglo-American army were qualitatively superior, and there is minimal evidence of any ideological differences affecting the rank and file. This is not to say that there was no tension or animosity among the senior officers themselves and between them and Washington, but the politics of command on the US side was primarily to do with the personality, style and capacity of individual generals, most particularly Zachary Taylor and Winfield Scott.

Taylor was lionised at home by many more than James Fenimore Cooper, his adoring constituency in New Orleans and the company of Post and Lemon, which marketed its 'Manhattan Fresh Minted Horse-Radish Sauce' under the motto 'Rough and Ready'; the general's nickname was borrowed to sell a range of commodities. As a man belonging to no political party in a long life during which he contrived to cast not a single vote in a national election, Taylor went on to win the presidential poll of 1848 by a comfortable margin – and with the highest number of votes (1.4 million) ever cast for an individual in the history of the USA (and the world) – over the populist and fiercely expansionist Democrat Lewis Cass. From the start, Polk had nurtured suspicions about Taylor's politics, even though the general held over 100 slaves on his plantations in Louisiana and had a markedly cold relationship with Scott, whose Whig affiliation was proudly public. But once Taylor was appointed and the campaign under way, the president's deeper concern was that 'General Taylor, I fear, is not the man for command of the army. He is brave but he does not seem to have resources or grasp of mind enough to conduct such a campaign.'[128] It was the conflict

---

128. *Diary of a President*, p. 144. *Zachary Taylor*, born Montebello, Virginia 24 Nov. 1784, and taken to Jefferson County, Kentucky, in his first year. Only formal education from a private tutor; volunteer, 1806; 1808, commissioned as ensign in regular army, catching yellow fever when he reported to general James

between Taylor and Quartermaster General Jesup over supply trains which occasioned this remark, but Polk's sharpest objections to Taylor's conduct related to his caution and lack of aggression in the northern campaign, where the president was looking for a decisive victory and where the general conducted his operations in terms of establishing a strategic position that was conducive to the opening of negotiations with the Mexicans. Military historians like Bauer have tended to side with Polk, criticising Taylor's reluctance to advance beyond Saltillo and occupy San Luis Potosí.[129] Certainly, Taylor never ran the risk embraced by Scott in deliberately driving a deep salient well beyond established supply lines ('Scott is lost' was Wellington's remark upon learning of the advance). But it was as a result of Buena Vista and the subsequent holding down of the north of the country that the Veracruz landings and subsequent offensive against the capital were made possible.

There was a clear political aspect to this issue because in February 1847 – both before and after Buena Vista – Calhoun had strongly advocated in the Senate a policy of holding a defensive line, occupation of only the north of Mexico, and negotiation with Mexico: all positions with which Taylor was in instinctive sympathy and which threatened the administration's plans. However, Taylor was more immediately concerned – and with good reason – that the transfer of regular troops from his to Scott's army had limited the viable strategic options open to him, and he complained that if he had been removed, as the patrician commander had wished, 'Santa Anna would have swept the country.... If Scott had left me 500 or 1,000 regular infantry the Mexican army would have been completely broken down [at Buena Vista], and the whole of their artillery and baggage taken or destroyed.' Although Buena Vista made Taylor's reputation with the US public, following the battle he was subjected to almost as much criticism within the government as Santa Anna would be on his side. Notwithstanding his notable lack of 'airs and graces', Taylor was as prickly as any public figure, and just before Veracruz fell to Scott he wrote that,

> I am satisfied that Scott, Marcy and company have been more anxious to break me down than they have been to break down Santa Anna and the Mexicans, for never was an officer left so completely bound hand and foot under all the circumstances of the case, at the mercy of the enemy after the most uncourteous, and I may say insulting course having being pursued against me by the party referred to. But through the blessings of divine providence I have disappointed their expectations if not defeated their nefarious schemes; and feel proud however in knowing that by pursuing the course I did, I saved the honor of my country and our glorious flag from trailing in the dust.[130]

Wilkinson at New Orleans. 1810, captain; 1819, lieutenant-colonel commanding 4th infantry at New Orleans; 1832, Black Hawk War; 1838, command of expedition against Seminoles, Florida. 1849, president of USA. Died Washington, 9 July 1850, following 4 July ceremony for construction of Washington Monument, when 'he felt the heat, drank much cold water, and afterwards ate cherries and drank iced milk. That night he was attacked by cholera morbus and fever.'

129. *Mexican War*, pp. 96–7, 219.

130. Taylor, Monterrey, to Wood, 20 Mar. 1847, in *Letters of Zachary Taylor*, pp. 90–91.

Seven months earlier, Taylor, flush from his undoubted victories at Palo Alto and
Resaca de la Palma, still commanding a substantial force of regulars, and having
received no direct criticism from Scott, had given his frank opinion of that general:

> General Scott is a man of strong impulse, both writes and speaks with great flippancy and
> frequently without due reflection as regards both, which has gotten him into many scrapes;
> but he means well on all occasions and is entirely mistaken if he supposes I am unfriendly
> to him.[131]

This was much more the attitude associated with a man who was averse to uniforms
and who was once treated as an orderly by a young subaltern who did not know him
– Taylor did nothing in response – but who was also sensitive enough to put on a
uniform especially for a meeting with Commodore David Conner, known to be
something of a dandy (Conner, no less perceptive, had deliberately dressed in mufti to
attend the conference). For a few of his men Taylor was not much more than 'a
heavy-set, corpulent and old-looking man'. For many more his popularity resided
precisely in the fact that he was 'plainly dressed but well enough for a hard journey.
He wore a plain forage cap, overcoat, black pants, shoes and spurs. He was riding an
indifferent horse with plain saddle and bridle and in every way was one of the
plainest men I have seen.'[132] A man who did his own darning was one who could be
trusted and who could lead men to their death. And it was this quality that Scott
found so aggravating:

> When the victory at Buena Vista reached Major General Brooke (a noble old soldier) com-
> manding at New Orleans, and a friend of General Taylor, he rushed with the report in his
> hand, through the streets to the Exchange, and threw the whole city into a frenzy of joy.
> By and by, came the news that the Stars and Stripes waved over Veracruz and its castle, and
> Brooke, also a friend of mine, was again eager to spread the report. Somebody in the crowd
> early called out: 'How many men has Scott lost?' Brooke was delighted to reply, 'Less than
> a hundred.' 'That won't do.' was promptly rejoined. 'Taylor always loses thousands. He is the
> man for my money.' Only a few faint cheers were heard for Veracruz. The long butcher's bill
> was wanted. When I received friend Brooke's letter giving me these details, I own that my
> poor human nature was piqued for a moment; and I said, 'Never mind. Taylor is a Louisianan.
> We shall, in due time, hear the voice of the Middle, the Northern, the Eastern States. They
> will estimate victories on different principles.' But I was mistaken. The keynote raised in
> New Orleans was taken up all over the land. Mortifications are profitable to sufferers, and
> I record mine to teach aspirants to fame to cultivate humility; for blessed is the man who
> expects little, and can gracefully submit to less.

Scott's candid recording of his envy, including mortification at popular expectations
of generalship, might well constitute his own sight of the elephant. The account was,
of course, written well after the event, and after the death of Taylor in 1849, when he
was serving as president – something that Scott could never quite forgive, even when
discussing his appointment to lead the initial expeditionary force:

---

131. Taylor, Camargo, to Wood, 23 Aug. 1846, in ibid., p. 48.
132. *Mexican War Diary of Thomas D. Tennery*, p. 58; Curtis, *Mexico under Fire*, p. 157.

This selection [of Taylor] was made with the concurrence of the autobiographer, who, knowing him to be slow of thought, of hesitancy in speech, and unused to the pen, took care, about the same time, to provide him, unsolicited, with a staff officer, Captain Bliss, his exact complement, who superadded modest, quiet manners, which qualities could not fail to win the confidence of his peculiar commander.... General Taylor's elevation to the Presidency, the result of military success, though a marvel, was not a curse to his country. Mr Webster, in his strong idiomatic English, said of the nomination that it was 'not *fit* to be made'; but probably he would have been equally dissatisfied with any candidate other than himself.

With a good store of common sense, General Taylor's mind had not been enlarged and refreshed by reading or much converse with the world. Rigidity of ideas was the consequence. The frontier and small military posts had been his home. Hence he was quite ignorant, for his rank, and quite bigoted in his ignorance. His simplicity was childlike, and with innumerable prejudices – amusing and incorrigible – well suited to the tender age.... Yet this old soldier and neophyte statesman had the true basis of a great character – pure, uncorrupted morals combined with indomitable courage. Kind-hearted, sincere and hospitable in a plain way, he had no vice but prejudice, many friends and left behind him not an enemy in the world.[133]

If we gain the sense that Scott is here having his cake and eating it, the overall picture is persuasive, and it is all the more so for being painted in the primary colours of the political palate, with a notionally equitable distribution of praise and condemnation beautifully subverted by its phrasing and sequence.

In fact, the 'old soldier' was only two years older than Scott, who landed at Veracruz in his sixty-third year and had enlisted before Taylor. A physically imposing man – at the age of nineteen he stood 6 foot 2 inches tall and weighed 230 pounds – Scott's early years in the army were, like Taylor's, dominated by the presence of Daniel Clark's nemesis, General James Wilkinson, as well as by service in the War of 1812. In both cases, though, Scott's experience was the more emphatic of the two. Prominent in operations on the Canadian border, twice severely wounded, and placed in command of the US forces at Lundy's Lane in July 1814, he was promoted brigadier in that year, aged twenty-eight. The promotion was all the more remarkable because Scott had never gone to West Point, and in 1808, having sat in on the trial of Vice-President Aaron Burr, he became convinced that Wilkinson, then general commanding the US army, was guilty of conspiracy to commit treason:

Wilkinson was the favorite of the new officers (all republicans) because, as brother-conspirator, he had turned *state's evidence* or 'approver' against Burr, and Burr's treason had been prosecuted with zeal at the insistence of Mr Jefferson. Some of these excited partisans had heard me, in an excited conversation the preceding summer, just before I sailed for the North, say that I knew, soon after the trial, from my friends Mr Randolph and Mr Tazewell, as well as others, members of the grand jury who found the bill of indictment against Burr, that nothing but the influence of Mr Jefferson had saved Wilkinson from being included in the same indictment, and that I believed Wilkinson to have been equally a traitor with Burr. This was in New Orleans, the Headquarters of Wilkinson, commanding the department. The expression of that belief was not only imprudent but, no doubt, *at that time* blameable

133. *Memoirs of Lt. General Scott*, pp. 425, 381–3.

inasmuch as the 6th article of war enacts that, 'any officer ... who shall behave with contempt or disrespect towards his *commanding* officer, shall be punished.' ... This officer, a violent partisan who lived and died a reprobate, as a blind to cover his instigator, trumped up another matter as the leading accusation, viz.: withholding money for the payment of the company.[134]

Scott was charged with ungentlemanly conduct and suspended for a year but exonerated from all suspicion of dishonesty with respect to the finances of his unit. Perhaps Wilkinson thought that his own attitude towards the army's monies was shared throughout the officer corps? Certainly Scott, whilst establishing his lifelong reputation as being impulsive and injudicious, was convinced that the Jeffersonian army which he had joined was both excessively politicised and in danger of professional decomposition:

> ... many of the appointments were positively bad and a majority of the remainder indifferent. Party spirit of that day knew no bounds, and, of course, was blind to policy. Federalists were almost entirely excluded from selection though great numbers were eager for the field, and in New England and some other States there were but few educated republicans. Hence the selections from those communities consisted mostly of coarse and ignorant men. In the other States, where there was no lack of educated men in the dominant party, the appointments consisted generally of swaggerers, dependants, decayed gentlemen and others 'fit for nothing else', which always turned out utterly unfit for any military purpose whatever.[135]

Over the following thirty years Scott strove to rectify this legacy, drawing up the first standard American drill regulations in 1815, travelling to Europe in that year and 1829 to study, and revising the three-volume manual of infantry tactics in 1835. Never a narrow theoretician, he took a leading role in the campaigns of the 1830s to 'pacify' the tribes, but his clear Whig sympathies and outspoken nature meant that he was not appointed general-in-chief of the army until 1841.[136] Scott, a stickler for protocol and ceremony, was known by the troops as 'Fuss and Feathers', although he was sensible enough to use a sombrero in the Mexican campaign, and his love of display certainly did not betray any surreptitious monarchist sympathies. Indeed, during the US occupation Scott sought to retain in operation as much as possible of the apparatus of the Mexican republican state, and, as we have seen, he held strong convictions as to what constituted modern, professional and civilised conduct of

---

134. Ibid., pp. 37–8.

135. Ibid., pp. 34–5. In 1846 Scott revived his reputation for maladroit utterances by pointedly explaining to the cabinet that, on account of taking a swift bowl of soup, he could not join them from the office where he was drawing up the plans for the Veracruz landing.

136. *Winfield Scott*, born Petersburg, Virginia, 13 June 1786, of a family that had moved to the colonies following the Battle of Culloden. 1807, enlisted as private in cavalry; 1808, captain; 1809, charged with 'ungentlemanly conduct'; 1812–14, active in operations against British; 1814, brigadier; 1815, *Rules and Regulations for the Field Exercise and Manoeuvres of Infantry*. 1817, married Maria May; action in Black Hawk War (1832), expedition against Seminoles (1835) and Cherokees (1838). Talked of as Whig presidential candidate, 1839. 1841, succeeded General Macomb in command of US army; 1852, appointed lieutenant-general; Whig presidential candidate, defeated by Pierce. Retired 31 April 1861; died 29 May 1866.

warfare. For this he enjoyed appreciable support amongst the Anglo-American intelligentsia of the day, and his subsequent reputation stands high both as the father of the modern US army and as the general who delivered victory in Mexico within the space of two harvests (and volunteer cycles). There were always, however, those, like Karl Marx, who were disinclined to engage in any form of hero worship, and particularly so of generals:

> I have now read the whole of Ripley (curiosity, of course, being sufficient for my purpose). I am no longer in any doubt – and Ripley in his 'restrained' sarcastic style of pen makes it plain – that the great Scott is nothing more than a common, petty, untalented, carping, envious cur and HUMBUG who, aware that he owed everything to the bravery of his soldiers and the SKILL of his commanders, played dirty tricks in order to reap the renown himself. He appears to be as great a general as the MANY-SIDED Greeley is a great philosopher.... But he is America's foremost (in terms of rank) general. Which is doubtless why Dana believes in him.[137]

Here Marx is having a crack at not only his editors but also the predilection for rank and personality in the peculiar ethos of American republicanism: in 1852 Scott became the first man appointed to the rank of lieutenant-general since George Washington. Had Marx read more fully he would probably have attributed success in the campaign directly to commanders like Wool, Worth, Kearny, Shields, Doniphan, Cadwalader, Twiggs, Lane and Quitman, who had either already risen to the rank of general through manifest merit or were now able to do so through the legislation of March 1847 which expanded the permitted number of generals (but only by three new brigadiers and two major-generals) as well as allowing officers of general rank to command volunteer units. Yet not even Marx, in all his upper- and lower-case causticism, could have included Gideon Pillow, Polk's law partner in Columbia, Tennessee, and the man responsible for the nomination of president to the Democratic candidature in 1844. Pillow had absolutely no military experience prior to his appointment to command a division, and the Battle of Cerro Gordo was won despite his incompetent conduct, which enabled the Mexican right to sustain its position throughout the encounter. Indeed, it was Pillow rather than Scott who tried to take credit for the achievements of others once the capital was taken, Scott laying charges against him for fabricating reports, leaking information to the press, and misappropriating government property (two captured howitzers were found in his baggage train). But after the conflict Pillow was exonerated by a court martial, going directly to the White House to dine with Polk in celebration. This highly politicised aspect of the US campaign was further underlined by the fact that when Scott wrongly accused General Worth – an officer of high professional reputation – of infractions similar to those allegedly committed by Pillow, Worth felt obliged to send Polk heated missives over this 'infamy'.

---

137. Marx, London, to Engels, 2 Dec. 1854, in *MECW*, XXXVIII, London 1985, p. 503.

Polk finally contrived to remove Scott from his command on 13 January 1848, on the grounds that he had in July 1847 offered the Mexicans a bribe of $1 million (and paid $10,000 of it) to end the conflict. The charge was levelled despite the fact that Polk's confidant Pillow had strongly supported the scheme whilst Quitman, Shields, Twiggs and Cadwalader, who were also present at the council, had either abstained or recommended caution. At the court of inquiry held at Frederick, Maryland, from June to July 1848, Pillow gave his evidence as if he were prosecuting attorney, but Scott and Trist refused to testify, and none of the information provided by the other generals proved that the offer had affected the conduct of operations. Scott retained his rank and position, and he was pointedly voted a medal by Congress. His record was recognised by those, like Zachary Taylor and William Worth, who came to dislike him personally and who had cause to resent his actions and opinions. Despite the vociferous campaign against all Whig commanders waged by Senator Thomas Benton, the deep prejudice of Polk himself and the lack of Taylor's populist touch, Scott's achievement was to conduct the most efficient military campaign possible within the technological and political constraints of the era.

These limits had never included a clear proscription of military leaders from political office. After Washington, whose status was almost by definition ambiguous, Jackson served two terms as a general-president (and, of course, Jefferson's first vice-president, Aaron Burr, was a colonel). Taylor – as Scott himself noted in dry envy – obtained the office through his record on the battlefield. In a much less impressive manner, the Democrat Franklin Pierce was able to exploit his service as a commander of New Hampshire volunteers – when he was frequently absent from action, sick or recovering from injuries falling from his horse – to take the 1852 presidential poll by winning 1,601,117 votes against the 1,385,453 garnered by Winfield Scott himself. Having finally obtained the Whig candidature (after fifty-three ballots), Scott had to suffer the indignity of being defeated by an erstwhile subordinate who traded on his good looks and had little difficulty in exploiting the elderly general's awkward combination of nativism, anti-slavery and outspoken condescension. In 1856 Pierce would be followed in office by James Buchanan, Polk's secretary of state, throwing the presidential succession from 1844 to 1860 – Democrat and Whig alike – very much under the shadow of the Mexican War. But never again would a soldier of such mediocre quality obtain the US presidency; both Grant and Eisenhower were in a different class. And whilst that office cannot be viewed as entirely immune to military pretension (one thinks of the overtures made to General Colin Powell and – with markedly less equanimity – the pretensions nurtured by General Alexander Haig), it was quite distinct to the Mexican presidency (at least until 1946, when the Mexican army lost its status as a sector of the governing PRI) by virtue of the fact that no individual military aspirant could expect organised corporate support to gain it.

Political division over the Mexican War within US society as a whole rarely reached the point of popular demonstration, let alone street-fighting. But, as has been seen, there was opposition, particularly in New England and especially from an intelligentsia discomforted by the manner in which O'Sullivan and Polk had purloined the language and motifs of republican idealism to justify foreign conquest. For some of the younger generation this was cause enough for individual protest: Thoreau spent a night in jail for refusing to pay a poll tax which, because it supported the war effort, he saw as worthy of civil disobedience. Writing from Rome for the *New York Tribune* early in May 1848, Margaret Fuller, full of expectations about a new European order in the wake of the Pope's abdication from temporal office, perceived the Mexican War as part of a pattern of corruption of American society, albeit not one of irreversible decay:

> My country is at present spoiled by prosperity, stupid with the lust of gain, soiled by crime in its willing perpetuation of slavery, shamed by an unjust war, noble sentiment much forgotten even by individuals, the aims of politicians selfish or petty, the literature frivolous and venal. In Europe, amid the teachings of adversity, a nobler spirit is struggling – a spirit which cheers and animates mine. I hear earnest words of pure faith and love. I see deeds of brotherhood. This is what makes *my* America. I do not deeply distrust my country. She is not dead, but in my time she sleepeth, and the spirit of our fathers flames no more, but lies hid beneath the ashes. It will not be so long; bodies cannot live when the soul gets too overgrown with gluttony and falsehood. But it is not the making a President out of the Mexican War that would make me wish to come back.[138]

With the defeat of this European utopia, Fuller set off two years later on the fateful voyage back to a tarnished America. But at the time that she wrote this dispatch there was, in fact, still one survivor from the founding generation who, although weakened by age and reconciled to the physical outcome of the war, sought to revive the original republican spirit. The unalloyed prose of Albert Gallatin's pamphlet is both more modern and more archaic than that of Fuller as he inveighs against annexation and condemns the racist nostrums of the day as intrinsically anti-democratic:

> Your mission was to be a model for all other governments and for all other less favored nations, to adhere to the most elevated principles of political morality, to apply all your faculties to the gradual improvement of your own institutions and social state, and by your example to exert a moral influence most beneficial to mankind at large. Instead of this, an appeal has been made to your worst passions; to cupidity; to the thirst of unjust aggrandizement by brutal force; to the love of military fame and of false glory; and it has even been tried to pervert the noblest feelings of your nature. The attempt is made to make you abandon the lofty position which your fathers occupied, to substitute for it the political morality and heathen patriotism of the heroes and statesmen of antiquity.
>
> In the total absence of any argument that can justify this war … it is said that the people of the United States have a hereditary superiority of race over the Mexicans, which gives them the right to subjugate and keep in bondage the inferior nation. This, it is also alleged, will be the means of enlightening the degraded Mexicans, of improving their social state, and ultimately increasing the happiness of the masses.
>
> Is it compatible with the principle of democracy, which rejects every hereditary claim of individuals, to admit to an hereditary superiority of race? … At this time the claim is but

---

138. *New York Tribune*, 7 May 1848, reprinted in Bell Gale Chevigny, *The Woman and the Myth: Margaret Fuller's Life and Writings*, New York 1976, p. 452.

a pretext for covering and justifying unjust usurpation and unbounded ambition.... Among ourselves the most ignorant, the most inferior, either in physical or mental faculties, is recognized as having equal rights, and he has an equal vote with anyone, however superior to him in all these respects. This is founded on the immutable principle that no man is born with the right of governing another man. The same principle applies to nations.[139]

It was in almost total opposition to these convictions that John Calhoun could also oppose the war, as threatening to dilute the racial balance and institutional integrity of Anglo-America. On 4 January 1848 Calhoun, fearing wholesale annexation of the conquered territories, told the US Senate:

> We make a great mistake in supposing all people are capable of self-government. Acting under that impression, many are anxious to force free governments on all the people of this continent, and over the world, if they had the power. It has lately been urged in a very respectable quarter that it is the mission of this country to spread civil and religious liberty all over the globe, and especially over this continent – even by force if necessary. It is a sad delusion. None but a people advanced to a high state of moral and intellectual excellence are capable, in a civilized condition, of forming and maintaining free governments.[140]

Here we have the case for non-intervention pitched in terms of cultural relativism and isolationism. In a speech to the Senate a year earlier Calhoun had painstakingly tied the government's explanation for the opening of hostilities into a more pragmatic argument against expansionism, assailing Polk on both the high ground and the low:

> If I rightly understand the objects for which the war was declared ... for, strange as it may seem, those objects even at this day, are left to inference ... they appear to have been threefold: first, to repel invasion; next, to establish the Rio del Norte [Rio Grande] as the western boundary of Texas; and thirdly, to obtain indemnity for the claims of our citizens against Mexico. The first two appear to me the primary, and the last only the secondary object of the war. The President, in his messages, did not recommend Congress to declare war. No. He assumed that war already existed, and called upon Congress to recognise its existence. He affirmed that the country had been invaded, and American blood spilt upon American soil.... The President, in addition, recommends that we shall prosecute the war in order to obtain indemnity for its expenses; but that, in no sense, can be considered as one of its objects, but a mere question of policy; for it can never be supposed that a country would enter upon a war for the mere purpose of being indemnified for its cost.
>
> I hold, then, Mr President – such being the objects of the war – that all of them can be accomplished by taking a defensive position. Two have already been thoroughly effected. The enemy has been repelled by two brilliant victories. The Rio del Norte is held, from its mouth to its extreme source, on the eastern side, by ourselves. Not a Mexican soldier is to be found there. As to the question of indemnity to our citizens, such has been the success of our arms that we have not only acquired enough for that, but vastly more.

---

139. 'Peace with Mexico', *Writings of Albert Gallatin*, IV, pp. 583–5. *Albert Gallatin*, born Geneva, 29 Jan. 1761; orphaned at nine; graduated 1779. Refused family offer to serve in Hessean mercenaries raised to fight for George III in the American colonies. 1780, travelled to Massachusetts to establish a business: 'I have not the slightest claim to military services.' 1789–90, member, Pennsylvania constitutional conference; 1793, married Hannah Nicholson; 1794, member of House in 4th Congress, subsequently serving two more terms; 1797, leader of Republican minority. Secretary of Treasury, May 1801 to Feb. 1814 (last year of which he acted as Peace Commissioner at Ghent). 1816, ambassador to France. Died, 12 Aug. 1849.
140. *The Essential Calhoun*, p. 114.

Having established these positions, Calhoun drove on to make the case – on grounds that are more familiar in our day than his – for peaceful coexistence with Mexico:

> I go further ... in aiming to do justice to ourselves in establishing the line we ought, in my opinion, to inflict the least possible amount of injury on Mexico. I hold, indeed, that we ought to be just and liberal to her. Not only because she is our neighbor; not only because she is a sister republic; not only because she is emulous now, in the midst of her difficulties, and has ever been, to imitate our example by establishing a federal republic; not only because she is one of the two great powers of this continent ... [but because] there is a mysterious connection between the fate of this country and that of Mexico; so much so, that her independence and capability of sustaining herself are almost as essential to our prosperity, and the maintenance of our institutions, as they are to hers. Mexico is to us forbidden fruit; the penalty of eating it would be to subject our political institutions to political death.[141]

There is some irony in the fact that it was Abraham Lincoln, the man finally responsible for abolishing that institution – slavery – Calhoun was most intent upon preserving, who picked up on Calhoun's implied doubt as to whether any 'invasion' had really taken place at all. On 22 December 1847, less than three weeks after entering Congress, Lincoln tabled a series of resolutions in the House requiring Polk to provide it 'with all the facts which go to establish whether the particular spot of soil on which the blood of our *citizens* was so shed, was, or was not, our own soil'.[142] Lincoln did not prosper in his effort to show that US forces had made an unprovoked attack on a Mexican settlement – the fighting had effectively ended by this time – but his resolutions formed part of a wider politicisation of the war that took in the issue of slavery. This had begun in earnest on 8 August 1846, when a new representative from Pennsylvania, David Wilmot, a member of Polk's own party and a supporter of expansionism (including the annexation of Texas as a slave state), borrowed from the 1787 Northwest ordinance to add to the president's appropriations bill the stipulation that in lands acquired from Mexico 'neither slavery nor involuntary servitude shall ever exist'.[143] Polk, ever impatient at obstacles in the legislature, noted in his diary,

> Late in the evening of Saturday the 8th, I learned that after an exciting debate in the House a bill passed that body but with a mischievous and foolish amendment to the effect that no

---

141. Speech on War Appropriations Bill, Senate, 9 Feb. 1847, in ibid., pp. 131–2. The government forced the declaration of war vote through the House on 11 May 1846 by limiting debate to two hours, three-quarters of which was taken up with the reading of Polk's message and the attached documents. The Whigs and Calhounites lost by 123 to 76 votes a resolution to separate the preamble, which blamed Mexico for the outbreak of hostilities ('whereas by the act of ... Mexico, a state of war exists between that government and the United States'), from the rest of the bill. On the final vote 174 congressmen backed the declaration, 20 abstained, and 14, led by John Quincy Adams, opposed it.

142. Quoted in Donald, *Lincoln*, p. 123.

143. The Northwest ordinance was passed with the primary aim of providing a transitional administration prior to statehood to the 'Old Northwest' (roughly, today's Ohio, Michigan, Indiana, Illinois and Wisconsin); it permanently excluded slavery from this territory. The Democrats controlled the 29th Congress by 30 to 25 in the Senate and 142 to 74 in the House; the 'Proviso' tabled by Wilmot passed the House by 83 to 64 but was talked out in the Senate.

territory which might be acquired by treaty from Mexico should ever be slaveholding country. What connection slavery had with making peace with Mexico it is difficult to conceive.[144]

The president must have been befuddled by irritation or writing with heavy disingenuousness. The connection was clear to almost all concerned about the 'peculiar institution' and the relation between the sections that was now threatened by the addition of new territories, which, apart from expanding or excluding the practice of slavery, would sooner rather than later return congressmen and senators to Washington, thereby affecting the precarious federal balance. Polk himself would die in 1849 and so never witnessed the compromise of 1850, but if the Mexican War was only the final event that made that fragile trade-off necessary, it still revived suspicions and drove distrust to unprecedented levels.

Calhoun's 'forbidden fruit' was Emerson's 'arsenic', but, as we have seen, Emerson was disinclined to challenge the long-term 'law of things', even if this was strenuously contested within the more immediate 'law of men'. Thus, whilst he stooped to sneer at Polk and his team, the transcendentalist seer recognised that the force was with them, and he could not overlook the temporising of those who opposed the war:

> These – rabble – at Washington are really better than the snivelling opposition. They have a sort of genius of a bold and manly cast.... Mr Webster told them how much the war cost, and sends his son to it. They calculated rightly on Mr Webster. My friend Mr Thoreau has gone to jail rather than pay his tax. On him they could not calculate. The Abolitionists denounce the war and give much time to it, but they pay the tax.[145]

Although this was one of Emerson's more callow pronouncements – Webster's son Ned joined the Massachusetts volunteers on his own account in the wake of his father's condemnation of the declaration of war as 'universally odious' and an 'impeachable offence' (he would die of typhoid at San Angel in January 1848) – it did reflect the inevitable difficulty of opposing the conflict at home as well as Emerson's conviction that the abolitionists had latched onto it opportunistically. Of the very few who outdid his sonorous public protests was Horace Greeley, who campaigned in the *New York Tribune* against the vote for war in language as robust as any (including that of his traducer and columnist Karl Marx). On 12 May 1846 Greeley set his pen against the 'stampede' to war on the basis of short-term exaltation:

> We can easily defeat the armies of Mexico, slaughter them by thousands, and pursue them perhaps to their capital; we can conquer and 'annex' their teritory; but what then? Have the

---

144. *Diary of a President*, p. 138.

145. *Journal*, VII, p. 219, quoted in Anderson, 'Emerson on Texas and the Mexican War', p. 196. This, of course, was a sentiment expressed privately, but Emerson was only slightly more modulated in public:

> We have had a bad war, many victories, each of which converts the country into an immense chanticleer; and a very insincere political opposition. The country needs to be delivered from its delirium at once. Public affairs are chained to the same law with private; the retributions of armed states are not less sure and signal than those which come to private felons.

North American Review, quoted in ibid., p. 198.

histories of the ruin of Greek and Roman liberty consequent upon such extensions of empire by the sword no lessons for us? Who believes that a score of victories over Mexico, the 'annexation' of half her territories will give us more liberty, a purer Morality, a more prosperous Industry than we have now? ... Is not life miserable enough, comes not Death soon enough, without resort to ... hideous ... war?

The next day, when Congress voted through the declaration, Greeley adopted a rather different tack:

Grant the Father of Lies his premises and he will prove himself a truth-teller and a saint by faultless logic. Shut your eyes to the whole course of events this last twelve years ... and it will become easy to prove that we are a meek, unoffending, ill-used people, and that Mexico has kicked, cuffed and grossly imposed upon us. Only assume premises enough, as Polk does, and you may prove that it is New Orleans which has been threatened with a cannonade instead of Matamoros, and that it is the Mississippi which has been formally blockaded by a strange fleet and army instead of the Rio Norte.[146]

This was neither a popular voice nor one likely to survive the string of victories that ensued. James Russell Lowell's adoption of a rustic New England argot in 'The Biglow Papers', on the other hand, flourished by fortifying the same sentiments with humour:

> They may talk o' Freedom's airy
>   Tell they're pupple in the face –
> It's a grand gret cemetary
>   For the barthrights of our race;
> They just want this Californy
>   So's to lug new slave-states in
> To abuse ye, an' scorn ye,
>   An' to plunder ye like sin.

Such vocal slapstick was better than Puritan fulmination for projecting beyond the abolitionist community Gallatin's views on the social and racial threats posed by the war:

> Afore I come away from hum I had a strong
>   persuasion
> Thet Mexicans worn't human beans – an ourang outan
>   nation –
> A sort o' folks a chap could kill an' never dream
>   on't arter ...
> But when I jined I worn't so wize ez that air queen
>   o'Sheby,
> For, come to look at 'em, they aint much diff'rent
>   from wut we be,
> An here we air ascrougin' 'em out 'o their own
>   dominions,

---

146. *New York Tribune*, 12 and 13 May 1846, quoted in Morison, *Dissent in Three American Wars*, pp. 44, 40–41.

> Asheltevin' 'em, ez Caleb sez, with air eagles'
>   pinions,
> Wich means to take a feller up just by the slack
>   o' 's trousis,
> An' walk him Spanish clean right out o' all his
>   homes an' houses;
> It must be right, for Caleb sez it's reg'lar
>   Anglo-Saxon.[147]

In the same vein, 'Major Downing', the military adviser to Polk invented by Maine humourist Seba Smith, goes straight and unflustered to the bottom line:

> we got ten to one for our outlay … cost us only two or three thousand men to annex … 150,000 Mexicans…. They ought to remember that in a Government like ours, where the people is used for voting, and where every nose counts one, it is the number that we are to stan' about in annexin' and not the quality.[148]

Whatever the difficulties between the president and his generals, the war laid him open to the charge of propagating 'caesarism', obnoxious to republican traditionalists like Philip Hone:

> Annexation is now the greatest word in the American vocabulary. Veni-vidi-vici! is inscribed on the banners of every caesar who leads a struggling band of American adventurers … into the chaparral of a territory which an unprovoked war has given them the right to invade.

And Polk's dismissal of his opponents as lacking in patriotism took such a partisan form that many, like Tennessee congressman Meredith Grey, welcomed the implied treason: 'Because we will not crouch, with spaniel-like humility, at his feet, and whine an approval of *all his acts*, we are met … with the grateful compliment from the President that we are traitors to our country.'[149] Some went so far as to write letters of solidarity to the Mexican government, raising the cry of betrayal for real when a bunch were discovered by Scott's troops in the main post office of the enemy capital.

Such pressures did not stop the campaign, but they did put the government on the defensive and increased the caution of those who had reconciled themselves to the war. Probably the most celebrated of these was Prescott, whose *History of the Conquest of Mexico* had been published less than three years before the war, and started selling heavily once hostilities broke out. Although Prescott resisted the admission that his

---

147. *The Biglow Papers*, pp. 6–7, 23–5, quoted in Schroeder, *Mr Polk's War*, pp. 37, 103. Compare this with the language aimed at Cushing and his like by Massachusetts congregationalists:

> While Humanity is outraged, our country disgraced, the Laws of Heaven suspended, and those of Hell put in force, by the conduct and continuance of the Mexican War, we shall not cease (to attempt at least) to rouse the public mind to a sense of the awful guilt brought upon this nation by what has deservedly been called 'the most infamous war ever recorded upon the page of history'.

Boston Recorder, 12 Aug. 1847, quoted in Ellsworth, 'American Churches and the Mexican War', p. 315.
148. Quoted in Schroeder, *Mr Polk's War*, p. 97.
149. Quoted in ibid., pp. 54, 75.

royalties were bulging on the back of the slaughter, he could scarcely avoid the analogies between Cortés and Scott when George Bancroft ordered that a copy of the book be placed in the library of every ship of the navy or when Caleb Cushing wrote from San Angel congratulating him on the accuracy of his descriptions and the beauteous prose of a book being read throughout the army.[150] Nor would Prescott have missed the bitter irony coursing beneath Lucas Alamán's offer to help Cushing with researches for his own book. Indeed, despite his visceral anti-Americanism, Alamán felt the calling of history strongly enough to accept visits from US soldiers inspired by Prescott, showing them the Cortés family archive, of which he was the official custodian.[151] Winfield Scott had observed this, was a keen reader, and shared Cooper's estimation of the power of writing to affect political fortune. Although he eventually wrote his own memoirs, he would scarcely have balked at having Prescott as his biographer. According to Prescott's own biographer, George Ticknor, the historian was at work on a study of Ferdinand II when

> he was surprised by a tempting invitation to write a history of the Second Conquest of Mexico – the one, I mean, achieved by General Winfield Scott in 1847. The subject was obviously a brilliant one, making, in some respects, a counterpart to the first conquest under Cortés, and, as to the bookselling results that would have accrued from such a work glowing with the fervent life Mr Prescott's style would have imparted to it, and devoted to the favorite national hero of the time, there can be no doubt they would have exceeded anything he had ever before dreamed of as the profits of authorship. But his course in another direction was plainly marked out.... Contemporary events, transient and unsettled interests, personal feelings and ambitions, had never entered into his estimates and arrangements for a literary life. He felt that he hardly knew how to deal with them. He therefore declined the honor – and honor it certainly was – without hesitation. 'The theme,' he said, 'would be taking; but I had rather not meddle with heroes who have not been underground two centuries at least.'[152]

Ticknor would have sympathised with this choice: he took thirty years to produce his *History of Spanish Literature*, published the year after the war ended. One cannot, however, quite suppress the suspicion that Prescott was hiding awkwardly behind his antiquarian vocation, standing at the head of a long line of learned persons for whom the Mexican War was the most barbaric expression yet of American civilisation. Even Albert Gallatin found some solace in the reports on local customs, artefacts collected and ruins visited sent to the American Ethnological Society (which he had helped to found in 1842) by soldiers engaged in amateur archaeology and ethnography. He was not alone: George Squier's work on the Aztec calendar, for example, draws directly on the observations of Lieutenant William F. Emory, an engineer in Kearny's force. Squier had been appointed as chargé d'affaires in Nicaragua on Prescott's recommendation, and we know from more than his exchange with Padre Cartine, the clocksmith

---

150. Johannsen, *To the Halls of the Montezumas*, pp. 150, 245–6.
151. Ibid., p. 247.
152. George Ticknor, *The Life of W.H. Prescott*, London 1863, p. 272.

of León, that he felt that 'time ... in these regions is not regarded as of much importance'.[153] Perhaps by harking back to distant epochs, when indigenous empires were raised and time rigorously observed and measured, the thrill of scholarship could combine with the thrall of ancient greatness to cast a veil over the unlovely making of modern America?

SIGHTS ON THE MOSQUITO SHORE

In his film *Walker* (1988), Alex Cox plays around with time. Most of the movie treats the adventurer from Tennessee in the 'real time' of 1855–60 and the 'right place' of Nicaragua. But every now and again Cox reminds the audience that their belief has been suspended by quietly introducing into the scene a contemporary object, such as a radio or bottle of Coca Cola. The director was certainly making a political point about the US government's campaign against the Sandinistas that was at its peak when he was shooting. However, because Nicaragua has long had a special relationship with modernity as well as with the USA, Cox's device appears less intrusive than might otherwise be the case. Indeed, as Perry Anderson reminds us at the beginning of *The Origins of Postmodernity*, the term 'modernism' was itself coined in 1890 by a Nicaraguan poet, Rubén Darío, to identify an aesthetic movement. Assessing the work of the Peruvian poet and historian Ricardo Palma, Darío wrote that he

> understands and admires the new spirit which today animates a small but triumphant and proud group of writers and poets of Spanish America: the spirit of Modernism. This implies: elevation and factual accuracy in criticism, in prose, freedom, imagination and the triumph of the beautiful over the didactic; originality in poetry and the infusion of colour, life, air and flexibility to old verse forms which suffered from repression for they were pressed between imitated iron moulds.[154]

In the same year Darío dedicated a poem to Walt Whitman, now slowed by a stroke and approaching death, where the new is given an activist voice and future tense but also drawn from the most ancient of patriarchies – that of prophets:

> The old man lives in his country of iron,
> handsome, saintly and serene patriarch.
> The olympian furrow of his brow
> commands and conquers with its nobility.

---

153. *Nicaragua: Its People, Scenery, Monuments*, I, New York 1852, p. 82.
154. 'Ricardo Palma', in *Obras Completas*, II, Madrid 1950, p. 21.

His infinite soul seems a mirror;
his tired shoulders deserving of the gown,
and with a harp of ancient oak,
he sings his song like a new prophet.

Priest who draws divine breath,
he announces for the future a better time.
he says to the eagle: 'fly!'; 'row!' to the oarsman,
and 'work!' to the hearty labourer.

That's the road taken by their poet
with his stern emperor's face.

Some fifteen years later, at the end of Theodore Roosevelt's first administration, with US dominion over the Caribbean basin apparently as secure as it was confident, the audible ambivalence of Darío's earlier eulogy to its premier poet has hardened into premonition as, donning the prophetic mantle himself, he addresses its first twentieth-century president:

It takes the voice of the Bible, or the verse of Walt Whitman,
      to reach you, Hunter!
Primitive and modern, simple and complex,
one part Washington, four parts Nimrod!

You are the United States,
You are the future invader
of that ingenuous America with indigenous blood
that still prays to Jesus Christ and still speaks in Spanish.

Darío's poetry is scarcely 'historical' in the sense of providing a critical narrative of the past, but it is certainly retrospective and wistful – just the qualities that he saw as being at the heart of modernism:

… you will see in my verses princesses, kings, imperial objects, visions of distant or im-possible countries; what do you want! I detest the life and the times I have to live in…. If there is any poetry in our America it is in the old things; in Palenque and Utatlán, in the Indian of legend, the fine and sensual Inca, and in the great Moctezuma on his golden throne.

These lines, from the preface to *Prosas Profanas*, were written in 1896, before the US invasion of Cuba but with that experience made conceivable by an authoritative US industrialisation and assertion of the nature of progress.[155] Darío, then, not only recognises the jagged counterflows between modernism and modernity; he positively insists upon them. In part they do simply correspond to the times in which he lived – he was born in 1867, ten years after William Walker was driven out of Nicaragua, and he died in 1916, when the world of kings and princesses was just as mired as that

---

155. This translation by Mike González in Mike González and David Treece, *The Gathering of Voices: The Twentieth-Century Poetry of Latin America*, London 1992, p. 8. 'Walt Whitman' and 'A Roosevelt' in Guillermo de Torre (ed.), *Rubén Darío: Antología Poética*, Buenos Aires 1966, pp. 97–8.

of factories and bourgeois sobriety in a conflict of unparalleled slaughter. However, the simultaneous recognition and expression of the flawed figure of actuality also corresponds to Darío's movement through space: in the voyage from his birthplace in the village of Metapa in the province of Matagalpa to the town of León, to Chile, Argentina and on to Europe, returning home – effectively to die – after an absence of eighteen years.

According to Luis Orrego, when Darío arrived in Santiago at the age of twenty-one,

> [his] ignorance was almost total; he could barely distinguish between a coach and a house, and he couldn't tell the difference between a painting and a print. His literary baggage was limited to Victor Hugo, who was his maestro and God; he knew of nothing and nobody beyond the great poet.[156]

If this is a knowing exaggeration, Darío himself recounts how the Chileans made him feel every inch the backward rustic, and no more so than in his clothes. When he went in person to follow up one of the two letters of introduction that he had been able to obtain in Nicaragua, he was met with incredulity:

> 'Would you, by any chance, be Señor Rubén Darío?' In a tone somewhere between aghast, fearful and hopeful, I asked, 'Would you, perhaps, be Señor C.A.?' I then watched as a veritable Jericho of illusions collapsed to the ground. He looked me up and down in one go, taking in my poor boy's thin body, my long hair, the rings under my eyes, my little jacket from Nicaragua, a pair of narrow little trousers that I had thought so elegant, my problematic shoes, and, above all else, my suitcase.[157]

Darío was staring at Santiago less as a *flâneur* than in awe, and if he was to find here, in Buenos Aires, Madrid and Paris, an audience and fame, these themselves were created by his versified voyage from the margins. Most of Darío's adult life was spent 'abroad', out of Nicaragua, which he served as a diplomat but remembered as a childhood. As Alvaro Salvador has noted, Darío shares with Gabriel García Márquez the wonder of a child from the tropical provinces at the phenomenon of ice, learning from Colonel Félix Ramírez, who was his great-uncle and served as his step-father, 'how to ride, how to recognise ice, and how to read children's painted books as well as a taste for Californian apples and French champagne. God will have given him a special place in one of his heavens.' This was a childhood also enriched by his aunt Josefa, 'lively, talkative, a great lover of crinoline, a little bit bonkers, who once – on the day of her mother's death – appeared in a pair of red shoes'.[158] However, between the death of the colonel and that of the matriarch Rubén experienced moments of sheer terror that are common to all children but much less readily given adult imprimatur in modern urban society:

---

156. Rubén Darío, *Azul... Cantos de Vida y Esperanza*, ed. Alvaro Santander, Madrid 1992, p. 15.

157. *Autobiografía*, Madrid 1945, p. 67.

158. Ibid., pp. 9, 21.

The house was a fearful place for me at night. Owls nested in the eaves. The only servants – Serapia and the Indian Goyo – told me tales of apparitions and souls burning in hell. The mother of my aunt was still alive; an ancient creature white with age and afflicted by continuous shakes. She filled me with terror as well, telling me about a decapitated friar and a hairy hand that chased after you like a spider…. She pointed out the window, not far from our house, through which Juana Catina, a very sinful woman and mad in body, had been carried off by the demons.[159]

Darío's great-uncle, Colonel Ramírez, known to his compatriots as '*bocón*' ('the mouth'), was, as a leading patriarch of León, a 'Democrat' or Liberal. In June 1855 he had been designated by his correligionists to travel to the port of Realejo and receive William Walker, whom they had contracted to help them in the civil war against the 'Legitimists' or Conservatives, largely based in the town of Granada. Ramírez is simply described by Walker as 'swarthy', the North American recognising the Nicaraguan's personal authority and military capacity as much as he did of any other local figure. The colonel, quickly grasping the drift of events, withdrew from the campaign after fighting alongside the foreign mercenaries in their first fight at Rivas.[160] Nevertheless, Ramírez was very publicly implicated in the initial Anglo-American incursion – something that Darío registers briefly and vaguely in his autobiography, and which may account for his failure to address the experience in verse even when, in 1909, the USA openly assisted the overthrow of the Zelaya government which the poet had served for almost its entire seventeen-year span.

Darío's job was eventually cancelled by the new, Washington-backed Estrada government, and when he landed back from Europe in Mexico he was greeted with cheers of 'Viva Rubén Darío! Down with the Yankees!' His vilification of Estrada as a traitor would seem to fit well with the general description of the modernist writers as 'nationalists and anti-imperialists'.[161] Yet there is little on Nicaragua itself in Darío's poems. Like Yeats – two years his senior – he revisits several times the myth of Leda and the swan to confront transience through an erotic voice, celebrate coitus (thereby sealing his break with the Catholic Church), and express a profound insecurity about the passage of time. Like Yeats, he draws on Whitman, and he circles around the adoration of the Magi as a motif. But Darío's poetry is never nationalist in the same way as is that of Yeats; arguably not at all. *Cantos de Vida y Esperanza* is dedicated to Nicaragua (and Argentina), but the country (like León and his '*tierra natal*') is mentioned just once in all the poems in the standard anthology. Darío cannot be accused – as, in 1913, Yeats accused John Mitchel – of promoting hate of the empire before love of the nation, but as a writer he is an anti-imperialist and American before he is a patriot and Nicaraguan. Certainly, none of his work remotely approaches Yeats's 'Under Ben Bulben' for directness of political injunction:

---

159. Ibid., pp. 10–11.
160. Walker, *War in Nicaragua*, pp. 39, 50, 85.
161. Gerald Martin, 'The Literature, Music and Art of Latin America, 1870–1930', in Leslie Bethell (ed.), *Cambridge History of Latin America*, IV, Cambridge 1986, p. 456.

Irish poets, learn your trade,
Sing whatever is well made,
Scorn the sort now growing up
All out of shape from toe to top,
Their unremembering hearts and heads
Base-born products of base beds.
Sing the peasantry, and then
Hard-riding country gentlemen,
The holiness of monks, and after
Porter-drinkers' randy laughter;
Sing the lords and ladies gay
That was beaten into the clay
Through seven heroic centuries;
Cast your mind on other days
That we in coming days may be
Still the indomitable Irishry.[162]

Like his Uruguayan friend Rodó, Darío generated a pan-American identity and vocation out of a small country upbringing. This sets him apart from both Neruda, who was both nationalist and anti-imperialist, and most of the Nicaraguan poetic tradition that followed him and combined his sensualism with an acute sense of place. Indeed, it is a mark of both the strength of that tradition and the weakness of orthodox historiography in Nicaragua that the country's past is best known through the pens of its poets and politicians.

Nicaraguan nationalism registered as a rhetoric in Darío's lifetime. There was not only the Walker episode but also the closely linked controversy over the protectorate of Mosquito Indians upheld by the British – and challenged by the USA – on the country's Caribbean or Atlantic coast. That conflict flared up in the 1840s, the decade after the collapse of the Central American Confederation, when Nicaragua, one of its constituent states, was striving to transform itself into an independent republic with all the evocation of cultural separateness and constitutional sovereignty that attends such a process. Fifty years later US intervention served to harden the nationalist voice just as it also generously underwrote the appeal of geographical fatalism and eager compliance. Yet baseball did not become the national game until after the US Marine Corps had been redeployed in the 1920s to suppress the guerrilla campaign waged by Augusto César Sandino.

Just as they labelled him a 'bandit' or 'brigand', Sandino often referred to the US forces as 'filibusters' or 'pirates':

Take heart Nicaraguans! They, barbarians of the north, would bid you farewell leaving the mark of their blows on your faces. Then so be it! Do not let retribution be delayed; square the account blow for blow, eye for eye, so that the yankees may learn the respect due to free peoples. There will be no forgiveness for you, Nicaraguans, if you turn the other cheek to the invader. Your hands should fall like thunderbolts upon the descendants of William Walker.

---

162. Augustine Martin (ed.), *W.B. Yeats: Collected Poems*, London 1990, p. 343. For Yeats's accusation of Mitchel, see Roy Foster, *W.B. Yeats: A Life. The Apprentice Mage*, Oxford 1997, p. 524.

Our autonomist army has amply demonstrated what the force of right can do against the right of force.[163]

By the start of 1930 Sandino had moved beyond the position – common amongst the Latin American left – that the ordinary people of the United States should be distinguished from Washington because they did not share the imperialist ambition of their government. Now he saw the 'descendants of William Walker' as no mere dupes or victims of machine politics and propaganda but supporters of the invasion of Nicaragua and so a people bereft of principle:

> We in Nicaragua also believed in the famous democracy of the Yankee people – there are some who still do – and we believed that the abuses committed by the White House govern-ments were not looked upon with approval by the North American people. Later ... still believing in a remnant of virtue among the avalanche of Walker's descendants, I said ... referring to the construction of the Nicaraguan canal, that the $3 million with which they aspired and still aspire – contrary to all international decency – to possess the right to intervene in our internal and external affairs, could be looked upon as shares of stock in the construction of that project. Although my earlier statement attributing to the North American people the same imperialist attitude held by their leaders has provoked opposition to my position, I am entirely convinced that the North American people support and will always support the expansionist policies of their unprincipled governments.[164]

Ernesto Cardenal, who would serve as minister of culture in the Sandinista govern-ment of the 1980s and who as a child walked daily past Darío's house in León when the US marines were still occupying Nicaragua, is able to hold on to the populist elements of the original filibustering campaign without pathologising the entire North American people in his poem 'Los Filibusteros', written in the early 1950s:

> There were ruffians, thieves, cardsharps and pistoleros.
> There were also brave, gentle and valiant men.
> Recruited by need and by dreams:
> One had no work and was on the dock
> When Walker's agent arrived with a free ticket
> to Nicaragua.
>   From where there was no return passage.
> Or they came for 160 acres of Central American land
> (to sell it) and 25 dollars a month,
> and they fought for nothing a month, and six square feet of earth.
> Or they came in search of glory: a name
> which would be inscribed in the annals of History.
> And their names remain forgotten,
> in barracks with the planks torn down for coffins
> and the sergeant drunk, pigs, excrement;
> or in those hospital of mangos, coconuts and almonds,
> delirious amongst the black men and magpies

---

163. Manifesto of 6 Sept. 1929, in Gregorio Selser, *Sandino*, New York 1981, p. 131.
164. Communiqué of 9 Jan. 1930, in Robert Conrad (ed.), *Sandino: The Testimony of a Nicaraguan Patriot, 1921–1934*, Princeton 1990, p. 291.

chilled by the winds of the Lake.
And the most fortunate were those who died in battle
or night ambushes on strange roads as if in a dream,
or by accident a violent death.
And 'The Transit Company' always brought more
filibusters and more filibusters
to San Juan del Sur
    and to San Juan del Norte.

Not yet thirty years old, Cardenal had lived in New York and made a pilgrimage to Walden Pond and Emerson's Concord home in the company of the dean of Nicaraguan poets, José Coronel Urtecho (1906–94), before embarking on this series of poems dedicated to the events of the 1850s. At the start of 'Greytown' (San Juan del Norte) he reminds us of the global character of the experience that was about to sweep over Nicaragua:

Greytown! Greytown!
Americans, Germans, Irishmen,
Frenchmen, mulattoes, Chinese, Spaniards,
they'd all come, meet each other here, and leave.
What's the news from New York? New Orleans? Havana?
They paid for guavos in marks; a bottle of rum
with dollars, francs, pounds.
    Any new annexation?
And breaking up the reflection of leaves,
    the *Daniel Webster* would pull away.

A similarly unblaming précis in verse of George Squier's 1849 book reflects Cardenal's capacity to comprehend the peculiarly catalytic effect of the exotic on the brutal innocence of Anglo-America. However, by far the strongest of these early poems is the thirty-page 'With Walker in Nicaragua', which in 1952 won the prize to celebrate the centenary of Managua's establishment as national capital.[165] Cardenal writes from the standpoint of Clinton Rollins, one of Walker's North American soldiers, and so provides himself with a voice that is inside the filibuster mind and unheated by patriotic hatred. The poem was composed five years before Cardenal entered the Trappist Monastery of Our Lady of Gethsemane in Kentucky, but one can find within it a disposition to distinguish the sinner from the sin; Cardenal's Walker is a peculiar man set on an evil course, not a peculiarly evil man:

I saw Walker for the first time in San Francisco;
I remember him as if I were seeing his blond face like a tiger's;
his grey eyes, without pupils, fixed like a blind man's,

---

165. All are translated by Jonathan Cohen in Ernesto Cardenal, *With Walker in Nicaragua and Other Early Poems, 1949–1954*, Middletown, Conn., 1984: 'With Walker in Nicaragua', pp. 42ff.; 'Los Filibusteros', p. 73; 'Greytown', p. 79. The *Antología Nueva* issued in 1996 by Editorial Trotta in Madrid includes the early epigrams that landed Cardenal in jail the same year he won the prize but excludes the longer works on Squier and Walker.

but which had expanded and flashed like gunpowder in combat,
and his skin faintly freckled, his paleness, his clergyman's ways,
his voice, colourless like the eyes, cold and sharp,
in a mouth without lips.
And a woman's voice was hardly softer than his:
that calm voice of his announcing death sentences ...
that swept so many into the jaws of death in combat.
He never drank or smoked and he wore no uniform.
Nobody was his friend.
And I don't remember ever seeing him smile.

Here Cardenal wraps a cool paraphrase of the several contemporary accounts of the US 'general' into the concern for physicality that bonds the Nicaraguan poetic tradition from Darío onwards. For Walker's death before a Honduran firing squad at Trujillo in 1860, the poet had to draw on different sources to sustain Rollins's reported account, ending with the final words attributed to the adventurer that he would use in other poems (most notably 'Zero-Hour' [1960], the wonderful and politically unrestrained homage to the victims of the Somoza dictatorship):

When they halted
the officer commanding the guard
read a paper in Spanish,
   surely his order.
And then Walker, in a calm and dignified voice,
without trembling,
spoke in Spanish.
And the filibusterers didn't know what he said.
They could see from where they stood
a newly made grave in the sand,
and Walker, who kept speaking, calm and dignified,
beside the grave.
And the man said:
   'The President
the President of Nicaragua, is a Nicaraguan...'
There was a drum roll
and gunfire.
All the bullets hit the mark.
Out of the 91 men only 12 made it back.
And there, by the sea, with no wreaths or epitaph, remained
William Walker of Tennessee.[166]

This calm reassertion that Walker was no Nicaraguan might explain his absence from the pantheon of traitors in *Canto General*, where Neruda, who published Cardenal's banned epigrams in Chile, upholds the orthodox chronology of Nicaraguan patriotism by commemorating Sandino's martyrdom at the hands of Somoza. Walker is inverted in the person of Somoza – the Nicaraguan hired from without (and dubbed 'the last American marine' by his enemies):

---

166. *With Walker in Nicaragua*, pp. 47, 71.

But when fire, blood,
and dollar didn't destroy
Sandino's proud tower,
and Wall Street guerrillas
made peace, invited
the guerrilla to celebrate,

and a newly hired traitor

shot him with his rifle.

His name is Somoza. To this day
he's ruling Nicaragua:
the thirty dollars grew
and multiplied in his belly.[167]

'Zero-Hour' is a kind of national *Canto General* and does in many ways prefigure Cardenal's *Canto Nacional* (1973), dedicated to the FSLN (the Sandinistas), with whom he sympathised whilst sustaining the contemplative community of Our Lady of Solentiname (1966–77, when it was destroyed by Somoza's National Guard) on Mancarrón Island in the south-east corner of Lake Nicaragua. There Cardenal expressed his 'exteriorist' poetics ('objective poetry, narrative and anecdotal' – not so different from Darío's modernist ambitions) to promote a form of liberation theology that radicalised his voice further still. At the same time, his geographical compass expanded well beyond the lake and the country to which it gave its name – through *Homenaje a los indios americanos* (1969) to *Cántico Cósmico* (1989), where the entire universe is taken for the theatre of a 550-page epic. Here, amidst talk of Einstein, Gaia, the second law of thermodynamics, Meister Eckhart and Schrödinger, there is not only a revindication of the sacrifices made to forge a revolution then about to end, and the necessary priest's allusion to the beginning being the Word (and that Word being light); there are also lines that would have appealed to Yeats:

Only love is revolutionary.
Hatred is always reactionary.

(Cardenal also notes how as a minister Guevara signed the first Cuban revolutionary banknotes simply 'Che'; Yeats only got to design the currency of the Free State. If money is indeed 'frozen desire', then revolutionary dreamers must play their part.[168])

In the early stages of *Cántico Cósmico*, though, there is a passage of nostalgic, almost 'interiorist' verse that overrides Cardenal's debts to the likes of Pound and Merton to conjure up the Walt Whitman of 'Crossing Brooklyn Ferry':

---

167. *Canto General*, trans. Jack Schmidt, Berkeley 1991, p. 127.

168. *Cántico Cósmico*, Managua 1989, p. 81. James Buchan, *Frozen Desire: An Inquiry into the Meaning of Money*, London 1997. In November 1940 Dr Erwin Schrödinger was appointed Director of the School of Theoretical Physics of the Institute of Advanced Study, Dublin. The other School of the Institute, set up in June 1940, is for Celtic Studies. My thanks to Neil Belton for reminding me of the interest of de Valera – born in the USA of a Spanish father – in mathematics and for drawing my attention to this singular moment in the development of Irish intellectual life.

I remember that branch of Woolworths on Broadway,
by 102nd street,
and the little assistant of seventeen or eighteen, looking after some cheap goods,
surrounded by demanding ladies,
   she retorted briskly to another, she was tired
(it was near closing-time,
   she was all day on her feet)
and her sternness broke into a broad smile
when she saw me, twenty-three years of age, at the entrance.
She smiled at me. A warm smile as if to say I'm tired.
   Slender, golden hair and roseate skin.
Instead of that job, she could have been in the movies.
Or I could have waited for her at closing-time.
I carried on down Broadway. Lower Broadway.
   Exactly thirty-eight years ago.
There on 102nd and Broadway
on the right-hand side coming from Columbia
about closing-time,
that is, about quarter to six.
   Now I am sixty-one years old.
Space–time has rushed by like an electric train
in a reality as illusory as a film.

Here Cardenal plays the *flâneur*, but at the end of his gigantic poem he is as direct and Whitmanesque a lover as any:

Our kisses between the butterflies
on a bed of fern.
Your thighs smelling of the ham-zah flower.
Your body with a panoply of colour
distilling coconut water.
   I sucked your breasts.
The fragrance of your semen like the milky kassaman flower.[169]

Cardenal is an inclusive poet. Although the Trappists required him not to publish whilst he was undergoing instruction, they did not stop him taking notes, and we can trace a writing career of nigh-on fifty years. Even before he became minister, Cardenal travelled widely – particularly in Latin America – amassing the facts and experiences that teem through his poems. Some affect to find his political beliefs overconfident,[170]

---

169. *Cántico Cósmico*, pp. 57–8, 540–41.
170. He came on stage like Che Guevara, and in the question-and-answer session he responded to the demagoguery of some agitators in the audience with more demagoguery than even they wanted to hear. He did and said everything necessary to earn the approbation and applause of the most recalcitrant: there was no difference between the Kingdom of God and communist society; the Church had become a whore, but thanks to the revolution it would become pure again, as it was becoming in Cuba; the Vatican, a capitalist cave which had always defended the powerful, was now the servant of the Pentagon; the fact that there was only one party in Cuba and in the USSR meant the elite had the task of stirring up the masses, exactly as Christ had wanted the Church to do with the people; it was immoral to speak against the forced-labour camps in the USSR – how could anyone believe capitalist propaganda?

but, just as the more measured Darío was parsimonious in the extreme with respect
to a poetic 'Nicaragua', so is Cardenal over the Mosquito coast and what are today
generally referred to as the Miskito people (often also taken to include the rest of the
population of the Atlantic coast which is not mestizo; that is, the black Creoles,
Caribs, Sumos and Ramas). They do not appear at all in his 'Indian poems', which
extend from the Pawnees and Iroquois through the Náhuatl to the Quechua and
Guaraní. Perhaps, numbering less than 100,000, the Mosquito might not merit greater
attention either as a distinct ethnic group of the Americas or as a constituent group of
Nicaragua, but Cardenal pays greater attention to the fewer Kuna people of Panama.
The Mosquito certainly played a very marginal role in national affairs before the
revolution (although Sandino's experimental commune of the 1930s abutted their
historic lands), and after it a combination of unresolved historical claims, clumsy
Sandinista policies and US-sponsored agitation encouraged many to join the counter-
revolutionary Contra in neighbouring Honduras. This may help to explain both the
lack of attention and a discernible sense of ambivalence, reaching back to a deeper
piratical past and extending beyond the borders of the republic, when the Mosquito/
Wanki are addressed by Cardenal:

> The indios of the Coco never reach the mysterious lake
> for fear of the voices they hear on its banks.
> Because the spirits of the cruel still guard the booty
>   and still fight,
> and shrieks (like toucans) and shots are heard,
> and at night the clank of chains, as if weighing anchor.
>   Every now and again the thrashing of an alligator
>   fighting with another alligator ...
> Some fin cutting through the quiet waters of the lake:
> a shark that like the pirates came in by the Patuca
> or perhaps it's a swordfish.
> When the rainy season comes there is no longer a lake of Apalka
>   and there is no longer a plain,
> just a lake reaching to the horizon
> that has removed the place where Apalka lake exists,
> with galleons loaded with silver, gold and pearls
> and the skeletons of pirates
>   all – skeletons and treasure – sunk in the mud.
> But perhaps there is a moon, and the infinite lake
> which none of the Wanki visit
> returns (the pirates' excited voices in the wind)
> to the light of the moon of an Atlantic night, a
> lugubrious lake of silver coin.[171]

And the final act of pure theatre: waving his hands, he announced to the world that the recent
cyclone that hit Lake Nicaragua was the result of some ballistic experiments carried out by the
United States.... I still have a vivid impression of his insincerity and his histrionics.

Mario Vargas Llosa, *The Real Life of Alejandro Mayta*, London 1986, pp. 79–80.

171. 'Apalka', in *Antología Nueva*, pp. 130–31. Lake Apalka lies in Honduras on the previously contested
Plains of Auka, across the Río Coco/Wanki/Segovia, which in 1906 was ruled to be the frontier between

The contrasts in peoples and place is brought out more strongly still by Eduardo Galeano in the context of the violence of the 1980s:

> I arrived in Bluefields, on the Nicaraguan coast, the day after an attack by the Contras. There were many dead and wounded. I was in the hospital when one of the survivors of the skirmish, a young boy, awoke from anaesthesia. He woke up without arms, looked at the doctor, and said:
> *'Kill me.'*
> I felt a knot in my stomach.
> That night, an atrocious night, the air was boiling ...
> I threw myself down on a terrace, alone, face to the sky. Not far from there, music rang out loudly. In spite of it all, the people of Bluefields were celebrating the traditional fiesta of the Maypole. The people were dancing jubilantly around the ceremonial tree. But I, stretched out on the terrace, didn't want to hear the music, or anything at all, and I was trying not to feel, not to remember, not to think about anything, anything whatsoever. And there I was, swatting away sounds, sadness and mosquitoes, my eyes fixed on the night sky, when a child of Bluefields whom I didn't know lay down beside me and began looking at the sky as I was, in silence.
> Then a shooting-star fell. I could have made a wish but it didn't occur to me.
> And the child explained:
> 'Do you know why stars fall? It's God's fault. God sticks them up badly. He sticks the stars on with rice water.'
> I greeted the dawn dancing.[172]

KINGS AND CONSULS

Ten years before William Walker first arrived in Nicaragua the idea of a powerful US presence in the region was almost unthinkable. As we have seen, prior to the war with Mexico the gap between the ambitions of the Monroe Doctrine and the logistical capacity of the US state was very wide. Even in Central America, which a century later would be considered to be under US tutelage almost as a matter of course, Washington had experienced exceptional difficulty even in establishing a diplomatic presence. If the account presented by Joseph Lockey is exaggerated, it is not by much, and his numbers are correct:

> Futility marked the early relations of the United States with Central America. Nothing went right; everything went wrong. The very agents of the Washington government seemed to move under an evil star. Physical hardships, vexations of spirit, dread diseases, and in some cases death itself attended them. Of the eleven appointees before 1849, three died en route;

Nicaragua and Honduras by the King of Spain. In 1960 the International Court of Justice in The Hague confirmed this ruling, and Nicaragua was finally obliged to cede the territory in dispute.

172. 'Heaven and Hell', in *The Book of Embraces*, New York 1991, p. 253.

another succumbed before he started on his mission; one escaped with his life by being dismissed before he embarked; another survived by contriving to draw his salary for more than a year without going near the Central American capital; and another travelled over the length and breadth of the country, unable to find a government to receive him. Though the remaining four reached their destination and were received, only one of these prolonged his stay beyond a few months, and he committed suicide soon after his return to the United States.[173]

For six years after the departure in 1841 of William Murphy, who suffered from yellow fever throughout his twelve-week stay in Guatemala, there was no US diplomatic representative at all. In March 1848 Elijah Hise of Kentucky was commissioned as chargé to Guatemala and empowered to conclude a treaty with Salvador, now an independent state. Although he could have travelled via San Juan del Norte and Lake Nicaragua, Hise decided to take the route via Panama, where, having already been shipwrecked off the Bahamas, he and his family fell ill and had to wait several weeks for a passage to Jamaica.

From Jamaica he wrote a doleful account of his sufferings; but he was not disposed to give up his mission. He had determined to send his wife and nephew back to the United States and then proceed by sea to the 'Gulph of Dolce', from which he declared, 'I will if I live make my way by land to Guatemala.' Yet he had the feeling that too much was expected of him. 'If the mission is important,' he complained, 'the Government should enable me to get there or recall me.' While waiting in Jamaica he was again prostrated with fever 'and brought to the verge of the grave'. Reduced to a mere skeleton, he 'tottered on board' a vessel bound for Havana where he expected to find an opportunity to proceed on his journey; but he thought it was 'due to truth and candour' to say that he almost despaired of reaching his destination alive. He expressed the hope that on account of the wretched state of his health the president would conceive it proper to recall him. Then, as if by magic and much to the credit of Havana, his health improved. He embarked for Omoa. On his way his health continued to improve and as his spirits rose correspondingly, he began to ponder the destiny of his country. 'By the by,' he volunteered, 'I should like to say something on the Cuba Question. A question upon which I think I am pretty well informed, but it would be out of place here; I would certainly give my support most cordially to an administration that should be in favour of – and knew how to EFFECT the ANNEXATION of Cuba to the United States.'[174]

As soon as he arrived at Omoa, Hise wrote to Secretary of State Buchanan, giving full vent to his atrocious grammar and spelling as well as untempered opinions:

Yet The Very best Portion of this Valuable Country has been Appropriated by Great Britain to herself, Including the Islands In Violation of the plain Terri Torrial rights of the states Honduras and Nicaragua. The Island of Roattan is one of the most Beatifull and Valuable in the World of the same Extent. I have seen a map at Truxhillo, Prepared by direction of the British Government in which is Laid down the Boundry of the Country which the English Government Occupy in part and Intend to Occupy altogether and claim the right to Occupy as the allies and Protectors of the Musquito Indians, a besotted, brutal Ignorant race of Indians who never had such a thing as a Government since the days of the Dominion of Old Spain commenced.... The English claim the right to occupy this country above described

---

173. Joseph Lockey, 'Diplomatic Futility', *HAHR*, 10:3, 1930, p. 265.
174. Ibid., pp. 291–2.

by Virtue of a Pretended treaty, with a trumped up pretended King of a *pretended* Kingdom of the Musquito Tribe of Indians.... Now will the U.S. suffer Great Britain to Enact on the Stage of North America the Same Bloody tragedy which it has allready performed in Hindostan and Elsewhere and Stand by and Endure that She shall have a commercial Monopoly in all these fertile regions on this very continent of North America where in our Days of Weakness we shook her dominion.[175]

Here Hise is not just expressing a Monrovian instinctive distrust of the British. He is also registering the downside of the victory in Mexico: although the weak and divided states of the isthmus now stood in full awe of Anglo-American military might, some also resented it deeply and were on the lookout for alternative international alliances. Even in Nicaragua, the country that stood to do best out of the Gold Rush with a new canal, opinion was sharply divided; and the president of the region's weakest state, Honduras, did not desist from making his views known to his citizens just as Scott was closing on Mexico City and defeat widely seen as imminent:

The beautiful, rich and powerful land of Mexico has been most unjustly humiliated by the foot of the foreigner, and the enemies of that Republic, the sister of Central America, have brought desolation, extermination and death with their armies, even going to the length of singing hymns of victory over the ruins of liberty, and, together with slavery, to bring in Protestantism, freedom of worship, to injure and undermine, if possible, the principles of our ancestors and which we profess and have sworn to defend at any risk, as the firmest foundation of a free and enlightened society. The cause of Mexico is, we may say, our own, and therefore to look upon it with indifference would be a crime meriting opprobium and execration.... I protest to you in the most solemn manner that I am ready to seal with my own blood my love for my religion, my fatherland, and for liberty; and that, far from humiliating myself before impiety and tyranny, I shall gladly descend into the grave with the satisfaction of not having betrayed my belief, of not being a slave, and of having secured the most rightful enjoyments for my fellow-citizens.[176]

This, of course, was full-blooded rhetoric, but it was not completely vacuous. After all, it was the Hondurans who would shoot Walker in 1860, and they did so, one should note, after he had been handed over to them by a British warship.[177]

---

175. Hise, Omoa, to Buchanan, 26 Oct. 1848, in W.R. Manning (ed.), *Diplomatic Correspondence of the United States: Interamerican Affairs, 1831–1860: III. Central America, 1831–50*, Washington 1933, pp. 289–90.

176. Proclamation of President Manuel Quijarro, Comayagua, 2 June 1847, in ibid., pp. 248–9.

177. Nearly a decade after Quijarro's sterling declaration and when Walker was at his most destructive in Nicaragua, the Honduran government was again complaining, but in a discernably more modern vein:

When one considers the ideas expressed by our colleagues *El Heraldo* of New York and the *Unión* of Washington, one can see that we have not advanced one step towards tranquillity or individual and territorial security. According to the *Unión*, the present US administration proposes to exclude all intervention by Great Britain in Central American affairs and to ignore the treaties existing between both governments, arrogating to itself the exclusive right to mind our affairs without intervention from any other country on earth. Who has given the United States such rights over us? Does a nation, or do individuals, perchance have more right to butt into a neighbour's affairs than does a more distant friend.... If the North Americans have honest intentions, what is it to them that another nation also mixes in our affairs, when we have the same friendly relations with both and participation in our well-being is equally open to all? The only logical conclusion is that their insidious policy conceals a direct interest of little advantage to us.

Gaceta Oficial de Honduras, 30 May 1857, cited in Selser, *Sandino*, pp. 209–10.

Relations between the USA and Great Britain in and over Central America oscillated quite wildly in the 1840s and 1850s and were understandably affected by the personalities of the 'diplomats' involved. At no stage, though, did they ever return to the amity prevailing at the start of the 1840s – before the annexation of Texas and the Mexican War. It is probable that the absence from the region in 1840–42 of Frederick Chatfield – who had been appointed British consul in June 1834 and acquired an unenviable reputation for ill-tempered arrogance – helped this relaxation. However, the warm reception given at the end of 1839 to the new US agent, John L. Stephens, by the superintendent of Belize, Colonel Macdonald, reflected a deeper sense of communion over Anglo identity and values that had survived the cold Jacksonian period and would be all but extinguished by the rivalry over the region after 1848 as the isthmus, and Nicaragua in particular, was pulled partially into the North American system:

> The large window of the dining room opened upon the harbour; the steamboat lay in front of the Government House, and black smoke, rising in columns from her pipe, gave notice that it was time to embark. Before rising, Colonel Macdonald, like a loyal subject, proposed the health of the Queen; after which he ordered the glasses to be filled to the brim and, standing up, he gave, 'The health of Mr Van Buren, President of the United States', accompanying it with a warm and generous sentiment, and the earnest hope of strong and perpetual friendship between England and America. I felt at the moment, 'Cursed be the hand that attempts to break it'; and albeit unused to taking the President and the people upon my shoulders, I answered as well as I could. Another toast followed to the health and successful journey of Mr Catherwood [Stephens's English artist] and myself, and we rose from the table. The government dory lay at the foot of the lawn. Colonel Macdonald put his arm through mine, and, walking away, told me that I was going to a distracted country; that Mr Savage, the American consul at Guatimala [sic], had, on a previous occasion, protected the property and lives of British subjects; and, if danger threatened me, I must assemble the Europeans, hang out my flag, and send word to him. I knew that these were not mere words of courtesy, and, [given] the state of the country to which I was going, felt the value of such a friend at hand.[178]

As with the debate over 'informal empire' in general, it is very hard to disentangle the economic and political motives of British policy towards Central America in the 1840s and 1850s.[179] These were just as strongly linked as they were on the US side, and in both countries important changes of government in those decades prompted alterations of tone and substance, occasionally raising the spectre of an official armed conflict. In general, though, it would seem that 'neither side ... aimed at exclusive control but each feared that this was in fact the other's real intention'.[180] After the US

---

178. John L. Stephens, *Incidents of Travel in Central America, Chiapas and Yucatán*, I (1841), New York 1969, p. 22.

179. See, especially, the debate between Robert A. Naylor, 'The British Role in Central America prior to the Clayton–Bulwer Treaty of 1850', *HAHR*, 40:3, 1960, and Mark J. Van Aken, 'British Policy Considerations in Central America before 1850', *HAHR*, 42:1, 1962. Also: Richard W. Van Alstyne, 'The Central American Policy of Lord Palmerston, 1846–1848', *HAHR*, 16:3, 1936, and 'British Diplomacy and the Clayton–Bulwer Treaty, 1850–60', *Journal of Modern History*, 11:2, 1939.

180. Kenneth Bourne, *Britain and the Balance of Power in North America, 1815–1908*, London 1967, p. 177.

victory in Mexico even Palmerston, who returned to the Foreign Office in 1846, had to recognise that it was impossible to face down Washington like most other governments, and yet the sharp differences in political culture and institutions could not be brushed aside when London held vital colonies in Canada and the Caribbean. Thus, in October 1848, Earl Grey, the colonial secretary, argued for a policy of containment founded on ideological grounds:

> The more I see and hear of the affairs of the United States, the more convinced I am of the extreme importance of consolidating in British America a system of government that is really popular and at the same time not so ultra-democratic in principle as that of the great republic. As the effect of the institutions of the United States becomes more and more developed, the more dangerous I think them to the peace of the world, and though otherwise perhaps I would not attach so much value to our possessions in America, I do think it of the utmost consequence that we should at least retain them long enough to raise them to a constitution in which they might maintain their own independence instead of being absorbed in the Union.[181]

Within such a perspective Central America presented London with an evident problem since it had only one small colony there in British Honduras (Belize), and otherwise its direct political and economic presence was distinctly modest: in 1850 London had one consul and two unpaid vice-consuls in the five states, where there were only sixteen British residents classified as merchants and nine as small traders.[182] Of course, the presence of the British navy, which had important bases in Jamaica and St Lucia, compensated to a considerable degree for the lack of direct possessions and the vulnerability of the few British commercial interests in the area. None the less, the Mosquito protectorate now took on greater importance than at any time since the treaty of 1783 with Spain that had ended the British suzerainty originally established over the area in 1740 by Robert Hodgson, a leading Belizean merchant. Under the 1783 treaty most of the 3,000 British subjects left the Mosquito Shore for Belize, but a number stayed on and were granted favourable concessions by the Spaniards. Equally, the Mosquito chiefs kept their close ties with both Belize and Jamaica, just as their relations first with the Spanish authorities and then with those of the Central American Confederation and Nicaragua remained distinctly cold. In 1816 King George Frederick II was crowned at Belize with the rites of the Anglican Church, as was Robert Charles Frederick in 1825, each sending his sons to be schooled in Kingston and making concessions of land to speculators and local merchants with great largesse and minimal attention to detail or economic consequence.

It was this linkage that Palmerston picked up in 1840 as an element of continuity and commitment which might override international treaties:

---

181. Grey, London, to Lord Elgin (governor-general of Canada), 11 Oct. 1848, quoted in ibid., p. 171.
182. Naylor, 'British Role', pp. 6–7. Until at least 1844, London, under pressure from the Belizean merchants, viewed its commercial monopoly over the Bay Islands off Honduras (Roatán and Guanaja, both claimed by Honduras) as vital to the economic survival of British Honduras.

When a British authority has with the sanction of the British government placed a crown upon the head of a foreign chief, the British government does seem to be bound in honour to keep that crown, such as it may be, upon the head on which it has been so placed, and to protect in his rights the chief who wears it.[183]

However, in London the Colonial Office was opposed to any such slippage towards an effective protectorate, and when Robert Charles Frederick died in 1842 with three sons under the age of majority, it disavowed his will that appointed Colonel Macdonald, the superintendent of Belize, to act as regent. As a consequence a power vacuum opened up on the shore, and by June 1842 the situation had deteriorated so far that the British felt themselves obliged to intervene in the form most fitting to the time and the place:

> I hereby declare the port of San Juan de Nicaragua, situated in the mouth of the river of that name, to be blockaded, and that all commercial intercourse with the said port shall be prevented and cease. I hereby give public notice of the same to all whom it may concern; and that all ships and vessels, under whatever flag they may be, will be turned away ... and if after any ship or vessel has been warned not to enter the said port, then and in that case any ship or vessel that may attempt to break the blockade will be seized and be dealt with according to the rules established for the breach of a *de facto* blockade.[184]

The blockade was raised in January 1843, but by June of that year matters had again deteriorated so far that it was reimposed for nearly fifteen months. By the time that it was finally lifted at the end of 1844 Lord Aberdeen had agreed to the appointment of Patrick Walker as consul-general to the Mosquito Shore in the mistaken belief that he was restoring a lapsed appointment rather than consolidating Palmerston's sleight of hand by creating an entirely new diplomatic post and relationship. Walker, who had previously served as colonial secretary in Belize, was dispatched to Bluefields in April 1844, a move the Foreign Office deemed absolutely vital to restore order in the area. However, the Colonial Office continued to resist the consequences for years after: 'we really must not allow ourselves to be dragged into the expense and trouble of protecting this mock king in the occupation of this territory which he cannot defend himself'.[185]

Consul Walker went straight about his business, arranging for the young prince George Augustus Frederick to be crowned so that he himself could play the part of regent. However, he was to discover that Palmerston's reservations about the quality of the crown involved ('such as it may be') were justified:

183. Minute on Colonial Office to Foreign Office, 27 Nov. 1840, quoted in R.A. Humphreys, 'Anglo-American Rivalries in Central America', in *Tradition and Revolt in Latin America and Other Essays*, London 1969, p. 168.

184. Proclamation by Vice-Admiral Sir Charles Adam, Commander-in-Chief, Navy, North America, West Indies and Seas Adjacent, 19 June 1842, in *BFSP, 1845–46*, XXXIV, p. 1263.

185. Lord Grey, London, to Lord John Russell, 6 March 1848, reproduced in Van Alstyne, 'Central American Policy of Lord Palmerston', p. 357.

I sent for the Regalia of the Kingdom from Wank's River, where it had been deposited by the King. I received a sort of crown formed of silver gilt and studded with crystal ornaments.... I have sent it to Jamaica to be cleaned and repaired, but as it is, in my humble opinion, unworthy of its destiny, I have most respectfully to suggest to your Lordship's consideration the propriety of the Government presenting the young King with a new crown and adding thereto a sceptre and sword.[186]

Following Palmerston's insistence upon the monarchical form, which now came to the centre of the British defence of its presence in eastern Nicaragua, Walker had a council of state appointed by the young king, who at the court-house on Bidwell Street in Bluefields dutifully mimicked British pageantry:

Whereas it being necessary for the welfare of our kingdom that a Supreme Local Government be established therein, and to that end, that a Council of State be appointed. Now Know ye, That we reposing especial Trust and Confidence in the friendly feeling towards our kingdom of Alexander Macdonald, Colonel British Royal Horse Artillery, Companion of the most Honourable Military Order of the Bath, Knight of St. Anne of Russia etc., have nominated, constituted and appointed, and do by these Present nominate, constitute and appoint the said Alexander Macdonald to be an honourable Member of our Council of State during our life.[187]

It had been an essential prerequisite for such political theatre that Walker put a stop to the confusion and swindling that ensued from the land grants made by the late king. Many of these partially overlapped or conflicted with each other, but three of them were large enough to cover the entire Shore and a good part of inland Nicaragua in which there had never been a Mosquito presence. One of the grants, made in 1841 for payment of $150 by Captain Willock of Belize and Mr Alexander of Liverpool, was for 2 million acres along the coast from Cape Gracias a Díos. The extent of the profits expected of this speculation may be gauged from the fact that Prince Charles of Prussia was negotiating a loan of £32,000 in London to finance his purchase of this land; it took some serious pressure from the Foreign Office to make him drop the plan.

However, it was the largest of the concessions – made to Peter and Samuel Shepherd of San Juan del Norte in 1839 – that proved to be the most problematic, not least because it exchanged the entire coast south of the Rio Grande (itself sixty miles north of Bluefields) through San Juan to the Chiriqui lagoon, which was claimed by Costa Rica as well as Nicaragua and which the brothers and their associate J.T. Haly planned to offer to the British as a naval base for the sum of £4,000. Over previous years Peter Shepherd had ensured that the king had been taken to and landed in the more remote zones so that they could be publicly claimed for Mosquitia and thus ceded in style. The entire extent was made over in exchange for the cancellation of

186. Walker, Bluefields, to Aberdeen, 9 Jan. 1845, quoted in Craig L. Dozier, *Nicaragua's Mosquito Shore: The Years of British and American Presence*, Birmingham, Ala., 1985, p. 54.

187. Royal Proclamation, 10 Sept. 1846, quoted in Eleonore von Oertzen (ed.), *The Nicaraguan Mosquitia in Historical Documents, 1844–1927*, Berlin 1990, p. 107.

the debts run up by the king with the merchant house which the Shepherds had run in San Juan since 1811 and which was now itself badly in debt to Kingston and Liverpool after the collapse of the tortoise-shell, mahogany and sarsaparilla markets in the 1830s. The monarch had been drunk when he signed the deal, and Colonel Macdonald had expended much effort in attempting to have it revoked, but under the treaty of 1783 he lacked any powers to do this, and it was only when Patrick Walker − previously Macdonald's secretary and so fully informed about the case − assumed the regency that a formal cancellation could be effected.

The British authorities were, however, unable to prevent the elderly Captain Samuel Shepherd from selling his grant to some 22 million acres outside their own dominions. They could do nothing at all in the USA, where the title was brought up a few years later by one Henry Kinney, a major in the Texas volunteers in the Mexican War and a founder of the town of Corpus Christi. Kinney was an energetic speculator who floated an issue of some 225,000 shares at $25 each to fund a colonisation scheme, tempting Daniel Webster's son Fletcher to get involved. Although no William Walker, Kinney caused almost as much trouble in the mid 1850s through his acquisition of the Shepherd claim since it was opposed by all Nicaraguan factions − none of which recognised the rights of the Mosquito chiefs to make grants of land − as well as by Cornelius Vanderbilt, whose Accessory Transit Company was reliant upon a concession from the government of Nicaragua to run its passenger steamers up from San Juan del Norte and across Lake Nicaragua. Thus, ten years after Patrick Walker's 1844 cancellation of the Shepherd claim it would be at the heart of the international conflict over the Mosquito coast, complicating relations not just between London and Washington but also among the three main North American enterprises in Nicaragua: those of William Walker, who was heavily armed; Kinney himself, who was lightly armed; and Vanderbilt, who relied upon the protection of the US navy.[188]

The character of the conflict over Mosquitia was also affected by the fact that neither Nicaragua nor Honduras had lodged formal claims to the Caribbean coast between San Juan del Norte and Cape Honduras until 1845 − a year after the protectorate had been formally announced by London and six years after the dissolution of the Central American Confederation to which they had belonged. The argument that these states lacked the juridical status to stake claims on the territory was used strenuously by Frederick Chatfield (who was promoted to chargé d'affaires in 1849) but used much more sparingly and tentatively by London, which enjoyed good relations with Guatemala and Costa Rica and was itself divided over the degree to which the protectorate should be allowed to determine policy towards Central America, let alone the USA. It is, then, important not to confuse Chatfield's position with that of the Foreign Office, just as Hise and his successor Ephraim George Squier

188. Van Alstyne, 'Central American Policy of Lord Palmerston', pp. 342–3; Squier, *Nicaragua*, I, p. 86; W.O. Scroggs, *Filibusters and Financiers: The Story of William Walker and his Associates* (1916), New York 1969, pp. 96–101.

often differed in detail and sometimes general approach from the Department of State.[189] On both sides the local representatives proved to be much more pugnacious than their ministries at home, and, of course, this mattered a great deal since news (and instructions) travelled slowly, isolation bred over-confidence and an instinct for action, and events on the ground drove policy as much as vice versa. Moreover, these diplomatic agents often found themselves chasing developments set in train by allies who eagerly interpreted policy according to their own lights.

Once Patrick Walker had cancelled the old king's land grants and settled the new monarch in with his council, he addressed the question of the Nicaraguan presence in San Juan del Norte, the control of which was vital to access to the San Juan river and the trans-isthmian route through San Carlos, across Lake Nicaragua, and finally over a few miles to the Pacific port of San Juan del Sur. It is, perhaps, not an entire coincidence that Walker began to increase the pressure on the small port's commander, Antonio Salas, in September 1847, when US forces were closing on the capital of Mexico. At the start of the month Walker made a diplomatic approach to Salas that was laced with polite and easy threat:

> I have to notify you that I have received from M. de Barruel, senior, information that his son (who is likewise his associate in business) has been imprisoned by your orders, for refusing to accept as legal tender, certain moneys of a spurious nature. M. de Barruel, at a distance from his Consul, has requested my interposition, as the functionary of a friendly nation, and I have now to demand from you the instant release of M. de Barruel, junior. Should this demand not be immediately complied with, you must hold yourselves responsible for the consequences.
>
> This dispatch will be presented to you by Commander Wilson of the Mosquito navy, who proceeds to San Juan in the Mosquito cutter-of-war *Sun* to deliver it into your hands. Some doubt, it appears, existed in your mind as to the recognition of the Mosquito flag; I have consequently to advise you that the Mosquito flag and nation are under the particular protection of the British Crown.
>
> Having now, Sir, discharged a necessary duty, I trust that you will not receive otherwise than friendly the remarks I now offer you. By resorting to extreme measures with M. de Barruel you have drawn down on your Government the resentment of one of the most powerful nations in the world: a nation most sensitively alive to the slightest dishonour passed on her subjects, and for which, should injustice be apparent, she will exact ample indemnity. The act has also been perpetuated within the dominions of the King of Mosquito.

Given the fact that Salas's reply five days later was written after the visit of a warship that he knew had replaced the white ensign with the Mosquito flag as a piece of pure pantomime, it is more impressive still:

> The commander of the cutter *Sun* has placed in my hands the letter which you were pleased to address to me in the first current, relative to an intervention on account of the youth Barruel, for faults that he has committed and to which there is no necessity to refer further

189. The (unsubstantiated) notion that Chatfield enjoyed a particularly close relationship with Palmerston underlies the argument that he was critically influential both in the breakdown of the Central American Confederation and in the developments of the 1840s: Mario Rodríguez, *A Palmerstonian Diplomat in Central American: Frederick Chatfield, Esq.*, Tucson, Ariz., 1964.

[other than to say that] it was done according to the rules of the State to which all the inhabitants under my authority are subject....

The same reclamation on your part in favour of a French Viscount, who ought to know the Law of Nations and whose long residence in the State should have acquainted him with our legislation, is surprising, as you cannot be ignorant [of the fact] that in case I have exceeded my functions, there is only one authority in the State with the power to judge me, and to which I would be called upon speedily to reply in any case. I appreciate the friendly notice which you have given me as to the particular protection which the British Crown is disposed to afford the flag of the Mosquito nation, but without entering into the question of its legitimacy, or of its territorial limits, which is the province of Governments, I can only obey the orders that I receive from my superiors.[190]

A month later, George Hodgson, who with his brother Alex upheld a century-old family influence over the Shore by sitting on the Mosquito Council of State, sent an ultimatum inland:

The King in Council hopes that his Excellency the President and the Government over which he presides, in order to insure those friendly relations between Mosquito and Nicaragua which are so important to their mutual benefit, will give orders to remove the Nicaraguan establishment from its present position at the mouth of the River San Juan [by 1 January 1848].... After that date, notice is hereby, openly and expressly given that strong measures will be employed.

Again, the Nicaraguan response was officially resolute, this time taking the form of a proclamation issued in León:

... it is pretended to consummate the scandalous spoliation of a part of the territory of Nicaragua. A faction of that State, the nomadic tribe of Mosquitos, at whose head is placed an imbecile child with the title of king, surrounded by a council composed of native ignorants and astute agents who direct everything, has intimated to this Supreme Government the evacuation of the port of San Juan del Norte by first of January next, threatening that unless by that date the establishment there shall have quitted the place, strong measures will be employed.... On effecting this act, the whole world will see how, in the obscurest and most violent manner, it is designed to convert our inexperience and misfortune to the benefit of the strongest.

No power has acknowledged for a *Nation* the tribe in question ... so far is the tribe from deserving the consideration of a kingdom, and still less the alliance and protection of a nation of the first class as is Great Britain.... Thus it is that a civil war is stirred up by the savage against the civilized part of Central America, to tear away by force from Nicaragua the only and the best port in the north, possessed since time immemorial without dispute, acknowledged as its property by all the nations of the globe, and even by Great Britain.[191]

Here the language of progress and protestation against illegal acts is underpinned by resignation in the face of the undoubted ability of the steamer HMS *Vixen* (Ryder) to take the port. Consul Walker and Captain Ryder duly rebuffed all efforts at

---

190. Walker, Bluefields, to the Commander of San Juan, 1 Sept. 1847; Salas, San Juan del Norte, to Walker, 6 Sept. 1847, in *BFSP, 1859–50*, XXXVIII, pp. 695–7.

191. Hodgson, Bluefields, to Salinas, 25 Oct. 1847; Guerrero, León, 12 Nov. 1847, in ibid., pp. 722, 734–5.

negotiation over San Juan and, as Walker reported to Palmerston a fortnight later, put into effect on 31 December 1847 a plan devised in Jamaica:

> An officer of the militia … immediately came off with the information that General Muñoz and his troops had evacuated the town the night before, retiring to Serapaqui, which he has fortified and leaving only a very small detachment behind. Acording to the arrangement previously made, I landed with Captain Ryder in his gig, the paddle-box boats of the *Vixen* following with marines, sailors and the militia. Having formed in column, they marched up to the flag-post and, facing round, deployed into line with great precision and correctness. The Nicaraguan flag was immediately hauled down. The Mosquitian, being then run up on shore, was at the same time hoisted on board the *Vixen*, and a royal salute was fired while the King proceeded from the cutter on shore.

When the few officials left behind by Muñoz refused to recognise as 'an independent prince' the supposed author of this gunboat diplomacy by proxy, Walker displayed the magnanimity of the victorious:

> I informed them that they removed all basis for a negotiation, and that we must proceed to put into execution our orders, and remove them from the Customs House for the purpose of installing a Mosquito administration therein. I stated to them, however, that we did not wish to put them to inconvenience, and would allow them until Monday to clear out of the Customs House or that receipts would be given for whatever goods they chose to leave behind. Everything was managed with the utmost courtesy on both sides.… After this proceeding the Nicaraguan officers, with ourselves, sat down to an entertainment which I had provided for the occasion.[192]

Walker then installed 'Major' George Hodgson as the governor of the renamed 'Greytown' (after Sir Charles Grey, governor of Jamaica) and another of the council, John Dixon, as its mayor, returning on 4 January to Bluefields on the *Vixen* in the company of the king. This move – made presumably on the understanding that the Nicaraguan refusal to defend the port betokened complete acquiescence in occupation – was badly mistaken. Colonel Salas, discovering that Walker had left only the Mosquito 'militia' in charge of the town, retook it easily on the 9th with only fifty men. In addition to the considerable propaganda value of restoring San Juan to Nicaraguan control, Salas provided the Nicaraguan government with a prized prisoner – a Hodgson. In this case it was George, whose leadership of the port had lasted all of five days and who, under public interrogation, told a story rich even by the formidable standards of the dealers of the Mosquito Shore:

> I had Mr George Hodgson brought before me, who, through the interpreters, Señores Don José Dolores Bermúdez and Pedro Yginio Silva, sworn to perform their duties faithfully, was questioned as to his name, age, profession, birthplace, residence, business or employment, and religion, and said: that his name is George Hodgson, his age 54 years, planter, Corn Island; his residence Bluefields; his business or employment, Senior Counsellor of the King and Adjutant Major General of the Militia. Asked when he arrived in this city, who conducted him, and from where, he said: that he arrived on the night of the 20th of this month; that

---

192. Walker, Bluefields, to Palmerston, 15 Jan. 1848, in ibid., pp. 737–8.

he was conducted by Adjutant Domingo Murillo, who is present. Asked his object in coming to San Juan, and by whose order, he said: that the object was to take possession of the Port of San Juan by order of Mr Patrick Walker, Regent of the Mosquito King and Consul General of Her Majesty's Government on the Mosquito Coast, which gentleman brought the declarer, Mr J.W. Little and another officer named John Dixon, who escaped, telling them: that they were going to take possession of San Juan without any opposition; and that he appointed the declarer Governor of the said Port for a period of one month; that he obliged him much to his distaste in the Custom House of the Port of San Juan; that the order to remain was oral, not written, for which reason he does not exhibit it. Asked whether it was he who authored the note which the pretended King of the Mosquitos handed to the Government of the State intimating the evacuation of the Port of San Juan by the first of January, he said: that in truth he cannot remember to have signed it, but if his full name appears it is possible that he signed it since he was forced to affix his signature many times, and he will have no difficulty in recognising it if presented to him. Asked what force they brought in for the occupation of the Port of San Juan and in what ships; who commanded the force, and from whence they proceeded, he said: that the whole force consisted of probably 150 men, 70 of them from Bluefields, who were brought by deceit, Mr Walker telling them that they were coming only to accompany the King to the Port of San Juan; that one of the ships was called *Cutter* and the other *Vixen*, a warship of Her Majesty's Government, being the first of the Mosquito navy; that Mr Walker commanded the force; Mr Rydder [*sic*] is Captain of the War Ship and Mr Harry of the other ship ... asked who composed the Council of the titular Mosquito King, and of what nationality they are, he said: that it is composed of himself, Mr Alexander Hodgson of Bluefields, John Dixon of Bluefields, Mr Halstead of Jamaica, Mr James Green of England, and Mr William Scott, secretary, a Scotchman.[193]

Having been badly outmanoeuvred by Salas's counterattack, Walker and Ryder rushed back to a once-again evacuated Greytown, but there they paused to take stock and confer with Kingston, the naval officer, who now naturally bore the leading responsibility, dispatching a predictable ultimatum to Muñoz:

I take this opportunity of informing you that I shall hasten to report to the Militia and Naval authorities at Jamaica this set of willful aggressing on the part of the Nicaraguan Government and which I have little doubt will be considered by them as a declaration of war against the Queen of England and the King of Mosquito. I am still in hopes that Colonel Salas has acted without orders from you or his government. Should this be the case I recommend you as the only means of averting the vengeance of their Britannic and Mosquito Majesties to visit this port *without a day's delay – to rehoist the flag of His Mosquitan Majesty and to restore in their positions the Captain of the Port, Captain Little, and the Governor, Major Hodgson.*[194]

---

193. Enclosure to Salinas, León, to Savage, 24 Jan. 1848, in Manning, *Diplomatic Correspondence*, III, p. 269. A description of George's brother Alex by Walker's successor as consul, W.D. Christie, raises the possibility that the Hodgson line on signatures was not quite so disingenuous as it seems to the modern eye:

Mr Alexander Hodgson [is] one of a large family of natural children of Colonel Hodgson, the former superintendent [Robert the Younger], by an African woman – his appearance is quite that of an African. He can sign his name but can write nothing else, and, when called on to append his signature to a document in the Council, it takes him five minutes to do so.

Christie, Bluefields, to Palmerston, 5 Sept. 1848, quoted in Dozier, *Nicaragua's Mosquito Shore*, p. 60.
194. Ryder, Greytown, to Muñoz, 16 Jan. 1848, quoted in Dozier, *Nicaragua's Mosquito Shore*, pp. 56–7.

With the whole project of the Mosquito protectorate being unravelled before them in what was effectively a guerrilla raid, the British authorities in Kingston, Sir Charles Grey and Vice-Admiral Sir Francis Austen (brother of the more famous Jane), sent an extra warship, HMS *Alarm* under Captain Granville Loch, but allowed Walker to hold notional command of a punitive expedition up the San Juan river. This force of 260 men in twelve flat-bottomed boats captured the fort which guards the entrance to Lake Nicaragua at San Carlos with only three men killed. However, it took another three weeks for Loch to agree a truce with the Nicaraguan authorities, who squabbled over the form of words to explain their 'outrage' even after they had released Hodgson and Little in return for the prisoners taken by the British marines. Eventually, Foreign Minister Sebastián Salinas agreed that San Juan del Norte (Grey-town) would not be disturbed and that Nicaragua would not seek to maintain a customs house at that port, but he wrote directly to Palmerston insisting that the truce in no way prejudiced his country's sovereignty over San Juan even as he signed up to the most craven form of words drafted by Captain Loch:

> Explanation. The Nicaraguan Government were ignorant that the Mosquito flag was so connected with that of England as that an outrage to it should involve an insult to that of Great Britain. They are most anxious to explain that so far from desiring to excite the anger of that Power, it is on the contrary their earnest will to cultivate the most intimate relations with it.

This brought an end to military efforts by the Nicaraguans to uphold their claim on San Juan, but it certainly did not consolidate the protectorate because on 11 February – the day before the attack on San Carlos – Patrick Walker, in attempting to save a man who had fallen overboard into the river, was himself dragged under and drowned. As Loch reported to Admiral Austen, 'the King of Mosquito is left without a protector or adviser, and the Port of San Juan without either a British or a Mosquitan inhabitant'.[195] In an emergency measure Major J.P. Sparks of the marines was sent to take charge of San Juan, where he found 'not a single privy' and less than sixty inhabitants, none of them British. When Walker's replacement as consul and regent, W.D. Christie, arrived at Bluefields in June he discovered a mere six shillings in the Mosquito treasury and an active anti-British lobby forming around Princess Agnes, who, amidst the natural confusion over royal succession in a polygamous society, threatened to undermine the entire façade of the protectorate. As a result, the appalled Christie was happy to fall behind Frederick Chatfield's proposal to drop the whole pretence of a separate monarchy and openly annex the Mosquito Shore as a colony. However, not even Palmerston was prepared to take such a step, which was resolutely opposed by the Colonial Office and scarcely viable when, two years after the taking of Greytown, there were still only a dozen Britons living on the Shore.[196]

---

195. Loch, Greytown, to Austen, 15 Mar. 1848, in *BFSP, 1849–50*, XXXVIII, pp. 753–7.
196. Robert A. Naylor, *Penny ante Imperialism: The Mosquito Shore and the Bay of Honduras, 1600–1914*, Rutherford, N.J., 1989, pp. 170–78.

Testing the Balance of Power

Such was the precarious position of British-backed Mosquitia in the wake of the Mexican War and the discovery of gold in California, the latter qualitatively transforming US interest in the isthmus and particularly in Nicaragua because of its manageable existing route and obvious potential for a canal. Under the Polk administration there was a general disposition to take seriously the conviction of Elijah Hise, the US agent in Guatemala, that 'Great Britain designs to become the owner and occupant by force or Strategem of the Ports of the Atlantic and Pacific coasts of Nicaragua'.[197] And yet, as shown by Hise's correspondence with the Guatemalan foreign minister, he was not quite the right man to be conducting the US diplomatic response to the British:

> Your acceptable Note of the 11th Inst. is received. I regret that Your Excellency is not now prepared or at Leisure to consider and determine upon the proposition, contained in my note of the 3rd inst. The proposition is Simple, not complicated, and does not require a protracted Correspondence, or numerous conferences. The question is simply will Your Government agree or not agree to adopt the Treaty referred to in my last note? The treaty is just, equal and reciprocal in its provisions. It can be examined in an hour, and the design of Your Excellency in relation thereto [should] be without delay known to me. Pardon me For being apparently importunate on this subject, My Excuse is that my residence in this city will be short.[198]

Hise was in a hurry not just out of natural exasperation or because the British navy was 'constantly hovering on the coasts' but also because in the previous year's election Lewis Cass, the Democrat candidate, had been beaten by Zachary Taylor, and Hise – to his evident relief – was to be replaced in his post. But he failed to take an acceptable treaty back to Washington, as did his successor, the 28-year-old Ephraim George Squier, who was markedly more literate than Hise, but if anything even more suspicious of the British. Unlike Hise, Squier spent most of his time in Nicaragua, first arriving at San Juan del Norte in June 1849, when he informed the new secretary of state, John Clayton, in no uncertain terms about the state of the Mosquito coast under Consul Christie:

> No written laws or regulations have been promulgated, and this gentleman is *defacto* a Dictator.... He has made himself extremely obnoxious to the inhabitants without exception, and his arbitrary conduct is the subject of complaint on every hand.... From all I can learn, the hostility of the Nicaraguans towards the English knows no bounds.

---

197. Hise, Guatemala, to Buchanan, 20 Dec. 1848, in Manning (ed.), *Diplomatic Correspondence*, III, p. 294.
198. Hise, Guatemala, to Rodríguez, 14 Feb. 1849, in ibid., pp. 308–9.

However, Christie was just leaving the Shore, and when, two months later, Squier reached León, he encountered in Frederick Chatfield, a far more repugnant representative of Albion's arrogance:

> My arrival here has been the signal for renewed insolence towards this State, the Government of which is in the weekly receipt of communications from the above-named official, making all kinds of demands, and loaded with threats in case they are not complied with. The tone of the communications is disgraceful in the extreme, and discreditable to the country of which Mr Chatfield is representative.[199]

In Nicaragua Squier encountered an extra problem in that Hise had, entirely on his own initiative, signed a treaty with that country pledging the USA to guarantee the integrity of its existing boundaries — a plainly dangerous commitment that the Taylor administration disowned immediately but with which Squier himself was in full agreement. As a result, he tried simultaneously to alleviate Clayton's concern about his motives, emphasise the threat posed by the British, and urge greater commitment to the region on Washington's part. On 12 September 1849, having settled in at León, Squier wrote a private letter to the secretary of state that reflected the excitement caused by the signing on 26 August of the contract between the Nicaraguan government and Cornelius Vanderbilt for the construction of a trans-isthmian canal:

> You will receive herewith, by special bearer of Despatches, a mass of documents, which Heaven assist you in wading through. I have had *no time*, as an eminent somebody once said, to make them *shorter*. But I beg, in the first place, that you will not, in consequence of the prominence I have given to British intrigues and operations in these quarters, think me afflicted with *Anglo-Mania*. Far from it. Still, I must repeat that no person, not on the spot, can credit the extent and intricacy of these intrigues. What under Heaven my predecessors have been about, passes my comprehension.... Chatfield, the British Consul General, who has practically the whole weight of British influence in his hands, is a man of small calibre, easily excited, and more by little than great things. There is no difficulty in managing him. It is only necessary to keep him in a rage about idle expressions from Tom, Dick and Harry to divert his attention from what is going on in earnest. There are others, however, who are quicker-witted, and more to be guarded against. Now, if it is desired, I feel confident that I can destroy British influence in these States, and even procure their after expulsion from this part of the continent. But I cannot do it single-handed; these people are greatly taken by appearances, and a little display of power now and then will convey immense weight and exercise an important influence in our favor. Let some portion of the Pacific Squadron 'be about', as they say of the Indians upon the western frontier, looking in occasionally here and there. It will make a material difference in the tone of the English, and make them hesitate how they resort to unauthorized measures. I feel quite sure that the attempt to confederate San Salvador, Honduras and Nicaragua will be successful. This will strengthen the hands of Carrera's enemies in Guatemala, and he will go down with the English party. Guatemala will then come into the arrangement, and Costa Rica will not be able to hold out for any considerable time. The nucleus will be Nicaragua, but Salvador will furnish the *brains* and the *soul*. The people of that state will stick to Union to the last. No British agent dares venture its borders.... I shall arrange things if possible so that I can interfere if necessary, but

199. Squier, San Juan del Norte, to Clayton, 10 June 1849; Squier, León, to Clayton, 20 Aug. 1849, in ibid., pp. 331, 349.

shall only act *when* necessary. I know this step may seem somewhat extraordinary; but the Gulf of Fonseca *must* be *free* or the Canal will be worthless.[200]

This last remark corresponded to confidential information that Squier had received indicating that Chatfield planned to seize Tiger Island (Tigre), a Honduran possession in the Gulf of Fonseca, under the pretext of securing payment of compensation for some mahogany taken from Belizean traders but with the real purpose of establishing a British military presence on the Pacific as well as Atlantic coast of the probable canal route. The cautious Clayton would probably have dismissed such a notion as a wild fancy (and somewhat at odds with Squier's own disparagement of Chatfield's worth) had this letter not been followed by a dispatch reporting precisely such action, undertaken on 16 October by the steamer HMS *Gorgon*. Moreover, Squier's stock in Washington could not have been damaged by the fact that he was able to enclose with his own report the original account of the occupation by the Honduran commander, Vicente Lechuga:

> At a quarter before two o'clock this day, I observed at the entrance of this harbour five long-boats filled with armed people, each boat carrying a cannon with corresponding ammunition. The people in the boats were dressed in uniform and armed; their number, as far as we could make out, about eighty, together with a boat in which were two officers and a civilian. Observing this, I immediately mustered my little picket of soldiers, hoisted the flag of Honduras and that of the Republic, and ordered my men to present arms, but not to attempt resistance as it was obviously hopeless against the superior force that was approaching. Under these circumstances, I allowed the officers to land, when I observed that the flag in their boat was English, and seeing the colours of a civilized nation, I presented myself to the officers, demanding the *cause* of this display of force and this hostile attitude.... An interpreter then requested me, by order of the Commander of the invading forces, to lower the colours of the republic so that the English flag might be raised; to which I answered that I would in no wise be party to any such act, and nothing but my weakness prevented me from driving him away by force of arms. The Commander then ordered his troops to advance, and directed an officer to lower our flag and hoist the English colours. This was done, with a British national salute, and a discharge of musketry, and with many cheers for Queen Victoria.[201]

Fired up by his mini-invasion – which was unauthorised by the Foreign Office and so soon disowned and reversed – Chatfield took it upon himself to warn Squier off his own plan to provide US guarantees for any canal that opened into the Gulf of Fonseca by sponsoring the pact betwen El Salvador, Honduras and Nicaragua and by assuming responsibility for the sovereignty of Tiger Island through a bilateral treaty with Honduras. The patronising approach of the British diplomat was, though, certain to provoke the bullish young New Yorker further still:

---

200. Squier, León, to Clayton, 12 Sept. 1849, reprinted in 'Letters of E. George Squier to John M. Clayton, 1849–50', *HAHR*, I:1, 1918, pp. 427–8. The contract gave Vanderbilt's company exclusive rights to build a canal at its own expense. The canal was to be open to vessels of all nations. The company was to make an initial payment of $10,000 and $10,000 every year until completion.

201. Enclosure in Squier, León, to Clayton, 25 Oct. 1849, in Manning (ed.), *Diplomatic Correspondence*, III, p. 418.

Owing to your recent arrival in this country you may not have had enough time to acquire a just knowledge of its political position in regard to other States, so as to be able to distinguish between fact and the misstatement of impassioned and prejudiced political partisans. These states cherish the erroneous belief that their weakness exempts them from the necessity of acting with decorum and regularity in their foreign relations, and they therefore constantly clamour against the superiority of any nation which requires them to perform the duties which they undertook to discharge on assuming the character of constituted political Bodies. This mistaken view of their true position prevents them from appreciating the forebearance of Her Majesty's Government.[202]

By now it was plain in both London and Washington that matters were getting out of hand locally and that Central America was rapidly acquiring great strategic importance, necessitating an agreement of corresponding breadth. At the end of September – well before Chatfield's seizure of Tiger Island – Clayton raised the whole issue with John Crampton, the British ambassador to Washington, who reported to Palmerston:

The junction of the two oceans by a canal, Mr Clayton observed, was an object so important to the whole of the commercial world that it was matter for surprise that an attempt had not long since been made to effect it. The increase of population on the western coast of this continent had, however, rendered it certain that such an attempt would ere long be made. The Government of the United States are strongly in favour of such an undertaking; but they are as earnestly opposed to its execution being made an object of jealousy by an attempt on the part of any one nation to monopolise to itself the credit due to such an enterprise or the advantage to be derived from it when effected. It should, in their view, be rather made a bond for peace and good understanding by being brought about by a combined effort and for the general benefit of mankind.

Clayton then suggested that the USA and UK sign a joint treaty with Nicaragua, although he recognised that the Mosquito question was a major impediment to the whole endeavour: 'You affirm the Mosquito title; we deny it. There we are at issue; and if that controversy be not arranged amicably, the canal will probably never be made by either of us.'[203] In the same vein, when a fortnight later Clayton heard that Squier had indeed signed the 'Chinandega Pact' with three of the five Central American states, he called in Crampton immediately to tell him that he disowned these actions. The indefatigible Squier forged on regardless, ostentatiously appropriating Tiger Island for Honduras (and the USA) upon its evacuation by the British, again earning an admonition from Clayton, who had been trying to rein him in for months:

In all your correspondence with the Central American states, you are desired to avoid the slightest exhibition of discourtesy or disrespect. It will, I am sure, be most agreeable to your own feelings as well as most conducive to the interests which it is your duty to promote, to

---

202. Chatfield, HMS *Gorgon*, to Squier, 25 Oct. 1849, in ibid., p. 427. On 26 December the British navy evacuated Tiger Island, hoisting the Honduran flag, which was given a 21-gun salute on the orders of Sir Phipps Hornby – a gesture which may have mollified Colonel Lechuga a little and certainly marked a turning point in Anglo-Honduran relations, which now improved in direct proportion to the activity of North Americans in Nicaragua.

203. Crampton, Washington, to Palmerston, 1 Oct. 1849, in *BFSP, 1850–51*, XL, London 1863, p. 956.

avoid all angry discussion or unpleasant controversy.... Negotiations are in progress with Great Britain which it is trusted will terminate in an amicable adjustment of all controversies between her and us in regard to the Central American states through which it is proposed to build a canal. If we should succeed according to our wishes and expectations, there will be no British colonization within the limits of either Nicaragua or Costa Rica.... In the meantime, you will carefully avoid all discussions or exhibitions which can possibly tend, by irritating British agents in Central America, to embarrass our negotiations with the British ministry. We shall never admit the Mosquito claim to sovereignty over any part of Nicaragua.[204]

Here Clayton may well have been asking the impossible, not just of Squier but of most North Americans caught up in the post-war, Gold Rush wave of Manifest Destiny. However, the higher needs of US diplomacy patently could not be fulfilled simply by muscular reiterations of the Monroe Doctrine, even when figures such as Louis Napoleon Bonaparte had become inveigled in plans for a French protectorate in Nicaragua, enthusiastically promoting the country as the vital global entrepôt of the future:

As Constantinople is the centre of the ancient world, so is the town of León, or rather Masaya, the centre of the new; and if the tongue of land which separates its two lakes from the Pacific Ocean were cut through, she would command, by her central position, the entire coast of North and South America. Like Constantinople, Masaya is situated between two extensive natural harbours, capable of giving shelter to the largest fleet, safe from attack. The state of Nicaragua can become, better than Constantinople, the necessary route for the great commerce of the world.[205]

Although Bonaparte's efforts to obtain a canal contract in Nicaragua in 1846 had come to nought – and he was not in power when Clayton was looking for a deal with the British – the Revolution of 1848 made the position of France, an important power in the Caribbean, most unpredictable.[206] In the event, Louis Napoleon set his political sights on Mexico, where the imperial project would collapse in disaster. Nevertheless, he retained an interest in both Costa Rica and Nicaragua, where the French presence was sustained in the 1850s by the journalist Félix Belly, almost as exotic as his collaborators Prince Polignac and the O'Gorman Mahon.

Clayton was unchallenged in Washington as to his identification of London as the power with which a deal needed to be done over Central America, but the terms of that deal proved highly controversial. This was not simply because soon after it had

---

204. Clayton, Washington, to Squier, 20 Nov. 1849, in Manning (ed.), *Diplomatic Correspondence*, III, pp. 55–6.

205. *Canal of Nicaragua: Or a Project to Connect the Atlantic and Pacific Coasts by Means of a Canal*, London 1846, p. 6.

206. Bonaparte had been in contact with the Central Americans since 1842 even though he was imprisoned in the fortress of Ham following his coup attempt in Boulogne. In 1844 he held talks with the Nicaraguan envoy Francisco Castellón, who had failed to get Guizot's help in persuading the British to lift the blockade of San Juan del Norte. E.W. Richards, 'Louis Napoleon and Central America', *The Journal of Modern History*, XXXIV, 1962. By 1850 Castellón, a leading Liberal, was convinced that Nicaragua would lose out to one North American group or another, but it was he who hired Byron Cole to contract mercenaries, and by the time he died in September 1855 Walker's capacity for destruction was already clear.

been signed Zachary Taylor died and Clayton was replaced as secretary of state by Daniel Webster, nor because the Democrats won the elections of 1852, under Franklin Pierce's platform for a more aggressive foreign policy (with Polk's secretary of war, W.L. Marcy, serving as secretary of state), and those of 1856, under Buchanan (Polk's secretary of state and Pierce's ambassador to London). Nor, indeed, did it stem from the fact that Palmerston ceased to be foreign secretary at the end of 1851, the Tories and Peelites holding power in Britain through the years of the Crimean War until the great imperialist himself took office as prime minister in February 1855 at the age of seventy-one.

At the heart of the problem in 'updating' the Monroe Doctrine for Central America at mid century was the difficulty in distinguishing, in the search for detente, between formal and informal empires and of adjusting the US anti-colonial ethos when Great Britain held almost all of its American power in colonial form. If a balancing act was genuinely sought by both governments, it proved impossible to secure an agreement with sustained bipartisan support in Washington. This, in turn, made it more difficult for London to withdraw from the Mosquito Shore – a withdrawal that became the real sticking point once it was clear, by late 1850, that no canal would be built quickly. Although both major parties in London agreed that the Shore's status as a protectorate was something of an embarrassment and certainly negotiable, those negotiations were unlikely to prosper whilst US politicians inveighed against the monarchical form of the protectorate and upped the anti-colonialist ante by challenging British possession of Belize. As a result, London clung on to its pseudo-possession in Nicaragua for a further decade, but solely by dint of naval power, and at the price of growing in-stability within the country as a whole as various governments sought to barter up the terms of an international stalemate at a time when tens of thousands of North Americans poured through the country. 'William Walker' is, then, the name attached to an accident that was waiting to happen, probably from 1849 onwards and certainly after 19 April 1850, when John Clayton signed what appeared to be a comprehensive treaty over Central America with Sir Henry Bulwer, formerly British ambassador to Madrid and Washington, whom Palmerston sent to the USA as a special plenipotentiary.

The Clayton–Bulwer treaty has only eight articles, covering three pages. It is the first article that was most important and almost immediately subjected to sharply different interpretations, raising the charge that it was – just like the compromise over slavery being assembled in Washington at the same time – a deliberate fudge:

> The Governments of Great Britain and the United States hereby declare that neither the one nor the other will ever obtain or maintain for itself any exclusive control of the said Ship-Canal, agreeing that neither will ever erect or maintain any fortifications commanding the same, or in the vicinity thereof, or occupy or colonize either Nicaragua, Costa Rica, the Mosquito Coast or any part of Central America; nor will Great Britain or the United States assume or exercise any dominion over the same, or take advantage of any intimacy, or use any advantage, connection or influence that either may possess with any State or people through or by whose territory the said canal may pass, for the purpose of acquiring or holding, directly or indirectly, for the subjects or citizens of the one, any rights or advantages

in regard of the commerce or navigation through the said canal, which shall not be offered on the same terms to the subjects or citizens of the other.[207]

Despite all the legalistic reiterations of this article, it was quite possible to read it as applying either exclusively to future colonisation or equally to present and future colonies, possessions and alliances.[208] Certainly, Palmerston did not intend Bulwer simply to stitch up a form of words that codified the status quo, and although Bulwer did negotiate the treaty very much on his own, by the end of the year Palmerston was persuaded that Nicaragua might be allowed both terminals of any canal. In agreeing to this he effectively withdrew his earlier plan to cede Greytown/San Juan del Norte to Costa Rica and instead declared it a free port. Even before the treaty Palmerston had believed that if an agreement over limits could be reached between Nicaragua and Mosquito the British would be able to withdraw their protection of the Shore, which he, like most other leading British politicians, now felt to be an onerous commitment.[209] Consul Christie had gone on leave in June 1849, did not return to Bluefields and was never replaced; the post was abolished altogether in September 1851.

However, the foreign secretary was initially of the firm view that the Clayton–Bulwer treaty simply did not apply to the Mosquito Shore, Belize or the Bay Islands (which he treated as its natural dependencies) – a position that Clayton only officially confirmed for the case of Belize (British Honduras) following the debate in the US Senate, which ratified the treaty by forty-two votes to twelve, apparently without great discussion of Belize.[210] Equally, from London's viewpoint the treaty could be

---

207. *BFSP, 1850–51*, XL, p. 1008.
208. For example, it was the opinion in April 1853 of Sir John Harding, queen's advocate, that

> The First Article expressly recognizes the fact that Great Britain has, and may have, alliances with, and affords and may afford, protection to States and Peoples in Central America.... Great Britain ... may in my opinion protect any State or people (including Indian tribes) in Central America, even by force of arms if needful without violating the Treaty.

Quoted in Van Alstyne, 'The Clayton–Bulwer Treaty', p. 158.
209. According to R.A.Humphreys,

> No one, plainly, had much regard for the Mosquito protectorate. Bulwer thought it a 'rotten affair'; Addington, the permanent under-secretary at the Foreign Office, 'a millstone around our neck'; Palmerston, of 'no earthly advantage' to Britain. In Russell's view the Indians were 'wretched savages', in Aberdeen's their territory had been extended 'beyond all just bounds'. But nobody was prepared to abandon them altogether. For one thing, British prestige, as Bulwer pointed out, would be seriously damaged. For another, a duty to the Mosquito Indians had been incurred and Britain was bound to discharge it. The only question was how. Greytown, it was agreed, was a separate problem.

Tradition and Revolt, p. 178.
210. In late June 1850 Clayton sent Bulwer a declaration that the treaty was not intended by either party

> to include the British settlement in Honduras (commonly called British Honduras, as distinct from the State of Honduras), nor the small islands in the neighborhood of that settlement, which may be known as its dependencies. To this settlement and these islands, the treaty negotiated was not intended by either of us to apply. The title to them it is now and has been my intention, throughout the whole negotiation, to leave, as the treaty leaves it, without denying, affirming or in any way meddling with the same, just as it stood previously. The Chairman of the Committee on Foreign

seen as a significant withdrawal from the position established by Canning thirty years earlier, an unprecedented concession of equal rights and partnership to the USA, including a most unusual abstention from future colonisation (which Palmerston interpreted in the strict sense of applying equally to private and state schemes, all proposals for which were henceforth rejected).

For many in Washington, by contrast, the agreement appeared not only to be a decisive retreat from the Monroe Doctrine and a tacit recognition of British rights over Belize, the Bay Islands and the ridiculous protectorate sustained within Nicaragua but also the surrender of a commercial advantage vital to the development and defence of the new trans-continental USA. For some Democrats, such as James Buchanan, it was less the ambiguity over past or present colonies that mattered than the circumscription of future expansion by the USA:

> ... the first two articles ought to be resisted to the utmost extremity. They are neither more nor less than a solemn stipulation on the part of the United States to Great Britain that at no future period shall we ever annex to our Country, under any circumstances, any part of the vast country of Central America.... Nay, more, it is a stipulation by which Great Britain, in fact, guarantees as against the United States, the integrity of the different states of Central America.... Instead of the protectorate of the Mosquito king, which Great Britain had assumed without a particle of right, she will become the protector of all the five states.... If Sir Henry Bulwer can succeed in having the first two articles of this Treaty ratified by the Senate he will deserve a British peerage.... The Treaty altogether reverses the Monroe Doctrine, and establishes it against ourselves rather than the European governments.[211]

Squier, whom Clayton sensibly withdrew from the region in June 1850, returned to Washington to find a new secretary of state in Daniel Webster, who, to his incredulity and indignation, was quite sympathetic to Bulwer's interpretation of the treaty. Still clinging to the notion that his own treaty might be given life, Squier fired off an anguished missive to Clayton himself – the very man who had been holding him back for eighteen months:

> Mr Bulwer insists on the most sweeping modifications of my treaty, and assures Mr Webster that you promised an infinity of things in respect of it, and amongst others that there should not be any thing suffered to remain implying a denial of the *actuality* of British protection on the Mosquito Shore! He says that the treaty negotiated between yourself and him 'was intended *in no way to affect* the Mosquito question', which was (I use his precise words) 'left *entirely out of view*, and in its original state'! He objects to the recognition of the right of Nicaragua to the line of the Canal, on the ground that it brings up the Mosquito pretensions,

Relations of the Senate, the Hon. William R. King, informs me that, 'the Senate perfectly understood that the treaty did not include British Honduras'.

Quoted in R.A. Humphreys, *The Diplomatic History of British Honduras, 1638–1901*, London 1961, pp. 53–4. The Senate debate was in executive session and so not publicly minuted.

211. Buchanan, Wheatland, to McClernand, 2 April 1850, in George E. Belknap, 'Letters of Bancroft and Buchanan on the Clayton–Bulwer Treaty, 1849–50', *AHR*, 5, 1899, pp. 99–100. The fact that Buchanan would go on to be ambassador to London and then president made his views particularly important, although they did mellow somewhat by the mid 1850s. Buchanan's estimation of Bulwer's worth eventually proved correct – he was created Baron Dalling and Bulwer in 1871, the last year of his life.

with which he pretends it was understood with you, the U.S. was in no way to meddle.... I deem it my duty to inform you of these facts, although it is probable your Washington Correspondents have kept you advised of what is going on. I am convinced the whole of the movement in Central America will come to a most 'lame and impotent conclusion' unless the Senate put an estopper on the cockney diplomatist.... Mr Webster is profoundly ignorant of the events of the case and too indolent to investigate it. Besides, his hostility to you personally will, as I have already said, rather lead him to wish an unfavourable issue.[212]

The pace of developments in California and Central America ensured that these differences of interpretation would be put to the test sooner rather than later. On 14 July 1851 Cornelius Vanderbilt's Accessory Transit Company inaugurated its steamer service from New York to San Francisco via Nicaragua. This route took ten days on the Atlantic from New York to San Juan del Norte/Greytown, and fifteen on the Pacific from San Juan del Sur to San Francisco. Within Nicaragua itself the travelling time initially varied widely because of the need to wait for the steamers plying the oceanic routes, sometimes requiring passengers to spend three weeks in the country. However, once extra vessels had been laid on, it was quite possible to cross Nicaragua in two days and undertake the whole trip inside a month. The optimum trans-isthmian passage from San Juan del Norte was fourteen hours in steamer (thirty in sailboat) to San Carlos; six hours from San Carlos across the lake to Virgin Bay; and four hours from Virgin Bay to San Juan del Sur. In 1851 this portion of the trip cost $40 ($27 by sailboat), when a steerage ticket for the entire voyage was $180, which was not so high when compared with the fortunes that might be made in the goldfields of California. Within a year of the service opening, the proportion of travellers to California who took the Nicaraguan route rose from one out of fifteen to one of every two. Within months the population of San Juan del Norte/Greytown rose to over 3,000, and by 1854 over 2,000 passengers were crossing Nicaragua every month, Vanderbilt's efficient steamer service marginalising talk of the canal and reaping very considerable profits for the company – over $1 million in 1855.[213]

John Mitchel made this trip over four days in November 1853 – the only occasion in which he set foot on Latin American soil:

> 14th. *Castilla Rapids*. Yesterday we traversed the Lake, about ninety miles from Virgin Bay to the outlet of the San Juan River – a vast and lovely lake, surrounded with untamable forests, and here and there a lofty mountain peak. Thus far we have come down in the lake steamer; but here rapids occur, where a transfer must be made; a walk of a quarter of a mile, and re-embarkation on another steamer below the rapids. We are housed in a most comfortless hotel for the night.
>
> 15th. This morning we floated down the San Juan to its mouth on the Atlantic side. It is a rapid, full, and powerful stream, bordered close to the water's edge, not by hedges but high walls of most luxuriant tropical foliage; the lofty trees bound together and festooned by all manner of trailing vines, making the whole a chaotic mass of almost solid verdure. No living

212. Squier, New York, to Clayton, 2 Sept. 1850, in 'Letters of E. George Squier', pp. 433–4.

213. E. Bradford Burns, *Patriarch and Folk: The Emergence of Nicaragua, 1798–1858*, Cambridge, Mass., 1991, pp. 180–83.

thing but alligators, wallowing in the shallow water, and occasionaly diving when gently titillated by a ball from a revolver. At last, we glide into the calm expanse of the bay of San Juan del Norte, called by the British 'protectors' Greytown, after an illustrious but roguish statesman, of the name of Grey. The town stretches and straggles about a mile along the shore, backed by wooded heights; seems to contain sixty or seventy houses, and one or two large hotels. We came ashore, and the *Prometheus*, an Atlantic steamer, not having yet arrived, we secure with difficulty, at an extortionate price, two bed-rooms at Lyon's Hotel, a large wooden house. Lyon is an American; and indeed, all the good houses in this place seem to be American; but there are also some English, and a few French. The non-arrival of the *Prometheus* seems to these people an interposition of Providence in their behalf, because they have 700 passengers delivered over to their tender mercies, to threat them at discretion and mulct them as much as they will bear....

There is a sort of municipal government established in the town, the mayor being an American, and the British never interfere now with the domestic concerns of Greytown. It is an anomalous species of government; for the ground undoubtedly belongs to the State of Nicaragua, and Greytown in its present condition must, ere long, breed quarrels. It was here that an English ship fired into the *Prometheus* two or three years ago, while insisting on the payment of harbour dues, payable by the American steamer in Greytown, as a British port, and although the dues are not now levied or claimed, yet it will depend entirely on England's convenience and strength, whether and how soon they be demanded again.[214]

In fact, the incident noted by Mitchel marked the beginning of the end for British claims on Greytown – something that even he, so keen to find the hand of imperialism, seems here half to accept. It took place two years before his visit – on 21 November 1851, when Captain Henry Churchill, the commander of the *Prometheus*, refused to pay harbour dues on the grounds that these were not admissible under the Clayton–Bulwer treaty, and James Green, the British consul in the town, called upon the support of HMS *Express*. According to the protest lodged with Palmerston a month later by US Ambassador Abbott Lawrence,

It appears that the *Prometheus* was at weigh at San Juan with about five hundred passengers, when the city authorities of San Juan boarded her with a police force, and served a process of attachment on the ship and captain for $123, claimed by these authorities as port dues, which the captain refused to pay. Thereupon, the *Express* immediately got under weigh, made sail for the steamer, and when within a quarter of a mile of her fired round shot over her forecastle, and a few minutes afterwards another shot over her stern, which passed so near that its force was distinctly felt by several persons on board. The captain of the steamer then sent a boat on board the brig to inquire the cause of the firing. The commander of the brig replied that it was to protect the authorities of Greytown in their demands, and that if the steamer did not immediately anchor, he would fire a bomb-shell into her, and he ordered his guns to be loaded with grape and canister. The steamer then proceeded to the anchorage and anchored. The brig anchored very near her, and sent a boat on board with orders that fires should be extinguished, and to say that an officer would be sent to see that this was done. The authorities then came aboard, and the amount demanded was paid under protest, and the steamer was permitted to proceed.[215]

---

214. *Jail Journal*, Glasgow 1876, pp. 309–10.
215. Lawrence, London, to Palmerston, 19 Dec. 1851, in *BFSP, 1850–51*, XL, pp. 1081–2. At the start of the decade Consul Green was resolutely opposed to the North Americans, calling them 'interlopers' who

This was not the final instance of aggressive naval action by the British on the Mosquito Shore, but it was the last directed specifically against a US target on behalf of London's officers. Washington's complaints in this instance were fully registered by the Foreign Office, which apologised with the assurance that British ships were only present to protect the port, not collect dues. The very day Lawrence sent his letter Palmerston was dismissed as foreign secretary for having congratulated Louis Napoleon on the coup he staged in Paris on 2 December. But the likelihood is that he would have taken a course similar to that adopted by his successor Lord Granville in recognising the much enhanced US presence in Greytown, ordering the British ambassador in Washington, John Crampton, to negotiate an extension of the Clayton–Bulwer treaty, and directing Green to report directly to Crampton and avoid any possible misunderstandings with the North Americans on the ground.[216] Bulwer himself wrote to the foreign secretary reiterating his now familiar point that, however burdensome Greytown had become to London and however fragile the British presence in the port, circumstances had contrived to make it a symbol of British authority:

> It is unfortunately out of our power to vacate Greytown and give it up to the first comers, Nicaragua or others, without, after all that has passed in writing and otherwise ... creating an impression throughout South and Central America very detrimental to our moral and commercial influence.[217]

It was, though, quite within the power of the American majority in Greytown to marginalise the British, and in February 1852 they sought to do this precisely by pushing for incorporation into Nicaragua, exploiting Green's 'diplomatic' absence in Bluefields:

> The British Consul is in Blewfields. Of the Town Council some of the members wish to withdraw, and most pleaded excess of business as an excuse for not attending. The police, consisting of some half dozen, are unpaid since December, and everything is in a most unsettled and unsatisfactory state. A large meeting was held on Saturday last by a large number of persons, almost all Americans, when resolutions were passed to send delegates to Nicaragua to petition for a corporation from that State for the Port of Greytown. These persons, so says public report, stated that if the Nicaraguan government accepted their demands, they would on their return hoist the Nicaraguan flag. Further, that they had been told on

---

have no care or fear of anything nor from anybody. They seem lords of the soil wherever they go, and they plainly tell us they guess this place belongs to Nicaragua, and that Nicaragua must have it, and they guess their rifles would lend them good aid if the Nicaraguans want it.

Green, Greytown, to Smart, 13 Sept. 1850, quoted in Naylor, *Penny ante Imperialism*, p. 189.

216. Granville, London, to Lawrence, 10 Jan. 1852; Granville to Crampton, 23 Jan. 1852, in *BFSP, 1851–52*, XLI, London 1863, pp. 768–80. The unstable nature of British party politics in the early 1850s made for a quick succession of foreign secretaries being appointed when the Mosquito question was at its most acute: Granville (26 Dec. 1851); Earl of Malmesbury (27 Feb. 1852); Lord John Russell (28 Dec. 1852); Earl of Clarendon (21 Feb. 1853); Earl of Malmesbury (26 Feb. 1858); Lord John Russell (18 June 1859) – but these were experienced men, and since the post of prime minister exchanged just between Derby, Aberdeen and Palmerston between February 1852 and June 1865, the degree of institutional continuity was as high as familiarity with the case.

217. Bulwer to Granville, February 1852, quoted in Van Alstyne, 'Clayton–Bulwer treaty', p. 159.

the quarter-deck of an American man-of-war, that if the Nicaraguan flag was hoisted the American man-of-war would salute it, and prevent the interference of English force.[218]

In the face of this danger, Green acceded almost immediately to a species of self-government in the town based on the common law of England, 'together with the admission of the decisions of the Supreme Courts of the United States in all trials' – not only the anomaly that Mitchel was to note some months later but also something of a precedent for William Walker, who would try in 1856 to implant an Anglo-American political system in the Nicaraguan heartland.

Elections were held under this hybrid constitution for a mayor, three judges of a supreme court, five aldermen, a health officer, a captain of the port, city attorney and city marshal, most of whom were Americans and all of whom were sworn in at the end of April 1852. Perhaps rather surprised at this achievement, James Green reported back to London:

> Since then everything has gone on very well, a very efficient police has been organised, taxes levied, and various salutary measures passed. Within the last week an opportunity presented itself of testing their efficiency. The bedroom of a returning Californian had been entered forcibly, and large amount of gold-dust plundered by a gang of desperadoes who had lately arrived from Chagres. Although the thieves had displayed consummate skill in their arrangements, the police soon discovered and arrested the parties. In the meantime, the Californians attempt to gain possession of the prisoners, for the purpose of lynching them. The citizens, however, armed themselves, turned out and formed a guard around the station-house, determined that the law should be carried into effect, and a fair trial given to them. A jury of twelve of the most responsible citizens of the place was then summoned, and, in fact, every form of law complied with.
> After a fair and remarkably well conducted trial, three persons were sentenced to be hung. After conviction, however, two of the number confessed, and gave information which tended to the recovery of a small portion of the plunder; the other prisoner was executed this morning. The two who confessed were reprieved; their punishment being commuted to branding.... Before his execution, the culprit confessed his participation in many robberies and murders.
> The firmness of the City Government has astonished the passers-through. They say: 'Greytown is sure to thrive while the laws are firmly administered, and life and property protected.' The inhabitants have declared their intention of resisting any attempt by Nicaragua to occupy this place, and have already informed the Commissioners that they are unanimous in their dislike to that Government.[219]

---

218. Cochrane, Greytown, to McQuhae, 2 March 1852, in *BFSP, 1851–52*, XLI, p. 831.
219. Green, Greytown, to Crampton, 31 May 1852, in ibid., p. 847. The first article of the Greytown constitution reads:

> 1. All men are by nature possessed of certain inalienable rights, among which are those of enjoying and defending life and liberty, acquiring and protecting property, and securing happiness. 2. All political power is inherent in the people. Government is instituted for their protection, security and benefit; and they have the right to alter and reform the same, whenever they deem it requisite for the public welfare.

Ibid, p. 849.

This remarkable volte-face was not only because the Americans had reached a *rapprochement* with Green, who had himself invested in local real estate, and because the town council could now claim the harbour revenues for itself. Many of the citizens were also losing sympathy with Vanderbilt's company, which was justifiably seen to be exploiting its monopoly. Over the coming months this tension would grow as the company sought to evade the payment of taxes by shifting much of its establishment across the harbour to Punta Arenas. The company was, of course, dependent upon its concession from Managua, and it seemed to many inhabitants of Greytown that the government in the new Nicaraguan capital was about to be handed back control of their town by a unilateral agreement between London and Washington.[220]

That agreement was negotiated over the spring of 1852 between John Crampton and Daniel Webster, after whom Vanderbilt had artlessly named one of his steamers. Webster, who in February successfully defended the case of Relf and Chew against Myra Clark in the Supreme Court, was not quite as amenable to the British case as George Squier had protested, and he made his main pitch the direct incorporation of the Mosquito Shore into Nicaragua with payment of compensation. Crampton, however, successfully resisted this on grounds of different cultures of citizenship and policies towards native populations:

> I told Mr Webster frankly that I did not think that these proposals were admissible.... The mere recommendation of an incorporation of the Mosquitos with the Nicaraguans amounted, in fact, to nothing more than the cession of the territory of the latter to the former; for the notion that Mr Webster seemed to entertain, that the reception of the Mosquitos as citizens of Nicaragua on the purchase of their 'possessory rights', would constitute by implication a sort of recognition of their independence and of our Protectorate, was not, I remarked, applicable to the case, being founded on the supposition that the condition of the Mosquitos was similar to the condition and status of Indian tribes in the territories of the United States, and to be dealt with on principles upon which the Indians are dealt with by the United States Government. This, however, is not the case; the constitutions of the Spanish American Republics not admitting the application of those principles.... In the United States the State regards all territories within its limits as appertaining to itself, as far as foreign nations are concerned; but, nevertheless, it makes Treaties with Indian tribes within those territories for the purchase of what are called their 'possessory rights' and for their removal from one district and their settlement in another; thus implying the recognition of a 'quasi' independence, but not adopting them as citizens of the United States – at least, not without the

---

220. The flag of the Mosquito King is still flying here, but that is the only evidence of his sovereignty. The control of the town is in the hands of the foreign residents, principally Americans, who recently elected a Constitution for themselves ... the mayor is an American named Martin, who appears to possess a kind of energy and talent well adapted to his anomalous and difficult position – a position in which Justice, while wielding her sword with one hand, is obliged to point a revolver with the other.... The object of the foreigners here is avowedly to establish a free port with as much circumajacent [*sic*] territory as possible; and they loudly proclaim that they will never submit to the rule of any native Power. To Nicaragua they bear especial hate, which may prove a source of trouble.

Walsh, Greytown, to Webster, 28 May 1852, in W.R. Manning (ed.), *Diplomatic Correspondence of the United States: Interamerican Affairs, 1831–1860: IV. Central America, 1851–60*, Washington 1934, p. 279.

fulfillment on their part of other conditions. In Spanish America, on the other hand, every inhabitant of a State, Indian or Spaniard, is *ipso facto* a citizen thereof.[221]

The final convention signed on 30 April reflected a compromise over these positions: a reservation of defined territory for the Mosquitos under Nicaraguan guarantee; later union of the Mosquitos, on their own option, with Nicaragua under full guarantees of citizenship; the cession of Greytown to Nicaragua for an indemnity to be paid out of the port dues. This proposal was, however, rejected by the Nicaraguan government, which was putting pressure on Vanderbilt over non-payment under the initial contract and which seemed to believe that it could extract still better terms if it held out until any possible Democrat victory in the November elections in the USA. Webster himself sneered at the ungrateful response: 'a mere matter of dollars and cents, the general good of the world being a mere feather in the balance against any violation of the eminent domain of Nicaragua'.[222]

The prolonged stalemate was now deepened by a shifting of positions – those of Washington and London coming together, whilst those of the Nicaraguan government, the townsfolk of Greytown and Vanderbilt separated. As a result of the Nicaraguan rejection of the Webster–Crampton accord the British government decided that it could withdraw its principal offer – the return of Greytown to Nicaraguan sovereignty – although it kept an open mind over the town's relationship with the protectorate:

> Her Majesty's Government would naturally prefer … that Greytown should remain precisely as it is now, nominally under the supremacy of Mosquito but really independent, and that both Great Britain and the United States should unite in affording protection to Greytown thus constituted, leaving it open to the now free port to work out its own future absolutely independent of all foreign control, or to become itself the head of Mosquito State, as time and circumstances may hereafter determine.[223]

---

221. Crampton, Washington, to Malmesbury, 28 March 1852, in ibid., p. 847.

222. Quoted in Robert Rimini, *Daniel Webster: The Man and His Time*, New York 1997, p. 716. According to the US chargé, John Kerr, the Nicaraguan rejection stemmed from a conviction that out of 'a jealousy, natural in their view, to two great maritime powers, something sooner or later may be elicited for the advantage of Nicaragua'. Kerr, León, to Webster, 28 July 1852, in ibid. The Nicaraguan government was prepared to concede a five-year franchise of Greytown, but it proposed a categorical revision of the first article of the treaty: 'The Mosquito Indians, and the territory of that name, remain for ever incorporated and united with that of Nicaragua, enjoying the same rights, and being subject to the same duties, as the other inhabitants of the state, according to the terms of the fundamental charter.' *BFSP, 1851–52*, XLI, p. 884.

223. Malmesbury, London, to Crampton, 16 July 1852, in *BFSP, 1851–52*, XLI, pp. 857–8. When the Whigs took back control of the Foreign Office in December 1852 the position remained much the same:

> … the Committee of Government of Greytown are, in fact, the real power which exercises authority in that part of Central America…. to Her Majesty's Government it would be a matter of indifference whether that authority was exercised in the name of the King of Mosquito or in the name of Greytown itself; but it is desirable that what is apparent should be made to conform, as far as possible, to what is real. What is apparent is that the King of Mosquito exercises sovereignty over Greytown; what is real is that he has no authority whatever.

Russell, London, to Crampton, 19 Jan. 1853, in *BFSP, 1852–53*, XLII, p. 156.

However, in Greytown itself the conflict between the town council and the Transit Company was becoming so sharp that it had overtaken the Anglo-US rivalry, escaping any ready diplomatic solution. Moreover, the new Democratic administration followed the US Whigs in backing Vanderbilt against a council that it saw as increasingly out for itself, intractable and sympathetic to the British. In February 1853 the council decided to face the company down, demanding that it move all its installations to the north of the harbour (and so unambiguously within Greytown's jurisdiction) and that it restrict itself exclusively to the transit business. The final straw, however, was rather more prosaic and will be readily appreciated by anybody who has suffered at the whim of any transport company (although it does come as a slight surprise to find George Squier amongst the passengers protesting to the Greytown council):

Gentlemen,

The Undersigned, passengers in the steamer *Prometheus*, beg leave to represent to your honorable body, that they have been refused passage to the interior in the steamer of the Nicaragua Transit Company, under the plea that there was no room for any except persons holding through tickets to California. But the Undersigned have reason to believe that a considerable number of persons, not holding through tickets, were allowed passage in said steamers, and that the exclusion of the Undersigned was an act of personal malice on the part of the aforesaid Nicaragua Transit Company. Regarding this Company as commercial carriers, pursuing their business in part within the jurisdiction of the corporation of San Juan, the Undersigned deem it their duty to complain to your honorable body of this violation of the common law and of the plain duties of Companies thus organized, especially as this act of exclusion operates greatly to the detriment of both their public and private interests, and with the view of calling your attention to the arbitrary, oppressive and illegal conduct of the aforesaid Nicaragua Transit Company, in order to its future prevention and punishment.

We have, etc.,

E. George Squier,
Wm. A. Jeffery, U.S. Navy,
S.W. Woodhouse, U.S. Army,
D.C. Hitchcock,
C.R. Follen.[224]

---

224. *BFSP, 1856–57*, XLVII, London 1865, p. 1008. Squier had never got on with the company. In 1850 – when still ambassador – he wrote to Clayton,

> The seeming inactivity of the Canal Company does not ... give encouragement. In fact, I suspect that certain members of that Company are fitted for little beyond talking and that they exercise this facility to an unnecessary and injurious extent. The letters from Mr Joseph L. White and his brother lately here, and which were exhibited to all the officers of the state and the leading citizens in a most ostentatious manner, were past all precedent egotistical. 'I stipulated this', and 'I did that' are the burthen of every sentence. Mr White is unquestionably what the Yankees term a 'smart man', but a most inveterate, indiscriminating and indiscreet talker.... In making these observations I need not say that they are dictated by no personal considerations for Mr White is nothing to me one way or another.

Squier, León, to Clayton, 8 May 1850, in 'Letters of E.G. Squier', p. 420.

Vanderbilt's harassed local agent, George McCewan, requested protection from the US consul but was told that he had no power to intervene, which seems to have been taken as a signal for action by the town's leaders:

> At about noon, the employés being at dinner, a party of thirty persons, of all nations and colors, headed by the City Marshal and commanded by Major James Lyon (a colored gentleman) and Captain Benjamin Mooney, arrived at this point to commence their work of destruction, being provided with all the necessary instruments for such purposes; which destruction they commenced by tearing down the American flags that were waving about the house and other buildings, and then wantonly destroyed the whole of the property, not even giving my employés time to save the articles in the houses, with the exception of the very few. In tearing down the buildings, these persons looked more like tigers falling upon their prey than human beings. Resistance could not be offered, because a leader and arms were wanting, and all had to look in silence on the destruction until the work was finished, which left all of us homeless, without the means of providing for our men the necessaries of life, and exposing them to the inclemencies of the weather at this season of the year, and in such a sickly country as this. What have we, then, to expect at the expiration of the term set by the [council's] ordinance of ejecting us from all the balance of the property, which time will expire in a very few days? The worst! The worst! Here we are without arms, and without protection, and anyway whatsoever subjected to be robbed by a set of unprincipled men, who have nothing to lose, and who act as, and who are *de facto*, the authority of the city of San Juan del Norte or Greytown.[225]

In fact, McCewan could rely on greater protection than his understandably distressed account suggests. Within days the USS *Cyane* under Captain George Hollins entered Greytown harbour and enforced the return of the company's property by the councillors, who in protest handed over the formal government of the place to the US officer. On this occasion the British response was simply to have the Mosquito flag rehoisted and to request that Washington clarify and tighten its instructions to naval commanders. When, a year later, Hollins revisited Greytown as a result of another assault on the Transit Company, Washington felt able to insist on the payment of $24,000 in reparations to the Vanderbilt concern. Squier's desire to see the US navy in action off Central America was finally realised, albeit against the stout burghers of Greytown rather than the impressionable citizens of Nicaragua, and with the British tellingly engaged in preparations for war against Russia. Moreover, by mid 1854 the interior of Nicaragua had collapsed into full civil war between Conservatives (Legitimists) and Liberals (Democrats), and the Greytown council saw no possible advantage in paying compensation to a company which no longer enjoyed protection – still less an unchallenged contract – for its operations inland. As a result, Lyon, Mooney, Kirkland, Shepherd and the others refused to obey Hollins's demands and called his bluff with regard to the threat to bombard the town. After five years of brinkmanship, high rhetoric and backroom deals, they probably figured that they were taking but one more pirouette through a token display of force.

---

225. McCewan, San Juan del Norte, 3 March 1853, in *New Orleans Delta*, 16 Mar. 1853, in *BFSP, 1852–53*, XLII, p. 215.

This attitude might well have paid off had there not occurred a few days later an incident on the San Juan river between the Transit Company steamer *Routh* and a small Nicaraguan craft in which the captain, T.T. Smith, shot dead Antonio Paladino without apparent provocation. Smith was detained at Greytown for murder despite the fact that the new US ambassador, Solon Borland, had been aboard his vessel and tried to stop the arrest. In the scuffle that followed somebody threw a bottle, which grazed Borland's head, the effusion of ambassadorial blood being enough to persuade Pierce to dispatch the *Cyane* once more, this time with unambiguous instructions. Having removed all its inhabitants, Hollins turned his cannon on Greytown, which, after the marines finished off with their torches those buildings missed by the gunfire, was, in John Mitchel's words,

> all blown to atoms now, burned down, reduced to ashes, and the ashes scattered on the wind – razed, trampled, sown with salt and become even as Sodom and Gomorrah by reason of the impious irreverence of some of the inhabitants towards one Solon Borland, august representative of a first-rate power.[226]

Lord Clarendon perhaps described the destruction of Greytown as 'an outrage without parallel in the annals of modern times' because it matched (and went well beyond the operational norms of) British gunboat diplomacy. Palmerston, himself plainly outraged at the effrontery of the challenge thrown down by Pierce and Marcy, railed at them in a manner so many had displayed towards him. Yet he did so in anguished recognition of the constraints imposed by the war in the Crimea as well as the fact that he – banished to the Home Office – could only draft cabinet memos, not issue directives to naval commanders:

> A quarrel with the United States is at all times undesirable, and is especially so when we are engaged in War with another Power but though at War, we are crippling effectually the naval means with which we are at War, and what is of great Importance we are sure at present of not having France against us, as an ally of the United States.
>
> In dealing with Vulgar minded Bullies, and such unfortunately the people of the United States are, nothing is gained by submission to Insult and wrong; on the contrary the submission to an Outrage only encourages the commission of another and a greater one – such People are always trying how far they can venture to go; and they generally pull up when they find they can go no further without encountering resistance of a formidable Character.
>
> In the present Instance we have many advantages on our side.
>
> We are successful in our War against Russia, which the United States Govt., when it sent the *Cyane* to Grey Town thought would hamper and embarrass us, and when we have taken Sebastopol and have knocked down Sweaborg and Cronstadt as we shall do with the Lancaster Guns, our naval force will to a great Degree be let free. We have France so bound up with

---

226. *Jail Journal*, p. 310. Mitchel added,

> a certain amount of punishment these Greytown people assuredly deserved for their uneatable dinners and their extortion; but the human mind, even of one who has suffered by their practices, would, perhaps, have been satisfied with some less condign and signal vengeance than that which has fallen upon them.

us that she cannot join the United States against us, we have North American Provinces now united and loyal, and dissatisfied with the United States, we have public opinion in the United States on our side, and we have the United States Government itself ashamed of what it has done and not daring to avow its act, though hesitating to disavow and atone for it.

The U.S. have no navy of which we need to be afraid, and they might be told that if they were to resort to privateering, we should however reluctantly be obliged to retaliate by burning all their Sea Coast Towns.

If we are not firm on this occasion I don't see on what occasion we could ever take our stand. If the Parts had been reversed we should long before this Time have seen Buchanan take his Passage Home unless we had yielded to an imperative Demand for the most ample satisfaction.[227]

Palmerston was right about the adverse popular reaction inside the US and the resultant hesitation of the Pierce government, which now had few practical options with which to follow up the actions of the *Cyane*. He was, however, equally wrong about the ease of operations in the Crimea, where, as he drafted this memo, British and French troops had just landed to great euphoria. The campaign in Russia rapidly bogged down British naval as well as ground forces in a conflict of infamous incompetence and mindless destruction. Nevertheless, the outbreak of that war was too eagerly seized upon by ambitious US diplomats in Europe as an opportunity to press home claims in the Caribbean. In April 1854 Washington had formally and forcibly offered Spain a price of $130 million for Cuba after a US ship, the *Black Warrior*, had been detained in Havana for infringement of customs regulations. Now Buchanan and his colleagues in Paris and Madrid, spurred on by Pierce's inaugural commitment 'not to be controlled by any timid forebodings of evil from expansion', drafted a rashly worded and immediately leaked 'despatch', which declared that if Spain, 'actuated by stubborn pride', would not sell Cuba, and if the island 'seriously endanger[s] our internal peace and existence of our cherished Union', then, 'by every law, human and divine, we shall be justified in wresting it [from her]'. This 'Ostend Manifesto' of October 1854 caused an immediate and combined protest from the major European powers, and, unlike the *Cyane* affair, it had to be disavowed in forthright fashion by the Pierce administration, which found itself thwarted in its efforts to exploit British distraction in Russia just as London was eventually obliged to recognise the limits the Crimean conflict placed on its capacity in the *Cyane* incident: 'Perhaps the least degrading course would be to let the matter drop at least until we have taken Sebastopol.'[228]

---

227. Clarendon, London, to Crampton, 31 Aug. 1854; Palmerston, 'Memorandum on a Draft of Despatch from Clarendon to Mr Crampton', 10 Sept. 1854, quoted in Bourne, *Britain and the Balance of Power in North America*, pp. 132–3.

228. Clarendon, London, to Palmerston, 31 July 1855, quoted in Humphreys, *Tradition and Revolt*, p. 179. Sebastopol finally fell on 9 Sept. 1855.

Even if it did seem misguided to bombard Charleston, San Francisco or Mobile in return for the destruction of Greytown, London could, of course, still send warships to invigilate the reconstruction of the Central American port through late 1854 and early 1855. To the eyes of John Wheeler, Borland's successor as US ambassador, this was a process 'without any government, or law or rule whatever'. However, Washington was now held responsible for that fact by Nicaraguans and foreign inhabitants alike, the 'swindling character' of all the locals accounting for the fact that the claim for damages presented by James Green on their behalf amounted to '$1,182,678.92, when the whole town in its palmiest days was not worth more than $100,000'.[229] Moreover, Wheeler felt all the prejudice caused by the punitive action without deriving any advantage from subsequent protection:

> A large portion of this community is composed of men of the most lawless character; without any visible means of living; whose tastes and temper delight in scenes of tumult, crime and blood. Daily, at this place within my hearing, are outrages committed; and my repose is broken by their bacchanalian orgies, 'making night hideous'.... Nothing but a sense of duty, and instructions from your Department, could compel me to remain two more months here; for there has not been an hour that the safety of myself and my family has not been jeopardized. Since I have no other protection than the Flag of my country (which these outlaws little respect) and (humiliating as the feeling may be to an American Minister) the guns of Her Britannic Majesty – ships-of-war in this Harbour which if ready to protect, as far as convenient, personal safety, are not to be used to avenge injury to our citizens, or insults to our flag.[230]

The *Cyane* incident, then, had not just shifted feelings against the USA; it had also unhinged the effort to forge at Greytown a stable enclave founded on North American political culture and the expectation of favourable regulation of competition by Washington. The resulting stand-off with Britain only accelerated the 'Californian-isation' of the township, encouraging Henry Kinney to set sail in the *Emma* and cash in on the Mosquito land claim he had bought off the Shepherd brothers. The first time that he tried to sail from New York Kinney was detained on a charge of fitting out a military operation, and when he was eventually able to break bail and clear coastal waters with thirteen companions, the *Emma* was shipwrecked off Turk's Island, forcing the adventurers to make a less than heroic entrance at Greytown as passengers on a British steamer. None the less, at public meetings on 6 and 7 September 1855 Kinney was appointed by acclaim as civil and military governor of the town, charged

---

229. Wheeler, San Juan del Norte, to Marcy, 22 Jan. 1855, in Manning, *Diplomatic Correspondence*, IV, p. 434. When, in August 1854, the Nicaraguan government had demanded reparations for the destruction wrought by the *Cyane*, Secretary of State Marcy retorted testily to Ambassador Marcoleta,

> These citizens for whom you make reclamation must have lived in treasonable association with the open and armed enemies of your country. They knew, for notice had repeatedly been given, that the town would be punished for its misdeeds, and they had every oportunity to withdraw from it.

Marcy, Washington, to Marcoleta, 2 Aug. 1854, in ibid., pp. 59–60.
230. Wheeler, San Juan del Norte, to Marcy, 10 Feb. 1855, in ibid., p. 445.

along with a new council that included Samuel Shepherd and his business partner T. Haly to draw up a fresh constitution. The British refused to recognise these new authorities but, in line with their practice of recent years, they also refused to intervene. Moreover, at the same time as Kinney had sailed in the *Emma* on the Atlantic route to Nicaragua, so on the Pacific coast had the *Vesta* set a course from San Francisco to Realejo. Here comes William Walker.

THE GREY-EYED MAN (AND THE TALL FELLOW)

The person who directly hired Walker to lead a military force of foreigners on behalf of the Liberals in the Nicaraguan civil war was one Byron Cole, a former newspaper editor from San Francisco who had first visited the country in mid 1854. Cole signed a contract with Francisco Castellón in December 1854 to provide 200 fighters, but he himself did not see action until 14 September 1856, when, commanding 300 men at San Jacinto, he was defeated by a force half the size, captured by local peasants and hanged from a tree. Cole is one of the very small number of people praised by Walker in the book that he published in March 1860, six months before he himself would be shot. Indeed, few of the names that figure in an unusually detailed account lived beyond the 1850s: the Conservative dictator Fruto Chamorro died in March 1855, before the lifting of the eight-month siege of Granada that opened the civil war; Castellón expired of cholera that September; and barely a dozen of the initial contingent of sixty on the *Vesta* survived the conflict. There is a real sense in which memory of the *Guerra Nacional* of May 1854 to May 1857 died with its principal participants, although between March 1856 and May 1857 – when the remaining Anglo-American mercenaries finally fled the country – the war was effectively international in its character, pitching forces from all the Central American countries against the Americans and a small coterie of local figures who stuck by them even after Walker declared himself president, reintroduced slavery, and destroyed the centre of the historic city of Granada. By that stage the conflict had been transformed from its early ideological and localist nature into a campaign devoted exclusively to expelling the foreign 'filibusterers' – a term derived from the Dutch '*vrijbuiter*' or freebooter, applied to the pirates who plundered Central America so energetically in the seventeenth century.

One signal result of the Walker episode was that whereas elsewhere in Central America the forces of liberalism took control in the 1860s and 1870s, in Nicaragua they were not able to do so until the 1890s, when José Santos Zelaya came to power (and was so faithfully served by Rubén Darío). After the 1850s the Nicaraguan Liberals struggled to retrieve a nationalist profile that had been so tarnished by their association with Walker. In some cases, such as Zelaya and Sandino, this resolution was maintained against the odds; in others, such as Moncada and Somoza, it was dropped with some alacrity. Liberalism in Nicaragua, then, was more protean than in most Latin American countries long before the Sandinistas and the Contras rehearsed its principal motifs in the even bloodier internationalised civil war of the 1980s. That conflict involved names – Argüello, Chamorro, Cuadra, Ramírez – which were just as prominent 130 years earlier, underlining the extent to which the political history of the country may be understood as a family affair. If this is still the case in a globalised world (both pre- and post-Cold War), it is not difficult to appreciate the force of kinship and local community in a world where the steamship was a novelty, agriculture rudimentary and largely dedicated to subsistence, foreign trade in the hands of a couple of dozen people, and where, as in the elections of 1853, only 490 people cast votes (two each – one having to be for a candidate from another district) for a Supreme Director of some 200,000 people.[231] Few would go so far as Costa Rican sociologist Samuel Stone, who has proposed genealogy as the primary factor in understanding political power in the isthmus since the conquest, but many have been at least partly persuaded by the thesis of Bradford Burns that the history of Nicaragua until the end of the *Guerra Nacional* and the onset of thirty-five years of Conservative rule is best understood as a bonding conflict between patriarchs and folk.[232]

The primacy of the family in pre-industrial Hispanic society is little more contested than is the primacy of the father within that family. On the eve of the revolution that would overthrow the third president of the Somoza dynasty, Humberto Belli published a telling hypothesis of conflict in the nineteenth century derived from the traits of a patriarchal family structure: 'an approbation of authoritarianism and personalism; limitations on compromise, dialogue, freedom, democracy and equality'.[233] Burns correctly insists upon the values of the time, distinguishing the head of household from all other adult males, even those who were married, who continued to owe submission. Equally, while some patriarchs dedicated themselves to siring children on any available occasion – Jesús de la Rocha (1812–81) boasted of eighty-two offspring despite being married just twice – great value was placed upon the form of marital propriety and legitimacy. Thus, when in 1851 Alejandro Manning, the youngest son of Don Tomás, a León merchant of British birth, ran off with Francisca Sanzón and got married 'clandestinely' in El Viejo, such was the scandal that the patriarch demanded an annulment not just from the archbishop but also from the city council.

231. Carlos Vilas, 'Family Affairs: Class, Lineage and Politics in Contemporary Nicaragua', *JLAS*, 24:2, 1992.

232. Samuel Z. Stone, *The Heritage of the Conquistadores: Ruling Classes in Central America from Conquest to the Sandinistas*, London 1990; Burns, *Patriarch and Folk*.

233. 'Un Ensayo de Interpretación sobre las Luchas Políticas Nicaraguenses', *Revista de Pensamiento Centroamericano*, 157, Dec. 1977. I have used Burns's admirable paraphrase.

Alejandro hired a lawyer to plead his case, but he was never going to win over the likes of 'The Students of Confucius', who distributed throughout a town that was ideologically 'Liberal' a pamphlet which denied 'class struggle' and decried 'innovators' who corrupted the youth with 'erroneous and seditious doctrines':

> Young people: you are obliged to respect your father whose will is law in domestic society.... This obligation falls on all social classes. It is a common and invariable rule founded on principles of religious morality and social harmony.... Public order rests on the respect due to the father and on the subsequent peace and tranquillity of the family.[234]

For Fruto Chamorro, election as Director in April 1853 presented an opportunity to institutionalise these values by replacing the constitution of 1838, which was marked by

> excessive extension of individual guarantees and extreme limitations on public power.... The destruction and prostration of public power stimulates the audacity of the ambitious; it has eroded among us any respect for law and weakened social bonds.... We need ... to strengthen the principle of authority, so deprecated and maligned among us. We can achieve this end by conferring consistently greater power on the executive. Furthermore, it is essential to surround the executive with greater pomp and majesty in order to command respect and to attract the admiration which that high office deserves.[235]

The authority sustained by Dr Francia for nigh-on thirty years in Paraguay and by Rosas for twenty in Argentina had proved highly elusive in Nicaragua, notwithstanding its similar colonial and religious inheritance; the 'monism' perceived throughout the sub-continent by Professors Wiarda and Dealy proves in practice to be alarmingly variable.

On the other side from Chamorro were those who argued that it was the lack of education, experience and creativity that accounted for the country's ills. In 1847 the anonymous 'S.C.' bemoaned the fact that the political system elevated paternal authority over technical skill:

> He who knew nothing about legislating was to govern in a political system that he did not even understand; he who did not even know how to count was to manage the public finances, and what is more to improve them; he who did not even know his neighbors in the next village was to direct our foreign relations; he who did not know how to read and write was to sit as judge.... In short, the ignorant were called to deliberate and the impotent to command and create. One can easily understand the results.

Amongst the worst of these was negativity and conflict:

---

234. *Primera Amonestación*, León 1851, quoted in Burns, *Patriarch and Folk*, p. 67.
235. *Mensaje a la Asamblea Constituyente Instalada el 22 de Enero de 1854*, Managua 1854, quoted in ibid., p. 29.

The rival politicians told the people what and whom they should hate.... They told the people that they had enemies and that to defeat them it would be necessary to lay waste the fields, to burn houses, and once having defeated the enemy, to place him outside the protection of the law.[236]

On the other hand, this system of polarisation and 'zero-sum' competition in which losers lost everything required the great bulk of the population excluded from the cabals of the elite to be very careful in their partisanship. Walker was given a lesson in this soon after his arrival in Nicaragua:

> The Leonese revolutionists styled their Executive Provisional Director, and asserted their resolution to maintain the organic act of 1838. They took the name of Democrats, and wore as their badge a red ribbon on their hats. Chamorro was called by his friends President – they thus declaring their adhesion to the new constitution [of April 1854]; and calling themselves Legitimists, they mounted the white ribbon.... Two or three times in their wanderings through plantations, the retreating party came upon native laborers, who are accustomed to fly at the sight of armed men, through fear of being pressed into military service; and once overtaking a slow, cautious old man who, after some hesitation, half opened his jacket, to show a red rose under it, they were amused by seeing a white rose at the same time fall to the ground.[237]

Likewise, foreigners had to equivocate if – unlike Walker – they were not safely armed:

> At the Halfway house a halt was ordered, and the owner of the establishment brought water to the door, the soldiers not being allowed to enter as there was liquor within. The keeper of this house was, perforce, a model trimmer. He was an American; but having witnessed various political changes since his residence in the Isthmus, and his place often being visited the same day by scouting parties belonging to adverse parties, he had acquired the habits of a man born in the midst of revolutions. He had in perfection all the little arts by which a man manages to maintain his neutrality though constantly surrounded by circumstances tending to endanger it.[238]

Here Walker is being more perceptive than many modern academics, and in observing that, 'in what might be termed minor diplomacy, the Central Americans are not to be surpassed', he picks up on the other side of Belli's model based on a patriarchal authoritarianism: the need to mollify, placate, temporise and flatter through words. Walker, a man of no smile and few words (although he died uttering them before the

---

236. 'Estado de los Pueblos al Establecerse la República Democrática', *Registro Oficial*, 1847, reproduced in *Revista de la Academia de Geografía e Historia de Nicaragua*, 11:1, April 1951, pp. 73–5, quoted in ibid., pp. 37–8.

237. *War in Nicaragua* (1860), Detroit 1972, pp. 15. 54.

238. Ibid., p. 90. Walker was even prepared to qualify his views on race to accommodate a political sociology of Machiavellianism:

> ... long civil war seems to have the power of creating this type of politicians, even among races least affected toward it; for the English Wars of the Roses produced the subtle genius of the third Richard, who vied with the best Italian of them all in his adherence to the maxims of the illustrious author of *The Prince*.

Honduran firing squad), came to appreciate this as he confronted the demands of governing a Spanish American people rather than simply subduing it with his superior guns:

> Don Carlos Thomas, a foreign merchant long resident in the place ... rendered much service to Walker, by his knowledge of men and things in Granada; and among other functions he performed that of writer of proclamations. He spoke and wrote English, French and Spanish with equal facility, and probably equal elegance, his English being, however, more Johnsonese than idiomatic, and his French and Spanish probably tinged with the same fault. The swell of his sentence was perfectly Ciceronian, when, with a glass or two of brandy in his head, he began to dilate on the grandeur of the present crisis in Nicaragua; and the exuberance of his feelings overflowed in a proclamation he wrote out for Walker, and had published, somewhat to the annoyance of the latter, when he saw his signature appended in print to an address teeming with the rhetoric which characterises Spanish American productions. The proclamation, however, though offensive to taste, did some good; for the purport of it was that protection would be given to all interests.[239]

Although he had died before Walker reached the country, Fruto Chamorro, who insisted that Nicaragua be converted from a state to a republic, would have sympathised with this passage:

> Words are always the expression of ideas, and sometimes they lend value to intentions. Nicaragua believes that the title Republic will shield it from some of the incalculable harm it has experienced in international relations because it has not properly expressed its status.... The new designation reflects reality and will benefit the nation.[240]

None the less, Walker, who prided himself on his command of political economy and was an enthusiastic advocate of free trade, preferred a materialist to a cultural explanation of the Nicaraguan conflict:

> The rivalry between the towns of León and Granada was a rivalry of trade and of interests as well as of social and political power. True, the political principles prevalent at Granada naturally led to high tariffs, while those of León tended to free trade; but the geographical position of the two towns did most to beget the commercial contest between them. Granada received its goods from the Atlantic, by the way of the lake and San Juan river, while León was supplied by vessels obliged to pass Cape Horn. It was difficult, however, to carry on smuggling by the river, while the facilities for contraband on the Pacific side were great. Thus León was able to compete with Granada by making up in smuggling what she lost by the voyage round the Horn.[241]

Walker wrote these lines in 1858–59, in between an abortive attempt to return to Nicaragua late in 1857 and his denouement at Trujillo in 1860. He was just thirty-six years old when the Honduran firing squad terminated a life that had been as restless and impetuous as it was studious and reflective. Born in Nashville and raised in a

---

239. Ibid., p. 116.

240. *Círculo a Todos los Gobiernos, Dándoles Conocimiento de los Motivos que Ha Tenido Nicaragua para Tomar el Nombre de República*, Managua 1854, quoted in Burns, *Patriarch and Folk*, p. 190.

241. *War in Nicaragua*, pp. 171–2.

household where his father – a comfortable merchant of Scottish presbyterian stock – refused to hold slaves, Walker was a fair-haired and slight child of sharp features and strong grey eyes. He was thought highly sensitive, close to his mother, and dubbed 'honey' and 'missy' at school. At the age of sixteen he obtained a degree in classics from the local university, and at nineteen he graduated in medicine from the University of Pennsylvania, writing his dissertation on the iris. Two years travelling in Europe, including further medical study at the Sorbonne, instilled in him a sharp dislike of the decadence of the old continent, and he was for a while hopeful that the revolutions of 1848 would inject a republican rigour into Europe. Returning to the USA to find his mother dying, Walker never practised medicine, instead seeking fortune as a lawyer and radical politician in New Orleans, where he became an editor of the *Delta* newspaper. It was in that city that there took place the only love affair that he is known to have had with a woman – Ellen Martin, the beautiful deaf-mute daughter of an aristocratic family. Walker learned sign language for Ellen, and they became engaged, but within a year of their meeting she died in the same cholera epidemic that killed Edmund Pendleton Gaines. Walker, despondent, moved on to California to write for papers and fight duels before staging a desultory filibustering expedition into northern Mexico in 1853. His account of that episode makes it clear that, aside from being one of the few lucky to escape with their lives, he had lost his earlier radical views on race, gender and slavery.

A Guatemalan officer who fought against Walker in Nicaragua thought him asexual and addicted only to the 'sensuality of power', but in describing the death of Timothy Crocker in the first of the engagements of the American 'Falange' in Nicaragua, Walker displays an expression worthy of Walt Whitman, who was working on the New Orleans *Crescent* at the same time as Walker was on the *Delta* and may well have known him:

> A boy in appearance, with a slight figure, in a face almost feminine in its delicacy and beauty, he had the heart of a lion; and his eye, usually mild and gentle, though steady in its expression, was quick to perceive a false movement on the part of an adversary, and then its flash was like the gleam of a scimitar as it falls on the head of the foe.[242]

Walker did not take the government of Nicaragua for himself for more than a year after the *Vesta* docked at Realejo in June 1855, and at no stage in his two-year stay was he able fully to control both León and Granada. Indeed, his forces were rarely able to score a conclusive victory over the Conservatives or, after September 1856, the combined Central American forces ranged against them. By March 1856 there were over 1,200 Anglo-Americans notionally under Walker's command, but they were a very mixed bunch, as he himself recognised, soon dispatching as ambassador to Washington 'with a view to getting him out of the country', one Parker French,

---

242. Ibid., p. 53.

who had arrived in California about 1852, under very suspicious circumstances. No one in California in those days, however, scrutinized too closely his neighbor's past, and as French was a clever and polished individual, he secured a seat in the legislature. All who had financial dealings with French had cause to regret it, and he soon acquired the reputation of being one of the cleverest rascals on the Pacific coast. Moreover, he was a megalomaniac. It was his morbid desire to do big things that accounted for his presence in California. Constantly devising great enterprises and with only his tongue easily persuading large numbers of people to enter into his schemes, he lacked the honesty and strength of purpose to carry his plans to a successful conclusion, and usually abandoned the undertaking as soon as he had filched from his associates all the money they were willing to entrust to his care.... In March 1855 French was accidentally shot in the leg while trying to separate two quarrelling companions in a steamboat bar. A few days after the accident the *State Journal* expressed the gratification that French was recovering *slowly*.[243]

Native Nicaraguans – Walker was insistent on the naturalisation clauses of the 1838 charter – could rarely expect the chance of a diplomatic exile if they were not trusted. Walker quickly revealed the ruthlessness that followed his suspicion, most infamously in the case of the defeated Conservative general Ponciano Corral, who, soon after he signed a truce with the American on 23 October 1855, wrote a letter to the Honduran leader Santos Guardiola that was seized and handed over to Walker, now formally commander-in-chief of the army. Corral's letter expressed directly the desperation to be expected of a beaten and disillusioned man:

> My esteemed friend: It is necessary that you write to friends to advise them of the dangers we are in, and that they work actively. If they delay two months there will not be time. Think of us and of your offers. I salute your lady; and commend your friend who truly esteems you and kisses your hand, P. Corral. Nicaragua is lost, lost Honduras, San Salvador and Guatemala if they let this get body. Let them come quickly if they would meet auxiliaries.

We only have Walker's maladroit translation as a source here, but however it read in the original, he saw it as out-and-out treason. His laconic account of the subsequent proceedings skims over the outrage felt in Granada, as Liberals and Conservatives alike began to register the awful fact that the man hired by one side had escaped control and was working to his own agenda:

> The leading Legitimists at Granada were placed under guard; and charges were made out against Corral for treason and conspiracy to overthrow the Government of the Republic. A court martial was ordered to try him, on the charges and specifications; for there was no existing civil tribunal before which to arraign him, and besides, being a military officer, he could, according to the law of the country, be called on to answer only in the military form. The court consisted of Americans, for there were few other officers of the army in Granada; and Corral, far from objecting to the court, preferred the naturalized to the native Nicaraguans as his judges. Colonel Hornsby was president of the court; Colonel Fry, judge advocate; and French acted as counsel for the prisoner. Don Carlos Thomas was sworn as interpreter of the court.

---

243. Ibid., p. 166; Scroggs, *Filibusters and Financiers*, p. 89. French did endeavour to gain diplomatic recognition from the State Department, but Marcy refused to accept either him or other 'ministers' dispatched by Walker until May 1856.

The court martial met on the 6th [November 1855] and the testimony was short but conclusive. The accused scarcely denied the charges; he asked only for mercy. The condition of his family was brought before the court; in order, if possible, to enlist its sympathy. The prisoner was found guilty on all charges and specifications, and the sentence was 'Death by shooting'; but the court unanimously recommended him to the mercy of the commander-in-chief.

The general-in-chief, however, considered that in this case mercy to one would be injustice to many. Walker had solemnly sworn, with bended knee and on the Holy Evangelists, to observe and have observed the treaty of 23 October; and he was responsible before the world, and especially to the Americans in Nicaragua – as well as before the throne of Heaven – for the faithful observance of his oath. How could the treaty continue to have the force of law if the first violation of it – and that too by the very man who had signed it – was permitted to go unpunished?

This was the same logic as that deployed by Robert Patterson in executing Antonio García and Ambrosio Alcalde for breaking their parole in the Mexican War, albeit now applied to words rather than deeds. But the execution of Corral has gone down in Nicaraguan history as a particularly infamous act because of the way Walker responded to the pleas for mercy from the womenfolk of Granada and the daughters of the condemned man. Walker's own account makes clear that a proclivity for mercy of the type exhibited by Mariano Donato Muñoz towards Anselma Condori and the victims of the Melgarejo regime in Bolivia was completely alien to him:

> … he who looks only at present grief, nor sees in the distance the thousand-fold sorrow a misplaced mercy may create, is little suited to the duties of public office; and hard as it was to resist such entreaties as the daughters if the prisoner pressed, Walker promised them to consider the pleas they had urged, and closed the painful interview as soon as kind feeling permitted.
> The next day the hour of execution was postponed from 12 to 2 pm.[244]

In *With Walker in Nicaragua*, this extension of a life by two hours is taken by Ernesto Cardenal as an act of calculated cruelty and a source of mirth for the filibusters. One who felt it deeply was 'Niña Yrena', who was Walker's first landlady in Granada and who had earlier counselled caution on Corral:

> Her family name was Irish, and she was probably the descendant of an Irish officer in the Spanish service, sent to the colonies before independence. A quick and minute observer, with all the gravity and apparent indifference of the native race, she had rendered much service to the legitimist party in days past; and even the stern nature of Fruto Chamorro owned her sway and yielded to her influence, when all others failed to move him. The private relations which it is said, and probably with truth, existed between her and D. Narciso Espinosa, a leading man among the Legitimists, enabled her to breathe her spirit into the party after the death of Chamorro had taken away the unity it before possessed. The Niña was fertile in resources for sending intelligence to her friends; and hence the headquarters of the force occupying Granada was soon [moved to] the government house on the Plaza.[245]

---

244. *War in Nicaragua*, pp. 138–9.
245. Ibid., p. 117.

The Niña was astute enough not to commit any of her intelligence to paper that fell into Walker's hands. This mistake was made in July 1856 by Tomás Manning, the British consul in León who only a few years before had undergone such perturbation over the unauthorised marriage of his son Alejandro and whose dislike of Walker was fully reciprocated because he was suspected of tipping off the Conservatives about a planned attack. Manning had entrusted a letter to Mariano Salazar, whom Walker arrested for non-payment for taxes on a consignment of brazil wood and then executed for treason when he tried to flee the country. Judging by the tone adopted by Walker's bi-lingual paper *El Nicaragüense* in publicising the captured missive, Manning would also have suffered that fate had he been apprehended:

> Among the many valuable documents found on the person of Señor Salizar was a letter from the British consul at León to Florentine Souci at San Miguel, San Salvador. This is another evidence of British agents relative to the affairs of this country.
>
> What, we would ask, in the name of philanthropy and our common humanity does Great Britain expect to gain by permitting her agents to encourage the half-civilized natives of this country to butcher each other; or by what species of sophistry does she expect to justify or excuse herself before the tribunal of Christendom, for sending to one part of the world agents who stir up strife and cause the ignorant natives to outrage human nature, while she sends missionaries of peace with the bible in one hand and flannel shirts in the other, that both the moral and physical condition of the heathen may be improved. To those who do not understand the Red Flannel Christianity of England, we respectfully submit the following letter of Mr Manning, her agent at León, of which we give a hurried translation:
>
>> León July 24 1856.
>>
>> Dear Friend: I am here, without knowing where to go, since Walker will not give us a passport to go through Granada. I understand that that man is furious with me, attributing to me the change. It is certain that all his acts are rapid; and we have not passed here without great apprehension that he will make an attack on León.... If this man receives forces and money, I assure you that it will not be easy to drive him out of the State; for as the forces come from the other States in handfuls of men nothing is accomplished and sacrifices are made in vain .... Altogether affairs are wretched in Nicaragua and very distressing, and if I remain here much longer I shall not have one shirt I can put on.... The troops here go altogether naked. If you have any drilling you can sell at 12.5 cents a yard, I will take ten bales. Don't forget my request in favor of my adopted son, Mr George Brower, to have him appointed to represent San Salvador in Liverpool.[246]

Walker later described these last two sentences as a 'lady's postscript', noting that Manning 'could not let slip the chance of making some money'.[247] He himself, however, could scarcely afford to alienate all the local business interests, especially since he had in February 1856 persuaded President Rivas to revoke the charter of the Accessory Transit Company on the (entirely justified) grounds that it had never paid to the state the agreed 10 per cent of its profits, which Walker put at $400,000 since 1851. In 1853 Cornelius Vanderbilt, greatly satisfied with the success of the company

---

246. *El Nicaraguense*, 9 Aug. 1856, enclosed in Wheeler, Granada, to Marcy, 12 Aug. 1856, in Manning (ed.) (no apparent relation), *Diplomatic Correspondence*, IV, pp. 562–3.
247. *War in Nicaragua*, p. 237.

and its eight new steamers, had treated his whole family to a celebratory holiday tour of Europe, putting the management of the firm in the hands of Charles Morgan and Cornelius Garrison, who promptly manipulated the stock and took complete control. Vanderbilt, 'apt to be loud, rustic and coarse in speech', may have alienated his erstwhile managers sufficiently to encourage them to steal his fortune, but he was also sufficiently shrewd and aggressive to win it back, trading in the market so that within months he had regained possession of the company. Nevertheless, Morgan and Garrison did a deal with Walker, who now directed Rivas to award the concession in Nicaragua to them. When news of this reached Wall Street, Accessory Transit shares fell from 23.25 cents on 14 February to 13 on the 18th. Vanderbilt immediately withdrew his steamers from service, began a fierce lobby of the State Department, and subsidised the purchase of arms by Costa Rica, which declared war on 1 March whilst Walker found himself deprived of supplies and reinforcements for weeks.[248] Although few Nicaraguans had harboured affection for Vanderbilt, the fact that Walker had tried to expropriate him for the benefit of his own associates deprived the action of any real appeal to them. Moreover, the Yankee robber baron now threw his appreciable resources behind the Central American campaign against Walker, and, with tacit support from both the US and British navies, his oceanic operations soon resumed.

According to Walker,

> The control of the Transit is, to Americans, the control of Nicaragua: for the lake, not the river as many think, furnishes the key to the occupation of the whole state. Therefore, whoever desires to hold Nicaragua securely must be careful that the navigation of the lake is controlled by those who are his staunchest and most reliable friends.[249]

For as long as he was able to hold Granada he could control the lake and so disrupt the trans-isthmian passage of thousands. None the less, Walker's wider strategy could not flourish without eventual control of San Juan del Norte/Greytown, now under the governorship of H.L. Kinney. Walker, recognising that no Nicaraguan government could countenance Kinney's concession of land derived from the Mosquito king via the Shepherds, and knowing that Washington was likewise set against him, was in something of a dilemma over the popular Texan, who 'had acquired that sort of knowledge and experience of human nature derived from the exercise of the mule trade'.[250] However, Kinney also needed him, and late in 1855 sent some emissaries up to Granada to thrash out a mutually beneficial accord. Confident of his position and sensing that Kinney was on weaker ground, Walker faced them down: 'tell your Governor Kinney, or Colonel Kinney, or Mr Kinney, or whatever he chooses to call himself, that if I ever lay hands on him on Nicaraguan soil I shall surely hang him'.[251]

248. Ibid., pp. 247–8; Scroggs, *Filibusters and Financiers*, pp. 152–3; *Dictionary of American Biography*.
249. *War in Nicaragua*, p. 157.
250. Ibid., p. 147.
251. Scroggs, *Filibusters and Financiers*, p. 129.

In the immediate wake of the execution of Corral, this was a sufficiently realistic prospect that the ambassadors decided to throw in their lot with Walker. However, Kinney's later offer to recognise Walker's military authority over the Mosquito Shore if he was permitted to retain his civil position and land claim was a very tempting means of securing Greytown and the San Juan. Had this deal lasted it might have substantially prolonged the Anglo-American occupation of Nicaragua, but the parties involved were not of the stature to maintain serious political agreements: the worse for wear through ingestion of rum, Kinney bragged in Rivas that one of his colonists was worth five of Walker's soldiers, and when news of this got back to 'the general' it required much popular supplication for the charge of treason against Kinney to be dropped.[252]

Walker never gained control of the river. Six months after arriving in the country he had established a power of veto over the trans-isthmian route but could not guarantee it for his friends. In the same vein, his American 'Falange' had captured Conservative Granada for the Liberals and controlled the puppet government established there, but it was losing support in León, and elsewhere Walker's writ ran no further than the patrols of his men, heavily armed but increasingly vulnerable to disease, particularly cholera, and seldom dissuaded from the consumption of debilitating quantities of liquor.

There is more than a little irony in the fact that, having resisted recognition of the increasingly puppet regime of Patricio Rivas for a year, the Pierce administration should extend it just before Rivas broke from Walker and threw his lot in with the emerging anti-filibuster alliance. Washington's ambassador, John Wheeler, found it hard to contain his enthusiasm for Walker's project, urged recognition with some insistence, and had to be admonished by Marcy for exceeding his brief and intervening in domestic affairs. The State Department was also confused by different – and often directly contradictory – accounts of developments in Nicaragua as it was lobbied by representatives of the previous Conservative government, the Rivas–Walker regime, the Accessory Transit Company and Greytown/San Juan del Norte. The decision to recognise Rivas was taken in May 1856 largely to help find a solution to 'the Transit question', which was now posing a major strategic difficulty for the USA.[253] Yet, even beyond diplomatic circles, there was profound scepticism as to Pierce's formalistic explanation of the move:

> It is the established policy of the United States to recognize all governments without question of their source, or organization, or of the means by which the governing persons attain their

---

252. Ibid., pp. 131–2. Kinney was kicked out of the country, but in 1857 he managed to interest some English Mormons in taking half his concession. On the strength of this he borrowed enough cash in Panama to be able to return to Greytown in April 1858. He was, though, immediately arrested and returned to the USA on the USS *Jamestown*. Unable to settle in Corpus Christi, he was shot dead in Matamoros in 1861, having got involved in the conflict between the *rojos* and the *crinolinos*.

253. Marcy, Washington, to Wheeler, 3 June 1856, in Manning (ed.), *Diplomatic Correspondence*, IV, pp. 85–6.

power.... We do not go behind the fact of a foreign government's exercising actual power to investigate questions of legitimacy.[254]

As is so often the case, this expression of *realpolitik* proved to be exceedingly convenient in the short term only to store up a host of problems over the immediate horizon. By 25 June – six weeks after being recognised by Washington – Rivas's preparedness to serve as Walker's puppet was exhausted. He denounced the North American as a usurper, traitor and enemy, and extended these charges to all who continued to serve the 'commander-in-chief'; henceforth there would be few prisoners taken in the war. Breaking a longstanding tradition of separating the celebration of party and that of patriotism, on 1 July Rivas made a logical appeal – that sectarian differences be set aside in a combined effort to meet a greater danger:

> For the past two years we spoke and acted in the name of two parties, Liberals and Conservatives. Now, fortune seems to have joined those two parties guilty of fostering so much unhappiness and to have created yet a third party that is both anti-national and anti-religion. The appearance of this new party causes us to forget once and for all the names of Liberal and Conservative to join together in eternal unity.[255]

However, the local military forces that had either fought against Walker or deserted his cause had been dispersed into disparate groups, plainly incapable of subjecting 'the Falange' to a decisive defeat. Rivas was, then, obliged to accept a need long recognised by the Conservatives – that of inviting an invasion by the armies of the other Central American states, which were not ideologically allied (except against Walker), and in the case of Costa Rica distinctly unsympathetic to both Nicaraguan factions. Rivas had helped to revive a nationalist rhetoric, but the strategic reality of the region encouraged the type of 'domino theory' urged by Ponciano Corral and Tomás Manning; and in the 1850s this was made much more telling by internal collapse than it would be in the 1900s (Zelaya against Chamorro), 1930s (Sandino against Somoza) or the 1980s (the Sandinistas against the Contras).

Having descended upon Nicaragua in the name of civilisation, free trade and democracy, Walker was now obliged to reveal his political hand fully. Elections had already been called for three days at the end of June before Rivas decided to desert the cause. Accordingly, on the last day of the month Wheeler reported to Marcy, 'nearly a unanimous vote has been given for William Walker', although the secretary of state also received an account of the poll from the opposition in León that was disturbingly plausible:

> The *Nicaragüense*, no. 36 of 12 July, published a list of votes, fabricated at Granada by the adventurer William Walker, assisted by two or three unnatural Sons of Nicaragua to bear out his claim to the presidency. Under the pretext of so solemn an imposture he claims for himself 15,835 votes, but in the absence of statistical facts he does not lay down all the

---

254. Message to the Senate, 15 May 1856, quoted in Burns, *Patriarch and Folk*, p. 201.
255. Quoted in ibid., p. 203.

population of the Republic [and] he presupposes others.... The whole list is but a tissue of imposture and fraud, but as so brave-faced a proceeding may meet with some credence abroad [I am instructed to tell you that] the acts are mere fictions.[256]

In his own book Walker glosses quickly over the details of the matter, not least because he had dismissed earlier polls as being flawed by the turmoil in the country. However, at the time, the *Nicaragüense* rather artfully introduced the concept of mass democracy by allowing some 8,000 votes of those counted not to be cast in favour of the American, who himself claimed only a 'large majority', rather than Wheeler's 'nearly unanimous vote'.[257] Fraud is too narrow a word for Walker's theatre, which now naturally moved on in the form of an inaugural address, duly delivered on 12 July:

> The principles which shall guide me in the administration both of the foreign and domestic affairs of the government are few and simple. To allow the utmost liberty of speech and action compatible with order and good government, shall be the leading idea of my political conduct. Therefore the greatest possible freedom of trade will be established, with the view of making Nicaragua what nature intended her to be – the highway for commerce between two oceans. And with this freedom will come the arts of civilization which grows and increases by the wants and necessities it itself creates.[258]

This line – quite standard Southern fare of the time – possessed a certain logic, even if it was, by the stage Walker enunciated it, impossible for him to apply beyond Granada and the steamer terminals at Virgin Bay on the lake and San Juan del Sur. More serious in terms of practical activity was the acceleration of the confiscation of lands belonging to 'enemies of the state', whose numbers had themselves naturally accelerated with Walker's election and who would expand further still when, on 12 September, the two political parties finally signed a pact to expel the filibusterers. Perhaps it was this move that finally encouraged Walker to reintroduce into Nicaragua slavery, which had been abolished in the municipality of Granada as early as 1811. John Wheeler, the one person who might have held Walker back from this move, on the grounds that (even under a Democratic presidency) it would totally jeopardise relations with Washington, signally failed to do so. Indeed, a week after the decree was published Wheeler wrote to Marcy that Nicaragua could 'never be developed without slave labor. This therefore is an important and necessary decree.'[259] Moreover, Walker was now absolutely pledged to slavery as a socio-economic system:

> With the negro-slave as his companion, the white man would become fixed to the soil; and they together would destroy the power of the mixed race which is the bane of the country. The pure Indian would readily fall into the new social organization; for he does not aim at

---

256. Wheeler, Granada, to Marcy, 30 June 1856; Salinas, León, to Marcy, 1 Aug. 1856, in Manning (ed.), *Diplomatic Correspondence*, IV, pp. 537; 550.
257. *War in Nicaragua*, p. 228; Burns, *Patriarch and Folk*, p. 203.
258. Enclosed in Wheeler, Granada, to Marcy, 15 July 1856, in Manning (ed.), *Diplomatic Correspondence*, IV, p. 545.
259. Wheeler, Granada, to Marcy, 30 Sept. 1856, quoted in Burns, *Patriarch and Folk*, p. 208.

political power, and only asks to be protected in the fruits of his industry.... The advantage of negro slavery in Nicaragua would, therefore, be two-fold; while it would furnish certain labor for the use of agriculture, it would tend to separate the races and destroy the half-castes who cause the disorder, which has prevailed in the country since independence.

Not only was he now prepared for the Northern opposition to his measure; he seems almost to have relished it as a vindication of his argument that the seizure of power in Nicaragua was an extension of the sectional dispute within the USA:

> ... the manner in which the free labor democracy of the North received the decree re-establishing slavery in Nicaragua is proof of the hollowness of its professions of friendship for Southern interests. There was scarcely a voice raised in defense of the measure north of the Potomac; though the free-labor States may find, when it is too late, that the only way to avoid revolution, and a conflict of force between the Northern and Southern states of the Union, is by the very policy Nicaragua proposed to establish.[260]

These lines were written after John Brown's raid on Harper's Ferry – the last major slavery-related crisis before Lincoln's election – and so they might be treated as more extensively self-serving than the rest of Walker's apologia. However, at the time of the decree he was clear that it meant that any annexation of Nicaragua which might take place could not be with the North or the Union as a whole. Accordingly, he sent his Cuban ally Domingo de Goicoura as an emissary to London,

> to explain that the necessities of Nicaragua required 'a republic based on military principles', such a republic being clearly unfit for admission into the northern Union. The English would readily perceive the growth of such a republic towards the southern limits of the United States would tend to restrain the territorial extension of the latter power. Walker conceived that by such a policy he would promote the welfare of his native no less than his adopted country; for the acquisition by the United States of any territory covered by a Spanish American population would be fertile of troubles and dangers to the confederacy ... above all, the acquisition of territory on the south would be fatal to the slaveholding States; for it would complete the circle of free-labor communities now girdling them on almost every side.[261]

Even in retrospect this was wishful thinking of the highest order. Although he was not to know it until several weeks after the slavery decree was issued, London and Washington were now acting together in a belated effort to deal with Walker, resolve the Mosquito question, and clear up the anomalies left by the Clayton–Bulwer treaty. In August George Dallas, who had been sent as a special envoy to London by Marcy, had agreed a draft treaty on Central America with Clarendon. The recent British role in the Nicaraguan debacle had been modest, and it was the Pierce administration that made the opening offer in conceding that the British colony in Belize was not included in the stipulations of the 1850 treaty, on the understanding that the Bay Islands – generally considered as its dependencies – would revert to Honduras.

---

260. *War in Nicaragua*, pp. 261–2, 265.
261. Ibid., pp. 268–9.

The key outstanding issue, then, was the extent and status of the Mosquito Shore and Greytown. Once again, no representative of Nicaragua participated in the negotiation of a treaty to which that state had necessarily to become a party. On the other hand, given the chaos that reigned inside the country in mid 1856, such an absence was more understandable than in 1850 or 1852. Despite the fall-out of the *Cyane* affair and Kinney's subsequent antics, Dallas and Clarendon agreed to retain Greytown as a 'free town (though under the sovereign authority of the Republic)', self-governing in every respect, with religious freedom, trial by jury and subject to no fiscal regime other than that established by its elected representatives. Washington haggled somewhat over the setting at the Rio Coco/Wanx as the northern frontier of the Mosquito country, but the western limit was quickly fixed at 84° 15', and the southern as starting at the Rio Rama, which opens into Bluefields Lagoon. Within these limits, which amounted to over 5 million acres, it was agreed that

> the Mosquito Indians ... shall enjoy the right to make, by their national Council or Councils, and to carry into effect all such laws as they may deem necessary for the government and protection of all persons within the same, and of all property therein belonging to their people or to such persons who have connected themselves with them. Their rights of property and of local government within the territory ... shall be recognised, affirmed and guaranteed by the Republic of Nicaragua in Treaties to be made by that State with Great Britain and the United States. The Mosquito Indians shall not be able to cede their territory or rights to any other State without the consent of Great Britain and the United States, by each separately expressed; it being, however, understood, that nothing shall preclude the consolidation of such voluntary compact and arrangements between the Republic of Nicaragua and the Mosquito Indians by which the latter may be definitively incorporated and united with the former.[262]

In some ways this was a step backwards from Webster–Crampton for the USA – Greytown was not to be transferred back to Nicaragua and those private concessions previously made on the Shore were now guaranteed, provided they fell within the limits now more clearly demarcated than ever before. However, the Democrats were signing up to the same partnership they had repudiated in 1853. There was no talk of any Mosquito monarchy and no permitted transfer of territory to other states, but also there was no force in Nicaragua capable of rejecting this imposition of the reservation option in the same way as the Conservatives had done four years earlier. The objection came from a different quarter: the US Senate, which the Democratic executive could not persuade to accept one apparently minor feature of the Dallas–Clarendon accord – that the Bay Islands would retain a self-governing status in the same fashion as the Mosquito Shore and Greytown. In April 1857, when a British general election gave Palmerston a majority of eighty-five, London rejected the Senate's amendment on this point, and the treaty therefore fell. At that stage, though, the precise status of British dependencies in the Caribbean seemed to be thoroughly marginal compared to the final struggle for the control of inland Nicaragua.

---

262. Article III, *BFSP, 1856–57*, XLVII, London 1865, pp. 677ff.

Walker's enterprise rested centrally upon the presumption that racial difference could only be resolved through the imposition of the strongest through force:

> They are but drivellers who speak of establishing fixed relations between the pure white American race, as it exists in the United States, and the mixed Hispano-Indian race, as it exists in Mexico and Central America, without the employment of force. The history of the world presents no such Utopian vision as that of an inferior race yielding meekly and peacefully to the controlling influence of a superior people. Whenever barbarism and civilization, or two distinct forms of civilization, meet the result must be war.[263]

On occasions, as with Parker French, Walker was prepared to admit that his men were hardly the best standard-bearers for civilization. When, shortly after Cole's defeat at San Jacinto in September 1856, some 200 new men landed from New York,

> they showed from the beginning how worthless they were for military duty. A very large proportion of them were Europeans of the poorest class, mostly Germans who cared more for the contents of their haversacks than of their cartridge-boxes. With the exception of Captain Russell and Lieutenants Nagle and Northedge, the officers were as trifling as the men; and these New York volunteers, as they called themselves, had not been in the country ten days before they began to desert in numbers. The promise of free quarters and rations seemed to have carried the most of them to Nicaragua; and the idea of performing duty could scarcely have entered their minds when they left the United States. Of course, such trash as these men proved to be far worse than no men at all; for their vices and corruptions tainted the good materials near them.[264]

Nevertheless, Walker placed a considerable store on appearances, and any new bunch of recruits could be used to show up mestizo vanity:

> The night before the recruits arrived a bearer of despatches from San Salvador, Colonel Padilla, had reached Granada; and on the morning of the 9th, dressed in a ludicrous uniform, and wearing a cocked hat he had brought all the way over the mountains from Cojutepeque, he sallied forth on a visit to the general-in-chief. The new men had just reached the Plaza, and were drawn up as to show their numbers to best advantage, when Padilla entered the general's quarters. The surprise of the San Salvadorian, at the sight of so many strange-looking men, was equal to the amazement the Americans found in his long, lank person, run into trowsers too short for his legs, and with the chest and arms tightly encased in a small military coat, buttoned up to the throat, and obstinate in the habit of slipping its lower edges above the pit of the stomach.[265]

Although Walker was no admirer of uniform, he was very keen on rank, and throughout the two-year campaign he refused to be drawn into anything resembling a guerrilla strategy. His insistence upon concentrating forces for formal engagements might have yielded a small-scale version of the success enjoyed by the Anglo-Americans in Mexico had the quality of his troops and ordnance been better and if he himself had possessed a modicum of the skill displayed by Taylor and Scott a decade earlier.

---

263. *War in Nicaragua*, p. 430.
264. Ibid., p. 287.
265. Ibid., pp. 179–80.

He had, though, never been trained as an officer, and even in the mid 1850s the advances in weaponry were still too slight to give the Americans a marked advantage:

> The night was dark and dismal, the rain falling now slowly and like a heavy mist, then rapidly and in drops nearly as big as a revolver bullet; but the men stood to their places, sheltering themselves under the large trees which cover the sides of the hill, and being careful to keep their cartridge-boxes dry, drawing them, for this purpose, to the front part of the belt, and bending over so as to protect the precious powder with their bodies.[266]

Moreover, although at the end of the campaign Walker boasted of the fact that his men had cast the first Central American cannonballs, this was an achievement in adversity, and it mattered much more that the 'Falange' could not press home the advantages of possessing artillery shells:

> From time to time Captain Schwartz tried to throw shells into the main Plaza, but the fuses were too short-timed, and the shells, for the most part, burst in the air. Besides the unfitness of the fuses, one of the howitzers was dismounted after a few discharges, and the carriage of the other was ill-adapted for its purposes.[267]

However, news of an enterprise such as the filibuster of Nicaragua was bound to attract some men of capacity and ruthlessness, especially in the wake of the 1848 revolutions and the Crimean War, which threw a great many jobbing warriors onto the open market. Walker's prize catch from this contingent was Charles Frederick Henningsen, a forty-year-old Briton of Belgian origin who had served in the Carlist wars in Spain and with Kossuth in the Hungarian revolution of 1848, accompanying the radical leader on his 1851 tour of the USA. Like Walker, Henningsen had a keen pen, and by the time he arrived in Nicaragua in October 1856, he had written eight books on his experiences. More importantly, he arrived with a large consignment of muskets that had been converted into Minié rifles, thanks to a donation of $30,000 from his new wife Williamina ('Belt') Connelly, the daughter of a leading Georgia family. Henningsen, then, brought the experience and equipment that was previously lacking and might have turned the war in Walker's favour. But he came too late and with too little, being able only to hold Granada against the accumulating Central American forces, which closed on the filibuster capital in the last week of November 1856.

Had Walker entertained the prospect of an irregular campaign he might have escaped the inevitable pincer movement by the Salvadorean and Guatemalan forces to the north and the Costa Ricans to the south (although his men would have been readily identifiable in the countryside, and by this stage small boys were brave enough to shout directly at the Anglo-Americans, '*Quieren por Walker? Yo no quiero al filibustero god-damn*'[268]). Henningsen held out for over a fortnight, but the breakdown of his

---

266. Ibid., p. 103.
267. Ibid., p. 292.
268. Burns, *Patriarch and Folk*, p. 214.

casualties indicates the real nature of the trap into which he had been locked: of his 419 men, 120 died of cholera and typhus, 110 were killed or wounded, some 40 deserted, and 2 were taken prisoner.[269] After a failed effort to relieve the city on 12 December, Walker ordered his commander to fire the centre of the town prior to evacuating it with his remaining men. Walker claims lamely that this was designed to revitalise the conflict between the Conservatives and Liberals, the latter still hating the city, but he had to acknowledge that

> it has been denounced as an act of vandalism, useless in its consequences to the authority which ordered it. As to the justice of the act, few can question it; for its inhabitants owed life and property to the Americans in the service of Nicaragua, and yet they joined the enemies who strove to drive their protectors from Central America. They served the enemies of Nicaragua in the most criminal manner; for they acted as spies on the Americans, who had defended their interests, and sent notice of all their movements to the Allies. By the laws of war, the town had forfeited its existence; and the policy of destroying it was as manifest as the justice of the measure.[270]

Henningsen had driven home the purely punitive motive of an incendiarism that razed seven churches by leaving a notice stuck on a lance: '*Aqui fue Granada*' ('Here was Granada'). Yet to conduct such a scorched-earth campaign without greatly superior resources was to ensure defeat, and although Walker held on – not least by dint of requisitioned steamers – for another six months, he was always in retreat, and had it not been for the virtually continuous presence of US and British warships in San Juan del Sur in the first half of 1857 he would – like most of the filibusters – have surely lost his life.

The penultimate scene of Alex Cox's portrait of Walker has the most striking anachronism of the whole film – the landing of a helicopter to rescue the surrounded US forces. Walker (Ed Harris, who a decade later would take the part of Prospero in Peter Weir's *The Truman Show*) staunchly refuses to be taken off, shouting that he is 'President of Nicaragua'. These are also the words with which Cardenal closes the curtain on him, on the beach at Trujillo. The fact is that Walker lived for three years after his humiliating evacuation from San Juan del Sur on the USS *St Mary's*, trying several times to get back to the isthmus. Many responded to his enterprise in the same vein as Lewis Cass, who would shortly become Buchanan's secretary of state:

> I am free to confess that the heroic effort of our countrymen in Nicaragua elicits my admiration, while it engages all my solicitude. I am not deterred from the expression of these feelings by sneers, or reproaches, or hard words.... The difficulties which General Walker has encountered and overcome will place his name high on the roll of the distinguished men of his age.[271]

---

269. *War in Nicaragua*, p. 339.
270. Ibid., p. 340.
271. *New York Times*, 24 May 1856, quoted in Burns, *Patriarch and Folk*, p. 281.

Others, like Horace Greeley, were markedly less impressed: 'In his whole career we look in vain for a single act of wisdom or foresight. All the successes he had he owed to the total exhaustion of the Nicaraguan population by civil war, and the desire for peace at any price.'[272]

There now seems to be agreement that Walker's insistence that he was a Central American president and not a US citizen was directed at the captain of HMS *Icarus*, which had rescued him off the coast of Honduras in September 1860, when a further effort to invade the region had collapsed in bloody confusion within weeks. Walker's remonstration was elicited by the captain's offer of safe passage to New Orleans. As a result, the commander – whose rare name of Norvell was the same as that of Walker's mother – handed him over to the Honduran forces, who shot him. No protest was ever lodged by the US government.

Walker had received particularly strong support from the transplanted exiles of Young Ireland John Mitchel and Thomas Meagher, for whom the adventurer from Tennessee had represented not only an ally in the struggle against the British but also 'a brave soldier of republicanism.... Nicaragua shall be free! The Democracy of America increased!'[273] Upon his return to the USA in 1857 Walker was warmly interviewed by Mitchel in New Orleans, and the radical Irishman also struck up a literary acquaintance in New York with Henningsen. Young Johnnie Mitchel was all set to join Henningsen's next campaign – to 'colonise' the Mexican state of Sonora – before the State Department forced its cancellation.[274]

However, it was Meagher who had become particularly enamoured of Central America, following the gift from Vanderbilt of a free passage from New York to San Francisco in 1853. Meagher threw himself wholeheartedly into support for the filibuster cause, risking powerful political friendships in the process despite the fact that he had not yet obtained either a pardon from the British or citizenship from the Americans. In February 1857, having recently graduated in law, he volunteered to act as defence attorney for 'Colonel' Farbins, Walker's 'Director of Colonisation', who had been arrested in New York for violation of the 1818 Neutrality Act. Facing down the outgoing president, Pierce, and his attorney-general, Caleb Cushing, Meagher threatened to produce incriminating documents in court unless the charges were withdrawn. Cushing called his bluff, and Meagher duly presented a letter from Pierce's private secretary Sydney Webster 'reporting a peculiar interest in Nicaraguan lands and colonization' as well as a deed transferring lands confiscated from Walker's enemies to

272. Quoted in Scroggs, *Filibusters and Financiers*, p. 306.

273. Meagher's *Irish News* quoted in Thomas Keneally, *The Great Shame: A Story of the Irish in the Old World and the New*, London 1998, p. 303.

274. In 1857 Henningsen had settled in his wife's home state of Georgia, perhaps knowing that for the first time in his life trouble would come looking for him. In 1861 he joined the Confederate forces, serving as a colonel in the 59th Virginia infantry, but his record was far from distinguished and he resigned at the end of 1862. He spent his last years destitute in the capital, dying in 1877 and being buried in the congressional cemetery.

Webster. The government could not plausibly deny that it was involved in the filibuster well beyond the diplomatic formalism enunciated by Pierce the previous year. Farbins left the court a free man, Pierce's embarrassment over the Nicaraguan affair intensified further still at the very death of his presidency, and Meagher, whose legal and journalistic career was otherwise in the doldrums, set his cap firmly towards the Latin section of the continent.

In January 1857, with Buchanan recently elected but not yet inaugurated, Meagher had succumbed to the lures of office: 'my disinclination to "place-hunting" no longer exists.... The same feelings which induced me to regard such gifts with contempt and emnity in Ireland, operate in a contrary direction here. I would rejoice and feel proud in serving the American Republic.' On this basis Meagher, who would only obtain his citizenship in May, proposed to the incoming president that he might be sent as an envoy to Quito, Bogotá, Guatemala, Honduras or even Rio. Despite the generous choice of offer, Buchanan, whose father hailed from Donegal, was astute enough to annotate the petition – 'incompatible with national interest'.[275]

As a result, Meagher returned to Central America in the spring of 1858 as a private US citizen, protesting hotly in Mitchel's Knoxville paper *Southern Citizen* that his visit to Costa Rica had no political purpose and was being undertaken with purely literary, botanical and artistic objectives. In making this trip Meagher was certainly courting risk because he was well known as a supporter of Walker, of whom the Costa Ricans had been first and fiercest enemies. In the event, the Irishman's letters of introduction to President Mora and the country's archbishop were well received, and he attended a presidential ball in a new suit. On the other hand, Meagher was depressed and annoyed to discover that the true purpose of his expedition – to reopen the search for a trans-isthmian route under US control – was under direct threat from Félix Belly, the French adventurer who had picked up on Louis Napoleon's enthusiasm for the same project and reached San José some two months earlier (although it was far from clear whether Belly carried any official French appointment or instructions).[276]

Belly had become interested in the idea of a canal after reading reports of the bombardment of Greytown by the *Cyane*. Recognising that any route depended upon an agreed and secure border between Nicaragua and Costa Rica, the Frenchman had purposefully cultivated the new Conservative president of Nicaragua, Tomás Martínez, playing quite a prominent role in the signing of a treaty between the two countries in April 1858 whereby Nicaragua was confirmed in its ownership and control of the San Juan river but pledged to allow Costa Rica unencumbered access to it. At the same time, in the face of fears about renewed filibuster incursions, Belly prompted the two states to apply to Great Britain and France for guarantees of protection.

---

275. Meagher, New York, to Buchanan, 28 Jan. 1857; Buchanan's annotation dated 15 March 1857, quoted in Keneally, *The Great Shame*, p. 305.
276. Cyril Allen, 'Félix Belly: Nicaraguan Canal Promoter', *HAHR*, 38:1, 1957, pp. 48–9.

Even though Belly's politico-speculative activities were taking in the not inconsid-
erable services of Irish patriots like the O'Gorman Mahon, they represented a serious
challenge for Meagher. Perhaps, though, he sensed that Belly lacked the money to
fund the concession that he had obtained. Meagher's description of the Frenchman
does suggest that he was less than impressed by appearances: 'Closely-shaved head,
finikin figure, spy-glass and spiderlike legs ... exquisitely booted and gloved ... bowing
himself constantly into profuse perspirations.'[277] Certainly, between these two men
transplanted to the tropics by ambition there was little of the affection evoked in verse
by another Belli – Gioconda:

> And there is reborn
> the excuse to speak your name
> in the wet night,
> gentle and humid ...
> and I return to the girl
> who will hear histories
> of like nights in Nicaragua.[278]

Beaten to the post, Meagher, who ruefully referred to the 'casus Belly', dedicated
himself to the avowed ends of his trip, although he did lend support to two Irish boys
from New York who had served under Walker and were being cared for by a Dr
Hogan in his San José home because of the severe ulcers they had picked up in the
last weeks of the campaign.

Belly, however, overplayed his hand in encouraging Mora and Martínez to redouble
their defences against filibustering. This was of slight consequence when limited to
the new Nicaraguan Penal Code Concerning Traitors, which identified any Nicaraguans 'who aided, abetted and allied with foreigners' in 'making war detrimental to
the national security of the Republic, whether it compromises independence, the
constitution or liberty' – terms broad enough to be comparable with the statute
under which Meagher himself had been tried in 1848. However, when the presidents
publicly cited at some length the misdeeds of the USA in Central America and
expressed their trepidation about the future, there was little chance that Washington
would take a relaxed view about Belly's activities, official or otherwise. Days after the
joint proclamation he rushed to Washington in an effort to explain to Buchanan how
his concession was not a breach of the Monroe Doctrine. In that he failed, but so also
did he fail to raise the funds to finance his canal project, only narrowly evading arrest

---

277. 'Holidays in Costa Rica', *Harper's New Monthly Magazine*, XX, Dec. 1859, Jan.–Feb. 1860, pp. 151–
61. Lord Napier, the British ambassador in Washington, found Belly to be, 'a person of great intelligence
but also of prodigious volubility and impetuosity. It is difficult not to be interested in his speculative
enthusiasm, while it is apparent that he is ill-fitted to conduct a negotiation in which patience and discretion are equally necessary.' Napier, Washington, to Malmesbury, 10 July 1858, quoted in Allen, 'Félix
Belly', p. 52.
278. 'Y...' (1974), in *El Ojo de la Mujer*, Madrid 1995, p. 45. Gioconda Belli moved from Nicaragua to
California in the 1990s.

for debt when he returned from the USA to France by escaping to El Salvador via Algeria. Belly, who returned to the region one last time in 1868, was, like Kinney, an adventurous freelancer capable of causing great nuisance rather than a resourceful entrepreneur able to realise the dream of transforming the isthmus. Yet his nautical illusions were always closer to the material world than were those of Louis Althusser, and he resisted all temptations to surrender his dream – even when the boiler of a steamer crossing the lake blew up, sinking the ship and leaving him in a lifeboat for three days and nights whilst his engineers and surveyors, wracked with yellow fever and believing the pioneer to be dead, struck camp and prepared to return to France. Belly was one of those people who apparently never stop of their own volition.[279]

Belly's failure helped to clear the space for the efforts of the British to regularise their position on the Mosquito Shore – finally effected not by treaty with the USA but directly with Nicaragua and Honduras in 1860 through agreements that would last until the 1890s (the regular passage of steamers through Nicaraguan waters was not resumed until 1864). It also gave Meagher an opportunity to try again. He returned to Costa Rica in 1859, this time bearing State Department documents and instructions, which helped him to persuade President Mora to settle the dispute that had blown up between the Panama Railroad Company and Meagher's new associate Ambrose Thompson, who had set up a Chiriqui Improvement Company to construct a rival trans-isthmian railway across Costa Rica. Once Mora had extracted promises that the US navy would make advance payments for the use of ports to be built on both coasts, the concession was approved, being rubber-stamped by the US Congress in July 1860. The exaltant Meagher set about surveying the Chiriqui route, albeit in a manner more rhetorical than trigonometrical: 'perfectly free of swamps – the writer having crossed from sea to sea without once wetting the sole of his shoe except, indeed, when he had to ford the rivers – not a dollar would have to be sunk, at any point, in the construction of artificial foundation'.[280]

The railway was not built, and the search to complement and compete with the Panama line continued. Amongst the most energetic of those engaged in that search was George Squier, who by the 1860s had set aside his Anglophobia and was promoting a railway across Honduras to British financiers on the grounds that, 'although *time*, not distance, is the true measure of the relation of places, yet as the saving of time depends more or less on the distance to be traversed, a shortening of distance must always be an important element'.[281]

---

279. *Félix Belly*, born Grenelle, Oct. 1816; brought up in Turin by his uncle, a priest. Married in Turin for three months; 1848, editor of *L'Impartial*, Rouen; *Des finances de la république*, Paris 1849; Constantinople correspondent of the *Morning Chronicle*, 1853; 1856–8 abortive effort to establish a museum of science in Paris; *A travers l'Amérique centrale: le Nicaragua et le canal interocéanique*, Paris 1867; supporter of the Paris Commune; professor of literature, University of Buenos Aires, 1873; afflicted by lupus of the face, he made two suicide attempts before dying in November 1878. The *Dictionnaire de Biographie Français* makes no mention of children in any spelling of his surname.
280. 'The New Route through Chiriqui', *Harper's New Monthly Magazine*, XXI, Jan. 1861.
281. *Honduras; Descriptive, Historical and Statistical*, London 1870, p. 248.

Once more, the project would come to nought, preserving for decades a pre-industrial unhurried activity that Squier himself had depicted two decades earlier, although anticipating the presence of people like himself conveying an Anglo-American tempo:

> Here were women seated on little stools beside snow-white sheets, or in the center of a cordon of baskets, heaped with cacao or coffee, starch, sugar, and the more valuable articles of common use; here a group with piles of hats of various patterns, hammocks, cotton, yarn, thread of pita, native blankets, petates, and other various articles which Yankees call 'dry goods'; here another group, with water jars, plates and candlesticks of native pottery; there a sillero or saddler exposed the products of his art, the zapatero cried his shoes, the herrero his machetes, bits for horses, and other articles of iron; girls proclaimed their dulces, boys shouted parrots and monkeys, and in the midst of all a tall fellow stalked about bearing a wooden clock from Connecticut in his arms.[282]

---

282. *Nicaragua*, II, p. 431.

APPENDICES

APPENDIX I

THE COURSE OF THE MEXICAN–AMERICAN WAR

1845	Mar.	1	Tyler signs annexation of Texas.
		4	Polk inaugurated.
	June	3	Santa Anna leaves for exile in Cuba.
		7	Uprising against Herrera regime.
	July	25	General Taylor ordered to Corpus Christi.
	Dec.	15	General Paredes 'pronounces' against Herrera regime.
		30	Paredes takes power in Mexico City.
1846	Jan.	13	Taylor ordered to Rio Grande.
	Mar.	21	Slidell mission fails.
		28	Taylor reaches Rio Grande.
	Apr.	25	Mexican forces attack Thornton's detachment.
	May	8	Battle of Palo Alto.
		9	Battle of Resaca de la Palma.
		13	USA declares war.
		18	Taylor occupies Matamoros.
	June	5	Kearny starts march to New Mexico.
	July	4	Bear Flag republic declared in California.
		7	Sloat seizes Monterey.
		15	Paredes ousted from power.
	Aug.	12	Stockton occupies Los Angeles.
		16	Santa Anna returns from Cuban exile.
		18	Kearny occupies Santa Fe.
	Sept.	20–24	Battle of Monterrey.
	Oct.	29	Wool occupies Monclova.
	Nov.	16	Taylor occupies Saltillo.
		18	Scott appointed to command Veracruz expedition.
	Dec.	12	Kearny reaches San Diego.
		27	Doniphan occupies El Paso.
1847	Jan.	3	Scott withdraws regular troops from Taylor.
		8	*Californios* defeated at San Gabriel.
		10	Stockton reoccupies Los Angeles.
		11	Gómez Farías decrees seizure of Church property to fund war effort.
	Feb.	22–23	Battle of Buena Vista.
		27	Revolt of the '*polkos*' against Gómez Farías.
		28	Battle of Sacramento.
			Gómez Farías and *puros* removed from power.

Mar.	1	Doniphan occupies Chihuahua.
	9	Scott's expedition lands.
	29	Surrender of Veracruz.
Apr.	8	Scott's inland advance begins.
	15	Trist appointed peace commissioner.
	18	Battle of Cerro Gordo.
May	15	Worth occupies Puebla.
Aug.	19	Battle of Contreras.
	20	Battle of Churubusco.
Sept.	8	Battle of Molina del Rey.
	13	Battle of Chapultepec.
	14	Scott occupies Mexico City.
	16	Santa Anna relinquishes presidency.
Oct.	6	Polk recalls Trist.
Nov.	16	Trist receives recall order.
Dec.	4	Trist decides to continue negotiating.

1848	Jan.	13	Polk relieves Scott of his command.
	Feb.	2	Treaty of Guadalupe Hidalgo signed.
	June	12	US troops evacuate Mexico City.

Appendix 2

The Mosquito Shore and Nicaragua, 1844–60

1844 Apr. Patrick Walker appointed British consul-general to Mosquito protectorate.

1845 Jan. León sacked; first Conservative president of Nicaragua takes office.
Fruto Chamorro's tax on *aguardiente* (liquor) provokes popular uprisings.

      May Mosquito Prince George Augustus Frederick taken from Bluefields to Belize on HMS *Hyacinth* and crowned king.
Coffee introduced into Nicaragua.

1846 Apr. US and Mexican forces clash on Rio Grande.

      May USA declares war on Mexico.

      June Palmerston pronounces the settlement of the Oregon frontier at the 49th parallel 'equally favourable to both parties'.

      July Managua raised to status of city.

      Oct. Consul Walker obtains repeal of land grants improperly obtained from Mosquito government by Shepherd brothers.

1847 Mar. US forces land at Veracruz.

      June Palmerston decides to fix southern limit of Mosquito kingdom at the San Juan river, bordering Costa Rica.

      Sept. Fall of Mexico City to US forces.

      Oct. HMS *Alarm* advises Nicaraguan authorities at San Juan del Norte that Mosquito sovereignty will be assumed there on 1 Jan. 1848.

1848 Jan. British troops occupy San Juan del Norte/Greytown (1st), which is retaken by Nicaraguan forces from León under Col. Salas a week later; the British return (25th) and advance up the San Juan river.

      Feb. Patrick Walker drowned in San Juan river, leaving political vacuum; British forces under Capt. Loch occupy San Carlos on Lake Nicaragua;
Treaty of Guadalupe Hidalgo between Mexico and USA.

      Mar. Armistace between British and Nicaraguan forces; Greytown remains in Mosquito hands.

      June British minister to Central America, Chatfield, and new consul to the Mosquito protectorate, Christie, agree that annexation is preferable to a protectorate.

      Nov. Palmerston instructs Chatfield to oppose any US efforts towards a Central American alliance threatening status of Mosquitia; he informs Christie that London wants no new colonies.

      Dec. Palmerston considers establishment of British naval refitting station for the Pacific squadron at San Juan del Sur.

1849   Mar.   Zachary Taylor inaugurated president of USA.

   June   Squier replaces Hise as US agent in Central America; Christie leaves post as British consul to Mosquito coast.

   Aug.   Vanderbilt signs contract with Nicaragua for canal route proposed to have Atlantic terminal at San Juan del Norte.

   First group of Anglo-Americans cross Nicaragua *en route* for California.

   Oct.   HMS *Plumper* enters Trujillo in demand of reparations for mahogany supplies seized by Honduran authorities from Belizean lumber companies.

   Chatfield directs seizure of Tiger Island by HMS *Gorgon*; disavowed by London.

   Nov.   Squier drafts and agrees 'Chinandega Pact' of Nicaragua, Honduras, El Salvador, to oppose British influence; disavowed by Washington.

1850   Jan.   Squier directs US-backed seizure of Tiger Island; disavowed by Washington.

   April   Clayton–Bulwer treaty signed in Washington (19th).

   July   President Taylor dies; replaced by Vice-President Fillmore.

   Spain recognises Nicaragua.

   Sept.   California admitted as a state of the Union.

   Nov.   Palmerston accepts privately that Greytown, now declared a 'free port', should eventually be ceded to Nicaragua.

1851   Jan.   British naval commanders in Jamaica oppose permanent military presence on Mosquito Shore.

   Steamer service inaugurated on Lake Nicaragua.

   July   Vanderbilt opens steamer service from New York to San Francisco via Greytown.

   Sept.   London abolishes post of consul-general to Mosquito Shore.

   Nov.   HMS *Express* fires shot across bow of US steamer *Prometheus* on San Juan river for non-payment of port dues at Greytown.

1852   Feb.   Managua made permanent capital of Nicaragua.

   Lord John Russell's ministry resigns after criticism from Palmerston; replaced by minority Conservative administration headed by Lord Derby.

   Mar.   Americans displace British leadership of Greytown town council.

   Establishment of British Colony of Bay Islands surprises Foreign Office.

   April   Webster–Crampton convention on Mosquito coast; rejected by Nicaragua.

   Chatfield replaced as British chargé to Central America.

   Dec.   Derby ministry replaced by Whig–Peelite coalition headed by Aberdeen.

1853   Mar.   Democrats return to power in Washington under presidency of Franklin Pierce.

   Conflict between Greytown council and Accessory Transit Company.

   April   Fruto Chamorro becomes supreme director.

   June   British Mediterranean fleet ordered off Dardanelles after Russian threats against Turkey.

   July   Buchanan sent to London as US ambassador.

1854   Jan.   Constitutional convention in Nicaragua; Liberal leaders go into exile; republic declared.

            Mar.   Britain and France declare war on Russia.

            Apr.   Washington presses Madrid to sell Cuba (for $130 million) following seizure of US ship *Black Warrior* at Havana for violating customs regulations.

            May   Nicaraguan Liberals land at Realejo; regional/civil war (*Guerra Nacional*) starts.

            June   US–British treaty of reciprocity reduces tension in Canada.

            July   Greytown bombarded and destroyed by USS *Cyane*.

            Aug.   Clarendon tells Crampton that the *Cyane* affair is 'an outrage without parallel in the annals of modern times'.

            Sept.   Franco-British force lands in Crimea.

            Oct.   'Ostend Manifesto' by US diplomats threatening force if Spain refuses to sell Cuba provokes European backlash; disavowed by Washington.

            Dec.   Castellón signs contract with Byron Cole for 200 US filibusterers under William Walker.

1855   Feb.   Palmerston, leading coalition, succeeds Aberdeen as prime minister; Bright urges peace in Crimea.

                    Nicaraguan Liberals lift siege of Granada after thirty-four weeks.

            June   Walker lands at Realejo with fifty-eight men; defeated by Conservatives at Rivas.

            Aug.   British drop complaints about *Cyane* affair.

                    US filibusterer Kinney lands at Greytown.

            Sept.   Sebastopol falls to British and French troops.

            Oct.   Walker captures Granada and sets up provisional government under Patricio Rivas.

            Nov   Walker executes Minister of War Corral for treason.

                    Guatemala approaches Britain and France to explore protectorate status.

1856   Feb.   Walker revokes Vanderbilt concession.

            Mar.   Treaty of Paris confirms peace between Russia and allies.

                    Walker's forces defeated by Costa Ricans at Santa Rosa (20th); repulsed from Rivas.

            May   Washington recognises Rivas government.

            June   Rivas declares Walker a traitor (25th); Walker stages and wins presidential poll (29th).

                    Palmerston considers deploying Royal Navy off Greytown.

            July   Walker inaugurated president of Nicaragua (12th); Cole defeated and hanged at San Jacinto (14th).

            Sept.   Slavery reintroduced to Nicaragua; Liberals join Conservatives against Walker.

                    Costa Rica and Nicaragua approach Britain and France for arms and protectorate status.

            Oct.   Clarendon–Dallas convention for British withdrawal from Mosquitia: establishment of its reservation status within Nicaragua; retention of Belize as a colony; transfer of the Bay Islands to Honduras.

Nov.   Walker's forces beaten back from Masaya.

Dec.   Walker evacuates Granada, destroying a large part of the town, including seven churches.

1857   Mar.   US Senate amends Clarendon–Dallas accord to cancel self-governing status of Bay Islands.

Buchanan inaugurated as US president, leading Democrat administration.

Apr.   British general election gives Palmerston a majority of 85.

London rejects amendments to Clarendon–Dallas accord, which fails.

May   Walker defeated at third Battle of Rivas, surrenders to USS *St Mary's* and is returned to USA; *Guerra Nacional* ends; Nicaragua ruled by joint executive.

Nov.   US warship prevents Walker landing in Nicaragua; he is later acquitted of violating neutrality act.

Dec.   Palmerston privately accepts US superiority in Central America.

1858   Feb.   Derby replaces Palmerston as prime minister.

Apr.   Treaty of limits between Nicaragua and Costa Rica, which obtains Guanacaste.

1859   June   Palmerston returns as prime minister; Gladstone is foreign secretary.

Nov.   Agreement for transfer of Bay Islands by London to Honduras in July 1860.

1860   Jan.   Treaty of Managua under which London surrenders all claims on Mosquito Shore, which becomes a reservation ruled by hereditary chieftain within limits of Nicaragua.

June   Walker leaves Mobile with sixty men to separate Bay Islands from Honduras.

Aug.   Walker declares himself president of Honduras in Trujillo.

Sept.   Walker surrenders to HMS *Icarus* (3rd), is handed over to Honduran authorities, who execute him (12th).

THANKS

This text is much the poorer for the fact that two clocks stopped before it was completed. They belonged to very different experts in marking time. Nick Richardson had a tongue that was far too sharp to hold down a job and a mind that feasted freely on the comfortably spoon-fed. David Cox was the epitome of the gentle don, always on the look-out for a shaft of wisdom in the midst of Oxbridge cleverness. Over eighty years of scholarship these two brilliant men published just one book and three scholarly articles between them, which puts the expansive expression of the present work into proper and sober perspective. Each of them, however, had convinced me that the Americas of 1850 would have been just as recognisable from the standpoint of 150 years earlier as of 150 years later, albeit for different reasons and in different ways. 'Modernity' has a deeper reach and a more tenuous grasp than is often recognised by its heirs and successors.

I am most grateful to the British Academy and the Leverhulme Trust for a Senior Research Fellowship, which, awarded for an allied project, enabled the completion of the present one away from the demands of teaching. Leslie Bethell, Paul Preston and Trevor Smith were characteristically generous in their support for the endeavour and in enduring my efforts to describe it. None of them believes that explanation is the exclusive source of understanding or that understanding is best achieved through tidiness, but my exploration of old-fashioned structuralist preoccupations by taking such a leisurely meander across academic disciplines has certainly taxed their patient pluralism.

I owe apologies of a rather different type to the Coordinadora de Historia of Bolivia because, having accepted an invitation to present a paper on nineteenth-century liberalism to a 1994 conference it had organised in Sucre, I opted to chase more than one hare over a longer course and ducked out of that event. The volume resulting from it – Rossana Barragán, Dora Cajías and Seemin Qayum (eds), *El Siglo XIX: Bolivia y América Latina*, La Paz 1997 – is far too strong for this to matter, but there are few things in academic life more irritating than the vain and pusillanimous reneging on their conference commitments. I hope, then, that the editors and Ana María Lema will accept *en lieu* both the continental and the local offerings made here. Equally, I must register my thanks to René Arze Aguirre, then Director of the Archivo Nacional de Bolivia in that same capital, for his help in developing the strange case of Mariano Donato Muñoz.

Few are so temperamentally averse as Malcolm Deas to a 'condescension of posterity' that sees the past and the dead as little more than stepping stones to the glowing-future-that-is-us-in-the-uniquely-challenging-present. Amongst his peers, and no less dedicated to improving and enjoying the present, is Alex Wilde, who also shares a love for that peculiarly modern nineteenth-century country, Colombia. The general support of both men has encouraged me to undertake a project that they are too wise to have recommended, but they never quite knew what I was up to. The number of friends, colleagues and generous strangers who provided advice, comment, documents, illustrations or a ready ear is greater than I dare list, but I should register my gratitude to Anastasia Bermudez, Jorge Brun Sanjinés, Alberto Crespo Rodas, Ken Duncan, Angela Gruenberg, Lisa Jardine, Erick Langer, Marci López Levy, Harry Lubasz, H.C.F. Mansilla, Rory Miller, Maxine Molyneux, Guillermo Nañez Falcón, Brendan O'Cathaoir, David Parsons, Anne Pérotin-Dumon, Eduardo Posada-Carbó, Natalia Sobrevilla and Eduardo Trigo O'Connor d'Arlach.

Those who recognise the acronym 'RAE' will instantly understand why I offer thanks to my heads of department during the preparation of the present text – Raymond Kuhn at Queen Mary and Westfield College and Victor Bulmer-Thomas at the Institute of Latin American Studies. Both are friends but neither needed to be so brave and absolutely uncomplaining when they discovered that they weren't going to get a secure and sensible supplement to the scholarly corpus. Anna Hayes and Jasmin Salucideen, who know more than most about the processing of texts and handling of persons, ensured its arrival and integrity, whilst the library staffs of the University of London's School of Advanced Study – particularly those of the Institute of Advanced Legal Studies, the Institute of Historical Research and the Institute of Latin American Studies – were exemplary in their support. Mina Moshkeri drew beautiful maps to the vaguest of directions. The man who guides my own Institute, Tony Bell, has been generous and helpful so far beyond the call of duty that the very least I can do in recompense is to defenestrate myself from the cosily coded blue universe of DOS into the brave new world of iconic grey.

John King generously volunteered to peruse the whole before anyone else. The fact that his knowledge of Poe and Cooper is as deep as that of Borges and Martí – and that he knows how properly to present poetic translations – meant that I benefited hugely from his forgiving advice. Dylan Martínez sportingly tested the passages on time in between assignments in Afghanistan, Indonesia and Kosovo even as he laboured locally and subversively to transform me into a grandfather. Colin Robinson has for years urged me to 'write some stories', and although he definitely did not mean them to take such a peregrinatory form, I doubt that there could be another publisher for this book. The same goes for Robin Blackburn, whose learned commentary on the typescript dug out many errors and made a rich set of suggestions, some of which I have been sensible enough to follow. The debt I have incurred with the Verso team directly responsible for producing the book you have before you is no less great. Justin Dyer, Lucy Morton, Sophie Arditti and Jane Hindle, my editor, have been wonderfully professional colleagues, adding a great deal to the book and in no way to be held accountable for those blemishes they could not persuade me to banish from it.

Neil Belton immediately recognised the first draft of the text for what it was, even though he had something very different in mind at the outset. His knowledge of and sympathy for Hibernian Atlanticism means that we might well have a second, enjoyable dander through the same world. Sharon Duncan, enthusiastic proponent of that vision and ardent liver of that life from the hills above Drumquin to those around Jalapa, went with me on the coldest of Armagh days to find John Mitchel's tomb. Ana María Aguilar ensured that similar excursions to Tarija and Tarata did not descend into abject antiquarianism, sensibly invigilating visits to both cemeteries and archives. Her selfless pursuit of lost-cause references has been crucial in the reconstruction of the life and world of General Francisco Burdett O'Connor – a story that deserves a much fuller rendition than could be managed here. Although Penny Woolcock narrowly missed the dubious delights of a search for Daniel Clark's last resting place in New Orleans, I cannot thank her enough for the exceptional patience and good humour shown in the face of extreme and varied provocation during the genesis of the book. It is a marvel that she has contributed so much and remained so loyal to a project that drew as many neuroses as it did wondrous ghosts into a home where she deserved respite from the different loopiness that is the world of television. The errors and shortcomings in the preceding pages are, notwithstanding these several and substantial debts, all my own work.

PICTURE CREDITS

The author and publisher are grateful to the following institutions and individuals for the reproduction of images held by them.

'El Camuati': English Club, Buenos Aires. Squier: Latin American Library, Tulane University. Parisian barricades: Bibliothèque Historique de la Ville de Paris. Olmsted: National Park Service, Brookline, Massachusetts. Trollope, by Julia Margaret Cameron: National Portrait Gallery, London. Kahkewaquonaby, by David Octavius Hall: Amon Carter Museum. Little Six, by Shindler: Smithsonian Institution (3509–A). Kickapoo: Smithsonian Institution (741–A). Gaucho dwelling, by Samuel Boote: Hack Hoffenberg, New York. Young John Mitchel: courtesy of the *Irish Times*. Older John Mitchel: Brendan O'Cathaoir. Smith O'Brien and Meagher: Kilmainham Jail Museum. Meagher: Montana Historical Society, Helena. Broadway: US Army Military History Institute. Rio, by Augusto Stahl: Gilberto Ferrez Collection. Buenos Aires, by Benito Panunzi: Hack Hoffenberg, New York. Sarmiento, by Franklin Rawson: Museo Histórico Sarmiento. Alberdi, by William Helsby, Valparaiso 1851, and San Martín: Fundación Antorchas and Museo Histórico Nacional, Buenos Aires. Emerson, by Black: Concord Free Public Library. Thoreau, by Maxham: Concord Free Public Library. Prescott: Library of Congress, Washington D.C. (LC–USZ62–110154). Fuller: Courtesy, Museum of Fine Arts, Boston. Reproduced with permission. © 1999 Museum of Fine Arts, Boston. All Rights Reserved. 'La Saya y Manto': Archivo Courret, Biblioteca Nacional, Lima. Gauguin's descendents: Musée de Pont-Aven. Greeley, by Matthew Brady: Library of Congress, Washington D.C. (LC–USZ62–110105). Bolívar and Sucre: Archivo Nacional de Bolivia, Sucre. Jenny and Karl Marx: Instituut voor Sociale Geschiedenis, Amsterdam. Myra Clark Gaines: courtesy of The Historic New Orleans Collection. Taney: United States National Archives (111–B–4208). Justices of the Supreme Court, 1865: Library of Congress, Washington D.C. (LC–USZ62–9906). Canal Street, New Orleans: from the collection of the Louisiana State Museum. Douglass: Chester County Historical Society, West Chester, Pennsylvania. Slave advertisement: Chicago Historical Society (ICHi-22003). Slave family in Savannah: Collection of the New York Historical Society (50482). Gordon, a slave: US Army Military History Institute. Calhoun, by Mathew Brady: Beinecke Rare Book and Manuscript Library, Yale University. Webster: courtesy, Museum of Fine Arts, Boston. Reproduced with permission. © 1999 Museum of Fine Arts, Boston. All Rights Reserved. Carlyle, 1854: Rare Book and Manuscript Library, Columbia University. Palmerston: National Portrait Gallery, London. Muñoz: Archivo Histórico, La Paz, Universidad Mayor de San Andrés (UMSA). Melgarejo: Archivo

Histórico, La Paz, UMSA. Franciscans: Padre Lorenzo Calzavarini O.F.M. Muzzani: Padre Lorenzo Calzavarini O.F.M. O'Connor: Eduardo Trigo O'Connor d'Arlach. Francisca Ruyloba: Eduardo Trigo O'Connor d'Arlach. Belzu: H.C.F.Mansilla. La Paz barricades: Archivo Histórico, La Paz, UMSA. Buchanan: courtesy of National Portrait Gallery, Smithsonian Institution. Polk: Library of Congress, Washington D.C. (LC–USZ62–110137). Gallatin: Library of Congress, Washington D.C. (LC–USZ62–110017). Taylor: Library of Congress, Washington D.C. (LC–USZ62–71730). Scott, by Mathew Brady: courtesy of National Portrait Gallery, Smithsonian Institution (NPG.78.245). Volunteers: William Dunniway Collection. Californian family: Seaver Center. Chester veterans: courtesy of South Carolina Library, University of South Carolina, Columbia.

Every effort has been made to obtain permission to use copyright material, both illustrative and quoted, in this book. Should there be any omissions in this respect we apologise and will be pleased to make the appropriate acknowledgements in any future edition of the work.

INDEX